W9-BZM-201

Simpson's Contemporary Quotations

Other works by James B Simpson

Best Quotes

Contemporary Quotations

Simpson's Contemporary Quotations

Veil and Cowl: Writings from the World of Monks and Nuns

The Hundredth Archbishop of Canterbury

Regent of the Sea

The Long Shadows of Lambeth X
with Edward M. Story

Stars in His Crown: Anglican Religious Orders
with Edward M. Story

Discerning God's Will: Lambeth XI
with Edward M. Story

Seasons of the Spirit
with Robert A. K. Runcie

SIMPSON'S CONTEMPORARY QUOTATIONS

THE MOST NOTABLE QUOTES FROM 1950 TO THE PRESENT

EDITED BY

JAMES B SIMPSON

HarperCollins*Publishers*

HarperCollins books may be purchased for educational, business, or sales promotional use. For information, please write to: Special Markets Department, HarperCollins Publishers Inc., 10 East 53rd Street, New York, New York 10022.

FIRST EDITION

Designed by Alma Orenstein

Library of Congress Cataloging-in-Publication Data
Simpson, James Beasley.
Simpson's contemporary quotations : the most notable quotes from 1950 to the present / edited by James B. Simpson. — Rev. ed.
p. cm.
Includes indexes.
ISBN 0-06-270137-1
1. Quotations, English. I. Title.
PN6083.S53 1997
082—dc21 96-51910

---

98 99 00 01 ❖/RRD 10 9 8 7 6 5 4 3

To Billye and Erleen
and to my far-flung Godchildren,
Janice Hind in Mexico,
Garrett Ruley in Alaska,
and Jennifer Ann Skinner in Japan,
whose generation will voice the contemporary quotations of the future.

He that giveth his mind...will keep the sayings of the renowned, and where subtle parables are, he will be there also. He will seek out the secrets of grave sentences, and be conversant in dark parables. He shall serve among great men, and appear before princes; he will travel through strange countries...When the great Lord will, he shall pour out wise sentences, and give thanks unto the Lord in his prayer.

Ecclesiasticus 39:1-4,6

CONTENTS

FOREWORD

Continuing my deep interest in the profundities, bon mots, witticisms, and epigrams of the lively last half of the 20th century, this book bundles together approximately 11,300 quotations with special emphasis on the years since 1988.

A fuller record of the earlier years may be found in the first three editions—*Best Quotes*, *Contemporary Quotations*, and *Simpson's Contemporary Quotations.* I eagerly anticipate bringing them together in a blockbuster of more than 20,000 quotes to mark the millennium.

The veteran news commentator H. V. Kaltenborn set the tone for my research in a preface to the first volume 39 years ago when he wrote that *the words* of the newsworthy and notable are the most newsworthy or defining thing about a person or event.

In a second edition, I noted my agreement that pronouncements of both the prominent and obscure constitute the essence of newsprint and sound.

In a foreword to a third edition, Daniel J. Boorstin, emeritus head of the Library of Congress, saw my compilation as "a documented retort to doomsayers who find wit and eloquence only in the deeper past."

These comments appear to come together in declaring a war of liberation against the inaccessibility of significant quotations otherwise lost on the wafting airwaves or buried in forests of newsprint and slippery surfaces of microfiche.

Once again I reaffirm that our era does, indeed, boast articulate spokespersons from every level of society and that their words can continue to interest and serve us.

Special thanks go to David Replogle, a former vice president of Houghton Mifflin, who gave another international dimension to my work by arranging for me to be a consultant to Britain's LaRousse Books with offices in Edinburgh; and to those who make *Simpson's* available in software in the U.S. and Germany.

I extend my appreciation to two well-versed men who reviewed the sections on sports and law—the eagle-eyed anthologist and author Paul Dickson and the able lecturer in legal research and assistant for legal services in the Yale University Library, Fred R. Shapiro.

At HarperCollins, I am grateful for the interest of Linda Cunningham and Robert A. Kaplan and their associates, the computer wizards John Day and Brian Desmond as well as Mary O'Shaugnnessy, Jay Papasan, Jeremie Ruby-Strauss, Helena Schwarz, and Elaine Verriest. Overseeing all of it has been my valued legal counsel and agent, Ronald L. Gordfarb, and his law partner, Nina Graybill.

I esteem the camaraderie that has developed with the Washington Library System, especially Alexander W. Geyger, Marian Holt, Mineta Rozen, Judy Zvonkin, and Betsy Fowler. They have been frequent telephone acquaintances, but the staff of the Georgetown branch has personally and patiently contended with my borrowing books and a staggering stack of magazines every Thursday morning.

A flattering nomination to the Cosmos Club by Professor Calhoun Winton of the University of Maryland and Daniel J. Boorstin, led to the use of a magnificent library and the vigilant, invaluable assistance of librarian Lura Young on Thursday afternoons.

Thanks, too, to columnist Bill Safire, a long-time friend of my books, and to his associate Dr. Jeff McQuain.

Through it all, my personal collection of quotation books stands at 200 in a handsome Biedermeier bookcase. They range from Adam Woolever's *Encyclopedia of Quotations: A Treasury of Wisdom, Wit and Humor, Odd Comparisons and Proverbs* to *Poetical Quotations With Copious Indexes* compiled in 1870 by S Austin Allibone to *Bartlett's* 16th edition edited by Harvard Professor Justin Kaplan.

As for modern quotations, the best of what's been said and written, flashed around the world, verified, analyzed, and recorded, comes back to us between the covers of this book. Short of an unlikely canonization, it is as good a tombstone or egotistical self-memorial as I can imagine.

Pausing in the newly learned technique of surfing the Internet, I offer my fax number, 202 244-5005, and invite readers to send me worthwhile quotations from the serious to the hilarious.

Most of all, I renew my indebtedness to a fellow priest, Edward M. Story, for wise counsel and careful indexing; to Anne H. Soukhanov who named the book *Simpson's* and brought to it the insights that distinguishes her editorship of the *American Heritage Dictionary*; and to Machiko Kumabe who translated it into four volumes for Shingo Funuya of Kodansha, Tokyo.

Lastly, I thank Robert E. Cleary, Professor of Political Science at American University, and Sanford J. Ungar, Dean of the School of Communications, for assistance in creating an endowment for fellowships to permanently continue research in the literature of modern quotations.

I commend these quotations for their power to help you formulate your own thoughts and tailor them to your particular situation; then you will have an unbeatable combination, the words of authority augmented by your own views, all expressed in a way that arrests attention and may gain a certain permanence.

All of the persons named in this preface may well join the weary printer of 18th century London who, on completing long hours of work on Dr. Johnson's dictionary, was heard to exclaim, "Thank *God* I am done with him!"

Supporting and goading us on is the abiding interest and affection that we continue to share for the ever present, energizing question, "Who said that?" And to that question, this book once again replies.

JAMES B. SIMPSON
Washington DC
Epiphanytide 1997

ON BEING USER-FRIENDLY

The broad outline and thrust of *Simpson's Contemporary Quotations* is readily seen in the three major categories highlighted in the Table of Contents:

The World
Humankind
Communications and the Arts

This trio of major headings is divided into fifty-five subsections, sixteen of which include areas specifically devoted to critical comment. Section titles also appear in the upper left and right corners of each page as a guide to discovering quotations about a specific topic or for browsing in pleasurable search.

PERSONS QUOTED

Within each section, the name of the speaker or writer is presented alphabetically. Brief identification usually reflects the person's status at the time his or her words were written or spoken.

SOURCES

Sources are offered for verification and for locating the quotation in fuller context. An attribution to "news reports" indicates that the quotation was carried by several wire services and other media; "news summaries" means that it appeared in publications or broadcasts at the end of a week, a month, or a year. Also note that authors and sources frequently appear in more than one section; for instance, versatile, articulate contemporaries such as the gadabouts Russell Baker and Brendan Gill turn up in numerous areas of interest in print or the vapors of video.

DATES

All quotations are dated. Use of the date only, usually from major addresses and judicial opinions, and statements recalled in obituaries, include, where possible, the actual date of the opinion or speech or the actual date of death. Months and years appear in shortened form with the day, month, and year in inverted order, ie, 13 Sep 88. Use of the date alone points to the quotation's appearance throughout the media on that date or the day following. Again, the date is the key to locating fuller context.

ORDER OF ENTRIES

Multiple quotations from an individual author or source within a particular section are in chronological order, with the earliest quote appearing first. Quotes from daily media are primary, followed by quotes from weekly or monthly magazines and from books. Several quotes from a book generally appear in the order in which they are to be found in the book; publisher and year of publication are included in attributions.

OTHER ASPECTS OF ATTRIBUTION

In addition to source and date, attributions usually give some information to pinpoint the quotation. The abbreviations *ib*, short for *ibidem*, "in the same place," is used when a quotation has the same author and the same attribution as the preceding quote. It may also be used when the author and publication are the same as in the preceding quotation, even though the date of publication is different. Standard abbreviations are used for professional titles (such as Dr for Doctor, an identification herein reserved for medical doctors); NYC for New York City, and CA for California. Radio and television networks are also abbreviated.

INDEXES

Since *Simpson's* is organized by categories, many quotations will be found by simply consulting the Table of Contents for the subject you want. To aid you further in searching out just the right quotations, there are two fulsome indexes—first Sources, then Subjects—at the end of the book. (For the first time, an inviting index of dozens of quotable lines is offered separately.) Each quote has its individual number appearing to the left of the individual quotation, beginning on page one, and running into the 11,000's by the end of the book. Index use of *see* and *see also* indicate a cross-reference. *Anon* is the mark of that elusive fellow, Anonymous. All in all, these indexes, used in conjunction with the list of categories given in the Table of Contents, will yield a fascinating sweep of the most significant and reflective quotations of our time.

THE WORLD

GOVERNMENT

Heads of State

Konrad Adenauer Chancellor of West Germany

1 The rare case where the conquered is very satisfied with the conqueror.

On allied occupation of West Berlin *NY Times* 21 Mar 60

2 We watched the resurrection of a nation under his evoking will.

On General Lucius D Clay as military governor of the American zone of Germany 1947–49, quoted by US Secretary of State Dean Acheson *Sketches from Life* Harper 61

3 Only the stupidest calves choose their own butcher.

On Western wheat shipments to Soviet Russia *NY Herald Tribune* 6 Oct 63

4 Adenauer, Eisenhower, and Diefenbaker—what a threesome!

On Germanic names among NATO leaders, cited by Canadian Prime Minister John G Diefenbaker in his book *One Canada* Macmillan of Canada 75

5 History is the sum total of things that could have been avoided.

Kansas City Times 9 Dec 78

6 I tell you, what I could not say to any German. . . . I hate uniforms, the curse of Germany.

On British Prime Minister Harold Macmillan's visit to Bonn 8 May 57, quoted by Alistair Horne *Harold Macmillan* Vol II Viking 89

7 How improvident of the Almighty to limit man's intelligence without limiting his stupidity!

To US Secretary of State Dean Acheson, quoted by David Acheson *Acheson Country* Norton 93

Raul Alfonsin President of Argentina

8 The house is in order, and there is no bloodshed!

To a crowd of 200,000 after surrender of rebellious officers *NY Times* 20 Apr 87

9 Go home and kiss your children and celebrate Easter in peace.

ib

Yasir Arafat Palestine Liberation Organization (PLO)

10 The sanctity of Jerusalem. . . dictates that we make it the joint cornerstone and capital of peace. . . a beacon for believers all over the world.

At White House signing of an accord of peace with Israel *NY Times* 29 Sep 95

11 We are betting everything on the future.

ib

Jean-Bertrand Aristide President of Haiti

12 These elections are the wheel of the machine of democracy that will take Haitians where they want to go.

At the polls a year after President Clinton sent troops to restore Aristide to office *NY Times* 20 Sep 95

Owen Arthur Prime Minister of Barbados

13 A rising tide can also overturn small boats.

Voicing fear of Caribbean summit of 34 Western Hemisphere nations that rapid market liberalizations could be overwhelming *NY Times* 12 Dec 94

Clement Attlee Prime Minister of Britain

14 [Communism is] the illegitimate child of Marx and Catherine the Great.

At Aarhus University, Aarhus, Denmark *London Times* 12 Apr 56

15 Democracy means government by discussion, but is only effective if you can stop people talking.

At Oxford *ib* 14 Jun 57

16 Broadly speaking the thing went off well, I think.

On Britain's hurried withdrawal from India at the cost of civil war and massacre of thousands, quoted by Andrew Roberts *Eminent Churchillians* Simon & Schuster 95

Baudoin I King of Belgium

17 Does everyone have freedom of conscience except the King?

On constitutional requirement that he sign abortion legislation passed by Belgium parliament *NY Times* 8 Apr 90

Menachem Begin Prime Minister of Israel

18 For the first time, I drank in the odor of the motherland.

On 1942 posting to Transjordan which, in Begin's eyes, was part of Eretz Israel, recalled on Begin's death 9 Mar 92

19 The life of every man who fights in a just cause is a paradox. . . . We fight, therefore we are.

The Revolt Nash 1948 and 77

20 Any idea of demilitarization. . . under foreign sovereignty would be a hoax because you can keep a gun in every garage.

Washington news conference 22 Mar 78

21 We have never asked anybody to recognize our right to exist. . . . [It] was given by the God of Abraham, Isaac and Jacob.

NY Times 20 Jun 78

22 Our brave, perhaps most hardened soldiers . . . embraced with tears and kissed the ancient stones of the remnants of the wall destined to protect the chosen place of God's glory.

On Jerusalem becoming a united city *ib* 31 Mar 79

23 This "flooral" arrangement is totally unacceptable to us.

On US reference to keeping Middle East peace negotiations on an upper floor while locating Lebanese and terrorist representatives on a lower one, quoted by former US Secretary of State George P Shultz *Turmoil and Triumph* Scribner 93

David Ben-Gurion Prime Minister of Israel

24 Without Jerusalem, we are a body without a soul.

Recalled in *US News & World Report* 18 Dec 95

Benazir Bhutto Prime Minister of Pakistan

25 For dictators across the world, democracy is the greatest revenge.

To US Congress *LA Times* 8 Jun 89

Willy Brandt Chancellor of West Germany

26 What belongs together will now grow together.

On demolition of the Berlin Wall, recalled on Brandt's death *Time* 19 Oct 92

Leonid I Brezhnev Soviet Premier

27 I. . . wish you energy and success in overcoming all kinds of difficulties; the causes of which are not easily seen at a distance.

Confidential message to President Nixon during the Watergate crisis, quoted by former Soviet Ambassador Anatoly Dobrynin *In Confidence* Times Books 95

Gro Harlem Brundtland Prime Minister of Norway

28 Some Norwegians think we can stand alone up here. They are stuck in their ways, suspicious of the outside world and scared of change. . . [and] that simply won't do.

On her "Yes to Europe" campaign for membership in the European Community *London Times* 28 Nov 94

29 There simply isn't time to be a mother, a wife and a politician. I like being a politician best.

ib

George Bush 41st US President

30 We meet on democracy's front porch.

At inaugural at US Capitol 20 Jan 89

31 The totalitarian era is passing, its old ideas blown away like leaves from an ancient lifeless tree.

ib

32 The future seems a door you can walk right through—into a room called tomorrow.

ib

33 We are the sum of our possessions. They are not the measure of our lives.

On values beyond materialism *ib*

34 America is never wholly herself unless she is engaged in high moral principle.

ib

35 We as a people have such a purpose. . . to make kinder the face of the nation and gentler the face of the world.

Statement of a new policy that editorialists interpolated as "a kinder, gentler America" *ib*

36 We bless them for choosing life.

On opposition to abortion *ib*

37 We have more will than wallet; but will is what we need.

ib

38 The final lesson of Vietnam is that no great nation can long afford to be sundered by a memory.

ib

39 This is the age of the offered hand.
On cooperation with Congress *ib*

40 The "offered hand" is a reluctant fist.
On protecting world peace *ib*

41 When America says something, America means it, whether a treaty or an agreement or a vow made on marble steps.
ib

42 We will always try to speak clearly, for candor is a compliment.
ib

43 There cannot be a common European home until all within it are free to move from room to room.
At Mainz, West Germany 31 May 89

44 This is more than a fleeting season of freedom. It is Hungary returning to its normal, traditional values. It is Hungary returning home.
At Karl Marx University, Budapest 12 Jul 89

45 The teaching of English is one of the most popular American exports.
On sending Peace Corps volunteers to Hungary *ib*

46 It would be inappropriate. . . to try to fine-tune for the people of Hungary how they ought to eat—how the cow ought to eat the cabbage, as we say in the United States.
On whether the US would continue to support a new Hungarian government if the next election brought "a leftist Communist-Socialist coalition" *ib*

47 Within our life time, the human race has traveled from the dunes of Kitty Hawk to the dust of another world.
On 20th anniversary of first moon landing 20 Jul 89

48 What was once improbable is now inevitable.
On future explorations of space *ib*

49 We must commit ourselves to. . . the permanent settlement of space.
ib

50 Our goal is nothing less than to establish the United States as the preeminent spacefaring nation.
ib

51 Trees can reduce the heat of a summer's day, quiet a highway's noise, feed the hungry, provide shelter from the wind and warmth in the winter.
At Sioux Falls SD 18 Sep 89; also see *Life* May 90

52 The forests are the sanctuaries not only of wildlife, but also of the human spirit. And every tree is a compact between generations.
ib

53 Hot-dogging? Well, you know, these charismatic, macho, visionary guys—they'll do anything.
On weighing risk in transferring to a launch on choppy seas during summit meeting off Malta 4 Dec 89

54 [He is] a bad guy in a pulp crime novel. . . a narcoterrorist.
On Panamanian General Manuel Antonio Noriega 20 Dec 89

55 A line has been drawn in the sand.
On sending troops to Persian Gulf after Iraq's invasion of Kuwait 8 Aug 90

56 That's not a threat, or a boast. That's just the way it's going to be.
To joint session of Congress, reaffirming determination to drive Iraq from Kuwait 11 Sep 90

57 I will do my level best to bring you home without a single shot fired.
Christmas message to troops in the Persian Gulf 24 Dec 90

58 Don't be misled by these rabbit trails running through the snow out there.
On reports that US troops were not ready to fight Iraq 27 Dec 90

59 The United States has moved under the code name Operation Desert Storm to enforce the mandates of the United Nations Security Council.
On commencing war against Iraq and replacement of the name Operation Desert Shield under which five months of preparation had been carried out 16 Jan 91

60 The coalition will give Saddam Hussein until noon Saturday to do what he must do—begin his immediate and unconditional withdrawal from Kuwait.
Statement 22 Feb 91

61 I have. . . directed General Norman Schwarzkopf, in conjunction with coalition forces, to use all forces available, including ground forces, to eject the Iraqi Army from Kuwait.
Statement 23 Feb 91

62 The liberation of Kuwait has now entered a final phase.
ib

63 Kuwait is liberated. Iraq's army is defeated. Our military objectives are met.
Statement 27 Feb 91

64 Kuwait is once more in the hands of Kuwaitis in control of their own destiny. . . . Its flag once again flies above the capital of a free and sovereign nation and the American flag flies above our embassy.
On the freeing of Kuwait City

65 At midnight tonight, Eastern standard time, exactly 100 hours since ground operations commenced and six weeks since the start of Operation Desert Storm, all United States and coalition forces will suspend offensive combat operations.
ib

66 When we say something that is objectively correct. . . people are going to listen. . . [or] let's put it this way: a re-established credibility for the United States of America.
On US's global role 1 Mar 91

67 There is something noble and majestic about patriotism in this country now. . . and part of this is the new-found viability of the United Nations.

ib

68 The specter of Vietnam has been buried forever in the desert sands of the Arabian Peninsula.

Radio address to US troops 2 Mar 91

69 We've kicked the Vietnam syndrome once and for all!

On the larger victory of the Persian Gulf War *Newsweek* 11 Mar 91

70 His credibility is zilch, zero, zed.

On the possibility of normalized relations with Saddam Hussein 16 Mar 91

71 Americans are a caring people. . . a good people, a generous people. . . [and] we went halfway around the world to do what is moral and just and right. And we fought hard, and—with others—we won the war.

To joint session of Congress *Time* 18 Mar 91

72 I will keep it the way it was when I was there. . . . He will be at the table when we need the intelligence to make critical decisions on foreign affairs. He will not be a politician, trying to shape policy.

On appointing Robert M Gates as director of the Central Intelligence Agency, a post Bush formerly held 14 May 91

73 It's very hard to ask the American people, "Please send money". . . when there's this dictatorship just 80 miles away.

On Communist Cuba as a bar to helping Russia *International Herald Tribune* 18 Jul 91

74 We reverse a half century of steadily growing strategic arsenals.

On joining Russia in signing the Strategic Arms Reduction Treaty 31 Jul 91

75 You must define your own branch of democratic capitalism.

On pressing Russia for economic change as a condition for large-scale US assistance *ib*

76 People must be free—to work, to save, to own their own homes, to take risks, to invest in each other and, in essence, to control their own lives.

ib

77 What is it with August?

On uprising against Russia's Mikhail S Gorbachev as compared to other significant historical events that have occurred during the month of August *London Times* 21 Aug 91

78 The world has changed at a fantastic pace with each day writing a fresh page of history before yesterday's ink has even dried.

To the nation, on reducing US and Soviet nuclear weapons 27 Sep 91

79 Our enemies have become our partners, committed to building democratic. . . societies. They ask for our support, and we will give it to them.

On Mikhail S Gorbachev's resignation as Russian premier *Washington Post* 26 Dec 91

80 The most compelling legacy of this nation is Jefferson's concept that we are created equal. It doesn't say "born" equal. He says "created." From the moment the miracle of life occurs, human beings must cherish that life, must hold it in awe, must preserve, protect and defend it.

To anti-abortion demonstrators 22 Jan 92

81 Communism died this year. . . [and] the Cold War didn't "end," it was won.

State of the Union 28 Jan 92

82 With imperial communism gone. . . we will shut down further production of the B–2 bomber. . . cancel the small ICBM program. . . cease production of new warheads for our sea-based ballistic missiles. . . stop all new production of the peacekeeper missile. . . [and] not purchase any more advanced cruise missiles.

ib

83 For half a century, American presidents have longed to make such decisions and say such words.

ib

84 The Soviet Union did not simply lose the cold war. The Western democracies won it.

At Texas A & M University in what was considered the valedictory of the Bush administration 15 Dec 92

85 The failure to respond to massive human catastrophes like that in Somalia would scar the soul of our nation.

On sending troops to hunger-plagued Somalia *ib*

86 [The Iran-Contra arms sales involvement has been] for more than six years. . . the most thoroughly investigated matter of its kind in our history. . . and it has cost more than $31 million.

On pardoning Defense Secretary Casper W Weinberger and five others 24 Dec 92

87 Prosecutions of the individuals I am pardoning represent what I believe is the most profoundly troubling development in the political and legal climate of our country: the criminalization of policy differences.

ib

88 These differences should be addressed in the political arena, without the Damocles sword of criminality hanging over the heads of some of the combatants.

ib

89 Presidents have historically used their power to pardon to put bitterness behind us and look to the future.

ib

90 For the first time in history, an American President has set foot in a democratic Russia.

On Moscow visit to sign START II, the Strategic Arms Reduction Treaty calling for Russia and the US to eliminate by the year 2003 almost three-quarters of their 20,000-odd nuclear warheads 3 Jan 93

James Callaghan Prime Minister of Britain

91 We've got to stop the loser mentality.
Time 24 May 78

Jimmy Carter 39th US President

92 This agreement. . . ensures. . . that this vital waterway. . . will continue to be well operated, safe and open to shipping to all nations.
On signing of treaty returning to Panama the control of the Panama Canal 7 Sep 77

93 Democracy is like the experience of life itself—always changing, infinite in its variety, sometimes turbulent and all the more valuable for having been tested by adversity.
To Parliament of India 2 Jun 78

94 If you fear making anyone mad, then you ultimately probe for the lowest common denominator of human achievement.
To Future Farmers of America, Kansas City 9 Nov 78

Fidel Castro President of Cuba

95 I am a Marxist-Leninist and I shall be a Marxist-Leninist until the last day of my life.
Statement 2 Dec 61, quoted by Arthur M Schlesinger Jr *A Thousand Days* Houghton Mifflin 65

96 How can the rope and the hanged man understand each other or the chain and the slave? Imperialism is the chain. Understanding is impossible. . . [but] someday there will be links—when there is a revolution in the United States.
On the limits of a *modus vivendi ib*

97 At least Kennedy was an enemy to whom we had become accustomed.
On learning of President Kennedy's assassination

98 [We are] this small country in the middle of the Yankee patio, the Caribbean.
At 26 July celebration, Havana 26 Jul 72

99 [It is] a dagger plunged into Cuban soil.
On American base established more than 90 years ago at Guantanamo Bay, Cuba *NY Times* 31 Mar 91

100 Time passes, and marathon runners get tired. This has been a very long race—too long. I feel I am a slave to the revolution.
On being asked if he expected to be President of Cuba in five years *Time* 8 Mar 93

Violeta Barrios de Chamorro President of Nicaragua

101 This is the dawn of a new republic. . . born not of screams and bullets, but of the deepest silence of the Nicaraguan soul—the conscience.
Inaugural statement *NY Times* 26 Apr 90

Chiang Kai-Shek, Generalissimo of Free China

102 Be firm with dignity, be self-reliant with vigor, do not be disquieted in time of adverse change.
Statement in Taiwan on loss of UN seat by his exiled government *NY Times* 22 Mar 72

Jacques Chirac President of France

103 One can understand that soldiers can be wounded, or even killed, but one cannot allow soldiers to be humiliated.
On reinforcing troops in Bosnia after Bosnian Serbs handcuffed hostages to military targets to avoid being bombed *NY Times* 23 Jul 95

Chou En-Lai Premier of Communist China

104 All diplomacy is a continuation of war by other means.
Saturday Evening Post 27 Mar 54

105 I shall soon be seeing Marx.
Deathbed remark quoted in Hugh Rawson ed A *Dictionary of Euphemisms and Other Doubletalk* Crown 81

Jean Chrétien Prime Minister of Canada

106 You end up looking like the fish.
On dislike for fishing with American presidents *NY Times* 25 Feb 95

Winston S Churchill Prime Minister of Britain

107 I went to sleep and slept the sleep of the saved and thankful.
On Japanese attack on Pearl Harbor that plunged the US into World War II *The Grand Alliance* Houghton Mifflin 50

108 When you have to kill a man, it costs nothing to be polite.
On ceremonial declaration of war with Japan *ib*

109 Surely you can make room for Britain to play her historic role upon that western sea whose floor is white with the bones of Englishmen.
Plea for a share of NATO's Atlantic Command 18 Jan 52, quoted by Dean Acheson *Present at the Creation* Norton 69

110 Remember that we are Greeks in their Roman Empire: it is our job to change their minds without their realizing it.
On asking Harold Macmillan to become World War II resident minister in Algiers, recalled by Anthony Sampson *The Anatomy of Britain* Hodder & Stoughton 62

111 Stupendous issues are unfolding before our eyes, and we are only specks of dust that have settled in the night on the map of the world.
On Allies' 1943 Teheran meeting, later quoted by James MacGregor Burns *Roosevelt: The Soldier of Freedom* Harcourt Brace Jovanovich 70

112 Never deal with the monkey when the organ grinder is in the room.

To a British diplomat who asked if he should confer with Count Geleazzo Ciano, Italian Prime Minister, or Ciano's father-in-law, Benito Mussolini, later recalled in *NY Times* 1 Apr 90

113 I can work here much better than in that center of effervecence and unrest called Westminster.

On preference for Checquers, the Prime Minister's residence in Kent *ib* 28 Aug 88

114 I have come here to ask not for gold but for steel; not for favors but equipment.

On growing Communist threats to peace, address to joint session of US Congress *ib* 16 Jan 52

115 The foundations. . . for preserving peace. . . stand now, not on paper but on rock.

On US support of the UN bearing "nine-tenths of the burden in Korea" *ib*

116 I, whose youth was passed in the august, unchallenged, and tranquil glare of the Victorian Era, may well feel a thrill in invoking once more the prayer and anthem, "God Save the Queen!"

On Elizabeth II's succession to the throne on the death of her father, George VI, 6 Feb 52, later quoted by Harold Macmillan *Tides of Fortune* Harper & Row 69

117 She is my monarch; my duty is the same.

On continuing weekly conference he had held with George VI, later quoted by Dean Acheson *Sketches from Life* Harper 61

118 I think she will listen. She has a good head.

On Elizabeth II *ib*

119 I call for a meeting at the summit.

Introducing "summitry" after the death of Joseph Stalin 5 Mar 53, quoted by by Evan Thomas and Walter Isaacson *The Wise Men* Simon & Schuster 86

120 The day may come when fair play, love for one's fellow-men, respect for justice and freedom, will enable tormented generations to march forth serene and triumphant from the hideous epoch in which we have to dwell. Meanwhile, never flinch, never weary, never despair.

Last address to Commons as Prime Minister 1 Mar 55

121 A conference should not be overhung by a ponderous or rigid agenda. . . drawn up in a vast cumbrous array.

At Geneva 20 Jul 55

122 He is the only bull who brings his own china shop with him.

On US Secretary of State John Foster Dulles, quoted by William Manchester *The Last Lion* Little, Brown 83

123 Dull, duller, Dulles.

ib

124 [Their] insatiable lust for power is only equaled by their incurable impotence in exercising it.

On opposition government after World War II, quoted by John Colville *The Fringes of Power* Norton 85

125 It was one of those cases in which the imagination is baffled by the facts.

On crash-landing in Scotland 10 May 1941 of the Nazi Rudolph Hess as a self-appointed peace emissary, recalled on Hess's death after life imprisonment in West Germany 17 Aug 86

126 Tangle within tangle, plot and counter-plot, ruse and treachery, cross and doublecross, true agent, false agent, double agent, gold and steel, the bomb, the dagger and the firing party.

Summing up the life of the secret agent, quoted by John le Carré *Our Gang* Knopf 95

William J Clinton 42nd US President

127 There is nothing wrong with America that cannot be cured by what is right with America.

Inaugural 20 Jan 93

128 This beautiful capital, like every capital since the dawn of civilization, is often a place of intrigue and calculation.

ib

129 I'd like for us to shift [our programs] from entitlement to empowerment. In the end, we want people not to need us anymore.

State of the Union 17 Feb 93

130 We must scale the walls of the people's skepticism, not with our words but with our deeds.

ib

131 Tell your stories. Tell the real stories, talk about the real lives—that's what gets to people.

To the first group of gay and lesbian leaders ever assembled at the White House *NY Times* 17 Apr 93

132 [It is] a place of deep sadness and a sanctuary of bright hope.

On dedicating the US Holocaust Memorial Museum in a mood described by reporter Henry Allen as "a bleak wintry day in the heart of spring" *Washington Post* 23 Apr 93

133 A lot of Americans have come here asking for a climate that is free of discrimination. . . to be able to work hard and live by the rules and be treated like other American citizens.

On the Gay Pride march on Washington, news conference 23 Apr 93

134 There is a permanent government here, but there's also a permanent political culture. And. . . it is my job as president to learn to make the most of that instead of letting it make the most of me.

On the atmosphere of "the permanent government. . . [that] puts an enormous extra burden on the process of change" *NY Times* 16 May 93

135 This has nothing to do with the political center; this has to do with my center!

On withdrawing the nomination of liberalist professor Lani Guinier to be Assistant Attorney General for Civil Rights 3 Jun 93

136 Surely, we can do it without the kind of rhetoric and air-filling bull that we hear so often.

On hoping to pass his health care package despite politics, at Tulsa 16 Aug 93

137 Today we bear witness to an extraordinary act in... a drama that began in a time of our ancestors when the word went forth from a sliver of land between the River Jordan and the Mediterranean Sea.

On White House signing of Palestinian-Israeli peace accord 13 Sep 93

138 We started this mission for the right reasons and we're going to finish it in the right way.

On US military intervention in Somalia 7 Oct 93

139 They may walk with a little less spring in their step, and their ranks are growing thinner, but let us never forget, when they were young, these men saved the world.

At Colleville-sur-Mer, France, on 50th anniversary of Allies' D-Day invasion *Washington Post* 7 Jun 94

140 Character is a journey, not a destination.

NY Times 31 Jul 94

141 The message of the United States to the Haitian dictators is clear: Your time is up. Leave now, or we will force you from power.

To the nation 15 Sep 94

142 This vast bleak desert hides great signs of life... for peace between Jordan and Israel is no longer a mirage.

At Arava Crossing, Israel, on the signing of peace treaty to end 46 years of war 26 Oct 94

143 Fifty years ago, an American president proposed a GI bill of rights.... Tonight, I propose a middle-class bill of rights.

To the nation in plea for tax breaks and new incentives, a step regarded as the opening of a battle with a new Republican Congress and a bid for reclaiming a disgruntled electorate 15 Dec 94

144 I can't stop being President.

On a suicide plane attack and two incidents of gun-fire on the White House *NY Times* 18 Dec 94

145 Once again our democracy has spoken... [but] we didn't hear America singing, we heard America shouting.

Acknowledging a new Republican majority, State of the Union 24 Jan 95

146 We are moving from an industrial age built on gears and sweat to an information age demanding skills and learning and flexibility.

ib

147 It's hard to remove ticks. Some of us who've had them, we know.

Asking for the power of a line-item veto *ib*

148 Pennsylvania Avenue has been routinely open... through four presidential assassinations and eight unsuccessful attempts... through a civil war, two world wars, and the Gulf War, it was open. But now it must be closed.

On blocking off the White House after several violent incidents 20 May 95

149 If a bullet can rip through metal like a knife through hot butter, then we should ban it.

On gun control NPR 30 Jun 95

150 Affirmative action is a moral imperative, a constitutional mandate and a legal necessity... [but] it should not go on forever... and it should be retired when its job is done.

On the 25th year of affirmative action 19 Jul 95

151 The rift... that is tearing at the heart of America exists in spite of the remarkable progress black Americans have made in the last generation.

At University of Texas 16 Oct 95

152 One million men do not make right one man's message of malice and division.

On the attendants of the Million Man March on Washington, some of whom had "a history that is far from its message of atonement and reconciliation" *ib*

153 There are still times when America and America alone can and should make the difference for peace.

To the nation on its role "as NATO's leader and the primary broker of the peace agreement" for Bosnia 27 Nov 95

154 By making an overwhelming show of force they will lessen the need to use force.

On sending forces to Bosnia for a year, "under the direction of an American general, to act not as war-makers but as peacemakers" *ib*

155 We will send you our most precious resource—the men and women of our armed forces.

On signing of Balkan peace accord in Paris 14 Dec 95

156 Today with a stroke of a pen our laws will catch up with the future.

On signing a bill for a sweeping overhaul of the telecommunications industry 8 Feb 96

Alfredo Nobre de Costa Prime Minister of Portugal

157 Every morning I first have to make an effort not to laugh at myself. Then I have to make an effort not to cry. Then I have to do the job.

On considering himself "completely inadequate" *LA Times* 30 Aug 78

Rene Coty President of France

158 The first among the French is now the first in France.

On being succeeded by Charles de Gaulle 9 Jan 59, quoted by Jean Lacouture *de Gaulle the Ruler* Norton 92

Edith Cresson Prime Minister of France

159 I'm not one of the elephants, and when I want to see them, I'll see them.
On canceling secret breakfast meetings with various political leaders *Le Monde* 19 May 91

160 You can replace men everywhere except in private life, but it's the only place.
Prime Time Live interview ABC TV 18 Jul 91

161 The Japanese are ants, little yellow men... who stay up nights thinking of ways to screw us.
Tokyo Iomturi 3 Sep 91

Charles de Gaulle President of France

162 At the Ministry of War, the look of things remained immutable. Nothing was missing except the State.
When France "virtually collapsed" *The Complete War Memoirs of Charles de Gaulle* Simon & Schuster 55

163 Mr Churchill and I agreed modestly... [that] when all is said and done, Britain is an island; France, the cape of a continent; America, another world.
On conference with Winston S Churchill

164 Nudity for a beautiful creature is natural enough, and for those around her is rather satisfying.
Denial that he wanted Britain "stripped naked" before joining the Common Market 8 Dec 57

165 In the tumult of great events, solitude is what I hoped for. Now it is what I love... [but] how is it possible to be contented with anything else when one has come face to face with History?
On concluding the third volume of his war memoirs 31 Dec 59

166 The so-called parties would, of course, have preferred to go on playing *belote.* But I forced them to play poker. And nobody is better at it than me.
On the election of 18 Nov 62 that biographer Jean Lacouture was to hail for turning "the monarchial republic into a republican monarchy" *Memoirs of Hope* Weidenfeld & Nicolson 71

167 Treaties are like roses and young girls. They last while they last.
Time 12 Jul 63

168 A great government such as yours does not act without evidence.
Commending US Secretary of State Dean Acheson on exposure of Soviet missiles in Cuba, quoted by Robert F Kennedy *Thirteen Days* Norton 69

169 Germany remains Germany... a great people... [but] she must be so placed that she may not become either tempted or tempter. If not, woe be the sons and daughters of men!
On the "lifetime of a single man" that saw invasion "three times by our neighbors across the Rhine," recalled on de Gaulle's death 9 Nov 70

170 Like a ship that puts out to sea having hardly touched port, so our country, having a victory, finds itself again faced with the necessity of struggling.
ib

171 An English farm in the Pacific.
On New Zealand, quoted by British Prime Minister Harold Macmillan *At the End of the Day* Macmillan 73

172 Is the Minister of Finance suggesting that when we shut the brothels, we should hand out the *Legion d'honneur* to the pimps?
Quoted by Jean Lacouture *De Gaulle the Ruler* Norton 92

173 I prefer my legend to power.
On nearing the end of his first term in office *ib*

174 The three levers controlling foreign policy are the diplomacy that expresses it, the army that sustains it and the police that protect it.
On what he reserved from control by Communist party participation in government *ib*

175 I would never have thought that I would be asked to delegate my constituent power twice in my life and that the man who was asking me to do so for the second time was he who had punished me for having done so the first.
On Marshal Henri Philippe Pétain and his contrasting roles as head of the French army in World War I and of the Occupation government in World War II *ib*

176 The high dignity of the leader is combined with the heavy chains of the servant!
On forming a new government *ib*

177 I heard all the doors of the palace closing behind me. But at the same time, I saw the prospect of a great undertaking open up before me.
On arriving at Élysée Palace 8 Jan 59 *ib*

178 In this sort of thing one has to keep walking or die. I have chosen to walk, but that doesn't mean that we may not also die.
To his Council of Minsters during the Algerian crisis 26 Aug 59 *ib*

179 It is entirely natural that one should feel nostalgia for what was the Empire, just as one may regret the gentle light of oil lamps, the splendor of the navy under sail.
On reaction to Algerian independence 14 Jun 60 *ib*

180 There is no valid politics outside realities.
On inappropriateness of negotiations while various factions courted Algeria *ib*

181 One does not talk if one does not leave one's knives in the cloakroom.
Statement at news conference on inappropriateness of negotiation while various factions courted Algeria *ib*

182 From the speculative and historical point of view, perhaps it would have been better than dying in one's bed or in an accident.

On alternatives to assassination *ib*

183 Gentlemen, hold tight to the mast, it's going to be a rough passage!

On France's fight to remain in the Sahara *ib*

184 You say that it is dangerous for me to know what a thousand corporals already know!

To President Einsenhower on the MacMahon Act forbidding the sharing of nuclear secrets with foreign powers *ib*

185 All those lawyers know is how to drown themselves in their own spit.

On great reform ending in an ordinance *ib*

186 [You are the] darling baby of Mother France. We will never abandon you.

On three tiny islands off the Newfoundland coast, France's foothold in North America 230 years after its loss of Canada *NY Times* 28 Apr 94

F W de Klerk President of South Africa

187 Today will be written up... as one of the most fundamental turning point days in the history of South Africa. Today we have closed the book on apartheid.

NY Times 19 Mar 92

188 I shall be surrendering power—not to the majority of the moment, but to the South African people... with the strong conviction that henceforth sovereignty will ultimately lie with them in the constitution.

On Nelson Mandela, successor to de Klerk in election that ended three centuries of white minority rule *Washington Post* 3 May 94

Deng Xiaoping Chinese Premier

189 There is great disorder under heaven, and the situation is excellent.

Toast that was regarded as "both appropriate and inscrutable" during President Ford's meeting with Mao Zedong, quoted by Walter Isaacson *Kissinger* Simon & Schuster 92

John G Diefenbaker Prime Minister of Canada

190 We are a power, not a puppet!

Reply to President Kennedy's bid for solidarity in resisting Fidel Castro, recalled in the sealing of the 1961 "Difenbunker," a 350-room, Carp, Ontario underground fortress secretly built during an uneasy Canadian era on the sidelines of the Cold War l6 Oct 95

Alec Douglas-Home Prime Minister of Britain

191 There are two problems in my life. The political ones are insoluble and the economic ones are incomprehensible.

NY Times 9 Jan 64

Abba Eban Prime Minister of Israel.

192 Chamberlain and Halifax were men of principle, but one of their principles was expediency.

On Britain's Prime Minister and Foreign Secretary *Israel Through My Eyes* Putnam 93

193 Dulles often wrestled with his conscience and always won.

On US Secretary of State John Foster Dulles *ib*

194 The Arabs often define themselves as a "family," and the speed of their transitions from mutual abuse to reconciliation conforms with this metaphor.

ib

Anthony Eden Prime Minister of Britain

195 We are not at war with Egypt. We are in an armed conflict.

To Commons 4 Nov 56

Dwight D Eisenhower 34th US President

196 A soldier's pack is not so heavy a burden as a prisoner's chains.

At inaugural 20 Jan 53

197 I just won't get into a pissing contest with that skunk.

To his brother, Milton, in 1953, refusing to publicly contend with Senator Joseph R McCarthy, quoted by Piers Brendon *Ike* Harper & Row 86

198 Just what does he think the Presidency is?

On a physician's warning to avoid "irritation, frustration, anxiety, fear, and above all else, anger," quoted by Michael R Beschloss *Eisenhower* HarperCollins 90

199 Now, on Friday noon, I am to become a private citizen. I am proud to do so. I look forward to it.

To the nation 17 Jan 61

Elizabeth II Queen of England

200 I have in sincerity pledged myself to your services, as so many of you are pledged to mine. Throughout all my life and with all my heart I shall strive to be worthy of your trust.

Address on the evening of her coronation 2 Jun 53

201 [The Commonwealth is like] an iceberg, except that it is not cold... and at the base of the iceberg, the part which keeps the rest afloat, is friendship and communication, largely in the English language.

Silver Jubilee address 7 Jun 77

202 It is a job for life.

National telecast on 40th anniversary of her accession, declaring an intention to continue on the throne 6 Feb 92

203 It's a question of maturing into something that one's got used to doing and accepting the fact that

it's your fate, because I think continuity is very important.

On weekly conferences with a series of nine Prime Ministers since 1952

204 The job and the life go together—you can't really divide it up.

ib

205 They unburden themselves and they tell me what's going on.

ib

206 It's rather nice to feel that one's a sort of sponge and everybody can come and tell one things.

London Times 6 Feb 92

207 Some things stay there and some things go out the other ear and some things never come out at all. Occasionally you can put one's point of view when perhaps they hadn't seen it from that angle.

ib

208 In the words of one of my more sympathetic correspondents, it has turned out to be an *annus horribilis.*

At the Lord Mayor's luncheon marking her 40th anniversary in a rare public acknowledgment of stress in national and family life 24 Nov 92

209 We are all part of the same fabric of our national society, and that scrutiny, by one part of another, can be just as effective if it is made with a touch of gentleness, good humor and understanding.

On criticism *ib*

210 I have enough experience. . . to restrain me from laying any money down on how many countries will be in the Commonwealth in 40 years' time.

On her meeting on Malta with 50 Commonwealth leaders, excepting South Africa and Fiji *London Weekly Telegraph* 29 Oct 93

211 [In the future] I suppose. . . there will be three absentees: Prince Philip, Britannia and myself. But you never know.

ib

212 You and I have spent most of our lives believing that this evening could never happen.

Toast to President Yeltsin at the Kremlin's first black-tie occasion since 1917 *NY Times* 20 Oct 94

213 There were no forgotten armies. There was just a vast number of men and women who fought for—and saved—the future of the free world.

At the Horseguards' Parade, London, on 50th anniversary of victory over Japan *Guardian Weekly* 27 Aug 95

Gerald R Ford 38th US President

214 I am a Ford, not a Lincoln!

To Congress after confirmation as vice president to replace Spiro Agnew 6 Dec 73

215 [I grant] a full, free and absolute pardon. . . for all offenses against the United States which he. . . has committed or may have committed or taken part in during the period from January 20, 1969, through August 9, 1974.

Official pardon given President Nixon 8 Sep 74

216 He has paid the unprecedented penalty of relinquishing the Presidency.

ib

217 If strange, whimsical and unexpected things were what Dorothy was really interested in, she wouldn't have gone to Oz. She would have come to Washington.

Recalling *The Wizard of* Oz in an address to Kansas legislature, Topeka 11 Feb 75

218 When we are able to look on the brighter side of our troubles and the lighter side of our struggles we Americans are at our very best.

To Washington's Gridiron Club 22 Mar 75 Harold Brayman ed *The President Speaks Off-the-Record* Dow Jones 78

219 I saw a hand come through the crowd in the first row. . . [and] in that hand there was a weapon.

On Lynette Fromme's assassination attempt *NY Times* 15 Nov 76

Indira Gandhi Prime Minister of India

220 I don't mind if my life goes in the service of the nation. If I die today, every drop of my blood will invigorate the nation.

NY Times 5 Nov 71, recalled on her assassination 31 Oct 84

Mikhail S Gorbachev Soviet Premier

221 The era of nuclear disarmament has begun.

On Moscow talks with President Reagan *Christian Science Monitor* 2 Jun 88

222 *Glasnost*. . . comrades, will undergo a serious test.

On democratization and change in the functions of Communist party committees *NY Times* 2 Jul 88

223 Having embarked upon the road of radical reform, the Socialist countries...have abandoned the claim to have a monopoly on the truth.

On an unprecedented visit to the Vatican *Time* 11 Dec 89

224 We need spiritual values, we need a revolution of the mind. It is only now that the real *perestroika* begins.

ib

225 I guess that these letters N-A-T-O may stand for Navies, Aircraft, Tanks, Obsolete.

On outdatedness of the North Atlantic Treaty Organization *NY Times* 4 Jun 90

226 The Cold War is behind us. Let us not wrangle over who won it.

At Stanford University 5 Jun 90

227 Look, Valentin Ivanovich, society is no army batallion and you can't put it in ranks and files.

To Deputy Defense Minister Valentin I Varennikov who was attempting a coup d'etat to overthrow Gorbachev 18 Aug 91 *Time* 7 Oct 91

228 We are flying into a new era.

To companions aboard aircraft returning to Moscow after the attempted coup *ib*

229 They... wanted to turn us into meat... to annihilate us!

To Russian Parliament *NY Times* 24 Aug 91

230 Dismembering this country... disuniting the state... I cannot agree.

On resigning from office 25 Dec 91

Vaclav Havel President of Czechoslovakia

231 For decades our statesmen and political leaders did not want to look out the windows of their airplanes.

On blindness to the progress of neighboring countries, address on assuming the presidency 1 Jan 90

232 Notions such as love, friendship, compassion, humility, or forgiveness have lost their depth and dimension; for many of us they represent nothing more than psychological idiosyncracies.

On 40 years of Communist domination *ib*

233 My people, your government has returned to you!

ib

234 The entire revolution is a peculiar drama, which no earthling could have written... an absurd play... a Greek tragedy ... a Goldonian farce... a fairy tale... and I am only a second assistant to the director, or maybe one of the actors.

US News & World Report 26 Feb 90

235 The Velvet Revolution.

On the Czechoslovakian overthrow of Communists *Newsweek* 30 Apr 90

236 I prefer to resign before I sign something bad.

On leaving office after one term *Wall Street Journal* 31 Jul 92

Edward Heath Prime Minister of Britain

237 I will not emulate those many Prime Ministers broken on the wheel of their obsession.

Quoted by John Campbell *Edward Heath* Jonathan Cape 93

238 What on earth do you want to go down a coal mine for? I shouldn't bother with the miners.

In 1973 to the newly appointed Archbishop of York, John Habgood, a year before a coal strike drove Heath from office, recalled in *Church Times* London 26 May 95

Omar Torrijos Herrera Chief of Government, Republic of Panama

239 Imagine that, 2,500 years of the Persian Empire reduced to ten people and two dogs.

On granting political asylum in 1980 to the Shah of Iran, recalled on Herrera's death 31 Jul 81

Hirohito Emperor of Japan

240 The ties between us and our people... do not depend upon mere legends and myths... predicated on the false conception that the Emperor is divine and that the Japanese people are superior to other races and fated to rule the world.

Address 1 Jan 1946 denying his divinity, a defining statement recalled on Hirohito's death 7 Jan 89

241 I told them I am not a god for the structure of my body is no different than that of a normal human being. I continued to tell them that it is a nuisance to be called such.

On breaking a Cabinet deadlock to end World War II in August 1945, disclosed in oral history made public 22 months after Hirohito's death *NY Times* 15 Nov 90

Lord Home (Alexander Frederick Douglas-Home) British Foreign Secretary 1960–63, Prime Minister 1963–64

242 You don't buy a canary and sing yourself.

On refraining from ambassadorial duties *NY Times* 21 Apr 61

Hussein I King of Jordan

243 [We will stop] signaling and hooting at each other like ships across a channel in a fog.

On differing positions of US and Jordan during Persian Gulf War *NY Times* 13 Mar 91

244 Mr Speaker, the state of war between Israel and Jordan is over.

To a joint session of the US Congress in an unprecedented appearance with another world leader, Israel's Prime Minister Yitzhak Rabin, on the reconciliation of the two countries *ib* 27 Jul 94

245 The two Semitic peoples, the Arabs and the Jews, have endured bitter trials and tribulations during the journey of history... [but now] I come before you fully conscious of the need to secure a peace for all the children of Abraham.

ib

246 I am determined to fulfill that part of my grandfather's legacy and leave my own.

Letter to President Clinton 20 Jun 93 on Hussein's forebearer, King Abdullah, who was assassinated in 1951 by a Palestinian as the young Hussein stood by, remarks made public *ib* 31 Jul 94

247 What is life all about? What is my responsibility? What will I be remembered for?

Continuing letter that followed White House meeting 14 Jun 93 which initiated US financial backing that made it possible for Jordan and Israel to secure peace *ib*

248 I was alone in my bedroom, looking at the swans on the lake. . . when there was a knock on the door and a hotel page came in with an envelope on a silver salver.

On learning while on holiday in 1952 in Geneva at age 17 that his father, King Talal, suffering from extreme schizophrenia, had abdicated, recalled in *London Times* 22 Jul 95

249 I did not need to open it to know my days as a schoolboy had ended. It was addressed to "His Majesty, King Hussein."

ib

250 The latest Pharaoh across the Nile.

On Egypt's President Gamal Abdel Nasser *ib*

251 So cunning and varied and constant have been the plots against my person that sometimes I feel like the central character in a detective novel.

ib

Saddam Hussein President of Iraq

252 Yours is a society which cannot accept 10,000 dead in one battle.

To the West on eve of invading Kuwait 25 Jul 90

253 [If the US attacks] there will be columns of dead bodies which may have a beginning but will have no end.

On UN resolution for economic embargo *NY Times* 26 Aug 90

254 They will swim in their own blood.

To Arab Baath Socialist Party on US intervention 10 Jan 91

255 If I am killed, there will be no part of me left bigger than the tip of my finger.

On surviving ten assassination attempts *Time* 7 Jan 91

256 Dogs will crush their skulls and walk on them.

On Israel, recalled on NPR 20 Jan 91

257 The great duel, the mother of all battles, has begun.

On outbreak of fighting with US and coalition forces *Newsweek* 11 Mar 91; in its wake, the *Toronto Star* spoke of "the mother of retreats"; the *London Times* of "the mother of all routs"; *Newsweek* 18 Mar 91 of what was "truly the mother of all cliches"

258 Fight them because with their defeat you will be at the last entrance of the conquest of all conquests.

Address to his troops 24 Feb 91

Arturo Umberto Illía President of Argentina

259 Eight days before they threw me out, I received a signed declaration of loyalty from all top military leaders. Three days before the coup, the commanders of the army, navy, and air force gave me another signed pledge. . . [and] on the day of the coup, I felt as secure as I ever did.

On deposition after three years in office *NY Times* 16 Sep 66

Alija Izetbegovic President of Bosnia

260 My government is taking part. . . without any enthusiasm but as someone taking a bitter yet useful potion or medication.

On joining the presidents of the US, Serbia and Croatia in signing a treaty for peace in the Balkans *NY Times* 15 Dec 95

261 The battle. . . is neither won nor lost. . . [but] will develop with different means, thanks to the force of ideas and action. . . [without] hatred. . . [or] revenge.

ib

Lyndon B Johnson 36th US President

262 I want to be progressive without getting both feet off the ground at the same time. . . a progressive who is prudent.

Interview 16 Mar 64

263 I am the king! I am the king!

Overheard on Air Force I by UPI correspondent Helen Thomas, later reported in her book *Dateline: White House* Macmillan 75

264 Like Grandma's nightshirt—it covered everything.

On US Congress's Gulf of Tonkin resolution authorizing Johnson "to take all necessary measures to repel attacks against US forces [in Vietnam]" 6 Aug 64

265 When a Southerner can sit in the White House, when a negro can aspire to the highest offices in the land, when a man of deep Jewish background can be the spokesman of this country to the world—that's what America is all about.

On himself as a Texan, on the possibility of an African American on the Supreme Court, and on appointing Associate Justice Arthur J Goldberg to be ambassador to the UN *Time* 30 Jul 65

266 Some nervous Nellies. . . will turn on their own leaders and their own country, and on our own fighting men.

On critics of Johnson's Vietnam policy; "nervous Nellies" was soon applied to all anti-involvement and anti-escalation forces and was eventually synonomous with Johnson's reference to "cussers and doubters" of his policy 17 May 66

267 It is our will and not our strength that is being tried.

On the Vietnam War, State of the Union 17 Jan 68

268 It's the rightest thing I've ever done.

To Press Secretary George Christian moments before Johnson announced to the nation that he not would seek another term 31 Mar 68, later reported in *Newsweek* 15 Apr 68

269 Leaks can kill you.

To President-elect Nixon, later quoted by Fred Emery *Watergate* Times Books 94

270 If it hadn't been for Edgar Hoover, I couldn't have carried out my responsibilities as Commander-in-Chief. Period. Dick, you will come to depend on Edgar. . . a pillar of strength in a city of weak men.

On FBI Director J Edgar Hoover *ib*

Juan Carlos I King of Spain

271 Let no one believe that his cause will be forgotten; let no one expect an advantage by a privilege.

On investiture as king *NY Times* 23 Nov 75

John F Kennedy 35th US President

272 United, there is little we cannot do in a host of cooperative ventures. Divided, there is little we can do—for we dare not meet a powerful challenge at odds and split asunder.

To allied nations, inaugural address 20 Jan 61

273 If a free society cannot help the many who are poor, it cannot save the few who are rich.

ib

274 Civility is not a sign of weakness, and sincerity is always subject to proof.

ib

275 Ask not what your country can do for you—ask what you can do for your country.

ib

276 You don't fire God.

On disinclination to replace FBI Director J Edgar Hoover, quoted in Senate committee findings on US intelligence activities 1976

277 I wonder how it is with you, Harold? If I don't have a woman for three days, I get a terrible headache.

To Prime Minister Harold Macmillan who recorded it in his diary 5 Mar 61, quoted by Alistair Horne *Harold Macmillan* Vol II Viking 89

278 I feel at home with Macmillan because I can share my loneliness with him. The others are all foreigners to me.

On foreign ministers *ib*

279 There's an old saying that victory has a hundred fathers and defeat is an orphan.

On the ill-fated invasion of Cuba, news conference 21 Apr 61. "The line. . . turned out to be just about the only positive contribution CIA Director Allen Dulles made to that week of disaster," wrote Peter Grose in tracing the remark to diaries of Count Galeazzo Ciano, Mussolini's foreign minister, that Dulles had unearthed in Switzerland *Gentleman Spy* Houghton Mifflin 94

280 I probably made a mistake in keeping Allen Dulles on. . . . It's hard to operate with legendary figures.

On Allen Dulles' continuing as CIA Director after the Bay of Pigs *ib*

281 McNamara has dealt with Defense; Rusk has done a lot with State; but no one has dealt with CIA.

On reigning-in government agencies in 1961, quoted by Arthur M Schlesinger Jr *A Thousand Days* Houghton Mifflin 65

282 Those families which are not hit in a nuclear blast can still be saved.

Urging acquisition of defense shelters in US 11 Mar 61

283 Too long we have fixed our eyes on armies prepared to cross borders, on missiles poised for flight. Now it should be clear that our security may be lost piece by piece, country by country, without the firing of a single missile or the crossing of a single border.

To American Society of Newspaper Editors, news summaries 30 Apr 61

284 I believe that this nation should commit itself to achieving the goal, before this decade is out, of landing a man on the Moon and returning him safely to Earth.

To Congress 21 May 61

285 He intends to bring to an end, through a stroke of the pen, first our legal rights to be in West Berlin—and secondly our ability to make good on our commitment to the two-million free people of that city. That we cannot permit.

To the nation on returning from his first meeting with Soviet Premier Nikita S Khrushchev 25 Jul 61

286 You never know what's hit you. A gunshot is the perfect way.

On presidential assassinations, quoted by Peter Collier and David Horowitz *The Kennedys* Summit 84

287 [It is] primarily a form of atomic blackmail.

On Soviet decision to resume nuclear testing, news summaries 31 Aug 61

288 What your government believes is its own business; what it does in the world is the world's business.

Letter to Nikita S Khruschev, later quoted by Theodore C Sorensen *Kennedy* Harper & Row 65

289 A strong America depends on its cities—America's glory and sometimes America's shame.

State of the Union 11 Jan 62

290 Those who make peaceful revolution impossible will make violent revolution inevitable.

To Latin American diplomats 12 Mar 62

291 They look like little footballs on a football field.

On studying aerial photos of Soviet missiles in Cuba, quoted by Sorensen *op cit*

292 It shall be the policy of this nation to regard any nuclear missile launched from Cuba against any nation in the Western Hemisphere as an attack by the Soviet Union. . . requiring a full retaliatory response upon the Soviet Union.

On sea blockade of Soviet ships delivering missiles to Cuba, address to the nation 22 Oct 62

293 I call upon Chairman Khrushchev to halt and eliminate this clandestine, reckless, and provocative threat.

ib

294 The cost of freedom is always high, but Americans have always paid it. And one path we shall never choose, and that is the path of surrender, or submission.

ib

295 I think your attention might well be directed to the burglar rather than to those who caught the burglar.

To Bertrand Russell on Russell's messages praising Khrushchev and castigating Kennedy for the latter's warlike attitude on Cuba 24 Oct 62; a similar exchange took place between UN Ambassadors Adlai E Stevenson and Valerian A Zorin 25 Oct 62

296 We are prepared to discuss a détente affecting NATO and the Warsaw Pact.

Message to Khrushchev in October 62 after the Cuban missile crisis, introducing the French word *détente* as a term for the loosening of a taut string, translated in Russian as *razrvadka*; later a by-word of Secretary of State Henry A Kissinger, see Walter Isaacson's *Kissinger* Simon & Schuster 92

297 His stately ship of life. . . is anchored in tranquil waters, proof that courage and faith and zest for freedom are truly indestructible.

On conferring honorary citizenship on Winston S Churchill 9 Apr 63

298 Equality of opportunity does not mean equality of responsibility.

On the duty of the educated to help safeguard the rights of all Americans, address at Vanderbilt University 19 May 63

299 The rights of every man are diminished when the rights of one man are threatened.

On sending national guardsmen to ensure peaceful integration of the University of Alabama, address to the nation 11 Jun 63

300 No one has been barred on account of his race from fighting or dying for America—there are no "white" or "colored" signs on the foxholes or graveyards of battle.

ib

301 Let it not be said of this Atlantic generation that we left ideals and visions to the past, nor purpose and determination to our adversaries.

To West German Parliament, Frankfurt 25 Jun 63

302 All free men. . . are citizens of Berlin. And. . . I take pride in the words, *Ich bin ein Berliner.*

Address in Berlin's Rudolf Wilde Platz 26 Jun 63

303 The greatest art of the world was the work of little nations. The most enduring literature. . . heroic deeds. . . and, yes, the salvation of mankind came through a little nation.

To Irish Parliament, Dublin 28 Jun 63

304 It honors those whose talent enlarges the public vision of the dignity with which life can be graced and the fullness with which it can be lived.

On reviving award of the Medal of Freedom to honor American artists 4 Jul 63

305 For the first time, we have been able to reach an agreement which can limit the dangers of this age.

On ratification of treaty to limit nuclear testing 7 Oct 63

306 The definition of happiness of the Greeks. . . is full use of your powers along lines of excellence. I find, therefore, the Presidency provides some happiness.

News conference 31 Oct 63

307 The three most overrated things in the world are the state of Texas, the FBI, and hunting trophies.

Quoted by William Manchester *The Death of a President* Harper & Row 67

308 We're heading into nut country today.

In Fort Worth to his wife a few hours before the assassination in Dallas 22 Nov 63 *ib*

309 You know, last night would have been a hell of a night to assassinate a President. There was the rain. . . the night, and we were all getting jostled.

ib

310 We in this country, in this generation, are—by destiny, rather than choice—the watchmen on the walls of the world.

Address prepared for Dallas luncheon on day he was assassinated 22 Nov 63

311 The righteousness of our cause must always underlie our strength. For as was written long ago: "Except the Lord keep the city, the watchman waketh but in vain."

ib

Ayatollah Ruhollah Khomeini spiritual leader of Iran

312 I am ready to sacrifice myself to perform the divine duty of defending Moslems and am looking forward to attaining the grand honor of martyrdom.

At 86, to Moslem pilgrims *NY Times* 2 Aug 87

313 If someone runs over a dog belonging to an American, he will be prosecuted. . . but if an American cook runs over the Shah, the head of state, no one will have the right to interfere with him.

On denouncing 1964 Status of Forces Agreement seen as an exemption of a vast number of Americans from

Iranian law, quoted by James A Bill *The Eagle and the Lion* Yale 88

314 Taking this decision was more deadly than taking poison. I submitted myself to God's will and drank this drink for His satisfaction.

On ending an 8-year war against Iraq *NY Times* 21 Jul 88

315 Leave the Persian Gulf before it is too late and you are drowned in quagmires of death.

Warning to US and European military forces *ib*

316 God has formed the Islamic Republic. . . the only government accepted by God on Resurrection Day.

Recalled on Khomeini's death 5 Jun 89

317 We don't say that the Government must be composed of the clergy but that the Government must be directed and organized according to the divine law, and this is only possible with the supervision of the clergy.

ib

Nikita S Khrushchev Soviet Premier

318 We will bury you!

Boasting of Soviet prowess to Western ambassadors at a reception in Moscow 17 Nov 56

319 Support by United States is rather in the nature of the support that the rope gives to a hanged man.

Interview in Egyptian newspapers 25 Nov 57

320 You may be my guest but truth is my mother.

To Vice President Richard M Nixon during visit to a Moscow exhibit of a model American home and an ensuing "kitchen debate" on the two countries' capabilities 25 Jul 59

321 We have the remnants of the plane—and we also have the pilot, who is quite alive and kicking!

Announcement that a US spy plane had been shot down 5 May 60

322 The Monroe Doctrine. . . has died, so to say, a natural death. . . [and] should best be buried as every dead body is so that it should not poison the air by its decay.

Kremlin news conference 13 Jul 60

323 If people do not show wisdom. . . they will come to a clash, like blind moles, and then reciprocal extermination will begin.

Letter to President Kennedy 22 Oct 62 on US protest against installation of nuclear missiles in Cuba, quoted by Robert F Kennedy *Thirteen Days* Norton 69

324 We are of sound mind and understand perfectly well that if we attack you, you will respond the same way. . . [but] only lunatics and suicides. . . could do this.

ib

325 The Soviet Government. . . has given a new order to dismantle the arms which you described as offensive, and to crate and return them to the Soviet Union.

Letter to President Kennedy *ib* 28 Oct 62

Vytautas Landsbergis President of Lithuania

326 The ghost of Stalinism is walking in the Kremlin, and the shadow of it lies far to the West.

On the possibility of Russian force against Lithuanian independence *NY Times* 22 Mar 90

Lee Teng-Hui President of Taiwan

327 We are so rich, but. . . our voice is so low that no one can hear it.

On drawing world attention to the major reason he was kept in office—a strong stance against militaristic, mainland China *NY Times* 29 Aug 95

Li Peng Prime Minister of China

328 China will never accept the US human rights concept. History has already proven that it is futile to apply pressure on China.

On meeting with US Secretary of State Warren Christopher *NY Times* 13 Mar 94

Harold Macmillan Prime Minister of Britain

329 It is. . . trite. . . to say that we live "in a period of transition". . . . Adam may well have made the remark to Eve on leaving the Garden of Eden.

NY Times 9 Jun 58

330 A man who trusts nobody is apt to be the kind of man nobody trusts.

NY Herald Tribune 17 Dec 63

331 The oldest among us can recall nothing to compare with him, and the younger ones among us, however long we live, will never see the like again.

On Winston S Churchill *NY Times* 29 Jul 64

332 It is as if we had employed a surgeon to perform a delicate operation and had then arranged that his elbow should be jogged at the most critical moment.

On harassment of heads of state by "every form of obstruction and vituperation"; US President Lyndon Johnson had the statement framed and placed on a wall near his bed *Newsweek* 28 Nov 66

333 [The German invasion of Russia] determined the character and issue of the war itself and formed the mould into which the life of Europe has since been poured.

The Blast of the War 1939–45 Harper & Row 68

334 A Foreign Secretary. . . is always caught by a cruel dilemma—hovering between the cliche and the indiscretion. . . either dull or dangerous.

To the Commons 17 Jul 55 *Tides of Fortune* Harper & Row 69

335 Americans [are] much as the Greeks found the Romans—great big, vulgar, bustling people more vigorous. . . more ideal. . . with more unspoiled virtues but also more corrupt.

War Diaries St Martin's 84

336 When one lives on Vesuvius, one takes little account of eruptions.

To President Kennedy on Russian missles trained on Europe as compared to 20 or 30 in Cuba *At the End of the Day* Macmillan 73

337 Although the proposed British marriage. . . was not exactly a shotgun wedding, the virginity of the lady must now be regarded as doubtful.

On Skybolt rockets supplied by the US *ib*

338 [It is] like bicycling along a tightrope.

On balancing the British economy, quoted by Alistair Horne *Harold Macmillan* Vol II Viking 89

339 In America, he is half King, half Prime Minister.

Defining the US presidency, diary entry 20 Mar 57

340 She has buried George III for good and all.

On Elizabeth II's US visit for Virginia's 350th anniversary *ib* 23 Oct 57

341 I am always hearing about the Middle Classes. What is it they really want? Put it down on a sheet of notepaper, and I will see whether we can give it to them.

Memo to Michael Fraser, head of the Conservative Research Dept, who replied that the Middle Class' unobtainable desire was to return to the comfortable standards of pre-war days *ib*

342 I thought the best thing to do was to settle these little local difficulties and then to turn to the wider vision of the Commonwealth.

Statement 7 Jan 58 on leaving London for his first long foreign tour; regarded as a put-down on recent Treasury resignations, it was recalled by Macmillan 13 years later as a seemingly casual but carefully calculated manner of establishing "a sense of proportion" *ib*

343 This is pure Chamberlainism. It is raining umbrellas.

Diary entry 21 Feb 57 at end of first year in office when public opinion decried Macmillan's failure to meet with Soviet Premier Nikita Khrushchev *ib*

344 [Africa was] like a sleeping hippo in a pool. . . suddenly it gets a prod from the white man and wakes us; and it won't go to sleep again.

ib

345 [They] have ceased to be on speaking terms—they are only on bawling terms.

On Colonial Secretary Alan Lennox-Boyd and the Board of Trade's David Eccles, diary entry 13 Jul 58 *ib*

346 I can see the helicopter now, sailing down the valley above the heavily laden, lush foliage of oaks and beech at the end of June.

On President Kennedy's departure from Macmillan's country house *ib*

347 Before those leaves had turned and fallen he was snatched by an assassin's bullet from the service of his own country and the whole world.

ib

John Major Prime Minister of Britain

348 I think we'd better begin again somewhere else.

To cabinet meeting after mortar explosion set off by Irish Republican Army narrowly missed 10 Downing St *London Times* 8 Feb 91

349 Modestly dramatic. . . landed in the garden, demolishing a rather attractive cherry tree en route.

On the IRA attack on 10 Downing St *NY Times* 28 Feb 91 and 29 Mar 92

350 More a lifebelt than a strait-jacket.

On the European monetary system *ib*

351 I want to see wealth cascading down the generations.

On possible change in the inheritance tax *New Yorker* 6 Jan 92

352 I sense a growing fear that we may lose so much that is precious to this country. . . that our deepest values as a civilized nation are being threatened.

On attacks on the monarchy and other "institutions that embody our nationhood" *Washington Times* 3 Mar 93

353 Time after time you'll find solutions are reached at the 59th minute of the 11th hour.

On the European Union *Guardian Weekly* 3 Apr 94

354 I am more a European in my head than in my heart, but I want to see Europe succeed.

ib

355 The Prince of Wales is the heir to the throne. He remains heir to the throne and when the time comes he will be King.

Statement reaffirming right to succession despite divorce *London Times* 1 Jul 94

356 I don't believe that any Prime Minister. . . could or should sit in Downing Street without actively trying to find a way out of the problems that have existed for so long.

On presenting in Belfast a plan known as the Joint Framework Document that would end "the dialogue of the deaf" and guarantee peace and greater independence in Northern Ireland *ib* 23 Feb 95

357 The next generation may not face the privations, the murders, the sorrow, the hardship, the deaths and the funerals. . . [but] it has to be by consent, by agreement; slow, difficult, painful. . . the only way.

On lessening of political violence in Ireland *ib*

358 We will need to carry opinion. . . with us whichever way we proceed, most definitely if we decide to go into a single currency.

On the necessity of a national referendum on a common European currency *ib* 2 Mar 95

Nelson Mandela President of South Africa

359 Out of the experience of an extraordinary human disaster that lasted too long must be born a society of which all humanity will be proud.

At inauguration as South Africa's first black president, *NY Times* 11 May 94

360 Each of us is as intimately attached to the soil. . . as the famous jacaranda trees of Pretoria and the mimosa trees of the bushveld.

ib

361 Humanity has taken us back into its bosom. . . . Never, never and never again shall it be that this beautiful land will. . . suffer the indignity of being the skunk of the world.

ib

Mao Zedong Chinese premier

362 If you want to know the taste of a pear, you change the pear by eating.

The Quotations of Chairman Mao Foreign Languages Press 67

363 Every Communist must grasp the truth, "Political power grows out of the barrel of a gun."

"Problems of War and Strategy" *ib*

364 Our principle is that the Party commands the gun, and the gun must never be allowed to command the Party.

ib

365 All reactionaries are paper tigers.

ib

366 Letting a hundred flowers blossom and a hundred schools of thought contend is the policy for promoting the progress of the arts and the sciences and a flourishing socialist culture in our land.

"On the Correct Handling of Constitutions Among the People," remarks that gave rise to the falsely tolerant slogan, "Let a hundred flowers bloom" *ib*

367 Comrades, you should analyze your responsibility and your stomachs will feel much more comfortable if you move your bowel and break wind.

On failure of "the Great Leap Forward" 23 Jul 59, quoted in papers made public in *NY Times* 1 Mar 70

368 The people are like water and the army is like fish.

On "China and the anti-Japanese struggle" of 1948, recalled on Mao's death 9 Sep 76

369 The East wind is prevailing over the West wind

Newsweek 20 Sep 76

370 [It is] the iron rice bowl.

On the symbol of life-time employement *Time* 6 Jan 85

371 If you fail, you will plunge into a fathomless abyss. Your body will shatter. Your bones will break.

To wife, Jiang Quing, on her duty to carry on the Communist cause, recalled on her suicide *Time* 17 Jun 91

Golda Meir Prime Minister of Israel

372 Israel's policy is peace, theirs is to throw us into the sea.

On Egypt *NY Journal-American* 19 Mar 61

373 The man feels he is God. Many disagree.

On Egyptian President Gamal Abdel Nasser *ib*

374 I won't be here but I see peace with our neighbors, a society with social justice, a high standard of culture, and an Israeli woman who reflects the best qualities of the peoples of nearly 100 nations which have come here.

ib

375 We intend to remain alive. Our neighbors want to see us dead. . . not a question that leaves much room for compromise.

Reader's Digest Jul 71

376 Women's liberation is just a lot of foolishness. It's the men who can't bear children. And no one's likely to do anything about that!

Newsweek 23 Oct 76

377 I've had enough.

On resigning as Prime Minister 11 Apr 74, recalled on Meir's death 6 Dec 78

378 We do not rejoice in victories. We rejoice when a new kind of cotton is grown and when strawberries bloom in Israel.

ib

379 Above all, this country is ours...(and) being a Jew is no problem in Israel.

Recalled on 30th anniversary of Israel's founding *International Herald Tribune* 11 May 78

380 Don't be humble, you're not that great!

To Kennedy Press Secretary Pierre Salinger, quoted by Diana McLellan *Washington Post* 24 Sep 95 reviewing Salinger's *PS: A Memoir* St Martin's 95

Carlos Menem President of Argentina

381 The mattress doesn't pay interest.

Imploring people to "keep money in their banks rather in their beds" *Wall Street Journal* 6 Apr 95

François Mitterrand President of France

382 There is a galloping horse of history and you just have to get on.

Quoted by Israeli Foreign Minister Shimon Peres on implementation of Israeli-Palestinian peace accord *US News & World Report* 27 Sep 93

383 I think it will be obliging enough to let me finish my term of office.

In nationally televised interview at 77 after two operations and chemotherapy for prostate cancer 26 Sep 94

384 The USA has held Cuba by the throat for decades.

Welcoming Fidel Castro to Paris and characterizing the American embargo on Cuba as "stupid" for a country that offered "no threat to world peace" *International Herald Tribune* 14 Mar 95

385 The first common victory should and will be the victory of Europe over itself.

On the importance of continental unity, address in Berlin on 50th anniversary of the end of World War II *US News & World Report* 22 May 95 World War II

Kiichi Miyazawa Prime Minister of Japan

386 [American determination] to produce goods and create value has loosened sharply... and lacks a work ethic, to live by the sweat of the brow.

To budget committee of the Diet in testimony on US labor *Washington Post* 4 Feb 92

Hosni Mubarak President of Egypt

387 Political missiles can trigger a misguided demonstration, but they never win a war.

Life Mar 91

P V Narashima Rao Prime Minister of India

388 Decisions are easier, you know, when there are no choices left.

On being asked if his tough measures were forged in determination or desperation in light of India's spectacular problems *London Observer* 7 Jul 91

Jawaharlal Nehru Prime Minister of India

389 At the stroke of the midnight hour, when the world sleeps, India will awake to life and freedom.

To India's Constituent Assembly on winning independence from Britain 14 August 1947, recalled on Nehru's death 27 May 64

Nguyen Van Thieu President of South Vietnam

390 America has been looking for a better mistress, and now Nixon has discovered China. He does not want to have the old mistress hanging around... old and ugly.

On President Nixon's visit to China, quoted by Walter Isaacson *Kissinger* Simon and Schuster 93

Richard M Nixon 37th US President

391 The greatest honor history can bestow is the title of peacemaker.

At inaugural 20 Jan 69, later chosen as inscription on Nixon's gravestone *NY Times* 25 Apr 94

392 Until he has been a part of a cause larger than himself, no man is truly whole. This is the way civilizations begin to die.

On student demonstrations against the Vietnam War 22 Mar 69

393 If we take the route of the permanent handout, the American character will itself be impoverished.

To the nation, on proposal to reform welfare programs 8 Aug 69

394 Tonight—to you, the great silent majority of my fellow Americans—I ask for your support.

To the nation in appeal to get behind the Vietnam War 3 Nov 69

395 The average American is just like the child in the family. You give him some responsibility and he is going to amount to something. He is going to do something.

Interview on the eve of his second successful campaign for the presidency, quoted by Stephen E Ambrose *Nixon: Ruin and Recovery* Simon & Schuster 91

396 On the other hand if you make him completely dependent and pamper him and cater to him too much you are going to make him soft, spoiled, and eventually a very weak individual.

ib

Sam Nujoma President of Namibia

397 As of today, we are masters of this pastoral land of our ancestors. The destiny of this country is now in our own hands.

On taking office after 23-year war against South African control *NY Times* 21 Mar 90

Olav King of Norway

398 But I have four million bodyguards.

When asked if he was afraid to walk alone in Oslo, recalled on Olav's death *London Times* 31 Jan 91

Vittorio Emanuele Orlando Prime Minister of Italy

399 The profound oblivion... descended on my name is the rational necessity of a historical situation imposed by destiny.

On his survival as the last of World War I's Big Four *Time* 8 Dec 52

400 Oratory is just like prostitution: you must have little tricks. Start a sentence and leave it unfinished. Everyone racks his brains and wonders what I was going to say.

ib

Lester B Pearson Prime Minister of Canada

401 A few Americans know Canada well, but many do not know it even a little. This irks us. Indeed a major irritant in our relations with the United States is the tendency of some Americans simply to take Canadians for granted.

Foreign Affairs Jan 65, quoted by US Secretary of State Dean Acheson *Grapes from Thorns* Norton 75

Shimon Peres Foreign Minister of Israel

402 What we are doing today is more than signing an agreement; it is a revolution. Yesterday a dream, today a commitment.

At White House signing of Palestinian-Israeli peace accord 13 Sep 93

403 We live in an ancient land and as our land is small, so must our reconciliation be great. As our wars have been long, so must our healing be swift. Deep gaps call for lofty breezes. Let all of us turn from bullets to ballots, from guns to shovels.

ib

404 We shall offer you our help in making Gaza prosper and Jericho blossom again.

ib

405 We have to build a new commonwealth on our old soil: a Middle East of the people and a Middle East for their children.

ib

406 The Syrians will have to understand that nobody can pick fruit unless he plants trees.

On Syria's need for deeper roots in international negotiations *NY Times* 19 Sep 93

407 If you walk up political steps, you must have an economic hand rail or else you'll fall down.

On transforming the Middle East from a permanent battleground to a common market *ib*

408 Many countries that gained independence failed because they thought that the story of nations is the story of flags. . . [but] it is really the story of people.

ib

409 As we leave a world of enemies, we enter a world of dangers. . . where dialogue is the only option for our world.

On receiving the Nobel Peace Prize *Washington Post* 11 Dec 94

410 The wars we fought. . . we won. . . but we did not win the greatest victory that we aspired to: release from the need to win victories.

ib

Georges Pompidou President of France

411 These talks were more like conception than delivery. And, after all, conception is more pleasurable than delivery.

On concluding Icelandic meeting on possibility of new declaration of Atlantic principles *NY Times* 2 Jun 73

412 Everytime someone shakes my hand, I think they are trying to take my pulse.

To US Secretary of State Henry A Kissinger on rumors of ill health, recalled on Pompidou's death five years later 2 Apr 74

Kazimiera Prunskiene Prime Minister of Lithuania

413 Even the world's darling does not have the monopolistic right to decide the fate of other nations.

On visiting US to protest Soviet reluctance to grant Lithuanian independence *NY Times* 4 May 90

414 Freedom, like a genie that's been let out of the bottle, doesn't necessarily want to listen to the dictates of the person who uncorked the bottle.

ib

Muammar Quaddafi Libyan head of state

415 The evidence against Libya is less than a laughable piece of a fingernail.

On charges that Libyan agents caused the explosion of Pan Am flight 103 over Scotland *USA Today* 29 Nov 91

Yitzhak Rabin Prime Minister of Israel

416 You don't make peace with friends. You make it with very unsavory enemies.

On eve of White House signing of Palestinian-Israeli peace accord *NY Times* 10 Sep 93

417 We have come from Jerusalem, the ancient and eternal capital of the Jewish people. . . from an anguished and grieving land. . . from a people, a home, a family that has not known a single year, not a single month, in which mothers have not wept for their sons.

On signing peace accord 13 Sep 93

418 Let me say to you, the Palestinians. . . in a loud and a clear voice: enough of blood and tears! Enough!

ib

419 You are not part of the national democratic camp. . . . You are not partners in the Zionist enterprise. You are a foreign transplant. . . an errant weed. Sensible Judaism spits you out.

To Israeli settlers who favored violence against Palestine 1 Mar 94

420 I. . . come. . . in the name of the children, who began their lives with great hope and are now names on graves and memorial stones, old pictures in albums, fading clothes in closets.

To US Congress in unprecedented appearance with a former enemy, King Hussein of Jordan *Washington Times* 27 Jul 94

421 The sight you see before you. . . was unthinkable just two years ago. Only poets dreamed of it and to our great pain, soldiers and civilians went to their deaths to make this moment possible.

On returning to the White House with PLO Chair Yasir Arafat to sign an accord transferring their reconciliation into a concrete plan to transfer much of the West Bank to the control of its Arab citizens 29 Sep 95

422 Peace has no borders.
ib

423 What Jewish boy or Jewish government could expect more, to be born in Jerusalem, and to fight the two major wars that decided the fate of Jerusalem.
Interview in 1987 recalled on Rabin's assassination *NY Times* 5 Nov 95

Ronald Reagan 40th US President

424 In your discussions of the nuclear freeze proposals, I urge you to beware the temptation of pride... and the aggressive impulses of an evil empire.
To National Association of Evangelicals, introducing an often quoted reference to "the evil empire" 8 Mar 83

425 Here, death ruled, but... we found that death cannot rule forever... [and] humanity refuses to accept that freedom of the spirit of man can never be extinguished.
At World War II concentration camp Bergen-Belsen 6 May 85

426 There is a Russian saying: *doveryai no proveryai*, trust but verify. How will we know that you'll get rid of your missles as you say you will?
To Premier Mikhail S Gorbachev at Reykjavik summit 11 Oct 86.

427 A few months ago, I told the American people I did not trade arms for hostages. My heart and my best intentions still tell me that is true, but the facts and evidence tell me it is not.
To the nation, admitting that he had knowledge of Iran arms sales 13 Nov 86

428 I cannot recall anything whatsoever about whether I approved an Israeli sales in advance or whether I approved replenishment of Israeli stocks... the simple truth is, I don't remember—period.
Letter to Tower Commission investigating Iran-Contra arms sales *NY Times* 27 Feb 87

429 As personally distasteful as I find secret bank accounts and diverted funds, as the Navy would say, this happened on my watch.
ib 4 Mar 87

430 I reject a potted-plant presidency.
On his capability as president *Time* 10 Aug 87

431 The American people believe that a stranger is a friend they have yet to meet.
On welcoming Premier Mikhail S Gorbachev to the White House 8 Dec 87

432 We don't know where that money came from and we don't know who had it and we don't know where it went.
Reaffirming belief that no laws were broken in Iran-Contra funding *NY Times* 17 Mar 88

433 It is a time when the first breath of freedom stirs the air and the heart beats to the accelerated rhythm of hope, when the accumulated spiritual energies of a long silence yearn to breathe free.
To students at Moscow State University on unprecedented new openess at summit conference *ib* 5 Jun 88

434 [He is a] dictator in designer glasses.
On Sandinistas' Daniel Ortega *Time* 21 Nov 88

435 A triangle of institutions—parts of Congress, the media, and special interest groups—is transforming and placing out of focus our constitutional balance, particularly in the areas of spending and foreign policy.
On an "iron triangle" in government, farewell address on domestic policy 3 Dec 88

436 Washington is a sieve... it was virtually impossible to find out who was doing the leaking and shut them up.
Deposition on the Iran-Contra arms sales *NY Times* 23 Feb 90

437 My average of meeting with people was about 80 a day for eight years.
On inability to recall details *ib*

438 Visitors to this mountaintop will see a great jagged chunk of the Berlin wall, hated symbol of, yes, an evil empire, that spied on and lied to its citizens, denying them their freedom, their bread, even their faith. Well, today, that wall exists only in museums, souvenir collections and the memories of a people no longer oppressed.
At dedication of Reagan Library 4 Nov 91

Mary Robinson President of Ireland

439 The women of Ireland, instead of rocking the cradle, rocked the system.
On winning presidential election *LA Times* 10 Nov 90

Anwar El-Sadat President of Egypt

440 Russians can give you arms but only the United States can give you a solution.
Newsweek 13 Jan 75

441 I am taking off my military uniform. I never expect to wear it again except for military occasions. Tell her that is the answer to her letter.
To Israeli Prime Minister Golda Meir on the signing of peace treaty between Israel and Egypt, quoted by Walter Isaacson *Kissinger* Simon & Schuster 92

Joseph Stalin Soviet Premier

442 Print is the sharpest and the strongest weapon of our party.
Address 19 April 1923, recalled on Stalin's death 5 Mar 53

443 How many divisions does the Pope have?
To Winston S Churchill at Potsdam Conference on Communist takeover of Poland, quoted by Harry S Tru-

man to American Association for Advancement of Science 13 Sep 1948 *ib*

444 If any foreign minister begins to defend to the death a "peace conference," you can be sure his government has already placed its orders for new battleships and airplanes.

ib

445 No greater instrument for counter-revolution and conspiracy can be imagined.

Opposing modern telephone system in the USSR, quoted in Ithiel de Sola Pool ed *The Social Impact of the Telephone* MIT Press 77

446 Lenin left us a state and we turned it to shit.

Quoted by Nikita S Khrushchev *Khrushchev Remembers* Little, Brown 90

447 Death solves all problems. No man, no problems.

Quoted by Robert Conquest's *Stalin* Viking 91

448 Well, that's fine. Let's use it. What's the next item on the agenda?

On being told of US development of the atomic bomb, quoted by James B Reston *Deadline* Random House 91

Levon Ter-Petrosyan President of Armenia

449 The center is dead. The center has committed suicide.

To Russian parliament on 15 former Soviet republics moving toward independence *NY Times* 27 Aug 91

Margaret Thatcher Prime Minister of Britain

450 Whenever the rule of force as distinct from the rule of law is seen to succeed, the world moves a step closer to anarchy.

Address on why Britain defended the Falkland Islands from Argentine take-over 26 May 82

451 We cling not to colonialism but to self-determination.

ib

452 We have ceased to be a nation in retreat.

On victory in the Falklands, a sign of Britain's over-all strength 3 Jul 82

453 It may be the cock that crows but it is the hen who lays the eggs.

On addressing a London inner of businessmen and industrialists *Wall Street Journal* 12 May 87

454 There prevailed. . . what I would call a censorship of fashion.

On prevailing attitude when she entered office that derided anyone who challenged conventional wisdom *ib*

455 It was far deeper than trembling because it mattered more. I knew it was one of the most important days of my life and wondered how it would go.

Recalling first Kremlin confrontation with Mikhail S Gorbachev *Life* Oct 87

456 It's rather like a military campaign. Time spent on reconnaissance is seldom wasted.

ib

457 The adrenalin flows when they come out fighting at me. I stand there and I know: Now come on, Maggie, you are wholly on your own. No one can help you. And I love it.

Reader's Digest Nov 87

458 I think it's a little bit optimistic. It's quite optimistic. It's very optimistic.

On George Bush's shortening by five years of Soviet timetable for reductions of conventional forces *Time* 12 Jun 89

459 Advisers advise, and ministers decide.

To the Commons when pressed to say that advisers should keep their advice private *NY Times* 27 Oct 89

460 Remember, George: this is no time to go wobbly.

To President Bush during Persian Gulf War 8 Mar 91 in what a senior Thatcher aide called "a backbone transplant" *New Yorker* 7 Dec 92; four years after leaving office, when the West failed to strongly support Bosnia, she told friends, "I should be in the rent-a-spine business" *NY Times* 27 Jul 95

461 We were running up the "Down" escalator, and we would have to run a great deal faster if we were ever to get to the top.

On taking office, recalled in her biography *The Downing Street Years* HarperCollins 93

462 Each sentence was my testimony at the bar of History.

On her final address to Commons *ib*

463 Consensus is the negation of leadership.

Reader's Digest Jan 95

Harry S Truman 33rd US President

464 Jesus Christ and General Jackson!

On receiving a call 12 Apr 1945 to come immediately to the White House where he was to learn of President Roosevelt's death, quoted by David McCullough *Truman* Simon & Schuster 92

465 Mrs R told me what had happened. Maybe it will come out all right.

ib

466 It may be the fire destruction prophesied in the Euphrates Valley era, after Noah and his fabulous ark.

On the atomic bomb 25 Jul 45, diary entry released 35 years later by the Truman Library *NY Times* 2 Jun 80

467 I told him to fire away. He did and it is dynamite.

On asking Joseph Stalin for the Soviet agenda at the Potsdam Conference *ib*

468 I have some dynamite, too, which I'm not exploding now.

On not immediately telling Stalin of the atomic bomb and plans for its use *ib*

469 Russia had no program except to take over the free part of Europe, kill as many Germans as possible, and fool the Western Alliance. Britain only wanted to control the Eastern Mediterranean, keep India, oil in Persia, the Suez Canal, and whatever else was floating loose.

ib

470 I felt myself an innocent idealist at one corner of that round table. . . what a show that was! A large number of agreements were reached in spite of the set-up—only to be broken as soon as the unconscionable Russian dictator returned to Moscow. And I liked the little son of a bitch.

ib

471 You must not ask the President of the United States to get down in the gutter with a guttersnipe.

On Senator Joseph R McCarthy charge 20 Feb 50 that there were 105 Communists in the State Department; as an alternative to a presidential response, Truman suggested that a confidential file on McCarthy be leaked to the press, later quoted by John Hersey *Aspects of the Presidency* Ticknor & Fields 80

472 Nobody, not even the President, can approach too close to a skunk, in skunk territory, and expect to get anything out of it except a bad smell.

ib

473 If you think somebody is telling a big lie about you, the only way to answer is with the whole truth.

ib

474 The attack on Korea makes it plain that Communism has passed beyond the use of subversion to conquer independent nations and will now use armed invasion and war.

On North Korean invasion of Republic of Korea 27 Jun 50

475 The only thing you have to worry about is bad luck. I never had bad luck.

On assassination attempt 1 Nov 50

476 I was the only calm one in the house. You see, I've been shot at by experts.

Recalling World War I after assassination attempt, quoted by Margaret Truman in biography of her mother *Bess W Truman* Macmillan 86

477 When I was a little boy I read about a fairy princess, and there she is.

On Princess Elizabeth's first visit to Washington 12 Nov 51

478 Can't somebody bring me a one-handed economist?

On economic adviser Edwin Nourse who favored the expression "on one hand, but on the other," recalled on Nourse's death 7 Apr 74

479 Anything going up there bearing my name will quiver a couple of times, turn belly up and die.

On the position of a Democratic president submitting legislation to a largely Republican Congress, later quoted by Clark M Clifford *Counsel to the President* Random House 91

480 In my opinion eight years as president is enough and sometimes too much for any man to serve in that capacity.

Announcement that he would not seek re-election 29 Mar 52

481 That precedent should continue—not by a Constitutional amendment but by custom based on the honor of the man in the office. Therefore, to re-establish that custom, although I could quibble and say I've only had one term, I am not a candidate and will not accept the nomination for another term. There are probably a million people who could have done the job better than I did it but. . . I always quote an epitaph on a tombstone in a cemetery in Tombstone, Arizona: "Here lies Jack Williams. He done his damndest."

Time 28 Apr 52

482 He'll sit here and he'll say, "Do this! Do That!" and nothing will happen. Poor Ike—it won't be a bit like the Army.

On his successor, General Dwight D Eisenhower, later quoted by Charles Krauthammer *Time* 20 Jun 88

483 The objective is to give the youngsters of this country some idea of what they have in the way of a government and what they have to do to keep it.

On the Truman Library in welcome to Dr Takuo Matsumoto, spokesman for the Japanese Good Will Ambassadors of the World Peace Study Mission 5 May 64

484 Well. . . you know, when you're running a war, the objective is to win it.

On battle and civilian casualties *ib*

485 We're the only country in history who. . . helped to revive the country which had been our enemies. And they weren't our enemies, they just thought they were.

ib

486 Some people simply cannot get it through their heads that the bombs were dropped to save a half million lives on both sides and twice that many on each side from being maimed for life.

Relpy to a Boston University official who wrote Truman regarding use of the atomic bomb, Truman Library archives 23 Sep 63

487 Too many. . . pass judgment on wartime decisions in the luxury of a peacetime environment. You should do your weeping at Pearl Harbor where thousands of American boys are underneath the water [because of] a Japanese sneak attack while we were at peace with Japan.

Written postscript to the letter *ib*

488 I sit here all day trying to persuade people to do the things they ought to have sense enough to do without my persuading them. . . . That's all the powers of the President amount to.

Quoted by Richard E Neustadt's *Presidential Powers and the Modern Presidents* Free Press/Macmillan 90

489 The buck stops here.

Truman's motto displayed on a sign on his desk, seen by columnist William Safire as "especially appropriate for Truman's momentous decisions to drop the first atomic bomb, order US forces to South Korea, and fire General Douglas MacArthur" *Safire's New Political Dictionary* Random House 93

Getulio Vargas President of Brazil

490 To the wrath of my enemies I leave the legacy of my death. I take the sorrow of not being able to give to the humble all that I wished.

Suicide note after 58 generals forced him to resign, news reports 25 Aug 54

Lech Walesa President of Poland

491 Here in Israel, the land of your culture and revival, I ask for your forgiveness. . . . I cannot weigh with a human scale 20 centuries of evil for both our people.

To Israeli Parliament on anti-Semitism in Polish history *NY Times* 21 May 91

492 There's no room for democracy when you are driving a bus. . . where everyone wants to grab the steering wheel. The first tree will finish you off.

On the need for a strong chief executive *Washington Post* 1 Nov 91

493 The thorn has been removed but the wound is still there.

On Russia's admission of guilt in Katyn massacre of 14,500 officers in the 1939 invasion of Poland *London Times* 6 Jun 95

Queen Wilhelmena Queen of the Netherlands

494 When we open our dykes, the water is ten feet deep.

To Wilhelm II who bragged that his guardsmen were seven feet tall, recalled on Wilhelmena's death 28 Nov 62

Harold Wilson Prime Minister of Britain

495 He who rejects change is the architect of decay. The only human institution which rejects progress is the cemetery.

To the Commons on US involvement in Vietnam *NY Times* 5 Jan 66

496 Given a fair wind, we will negotiate our way into the Common Market, head held high, not crawling in. Negotiations? Yes. Unconditional acceptance of whatever terms are offered us? No.

Address in Bristol 20 Mar 67

497 The greatest asset a head of state can have is the ability to get a good night's sleep.

BBC Radio 16 Apr 75

498 If you have ever been dead by lunchtime and even worse by nightfall—well, you know others have been through it before you and you can get a sense of perspective.

The Governance of Britain Harper & Row 77

499 This place is like a tremendous organ; anything you play comes out at the other end.

On 10 Downing Street, quoted by Anthony Sampson *The Changing Anatomy of Britain* Random House 82

Roh Tae Woo President of South Korea

500 [I address] my dear 60-million compatriots.

Broadcast to both North and South Korea on hopes of bringing them closer together *NY Times* 9 Jul 88

Boris N Yeltsin President of Russia

501 It's impossible to combine a hedgehog and a snake.

On merging Bolshevism with economic reform *NY Times* 9 Sep 90

502 I absorbed a lot from the system that is now so sick. I'm in the process of a self-revision.

ib 21 Sep 90

503 A rusty nail is still lodged in my heart.

On personal bitterness against Mikhail S Gorbachev *ib*

504 Great Russia is rising from her knees.

On inauguration as Russia's first freely elected president *International Herald Tribune* 11 Jul 91

505 You may build a throne of bayonets, but you cannot sit on it.

On attempted overthrow of Mikhail S Gorbachev, paraphrasing a remark by William Ralph Inge ABC TV 21 Aug 91

506 The enemies are already like cockroaches in a bottle, trying to eat each other.

On attempts to overthrow Gorbachev/Yeltsin government, news reports 24 Aug 91

507 On a lighter note, shall we now sign a decree suspending the activities of the Russian Communist Party?

NY Times 24 Aug 91

508 Muscovites. . . tens of thousands. . . spent three day in the rain. . . the thing that the coup organizers failed to take into account.

ib 26 Aug 91

509 I trust him. . . much more so than three weeks ago when he was still capable of maneuvering and meandering.

On Mikhail S Gorbachev *ib* 4 Sep 91

510 There were times when Gorbachev thought I was a bit of a corpse.

ib 5 Sep 91

511 The international community and leaders of foreign states have finally overcome the syndrome of vagueness.

On Russia's agreement to cut armaments *ib* 29 Sep 91

512 There will be no more red flag.

Announcing that the Soviet Union would cease to exist at midnight *ib* 18 Dec 91

513 They made a mistake by not shooting me.

Reflecting on "putschists" coup of the previous August to overthrow Gorbachev *Newsweek* 30 Dec 91

514 We have left behind the period when America and Russia looked at each other through gunsights, ready to pull the trigger at any time.

To US Congress 17 Jun 92

515 We are firmly resolved not to lie any more. We are inviting the cooperation of the United States and other nations to investigate these dark pages.

On opening archives of the KGB and Communist Party Central Committee *ib*

516 [Opponents are] a theater of shadows in which the ghosts of the past are giving their farewell performance.

To the British Parliament *London Times* 11 Nov 92

517 The walls of this hall reddened from the endless insults, the hatred and the rudeness, from the filth that flows over at the Congress because of the morbid ambitions of bankrupt politicians.

On barring concessions to Russian Congress *NY Times* 11 Dec 92

518 This treaty... becomes the core of the system of global security guarantees.

On joining President Bush in signing Start II, the second Strategic Arms Reduction Treaty calling for Russia and the US to eliminate by the year 2003 almost three-quarters of their 20,000-odd nuclear warheads *ib* 3 Jan 93

519 For the first time in more than 1,000 years of our history, the choice was made, the choice of a head of state... either go on crawling to the Communist impasse or undertake deep reform to follow the road of progress, which the human race is following.

Address to the Russian people declaring his duty "as a citizen, as a patriot and as a decent man" to assume virtually unlimited power and to order national balloting to decide how and by whom Russia should be governed 21 Mar 93

520 I have a telephone and I will run the country myself.... I am not abandoning the controls.

To reporters covering his departure from Moscow for his first summit with President Clinton *Washington Times* 3 Apr 93

521 Remember that Germany, to get rid of the Communist monster, needed $100 billion.

When asked whether one billion dollars in US aid would be sufficient for Russia *ib*

522 If there is no president, the power will be assumed by the most extremist forces, and the entire world will shudder.

On national referendum on his leadership *ib* 10 Apr 93

523 The current corps of deputies has lost its right to be in control of crucial levers of state power.

On disbanding the legislature and discrediting its attempt to oust him *NY Times* 22 Sep 93

524 They're on the last 100 meters after a 3,000-meter race.

On rebels' hold-out in the parliament building 26 Sep 93

525 Shots are thundering in Russia's capital and blood has been spilled.... Those waving Red flags have once again covered Russia with blood.

Address to the nation as overthrow attempt was brought under control *ib* 5 Oct 93

526 We have all been scorched by the deadly breath of fratricide.

ib 7 Oct 93

527 Someone is always trying to take you by the arm, to suggest something, to make things comfortable, more comfortable, and still more comfortable. A kind of psychological numbness sets in.

The Struggle for Russia Times Books 94

528 Today is the last day of the past.

On withdrawal of Russian troops from Berlin after 50 years military occupation *Washington Post* 1 Sep 94

529 Europe is in danger of plunging into a cold peace.

Address to 52-nation Budapest summit meeting that had hoped to hasten NATO expansion and strengthen Europe's security *NY Times* 6 Dec 94

530 History demonstrates that it is a dangerous illusion to suppose that the destinies of continents and of the world community in general can somehow be managed from one single capital.

Comment regarded as a thinly veiled criticism of what Russia perceives as Washington's emergence as the only global power *ib*

Officials and Other Personages

Diane Abbott Member of Parliament

531 [It is] forests of middle-aged men in dark suits all slightly redfaced from eating and drinking too much... a nightmare of elderly white males.

On being seated as the first black woman member in seven centuries of British Parliament *NY Times* 3 Jun 88

532 "If you look down you can see darkies talking"... that will be the title of my biography.

Quoting a guard conversing with visitors in the gallery *ib*

Elliott Abrams US Assistant Secretary of State for Inter-American Affairs

533 There isn't any way for the people of Nicaragua to find out what's going on in Nicaragua.

On US technical aid to Nicaraguan rebels for a powerful radio station to promote anti-Sandinistan ideas *NY Times* 9 Nov 86

534 I was careful not to ask Colonel North questions I did not need to know the answers to.

On avoiding references to Oliver L North's covert actions in sale of arms *ib* 4 Jun 87

535 I never said I had no idea about most of the things you said I said I had no idea about.

To Special Prosecutor Lawrence E Walsh, news reports 3 and 4 Jun 87

536 They want a cease-fire because the Contras cease fire when they're dead—that's the kind of cease-fire they need.

On sending US troops to Honduras after Nicaraguan invasion *Nightline* ABC TV 16 Mar 88

537 Questions were weapons and answers were shields.

On Congressional hearings as battlegrounds between the executive and legislative branches of government *Undue Process* Free Press 93

538 Walsh had been a neutron bomb kind of lawyer: the neutron bomb that kept the buildings, the factories and the bridges intact, and only killed the people in them.

On Iran-Contra special prosecutor Lawrence E Walsh's vigor in defending the government despite the cost to persons who testified *ib*

539 He would tell you he was defending the institution or the Constitution... and the mere people he ran up against could not be permitted to get in the way. Crunch!

ib

Dean Acheson US Secretary of State

540 Whatever the outcome of the appeal, I do not intend to turn my back on Alger Hiss.

On accusations that a former aide had been a Communist spy and had perjured himself in investigations of the charge *NY Times* 25 Jan 50

541 These principles... were stated for us a very long time ago... on the Mount of Olives.

ib

542 The attack upon Korea makes it plain beyond all doubt that Communism has passed beyond the use of subversion to conquer independent nations.

Statement drafted for President Truman 25 Jun 50 at outset of Korean conflict, quoted by Gaddis Smith *The American Secretaries of State and Their Diplomacy* Vol XVI Cooper Square 72

543 The wise laborer will receive them with Joy and cherish them against the evil hours when no man may smile.

On the "humorous, sometimes comic, even ridiculous incidents" in diplomacy in *Sketches from Life* Harper 61

544 Don't give it a thought, me lad. If those blokes don't want yer, there's plenty as does.

On his thoughts when Republican congressmen urged his replacement *ib*

545 The *Garde Républicaine's* bugles and drums gave us flourishes... horsehair plumed helmets, breastplates, white knee breeches, and high black boots, flashed its sabers in salute. One missed a rollicking opening chorus by Victor Hugo.

On the Conference of Foreign Minister at the Palais Rose in Paris *ib*

546 All I can say to Mr Bevan is written in an English book, *The Book of Common Prayer:* "The remembrance of our sins is grievous unto us; the burden of them is intolerable."

On British Foreign Minister Ernest Bevan who had advocated forgiveness of actions before reconcilation was asked *ib*

547 He still had his glorious sense of words drawn from the special reservoir from which Lincoln also drew, fed by Shakespeare and those Tudor critics who wrote the first *Prayer Book of Edward VI* and their Jacobean successors who translated the Bible.

On Winston S Churchill in old age *ib*

548 "The conference at the summit"... begun as an attractive catch-phrase to mean a meeting of four heads of government, gradually seduced him, and countless others, into a transcendentalism, by which such a meeting took on spiritual and superhuman potentialities.

On Churchill becoming "entrapped by the illusion of his own words" *ib*

549 [A summit] would be held in the atmosphere of a political *Parnassus,* washed clean of propaganda and earthly purposefulness, where those godlike creatures could pursue, and perhaps attain goals beyond the reach of these same beings in their daily human environment.

ib

550 He smiled with the spontaneity of a mechnical tiger.

On Soviet Foreign Minister V M Molotov *ib*

551 Konrad Adenauer tasted the rich wine of wide popular acclaim.

On the German Chancellor's 1949 election as the first *Bundeskanzler* of the new Federal Republic of Germany *ib*

552 Great Britain has lost an empire and has not yet found a role.

At West Point 5 Dec 72, prompting Prime Minister Harold Wilson to reply, "Mr Acheson is a distinguished figure who has lost a State Department and not yet found himself a role" *NY Times* 23 Nov 69

553 The most important aspect of the relationship between the president and the secretary of state is that they both understand who is president.

Quoted by Secretary of State Dean Rusk NBC TV 26 Mar 69

554 I felt like a bartender announcing that the last drink before closing time would be cambric tea.

On his role as the final speaker at a demonstrative meeting of the National Council of Soviet-American Friendship *Present at the Creation* Norton 69

555 I had shown my colors. Those who took their red straight, without a chaser of white and blue, were not mollified.

On criticism of Soviets *ib*

556 The enormity of the task... only slowly revealed itself... as just a bit less formidable than that described in the first chapter of Genesis.

On postwar restructuring *ib*

557 Our name for problems is significant. We call them headaches. You take a powder and they are gone.

On a US tendency for passive involvement in foreign affairs, quoted by David S McLellan *Dean Acheson: The State Dept Years* Dodd, Mead 76

558 You can't argue with a river, it is going to flow. You can dam it up... put it to useful purposes... deflect it, but you can't argue with it.

On the fruitlessness of keeping Russians from fishing in waters that should be off-limits *ib*

559 From Vienna by way of Dakar we fly to Recife... and then to Rio... [and] after Rio knocks itself and us out, we go on to São-Paulo and do it all over again. The remains are then returned to Washington for interment in the State Department.

To Archibald MacLeish 21 Jun 52 David S McLellan and David C Acheson ed *Among Friends: Personal Letters of Dean Acheson* Dodd, Mead 80

560 Bright, quick, amusing and intelligent... this is quite a girl, as the Dutch will find out, if she has a chance to show them.

To Justice Felix Frankfurter after meeting Crown Princess Beatrix of the Netherlands 19 May 62 *ib*

561 Our weakness was Papandreou's weakness, a garrulous, senile windbag without power of decision or resolution.

On Greek Premier George Papandreou during Greek-Turkish dispute over Cyprus *ib* 7 Dec 64

562 Formosa is a subject which seems to draw out the boys like a red-haired girl on the beach. It appears that what you want most is what you ain't got.

On Free China's withdrawal to Formosa *ib*

563 Washington is like a self-sealing tank on military aircraft. When a bullet passes through, it closes up.

On Averill Harriman's move from Marshall Plan Administrator to National Security Director, quoted by Walter Isaacson and Evan Thomas *The Wise Men* Simon & Schuster 86

564 [It was] homage to plain dumb luck.

On US blockage of Soviet ships off Cuba *ib*

565 The Iraq is really not whacky/ Toady, perhaps, even tacky/ When they gave *him* the word/ He gave *us* the bird/ And joined with the Arabs, by cracky!

Limerick written during a dull meeting of Foreign Ministers *ib*

566 Charm never made a rooster.

On attempts to maintain peace by good intentions as opposed to poor military organization, quoted by James B Reston *Deadline* Random House 91

567 [I like] lopping off the heads of tall poppies.

On overcoming obstacles through careful research and definition *ib*

568 It is just as full of propaganda as a dog is full of fleas. In fact, I say it's all fleas and no dog.

On Russian Foreign Minister Andre Vishinsky's proposal that the US should withdraw from postwar Europe *ib*

569 With a nation, as with a boxer, one of the greatest assurances of safety is to add reach to power.

On American bases in Europe *ib*

570 He struck me as looking like a pear on top of two toothpicks.

Remembering his call on Charles de Gaulle 22 Oct 62 during the Cuban missile crisis, quoted by Douglas Brinkley *Dean Acheson: The Cold War Years 1953–71* Yale 92

571 The Canadians seem to be held together with string and safety pins.

ib

572 The damned cuss has brains and has thought a lot.

On Henry A Kissinger as national security adviser *ib*

573 [It was like] finding oneself pregnant and trying to fall in love as quickly as possible.

On the weekend of Richard M Nixon's inauguration *ib*

574 If the best minds in the world had set out to find us the worst possible location in the world to fight this damnable war, politically and militarily, the unanimous choice would have been Korea.

On the Korean War, quoted by Joseph Goulden *Korea* Times Books 82

575 It was not necessary to call in Price Waterhouse to discover that 1,500 Cubans weren't as good as 250,000 Cubans.

To President Kennedy after the ill-fated Bay of Pigs invasion of Cuba, quoted by Evan Thomas *NY Times* 8 Nov 92 reviewing Douglas Brinkley's book *op cit*

576 What in the name of God are 500,000 men doing out there? Chasing girls?

In White House meeting on hearing Joint Chief of Staff Earle Wheeler concede that the US could not win a "classic military victory" in Vietnam *ib*

Lord Addington (Dominic Bryce Hobard) House of Lords

577 It's a great privilege if you don't mind living off boiled rice.

On succeeding to the peerage at age 19 *Wall Street Journal* 9 Nov 93

Farouk Al-Sharaa Foreign Minister of Syria

578 If the entire world were to adopt such claims, it would have to encourage all Christians to emigrate to the Vatican and all Muslims to emigrate to Holy Mecca.

On Israel's statements on the migration of Jews *NY Times* 1 Nov 91

Aldrich H Ames CIA agent

579 It was as if neon lights and searchlights lit up all over the Kremlin, shone all the way across the Atlantic ocean, saying, "There is a penetration."

On setting off "bells and whistles" in giving Russia the names of persons spying for the US *NY Times* 28 Jul 94

580 [I was only] leveling the playing field.

On his belief that he was helping to end the Cold War *USA Today* 29 Jul 94

Meir Amit head of Mossad, Israel's foreign intelligence agency

581 The idea. . . was to create an impression of interminable search, of changing direction, of complexity and infinity, which is what intelligence gathering is all about.

On Israeli agents *International Herald Tribune* 27 Aug 85

Duane Andrews Congressional aide

582 [It's like] walking into a room full of china all on the floor—with people complaining that we were going to break up their rice bowl.

On combining British and US intelligence operations *London Times* 26 Jul 91

T Coleman Andrews Director, Internal Revenue Service

583 There is something wrong with any law that causes that many people to have to take a whole day off from their jobs to find out how to comply.

On help sought by 12-million taxpayers, news reports of 24 Oct 55

Anon

584 [He has] other cats to whip.

French diplomat on Ayatollah Ruhollah Khomeini's priorities beyond concern for public opinions in the West *NY Times* 16 Feb 89

585 All smoke and no steel.

A French official's comment on President Clinton's "Partnership for Peace" plan to hold off a definitive decision on whether former Soviet satellite countries should be allowed to Join NATO *ib* 9 Jan 94

586 If you want to know about scum, you have to recruit scum.

On US spy operations *Newsweek* 10 Apr 95

Georgi Arbatov Director, Moscow Institute for Study of USA and Canada

587 We are going to do something terrible to you—we are going to deprive you of an enemy.

On softening of Soviet policies *Time* 23 May 88

Jose Antonio Arbesu unofficial Cuban representative to the US

588 I am a non-person. I am the man who never was.

On his role in representing a government not recognized in Washington *NY Times* 5 Dec 90

Moshe Arens Israeli Ambassador to US

589 We have wiped PLO from the scene. Don't you Americans now pick the PLO up, dust it off, and give it artificial respiration.

On the Palestine Liberation Organization (PLO), quoted by Secretary of State George P Shultz *Turmoil and Triumph* Scribner 93

Lee Aspin Chair, US House of Representatives Armed Services Committee 1986–93, Secretary of Defense 93–94

590 Only the United States would fight a major war while figuring out how to take an ax to its military.

As chair of House Armed Services Committee on finalizing budget cuts in spite of Persian Gulf War *Newsweek* 18 Mar 91

591 Thin gruel became red meat.

On the US Navy's attempt to attribute an explosion aboard the battleship Iowa to a jealous homosexual lover, quoted by Randy Shilts *Conduct Unbecoming* St Martin's 93

592 Today we are here to observe another point of passage, which is the end of the "Star Wars" era. . . sealed by the collapse of the Soviet Union.

On relegation of weapons in space to small-scale research after ten years and nearly $30 billion as President Reagan's vision of a shield against nuclear attack *NY Times* 14 May 93

Tariq Aziz Foreign Minister of Iraq

593 The Iranian clergy are like the dinosaur coming up from the basement of history. They will never stop until they are wiped out.

On Persian Gulf War with religiously-dominated Iran *NY Times* 4 Oct 87

Bruce Babbitt US Secretary of the Interior

594 There is room in the west for wolves.

To House of Representatives Natural Resources Committee on controversial restoraton of wild life *Washington Times* 27 Jan 95

James A Baker III US Secretary of State

595 Sometimes you move publicly, sometimes privately. Sometimes quietly, sometimes at the top of your voice. And sometimes an active policy is best advanced by doing nothing until the right time—or never.

On statesmanship *Time* 19 Mar 90

596 The Iraqi invasion of Kuwait is one of the defining moments of a new era.

NY Times 23 Sep 90

597 [The] only thing that is for sure is that you should have gone out and bought some Rand McNally stock sometime ago.

On redrawing the map of Russia *ib* 22 Dec 91

598 Now your limousine is yellow and your driver speaks Farsi.

On leaving office, address to Washington's Alfalfa Club 30 Jan 93 *ib* 25 Apr 93

George W Ball US Under Secretary of State

599 [It was] like giving the keys of the world's largest liquor store to a confirmed alcoholic.

On oil profiteering that permitted arms-buying spree by Mohammed Reza Pahlavi, last shah of Iran, quoted by William Shawcross *The Shah's Last Ride* Simon & Schuster 88

600 Once on the tiger's back, we cannot be sure of picking the place to dismount.

To Secretary of Defense Robert S McNamara expressing skepticism on escalation of Vietnam War 5 Oct 64 a document that became known as "the tiger's back memo," quoted by Deborah Shapley *Promise and Power* Little, Brown 93

601 Never to be bored, never to be frustrated, never to be alone.

On what John F Kennedy wanted from the presidency, quoted by Richard Reeves *President Kennedy* Simon & Schuster 93

Le Van Bang Vietnam diplomat

602 Vietnam is not a war, but a country.

On renewing official ties to the US *Washington Post* 3 Oct 95

Bernard M Baruch US Adviser to UN Atomic Energy Commission

603 Let us not be deceived—we are today in the midst of a cold war.

To South Carolina legislature 16 Apr 1947, using an expression suggested to him by editor Herbert Bayard Swope, recalled on Baruch's death 20 Jun 65

604 The cold war is getting warmer.

To a Senate committee 1948 *ib*

Oded Ben-Ami spokesman for Israeli Prime Minister

605 It was a handshake with someone who just a moment ago was the devil in person.

On peace accord between Palestine and Israel *Time* 27 Sep 93

William J Bennett US Secretary of Education

606 After 10 AM, the average IQ [of a cabinet officer] drops a point every half an hour; by nightfall it is off the charts.

Time 19 Sep 88

Aneurin Bevan Member of Parliament and Minister

607 This island is almost made of coal and surrounded by fish; only an organizing genius could produce a shortage of both at the same time.

Statement as Minister of Health 18 May 45 recalled on Bevan's death 6 Jul 60

608 The ordinary man has been spending his life. . . for the last couple of generations. . . trying to get his hands on the levers of big policy, and trying to find out where it is, and how it was that his life was shaped for him by somebody else.

Quoted by Anthony Sampson *Anatomy of Britain* Hodder & Stoughton 62

Ernest Bevin British Foreign Minister

609 My [foreign] policy is to be able to take a ticket at Victoria Station and go anywhere I damn well please.

Spectator 20 Apr 51

610 If 'e 'adn't been so stupid, you wouldn't have been strong enough to come to our rescue in the war, and after it with Marshall aid.

On George III, quoted by US Secretary of State Dean Acheson *Sketches from Life* Harper 61

611 The trouble with my people is their poverty of desire.

Recalled in article on British values *NY Times* 9 Oct 85

Georges Bidault Prime Minister of France

612 I have plumbed the depth of human cowardice and I realized that there is only one way to be right and that is to be in power.

Statement in 1962 shortly before he was exiled for attempting to overthrow the de Gaulle presidency, recalled on Bidault's death 26 Jan 83

613 If we had not been dealing with the devil in person, we could have saved Algeria.

On Charles de Gaulle *ib*

614 Africa is destined to anarchy. It is turning into 36 Haitis with 36 Duvaliers, full of Cadillacs, beggars and snarling dogs.

ib

Frances Biddle US Attorney General

615 The constitution has never greatly bothered any wartime president.

In Brief Authority Doubleday 62

Alan Blinder Vice Chair, Federal Reserve Board

616 If you try to give an on-the-one-hand-or-the-other-hand answer, only one of the hands tends to get quoted.

On economic ambiguities *Wall Street Journal* 23 Jun 95

Charles E Bohlen US Ambassador to Soviet Union

617 A non-Communist premier with Communist ministers would be like a woman tryng to stay half pregnant.

On Winston S Churchill's suggestion that the West share spheres of influence with Joseph Stalin in the postwar development of the Balkans, quoted by Walter Isaacson and Evan Thomas *The Wise Men* Simon & Schuster 86

618 There are two ways you can tell when a man is lying. . . when he says he can drink champagne all night and not get drunk. . . [and] when he says he understands Russians.

Quoted by Serge Schmemann *NY Times* 26 Dec 93 reviewing Daniel Yergin and Thane Gustafson's *Russia 2010* Random House 93

Betty Boothroyd Speaker of the House of Commons

619 They want to change the flow of the Thames.

On new members in Parliament *NY Times* 27 Sep 93

620 I could understand it if I were in a soap opera. Maybe I am.

On becoming internationally known through television *ib*

621 [It is] a cross between train spotting and bungee jumping.

On her role as Speaker *Washington Post* 29 Sep 93

622 I have to smash them. . . [but] you've always got to have the one-liner. It takes the sting out when the tension builds up.

ib

623 We shall make use of the richness of the English language in select elegant phrases. . . without causing offence.

In severe rebuke to Prime Minister John Major for calling Tony Blair "a dimwit" and another for use of what was termed "an unprintable American epithet" *London Times* 9 Feb 95

Virginia Bottomley British Secretary of State

624 Women do not have the right to have a child. The child has a right to a suitable home.

On 58-year-old woman slated to become the world's oldest mother of twins through implanted eggs *London Times* 28 Dec 93

Lord Boyd-Carpenter (John Archibald Boyd-Carpenter) Member of Parliament

625 There is a feeling in the Lords that we must not funk the issue.

On establishing a law that a share in pensions should be awarded wives divorced in middle age *London Times* 22 Feb 95

Willy Brandt Chancellor of West Germany

626 From the bottom of the abyss of German history, under the burden of millions of victims of murder, I did what human beings do when speech fails them.

On an unplanned act of placing a wreath at a Warsaw holocaust memorial *Newsweek* 19 Oct 92

Kingman Brewster US Ambassador to Great Britain

627 It is satisfying for the descendant of a dissident refugee from Elizabeth I to present his credentials to Elizabeth II.

The Observer London 3 Jul 77

628 We all live in a televised goldfish bowl.

Lecture, St George's Chapel, Windsor 5 May 78

629 I'm very curious to know what the hell they're saying on the phone, but I'd be more worried if they weren't talking.

On direct contact between heads of state *The Observer* London 10 Jun 79

Styles Bridges US Senator

630 China asked for a sword, and we gave her a dull paring knife.

On China's collapse to Communism, quoted by David Halberstam *The Fifties* Villard 93

Richard H Bryan US Senator

631 Being chairman of the Senate Ethics Committee is like jumping off a cliff. The thrill is very short.

On charges of sexual misconduct against Senator Bob Packwood NPR 2 Nov 93

John Bryant US Congressman

632 After midnight, vampire-like, the communications bill rises each evening to be debated until dawn, when again we return to the regular order on the floor.

On accusing Republicans of staging "a nocturnal assault on consumers" to delay action on opening telephone and cable companies to free-wheeling competition *NY Times* 4 Aug 95

633 These issues are too important to be debated when America is sound asleep.

ib

Anne McGill Burford environmentalist

634 It's a nothingburger.

On withdrawing her nomination to head the National Advisory Committee on Oceans and Atmosphere *NY Times* 19 Aug 84

RA Butler Chancellor of the Exchequer

635 It takes two to make love and two partners to make trade agreements work.

Recalled on Butler's death 9 Mar 82

636 Unrequited trade or unrequited exports pay no better than unrequited love.

ib

Harold Caccia British Foreign Secretary

637 If you are to stand up for your Government you must be able to stand up to your Government.

Quoted by Anthony Sampson *The Anatomy of Britain* Hodder and Stoughton 62

Hattie Caraway US Senator

638 I haven't the heart to take a minute from the men. The poor dears love it so.

On why she never made a speech during 13 years as the first woman in the US Senate, 1931–44, recalled on Caraway's death 21 Dec 50; Winston S Churchill called her "the sitting hen," a UPI reporter and novelist spoke of her as the "the quiet grandmother, who won nothing, lost nothing and did nothing" *Washington Post* 31 Dec 50

William J Casey Director, Central Intelligence Agency

639 The ultimate covert operation.

On Iran-contra arms sales *US News & World Report* 20 Jul 87

640 If you have to write everything down, you don't belong in this business.

Ordering Oliver L North to stop taking notes on establishing clandestine bank accounts *Time* 28 Oct 91

Henry Catto US Chief of Protocol

641 Like being the captain of a mine-sweeper, if you do your job well, nobody notices. If you don't, there's a hell of an explosion.

Washington Post 22 Mar 88

Charles Prince of Wales

642 Quite awe-inspring to process slowly into the Chamber and make the obeisances and take the oath to the accompanying pregnant silence and occasional baronial cough or ducal splutter.

Diary entry 11 Feb 69 on being formally introduced to the House of Lords, quoted by Jonathan Dimbleby *The Prince of Wales* Morrow 94

643 I longed to blow up every glistening chrome and plastic symbol of a nation's materialism and conceit.

Diary entry on viewing 23 national pavilions at Japan's Expo '70 in Tokyo *ib* 11 Apr 70

644 Tears poured out of the corners of his bloodhound eyes.

On former Prime Minister Harold Macmillan seized with hay fever at a formal dinner *ib* 11 Nov 70

645 Peace o'er came him and he settled down to tell me in his inimitable and ponderous way how much he had enjoyed working for Mummy as PM.

ib

646 Endless African delegations swept down the aisle, rustling like a pile of stationery.

On Charles de Gaulle's memorial service at Notre Dame *ib*

Warren Christopher US Secretary of State

647 I wish the meeting had been as good as the lunch.

On beginning talks in Beijing with China's Prime Minister *NY Times* 13 Mar 94

648 Sometimes you have to learn how to give the right answer to the wrong question.

On Syrian President Hafez Assad's complaint that he had been put off by a hostile question in a news conference shared with President Clinton *US News & World Report* 19 Dec 94

Galeazzo Ciano Italian Foreign Minister

649 Victory finds a hundred fathers but defeat is an orphan.

Diary entry quoted from a 1951 film *The Desert Fox*, believed to have inspired President Kennedy's similar comment on the abortive 1961 invasion of Cuba, *NY Times* 1 Apr 90

Henry Cisneros US Secretary of Housing and Urban Development

650 [Our cities are] like piles of dry wood with red-hot coals underneath.

On the possibility of race riots *US News & World Report* 19 Apr 93

651 We have to be honest, we have to be truthful and speak to the one dirty secret in American life, and that is racism.

ib

Alan Clark British Minister of Trade

652 Faster than I can digest them, great wedges of documentation are whumped into my "In" tray.

On becoming Parliamentary Under-Secretary of State, Department of Employment *Mrs Thatcher's Minister* Farrar Straus Giroux 93

653 No time even to pee—always a favorite ploy of civil servants who are known to have fiber-glass bladders.

At a conference in Budapest 17 Oct 86 as Minister of Trade *ib*

654 [They are] auditioning for the All England Triteness Award.

On fellow guests at Prince Charles' country home *ib*

655 He's driving in from Heathrow, just back from some pointless and diverting voyage, when he should be tirelessly cigaretting at the very center of things.

On the absence of a key colleague during an attempt to unseat the Prime Minister *ib*

William S Cohen US Senator

656 You've slipped the surly bonds of public service.

Commending Donald T Regan for resigning as President Reagan's Chief of Staff *NY Times* 31 Jul 87

Constantine King of the Hellenes

657 It is the nature of my country that all Greeks are homesick.

On being stripped by Prime Minister Andreas Papadreou of passport, citizenship and property rights *London Times* 15 Apr 94

658 You can change your name but you cannot acquire one, by law. I have no surname. I can only be what I am.

ib

Richard G Darman US Budget Director

659 "Corpocracy"—large-scale corporate America's tendency to be like the government bureaucracy.

NY Times 9 Nov 86

660 I am now celebrating the 20th anniversary of the first request for my resignation. I look forward to many more.

To the White House press room, quoted by Brian Kelly *Adventures in Porkland* Villard 92

Moshe Dayan Israeli Foreign Minister

661 Whenever you accept our views, we shall be in full agreement with you.

To US Secretary of State Cyrus Vance during Arab-Israeli negotiations *London Observer* 14 Aug 77

Maurice Couve de Murville French Foreign Minister

662 The weak who know how to play on their weakness, are strong. This is the secret of women and of the developing countries.

London Observer 24 Jan 65

Bernadette Devlin Member of Parliament

663 It wasn't long before people discovered the final horrors of letting an urchin into Parliament.

On becoming at 21 the youngest woman to serve in Parliament since the 18th century *The Price of My Soul* Knopf 69

664 *The Price of My Soul* refers not to the price for which I would be prepared to sell out, but rather to the price we all must pay in life to preserve our own integrity. To gain that which is worth having, it may be necessary to lose everything.

On her autobiography news summaries 31 Dec 69

Carlo Ripa di Meana European Commissioner for Italy

665 Italy represents a laboratory where you can see what happens in a total absence of rules.

Wall Street Journal 20 Nov 88

Everett M Dirksen US Senator

666 The whole bosom of God's earth was ruptured by a man-made contrivance we call a nuclear weapon.

Senate address credited with assuring passage of the Limited Test Ban Treaty 10 Sep 63

Anatoly Dobrynin Soviet Ambassador to US

667 Deliberate use of an ambassador by his own government to mislead an American administration remained a moral shock to me for years to come and left me more cautious and critical of the information I received from Moscow.

On meetings with President Kennedy without knowledge of his country's build-up of missiles in Cuba *In Confidence* Times Books 95

668 Nixon's last friend.

On Soviet premier Leonid Brezhnev's behind-the-scenes backing of President Nixon during the Watergate crisis *ib*

Christopher J Dodd US Senator

669 Time is the 101st Senator. . . the ally of the people who want to do nothing.

On difficulty of passing President Clinton's health program when legislators were longing for vacation *NY Times* 26 Aug 94

670 Fewer people can stop more.

ib

Lewis Douglas US Ambassador to Britain

671 In the darkness of the night, each of the great ships would quietly slip into the sheltering harbors of the Clyde or New York.

On the decommissioning of the *Queen Mary* after gallant wartime service in the years she did not serve as a passenger liner *NY Times* 30 Oct 68

672 Within less than 72 hours, in the grayness of dawn or the blackness of midnight, unheralded and unsung, it would vanish into the vast spaces of the Atlantic, to run the gauntlet of the hostile German wolf-packs awaiting them.

ib

Hugh Dryden Director, National Aeronautical Space Admistration

673 [We were like] a piano player who didn't know what was going on upstairs.

On spy flights over Russia kept secret from NASA, the State Department and the Central Intelligence Agency quoted by Peter Grose *Gentleman Spy* Houghton Mifflin 94

John Foster Dulles US Secretary of State

674 The Soviets sought not a place in the sun, but the sun itself. Their objective was the world. They would not tolerate compromise on goals, only on tactics.

Quoted by Peter Grose *Gentleman Spy* Houghton Mifflin 94

Daniel Ellsberg military analyst

675 To see the conflict and our part in it as a tragedy without villains, war crimes without criminals, lies without liars, espouses and promulgates a view of process, roles and motives that is not only grossly mistaken but underwrites deceits that have served a succession of presidents.

On "the Pentagon papers," 40 volumes of classified reports that he made available to the media *Time* 28 Jun 71

Daniel J Evans US Senator

676 [It is] more than a red herring: I'd call it a crimson whale.

On Senator Jesse Helms' opposition to destruction of nuclear warheads *NY Times* 27 Jan 88

James Exon US Senator

677 I want to keep the information superhighway from resembling a red-light district.

On sponsoring a bill to prohibit obscene material on computer networks *Washington Post* 24 Mar 95

Lauch Faircloth US Senator

678 It was like eating ice cream with knitting needles to get something out of the White House and now it's worse than skinning a hippopotamus with a letter-opener.

On the Clintons involvement in Whitewater land sales NPR 26 Oct 95

679 It was like teaching a kangaroo to do the limbo.

NY Times 11 Feb 96

Guy Ferdinand Haitian Vice Counsel, Washington

680 He was a tree. People would come to the tree and take a piece of fruit.

On Haitian freedom fighter Wilson Desir *NY Times* 15 Sep 95

Hamilton Fish Jr US Congressman

681 Never put anybody on hold.

On telephone contact with constituents *US News & World Report* 9 Jan 95

Gerald R Ford US Congressman, 1949–73, US President 73–77

682 An impeachable offense is whatever a majority of the House of Representatives considers it to be at a given moment in history.

On leading the last of three unsuccessful attempts to impeach Supreme Court Justice William O Douglas, news reports 15 Apr 70

Gary E Foster Deputy Director for Planning and Coordination, Central Intelligence Agency

683 They tended to pour a little gas on every pilot light.

On negative concerns of staff during confirmation hearings for newly appointed director Robert M Gates, *NY Times* 12 Nov 91

Anthony Frank US Postmaster General

684 We make a house call on every home and every business six days a week... for 29 cents. Plumbers charge 58 bucks.

On delivering the mail *Time* 4 Mar 91

685 This is the biggest management challenge in the US.

On why he aspired to be Postmaster General *ib*

686 When I see a divorce, I see two postal deliveries instead of one.

On rising costs *Fortune* 10 Feb 92

Felix Frankfurter Associate Justice, US Supreme Court

687 The difference is... about the same as between French cooking and hardtack.

On Secretary of State Dean Acheson's fear that he would "go stale" on returning to private life *NY Times* 18 Jan 59

Oliver Franks British Ambassador to US

688 Dean began to do what he called "unachieving" the agreement.

On Secretary of State Dean Acheson's reaction to President Truman's promise that the US would not use the atomic bomb without consulting Britain, quoted by James B Reston *Deadline* Random House 91

John E Frohnmeyere Chair, National Endowment for the Arts

689 The eclipse of the soul will soon pass and with it the lunacy that sees artists as enemies and ideas as demons.

On resigning after fight over Congressional funding of controversial art *Washington Post* 22 Feb 91

690 Politicians demand that the only art that be funded is that which will not offend a mainstream person.

Newsweek 16 Mar 92

691 The 1st Amendment protects the speakers, not the listeners.

ib

J William Fulbright US Senator

692 Fearful and hostile behavior is not rational but neither is it uncommon, either to individuals or to nations, including our own.

On "arrogance of power" in American policy on Vietnam *New Yorker* 6 Mar 95

John Kenneth Galbraith economist and diplomat

693 I am reminded of a courtesan whose conquests have made her the cynosure of all men and the envy of all women and who at any critical moment in the conversation insists on the absolute importance of chastity.

On congratulating Treasury Secretary Douglas Dillon on his successful economic policy despite Dillon's tendency "to be so bent on your discredit that you plan for it," quoted by Arthur M Schlesinger Jr *A Thousand Days* Houghton Mifflin 65

694 They were unloaded in all the secrecy that would attend mass sodomy on the BMT at rush hour.

On a US carrier's delivery of a dozen supersonic jets for Karachi *American Heritage* Oct 69

695 My carefully coined phrase "the conventional wisdom" [referred to] the force that attempted to justify the disparity in well-being.

A Journey Through Economic Time Houghton Mifflin 94

John W Gardner US Secretary of Health, Education, and Welfare

696 We are all faced with a series of great opportunities—brilliantly disguised as insoluble problems.

On his role in the cabinet *Reader's Digest* Mar 66

697 We get richer and richer in filthier and filthier communities until we reach a final state of affluent misery—crocus on a garbage heap.

NY Times 9 Oct 69

Richard A Gephardt US Congress Minority Leader

698 With resignation but with resolve, I hereby end 40 years of Democratic control of this House.

On relinquishing gavel to Speaker Newton L Gingrich after Republican electoral victory *Washington Post* 5 Jan 95

Gennadi Gerasimov Spokesman, Russian Foreign Ministry

699 We buried the Cold War at the bottom of the Mediterranean Sea.

On Bush-Gorbachev meeting aboard ships off Malta 2 and 3 Dec 89, quoted by Michael R Beschloss and Strobe Talbot *At the Highest Levels* Little, Brown 93

German Unification Treaty

700 Only peace will emanate from German soil.

Stipulation of treaty that also promised limitation of arms and maintenance of present boundaries in a united Germany from which the Allied powers withdrew after 45 years of occupation *NY Times* 13 Sep 90

Newton L ("Newt") Gingrich
Speaker, US House of Representatives

701 The. . . purpose [of the "Contract With America"] has been to show that change is possible. . . [and that] even in Washington you can do what you say you're going to do.

Address to the nation on the work of the Republican majority *Washington Post* 5 Apr 95

702 No civilization can survive with 12-year-olds having babies. . . 15-year-olds killing each other. . . 17-year-olds dying of AIDS. . . 18-year-olds getting diplomas they can't read.

On "tragedies that have grown out of the current welfare state" *ib*

703 We must restore freedom by ending bureaucratic micromanagement here in Washington.

ib

704 The congressional voting card is the most expensive credit card in the world.

On two generations piling up trillions for future citizens to pay *ib*

705 It was once an American tradition to pay off the mortgage and leave the children the farm. Now we seem to be selling the farm and leaving our children the mortgage.

ib

706 I'm a hawk, but I'm a cheap hawk.

On spending less on national defense *ib*

707 This is not about green eyeshades and accounting; this is about forcing the scale of change necessary for America to be successful in the 21st century.

On balancing the national budget *NY Times* 11 Apr 95

708 Like three-dimensional chess. . . we're engaged in three or four revolutions at once.

On promoting a Republican "budget of hope" as opposed to a Democratic "budget of despair" in 1979, his first year on Capitol Hill *ib*

Françoise Giroud French Secretary of State for Women's Affairs

709 It is vital to understand that the question of women is not a matter of brassieres and dishwashing.

On accepting appointment to office *NY Times* 17 Jul 74

710 [A woman has the] right. . . not to become an ersatz for men.

Encyclopedia Britanniaca 75

711 I reject the term of equality between man and woman, when it claims to ignore biology.

ib

Arthur J Goldberg US Secretary of Labor

712 If the arts are to flourish, they must be relieved of total dependence upon the market place.

On settling a strike that threatened to shut down the Metropolitan Opera, quoted by Arthur M Schlesinger Jr *A Thousand Days* Houghton Mifflin 65

General Andrew Goodpaster
Eisenhower White House Military Aide

713 The President isn't in the business of using scapegoats.

Rejecting Allen Dulles' offer to resign as CIA Director to save embarrassment after the 1960 downing of a US spy plane was over Russia, quoted by Peter Grose *Gentleman Spy* Houghton Mifflin 94

Albert Gore Jr US Vice President

714 If we allow the information superhighway to bypass the less fortunate sectors of our society—even for an interim period—we will find that the information rich will get richer while the information poor get poorer with no guarantee that everyone will be on the network at some future date.

To National Press Club 21 Dec 93, borrowing the term "information superhighway" from his father, the Senator who spearheaded the Interstate Highway System *Wall Street Journal* 1 Feb 94

715 I'm not too proud to go to funerals.

Disputing "an apocryphal" that he was not fulfilling a customary role of less active Vice Presidents *NY Times* 19 Feb 95

Alan Greenspan Chair, Federal Reserve Board

716 The buck starts here.

Sign on his desk that was contrasted to Presidents Truman and Reagan's "The buck stops here," quoted by Bob Woodward *The Agenda* Simon & Schuster 94

717 The gut-feel of the 55-year old trader is more important than the mathematical elegance of the 25-year old genius.

On how the experience and wisdom of Barings executives in London might have saved the fall brought on by a young English trader in Singapore *NY Times* 6 Mar 95

718 Monetary policy never ends. It's like the luggage carousel in the airports.

To US Senate Banking Committee *Wall Street Journal* 23 Jun 95

719 I worry incessantly that I might be too clear.

On the might-and-might-not possibility of the Federal Reserve lowering interest rates *NY Times* 25 Jun 95

720 The color is still the same. The greenback will still be green.

On anti-counterfeiting imprints that do not change the appearance of currency *Washington Post* 28 Sep 95

Andrei A Gromyko Soviet Foreign Minister

721 [Whether Mr or Mrs or Miss So and So can or cannot leave such and such a country. . . .[is] a tenth-rate question.

In attempt to sidestep references to narrow immigration policies, quoted by former US Secretary of State George F Shultz *Turmoil and Triumph* Scribner 93

722 I am silent, like fish.

Remembering his non-participation 6 Jan 86 in summit talks at Geneva *ib*

Alexander M Haig Jr US Secretary of State

723 I take it as a compliment when an agent of the largest and most heinous bully of the century, the Soviet Union, accuses me of being a bully.

On how he was regarded by Soviet Ambassador Anatoly Dobrynin *Washington Post* 27 Oct 95

Albert Hakin Iranian arms dealer

724 It portrayed. . . dogs sitting around the table. . . one of the dogs taking a little nap and. . . this represented our Cabinet—and that was Mr Casey taking a nap. That broke the ice.

On a picture viewed during White House tour given Hakin and an Iranian official by Oliver L North during talks on secret sale of arms to Iran while William J Casey was head of the CIA *NY Times* 5 Jun 87

Robert B Hall Deputy Assistant Secretary of Defense

725 Environmental terrorism.

On Iraq's wartime flooding of Persian Gulf with oil, a term also used by Assistant Secretary Pete Williams, news reports 25 Jan 91

Nizar Hamdoon Iraqi Ambassador to US

726 They can sell you and buy you at the same time.

On Saudi Arabia *USA Today* 27 Aug 87

Des Hanafin Irish senator

727 The people. . . want to keep their constitutional right to lifelong marriage.

On voters' decision to retain restrictions against divorce *NY Times* 28 Jun 86, a decision reversed by a narrow vote nearly ten years later, news summaries 31 Dec 95

Suzan Shown Harjo Executive Director, National Congress of American Indians

728 We want the dead Indians out and the live Indians in.

On removal of Indian skeletal remains from Smithsonian Institution *Washington Post* 12 Sep 89

729 It's. . . a disgraceful situation where Indians are an archaeological resource of the US. . . [and] US property—not quite humans.

ib

730 We aren't snails, dinosaurs or elephants. We're Americans.

ib

Pamela Harriman US Ambassador to France

731 Too many. . . see him as a man who plays the saxophone by night and wears running shoes by day. Next week he needs to show them his brains, his scope, his leadership.

On eve of President Clinton's first European trip since taking office *NY Times* 9 Jan 94

732 Face-to-face is better than fax to fax. . . and nowhere is it more true than dealings between the French and ourselves.

Vanity Fair Feb 94

Frederick Brown Harris Chaplain, US Senate

733 Tenderly. . . we bear the worn, bodily tenement of the oldest chief executive to this highest pedestal of honor where so recently lay the martyred form of the youngest.

At funeral of President Hoover, age 90 *NY Times* 24 Oct 64

Mark O Hatfield US Senator

734 Now body bags are "human remains pouches". . . . Your sons and daughters and mothers and fathers will have their faces blown off. . . limbs torn apart. . . chests ripped open, but they won't come home in body bags. . . [but] in neat and tidy human remains pouches.

Opposing US intervention in Kuwait 12 Jan 91

Robert M Hayes NYC Coalition for the Homeless

735 You step over bodies to get to the gourmet food line.

On Grand Central Station's 400 to 500 homeless *NY Times* 2 Feb 88

Denis Healey Chancellor of the Exchequer

736 The Great She-Elephant, who must be obeyed.

On Margaret Thatcher *The Time of My Life* Norton 90

Joel Hefley US Congressman

737 It will help to eliminate so-called pork parks.

On legislation creating a National Park System Review Commission *Christian Science Monitor* 26 Jun 95

Jesse Helms US Senator

738 I've seen them come and go and the best thing about almost all of them is when they go.

On delaying all ambassadorial appointments until his recommendations for reform were taken more seriously *NY Times* 14 Sep 95

Smith Hempstone US Ambassador to Kenya

739 If you liked Beirut, you'll love Mogadishu.

To US Marines in Somalia some years after the Corps' losing battle against Kenyan terrorists *Guardian Weekly* 19 Dec 92

740 It will take five years to get Somalia not on its feet but just on its knees.

ib

741 [They] will keep tens of thousands of Somali kids from starving to death in 1993 who, in all probability, will starve to death in 1994.

ib

Lord Hesketh (Thomas Alexander Fermor-Hesketh]

742 It ill becomes those of us who have so greatly benefited from the... past to assist in... violence against the thread which links that past to the future.

On the 75-to–39 defeat of a bill to allow women the right to inherit a peerage *NY Times* 13 Mar 94

Rudolph Hess Nazi party leader

743 I was allowed for many years of my life to work under the greatest son that my people produced in their 1,000-year history. I regret nothing.

Statement on Adolf Hitler to Nuremberg war criminals tribunal, recalled on Hess's death at age 93 still imprisoned 28 Dec 87

Jim Hightower Texas Agricultural Commissioner

744 Little ol' boy in the Panhandle told me the other day you can still make a fortune in agriculture. Problem is, you got to start with a large one.

On the financial crisis of the American farmer, to Chamber of Commerce, Dallas *NY Times* 9 Mar 86

745 The only difference between a pigeon and the American farmer today is that a pigeon can still make a deposit on a John Deere.

ib

Richard Hirsch Rabbi, International Reform Movement

746 It came down to... six Arabs sitting in Jerusalem determining who is a Jew in New York, Melbourne, London and Johannesburg.

On efforts of Israeli parliament to define who is a Jew *NY Times* 7 Jul 87

Philip Hocker Director, Mineral Policy Center

747 This latest $1-billion boondoggle is only the first drop of a new torrent unless Congress acts to stop it.

On the need to amend an 1872 law allowing mining companies to patent or take title to property if they find minerals *US News & World Report* 18 Sep 95

Richard Holbrooke Assistant US Secretary of State

748 We've been talking about talking. Now we're going to be talking.

On negotiations to end the war in Bosnia CBS TV 2 Sep 95

749 If they leak, I'm sure they will leak inaccurately.

On keeping peace talks secret *NY Times* 5 Nov 95

750 We may have to do some corrective surgery.

On what might be leaked *ib*

J Edgar Hoover Director, Federal Bureau of Investigation

751 You are honored by your friends... distinguished by your enemies. I have been very distinguished.

To House Sub-Committee on Appropriations, quoted by Curt Gentry *J Edgar Hoover* Norton 91

C F Howe Canadian Minister of Trade and Commerce

752 I am busier than a whore working two beds.

PBS TV 12 Sep 88

Roman L Hruska US Senator

753 There are a lot of mediocre judges and people and lawyers, and they are entitled to a little representation.... We can't have all Brandeises, Frankfurters, and Cardozos.

On Supreme Court appointments *NY Times* 17 Mar 70

Reed E Hundt Chair, Federal Communications Commission

754 Your job as chair is to get things done. But if you are a commissioner, your primary power comes from being able to block things.

On public rebellion by three of the five-member commission against Hundt's desire to require television stations to carry at least three hours a week of educational programming, *NY Times* 20 Nov 95

Douglas Hurd British Foreign Minister

755 At long last we are bringing Charlie in from the cold.

On the abolishment of the Checkpoint Charlie crossing between East and West Berlin *London Times* 23 Jul 90

756 Are the US Congress, House of Commons, French Assembly, German Bundestag, solemnly ready to guarantee with the lives of their citizens the frontiers of, say, Slovakia? If not, or not yet, then it would be a deceit to pretend otherwise.

Cautioning against false guarantees on membership in NATO *NY Times* 13 Jan 94

757 I am today's man and have many tomorrows.

Denial that he was "yesterday's man" who would be replaced in the cabinet *London Times* 31 Jan 95

758 Is it really more in the public interests that I just sit on my backside and do nothing?

On accepting a $200,000 directorship in private industry 13 Sep 95

Ward Hussey Office of Legislative Council, US House of Representatives

759 A good draftsman must be a policy eunuch.

On codifying bills, especially tax legislation *Wall Street Journal* 22 Aug 86

Henry J Hyde US Congressman

760 You're going to get a million more abortions. We're awash in a sea of blood.

On successfully sustaining the objection that he raised in 1977 to federal financing of abortions for poor women except in cases of rape, incest or threats to health *NY Times* 1 Jul 93

Vitaly Ignatenko spokesman for Mikhail S Gorbachev

761 [He does not expect] black limousines filled to the brim with money.

On rumors that the Soviet president would ask a London summit conference for a $10 to $12 billion stabilization fund *USA Today* 17 Jul 91

Daniel E Inouye US Senator

762 The story is not of covert activity alone but of covert foreign policy. Not secret diplomacy, which Congress has always accepted, but secret policy-making, which the Constitution has always rejected.

On beginning work as co-chair of Congressional hearings on Iran arms sales *NY Times* 6 May 87

763 It is a tale of working outside the system and of utilizing irregular channels and private parties, accountable to no one, on matters of national security while ignoring the Congress and even the traditional agencies of executive foreign policy-making.

ib

764 How did this happen. . . how did life-long public servants, and patriotic Americans. . . mislead you. . . keep away from the Secretary of State and the Secretary of Defense, lie to Congress, withhold information from the President. . . [and] destroy government documents to hide or cover up their activities?

ib

765 [They involved] rather shady characters. . . in participating in the formulation of foreign policy and implementation. . . while. . . skirting around the people who should be doing that work.

To Secretary of State George Schultz 24 Jul 87

766 At best, casual.

On testimony from Attorney General Edwin Meese III 30 Jul 87

767 It was a fall-guy plan suitable for a grade-B movie, not a great power.

4 Aug 87

768 No times were more dangerous than when our country was born, when revolution was our midwife.

On Admiral John M Poindexter and Lieutenant Colonel Oliver L North's contention that their actions were greatly influenced by "a dangerous world"

769 A great nation betrayed the principles which have made it great, and thereby became hostage to hostage-takers.

ib

770 These hearings will be remembered longest not for the facts they elicited, but for the extraordinary and extraordinarily frightening views of government they exposed.

ib

Andy Ireland US Congressman

771 The experience with the A–12 is not an isolated incident that can be fixed by slitting the wrists of an admiral or two.

To former Navy Secretary H Lawrence Garett III at hearing on over-expenditure and failure of the Stealth bomber *Washington Post* 29 Oct 95

J H James Deputy Master of the British Mint

772 The lady doesn't sit well on the top of large numerals. She looks jolly uncomfortable.

On Britannia's absence from coins designed for transference to the decimal system *NY Times* 16 Feb 68

Peter Jay British Ambassador to the US

773 A national health plan is like sex—people get in a tiz about starting it, but once they have, they never go back.

NY Times 2 Jul 78

Barbara Jordan US Congresswoman

774 I felt somehow for many years that George Washington and Alexander Hamilton just left me out by mistake. But, through the process of amendment, interpretation and court decisions, I have finally been included in "We the people."

To House Judiciary Committee as the first black elected from Texas since Reconstruction *NY Times* 25 Jul 74

775 [Thank you] for the glorious opportunity of sharing the pain of this inquiry.

On consideration of impeachment of President Nixon

Hamilton Jordan Carter White House Chief of Staff

776 I've always wanted to see the pyramids!

On looking down the bodice of the Egyptian ambassador's wife *Washington Post* 18 Dec 77

Manohar Joshi Maharashtra State chief minister

777 Mumbai eliminates the last vestige of British imperialism and restores the original ethnic name.

On changing the name of Bombay to Mumbai as part of similar change over much of India *USA Today* 22 Aug 95

John R Kasich Chair, Budget Committee, US House of Representatives

778 What's the difference between the B–2 and Dracula? Even if you put a stake through the heart of the Stealth, it won't die.

On the resilience of the Stealth bomber, the most expensive aircraft in aviation history, as a symbol of preparedness despite efforts to cut defense spending *Washington Post* 24 Sep 95

George F Kennan US diplomat

779 An unduly high percentage. . . became, at best, empty bundles of good manners and, at worst, rousing stuffed shirts.

On Foreign Service officers, quoted by Arthur M Schlesinger Jr *A Thousand Days* Houghton Mifflin 65

780 [One sometimes feels] a guest of one's time and not a member of the household.

On view of himself as a pragmatist, quoted by Walter Isaacson and Evan Thomas *The Wise Men* Simon & Schuster 86

781 [They were] fig leaves of democratic procedure to hide the nakedness of Stalinist dictatorship.

On postwar agreements on governing Eastern Europe *ib*

Edward M Kennedy US Senator

782 There are few more vivid symbols of the disgrace of our current tax laws than the martini lunch.

On write-offs for business entertaining, quoted by William Safire *Safire's Political Dictionary* Random House 78

Robert F Kennedy US Attorney General

783 Many times. . . I had heard the military take positions which, if wrong, had the advantage that no one would be around at the end to know.

On Russian placement of nuclear missiles in Cuba *Thirteen Days* Norton 69

784 The meeting droned on. But everyone looked like a different person. For a moment the world had stood still, and now it was going around again.

On a meeting interrupted by news that Russian ships had stopped at the naval blockade off the coast of Cuba *ib*

Kerner Commission

785 What white Americans have never fully understood—but what the Negro can never forget—is that white society is deeply implicated in the ghetto.

On the ghetto as white-created, maintained and condoned *ib*

Lord Kilbracken (John Robert Godley)

786 I would have to support abolishment of the House of Lords on principle, but I would hate to lose use of its library.

Wall Street Journal 9 Nov 93

Henry A Kissinger National Security Advisor 1969–73 US Secretary of State 1973–77

787 We lost sight of one of the cardinal maxims of guerrilla war: the guerrilla wins if he does not lose. The conventional army loses if it does not win.

On the Vietnam War *Foreign Affairs* Jan 69

788 [The] American temptation is to believe that foreign policy is a subdivision of psychiatry.

At University of South Carolina commencement *Time* 17 Jun 86

789 Power is the ultimate aphrodisiac.

Quoted by Walter Issacson *Kissinger* Simon & Schuster 92

790 Behind the trees. . . the jockeys decide who will win. . . and we're behind the trees!

To North Vietnam's Le Duc Tho, likening the race track at Auteuil, near Paris, to the October 1972 Vietnam peace talks in Paris *ib*

791 Peace came in the guise of the droning voice of an elderly revolutionary wrapping the end of a decade of bloodshed into legalistic ambiguity.

On negotiations that Kissinger saw as "the most thrilling moment" of his entire career *ib*

792 Ask him if he's ever been kissed on the mouth by Brezhnev.

To UN Ambasssdor Yakov Malik on Kissinger's close acquaintance with Soviet Premier Leonid I Brezhnev *ib*

793 It was a fate of Biblical proportions.

On Richard M Nixon's resignation as President *ib*

794 Any people who have been persecuted for 2,000 years must be doing something wrong.

On Israel's attack on Egypt, adding that "if it were not for the accident of my birth, I would be anti-Semitic!" *ib*

Andrei V Kozyrev Russian Foreign Minister

795 For the first time ever, I flew from Moscow to New York feeling free from being targeted by my own missiles. And going back, I am sure also that I am not targeted by American missiles.

On progress in arms control *NY Times* 25 Apr 95

Bert Lance Carter White House Budget Director

796 Turn over the *Washington Post* with your big toe, and if your name's above the fold, you know you're not going to have a good day.

Washington Post 6 Oct 93

Wayne Lapierre Executive Vice President, National Rifle Asssociation

797 Jack-booted government thugs wearing Nazi bucket helmets and storm-trooper uniforms.

On federal efforts to control gun sales new reports 1 May 95

798 [This is] a battle to retake the most precious, most sacred ground on earth.

On gun control laws as infringements on the 2nd Amendment right to keep and bear arms *US News & World Report* 22 May 95

Salvador Laurel Vice President, Philippines

799 [He suffers] the cobwebs of doubt.

On Ronald Reagan's reservations on new government *NY Times* 2 May 86

Jim Leach US Congressman

800 The only thing the Balkans export is history.

On war in Bosnia Station WAMU Washington 25 Nov 95

Bernard H Levi Professor of Law, University of Chicago

801 It needs a soul.

To President Ford on the post of Attorney General to which Levi was subsequently appointed, recalled in *NY Times* 29 Jul 87

Ken Livingstone Chair, Greater London Council

802 Vandals in ermine.

On the House of Lords *NY Times* 27 Oct 84

Albert John Luthuli Zulu leader

803 The laws of the land virtually criticize God for having created men of color.

Accepting Nobel Peace Prize *Time* 22 Dec 61

V I Malkevich Soviet First Deputy Minister of Foreign Trade

804 We are not Ivans who do not remember our relatives.

Acknowledging American help on becoming computer literate *NY Times* l7 May 90

George C Marshall US Secretary of State

805 Our policy is directed not against any country or doctrine but against hunger, poverty, desperation, and chaos.

At Harvard commencement 5 Jun 1947 announcing European Recovery Plan (ERA) that became known as the Marshall Plan, recalled on Marshall's death 16 Oct 59

Charles M Mathias Jr US Congressman

806 Most of us are honest all the time, and all of us are honest most of the time.

On congressional ethics *Time* 31 Mar 67

Joseph R McCarthy US Senator

807 I have here in my hand a list of 205. . . members of the Communist Party. . . still working and shaping the policy of the State Department.

At Wheeling W VA beginning a period of unfounded accusations 9 Feb 50, quoted by Richard H Rovere *Senator Joe McCarthy* Harcourt Brace 59

Robert C McFarlane National Security Adviser

808 He knows so little and accomplishes so much.

On President Reagan, quoted by former Secretary of State George P Shultz *Turmoil and Triumph* Scribner 93

Edwin Meese III White House Counsel, 1981–85 Attorney General 1985–89

809 Is there anything else that can jump up and bite the President on the ass?

To Oliver L North on Iran-contra arms sales *Time* 28 Oct 91

Walter Momper Mayor of West Berlin

810 This is where the old heart of Berlin used to beat, and it will beat again.

On greeting East Berlin's mayor at Potsdamer Platz as demolition began on the Berlin wall *NY Times* 13 Nov 89

Daniel P Moynihan US Senator

811 They live off secrecy. . . . [it] keeps the *mistakes* secret.

On government intelligence agencies quoted by Richard Reeves *President Kennedy* Simon & Schuster 93

812 How many millions of infants we will put to the sword is not clear. There is dickering to do.

On efforts to deny cash assistance to children born to unmarried mothers under 18 or those on welfare *NY Times* 25 Oct 95

813 A culture of secrecy took hold of the government.

On disclosure of Venona, the successful effort to break the Soviet code on theft of atomic blueprints *International Herald Tribune* 13 Jul 95

Malcolm Muggeridge essayist

814 Secrecy is as essential to intelligence as vestments to a Mass, or darkness to a spiritual seance.

Contrasting his wartime work in intelligence with the openness of Britain's M-I6 unit *NY Times* 22 Aug 93

John P Murtha US Congressman

815 [It] has been failing the American people and rewarding itself for the effort.

On Congress' increase of its own pensions, far higher than those of most citizens *Washington Post* 11 Mar 95

Lieutenant Colonel Oliver L North US Marine Corps

816 I thought using the Ayatollah's money to support the Nicaraguan resistance. . . was a neat idea.

On clandestine Iran arms sales and subsequent aid to Nicaragua 8 Jul 87

Gerald P Nye US Senator

817 A bird of prey on the masses.

On the blue eagle symbol of the 1930s National Recovery Adm (NRA), recalled on Nye's death 17 Jul 71

Bob Packwood US Senator

818 I am accused of kissing women. . . perhaps overeagerly kissing women. And that is the charge, not drugging, not robbing, kissing!

On his exasperation on charges of sexual misconduct, lobbying, and editing diaries subpoenaed by Senate Ethics Committee *NY Times* 7 Sep 95

819 More than Francis of Assisi. . . less than Wilt Chamberlain.

Invoking the name of the Italian saint and an American basketball star in estimating the amount of sex in his diaries 9 Sep 95

David Pryor US Senator

820 It's. . . like. . . cutting the top off the flagpole when the flag is stuck halfway up.

On reducing postal standards to speed up mail *Wall Street Journal* 30 Jan 91

Dan Quayle US Vice President

821 It doesn't help. . . when primetime TV has a character. . . bearing a child alone. . . just another lifestyle choice.

On criticism of a sitcom character, Murphy Brown, played by Candice Bergen, which set off a widespread defense of single mothers and freedom of choice *Washington Post* 21 May 92

Janet Reno US Attorney General

822 Nothing can make me madder than lawyers who don't care about others.

To American Bar Association *NY Times* 9 Aug 93

823 The right thing to do can produce debate, and I want it to be spirited debate.

On the value of public discussion *ib* 15 May 94

824 I want lawyers to call me and tell me: Janet, have you lost your mind?

ib

825 Reckless comparisons are despicable. . . to spread the poison that the government was responsible for the murder of innocents.

Denouncing "a moral equivalency" between the government raid on Waco's Branch Davidians 19 Apr 93 and the Oklahoma City bombing on the same date two years later *Newsweek* 15 May 95

826 I made the decision long ago that to be afraid would be to diminish my life.

NPR interview 18 Jul 95

William P Rogers Secretary of State 1969–73

827 Making foreign policy is like pornographic movies. . . more fun doing it than watching it.

On becoming Under Secretary of State for Economic Affairs 7 Jun 82

George W Romney Governor of Michigan

828 I didn't say I didn't say it. I said I didn't say I said it. I want to make that very clear.

On clarification of policy *National Review* 12 Dec 67

William P Roth Jr Chair, US Senate Governmental Affairs Committee

829 If only trimmed, it inevitably creeps back. . . thicker and more deeply rooted than before.
Comparing bureaucracy to crab grass *Washington Times* 19 May 95

William D Ruckelhaus former Director, Enviromental Protection Agency

830 Everybody wants you to pick it up, and nobody wants you to put it down.
On disposal of garbage *Fortune* 21 Nov 88

Eduard A Shevardnadze Soviet Foreign Minister

831 They should be buried at the Kremlin wall. If there is no room there, there are some people who can be dug up.
On honoring those who died in fighting the attempted overthrow of Mikhail S Gorbachev *Japan Times* 23 Aug 91

George P Shultz US Secretary of State, 1982—88

832 He made a combative apology.
On ability of Elliott Abrams, Assistant Secretary for Inter-American Affairs, to acknowledge a sensitive question without giving a definite reply *NY Times* 25 Jul 87

833 Gardening. . . is one of the most underrated aspects of diplomacy. . . . [and] the way to keep weeds from overwhelming you is to deal with them constantly and in their early stages.
On meeting people "on their own turf" *Turmoil and Tragedy* Scribner 93

834 Lightswitch diplomacy.
On Carter administration's individual trades that could be turned on and off to induce changes in government policy *ib*

835 The Soviet game is chess. . . ours is poker. We will have to play a creative mixture of both games.
To President Reagan *ib*

836 The Strategic Defense initiative. . . proved to be the ultimate bargaining chip.
On Soviet alarm at the prospect of American science "turned on" and venturing into the realm of space defense *ib*

837 Better to use force when you should rather than when you must.
ib

838 [To be last] means. . . the level of force and the risk involved may have multiplied many times over.
ib

839 The president was a prisoner of his own staff.
Expressing belief that three years before the Iran arms sales President Reagan was being manipulated in the withholding of information from others in the White House *ib*

840 Ballistic missiles. . . represented the first real external threat to our homeland since the time of the American Revolution.
On "the only area of Soviet advantage" *ib*

841 This snake has never died, no matter how many times I hacked at it.
On repeated efforts to stop US arms sales to Iran *ib*

842 A "staffocracy" had been created.
On the National Security Council operating as "government by a unit of government that was totally unchecked but which functioned with the implied authority of the presidency" *ib*

843 Not far from Ronald Reagan's small town of Dixon, Illinois, is Jane Addams's Cedarville. . . Ulysses Grant's Galena. . . Carl Sandburg's Galesburg. Reagan had something of them all; his heart going out. . . his will ready to fight. . . his voice able to move the nation.
ib

Gerry Sikorski US Congressman

844 [It functioned] like a toothless terrier on Valium.
On chairing the House panel with the oversight of the Office of Government Ethics *NY Times* 8 Jul 87

Henri Simomet Belgian Foreign Minister

845 If the leadership is not always understood, it is because there has not always been much to understand.
On Soviet aggression in Afghanistan *NY Times* 15 May 80

Alan K Simpson US Senator

846 I come from a state where gun control is just how steady you hold your weapon.
Fortune 30 Dec 91

Joseph John Sisco US diplomat

847 Welcome to shuttle diplomacy!
To newsmen Marvin Kalb and Ted Koppel on hurrying between capitals by jets as part of Henry A Kissinger's first trip to the Middle East after the Yom Kippur War *NY Times* 29 Oct 95

Judy Smallwood Prime Minister of Newfoundland

848 We are not a nation. We are a medium-sized municipality left far behind the march of time.
On persuading Newfoundlanders to join the union that became an independent Canada, recalled on Smallwood's death 18 Dec 91

Margaret Chase Smith US Senator

849 The greatest deliberative body in the world. . . has too often been debased to the level of a forum of hate and character assassination sheltered by the shield of congressional immunity.

"Declaration of Conscience" delivered on the floor of the Senate in denouncing unsubstantiated accusations by Sen Joseph R McCarthy 1 Jun 50

850 [We] ignore some of the basic principles. . . of the right to criticize. . . to hold unpopular beliefs. . . to protest. . . [and] the right of independent thought.

ib

851 The exercise of these rights should not cost one single American citizen his reputation or his right to a livelihood. . . merely because he happens to know someone who holds unpopular beliefs. Who of us does not?

ib

852 I do not want to see the Republican party ride to political victory on the Four Horsemen of Calumny—fear, ignorance, bigotry, and smear.

ib

853 If I can't trust you on little lies, sir, how will I ever believe you on the big ones?

To Defense Secretary Robert S McNamara who confessed a falsehood on a shipyard closing, recalled on Smith's death 29 May 95

Ted Stevens US Senator

854 It is not a pay raise, it is a pay equalization concept.

On the Senate's raising of its salaries, cited for a Doublespeak Award of the National Council of Teachers of English *US News & World Report* 18 Nov 91

Henry L Stimson US Secretary of State

855 Gentlemen do not read each other's mail.

On closing "Black Chamber" code-breaking office that intercepted secret messages between governments in 1929, recalled on Stimson's death 20 Oct 50

Robert S Strauss business executive and diplomat

856 I don't know what it is that I'm ambassador to.

On becoming Ambassador to Russia coincidental to disappearance of the Soviet Union CBS TV 11 Dec 91

857 Don't pray with him! Jim Wright can outpray anybody!

To Secretary of State George P Shultz on House Speaker James C Wright Jr's interference in Central American policy, recalled by Shultz in *Turmoil and Triumph* Scribner 93

Xavier Suarez Mayor of Miami

858 "Give us your tired and your poor, and . . ." but don't give us Haitians.

On rejecting Haitian "boat people" *Sunday Morning* CBS TV 14 Jun 92

James W Symington US Chief of Protocol

859 A number of incidents and threats. . . caused the Secret Service. . . to treat a state visitor more like an endangered species than an honored guest.

On security precautions at Blair House *Washington Post* 4 Jun 95

Robert A Taft US Senator

860 Lending arms is like lending chewing gum. You don't get it back.

On lend-lease, recalled by David Brinkley *Washington Goes to War* Knopf 88

John G Tower US Senator

861 One thing is very, very clear: that members of the system who were privy to what was going on failed the President. . . to advise him. . . to insist on periodic review. . . to expose him to expert judgments and briefings.

On release of the Tower Report on the National Security Council and Iran-contra arms sale *NY Times* 27 Feb 87

Jacques Trémolet de Villers Chief Defense Attorney

862 You are France, not the man in the dock. . . and you will give a historic verdict, but not a verdict on history.

To jury in trial of pro-Nazi militiaman Paul Touvier for deaths of seven Jews near Lyons in World War II *NY Times* 20 Apr 94

863 The dead do not deserve an unjust condemnation.

ib

John Turner Canadian Minister of Finance

864 We are walking along a tightrope, backwards.

On inflation *Toronto Star* 2 Nov 74

Stansfield Turner Director, CIA

865 [It's] almost like asking a fighter pilot to leave his supersonic jet and become a crop duster in a propeller-driven biplane.

On post-cold-war expectations of the CIA *Washington Post* 2 Nov 91

Rupert Uloth essayist

866 This role is as fixed as a flag-pole over Buckingham Palace.

On England's Lord Lieutenants as regional representatives of the monarch *Country Life* 21 Sep 95

US National Archives

867 To promote a more perfect union between the ancient inks and the cracking parchment.

On construction in 1952 of special storage areas for the Constitution and Bill of Rights *Life* Special Issue 87

US Senate Sub-Committee, Democratic Majority Report

868 We are constrained fearlessly and frankly to call the charges. . . what they truly are: a fraud and a hoax perpetrated on the Senate of the United States and the American people.

On Senator Joseph R McCarthy's charges of Communist infiltration *Time* 24 Jul 50

Yuri P Vlasov Congress of the Soviets

869 The KGB. . . hasn't divulged its secrets yet—except for some excavated graves.

On assessing the cruelties of the secret police in an address that stunned Russian legislators *NY Times* 1 Jun 89

Lord Wakeham (John Wakeham)

870 I sometimes feel as though I were appearing before 400 headmasters and headmistresses.

To the House of Lords *London Times* 4 Nov 93

Caspar W Weinberger US Secretary of Defense

871 Wishful thinking is equally as effective for arms control as it is for birth control.

USA Today 6 Oct 86

872 This is almost too absurd to comment on. . . like asking Qaddafi over for a cozy chat.

Notation on National Security Council's proposal to sell arms to Iran, later confirmed by Weinberger in congressional investigation *NY Times* 1 Aug 87

873 I believe this baby has been strangled in the cradle.

Recalling his presidential advisory against arms sales to Iran *ib*

874 You have. . . to do what bank examiners do.

On verification of arms reductions by US and Russia 11 Oct 87

David Wessel reporter

875 Something about monetary policy tantalizes the poet that lurks deep. . . with central bankers.

On Federal Reserve Chair Alan Greenspan's "ability to obfuscate" *Wall Street Journal* 23 Jun 95

David Whipple CIA agent

876 You could call it a lie, but for us, that's keeping cover.

On testifying to congress, winner of Doublespeak Award of the National Council of Teachers of English *US News & World Report* 18 Nov 91

Christine Todd Whitman Governor of New Jersey

877 The states are the laboratories of democracy.

Republican Party reply to President Clinton's State of the Union *NY Times* 29 Jan 95

Charles E ("Engine Charlie") Wilson President, General Motors Corporation

878 What was good for our country was good for General Motors, and vice versa. . . [but] the difference does not exist. Our company is too big. It goes with the welfare of the country.

Reflecting on what he had said 15 Jan 53 ("What's good for General Motors is good for the country.") on becoming Secretary of Defense *American Heritage* Feb 95

R James Woolsey CIA Director

879 We have slain a large dragon, but now we must live in a jungle filled with a bewildering variety of poisonous snakes, and in many ways the dragon was easier to keep track of.

On the CIA after the Cold War *Forbes* 25 Oct 93

880 There are some important differences between Benedict Arnold and Ames. . . all in Arnold's favor.

On the CIA's Aldrich H Ames' betrayal of at least 12 secret agents in Russia *NY Times* 19 Jun 94

881 A polygraph exam is no substitute for judgment.

On inconclusive lie detector tests *ib*

James C Wright Jr Speaker, US House of Representatives

882 Now I know how that pancake feels when you pour the syrup over it.

On unveiling of his official portrait two years after he was forced to resign *International Herald Tribune* 12 Jul 91

Rufus Yerxa US Trade Representative

883 There is not enough caffeine in the world to make a. . . panel proceeding interesting.

On why the public would not be drawn to hearings of the World Trade Organization *Wall Street Journal* 19 May 95

Courtney Young British Intelligence Officer

884 A hotbed of cold feet.

On the British Foreign Office, quoted by Peter Wright *Spycatcher* Viking 87

Warren Zimmerman US Ambassador to Rumania

885 This is not openness. This is closedness.

On reversal of press access to Rumania *Time* 8 Jun 87

Andrei Zyrianov Second Secretary, Russian Foreign Ministry

886 It's like the grass in Hyde Park. . . beautiful and smooth, but it's taken 200 years to grow.

On British diplomacy *London Times* 28 Oct 91)

Politics

Dean Acheson US Secretary of State

887 A real Centaur—part man, part horse's ass. A rough appraisal, but curiously true.

On President Johnson 13 Apr 68 David S McLellan ed *Dean Acheson: The State Dept Years* Dodd, Mead 76

888 No one rises above the level of what we used to expect of respectable mayors.

On international leadership *ib*

Spiro Agnew US Vice President

889 I was just one of the worst complications he could have had. . . [and] I felt totally abandoned.

On resigning after entering a no-contest plea to tax evasion and never again speaking to President Nixon *Go Quietly or Else* Morrow 80, and comment at Nixon's funeral *NY Times* 28 Apr 94

Lamar Alexander US Secretary of Education

890 I've been vaccinated but not infected.

On knowing Washington as a cabinet member before seeking Republican presidential nomination, news reports 9 Nov 95

Anne Princess Royal

891 I was often pictured as a second cousin to a horse.

On a toothsome public image that changed through her work for children's welfare *People* 14 Nov 88

Anon

892 A knight looking for a liege lord to serve.

Comment at the Department of Justice on Watergate break-in leader G Gordon Liddy, quoted by Fred Emery *Watergate* Times Books 94

893 Running a cemetery is just like being President: you got a lot of people under you and nobody's listening.

Quoted by President Clinton 10 Jan 95

894 Hussein isn't just sitting on the fence; he is the fence.

An American diplomat on Jordan's King Hussein prior to making peace with Palestine *London Times* 22 Jul 95

895 The fear for some Europeans is Teutonic knights in three-piece suits.

A diplomat speaking of the suspicion of Germans *NY Times* 16 Sep 95

896 Perpetual optimism is a force multiplier.

Aphorism kept under glass on Gen Colin L Powell's desk 17 Sep 95

897 They were the White House's Berlin Wall.

On control by advisers H R Haldeman and John R Ehrlichman of access to President Nixon, quoted on *Nixon* PBS TV 8 Jan 96

Dick Armey Majority Leader, US House of Representatives

898 Entitlement spending—the politics of greed wrapped in the language of love.

On President Johnson's legacy to the Democratic party *US News & World Report* 12 Dec 94

Paddy Ashdown Member of Parliament

899 Pompous, stuck up, separated, archaic. . . I detest it.

On the Commons as seen by its longest-serving Liberal Democrat *Country Life* 2 Mar 95

Nancy, Lady Astor Member of Parliament

900 Superiority we've always had; all we ask is equality.

On becoming the Commons' first woman member, recalled on Lady Astor's death 2 May 64

901 I had certain disagreeable qualities and a shameful audacity very much needed.

ib

Lee Atwater Advisor to Bush White House

902 You were the best rabbit we had. Let them chase you and they'll stay off the important things.

To Vice President Dan Quayle *Washington Post* 7 Jan 92

Bruce Babbitt Governor of Arizona

903 George Bush reminds every woman of her first husband.

On opposing Bush for presidential nomination *Newsweek* 13 Jun 88

James A Baker III US Secretary of State

904 This has all the ingredients that brought down three of the last five Presidents: a hostage crisis, body bags and a full-fledged economic recession caused by $40 oil.

To President Bush in 1991 on the effect of the Persian Gulf War on winning a second term *The Politics of Diplomacy* Putnam 95

Howard H Baker Jr US Senator

905 The cloakroom becomes my office, the floor my domain.

On his role as Senate majority leader *Time* 26 Apr 82

906 Never speak more clearly than you think.

On becoming President Reagan's third Chief of Staff *NY Times* 6 Sep 87

Tony Banks Member of Parliament

907 [You are] an inflated pig's bladder on a stick.

In Commons debate with conservative member Terry Dicks *London Times* 9 Feb 95

Marion Barry Mayor of Washington, DC

908 Bitch set me up!

On his arrest on possession of drugs *Washington Post* 19 Jan 90

909 There are two kinds of truth. . . real truths and made-up truths.

13 May 90

Bernard Baruch presidential advisor

910 Let us not be deceived—we are today in the midst of a cold war.

To South Carolina legislature 16 Apr 1947, naming an era that was to continue until the 199Os, recalled on Baruch's death 20 Jun 65

William J Bennett US Secretary of Education

911 There is no dead time in this town.

Advising the new Congress for a continual offensive alert *NY Times* 12 Dec 94

Lloyd Bentsen Jr US Senator

912 America has just passed through. . . an eight-year coma in which slogans were confused with solutions and rhetoric passed for reality.

Recalling the Reagan White House as he accepted the Democratic nomination for Vice President 21 Jul 88

913 Senator, I served with Jack Kennedy. I knew Jack Kennedy. Jack Kennedy was a friend of mine. Senator, you're no Jack Kennedy.

On opponent Dan Quayle's contention that his congressional experience equaled that of President Kennedy *NY Times* 9 Oct 88

Aneurin Bevan Member of Parliament

914 A speech by Chamberlain is like paying a visit to Woolworth's; everything in its place and nothing above sixpence.

On Neville Chamberlain, quoted by Michael Foot *Aneurin Bevan* Atheneum 62

915 The right kind of leader for the Labor Party is a desiccated calculating machine who must not in any way permit himself to be swayed by indignation.

ib

Betty Boothroyd Speaker, House of Commons

916 Elect me for who I am, and not for what I was born.

On successful bid to become the Commons' first woman speaker *London Times* 28 Apr 92

George Bush US Vice President, 1981-88; 41st US President, 1989-93

917 Competence makes the trains run on time but doesn't know where they're going.

On Democratic charges of incompetence 19 Aug 88

918 This is America—a brilliant diversity spread like stars, like a thousand points of light in a broad and peaceful sky.

Acceptance speech, New Orleans 18 August 88

919 Read my lips: no new taxes!

ib

920 [I would not be surprised if he] thought a naval exercise is something you find in a Jane Fonda workout book.

On opponent Michael S Dukakis *Time* 19 Sep 88

921 My ancestors came over on the Mayflower carrying Bloomingdale's shopping bags.

Contrasting his background to immigrant opponent *NY Times* 18 Jul 89

922 Some of the journalists have had flu, and people in our country have had it, so why isn't the President entitled to 24 hours?

On political effect of his fainting at a state dinner in Tokyo 9 Jan 92

923 I think Democrats get the flu from time to time.

ib

924 Let's finish the job with style.

On defeat for a second term 4 Nov 92

925 [A defeated] Winston S Churchill said "I have been given the Order of the Boot". . . the exact position in which I find myself today.

Address to the nation 7 Nov 92

926 It's back to the real world for the Bushes... it's been one hell of a ride.

On arriving home in Houston 20 Jan 93

927 Now I understand why he's inside looking out and I'm outside looking in.

On returning to the White House as President Clinton's guest for Palestine-Israeli peace accord signing *Washington Post* 15 Sep 93

George W Bush Governor of Texas

928 I've inherited 100 per cent of his enemies and only 50 per cent of his friends.

On his father's influence on gubernatorial campaign *Washington Times* 12 Oct 94

Larry Bush press secretary to San Francisco Mayor Art Agnos

929 To "out" someone is to show that they're powerless.

On identifying homosexuals in public life *Washington Times* 13 Sep 90

Gatsha Buthelezi Chief Minister of Kwazulu

930 His head is so deeply buried in the sand that you will have to recognize him by the shape of his toes.

On South African President Pieter Botha's stand on Apartheid *NY Times* 9 Apr 87

Jimmy Carter 39th US President

931 My role is one of filling vacuums.

On work with 105 countries since leaving the White House ABC TV 13 Dec 94

932 I feel truer to myself... more of a missionary than a politician.

On the Carter Library as a center of study of international issues *Life* Nov 95

Rosalynn Carter First Lady

933 We sat in rocking chairs on the Truman balcony at 4:30 every afternoon and we talked.

On sharing the presidency with her husband *NY Times* 14 Jun 83

934 I knew it was a man's world, but I needed to know. I'd be damned if I'd leave.

On attending cabinet meetings *ib*

935 He made us safe for our bigotry.

On President Reagan Station WAMU Washington 5 Mar 91

James Carville Clinton campaign strategist

936 Even a broken clock is right twice a day.

On Washington officialdom *NY Times* 2 Feb 92

937 Every campaign's a door and you don't know what's behind it when you kick it in.

ib 2 Sep 95

Dick Cheney Chief of Staff, Carter White House

938 The value of the experience in Washington depends on being able to know when it's over.

On "ghosts" waiting to be called again to government service, quoted by Haynes Johnson *In the Absence of Power* Viking 80

Madame Chiang Kai-Shek First Lady of Free China

939 [American politics is] clodhopping boorishness and uncivilized geste.

Recalled on her return at age 98 to again address Congress *NY Times* 24 Jul 95

Shirley Chisholm US Congresswoman

940 One thing they're afraid of in Shirley Chisholm is her mouth!

Assessing her role as the first black congresswoman *NY Times* 13 Apr 69

Winston S Churchill Prime Minister of Britain

941 Just before dawn I woke suddenly with a sharp stab of almost physical pain. A hitherto subconscious conviction that we were beaten broke forth and dominated my mind.

On losing postwar re-election as Prime Minister *Triumphs and Tragedies* Houghton Mifflin 53

942 A sheep in sheep's clothing... a modest man with plenty to be modest about.

On Prime Minister Clement Attlee *Time* 7 Aug 64

943 Anybody can rat, but it takes a certain amount of ingenuity to re-rat.

On re-embracing the Conservative Party *ib*

944 It is time to pierce the bloated bladder of lies with the poignance of truth.

On Aneurin Bevan, recalled on Churchill's death 24 Jan 65

945 It is never necessary to commit suicide, especially when you may live to regret it....and sometimes it need more courage to decline to jump a fence...then to go for it.

Quoted by Harold Macmillan *Tides of Fortune* Macmillan 69

946 The most dangerous moment for evil governments is when they begin to reform.

On Joseph Stalin's death *ib*

947 A merchant of discourtesy.
On Laborite Aneurin Bevan *London Times* 30 Apr 82

948 A sea of hard little hats on hard little heads.
On his constituency as a member of Parliament, quoted by William Manchester *The Last Lion* Little, Brown 83

949 When the mouse is away, the cats will play.
On Laborites during Clement Attlee's visit to Moscow *ib*

950 Politics is like waking up in the morning. You never know whose head you will find on the pillow.
ib

951 The plight of the *genus politicus* is that he is asked to stand, and he is expected to lie.
ib

952 Politics is very much like war. We use poison gas at times.
ib

953 [My policy will be] houses, red meat, and not getting scuppered.
On platform after the 1951 election, quoted by Alistair Horne *Macmillan* Vol 1 Viking 89

954 Some socialists see private enterprise as a tiger... others as an old cow to be milked... but Conservatives see it as a sturdy horse that pulls along our economy.
Quoted by Nigel Everett *The Tory View of Landscape* Yale 94

Clark Clifford Special Counsel to Truman White House

955 [He was] the amiable dunce.
On Ronald Reagan, quoted by Haynes Johnson *Sleep Walking Through History* Norton 91

Hillary Rodham Clinton First Lady

956 I'd be a terrific governor... a terrific president.
Statement during 1992 presidential campaign *Washington Post* 25 Feb 95

957 I'm sitting here because I love him, and I honor what he's been through, and what we've been through together, and you know, if that's not enough for people, then, heck, don't vote for him.
In joint appearance with her husband after he was accused of marital infidelity *60 Minutes* CBS TV 26 Jan 92

958 I suppose I could have stayed home, baked cookies, and had teas.
Defending charges of conflict of interest between politics, domesticity, and her legal career *NY Times* 18 May 92

959 [America suffers from a] sleeping sickness of the soul... that we lack... that sense that our lives are part of some greater effort.
Address at Austin TX *ib* 23 May 93

960 I'm holding up fine except that it's lonely in the bunker.
On investigation of Whitewater land sales *USA Today* 21 Mar 94

961 The heart and soul of the American economy... is risk-taking and investing in the future.
At unprecedented news conference called to discuss political collusion behind her stock market earnings *NY Times* 23 Apr 94

962 It is time for us to say here in Beijing, and the world to hear, that it is no longer acceptable to discuss women's rights as separate from human rights.
Addressing the 4th World Conference on Women *ib* 6 Sep 95

William J Clinton 42nd US President

963 I experimented with marijuana a time or two.... [but] I didn't inhale and I didn't try it again.
CBS TV 29 Mar 92

964 Cash for trash.
On supermarket tabloid payments for Gennifer Flowers' allegations of a long affair ABC TV 23 Jan 92

965 The American people—at least, people that have been married for a long time—know what it means and know the whole range of things it can mean.
On charges of marital infidelity *60 Minutes* CBS TV 26 Jan 92

966 I've been reclined on the national couch.
On discussions of his character *US News & World Report* 20 Jul 92

967 Bean counters!
On women's groups whom he regarded as more interested in quotas than competence *NY Times* 22 Dec 92

968 I want a cabinet that looks like the face of America.
25 Dec 92

969 Don't stop thinking about tomorrow.
When asked for his motto *Prime Time* ABC TV 14 Jan 93

970 I'm a lot like Baby Huey... fat... ugly... [but] if you push me down, I keep coming back. I just keep coming back.
Time 7 Feb 94

971 If everybody... had a character as strong as hers, we wouldn't have half the problems we've got.
On his wife's role in Whitewater land sales 7 Mar 94

972 Don't drink in public; you might act like yourself.
Quoted by Meredith Oakley *On the Make* Regnery 94

973 If something makes you cry, you have to do something about it. That's the difference between politics and guilt.
ib

John Colville British diplomat

974 Few of our island kith and kin/ Are totally immune to sin./ Yet, when some man the public knows/ Is caught *flagrante delicto*/ With feigned regret and hidden spite/ The sepulchres are painted white.

Letter to *London Times* during charges of sexual misconduct against Minister of War John Profumo, quoted by Alistair Horne *Harold Macmillan* Vol II Viking 89

975 Sometimes the plea's security;/ Sometimes it's national purity./ Unleashing bloodhounds; splendid sport/ For those who've not themselves been caught.

ib

John B Connally Governor of Texas

976 All hat and no cattle.

On President Bush's claim of being a Texan *NY Times* 14 Feb 89

Nellie Connally Governor's wife

977 You can't say Dallas doesn't love you, Mr President!

To John F Kennedy moments before he was assassinated, quoted by William Manchester *The Death of a President* Harper & Row 67

Mario Cuomo Governor of New York

978 Ever since the Republican landslide on Nov. 8, it's been getting dark outside a little earlier every day. You notice that?

NY Times 17 Dec 94

979 Dog eat dog produces, inevitably, just one dog.

Disdaining "everyone for himself" on leaving office as governor after 12 years *ib* 31 Dec 94

John W Dean III Special Counsel, Nixon White House

980 I began by telling the President that there was a cancer growing on the presidency.

On advising President Nixon of blackmail money sought by the Watergate burglars, testimony at Watergate hearings 25 Jun 73

981 He asked me how much and I chose a figure—a million dollars. He said that was no problem.

ib and *Nixon* PBS TV 8 Jan 96

Somerset de Chair former Member of Parliament

982 I've been a rebel without a pause.

Reflecting at age 83 on his years as politician, war veteran, and author *London Times* 29 Nov 94

Charles de Gaulle President of France

983 I thought the French would recall me very quickly. . . [but] they. . . wasted several years.

On time out of office, quoted by Jean Lacouture *De Gaulle the Ruler* Norton 92

984 A coup. . . simply replaces one sergeant-major with another.

On ineffectiveness of overthrowing government *ib*

985 Nothing more enhances authority than silence. . . the crowning virtue of the strong.

On a political eclipse, quoted by Peter Vansittart *In the Fifties* John Murray 95

986 Long live Free Quebec!

At Montreal in unparalled intrusion into Canadian politics 24 Jul 67

Valéry Giscard d'Estaing President of France

987 I do not like her. She is not like a man and not like a woman.

On Margaret Thatcher, quoted by Bernard Garfinkel *World Leaders Past and Present* Chelsea House 85

John G Diefenbaker Prime Minister of Canada

988 Dogs. . . are the one animal that know the proper treatment to give to polls.

Bill McNeil ed *Voice of the Pioneer* Doubleday of Canada 78

Everett M Dirksen US Senator

989 What a spectacle as some sturdy, eloquent Texan with the right mixture of the spirit of the Alamo and a little corn tranquilizer in his fevered veins moves into the nominating peroration.

To Washington's Gridiron dinner 11 Mar 60 on Lyndon B Johnson's presidential candidacy, quoted by Harry Brayman *The President Speaks Off the Record* Dow Jones 76

990 We love you for what you are—logically illogical, regularly irregular, frugally unfrugal.

Farewell toast to President Eisenhower *ib*

991 The oil can is mightier than the sword.

On political leadership *Life* 5 Jun 64

992 I am a man of fixed and unbending principles, the first of which is to be flexible at all times.

Recalled on Dirksen's death 7 Sep 69

993 To my bedridden amazement, my pajama-ruffled consternation, yes, my pill-laden astonishment, I learned they were victims of that new White House telephonic half-Nelson known as the Texas twist.

On President Johnson's successful defeat of three bills during a Dirksen hospitalization *ib*

994 You don't mind if we denounce you once in a while, do you, Lyndon? You can explain that better than when someone on your side of the aisle denounces you.

Quoted by Claudia ("Lady Bird") Johnson *A White House Diary* Holt Rinehart Winston 70

995 A billion here, a billion there. Pretty soon it runs into real money.

"Half a Trillion in Real Money" quoted in editorial *NY Times* 2 Dec 79

Thomas J Dodd US Senator

996 Is there anyone alive who has not felt... that goodness has suddenly fled the world... when, without deserving it, you come under general attack; when you know the attack is unjust, yet others deny or doubt what you know?

At opening of Senate debate on his private use of campaign funds *NY Times* 14 Jun 67

997 Be done with it!... In the twilight of my life! And that will be the end of me! But give me a night's rest either in sorrow or relief.

Appeal to the Senate to conclude censure hearings *Newsweek* 3 Jul 67

Elizabeth Dole US Secretary of Transportation

998 Sometimes I think we're the only two lawyers in Washington who trust each other.

On marriage to Senator Robert J. Dole *Newsweek* 3 Aug 87

Robert J Dole US Senator

999 It is inside work with no heavy lifting.

On the Vice Presidency ABC TV 24 Jul 88

1000 Contrary to reports that I took the loss badly, I slept like a baby—every two hours I woke up and cried.

On losing presidential nomination 14 Aug 88

1001 Putting a majority together is like a one-armed man wrapping cranberries.

Quoted by Hedrick Smith *The Power Game* Random House 88

1002 It only takes one vote to win the Vice Presidential nomination.

On the ultimate decision of the Presidential nominee CNN 15 Jun 91

1003 There they were, See No Evil, Hear No Evil, and Evil.

On former President Nixon with Gerald Ford and Jimmy Carter at Washington Gridiron Club dinner 26 Mar 83; also see Stephen E Ambrose *Nixon: Ruin and Recovery* Simon & Schuster 91

1004 The man who won't take yes for an answer.

On Senator Alphonse D'Amato's enthusiasm for raising specific sums in high figures beyond promises of support for Dole's presidential campaign *Time* 11 Sep 95

John Donahue Professor of Political Science, Harvard

1005 They take a lot of their pay in sunsets.

On National Park Service rangers *US News & World Report* 3 Apr 95

Alec Douglas-Home Prime Minister of Britain

1006 [We shall] only harry the new government when it deserves harry.

Christian Science Monitor 19 Oct 64

1007 Meet her positive politics with a positive attitude... [or] we shall fall into that deep pit which is the middle of British politics.

On the Labor party and Margaret Thatcher *London Sunday Times* 6 Sep 81

Thomas E Eagleton US Senator

1008 A little perjury is okay, but not too much.

To Avrom Landesman, a rabbi and veteran civil servant, on testifying on influence pedaling by Joseph R Wright Jr of the Office of Management and Budget *Wall Street Journal* 8 Nov 85

Abba Eban Prime Minister of Israel

1009 Israel is not an aviary.

When asked if his country's policy was hawkish or dovish, *NY Post* 8 Jul 67

1010 I think that this is the first war in history that on the morrow the victors sued for peace and the vanquished called for unconditional surrender.

NY Times 9 Jul 67

1011 Men and nations do behave wisely, once all other alternatives have been exhausted.

Vogue 1 Aug 67

1012 Chamberlain and Halifax were men of principle, but one of their principles was expediency.

On Britain's Prime Minister and Foreign Secretary, quoted by Howard M Saecher *Guardian Weekly* 28 Feb 93 reviewing Eban's *Israel Through My Eyes* Putnam 93

Anthony Eden Prime Minister of Britain

1013 I would not hesitate to go tiger hunting with him.

On the social acceptance of US Secretary of State Dean Acheson, quoted by Walter Isaacson and Evan Thomas *The Wise Men* Simon & Schuster 86

Edward Duke of Windsor

1014 British life... affords a series of nursery slopes down which a diffident and inarticulate royal apprentice may be conducted. . . without imposing too much embarrassment upon the people.

A King's Story Putnam 51

John R Ehrlichman Special Counsel to Nixon White House

1015 He's the Big Enchilada.

On possibility of placing Watergate blame on Attorney General John Mitchell, taped conversation 27 Mar 73

1016 [We want] modified, limited hangout.

On Watergate *The Company* Simon & Schuster 76

Dwight D Eisenhower 34th US President

1017 No soldier. . . was ever struck in his emotional vitals by a President with such an apparently sincere and certainly astounding proposition.

On President Truman's promise that "there is nothing that you may want that I can't try to help to get and that definitely and specifically includes the Presidency" *NY Times* 13 Jan 52

1018 I don't want my Vice President to be a throttlebottom.

On giving more responsibility to Richard M Nixon, quoted by Julie Nixon Eisenhower *Pat Nixon* Simon & Schuster 86

1019 Either this Republican party will reflect progressivism or I won't be with them any more.

News summaries 31 Oct 54

1020 He just hasn't grown. He will never be president. People don't like him.

To Republican Chair Leonard Hall in 1956, reluctantly agreeing to again have Richard M Nixon as a running mate, quoted by William Ewald *Eisenhower the President* Prentice Hall 81

1021 What is that monkey waiting for? Polishing his prose?

On Adlai E Stevenson's delay in conceding loss after carrying only seven states to Eisenhower's 41, news reports 6 Nov 56

1022 The political strength that these people could generate. . . could not elect a man who was committed to giving away $20 gold pieces to every citizen. . . for each day of the calendar year.

On overly conservative Republicans, news summaries 30 Nov 56

1023 Douglas MacArthur was running for the Presidency—all his life.

Recalled on Eisenhower's death 28 Mar 69

1024 Nixon went from a political cadaver to political marvel.

On Richard M Nixon's "Checkers" speech that saved his candidacy as Eisenhower's running mate in 1952 *ib*

1025 A fine man who, in the middle of a stormy lake, knows nothing of swimming.

On his initial impression of Harry S Truman while Eisenhower was military chief of staff, quoted by Michael R Beschloss *Eisenhower* HarperCollins 90

1026 A repudiation. . . [a] hit in the solar plexus with a ball bat.

On Nixon's 1960 defeat by John F Kennedy *ib*

1027 Worst damn fool mistake I ever made.

On appointment 30 Sep 53 of Earl Warren to be Chief Justice of the Supreme Court *ib*

1028 It could not have happened in my administration.

On Kennedy's Bay of Pigs fiasco after rejecting as "small-minded" the suggestion of Eisenhower's son, John, that Kennedy simply say "I don't run no bad invasions" *ib*

1029 There is bound to be a psychotic sort of accident sometime.

On President Kennedy's assassination *ib*

1030 I want. . . the $60 GI job and no medals on my chest.

To President Harry S Truman a few hours after President Kennedy's funeral that Truman viewed as "Hollywood theatrics" 25 Nov 63

Dr Joycelynn Elders US Surgeon General

1031 I came here as prime steak and now I feel like low-grade hamburger.

On a prolonged time between her nomination by President Clinton and confirmation by the Senate *Newsweek* 20 Sep 93

Sam J Ervin US Senator and Chair, Watergate Hearings

1032 Divine right went out with the American revolution and doesn't belong to the White House aides. What meat do they eat that makes them so great?

News conference during Watergate investigation *Time* 16 Apr 73

1033 I'm not going to let anybody come down at night like Nicodemus and whisper something in my ear that no one else can hear. That is not executive privilege; it is poppycock.

At Senate Watergate hearings *US News & World Report* 28 May 73

1034 If the many allegations made to this date are true, then the burglars who broke into the headquarters of the Democratic National Committee at the Watergate were, in effect, breaking into the home of every citizen.

ib

1035 There is nothing in the constitution that authorizes or makes it the official duty of a president to have anything to do with criminal activities.

At Senate Watergate hearings *Washington Post* 12 Jul 73

1036 I used to think that the Civil War was our country's greatest tragedy, but I do remember that there were some redeeming features in the Civil War in that there was some spirit of sacrifice and heroism displayed on both sides. I see no reedeming features in Watergate.

ib 24 Jul 73

General Romulo Escobar Bethancourt President, Panamanian Democratic Revolutionary Party

1037 The treaty is like a small stone in a shoe that one must suffer for 23 years in order to remove a nail from one's heart.

On the 1977 treaty for the US to relinquish control of the Panama Canal by the year 2,000, recalled on Escobar's death, *NY Times* 30 Sep 95

Lord Esher (Oliver S B Bret), National Trust

1038 We... have inherited an institution which we certainly should never have had the intelligence to create. We might have been landed with something like the American Senate.

On the House of Lords *Wall Street Journal* 2 May 63

Robert Evans Professor at University of British Columbia Center for Health Services and Policy Research

1039 It's not so much being attacked by a leopard... [but] being yawned at by a higher ranking male, showing very large canine teeth.

On comparative studies of East African baboons and 10,000 persons in the Whitehall ecosystem *Guardian Weekly* 11 Sep 94

Nicholas Fairbairn Member of Parliament

1040 One of the great difficulties of Christianity is that it falls into the hands of the wrong people.

London Times 20 Feb 95

Orville Faubus former Governor of Arkansas

1041 When you start your campaigning, don't let your shirttail hit your back until it's over.

Advice to Bill Clinton *Washington Times* 15 Dec 94

Dianne Feinstein US Senator

1042 Their blue suits mean business as usual. I say elect this dress.

On her male opponents *NY Times* 26 Mar 95

Tom Fenton foreign correspondent

1043 Going back to communism is as incomprehensible as trying to unring a bell.

On the mind of many Russians in the wake of national elections *Sunday Morning* CBS TV 9 Jun 96

Ralph Flanders US Senator

1044 He dons his war paint... goes into his war dance... goes forth to battle and proudly returns with the scalp of a pink Army dentist.

On Senator Joseph R McCarthy's search for Communists in government, quoted by David Oshinsky *A Conspiracy So Immense* Free Press 83

Gerald R Ford 38th US President

1045 That's a categorical inaccuracy.

On rumors he was in psychotherapy *NY Times* 17 Oct 73

1046 It's like being invited to listen to the eulogies at your own funeral, plus the lies people tell about you at the wake.

On presidential scholars discussing his administration *ib* 8 Apr 89

Vincent W Foster Jr Deputy Counsel, Clinton White House

1047 I was not meant for the spotlight of public life in Washington. Here running people down is considered sport.

In note found after his suicide *NY Times* 13 Aug 93

Felix Frankfurter Associate Justice, US Supreme Court

1048 [He counteracts] the notion that conscience is something a public man checks in the cloakroom of prudence.

On US Secretary of State Dean Acheson's refusal to turn his back on accused spy Alger Hiss, quoted by David S McLellan *Dean Acheson: The State Dept Years* Dodd, Mead 76

J William Fulbright US Senator

1049 To be a statesman, you must first be elected.

On keeping his Arkansas constituency by voting against civil rights, a stand that barred his appointment as Secretary of State, recalled in *New Yorker* 6 Mar 95

John Kenneth Galbraith economist and diplomat

1050 It is now widely believed that God is a conservative.

Toronto Star 15 Nov 80

John Nance ("Cactus Jack") Garner
US Vice President

1051 I gave up the second most important job in Government for eight long years as Roosevelt's spare tire.
On resigning his post as Speaker of the House of Representatives *Saturday Evening Post* 2 Nov 63

John Gavin US Ambassador to Mexico

1052 If he had an affair while in office I misjudged him. I thought he was just doing that to the country.
On Richard M Nixon *Newsweek* 26 May 86

Richard Gephardt US Congress Minority Leader

1053 The secret to our democracy is that the losers in any argument are willing to accept the loss.
At Capitol Hill meeting of former speakers and leaders, *Washington Tmes* 24 May 95

David Gergen White House Advisor

1054 Fred, there are moving vans in Executive Drive!
To Fred Emery of *The Times* of London 7 Aug 74 who needed confirmation of President Nixon's resignation in order to meet an early deadline, quoted by Emery *Watergate* Times Books 94

1055 When he hung up on Nancy Reagan, that's when he crossed the final threshold.
On White House Chief of Staff Donald T Regan *Nightline* ABC TV 27 Feb 87

1056 You only have one 4-star general, but you have got a lot of lieutenants who can give blood.
On White House associates who can take responsibility for presidential actions, quoted by John Maltese *Spin Control* University of North Carolina Press 92

1057 We are making politics a spectator sport in which our only duty is to vote somebody into office and then retire to the grandstands.
US News & World Report 10 May 93

1058 There was. . . a feeling that if you didn't control. . . they would control it—they, the great outside they.
On working as a speechwriter in the Nixon White House *NY Times* 31 Oct 93

1059 [Nixon taught us that] about the time you are writing a line you have written so often you want to throw up, that is the first time the American people will hear it.
ib

Kathleen Gingrich Congressman's mother

1060 He said, "Mother, she's a bitch!"
Confiding to reporter Connie Chung ("Whisper in my ear, just between you and me") what her son said about Hillary Rodham Clinton *Washington Times* 9 Jan 95

Newton L ("Newt") Gingrich
US Congressman

1061 In America, power comes from God to the individual and is loaned to the state.
Quoted by former Prime Minister Margaret Thatcher *Wall Street Journal* 13 Jul 95 reviewing Gingrich's *To Renew America* HarperCollins 95

1062 Clinton will do the Arkansas two-step: veto, then sign.
On legislation to balance the budget *Fortune* 18 Sep 95

Barry M Goldwater US Senator

1063 He had probably been vaccinated with a phonograph needle.
On the windy Senator Hubert Humphrey as a presidential candidate *With No Apologies* Morrow 79

Mikhail S Gorbachev Soviet Premier

1064 We should not be afraid of it, the way the devil is of incense.
On the possibility of a multi-party system *NY Times* 14 Jan 90

1065 I have no intention of hiding in the *taiga*.
On giving up office, telephone call to President Bush *NY Times* 26 Dec 91

1066 Watch out for Russia. They will zig and zag.
ib

1067 I caught hell from it, but I kept silent because this was *kasha* I cooked myself.
On the demands of living in a democracy *ib*

Philip L Gramm US Senator

1068 I didn't come to Washington to be loved and I haven't been disappointed.
NPR 24 Feb 95

1069 Sophia Loren is not a citizen.
On being asked if he would choose a woman as a running mate for the Presidency *Newsweek* 13 Mar 95

1070 I'm carrying so much pork I'm beginning to get trichinosis.
NBC TV 12 Mar 95

1071 I have the most reliable friend that you can have in American politics—ready money.
On seeking presidential nomination *NY Times* 23 Apr 95

1072 When the voter speaks, I listen, especially when the voter is saying someone else's name.
On withdrawing from the presidential race 15 Feb 96

Mark Green NYC Public Advocate

1073 If hypocrisy were an Olympic event, Al would win the gold, silver and bronze.

On his 1986 senatorial opponent Alfonse M D'Amato *NY Times* 24 Jul 95

Alan Greenspan Chair, Federal Reserve Board

1074 If you can't deal every day with having people trying to destroy you, you shouldn't even think of coming down here.

To a New Yorker considering a top administrative job *Washington Post* 6 Jun 94

H R Haldeman Chief of Staff, Nixon White House

1075 The President wants to be sure... we make a list of all those people, lobbyists and lawyers, and after the election, cut them out forever... also... individual reporters and publishers.

Post-election memo *The Haldeman Diaries* Putnam 94

1076 The key now is to poison the Democratic well.

On political strategy 22 Jun 71, Haldeman with Joseph DiMona *The Ends of Power* Times Books 78

1077 He asked me to listen and take notes... and I ended up with a perjury charge.

On White House Special Counsel John W Dean III *ib*

Pamela Churchill Harriman US Ambassador to France

1078 If you do anything, they will say everything.

On the press and politics *Vogue* Aug 92

Robert Hartmann Counsel to Ford White House

1079 His compulsion to crow is as natural as a rooster's... to preen as normal as a peacock's. Ford... knew it was hopeless to fool with Mother Nature.

On Secretary of State Henry A Kissinger and President Ford *Palace Politics* McGraw-Hill 80

Roy Hattersley Laborite deputy leader

1080 She has the certainty of the second-rate, and that is a substantial piece of armor. It has never crossed her mind that she is wrong.

On Margaret Thatcher *Wall Street Journal* 14 May 87

Bob Hawke Prime Minister of Australia

1081 [He is] a shiver looking for a spine to run up.

On Deputy Prime Minister Paul Keating's disclosure that Hawke had broken a promise to endorse him as his successor *Newsweek* 17 Jun 91

Denis Healey Laborite leader

1082 It's like being savaged by a dead sheep.

On being criticized by Foreign Secretary Geoffrey Howe *NY Times* 3 Jul 87; on Healey's congratulations years later on becoming Foreign Secretary, Howe said it was "like being nuzzled by an old ram," quoted by Healey *The Time of My Life* Norton 90

Jesse Helms US Senator

1083 [There has been] a cacophony of carping.

On criticism of foreign policy on the Persian Gulf *Newsweek* 17 Dec 90

Herbert Hoover 31st US President

1084 People moved in hushed and anxious hours while his life lingered on. It was thus I learned that some great man was at the helm of our country.

On President Garfield's assassination *The Memoirs of Herbert Hoover* Vol I Macmillan 51

1085 [Some] uninformed persons recollect my term... solely as the period of the Great Depression... [and] that was indeed the nightmare of my years in the White House.

Preface to Vol II 52

1086 The only way out of elective office is to get sick or die or get kicked out. Democracy is not a polite employer.

Vol III 52

1087 The White House... a palace more comfortable than that of most kings.

ib

1088 A chameleon on plaid.

On his opponent Franklin D Roosevelt, quoted by James MacGregor Burns *The Lion and the Fox* Harcourt, Brace 56

1089 The humble decimal point... [has a] pathetic and heroic life wandering among regimented ciphers, trying to find some of the old places he used to know.

Recalled on Hoover's death 21 Oct 64

E Howard Hunt CIA officer and White House consultant

1090 Operation Gemstone.

To Attorney General John N Mitchell on code-name for the Watergate break-in, quoted by Fred Emery *Watergate* Times Book 94

Douglas Hurd British Foreign Secretary

1091 May you bring down every duck in the last flight of the shoot.

Election day cable to President Bush's campaign director *New Yorker* 7 Dec 92

Henry J Hyde US Congressman

1092 This is not a Christmas tree. This is the whole Emerald City of Oz.

On viewing passage of the Democratic administration's $30.2 billion anti-crime bill as a measure that he believed would not effectively fight crime and was filled with pork, *Washington Post* 29 Jul 94

Harold Ickes US Secretary of the Interior

1093 Lewisite is ordinarily thought of as a deadly poison gas.

On United Mine Workers President John L Lewis *Life* 23 Oct 50

1094 Dewey has thrown his diaper into the ring.

On NY Governor Thomas E Dewey's presidential candidacy at age 39 *ib*

1095 He is suffering from halitosis of the intellect. That's presuming he has an intellect.

On Senator Russell Long, quoted by Arthur M Schlesiger Jr *The Politics of Upheaval* Houghton Mifflin 88

Frank Ikard US Congressman

1096 He. . . knows how many thousands of flat-headed bolts were used in a Chevrolet and what it would do to the national economy if they took out three of them.

On Alan Greenspan's appointment as chair of Federal Reserve Board *Time* 5 Jun 87

Adm Bobby Ray Inman US Navy

1097 If you talk about your conversations you don't get invited to have other ones.

On relationships with US Presidents *NY Times* 19 Jan 94

Reverend Jesse Jackson civil rights leader

1098 Mend it but don't end it.

On continuation of affirmative action, a comment almost immediately incorporated in an address by President Clinton 19 Jul 95

Andrew Jacobs Jr US Congressman

1099 It's like saying that the patient died but the good news is that he's eating less.

On the Reagan administration's boast of reducing inflation *Washington Post* 6 Jun 82

Gary Jacobson Professor of Political Science, University of California, San Diego

1100 You don't convince people to support you for your reasons. You convince them to support you for their reasons.

On the need for candidates to adjust their positions to shifting public attitudes *NY Times* 17 Sep 95

Claudia ("Lady Bird") Johnson First Lady

1101 That immaculate woman, exquisitely dressed. . . caked in blood!

On Jacqueline Kennedy Onassis after the assassination *A White House Diary* Holt Rinehart Winston 70

1102 I. . . surveyed the room, picking out friend and foe and question mark.

On legislators assembled for State of the Union 10 Jan 67 *ib*

1103 I face the prospect of another campaign like an open-ended stay in a concentration camp.

ib

1104 Every half-hour you are thrust into confrontation with people who you think are smarter than you are.

At Radcliffe baccalaureate *ib*

1105 Mrs Kennedy is going to marry Aristotle Socrates Onassis! . . . I feel strangely freer! No shadow walks behind me down the halls of the White House.

ib

1106 The chariot has turned into a pumpkin and all the mice have run away.

On reaching the LBJ Ranch after six years in the White House, quoted by Julie Nixon Eisenhower *Pat Nixon* Simon & Schuster 86

1107 We were distant. But that suited both of us.

On Jacqueline Kennedy Onassis *Washington Post* 23 Mar 95

1108 This country needs to be united. And sadly, sadly, he wasn't the man who could do it.

On President Johnson's decision not to seek a second term during the Vietnam War *ib*

Lyndon B Johnson 36th US President

1109 Texas proudly casts its vote for the fighting sailor who wears the scars of battle.

On a short-lived nomination of John F Kennedy as vice presidential running mate for Adlai E Stevenson 17 Aug 56

1110 They've been peddling eyewash about themselves and hogwash about Democrats. What they need is a good mouthwash.

On Republican slurs against running mate John F Kennedy *Quote* 23 Oct 60

1111 Your daddy never let his Vice Presidents put their heads above water.

To Franklin D Roosevelt Jr, quoted by Arthur M Schlesinger Jr *A Thousand Days* Houghton Mifflin 65

1112 He wants to repeal the present and veto the future.

On presidential opponent Barry Goldwater, address at Cleveland 8 Oct 64

1113 They aren't walking around with their zippers unbuttoned.

On his staff's discreet political behavior *Quotations from Chairman LBJ* Jack Shepard and Christopher S Wren Ed Simon & Schuster 68

1114 It hurts good. I want to miss it.

On leaving the White House 2 Feb 69

1115 The difference between being a member of the House. . . and the Senate is the difference beteween chicken salad and chicken shit.

To George Bush, news summaries 31 Dec 70

1116 The presidency has made every man who occupied it, no matter how small, bigger than he was; and no matter how big, not big enough for its demands.

NY Times 26 May 72

1117 He could leave more dead bodies in the fields with less remorse than any politician I've ever seen.

On former Texas Governor John B Connally recalled on Johnson's death 22 Jan 73

1118 I knew from the start if I left a woman I really loved—the Great Society—in order to fight that bitch of a war. . . then I would lose everything at home. My hopes. . . my dreams.

On Vietnam, quoted by Doris Kearns Goodwin *Lyndon Johnson and The American Dream* St Martin's 76

1119 Let's press the flesh.

On shaking hands, quoted by Alistair Cooke *The Americans* Knopf 80

1120 I want every family in America to have a carpet on the floor and a picture on the wall. After bread, you've got to have a picture on the wall.

On visiting Pittsburgh's Polish-Czech area *ib*

1121 When things haven't gone well...call in a secretary or staff member and chew him out. You will sleep better and they will appreciate it.

People 2 Feb 87

1122 It's like necking, it's a hard neck but there's no going to bed.

On running for elective office *Lyndon* PBS TV 8 Apr 87

1123 I never trust a man unless I've got his pecker in my pocket.

Regardie's Apr 88

1124 [It is] about as much fun as throwing cow shit at the village idiot.

On Washington's annual Gridiron dinner, quoted by Hedrick Smith *The Power Game* Random House 88

1125 I felt I was being chased on all sides by a giant stampede.

On angry public protests, quoted by Charles Kaiser 1968 in *America* Weidenfeld & Nicolson 88

1126 I was being forced over the edge by demonstrating students, marching welfare mothers, squawking professors, and hysterical reporters.

ib

1127 If you have a mother-in-law and she has only one eye and it is in the middle of her forehead, you don't keep her in the livingroom.

On the Vietnam War and presidential elections, quoted in *LBJ: An American Experience* PBS TV 29 Sep 91

1128 It's like being a dog in the country. When you run, they're always snapping at your ass. When you, stop, they fuck you to death.

Time 23 May 94

1129 I am going to sit on this porch for two years, doze, and think. And then one day I will get up and get Walter Lippmann.

On one of the severest columnists on Vietnam *Remembering My Good Friends* HarperCollins 95

Lionel Joseph British Minister of Housing and Social Services

1130 The political center in France is like the Bermuda Triangle. Whoever approaches it disappears.

NY Times 18 May 91

Nancy Kassebaum US Senator

1131 Honk if you're not running for president.

Suggestion for bumper sticker *Wall Street Journal* 22 May 87

Mitchell Kaye Georgia State Legislature

1132 Every year they release two liberal Democrats in the wild so they don't become an endangered species.

On growing conservativism as seen in the election of Georgia's first Jewish Republican legislator *NY Times* 1 Aug 94

Edward M Kennedy US Senator

1133 I don't think about being President any more. I don't think about it any less either.

Newsweek 12 Oct 87

1134 I see Michael Harrington as delivering the Sermon on the Mount to America. . . . when the night was the darkest.

On Harrington's "war on poverty" in *The Other America* Penguin 81 *NY Times* 2 Jul 88

1135 Where was George?

Refrain taken up by conventioneers in attack on Vice President George Bush for disassociating himself with the Reagan administration's setbacks *ib* 20 Jul 88

1136 Racism in a business suit.

On former Ku Klux Klan member David Duke's candidacy for governor of Louisiana *ib* 26 Oct 91

1137 Today's rising tide is lifting only some of the boats, primarily the yachts.

Expressing belief that "Americans are working more and earning less" *ib* 9 Feb 96

Jacqueline Kennedy Onassis First Lady

1138 I cast only one vote—for Jack. It is a rare thing to be able to vote for one's husband for President and I didn't want to dilute it by voting for anyone else.

At the Hyannis Port MA family compound three days after the 1960 elections, quoted by Arthur M Schlesinger Jr *A Thousand Days* Houghton Mifflin 65

1139 He slumped in my lap, his blood and his brains were in my lap.

On the assasination to Theodore H White *In Search of History* Harper & Row 78

1140 All I keep thinking of is this line from a musical comedy, it's become an obsession with me. . . "Don't let it be forgot, that once there was a spot, for one brief shining moment, that was known as Camelot!"

On Frederick Lowe's lyrics from Alan Jay Lerner's *Camelot* which became synonomous with the Kennedy administration *ib*

1141 Later on when a series of disastrous Presidents and Prime Ministers. . . will have botched up everything—people will say "Do you remember those days—how perfect they were?" The days of you and Jack.

Letter to Harold Macmillan 31 Jan 64 quoted by Alistair Horne *Harold Macmillan* Vol II Viking 89

1142 Uncle Cornpone and his Little Porkchop.

On the Johnsons *Newsweek* 30 May 94

John F Kennedy 35th US President

1143 I just held it out. . . and he grabbed at it.

On offering Lyndon B Johnson the vice presidential spot on Kennedy's presidential ticket 12 Jul 60, quoted by Arthur M Schlesinger Jr *A Thousand Days* Houghton Mifflin 65

1144 [It is] like drafting a state document.

On composing a birthday telegram to Vice President Johnson *ib*

Joseph P Kennedy Ambassador to Britain

1145 With the money I spent, I could have elected my chauffeur.

On contributions to his son's presidential campaign, quoted by Nigel Hamilton *JFK: Reckless Youth* Century 92

Robert F Kennedy US Senator

1146 We Kennedys, we eat Rockefellers for breakfast.

On David Rockefeller's intervention in Peruvian tax dispute, quoted by Peter Collier and David Horowitz *The Rockefellers* Holt Rinehart Winston 76

J Robert Kerrey US Senator

1147 The Republicans would open him up like a soft peanut.

On President Clinton's restoration of relations with Vietnam as a political liability if he had been a candidate in 1991, NPR 15 Jul 95

Nikita S Khrushchev Soviet Premier

1148 Why found another party? That would be like voluntarily letting someone put a flea in your shirt.

To French Socialists *Der Monat* Jun 57

Martin Luther King Jr civil rights leader

1149 When the architects of our republic wrote the magnificent words of the Constitution and the Declaration of Independence, they were signing a promissory note to which every American was to fall heir.

At Lincoln Memorial during the March on Washington 28 Aug 63

1150 This is no time to take the tranquilizing drug of gradualism.

ib

1151 I have a dream that one day we will be able to join hands and sing to the words of the old Negro spiritual, "Free at last, free at last, thank God Almighty, we're free at last!"

ib

Neil Kinnock Member of Parliament

1152 They travel best in gangs, hanging around like clumps of bananas, yellow and thin-skinned.

On Tory critics *London Observer* 22 Feb 87

1153 She only went to Venice because somebody told her she could walk down the middle of the street.

On Prime Minister Margaret Thatcher news reports 9 Jun 87

Henry A Kissinger US Secretary of State

1154 Conservatives who hated Communists and liberals who hated Nixon came together in a rare convergence, like an eclipse of the sun.

On combined opposition to détente *Years of Upheaval* Little, Brown 82

1155 The blood feud with Nixon ran too deep. If Nixon was for détente, perhaps the Cold War wasn't all bad!

ib

1156 Intellectuals should make themselves heard by putting forward their perceptions of what is right. Then let the politicians worry about what is possible.

To an assembly of 76 Nobel laureates *NY Times* 24 Jan 88

1157 When Nelson buys a Picasso, he doesn't hire four housepainters to improve it.

On aides who revised an address Kissinger had prepared for Nelson Rockefeller, quoted by Walter Isaacson *Kissinger* Simon & Schuster 92

1158 I have not faced such a distinguished audience since dining alone in the House of Mirrors.

At the initial Washington meeting between Israeli and Egyptian diplomats *ib*

Alf Landon 1936 Republican presidential nominee

1159 I was an oilman who never made a million, a lawyer who never had a case and a politician who carried only Maine and Vermont.

Hundredth birthday recollections of 1936 race against Franklin D Roosevelt *NY Times* 7 Sep 87

Ivan Lawrence Member of Parliament

1160 It will be a broadcast surpassing impertinence.

On Jesse Jackson's address on British race relations scheduled for the same hour as the Queen's Christmas Day message *NY Times* 26 Dec 94

Nigel Lawson Chancellor of the Exchequer

1161 Her ideal Cabinet contains one person—herself.

Mantra on Prime Minister Margaret Thatcher *Illustrated London News* Oct 88

Jim Leach US Congressman

1162 Whitewater is. . . a metaphor for privilege for a government run by a new political class which takes shortcuts to power with end runs of the law.

On chairing investigaton of Clintons' roles in Whitewater land sales *NY Times* 27 Jul 94

Ann Lewis Political Director, Democratic National Committee

1163 Hillary Clinton is a national Rorschach test of how people feel about the changing roles of women and men.

Vanity Fair June 94

John L Lewis President, United Mine Workers

1164 No tin hat brigade of goose-stepping vigilantes or bibble-babbling mob of blackguarding and corporation-paid scoundrels will prevent the onward march of labor.

Address 3 Sep 1937, recalled on Lewis' death 11 Jun 68

John V Lindsay Mayor of New York

1165 Tides of acid debate. . . gusts of hot air, have played havoc with the paint job.

On redecoration of City Hall *NY Times* 23 Oct 73

1166 Like Zsa Zsa Gabor's fifth husband: I know what I'm supposed to do but I don't know how to make it interesting.

On introducing politicians 16 Apr 78

Mary Lindsay Mayor's wife

1167 That's not the man I sleep with!

On scanning an article on husband John Lindsay's New York City mayorial campaign *Time* 12 Nov 65

General Douglas MacArthur US Army

1168 He'll make a fine president. He was the best clerk who ever served under me.

On Dwight D Eisenhower's election as 34th US President news summaries 31 Dec 52

Harold Macmillan Prime Minister of Britain

1169 A wonderful little man—iron painted to look like wood.

On a successor, Alec Douglas-Home, quoted by John Gunther *Procession* Harper & Row 65

1170 We were told of the succession of Malenkov to the position of Augustus, with Beria (secret police) to Caesar.

Diary entry on Joseph Stalin's death *Tides of Fortune* Macmillan 69

1171 A very pale pasty face. . . large forehead . . . closely cut grey hair. . . respectable black suit. . . a head gardener in his Sunday clothes.

On Soviet Foreign Minister V M Molotov *ib*

1172 Bulganin looks like a Radical-Socialist Mayor of a French industrial town. . . *un bon papa*. . . [and] effects a jolly, friendly, but not undignified style.

On Soviet Prime Minister Nikolai Bulganin *ib*

1173 [I am] a fallen minister, fallen, like Satan, from the Whitehall of heaven, without hope of return.

Letter to a friend on leaving office *ib*

John Major Prime Minister of Britain

1174 I never describe myself as anything. People must make up their own minds.

On being asked if he was a Thatcherite *NY Times* 16 Mar 91

1175 Conservatism is giving people a hand up rather than a hand-out.

London Times 28 Jun 91

1176 I'm fit, I'm well, I'm here and I'm staying.

On attacks on his leadership 5 Jun 93

1177 He deserves a good kick up his endogenous zone.

On Labor's Gordon Brown *ib* 28 Oct 94

1178 You can't shake our constitution around as if it were a cocktail at an Islington dinner party.

3 Dec 94

1179 [A typically] engaging outburst of frankness and candor.

On Kenneth Clark's desire to move from being Chancellor of the Exchequer to Prime Minister "at a time of John Major's own choosing" *ib* 30 Nov 94

1180 A sound bite politician leading a soap powder party—everything pre-determined and pre-packaged.
On Labor's Tony Blair *London Sunday Times* 30 Apr 95

André Malraux French Minister of Culture

1181 France is like those great iron statues buried after ancient conquerors pass by and which suddenly, in time of cataclysms, are unearthed by a flash of lightning.
Quoted by Jean Lacouture *de Gaulle the Ruler* 92

1182 Take an archbishop, add some venerable member of a Masonic lodge, remove a plumber, multiply by a sub-mistress of a brothel and shake: you will have an "alliance deputy!"
Contrasting the "alliance system" as a challenge to the representative system in 1951 elections *ib*

Eugene J McCarthy US Senator

1183 The war in Vietnam. . . [is] of questionable loyalty and constitutionality. . . diplomatically indefensible. . . even in military terms. . . [and] morally wrong.
To Conference of Concerned Democrats in address noted for crystallizing dissent against the Vietnam War 2 Dec 67

1184 Being in politics is like being a football coach. . . smart enough to know the game and stupid enough to think it is important.
LA Times 7 Dec 91

Michael D McCurry Clinton White House Press Secretary

1185 The President, if he were not the President, would have delivered a more forceful response. . . on the bridge of Mr Safire's nose.
On columnist William Safire's charge that Mrs Clinton was "a congenital liar" *NY Times* 9 Jan 96

Raymond J McGrath US Congressman

1186 All sticks and no carrots.
On cabinet pressure to support bipartisan budget compromise *NY Times* 5 Oct 90

Ian McIntyre British Labor Party leader

1187 The First Person of the Soviet Trinity.
On Lenin *London Times* 2 Feb 95

John N Mitchell Nixon campaign chair and US Attorney General

1188 Let's not contribute any more than we have to, to the coffers of organized crime.
On former CIA senior officer G Gordon Liddy's plans to recruit underworld figures for Watergate break-in and other spying, quoted by Liddy *Will* St Martin's 80

1189 If you print that, Kay Graham's tit will be in a wringer.
On *Washington Post* publisher 29 Jun 72 on learning from reporter Bob Woodward of a slush fund to fight Watergate charges, quoted by Woodward and Carl Bernstein *All the President's Men* Simon & Schuster 74

François Mitterrand President of France

1190 The eyes of Stalin, the voice of Marilyn Monroe.
On Margaret Thatcher, quoted in Thatcher's *The Downing Street Years* HarperCollins 93

Robert Moses NYC Parks Commissioner

1191 Never give 'em a cheap ticket to immortality.
Advising successor Thomas Hoving to go after the multi-millionaires for contributions, quoted by Anthony Sampson *The Midas Touch* Hodder & Stoughton 89

Stanley Mosk Attorney General of California

1192 Little old ladies in tennis shoes.
On elderly activists, cited by William Safire *Safire's Political Dictionary* Random House 75

Roy Neel Deputy Chief of Staff, Clinton White House

1193 Her detractors. . . largely viewed as little more than gnats. . . have now become lions and tigers.
On criticism and firing of President Clinton's Surgeon General Joycelyn Elders *Washington Post* 12 Dec 94

Harold Nicolson Member of Parliament

1194 Which Indians? We educated ours. You massacred yours.
On being asked on a US lecture tour to justify British behavior in India, quoted by Peter Vansittart *In the Fifties* John Murray 95

Pat Nixon First Lady

1195 The hearings are just like a snake about to devour people.
On Watergate, letter to a friend, quoted by Julie Nixon Eisenhower *Pat Nixon* Simon & Schuster 86

Richard M Nixon 37th US President

1196 She's pink right down to her underwear.
On allegations of Communist sympathies in Representative Helen Gahagan Douglas whom he defeated in 1950 for the US Senate, recalled by Stephen E Ambrose *Nixon: The Triumph of a Politician* Simon & Schuster 87

1197 Within a few months he was attending every meeting and allowing the discussions to ramble on as if it were his duty to be bored for the country as well as to lead it.

On President Eisenhower's recovery from surgery *RN: The Memoirs of Richard Nixon* Grosset & Dunlap 78

1198 Let us begin by committing ourselves to the truth—to see it as it is, and tell it like it is—to find the truth, to speak the truth, and to live the truth.

Accepting Republican presidential nomination 24 Jul 68

1199 For years politicians have promised the moon. I'm the first one to be able to deliver it.

Radio message to astronauts 20 Jul 69

1200 There are no sacred cows. We will tear up the pea patch.

On dealing with political enemies after winning re-election in 1972, quoted by Stephen E Ambrose *Nixon: Ruin and Recovery* Simon & Schuster 91

1201 I'll pardon the bastards.

To Chief of Staff H R Haldeman on learning details of the Watergate break-in 30 Jun 72, quoted by Fred Emery *Watergate* Times Books 94

1202 They're all on drugs there anyway.

On rejecting the Department of Health, Education and Welfare in favor of the Justice Department in handling the problem of drugs 24 May 71, quoted by H R Haldeman's *The Haldeman Diaries* Putnam 94

1203 We must maintain the integrity of the White House, and the integrity must be real, not transparent.

On the resignations of aides Ehrlichman, Haldeman, Dean, and Attorney General Richard G Kleindienst 17 Apr 73

1204 During the week following the Pentagon Papers' publication, I approved the creation of a special investigation unit within the White House—which later came to be known as the "plumbers"... whose principal purpose was to stop security leaks.

Statement on allegations surrounding Watergate investigation 22 May 73

1205 Can you imagine Jerry Ford sitting in this chair?

On Gerald R Ford whom Nixon nominated to succeed Spiro T Agnew as vice president; remark quoted by Nelson A Rockefeller who later became Ford's vice president, Emery *op cit* 12 Oct 73

1206 To allow the tapes to be heard by one judge would create a precedent that would be available to 400 district judges.

On rejecting order from US Appeals Court to surrender tapes of conversations in the oval office 20 Oct 73

1207 In giving you these tapes, blemishes and all, I am placing my trust in the basic fairness of the American people.

Address to the nation on relinquishing Watergate tapes after the House Judiciary Committee, joined by 8 of the 17 Republicans in its membership, warned that refusal "might constitute a ground for impeachment" 30 May 74

1208 Well, I screwed it up real good, didn't I?

To Chief of Staff Alexander M Haig and Press Secretary Ronald L Ziegler 3 Aug 74 on setting to work on Nixon's resignation address, quoted in *Nixon* Emery *op cit*

1209 You know, Al, you soldiers have the best way of dealing with a situation like this.... You just leave a man alone in a room with a loaded pistol.

To Haig, Emery *op cit* 78

1210 We think that when someone dear to us dies... when we lose an election... suffer a defeat... that all is ended. Not true. It is only a beginning, always.

Farewell remarks to the White House staff 9 Aug 74

1211 Pat and I were happier on Nov 6, 1946, than we were ever to be again in my political career.

On "excitement and jubilation" of winning initial election to US Congress, *RN: Memoirs op cit* 78

1212 Jackson is a poet, Cuomo is a poet, and Dukakis is a word processor.

On Jesse Jackson, Mario Cuomo, and Michael S Dukakis, candidates for 1988 Democratic presidential nomination, news summaries 15 Apr 88

1213 Watergate was one part wrongdoing, one part blundering, and one part political vendetta by my enemies.

In the Arena Simon & Schuster 90

1214 Gorbachev is Wall Street and Yeltsin is Main Street; Gorbachev is Georgetown drawing rooms and Yeltsin is Newark factory gate.

Comparing Soviet leaders during interview in Moscow *Washington Post* 4 Apr 91

1215 I'm kind of allergic to taping, you know.

On spotting a trio of tape recorders that had been set rolling near his sleeve *ib*

1216 Some summits do not help an American president at home, as I am well aware.

At 78, advising Mikhail S Gorbachev against false hopes that another grand summit could help Gorbachev's sagging future *NY Times* 7 Apr 91

1217 If I could find a way to get him out of there, even putting out a contract on him, if the CIA still did that sort of thing, assuming it ever did, I would be for it.

On Saddam Hussein's continuance in office after the end of the Persian Gulf War *60 Minutes* CBS TV 14 Apr 91

1218 Bush will be like Ford. As soon as he leaves town, he'll no longer matter. I've been gone 20 years, but I still matter.

New Yorker 28 Dec 92

1219 There's no way that you could apologize that is more eloquent, more decisive, more finite, or to say that you are sorry, which would exceed resigning the Presidency of the United States. That said it all. And I don't intend to say any more.

In April 84 television interview with former aide Frank Gannon, recalled on Nixon's death *NY Times* 24 Apr 94

Kenneth O'Donnell Kennedy White House aide

1220 Mr President, the president is dead.

To Lyndon B Johnson after assassination of John F Kennedy 22 Nov 63

Thomas P ("Tip") O'Neill Speaker of the House

1221 You can teach an old dog new tricks—if the old dog wants to learn.

On working with President Reagan NPR 2 Jan 89

1222 I thought, poor Sil, four bells did ring for him but for those of us who spent a good part of our lives in Congress, it has another meaning.

On Representative Silvio Conte's death and the four bells that traditionally signify the House's final adjournment, Paul Dixon and Paul Clancy ed *The Congress Dictionary* Wiley 93

1223 Keep your left hand high.

Recommending the boxer's defensive posture to President Carter, recalled on O'Neill's death *NY Times* 7 Jan 94

1224 It was sinful that Ronald Reagan ever became President, but he would have made a hell of a king.

Time 17 Jan 94

George E Pataki Governor of New York

1225 I am me. I was me before I was Governor. I was me before the campaign. I don't want to change now that I'm Governor.

Giving assurance that he was "not playing a role" *NY Times* 23 May 95

John Patten British Secretary of Education

1226 I no longer care what anyone writes about me, save my dear wife in her diary and the recording angel in heaven.

On political criticism *London Times* 21 Jul 94

Eva Perón President's wife

1227 My only flag is Perón; my best reward the love of the Argentine people.

On withdrawing as vice presidential candidate while restating her loyalty to her husband, General Juan Perón, *NY Times* 1 Sep 51

Henry E Petersen Assistant US Attorney General for Prosecutions

1228 If I come up with evidence. . . I am just going to waltz it over to the House of Representatives.

Testimony on conversation with President Nixon, quoted by Fred Emery *Watergate* Times Books 94

Anton Pinay Prime Minister of France

1229 The Algerian personality does not exist.

On French control of Algeria, quoted by Jean Lacouture *De Gaulle the Ruler* Norton 92

General Colin L Powell US Army

1230 In one generation we have moved from denying a black man service at a lunch counter to elevating one to the highest military office in the nation and to being a serious contender for the Presidency.

At news conference announcing that he would not seek presidential nomination *NY Times* 9 Nov 95

Dave Powers aide to President Kennedy

1231 What do you suppose Nixon's doing while you're lying there in bed?

On surefire words for awakening John F Kennedy, quoted by John Bartlow Martin *It Seems Like Only Yesterday* Morrow 86

Dan Quale US Senator

1232 Fifteen thousand journalists. . . [want to] shake him by the ankles until something bad comes out.

On nominees for the vice presidency *USA Today* 17 Aug 88

Jeanette Rankin US Congresswoman

1233 As a woman I can't go to war, and I refuse to send anyone else.

On voting against US entry into World War I and World War II, high points in her career as the first woman to serve in Congress, quoted by Hannah Josephson *Lady in Congress* Bobbs, Merrill 74

Sam Rayburn Speaker, US House of Representatives

1234 Go along to get along.

On politics as a process of accomodation, recalled by former Speaker Gerald R Ford *Washington Times* 24 May 95

Nancy Reagan First Lady

1235 If the President has a bully pulpit, then the First Lady has a white glove pulpit. . . more refined, restricted, ceremonial, but it's a pulpit all the same.

NY Times 10 Mar 88

1236 I'm more aware if somebody is trying to end-run him. . . it just never occurs to him.

On protecting her husband *Time* 28 Nov 88

1237 For eight years I was sleeping with the President, and if that doesn't give you special access, I don't know what does!

On influence in the White House *My Turn* with William Novack, Random House 89

Ronald Reagan 40th US President

1238 I will not make age an issue. . . . I am not going to exploit for political purposes my opponent's youth and inexperience.

At age 73, on television debate with opponent Walter F Mondale 21 Oct 84

1239 I paid for this microphone!

To a New Hampshire moderator who tried to keep President Reagan from speaking in behalf of other candidates *Congressional Quarterly* 23 May 88

1240 Facts are stupid things, uh, stubborn things, I should say.

Slip from prepared text in farewell address to Republican National Convention *NY Times* 21 Aug 88

1241 Go ahead. . . make my day!

On the opportunity to veto tax increases, a remark carried over from Clint Eastwood's film *Dirty Harry ib* 4 Sep 88

1242 The most elegant lynching I have ever seen.

On the annual Gridiron dinner of the Washington press, quoted by Hedrick Smith *The Power Game* Random House 88

1243 You can get me to crap a pineapple but you can't get me to crap a cactus.

On House Speaker James C Wright's proposal to omit Social Security and postpone a tax-cut for a year in exchange for domestic spending cuts and other measures *ib*

1244 If he's Harry Truman, I'm Roger Rabbit!

On similarities drawn between opponent Michael S Dukakis and President Truman *Washington Post* 2 Jan 89

1245 John doesn't look you in the eye. He looks you in the tie.

On campaign strategist John Sears, quoted by Nancy Reagan *My Turn* with William Novack Random House 89

1246 There's our little bungalow down there!

On viewing the White House from a helicopter the day he left office, excerpted in *Washington Post* 22 Apr 91 from Lou Cannon's *President Reagan: The Role of a Lifetime* Simon & Schuster 91

1247 They're pointing to the wrong end of Pennsylvania Avenue.

To Republican National Convention on liberal Democrats pressing for change *NY Times* 18 Aug 92

1248 Politics is just like show business. . . a hell of an opening, you coast for a while, you have a hell of a closing.

ib 23 Apr 95

Ralph Reed Executive Director, Christian Coalition

1249 We're the McDonald's of American politics.

On registering the coaliton's 1,500th county chapter *Time* 15 May 95

Richard Reeves biographer

1250 He was an artist who painted with other people's lives, squeezed people like tubes of paint, gently or brutally, and the people around him—family, writers, drivers, ladies-in-waiting—were the indentured inhabitants serving his needs and desires.

President Kennedy Simon & Schuster 93

Robert Reischauer Director, Congressional Budget Office

1251 I'm standing in the kitchen and having my wife throw pots and pans at me.

On preparing to testify to Congress on the Clinton health plan *Newsweek* 2 Jan 95

Janet Reno US Attorney General

1252 I'm just an awkward old maid with a very great affection for men.

On rumors that she was a lesbian *Washington Times* 22 Feb 93

Ann Richards Texas State Treasurer, later Governor

1253 Poor George, he can't help it—he was born with a silver foot in his mouth.

On Republican candidate George Bush, keynote address to Democratic National Convention *NY Times* 19 Jul 88; later attributed to reporter Paul Crowell commenting on New York City Parks Commissioner Newbold Morris *ib* 1 Apr 66

1254 They have carved up this state like a non-union meat cutter working on a one-legged turkey.

On federal judges' role in redistricting 26 Jan 92

1255 You have got to prove your manhood down here whether you're a man or a woman.

On Ross Perot's bid for presidential nomination 8 Jun 92

1256 You can put lipstick on a hog, and it's still a pig.

On Republican attempts to enhance its candidates *Sunday Morning* CBS TV 25 Oct 92

1257 This is a knock-down, hide the kids in the barn, fight.

On opposing George W Bush for reelection as governor NBC TV 26 Oct 94

1258 You can stick a fork in Bush because he's done!

ib

1259 He don't know sic 'em from "come here."

ib

Donald Riegle US Senator

1260 I did not organize the meeting... decide who was going to attend... invite anybody... create the agenda... was not invited... and everybody knows I did not attend.

To Senate Ethics Committee on charges that he profited from conferences with savings and loan company *Wall Street Journal* 4 Mar 91

John D ("Jay") Rockefeller IV US Senator

1261 None of this works unless everyone is happy. It's like orchestrating a symphony of unhappiness.

On necessity of compromise on health care financing *Washington Post* 1 Jul 91

Arthur M Schlesinger Jr biographer

1262 Ceremony, circus, farce, melodrama, tragedy... nothing else offers all at once the whirl, the excitement, the gaiety, the intrigue, and the anguish.

On national political conventions *A Thousand Days* Houghton Mifflin 65

1263 At the time it is all a confusion; in retrospect... all a blur.

ib

1264 The Kennedy Presidency began with incomparable dash. The young President, the old poet, the splendid speech, the triumphant parade, the brilliant sky and the shining snow; it was one of the most glorious of inaugurals.

ib 20 Jan 61

Patricia Schroeder US Congresswoman

1265 He's just like a Teflon frying pan: Nothing sticks to him.

On President Reagan's ability to overcome charges of corruption *Boston Globe* 24 Oct 84

1266 Washington is awash in postwar testosterone.

On decision not to seek presidential nomination in the wake of victory in the Persian Gulf War *NY Times* 30 Jun 91

1267 I said, "Schroeder, you've gone from toilet-training your children to menopause in this place. You're getting real close to be a lifer."

On decision to withdraw after serving since 1973 *Newsweek* 18 Dec 95

George P Shultz US Secretary of State

1268 Washington is a resigning town. Nothing else holds the special excitement of a rumored resignation.

Turmoil and Triumph Scribner 93

Alan K Simpson US Senator

1269 [It was like] giving dry birth to a porcupine.

On passage of immigration reform bill *Washingtonian* Mar 89

1270 I get in a lot of trouble around here flapping my jaw and you will too unless you restrain yourself and she didn't and she's going.

On Surgeon General Joycelyn Elders *Nightline* ABC TV 9 Dec 94

1271 When they're after your butt, answer the phone.

To Hillary Rodham Clinton on confronting critics *US News & World Report* 9 Jan 95

Margaret Chase Smith US Senator

1272 I'd go right to Mrs Truman and apologize. Then I'd go home.

On being asked what she would do if she woke up one morning in the White House, recalled on Smith's death 30 May 95

Christopher Soames House of Lords

1273 I wouldn't even treat my gamekeeper like that.

In shocked reaction to former Prime Minister Margaret Thatcher's handling of her cabinet *London Times* 21 Oct 93

Anatoly A Sobchak Mayor of St Petersburg

1274 He tried to reform the unreformable.

On Soviet President Mikhail S Gorbachev *NY Times* 15 Dec 91

David Steel Chair, British Liberal Party

1275 We have acquired the reputation throughout Europe of being a race of off-shore barbarians, unsuccessful and uncouth, a violent people with a raucous ruler.

On Britain under Margaret Thatcher *Wall Street Journal* 12 May 87

George Stephanopolous Advisor to Clinton White House

1276 That ball has to go out of the park, over the river, and through an apartment window.

On campaign manager Bruce Lindsay's desire for total effectiveness in Clinton's public speaking *NY Times* 13 Jan 92

1277 We're always stuck in the small crawl space between "must win" and "can't lose."

On small congressional margins 23 Oct 94

Adlai E Stevenson Governor of Illinois

1278 [The Presidency's] potential. . . smothers exultation and converts vanity to prayer.

On becoming the Democratic nominee for the White House *Time* 4 Aug 52

1279 If Republicans will stop telling lies about the United States, we will stop telling the truth about them.

At Bakersfield CA 10 Sep 52

1280 Looking back, I am content. Win or lose I have told you the truth as I see it. I have said what I meant and meant what I said.

Concluding his presidential campaign, news summaries 10 Nov 52

1281 *Via ovum cranium difficilis est.* The way of the egghead is hard.

On charges that he was too intellectual *Call to Greatness* Harper 54

1282 Shouting is not a substitute for thinking and reason is not the subversion but the salvation of freedom.

ib

1283 He who slings mud generally loses ground.

Recalled on Stevenson's death 14 Jul 65

1284 You can't teach an underdog new tricks.

On presidential hopeful Estes Kefauver's replay of his anti-bossism theme *Newsweek* 1 Nov 71

1285 The best politics is good government.

Quoted by NY Gov Mario Cuomo *NY Times* 26 Aug 90

John Stokes Member of Parliament

1286 At last we saw the gentlemen of England in full cry, and really splendid they looked.

On survival of fox hunting by Commons' vote in what reporter Craig R Whitney referred to as "squirearchy 197, and foxes 175" *NY Times* 15 Feb 92

Noah S Sweat Jr County Judge, Corinth MS

1287 If by whisky you mean the water of life that cheers men's souls. . . smooths out the tensions of the day. . . gives gentle perspective to one's view of life, then put my name on the list of the fervent wets.

In "calculated ambivalence" in evading wet-vs-dry county options, misattributed in *NY Times* 14 Jul 92, corrected by William Safire *op cit* 12 Jan 92

1288 If when by whisky you mean the devil's brew that rends families, destroys careers and ruins one's ability to work, then count me in the ranks of the dries.

ib

Denis Thatcher Prime Minister's husband

1289 Margaret, it is time to go.

To his wife, Margaret, in crisis that forced her from office as Prime Minister after she had lost the loyalty of all but three of her ministers *Time* 3 Dec 90

Margaret Thatcher Prime Minister of Britain

1290 What Britain needs is an iron lady.

Campaign slogan quoted in *Newsweek* 14 May 79

1291 You turn if you want to. The lady's not for turning.

On belief that national decline would not turn if people believed government could alter its course 10 Oct 80

1292 Not sacred cows. . . just cattle to be slaughtered.

On nationalized industries *US News & World Report* 22 Jun 87

1293 It wouldn't have happened if they had had a woman Prime Minister at the time.

On losing the American colonies *NY Times* 4 Jul 87

1294 You don't do that to me, dear. I'm only in politics.

To a Spanish tourist who curtsied *US News & World Report* l6 Nov 87

1295 Cabinet ministers resign from time to time.

To the Commons when asked who in the Cabinet had been sacked *Vanity Fair* Jun 89

1296 There is no such thing as society.

On society as an abstraction and alibi for individual reponsibility, quoted by Hugo Young *The Iron Lady* Farrar Straus Giroux 89

1297 I fight on. I fight to win.

On reports that she would resign *Time* 3 Dec 90

1298 It is rather a funny old world.

On being forced out even though she had won three elections and still held party support

1299 When I looked at him and he looked at me, I didn't feel it was a man looking at a woman. More like a woman looking at another man.

On her opponent Edward Heath, recalled in *London Times* 29 Jun 91

1300 They choose to do that thing to me. . . when I was actually abroad negotiating and signing a treaty for my country. So be it! So be it!

On also relinquishing her seat in Parliament at the time of leaving office *ib*

1301 I am now free to live another life of practical use both to the people of this country and internationally.

ib

1302 You can't expect a person who's not been in the heat of the fire and teeth of the wind to have the same viewpoint as someone who has been through it all.

On her successor John Major *ib*

1303 It is a privilege to take my place on these distinguished and tranquil benches after 33 years before the mast in the other place.

To the Lords *Guardian Weekly* 12 Jul 92

1304 I always found the most effective weapon was "No" or sometimes "No, No, No!"

ib

1305 A typical Foreign Office view! That the European Community's cohesion is more important than that a person like Britain should get a fair deal!

On the charge that her methods alienated others *London Times* 21 Oct 93

1306 It pays to know the enemy—not least because at some time you may have the opportunity to turn him into a friend.

ib

1307 The fact that the baton unexpectedly passed to me. . . would perhaps have embittered or at least disheartened a lesser man.

On Keith Joseph stepping aside as a candidate for Prime Minister to become one of the principal architects of Thatcherism *ib* 19 Dec 94

1308 It would be the equivalent of having the Prime Minister of England invite the Oklahoma City bombers to 10 Downing Street to congratulate them on a job well done.

On President Clinton's White House welcome to Sinn Fein leader Gerry Adams *Newsweek* 15 May 95

1309 I got the distinct impression he felt. . . he was, in effect, being dismissed by his housemaid.

On relieving Christopher Soames as leader of the House of Lords *The Path to Power* HarperCollins 95

1310 Rocking the boat is a good thing if the boat is already adrift and threatened by total shipwreck.

Expressing belief that a party is less hurt by disagreements than by stifled debate *NY Times* 12 Jan 96

Mark Thatcher Prime Minister's son

1311 It's time to pay up for Mumsie.

On approaching a Hong Kong millionaire for a contribution to the Thatcher Foundation *New Yorker* 6 Jan 92

Clarence Thomas US Supreme Court nominee

1312 Unless you kowtow to an old order. . . you will be lynched, destroyed, caricatured by a committee of the Senate rather than hung from a tree.

To Senate Judiciary Committee on charges of sexual harrassment by Anita F Hill who had worked with Thomas on the Equal Employment Opportunity Commission *NY Times* 13 Oct 91

1313 This is high-tech lynching. I cannot shake off these accusations, because they play to the worst stereotypes we have about black men in this country.

ib

1314 I wasn't harmed by a racist group. . . [but] by this process. . . which accommodated these attacks on me.

ib

William Thomas US Congressman

1315 If a member. . . speaks words that under the rules could be taken down and no one asks that they be taken down, then in fact words could have been spoken that would have been taken down, but no one asked that they be taken down—is that correct under our rules?

On demand that Representative Carrie E Meek's remarks about Speaker Newton L Gingrich's book contract should be stricken from the record *NY Times* 19 Jan 95

James E Thompson Governor of Illinois

1316 It is not so much who you elect, it's who you throw out.

On cleaning up government *Chicago Tribune* 26 Jul 81

Jeremy Thorpe Member of Parliament

1317 Greater love hath no man than this, that he lay down his friends for his life.

On Prime Minister Macmillan's cabinet purge *Wall Street Journal* 20 Aug 62

1318 Edward Heath is the plum pudding around which no one ever succeeds in igniting the brandy.

On Prime Minister Heath *London Times* 1 Jun 93

Jacques Toubon French Minister of Culture

1319 You know what happens when you beat mayonnaise too hard—it turns.

On warning against too much enthusiasm for Jacques Chirac's presidential candidacy *London Times* 28 Feb 95

John G Tower US Senator

1320 I've not only been screened, I've been sifted.

On prolonged background check and rejection as Secretary of Defense *Forbes* 23 Jan 89

1321 The old political carcass hung by a lynch mob from an oak tree in Washington last March, has now been cut down and is still alive.

To Texas Republican Party which had nominated Tower to succeed Lyndon B Johnson as the first GOP senator from Texas since Reconstruction *NY Times* 5 Apr 90

1322 In Beirut they hurl a grenade. . . [but] up here. . . they kill you in a different way.

On Capitol Hill politics 6 Apr 91

Jim Trafficant US Congressman

1323 The House is a microwave and the Senate a crockpot; they operate differently.

CNBC 15 Feb 95

Pierre Trudeau Prime Minister of Canada

1324 We are a party of the extreme center, radical middle.

Responding in 1978 to a charge of a rightward turn by his Liberal party *NY Times* 14 Jun 92

Harry S Truman 33rd US President

1325 He looked as if he'd swallowed a hot stove.

On an isolationist senator the day after Pearl Harbor, quoted by David McCullough *Truman* Simon & Schuster 92

1326 There isn't a one of them has enough sense to pound sand in a rat hole.

On *Newsweek* poll of 50 writers, all of whom predicted that Thomas E Dewey would defeat Truman *ib*

1327 Why this fellow doesn't know any more about politics than a pig on Sunday.

On President Eisenhower's 1952 candidacy, quoted by Richard M Nixon *RN: Memoirs of Richard Nixon* Grosset & Dunlap 78

1328 If you can't stand the heat you better get out of the kitchen.

To Aero Club of Washington, quoting a colleague from Truman's days as a county judge 27 Dec 52

1329 It was the tragedy and shame of our time.

On charges of Communists in government *Memoirs: Years of Decision* Doubleday 55

1330 Party platforms are contracts with the people.

Memoirs: Years of Trial and Hope Doubleday 56

1331 It's not the Pope I'm afraid of, it's the Pop.

On John F Kennedy as a Roman Catholic candidate backed by a wealthy financeer-politico father, recalled by Alonzo J Hamby *Man of the People* Oxford 95

1332 The President hears a hundred voices telling him that he is the greatest man in the world. He must listen carefully indeed to hear the one voice that tells him he is not.

This Week 5 Apr 64

1333 How far would Moses had gone if he'd taken a poll in Egypt?

Show Nov 64

1334 Being criticized. . . he never did get it through his head that that's what politics is all about.

On President Eisenhower, Merle Miller ed *Plain Speaking* Berkley 74

1335 The first six months you wonder how the hell you ever got here. For the next six months you wonder how the hell the rest of them ever got here.

To a new Congressman, recalled on Truman's death 26 Dec 72

1336 If a man can accept a situation. . . with the thought that it's only temporary, he comes out all right. But when he thinks that he is the cause of the power, that can be his ruination.

ib

1337 A good politician has had to be 75 percent ability and 25 percent actor, but I can well see the day when the reverse could be true.

Quoted by Francis X Clines "Images: Roosevelt to Reagan" *NY Times* l4 Oct 84

1338 Being president is like riding a tiger. . . keep on riding or be swallowed.

Quoted in "A Guide to the 99th Congress" *NY Times* 28 Dec 84

1339 When you are President, the only future you have is in the memory of the people.

Life Dec 88

1340 I wasn't going to go down in history like Pierce or Buchanan or Chester Arthur or Benjamin Harrison. . . one of your arm-rolling cheek-kissing mollycoddles!

Quoted by William Safire *Safire's New Political Dictionary* Random House 93

1341 The only lobbyist the whole people have in Washington is the President.

ib

Stewart L Udall US Secretary of the Interior

1342 Once you've run for president, the only way to get that out of your system is with embalming fluid.

Quoted by commentator Ken Bode NBC TV 8 Nov 88

Jack Valenti Special Assistant, Johnson White House

1343 Speechwriters have a unique distinction in Washington—none of us has ever been indicted.

Quoted by Peggy Noonan *What I Saw at the Revolution* Random House 90

Colonel Harry Vaughn military aide to President Truman

1344 [Bess Truman] looked the way you do when you draw four aces.

On Truman's announcement that he would not seek another term, quoted by Margaret Truman *Bess W Truman* Macmillan 86

Gore Vidal novelist

1345 Two choleric below-the-title character actors, good for cutaways when the stars needed a rest.

On Pat Buchanan and Ross Perot in the Bush-Clinton presidential race *NY Times* 18 Sep 94

Dmitri Volkogonov historian

1346 He had always stood before us in the death-mask of the earthly God he had never been.

On Lenin *Lenin: Life and Legacy* HarperCollins 95

Robert F Wagner Mayor of NYC

1347 The most important appointment you make. . . is your telephone operator.

On running a campaign with trust and confidentiality *NY Times* 13 Feb 91

Lech Walesa Polish Solidarity leader

1348 They wanted us not to believe in God and our churches are full. . . to be materialistic and incapable of sacrifices but we are anti-materialistic, capable of sacrifice. . . to be afraid of the tanks of the guns, and instead we don't fear them at all.

On Communism's failure in Poland *London Sunday Times* 22 Mar 81

1349 Rushing is good only for catching fleas.

On orderly preparation for free and democratic elections *ib* 7 Jul 89

George C Wallace Governor of Alabama

1350 Talking about schools and highways and prisons and taxes. . . couldn't make them listen. Then I began talking about niggers—and they stomped the floor.

On 1958 Alabama gubernatorial race, quoted by Dan T Carter *The Politics of Rage* Simon & Schuster 95

1351 No son-of-a-bitch will ever out-nigger me again.
ib

1352 Segregation now, segregation tomorrow and segregation forever!

On continuing in office 14 Jan 63, *Life* 26 Dec 69

1353 Welcome to Montgomery. . . may your lessons never be forgotten.

Observing the 30th anniversary of a civil rights protest march, a complete reversal of his original positions 17 Mar 95

Benjamin Ward NYC Police Commissioner

1354 I think he thinks I'm important, and that may be as important as being important.

On Mayor Edward Koch *NY Times* 27 Oct 88

David Watkins Clinton White House Administrative Director

1355 I knew there would be hell to pay if I failed to take swift and decisive actions in conformity with the First Lady's wishes.

Memo on dismissals in the White House Travel Office *Washington Post* 5 Jan 96

Lowell P Weicker Jr Governor of Connecticut

1356 I am in the business, as you are, of where anyone can call you anything—and most of the time they do.

To commentator David Brinkley ABC-TV 12 Jan 92

Mark White Governor of Texas

1357 It will make the Alamo seem like a love-in.

On Ross Perot's bid for the presidency *NY Times* 8 Jun 92

Harold Wilson Prime Minister of Britain

1358 He immatures with age.

On Labor leader Anthony Benn, quoted by Anthony Sampson *The Changing Anatomy of Britain* Random House 83

1359 If you rattle along at great speed, everybody inside is too exhilarated or too seasick to cause any trouble. But if you stop, everybody gets out and argues about where to go next.

On heading the Labor Party *London Times* 9 Feb 95

Betsey Wright aide to President Clinton

1360 They're bimbo eruptions.

On charges of sexual misconduct against President Clinton *Washington Post* 30 May 94

James C Wright Jr Speaker, US House of Representatives

1361 The boiling, churning caldron of America!

On the legislators over which he presided *Life* Fall 87

Boris N Yeltsin President of Russia

1362 Rehabilitation after 50 years is habitual. . . but I am asking for it while I am alive.

To Communist Party Conference *NY Times* 2 Jul 88

1363 Policy making is not as easy as slurping down cabbage soup.

ib 3 Jul 88

Andrew Young Mayor of Atlanta

1364 If the comb can get through your hair without getting interrupted, *then you colored.* If the comb gets hung up, *then you black.*

Defining his role as a black candidate for governor of Georgia *Time* 16 Jul 90

David R Young Administrative Aide, Nixon White House

1365 I am a plumber. I fix leaks.

On participation in a special investigative unit known as the Plumbers, quoted by Theodore H White *Breach of Faith* Atheneum 75

Gennadi Zyuganov Russian presidential candidate

1366 Jesus was the first Communist.

On following Boris Yeltsin in attempting to curry favor with the Russian Orthodox Church *US News & World Report* 24 Jun 96

Political Criticism

Joel Achenbach reporter

1367 Witnesses sweat profusely... as they struggle to find a more reasonable-sounding lie.

On congressional hearings on Clinton involvement in Whitewater land sales *Washington Post* 27 Jul 94.

1368 Not exactly a live wire... a voice that could induce sleep in a shark... the perfect witness who couldn't possibly have witnessed anything.

On Clinton White House counsel Lloyd Cutler's testimony on Whitewater land sales *ib*

1369 Whenever you read that someone is an old friend of President Clinton's you immediately assume he's in trouble.

ib

Roger Ailes media consultant

1370 The public won't forgive you if you're not prepared... not committed... not comfortable and if you're not interesting.

To Republican senators, quoted by Hedrick Smith *The Power Game* Random House 88

1371 You... are the message, not just your words... your energy, your eyes, your clothes, your everything.

ib

1372 In general, the public likes commitment... a very winning trait.

ib

Saul Alinsky labor leader

1373 A racially integrated community is a chronological term timed from the entrance of the first black family to the exit of the last white family.

Rules for Radicals Random House 91

Henry Allen reporter

1374 They are a great tradition... gliding in and out of the corridors of power with the opulent calm of angelfish swimming through an aquarium castle.

On presidential advisers *Washington Post* 3 Jan 89

1375 They get trundled through the city like images of saints on medieval feast days while we toss garlands at them in the form of commission chairmanships, briefing papers, and memos.

ib

1376 He long ago learned to eschew the little turf-dances of human encounter.

On President Bush's National Security Council Adviser Brent Scowcroft

1377 There is also the modesty of a kid who grew up quite small and very, very smart in a place like Ogden, Utah.

ib

1378 It is unlikely that anyone will write his biography, but he will be enshrined in 10,000 indexes.

ib

Joseph W Alsop columnist

1379 There is a miasma of neurotic fear and internal suspicion.

On Washington as the beginning of the McCarthyism of unfounded charges of government disloyalty by supposed Communists *Saturday Evening Post* 29 Jul 50

1380 You should judge presidents like plumbing fixtures—by whether they flush.

W 26 Feb 82

1381 He was our very last frontier president as well as the first we had since Abraham Lincoln and Andrew Johnson

On Lyndon B Johnson *I've Seen the Best of It* Norton 92

1382 [It was] like a man marrying his mistress, long after the flames of passion have flickered and gone out, because he is used to her and needs someone to darn his socks.

On Adlai E Stevenson's second try for the presidency in 1956 *ib*

Jonathan Alter reporter

1383 Vice President Bush was derided as a "lap dog"... [but] by 1988, he was a pit bull.

On Bush's poltical image as president directing the Persian Gulf War *Newsweek* 20 May 91

Stephen E Ambrose historian

1384 This is the political story of the century... high drama and low skullduggery, lies and bribes, greed and lust for power, abuse and misuse of power... attack and counterattack, vicious infighting, and constant psychological warfare.

Forward to *Nixon: Ruin and Recovery* Simon & Schuster 91

1385 It includes fundamental questions of democracy, freedom, justice, and just plain decency.

ib

1386 At stake is the presidency of the United States, as it was in 1973–74 and as it would be in the future.

ib

1387 A classic example of Nixon at work. . . to make everything "perfectly clear," leaving everything opaque.

On Richard M Nixon's *RN: The Memoirs of Richard Nixon* Grosset & Dunlap 78

Yehuda Amichai poet

1388 A psychiatrist could do nothing to solve the city's problems—Jerusalem has no subconscious at all. . . [because] everything is out in the open, even the infighting.

NY Times 10 Sep 95

1389 Where else do you see Jews dressed like 19th-century Russians and Arabs dressed like Arabs and other people in modern dress, all at each other?

ib

1390 An open madhouse. . . but its great accomplishment is that it has succeeded in not being a museum.

ib

Anon

1391 Madly for Adlai.

Presidential campaign slogan for Adlai E Stevenson's nomination 26 Jul 52

1392 Be thankful only one can win.

Bumper sticker on the Nixon-Kennedy presidential race 60

1393 I'd rather be Red than dead.

Slogan of Britain's Campaign for Nuclear Disarmament *Time* 15 Sep 61

1394 [They] either go native, or go sour.

On aging career diplomats, quoted by Anthony Sampson *Anatomy of Britain* Harper & Row 62

1395 "What have you done?" cried Christine./ "You've wrecked the whole party machine./ To lie in the nude may be rude,/ But to lie in the House is obscene."

On War Minister John Profumo's acknowledgment to Commons of intimacy with Christine Keeler who had become known as "Britain's fastest rising fallen woman" *Time* 21 Jun 63

1396 All the Way with LBJ.

Bumper sticker for Lyndon B Johnson's presidential nomination 17 Aug 64

1397 [He looks like] an important senior faun.

On Prime Minister Harold Macmillan, quoted by John Gunther *Procession* Harper & Row 65

1398 Burn, baby, burn!

Radical cry in racial strife and torching in Watts CA and Newark NJ *Time* 11 Aug 67

1399 [He had] pissed on his last campfire.

On rightist revolt against Speaker of the House Sam Rayburn, quoted by William Manchester *The Death of a President* Harper & Row 67

1400 Who Else but Nelse?

Bumper sticker for Nelson A Rockefeller's New Hampshire write-in presidential primary 16 Mar 68

1401 [He was the] abominable no-man.

On Sherman Adams' role as Eisenhower White House Chief of Staff, quoted by William Safire *Before the Fall* Doubleday 75

1402 The Grin Will Win.

Bumper sticker for Jimmy Carter's presidential nomination 14 Jul 76

1403 Get behind a judge on Monday in case you find yourself in front of him on Tuesday.

LA Times 29 Nov 78

1404 To err is human; to blame it on the other party is politics.

Washingtonian Nov 79

1405 Fumbling silence in the White House seeps out over the country like a cold fog over a river bed where no stream runs.

On the Eisenhower administration, quoted by Dean Acheson writing to Harry S Truman 28 May 53, David S McLelland and David C Acheson ed *Among Friends: Personal Letters of Dean Acheson* Dodd Mead 80

1406 It was like the King's assassination, only in reverse—an unforgettable moment of absolute confidence and joy that remains with you all the rest of your life.

On televised address by King Juan Carlos of Spain after an unsuccessful fascist uprising, news reports 23 Feb 81

1407 The Great Communicator.

Frequently heard reference on President Reagan's acting ability to put a good spin on speeches prepared for him 81

1408 Don't report what he says, report what he means.

Editors' rule for covering Senator Barry Goldwater's campaign for presidential nomination, quoted by Robert MacNeil *The Right Place at the Right Time* Little, Brown 82

1409 History will recall, Reagan did the least of all.

Signboard carried by White House AIDS pickets, quoted by Randy Shilts *And the Band Played On* St Martin's 86

1410 Save something for the Third Act.

Show business adage applied by President Reagan to his final months in the White House *Time* 16 Mar 87

1411 There is no unemployment but no one works./ No one works but production goes up./ Production goes up but there is nothing in the stores./ There is nothing in the stores but there is everything in the home./ There is everything in the home but everyone is unhappy./ Everyone is unhappy but everyone votes yes.

Current quip in Moscow *US News & World Report* 20 Apr 87

1412 The future ain't what it used to be.

Iowa farmer quoted by President Bush NBC TV 10 May 87

1413 There are checks and balances in government—the checks go to candidates and the balance to the people.

Sunday Morning CBS TV 17 May 87

1414 I hear what he says and I believe what he says, but what I don't believe is what I hear he says.

An unidentified admiral on Admiral John M Poindexter's testimony in Iran arms sales *NY Times* 18 Jul 87

1415 Bill was a tropical fish. His native habitat was hot water.

On CIA Director William J Casey and his role in the Iran arms sales 19 Jul 87

1416 God bless Nanny, she thinks it wouldn't do for you to know about the naughty things that grown-up people do.

Ballad tweaking Prime Minister Margaret Thatcher *NY Times* 24 Aug 87

1417 They are rooming with Mrs Greenfield.

On England's homeless who sleep in the open, *NY Times* 26 Sep 87

1418 Democracy is the worst possible kind of government except any other kind.

Quoted by Ted Koppel in interview with Phil Donahue NBC 2 Nov 87

1419 I know one thing we did right/ Was the day we started to fight,/ Keep your eye on the prize,/ Hold on, hold on!

Civil rights song quoted by Juan Williams *Eye on the Prize* Viking 87

1420 Ain't gonna ride them buses no more,/ Ain't gonna ride no more./ Why don't all the white folk know/ That I ain't gonna ride no more.

On black boycott of Montgomery AL buses *ib*

1421 People: Don't ride the buses today. Don't ride it for freedom.

Sign posted on Montgomery bus shelters *ib*

1422 You fought a good fight. You were in it right up to the beginning.

Quoted by former Arizona Governor Bruce Babbitt to candidates seeking Democratic presidential nomination NBC TV 18 Feb 88

1423 Under capitalism, man exploits man. Under Communism, the situation is reversed.

Eastern European saying quoted at outset of editorial entitled "The Ides of Marx" *NY Times* 15 Mar 88

1424 I wonder each night what the monster will do to me tomorrow.

Belfast graffiti in wake of sniper shootings during IRA funerals 20 Mar 88

1425 Equality, brutality, stupidity.

Slogan proposed for fountain commemorating Bastille Day *Newsweek* 18 Jul 88

1426 Our wimp can beat your shrimp.

Democratic campaign button promoting George Bush's presidential campaign against Michael S Dukasis, news reports 18 Aug 88

1427 [It is] the sort of respect you get between an elephant and a rhino.

On Prime Minister Margaret Thatcher and Chancellor of the Exchequer Nigel Lawson *Illustrated London News* Oct 88

1428 [He is] Mr Elbows and Knees.

On Democratic presidential nominee Michael S Dukakis *Time* 21 Nov 88

1429 Reagan for Rushmore.

Slogan implying a Ronald Reagan immortality equal to other presidents carved into Mt Rushmore *Time* 21 Nov 88

1430 It's morning again in America.

Reagan slogan in 1984 presidential campaign, quoted by Hedrick Smith *The Power Game* Random House 88

1431 Poverty's where the money's at.

On President Johnson's anti-poverty program, quoted by Jimmy Breslin *He Got Hungry and Forgot His Manners* Ticknor & Fields 88

1432 Before you save the world, you've got to save your seat.

On legislators who need to keep in close touch with constituents *NY Times* 2 Jan 89

1433 We understand everybody.

Solidarity Party slogan seen in Warsaw shortly after the union gained legal status *ib* 13 May 89

1434 The 80-year-olds are calling meetings of 70-year-olds to decide which 60-year-olds should retire.

On reactions to sudden resurgence of octogenarian revolutionaries in Chinese government *Time* 12 Jun 89

1435 Arizona has the two best Senators money can buy.

On alleged campaign support from a savings and loan executive for John McCain and Dennis DeConcini *NY Times* 22 Dec 89

1436 Stagflation!

Westminster economists' term for Britain's stagnant economy and simultaneous inflation, quoted by Alistair Horne *Harold Macmillan* Vol II Viking 89

1437 All the egg heads are in one basket.

On President Kennedy's advisers, quoted by Prime Minister Macmillan in letter to the Queen *ib* 12 Apr 61

1438 He's like ugly on ape.

White House lingo on hard political stances *Newsweek* 26 Feb 90

1439 The bureaucracy Americans love to hate.

On the US Postal Service, quoted by Ted Koppel *Nightline* ABC TV 16 Mar 90

1440 [We may have a] peace dividend.

On reapportionment of defense funds to peaceful uses, defined by President Bush in NPR interview 17 Mar 90

1441 [They] are not particular monarchists, but they are becoming Juan Carlists.

On Spain's loyalty to its king *Town & Country* Apr 90

1442 The Americans have taken out the cancer but they have left the patient with so many problems that he still could die.

A Panamanian official's wife on US invasion in the wake of the Noriega dictatorship *Newsweek* 2 Jul 90

1443 She cannot see an institution without hitting it with her handbag.

A Conservative Member of the Parliament on Prime Minister Margaret Thatcher, quoted by George Will "The Successful Annoyer" *Newsweek* 2 Jul 90

1444 What's the difference between the US and Russia? The US will soon be the only one with a legal Communist Party.

NPR 2 Oct 90

1445 When the frog asked the scorpion why he was bitten, the scorpion said, "Well, you know the Middle East."

Discussion preceding the Persian Gulf War Station WAMU Washington 19 Oct 90

1446 Don't iron while the strike is hot.

Women's liberation slogan quoted on PBS 26 Jan 91

1447 Fused at the hip.

On national security adviser Brent Scowcroft and Secretary of State James A Baker III as the Siamese twins of the Bush White House *NY Times* 21 Feb 91

1448 I caught a bear./ Bring him here./ He won't go./ Then come here yourself./ He won't let me go.

Russian folk saying quoted by the weekly *Commersant* on the first national referendum that sought a mandate for Mikhail S Gorbachev's post-perestrokia era *ib* 20 Mar 91

1449 We're here./ We're queer./ Get used to it.

Motto of the homosexual liberation movement Queer Nation that rejected use of the term "gay" *ib* 6 Apr 91

1450 When these guys jump off a cliff, they like to hold hands.

On growing number of senators opposing Clarence Thomas' nomination to the US Supreme Court *ib* 28 Sep 91

1451 Twelve drawers full of political cancer.

Assessment by an FBI agent of the files of Director J Edgar Hoover *Newsweek* 23 Sep 91

1452 [It is] the heraldic equivalent of a pair of furry dice bouncing around in the back of a state coach.

On the title of Countess of Finchley bestowed on the still contentious former Prime Minister Margaret Thatcher *New Yorker* 6 Jan 92

1453 Excessive compartmentalization yields the Bay of Pigs.

On President Bush's tendency to treat some activities, notably the choice of Dan Quayle as a running mate, with the secrecy of the 1961 invasion of Cuba *Washington Post* 7 Jan 92

1454 Social Security is the third rail of American politics—touch it and you're dead.

Quoted by Social Security Commissioner Dorcas Hardy Station WAMU Washington 10 Jan 92

1455 The day Leningrad became St Petersburg again, every pretender in Europe took out his scepter and polished it.

Comment by an unidentified member of the Romanov family *Vanity Fair* Feb 92

1456 Clothes-pin voting: Hold your nose and press the lever.

On voting the party line Station WAMU Washington 28 Feb 92

1457 I am a citizen of a nonexistent state and I don't know where I live. . . the Commonwealth of Independent States, or is it the Russian Federated Republic? Is it Siberia, and is it the Sovereign Republic of Altai?

On confusion of many Russians after the Soviet Union was dissolved *NY Times* 14 Jun 92

1458 We expected a nice sound bite that evening. We got bitten instead.

An aide to President Bush *Time* 10 Aug 92

1459 It's election time in America, when politicians go off their medication.

On eve of the National Republican Convention, Station WETA Washington 15 Aug 92

1460 In politically conservative, repressive times, big breasts on women become very popular and in liberal, free-wheeling times, small breasts become popular. . . . Clearly we are in a repressive age.

Caller to San Francisco's KGO *Chris Clark Show,* "A New Boom and Bust Theory" *Harper's* Aug 92

1461 In a repressive age people feel the need for nurturing. That's why big breasts become popular. . . we get scared and we get conservative.

ib

1462 The economy, stupid!

Sign in Clinton headquarters that became a by-word for the central issue of the 1992 presidential campaign *Fortune* 19 Oct 92

1463 I don't think it's anything they hear. It's what they don't hear.

On false expectations of Clinton cabinet appointees *NY Times* 25 Dec 92

1464 Sometimes it's sort of circular. . . [and] as the process goes along, they believe it's true because they read it in the press.

ib

1465 It's easier to get a photograph of the Pope in the shower than a picture of her.

On Hillary Rodham Clinton's low profile in the period between her husband's election and inauguration *Newsweek* 25 Jan 93

1466 From the cradle to the grave,/ Even if I misbehave,/ There's a place for me/ On government subsidy.

Quoted by a Baltimore caller to Station WAMU Washington 15 Jun 93

1467 This is nonsense on stilts.

A phrase downplaying some official statements and political predictions *Washington Post* 16 Jul 93

1468 The baby born after a difficult labor grows healthy.

Proverb quoted by political analyst Kenzo Uchida after election of Japan's first Prime Minister in 38 years not drawn from the Liberal Democratic party *NY Times* 7 Aug 93

1469 She appeals to affection for Mum, deference to Miss, fear of Madam, and a male eye for Mademoiselle.

On Betty Boothroyd, Speaker of the House of Commons *Washington Post* 29 Sep 93

1470 It's not every day you learn the solution to one of life's great mysteries—how do horses get to sleep standing up?

On listening to an address by Prime Minister John Major *Guardian Weekly* 17 Oct 93

1471 Vote today, die tonight.

Guerilla slogan that failed to discourage 80 percent of El Salvadorans from voting for a free government, quoted by former US Secretary of State George P Shultz *Turmoil and Triumph* Scribner 93

1472 Behold the turtle, it only makes progress when it sticks its neck out.

A favorite saying of Harvard President James B Conant, quoted by James G Hershberg *James B Conant* Knopf 93

1473 It's the eggplant that ate Chicago.

On an inconsequential attack on something large, quoted by Suzanne Garment of the American Enterprise Institute on the call for a special prosecutor to investigate President Clinton's involvement in Whitewater land sales *Washington Times* 6 Jan 94

1474 A potato candidate. The best part of him is underground.

On Adlai E Stevenson's ancestors *Washington Post* 9 Jan 94

1475 If I be walking on the wrong side of the road when the bomb hits, I'll just vote from heaven.

An elderly black man on possible attack on his way to vote in South African election that ended three centuries of white minority rule *Washington Post* 3 May 94

1476 It's compassion fatigue.

On people who were weary of feeling sorry about character charges against President Clinton NPR 13 May 94

1477 In 1968 you could only find five homosexuals in America.

On growing acceptance of the gay community as seen in the thousands attracted to Gay Pride Week and New York's Gay Games *ib* 25 Jun 94

1478 He is the castor oil of the Palestinian peace movement.

On PLO Chair Yassir Arafat *ib* 4 Jul 94

1479 He looks like a homeless man in a thousand dollar suit.

On Senator Edward M Kennedy's campaign for re-election at age 62 *Washington Post* 1 Oct 94

1480 There came a generation that knew not Joseph. Nor Jack. Nor Bobby.

On Kennedy mystique's fading influence on voters *ib*

1481 He is. . . born on third base and thinks he hit a triple.

On President Bush's upper class world, a slur revived during his son's campaign to be governor of Texas *NY Times* 2 Nov 94

1482 The 30-Second TV Spot: The Chicken Pox of Politics.

Headline on 1994 political campaign 8 Nov 94

1483 The only poll that really counts happens on Election Day.

Time 14 Nov 94

1484 Home and dry before he started.

Cited by columnist Matthew Parris as one of the most favored political cliches when there is no opposition *London Times* 28 Nov 94

1485 Conservative back bench turkeys were never likely to vote for Christmas.

ib

1486 The President is a walking dead man. He just doesn't know it yet.

A senior legislator on President Clinton's political future as he entered the second half of his term of office *Nightline* ABC TV 6 Dec 94

1487 He was. . . on the "enemies list" of President Nixon. . . a Social Register of the liberal establishment.

On Leonard Bernstein's endorsement of the Black Panthers and boycott of Nixon's 1973 inaugural concert, quoted by Meryle Secrest *Leonard Bernstein* Knopf 94

1488 He won't stab you in the back—even if you deserve it.

On Al Gore as Clinton's running mate, quoted by Bob Woodward *The Agenda* Simon & Schuster 94

1489 The United States is a society which has passed from barbarism to decadence without any intervening phase of civilization.

Cited by London's *Economist* as "the best loved cliché of all" in thinking about America, quoted by Gerald Gunther *Learned Hand* Knopf 94

1490 The nigger in his place. . . the coolies out of the country.

National Party of Africa's double-barreled 1948 campaign theme, recalled by Nelson Mandela *Long Walk to Freedom* Little, Brown 94

1491 Has he reconnected with the angry middle?

Listener's question on President Clinton's rapport with

the middle class after his State of the Union NPR 26 Jan 95

1492 You British are just waving us goodbye.
An elderly Belfast woman expressing a loyalist view of Prime Minister John Major's plan for greater independence for Northern Ireland *London Times* 23 Feb 95

1493 I'm spending my children's inheritance.
Bumper sticker on the economics of Social Security *NY Times* 24 Feb 95

1494 Louisianans don't tolerate corruption; they demand it.
ib 5 Mar 95

1495 Welfare should be a safety-net, not a hammock.
NPR 12 Mar 95

1496 To avoid criticism, say nothing, do nothing, be nothing.
Inscription on pillow given Claudia ("Lady Bird") Johnson by her staff *Life* Apr 95

1497 The French want to attack, the Americans want to bomb, and the British want to have another meeting.
A US diplomat on war in Bosnia *NY Times* 27 Jul 95

1498 Where is Lesbian, a country or a place?
Question asked of a reporter by an English-language interpreter at the Fourth World Women's Conference *US News & World Report* 18 Sep 95

1499 Lincoln was the Christ figure of democracy's passion play.
Quoted by commentator David Gergen from among 5,000 books on Lincoln *McNeil-Lehrer Report* 17 Oct 95

1500 I refuse to deal with the organ-grinder. I want the monkey.
A Member of Parliament who wanted to by-pass the Commons' Speaker Betty Boothroyd, cited by Boothroyd as the most insulting remark in her experience CBS-TV 29 Oct 95

1501 If you are willing to run for president and do what it takes, you are not worthy of being president.
Quoted by commentator David Brinkley, Station WAMU Washington 7 Nov 95

1502 [His political style is] masterful inactivity.
On the skill of India's President Munester P V Narashimha in deferring difficult decisions *NY Times* 20 Dec 95

1503 She's going to do happy talk.
On speculation that Hillary Rodham Clinton would be more of an advocate for childrens' rights than for political causes as her husband's second-term campaign approached Station WAMU Washington 5 Jan 96

1504 Don't buy books by crooks.
On Richard M Nixon's memoirs that sold more copies than any other presidential memoir in history despite negative reviews *Washington Post* 30 Jun 96

R W Apple Jr Chief, Washington bureau *NY Times*

1505 Underdog, true believer, one man against the crowd: there was a lot of Gary Cooper in him, the lonesome cowboy, a lot of Jimmy Stewart, too, the honest man facing down the politicians, and quite a bit of Huck Finn.
Reporting on Lieutenant Colonel Oliver L North in hearings on Iran arms sales *NY Times* 12 Jul 87

1506 Pensive, passionate, sanctimonious, sincere, impatient, impenitent, articulate, aggressive, cocky, contrite—[North] was all of those things.
ib

1507 The good times are supposed to roll in New Orleans, a hedonistic Latin city, not in Minneapolis, an earnest Scandinavian one.
On charges against Minnesota Congressman Arlan Strangeland that seemed more reflective of Louisiana than a conservative state *ib* 30 Oct 90

1508 Behind all foreign policy there lurks, or ought to lurk, careful political calculation. What the folks at home will not support, the traveling potentate cannot afford to promise.
On President Clinton's Eastern European tour *ib* 13 Jan 94

1509 He was a Brobdingnagian among Lilliputians in Tokyo, viewed against the untested and the shop-worn leaders with whom he conferred.
On President Clinton, quoted by columnist James J Kilpatrick *Richmond VA Times-Dispatch* 20 Feb 94

1510 Twenty-three teenagers who could screw up a one-car funeral.
On the Clinton White House restaffing of its travel office *Washington Post* 28 Jun 94

1511 Foreign policy came calling at the White House today. . . a frequent visitor and lately an increasingly welcome one.
On the lessening of President Clinton's inclination to shun foreign policy in favor of personally managing a series of visible accomplishments overseas 29 Sep 95

1512 This afternoon's events. . . provided some badly needed political theatrics.
On signing of the Palestine-Israeli peace accord *ib*

1513 The United States played the mid-wife's role with skill and without too much self-praise, and the moment had the genuine aroma of history.
ib

1514 China has rejected the long-sought invitation for a meeting. . . because it did not come with a promise of 21-gun salutes, a state dinner and Chinese flags fluttering along Pennsylvania Avenue.
On an international exchange that fell short of a summit between President Clinton and President Jiang Zemin *ib*

1515 The day was entangled in ambiguity and illuminated by ardor.

On conflicting messages of peacefulness and agressiveness in black speakers addressing the Million Man March on Washington 17 Oct 95

W H Auden poet

1516 Were one to deprive them of all their igneous figures of speech. . . instead of stamping out flames or consuming stubble with fire, they would only shut out a draught or let in a little fresh air.

On politicians, quoted in Edward Mendelson ed *W H Auden* Vintage 91

David Axelrod media consultant

1517 While George Bush putts, America goes down the hole.

On the listless Bush campaign for presidential reelection *NY Times* 23 Jan 92

Russell Baker columnist

1518 That night, image replaced the printed word as the natural language of politics.

On the Kennedy-Nixon debates 26 Sep 60, forerunners of a standard fixture of US presidential contests, recalled by David Halberstam *The Fifties* Villard 93

1519 A new star of tremendous national appeal, the skill of a consummate showman.

On President Kennedy at his first televised press conference *NY Times* 26 Jan 61

1520 The search for perfect security has uglified Washington....Uniforms everywhere. Ugly concrete excrescences. Barricades, metal detectors, official guns...an air of penitentiary about the place...security so palpable it gave me the fantods, which is what ghostly encounters gave Huckleberry Finn.

On as uneasy Washington that reflected, Baker believed, "the national insecurity" *ib* 16 Mar 91

Moustapha Bakry Editor, *Al Wafd* weekly magazine

1521 The trees sway in anger and the birds fly away to avoid smelling your hated fragrance.

On Benjamin Netanyahu's first visit to Cairo after becoming Prime Minister of Israel *NY Times* 19 Jul 96

Julian Barnes foreign correspondent

1522 He is the only political interviewer. . . who doesn't approach the Prime Minister on all fours while loosening the collar to allow easier entry of the stiletto heel between the neck vertebrae.

On commentator David Dimbleby and Prime Minister Margaret Thatcher *New Yorker* 5 Mar 90

1523 She resembles the figurehead on the prow of some antique sailing ship, emblematic as much as decorative. . . [but is] cast as Matron. . . who supervises the dinners and hands out the cod-liver oil.

On Mrs Thatcher *ib*

1524 When accused of the worst crimes under the sun, she merely frowns slightly as if it is yet another complaint about the quality of her custard.

ib

1525 She has seen generations of boys come and go, some well groomed and courteous, others rough and uppity, and she knows that all of them, in the long run, will look back fondly on her legendary strictness.

ib

1526 To the liberal, snobbish, metropolitan, cosmopolitan, she displayed a parochial, small-shopkeeper mentality, puritanical and Poujadiste, self-interested and xenophobic, half sceptred-isle nostalgia and half count-your-change bookkeeping.

ib 15 Nov 93

1527 Notions of British sovereignty, honor, and independence. . . bray out like trumpet cadenzas from these pages.

ib

Laurence I Barrett *Time* magazine

1528 [He had] a teatime snack of crow.

On presidential adviser David Gergen's revising of a press briefing that he had given a few hours earlier in the Reagan White House *Gambling With History* Doubleday 83

Felicity Barringer reporter

1529 They wanted. . . justice, written not just in words but in stone. . . to create from a past bounded by forgetfulness a future guarded by memory.

On groups campaigning in Moscow for memorials for victims of Stalin *NY Times* 3 Jul 88

Lord Beaverbrook (William Maxwell Aiken) Publisher

1530 He did not care in which direction the car was traveling, so long as he remained in the driver's seat.

On Prime Minister Lloyd George *New Statesman* 14 Jun 63

1531 With the publication of his private papers in 1952, he committed suicide 25 years after his death.

On Field Marshall Earl Haig's *Men and Power* Duell Sloan Pearce 57, recalled on Beaverbrook's death 9 Jun 64

Hilaire Belloc essayist

1532 If you reject me on account of my religion I shall thank God that he has spared me the indignity of being your representative.

In unsuccessful race for Parliament, recalled on Belloc's death 16 Jul 53

Irving Berlin composer

1533 I Like Ike.

Lyrics that Berlin based on the song "They Like Ike" in his Broadway musical *Call Me Madam* and personally introduced to an Eisenhower rally at Madison Square Garden 8 Feb 52, quoted by Laurence Bergreen *As Thousands Cheer* Viking 90

Berliner Illustrierte magazine

1534 Refugees—people who vote with their feet.

On crowds fleeing East Germany, Special Issue 61

1535 The last freedom—freedom to flee.

ib

Barton Bernstein Professor of History, Stanford

1536 It's been an intellectual bloodletting.

On the controversial documentation and ultimate cancellation of the Smithsonian Institution's 50th anniversary exhibition of the Hiroshima bombing *USA Today* 31 Jan 95

Jeffrey H Birnbaum *Time* magazine

1537 Ross Perot's memory is in direct proportion to his height.

On 5'5" Texas gadfly presidential candidate Ross Perot, Station WAMU Washington 1 Aug 94

1538 If money is the milk of politics, California is the cash cow.

On generous contributions for which candidates vied after Governor Pete Wilson dropped out of the presidential race *Time* 9 Oct 95

Edward Bliss Jr CBS producer

1539 It promoted harassment by subpoena.

On Nixon administration's media relationship *Now the News* Columbia University Press 91

Sidney Blumenthal staff writer

1540 Filled with shards of kitsch, ripped from the context of popular culture.

On Ronald Reagan's presidential rhetoric *Washington Post* 3 Jan 89

Ken Bode *Washington Week in Review*, Station WETA

1541 [It constitutes] one-ninth of one-third of the Government.

On the significance of a US Supreme Court appointment *NY Times* 26 Jun 94

Vernon Bogdanor Fellow, Brasenose College, Oxford

1542 The Lords. . . appear likely to slumber on.

On unsuccessful attempts to reform the House of Lords *London Times* 7 Nov 94

Jorge Luis Borges Argentine writer and poet

1543 The Falklands thing was a fight between two bald men over a comb.

On Argentina's attempt to take over British-held islands *Time* 16 Feb 83

Peter G Boyle biographer

1544 They are the last drops of vintage wine from a musty old bottle.

On Winston S Churchill's letters to President Eisenhower, Peter G Boyle ed *The Churchill-Eisenhower Correspondence 1953–1955* University of North Carolina 90

Nicholas F Brady US Secretary of the Treasury

1545 If you want to be vice president, stand out here in the rain in your underwear and let everybody see what you're made of.

On the need to strip the secrecy from selection of vice presidential candidates *Washington Post* 28 Aug 88

H L Brands Professor of History, Texas A & M University

1546 No country is heroic to its historians.

The Devil We Knew Oxford 93

Jimmy Breslin columnist

1547 Many city commissioners marched in great pain. . . [from] damaged lumbars from leaning over to pick up all the money.

On political graft reflected in Manhattan's St Patrick's Day Parade *NY Daily News* 16 Mar 86

1548 Mirrors and. . . beautiful blue smoke rolling over the surface of highly polished mirrors, first a thin veil. . . then a thick cloud. . . the mirrors catching it all and bouncing it back and forth.

On illusions of political power *NY Times* 24 May 87

1549 There can be seen in the smoke great, magnificent shapes, castles and kingdoms, and maybe they can be yours.

ib

Alan Brinkley Professor of History, City University of New York

1550 Britain may imagine itself a new Greece to America's Rome.

Quoted by Christopher Hitchens *Blood, Class, and Nostalgia* Farrar Straus Giroux 90

David Brinkley commentator

1551 Most delegates have an Elks Club mentality.

On the national political conventions *This Fabulous Century* Time-Life Books 70

1552 If you turn on your set and see nothing is happening. . . do not call a serviceman. You have tuned in the US Senate.

ABC TV 1 Jun 86, quoted by Edward Bill Jr *Now the News* Columbia University Press 91

1553 [They] will fearlessly commit both parties to favor mother love and the protection of the whooping crane, and to oppose the man-eating shark and the more unpopular forms of sin.

On party platforms, quoted by Marc Gunther *The House That Roone Built* Little, Brown 94

1554 Safely and reliably conservative. . . from the Ohio heartland. . . all blue suits, white shirts, bare scalp, rimless glasses, vest and gold watch chains. It was said he looked like "a composite picture of 16 million Republicans."

On Senator Robert A Taft as a 1952 candidate for presidential nomination *David Brinkley: A Memoir* Knopf 95

Vera Brittain novelist and biographer

1555 Politics are usually the executive expression of human immaturity.

Rebel Passion Allen & Unwin 64

Joseph Brodsky poet

1556 Illness and death. . . the only things that a tyrant has in common with his subjects. . . [and] in this sense alone, a nation profits from being run by an old man.

"On Tyranny" *Less Than One* Farrar Straus Giroux 86, recalled on selection of the Russian-born, exiled Brodsky as a Nobel laureate *NY Times* 23 Oct 87

Tom Brokaw commentator

1557 More questions than a three-year old at bedtime.

On voters of the mid-80s NBC TV 4 Nov 86

Richard Brookhiser *National Review*

1558 Mr Dukakis's biggest investment. . . is his son-of-immigrants portfolio. . . . [which] cleanses him of that great peril for post-McGovern Democrats, the whiff of Freak House: what Chuck Colson dubbed, "acid, amnesty, and abortion."

On Michael S Dukakis's presidential nomination, quoted by John Kenneth White *The New Politics of Old Values* University Press of New England 88

Ronald Brownstein *LA Times*

1559 The maximum in glamour was married to the maximum in power.

On the Hollywood-Washington friendship of John F Kennedy and Frank Sinatra *The Power and the Glitter* Pantheon 91

Patrick E ("Pat") Buchanan presidential aspirant

1560 The upholstered playpen of the arts and crafts auxiliary of the Eastern liberal establishment.

On the National Endowment for the Arts *NY Times* 22 Feb 92

1561 There will be no peace in the valley.

Pledge to fight all pro-abortion candidates in race for presidential nomination NPR 2 Aug 96

Art Buchwald columnist

1562 This is not an easy time for humorists because the government is far funnier than we are.

At international meeting of satirists and cartoonists *NY Times* 28 Jun 87

Christopher Buckley writer and editor

1563 I don't have conservative credentials. What I have are conservative genes.

On inheriting his father's political stance, quoted by Peter Occhiogrosso ed *Once A Catholic* Houghton Mifflin 87

William F Buckley Jr columnist

1564 [Conservatism is] a paradigm of essences toward which the phenomenology of the world is in continuing approximation.

Wall Street Journal l8 Dec 67

1565 Being America's foremost Socialist is like being the only tall building in Topeka, Kansas.

Quoted by Michael Harrington *The Long-Distance Runner* Holt 88

Elisabeth Bumiller reporter

1566 A perfumed herd of thousands drank beer and wore emeralds . . . a bacchanalia of the haves.

On the Reagan administration's pre-inaugural parties *Washington Post* 19 Jan 81

William Bundy governmental official

1567 Vietnam really rang his Korea bell.

On insistence of Secretary of State Dean Acheson, that Truman's see-it-through Korean War policy be applied to Vietnam, quoted by Douglas Brinkley *Dean Acheson: The Cold War Years 1953–71* Yale 92

James McGregor Burns historian

1568 He would use the tricks of the fox to serve the purposes of the lion.

On Franklin D Roosevelt's belief that gaining power by winning elections was the first, indespensable task *Roosevelt: The Lion and the Fox* Harcourt, Brace 56

Kenneth L Burns historian

1569 Over 10,000 men and women have served [in the Congress]: farmers and housewives, Rhodes scholars and ex-slaves, astronauts and priests, basketball stars and convicted felons, school teachers and playwrights. And lawyers, always lawyers.

In television profile *The Congress* PBS TV 4 Jul 90

1570 He was a slow moving giant hulk... out of whose collar rose an enormous, round, clean shaven baby face like a Casaba melon from a fat black stalk.

On the pre-Civil War black Congressman George White *ib*

Ian Buruma *The Spectator*

1571 [Japan is] a nation of people longing to be 12-year-olds or even younger.

The Wages of Guilt Farrar Straus Giroux 94

1572 There they sit... glassy-eyed in front of pinball machines ... while listening to the din of the *Battleship March* beating away in the background.

ib

1573 German memory was like a massive tongue seeking out, over and over, a sore tooth.

ib

Dr Helen Caldicott President Emeritus, Physicians for Social Responsibility

1574 [Mickhail S Gorbachev] established that Russian flesh burned at the same rate as American flesh.

On reduction of atomic weapons, Station WAMU Washington 15 Apr 92 on her book *A Plan to Heal the Earth* Norton 92

David Cannadine reporter

1575 Prince Albert... discovered the impotence of being earnest.

On Queen Victoria's consort *The Pleasure of the Past* Norton 91

1576 Neville Chamberlain had greatness thrust upon him—and in trying to prove he could bear it, collapsed under the weight.

ib

Lou Cannon reporter

1577 He was... simply an actor on loan from Hollywood who had entered politics because he wanted to restrain the power of an increasingly intrusive government.

President Reagan: The Role of a Lifetime Simon & Schuster 91

1578 [He] may have been the one president in history... who saw his election as a chance to get some rest.

ib

Stokely Carmichael Chair, Student Nonviolent Coordinating Committee

1579 We want black power! We want black power! That's right—that's what we want. Black power!

At Greenwood MS rally following ambush shooting of freedom marcher James Meredith *Christian Science Monitor* 11 Jul 66

General Michael P C Carns US Army

1580 In today's confirmation proceedings, one is innocent until nominated. Thereafter one must struggle to prove innocence.

On declining to face "venomous and abusive" congressional hearings to be confirmed as director of the CIA *Newsweek* 20 Mar 95

Robert Caro biographer

1581 He was a builder on Moses' scale... [and] his arrogance was also on the Moses scale.

On comparing NY Governor Nelson Rockefeller with NYC Parks Commissioner Robert Moses *The Power Broker* Knopf 74

Nippy Carville Clinton aide's mother

1582 She was better copy than all of us put together. You've got a racehorse like that, partner, you've got to let her run.

On President Clinton's mother, Virginia Clinton Kelley *NY Times* 9 Jan 94

Barbara Chase-Riboud historian

1583 She should be able to walk through the front door of American history.

On Sally Heming as Thomas Jefferson's black mistress in Chase-Riboud's book *The President's Daughter* Crown 94 Station WAMU Washington 21 Nov 94

Marquis Childs columnist

1584 [He is] an Iago of Iagos.

Likening William C Bullitt, US Ambassador to Russia and France, to a Shakespearian character who appeared to be the epitome of trust but was driven by bitterness to compromise his cause *Witness to Power* McGraw-Hill 75

George J Church reporter

1585 Nothing in Biden's campaign became him like the leaving of it.

On Senator Joseph Biden's withdrawal from race for presidential nomination *Time* 5 Oct 87

Deborah Churchman essayist

1586 [She had] desert-dry wit within the confines of a deadpan delivery.

On Clare Boothe Luce *Christian Science Monitor* 9 Dec 80

William L Clay US Congressman

1587 Rule 1 is take what you can, give up what you must. Rule 2 is take it whenever, however, and from whomever. Rule 3 is, if you are not ready to abide by the first two rules, you are not qualified for a career in politics.

Advice to blacks in politics *Just Permanent Interests* Amistad 93

Eleanor Clift reporter

1588 He is the Prince of Pork. Cross him and you pay; praise him and you play.

Reporting on Senator Robert Byrd *Newsweek* 15 Apr 91

1589 She'll hit all the media's stations of the cross.

On Hillary Rodham Clinton's talk-show appearances to sell the presidential health plan *ib* 20 Sep 93

1590 It's a feather dropped from the wind.

On Vice President Dan Quayle's withdrawal from race for presidential nomination Station WAMU Washington 10 Feb 95

Francis X Clines reporter

1591 Here is a monument to American politics, a tower of talk built of 900 five-inch reels of tape kept in a vault in the same building that houses the Constitution.

Reporting on the US Archives' public airing of Nixon tapes *NY Times* 17 Jun 80

1592 It is as if Hogarth played a joke on Constable and stippled a band of lively, hope-worn vulgarians across a pristine English landscape.

On welfare recipients in a fourteenth-century manor house *ib* 26 Sep 87

1593 A Caribbean flower amid Anglo-Saxon evergreens.

On Diane Abott as first black woman elected to the British Parliament in its 700-year history *ib* 5 Jun 88

1594 By all the whimsy of history, the bold plan deserves to be called the Capitalist Manifesto, so completely would it undo Marx and Engels.

On Stanislav S Shatalin's scheme to junk Communism in 500 days *ib* 9 Sep 90

1595 The remarkable proposal drifted out into a capital increasingly ominous for the sight of bread lines actually longer than the vodka lines.

On emergence of the possibility of dropping Communism *ib*

1596 They were busy moving ever deeper down Manichaean corridors of irrelevant debate.

ib

1597 The sprawling city's... flirtation with democracy had to suffer a total of 5,000 chaperones—5,000 lawmakers daily at the business of talking, warning, despairing, proposing, voting and even outright seceding.

On Moscow's plethora of neighborhood councils 3 Mar 91

1598 They bear the terrible burden of being designer clones of the parents, displayed for genealogical appreciation.

ib

1599 Mr Agnew emerged... after long absence for a bit of ceremonially controlled limelight.

On the unveiling of a marble bust near the US Senate gallery of Vice President Spiro Agnew, 22 years after he left office with a felony plea bargain 28 May 95

ib

1600 Another Vice President, staring out in petrified whiteness, is recalled as having most likely died in *flagrante delicto* after he left office.

On Nelson A Rockefeller *ib*

1601 [Mr Agnew invests] the gallery with more of the ragged human truth of politics than is ever hinted at in all the daily heights of C-Span oratory.

ib

1602 Calvin Coolidge, the Vice President who ate lunch alone every day, is pinned behind an open door, sharing his niche with a fire extinguisher.

ib

1603 Flesh and stone, hubris and humility mingle uneasily in the Senate corridors: life is in the blur, history in the marble.

ib

1604 Tantalizing bits broadcast... before the Capital's ever-ravenous political cast... bordered on a lampoon of all the long Washington culture of hearings past, from pumpkin papers to smoking gun... erased tapes and White House plumbers.

On investigation of the Clintons' involvement in Whitewater land sales 19 Jul 95

1605 Laboring somewhere short of tumult, the joint panel. . . allowed Mr Schumer. . . the sudden brandishing of an AK-47 assault weapon wielded as authoritatively as a bishop's crook.

On Congressman Charles E Schumer's display of arms amassed for the government's attack on the Waco Branch Davidians 20 Jul 95

1606 No forum outdid the Waco hearing [in] ranging from religion's apocalyptic certainties to democracy's conspiratorial doubts.

ib

1607 [He] pleaded for the record, bobbing amid the white-capped ocean of rhetoric.

On Congressman Bill Zeliff urging colleagues to "back away from the attraction of political rhetoric" *ib*

1608 The D'Amato image. . . gauche, lippy, brazen populist—is hardly a full picture here, where his many strands of power are gathered easily in his restless, far-reaching hands.

On Senator Alfonse M D'Amato and his "soft-spoken gravity" in chairing the hearings on Whitewater land sales 30 Jul 95

1609 His new sass-and-tell autobiography. . . burnishes his scrapper's image banking bill arcana that leave critics suspicious; his soaring love life; Whitewater's intriguing political rapids, and his growing role in national politics.

On publication of D'Amato's *Power, Pasta, and Politics* Hyperion 95 *ib*

1610 [It was] a 10-volume, 40-pound tome released. . . with all the heft of a millstone.

On Senator Bob Packwood's diaries made public by the Senate Ethics Committee 8 Sep 95

1611 He patted the huge indictment as gingerly as an executioner's gurney.

On Senator Mitch McConnell's chairing the Senate Ethics Committee against Packwood 10 Sep 95

James B Conant President, Harvard University

1612 It seems as though I were in a lunatic asylum, but I am never sure who is the attendant and who the inmate.

Letter in 1950 to Bernard Baruch on secret consultations on the atomic bomb, quoted by James G Hershberg *James B Conant* Knopf 93

1613 What irony. First we were afraid the Germans would rearm, now we are afraid they won't.

Diary entry 23 Jul 66

James Cone theologian

1614 Black power is an affirmation of the humanity of blacks in spite of white racism. . . an attitude, an inward affirmation of the essential worth of blackness.

Black Theology Orbis Books 93

Cyril Connolly essayist

1615 Sometimes I think the England I know now is like a parent that has had a first stroke.

Arthur Koestler ed *Suicide of a Nation* Macmillan 64

William Connor historian

1616 To have been alive with him was to have dined at the table of history.

On Winston S Churchill, recalled on Connor's death 6 Apr 67

Alistair Cooke commentator

1617 All Presidents start out pretending to run a crusade, but after a couple of years they find they are running something much less heroic, much more intractable: namely, the Presidency.

Writing in *The Listener* 1963, quoted by William Safire *Safire's Political Dictionary* Random House 93

1618 [It was] an episode out of George Orwell rewritten by Charles Dickens.

On Gerald R Ford's succession to the US presidency on Richard M Nixon's resignation *The Americans* Knopf 79

1619 [Elections are] like a christening, a wedding, a graduation ceremony, a holy war, a revolution even. . . a fireworks display, a gaudy promise of what life ought to be, not life itself.

ib

1620 [After elections] we settle down to the long, gray pull of mending-and-making-do, the day-to-day duties and favors and shenanigans and small kindnesses, and the grumbles and chores of life.

ib

Matthew Cooper essayist

1621 In an age when revelation is revered, with talk shows serving as confessionals and bestsellers urging us to connect with the child within, biography seems more important than ever.

"Words and Pictures Larger Than Life," essay on the place of President Clinton's personal history in the presidential campaign *US News & World Report* 27 Jul 92

1622 Without the oxygen of ideas, the flame of personality quickly dies.

On the importance of substantial thinking to support interest in a colorful personage *ib*

David Corn Washington editor, *The Nation*

1623 Dulles stood as the symbol. . . a tweedy, pipe-smoking, blue-blooded diplomat. . . "a gentleman spy."

Washington Post 27 Nov 94 on CIA Director Allen Dulles as the epitome of the spy masters in Peter Grose's *Gentleman Spy* Houghton Mifflin 94

Country Life magazine

1624 He is not quite a one-man band, but he is the only man in the band who matters much. He knows it; everyone knows it; it is said not to endear him to his colleagues.

On Liberal Democrat Paddy Ashdown 2 Mar 95

1625 People want to believe that they live in a nation that can afford a royal yacht.

"Let Them Eat Lollipops" editorial on retention of the *Britannia* 13 Jul 95

1626 The public might even feel that a government whose instincts are right about small things may be equally trusted with large ones.

ib

1627 Lollipop deprivation is now so acute that the idea tasted sweet on the tongue.

ib

George Creel journalist

1628 While talking to her—as nice a way to pass an hour as could be imagined—one expects her to start shelling peas.

On interviewing Arkansas' Hattie Caraway, first woman elected to a full term in the US Senate, quoted by David Brinkley *Washington Goes to War* Knopf 88

Ivor Crewe Professor of Political Science, University of Essex

1629 She hasn't been dealt a very good hand, but she's a skilled player and the rest of the people around the table are such poor players they allow her to win.

On Margaret Thatcher's bid for a third term *Wall Street Journal* 14 May 87

Julian Critchley Member of Parliament

1630 Thirty-five years ago you could tell a Tory just by looking at him. . . pre-war sleekness: elderly gentlemen in Trumper's haircuts, wearing cream silk shirts and dark suits, Brigade or Old Etonian ties. They were all called Charlie; today they all seem to be called Norman.

A Bag of Boiled Sweets Faber & Faber 95 quoted by Matthew d'Ancoa *London Times* 21 Nov 94

E M Dealey Chair, *Dallas Morning News*

1631 We need a man on horseback to lead this nation, and many people in Texas and the southwest think that you are riding Caroline's bicycle.

To President Kennedy, echoing the opposition to him on the eve of the visit climaxed by the Kennedy assassination, quoted by Arthur M Schlesinger Jr *A Thousand Days* Houghton Mifflin 65

Ralph De Gennaro Director of Appropriations Project, Friends of the Earth

1632 [We need] green scissors.

On cutting government subsidies in order to protect the ecology *Washington Post* 31 Jan 95

Ann Devoy reporter

1633 They were stuck with a lemon of a candidate that they were trying to sell as lemonade.

On Republican Vice President Dan Quayle *Washington Post* 16 Jul 89

Richard Dimbleby BBC commentator

1634 Moving through the darkness of the night is an even darker stream of human beings. . . . They are the people, and to watch them pass is to see the nation pass.

On the long lines at the bier of George VI in London's Westminster Hall, quoted by Jonathan Dimbleby *Richard Dimbleby: A Biography* Hodder & Stoughton 75

Phil Donohue talk-show host

1635 It could turn Congress into the Mormon Tabernacle Choir.

On government censorship of art NBC TV 19 Sep 90

Maureen Dowd columnist

1636 The Senator talked to the Attorney General as though he were the driver of a fire engine who had decided to take the scenic route to a five-alarm blaze.

On Senator Warren Rudman's questioning of Attorney General Edwin Meese III on Iran-Contra arms sales *NY Times* 28 Jul 87

1637 She showed the value of contrition as a political weapon in the television age.

On Hillary Rodham Clinton's news conference on Whitewater land sales and stock market investments 23 Apr 94

1638 President Clinton returned today. . . to the university where he didn't inhale, didn't get drafted, and didn't get a degree.

On President Clinton's visit to Oxford where as a Rhodes scholar he had tried marijuana, avoided conscription, and left to attend Yale Law School *NY Times* 9 Jun 94

1639 He can talk like Cotton Mather and write like Jacqueline Susann.

ib 4 Dec 94 on Speaker of the House Newton L Gingrich's novel *1945* Baen Books 94

1640 Don't write anything down, but save everything that anyone else writes down.

On political survival in Washington *US News & World Report* 9 Jan 95

1641 The only focus is the unfocusability.
On President Clinton *ib*

1642 The graceful, hard male animal who did nothing overtly to dominate us yet dominated us completely, in the exact way we wanted that to happen at this moment, like a fine leopard on the veld, was gone.
On Colin Powell's withdrawal from consideration for presidential nomination *NY Times* 9 Nov 95

1643 He offered Mr Clinton a two-page strategy on acting like Nixon without looking like Nixon.
On attorney James Hamilton's counsel on questions about Whitewater land sales l7 Dec 95

1644 Mrs Clinton is accustomed to stepping behind an apple-pie-and-motherhood scrim.
On the First Lady's emphasis on interest in wholesome issues to transcend what she decribes as "all the spiderwebs that are spun" about political influence 7 Jan 95

1645 She has taken to the hearth with a vengeance... using rituals of domesticity to make her desire for "systemic" change seem less threatening.
ib

Slavenka Drakulic Croatian editor and feminist

1646 [It has] turned into... an ill-fitting shirt... sleeves too short, collar too tight. You may not like the color, and the cloth might itch. But... there is nothing else to wear.
On nationalism's distortion of Yugoslavia's moral compass after 45 years of Communism *The Balkan Express* Norton 93

Susan Dunn Professor of French Literature and History, Williams College

1647 How could the hegemony of English as the new international language of finance, science and popular culture not be a bitter blow to the collective narcissism of the French?
Letter in reply *NY Times* 10 Apr 94 to French Minister of Culture Jacques Toubon's salute to proposed law to ban foreign words, especially English, from the public domain "Tempest in a Demitasse" *op cit* 4 Apr 94

1648 The cult of the French language tells us that the key to the national identity of the French is not a religion, geography, a common past or a Constitution. The key to France is French.
ib

Bob Dylan musician and lyricist

1649 How many roads must a man walk down before you can call him a man?... The answer, my friend, is blowin' in the wind, the answer is blowin' in the wind.
"Blowin' in the Wind" song from which a radical youth movement known as the Weathermen took its name, copyright H Witmark & Sons 84

Terry Eagleton Warton Professor of English Literature, Oxford University

1650 "British" is a political concept, "English" a cultural one. Britain means Crown, State, and Empire. England means tea shops, lager louts, and sun-drenched cathedral closes.
Literary Englands David Gervais Ed Cambridge University Press 93

The Economist London

1651 They snigger and smirk... sneer and jeer... murmur and yawn... gossip salaciously in the bars... honk and cackle when the Prime Minister or his opposite number is trying to talk.
On Speaker Betty Boothroyd's task of bringing politicians to order in the House of Commons *NY Times* 27 Sep 93

1652 They are like unruly schoolchildren, egged on by the frisson of a chance of being spanked by Madam Speaker but knowing they will usually get away with naughtiness.
ib

Robin Edmonds British Foreign Service

1653 It was as if all the resources and treasures which in the days of her pre-eminence had been built up by Victorian thrift and enterprise had now been flung, with a kind of calculated prodigality, upon the pyre of total war.
On Britain's World War II expenditures of a quarter of its national wealth *Setting the Mould* Norton 86

India Edwards Chair, Citizens for Johnson

1654 A spavined little hunchback.
On John F Kennedy as Lyndon B Johnson's opponent, a deprecatory characterization avoided by the press, recalled by *Washington Post* editor Ben Bradlee *A Good Life* Simon & Schuster 95

T S Eliot poet

1655 Your pigs are far more intelligent than the other animals, and therefore the best qualified to run the farm... [but] what was needed (someone might argue) was not more communism but more public-spirited pigs.
Rejecting George Orwell's *Animal Farm* manuscript, quoted by Michael Shelden *Orwell* HarperCollins 91

Geoffrey Elton Professor of History, Clare College, Cambridge

1656 When I meet a historian who cannot think that there have never been great men, great men moreover in politics, I feel myself in the presence of a bad historian.

On "the belittling of great men" *Political History* Garland 84

1657 There are times when I incline to judge all historians by their opinion of Churchill—whether they can see that. . . he still remains, quite simply, a great man.

ib

Ron Elving Political Editor, *Congressional Quarterly*

1658 They don't have to sit down and write a long letter that would pass the 4th grade teacher for penmanship.

On the convenience of E-mail in the increasing number of letters to legislators, Station WAMU Washington 4 Jul 95

1659 It doesn't have to be long, or be eloquent, or be Wordsworth.

ib

Fred Emery Washington Bureau Chief, *The Times of London*

1660 Watergate loomed important, but as distant as the Napoleonic wars.

On proposing and narrating the BBC retrospective on Watergate as the "greatest political scandal in American history" *NY Times* 16 May 94

1661 It's the sequential worsening, the way it is drawn out and unfolds slowly over time, that makes it so compelling. You watch, gripped and amazed, wondering not only how could this have happened, but will they get him in the end?

ib

Guillermo Endara Panamanian attorney

1662 If father will fix it, why should we?

On US intervention in reign of General Manuel Antonio Noriega *NY Times* 27 May 88

Gordon Englehart reporter

1663 He could peck corn with the chickens.

On Vice President Dan Quayle's common touch "RX for the Veep" *Newsweek* 20 May 91

David Ensor foreign correspondent

1664 He has descended upon Russia like an avenging Old Testament prophet.

On Alexandr Solzhenitsyn's return to his homeland *Nightline* ABC TV 18 Jul 94

Steven Erlanger reporter

1665 It all reminds Russians that the collapse of the Soviet Union was like a sudden shotgun blast that caused all the crows to fly up out of the tree, hover for a time to look around, and then quietly resettle, though sometimes on different branches.

On the rebuilding of Moscow's 19th century Cathedral of Christ the Savior *NY Times* 26 Sep 95

Robert Evans Professor of Health, University of British Columbia

1666 What really bothers subordinates is not so much worrying about being attacked by a leopard. . . [but] being yawned at by a higher ranking male, showing very large teeth, whenever one is trying to enjoy one's dinner or one's mate.

On comparative studies of East African baboons and 10,000 persons in the British civil service ecosystem *Guardian Weekly* 11 Sep 94

Charles Evers Mayor, Fayette MS

1667 We're not going to do you like you done us, white folks. We just gonna make damn sure you don't do us no more.

On becoming the first black to head a municipality since Reconstruction *Time* 18 Jul 69

James Farrands Imperial Wizard, Ku Klux Klan

1668 If I were a black man, I guess I'd be heavily involved in the black movement. I'm the natural leader type.

Life Jan 87

Louis Farrakhan President, Nation of Islam political party

1669 There's a new black man in America today. . . you don't have to bash white people. . . [and] all we got to do is go back home and turn our communities into productive places.

To the Million Man March on Washington marked by upbeat positivism *NY Times* 16 Oct 95

William Farrell Chief of Albany Bureau *NY Times*

1670 Nelson is a true democrat. He has contempt for everyone.

On Vice President Nelson A Rockefeller, quoted by Peter Collier and David Horowitz *The Rockefellers* Holt Rinehart Winston 76

Jules Feiffer cartoonist

1671 As a matter of racial pride we want to be called blacks. Which has replaced the term Afro-American. Which replaced Negroes. Which replaced colored people. Which replaced darkies. Which replaced blacks.

Quoted by William Safire *Language Maven Strikes Again* Doubleday 90

Patrick Fenton political analyst

1672 Once, in the 1950's, their fathers sat quietly and listened whenever the President spoke on television.

On apathy of non-voters in a Brooklyn bar to White House broadcasts *NY Times* 15 Mar 88

1673 John F Kennedy for a brief time gave their fathers an America where the words of a President were once so grand that they hung in the kitchens of the working class.

ib

Millicent Fenwick US Congresswoman

1674 The gentle and respectful ways of saying "To hell with you" are being abandoned.

Recalled on Fenwick's death 16 Sep 93

Don Ferguson Canadian radio satirist

1675 [It is a way] to prick the balloon of pomposity.

On political cartoons *NY Times* 28 Jun 87

Howard Fineman political correspondent

1676 The vice presidency is the sand trap of American politics.

"RX for the Veep" on Dan Quayle's image problems *Newsweek* 20 May 91

Johannes Fink parish priest

1677 Short speeches, long sausages.

Advice to a post-war youth group that included future West German Chancellor Helmut Kohl *Vanity Fair* Dec 90

Mary D Fisher AIDS victim

1678 I am one with a black infant struggling with tubes in a Philadelphia hospital. . . [and] with the lonely gay man sheltering a flickering candle from the cold wind of his family's rejection.

To the Republican National Convention 19 Aug 92

1679 If you do not see this killer stalking your children, look again. There is no family or community, no race or religion, no place left in America that is safe. Until we genuinely embrace this message, we are a nation at risk.

ib

Marshall Fishwick Professor of American Studies, Washington & Lee

1680 His aloof alabaster face stares at me from monuments, paintings, coins, and postage stamps.

On George Washington *Saturday Review* 20 Feb 60

1681 Towns named after him are everywhere. Beds he slept in are relics, stones he stepped on are sacred, battles he lost are victories. . . the Man in the White Marble Toga.

ib

1682 His body may be at Mount Vernon, but his spirit looks down from Mount Olympus.

ib

Kellyanne Fitzpatrick professional pollster

1683 People have accused us of being media whores. If that is true, then it's because we cater to a very horny clientele.

Washington Times 24 Oct 94

Janet Flanner *New Yorker* correspondent

1684 It was. . . the words and voice of an aged patriot, ripe in civilization, wounded in heart and mind, angered by the treachery of former friends, emptying the classic phials of his disdain upon the evil. . . in an outburst of scorn as old as the antiquity of power itself.

On Charles de Gaulle's broadcast against 1961 Algerian uprising *Paris Journal 1944–65* Atheneum 65

1685 It was the male voice of French tragedy.

ib

Michael Foot Member of Parliament

1686 A Royal Commission is a broody hen sitting on a china egg.

Laborite speech to House of Commons, news summaries 31 Dec 64

1687 It is always his desire to give an imitation of a semi-house-trained polecat?

On Conservative Party Chair Norman Tebbit, news summaries 31 Dec 83

Carl Friedrich historian

1688 To be an American is an ideal, while to be a Frenchman is a fact.

Time 9 Nov 87

Al From Executive Director, Democratic Leadership Council

1689 He must govern more grandly and dance again with those who brung him.

Warning against a compromise between centrist views on which President Clinton won office and the liberalism of special interests *Time* 12 Dec 94

David Fromkin Professor of International Relations, Boston University

1690 Arriving early, they stayed late. Theirs was a long day in the sun.

On the defining US role in international politics— Roosevelt, Truman, Eisenhower, Marshall and MacArthur *In the Time of the Americans* Knopf 95

Robert Frost poet

1691 Summoning artists to participate/ In the august occasions of the state/ Seems something artists ought to celebrate.

For John F Kennedy: His Inauguration poem written at age 87; snow-blindness prevented the aged poet from going beyond the first three lines 20 Jan 61

1692 Today is for my cause a day of days,/ And his be poetry's old-fashioned praise,/ Who was the first to think of such a thing.

On Kennedy's invitation *ib*

1693 Courage is in the air in bracing whifts./ A golden age of poetry and power/ Of which this noonday's the beginning hour.

ib

Suzanne Garment American Enterprise Institute

1694 [They] produced a higher-up who was not your average sweaty-palmed witness but a pit bull of an adversary.

On Senatorial committee's questioning of Avrom Landesman, Harvard Law graduate, rabbi, and veteran civil servant *Scandal* Times Books 91

1695 Scandals take hold particularly well when they reinforce a pre-existing idea.

NY Times 13 Mar 94

Romain Gary novelist

1696 Never before has Sancho Panza worked so hard for Don Quixote and both were united in the same man.

On Charles de Gaulle *Life* 20 Nov 70

Henry Louis Gates Jr Chair, African-American Studies, Harvard

1697 Richard Wright wrote famously that the negro is America's metaphor. Now we have Colin Powell as a metaphor for consolidation and O. J. as a metaphor for division.

On the US Army general and famous athlete coming into celebrated and controversial headlines at the same time, quoted by columnist Maureen Dowd *NY Times* 5 Oct 95

Nancy Gibbs Senior Editor *Time*

1698 All honey and suckle.

On Elizabeth H Dole as a presidential campaigner for her husband, Robert J Dole *Time* 1 Jul 96

Franz-Olivier Giesbert biographer

1699 Jacques Chirac acts with conviction. But he lacks convictions.

On completing a biography of France's Prime Minister and future president *NY Times* 16 Mar 88

Brendan Gill *New Yorker* critic

1700 [It was] a vain attempt to subdue that unsubduable country.

On Cromwell's settlement of Scots in the north of Ireland *A New York Life* Poseidon 90

Françoise Giroud biographer

1701 With his air of being entirely enclosed in a first-quality thin cloth, the all-wool and fresh complexioned Pinay is the spitting image of many Frenchmen of his age who daily curse the government.

On Prime Minister Antoine Pinay at age 61 in 1953, recalled on Pinay's death *London Times* 14 Dec 94

Harry Goldman Editor, *Carolina Israelite*

1702 I always knew the first Jewish President would be an Episcopalian.

On Barry Goldwater's candidacy, recalled on Goldman's death 17 Mar 61

Sheldon R Goldstein Executive Director, National Association of Social Work

1703 The American people are getting tired of being trickled on.

On the theory of "trickle-down economics" Station WAMU Washington 13 May 95

Ellen Goodman columnist

1704 They were reading a thousand miles of bad road on his 62-year-old face.

On Senator Edward M Kennedy's hard fight for re-election *Washington Post* 1 Oct 94

1705 Kennedy not only carries baggage from the past, he carries shrapnel, some of it from self-inflicted wounds.

ib

1706 "Character" has become a household word.

ib

Walter Goodman television critic

1707 "Frankly". . . invariably precedes a statement that comes right out of their prepared package.

Reporting on presidential election-year talk shows *NY Times* 28 Aug 92

1708 "The American people"... [a] phrase that is waved each week by representatives of both parties like warriors who have run out of ammunition.

On Secretary of State Henry A Kissinger's Nixon funereal tribute that it was "a privilege to have been allowed to help him" *ib*

1709 It was like watching Metternich deferentially nudge aside a mere emperor.

On Henry A Kissinger's funeral tribute to Richard M Nixon *ib* 29 Apr 94

Paul Greenberg columnist

1710 [There is a] disturbing similarity between Slick Willie and Old Orv.

On former Arkansas Governor Bill Clinton and Orville Faubus, a predecessor who resisted desegregation in 1957; first use of the reference Clinton as "Slick Wille," Pine Bluff AR *Commercial* 20 Sep 80

Jeff Greenfield critic

1711 He's drawn enough lightning to power a major American city for a year.

On Attorney General Edwin Meese III *Nightline* ABC TV 20 Nov 87

1712 It's like a big elephant sitting in the livingroom.

On charges of marital infidelity against presidential candidates 23 Jan 92

Meg Greenfield *Newsweek* columnist

1713 Between Iraq and A Hard Place.

A title considered but not used for a 1974 *Washington Post* editorial; with the problem posed in the early 1990s by Iraq's Saddam Hussein, the pun was widely used according to William Safire *Safire's New Political Dictionary* Random House 93

1714 Shamed people in the modern ambience don't kill themselves, they make a killing.

On the propensity for publishing books instead of committing suicide *Washington Post* 26 Jul 93

Fred Greenstein Professor of Government, Princeton

1715 It hasn't been good for the nation, but it's been good for political science.

On the Reagan presidency *NY Times* 7 Sep 87

William Greider political analyst

1716 If the secrets of the temple were revealed... [the people] would stand before the awesome authority to which free citizens deferred. They would know at last what it was they really believed in.

Secrets of the Temple: How the Federal Reserve Runs the Country Simon & Schuster 88

Matthias Griebel Curator, Dresden City Museum

1717 A fire went out from Germany and went around the world in a great arc and came back to Germany.

On the 50th anniversary of the Allies' fire bombing of Dresden *NY Times* 11 Feb 95

Sergei I Grigoryants Editor, *Glasnost* magazine

1718 We stand between a glass of water and the sea. The glass of water can't be the sea but it can keep itself pure.

On belief that conciliation can only muddy the human rights movement's "purity and clarity" of reform *NY Times* 16 Dec 87

Lloyd Grove *Washington Post* staff writer

1719 When you're a gruff-talking, steak-eating, cigar-sucking, martini-chugging, unmade king-size bed of a Chicago politician like Dan Rostenkowski—wearing a tweed sport coat of chemical-fire blue, with a face like a caved-in medicine ball—the word "sorry" doesn't dare to pass your puckered lips.

On the reluctance of the chair of Congressional Ways and Means Committee to plead guilty to felony charges *Washington Post* 11 Apr 96

Guardian Weekly

1720 If some palm-fringed atoll were available, might not even Britain be tempted to indulge in one last bang?

"For Whom the Atoll Tolls" editorial on the French *folie de grandeur* in a nuclear test explosion in Tahiti 17 Sep 95

Olivier Guichard De Gaulle Chief of Staff

1721 He remained master in the game, but it was the game itself that eluded him.

On Charles de Gaulle's disposition of "the enormous fish that History had stuck on the end of his line," quoted by Jean Lacouture *de Gaulle the Ruler* Norton 90

John Gunther biographer

1722 Clothes and hair were neat and gray... [and] gray-framed spectacles magnified the gray hazel eyes, but there was no grayness in the mind.

On Harry S Truman, quoted by David McCullough *Truman* Simon & Schuster 92

Richard Gwyn political analyst

1723 Politics... it's our substitute for national theater, mostly vaudeville.

Toronto Star 29 Dec 84

1724 [She] is like some unknown pop singer, who lucks into one song that captures the public imagination, but who never gets back on the charts.

On Kim Campbell's defeat after brief term as Canadian Prime Minister *NY Times* 31 Oct 93

Clyde Haberman foreign correspondent

1725 Surrounded by government bureaucrats of various pinstripes, shepherded to and from by chamberlains, they looked about as free as glass-encased butterflies.

Reporting from Tokyo on Crown Prince Akihio and Crown Princess Michiko *NY Times* 3 Oct 87

1726 He talks about an economic common market where. . . swords are beaten into microchips.

On Israeli Prime Minister Shimon Peres' vision of a peaceful Middle East *ib* 19 Sep 93

Alan Hamilton reporter

1727 The Princess of Wales clearly saw eye to eye with the president of Argentina, but only when they sat down to lunch.

On the willowey Princess Diana's meeting with 5'3" President Menen *London Times* 25 Nov 95

1728 She offered a tentative paw for a shake but not a kiss.

On Diana's ruefully extended hand, which British protocol, remembering the Falkland Islands War, sanctioned *ib*

Miklos Haraszti Hungarian journalist

1729 [It was] a sculpture of tyrannicide.

On bronze boots from Budapest's felled statue of Joseph Stalin *NY Times* 13 Dec 87

1730 There remains only the old platform, reeking of the old boots.

ib

Yehoshafat Harkabi Professor of International Relations, Hebrew University

1731 Israel cannot defend itself if half its popualton is the enemy.

On Arab population, quoted by Lance Morrow "Israel: At 40, The Dream Confronts Palestinian Fury and a Crisis of Identity" *Time* 4 Apr 88

1732 We need a Zionism of quality, not of acreage.

ib

Richard Harkness commentator

1733 [A committee is] a group of the unwilling, picked from the unfit, to do the unnecessary.

NY Herald Tribune 15 Jun 60

Lord Harlech (David Ormsby-Gore) British Ambassador to the US

1734 In the end it may well be that Britain will be honored by historians more for the way she disposed of an empire than for the way in which she acquired it.

NY Times 28 Oct 62

E Roland Harriman Chair, Union Pacific Railroad

1735 I don't belong to any organized party. I'm a Republican.

NY Times 28 Jun 64

Roy Hattersley Labor Party deputy leader

1736 She has the certainty of the second-rate and that is a substantial piece of armor. It has never crossed her mind that she is wrong.

On Prime Minister Margaret Thatcher *Wall Street Journal* 14 May 87

Vaclav Havel President of Czechoslovakia

1737 I fear the price we are all bound to pay for the drastic suppression of history. . . banishment. . . [and] the new compulsory "deferral" of every opportunity for society to live in anything like a natural way.

Letter in Apr 1975 to the Communist leader he was to succeed as president 15 years later *NY Times* 30 Dec 89

Denis Healey Chancellor of the Exchequer

1738 Mrs Thatcher is doing for monetarium what the Boston Stranger did for door-to-door salesmen.

Recalled in *London Times* 28 Nov 95

Lillian Hellman playwright

1739 I cannot and will not cut my conscience to fit the year's fashions.

Letter to the House Committee on Un-American Activities at height of accusations of Communist party membership among writers and artists, news reports 20 May 52

Ernest Hemingway novelist

1740 All the contact I have had with politics has left me feeling as though I had been drinking out of spittoons.

NY Times 17 Sep 50

Dennis Henigan Director, Legal Action Project, Center to Prevent Hand Gun Violence

1741 The NRA has never seen a gun it didn't like.

On lobbying against National Rifle Association NPR 14 Dec 90

William A Henry III Senior Editor *Time*

1742 The most basic fact of American life is that sometime within the next 50 or so years, non-Hispanic white people will become demographically just another minority group . . . collectively outnumbered by Hispanics of all races, blacks, Asians, Indians, and assorted other ethnic groups not associated with western Europe. . . an ethnic evolution.

In Defense of Elitism Doubleday 94

Seymour Hersch journalist

1743 It was the daily decay of integrity.

On Watergate *The Price of Power: Kissinger in the Nixon White House* Summit 83

James C Hershberg biographer

1744 They were gray men in gray suits with a gray message, solemnly reprinted in the good gray pages of *The New York Times.*

On top social, professional, and corporate members of the Committee on the Present Danger formed in 1950 to lobby for an ideological approach to winning the Cold War *James G Conant* Knopf 93

Stephen Hess Senior Fellow, Brookings Institution

1745 We really do elect a president to be our very own sonofabitch.

On the office of president as a target for criticism *NY Times* 17 Jul 94

Charles Higham biographer

1746 [Richard M Nixon] was pressing with hobnailed boots the wine of sour grapes.

On John F Kennedy's successful race for president *Rose* Pocket Books 95

George Hill political analyst

1747 She is. . . inclined to cough noisily when he goes on too long. . . a traditional prerogative of the political wife, and rather more necessary in this instance.

On Labor's Neil Kinnock's wife, Glenys *London Times* 19 Feb 87

1748 [He] stirred whiskey with a thick forefinger, his socks drooped, his suits were green-hued, his ties indifferent, and his breath chronically bad.

On US Secretary of State John Foster Dulles *ib*

Alger Hiss former President, Carnegie Endowment for International Peace

1749 It was fabricated by an unholy trinity bound together by the theology of anti-communism.

On Richard M Nixon and J Edgar Hoover's pursuit of Whittaker Chambers' accusations that led to Hiss's conviction on charges of perjury *Recollections of a Life* Holt 88

Godfrey Hodgson Foreign Editor, *London Independent*

1750 His whole life has been one sustained career of escapology.

On Richard M Nixon *NY Times* 10 Mar 91 reviewing Tom Wicker's *One of Us: Richard Nixon and the American Dream* Random House 91

Joan Hoff historian

1751 [He was] half of the odd couple. . . an American Quaker and a German Jew.

On Richard M Nixon as US President with Henry A Kissinger as Secretary of State *Nixon Reconsidered* Basic Books 94

1752 [They] shared their worst characteristics.

ib

Abbie Hoffman social activist

1753 I always held my flower in a clenched fist.

On his role as a 1960s flower child *Soon to Be a Major Motion Picture* Putnam 80, recalled on Hoffman's death 14 Apr 89

Richard Hofstadter Professor of American History, Columbia University

1754 It has been our fate as a nation not to have ideologies but to be one.

NY Times 2 Jul 89

Simon Hoggart political analyst

1755 It wasn't a great speech—it never is—but it was rousingly adequate, even thrillingly average. . . jokes are almost funny, the tone almost assured, the peroration almost moving. . . [and] it may have been the best speech he has ever made.

On John Major's address at Blackpool a year before his re-election as Prime Minister "A Range of Duck-Billed Platitudes" *Guardian Weekly* 17 Oct 93

Anthony Holden biographer

1756 [It is] a comfortable form of inherited imprisonment.

On the British monarchy *Prince Charles* Atheneum 80

Bob Hope entertainer

1757 I don't know what people have got against Jimmy Carter. He's done nothing.

Campaign speech, news reports 2 Nov 80

Alistair Horne biographer

1758 A ceremony richly encrusted with pageantry and ermine.

On Prime Minister Harold Macmillan's formal seating in the House of Lords *Harold Macmillan* Vol II Viking 89

Anthony Howard *Observer* columnist

1759 [It is] the politics of evangelism, the faith that individual men are cast to be messiahs.

Expressing a British view of favoritism that sometimes marks the first years of a presidential term *NY Times* 27 Jan 89

Michael Howard Regius Professor of Modern History, Oxford

1760 We were *noblesse oblige* like crazy for about three decades. At last there was nothing left to oblige with.

On the sense of obligation in national life, quoted by Richard Critchfield *An American Looks at Britain* Doubleday 90

Philip Howard *London Times* columnist

1761 If you add the concealed costs of the monarchy, and subtract the concealed profits, you arrive at the conclusion that such arithmetic is not worth the calculation.

The British Monarchy in the 20th Century Hamish Hamilton 77, quoted in *Fortune* 25 Mar 91

James Humes President, Winston Churchill Institute

1762 In wars you can be killed once but in politics many times.

Churchill: Speaker of the Century Stein & Day 80

1763 We see in Carter sometimes a microscopic examination of twigs, but no view of the forest.

On President Carter *ib*

Samuel Hynes Professor of English, Princeton

1764 [His political theory] was as English as bitter beer and toad-in-the-hole.

On George Orwell's belief that "every political opinion has a certain regional tinge to it" as seen in Michael Shelden's *Orwell: The Authorized Biography* HarperCollins 91

India Today

1765 Rajiv Gandhi is not just in crisis. He is the crisis.

On Prime Minister Rajiv Gandhi *Time* 10 Aug 87

Irish Independent

1766 After three generations, a young man of fully Irish stock has reached the last point of integration into American life.

On President Kennedy *National Observer* 1 Jun 63

Irish Republican Army militant protest group

1767 While nationalist people are forced to live under British rule, then the British cabinet will be forced to meet in bunkers.

Statement after the shelling 10 Downing St while cabinet was meeting *Washington Post* 8 Feb 91

Walter Isaacson Asst Mgr Editor, *Time*

1768 No one could shine his shoes, much less fill them.

On President Nixon's self-image at the time of his resignation *Kissinger* Simon & Schuster 92

Aldon O James Jr President, National Arts Club

1769 She came in like a little church mouse. Now, she's an attack rat.

On Sharon S Benenson, Chair, Gramercy Park Board, and her desire to cut down some of the trees in the mid-Manhattan square *NY Times* 23 May 95

Kathleen Hall Jamieson Dean, Annenberg School of Communications, University of Pennsylvania

1770 What causes a scandal to take root is what involves a reader in an Agatha Christie novel: the anticipation that a full-blown plot is going to be revealed that is going to explain something basic to mankind, like human venality, thwarted love or the corrupt use of power.

On President Clinton and Whitewater land sales *NY Times* 13 Mar 94

Peter Jenkins columnist

1771 [He] led his supporters up the Himalayas and down again; they stood with him in the last ditch to defend sterling . . . set on the see-saw of rising unemployment and wage restraint and watched him herd sacred cows up to the sacrificial altar.

On British Labor Prime Minister Harold Wilson *Guardian* editorial recalled on Wilson's death 27 May 92

Simon Jenkins columnist

1772 His eyes drooped at the bottom not at the top, the droop of worldly wisdom. Each office of state adds a new bag to his cheek, like rings on a tree.

On Kenneth Clarke, Chancellor of the Exchequer, who pressed on in hopes of succeeding Prime Minister John Major "at a time of Mr Major's own choosing" *London Times* 30 Nov 94

1773 As Westminster nights lengthen, the suit rumples, the speech slurs, the gaffes become more endearing.

ib

Ivor Jennings historian

1774 The path to political preferment passes through the field of party orthodoxy.

Quoted by Anthony Sampson *Anatomy of Britain* Hodder & Stoughton 62

Jiang Quing Member of the Gang of Four

1775 I was Chairman Mao's dog. When he told me to bite, I bit....[and] if I had known it was permitted to shoot people in Tiananmen Square, I would have done it years ago.

NY Times 13 Dec 80, also recalled on Jiang Quing's death 14 May 91

1776 Man's contribution to human history is nothing more than a drop of sperm.

Newsweek 20 Feb 84

Pope John Paul II Archbishop of Crakow 1964–78; Pope 1978–

1777 In a certain sense Communism as a system fell by itself . . . as a consequence of its own mistakes and abuses.

Crossing the Threshold of Hope Knopf 94

Gerald W Johnson journalist

1778 Lerner's great distinction is the enemies he has made. Few. . . are so bitterly hated by so many of the right people.

NY Times 14 Feb 60 reviewing Max Lerner's *Unfinished Country* Simon & Schuster 59

Patricia Sill Johnstone Secretary to Member of Parliament Nicholas Scott

1779 What are you worried about? The child's not dead. He's not even English.

To the father of a 3-year-old boy after Scott left the scene of an automobile accident; he subsequently faced demands that he resign from parliament *London Times* 6 Jun 95

Lionel Joseph French socialist

1780 The political center in France is like the Bermuda Triangle. Whoever approaches it disappears.

Quoted by Flora Lewis "France, Where the Center Holds" *NY Times* 18 May 91

Ward Just novelist

1781 [Chicago is] the place where bulls and foxes dine very well, but lambs end up head down on the hook.

Jack Gance Houghton Mifflin 88

1782 The world behind the curtains was turbulent, dangerous and unpredictable as a man's heart, and as unknowable.

ib

Vladimir P Kabaidze factory export manager

1783 It's useless to fight the forms. You've got to kill the people producing them.

To Communist Party Conference *NY Times* 1 Jul 88

Henry Kamm foreign correspondent

1784 The people of this capital city did something they said they had never done—they flocked to Communist Party headquarters. Then they stood there and laughed.

On removal of a larger-than-life bronze statue of Lenin from Tallinn, Estonia *NY Times* 24 Aug 91

Bachi Karkaria *Bombay Times*

1785 Mumbai harks back to a past that is glorious. Bombay, on the other hand, represents grit, gumption and a go-getting spirit that's perfectly suited to the present.

Opposing order of the right-wing Hindu party Shiv Sena to change the name of Bombay to that of the Hindu goddess, Mumbai, to eliminate vestiges of British rule *USA Today* 22 Aug 95

Elizabeth Kaye journalist

1786 Within a few months the Deans entered into that epic mutual disgust which more ordinary couples accumulate only after a number of years.

On Nixon White House counsel John W Dean III and his wife, Maureen *George* Dec 95

Bill Keller foreign correspondent

1787 [His] enigmatic scowl was the face of Soviet foreign policy.

Reporting on death of Foreign Minister Andrei A Gromyko *NY Times* 4 Jul 89

Kitty Kelley biographer

1788 Deaver became a social mountaineer.

On Michael Deaver as Reagan White House Deputy Chief of Staff *Nancy Reagan* Simon & Schuster 91

Michael Kelly reporter

1789 [It] draped the old dream of pure democracy with the glossy promise of technology: "the electronic town hall."

On presidential hopeful Ross Perot's proposal for television programs with reply cards from listeners that would establish a national consensus *NY Times* 6 Jun 92

1790 By Election Day 1968, Nixon had been so thoroughly repackaged that he became, in a sense, the first President to win the office by suicide.

ib 31 Oct 93

1791 Bill Clinton, who is as surely of the apex of the image age as John F Kennedy was of its dawn, looms over the video landscape, cordless microphone in hand, forever talking, listening, empathizing. His is the Presidency as public-access television: everyone gets on the air with him sooner or later.

On public perceptions of US Presidents 31 Jul 94

1792 Lincoln is honest, Carter is weak, Reagan is decent but doddering. Bush is a wimp.

ib

Murray Kempton columnist

1793 His only vanity is his manners.

On civil rights leader A Philip Randolph *Rebellions, Perversities, and Main Events* Times Books 94

1794 Matthew Ianniello has been lost to Mulberry Street and on long-term lease to the federal prison system since 1986.

On the proprietor of the Umbertos Clam House in Manhattan's Little Italy *ib*

1795 For touching a people who want to forget ugly problems, no politician equals the one who has already forgotten them himself.

On Ronald Reagan *ib*

Lauren Kirk Little Rock model

1796 [She] pumped up her affair with Clinton to make it look long and passionate. . . [and] just can't accept the fact that he came, wiped himself off, zipped up, and left.

On Bill Clinton and Kirk's former roommate, Gennifer Flowers, quoted by Meredith L Oakley *On the Make* Regnery 94

Ivan Kitayev Soviet archivist

1797 One must not dance on the bones of the ones who built history, who created a great state.

Warning against abuse of undeniable Bolshevik history in frenzy of pro-democratic iconoclasm *NY Times* 22 Jan 92

Elizabeth Kolbert reporter

1798 [He is] a rare political breed: a man who can speak both the language of the Christian right and the language of Washington insiders.

On political adviser Gary L Bauer *NY Times* 1 Nov 95

Komsomolskaya Pravda

1799 [He had] been unable to change the life of the people for the better but has changed the people themselves. This is both his drama and his achievement.

Editorial on Mikhail S Gorbachev *Washington Post* 25 Dec 91

Baruch Korff founder, National Citizens Committee for Fairness to the Presidency

1800 You will be sinning against history if you allow the partisan cabal in Congress and the jackals in the media to force you from office.

To President Nixon on White House visit 6 Aug 74 the day Nixon decided to resign from office, recalled on the death of Korff, a Ukrainian-born Orthodox rabbi *NY Times* 27 Jul 95

Charles Krauthammer columnist

1801 US politicians routinely vie with each other for the Lil' Abner prize for the most humble, most miserable upbringing.

"The Pornography of Self-Revelation" on Clinton and Gore's addresses at the Democratic National Convention *Time* 10 Aug 92

1802 After four days of speeches a foreign visitor could be forgiven for thinking indoor plumbing was a Reagan-era innovation.

ib

1803 Exposing oneself and exploiting one's family are. . . simply other forms of debasement that a modern democratic public now demands before it is prepared to confer high office on anyone.

ib

1804 While nonproliferation is a vital American goal, denuclearization is a simple folly.

ib

Charles Kuralt commentator

1805 The trouble in that part of the world is as old as the Old Testament.

On signing of the Israli-PLO peace accord CBS TV 12 Sep 93

Jean Lacouture biographer

1806 [He was] the boldest manipulator of that raw material of politics, known as circumstances.

de Gaulle the Rebel Norton 90

1807 A small General Staff... possessed of innumerable ears and capable of discreet initiatives... [whose] contacts and acts were on the border of legality... lived and acted at this time on the frontier of sedition.

On de Gaulle's efforts to return to power *de Gaulle the Ruler* Norton 92

Wayne LaPierre Executive Vice President, National Rifle Association

1808 [It is] like saying the weather report... caused the damage, rather than the hurricane.

On possession of weapons as compared to terrorist activities *Nightline* ABC TV 1 May 95

1809 [They are] jack-booted government thugs wearing Nazi bucket helmets and storm-trooper uniforms.

Statement on federal agents 1 May 95 that was widely denounced in the light of the Oklahoma City explosion a month earlier *Washington Times* 19 May 95

1810 We do not do battle with bullets, we fight with ballots.

To NRA's national convention in Phoenix AZ *NY Times* 21 May 95

1811 We're the people who helped clean out Congress in 1994, and we're going to help clean your clock in 1996....[This is] a battle to retake the most precious, most sacred ground on earth.

To President Clinton *ib*

1812 If there's one thing we've learned over the years, it's that when you feed the alligator, it comes right back for the next bite.

On futility of cooperating with gun-control legislation and its alleged constitutional violation of "the right to bear arms" *US News & World Report* 22 May 95

Jim Lehrer commentator

1813 Some say it is the only job in American government for which you have to be really smart.

On Daniel J Boorstin's retirement as Librarian of Congress *McNeil-Lehrer Report* PBS TV 8 Sep 87

Eugene Lehrmann President, American Association of Retired Persons

1814 I saw neighbors take a horse and buggy and drive to the poor house.

At age 78, looking back on the 1930s *NY Times* 27 Aug 95

Michael Lerner editor and publisher, *Tikkun* magazine

1815 [The politics of meaning] addresses the psychological, ethical and spiritual needs of Americans... [and] incorporates the liberal and progressive agenda, but it puts this agenda in a much deeper context.

On his "politics of meaning" theory popularized by Hillary Rodham Clinton *Washington Post* 9 Jun 93

C S Lewis novelist

1816 A sick society must think much about politics, as a sick man must think much about his digestion.

The Weight of Glory Macmillan 80

David Levering Lewis Professor of History, Rutgers

1817 Robinson is a hawk with the personality of a dove and the pen of a social worker.

Review of Robert Robinson's *Black on Red: A Black American's 44 Years Inside the Soviet Union* Acropolis 88, *Washington Post* l5 May 88

John Lewis US Congressman

1818 The spirit of history just tracked us down and used us.

On non-violent confrontation of racial hatred, quoted by Fred Powledge *Free at Last* Little, Brown 91

Robert Lichter political analyst

1819 Washington is quiet now except for the background hum of knives being sharpened.

Of the interim between the Reagan and Bush administrations *NY Times* l8 Jan 89

Anne Morrow Lindbergh diarist

1820 Thoughts die and are buried in the silences between sentences.

On the conversational style of US Secretary of State John Foster Dulles *War Within and Without* Harcourt Brace Jovanovich 80

Edward Linenthal Professor of Religion and American Culture, University of Wisconsin

1821 The commemorative membrane is so sensititve to any perceived act of desecration, it immediately becomes an event.

On disputes on mutually agreeable language on Auschwitz and Hiroshima's 50th anniversaries *NY Times* 29 Jan 95

1822 Fiftieths... intensify arguments over any form of rememberances... are the last time when you have massive groups of veterans or survivors who are able to put their imprint on the event.

ib

Jules Loh Associated Press writer

1823 Twice before over the past century the Klan has seemed. . . missing and presumed dead. Both times its hooded head rose from the cold ashes of burnt crosses to burn and flog and kill again.

On the KKK's former Imperial Wizard Robert Shelton's statement that the Ku Klux Klan will never return *Washington Times* 21 Dec 94

London Financial Times

1824 To ask Mumford's views on a planning issue is like calling down Moses to advise the president of Israel.

On retention by Christ Church, Oxford, of city planner Lewis Mumford to defeat plans to build a highway through Christ Church Meadows, quoted by Donald L Miller *Lewis Mumford* Weidenfeld & Nicolson 89

London Daily Mirror

1825 The bomb may have been planted by an Irish terrorist, but the fingerprints upon it were American.

Editorial alleging that US money financed the Irish Republican Army's placing of bombs in a Brighton hotel where Prime Minister Margaret Thatcher and the Conservative Party were convening *NY Times* 16 Oct 84

London Times

1826 The opulent blue and gold design of the British passport is being replaced by the regimented purple document of the European Community.

"Passport to the Past" editorial on a "change lamented by the patriots who cherish the few outward signs that distinguish these islands from the Continent" 3 Apr 91

1827 Hierarchical, huge, craftily networked, a pretty pyramid of baubles to reward the boys and girls who have pleased their political masters. . . outward and visible symbols of a class-riven society.

"The New Year's Honors List" editorial 31 Dec 92

1828 Few have aspired to grasp a larger mantle: to inspire the populace, to articulate what it means to be British, to make people feel good about their country.

"Lady in Purple" editorial on Margaret Thatcher's memoirs 21 Oct 93

1829 Heraldry is a science of great complexity which the British employ with passionate snobbery. . . a powerful expression of the bourgeois individualism which has become the bedrock of Western culture.

"Arms and the Lady" editorial on the granting of a coat-of-arms to Thatcher 19 Nov 94

1830 To celebrate the minor icons of everyday British life—red pillar boxes, black cabs, old-fashioned telephone boxes—is to risk being called a reactionary.

"Old Hat" editorial on moves to retire the highdomed hat worn by police 28 Nov 94

1831 A form of collective insanity—mad MP disease, perhaps, has broken out at Westminster. . . brought on by giving firmly held beliefs precedence over the interests of the party.

"The Tory Sickness" editorial on the Conservative Party's position as Prime Minister John Major appeared to be losing authority 7 Dec 94

1832 There is on Sark neither income tax nor bureaucrats, nor even—*mon dieu!*—motor cars. . . a speck on the map that wants to remain a speck, that wishes to remain self-governing rather than give in to the European Union.

"The Conquering Sarkeese" editorial on the politics of the doughty island called Sark 18 Feb 95

1833 However great the provocation, the estranged wife of the future monarch should not debate in public his fitness and preparedness to rule.

"The Royal Individuals" on Princess Diana's most revealing telecast interview 22 Nov 95

John Lukacs historian

1834 A great statesman prevailed over a great revolutionary; the writer over the orator; a cosmopolitan over a racist; a democratic aristocrat over a populist demagogue; a traditionalist over a radical; a patriot over a nationalist.

On Winston S Churchill and Adolf Hitler *The Duel* Ticknor & Fields 91

Roger Lyons General Secretary, Manufacturing, Science and Finance Union

1835 Like putting Dracula in charge of a blood bank.

On Lyon's transfer from his position as Treasury Chief Secretary to Secretary of Employment *London Times* 21 Jul 94

Dwight MacDonald critic

1836 Large foundations, like large corporations, are timid beasts, and when they are frightened by some small but vocal minority they envelop themselves in clouds of public relations.

On "philanthropoids'" conventional, non-risk grants *The Ford Foundation* Reynal 56

Roderick Macleish commentator

1837 People who write or ghostwrite. . . while the President [of the US] is still in office, are. . . fools if they don't understand the system, scoundrels if they do.

"Power Books" *Connoisseur* Sep 88

John Maginnis reporter

1838 Edwin Edwards is a very proud man who has everything in life except his good name, and he wants it back, even if he has to give good government to do it.

On Edwin Edwards' campaign for re-election as governor of Louisiana *NY Times* 11 Nov 91

Norman Mailer novelist

1839 He had a strong decent face and something tough as rubber in a handball to his makeup, but his eyes had been punched out a long time ago.

On Nelson A Rockefeller's political life as governor of New York state and US Vice President *Harper's* Feb 88

1840 [His eyes had] the distant lunar glow of the small, sad eyes you see in a caged chimpanzee or a gorilla.

ib

Malcolm X human rights activist and Muslim leader

1841 We didn't land on Plymouth Rock. It landed on us.

Life Fall 90

Thomas Mallon diarist

1842 [Journal keeping can enforce the political impulse] to explain, to justify, to plead a case before history.

A Book of One's Own Ticknor & Fields 84

1843 Most politicians can't resist the opportunity to use their journals as posthumous press releases.

ib See also NY Times 31 Oct 93

William Manchester biographer

1844 Each county was an autonomous duchy, each was faction-ridden... raiding one another's castles and swatting innocent vassals.

On Texas at the time of John F Kennedy's assassination there *The Death of a President* Harper & Row 67

1845 They were political cannibals, and a naive outsider venturing among them could be eaten alive.

On Governor John B Connally Jr *ib*

1846 They now had a leader cut from whipcord.

On Governor Connally *ib*

1847 Both in public and in private, Kennedy had been as direct as his pointed finger at televised press conferences.

On John F Kennedy's political style *ib*

1848 Johnson approached a strongly fortified position by outflanking it, or burrowing under it, or surprising the defenders from the rear, or raining down obstacles upon them from the sky, or starving them into submission.

On Lyndon B Johnson *ib*

1849 Rarely, and then only reluctantly, would he proceed directly from A to B. To him the shortest distance between two points was a tunnel.

ib

1850 When the circus catch was made, he wanted the fans to note the LBJ brand on the fielder's glove.... His critics called him a wheeler-dealer. They overlooked the subtlety of Johnsonian strategy, his use of wheels within wheels.

ib

1851 Put him within reach of a console switchboard and he became an octopus, clutching telephone receivers like bunches of black bananas.

ib

1852 The telephones began ringing in Whitehall as the first olive moments of daybreak revealed the majestic buildings towering against a darkling, still starry sky—vast cathedrals of an empire whose celebrants had been dwindling year by year since what had been called, and was now known to be, the Armistice.

On Winston S Churchill and London at the time of the fall of France in World War I *The Last Lion* Little, Brown 88

1853 [Churchill] resolved to lead Britain and her fading empire on one last great struggle... to arm the nation, not only with weapons but also with the mace of honor, creating in every English breast a soul beneath the ribs of death.

ib

Thomas Mann Director of Governmental Studies, Brookings Institution

1854 He's a great ex-president. It's a shame he couldn't have gone directly to the ex-presidency.

On Jimmy Carter's visit to Korea *Newsweek* 27 Jun 94

Attalah Mansour Israeli journalist

1855 Instead of stepping on the snake that threatened them, they swallowed it. Now they have to live with it, or die from it.

On Israel's relationship with Arabs *Time* 4 Apr 88

David Maraniss *Washington Post* reporter

1856 Luck and fate always seem to appear at the edge of the road as Bill Clinton drives along the highway of ambition, two friendly hitchhikers, thumbs out, ready to be picked up for stretches here and there when other passengers appear less attractive.

First in His Class Simon & Schuster 95

1857 In the fall of 1970, luck and fate not only went along for the ride, they crowded him out of the driver's seat and took over the steering wheel.

On Clinton's avoidance of Vietnam conscription and departure from Oxford for Yale Law School and meeting his future wife *ib*

1858 Slowed by heart attacks, his rugged visage blurred by extra pounds and stringy long hair, LBJ played out his final days along the Pedernales as a phantasmagoric presence, not all there but not yet gone.

On President Johnson's 1972 meeting at the LBJ ranch with presidential nominee George McGovern *ib*

1859 Clinton would study the two men, borrow a colloquialism from one, a hand gesture from the other, and incorporate them in his routine.

On Clinton's work for David Pryor and Dale Bumpers as they stumped Arkansas for election to the US Senate *ib*

1860 [Clinton] was both a natural politician and an artful imitator, for those two types may in fact be one and the same.... At 34, he fit the ironic description of the quintessential Rhodes Scholar: someone with a great future behind him.

On Clinton as the youngest governor in US history to be defeated after one term *ib*

1861 He is a congenital campaigner.

Prediction that Clinton will always be a candidate for some office or an advocate CNBC 7 Mar 95

John Mariotta Welbilt Electronic Die Corp engineer

1862 [I am] a New York Rican... an individual that cannot speak English and cannot speak Spanish.

Too Good to be True Doubleday 90

Tom Mathews senior editor *Newsweek*

1863 His mistress Alice Glass... played swan to Lady Bird's loyal mud hen.

Newsweek 19 Mar 90 comparing President Johnson's mistress to his wife in reviewing Robert Caro's *The Years of Lyndon Johnson: Means of Ascent* Knopf 90

Christopher J Matthews President, Government Research Corp

1864 Hang a lantern on your problem.

Advice to political candidates to expose personal frailties before the press learns of them *NY Times* 10 Jul 87

1865 The key is to be a porcupine—have a reputation for being difficult.

Quoted by Hedrick Smith *The Power Game* Random House 88

François Mauriac novelist

1866 So it was to be the hour of Pilate.

On France's rejection of Charles de Gaulle's leadership, quoted by Jean Lacouture *de Gaulle the Ruler* Norton 92

1867 [He] would no longer be on our horizon, standing at his lookout post, that strange character who is of the stature of nobody else, that individual whose "greatness" we had finally grown tired of.

ib

Alex Mayhew Professor of Political Science, Georgetown University

1868 The future of America is based on one generation sacrificing for the next.

Expressing a belief most quoted by Mayhew's former student, President Clinton; cited in interview with Clinton biographer David Maraniss CNBC 7 Mar 95

Ann McBride President, Common Cause for Accountability in Government

1869 [I]t isn't a scandal waiting to happen. It's a scandal right now.

On Senator Alphonse D'Amato dual role as political fundraiser and Senate Banking Committee chair *Time* 11 Sep 95

1870 D'Amato is concentrating on soft money, which packs the biggest potential for abuse.

Defining "soft money" as huge, hard-to-track donations, not limited by law, that are used for polling, TV spots, get-out-the-vote drives, and other activities ostensibly unrelated to a specific candidate *ib*

David McCullough biographer

1871 [They were] old habits of the mouth.

On Harry S Truman's racial slurs as custom rather than conviction Station WAMU Washington 7 Sep 92

Michael D McCurry Clinton White House Press Secretary

1872 There are people around here who think Hillary Clinton is responsible for the weather.

On blaming the First Lady for a snowfall as well as behind-the-scenes activities *NY Times* 7 Jan 95

Robert D McFadden reporter

1873 The ringing inspirations of Winston S Churchill and the patrician visions of Harold Macmillan were not his style.

On Prime Minister Harold Wilson as "that rarest of political creatures—a Labor leader who could actually win elections" *NY Times* 25 May 95

1874 Rotund, provincial, resolutely middle-class, studiously ambiguous... Wilson was a fixture for 30 years, a solid workingman's socialist in a rumpled ready-to-wear suit and his trademark Gannex mackintosh.

ib

1875 The silver-haired, pipe-smoking northerner was a consummate British politician: tenacious, shrewd, manipulative, a blend of homespun tastes, acid wit and pragmatic, often shifting policies... the symbol of an emerging middle-class Briton.

ib

William S McFeely biographer

1876 By his very presence he not only announced that he was black but also instructed all who looked at him that they were not to see that face pejoratively.

On the former slave who became a heroic symbol of freedom *Frederick Douglass* Norton 91

1877 Douglass sang of himself, and he did so just by standing on the platform... that neither color nor previous condition of servitude was relevant to his aspirations, either for himself or for others.

ib

Robert McGeehan Assistant Professor of Political Science, City College CUNY

1878 [The French assured that] considerable time would pass before a German in uniform would appear—and if he did, he would not be in a German but a European uniform.

On the 1950 Pleven Plan that made German rearmament virtually dependent on the birth of a politically unified Europe *The German Rearmament Question* University of Illinois Press 71

1879 [He compelled them] to pull a rabbit from a hat quickly .... Little wonder that Pleven's animal was a close relative of Schuman's lapin.

On influence of US Secretary of State Dean Acheson *ib*

Ralph McGill editor, *Atlanta Constitution*

1880 We love the South with a fierce, protective passion such as parents have for a crippled child... the courage and the courtesy that survived the wounds: the rare, bright flower that was not twisted by defeat or occupation, the intelligence that knows we must move with time and does not want to be let alone.

Quoted in Barbara Binswanger and Jim Charlton ed *On the Night the Hogs Ate Willie* Dutton 94

Peter McGrath essayist

1881 Treason is an emotional threshold past which there is no looking back.

On the death in Moscow of double agent Kim Philby *Newsweek* 23 May 88

Mary McGrory columnist

1882 The haircut is the most celebrated incident in barbering since the encounter between Samson and Delilah.

Reporting on what critics alleged to be President Clinton's $200 haircut aboard Air Force One that tied up Los Angeles air traffic *Washington Post* 25 May 93

1883 He had an infinite capacity for inclusion, for boomers, boll weevils, the blow-dried and the bewildered.

Eulogy for House Speaker Thomas P "Tip" O'Neill *ib* 9 Jan 94

1884 He was the ultimate Himself, the man of the house who looks after his own, a national patriarch disguised as a politician.

ib

George Meany President, AFL-CIO

1885 We heard from the abortionists, and we heard from the people who looked like Jacks, acted like Jills and had the odors of johns.

On 1972 Democratic National Convention recalled in *Wall Street Journal* 11 Jul 84

H L Mencken humorist

1886 He is a man who sits in the outer office of the White House hoping to hear the President sneeze.

On US Vice Presidents, recalled on Mencken's death 29 Jan 56

1887 The varnishers and veneerers have been busily converting Abe into a plaster saint... to pump all his human weaknesses out of him, and so leave him a mere moral apparition, a sort of amalgam of John Wesley and the Holy Ghost.

On Abraham Lincoln, quoted by Fred Hobson *Mencken: A Life* Random House 94

1888 Until he emerged from Illinois they always put the women, children and clergy to bed when he got a few gourds of corn aboard.

On US President Grover Cleveland *ib*

1889 His whole huge carcass seemed to be made of iron... [and] he sailed through American history like a steel ship loaded with monoliths of granite.

ib

1890 [He is] a third-rate political wheel-horse, with the face of a moving-picture actor, the intelligence of a respectable agricultural implement dealer, and the imagination of a lodge joiner... a benign blank—a decent, harmless, laborious, hollow-headed mediocrity.

On US President Warren G Harding *ib*

1891 [His] English reminds me of tattered washing on the line... of stale bean-soup, of college yells, of dogs barking idiotically through endless nights. It is so bad that a sort of grandeur creeps into it. He slept more than any other president, whether by day or by night.... He had no ideas, but he was not a nuisance. Nero fiddled but Coolidge only snored.

On US President Calvin Coolidge *ib*

George Miller US Congressman

1892 [Calculating fair market value] without regard to the mineral deposits in the land is like selling Fort Knox for the value of its roof.

On a bill allowing mining companies to purchase government land *Wall Street Journal* 6 Nov 95

Jonathan Miller London computer enthusiast

1893 Owning a bulldog is a bit like driving an ancient Bentley with woodworm in the dashboard. They carry a slight political incorrectness.

On the bulldog as a symbol of British strength *Wall Street Journal* 27 Dec 94

Kenneth R Minogue political philosopher

1894 Most of us are, in some degree or other, liberal. It is only the very cynical, the unassailably religious, or the consistently nostalgic, who have remained unaffected.

Quoted by Richard Brookhiser "Being Right in a Post-Postwar World" *Time* 11 Dec 89

Emily B Minor critic

1895 The next thing we know there'll be a movement to make Mt Everest accessible to handicapped persons.

One Person's Opinions privately published 91

Lee Miringoff Director, Marist Institute of Public Opinion

1896 It's very hard to get a new set of teeth.

On NY Governor Mario Cuomo's "political teeth" cut on two previous terms in office *NY Times* 23 Jun 91

Martha Mitchell wife of US Attorney General

1897 [Nixon] bleeds people. . . draws every drop of blood and then drops them from a cliff. He'll blame any person he can put his foot on.

Late-night telephone call to UPI White House reporter Helen Thomas *LA Times* 26 Aug 73

Herbert Mitgang critic

1898 A speeechwriter placing semi-precious words within a hollow crown.

On Peggy Noonan's work for Ronald Reagan *NY Times* 31 Jan 90

Tom Morgan essayist

1899 She. . . happens to stick out a foot just as history is rushing by.

On Fawn Hall, the secretary who helped Oliver L North dispose of top-secret papers on Iran arms sales, as "the archetype of the accidental celebrity" *Newsweek* 9 Mar 88

Hank Morris Dukakis campaign aide

1900 George Bush thinks a domestic policy is how much he pays his maid.

Quoted in study of effective sound bites *NY Times* 22 Jan 92

Leonard Mosley biographer

1901 A man of charm, charm, charm, and luck, luck, luck.

On Lord Louis Mountbatten *The Last Days of the British Raj* Harcourt, Brace 62

Stanley Mosk Attorney General of California

1902 They are little old ladies in tennis shoes.

On elderly activists in the 1960s, William Safire ed *Safire's Political Dictionary* Random House 75

Bill Moyers Johnson White House press secretary

1903 He may have lost his ambition, but he remembers where he put it.

On presidential hopeful Nelson A Rockefeller *NY Times* 26 Nov 67

Malcolm Muggeridge humorist

1904 He is not only a bore but he bores for England.

On Anthony Eden, from a study on new statesmanship recalled on Muggeridge's death 14 Nov 90

Deroy Murdock media consultant

1905 [He is] a riddle wrapped in a mystery inside a uniform.

On speculation on political candidacy of General Colin L Powell, former chair of the Joint Chiefs of Staff *NY Times* 1 Feb 95

Edward R Murrow commentator

1906 No one can terrorize a whole nation, unless we are all accomplices.

On Senator Joseph R McCarthy's accusations of Communists in government, regarded as the beginning of proof that the charges were unsubstantiated CBS TV 7 Mar 74

1907 The people you have seen have the strength to harvest your fruit and vegetables. They do not have the strength to influence legislation. Maybe you do.

Concluding documentary telecast on migrant labor *Harvest of Shame* CBS TV 25 Nov 60

National Advisory Commission on Civil Disorders

1908 Discrimination and segregation have long permeated much of American life; they now threaten the future of every American.

Response to President Johnson's request to find the cause of race riots *NY Times* 1 Mar 68

National Public Radio

1909 In a place where things could hardly get worse, today they did.

Reporting on Haiti 14 Dec 93

Enid Nemy reporter

1910 Power brokers, actual and aspiring, the merely rich, butterflies and hangers-on of society, the stars and the satellites. . . they would show up at the opening of an envelope.

On Democratic National Convention *NY Times* 11 Aug 80

Benjamin Netanyahu Likud party leader, later Israeli Prime Minister

1911 The coalition is standing on chicken legs.

Invoking a Hebrew idiom to describe the shakiness of "a shriveled majority, 61 out of 120," supporting the Israeli-Palestinian peace accord *NY Times* 24 Sep 93

Richard E Neustadt Emeritus Professor of Government, Harvard

1912 Never let your Nancy be immobilized, could be a rule of thumb for future Presidents.

On Nancy Reagan and other advisers *Presidential Power and the Modern Presidents* Free Press/Macmillan 90

Newsweek

1913 Adlai E Stevenson, no matter how many holes his shoe soles bore, no matter how steeped he was in the lore of Lincoln, couldn't fool them, he wasn't folks.

Recalling on Stevenson's death, his loss to Dwight D Eisenhower in 1952 presidential race 26 Jul 65

1914 At the. . . tap-tap of a computer keyboard, he had become a man of hitherto unrealized size, strength, wit, grit and compassion.

On George Bush's new public image achieved by speechwriters and others 21 Nov 88

The New York Times

1915 In effect former President Nixon himself was also on trial . . . [and] the jury's "guilty" verdict in effect applies, to Mr Nixon as well as to the luckless subordinates who acted in his behalf.

"Guilty" editorial on conviction of Attorney General John N Mitchell, and White House aides John D Ehrlichman and H R Haldeman 2 Jan 75

1916 Who owns history? The public servants who make it, or the people who hire them and to whom they are accountable?

"Who Owns History?" editorial holding that records are not the exclusive property of presidents and other officials who are writing memoirs 19 Nov 83

1917 [They] may market. . . their personal insights and integrity. But the facts that might have to be secret for a time should not be theirs alone to sell.

ib

1918 Armed with a notebook, ingratiating grin and fine intelligence, he grew to be a most discerning witness of America's most distinctive rite, not just the election but the making of our presidents.

"Teddy White, the Maker of Epics" editorial on journalist Theodore H White 17 May 86

1919 He had an acute eye for important bit players, and if his heroes tended to be a bit larger than life, they inhabited epics.

ib

1920 Diplomacy abhors a vacuum.

"The Speakers of State" editorial on Reagan administration's lack of policy for Central America 17 Nov 87

1921 For Palestinians, PLO is a Homeland of the Mind.

Headline on militancy of Palestinian Liberation Organization 20 Mar 88

1922 A crook he was not, but this is not the only basis for holding high office.

"Mr Meese Judges Mr Meese" editorial on resignation of US Attorney General Edwin Meese III 6 Jul 88

1923 His friend Ronald Reagan gave more faithful loyalty down than Ed Meese gave lawyerly loyalty up.

ib

1924 Empty luggage may be easier to carry, but it's still empty.

"The Painless Platform" editorial on Michael S Dukakis' presidential campaign promises 20 Jul 88

1925 Lightning rods have had it better than Nancy Reagan.

"Scratching at the Teflon" editorial on publication of Kitty Kelley's *Nancy Reagan* 10 Apr 91

1926 Who is quickest on the drawl?

On claims to Texas by both George Bush and rival presidential aspirant Ross Perot 8 Jun 92

1927 They doomed themselves to arguing with history.

"Justice and Mercy in Arkansas" editorial on the death of Governor Orville Faubus and "his generation of segregationist politicians" 17 Dec 94

1928 History has decreed, beyond argument and beyond appeal, that they will be remembered for the one big thing they got wrong. . . .[and] when it comes to the final judgments on political conduct, history is not merciful. It is just.

ib

Reinhold Niebuhr theologian

1929 The whole art of politics consists in directing rationally the irrationalities of men.

Recalled on Niebuhr's death 1 Jun 71

Peggy Noonan speechwriter

1930 [He is] a comma in an easy chair.
On working with George Bush *Washington Times* 18 Jan 89

1931 A speech is poetry: cadence, rhythm, imagery, sweep. . . and reminds us that words, like children, have the power to make dance the dullest beanbag of a heart.
What I Saw at the Revolution Random House 90

1932 Speechwriters are, somehow, the kids of politics, itself in some ways a kid's game.
ib

1933 Rhetoric is only a small stream off the river of American prose—but in terms of politics it is the ocean you sail on or sink in.
ib

1934 I first saw him as a foot, a highly polished brown cordovan wagging merrily on a hassock.
On President Reagan *ib*

1935 They're. . . guys with ambition so strong it's like a steel rod sticking out of their heads. . . . Steel with an overlay of tennis.
On political alliances of George Bush and Secretary of State James A Baker III *NY Times* 6 May 90

1936 Oh, hell—I'm a writer. I don't have to put on makeup when I write.
Declining invitations to do television commentary *Washington Post* 11 Aug 92

1937 They looked at him and saw a hand grenade with a bad haircut.
On voters' view of independent presidential candidate Ross Perot *Forbes* 14 Sep 92

Oliver L North US Senatorial candidate

1938 Most people don't give a rat's patootie.
On voters' regard for his role in the Iran-Contra arms sales *NY Times* 28 Jan 94

1939 This is my best friend, Betsy, and the four children God loaned us.
Introducing his wife and family during campaign for US Senator from Virginia *Washington Post* 20 Mar 92

Michael Novak American Enterprise Institute

1940 Woodstock in a tuxedo.
On the Clinton presidential inauguration *Washington Times* 19 Jan 93

John J O'Brien Washington correspondent, *Philadelphia Inquirer*

1941 The only candidate who can whistle "Dixie" while humming the "Battle Hymn of the Republic."
On President Johnson in Harold Brayman ed *The President Speaks Off the Record* Dow Jones 76

P J O'Rourke Editor, *Rolling Stone* magazine

1942 Communism doesn't really starve or execute that many people. Mostly it just bores them to death.
Holidays in Hell Atlantic Monthly Press 88

1943 Republicans are the party that says government doesn't work, and then they get elected and prove it.
Parliament of Whores Atlantic Monthly Press 91

George Orwell novelist and critic

1944 One could not even dignify him with the name of stuffed shirt. He was simply a hole in the air.
On Prime Minister Stanley Baldwin *The Lion and the Unicorn* 1940, recalled on Orwell's death 21 Jan 50

1945 The great enemy of clear language is insincerity.
Politics and the English Language 1946

1946 Political language. . . is designed to make lies sound truthful and murder respectable, and to give an appearance of solidity to pure wind.
ib

1947 It was a bright cold day in April, and the clocks were striking thirteen.
1984 1949

1948 Big brother is watching you.
ib

1949 Doublethink means the power of holding two contradictory beliefs in one's mind simultaneously and accepting both of them.
ib

Matthew Parris columnist

1950 Sincerity in the Commons is so rare it's shocking.
London Times 22 Feb 95

1951 Tony Blair has been lobbing freeze-dried, low-fat, vacuum-packed, reduced-calorie, monosodium glutamate-enhanced sound bites.
On Labor's Opposition Leader at Question Time with Prime Minister John Major *ib* 26 Apr 95

1952 Black Rod in silk lace, with a billiard cue. . . Lord Chancellor and Madam Speaker in funereal hose and gilded brocade, knocking 'em cold in black and gold.
On President Clinton's visit to Parliament as a "straight man" to its "pantomine show" *ib* 30 Nov 95

1953 All the ridiculous flim-flam of invented British antiquity. . . the backgroup of unspeakable Victoriana.
ib

Landon Parvin speechwriter

1954 What you do is take the truth and just skew it a bit.
On political wit for the Washington press's annual Gridiron dinners *NY Times* 29 Mar 91

1955 When someone becomes President they automatically are funnier because people are readier to laugh.

ib

Boris Pasternak novelist

1956 Reality, like a neglected daughter, ran off half-dressed and presented legitimate history with the challenge of herself just as she was—from head to toe illegitimate and dowryless.

On the Russian revolution *NY Times* 1 Jan 78

Alan Paton South African novelist

1957 Cry, the beloved country, for the unborn child that is the inheritor of our fear.

Cry, the Beloved Country Scribner's 50, recalled on Paton's death 12 Apr 88

1958 I have one great fear in my heart. One day when they [the whites] have turned to loving they will find we are turned to hating.

Lines for central figure, Kumalo *ib*

Laurence J Peter psychologist and educator

1959 In a hierarchy, every employee tends to rise to his level of incompetence; the cream rises until it sours.

The Peter Principle Morrow 69

1960 Bureaucracy defends the status quo long past the time when the quo has lost its status.

San Francisco Chronicle 29 Jan 78

Kevin Phillips columnist

1961 For middle-class taxpayers to believe there's going to be a cut is like chickens trusting Colonel Sanders.

NPR 13 Aug 93

Ralph Picardo FBI labor informant

1962 Swans don't swim in the gutter.

Demanding a more extensive probe of Reagan campaign worker Raymond Donovan on his appointment as Secretary of Labor, quoted by Suzanne Garment *Scandal* Times Books 91

Enoch Powell Member of Parliament

1963 The greatest of the Might-Have-Beens.

On RAB Butler who never progressed to Prime Minister from appointment as Minister of Education, Chancellor of the Exchequer, and Foreign Secretary *London Daily Telegram* 12 Jul 71

Thomas Powers historian

1964 She did not spill the milk; the cat spilled the milk, her friend spilled the milk, the milk only looked spilled, it is not actually milk.

On tendencies to label Hillary Rodham Clinton as a liar while missing the character trait "of a little girl determined to be perfect" *NY Times* 24 Mar 96

Pravda

1965 Russian-Chinese friendship is as firm and indestructible as the Himalayas. . . deep as the Pacific . . . vast as the Yangtze and the Volga.

Quoted by Marvin Kalb *Dragon in the Kremlin* Dutton 61

Michael H Prendergast Chair, NY State Democrats

1966 So light he could tap-dance on top of a Charlotte Russe.

On Robert F Wagner's candidacy for mayor of New York, recalled on Wagner's death *NY Times* 13 Feb 91

Mario A Procaccino mayoral candidate

1967 Limousine liberals.

On the alienation of many New Yorkers to Manhattan's more opulent residents *NY Times* 21 Dec 95

1968 It's safer to be in the Vietnam War than to be in New York at 3 o'clock in the morning.

ib

Wesley Pruden columnist

1969 Wombats, wampus cats and geezilbillies of all kinds, each uglier than the others, will be crawling over hill and hollow and out of the swamps and bayous.

On a special counsel's investigation of Whitewater land sales *Washington Times* 19 May 95

1970 The [special counsel wants to] count the ways the officers and gentlemen (and some of the ladies). . . assisted, expedited, facilitated, attended, sustained and otherwise folded, spindled and mutilated the efforts. . . to investigate.

ib

Todd S Purdum columnist

1971 How can a culture that picks apart its presidents' infirmities, infidelities and infelicities. . . compete with a fable about a cherry tree and the truth?

Comparing George Washington's "I cannot tell a lie" to press preoccupation with "dye in the hair or clay on the toes. . . *roman a clef* on dysfunctional First Families and graphic sex with Marilyn Monroe" *Washington Times* 22 Feb 95

1972 She remains a one-woman flying fortress, jetting around the country beneath the radar.

Reporting on Hillary Rodham Clinton's tempered activism after losing out on revision of health insurance legislation *NY Times* 24 Jul 95

Nizar Qabbani Syrian poet and former diplomat

1973 Our culture? Nothing but bubbles in washtubs and chamberpots.

Quoted by Albert Hourani *A History of the Arab People* Harvard University Press 91

Dorothy Rabinowitz critic

1974 She decided at an early age that she wanted to make her life and career in Alaska or some other wild and strange place. She managed the same thing by marrying Lyndon B Johnson.

On a televised biography of Claudia ("Lady Bird") Johnson *Wall Street Journal* 17 Jun 93

Martha Raddatz reporter

1975 He is hot tea and honey, instant relief for what ails the Pentagon.

On nomination of William Perry to be US Secretary of Defense NPR 25 Jan 94

Howell Raines Washington editor *NY Times*

1976 The defining moment is that point at which the essential character of a candidate or campaign stands revealed to the individual or political organization and to the external world.

On originating the term "defining moment," cited by William Safire *NY Times* 23 Sep 90

1977 The redneck Riviera.

On the Central Gulf Coast of Florida *ib*

Michael Ramsey Archbishop of Canterbury

1978 Liberalism alone is the great Lady Surgeon of national maladies, and while she is temporarily abed with a broken limb, the nation is the sufferer.

On Britain's 1927 "great strike," quoted by Owen Chadwick *Michael Ramsey* Oxford 90

Dan Rather commentator

1979 A Republican governor in Texas is as rare as a mild bowl of chili.

CBS TV 20 Sep 82

1980 A president who plays the saxaphone was welcomed today by the trumpets of state.

On the Clinton inauguration 20 Jan 93

1981 A walking national monument to himself.

On Cuban dictator Fidel Castro *The Last Revolution* 18 Jul 96

Wendell Rawls Jr reporter

1982 The inevitable new sun crawled over the tall pines and bathed a tired black dog lying in the street of the wilted hometown of a defeated president.

On Plains GA the day after President Carter's losing bid for re-election *NY Times* 6 Nov 80

1983 Little moved. . . save an early pulpwood truck with a snaggled grill, a yellow school bus picking up children, an elderly couple in a camper from Idaho, and a half empty coach of tourists.

ib

1984 Now it was as quiet as it used to be, in the yesteryears before the yesterdays.

ib

Andrew Rawnsley reporter *Guardian*

1985 She was paraded into the mock-Gothic slap and tickle of the Upper House dressed in scarlet, gold braid and black cap, the pelts of several small animals hanging from her shoulders, like a cross between Little Red Riding Hood and the wolf.

On Margaret Thatcher's seating in the Lords as Baroness Thatcher of Kesteven *Guardian Weekly* 12 Jul 92

1986 In poop-deck hats, Lord Boyd-Carpenter, her first ministerial boss, and Lord Joseph, her ideological guru, marched fore and aft, like two tugs guiding an old liner to its final harbor.

ib

1987 A little shiver went up the old wet spine of Lord Pym, withdrawing his tortoise-like head into his shoulders. Lord Callaghan was descending into a deep sulk, clearly thinking that they were letting in anybody these days.

ib

1988 Lord Whitelaw gently rolled those weary oyster eyes at what she might do to their sleepy, exquisitely well mannered club where *noblesse* was still *oblige.*

ib

William Rees-Mogg Editor *London Times*

1989 Men of the finest intellect do not necessarily make the best political leaders. . . [because] crude vigor or brazen self-confidence are useful in the sweaty cockpit of the House of Commons.

Quoted by John Russell *London* Abrams 94

Richard Reeves biographer

1990 Politics is sex in a hula-hoop.

NY Post 14 Jun 76

1991 He wanted to make sure she looked dark enough.

On why John F Kennedy thrice repeated a photo session with a black campaign worker *President Kennedy* Simon & Schuster 93

James B Reston Chief, Washington Bureau, *NY Times*

1992 Smarter than most of his colleagues in the Truman cabinet, but not smart enough to hide it.

On Secretary of State Dean Acheson *Deadline* Random House 91

1993 His intelligence was matched only by his unpopularity, and his guess was that anything with his name on it would probably be defeated.

On George F Kennan as ambassador to the Soviet Union and later head of the State Department's policy-planning staff *ib*

1994 He could strut sitting down.

On Senator Arthur Vandenberg *ib*

1995 They wanted him on tap and not on top.

On desire of the Kennedy and Johnson White House to have Adlai E Stevenson remain at the UN rather than becoming Secretary of State *ib*

1996 They were always... getting more credit than they deserved more sorrow than they could bear, climbing into jobs before they were ready and failing just when they were succeeding.

On John F, Robert F, and Edward M Kennedy *ib*

1997 The most successful... were the cheerful optimists, who appointed competent advisers and listened to them: Roosevelt, Truman, and Eisenhower.

On US presidents *ib*

1998 The least successful presidents were the pessimists who assumed the worst in everybody and didn't listen to anybody: Nixon and Johnson.

ib

1999 He not only knew a lot about foreign affairs, he was a foreign affair.

On Secretary of State Henry A Kissinger *ib*

2000 The American people... were like him: cheerful, optimistic, patriotic, inconsistent, and casually inattentive.

On President Reagan *ib*

2001 The wives of presidents should be authorized and even encouraged to ask their husbands at least once a month: "What on earth did you think you were doing?" And on occasion to tell him what nobody else would, namely, "I love you, but sometimes think you're a certified fathead."

ib

Walter Reuther President, Congress of Industrial Organizations (CIO)

2002 If it walks like a duck and it talks like a duck, then it must be a duck.

On recognizing a Communist, in William Safire ed *Safire's Political Dictionary* Random House 78

Frank Rich columnist

2003 Mr Altman... has already shot himself in both feet and every other appendage.

On US Deputy Secretary of the Treasury Roger C Altman's testimony on Clinton involvement in Whitewater land sales *NY Times* 4 Aug 94

Sam Richardson Chief Lobbyist, United Mine Workers (UMW)

2004 The issue is an incredibly contentious little pimple on the backside of a huge budget bill.

On opposing repeal of a 1992 retroactive federal mandate requiring 300 companies to pay premiums for miners' health benefits *NY Times* 6 Nov 95

2005 It's like taxing me for something my grandfather did 40 years ago.

ib

Peter Riddell political editor *London Times*

2006 Ministerialitis—an illness of ministers of state in office for many years. Its symptoms are an exaggerated liking for red boxes, government cars and other trappings of office; and, in its extreme form, a belief that you can never lose your job.

London Times 28 Oct 91

2007 It is more traditionally known as hubris; which can lead to nemesis.

ib

Don Ritchie Associate Historian, US Senate

2008 He feared no one would recognize him with his eyeglasses off, and now... no one recognizes him with his eyeglasses on.

On little-known US vice president, James S Sherman, whose marble bust is the only one with spectacles *NY Times* 28 May 95

Roxanne Roberts reporter

2009 Lady Thatcher co-starred in her third Reagan birthday since they won the Cold War and lost their jobs.

On President Reagan turning 83 *Washington Post* 4 Feb 94

2010 Thatcher kept heaping praise on her buddy "Ron," but there was just something that sounded like a big sister telling him to go clean his room.

ib

Steve Roberts journalist

2011 There are a lot of legislators who thought Mr Chairman was their first name.

Reporting on the vanity of heading a Congressional committee Station WAMU Washington 7 Mar 95

Lawrence S Rockefeller Member of the Board of Eastern Airlines

2012 Lyndon gave me that instead of the Hawaii air route.

On President Johnson's bestowal of the Medal of Freedom after Eastern Airlines failed to receive permission to fly a coveted route, quoted by Peter Collier and David Horowitz *The Rockefellers* Holt Rinehart Winston 78

Llewellyn Rockwell Ludwig von Mises Institute

2013 It's enough that he has [his likeness] on the dime, which thanks to him is worth about 2 cents.

Objecting to a Franklin D Roosevelt memorial *Washington Times* 14 Oct 94

The Rolling Stones rock music group

2014 We sell 'em missiles, we sell 'em tanks./ We give 'em credit, you can call up the banks./ It's just a business, you can pay us in crude./ You'll love these toys, just go play out your feuds./ We got no pride, don't care whose boots we lick./ We act so greedy, makes me sick, sick, sick.

Haywire song on arms sales to the Middle East *NY Times* 27 Feb 91

Ed Rollins political consultant

2015 An extremely dangerous demagogue with delusions of adequacy. . . he'd treat nickels like they were manhole covers.

On presidential aspirant Ross Perot and his economies as compared to his excesses *Bare Knuckles and Back Rooms* with Tom DeFrank Broadway Books 96

2016 They were masters of the black art of using somebody else's phrase with reporters so somebody else got fingered for their leaks.

On associates of Secretary of State James A Baker III—"an unbelievable control freak"—in the Reagan White House *ib*

William Rosenberg VP, American Historical Assn

2017 A political appointment is implicitly corrupt because it it raises questions about whether the materials made available to the public constitute the full record.

On President Clinton's nomination of former Governor John Carlin of Kansas as national archivist instead of a professionally-trained historian *NY Times* 21 May 95

Roger Rosenblatt contributing editor *Time*

2018 The candidate. . . who is willing to take the country problem by problem, perhaps to discover a vision by deduction, will not bring down the house with a speech. . . but he could grow up to be president.

"A Candidate with a Vision" *Time* 1 Feb 88

2019 The 1st Amendment has always been dearest to our hearts because it allows us to see where our hearts are located.

On guaranteed freedom *Life* Fall 91

2020 [He] is known as the brains of the outfit. That gives you an idea of the outfit.

On Bush White House Chief of Staff John Sununu *NY Times* 18 Nov 91

A M Rosenthal columnist

2021 The new threat-word is Lebanonization. . . the activity within a single country so riven with religious and other disputes that the country becomes impossible to govern.

On Lebanon's subjectivity to invasion by Palestinians and Syrians *NY Times* 21 Apr 91

Leo Rosten writer and lecturer

2022 Dissenters have no greater moral or physical rights than non-dissenters. Complaint contains no *carte blanche* security; if it did, hypochondriacs should be kings.

A *Triumph for Reason* Doubleday 70

Polly Rothstein Director, NY Coalition for Legal Abortion

2023 Why is it that you owners are so powerful? There are more uterus-owners than gun-owners.

On the gun lobby's concentration on arms control to the neglect of other issues concerning women and the general poulation *Newsweek* 17 Jul 89

Clayton Ruby Toronto lawyer

2024 We have left the postmodern age and entered the post-human.

Expressing belief that the bonds of common humanity and mutual obligations "are no longer reflected by government" *NY Times* 17 Sep 95

Norman Rush novelist

2025 Socialism is like knitting with oars.

Mating Knopf 91

Marty Ryall Executive Director, Arkansas Republican Party

2026 Arkansas is the only bureaucracy in the world that destroys more paperwork than it creates.

On difficulty of documenting President Clinton's years as governor *NY Times* 20 Mar 94

Larry J Sabato
Professor of Political Science, University of Virginia

2027 When you're chairman of Ways and Means for so many years, you rarely meet a person who doesn't tell you you're the second cousin to God.

On Representative Dan Rostenkowski's conviction of mail fraud after 14 years as head of the US Congress's most powerful committee *Washington Post* 11 Apr 96

Morley Safer commentator

2028 [She is] Mary Poppins with a hammer. . . never married to anyone but the Commons.

On House of Commons Speaker Betty Boothroyd *60 Minutes* CBS TV 29 Oct 95

William Safire columnist

2029 The new, old, and constantly changing language of politics is a lexicon of conflict and drama. . . ridicule and reproach. . . pleading and persuasion.

Introduction to *Safire's Political Dictionary* 1st Ed Random House 68

2030 Color and bite permeate a language designed to rally many men, to destroy some, and to change the minds of others.

ib

2031 Oddly romantic, loyal, and benumbed. . . dour, pipe-smoking, bloodhound-visaged "heavy". . . John Mitchell was the rock upon which Nixon built his church.

On Nixon's Attorney General *Before the Fall* Doubleday 75

2032 Cover your ass—the bureaucrat's method of protecting his posterior from posterity.

Safire's Political Dictionary 3rd Ed Random House 78

2033 President Reagan is a rhetorical roundheels, as befits a politician seeking empathy with his audience.

Language Maven Strikes Again Doubleday 90

2034 The color of the voter's light is amber, not green.

On France's reluctance to join a union of European currencies *NY Times* 21 Sep 92

2035 [He is] a living example that still waters could run shallow.

On Under Secretary of State William Clark, quoted by Eric Alterman *Sound & Fury* HarperCollins 92

2036 George Bush is patrician, not folksy, and he clanks falsely when he puts on Joe Sixpack nonairs.

NY Times 18 Oct 92

2037 Kick 'em while they're up, not while they're down.

On political criticism, quoted by Edwin Diamond *Behind the Times* Villard 93

2038 The silent majority, like a great soaking-wet shaggy dog banished from the house during the Watergate storms, romped back into the nation's parlor and shook itself vigorously.

Recalling President Nixon's reference 3 Nov 69 to Vietnam War supporters he identified as "the silent majority" *Safire's New Political Dictionary* Random House 93

2039 [The silent majority] is the remarkable legion of the unremarked, whose individual opinions are not as colorful or different enough to make news, but whose collective opinion, when crystallized, can make history.

ib

2040 Here sits America, with no appetite and in the wrong restaurant, served up a costly, tasteless, warmed-over dish it didn't order and cannot send back.

On sexual harassment charges against President Clinton *NY Times* 5 May 94

2041 A pipsqueak principality in a war of nerves.

On Haiti *ib* 15 Sep 94

2042 I was egregiously wrong.

On serving as a speechwriter for President Nixon *USA Today* 30 Aug 95

2043 Americans of all political persuasions are coming to the sad realization that our First Lady. . . is a congenital liar.

On examining Hillary Rodham Clinton's explanations of her stock market gains, Whitewater land sales, and White House firings *NY Times* 8 Jan 96

Harrison E Salisbury foreign correspondent

2044 Roosevelt thought he was putting a superfox to watch the smaller foxes.

On Franklin D Roosevelt's appointment of Joseph P Kennedy as first chair of the Securities and Exchange Commission *Heroes of My Time* Walker 93

Anthony Sampson journalist

2045 Secrecy is one of the British obsessions, like class, which seems to express a deeper psychological need, as if it were a substitute for the mystery of a religion.

The Anatomy of Britain Harper & Row 62

2046 A life-size white marble statue of the young Queen Victoria, sitting on the Coronation chair and crowned with laurels, looks down on elderly peers sitting at hexagonal tables, writing letters on gothic writing paper.

On the House of Lords *ib*

2047 The name of the visitor is called, and the Member strides up to him with a sudden transformation of expression—arm outstretched, face beaming to welcome this single voter, this sixty-thousandth part of his electorate.

On members of Parliament greeting constituents *The New Anatomy of Britain* Hodder & Stoughton 71

2048 The visitor, looking down from the gallery, sees his MP in his own habitat, as if coming suddenly upon a pride of lions in their own lair, overheard as if no one were watching.

ib

2049 On its dullest days the house sounds like a federation of bores who. . . have finally found their resting place in a club which has a basic bargain: if I listen to you, you must listen to me.

On the House of Commons *ib*

2050 However much the Prime Minister may nod, bow and hover, he knows that he is the embodiment of parliament's power, and that in theory. . . if a bill were passed for the execution of the Queen, the Queen would have to sign it.

On the Prime Minister's relationship to the monarch *ib*

2051 [Their weekly meetings] are dreaded by at least one of them.

On Prime Minister Thatcher and Elizabeth II *The Changing Anatomy of Britain* Harper & Row 83

Paul A Samuelson Professor of Economics, MIT

2052 He checked the ice in front of him all the time.

Debunking President Kennedy's reputation as "a dashing, deciding type" *NY Times* 31 Oct 93

Claire Sargent woman candidate

2053 It's about time we voted for Senators with breasts. After all, we've been voting for boobs long enough.

On running for US Senate from Arizona *Time* 5 Oct 92

Jean-Paul Sartre philosopher and novelist

2054 I do not believe in God but if I had to choose between Him and the present incumbent, I would choose God. He is more modest.

On Charles de Gaulle, quoted in *de Gaulle and France* PBS TV 30 Nov 92

Simon Schama historian

2055 In the ebullient infancy of the British Empire, beef was not just the dinner of choice; it was an entire gastronomic constitution, the marrow of political freedom.

On belief that "Britannia ruled the waves just as long as her belly was full of beef" *New Yorker* 8 Apr 96

Serge Schmemann foreign correspondent

2056 With a fanfare of trumpets, a patriarchal blessing and a dollop of politics, Boris N Yeltsin was inaugurated. . . as Russia's first freely elected president.

International Herald Tribune 11 Jul 91

2057 The Soviet state, marked throughout its brief but tumultuous history by great achievement and terrible suffering, died today after a long and painful decline. It was 74 years old.

NY Times 26 Dec 91

2058 A flourish of oratory and a dash of wistfulness . . . marked Mr Bush's last curtain call in the East-West drama that defined so much of his presidency.

On President Bush's signing with Boris Yeltsin a new Strategic Arms Reduction Treaty calling for Russia and the US to eliminate by the year 2003 almost three-quarters of their 20,000-odd nuclear warheads *ib* 4 Jan 93

Billie Schneider Arkansas restauranteur

2059 What is this William J Clinton? You're not gonna run as William J Clinton. You're Bill Clinton. And you're gonna run as Bill Clinton!

Counsel supplied by the proprietor of Clinton's favorite northwest Arkansas cafe, quoted by David Maraniss *First in His Class* Simon & Schuster 95

Thomas J Schoenbaum Professor of Political Science, University of Georgia

2060 [He] made himself the rock against which crashed the successive waves of dissent.

On US Secretary of State Dean Rusk during the Vietnam War *Waging Peace and War* Simon & Schuster 88

2061 [He was] widely regarded as the chief hawk in the aerie of Vietnam advisers.

ib

Daniel K Schorr commentator

2062 Not to know Ross Perot is to love him.

On a Democratic presidential hopeful NPR 9 Jun 92

2063 She cannot be dropped off the back of the sled to slow the pursuing wolves.

On Hillary Rodham Clinton's position as First Lady in relationship to Whitewater land sales 7 Mar 94

2064 As I learned in high school, magnetic north is not true north.

On President Reagan's letter to Senator Paul Lexalt denying endorsement of Oliver L North's senatorial candidacy 18 Mar 94

2065 Now we have all our eggs in one basket and that basket is Aristide.

On US backing of Haiti's President Jean-Bertrand Aristide 8 Oct 94

2066 Terrorism is the poor man's way of making war.

On bombing of the Oklahoma City federal building, interviewed Station WAMU 21 Apr 95

2067 We have two ways of demolishing our country. One is the Oklahoma City bombing and the other is Republicans in Congress.

ib 5 Jun 95

William Seale historian

2068 Those who see the White House at close hand. . . learn that in reality it has only one resident. Each enters in triumph.

The White House: The History of An American Idea AIA Press 93

2069 The White House has been pulled apart, rearranged, gutted by fire and renovation, reassembled; yet it is always the same.

ib

2070 Its idea has become its essence.

ib

Francis Sejersted Chair, Nobel Prize Committee

2071 These are not saints. They are politicians in a complicated reality and it is the total picture that was decisive.

On awarding Nobel Peace Prize to two men with widely differing viewpoints, South Africa's President F W de Klerk and his former prisoner Nelson Mandela *NY Times* 18 Oct 93

Eric Sevareid commentator

2072 Mr Agnew preached the old fashioned virtues and practices old fashioned vices.

On Vice President Spiro Agnew's 1973 acceptance of a plea bargain for taking bribes, quoted by Raymond A Schroth *The American Journey of Eric Sevareid* Steerforth Press 95

2073 The last mighty effort of the original Samson. . . brought the whole temple down upon himself and everyone else.

Broadcast 22 Oct 73 on President Nixon's "Saturday night massacre" in the firing of key figures in the Watergate investigation *ib*

Walter Shapiro contributing editor *Time*

2074 Seven Democrats gazed into the double mirrors of the slate-gray dressing rooms, and each saw the next President of the US.

On televised debate of seven candidates for Democratic presidential nomination *Time* 13 Jul 87

George Bernard Shaw playwright

2075 The man who knows nothing and thinks he knows everything is pointed clearly to a political career.

Recalled on Shaw's death 1 Nov 50

Gail Sherry essayist

2076 Thatcher's initial warmed-milk voice turns instantly to a scald.

On the Prime Minister taking questions in the Commons *Vanity Fair* Jun 89

2077 Then there's the nanny voice, all-knowing, simply telling you what's best for you, a throwback to the primal authority figure who marked many of those men more powerfully than their mothers.

ib

2078 A sort of decaffeinated Noel Coward.

On Thatcher speechwriter Robert Millar *ib*

Robert Shelton Imperial Wizard, Ku Klux Klan

2079 The Klan will never return. . . with the robes and the rallies and the cross lightings and parades, everything that made the Klan the Klan, the mysticism, what we called Klankraft.

On 30th anniversary of Freedom Summer in the American South that marked the start of the Klan's decline *Washington Times* 21 Dec 94

2080 I'm still a Klansmen, always will be. The Klan is my belief, my religion. But it won't work anymore. The Klan is gone. Forever.

ib

Eduard A Shevardnadze Foreign Minister in the Gorbachev Kremlin

2081 Cowards almost always die. If they survive you can't really call it living.

On returning to his native area of Tbilisi, Georgia on the edge of the former Soviet Union *NY Times* 19 Oct 95

2082 For us in Georgia, the sun rises not in the East but in the North, meaning in Russia.

Recalling a statement that angered Georgians and, he conceded, "caused a certain amount of distress among astronomers. . . but I was simply expressing the fact that Russia is a very big factor in our lives" *ib*

Dave Shiplett Assistant editorial page editor *Rockey Mountain News*

2083 The year's most nonawaited book.

Wall Street Journal 20 May 94 on former US Vice President Dan Quayle's *Standing Firm* HarperCollins 94

2084 His strong wife Marilyn could sit a roomful of congressional wimps back on their seats with one flash of her incisors.

ib

Randy Shilts reporter *San Francisco Chronicle*

2085 Don't offend the gays and don't inflame the homophobes. . . the twin horns on which the handling of this epidemic would be torn from the first day of the epidemic.

On the politics of AIDS *And the Band Played On* St Martin's 87

Hugh Sidey White House Correspondent

2086 When a bureaucrat makes a mistake and continues to make it, it usually becomes the new policy.

Time 29 Nov 76

2087 The Washington Establishment... is the big, raw nerve end of the US. Curse it, attack it, defy it indefinitely, and a President almost always ends up diminished.

ib 23 Nov 87

2088 Washington is... politicians, lobbyists, journalists, tycoons, labor skates, hustlers, social climbers, clergy, judges, tourists, professors, bureaucrats and any number of crooks, white collar and otherwise. In short, it has served as America come to the front office to complain.

ib

2089 They are fragments of silver in a year of political dross.

On Peggy Noonan's speechwriting for the Bush presidential campaign *ib* 2 May 88

2090 There is a portion of the character of any president, never glimpsed before, that emerges under the pressure of his office.

ib 27 Jul 92

2091 That Godlike hold over life and death vanished from his fingers and into a military aide's hands and later to Bush's pocket.

On the code card for nuclear attack that President Reagan fished from his pocket at Bush's inaugural with the question, "What do I do with this?" *ib* 16 Nov 92

2092 There is irony in... that he may never have understood that so many others were not so blessed by Providence, and that is one of the reasons he lost this election.

On President Bush's defeat *ib* 30 Nov 92

2093 A jubilant but strange pledge of peace. No large armies lying smashed and smoking in the far deserts. No victors, no vanquished.

On Yitzhak Rabin and Yasir Arafat's signing of the Palestinian-Israeli peace accord *ib* 27 Sep 93

2094 This was a search for peace in quieted minds and hearts, though no less perilous for that. It was a profound statement of hope, this singular coming together... on the broad green South Lawn of the White House, with chrysanthemums in bloom and robins calling.

ib

2095 She was a butterfly caught in the political torrents of Washington, detesting many of its coarse rituals but fascinated by its drama.

Recalling Jacqueline Kennedy Onassis *ib* 30 May 94

Paul Simionescu Technical Manager, Romlux

2096 It's like in an American movie where a very well-trained herd of cattle finds itself walking in... a 45-year-long canyon, and when it finally opens out into a valley everyone is just bewildered, like animals having too many possibilities.

On freed Rumania's drop in productivity *NY Times* 25 Feb 91

Kirke L Simpson columnist

2097 [He] was chosen by a group of men in a smoke-filled room.

Associated Press dispatch coining the "smoke-filled room" on presidential nomination of Warren G Harding, recalled on Simpson's death *NY Times* 17 Jun 72

Frank Sinatra entertainer

2098 If I had a son, I'd like him to be like Pat Boone—till he was three hours old.

On the singer Pat Boone who campaigned for Ronald Reagan while Sinatra worked for Jerry Brown in 1966 California gubernatorial race, quoted by Kitty Kelley *His Way* Bantam 86

Upton Sinclair writer and activist

2099 I aimed at the public's heart and by accident I hit its stomach.

On *The Jungle* 1903, credited with passage of the Pure Food and Drug Act, recalled on Sinclair's death 25 Nov 68

Damu Smith Greenpeace

2100 [We] must lay down our Uzis and Tech-9's and not kill each other anymore.

At the Million Man March on Washington *NY Times* 17 Oct 95

Hedrick Smith foreign correspondent

2101 The cat is out of the bag—but it's not one cat, it's a zillion cats.

On the democratizing of Russia, Station WAMU Washington 18 Dec 90

Linda Smith US Congresswoman

2102 You can't perform surgery in a dirty operating room and with a team that hasn't scrubbed.

On the need for radical campaign finance reform that would ban money from the Political Activities Committee as well as out-of-state contributions *Time* 25 Dec 95

Alexander Solzhenitsyn Russian writer and activist

2103 An amicable agreement of diplomatic shoves will bury and pack down corpses still breathing in a common grave.

On US policy of détente and an approaching Helsinki summit conference *NY Times* 15 Jul 75

2104 [It is a] great petrified tear.

On the Gulag Archipelago *Wall Street Journal* 2 Oct 84

2105 The death knell has sounded for Communism. But... we face the danger of being crushed by the debris.

Fear expressed in the first Solzhenitsyn article to appear in an official Soviet publication in three decades *NY Times* 19 Sep 90

2106 All the dirty mouths that for decades served totalitarianism have rushed into the new *glasnost*. . . [but] who among them has said at least one word of repentance?

Washington Post 19 Sep 90

2107 Woe to that nation whose literature is interrupted by force. This is the amputation of its memory.

Quoted by Harrison E Salisbury *Heroes of My Time* Walker 93

2108 The nation cannot long remember itself. . . it is deprived of spiritual unity.

ib

2109 Silent generations grow old and die without ever talking about themselves, either to each other or to their descendents. . . a danger to the whole of mankind when the whole of history ceases to be understood as a result of such a silence.

ib

2110 The scum of triviality has cleared, and the people have ripened enough to become conscious of their fate in its essence and its depth.

On the timeliness of Solzhenitsyn's return to Russia *NY Times* 29 May 94

2111 What unifying idea will come, I don't know but the thought that comes naturally to mind is love for one's nation without servility, without false claims, with acknowledgment of sins and failings.

ib

Yasunori Sone Professor of Political Science, Keio University, Tokyo

2112 There is a vacuum of voices.

On lack of choices offered voters because of the similarities of the two leading parties *Christian Science Monitor*

Theodore C Sorensen counsel to Kennedy White House

2113 In the distance the dome of the Capitol covers a milieu of wisdom and folly, Presidential ambitions and antagonisms, political ideals, and ideologies.

Prologue to *Kennedy* Harper & Row 65

2114 Away to the left, in white sandstone hidden behind a screen of greenery, is the seat of executive power, the scene of more heroic dramas, comedies and tragedies than any stage in the world.

On the White House *ib*

2115 He knew that he had always been too junior, too liberal, too outspoken and too much in a hurry to be accepted in their inner ruling circles; and they knew that he spoke a different language and seemed more at home with a different breed of friends.

On President Kennedy's reference to legislators in his 1961 State of the Union *ib*

Michael Specter foreign correspondent

2116 These are lonely days for the grim, white-haired man who runs this country. . . who helped create the epoch he must now endure.

On Eduard A Shevardnadze, Foreign Minister in the Gorbachev Kremlin, who aided in the fall of Communism and then retreated to his native Georgia *NY Times* 19 Oct 95

2117 His dark green eyes stopped twinkling a long time ago. He shuffles when he walks, as if he were wearing leg irons. . . [and] lives wrapped in a paramilitary cocoon. Ambivalent, undecided and deeply emotional, they have insisted that he fix their broken country.

On Shevardnadze's fellow Georgians *ib*

Keith Spicer Canadian broadcasting executive

2118 There is the habit of politicians in democracies to take on priestly attitudes, to believe they are demigods, to play in the sandbox of power and throw sand in the eyes of the citizens who put them there.

On officials too long in office *NY Times* 31 Oct 93

Sergei B Stankevich Deputy Mayor of Moscow

2119 This city has too much democracy per square kilometer.

On Moscow's 5,000 neighborhood councils *NY Times* 3 Mar 91

Wallace Stegner novelist

2120 A political animal can be defined as a body that will go on circulating a petition even with its heart cut out.

Quoted by T H Watkins *Righteous Pilgrim* Holt 90 from Stegner's *Beyond the Hundredth Meridian* Houghton Mifflin 54

Richard Stengel senior writer *Time*

2121 Those who live by the image die by the unmaking of it.

On plethora of books on the Reagan White House *Time* 23 May 88

Abdel Rahim Sukar Palestinian nationalist

2122 I cried. . . but. . . when I saw the flesh and blood of Jews, I was happy.

On his brother, Anwar, who blew himself up in a crowd of Israelis *Newsweek* 6 Feb 95

Kevin Sullivan foreign correspondent

2123 [He] was as invisible as a flashlight on a sunny beach.

On Japanese politician Naoto Kan's hopes to become prime minister *Washington Post* 10 Jul 96

Michael Tankersley Public Citizen lobby group

2124 The archivist is the custodian of the historical memory of the country.

On President Clinton's nomination of Kansas Governor John Carlin instead of a professional historian to be the national archivist *NY Times* 21 May 95

A J P Taylor Socialist Party leader

2125 Politics express the activities of "man in society," as the theme of history has rightly been called. All other forms of history seem to me history with the history left out.

London Times 8 Sep 90

Elizabeth Taylor actress

2126 You help them get elected, and then the Senate becomes the wife, the mistress. That was one lady I couldn't begin to fight. She was too tough.

On her divorce from Senator John Warner *Cosmopolitan* Sep 87

Pierre-Henri Teitgen cabinet minister

2127 [It was just] a little party that made its own little soup in its own little corner.

On Charles de Gaulle's attitude towards political parties, especially the Mouvement Republicain Populaire (MRP), quoted by Jean Lacouture *op cit*

Shabtai Teveth historian

2128 The blessing of 1967 was that Israel proved again that it was viable and not, as the Arabs imagined, something that could be wiped off the map without much effort.

On 25th anniversary of the Six Day War *NY Times* 8 Jun 92

2129 It was a return to the land of the Bible. Suddenly, Israel became the Land of Israel.

ib

Evan Thomas White House correspondent

2130 This maladroit middle-aged man with thinning, blow-dried hair sticking his tongue down the throat of a startled young campaign aide became a sick joke.

On Senator Bob Packwood on the eve of US Senate censure *Newsweek* 18 Sep 95

2131 Safe in the strangely cosseted world of the Senate, he was free to play the Lothario.

ib

Time magazine

2132 The old man puffed into sight like a venerable battlewagon pressing up over the horizon... a smudge of smoke, then the long cigar, then the familiar, stoop-shouldered hulk that a generation has come to know as the silhouette of greatness.

On Winston S Churchill disembarking from the Queen Mary 14 Jan 52

2133 In place of many of the old stereotypes of the Jew emerged a bronzed and bare-chested figure somewhat larger than life; the sabra (native-born Israeli).

On Israel 9 Jun 67

2134 [The sabra] takes that name from the fruit of the cactus that thrives in his land, a handsome, romantic idealist who furrowed his fields rather than his brow and was equally adept at digging wells for his country and graves for its enemies.

ib

2135 His career was a text book example of the rise of a patrician in the snug embrace of the American establishment.

On Dean Acheson 25 Oct 71

Luther Henry Tindal fruit picker

2136 Hell, I fruit tramp to survive.... Fruit tramp says what I am. Migrant don't.... [It's] a statistic.

Quoted by Herman LeRoy Emmet *Fruit Tramps* University of New Mexico Press 90

Henry Tizard British radar developer

2137 We are a great nation, but if we continue to behave like a great power, we shall soon cease to be a great nation.

Time 18 Mar 91

Toledo Blade

2138 A wonderful mind which knows practically everything and understands practically nothing.

On Ohio's Senator Robert A Taft 31 Jul 53

Garry Trudeau satirist

2139 Criticizing a political satirist for being unfair is like criticizing a nose guard for being physical.

Newsweek 15 Oct 90

Charles Trueheart Canadian correspondent

2140 With apolgies to the beaver, no Canadian symbol bestrides the world so formidably as the Mountie, the red-serge-suited, wide-brim-hatted, high-booted, high-boot shod constable of the Royal Canadian Mounted Police.

Guardian Weekly 26 Feb 95

Leon Uris educator and author

2141 A republic eventually came to pass but the sorrows and troubles never left that tragic, lovely land. For you see, in Ireland there is no future, only the past happening over and over.

Trinity Doubleday 76

US News & World Report

2142 A think tank in cowboy boots.

On Texas Representative Dick Armey as house majority leader 12 Dec 94

Peter Vansittart novelist and historian

2143 A fortnight, a single shrieking afternoon, had sufficed to implement the message. . . that civilization was a fragile crust.

On the Suez crisis *In the Fifties* John Murray 95

2144 Great art, major science and profound wisdom had for most of us shrivelled to irrelevance. Eden himself faded away, reviving later, in the English manner, as Lord Avon.

On Prime Minister Anthony Eden *ib*

Pierre Viansson-Ponté historian

2145 To say he mingled with the crowd would be an understatement: he plunged into it, he wallowed in it, he was literally dissolved in it.

On Charles de Gaulle in political gatherings, the "'*bain de foule*,' the act of bathing in the crowd" quoted by Jean Lacouture *op cit*

2146 He led a charmed life, believed in it and needed contact with the crowd as an ever renewed demonstration of his invulnerability, as proof of his ascendancy, like a bathe in the Fountain of Youth.

On De Gaulle's fearlessness despite "Algerians carrying retractable knives, activists armed with loaded revolvers and even madmen carrying hypodermic needles" *ib*

Gore Vidal novelist and critic

2147 Astronauts! Rotarians in space!

Myra Breckinridge Little, Brown 68

2148 She was contemptuous of. . . those politicians prone to the Ciceronian vice of exaggerating their contribution to history, a category in which she firmly placed that quaint Don Quixote of the cold war, Dean Acheson.

On Eleanor Roosevelt *United States Essays: 1952–92* Random House 93

2149 Eisenhower [was] reading a speech with his usual sense of discovery.

On President Eisenhower *ib*

2150 Nancy's career is now one of wifedom. . . and, in due course, social climbing. She was born with a silver ladder in her hand.

On Nancy Reagan *ib*

2151 [It]. . . added Pat Buchanan and Ross Perot, two choleric below-the-title character actors, good for cutaways when the stars needed a rest.

On the Clinton presidential race *NY Times* 18 Sep 94

Peter Viereck poet and historian

2152 McCarthyism is the revenge of the noses that for 20 years of fancy parties were pressed against the outside window pane.

Editorial on charges of Communists in government as an expression of class differences, quoted in *This Fabulous Century* Time-Life Books 70

Dmitri Volkogonov historian

2153 He had always stood before us in the death-mask of the earthly God he had never been.

On Vladimir Ilyich Lenin *Lenin: Life and Legacy* HarperCollins 95, quoted by reviewer Ian McIntyre who saw Lenin as "the first person of the Soviet Trinity," *London Times* 2 Feb 95

Nicholas Von Hoffman columnist and biographer

2154 Lincoln's answer was to more or less abolish the Bill of Rights and win the war; Nixon's was to keep the Bill of Rights and lose the war.

On Richard M Nixon and Vietnam *Japan Times* 16 Jun 91

2155 The old boy died neither from rage or shame and like the amiable vampire of our politics that he is, threw back the coffin lid yet one more time.

On Nixon *ib*

Richard Wade Professor of History, City College of New York

2156 If you sit in the governor's office, you'll see that the chair faces Washington.

On presidential ambitions of governors of New York NPR 7 Oct 94

John Walcott Assistant managing editor *US News & World Report*

2157 The Republican and Democratic conventions survive, like the running of the bulls in Pamplona or the Apache devil dance, mostly as a ritual link to the past. . . and an excuse to party.

On the "tribal rites" of the major political parties *US News & World Report* 26 Aug 96

Martin Walker US Bureau chief, *The Guardian*

2158 An extraordinary woman whose grandeur has always carried just a touch of antique farce, Lady Thatcher begins her memoirs with cadences that blend the Shakespearian with Monty Python.

Review Margaret Thatcher's *The Downing Street Years* HarperCollins 93 *Washington Post* 31 Oct 93

2159 She was a woman of another era, a true Iron Lady who tried and ultimately failed to bend the age of silicon to her monstrous and seductive will.

ib

2160 I inquired whether knee-cap soup and blood-sausage were on the menu.

On a dinner party honoring Jerry Adams, president of Shinn Fein, political arm of the Irish Republican Army NPR 4 Oct 94

Wyatt Tee Walker aide to Martin Luther King Jr

2161 The most important thing that happened in that whole period was that people decided that they were not going to be afraid of white folks anymore.

Quoted by Fred Powledge *Free at Last?* Little, Brown 91

Wall Street Journal

2162 If you don't provide loyalty down, you can't expect loyalty up.

"On Loyalty" editorial on the degree of support owed a president by former aides 11 May 88

2163 The already debilitated Reagan presidency will now suffer the death of a thousand snickers.

On Nancy Reagan's dependence on astrology in approving her husband's travel schedule and other matters as disclosed by former Chief of Staff Donald Regan *ib*

2164 The Reagan people were consumed by the Beltway maw, a corrosive brew of ideological hostility, partisan sharp-shooting, congressional arrogance, company-town rumor-mongering and pack journalism.

On the Washington ambience *ib*

2165 God is registered to vote in Hollywood as a Republican. However, Jesus Christ is a Democrat from Santa Monica.

"God Lives in Hollywood" editorial on California's voter registration lists 12 Jul 95

Robert D Waller Conservative Party pollster

2166 Among the people as a whole, as long as she can deliver bread and circuses. . . she can go on.

On Prime Minister Margaret Thatcher *NY Times* 5 Jan 88

Margaret Garrard Warner Washington correspondent

2167 No matter how hard he tries to sound like a member of the red-meat right, he seems like an Episcopalian, which he is, at a fundamentalist tent meeting.

On George Bush as US presidential candidate *Newsweek* 19 Oct 87

2168 "You'll be bored beyond belief," Kissinger told him, then set about to make that true.

On Bush's relationship with Henry A Kissinger as US Secretary of State *ib*

Washington Post

2169 The "testimonial dinner" is a political fraud, a gastronomical affront, an ethical outrage, a colossal bore, an insufferable social disaster and financial shakedown.

Editorial quoted in *Wall Street Journal* 19 Sep 67

2170 The Closest of Strangers.

Headline on sharing the Nobel Peace Prize by South Africa's F W de Klerk and Nelson Mandela 9 Jan 94

Washington Times

2171 Cool is Hot.

On Massachusetts Governor Michael S Dukakis's low-key campaign for Democratic presidential nomination *Wall Street Journal* 3 May 88

T H Watkins biographer

2172 A parade started and soon there was exhibited in full force that peculiarity of American convention politics—the absolutely genuine planned spontaneous demonstration.

On the 1940 Democratic convention *Righteous Pilgrim* Holt 90

Auberon Waugh contributing editor *The Spectator*

2173 Intelligent, educated and literate Englishmen are neither left-wing or right-wing, but are bored by politics and regard all politicians with scorn.

Brideshead Benighted Little, Brown 86

2174 As a natural romantic, I had hoped to find the House of Commons like a cornrick where every sheaf lifted will reveal a family of rats fighting, eating and copulating and dashing for cover when exposed to the light of day. Instead, I found an assembly of dirty-minded but torpid and inadequate drunks.

ib

Theodore H White journalist and historian

2175 Eisenhower has. . . a magic in American politics that is peculiarly his: he makes people happy.

On Dwight D Eisenhower's appearances during Richard M Nixon's 1960 presidential campaign, recalled by Michael R Beschloss *Eisenhower* HarperCollins 90

2176 Chafing in action when his nature yearned to act, conscious of indignities real and imagined, Johnson went through three years of slow burn.

On Lyndon B Johnson as John F Kennedy's vice president, quoted by Arthur M Schlesinger Jr *A Thousand Days* Houghton Mifflin 65

2177 He is like a good pre-war house... [which] they don't build that way anymore. He's also been repainted several times.

On Richard M Nixon's return to presidential politics after 1960 loss to John F Kennedy *Time* 16 Feb 68

2178 [Nelson A Rockefeller] was almost a force of nature, like a slumbering volcano, wreathed in clouds, occasionally emitting smoke which soothsayers attempted to interpret.

The Making of the President 1968 Atheneum 69

2179 The best time to listen to a politician is when he's on the stump on a street corner in the rain late at night when he's exhausted. Then he doesn't lie.

NY Times 5 Jan 69

2180 His passion has aroused the best and the beast in the man, and the beast waited for him in the kitchen.

On Robert F Kennedy's presidential candidacy and assassination as he took a short cut to exit Los Angeles' Ambassador Hotel *The Making of the President 1968* Atheneum 69

2181 The epitaph on the Kennedy Administration became Camelot—a magic moment in American history, when gallant men danced with beautiful women, when great deeds were done, when artists, writers and poets met at the White House and the barbarians beyond the walls were held back.

On President Kennedy's favorite musical *Camelot* which gave its name to his term in office *In Search of History* Harper & Row 78

2182 The flood of money that gushes into politics today is a pollution of democracy.

Time 19 Nov 84

2183 There is no excitement anywhere in the world, short of war, to match the excitement of an American presidential campaign.

On his role as "a storyteller of elections" in his series of books on campaigns, recalled on White's death 15 May 86

2184 Politics in America is the binding secular religion.

ib

Walter White Secretary, National Association for the Advancement of Colored People

2185 Oh, my God, if we could have her sing at the foot of Lincoln!

On learning of plans for Marian Anderson to transcend the Daughters of the American Revolution's refusal for space in Constitution Hall by singing from the steps of the Lincoln Memorial, quoted by T H Watkins *Righteous Pilgrim* Holt 90

Tom Wicker *NY Times* columnist

2186 In the dark of his soul, Americans could have seen their mirror, seen themselves as they knew they were, not as they frequently dreamed of being.

On the Watergate crises *One of Us* Random House 91

Thornton Wilder playwright

2187 [It created] a whole new world of surprised self-respect.

On President Kennedy's invitations to artists for readings, recitals, and dramatic performances at White House dinners, quoted by Arthur M Schlesinger Jr *op cit* Houghton Mifflin 65

Roy Wilkins Executive Director, National Association for the Advancement of Colored People

2188 The term "black power" means anti-white power... a reverse Mississippi, a reverse Hitler, a reverse Ku Klux Klan.

To NAACP's 57th annual convention *Wall Street Journal* 8 Jul 66

2189 Though it be clarified and clarified again, "black power" in the quick, uncritical and emotional adoption it has received from some segments of a beleaguered people can mean in the end only black death.

ib

2190 If, through some miracle, it should be enthroned briefly, the human spirit, which knows no color, or geography, or time, would die a little, leaving for wiser and stronger and more compassionate men the painful beating back to the upper trail.

ib

George Will columnist

2191 He is a friendly man with few close friends. Perhaps only one. He married her.

On Ronald Reagan *Newsweek* 9 Jan 89

2192 What the federal government does basically is borrow money from people and mail it to people.

On entitlement programs ABC TV 19 Sep 93

Edward Bennett Williams attorney

2193 They don't realize what power really is. I'm about to see true power.

On being shown a press clipping naming him one of the most powerful men in Washington even as he lay dying, quoted by Evan Thomas *The Man to See* Simon & Schuster 91

James Williams National Association for the Advancement of Colored People

2194 The initials NAACP are part of the American vocabulary.

Quoted by William Safire "People of Color" *NY Times* 20 Nov 88

Garry Wills Adjunct Professor of History, Northwestern University

2195 He is as simple as a declarative sentence written in an unknown language.

On Democratic presidential nominee Michael S Dukakis *Time* 25 Jul 88

2196 He is enigmatic precisely because he seems to contain no mysteries.

On Louisiana Governor Earl Long and his influence on Bill Clinton's aide James Carville *New Yorker* 12 Oct 92

2197 Earl Long disintegrated in a shower of epigrams, some shrewd, some absurd.

ib

2198 He is at the mercy of the breath of every fool.

On criticisms of a US President, Station WAMU Washington 4 Jul 94

Michael Wines reporter

2199 America boasts no grander generals in public-opinion wars than its politicians, who make people like them against long odds, and its tobacco company executives who make people like a product that science says can kill them.

On congressional hearings on cigarette manufacturers *NY Times* 15 Apr 94

2200 [It is] a job that, amid the Republic's single most concentrated collection of egos, is the Orient Express of ego trips.

On the struggle for "one of the most eminent and visible posts in politics," majority leader of the US Senate *ib* 24 Jun 94

David Wise reporter

2201 The administration is discovering. . . that when the gap between a government's actions and its words become discernible, it is in trouble.

"Dilemma in Credibility Gap" believed to be first use in print of "credibility" and "credibility gap" *NY Herald Tribune* 13 May 65; see also *Washington Post* 5 Dec 65

James Wolcott essayist

2202 By the time she reached the White House, she had Political Wife down pat. She simply settled more comfortably into herself. She became her own official residence.

On Barbara Bush *New Yorker* 3 Oct 94

Tom Wolfe novelist

2203 Radical chic invariably favors radicals who seem primitive, exotic and romantic.

On backing of radical political groups by wealth and prominence *Radical Chic* Farrar Straus Giroux 70

2204 [Radical chic includes] the grape workers who are not merely radical and "of the soil" but also Latin, the Panthers, with their leather pieces, Afros, shades and shoot-outs; and the Red Indians, who, of course, had always seemed primitive, exotic and romantic.

ib

Jane Wyman actress

2205 Ask him what time it is and he'll tell you how the watch was made.

On Ronald Reagan as seen by his first wife, quoted by Jack Finney *From Time to Time* Simon & Schuster 95

Ralph Yarborough US Senator

2206 The only case on record of a man swimming toward a sinking ship.

On Texas Governor John Connally's 1973 switch from Democratic to Republican party in bid for presidential nomination *Washington Post* 18 Jan 88

Grigory A Yavlinsky Russian economist

2207 We have liberated the Soviet system instead of liberating society from the Soviet system.

On seeking election to the Russian parliament *NY Times* 1 Dec 95

Jack Yellen lyricist

2208 Happy days are here again!

Refrain of 1929 song that became the Democratic Party campaign theme, recalled on Yellen's death 17 Apr 91

Hugo Young biographer

2209 The ritual roasting was not necessarily followed by terminal immolation.

On encounter between the head of the Central Policy review staff, Kenneth Berrill, and Prime Minister Thatcher *The Iron Lady* Farrar Straus Giroux 89

2210 By common repute the only one of the eight prime ministers of the present reign with whom the monarch never succeeded in developing an easy relationship was not Mrs Thatcher but Edward Heath: a failing which gave Her Majesty something in common with much of the human race.

ib

James E Young Professor of English and Judaic Studies, University of Massachusetts

2211 By themselves, monuments are of little value, mere stones in the landscape. But as part of a nation's rites or the object of a people's national pilgrimage, they are invested with national soul and memory.

Quoted by Gustav Niebuhr *NY Times* 29 Jan 95 from Young's *The Texture of Memory* Yale 93

Zhang Xiaogan journalist

2212 Tiananmen Square is China's state cathedral.

On Peking's center or what journalist Orville Schell called "China's ultimate political reference point" that transcended Mao Zedong's refashioning of it as a secular shrine to the party and the revolution, quoted by Schell in *Mandate of Heaven* Simon & Schuster 94

Nora Ziegler homeless person

2213 It's a metaphor made concrete.

On the homeless' occupancy of Manhattan's City Hall Park *NY Times* 28 Nov 88

Peter Zimroth legal consel for New York City

2214 [It is] the politics of exclusion.

Asserting NYC's case against George Bush's use of original figures rather than updated ones, especially on minorities, in decisions based on the 1990 census *NY Times* 10 Aug 94

UNITED NATIONS

Officials and Delegates

Madeleine K Albright United States

2215 You can depart voluntarily and soon, or you can depart involuntarily and soon.

To the Haitian military junta on the meaning of the UN Security Council's authorization of a US invasion and occupancy of Haiti *NY Times* 1 Aug 94

2216 Words are cheap; actions are the coin of the realm.

On Iraq's massing of 80,000 troops while accusing the US of ill will *Time* 31 Oct 94

2217 I meet more foreigners per square inch than anybody.

NY Times 25 Nov 94

2218 I can be at the takeoff and the flight, not just the landing.

On participating in biweekly White House meetings that helped Albright get the whole picture *US News & World Report* 13 Feb 95

2219 The silver lining is that people no longer think it's preposterous for there to be a woman Secretary of State.

On the future *ib*

Kofi Annan UN Under Secretary General

2220 The impression is that the easiest way to disrupt a peacekeeping operation is to kill Americans.

On White House failure to prepare the public for US casualties during withdrawal of troops from Somalia *NY Times* 30 Jan 94

Anon

2221 The UN is a collection of all the world's chauvinisms.

On difficulties with male colleagues *NY Times* 10 Apr 95

Warren R Austin United States

2222 Below the 38th Parallel the light of day has shown. . . above that line—all was darkness.

On the defining gulf between free and Communist-dominated Korea *NY Times* 11 Aug 50

2223 The only voice. . . was an echo of a greater voice that had come rolling and rumbling upon steppe and tundra and mountain from a far-away place.

On Soviet influences *ib*

Bernard M Baruch US representative to UN Atomic Energy Commission

2224 We are now facing a problem more of ethics than of physics

On presenting US proposals for control of atomic energy, recalled on Baruch's death 20 Jun 65

Boutros Boutros-Ghali Egypt, UN Secretary General

2225 I survived the Egyptian bureaucracy. If you can do that you can run the UN.

NY Times 16 Oct 93

2226 Tomorrow they can destroy the UN.

On the power of member nations to vote the UN out of existence *ib*

2227 Peacekeeping has been. . . put into this "Don't just stand there, do something" syndrome. . . [but] has often worked best when it's "Don't do something, just stand there!"

ib 2 Jan 94

2228 This is the rule of the game. . . if you are successful, you must disappear, to let the other people say, "We have done this on our own." And in the case you fail you must accept that you will be accused of all the failures.

On the role of the scapegoat *ib*

Richard Butler Australia

2229 This bureaucracy was designed in hell.

On wasteful management that marked the UN 50th anniversary *International Herald Tribune* 24 Jun 95

Lord Caradon (Hugh Mackintosh Foot) Great Britain

2230 Now that he has changed the weather/ Lion and lamb can vote together./God bless the Russian delegation,/I waive consecutive translation.

Poem read to Security Council in tribute to Soviet representative Vasily V Kuznetsov *NY Times* 20 Jun 68

2231 Better to make prime ministers out of prisoners than prisoners out of prime ministers.

Reply to criticism by Soviet representatives *International Herald Tribune* 5 Jun 79

2232 I wanted to say in the Security Council, "There is no cause for alarm. The rumbling sound that you hear is the normal noise of the Soviet ambassador being lowered and locked into a fixed position." But I never got to say it, the time was never quite right.

Mimicking British pilots' explanation to passengers on lowering of landing gear *ib*

Andrew Cohen Great Britain

2233 To campaign against colonialism is like barking up a tree that has already been cut down.

Quote 23 Feb 58

Jose Correa Nicaragua

2234 We do not believe in having happiness imposed upon us.

Reply to Soviet representative *NY Times* 20 Jul 60

Declaration of the Rights of the Child

2235 Mankind owes to the child the best it has to give.

NY Times 20 Oct 59; resolution adopted 19 Jul 60

Francisco A Delgado Philippines

2236 You can discuss, argue and talk back to the Americans, as we have discussed, argued and talked back during all the years of our subjugation, and since—without being shot at dawn.

NY Times 6 Oct 60

Guido De Marco Malta, General Assembly President

2237 [It is a] town meeting of the world.

NY Times 19 Sep 90

Nizar Hamdoon Iraq

2238 She calls, we meet, she hands me a note. For me, this is the lowest form of diplomacy.

On going from mid-1980s cordiality to formalized communications with US Ambassador Madeleine K Albright *Time* 16 Oct 95

Dag Hammarskjöld Secretary General

2239 Don't move without knowing where to put your foot next. . . without having sufficient stability to enable you to achieve exactly what should be the next step.

On applying his sport of mountain climbing to the UN, recalled on Hammarskjöld's death 18 Sep 61

2240 I am the curator of the secrets of prejudices of 79 nations.

Quoted by Alistair Cooke *Talk About America* Knopf 68

David Hannay Britain

2241 They're trying to do deals all the time. But we're not buying carpets.

On Iraq's proposal that the UN close its files on Iraqi armaments in exchange for more details on biological weapons *NY Times* 21 Jun 95

Jeane J Kirkpatrick United States

2242 We have war when at least one of the parties to a conflict wants something more than it wants peace.

US News & World Report 27 Dec 82

Jose Maza Chile, General Assembly President

2243 The same Scotch. . . the same Manhattan. . . the self-same shrimps. . . the same people. . . that is why I favor longer receptions so that people have time to talk. . . and receptions to which fewer people would be invited.

On the need for more time to meet a smaller group, news summaries 31 Dec 55

Antonio Monteiro Portugal

2244 It's group therapy for the world.

On the series of debates that mark the General Assembly's annual reconvening *NY Times* 27 Sep 86

Eleanor Roosevelt United States

2245 Where, after all, do universal human rights begin? In small places, close to home. . . the world of the individual person. . . [and] unless these rights have meaning there, they have little meaning anywhere.

To UN Commission on Human Rights 27 Mar 58

Jan Christian Smuts South Africa

2246 This time we will put it off. We have learned our lesson.

On future threats of war, quoted by Alfred Eisenstaedt *Witness to Our Time* Viking 66

Paul Henri Spaak Belgium

2247 Our agenda is now exhausted. . . the Secretary General. . . all of you are exhausted. I find it comforting that with our very first day, we find ourselves in such complete unanimity.

Concluding the first meeting of the UN General Assembly, recalled on Spaak's death 31 Jul 72

Adlai E Stevenson United States

2248 Let this be remembered, not as the day when the world came to the edge of nuclear war, but as the day when men resolved to let nothing thereafter stop them in their quest for peace.

To UN General Assembly on resolution of the Organization of American States that the US should take action against Soviet placement of nuclear missiles in Cuba 22 Oct 62, quoted by Arthur M Schlesinger Jr *A Thousand Days* Houghton Mifflin 65

2249 We struggle to inject into the discourse—the often rough, fierce, intemperate dialogue of the nations—those elements of order without which we are condemned to stand in fearful exposure on that last fatal brink that overlooks Armageddon.

On receiving the American Jewish Committee's Liberties Medallion *NY Post* 26 May 63

2250 The only worthy response to danger and failure is a renewed dedication to success, and I trust it will be written of the American people in our time, not that we refused to soil our hands with the imperfections of ourselves and of the world, but that we grew stronger, striving to overcome them.

ib

2251 I believe in the forgiveness of sin and the redemption of ignorance.

To a heckler at a UN Day address in Dallas, TX, who asked Stevenson to state his beliefs *Time* 1 Nov 63

2252 Are these human beings or are these animals?

On being hit and spat upon in Dallas, an incident that caused Stevenson to warn President Kennedy against going there, quoted by Arthur M Schlesinger in *A Thousand Days* Houghton Mifflin 65

2253 We travel together, passengers on a little space ship, dependent on its vulnerable reserves of air and soil; all committed for our safety to its security and peace; preserved from annihilation only by the care, the work, and I will say, the love we give our fragile craft.

Last major address to UN Economic and Social Council 9 Jul 64

2254 We cannot maintain it half fortunate, half miserable, half confident, half despairing, half slave—to the ancient enemies of man—half free in a liberation of resources undreamed of until this day.

ib

U Thant UN Secretary General

2255 Today the UN faces a moment of great responsibility. . . the very fate of mankind. If today the UN should prove itself ineffective, it may have proved itself so for all time.

To UN Security Council on Soviet missiles in Cuba 24 Oct 62

Tim Trevan UN Special Commission

2256 We retain the right to designate any location in Iraq. And when we have the need to, we shall visit any location.

On cancellation by UN inspectors in Baghdad of an inspection tour of a military ministry considered off-limits by Iraq *NY Times* 18 Aug 92

Dawa Tsering Himalayan Buddhist Kingdom

2257 Speeches are the price we pay for events. . . .[but] I found out that Uruguay had 3 million people and 10 million cows. . . .and Castro is a real folk hero, maybe the last one left.

On attending a UN 50th anniversary dinner *NY Times* 25 Oct 95

United Nations Report

2258 No one can escape the unwanted sound that is called noise, a disturbance to our environment escalating so rapidly as to become one of the major threats to the quality of human life.

The State of the Environment *NY Times* 16 Dec 83

United Nations Resolution

2259 The Security Council. . . noting that despite all efforts by the UN, Iraq refuses to comply with its obligation. . . decides, while maintaining all its decisions, to allow Iraq one final opportunity, as a pause of good will, to do so.

Authorization to US and its allies to expel Iraq from Kuwait by force if it did not withdraw within 47 days *NY Times* 30 Nov 90

Brian Urquhart UN Under Secretary General

2260 The UN's relationship with the city is like a long, rather positive marriage. . . tremendous ups and downs and the partners occasionally get tremendously fed up with each other.

Looking back on his 40 years at the UN on its 50th anniversary, *NY Times* 20 Oct 95

2261 It is the world's Number 1 fig leaf and scapegoat.
On the UN 21 Oct 95

Vernon Walters United States

2262 People. . . can't give in to one another, but they can give in to the UN.
Life Dec 88

Richard A Woolcott Australia

2263 Apart from a good mind, the two most important assets for a United Nations diplomat are a good tailor and a strong liver.
NY Times 4 Oct 85

Andrew Young United States

2264 That was not a lie, it was just not the whole truth.
On disclosing an unauthorized meeting with the Palestine Liberation Organization that resulted in Young's resignation 14 Aug 79

Valerian A Zorin USSR

2265 I am not in an American courtroom, sir, and therefore do not wish to answer a question that is put to me in the fashion in which a prosecutor puts questions. In due course, sir, you will have your reply.
To US Ambassador Adlai E Stevenson when challenged to deny that the USSR had offensive missiles in Cuba 25 Oct 62

Critics

Dean Acheson US Secretary of State

2266 In the Arab proverb, the ass that went to Mecca remained an ass; hence a policy has little added to it by the place of utterance.
Dept of State Bulletin 16 Jun 46, quoted by David S McLellan *Dean Acheson: The State Dept Years* Dodd, Mead 78

2267 My job was to be the John the Baptist of the Marshall Plan without giving the receivers of relief an unrestricted drawing account on the US Treasury.
On formation of the UN Relief and Rehabilitation Administration *Grapes from Thorns* Norton 75

Anon

2268 Would it be correct to call this a police action?
Unidentified reporter's question to President Truman whose affirmative reply made "police action" the preferred political term for the Korean War, quoted by Eric Goldman *The Crucial Decade* Knopf 56

2269 It's the type of language you can drive a truck through. Or a helicopter. Or a missile.
On US-backed resolution for "humanitarian intervention" permitting nations to use force if citizens are mistreated while being held hostage *Time* 29 Oct 90

2270 The most impossible, daunting, challenging, rewarding, fascinating, clearly unique job on earth.
On search for a new UN Secretary General as described by a former holder of the office *NY Times* 17 Mar 91

Corazon Aquino President of the Philippines

2271 One must be frank to be relevant.
Chiding UN for lack of support in opposing the Ferdinand Marcos regime 22 Sep 86

Jean-Bertrand Aristide President of Haiti

2272 We will prepare our reconciliation coffee with the filter of justice, so that no traces of violence or vegeance will be found.
To General Assembly on promise to follow its intervention with reconciliation in a judicial process *NY Times* 5 Oct 94

2273 The first black republic on earth. . . is marching resolutely. . . toward the establishment of a democratic society.
ib

Bernard M Baruch economic adviser to Franklin D Roosevelt

2274 We are now facing a problem more of ethics than of physics.
On presenting US proposals for control of atomic energy, recalled on Baruch's death 26 Jun 65

George Bush 41st US President

2275 In the waning weeks of one of history's most hopeful summers, the vast, still beauty of the peaceful Kuwaiti desert was fouled by the stench of diesel and the roar of steel tanks.
To the UN on Iraqi invasion of Kuwait 1 Oct 90

2276 Once again, the sound of distant thunder echoed across a cloudless sky. And once again, the world awoke to face the guns of August.
ib

2277 So let it be said of the final decade of the 20th century, this was a time when humankind came into its own. . . [and] emerged from the grit and the smoke of the industrial age to bring about a revolution of the spirit and the mind and began a journey into a new day. . . new age. . . and new partnership of nations.
ib

2278 The UN is now fulfilling its promise as the world's parliament of peace.

ib

William J Clinton 41st US President

2279 Let us establish a strong mandate for an Office of Inspector General. . . and a reputation for toughness. . . integrity. . . effectiveness.

To the UN on aftermath of US intervention in Somalia 27 Sep 93

Mikhail S Gorbachev Soviet Premier, later President of Russia

2280 We are not abandoning our convictions. . . but neither do we have any intention to be hemmed in by our values.

To UN 7 Dec 88, recalled on fall of the Soviet Union 19 Aug 91

2281 Paraphrasing the words of the English poet that Hemingway took as an epigraph to his famous novel, I will say this: The bell of every regional conflict tolls for all of us.

ib

2282 The Soviet Union has taken a decision to reduce its armed forces.

On cutting manpower and armaments plus withdrawal of some forces from East Germany, Czechoslovakia and Hungary *ib*

2283 God is on your side.

To UN Secretary General Perez de Cuellar *Time* 19 Dec 88

Douglas Hurd British Foreign Secretary

2284 Preventive diplomacy is quicker and more helpful. . . than the most successful peacekeeping or peacemaking operation which follows.

To UN on behalf of the 12 member-nations of the European Community *NY Times* 23 Sep 92

John F Kennedy 35th US President

2285 To the UN, our last best hope. . . we renew our pledge. . . to prevent it from becoming merely a forum for invective—to strengthen its shield of the new and the weak—and to enlarge the area in which its writ may run.

Inaugural speech 20 Jan 61

2286 Even the three horses of the troika did not have three drivers, all going in different directions.

To UN on rejecting Soviet plan to replace the Secretary General with a trio of powers sharing equal responsibilities 25 Sep 61

2287 To permit each power to decide. . . its own case would entrench the Cold War in the headquarters of peace.

ib

2288 We far prefer world law, in the age of self-determination, to world war, in the age of mass extermination.

ib

Nikita S Khrushchev Soviet Premier

2289 All the sparrows on the rooftops are crying about the most imperialist nation that is supporting the colonial regime in the colonies in the United States of America.

To the General Assembly 1 Oct 60

2290 What innocence, may I ask, is being played here when it is known that this virtuous damsel has already got a dozen illegitimate children?

ib

2291 We. . . have ordered the masters of Soviet vessels bound for Cuba but not yet within the area of the American warships' piratical activities to stay out of the interception area.

To the Secretary General on the US blockade of Soviet ships approaching Cuba 25 Oct 62, quoted by Robert F Kennedy *Thirteen Days* Norton 69

Golda Meir Foreign Minister of Israel

2292 We who have such an intimate knowledge of boxcars and deportation. . . cannot be silent.

To the General Assembly on Soviet actions in Hungary, news summaries 21 Nov 56

V S Krishna Menon Defense Minister for India

2293 The expression "positive neutrality" is a contradiction. . . [like] a vegetarian tiger.

To General Assembly *NY Times* 18 Oct 60

Archibald MacLeish poet and statesman

2294 It has all the raisins in the original but an attempt has been made to combine them into some kind of pudding.

On submitting to the US State Department a second draft of his preamble for the UN Charter, quoted by Scott Donaldson *Archibald MacLeish* Houghton Mifflin 92

Harold Macmillan Prime Minister of Britain

2295 A vast edifice filled with people throwing stones at each other.

On his first visit to the UN, recalled in Macmillan's book *Tides of Fortune* Macmillan 69

James Morris essayist

2296 Ablaze, like a slab of fire. . . its parade of white flagstaffs gleaming in the street light, and the humped black limousines patient at the door.

On the UN building *NY Times* 2 Oct 60

2297 When at last you cross the road to the UN... it is like traversing some unmarked but crucial frontier.

ib

James B Reston reporter

2298 He outshouted, outcharged, outchallenged and outraged [every other delegation].

On Polish delegate Stefan Wierblowski's support of Soviet motion for seating of the Chinese People's Republic *NY Times* 6 Sep 50

Nelson A Rockefeller Member of UN Building Site Committee

2299 Pa... wants to know how much that site along the East River would cost! He wants to give it to them!

To architects planning the UN headquarters 12 Dec 1946, quoted by Victoria Newwhouse *Wallace K Harrison, Architect* Rizzoli 89

Arthur M Schlesinger Jr historian

2300 The great glass tower glittering above the East River... a world of its own, separate, self-contained and in chronic crisis.

On the UN during the Kennedy presidency *A Thousand Days* Houghton Mifflin 65

2301 A dozen unrelated emergencies might explode at once, demanding immediate reactions.

ib

2302 Its own ethos... rules... language: delegates would argue interminably over whether to "note" or to "reaffirm" a past resolution, to "deplore or regret" or "condemn" a present action.

ib

Haile Selassie Emperor of Ethiopia

2303 Today I stand before the world organization which has succeeded to the mantle discarded by its discredited predecessor.

On becoming the first ruler to address both the League of Nations and the UN 4 Oct 63

2304 Throughout history it has been the inaction of those who could have acted, the indifference of those who should have known better, the silence of the voice of justice when it mattered most, that has made it possible for evil to triumph.

ib

Thomas Sheehy Heritage Foundation

2305 Sometimes intervention is not the answer ... sometimes these conflicts just have to play out.

On UN forces in Bosnia *Christian Science Monitor* 26 Jun 95

Kevin Starr California State Librarian

2306 San Francisco lost its best shot at becoming the Geneva of the Pacific... a crossroads city.

On recalling the UN's founding in San Francisco and rejection of the 1,500-acre Presidio for its home *Christian Science Monitor* 26 Jun 95

Time magazine

2307 One by one, the proud, solemn black men advanced through the murmuring chamber...carrying themselves with graven dignity, often combining ritual facial scars with impeccable European manners, they came from lands of jungle and desert whose very names were scarcely known to the West.

On UN's 15th General Assembly that "in the sweep of history...might be regarded as the time of the Africans" 15 Oct 60

Harry S Truman 33rd US President

2308 [We] sat down on paper the only principles which will enable civilized human life to continue to survive.

Recalled on 10th anniversary of UN's founding *NY Herald Tribune* 25 Jun 55

2309 If we support the UN, we won't have any trouble.... That's my theory and I set up the UN, as you know.

To Dr Takuo Matsumoto, spokesman for the Japanese Goodwill Ambassadors of the World Peace Study Mission, on a visit to the Truman Library 5 May 64

Boris Yeltsin President of Russia

2310 We are friends not for the moment but for the centuries.

On observing the UN's 50th anniversary with President Clinton *NPR* 27 Oct 95

ARMED FORCES

Officers and Enlistees

General Paul Dewitt Adams US Army, Commander in Chief, Unified Quick Assault Forces

2311 The man who creates the most violence in a military situation is the one who will win.

Time 17 Apr 64

Kenneth Adelman Director, US Arms Control and Disarmament Agency

2312 The history of arms control is a history of great visions eventually mugged by reality.

Newsweek 1 Dec 86

Captain Ayedh Al-Shamarant Saudi Arabian pilot

2313 First target, splash! Second target, splash!

Cockpit recording as the pilot became the first Allied airman to shoot down two Iraqis in Persian Gulf War *Newsweek* 4 Feb 91

Admiral George Anderson Jr US Chief of Naval Operations

2314 Now, Mr Secretary, if you and your deputy will go back to your offices, the Navy will run the blockade.

On brandishing a manual of procedures to Pentagon officials at the time of the Cuban missile crisis, recalled on Anderson's death 4 Mar 92

Anon

2315 Sir, a doolie is that insignificant whose rank is measured in negative units, one whose potential for learning is unlimited.

Self-description of Air Force Academy freshmen *Time* 19 Jan 62

2316 God and the soldier all men adore,/ In time of danger and no more,/ For when the danger is past and all things righted,/ God is forgotten and the old soldier slighted.

Lines scrawled on an old sentry box on Gibralter, quoted by President Kennedy in effort to show personal concern for troops by frequent visits to posts at home and abroad, quoted by Theodore C Sorensen *Kennedy* Harper & Row 65

2317 It became necessary to destroy the town to save it.

Unidentified major's comment on bombing and shelling of Bentre, South Vietnam *NY Times* 8 Feb 68

2318 The target is destroyed.

Soviet SU-15 pilot reporting demolition of Korean airliner that had strayed from its course; 269 persons died *ib* 7 Sep 83

2319 [For reading chests] disregard all Legions of Merit, Air Medals, Distinguished Service Medals. Discount Silver Stars if the officer was high-ranking when it was awarded and if unaccompanied by a Purple Heart.

US Marine Corps colonel's formula for interpretation of campaign ribbons on uniforms *Newsweek* 9 Jul 84

2320 [It began with] combat support.

US term for furnishing advisers to South Vietnam army, quoted by Charles Mohr "History and Hindsight: Lessons from America's Years of War in Vietnam" *NY Times* 30 Apr 85

2321 Our little tigers can beat their little tigers.

Initial American attitude in Vietnam war *ib*

2322 It is so accurate you could drop it down the Kremlin chimney.

NATO weapons expert on Pershing II mobile weapon capable of throwing a single nucleur warhead more than a thousand miles *US News & World Report* 27 Jul 87

2323 [You get to] see the world, meet interesting people and kill them!

US Marine Corps enlistment poster seen in Gustav Hasford's film *Full Metal Jacket*, quoted in *NY Times* 28 Jul 87

2324 [It is] global double zero.

Arms control term applied to Mikhail S Gorbachev's agreement for mutual elimination of intermediate and shorter-range missiles in Asia and Europe *Time* 3 Aug 87

2325 The only thing we have to do is tell the guy to get his feet off the console.

On readiness of Strategic Air Command's to meet enemy attack *NY Times* 10 Dec 87

2326 When you walk without footmarks. . . talk without a sound. . . cook without smoke, that is how you survive.

On enemy soldiers who hid in subterranean tunnels in Vietnam *Time* 18 Jan 88

2327 Grab them by the balls and the hearts and minds will follow.

Mess hall sign on dealing with Vietnam civilians, quoted by Hedley Donovan *Right Places, Right Times* Holt 89

2328 We're kuwaiting.

American serviceman posted to Persian Gulf after Iraq's invasion of Kuwait NBC TV 16 Aug 90

2329 They're candidates for the Order of the Pine Box.

On potential casualties if US declared war on Iraq NPR 7 Dec 90

2330 These sesame seed countries.

On warfare in the Middle East *ib*

2331 Yesterday's gone. Tomorrow will come if we survive today.

First rule of westerners in hiding in Kuwait *Time* 24 Dec 90

2332 I am trying to run away bravely.

British pilot over Iraq ABC TV 19 Jan 91

2333 I shot to the head./ My target is dead./ Walking in a sniper wonderland.

US Marine platoon song used in Saudi Arabia *NY Times* 3 Feb 91

2334 One minute you're a hawk in the skies, the next you are an ant on the ground.

On being shot down in the Persian Gulf War *Newsweek* 4 Feb 91

2335 To really live, you must almost die. To those who fight for it, life has a meaning that the protected will never know.

Sign in Special Forces camp recalled by Medal of Honor winner Gary Beikirch of the Green Berets *US News & World Report* 25 Feb 91

2336 Every night it is bomb, bomb, bomb. When we fought Iran, we had breakfast lunch and dinner every day. Here there is no water, hardly anything to eat.

Iraqi soldier on surrendering to Egyptian forces during Persian Gulf War *Time* 25 Feb 91

2337 Travel light, freeze at night.

Motto of front line troops in Persian Gulf War *ib*

2338 This may not be hell but you can see it from here.

101st Airborne soldier on alert in Kuwait NBC TV 3 Mar 91

2339 We are winning, this we know,/ General Harkins tells us so./ In the Delta, things are rough,/ In the mountains, mighty tough./ But we're winning, this we know./ General Harkins tells us so.

Song mocking General Paul Harkins, US commander in Vietnam, quoted by James B Reston *Deadline* Random House 91

2340 They dialed 911 and we answered.

An American colonel as US troops went ashore in Somalia, quoted by Dan Rather CBS TV 8 Dec 92

2341 It's 105 degrees in Saigon and rising.

Prearranged coded signal for Americans and dependents to assemble at evacuation points during Vietnam War, quoted by Walter Isaacson *Kissinger* Simon & Schuster 92

2342 Cheat and retreat.

On Iraq's repeated flouting and reluctant compliance to allied demands *Washington Post* 9 Jan 93

2343 Complete the mission, though I be the lone survivor. Never leave a fallen comrade to fall into the hands of the enemy.

The Ranger's Creed, quoted after the Rangers, a US Army unit, stayed to guard the body of a pilot fatally caught in a downed helicopter in Somalia *NY Times* 25 Oct 93

2344 What you see here,/ what you do here,/ What you hear here,/ When you leave here,/ Let it stay here.

Song urging confidentiality on medical experimentation *US News & World Report* 24 Jan 94

2345 Keeping track of this operation is like trying to paint a fast-moving train.

On internment of more than 2,000 Haitian refugees at Guantanomo Naval Base in Cuba NPR 2 Jul 94

2346 You're too old, you can't see and you're a woman. Maybe the "dogs" would take you.

A US Marine Corps recruitment officer to Hillary Rodham Clinton when she asked about enlisting in 1975 and was referred to the Army *Newsweek* 26 Dec 94

2347 It was death by 1,000 anecdotes.

A Pentagon official's comment on whether testimony given the Senate Armed Services Committee reflected isolated problems or systemic ones in a military still struggling to identify its post-Cold War missions *NY Times* 20 Jan 95

2348 Don't ask, don't tell.

Compromise policy, shortly expanded to "Don't ask, don't tell, don't pursue," formulated in response to Clinton campaign proposal disallowing disclosure of sexual orientation; within the armed forces it reportedly became, "Ask, pursue and harass" NPR 28 Feb 95

2349 Now, sir, a war is never even. Sir, a war is won.

Tank officer explaining military injustice to a man armed only with a knife *NY Times* 9 Jul 95

Admiral Jeremy ("Mike") Borda USN, Chief of Naval Operations

2350 We share a bond that is stronger than those who are bound to the shore can understand.

To fellow seafarers in 1994 shortly before becoming the US Navy's top-ranking officer *US News & World Report* 27 May 96

2351 Can the sailor commit suicide and not have the leader know that he or she was in distress? No.

Address at US Naval Academy outlining a new concept to make officers more responsible, recalled six months later on Borda's suicide over his eligibility to wear a combat decoration *ib*

General Omar N Bradley US Joint Chief of Staff

2352 The wrong war, at the wrong place, at the wrong time, with the wrong enemy.

On the Korean War news reports 24 May 51

2353 The best service a retired general can perform is to turn in his tongue along with his suit and to mothball his opinions.

News summaries 17 May 59

Lieutenant General Frederick Browning British Army, Deputy Commander, 1st Allied Airborne Army

2354 We might be going a bridge too far.

To Field Marshal Montgomery on plans to capture a sixth and crucial bridge over the Lower Rhine at Arnhem 10 Sep 1944, frontispiece quoted by Cornelius Ryan *A Bridge Too Far* Simon & Schuster 74

George Bush 41st US President

2355 The military of the United States is the greatest equal opportunity employer around.

On proportion of African Americans in armed forces 25 Feb 91

Lietenant William L Calley Jr US Army

2356 That was the order of the day. They were all enemy. They were all to be destroyed.

On 1968 Vietnam civilian deaths at My Lai, news summaries 23 Feb 71

Sergeant Scott Camil USMC

2357 The men would use their penises to probe them to make sure they didn't have anything hidden anywhere. And this was raping but it was done as searching.

On raiding Vietnam villages, quoted by Susan Brownmiller *Men, Women and Rape* Simon & Schuster 75

Brigadier General Sherian Grace Cardoria US Army

2358 By act of Congress, male officers are gentlemen, but by act of God, we are ladies.

On being singled out as highest-ranking black woman *US News & World Report* 13 Feb 89

Tom Carhart Vietnam veteran

2359 [It is] a black gash of shame.

On Washington's Vietnam War Memorial *USA Today* 12 Nov 87

Rear Admiral Arthur Cebrowski Commander, USS America

2360 It has the most awesome war-making potential in any one place. And we're ready to fight on arrival.

On Aegis guided-missile cruiser *US News & World Report* 28 Feb 94

2361 The information domain is the future battlefield.

On newly developed system that permits every ship's commander to see instantly what every other ship and plane can see *ib* 24 Oct 94

General Raoul Cedras Haitian military leader

2362 I will wash my bayonet in your blood.

To opposing forces in overthrow of Haitian government NPR 3 May 94

2363 I would rather take an American bullet in the chest than a Haitian bullet in the back.

On belief that he would be assassinated if he fled the country in response to US negotiation team of former President Jimmy Carter, General Colin Powell, and Senator Sam Nunn *Time* 3 Oct 94

Chad Military Communique

2364 [The raid] must be written in gold letters in the great book of victories.

On Chad's first invasion of Libya in border conflict that began in 1973 *Time* 21 Sep 87

Charles Prince of Wales

2365 They seem more nervous of me than I do of them—but I dare say the element of fear and subservience will soon return to me via the agency of a well-placed boot!

Confidential letter 18 Mar 71 quoted by Jonathan Dimbleby while training with the Royal Navy and RAF *The Prince of Wales* Morrow 94

2366 [I felt like] a retired tortoise while flocks of butterflies indulged in the biggest population explosion since Adam and Eve.

On wearing a parachute harness while waiting to make his first jump in July 1971

Richard Cheney US Secretary of Defense

2367 Colin, you're Chairman of the Joint Chiefs of Staff. You're not Secretary of State. You're not the National Security Adviser anymore. And you're not Secretary of Defense. So stick to military matters.

To General Colin L Powell after 1991 White House meeting on the Persian Gulf War, later quoted by Powell *My American Journey* Random House 95, excerpted in *Time* 18 Sep 95

2368 It's just a quaint little rule but we're not going to change it.

On not admitting homosexuals to the armed forces, quoted by President-Elect Clinton in his efforts to change the regulations *NY Times* 15 Nov 92

2369 I pilot a big ship. It takes a long time to turn it around.

On being pressed by US Congressman Barney Frank to rescind homosexual exclusions, quoted by Randy Shilts *Conduct Unbecoming* St Martin's 93

General Ben Chidlaw Commander, US Continental Air Defense

2370 It is better to have less thunder in the mouth and more lightning in the hand.

On protecting 3-million square miles of territory with 10,000 miles of border to guard and a fence to build, 10, 11 or 12 miles high *Time* 20 Dec 54

Winston S Churchill Prime Minister of Britain

2371 Really I feel less keen about the Army every day. I think the Church would suit me better.

Postscript on a letter home during early training at Sandhurst, quoted by William Manchester *The Last Lion* Little, Brown 83

2372 War is a game that is played with a smile. If you can't smile, grin. If you can't grin, keep out of the way till you can.

ib

2373 If Hitler invaded hell I would make at least a favorable reference to the devil in the House of Commons.

The Grand Alliance Houghton Mifflin 50

2374 Before Alamein we never had a victory. After Alamein we never had a defeat.

The Hinge of Fate Houghton Mifflin 50

2375 There was unanimous, automatic, unquestioned agreement around our table.

On Potsdam Conference approval of US use of the atomic bomb in Japan *Triumph and Tragedy* Houghton Mifflin 53

2376 When the war of the giants is over the wars of the pgymies will begin.

On the end of World War II *ib*

2377 In defeat unbeatable: in victory unbearable.

On Viscount Montgomery, quoted by Edward Marsh *Abrosia and Small Beer* Longman 64

2378 Don't talk to me about naval tradition. It's nothing but rum, sodomy, and the lash.

Quoted by Peter Gretton *Former Naval Person* Cassell 68, recalled in *Newsweek* 4 Feb 91

General Mark W Clark US Army

2379 I was the first American commander to put his signature on a paper ending a war when we did not win it.

On leading UN troops in Korea, his third and last war before retiring *NY Herald Tribune* 21 Oct 53

James Clavell British artillery officer

2380 So long as I remember Chang Yi, I know I'm living 40 borrowed lifetimes.

On World War II's Chang Yi prison camp where only 1 in 15 prisoners survived, an experience on which he drew for his novels *Shogun* and *Tai-Pan, US News & World Report* 19 Sep 94

William J Clinton 42nd US President

2381 We need everybody in America that has got a contribution to make, that's willing to obey the law and work hard and play by the rules.

On admitting homosexuals to the armed forces 12 Nov 92

2382 I don't think status alone, in the absence of some destructive behavior, should disqualify people.

ib

2383 The issue is not whether there are gays in the military. It is whether they can be in the military without lying about it.

ib

2384 He said what he thought but then he said, "You're the boss."

On initial discussion of gays with General Colin L Powell, Joint Chief of Staff 19 Nov 92

2385 Most Americans believe if you don't ask and you don't say and you're not forced to confront it, people should be able to serve.

On what became the "don't ask, don't tell" compromise that would allow gays to serve in the military if they weren't asked about their sexual orientation and did not themselves volunteer acknowledgment 26 May 93

2386 It certainly will not please everyone—perhaps not anyone—and clearly not those who hold the most adamant opinions on either side of this issue.

On homosexuals 12 Nov 92

General Moshe Dayan Israeli Army

2387 We were fighting to prevent the fall of the Third Temple.

On commanding Israeli forces in Six-Day War against Egypt *Time* 16 Jun 67

2388 If we lose this war, I'll start another in my wife's name.

Recalled on Dayan's death 16 Oct 81

Boatswain's Mate 3rd Class Doug Deboth US Coast Guard

2389 Now lower your butts, flangeheads, and haul away!

Orders to secure lines along the entire length of the Coast Guard cutter *Eagle Smithsonian* Aug 94

General Charles de Gaulle President of France

2390 I was France. France cannot be France without greatness.

On leadership of Free France and the resistance during World War II *The Complete War Memoirs of Charles de Gaulle* Simon & Schuster 54

2391 It was my duty to restore [the state]. I installed my staff at once and got down to work.

On arriving at the Ministry of State on cessation of hostilities *ib*

2392 And don't forget to get killed.

On permitting novelist Romain Gary to return to combat, recalled by Gary, "To Mon General" *Life* 9 May 69

2393 You'll live. Only the best get killed.

ib

2394 I kneaded heavy dough.

Recalling his direction of Free France forces during World War II, quoted by Don Cook *Charles de Gaulle* Putnam 83

2395 My own nature warned me and my experience taught me that, at the summit, one can preserve time and strength only by remaining on the remotest heights.

ib

2396 As for the soldiers, I shall do nothing until their leaders have devoured one another.

On Algerian attempts to break away from France, quoted by Jean Lacouture *de Gaulle the Ruler* Norton 92

De Haute Studes Militaire

2397 You've given us enough trouble with your paper tanks—now go and see what you can do with your metal ones.

Dispatch from the Center for Higher Military Studies to General de Gaulle as a young officer in a tank regiment, quoted by Don Cook *Charles de Gaulle* Putnam 93

Angus Deming US Marine Corps

2398 The terrain was as much an enemy as the one that was shooting at us. . . always another hill to climb, and the weather seemed of two kinds: unbearable heat or unbearable cold.

Recalling Korean War at the time of the dedication of its national memorial 45 years later *Time* 7 Aug 95

2399 So much bravery, so much uncomplaining devotion to duty, went unrecognized for so long. Now that lingering bitterness has been laid to rest at last.

ib

General Jimmy Doolittle US Army

2400 [Russia is] an implacable enemy. . . [to whom] acceptable norms of human conduct do not apply.

Quoted by Evan Thomas *Washington Post* 26 Feb 95 reviewing Christopher Andrew's *For the President's Eyes Only: Secret Intelligence and the American Presidency* HarperCollins 94

Thomas Downey US Congressman

2401 [A] precedent has now been set about verification that cannot be undone.

On Soviet permission for four Congressmen to prowl for four hours through secret radar facility *Time* 21 Sep 87

Rear Admiral James Doyle US Navy

2402 If MacArthur had gone on the stage you never would have heard of John Barrymore.

On General Douglas MacArthur's pitch to the Joint Chiefs of Staff for the landing at Inchon, Korea, quoted by William Manchester *American Caesar* Little, Brown 78

General John Draude US Marine Corps

2403 Love is what you use to overcome the feelings of fear, which are natural. What will cause a Marine to jump on a hand grenade, killing himself in order to save his fellow Marines? Love.

Addressing Marines during Persian Gulf War *Life* Mar 91

2404 Marines don't fight for their country, they don't fight for the Marine Corps, they don't fight for apple pie, motherhood, Sally Lou or Lost Overshoe, Iowa. They fight for their buddies. They fight for their buddies.

ib

Atif Dudakovic Commander, Bosnian Army V Corps

2405 The Balkan death house opened in 1913 and now the time has come for everyone to pay their bills.

On realization of Crotian writer Miroslav Krleza's 1917 prophecy that "our whole life is now a vast dying—climaxed in the 1990s war between Bosnia and Serbs" *NY Times* 24 Sept 95

General Dwight D Eisenhower 34th US President

2406 When you put on a uniform, there are certain inhibitions that you accept.

As US Army general on learning that President Truman had relieved General Douglas MacArthur of his command in Japan and the Far East 11 Apr 51

2407 The most terrible job in warfare is to be a second lieutenant leading a platoon when you are on the battlefield.

17 Mar 54

2408 That was not the biggest battle that ever was, but for me it always typified one thing—the dash, the ingenuity, the readiness at the first opportunity that characterizes the American soldier.

On 10th anniversary of the Battle of the Remagen Bridge 8 Mar 55

2409 The purpose is clear. It is safety with solvency. The country is entitled to both.

Urging unification of ground, sea and air commands 17 Apr 58

2410 The sergeant is the Army.

NY Times 24 Dec 72

2411 He's just a little man, and he's just as little inside as he is outside.

On publication of the memoirs of Field Marshal Bernard Law Montgomery, 1st Viscount Montgomery of Alamein, quoted by Nigel Hamilton *Monty* McGraw-Hill 87

2412 This embattled shore, portal of freedom, is forever hallowed by the ideals, the valor and the sacrifices of our fellow countrymen.

Inscription at American cemetery near St-Laurent, quoted by Stephen E Ambrose's *D-Day, June 6, 1944* Simon & Schuster 94

2413 It is an armistice on a single battleground, not peace in the world.

On the end of the Korean War, recalled by President Clinton on dedication of Korean War Memorial Washington 27 Jul 95

2414 You must be crazy. We can't use those awful things against Asians for the second time in less than ten years! My God!

To nuclear-minded advisers on taking the final decision not to go nuclear in Asia in 1954, recalled on 50th anniversary of the atomic bomb *Guardian Weekly* 6 Aug 95

2415 Never send a batallion to take a hill if you've got a division.

Recalled by Eisenhower biographer Stephen E Ambrose *New Yorker* 9 Oct 95

Brigadier General Thomas Farrell US Army engineer

2416 Jesus Christ, the longhairs have let it get away from them!

Quoted by Alfred Kazan *NY Times* 1 May 88 reviewing Spencer R Weart's account of witnessing the exploding of the first atomic bomb *Nuclear Fear* Harvard University Press 88

Major Francis Edward Foley British Secret Service

2417 He was a nasty piece of ignorance.

On interrogation over a 10-month period of the Nazi officer Rudolf Hess who landed in Scotland with peace plan, quoted on Hess's death after long imprisonment *NY Times* 29 Sep 87

James V Forrestal US Secretary of the Navy

2418 The raising of that flag on Suribachi means a Marine Corps for the next 500 years.

Quoted by Richard Severo *NY Times* 1 Oct 91, reviewing Karal Ann Marling and John Weterhell's *Iwo Jima* Harvard 91

Major General Paul Funk Commander, US 3rd Armored Division

2419 I don't eat salad. I eat beef and wear wool.

Self-description to reporters covering Persian Gulf War *NY Times* 19 Feb 91

General John Galvin Supreme Allied Commander, Europe

2420 There's a lot of iron around.

On lack of conventional arms-control agreement despite better relations with Russia *US News & World Report* 1 Jun 92

Lieutenant General Alfred M Gray US Marine Corps

2421 There's no such thing as a crowded battlefield. Battlefields are lonely places.

Address to officers *Newsweek* 9 Jul 84

2422 [I go] where the sound of thunder is.

On 14-year career that had given Gray more time in the field in Korea and Vietnam than most generals *ib*

2423 I don't run democracy. I train troops to defend democracy and I happen to be their surrogate father and mother as well as their commanding general.

To new officers *ib*

2424 All of you are assistant mothers and fathers. That is an awesome responsibility.

ib

Arlo Guthrie musician

2425 Proceeded on down the hall,/ Gettin' more injections./ Inspections, detections, neglections./ And all kinds of stuff/ That they was doin' to me.

From Vietnam-era song, *Alice's Restaurant* on US Army physical exams *Newsweek* 5 May 86

Philip Charles Habib Israeli Defense Minister

2426 Don't be caught by surprise if and when we do it. . . or if and when we do it, don't tell us that you are caught by surprise.

To US State Department prior to Israel's 1982 invasion of Lebanon, recalled on Habib's death 26 May 92

Admiral W F ("Bull") Halsey, US Navy

2427 The Third Fleet's sunken and damaged ships have been salvaged and are retiring at high speed toward the enemy.

Replying to claims that the Japanese had destroyed the US fleet in October 1944, recalled on Halsey's death 16 Aug 59; also see E B Potter's *Bull Halsey* Naval Institute Press 85

Lieutenant General Hubert R Harmon Superintendent, US Air Force Academy

2428 The academy's long-range mission will be to train generals, not second lieutenants.

Newsweek 6 Jun 55

Admiral Thomas B Hayward Chief of Operations, US Navy

2429 We are. . . a one-and-a-half ocean navy with a three-ocean commitment.

Congressional testimony *NY Times* 11 Apr 82

Commander David Hobbs Royal Navy

2430 We are not trying to save money but to redistribute it. . . and to provide good protective clothing with modern materials.

On abandoning bell-bottom trousers after 137 years, *London Times* 4 Nov 94

Lietenant Colonel Richard Holk
US Army

2431 By the purest schoolyard definition, it's snitching.

Announcing US Army's toll-free hot line to report suspected espionage—1-800-CALL-SPY *Newsweek* 11 May 87

Pierre Holmes BBC Broadcaster

2432 Long violin sobs rock my heart in monotonous languish.

Paraphrasing 19th century poet Paul Verlaine in coded radio message to France on 1944 Allied invasion of Normandy, recalled on Holmes' death 18 Dec 93

Rear Admiral Grace Murray Hopper US Navy

2433 From then on, when anything went wrong with a computer, we said it had bugs in it.

On the removal of a bug two inches long from an experimental computer at Harvard in 1945 *Time* l6 Apr 84

2434 In total desperation, I called over to the engineering building and I said, "Please cut off a nanosecond and sent it over to me."

On using a piece of wire to represent maxium distance that electricity could travel in a billioneth of a second *60 Minutes* 24 Aug 86

2435 At the end of about a week, I called back and said, "I need something to compare this to. Could I please have a microsecond?"

ib

2436 I handed my passport to the immigration officer, and he looked at it and looked at me and said, "What are you?"

On becoming the oldest officer on active duty *ib*

2437 A ship in port is safe but that's not what ships are built for.

Recalled on Hopper's death 1 Jan 92

Lieutenant General Charles A Horner US Air Force

2438 It provides a sheet of music that everybody sings the same song off.

On computerization of armed forces in Persian Gulf *NY Times* 21 Jan 91

2439 We couldn't have taken a pickup truck, put those bombs [in it] and laid them out there any more accurately.

On electronic-jamming of planes escorting a Saudi aircraft that left four craters on an Iraqi runway *US News & World Report* 28 Jan 91

2440 It is a target-rich environment.

ib 11 Feb 91

2441 The idea is to feed the enemy in bite-size chunks to the ground forces to devour.

Time 25 Feb 91

Lieutenant William Howey US Navy
pilot

2442 Once you put on a flight suit, you can't tell the difference, and the helicopter sure can't tell the difference.

On admitting women to combat *NY Times* 29 Apr 93

Lyndon B Johnson 36th US President

2443 Against such force, the combined destructive power of every battle ever fought by man is like a firecracker thrown against the sun.

On US capability with 1100 US strategic bombers, address at US Coast Guard Academy, New London CT 3 Jun 64

2444 We did not choose to be the guardians of the gate, but there is no one else.

To the nation on continued intervention in Vietnam 28 Jul 64

2445 The Air Force comes in every morning and says, "Bomb, bomb, bomb"... and then the State Department comes in and says, "Not now, or not there, or too much, or not at all."

To Adlai E Stevenson, quoted by Philip I Geyelin *Lyndon B Johnson and the World* Praeger 66

2446 Curtis LeMay wants to bomb Hanoi and Haiphong. You know how he likes to go around bombing.

To columnist Walter Lippmann, quoted by Ronald Steel *Walter Lippmann and the American Century* Atlantic-Little, Brown 80

2447 You wake up... at 3:30 to see if they're back.

On following news of attacks during Vietnam War, recalled by White House columnist Hugh Sidey "Lyndon Johnson's Personal Alamo" *Time* 15 Aug 85

2448 Hell, it's just like the Alamo... and I'm going to go and thank the Lord that I've got men who want to go with me, from McNamara right on down to the littlest private who's carrying a gun.

On Secretary of Defense Robert S McNamara *ib*

2449 If one little old general in shirt sleeves can take Saigon, think about 200 million Chinese comin' down those trails. No sir, I don't want to fight them.

On invading northward where a huge army was massed *ib*

2450 I don't know what it will take out there—500 casualties maybe, maybe 500,000. It's the aughts that scare me...it's always a strain when people are being killed....[and I am feeling] personally responsible.

ib

2451 Go out there and nail that coonskin to the wall.

To troops in Vietnam 27 Oct 66, quoted by Clark M Clifford *Counsel to the President* Random House 91

2452 What's endearing about this job is four hours sleep. Getting the crap beat out of you. Make you feel alive.

On service aboard the Coast Guard cutter *Eagle* four months after enlistment recalled in *National Geographic* Aug 95

John F Kennedy Jr 35th US President

2453 Only when our arms are sufficient beyond doubt can we be certain beyond doubt that they will never be employed.

Inaugural 20 Jan 61

2454 There is always inequity in life. Some men are killed in war and some men are wounded, and some men are stationed in the Antarctic and some are stationed in San Francisco.

To reservists anxious to be released from active duty 21 Mar 62

2455 It's very hard in military or personal life to assure complete equality. Life is unfair.

ib

2456 I look forward to. . . a future in which our country will match its military strength with our moral restraint, its wealth with our wisdom, its power with our purpose.

At Amherst College, his last major address 26 Oct 63

2457 If you take the wrong course. . . the President bears the burden of the responsibility quite rightly. The advisers may move on—to new advice.

To White House Special Counsel Theodore C Sorensen in December 1962 after the ill-fated Bay of Pigs invasion of Cuba, quoted by Sorensen *Kennedy* Harper & Row 65

2458 It's like taking a drink. The effect wears off and you have to take another.

On Joint Chiefs of Staff's call for show of military force in Veitnam, quoted by Arthur Schlesinger Jr, *NY Times* 29 Mar 92 reviewing John M Newman's *JFK and Vietnam* Warner 92

2459 If I tried to pull out completely now from Vietnam, we would have another Joe McCarthy scare on our hands, but I can do it after I'm re-elected.

On facing possibility of Republicans changing their cry of "Who lost Indochina?" to "Who lost China?"

ib

Rear Admiral Husband E Kimmel USN, Commander of Crusiers,Battle Force, Pacific

2460 The sky was full of the enemy.

On his initial reaction to Japanese attack on Pearl Harbor, quoted by Gordon W Prange *At Dawn We Slept* McGraw-Hill 81

Colonel Ryszard Kuklinski Polish General Staff

2461 I started to enter this world of secrets, and I gradually discovered, piece by piece, the most tragic plans for humanity. . . . My mission was to prepare war with the West.

On being assigned in 1964 to work with a Communist-dominated leadership *Washington Post* 13 Dec 92

General Aleksander I Lebed Russian Army

2462 This country has been without stern, sails and wind, and it needs someone at the helm.

At age 45, returning from Russian occupation of Afganistan to proclaim the need for restoration of old fashioned Soviet values *NY Times* 13 Oct 95

2463 We are doomed to live in an authoritarian state until genuine democracy, which should not be confused with anarchy, can be set up.

ib

2464 There should be at least one man in Russia who is sober.

On rejecting a life-style of dachas, drinking and limousines *ib*

2465 Comrade Commander, you know that I am ready to carry out any order. But I must understand its meaning.

On calling headquarters from a pay phone in August 91 after uprising against the Russian White House *ib*

2466 I tried to change something from the bottom. . . [but] to achieve anything, you have to act from the top.

ib

General Curtis E LeMay US Air Force Chief of Staff

2467 My solution to the problem would be to tell them frankly that they've got to draw in their horns. . . or we're going to bomb them back into the stone age.

On the North Vietnamese *Mission With LeMay* Doubleday 55

2468 A man should have dinner with his friends, and the commanding general has no friends.

On declining to dine with a group of colonels, recalled on LeMay's death 1 Oct 90

2469 I'll tell you what war is about. You've got to kill people, and when you've killed enough they stop fighting.

New Yorker 19 Jun 95

2470 You're going to deliver the biggest fire-cracker the Japanese have ever seen.

On fire-bombing Tokyo 10 Mar 1945 *ib*

2471 If you don't get the enemy, he gets you.
ib

2472 I suppose if I had lost the war, I would have been tried as a war criminal. Fortunately, we were on the winning side.
ib

2473 Everybody thought they were doing fine. The first thing to do was convince them otherwise.
On taking control of the Strategic Air Command *ib*

2474 Well, maybe if we do this overflight right, we can get World War III started.
To a reconnaissance pilot whose plane had been damaged by an MiG-17 while over Russia in 1954 *ib*

2475 The most radical effect of the changes in warfare is not upon how wars are won or lost, but upon how they will start.
National War College Lecture 1956 *ib*

2476 No nation can arrive at a deliberate decision to wage war today unless it is clear, beyond any doubt, that victory is assured.
ib

Ernst Lindemann Captain, German Navy

2477 I will not let my ship be shot out from under my ass.
On World War II's ill-fated Bismarck, recalled by Robert D Ballard with Rick Archbold *The Discovery of the Bismarck* Warner/Madison 90

Sergeant Clayton T Lonetree US Army

2478 I am an apple—red on the outside but white on the inside.
On charges of admitting Russian agents to US Embassy in Moscow *NY Times* 25 Aug 87

General Douglas MacArthur US Army

2479 The world has turned over many times since I took the oath on the plain at West Point... but I still remember the refrain of one of the most popular barracks ballads of that day which proclaimed most proudly that old soldiers never die; they just fade away.
Address to Congress after being relieved of duty by President Truman 19 Apr 51

2480 Like the old soldier in that ballad, I now close my military career and just fade away, an old soldier who tried to do his duty as God gave him the light to see that duty.
ib

2481 It has just about as much bearing on the problems of Korea today as would a report on the military operations of Bunker Hill.
On Lieutenant Albert C Wedemeyer's warning to President Truman to arm South Korea in 1947 prior to Communist invasion *NY Times* 2 May 51

2482 No more subordinate soldier has ever worn the American uniform.
Speaking of himself to Senate committee investigating his dismissal *ib* 4 May 51

2483 The Russian has never been a sea-going man. It has been his enormous weakness. His great strength has always been on the ground.
On belief that Russia could not conquer Japan *ib*

2484 You know that the first rule of bridge is to lead from your own strength.
To Senator Lyndon B Johnson on use of air and naval forces in Korea *ib*

2485 War never before in the history of the world has been applied as a piecemeal way, that you make half-war and not whole war.
On the Korean War *ib*

2486 I can recall no parallel in history where a great nation recently at war has so distinguished its former enemy commander.
On receiving one of Japan's highest decorations *ib* 23 Jun 60

2487 In my dreams I hear again the crash of the guns, the rattle of musketry, the strange, mournful mutter of the battlefield. But in the evening of my memory always I come back to West Point. Always there echoes and re-echoes: duty, honor, country.
Recalling West Point's motto on receiving the Academy's Sylvanus Thayer Award for service to the nation *ib* 12 May 62

2488 Where-oh-where... were those bright eyes and slim ankles that had been kidding us in our dreams?
On the Rainbow Division's unsung return home *Life* 24 Jan 64

2489 One little urchin asked us who we were and when we said—we are the famous 42nd—he asked if we had been in France
ib

2490 I've looked that old scoundrel death in the eye... but this time I think he has me on the ropes.
At Washington's Walter Reed Medical Center *ib*

2491 In war, you win or lose, live or die—and the difference is just and eyelash.
Posthumous memories *ib* 10 Jul 64

2492 They died hard, those savage men—like wounded wolves at bay. They were filthy, and they were lousy, and they stunk. And I loved them.
On troops who defended Bataan and Corregido in the winter of 1942 *ib*

2493 The chickens are coming home to roost, and you happen to have just moved into the chicken house.
To John F Kennedy on presidential crisis, a favorite remark the chief executive often quoted, cited by Theodore C Sorensen *Kennedy* Harper & Row 65

2494 My first recollection is that of a bugle call.

On growing up in a military family, quoted by William Manchester *American Caesar* Little, Brown 78

General George C Marshall US Army

2495 Morale is a state of mind. It is steadfast and courage and hope. It is confidence and zeal, and loyalty. It is élan, esprit de corps and determination.

Recalled on Marshall's death 16 Oct 59

2496 We want you to feel unhampered tactically and strategically to proceed north of the 38th parallel.

Telegram to General Douglas MacArthur on fighting the Korean War in September 1950, later used by MacArthur as justification for continuing operations after the Chinese had made their presence known, quoted by David S McLellan *Dean Acheson: The State Department Years* Dodd, Mead 76

2497 Don't fight the problem, decide it.

Favorite advice, quoted by Walter Isaacson and Evan Thomas *The Wise Men* Simon and Schuster 86

Sergeant Leonard Matlovich Air Force

2498 A gay Vietnam veteran. . . they gave me a medal for killing two men—and a discharge for loving one.

Tombstone for first active-duty soldier to openly acknowledge his homosexuality *Washington Post* 22 Apr 88

Major Harold McAdoo US Army

2499 We've got 50,000 people here. We couldn't tell them to leave their teeth behind.

On dentistry for troops in Presian Gulf *NY Times* 21 Feb 91

Vice Admiral J M McConnell US Navy Central Intelligence Agency

2500 The window of Venona was closed forever.

On the CIA's successful work in breaking Venona, the Russian World War II secret code for spying on atomic research, a short-lived victory that was dashed when the Soviets learned of the penetration *Washington Post* 12 Jul 95

Dave McKnight intelligence officer, US Special Operations Command

2501 When you replace him with an American soldier, you have a patriot watching the target.

On the military's preference for their own soldiers as spies over paid informants *Time* 29 My 95

Robert S McNamara US Secretary of Defense

2502 I wondered if I'd ever see another Saturday night.

On threat of nuclear war from Russian warheads in Cuba in October 62, quoted by Elie Abel *Missile Crisis* Lippincott 66

2503 I don't object to it being called "McNamara's war". . . . It is a very important war and I am pleased to be identified with it and do whatever I can to win it.

On Vietam War *NY Times* 25 Apr 64

2504 Neither conscience nor sanity itself suggests that the United States is, should or could be the global gendarme.

To American Society of Newspaper Editors *ib* 16 May 66

2505 Coercion, after all, merely captures man. Freedom captivates him.

ib

2506 One cannot fashion a credible deterrent out of an incredible action.

On nuclear weapons *The Essence of Security* Harper & Row 68

2507 We had a two-track approach, one political and the other military, and the military was designed to move us along the political track.

On the Vietnam War in late '67, quoted by Deborah Shapley *Promise and Power* Little, Brown 93

2508 We tend to justify our actions and in a sense we color history to acheive that objective.

On why he waited 30 years to write his autobiography, quoted by Robert Siegel ed *The NPR Interviews* Houghton Mifflin 94

2509 I am a problem-solver whether it be at Ford or the World Bank or Defense, but I am gradually learning some problems don't have solutions.

ib

2510 If the South Vietnamese were to be saved, they had to end the war themselves. Straying from the central truth, we built a progressively more massive effort on an inherenty unstable foundation.

Quoted by Thomas W Lippman, *Washington Post* 9 Apr 95 reviewing McNamara's *In Retrospect: The Tragedy and Lessons of the Vietnam War* Times Books 95

Commander James Meacham US Navy

2511 I'm not talking about confusion and inefficiency, which to a certain extent are products of all wars, but about muddle-headed thinking, cover-your-ass orders, lies and outright foolishness on the very highest level.

1968 letter from Vietnam to his wife, used by CBS TV in its 1982 documentary *The Uncounted Enemy: A Vietnam Deception*, which prompted General William C Westmoreland to sue CBS for $120 million *NY Times* 4 Jan 85

Golda Meir Prime Minister of Israel

2512 We don't thrive on military acts. We do them because we have to, and thank God we are efficient.
Vogue Jul 69

General John H ("Iron Mike") Michaelis US Army

2513 You're not here to die for your country. You're here to make those so-and-so's die for theirs.
To troops fighting in Korea *Time* 11 Nov 85

Captain Alfred Hart Miles US Navy

2514 Anchors aweigh, my boys,/ Anchors aweigh!/ Farewell to college joys,/ We sail at break of day, day, day!
Anchors Aweigh 1907 recalled on Miles' death 6 Oct 56

2515 Through our last night on shore,/ Drink to the foam!/ Until we meet once more,/ Here's wishing you a happy voyage home!
ib

Musa Mirzhuyev Military Advisor to Chechnya State of Russia

2516 The Russian empire was never capable of using a scalpel. It has always barged into other people's gardens with a bear's claw.
On invasion by Moscow-directed forces to quell Chechnya's attempted break-away, *NY Times* 19 Dec 94

Field Marshal Bernard Law Montgomery 1st Viscount Montgomery of Alamein

2517 Decisions! And a general, a commander-in-chief who has not got the quality of decision, then he is no good.
CBS TV 28 Apr 59

2518 If I am anxious, I don't fight them. I wait until I am ready.
On going into battle, recalled on Montgomery's death 24 Mar 76

2519 I've spent my life fighting the Germans and the politicians. It is much easier to fight the Germans.
ib

2520 I would as soon think of going into battle without my artillery as without my Chaplains.
On unveiling 8th Army Memorial Window in Cairo, quoted by Nigel Hamilton *Monty* McGraw-Hill 87

2521 There's only been one man who could walk upon the sea—and you're certainly not him!
To General A P Juin, Commander in Chief of French Forces. *ib*

2522 I've got to go meet God—and explain all those men I killed at Alamein.
In old age, unable to sleep *ib*

2523 If I had to express in a very few words the root of the whole problem. . . I would say it all depends on the full acceptance of four words: Don't march on Moscow.
Recommendation to NATO to concentrate on peacetime build-up of air and missile arms rather than land forces *ib*

2524 Irritate them one at a time—that's my motto.
On Whitehall's anxiety about his personal visits to world leaders *ib*

2525 Tell them that unconditional surrender comes first. . . . Otherwise we shall be delighted to go on fighting.
Recalled by Montgomery's interpreter as 50th anniversary of German capitulation neared *London Times* 7 Dec 94

Captain Frank Moreno US Army

2526 It can't be matched by a satellite that takes three to four hours to get information to a commander. An enemy tank column of 100 tanks can pass by and be eating dinner in Baghdad by then.
On the importance of infantry as opposed to air surveillance *US News & World Report* 11 Mar 91

Lieutenant Shigeharu Murata Japanese pilot

2527 Good morning, Commander! Honolulu sleeps!
To Captain Mitsudo Fuchida, leader of air attack on Pearl Harbor, quoted by Gordon W Prange from interview with Fuchida 10 Dec 63 *At Dawn We Slept* McGraw-Hill 81

Peter C Newman journalist and editor

2528 We could do nothing except send a mountie out in a Skidoo to give out parking tickets.
On possibility of foreign invasion of the Canadian Arctic *The True North: Not Strong and Free* McClelland & Stewart 83

Major Michael Davis O'Donnell 1st Aviation Brigade US Army

2529 And in that time/ When men decide and feel safe/ To call the war insane,/ Take one moment to embrace/ Those gentle heroes/ You left behind.
Inscription for the NY Vietnam War Memorial from lines written in 1970 three months before O'Donnell's death in battle *Newsweek* 20 May 85

Maurice Oldfield director of M-I6, British Military Intelligence

2530 Military intelligence has the same kind of relationship to real intelligence as military music has to real music.

Quoted by Michiko Kakutani, *NY Times* 19 Apr 83 reviewing Anthony Sampson's *The Changing Anatomy of Britain* Random House 83

Colonel Donald H E Opfer Air Attache, US Embassy, Phnom Penh, Cambodia

2531 You always write it's bombing, bombing, bombing. It's not bombing. It's air support.

To newsmen covering the Vietnam War in 1973, winner of the National Council of Teachers of English 1974 Doublespeak Award cited by Hugh Rawson ed *Euphemisms & Other Doubletalk* Crown 81

Thomas O Paine Deputy Administrator, National Aeronautics and Space Administration (NASA)

2532 I saw the tooth and claw simplicity of the sea.

On World War II service in the western Pacific, recalled on Paine's death 4 May 92

Major General Harold Parfitt US Army

2533 There will be no more tomorrows, only yesterdays, for the Canal Zone.

On relinquishing authority as last governor of Panama Canal Zone *Time* 15 Oct 79

Jonathan Jay Pollard US Naval Intelligence Analyst

2534 I feel as if I have metamorphosized into a twisted Zionist version of Alcibiades, never again to know the comfort of a homeland spiritual refuge.

On conviction of spying for Israel *Time* 16 Mar 87

2535 I never sold my soul to Mammon. . . . I would seem to have strangled my dreams on the altar of unbridled hubris.

ib

General Colin L Powell US Army, Chair, Joint Chiefs of Staff

2536 We have decapitated him from the dictatorship.

On evicting from office Panama's General Manuel Noriega, *Washington Post* 21 Dec 88

2537 We are required to pledge our sacred honor to a document that looks at the military. . . as a necessary, but undesirable, institution useful in times of crisis and to be watched carefully at all other times.

On the US Constitution, address to military from 34 nations a year before start of the Persian Gulf War, recalled in *US News & World Report* 4 Feb 91

2538 The American people do not want their young dying for $1.50-gallon oil.

Urging caution against interfering with Iraq's invasion of oil-rich Kuwait in White House meeting 2 Aug 90, quoted by Michael R Gordon and Bernard E Trainor *The General's War* Little, Brown 93, quoted in *NY Times* 23 Oct 94

2539 The decision is still in the hands of the defender to decide whether or not he has had enough punishment. Such strategies are designed to hope to win; they are not designed to win.

On reliance on use of air power only to defeat Iraq *NY Times* 4 Dec 90

2540 First we're going to cut it off, and then we're going to kill it.

On opposition to Operation Desert Storm *ib*

2541 We have a toolbox that's full of lots of tools, and I brought them all to the party.

On choice of weapons *Time* 4 Feb 91

2542 One of the fondest expressions around is that we can't be the world's policeman. But guess who gets called when suddenly someone needs a cop.

Life Mar 91

2543 As soon as they tell me it is limited, it means they do not care whether you achieve a result or not. As soon as they tell me "surgical," I head for the bunker.

On the Pentagon's devisive "all or nothing" doctrine for using force that some regarded as increasingly irrelevant to a world in which violent nationalism and ethnic conflict have supplanted superpower hostilities as in Bosnia and Herzegovina, *NY Times* 28 Sep 92

2544 It's sort of like the cavalry coming to the rescue.

On sending American troops to Somalia *Life* 5 Apr 93

2545 They fought what they thought foolish or irrelevant, and consequently did not survive to do what they considered vital.

On detecting "a commmon thread running through the careers of officers who ran aground even though they were clearly able," quoted by Richard Reeves *Guardian Weekly* 8 Oct 95 reviewing Powell's *My American Journey* Random House 95

2546 If I was to be confined to one end of the playing field, then I was going to be a star on that part of the field. . . not. . . emotionally crippled because I could not play on the whole field.

On beginning basic training at Ft Benning GA, book excerpted in *Time* l8 Sep 95

2547 No body, no credit. . . . Half an hour later he returned and handed me a handkerchief. I opened it and gasped at a pair of freshly cut ears.

On insisting that only a dead body could be accepted as evidence of an enemy casualty *ib*

2548 Beating them? Most of the time we couldn't even find them.

On witnessing a losing war in Vietnam's Shau Valley *ib*

2549 Under pressure... an active volcano... [but] my faith in Norman was total.

On General Norman Schwarzkopf in the Persian Gulf War *ib*

2550 I would have to be soul-dead not to marvel at the trajectory my life had followed.

On retiring from an army career that saw him rise to the highest-ranking officer in the US armed forces *ib*

General Tommy Powers Chief, US Strategic Air Command

2551 Restraint? Why... the whole idea is to kill the bastards.

To colleagues in the 1960s who wanted to confine nuclear bombing to Soviet missile bases in the event a strike was necessary *Guardian Weekly* 6 Aug 95

2552 At the end of the war, if there are two Americans and only one Russian, we win.

ib

Lewis B Puller Jr Vietnam amputee

2553 If I could now summon the courage to forgive my government, to forgive those whose views and actions concerning the war differed from mine and to forgive myself, I could perhaps... find the reason for which I had been spared, first in Vietnam and then, a second time, from an alcoholic death.

Quoted by Joseph L Galloway on Puller's suicide, "Last Week, the Vietnam War Killed This Man," *US News & World Report* 23 May 94, drawing on Puller's Pulitzer Prize book *Fortunate Son* Grove & Weidenfeld 91

2554 In dying, he took a part of my experience to his grave, and I felt cheated and betrayed that the man could no longer bear testimony to our ordeal.

On the death of a comrade *ib*

2555 Lieutenant Lewis B Puller Jr reporting for duty, Sir! I've already served my time in hell.

When asked what he would say to God when he arrived in heaven *ib*

Admiral Arthur W Radford US Navy, Chair, Joint Chiefs of Staff

2556 A decision is the action an executive must take when he has information so incomplete that the answer does not suggest itself.

Time 25 Feb 57

Radio Swan US broadcast

2557 Alert! Alert! Look well at the rainbow. The first will rise very soon.

Coded message alerting Free Cuba underground to attempted invasion by US forces, quoted by Haynes Johnson *The Bay of Pigs* Norton 64

2558 The fish will not take much time to rise. Chico is in the house. Visit him. The sky is blue. Place notice in the tree. The tree is green and brown. The letters arrived well. The letters are white. The fish will not take much time to rise. The fish is red.

ib

Keith Raisch US Coast Guard

2559 Ease starboard, haul port, handsomely port!

Orders issued in guiding the cutter *Eagle* as the only sailing master left in US services *Smithsonian* Aug 95

Ronald Reagan 40th US President

2560 We pray for the wisdom that this hero be America's last unknown.

At entombment of the unknown soldier of Vietnam 22 May 84

2561 Uninvited, unwanted, unyielding, almost 40 years after the war.

On Soviet troops remaining in France four decades after the Allied invasion of Normandy 6 Jun 84

2562 The only weapon we have is MAD—Mutual Assured Destruction. Why don't we have MAS instead—Mutual Assured Security?

On proceeding with Strategic Air Command build-up independent of whatever arms reduction agreement might be reached with Soviets *NY Times* 12 Feb 85

2563 We're talking about a weapon that won't kill people. It'll kill weapons.

On development of the Strategic Defense Initiative *Newsweek* 30 Sep 83

2564 He had four stars on his shoulder and 50 stars in his heart.

On dedication of Alabama aerospace and science center named for General Daniel James Jr, US Air Force's first black general *NY Times* 10 May 87

Colonel Russell Reeder US Army

2565 He was a 12th century knight with a 20th-century brain.

On General Matthew B Ridgway, quoted by Clay Blair Ridgway's *Paratroopers* Doubleday 85

General Matthew Ridgway US Army

2566 Sometimes, at night, it was almost as if I could hear the assurance that God the Father gave to another soldier, named Joshua: "I will not fail thee nor forsake thee."

Recalling his World War II command of 82nd Airborne Division *Time* 28 May 84

2567 I commanded the 18th Airborne Corps at the Battle of the Bulge. I am a soldier, and the president is in trouble. I am ready to come and lay that wreath myself.

Responding at age 90 to President Reagan's controversial visit to Bitburg, Germany, cemetery where both US and SS troops were buried, quoted by former Secretary of State George P Shultz *Turmoil and Triumph* Scribner 93

Sergeant Barry Sadler US Army

2568 Men who mean just what they say—the brave men of the Green Beret.

The Ballad of the Green Berets 1966 recording recalled during Persian Gulf War *Newsweek* 4 Mar 91

General H Norman Schwarzkopf III Commander, Allied Forces, Persian Gulf

2569 I don't consider myself dovish and I certainly don't consider myself hawkish. Maybe I would describe myself as owlish—that is wise enough to understand that you want to do everything possible to avoid war.

NY Times 28 Jan 91

2570 Once you're committed to war, then be ferocious enough to do whatever is necessary to get it over with as quickly as possible in victory.

ib

2571 You must be the thunder and lightning of Desert Storm.

To 450,000 troops in Operation Desert Storm *US News & World Report* 28 Jan 91

2572 Hold your first soldier who is dying in your arms, and have that terribly futile feeling that I can't do anything about it. . . . Then you understand the horror of war.

ib 11 Feb 91

2573 Any soldier worth his salt should be antiwar.

ib

2574 One hundred hours has a nice ring.

Urging a cease-fire 27 Feb 91 after the Persian Gulf War's first hundred hours, quoted by Michael R Gordon and Bernard E Trainor *The General's War* Little, Brown 94, quoted in *NY Times* 23 Oct 94

2575 Once we had taken out his eyes, we did what could best be described as the Hail Mary play in football.

On ground action that followed up on air warfare, news conference at Riyadh, Saudi Arabia *ib* 28 Feb 91

2576 When the quarterback is desperate for a touchdown at the very end, what he does is, he steps up behind the center, and all of a sudden every single one of his receivers goes way out to one flank, and they all run down the field as fast as they possibly can and into the end zone, and he lobs the ball.

Explaining the Hail Mary play *ib*

2577 It's a combination of desertions. . . of people that were killed. . . people that we captured. . . [and] some other people who are just flat still running.

Accounting for dispersal of 150,000 enemy troops *ib*

2578 As for as Saddam Hussein being a great military strategist, he is neither a strategist nor is he schooled in the operational art nor is he a tactician nor is he a general nor is he a soldier. Other than that, he's a great militaryman.

ib 28 Feb 91

2579 We had a completely robust strategic air campaign that was very executable, right down to a gnat's eyelash.

On preparation for the Persian Gulf War *Time* 11 Mar 91

2580 It will be miraculous to families of these people. . . but it is miraculous.

On low casualties *ib*

2581 Seven months ago I could give a single command and 541,000 people would immediately obey it. Today I can't get a plumber to come to my house.

On postwar life *Newsweek* 11 Nov 91

John M Shalikashvili Chair, US Joint Chiefs of Staff

2582 To own a country hardware store. To sit outside in the sun with my blue apron, waiting for a customer to come by, to rummage through little bins looking for a particular bolt a customer might want, and once found to go back out to my bench in the sun.

On the job of his dreams *Newsweek* 19 Sep 94

2583 You, the veterans, are the heroes of yesterday, the heroes of today, and the heroes of tomorrow.

At New York City ceremonies on the 50th anniversary of the end of World War II in Europe *ib* 22 May 95

General Henry H Shelton US Commander in Haiti

2584 We're not rent-a-cops.

On shifting some occupational responsibilities to United Nations forces *NY Times* 9 Oct 94

Major Randy Shoel US Army

2585 It's great, but it's like Noah's Ark. Who's going to clean out that thing?

On air-lift of ll4 mules from Kentucky to anti-Soviet guerrillas of Afghanistan *Wall Street Journal* 28 Apr 88

Jacques Soustelle French Minister of Information

2586 The orders they received. . . were always the same: "France remains and will remain". . . . It was the whole army that made that oath: an oath that no one had the right or power to untie.

On French forces in Algeria, quoted by Jean Lacouture *De Gaulle the Ruler* Norton 92

General Joseph W Stilwell US Army

2587 [They're] a nice crop of radishes. . . a sad epitome of China's fate.

On graves of Chinese soldiers, quoted by Barbara Tuchman *Stilwell and the American Experience in China* Macmillan 70

2588 "Can we produce better officers in five years?" So I tell them two generations might do it.

On the Chinese army *ib*

2589 [Military aides] are door-openers and coat-hangers . . . a swagger stick. . . a concept in conspicuous waste.

ib

2590 The higher a monkey climbs a pole, the more you see of his behind.

On promotions *ib*

Mary R Stout President, Vietnam Veterans of America

2591 "Veteran" is no longer a male word.

On becoming VVA's first woman president *NY Times* 3 Aug 87

General Gordon Sullivan Chief of Staff

2592 Smaller is not better, better is better.

On substitution of technology for raw mass of combat power *US News & World Report* 24 Oct 94

General Maxwell D Taylor US Army

2593 They didn't know how it ran, where you put in the gas, where you put in the oil, where you turn the throttle.

On the Kennedy White House and botched invasion of Cuba's Bay of Pigs, quoted by Ralph G Martin A *Hero for Our Time* Macmillan 83

2594 The first man I met in the darkness I thought was a German until he cricketed. . . [then] we threw our arms around each other and I knew we had won the war.

On recognizing fellow soldiers by a click in the night as the Normandy invasion began *Time* 28 May 84

2595 [It is] looking under bushes for the Vietnamese George Washington.

On White House attempts to pin-point a key person to be assassinated in Vietnam, quoted by Richard Reeves *President Kennedy* Simon & Schuster 93

Field Marshal Sir Gerald Templer British Army

2596 Dickie, you're so crooked that if you swallowed a nail you'd shit a corkscrew.

To Louis Mountbatten, quoted by Nigel Hamilton *Monty* McGraw-Hill 87

Irvin H Thesman 1st Electronics Mate, US Navy

2597 It was a deep, powerful feeling, like being dug out of your own grave.

On being rescued from the battleship *Oklahoma* more than 24 hours after it was bombarded in Japanese attack on Pearl Harbor, quoted by Gordon W Prange *At Dawn We Slept* McGraw-Hill 81

Paul W Tibbets Us Army Air Force

2598 I've never lost a night's sleep over it, and I never will. . . . I got nothing to be ashamed of.

At age 79 on his role as commander of the mission that dropped the atomic bomb on Hiroshima in 1945, *Washington Post* 30 Jan 95

2599 It was a beautiful military target. . . [and the] land-water contrasts were the best you could get. . . [on] the center of everything being done to resist an invasion.

On Hiroshima as a prime target *ib*

Harry S Truman 33rd US President

2600 The Marine Corps is the Navy's police force and as long as I am President that is what it will remain. They have a propaganda machine that is almost equal to Stalin's.

5 Sep 50

2601 I was ready to kick him into the North China Sea.

On General Douglas MacArthur's statement to Chinese troops in Korea in defiance of Truman's proposal that would have permitted them to withdraw without losing face, 24 Mar 51

2602 With deep regret, I have concluded that General of the Army Douglas MacArthur is unable to give his whole-hearted support to the policies of the United States government and of the United Nations in matters pertaining to his official duties.

On change of command in the Far East 5 Apr 51

2603 I always considered statesmen to be more expendable than soldiers.

Memoirs: Years of Decision Doubleday 55

2604 If there is one basic element in our Constitution, it is civilian control of the military.

Memoirs: Years of Trial and Hope Doubleday 56

2605 I could not worry about what history would say about my personal morality. I made the only decision I knew how to make. I did what I thought was right.

On decision to use the atomic bomb, statement in lecture in 1965 recalled in controversy on postage stamp marking the bomb's 50th anniversary *NY Times* 9 Dec 94

2606 I didn't fire him because he was a dumb SOB, although he was, but that's not against the law for generals. If it was, half or three-quarters of them would be in jail.

On Douglas MacArthur, quoted by Merle Miller *Plain Speaking* Berkley 74

2607 He was one of the men you could count on to be truthful in every way and when you find somebody like that, you have to hang onto them.

On General George Marshall *ib*

Lieutenant Colonel Bill Tucker US Army

2608 The Apache is the Mercedes of helicopters.

On army's combat use of "super" helicopter in Persian Gulf *Newsweek* 4 Mar 91

Captain James R Turner US Navy

2609 The white rat. . . hears all, sees all and tells all.

On independent scrutiny of submarine patrol tapes known as "white rat" *NY Times* 6 Dec 87 [p 48]

Petty Officer Tony Turner US Coast Guard

2610 It's the human touch. . . coming from a person's hand, through the air, into another person's ear—and there's no language barrier.

On the Morse Code in use for nearly a century until replaced by satellites *NY Times* 2 Apr 95 [p 19]

John Paul Vann US Army

2611 We had also, to all the visitors who came over there, been one of the bright shining lies.

To a US Army historian on the Vietnam War, quoted by Neal Sheehan *A Bright Shining Lie* Random House 88

Major General Mguyen Trong Vinh Vietnamese Publisher

2612 For 2,000 years, wars have seeded our land with the bones of the missing in action and the American war produced a particularly rich crop.

On extending help in locating the bodies of missing Americans *NY Times* 20 May 94 [p 1]

US Military Assistance Command

2613 The term "free fire zone" will not be used under any circumstances.

New rule for use of firepower in the Republic of Vietnam substituting "specified strike zone" for "free fire zone" and "prescribed fire zone," cited by Hugh Rawson ed *Euphemisms & Other Doubletalk* Crown 51

Field Marshal Walther Von Brauchitsch Commander in Chief,German Army

2614 Hitler was the fate of Germany and this fate could not be stayed.

Quoted by William Shirer in frontispiece to *The Rise and Fall of the Third Reich* Simon & Schuster 60

John Walker convicted spy

2615 K Mart protects their toothpaste better than the Navy guards their secrets.

The Spy Who Broke the Code PBS TV 10 Apr 90

General Walton Walker Commander, US 8th Army in Korea

2616 There will be no Dunkirk, there will be no Bataan, a retreat to Pusan would be one of the greatest butcheries in history. We must fight to the end.

On mounting a major attack in first weeks of the Korean War in July 50, quoted by Roy Appleman *South to the Naktong, North to the Yalu* Office of the Chief of Military History 61

2617 Any man who gives ground may be responsible for the deaths of thousands of his comrades.

ib

Colonel William Webber US Army

2618 It was the five-paragraph war, because that's all history gives it.

On the Korean War, quoted on dedication of Korean War Memorial, Washington, CBS TV 28 Jul 95

Major General Briant Wells US Infantry

2619 It was when decisions or actions taken were so obviously screwy but which nevertheless had to be endured, that developed on your countenance some of the pain that was in your soul.

Letter to General Joseph "Vinegar Joe" Stilwell on seeing a "sour" newspaper picture that typified situations that won him the nickname "Vinegar," quoted by Barbara W Tuchman *Stilwell and the American Experience in China* Macmillan 70

2620 It isn't vinegar, Joe—it's just something else that looks like it.

ib

Private Gregory White US 82nd Airborne Division Army

2621 Each shovel I scoop out means I might save an arm. The next shovel means I might save a leg.

On joining other privates as well as officers and chaplains in digging trenches along the northern line of Persian Gulf War *Time* 25 Feb 91 [p 37]

Colonel Alton Whitley US Army, Commander US F–117A Stealth Fighters

2622 You pick precisely which target you want. . . the men's room or the ladies' room.

On Persian Gulf bombing *Newsweek* 28 Jan 91

Lieutenant General John J Yeosock US Army, Commander Persian Gulf

2623 The cavalry is not a branch, it's an attitude.

US News & World Report 11 Feb 91

2624 I have fewer disciplinary problems commanding a third of a million troops now than I did in 1973 commanding 1,000 men.

On morale of volunteers as compared to draftees of Vietnam War *Time* 18 Mar 91

Dr Ken Yuasa Japanese physician

2625 First we removed the appendix; then we amputated both arms and legs.

On surgery on Chinese prisoners in World War II, disclosed as an act of public penance to encourage Japan to admit to some of history's most grotesque atrocities *Washington Times* 21 May 95

2626 I dutifully carried out these operations as my duty to the emperor. There was no conscience to say these were inhuman things.

ib

Observers and Critics

Anon

2627 Truman lost his temper, MacArthur lost his job, Acheson lost his war, a million and a half people lost their lives, and Stalin didn't even lose a night's sleep.

On the Korean War *NY Herald Tribune* 6 Apr 64

2628 Pearl Harbor never dies, and no living person has seen the end of it.

Counsel to Rear Admiral Husband E Kimmel, Commander of Cruisers, Battle Force, Pacific, quoted by Donald M Goldstein concluding introduction to Gordon W Prange's *At Dawn We Slept* McGraw-Hill 81

2629 This embattled shore, portal of freedom is forever hallowed by the ideas, valor and sacrifice of our fellow countrymen.

Inscription on Normady coast monument, quoted by John Vinocur "D-Day Plus 40 Years" *NY Times* 13 May 84

2630 Here lie German soldiers. God had the last word.

ib

2631 [Guerrilla warfare was] as fast as rabbits and cautious as virgins.

On Korean War, quoted by Vicki Goldberg *Margaret Bourke-White* Harper & Row 86

2632 He who lasts longest, laughs last.

A "golden rule of bureaucracies" quoted by the US Naval War College's Alvin H Bernstein *Wall Street Journal* 16 Feb 89 reviewing former Navy Secretary John F Lehman Jr's *Command of the Sea* Scribner 89

2633 I am a human being; do not fold, bend, or mutilate.

Demonstrator's sign at the Pentagon 22 May 66, quoted by Deborah Shapley *Promise and Power* Little, Brown 93

2634 There are no devils left in hell. They are all in Rwanda.

A missionary's comment on strife and warfare in Rwanda *Time* 16 May 94

2635 The military have so much to ask for in forgiveness that they're even trying to bribe Buddha.

On Burma, seven years after its military refused to accept the democratic opposition's victory *Le Monde* 14 Feb 95 quoted in *Guardian Weekly* 26 Feb 95

2636 I see your name on a black wall. A name I gave you as I held you so close after you were born, never dreaming of the too few years I would have you.

Note left at the black granite wall of Washington's Vietnam memorial *American Heritage* Feb 95

2637 Freedom is Not Free.

Inscription on the Korean War Memorial dedicated on the 42nd anniversary of the war's end *Washington Times* 22 Jul 95

2638 Our nation honors her sons and daughters/ Who answered their country's call to defend a country/ They did not know and a people they had never met.

Inscription at the Pool of Rememberance *ib*

W H Auden poet

2639 To save your world, you asked this man to die: Would this man, could he see you now, ask why?

Epitaph for the Unknown Soldier October 1953 *Collected Poems* Edward Mendelson ed Vintage 91

Robert D Ballard Oceanographic Institute, Woods Hole MA

2640 There was no time to abandon ship; the ship was abandoning them.

On German Navy's World War II sinking of the British ship *Hood, The Discovery of the Bismarck* Warner Madison Press 90

Homer Bigart World War II foreign correspondent

2641 The Sicilians are too friendly. Their attitude strengthens the impression that this island is a forgotten portion of Southern California, instead of a segment of enemy Italy.

Dispatch recalled on Bigart's death *NY Times* 17 Apr 91

2642 Generally, there is no mistaking the dead—their strange contorted posture leaves no room for doubt.

ib

2643 But this soldier, his steel helmet tilted over his face, seemed merely resting in the field. We did not know until we came within a few steps and saw a gray hand hanging limply from a sleeve.

ib

Sidney Blumenthal Senior Editor, *New Republic*

2644 The only historians who will profit... will be the ones who wish to know only what the Pentagon wished them to know.

On inside information on Persian Gulf War, *NY Times* 26 May 91, reviewing Bob Woodward's *The Commanders* Simon & Schuster 91

Artyom Borovik Russian journalist

2645 With each passing day, the war more and more resembled the sexual performance of an impotent.

On Soviet invasion of Afghanistan, quoted by Bill Keller *NY Times* 13 Jan 91 reviewing Borovik's *The Hidden War* Atlantic Monthly Press 91

David Brinkley commentator

2646 A cavalary commander... said he had just been given a thousand new men who had never seen a horse and a thousand horses who had never seen a man.

Washington Goes to War Knopf 88

2647 He was not troubled by the recent news that Poland's cavalry, the best in Europe, had been desroyed by Hitler's tanks in about a week.

ib

McGeorge Bundy Advisor, National Security Council

2648 The briefings... tend to be sessions where people try to fool him, and he tries to convince them they cannot.

On US Defense Secretary Robert S McNamara's press conferences on the Vietnam war, quoted by Leonard Bushkoff *Christian Science Monitor* 17 Apr 95 reviewing McNamara's *In Retrospect* Times Books 95

Max Cleland Administrator of Veterans Affairs

2649 Because of the war, and because of the outcome, a few years later the veteran becomes the guy in society responsible for terrorist activities, for crime and other bad things. And not just any veteran—the Vietnam veteran. Somehow the combination of losing the war and with My Lai and the drug scene, the Vietnam veteran has come to personify that which is wrong with the culture.

Washington Post 7 Aug 77; also see Baskir and Strauss's *Chance and Circumstance* Knopf 78 and Deborah Shapley's *Promise and Power* Little, Brown 93

Francis X Clines reporter

2650 The risky daylight rescue... culminated with Captain O'Grady... darting from the woods with a pistol in hand and deliverance in mind.

On Marine Capt Scott O'Grady helicopter rescue after his plane was shot down over Serb territory in Bosnia *NY Times* 9 Jun 95

Alistair Cooke commentator

2651 The more expert they become the more they look like lab assistants in small colleges.

On personnel of antiballistic missile complex *America* Knopf 73

2652 "Collateral damage".... It means civilians—old men, women young and old, and children—incinerated and gone for good.

On Pentagon briefings *Vanity Fair* Dec 92

Richard Corliss war correspondent

2653 He lacks the heroic mien—steel forged in Camelot—of central casting's great military strategists: Wellington, MacArthur, Cordesman.

On General Norman Schwarzkopf *Time* 11 Mar 91

2654 His stare, which can be ferocious, is undercut by a fretful brow; the small, almost gentle features are stranded in a moon of a face.

ib

2655 One suspects that this man's tone would be the same at the end of any war; a powerfully plainspoken mixture of triumph, requiem and relief.

ib

Robert Dallek Professor of History, University of California, Los Angeles

2656 What makes war interesting for Americans is that we don't fight war on our soil, we don't have direct experience of it, so there's an openness about the meanings we give it.

NY Times 24 Feb 91

2657 War for us is like a tabula rasa, a black slate which we can use to turn into a moral crusade, and that's what's happening now, particularly as a healing experience in relation to Vietnam.

ib

2658 It's Vietnam revisited as it should have been—Vietnam: The Movie, Part II, and this time it comes out right.

On the Persian Gulf War *ib*

Linda Grant DePauw Minerva Center

2659 [The Citadel] is preparing soldiers who might do splendidly at Gettysburg.

On the South Carolina institution which, with Virginia Military Institute, continued to exclude women *Newsweek* 22 Aug 94

Alan Dundes Professor of Anthropology and Folklore, University of California, Berkeley

2660 The tying of a ribbon to a tree. . . and there are all kinds of rituals involving knots—sacred knots, nuptial knots. This tying business is very, very old.

Quoted in "Yellow Ribbons," editorial on the custom begun for hostages in Iran in 1980 and continued as symbols of hope for Americans serving in the Persian Gulf *NY Times* 4 Feb 91

Joerg Duppler military historian

2661 [July 20, 1944] is the only thing we can be proud of during World War II and the Nazi regime.

On 50th anniversary of attempt to assassinate Adolf Hitler *Washington Times* 20 Jul 94

Thomas F Eagleton US Senator

2662 The Air Force immediately gave its cooperation. The Army begrudgingly gave its reluctant cooperation. The Navy stonewalled and got away with it.

On efforts of federal commission to close 86 costly bases *NY Times* 30 Dec 88

William Faulkner author

2663 It was that innocence again, that innocence which believed that the ingredients of morality were like the ingredients of pie or cake and once you had measured them and balanced them and mixed them and put them into the oven it was all finished and nothing but pie or cake could ever come out.

Absolom, Absolom! Random House 1936 quoted by Leonard Bushkoff in regard to Lyndon B Johnson and Robert McNamara's lack of imagination or awareness that the US could be thwarted in the Vietnam War *Christian Science Monitor* 17 Apr 95

Otto Friedrick news analyst

2664 More than 80 Japanese bombers caught the *Prince of Wales* on a glassy sea under a cloudless sky, vulnerable as a jeweled dowager surrounded by more than 80 switchblades.

On Japanese bombing of a battle crusier three days after Pearl Harbor *Time* 2 Dec 91

Robert Fuller physicist

2665 No matter how fast I ran, my shadow kept up with me. That's the arms race, a race with one's own shadow.

Christian Science Monitor 16 Dec 82

Newton L ("Newt") Gingrich Speaker, US House of Representatives

2666 Females have biological problems staying in a ditch for 30 days because they get infections. . . [but] men are basically little piglets; you drop them in the ditch, they will roll around in it.

On preference for men in combat *NY Times* 19 Jan 95

Vicki Goldberg author

2667 The wounded man's lips were pale as cigarette smoke, his breathing so shallow he seemed to have given up oxygen.

On wounded encountered in photographic coverage of Allied advance on Germany in World War II *Margaret Bourke-White* Harper & Row 86

2668 He whispered out a request for watermelon; the nurse said that was a sign he was near death.

ib

2669 The mules that trudged supplies up the steep slopes wore white sheets and pillowcases with eyeholes cut in them, like ragtag versions of horses in medieval jousts. . . like members of the Ku Klux Klan.

On US 88th Division's camouflage in deep snow near Bologna *ib*

Barry Goldwater US Senator

2670 You don't need to be "straight" to fight and die for your country. You just need to shoot straight.

On homosexuals in the military *Life* Dec 93

Nancy Gourley serviceman's survivor

2671 A single tooth does not a death make. . . [nor] validates a death. Anyone can lose a tooth.

Objecting to the burial with full military honors given to a fragment of the body of Mrs Gourley's brother, Warrant Officer Gregory S Crandall who died in Vietnam in 1971 *Washington Post* 19 Sep 93

Peter Grier reporter

2672 He smiles with the faraway, sea-remembering smile on all desk admirals.

On Admiral James D Watkins, first nuclear submariner to become Chief of Naval Operations *Christian Science Monitor* 4 Jun 86

2673 It looks like a condominium with a cannon and tracks.

On introduction of the US Army's 25-ton Bradley Fighting Vehicle *ib* 19 Aug 86

2674 A man with a book deal big enough to buy his own heavy armored division.

On General Colin L Powell's retirement *ib* 30 Sep 93

Jennifer Harbury serviceman's survivor

2675 It's a cover-up of a cover-up.

On search for the body of her husband after his capture as a guerilla in Guatemala *Newsweek* 10 Apr 95

Robert Harris author

2676 They lumbered along the fresh concrete runway, roaring with frustration, clawing at the air for liberation, until suddenly a crack of daylight appeared beneath them, and the crack widened, and they were aloft.

On the take-off of World War II Flying Fortresses, quoted by Dwight Garner *Washington Post* reviewing Harris' *Enigma* Random House 95

William Hickey reporter

2677 [They] didn't really want to hear about the present or the future. . . for this one night they want to wallow in memories—to capture the atmosphere of sand and sun, of furtive "brews" and filthy cigarettes.

On reunions of the British forces at Alamein *London Daily Express* 24 Oct 53

Richard Hough military historian

2678 No instrument of war has ever surpassed the battleship in its menacing grandeur and in its disastrous ability to condition man's mind to the destruction of his fellows.

Wall Street Journal 15 Jun 89

Intelligence Services Act

2679 [The job of the Government Communications Headquarters is] to monitor or interfere with electromagnetic acoustic and other emissions.

Official definition of eavesdropping *Guardian Weekly* 1 Jan 95

2680 Proliferation is a form of espionage.

On nuclear, chemical, and biological weapons as part of its bailiwick *ib*

John Keegan London Daily Telegraph correspondent

2681 In their deeps, new navies of submarine warships, great and small, will be exacting from each other the price of admiralty.

On the future of nuclear warfare at sea, quoted by Christopher Lehmann-Haupt, *NY Times* 6 Apr 89, reviewing Keegan's *The Price of Admiralty* Viking 89

2682 His generalship smelt of midnight oil, and his personality had a faint, musty odor of the bookish Wykehamist.

On Archie Wavell's World War II command in the Middle East, quoted by William Jackson *London Times* 27 Jul 91 reviewing Keegan's *Churchill's Generals* Weidenfeld & Nicolson 91

Edward M Kennedy US Senator

2683 This is the American journey at its best.

To Senate Armed Services Committee on proposed integration of blacks and women 31 Mar 93

Lore Kessibuki Bikini native

2684 We've learned to dry our tears of sorrow with dollar bills. But money never takes the place of Bikini.

On government compensation received by "Pacific atomic nomads," during 42-year period that their native atoll test site remained uncleared of nuclear waste *NY Times* 10 Aug 88

Henry A Kissinger US Secretary of State

2685 A conventional army loses if it does not win. The guerilla army wins if it does lose.

"The Vietnam Negotations" *Foreign Affairs* Jan 69

Esben Kjeldbaek Curator, Copenhagen Resistance Museum

2686 Many saw without seeing.

On World War II German officers who allowed nearly all of Denmark's Jews to escape to neutral Sweden *NY Times* 28 Sep 93

Jean Lacouture author

2687 [He was] mythically a general to all eternity, but legally a retired colonel.

On Charles de Gaulle *De Gaulle the Ruler* Norton 92

Bernard Levin columnist

2688 May the earth lie lightly on a soldier's bones.

Tribute to Field Marshal Bernard Law Montgomery *Montgomery of Alamein London Times* 31 Mar 76

Irwin Levine and L Russell Brown lyricists

2689 Tie a yellow ribbon 'round the old oak tree.

Tie A Yellow Ribbon song of rememberance in Vietnam War, Levine and Brown Music Inc 72

Life magazine

2690 There is still something to be divined from a conflict that leveled one country and bitterly divided another, that killed the body, seared the mind or crushed the soul of so many, that ennobled so few and brought suffering to all.

On a portrait gallery of personages of the Vietnam conflict seen as "the dreadful war that ended so ambiguously" Jun 95

2691 Gaze upon their faces—American and Vietnamese, men and women, young and old—and let us vow to do better next time.

ib

Eric Lomax war veteran

2692 I had just heard the British Empire begin to fall.

On the sound of a Japanese torpedo launched against "two of the mightiest, most invincible battleships, the *Prince of Wales* and *Repulse*," as Lomax stood on a beach near Singapore on 9 Dec 1941 quoted by Ian Jack *Guardian Weekly* 3 Sep 95 reviewing Lomax's *The Railway Man* Jonathan Cape 95

2693 Below me was a heavy web of iron and wood. . . parallel lines merging smoothly into other sets of tracks, ladders fixed to the earth, climbing into the distance.

On becoming a train buff at age 13 as he watched an engine and cars cross the Forth Bridge in Scotland. *ib*

2694 Oh, the joy of its sudden appearance on that dusty and degraded siding under the palm trees!

On his delight at seeing a rare old German engine in a prison camp in Burma *ib*

Melvin J Maas US Congressman

2695 If you want a Marine Corps because you believe it is essential to the security of the country, we want you to say so, gentlemen, in legislative language. Then it can only be changed by you and not by some executive order.

To Senate Commitee on the Armed Forces during post-war reorganization of armed forces that resulted in the 1947 National Security Act, recalled by Townsend Hoopes and Douglas Brinkley *Driven Patriot* Knopf 92

Robert MacLean Director, Britain's Vickers-Supermarine Aviation Co

2696 I wanted something quarrelsome and troublesome, spitting venom, a thoroughly nasty and unpleasant creature to meet.

On naming World War II Spitfire fighter planes *NY Herald Tribune* 11 Apr 64

William Manchester biographer

2697 He was a great thundering paradox of a man. . . with a pilot light of paranoia.

On General Douglas MacArthur, subject of Manchester's *American Caesar* Little, Brown 78

2698 Japanese naval officers in dress whites are frequent guests at [Pearl Harbor] officers' mess, [and are] very polite. They always were. Except, of course, for that little interval there between 1941 and 1945.

Goodbye, Darkness: A Memoir of the Pacific War Little, Brown 80

2699 I wondered vaguely if this was when it would end, whether I would pull up tonight's darkness like a quilt and be dead and at peace evermore.

On an enemy attack *ib*

2700 Men. . . do not fight for flag or country, for the Marine Corps or glory of any other abstraction. They fight for one another. [And] if you came through this ordeal, you would age with dignity.

ib

2701 The French had collapsed. The Dutch had been overwhelmed. The Belgians had surrendered. The British army, trapped, fought free and fell back toward the Channel ports, converging on a fishing town whose name was then spelled Dunkerque. Before them lay the sea.

On the evacuation of 340,000 troops in the wake of German advances on the continent 4 Jun 1940, preamble to *The Last Lion* Little, Brown 83

2702 It was England's greatest crises since the Norman Conquest, vaster than those precipitated by Philip II's Spanish Armada, Louis XIV's triumphant armies or Napoleon's invasion barges massed at Boulogne. This time Britain stood alone.

ib

2703 The forest seemed almost alive, a great squatting toad-like beast thrusting its green paws through ravines toward the shore, emitting faint whiffs of foul breath, a stench of rotting undergrowth and stink lillies.

On the 50th anniversary of the Battle of Guadalcanal *NY Times* 7 Aug 92

2704 High, spiky, golden grass feathered the slopes of this rugged hogback, leading down to. . . dense jungle.

On the fight for Bloody Ridge *ib*

David Maraniss biographer

2705 This letter would later emerge as the best known essay of Bill Clinton's life, the testament of a bright, troubled, manipulative young man struggling with his conscience and his ambition.

On President Clinton's letter as a graduate student 3 Dec 69 to arrange ROTC enlistment to avoid being drafted for the Vietnam war, a position that was to haunt his future campaigning *First in His Class* Simon & Schuster 95

2706 It is. . . classic Bill Clinton, sincere and deceptive at the same time, requiring a careful reading between the lines

ib

Bill Mauldin Pulitzer Prize cartoonist

2707 Combat soldiers and medical aid men with dirt in their ears. . . are rough and their language gets coarse because they live a life stripped of convention and niceties.

On warfare's nobility and dignity despite danger in squalid circumstances, quoted by Jonathan Yardley, *Washington Post* 24 May 95 reviewing Mauldin's *Up Front* Norton 95

2708 When they are fighting, despite their bitching and griping and goldbricking and mortal fear, they are facing cold steel and screaming lead and hard enemies, and they are advancing and beating the hell out of the opposition.

ib

John T McNaughton General Counsel to Defense Secretary Robert S McNamara

2709 It is not clear that we dominate the area militarily at the subnuclear levels, and honest opinion.

Memo 19 Jan 66 quoted by Deborah Shapley *Promise and Power* Little, Brown 93

James A Michener author

2710 [They were] a group of two dozen nurses completely surrounded by 100,000 unattached American men.

On the heroines he chose for his 1947 book *Tales of the South Pacific*, letter to James B Simpson 1951

2711 I was a Navy officer writing about Navy problems and I simply stole this lovely Army nurse and popped her into a Navy uniform, where she has done very well for herself.

On creation of the role played by Mary Martin when Michener's book became the Broadway hit *South Pacific ib*

2712 The fate of America was being determined by Frenchmen engaged in mortal collision with Englishmen.

Chesapeake Random House 78

2713 He watched the grand procession of stars as they rose from the waters: the Bull reared his horns above the sea, followed by the huddling Twins. At nine the Lion crept out, and at midnight he had a clear view of the bold star he had studied so longingly in the hours before dawn. . . red-gold Arcturus flaming like a beacon.

On a US Navy pilot awaiting take-off over the Sea of Japan *Space* Random House 82

2714 The warm-hearted camaraderie of men. . . had spent the last dozen years risking their lives and. . . hoped to spend the next dozen doing exactly the same.

On test pilots *ib*

Brian Moore novelist

2715 He bathes daily in a running tap of words.

On desk work of a colonel in Moore's novel *The Color of Blood* Dutton 87

2716 He did not look military, but professorial, his balding head laureled with a wreath of sandy hair.

ib

Lance Morrow essayist

2717 Like robots suffering an obscure sorrow, they carried the casket of the new Unknown Soldier, the one from Vietnam. . . a different kind of war. . . a shattering time, a bomb that originated a world away and went off in the middle of the American mind.

"War and Rememberance" on the burial of the Vietnam Unknown Soldier *Time* 11 Jun 84

2718 The crowds lining the route broke into applause, a sweet and deeply felt spontaneous pattering that was a sort of communal embrace. Welcome home.

ib

2719 The victory was as satisfying as anything Americans have done together since landing on the moon.

ib

2720 It was a re-run of their shining self, of Buffalo Bill, who (e.e. cummings wrote) could "ride a watersmooth-silver stallion and break onetwothreefourfivepigeonsjustlikethat."

"A Moment for the Dead" on victory in the Persian Gulf war *ib* 1 Apr 91

2721 Shooting a rabid dog, which is, down deep, what Americans feel the war was all about, exterminating a beast with rabies.

ib

John M Newman naval architect

2722 [It was] deception within deception.

On the Kennedy administration's false figures of Vietnam military and civilian fatalities, quoted by Arthur M Schlesinger Jr, *NY Times* 22 Mar 92 reviewing Newman's *JFK and Vietnam* Warner 92

The New York Times

2723 [They are] transfixed by the mysterious marble panels, glassy black windows reflecting the present and overlooking the past.

"The Black Gash of Shame" editorial on visitors to Washington's Vietnam Memorial 14 Apr 85

2724 A memorial at once national and personal. In each sharply etched name one reads the price paid by yet another family. In the sweeping patterns of names, chronologically by day of death, 1959 to 1975, one reads the price paid by the nation.

ib

2725 America may not yet comprehend the loss of those 58,000 lives; but it has at last found a noble way to remember them.

ib

Gordon W Prange historian

2726 Japanese luck held together, pinned by misunderstanding and tied with red tape.

On the success of surprise attack on Pearl Harbor *At Dawn We Slept* McGraw-Hill 81

2727 It was like Romeo taking Juliet to task.

On Secretary of the Navy Frank Knox's difficulties in criticizing the Navy's role in defending Pearl Harbor *ib*

Ivan Prashker historian

2728 In that world so brutalized where even children are taught to kill, can their... green coat of honor possibly avoid becoming a tattered rag of shame?

On West Point code in Vietnam setting, quoted by Harry G Summers Jr *Washington Post* 1 Jan 89 reviewing Prashker's *Duty, Honor, Vietnam* Arbor House 88

Charles S Robb US Senator

2729 The threat to morale comes not from the orientation of a few, but from the closed minds of the many.

On gays in the military *NY Times* 5 Feb 93

Sydney H Schanberg war correspondent

2730 Planes do not drop bombs, they "deliver ordnance"; Napalm is soft ordnance.

On the bland Vietnam war military briefings that were without "any sense, not even implicitly" of people being killed, homes being destroyed, thousands of refugees fleeing, "The Saigon Follies, or Trying to Head Them Off at the Credibility Gap" *NY Times* 12 Nov 72

Arthur M Schlesinger Jr Special Assistant to President Kennedy

2731 The only signal from the beach was a wail of SOS's.

On ill-fated US invasion of Bay of Pigs in Cuba *A Thousand Days* Houghton Mifflin 65

Patricia Schroeder US Congresswoman

2732 [I have been] working in a male culture for a very long time, and I haven't met the first one who wants to go out and hunt a giraffe.

On Speaker of the House Newton L ("Newt") Gingrich's belief that men are more fit than women for military combat *NY Times* 19 Jan 95

Scientific American magazine

2733 This is a moral tract on mass murder: how to plan it, how to commit it, how to get away with it, how to justify it.

Review of Herman Kahn's *On Thermonuclear War* Princeton 60, quoted in *Guardian Weekly* 6 Aug 95

Michael Shaara historian

2734 Soldiering has one great trap. To be a good soldier you must love the army. But to be a good officer you must be willing to order the death of the things you love.

Quoted in *Forbes* 19 Oct 92 reviewing Shaara's Civil War novel *The Killer Angels* American Heritage 92

John Skow essayist

2735 The faces of those old horse soldiers were lined and stories were written on the lines.

On the annual meeting of the US Horse Cavalry Association "In Kansas: Echoing Hoofbeats" *Time* 23 Nov 87

Theodore C Sorensen counsel to Kennedy White House

2736 A "surgical strike" had appeal to almost everyone.

On bombing of Cuban missile sites, a plan that was momentarily popular before a "quarantine" of Russian ships was decided upon *Kennedy* Harper & Row 65

Albert Speer Nazi architect

2737 As the rules demanded, most are lying on their backs on the blanket, heads turned to the inside of the cell... as though already laid in their biers.

On what Allied soldiers saw as they stared into the cells where Goring, Ribbentrop, Streicher and other leaders in the Hitler government awaited hanging, quoted by Peter Vansittart *In the Fifties* John Murray 95

Jocelyn Stevens Chair, English Heritage

2738 Battlefields are pages on which history's punctuation marks are written in blood.

On first steps to protect English battlefields ranging from the year 991 to 1715 *London Times* 7 Sep 94

Cyrus Sulzberger *NY Times* correspondent

2739 The mud was like glue at midday and like iron in the freezing nights.... Dead GI's lay in the crater valley they called Purple Heart, their throats eaten out by scavenger dogs.

On Allied advance in Italy *The American Heritage Picture History of World War II* American Heritage 66

Tatsugoro Suzuki "comfort woman"

2740 We were told that our mission was to be a sexual dike to protect the chastity of Japanese women.

Publicly recalling for the first time her government's decision in 1945, six days after surrender, in recruiting thousands of women to become prostitutes in government-established houses because of the fear that the conquering Americans would emulate Japanese soldiers in raping all women *NY Times* 27 Oct 95

Robert Timberg historian

2741 [The nightingale] has a template in its brain that contains all the notes for the music. . . [but] the bird cannot sing unless its song is first triggered by the song of another nightingale.

On men who could not take covert action until President Reagan seemed to reaffirm their patriotism by calling Vietnam "a noble cause" *The Nightingale's Song* Simon & Schuster 95

2742 At times the lyrics seemed to enter a scrambler once they issued from Reagan's lips, only to emerge in versions that resonated to the individual tastes of the listening audience.

ib

2743 Much like Reagan himself, the Nightingale's Song could be anything you wanted it to be.

ib

2744 [They were] metaphors for the emotions, motivations and beliefs of a legion of well-meaning but ill-starred warriors.

On US Naval Academy graduates John McCain, John M Poindexter, Robert C McFarlane, James Webb and Oliver L North *ib*

2745 [He was] a Holly Golightly in Marine green.

On Oliver L North *ib*

Time magazine

2746 The mighty US suddenly seemed as impotent as a beached whale.

On the fall of 28 of South Vietnam's 44 provincial capitals 15 Feb 68

2747 The rescuers had to rescue themselves.

On ill-fated helicopter attempt to free hostages in Iran 5 May 80

Barbara W Tuchman historian

2748 On history's clock it was a sunset, and the sun of the old world was setting in a dying blaze of splendor never to be seen again.

On "the muffled tongue of Big Ben tolling nine as the cortege left the palace," marking Edward VII's funeral procession and the dawning of World War I *The Guns of August* Macmillan 62

2749 A relentless talent for tactlessness.

On Germany's entry into World War I *ib*

2750 [Each of his commands had] its appropriate staffs, pomp and paperwork.

On posts held by General Joseph W Stilwell *Stilwell and the American Experience in China* Macmillan 70

2751 Since he hated palaver and loathed pretentions, it was understandable that he preferred war in the jungles of Burma among leaches, mildew, and outright enemies.

ib

2752 He was 61. . . [with] a deceptive appearance of physical fragility. He was, in fact, as fragile as steel wire.

ib

2753 The notorious war lord. . . [was] said to have the physique of an elephant, the brain of a pig, the temperament of a tiger and to be dangerous even to look at.

On Chang Su Chang *ib*

2754 On a lantern-lit Chinese barge poled by boatmen over the dark Pei Hai Lake in the Imperial City, a party from the American Embassy enjoyed a serene excursion under a full moon on the evening of July 7, 1937.

On eve of Sino-Japanese War *ib*

2755 They knew they stood in the presence of an Incident.

On finding the body of a Japanese soldier that marked the start of the Sino-Japanese War *ib*

2756 [Marine Captain Evans F Carlson] could not present a lily without gilding it.

On transmitting information to President Roosevelt from "mutual confidence obtained between the Generalissimo (Chiang) and Communist leaders of China's Communist Party" *ib*

2757 In deserted streets the only living creatures were dogs unnaturally fattened by feasting on corpses.

On Japanese invasion of the Yangtze delta *ib*

2758 The key city of the south fell like a ripe pear.

On Japanese capture of Canton, "China's last access by sea to the outside world" *ib*

2759 No awakening was ever to be more painful.

On pre-World War II view of Japan as an imitator which "continues to follow in the wake of Western progress"

2760 Grounded by deafness and feeling the sense of persecution that afflicts men with a mission when they are not listened to, he retired in 1936.

On Major General Claire L Chennault's withdrawal prior to joining the staff of Chiang Kai-skek *ib*

2761 Hard, wiry and weathered like Stilwell and about his size with a face scarred from the windstream of open cockpits, Chennault combined great professional skill with a touch of megalomania.

ib

2762 The days of November unrolled toward the most premonitored surprise attack in history.

On Japanese preparations for Pearl Harbor attack *ib*

2763 Innate fear and hate of Communism reasserted itself in America. On that dark yeast, grudge, ambition and vindictiveness could feed, and demagogues grow fat.

ib

2764 Most people are relieved to find a superior on whose judgment they can rest. That, indeed, is the difference between most people and Generals.

"Generalship" address at US Army War College, April 72 *Practicing History* Knopf 81

John Vinocur journalist

2765 At the edge of the cliffs, the wind is a smack, and D-Day becomes wildly clear: climbing that cutting edge into the bullets.

Reporting from the Normandy coast on 40th anniversary of Allied invasion *NY Times* 13 May 84

2766 At Saint Laurent-sur-Mer. . . a great lawn at the edge of the sea, white marble crosses and Stars of David against an open horizon. . . very American in the best sense; no phony piety, simple, easy.

On a US military cemetery *ib*

Curt Weldon US Congressman

2767 The new slogan of that battalion of 600 troops is to march together and say, "Clank, clank, I'm a tank."

On the 2nd Armored Division, Fort Hood TX, where insufficient funds for fuel and maintenance gave way to ten training exercises in which men walked together pretending they were in tanks *Washington Times* 22 Feb 95

John Wheeler historian

2768 It was the defining event. . . and remains a thousand degrees hot.

On the Vietnam War *Touched with Fire* Anon 85

Peter Wyden historian

2769 Cataclysms from the Old Testament came to Truman's mind: "It may be the fire destruction prophesied in the Euphrates Valley era after Noah and his ark.

Day One: Before Hiroshima & After Simon & Schuster 84

2770 Churchill also resorted to biblical terms. . . . He brimmed over with exuberance: "What was gunpowder? Trivial. What was electricity? Meaningless. The atomic bomb is the Second Coming in wrath.

ib

Lieutenant Colonel Yisrael Israeli patrol leader

2771 It is a battle of eyes—Israeli eyes against Palestinian eyes, looks meant to kill against looks meant to intimidate, darting glances versus blank stares, eyes begging for a little friendship meeting eyes round with fear.

On tensions between Palestinians and Israelis on West Bank *NY Times* 5 Jan 88

Edwin Yoder Jr journalist

2772 [Saddam Hussein is] protecting his military assets and lying doggo while US allied air power breaks over him.

Expressing a "let sleeping dogs lie" theory in Persian Gulf War, cited by William Safire *NY Times* 14 Jul 91

LAW

Attorneys and the Practice of Law

Leslie Abramson attorney

2773 It's a terrible thing having a client on the stand; it's like putting a baby out in traffic.

On her role as the defense in Los Angeles trial of Lyle and Eric Menendez for their parents' murder NBC TV 1 Feb 94

Dean Acheson US Secretary of State

2774 The Supreme Court is the oracle which. . . gives an answer requiring several decades of further elucidation.

Sketches From Life of Men I Have Known Harper's 61

2775 He lives in personal relationships as a fish lives in water. . . a man immersed in people.

On Supreme Court Justice Felix Frankfurter *Harvard Law Review* Nov 62

2776 Justice Brandeis' standard for our work was perfection as a norm, to be bettered on special occasions.

On serving as clerk to Louis Brandeis

Roger Akeley Commissioner of Planning, Dutchess County NY

2777 Whoever moved there last wants to pull up the drawbridge.

On zoning laws *NY Times* 17 Oct 86

American Civil Liberties Union (ACLU)

2778 Liberty is always unfinished business.

Annual Report 55/56

Anon

2779 Fraud is the homage that force pays to reason.

Quoted by Charles P Curtis *A Commonplace Book* Harper & Row 67

2780 The rain it raineth on the just/ And also on the unjust fella;/ But chiefly on the just, because/ The unjust steals the just's umbrella.

Quoted in Watergate hearings, Thad Stem Jr and Alan Butler eds *Sen Sam Ervin's Best Stories* Moore 73

2781 My duty is to speak and yours to listen, but if you finish before I do, please let me know.
On inattentive juries, quoted by Louis Nizer *The Implosion Conspiracy* Doubleday 73

2782 A law-suit is a fruit tree planted in a lawyer's garden.
Washington Post 6 May 79

2783 Doctors inhabit the first circle of hell, lawyers the second.
Quoted by heiress Barbara Hutton on firing her attorney of 20 years *Poor Little Rich Girl* NBC TV 17 Nov 87

2784 A liberal is a conservative who has been arrested.
Quoted by Tom Wolfe *The Bonfire of the Vanities* Farrar Straus Giroux 87

2785 [It was] acquaintance rape.
On charges growing out of parties at University of California at Berkeley NPR 30 Jun 88

2786 The Tortilla Wall.
On the easily penetrated US-Mexican border NPR 20 Dec 91

2787 Sue Someone You Love.
Giant blue fluorescent sign behind the desk of divorce attorney Raoul Felder *London Times* 4 Sep 92

2788 Trouble is my Business.
Metal deskplate displayed in Felder's office *ib*

2789 She played golf as she decided cases: aiming left, swinging right, and hitting down the middle.
On Judge Ruth Bader Ginsburg at time of her appointment to the US Supreme Court *NY Times* 25 Jun 93

2790 Compared with litigation, roulette is a game of skill.
London Times 17 Aug 93

2791 "A" made professors, "B" the judges, and "C" made the money.
On ranking students according to grades, a favorite saying while Richard M Nixon was enrolled at Duke University Law School, quoted by Jonathan Aitken *Nixon* Regnery 93

2792 Crofts are small parcels of land surrounded by legislation.
On legalities of land acquisition in the Scottish highlands *Country Life* 11 Aug 94

2793 Hit me. I need the money.
Bumper sticker reflecting a litigious age *London Times* 31 Jan 95

Lord Asquith Of Bishopstone [Cyril Asquith] House of Lords

2794 The Court of Appeals should not be slow, rude and right. . . that would be usurping the function of the House of Lords.
Quoted by Anthony Sampson *Anatomy of Britain* Hodder & Stoughton 62

Louis Auchincloss author

2795 It was the dark, hirsute thing behind the green leaves of the new prosperity.
On a trust's unfair division, quoted by Christopher G Dahl *Louis Auchincloss* Ungar 86

Arthur D Austin Professor of Law, Case Western University

2796 The straw that stirs the drink.
On the footnote's role in law *NY Times* 8 Jun 90

F Lee Bailey attorney

2797 My fees are sufficient punishment for anyone; The guilty never escape unscathed.
LA Times 9 Jan 72

Howard H Baker Sr US Congressman

2798 You've got to guard against speaking more clearly than you think.
On the first court appearance of his son, future US Senator Howard H Baker Jr *Washington Post* 24 Jun 73

Roger N Baldwin founder, American Civil Liberties Union

2799 Rights are. . . won only by those who make their voices heard. . . activists and militants.
Life Fall 91

Julian Barnes attorney

2800 He lies like an eye-witness.
On a client's cooperative friend *Talking It Over* Knopf 91

David L Bazelon Judge, US Court of Appeals, District of Columbia

2801 There goes a walking violation of the 6th Amendment.
On a court's regard for the quality of representation assigned to defendants *NY Times* 21 Feb 93

Melvin Belli attorney

2802 If you can tell. . . and show. . . let them see and feel. . . taste or smell the evidence, then you will reach the jury.
Celebrity Register Gale 90

Douglas Besharov American Enterprise Institute

2803 The atomic bomb of child-custody fights.
On allegations of sex abuse *Time* 4 Mar 91

Francis B Biddle US Attorney General

2804 The Constitution has never greatly bothered any wartime President.

On the chief executive as commander-in-chief *In Brief Authority* Doubleday 62

S Tupper Bigelow Ontario judge

2805 No witness except God could tell the truth, the whole truth and nothing but the truth, and up to now He has not appeared in my court as a witness.

On the need to abolish the oath taken by those giving testimony *Toronto Star* 1 Jul 76

Hugo L Black Associate Justice, US Supreme Court

2806 Harry, don't ask many questions and then you won't ask many foolish questions.

To Justice Harry A Blackmun, quoted by Blackmun on *Nightline* ABC TV 3 Dec 93

Harry A Blackmun Associate Justice, US Supreme Court

2807 The pall of Watergate with all its revelations of misplaced loyalties, of strange measures of the ethical, of unusual doings in high places, and by lawyer after lawyer after lawyer, is upon us...[and] our Jerusalem is in ruins.

To American Bar Association prayer breakfast at height of congressional hearings 5 Aug 73

2808 The writing of an opinion is the most creative part of the job, like an artist putting out a good painting.

On the work of the court *Life* Fall 87

2809 Nine separate kingdoms...fallible human beings trying to do our best.

Life fall 87

2810 [Welcome to] the good old number-three club...I was third choice in 1970 and you were third in 1987...keeps you humble...keeps you from getting too judgy.

To Justice Anthony M Kennedy *NY Times* 25 Jul 88

2811 From this day forward, I no longer shall tinker with the machinery of death.

Solitary dissent in the Court's refusal to hear a prisoner's appeal 23 Feb 94

2812 Rather than continue to coddle the Court's delusion...I...concede that the death penalty experiment has failed.

ib

Albert P Blaustein Professor of Law, Rutgers

2813 A constitution is...in many senses a nation's frontispiece...a rallying point for the people's ideals and aspirations, as well as a message to the outside world as to what the country stands for.

On three decades of drafting constitutions for nations in transition *NY Times* 23 Aug 94

2814 We cannot put constitutions together like prefabricated hen houses.

On the necessity of reflecting a country's culture and history

2815 When Mr Nixon left power, the only person with a gun was a policeman directing traffic.

On the US Constitution as a document that worked well in time of crises

Marlon Brando actor

2816 No, I will not swear to God because I do not believe in the conventionality...I will swear on my children and my grandchildren.

Refusing to be sworn at a son's murder trial *USA Today* 1 Mar 91

Robert Bray National Gay and Lesbian Task Force

2817 If it isn't ten toes up and ten toes down, heterosexuals risk going to jail too.

On anti-sodomy laws *Time* 1 Oct 90

William J Brennan Associate Justice, US Supreme Court

2818 Capital punishment...treats members of the human race...as objects to be toyed with and discarded.

To Hastings College of Law *LA Times* 19 Nov 85

2819 Clerks get into the damndest wrangles—which is the way they help me.

On exchange of views by clerks serving Justices *Life* Feb 87

2820 If you can't define it, you can't prosecute people for it!

On becoming over a 16-year period the Justice who wrote most of the opinions on obscenity suits *New Yorker* 12 Mar 90

2821 Five votes! Five votes can do anything around here.

On majority rulings on the nine-member court

Joe Freeman Britt District Attorney, Robeson County NC

2822 In all jurors, a small flame burns...a flame wanting to preserve human life. It's my job to extinguish that flame.

On winning 44 sentences for capital punishment, a Guinness record as the world's "deadliest prosecutor" *US News & World Report* 2 May 88

Susan Brownmiller author and activist

2823 Man's discovery that his genitalia could serve as a weapon to generate fear must rank as one of the most important. . . of prehistoric times, along with the use of fire and the first crude stone axe.

On rape *Against Our Will* Simon & Schuster 75

Warren E Burger Chief Justice, US Supreme Court

2824 The greatest strength of the court is how people react to it.

Connoisseur Jul 84

2825 I don't believe in the carry-off theory, that you stay there until you're carried off.

Interview a year after leaving the high court *NY Times* 16 Apr 87

2826 If you have a tire go flat on your car, you don't throw the car away.

On proposals for a new constitutional convention *ib*

Dick Burr NAACP Legal Defense and Educational Fund

2827 The test of innocence is a unicorn; everybody knows what it looks like, yet nobody has ever seen one.

Newsweek 6 Apr 92

James E Butler Jr attorney

2828 Give us a verdict that says never again!

Plea for a large punitive award on a death due to a truck's defective fuel tank; subsequent grant of $101 million was later cited in a bill to reduce the extraordinary amounts awarded by juries *Washington Post* 14 Sep 95

John J Byrne Chair, Fireman's Fund Corp

2829 Setting casualty loss reserves is like burying Dad in a rented suit. You think you've paid the bill, but the bills keep coming in.

On soaring cost of product liability suits *Fortune* 3 Mar 86

Frank Cammuso Syracuse, *NY Herald-Journal* Cartoonist

2830 Sir, the Supreme Court is here to polish the glass ceiling.

Cartoon of the Justices arriving at an office marked White Guy Inc *Newsweek* 16 Jun 95

John Wishart Campbell defense attorney

2831 He's a fair man who treats everyone the same. He's mean to everyone.

On Joe Freeman Britt, District Attorney for Robeson County NC, whose record for obtaining 44 capital punishment convictions won him a Guinness recognition as the world's "deadliest prosecutor" *NY Times* 8 Feb 88

Albert Camus novelist

2832 Justice of this kind is obviously no less shocking than the crime itself, and the new "official murder," far from offering redress for the offense committed against society, adds instead a second defilement to the first.

Quoted by US Supreme Court Justice William J Brennan Jr from Camus' *Reflections on The Guillotine* Fridtjos-Karla 60 in dissenting opinion on cases that upheld capital punishment 2 Jul 76

Jim Carrigan Judge, US Court of Appeals

2833 Creativity in the art of abusive epithet has all but disappeared.

On dismissing $12-million libel suit with ruling that calling someone a "sleaze bag" who "slimed up from the bayou" does not constitute slander Time 28 Aug 87

2834 It is all too rare today to hear the clear, clean ring of a really original insult.

ib

Michael A Chapnick Senior Partner, Lord, Day & Lord

2835 We had too many green cows with purple spots as opposed to cookie-cutter transactions.

On costly, one-time clients rather than retainers, a predominance that led to the closing of Manhattan's oldest law firm *NY Times* 2 Oct 94

Jesse Choper Dean, Law School, University of California at Berkeley

2836 He. . . continued to take thin slices of the salami.

On diverse viewpoints of US Supreme Court Associate Justice Lewis F Powell Jr *NY Times* 17 Jun 87

Marcia Clark Prosecuting Attorney, LA County

2837 A dream is a wish your heart makes.

On testimony that football star O J Simpson had told a friend that he dreamed of killing his wife *US News & World Report* 13 Feb 95

Tom C Clark Associate Justice, US Supreme Court

2838 We. . . don't want to go out on a picket line in our robes; we have to convince the nation by force of our opinions.

On desegregating schools, quoted by Richard Kluger *Simple Justice* Knopf 75

2839 [It is] bursting with words that go through so much and conclude with so little.

On Justice Felix Frankfurter's almost record 64-page dissent in a 6–2 decision holding a Tennessee reapportionment act to be unconstitutional 26 Mar 62

William J Clinton 42nd US President

2840 Sometimes, all the answers have to come from the values and the stirrings and the voices that speak to us from within.

Appeal to Memphis' African Americans to look to themselves for an end to black-on-black violence *Newsweek* 6 Dec 93

Adam Clymer newspaper executive

2841 [It is] a court system that seemed to look up from its slumbers to pound us down whenever we thought we were getting on our feet.

On a Vermont system that meted out an appeal sentence of only 30 months in prison for drunken driving in which Clymer's 20-year-old daughter was killed *NY Times* 2 Nov 86

William C Cobb Houston legal consultant

2842 When buffalo become scarce, buffalo hunters can come up with a better way of hunting, they can hunt something else, or they can nurture the buffalo they have.

On bringing in new clients *NY Times* 22 Oct 93

2843 Buffalo hunters cannot sit in bars waiting for the buffalo to return on their own.

missing source

Felix S Cohen attorney

2844 Like the miner's canary, the Indian marks the shifts from fresh air to poison gas in our political atmosphere.

"The Erosion of Indian Rights 1950–1953" *Yale Law Journal* 53

Roy M Cohn attorney

2845 I don't want to know what the law is, I want to know who the judge is.

On fixing cases *NY Times* 3 Apr 88

Alistair Cooke commentator

2846 This chamber is haunted by single sentences that have transformed the life of the American people.

On the US Supreme Court *Inventing A Nation* Maryland Public Television 18 Jul 89

2847 He was the missing giant of the convention.

On the influence of Thomas Jefferson who was serving abroad at the time of the constitutional convention

Edward D Cowart Judge, Florida Circuit Court

2848 Cripple that and walk it by me slow.

Request for clarification, quoted by Ann Rule *The Stranger Beside Me* Norton 80

John Cummings New Orleans trial lawyer

2849 He is a special kind of guy. Specially good and specially bad.

On attorney Melvin Belli *Wall Street Journal* 23 Nov 88

Mario Cuomo Governor of New York

2850 It's about as luxurious a life as you can imagine, intellectually.

Comment to Albany *NY Times Union* editorial board on the US Supreme Court *NY Times* 20 Mar 93

2851 All you have to do is listen, think, read, conclude and write.... They give you money... they give you respectability. It's heaven.

On imagining life as a U.S. Supreme Court justice *ib*

2852 They put you in this big room. They slam this mahogany door shut. And you're dead. You're entombed.

Expressing an opposite view of the high court *ib*

2853 When the World Trade Center collapses, you can't go on television and tell people not to worry about it.

On the restricted life of Supreme Court Justices *ib*

2854 You don't have to wear pants. You can live your life in a robe.

ib

2855 The best way to pick a judge is by picking someone who's good at doing what a judge is supposed to do, not at what a president, a governor or legislator is supposed to do.

On a standard that won him credit for almost single-handedly restoring the reputation of NY's highest court *More Than Words* St Martin 93

Charles P Curtis attorney

2856 A practicing lawyer will soon detect in himself a perfectly astonishing amount of sincerity.

On becoming thoroughly identified and in agreement with a client, quoted by Martin Mayer *The Lawyers* Harper 67

2857 You cannot very well keep your tongue in your cheek while you are talking.

On the peril of believing your own brief *ib*

Christopher Darden Deputy District Attorney, LA County

2858 It's the dirtiest, filthiest, nastiest word in the English language.

Request as proscecutor that the court bar the word "nigger" in the O J Simpson murder trial *Washington Post* 25 Jan 95

Lord Denning (Alfred Thompson Denning), Lord Justice

2859 A company... has a brain and a nerve center... [and] hands which hold the tools and act in accordance with directions from the center.

On acceptance of suits against corporations instead of individuals *London Times* 13 Dec 94

Alan Dershowitz Professor of Law, Harvard

2860 The courtroom oath—"to tell the truth, the whole truth and nothing but the truth"—is applicable only to witnesses... [because] the American justice system is built on a foundation of not telling the whole truth.

The Best Defense Random House 82

2861 He drives the defense crazy... couldn't care less about the ultimate result... [only] his little drops of blood.

On Dr Henry C Lee, forensic scientist *NY Times* 9 Dec 94

2862 I have great compassion for God now, because I think Bill is going to start filing lawsuits as soon as he gets to heaven.

On the death of radical lawyer William Kunstler *USA Today* 5 Sep 95

Patrick Devlin Justice of the High Court

2863 The judges of England have rarely been original thinkers or great jurists... [and] have needed the stuff of morals supplied to them so that out of it they could fashion the law.

Quoted by Ludovic Kennedy "The Legal Barbarians" *Spectator* 15 Sep 61

2864 It's like seeing... different parts of the stage, and finding that they're all Gerald du Maurier in the end.

On the similarity of judges, businessmen and civil servants *Anatomy of Britain* Hodder & Stoughton 62

Thomas Dickerson Judge, NY State Court

2865 [It is] educational malpractice; students are consumers.

On ordering Pace University to pay $1,000 each to students who were asked to figure price differences in a computer course not requiring a math background *Wall Street Journal* 9 May 95

Nick Doak spokesman for Lloyd's of London

2866 Trying to establish pecuniary loss would be damn near impossible.

On damages for a detached or dysfunctional penis *NY Times* 13 Feb 94

Robert J Dole US Senator

2867 I learned in law school, boys, bill 'em when the tears are still falling.

On collecting reimbursements from allies in Persian Gulf War, television interview 3 Mar 91

Frank J Donahue Judge, Massachusetts Superior Court

2868 While conducive to sleep, it is not conducive to a desire to sleep with a member of the opposite sex.

On ruling that Kathleen Winsor's novel *Forever Amber* could be sold in Massachusetts, Clifton Fadiman ed *The American Treasury* Harper 55

Phil Donahue TV host

2869 [This is] the bimbo factor.

On false accusations of rape NBC TV 25 Apr 92

William O Douglas Associate Justice, US Supreme Court

2870 The right to dissent is the only thing that makes life tolerable for a judge of an appellate court.

America Challenged Princeton 60

2871 Those who start down a water course may be strangers at the beginning but almost invariably are close friends at the end.

Farewell letter to colleagues 14 Nov 75

2872 No patent medicine was ever put to wider and more varied use than the 14th Amendment.

On the Civil War amendment that sustained states from abridging individual rights, quoted by Justice Hugo Black in biography of his parent *My Father* Random House 75

2873 At the end of a 25-mile hike, your work is pretty well done.

On the value of taking time off to think *NY Times* 29 Oct 79

Kevin T Duffy Judge, US District Court, Southern District of NY

2874 Jurors should go home every night and fight with their spouses like the rest of us!

On not sequestering jurors *NY Times* 3 Oct 93

Michael Durfee Child Abuse Prevention Coordinator, LA County

2875 We are yanking a whole lot of babies.

On removing children from homes where they were believed to be at risk *USA Today* 2 Mar 95

John P Eaton journalist

2876 Only time's passing would bring questions for which no answers had been provided, and answers whose questions had yet to be asked.

On claims of families and survivors *Titanic: Destination Disaster* Norton 87

Marian Wright Edelman President, Children's Defense Fund

2877 The crisis of children having children has been eclipsed by the greater crisis of children killing children.

On guns in public schools *Washington Post* 24 Jan 94

Adolf Eichmann Nazi official

2878 After a short while, gentlemen, we shall meet again. So is the fate of man.

Last statement before being hanged for war crimes, Ramleh Prison, Tel Aviv 1 Jun 62

Dwight D Eisenhower 34th US President

2879 These are not bad people. All they are concerned about is to see that their sweet little girls are not required to sit in schools alongside some big black bucks.

To Chief Justice Earl Warren on desegregation of schools, quoted by Bernard Schwartz and Stephen Lesher *Inside the Warren Court* Doubleday 83

Thomas I Emerson Professor of Law, Yale

2880 The function of the censor is to censor. He has a professional interest in finding things to suppress.

Recalled on Emerson's death 18 Jun 91

Richard A Epstein Professor of Law, University of Chicago

2881 The irreducible core of this body of law can be succinctly expressed: Keep off.

On ownership of property *Simple Rules for a Complex World* Harvard 95

Susan Estrich Professor of Law, University of Southern California

2882 NBC News jumped off the Empire State Building. So *The New York Times*, like any thoughtful toddler, decided it had to follow suit.

On the release of a rape victim's name after speculation on her morality and judgment *NY Times* 18 Apr 91

Myrlie Evers victim's mother

2883 I don't have to say accused assassin... now I can say convicted assassin.

On Byron De La Beckwith's conviction 31 years after the Jackson MS fatal shooting of civil rights leader Medgar Evers *NY Times* 6 Feb 94

Executive Order 10925

2884 The contractor will take affirmative action to ensure that applicants are employed... without regard to race, creed, color or national origin.

President Kennedy's landmark order stemming from the 1955 White House Conference on Equal Job Opportunity and formalizing the term "affirmative action" Mar 61, implemented by a young lawyer, Hobart Taylor Jr, *NY Times* 11 Jun 95; later translated in some political circles as "racial preference" NPR 5 Feb 96

Bruce Fein constitutional commentator

2885 Conservative castles of sand!

Expressing belief that US Supreme Court's reasoning could easily be washed away in the next liberal tide *NY Times* 27 Sep 91

2886 Comparing the [1930] membership... with its contemporary counterpart might suggest a new theory of evolution: survival of the unfit.

On the pre-New Deal court that included Charles Evans Hughes, Oliver Wendell Holmes, Louis D Brandeis and Harlan Fiske Stone *ib*

2887 [He is] gelatinous... unedifying... with splendid opacity and ponderousness... an earmark of ineptitude.

On Justice David H Souter *ib*

2888 [A single liberal vote would change] the incestuous sloppiness that goes on when people of the same ideology just talk to themselves.

ib

Esther Fein reporter

2889 Hundreds of letters, some squeezed and kissed for good luck... landed atop thousands of other letters in a bin outside the main post office.

On applications for special visas in a one-time-only chance to avoid years of red tape to immigrate and/or be employed in US *NY Times* 22 Jan 87

Raoul Felder attorney

2890 People who inherit their wealth are anally retentive about spending it, and people who make their money aren't. You know you can earn it again.

On his $450 an hour fee as divorce counsel *London Times* 4 Sep 92

2891 A videotape is powerful ammunition that shows a person's real mood.

On value of videotaping legal signings to avoid future charges of duress *Forbes* 23 May 94

Jean Fletcher American Dog Owners Assn

2892 It's gotten to the point where anything with four legs, tail on the south and teeth on the north, is a pit bull.

On establishment of Canine Defense Fund to fight pit bull ordinances *NY Times* 12 Jul 87

Percy Foreman attorney

2893 They may not always be right, but they are never wrong.

On loyalty to clients, including defense of James Earl Ray in assassination of Martin Luther King Jr *NY Times* 27 Aug 88

2894 In a murder... try... husband, lover, police,... or society generally. But never the defendant.

On handling 1,500 death-penalty cases, fewer than half of which ever went to trial *ib*

Felix Frankfurter Associate Justice, US Supreme Court

2895 Our society... is a legal state in the sense that almost everything that takes place will sooner or later raise legal questions.

Quoted by Martin Mayer *The Lawyers* Harper & Row 67

2896 Chief Justices... are rarer than Presidents.

On life appointments that continue while presidents come and go *ib*

2897 Being in on big political decisions was like getting used to French cuisine.

On Dean Acheson's years as law clerk, quoted by David C McClellan *Dean Acheson: The State Dept Years* Dodd, Mead 74

2898 Once Dean had dined on such rare meat it was painful to return to the hardtack of the law.

ib

2899 I despise a judge who feels God told him to impose a death sentence. I am mean enough to try to stay here long enough so that K will be too old to succeed me.

"To Judge Learned Hand" on Irving R Kaufman's statement that he had prayed for guidance before imposing the 1951 death sentence on convicted atomic spies Julius and Ethel Rosenberg, recalled on Kaufman's death 1 Feb 92

William Gaddis novelist

2900 Justice? You get justice in the next world, in this world you have the law.

Opening words of Gaddis' *A Frolic of His Own* Poseidon Press 94

William E Geist reporter

2901 They come by cab, by bike and on foot to claim their cars, to pay towing fees—perchance to hurl insults and attache cases at the cashiers.

Reporting on New York City auto pound *NY Times* 28 Feb 87

2902 [The] graffiti consists mainly of profane threats... [but] everyone pays.

ib

Glenn George US Postal Official

2903 Wearing it is the same as saying it.

On T-shirts with profanity or porn, Jackson MS *Clarion-Ledger* 25 May 94

Diane Giacalone Assistant US Attorney, Brooklyn NY

2904 I like the law—the more complicated the better.

On prosecution of racketeering *NY Times* 23 Sep 86

Stephen Gillers Professor of Legal Ethics, NYU Law School

2905 The public is always ready to vote for anything that is bad for lawyers.

On bill to curb large punitive damages awarded by juries *Washington Post* 14 Sep 95

Douglas H Ginsburg Judge, US Court of Appeals, Washington

2906 The memory of those... banished for... opposition to unlimited government, is kept alive by a few scholars... in the hope of a restoration, a second coming of the Constitution of liberty.

On two 5–4 rulings that invalidated federal law prohibiting possession of guns near schools and disallowed states' right to limit congressional terms *NY Times* 28 May 95

Ruth Bader Ginsburg Associate Justice, US Supreme Court

2907 This place specializes in reason.

On the Supreme Court *Prime Time* ABC TV 30 Dec 94

2908 I feel pretty good when I'm the fifth vote to decide the case... even better if I'm the fourth and pick up a fifth based on the writing.

Washington Post 7 Jun 95

I Leo Glasser Judge, Federal District Court, Brooklyn NY

2909 There has never been a defendant of his stature in organized crime who has made the leap he made from one planet to another.

On evidence offered against the Mafia by former mob member Salvatore "Sammy the Bull" Gravano *NY Times* 27 Sep 84

Carey Goldberg reporter

2910 The old law firms die with a crash of titanic egos, a splintering of stubborn partners, a skittish flight of lawyers.

On the closing of Wall Street's 126-year-old Mudge Rose Guthrie Alexander & Ferdon *NY Times* 1 Oct 95

2911 Donald Zoeller... the firm's new chairman... a man as seemingly serene as his lobby walls.

On Zoeller's appointment to preside over Mudge Rose's Wall Street offices of muted turquoise *ib*

Barbara Goldsmith biographer

2912 [There were] squadrons of lawyers from some of Wall Street's most prestigious firms... smug respectability, of infallible integrity.

On legal counsel in contested will of health-care tycoon J Seward Johnson *Vanity Fair* Nov 86

2913 They seem to belong to an exclusive club... hair crisply cut... suits Dunhill... ties predominantly the new power color, yellow.

ib

2914 This contest... gradually has been transmuted into a battle among lawyers, about lawyers, for lawyers.

ib

Gerald Goldstein President, National Association of Criminal Defense Lawyers

2915 How we treat the least of us—the most despicable—is how ultimately we can expect to be treated ourselves.

On prosecutors *Christian Science Monitor* 26 Jun 95

Arthur Goodhart educator

2916 The idea of a fair trial has been the greatest contribution made to civilization by our Anglo-American polity.

"Fair Trial and Contempt of Court in England" *NY Law Journal* 25 Jun 64

Linda Greenhouse reporter

2917 The court shelters its inhabitants from the relentless public exposure that is the modern trade-off for the exercise of great public power.

On covering the US Supreme Court *NY Times* 7 Mar 93

2918 The Justices are not about to give up the intimate and anachronistic little world where fate and politics have placed them for life.

ib

Steven Greenhouse reporter

2919 It honors ferocity.

On appointment of the Robins, Zelle law firm to represent the Government of India in negligence suit against Union Carbide Corp, for disaster at Bhopal *NY Times* 12 Mar 85

Antony Grey Secretary, Homosexual Law Reform Society

2920 Though being homosexual has affected the course of my life profoundly... I do not regard it as the most important or interesting thing about me (or anyone else).

Quest for Justice Sinclair-Stevenson, London 92.

2921 Sexual behavior has nothing to do with morals in the sense of what is laid down in the Bible or by some people in a committee room. It has everything to do with ethics... how people treat one another.

ib

2922 One knows what one is. You know by what makes you turn your head in the street.

ib

Roy Grutman reporter

2923 A lawyer is a utensil, like a knife or fork. It doesn't make any difference who ate with it last, only that it was sufficiently sanitized between meals.

On representing celebrities *Lawyers and Thieves,* with Bill Thomas, Simon & Schuster 90

2924 Think of the worst thing that could be said about you; now imagine hearing it announced in a courtroom by an attorney with a very loud voice whose job it is to tear you to shreds.

ib

2925 If all goes well, they will turn the deliberations into a shouting match, and... end with a hung jury and, with any luck, an out-of-court settlement.

On preference for nonconformists on juries *NY Times* 28 Jun 94

2926 For laywers, winning isn't everything—getting paid is.

ib

Lord Hailsham of Marylebone (Quintin Hogg) Lord Chancellor

2927 The only law in which there is any merit in obeying is the one you do not agree with because you think it is mistaken or operates against your interest.

NY Times 23 Apr 72

2928 The only law which there is any merit enforcing is the law which at least somebody would not obey if it were not enforced.

ib

Terence Hallinan San Francisco Board of Supervisors

2929 We are doing it here. We are creating a civil right.

On pioneering municipal legislation making it illegal to discriminate against cross-dressers, transsexuals, and other transgendered persons *Washington Times* 15 Dec 94

Learned Hand Senior Judge, 2nd Circuit, US Court of Appeals

2930 It is as craftsmen that we get our satisfactions and our pay.

On a lasting lesson learned at Harvard Law School, address at Harvard 6 Feb 58

2931 We hide our incapacity to dispose of a future controversy by deputing it to. . . that factitious ghost, "the reasonable man."

Quoted by Martin Mayer *The Lawyers* Harper & Row 67

2932 Drudgery, senseless bickering, stupid obstinacies, captious pettifogging. . . harass and befog the bench where like any other workman he must do his work.

On the life of a judge *ib*

2933 Your duty is to seek justice, not to act as a timekeeper.

To a prosecutor who pressed for the finality of the death penalty in the Rosenburg espionage trial, quoted by Leonard Nizer *The Implosion Conspiracy* Doubleday 73

Lord Charles Harman Justice of the High Court

2934 No one is employed to sit in the coffee room and eat roast mutton.

Disallowing appeal on tax-free entertaining, quoted by Anthony Sampson *Anatomy of Britain* Hodder & Stoughton 62

2935 It seems to. . . poison the wells of hospitality.

ib

Jonathan Harris Professor of Chemical Engineering, MIT

2936 The idea that you can question a child repeatedly, ignore every "no," and take every "yes" as valid—that's junk science.

On rallying support against suggestive, bizarre and improbable answers obtained from children in investigations of abuse in nursery schools *USA Today* 1 Sep 95

Gideon Hausner reporter

2937 In Maidanek, Poland, there was only one place where the children were treated kindly: at the entrance to the gas chambers each one was handed a sweet.

On indicting Eichmann *NY Times* 16 Apr 61

Ernest Hemingway novelist

2938 It's like having a pet cobra in the house to bite me once each day. . . like having a spastic outfielder.

On retaining lawyers, quoted by Charles Scribner Jr *In the Company of Writers* Scribner's 90

Russ M Herman attorney

2939 My Pinocchio doll with a cigarette for a nose. . . starts smoking whenever the tobacco companies lie.

On a doll called Cigarocchio that he said he would bring to court as one of the "legal buccaneers" banded together against the tobacco industry *NY Times* 4 Mar 95

Barbara Holland journalist

2940 The opinion of 11 jurors is merely an opinion, but the opinion of 12 is magic.

Reporting on the history of juries *Smithsonian* Mar 95

2941 We can't put them in jail anymore, but we can select them half to death.

Comparing Cromwellian practice and present procedures *ib*

2942 The modern juror doesn't know what it was designed to know—its neighbors—and a clever lawyer can sometimes play on it as upon a harp.

ib

2943 [He] was an enormous, lion-headed man. . . [who] convinced a jury that his client's trigger finger had accidentally slipped, not once but six times.

On attorney William Howe of rowdy post-Civil War New York *ib*

Herbert Hoover 31st US President

2944 Our country has deliberately undertaken a great social and economic experiment, noble in motive and far-reaching in purpose.

On the 18th Amendment prohibiting sale of alcoholic beverages, recalled on Hoover's death 20 Oct 64

J Edgar Hoover Director, FBI

2945 We of the FBI are powerless to act in cases of oral-genital intimacy, unless it has in some way obstructed interstate commerce.

New York 6 Oct 80

Roman Hruska US Senator

2946 Mediocre judges, people and lawyers. . . are entitled to a little representation aren't they, and have a little chance?

In defense of President Nixon's doomed nomination of G Harold Carswell to the Supreme Court in 1970, recalled in *NY Times* 27 Sep 91

Harold Hughes Justice, NY State Supreme Court

2947 New York is comprised of people and their offspring who left regimes where central government decreed all knowingly what was best for them.
NY Times 25 Apr 87

Derek Humphry Founder, Hemlock Society

2948 We're not lawbreakers, we're law reformers.
On assisted deaths for the terminally ill *Time* 28 Dec 92

Barbara Hutton heiress

2949 With one stroke of the pen I alienated an entire nation.
On following legal advice to take a foreign husband's citizenship to avoid high US taxes, quoted by David Heymann *Poor Little Rich Girl* Random House 84

Intelligence Services Act

2950 [The job of the Government Communications Headquarters is] to monitor or interfere with electromagnetic acoustic and other emissions.
Definition of eavesdropping by British intelligence *Guardian Weekly* 1 Jan 95

2951 Proliferation is a form of espionage.
On nuclear, chemical, and biological weapons *ib*

Lance A Ito Assistant Presiding Judge, LA Superior Court

2952 Rule 1: Be cautious, careful and when in doubt, keep your mouth shut. Rule 2: When tempted to say something, take a deep breath and refer to Rule 1.
On presiding at the O J Simpson murder arraignment *NY Times* 23 Jul 94

Alain Jakubovicz attorney

2953 I have the honor to represent six million ghosts.
On his role as prosecutor in trial of Nazi war criminal Klaus Barbie *NY Daily News* 17 May 87

Joe Jamail attorney

2954 Take exquisite facts and have dull lawyers. . . [and] you get a jury that makes up its mind based on which lawyer bored them the least.
On winning $10-million settlement, the largest in history, in Pennzoil suit against Texaco, CBS News 7 Nov 87

Neal Johnston Chief of Staff, NY City Council

2955 The screening process through which law firms choose new partners is perhaps as well considered as anything this side of a papal election.
NY Times 6 Mar 83

Lisa Kembler attorney

2956 What we have is Lorena Bobbitt's life juxtaposed against John Wayne Bobbitt's penis.
Defense presentation for wife who severed her husband's penis but ultimately won acquittal *Guardian Weekly* 16 Jan 94

2957 The evidence will show that in her mind it was his penis from which she could not escape, that caused her the most pain, the most fear, the most humiliation.
ib

2958 At the end of this case you will come to one conclusion. . . a life is more valuable than a penis.
ib

Anthony M Kennedy Associate Justice, US Supreme Court

2959 There is a zone of liberty. . . where the individual can tell the Government, "Beyond this line you may not go."
On where constitutional law draws the line and on what principles, dual topics that Kennedy raised in his confirmation hearings by the Senate Judiciary Committee *NY Times* 15 Dec 87

2960 The framers of the Constitution made a covenant with the future.
ib

2961 The Constitution isn't weak because we don't know the answer to a difficult problem. It's strong because we can find that answer.
ib

2962 An Orwellian rewriting of history.
On Justice Harry A Blackmun's majority opinion that permitted display of a Hanukkah menorah but barred a Nativity scene *ib* 28 Jul 89

2963 Perpetual disrespect for the finality of convictions disparages the entire criminal-justice system.
Newsweek 6 Apr 92

Edward M Kennedy US Senator

2964 It was a semantic misunderstanding.
On not talking with police because he thought his nephew was charged with sexual battery rather than rape *US News & World Report* 27 May 91

Robert F Kennedy US Attorney General

2965 Courage is the most important attribute of a lawyer.

To University of San Francisco Law School 29 Sep 62

2966 [Courage] can never be an elective in any law school... limited, dated or outworn, and it should pervade the heart, the halls of justice and the chambers of the mind.

ib

Martin Luther King Jr civil rights leader

2967 Life is breathed into a judicial decision by the persistent exercise of legal rights until they become usual and ordinary.

"The Case Against Tokenism" 62, James Washington ed *A Testament of Hope* Harper & Row 86

2968 One has not only a legal but a moral responsibility to obey just laws. Conversely, one has a moral responsibility to disobey unjust laws.

Why We Can't Wait New American Library 64

2969 Negroes have committed derivative crimes ... born of the greater crimes of the white society.

To Southern Christian Leadership Conference 16 Aug 67

Edward Koch Mayor, New York City

2970 The knife of corruption endangered life... the scalpel of law is making us well again.

State of the City address *NY Times* 28 Jan 87

Harold Hongju Koh Professor of Law, Yale

2971 Silence has a sound, and the sound is "no."

To US Senate Judiciary Committee on the presidential right to enter Persian Gulf War without congressional approval NPR 10 Jan 91

A J Kristol Judge, Federal Bankruptcy Court, Southern Florida

2972 It would be found in civil contempt and fined 50 megabytes of hard-drive memory and ten megabytes of random access memory.

On what should be imposed on a "rogue computer" that continued to send notices of a fine after it had been rescinded NPR 10 Apr 93

Philip B Kurland Professor of Law, University of Chicago

2973 This is a landmark case, but we don't know what it marks.

On Supreme Court decision upholding affirmative action, the impact of which he said would not be known for many years *Newsweek* 10 Jul 78

Gara Lamarche Executive Director, Texas Civil Liberties Union

2974 The finality of death makes unfairness irrevocable.

On reprieve received while the defendent was being executed *NY Times* 17 Jan 88

2975 Whatever is taking place in predawn hours, it certainly isn't justice.

ib

J Miller Leavy Los Angeles county prosecutor

2976 The corpus delicti is not the actual body of the deceased... [it] is the body of the crime.

On Leonard Ewing Scott's 1957 murder conviction that paved the way for successful prosecution where no body was found, quoted by Diane Wagner *Corpus Delicti* St Martin/Marick 86

Gerald B Lefcourt Vice President, National Association of Criminal Defense Lawyers

2977 If you please the government, you go free; if you don't, there are Draconian sentences for almost every crime.

On entrenching an informer system by giving only a five-year sentence to former Mafia member Salvatore "Sammy the Bull" Gravano despite admission of involvement in 19 murders *NY Times* 27 Sep 94

John Leo essayist

2978 Everything bad that happens to us is someone else's fault, and someone else must be made to pay.

Reporting on "the world's most litigious age" *US News & World Report* 22 May 95

Gershon Legman biographer

2979 Murder is a crime. Describing murder is not. Sex is not a crime. Describing sex is.

Censorship study quoted by Fred R Shapiro ed *American Legal Quotations* Oxford 93

Pierre S Leval Judge, US District Court, Southern District of New York

2980 The witness is not a truth-teller.

On Defense Secretary Robert S McNamara's testimony 26 Mar 84 recalling the possibilities of US victory in Vietnam, quoted by Debroah Shapley *Power and Promise* Little, Brown 93

William Levine Chair, Investors Arbitration Services Inc

2981 We know what's under the carpet because we used to be the carpet cleaners.

On former brokers offering representation for redress of legal counsel resulting in loss of investments *Wall Street Journal* 14 Nov 95

Wilmarth S Lewis educator

2982 When you're lying on your belly/ There's nothing like Shelley;/ Better, far, than drowning/ Is an evening with Browning;/ The tropics' torrid heats/ Are cooled with lines by Keats;/ And where ever you may go/ Read Edgar Allan Poe.

On a reading list sent to students entering Harvard Law School, quoted by Dean Acheson *Among Friends* Dodd Mead 80

Jutta Limbach President, German High Court

2983 The lasting contribution of Nuremberg was to make individuals responsible for the wars they start.

On 50th anniversary of the Nuremberg war criminals trial *NY Times* 20 Nov 95

Karl Llewellyn attorney

2984 Law. . . begins when someone takes to doing something someone else does not like.

Quoted by Martin Mayer *The Lawyers* Harper & Row 67

Randall Lockwood Director of Higher Education, Humane Society of the US

2985 Your right to own a vicious dog stops at the next person's throat.

On "growing propensity to have mean dogs in an age when we're increasingly distrustful of law enforcement" *NY Times* 12 Jul 87

London Daily Mirror

2986 The Brighton bomb may have been planted by an Irish terrorist, but the fingerprints were American.

Editorial on IRA bombing of a Brighton hotel where Conservative Party conference was taking place *NY Times* 16 Oct 84

Mary Lupo Circuit Judge, Palm Beach FL

2987 She's a walking mistrial.

On a potential William Kennedy Smith rape case juror who didn't care "who diddled who" *USA Today* 7 Nov 91

Patrick Lynch counsel for Exxon Corp

2988 If a minor mistake has very serious consequences, people will see the mistake as being greater than it was.

On the failure of a fully qualified third mate to make a turn that would have avoided North America's worst oil tanker spill that led to a federal court awarding $15 billion in punitive damages for some 10,000 persons *NY Times* 14 Jun 94

Archibald MacLeish poet and statesman

2989 Adjudicated quarrels of mankind,/ Brown row on row!—how well these lawyers bind/ Their records of dead sin—as if they feared/ The hate might spill and their long shelves be smeared/ With slime of human souls—brown row on row/ Span on Philistine span, a greasy show/ Of lust and lies and cruelty, dried grime/ Streaked from the finger of the beggar, Time.

"A Liberty of Law" recalled by Scott Donaldson *Archibald MacLeish* Houghton Mifflin 92

Norman Mailer novelist

2990 You don't know anything about a woman until you meet her in court.

Penthouse Nov 84

Emil Mannhart Chief Justice, Munich Palace of Justice

2991 Himmler found in him his bureaucrat of death.

On Nazi Lieutenant General Karl Wolff's conviction for "aiding and abetting murder in at least 300,000 instances" in World War II *Time* 9 Oct 64

David Margolick columnist

2992 Other lawyers of his ilk have died out or burned out or straightened out or sold out.

Reporting on the radical William Kunstler at 74 *NY Times* 6 Jul 93

2993 He is Snow White to Mr Fein's Seven Dwarfs.

On Supreme Court Justice Antonin Scalia's relationship to constitutional commentator Bruce Fein

Jimmy Marks Gypsy chief

2994 We are the hidden Americans. . . so invisible not even our tears are seen, and our cries are not heard.

On Gypsies' first lawsuit for civil rights *Life* Oct 92

Daniel Marshall attorney

2995 I doubt whether even a justice of the peace would call the meanest pimp before the bar on such short notice.

On special session of the US Supreme Court to rule on a stay of execution in the 1953 Rosenberg espionage case, quoted by Louis Nizer *The Implosion Conspiracy* Doubleday 73

Michael Marshall former Suffragan Bishop of Woolwich

2996 [It was] an absurdity of. . . retrospective scrupulosity.

On endangered elephants laws that prevented him exporting a piano to Britain *Episcopal News Report* 19 Aug 92

Thurgood Marshall Associate Justice, US Supreme Court

2997 The government they devised. . . required several amendments, a civil war and momentous social transformation to attain the system of constitutional government.

On the US Constitution *NY Times* 10 May 87

2998 I believe in the color-blind society—but it has been and remains an aspiration.

Life Fall 87

2999 If it's a dope case, I won't even read the petition. . . ain't giving no bread to no drug dealer. . . won't handle incest cases, either. Disgusting!

ib

3000 He did what he could with what he had.

On himself on retiring 28 Jun 91

3001 There's no difference between a white snake and a black snake. They both bite.

On being asked if his successor should be black *Newsweek* 8 Jul 91

Mark Masarsky Russian capitalist

3002 There is no higher law than private ownership of property. . . the same kind of brilliant human discovery as the wheel and fire.

On rejecting the Communist policy of collective ownership, *NY Times* 25 Feb 92

Robert Megarry Justice of the High Court of Britain

3003 Argued law is tough law.

Quoted by John Mortimer *Murders and Other Friends* Viking 95

Arthur Miller playwright

3004 The police station is where our liberties begin and end.

On forced confessions, quoted in *Superchief: The Life and Legacy of Earl Warren* PBS TV 2 Oct 89

Martha Minow Professor of Law, Harvard

3005 The country holds an ideal of the Court as a place where people sit down and reason together. It's really nine separate courts.

On US Supreme Court *NY Times* 28 Jul 89

Thomas A Moore counsel

3006 Pain and suffering is something that's inflicted on somebody; loss of enjoyment of life is something that's taken away.

On seeking additional compensation for brain-damaged client *NY Times* 6 Jan 89

Reed Morgan attorney

3007 Gross negligence. . . unreasonably dangerous . . . defectively manufactured.

On winning an award of $2.7 million for a 79-year-old woman scalded by McDonald's coffee *Newsweek* 20 Mar 95

Lance Morrow essayist

3008 In Texas lore, there is a defense for murder that goes like this: "He needed killing."

"A Moment for the Dead" essay on Persian Gulf War *Time* 1 Apr 91

John Mortimer attorney and playwright

3009 Given sufficient endurance you can bore a judge into submission by going on until he's in real danger of missing his train to Hayward's Heath and is ready to submit.

Murderers and Other Friends Viking 95

Michael B Mukasey Judge, NY Federal Court

3010 I am not going to order an open file just because you stomp your Buster Browns.

On Attorney John H Jacobs' desire to see evidence seized overseas in explosion at the NY Trade Center *NY Times* 15 Apr 95

Ralph Nader lobbyist

3011 [They are] unsafe at any speed.

Congressional testimony on the need for increased regulation of automobile design *Unsafe at Any Speed* Grossman 65

National Advisory Commission On Civil Disorders (Kerner Report)

3012 Our nation is moving toward two societies, one black, one white—separate and unequal.

On presidential inquiry on riots in US cities *NY Times* 1 Mar 68

3013 Discrimination and segregation have long permeated much of American life; they now threaten the future of every American.

ib

National Rifle Association

3014 Tell them what rape is. Be graphic. . . disgusting . . . obscene.

On laws seeking to limit sale and use of firearms *NY Times* 4 Dec 94

Louis B Nizer defense attorney

3015 Some people will believe anything if you whisper it to them.

Thinking On Your Feet Pyramid 63

3016 She was the darling of congressional committees who wanted the facts right from the bear's mouth.

On Elizabeth Bentley's role as a counter-spy against Russia *The Implosion Conspiracy* Doubleday 73

3017 Greenglass pounded his chest with *mea culpa*, so loud it was heard around the world.

On David Greenglass's confessions in Rosenberg espionage trial *ib*

3018 Excitement has never diminished, indeed it has grown: the challenge is ever new... contest is ever intense... surprise is ever present.

On more than six decades in the courtroom, recalled on Nizer's death at 92 *NY Times* 11 Nov 94

3019 I would pray, O Lord, never to diminish my passion for a client's cause, for from it springs the flame which leaps across the jury box and sets fire to the conviction of the jurors.

ib

Gerald Nunziato Director, Tracing Center, US Bureau of Alcohol, Tobacco, and Firearms [ATF]

3020 The gun is God; the NRA is the congregation; and ATF is the devil.

On the National Rifle Association's opposition to gun-control laws *Time* 24 Jul 95

Mary Hostetler Oakey Department of Correction, District of Columbia

3021 It doesn't and it hasn't.

On the electric chair as a deterrent to violent crime *Journey From the Gallows* University Press of America 88

David Obey US Congressman

3022 Would it be possible to bring the guillotine directly to the House floor?

Objection to restrictions on federal appeals by inmates on death row *NY Times* 5 Oct 90

Sandra Day O'Connor Associate Justice, US Supreme Court

3023 We aren't free to just apply a woman's intuition—if there is such a thing.

On judicial restraint in problem solving *London Times* 19 Oct 91

3024 If you think that I was happy when Justice Ginsburg was appointed, you should see how happy my husband was!

On welcoming a second woman justice to the Supreme Court bench ABC TV 29 Dec 94

Walter Olson journalist

3025 The unleashing of litigation in its full fury has done cruel, grave harm and little lasting good... clogs and jams the gears of commerce... torments the probably innocent and rewards the palpably irresponsible.

The Litigation Explosion Dutton 91

3026 [It] has sent the cream of a nation's intellectual talent into dubious battle.

ib

3027 What began as a page out of Dickens ended as a page out of Kafka.

ib

Brian O'Neill attorney

3028 You need to take a substantial bite out of their butt before they change their behavior.

On successfully representing some 10,000 people seeking huge compensatory and punitive damages from Exxon for North America's worst oil tanker spill *NY Times* 14 Jun 94

Florence Orbach prospective juror

3029 The worst thing I've heard about the Kennedys is that they're very smart but when they get horny, their penis takes over and their brain closes.

Reply to questioning as prospective juror in William Kennedy Smith rape trial *Washington Times* 6 Nov 91

Rosa Parks civil rights heroine

3030 All I was doing was trying to get home from work.

On refusing to move to the back of a Montgomery AL bus 1 Dec 55, a protest that ultimately achieved integration, quoted by Pamela R Fletcher *Rosa Parks* Dial 92

3031 My feet are tired, but my soul is rested.

ib

Richard N Parslow Superior Court, Orange County CA

3032 A three-parent, two-natural-mom situation is ripe for crazy-making. I refuse to split the child emotionally.

Denying parental rights to a surrogate mother *NY Times* 23 Oct 90

Robert Patterson Defense Counsel, Virginia Military Institute

3033 [They consider it] some big-game animal to be hunted down, tracked, caught, badgered, and killed so that some lawyer or some organization can go back up and hang a trophy on a wall in an office.

On efforts to make VMI co-educational *New Yorker* 5 Sep 94

Ian Percival Member of Parliament

3034 Of course there is no need for a death penalty in a civilized society—but first get your civilized society.

To Parliament in futile attempt to restore capital punishment in Britain *US News & World Report* 13 Apr 87

Stewart Pollock Justice, NJ Supreme Court

3035 Horizontal federalism. . . though untidy, invests the system with a vibrant diversity.

On states looking to each other instead of the US Supreme Court for guidance on constitutional law *NY Times* 4 May 86

Lord Ponsonby Of Shulbrede (Frederick Matthew Thomas) Labor peer

3036 It is an offense for a man to rape a woman or another man. . . if a person. . . at the time of the intercourse does not consent and at the time he knows that the person does not consent to the intercourse or is reckless as to whether that person consents.

On the House of Lords defining for the first time what constitutes male rape *Guardian Weekly* 17 Jul 94

3037 The purpose is to tidy up the law relating to penalties where buggery would remain an offense but would not be rape.

ib

Shirley Pope NYC Law Clerk

3038 Just calm down. . . this is happening to you. . . is not a dream. . . you are in New York. That will be $100.

On imposing fines for towing of automobiles, quoted by William E Geist "Citadel of Fury" *NY Times* 28 Feb 87

Thomas Reed Powell Professor of Constitutional Law, Harvard Law

3039 If you think that you can think about a thing, inextricably attached to something else, without thinking of the thing it is attached to, then you have a legal mind.

Recalled on Powell's death 15 Aug 55

William L Prosser Dean, University of California Law School

3040 The litigant has vital interests at stake. . . and the robed buffoon who makes merry at his expense should be choked with his own wig.

The Judicial Humorist Little, Brown 52

Henry Putzel Jr Chief, Voting and Elections Section, Civil Rights Division, US Department of Justice

3041 [One needs to be] a word nut and a double revolving peripatetic nit-picker.

On reporting court decisions *Yearbook of the Supreme Court* Historical Society 80

Harriett Schaffer Rabb Employment Rights Project, Columbia Law School

3042 If you call it a big yellow bus, it's a big yellow bus even if it looks like a wrist watch.

To *NY Times* counsel who preferred the word "annuities" for back pay equalizing women employees, quoted by Nan Robertson *The Girls in the Balcony* Random House 92

Jed S Rakoff attorney

3043 To federal prosecutors of white-collar crime, the mail fraud statute is our Stradivarius, Colt 45, Louisville Slugger, Cuisinart—and our true love.

On the 1872 statute barring use of mails to defraud *NY Times* 20 Nov 87

Lord Rea (Nicolas Rea) physician and Member of Parliment

3044 May I suggest the noble Lord, while rambling over many curious and peculiar arrangements which I did not understand, none the less was at times confusing friendship with homosexuality?

To the Lords during debate on whether gays should be allowed to adopt children *London Times* 25 Feb 91

Lord Reid (George Oswald Reid) Justice of the High Court

3045 Most experienced counsel would agree that the golden rule is—when in doubt, stop. Far more cases have been lost by going on too long, than by stopping too soon.

Quoted by John Mortimer *Murderers and Other Friends* Viking 95

Charles Rembar journalist

3046 Pornography is in the groin of the beholder.

The End of Obscenity Random House 68

William H Rehnquist Chief Justice, US Supreme Court

3047 [It is] a search for what the words used meant to them.

On the ongoing concern for the founding fathers' intent in drafting the US Constitution *Life* Fall 87

3048 [It is] a regrettably patronizing civics lecture.

On Justice William J Brennan Jr's majority opinion that burning the American flag could not be legally prohibited *NY Times* 28 Jul 89

3049 I assume they're all nervous—they should be.

On attorneys practicing before the US Supreme Court *Washington Times* 3 Jul 92

Daniel C Richman Clerk, US Supreme Court

3050 This is not a case about only homosexuals. All sorts of people do this kind of thing.

Memo in capital letters to Justice Thurgood Marshall on statute on sexual acts between individuals *NY Times* 25 May 93

Jeremy Rifkin geneticist

3051 Genetic privacy will be the major constitutional issue of the next generation.

On genetic engineering *Time* 17 Jan 94

Simon Rifkind NY judge

3052 Impartiality is an acquired taste, like olives. You have to be habituated to it.

Time 20 Aug 79

3053 Like an usher in a dark movie theater, holding the client by the hand, the lawyer guides him through the maze of law and regulation which now enmeshes all our lives.

NY Times 15 Nov 95

Roger Rosenblatt essayist

3054 The four sheets of parchment were vellum, the skin of a lamb or a calf, stretched, scraped and dried. The ink, a blend of oak galls and dyes. The light, an oil lamp. The instrument, a feather quill.

"Words on Pieces of Paper" on 200th anniversary Of US Constitution *Time* 6 Jul 87

3055 Amazing little artifact. . . . Sanctified in helium and watched over by an electronic camera.

On preservation of one of the nation's most cherished documents *ib*

Julius Rosenberg convicted spy

3056 He looks like a cross between a rabbinical student and an army sergeant.

On Federal Judge Irving Kaufman who was to preside at espionage trial of Rosenberg and his wife and sentence them to death, quoted by Louis Nizer *The Implosion Conspiracy* Doubleday 73

Paul Rothstein Professor of Law, Georgetown

3057 They might be able to argue that he was nuts, but not the kind of nuts that gets you off under the law.

On difficulty of proving that Francisco Martin Duran's shooting at the White House did not constitute an assassination attempt *Washington Times* 3 Nov 94

William Rubenstein Director, ACLU Lesbian and Gay Rights Project

3058 When a man is allowed to marry a woman, but a woman is not allowed to marry a woman, that is a form of discrimination.

On urging other states to follow the Supreme Court of Hawaii's ruling that gays may not be prohibited from marrying *Washington Post* 7 May 93

Carl Sandburg poet

3059 Why is there always a secret singing/ When a lawyer cashes in?/ Why does a hearse horse snicker/ Hauling a lawyer away?

"The Lawyers Know Too Much" 1920, recalled on Sandburg's death 22 Jul 67

3060 In the heels of the higgling lawyers, Bob/ Too many slippery ifs and buts and howevers./ Too much hereinbefore provided whereas,/ Too many doors to go in and out of.

ib

3061 When the lawyers are through/ What is there left, Bob?/ Can a mouse nibble at it/ And find enough to fasten a tooth in?

ib

Severino Santiapichi Chief Justice of Italy

3062 Let us return to the point, to the pistol.

At trial of Mehmet Ali Agca for attempted assassination of Pope John Paul II *NY Times* 1 Jun 85

Antonin Scalia Associate Justice, US Supreme Court

3063 Look, there are four possible answers: "Yes, No, I don't know and I'm not telling"—which is it?

On oral arguments heard by the court *Life* Fall 87

3064 Maybe it's just because I'm new. . . because I'm an ex-academic. Maybe it's because I'm right.

On lack of conferences between justices *NY Times* 22 Feb 88

3065 [Take] for example, the case of the 11-year-old girl raped by four men and killed by stuffing her panties down her throat. . . how enviable a quiet death by lethal injection compared with that!

Responding to Justice Harry A Blackmun's dissent on the death penalty 23 Feb 94

3066 Separation of powers, a distinctively American political doctrine, profits from the advice authored by a distinctively American poet: Good fences make good neighbors.

Law as related to poet Robert Frost *Washington Post* 2 Oct 95

Daniel K Schorr commentator

3067 Lawyers who used to chase ambulances now chase sexual harassment cases.

On proliferation of harassment charges against prominent persons Station WAMU Washington 6 May 94

Cathy Seibel Assistant US Attorney

3068 Just because you're rich doesn't mean you're not cheap.

On prosecution of hotel owner Leona Helmsley *NY Times* 24 Aug 89

Robert Seigel commentator

3069 Learned Hand—the most American jurist never to sit on the Supreme Court.

On interviewing Hand's biographer Gerald Gunther NPR 20 Jun 94

Fred R Shapiro Lecturer in Legal Research, Yale Law School

3070 Law is the intersection of language and power.

Preface to *The Oxford Dictionary of American Legal Quotations* Oxford 92

Irving S Shapiro Chair, E I du Pont de Nemours

3071 Litigation should be a last resort, not a knee-jerk reflex.

Christian Science Monitor 5 Dec 78

Robert Shilliday government prosecutor

3072 The genesis of the plan was confusion... murky... dark... without form... to put the estate of Newhouse on a collision course with the Internal Revenue Service.

On unsuccessful prosecution of the S I Newhouse estate for tax evasion, quoted by Thomas Maier *Newhouse* St Martin 94

Scott Simon commentator

3073 There's a new Olympic sport—litigation!

On Tonya Harding's battle for eligibility to skate in Norway NPR 12 Feb 94

David H Souter Associate Justice, US Supreme Court

3074 [It is] the work of a gladiator, but he thrusts at lions of his own imagining.

On Justice Antonin Scalia's judicial opinions *Washington Post* 4 Jul 94

Gerry Spence Wyoming attorney

3075 The natural enemy of a gopher is a rattlesnake ... of the NRA it is the ATF.

On the roles of the National Rifle Assn and the US Bureau of Alcohol, Tobacco and Fire Arms in a federal siege of the property of his client *Time* 24 Jul 95

Alessandra Stanley reporter

3076 Early every morning, braces of finely groomed men and women in Burberry raincoats slink past doormen and nannies and stealthily pace the well-swept streets of the Upper East Side.

On illegality of riding unmarked vans to work *NY Times* 25 Feb 91

Adlai E Stevenson statesman

3077 The sound of tireless voices is the price we pay for the right to hear the music of our own opinions.

Quoted in *The Guide to American Law* Vol 9 West Publishing Co 84

Thomas B Stoddard attorney

3078 I became the client as well as the lawyer... "they" became "we."

On contracting AIDS while serving as counsel to the Lambda Legal Defense and Education Fund *NY Times* 5 Feb 93

William Styron novelist

3079 It is a broiling process at intensely high temperature.

On death in the electric chair *NY Times* 10 May 87

3080 Pigs and cattle go more expeditiously into that good night.

ib

Donald Sullivan attorney

3081 Different and often contradictory... it didn't happen, we didn't do it, somebody else did it, you weren't hurt, you're not hurt as bad as you say you were, and besides, we weren't there.

Statement to the US Supreme Court on the variety of claims permissible under law, quoted by Peter Irons and Stephanie Guitton *May It Please the Court* New Press 94

3082 [A] guy will... say, my dog didn't bite you, besides, my dog is real friendly and never bites anybody and defense number three, I don't have a dog.

ib

Victor Sussman science writer

3083 These days they tend to arrest the equipment as well as the person.

On obscenity on computer networks Station WAMU Washington 21 Jul 94

3084 It is a cybrianic singles bar.

On meeting people via computer networks *ib*

Bernard Taple Minister of Urban Affairs for France

3085 I have lied in good faith.

On charge that he testified falsely in admission of fixing a soccer match *NY Times* 22 Mar 95

Hobart Taylor Jr minorities attorney

3086 I was torn between... "positive action" and... "affirmative action"... and I took "affirmative action" because it was alliterative.

On adopting "for a sense of positiveness" as a more appealing title than Executive Order 10925 that banned discriminatory hiring by federal contractors *NY Times* 11 Jun 95

Lord Taylor of Gosforth (Peter Murray Taylor) Lord Chief Justice

3087 It's a legacy from the 18th century and people might assume that anyone wearing one of them is likely to be thinking in an 18th century way.

On the fruitless hope that judges would relinquish their wigs *London Times* 23 Mar 93

Margaret Thatcher Prime Minister of Britain

3088 [It was] a dog that barely barked at the time.

On a statute little questioned in 1971 but later contentious on the rank of national law over community law *The Path to Power* HarperCollins 95

Clarence Thomas Associate Justice, US Supreme Court

3089 I'm going to be here for 40 years. For those who don't like it, get over it.

On allegations that he had made crude sexual references and relished pornography *US News & World Report* 14 Nov 94

3090 The mere fact that a school is black does not mean that it is a... constitutional violation.

On becoming the first high court justice to question the basis of the 1954 landmark *Brown* v *Board of Education* on school desegregation *Christian Science Monitor* 26 Jun 95

Fred Thompson US Senator

3091 This whole debate has been the battle of the anecdotes, and the anecdotes on either side are examples of rare happenings.

On voting in favor of bill to reduce large punitive damages awarded by juries *Washington Post* 14 Sep 95

John Tierney reporter

3092 It took effect a decade ago very quietly. But since then every New Yorker has heard its consequences.

On law granting insurance discounts for car alarms *NY Times* 19 Feb 91

3093 Sometimes the bystanders called the police... but twice as often their involvement consisted of helping the thief break in.

ib

Time magazine

3094 Each working day—from the first Monday of October until the end of June or early July—the Justices of the US Supreme Court are asked by specific litigants with particular problems, pray tell me, what does the Constitution mean?

"What They Say It Is" 6 Jul 87

3095 The final opinions are directed beyond the litigants to guide lower-court judges, sometimes to instruct the nation, occasionally even to address history.

ib

Titanic Preservation Trust

3096 Delving in the innards of the *Titanic*, two-and-a-half miles down in the Atlantic, is like trespassing with intent to do damage in a graveyard.

Protesting removal of artifacts from lost ocean liner, quoted by John P Eaton *Titanic: Destination Disaster* Norton 87

Robert Traver commentator

3097 For all its lurching and shambling imbecilities, the law—and only the law—is what keeps our society from bursting apart at the seams, from becoming a snarling jungle.

Anatomy of a Murder St Martin's 58

3098 Every jury trial in the land is a small daily miracle of democracy in action.

ib

3099 The very slowness of the law, its massive impersonality, its insistence upon proceeding according to settled and ancient rules—all this tends to cool and bank the fires of passion and violence and replace them with order and reason.

ib

Laurence H Tribe Professor of Constitutional Law, Harvard

3100 All it would take in some instances is one more vote for the extreme views they take to become the law of the land.

On conservative viewpoints of Supreme Court Justices Antonin Scalia and Clarence Thomas *Christian Science Monitor* 26 Jun 95

Scott Turow author

3101 "Torts" more or less means "wrongs" and. . . concern virtually the entire range of misfortune and hurts which human beings can blame on one another.

One L Putnam 77

3102 Torts. . . prove your mother was right.

ib

US Department Of Justice

3103 By annexing Texas, the US certainly did not commit itself to relinquish what has been a fundamental cornerstone. . . that would mean in effect that Texas was not annexed to the US, but that the US was annexed to Texas.

Brief filed with Supreme Court to secure rights to offshore oil *Time* 20 May 54

US Department Of State

3104 Nations are outmanned, outgunned and outspent by narcotics traffickers.

On inability to stop narcotics production and sales *NY Times* 2 Mar 88

Arthur T Vanderbilt Justice, NJ Supreme Court

3105 Life has never been completely charted and as long as change is one of the great facts of life, it never will be; and law, we must always remember, is but one aspect of life.

"A Report on Prelegal Education" *NY University Law Review* 25 Apr 50

Jacques Verges attorney

3106 I am honored to defend this lonely man at this national hanging.

On defense of Nazi war criminal Klaus Barbie *NY Daily News* 17 May 87

Dr Kanu Virani Chief Deputy Medical Examiner, Oakland County MI

3107 If a person takes her or his life entirely by her or himself, it's suicide. If someone actively participated in the procedure, that's homicide, not suicide.

Ruling on death of a multiple sclerosis patient through carbon monoxide and mask brought to her bedside by Dr Jack Kevorkian *NY Times* 6 Jun 92

William Von Raab Commissioner, US Customs Service

3108 Until I'm shown that an individual is not corrupt. . . my assuption is that he is.

On the Mexican government *Newsweek* 26 May 86

James Vorenberg Director, National Crime Commission

3109 Being a defense lawyer is like giving your life to the Boston Red Sox. You always lose.

Quoted by Martin Mayer *The Lawyers* Harper & Row 67

Jane Wallace reporter

3110 Jamail is a blunt, colorful man with a blunt, colorful mouth.

On Houston attorney Joe Jamail *West 57th* CBS TV 7 Nov 87

Lawrence Walsh US government counsel

3111 An independent counsel has no government agency behind him, they're all against him.

To news commentator Ted Koppell *Nightline* ABC TV 20 Jan 94

3112 The president of the United States is different: he cannot be accused of nitpicking and breaking the law.

ib

Byron R White Associate Justice, US Supreme Court

3113 Justice Brennan's proposed ending to this lawsuit is as unsatisfying as the conclusion of a bad mystery novel: we learn on the last page that the victim has been done-in by a suspect heretofore unknown, for reasons previously unrevealed.

On Justice William J Brennan's opinion that held that a black woman did not have a racial harassment claim because she did not make the proper allegation at trial *Washington Post* 24 May 93

Mary Jo White US Attorney

3114 [It was] a virtual supermarket for crack cocaine. . . permeated with violence.

On government seizure of Manhattan's Kenmore Hotel after drug sales, murders, prostitutes, and general breakdown *NY Times* 9 Jun 94

Randall Williams Director, Klanwatch

3115 When you called the law, the people who are supposed to protect you, they're the same people who are out to get you. Well, could life be more terrifying?

On 30th anniversary of the South's "Freedom Summer" *Washington Times* 21 Dec 94

3116 Kluxers show up here and there. . . [but] the back of the organized Klan is broken, and it will never come back.

On dissolution of the Ku Klux Klan *ib*

Charles E Wyzanski Jr Senior Judge, US District Court for Massachusetts

3117 Read in the daily press, studied in the common school, knotted into the rope of enduring history, they may well be the largest single contribution to the philosophy of the American way of life.

On judicial opinions of the Supreme Court *Atlantic* Nov 56

Donald Zoeller Chair, Mudge Rose Guthrie Alexander & Ferdom, NYC

3118 In good years, money papers over all your problems.

On the troubled economics of his 126-year-old Wall Street law firm *NY Times* 1 Oct 95

3119 Down years tell you whether people like each other and trust each other.

On departure of key partners *ib*

Judicial Opinions

Frank X Altimari Judge, US Court of Appeals, New York

3120 Whether intended as so, or not, begging in the subway often amounts to nothing less than assault creating in the passengers the apprehension of imminent danger.

Majority opinion in 2–1 ruling that begging is not a constitutionally protected right *NY Times* 11 May 90

Anon

3121 Not guilty if he returns the cows.

Verdict from New South Wales jury ruling on an allegation of stolen cows *Smithsonian* Mar 95

3122 Not guilty—and he doesn't have to return the cows.

On renewing its opinion in a stance called "pig-headed and mutinous" after rejection by an outraged judge *ib*

Sidney H Asch Judge, NY State Supreme Court, Appellate Division

3123 Where sexual proclivity does not relate to job function, it seems clearly unconstitutional to penalize an individual in one of the most imperative of life's endeavors, the right to earn one's daily bread.

Majority opinion in 3–1 ruling that upheld municipal authority to bar private agencies from discrimination on the basis of sexual orientation 7 May 85

Marianne O Battani Judge, Wayne County Circuit Court, Detroit MI

3124 We really have no definition of *mother* in our law books. *Mother* was believed to have been so basic that no definition was deemed necessary.

Ruling that the biological mother of an infant conceived outside the womb is the "true" mother as opposed to the woman who carries the child to term 14 Mar 86

David L Bazelon Judge, US Court of Appeals, District of Columbia

3125 The majority decision constitutionalizes a distinction between a red leather pouch and a paper bag that is necessarily based at least in some part on economic and class differences and perceptions.

Concurring in part and dissenting in part in 2–1 ruling that recognized luggage but not paper bags as a personal sanctuary 17 Apr 80

3126 In some of our subcultures paper bags are often used to carry intimate personal belongings. And, the sight of some of our less fortunate citizens carrying their belongings in brown paper bags is too familiar to permit such class biases to diminish protection of privacy.

ib

Joseph W Bellacosa Associate Judge, NY State Court of Appeals

3127 It is unwise for the judiciary to transmogrify newspeople into agents of the government to collect evidence.

Minority opinion in 4–3 ruling that journalists' notes or other materials obtained from confidential sources were not covered by state law protecting news organizations from disclosing information gathered for a news article *NY Times* 8 Jul 87

Hugo L Black Associate Justice, US Supreme Court

3128 State help to religion injects political and party prejudices into a holy field.

Dissenting opinion in 6–3 ruling allowing public schools to release students for religious instruction 28 Apr 52

3129 It too often substitutes force for prayer, hate for love, and persecution for persuasion.

ib

3130 Criticism of government finds sanctuary in several portions of the 1st Amendment. It is part of the right of free speech. It embraces freedom of the press.

Dissenting opinion in 5–4 ruling that forbade a person summoned before a congressional committee to refuse to answer the question, "Are you a member of the Communist Party?" 27 Feb 61

3131 Neither [state nor nation] can constitutionally pass laws or impose requirements which aid all religions against non-believers, and neither can aid those religions based on a belief in the existence of God as against those religions founded on different beliefs.

Unanimous decision that states cannot compel officeholders to believe in God 19 Jun 61

3132 In this country it is no part of the business of government to compose official prayers for any group of the American people to recite.

Majority opinion in 8–1 ruling that a prayer written by the NY Board of Regents and read aloud in public schools violates the 1st Amendment's "establishment of religion" clause 25 Jun 62

3133 The right of one charged with crime to counsel may not be deemed fundamental and essential to fair trials in some countries, but it is in ours. . . [but] this noble idea cannot be realized if the poor man charged with crime has to face his accusers without a lawyer to assist him.

Unanimous opinion that held that all states must provide lawyers to poor defendants in felony cases 18 Mar 63

3134 No right is more precious in a free country than that of having a voice in the election of those who make the laws. . . [because] other rights, even the most basic, are illusory if the right to vote is undermined.

Majority opinion in 6–3 ruling that the Constitution requires a state's congressional districts to be substantially equal 17 Feb 64

3135 An unconditional right to say what one pleases about public affairs is what I consider to be the minimum guarantee of the 1st Amendment.

Concurring opinion in 9–0 ruling that a public official cannot recover libel damages for criticism of his official performances unless he proves that the statement was made with deliberate malice 9 Mar 64

3136 I was brought up to believe that Scotch whisky would need a tax preference to survive in competition with Kentucky bourbon.

Dissenting opinion in 6–2 ruling that limited the power of states to tax and restrict the liquor business 1 Jun 64

3137 Sex is a fact of life. . . [and] while it may lead to abuses. . . no words need be spoken. . . for people to know that the subject is one pleasantly interwoven in all human activities and involves the very substance of the creation of life itself.

Dissenting opinion in 5–4 ruling that upheld conviction of publishers of erotic literature and held that "titillating" advertising could be proof of obscenity 21 Mar 66

3138 Our Constitution was not written in the sands to be washed away by each wave of new judges blown in by each successive political wind.

Dissenting opinion in 6–2 ruling that upheld federal law making possession of heroin sufficient evidence of legal importation of drugs 20 Jan 70

3139 Trial judges confronted with disruptive, contumacious, stubbornly defiant defendants must be given sufficient discretion to meet the circumstances of each case.

Unanimous opinion that a disorderly defendant may forfeit the constitutional right to be present in court 31 Mar 70

3140 The argument seems to run. . . that the city's closing of the pools to keep the two races from swimming together violates the 13th Amendment. To reach that result from the 13th Amendment would severely stretch its short simple words and do violence to its history.

Majority opinion in 5–4 ruling that Jackson MS closing of public pools did not constitute racial discrimination 14 Jun 71

3141 Paramount among the responsibilities of a free press is the duty to prevent any part of the government from deceiving the people and sending them off to distant lands to die of foreign fevers and foreign shot and shell.

Concurring opinion in 6–3 ruling that upheld the press's right to publish the smuggled documents known as the Pentagon Papers 30 Jun 71

3142 In my view, far from deserving condemnation for their courageous reporting, *The New York Times*, *The Washington Post* and other newspapers should be commended for serving the purpose that the Founding Fathers saw so clearly.

On newspaper publication of the Pentagon Papers despite the efforts of Nixon's Attorney General to stop them *ib*

3143 In revealing the workings of government that led to the Vietnam War, the newspapers nobly did precisely that which the Founders hoped and trusted they would do.

On exercising freedom of the press *ib*

Harry A Blackmun Associate Justice, US Supreme Court

3144 The States are not free, under the guise of protecting maternal health or potential life, to intimidate women into continuing pregnancies.

Majority opinion in 5–4 *Roe* vs *Wade* ruling that established the constitutional legality of abortion 22 Jan 73

3145 If there is any truth to the old proverb that "one who is his own lawyer has a fool for a client," the Court. . . now bestows a constitutional right on one to make a fool of himself.

Dissenting opinion in 6–3 ruling that allowed a defendant to refuse counsel 30 Jun 75

3146 In order to get beyond racism, we must first take account of race. . . and in order to treat some people equally, we must treat them differently.

Concurring in part and dissenting in part in 5–4 ruling that affirmed constitutionality of college admission programs that gave special advantage to minorities to remedy past discrimination 28 Jun 78

3147 It operates on a fundamentally mistaken premise that high solicitation costs are an accurate measure of fraud. . . [and] creates an unnecessary risk of chilling free speech.

Majority opinion in 5–4 ruling that struck down a Maryland statute regulating how much charities may spend on fund raising 26 Jun 84

3148 The Court really has refused to recognize. . . the fundamental interest all individuals have in controlling the nature of their intimate associations.

Dissenting opinion in 5–4 ruling that upheld the right to prohibit deviant sexual behavior 30 Jun 86

3149 Depriving individuals of the right to choose for themselves how to conduct their intimate relationships poses a far greater threat to the values most deeply rooted in our Nation's history than tolerance of noncomformity could ever do.

ib

3150 The right of an individual to conduct intimate relationships in the intimacy of his or her own home seems to me to be the heart of the Constitution's protection of privacy.

ib

3151 It is precisely because the issue raised by this case touches the heart of what makes individuals what they are that we should be especially sensitive to the rights of those whose choices upset the majority.

ib

3152 [Disapproval of homosexuality cannot justify] invading the houses, hearts and minds of citizens who choose to live their lives differently.

ib

3153 One wonders whether the majority still believes that race discrimination—or, more accurately, race discrimination against non-whites—is a problem in our society, or even remembers that it ever was.

Dissenting opinion in 5–4 ruling that under-representation of minorities can be rebutted by employers who show reasonable justification 5 Jun 89

3154 The plurality opinion is filled with winks, and nods, and knowing glances to those who would do away with *Roe* explicity, but turns a stone face to anyone in search of what the plurality conceives as the scope of a woman's right under the Due Process Clause to terminate a pregnancy free from the coercive and brooding influence of the State.

Minority opinion in 5–4 ruling that gave states the right to impose sharp new restrictions on abortions 3 Jul 89

3155 I fear for the future. . . for the liberty and equality of the millions of women who have lived and come of age in the 16 years since *Roe* was decided. . . for the integrity of, and public esteem for, this Court.

ib

3156 This "it-is-so-because-we-say-so" jurisprudence constitutes nothing other than an attempted exercise of brute force; reason, much less persuasion, has no place.

ib

3157 The viability line reflects the biological facts and truths of fetal development: it marks that threshold moment prior to which a fetus cannnot survive separate from the woman and cannot reasonably and objectively be regarded as a subject of rights or interests distinct from, or paramount to, those of the pregnant woman.

ib

3158 Thus, "not with a bang, but a whimper," the plurality discards a landmark case of the last generation and casts into darkness the hopes and visions of every woman in this country who had come to believe that the Constitution guaranteed her the right to exercise some control over her unique ability to bear children.

ib

3159 The government may acknowledge Christmas as a cultural phenomenon, but under the 1st Amendment it may not observe it as a holy day by suggesting that people praise God for the birth of Jesus.

Majority opinion in 5–4 ruling that a court house display of a nativity scene is unconstitutional 3 Jul 89

3160 The only Christmas the State can acknowledge is one in which references to religion have been held to a minimum.

ib

3161 Unlimited jury discretion. . . in the fixing of punitive damages may invite extreme results that jar one's constitutional sensibilities. . . [but the Court] need not, and indeed we cannot, draw a mathematical bright line between the constitutionally acceptable and the constitutionally unacceptable that would fit every case.

Majority opinion in 7–1 ruling that rejected a constitutional attack on punitive damages, leaving juries with broad discretion over awards for damage 4 Mar 91; also see *Time* 18 Mar 91

3162 Decisions about the welfare of future children must be left to the parents who conceive, bear, support and raise them rather than to the employers who hire those parents.

Unanimous opinion ruling that employers may not exclude women from jobs in which exposure to toxic substances could harm a developing fetus 20 Mar 91

3163 Women as capable of doing their jobs as their male counterparts may not be forced to choose between having a child and having a job.

ib

3164 I cannot remain on this Court forever, and when I do step down, the confirmation process for my successor well may focus on the issue before us today. That, I regret, may be exactly where the choice between the two worlds will be made.

On 5–4 opinion affirming right for abortion with Justice Blackmun concurring in part and dissenting in part 29 Jun 92

3165 The execution of a person who can show that he is innocent comes perilously close to simple murder.

Dissenting opinion in 6–3 ruling that strong, new evidence was not allowable in changing a murder conviction *Christian Science Monitor* 27 Jan 93

3166 We hold that gender, like race, is an unconstitutional proxy for juror competence and impartiality.

Majority opinion in 6–3 ruling that the Constitution's guarantee of equal protection bars exclusion of potential jurors on the basis of their sex 19 Apr 94

3167 Discrimination serves to ratify and perpetuate invidious, archaic and overboard stereotypes about the relative abilities of men and women. . . gross generalizations that would be deemed impermissible if made on the basis of race are somehow permissible when made on the basis of gender.

ib

3168 Tax legislation is not a promise.

Unanimous opinion that Congress did not violate the Constitution when it closed a tax loophole retroactively and collected back taxes from those who had relied on the original provision 13 Jun 94

Robert H Bork Judge, US Court of Appeals, District of Columbia

3169 By depriving the charged person of any defenses [the rulings] mean that sexual dalliance, however voluntarily engaged in, becomes harassment whenever an employee sees fit, after the fact, so to characterize it.

Dissenting opinion in 7–3 ruling that held employers responsible for sexual harassment of one employee by another 14 May 85

Brazilian Supreme Court

3170 Homicide cannot be seen as a normal and legitimate way of reacting to adultery.

Majority opinion in 3–2 ruling that a man cannot win acquittal on the grounds of "legitimate defense of honor" in the fatal knifing of his wife 29 Mar 91

3171 In this kind of crime what is defended is not honor, but vanity, exaggerated, self-importance and the pride of the lord who sees a woman as his personal property.

ib

William J Brennan Jr Associate Justice, US Supreme Court

3172 Sex and obscenity are not synonymous.

Majority opinion in 6–3 ruling that established a new legal standard for obscenity 24 Jun 57

3173 Sex, a great and mysterious motive force in human life, has indisputably been a subject of absorbing interest to mankind through the ages.

ib

3174 In a civilized society, government must always be accountable to the judiciary for a man's imprisonment.

Majority opinion in 6–3 ruling that in some circumstances a state prisoner may challenge his imprisonment by obtaining a federal writ of habeas corpus even if he had not appealed his conviction through the state court system 18 Mar 63

3175 The *Great Writ of Habeas Corpus* is simply a mode of procedure. . . inextricably intertwined with the growth of fundamental rights of personal liberty.

ib

3176 We consider this case against the background of a profound national commitment to the principle that debate on public issues should be uninhibited, robust, and wide-open, and that it may well include vehement, caustic, and sometimes unpleasantly sharp attacks on government and public officials.

Unanimous opinion that an official cannot recover libel damage for criticism of his official performance unless deliberate malice is proven 9 Mar 64

3177 The pall of fear and timidity imposed upon those who would give voice to public criticism is an atmosphere in which the 1st Amendment freedoms cannot survive.

On newspapers facing libel charges *ib*

3178 [Such a rule] dampens the vigor and limits the variety of public debate.

ib

3179 Speech concerning public affairs is more than self-expression; it is the essence of self-government.

Unanimous opinion that New Orleans District Attorney Jim Garrison had not libeled criminal court judges by saying that the withholding of investigative funds indicated the protection of "Canal Street clip joints" 23 Nov 64

3180 We today hold that the Constitution does not forbid the States minor intrusions into an individual's body under stringently limited conditions.

Majority opinion in 5–4 ruling that blood tests of drunken drivers do not constitute self-incriminating evidence 20 Jun 66

3181 If the right of privacy means anything, it is the right of the individual, married or single, to be free from unwarranted governmental intrusion into matters so fundamentally affecting a person as the decision of whether to bear or beget a child.

Majority opinion in 4–1 ruling that protection against conception should not be denied to single persons in the state of Massachusetts 22 Mar 72

3182 Death is an unusually severe and degrading punishment.

Concurring opinion in 5–4 ruling that outlawed States' right to impose capital punishment 29 Jun 72

3183 Our Nation has had a long and unfortunate history of sex discrimination. . . rationalized by an attitude of "romantic paternalism" which, in practical effect, put women, not on a pedestal, but in a cage.

Majority opinion in 8–1 ruling that spouses of servicewomen have the same right to benefits as spouses of servicemen 14 May 73

3184 Indeed, throughout much of the 19th century the position of women in our society was, in many respects, comparable to that of blacks under the pre-Civil War slave codes.

ib

3185 The law has progressed to the point where we should declare that the punishment of death, like punishment on the rack, the screw, and the wheel, is no longer morally tolerable in our inbred society.

Dissenting opinion in 7–2 ruling that upheld the death penalty 2 Jul 76

3186 Death is. . . unusual in its pain, in its finality, and in its enormity, but it serves no penal purpose more effectively than a less severe punishment: therefore the principle inherent in the Clause that prohibits pointless infliction of excessive punishment when less severe punishment can adequately achieve the same purposes invalidates the punishment.

ib

3187 [He is] a legitimate class of one.

Majority opinion in 7–2 ruling that overturned the 1974 law that established government control of Richard M Nixon's presidential papers and tape recordings 27 Jun 77

3188 We cannot. . . let colorblindness become myopia.

Dissenting opinion in 5–4 ruling that prohibited racial quotas in university admission policies 28 Jun 78

3189 It is difficult to understand precisely what the State hopes to achieve by promoting the creation and perpetuation of a subclass of illiterates. . . adding to the problems and costs of unemployment, welfare and crime.

Majority opinion in 5–4 ruling that young illegal aliens have a constitutional right to public schooling 15 Jun 82

3190 Whatever savings might be achieved by denying these children an education, they are wholly insubstanial in light of the costs involved to these children, the State and the Nation.

ib

3191 To suggest, as the Court does, that such a symbol is merely "traditional" and therefore no different from Santa's house or reindeer is not only offensive to those for whom the creche has profound significance, but insulting to those who insist for religious or personal reasons that the story of Christ is in no sense a part of "history" nor an unavoidable element of our national "heritage."

Minority opinion in 5–4 ruling that nativity scenes may be part of municipal observances 5 Mar 84

3192 Use of a mentally ill person's involuntary confession is antithetical to the notion of fundamental fairness.

Dissenting opinion in 7–2 ruling that confessions from the mentally ill may be used against them even if those confessions are not the product of free will 10 Dec 86

3193 Society's accumulated myths and fears about disability and disease are as handicapping as are the physical limitations that flow from actual impairment.

Majority opinion in 7–2 ruling that people with contagious diseases are covered by law that prohibts discrimination against the handicapped in federally aided programs 3 Mar 87

3194 When prisoners emerge from the shadows to press a constitutional claim. . . they speak the language of the charter upon which all of us rely to hold official power accountable.

Dissenting opinion in 5–4 ruling that religious rights of some prisoners could not be accomodated without creating bona fide security problems 9 Jun 87

3195 The freedom of individuals verbally to oppose or challenge police action without thereby risking arrest is one of the principal characteristics by which we distinguish a free nation from a police state.

Majority opinion in 8–1 ruling that the 1st Amendment protects the rights of individuals to verbally challenge police if conduct does not amount to "physical obstruction" 15 Jun 87

3196 [Educators have an] undeniable, and undeniably vital, mandate to inculcate moral and political values [but] not a general warrant to act as thought police.

Minority opinion in 5–3 ruling that a student newspaper is part of a high school's curriculum and subject to censorship 13 Jan 88

3197 Deities may be able to visit the sins of the father on the son but I cannot agree that courts should be permitted to visit the sins of the lawyer on the innocent client.

Dissenting opinion in 5–3 ruling that criminal trial judges may bar defense witnesses from testifying in order to punish attorneys for failing to disclose the witnesses' identities soon enough 25 Jan 88

3198 Today's ruling sacrifices a religion at least as old as the Nation itself, along with the spiritual well-being of its approximately 5,000 adherents, so that the Forest Service can build a six-mile segment of road that two lower courts found had only the most marginal and speculative utility.

Minority opinion in 5–3 ruling that upheld government plan to develop part of a national forest in California that was sacred to three Indian tribes 19 Apr 88

3199 [It is] cruelly surreal.

ib

3200 Scrutiny of another's trash is contrary to commonly accepted actions of civilized behavior.

Minority opinion in 6–2 ruling that police may freely search garbage bags left for collection 16 May 88

3201 A search of trash, like a search of the bedroom, can relate intimate details about sexual practices, health, and personal hygiene.

ib

3202 I suspect. . . that members of our society will be shocked to learn that the Court, the ultimate guarantor of liberty, deems unreasonable our expectation that the aspects of our private lives that are concealed safely in a trash bag will not become public.

ib

3203 What the Court declines to snatch away with one hand, it takes with the other.

Minority opinion in 5–4 ruling refusing to overthrow a major civil rights precedent that gave minorities the right to use a Reconstruction-era law to sue for private acts of racial discrimination 15 Jun 89

3204 We can image. . . no better way to counter a flag-burner's message than by saluting the flag that burns.

Majority opinion in 5–4 ruling regarded as a 1st Amendment landmark that burning the US flag could not be legally prohibited 21 Jun 89

3205 We do not consecrate the flag by punishing its desecration, for in doing so we dilute the freedom that this cherished emblem represents.

ib

Warren E Burger Chief Justice, US Supreme Court

3206 The hazards of churches supporting government are hardly less in their potential than the hazards of government supporting churches.

Majority opinion in 8–1 ruling that allowed church properties to be tax exempt 4 May 70

3207 It is indeed an old business that it has taken this Court nearly two centuries to "discover" a constitutional mandate to have counsel at a preliminary hearing.

Dissenting opinion in 6–2 ruling that declared right of the accused to court-appointed counsel at pretrial hearings 22 Jun 70

3208 What is required by Congress is the removal of artificial, arbitrary, and unnecessary barriers to employment when the barriers operate invidiously to discriminate on the basis of racial or other impermissible classification.

Majority opinion in 8–0 ruling that upheld the 1964 Civil Rights Act in prohibiting employers from requiring a high school diploma or intelligence test score as a condition of employment if neither test was related to job skills and if both tended to disqualify more black than white applicants 8 Mar 71

3209 It is hardly believable that a newspaper long regarded as a great institution in American life would fail to perform one of the basic and simple duties of every citizen with respect to the discovery or possession of stolen property or secret government documents.

Dissenting opinion in 6–3 ruling that freedom of the press would not have been violated if the *NY Times* had been prohibited from printing the leaked Pentagon Papers concerning the Vietnam War 30 Jun 71

3210 A way of life that is odd or even erratic but interferes with no rights or interests of others is not to be condemned because it is different.

Majority opinion in 6–1 ruling that freed members of religious sects from compulsatory school attendance 15 May 72

3211 It is neither realistic nor constitutionally sound to read the 1st Amendment as requiring that the people of Maine or Mississippi accept public depiction of conduct found tolerable in Las Vegas or New York City.

Majority opinion in 5–4 ruling that constituted new guidelines on obscenity to enable states to ban books, magazines, plays and motion pictures offensive to local standards 21 Jun 72

3212 The "sexual revolution" of recent years may have had useful by-products in striking layers of prudery from a subject long irrationally kept from needed ventilation. But it does not follow that no regulation of patently offensive "hard-core" material is needed or permissible; civilized people do not allow unregulated access to heroin because it is a derivative of medicinal morphine.

ib

3213 Editing is what editors are for and editing is selection and choice of material.

Majority opinion in 7–2 ruling that allowed radio and television stations to refuse to sell time for political or controversial advertisements 29 May 73

3214 Calculated risks of abuse are taken in order to preserve higher values.

ib

3215 Neither the doctrine of separation of powers, nor the need for confidentiality of high-level communications. . . can sustain an absolute, unqualified presidential privilege of immunity from judicial process under all circumstances.

Unanimous opinion in *US* v. *Nixon* holding that the needs of the judicial process may outweigh presidential privilege in regard to Watergate tapes 24 Jul 74

3216 Free speech carries with it some freedom to listen.

Majority opinion in 7–1 ruling that prohibited the closing of courtrooms to the press 2 Jul 80

3217 There can be no doubt that the practice of opening legislative sessions with prayer has become part of the fabric of our society.

Majority opinion in 6–3 ruling that both Congress and state legislatures may pay a chaplain to open sessions with prayer 5 Jul 83

3218 The Constitution. . . affirmatively mandates accommodation, not merely tolerance, of all religions, and forbids hostility toward any.

Majority opinion in 5–4 ruling that a city may include a nativity scene as part of a Christmas display 5 Mar 84

3219 To forbid the use of this one passive symbol, the creche, at the very time people are taking note of the season. . . would be a stilted overreaction contrary to our history and to our holdings.

ib

3220 Respondent's expectation that his garden was protected from such observation is unreasonable and is not an expectation that society is prepared to honor.

Majority opinion in 5–4 ruling that upheld aerial surveillance without a warrant of a fenced backyard where police suspected marijuana was growing 19 May 86

3221 To hold that the act of homosexual sodomy is somehow protected as a fundamental right would be to cast aside millennia of moral teaching.

Concurring opinion in 5–4 ruling that upheld the right to prohibit deviant sexual behavior 30 Jun 86

3222 To permit an officer controlled by Congress to execute the laws would be, in essence, to permit a congressional veto.

Majority opinion in 7–2 ruling striking down the central provision of a sweeping measure that Congress had devised to curb federal deficits 7 Jul 86

3223 Congress, in effect, has retained control over the execution of the Act and has intruded into the executive function. The Constitution does not permit such intrusion.

ib

3224 Once Congress makes its choice in enacting legislation, its participation ends.

ib

Canadian Supreme Court

3225 Kneeling to receive Communion is not a criminal offense.

Ruling against arrest of Roman Catholics in Nova Scotia for "disturbing the solemnity of a church service" by refusing to follow a new directive to stand while receiving the sacrament, news summaries 30 Sep 85

Tom C Clark Associate Justice, US Supreme Court

3226 The ignoble shortcut to conviction. . . tends to destroy the entire system of constitutional restraint on which the liberties of the people rest.

Majority opinion in 6–3 ruling reversing a 1949 landmark decison and holding that the Constitution forbids the use of illegally seized evidence in state criminal trials 19 Jun 61

3227 Having once recognized that the right to privacy embodied in the 4th Amendment is enforceable . . . we can no longer permit that right to remain an empty promise.

ib

3228 Our decision. . . gives to the individual no more than that which the Constitution guarantees him, to the police officer no less than that to which honest law enforcement be entitled, and, to the courts, that judicial integrity so necessary in the true administration of justice.

ib

3229 In the relationship between man and religion, the State is firmly committed to a position of neutrality.

Majority opinion in 8–1 ruling that religious exercises in public schools are unconstitutional 17 Jun 63

3230 The breach of neutrality that is today a trickling stream may all too soon become a raging torrent.

ib

3231 To so interpret the language of the Act is to extract more sunbeams from cucumbers than did Gulliver's mad scientist.

Dissenting opinion in 7–2 ruling that upheld the constitutionality of loyalty oaths 1 Jun 64

3232 To conjure up such ridiculous questions, the answers to which we all know or should know are in the negative, is to build up a whimsical and farcical straw man which is not only grim but Grimm.

ib

3233 A defendant. . . is entitled to his day in court, not in a stadium or a city or nationwide arena.

Majority opinion in 5–4 ruling that the principles of a fair trial are violated when telecasting is allowed 7 Jun 65

3234 Trial by television is. . . foreign to our system.

ib

Harold G Clarke Chief Justice, Georgia Supreme Court

3235 A nameless, faceless figure strikes terror in the human heart. But, remove the mask, and the nightmarish form is reduced to its true dimensions.

Majority opinion in 6–1 ruling that banned Ku Klux Klan hoods and masks *NY Times* 6 Dec 90

3236 The peace of society is not endangered by the profane or lewd word which is not directed at a particular audience.

Majority opinion holding that a state law banning bumper stickers with lewd or offensive messages is wrongfully restrictive of self-expression 25 Feb 91

Colorado Supreme Court

3237 Fundamental rights may not be submitted to a vote.

Majority opinion by Judge Robert H Jackson in 5–1 ruling that validated ordinances protecting homosexuals from discrimination in jobs and housing *NY Times* 20 Jul 93

Lynn D Compton Judge, California Court of Appeal, 2nd District

3238 Whatever choice Elizabeth Bouvia may ultimately make, I can only hope that her courage, persistence and example will cause our society to deal realistically with the plight of those unfortunate individuals to whom death beckons as a welcome respite from suffering.

Unanimous opinion that the right to refuse medical treatment is basic and fundamental in the case of a quadriplegic celebral palsy victim who requested she not be force-fed 16 Apr 86

Lawrence H Cooke Judge, NY State Court of Appeals

3239 Ordinarily, death will be determined according to the traditional criteria of irreversible cardiorespiratory repose. When, however, the respiratory and circulatory functions are maintained by mechanical means, their significance, as signs of life, is at best ambiguous.

Unanimous opinion that a person may be deemed legally dead when the brain has ceased to function, even if heartbeat and breathing are being maintained artificially 30 Oct 84

Richard L Curry Judge, Cook County Circuit Court, Chicago

3240 The scheme which has major-league baseball trashing a residential community and tinkering with the quality-of-life aspirations of countless households so that television royalties might more easily flow into the coffers of 25 distant sports moguls is not consonant with present-day concepts of right and justice.

Supporting citizens' protest against night baseball at Chicago's Wrigley Field 25 Mar 85

Martha Craig Daughtrey Justice, Tennessee Supreme Court

3241 Preembryos are not, strictly speaking, either "persons" or "property," but occupy an interim category that entitles them to special respect because of their potential for human life.

Unanimous opinion holding that a divorced man could prevent his former wife from using or donating frozen embryos and that he could not be compelled to become a father against his wishes *NY Times* 2 Jun 92

William O Douglas Associate Justice, US Supreme Court

3242 Free speech is not to be regulated like diseased cattle and impure butter.

Dissenting opinion in 5–4 ruling that banned sale of obscene books 24 Jun 57

3243 As I read the Constitution, one of its essential purposes was to take government off the backs of people and keep it off.

Dissenting opinion in 7–2 ruling that the constitutionality of registering as a Communist-front organization can be challenged in court 11 Dec 67

3244 If discrimination based on race is constitutionally permissible when those who hold the reins can come up with "compelling reasons" to justify it, then constitutional guarantees acquire an accordionlike quality.

Dissenting opinion in 5–4 ruling refusing to decide whether professional schools can give preference to admission of minority students at the expense of white applicants; Douglas held that the admission practices at issue were constitutional 23 Apr 74

Harry T Edwards Judge, US Court of Appeals, DC Circuit

3245 History, custom, and usage indicate unequivocally [that prior to 1974] Presidents exercised complete dominion and control over their Presidential papers.

Unanimous decision that Richard M Nixon was to be compensated for government seizure of his historically valuable White House papers and tapes, including the Watergate recordings *NY Times* 18 Nov 92

Federal Constitutional Court Of Germany

3246 Citizens of the former East Germany, who... spied for the secret services of their state exclusively from the territory of East Germany against West Germany, may no longer be prosecuted after reunification.

Majority opinion in 5–3 ruling that former East German spy masters cannot be prosecuted for conducting Cold War espionage against the West *NY Times* 24 May 95

Felix Frankfurter Associate Justice, US Supreme Court

3247 It would be a stratification... of constitutional history... to hold that in order to convict a man the police cannot extract by force what is in his mind, but can extract what is in his stomach.

Majority opinion in 8–0 ruling that evidence obtained by pumping a drug addict's stomach may not be used to convict him 2 Jan 52

3248 This is a horse soon curried.

Majority opinion in 7–2 ruling that drivers arrested in states other than their own do not waive their federal rights 9 Nov 53

John Marshal Harlan Associate Justice, US Supreme Court

3249 [Due process and liberty] stands. . . on its own bottom.

Concurring opinion in 7–2 ruling that prohibiting medical counsel on abortion infringed on married couples' constitutionally protected right to privacy 7 Jun 65

Robert H Jackson Associate Justice, US Supreme Court

3250 The petitioner's problem is to avoid Scylla without being drawn into Charybdis.

Majority opinion in 5–4 ruling that prohibited federal jurisdiction over utility rates 7 May 51

3251 We are not final because we are infallible, but we are infallible only because we are final.

Concurring opinion in 6–3 ruling that upheld the Supreme Court as the bench of last appeal 9 Feb 53

3252 He who must search a haystack for a needle is likely to end up with the attitude that the needle is not worth the search.

ib

3253 The validity of a doctrine does not depend on whose ox it gores.

Dissenting opinion in 5–3 ruling that upheld state laws setting statute of limitations on cases of wrongful death 18 May 53

Irving S Kaufman US Court of Appeals, 2nd Circuit

3254 We doubt that even so eminent a composer as plaintiff Irving Berlin should be permitted to claim a property interest in iambic pentameter.

Ruling that *Mad* magazine was not guilty of plagiarism in parody of Irving Berlin's music *NY Times* 24 Mar 64

Anthony M Kennedy Associate Justice, US Supreme Court

3255 Federalism was our nation's own discovery.

Concurring opinion in 5–4 ruling that despite advantages of limiting congressional terms, the change can only be made by constitutional amendment 22 May 95

Jackson L Kiser Judge, US District Court, Roanoke VA

3256 If VMI marches to the beat of a drum, then, Mary Baldwin marches to the melody of a fife, and when the march is over, both will have arrived at the same destination.

Ruling on equality of the dual education programs at Virginia Military Institute and a neighboring women's college, established by the latter as an alternative to admitting women to VMI *NY Times* 2 May 94

Lord Lane of St Ippollitts [Geoffrey Dawson] Lord Chief Justice

3257 A rapist remains a rapist subject to the criminal law, irrespective of his relationship with his victim.

Ruling that men can be found guilty of raping their wives *London Times* 24 Oct 91

Thurgood Marshall Associate Justice, US Supreme Court

3258 If the 1st Amendment means anything, it means that a State has no business telling a man, sitting alone in his own house, what books he may read or what films he may watch.

Unanimous opinion that the 1st Amendment guarantees the right to possess material that might be regarded as obscene in public 7 Apr 69

3259 Power, not reason, is the new currency of this court's decision making. . . [and] cast aside today are those condemned to face society's ultimate penalty.

Dissenting opinion in 6–3 ruling, reversing an opinion handed down in 1987, that held that prosecutors in death-penalty cases could introduce evidence about a victim's character and suffering caused by the crime 27 Jun 91

Sandra Day O'Connor Associate Justice, US Supreme Court

3260 The court today surveys the battle scene of federalism and sounds a retreat. . . but will in time again assume its constitutional responsibility.

Dissenting opinion in 5–4 ruling that removed virtually all federally-based constitutional limitations on Congressional power 19 Feb 85

3261 Multi-million dollar losses are inflicted on a whim.

Dissenting opinion in 7–1 ruling in which her fellow justices held that a million-dollar punitive-damage settlement did not violate the 14th Amendment's due-process clause 4 Mar 91, also see *Time* 18 Mar 91

Lewis F Powell Jr Associate Justice, US Supreme Court

3262 Because of the singular importance of the President's duties, diversion of his energies by concern with private lawsuits would raise unique risks to the effective functioning of government.

Majority opinion of 5–4 ruling that gave President Nixon absolute immunity from damage suits growing out of Watergate 24 Jun 82

William H Rehnquist Chief Justice, US Supreme Court

3263 A father's interest in having a child—perhaps his only child—may be unmatched by any other interest in his life.

Opinion concurring in part and dissenting in part in 6–3 ruling that prohibited states from requiring women to obtain their husbands' consent for abortion 1 Jul 76

3264 Pregnancy is of course confined to women, but it is in other ways significantly different from the typical covered disease or disability.

Majority opinion in 6–3 ruling that allowed private employees to refuse to compensate women for absences due to pregnancy 7 Dec 76

3265 This result. . . will daily stand as a veritable sword of Damocles over every succeeding president and his advisers.

Dissenting opinion in 7–2 ruling that upheld congressional seizure of President Nixon's presidential papers 28 Jun 77

3266 The Constitution requires that Congress treat similarly situated persons similiarly, not that it engage in gestures of superficial equality.

Majority opinion in 6–3 ruling that upheld military draft for males only 25 Jun 81

3267 [The majority has created] a scenario in which the government appears as the Big Bad Wolf and Pacifica as Little Red Riding Hood. A more appropriate analogy [would be] Faust and Mephistopheles.

Dissenting opinion in 5–4 ruling that lifted ban on editorializing by public broadcasting's Pacifica Foundation 3 Jul 84

3268 Allowing the presentation of views while forbidding the expenditure of more than $1,000 to present them is much like allowing a speaker in a public hall to express his views while denying him the use of an amplifying system.

Majority opinion in 7–2 ruling that Congress cannot limit independent spending by political action committees in presidential campaigns 18 Mar 85

3269 The considered professional judgment of the Air Force is that the traditional outfitting of personnel in standardized uniforms encourages the subordination of personal preferences and identities in favor of the overall group mission.

Majority opinion in 5–4 ruling that allowed the military to prohibit an Orthodox Jewish officer from wearing a yarmulke indoors while in uniform 25 Mar 86

3270 [Jury selection] is best based upon seat-of-the-pants instincts, which are undoubtedly crudely stereotypical and may in many cases be hopelessly mistaken.

Dissenting opinion in 7–2 ruling that increased the difficulty of excluding African Americans from juries that try African-American defendants 30 Apr 86

3271 Lincoln's tall, gangling posture, Teddy Roosevelt's glasses and teeth, and Franklin D Roosevelt's jutting jaw and cigarette holder have been memorialized by political cartoons. . . our political discourse would have been considerably poorer without them.

Unanimous ruling that overturned a $200,000 award to the Reverend Jerry Falwell for "emotional distress" over a magazine that portrayed him as an incestuous drunk; the Court broadly affirmed and extended the protection of criticism of public figures as free speech even if the criticism is "outrageous" and offensive 24 Feb 88

3272 Nothing in the Constitution requires States to enter or remain in the abortion business or entitles private physicians and their patients access to public facilities for the performance of abortions.

Majority opinion in 5–4 ruling that gave states the right to impose sharp new restrictions on abortion 3 Jul 89

3273 To the victor belong only those spoils that may be constitutionally obtained.

Minority opinion in 5–4 ruling that the Constitution bars most patronage-based hiring and promotion decisions 21 Jun 90

3274 The admission of an involuntary confession is a "trial error," similar in both degree and kind to the erroneous admission of other types of evidence.

Minority opinion in 5–4 ruling that what was once taboo will henceforth be merely a technicality 26 Mar 91

3275 Criminal conduct may be more heavily punished if the victim is selected because of his race or other protected status than if no such motive obtained.

Unanimous opinion upholding Wisconsin law that metes out long sentences for hate crimes 11 Jun 93

3276 The 1st Amendment does not demand that patients at a medical facility undertake Herculean efforts to escape the cacophony of political protests.

Majority opinion in 6–3 ruling limiting protests at abortion clinics 30 Jun 94

3277 Prisoners do not shed all constitutional rights at the gate. . . [but] discipline by prison officials in response to a wide range of misconduct falls within the expected parameters of the sentence imposed by a court of law.

Majority opinion in 5–4 ruling repudiating recent prisoners'-rights cases and making it substantially more difficult for prisoners to bring constitutional lawsuits challenging prison management 19 Jun 95

Charles R Richey Judge, US District Court, District of Columbia

3278 The court must admit that it is not comfortable with racially based distinctions. [But] "no decision of [the Supreme] Court has ever adopted the proposition that the Constitution must be colorblind."

Rejecting Justice Depepartment's argument that a 1984 Supreme Court decision "precludes the use of any race-conscious affirmative action plan" 1 Apr 85

Angelo P Roncallo Justice, NY State Supreme Court

3279 It matters little whether the ovum/sperm union takes place in the private darkness of a fallopian tube or the public glare of a petri dish.

Ruling that the woman who provides embryos has the sole right to determine their fate regardless of whether she has become divorced from the man who fertilized them *NY Times* 20 Jan 95

3280 To deny a husband rights while an embryo develops in the womb and grant a right to destroy while it is in a hospital freezer is to favor situs over substance.

Rejecting a former husband's wishes that the embryos be used for medical research *ib*

3281 Equating zygotes with washing machines and jewelry for purposes of a marital distribution borders on the absurd.

Rejecting arguments that the embryos were little more than marital property *ib*

Israel Rubin Associate Justice, NY Supreme Court, Appellate Division

3282 Between true yachtsmen, victory is pursued on the water and not in the courtroom.

Concurring opinion in 4–1 ruling that San Diego Yacht Club could keep the American Cup that it won in 1988 but lost after a legal challenge *NY Times* 20 Sep 89

H Lee Sarokin Judge, US District Court, Newark NJ

3283 If we wish to shield our eyes and noses from the homeless, we should revoke their condition, not their library cards.

Ruling that public libraries cannot bar the homeless *NY Times* 23 May 91

David B Saxe Acting Justice, NY State Supreme Court

3284 The context of music cannot be separated from the number of musicians and instruments needed to create a work of art.

Ruling that a NYC law that sets a limit of three musicians on stage at a time is unconstitutional because it abridges the 1st Amendment right of free expression *NY Times* 29 Jan 88

Antonin Scalia Associate Justice, US Supreme Court

3285 Frequently an issue of this sort will come before the court clad, so to speak, in sheep's clothing. . . but this wolf comes as a wolf.

Minority opinion In 7–1 ruling upholding federal law that provides for independent prosecutors to investigate suspected crimes by high-ranking officials 29 Jun 88

3286 The context of this statute is acrid with the smell of threatened impeachment.

ib

3287 This is somewhat like referring to shackles as an effective means of locomotion.

On an attorney general's power to remove an independent counsel for "good cause" *ib*

3288 We can now look forward to at least another Term with carts full of mail. . . and streets full of demonstrators, urging us—their unelected and life-tenured judges who have been awarded those extraordinary, undemocratic characteristics precisely in order that we might follow the law despite the popular will—to follow the popular will.

Concurring opinion in 5–4 ruling that gave states the right to impose sharp new restrictions on abortion 3 Jul 89

3289 It thus appears that the mansion of constitutionalized abortion law. . . must be disassembled doorjamb by doorjamb and never entirely brought down, no matter how wrong it may be.

ib

3290 Dying is personal. And it is profound. For many, the thought of an ignoble end, steeped in decay, is abhorrent. A quiet, proud death, bodily integrity intact, is a matter of extreme consequence.

Concurring opinion in 5–4 ruling that a person whose wishes are clearly known has a right to a discontinuance of life-sustaining treatment 25 Jun 90

3291 The purpose of Indiana's nudity law would be violated, I think, if 60,000 fully consenting adults crowded into the Hoosierdome to display their genitals to one another even if there were not an offended innocent in the crowd.

Concurring opinion in 5–4 ruling that enforcement of a public indecency statute to require that dancers in adult entertainment establishments wear pasties and a G-string did not violate the 1st Amendment 21 Jul 91

3292 Not only must mercy be allowed, but now only the merciful may be permitted to sit in judgment.

Dissenting opinion in 6–3 ruling that defendants have a constitutional right to have prospective jurors questioned on whether they would automatically vote to impose the death penalty if they decided the defendant was guilty 15 Jun 92

3293 Our belief is that burning a cross in someone's front yard is reprehensible. But [the city of] St Paul [MN] has sufficient means at its disposal to prevent such behavior without adding the 1st Amendment to the fire.

Majority opinion in 5–4 ruling that legislatures may not single out racial, religious or sexual insults for prosecution as "hate speech" 22 Jun 92

3294 How upsetting it is, that so many of our citizens. . . think that we justices should properly take into account their views, as though we were engaged not in ascertaining an objective law but in determining some kind of social consensus.

Concurring opinion in 5–4 ruling upholding the right to abortion 29 Jun 92

3295 Like some ghoul in a late-night horror movie that repeatedly sits up in its grave and shuffles abroad, after being repeatedly killed and buried, *Lemon* stalks our establishment clause jurisprudence once again, frightening the little children and school attorneys.

Concurring opinion with unanimous ruling that a public school district may not prevent a church group from using its classrooms after school hours despite 1971 *Lemon* v. *Kurtzman* ruling that honed more closely to the constitutional decree that government "shall make no law respecting an establishnment of religion" 7 Jun 93

3296 In the eyes of government, we are just one race here. It is American.

Concurring opinion in 5–4 ruling that federal programs that classify people by race, even for an ostensibly benign purpose such as expanding opportunities for minorities, are presumably unconstitutional, a significant statement against affirmative action 12 Jun 95

3297 Religious speech, far from being a 1st Amendment orphan, is as fully protected. . . as secular private expression.

Majority opinion in 7–2 ruling that the Ku Klux Klan had a free-speech right to erect a cross in a state-owned park in Columbus, Ohio, that operated as a public forum, open to varieties of private expression 29 Jun 95

3298 A free-speech clause without religion would be *Hamlet* without the prince.

ib

Harvey R Sorkow Judge, NJ Superior Court

3299 To make a new concept fit into an old statute makes tortured law with tortured results.

Ruling in the Baby M case that a surrogacy agreement was a valid consent and did not violate prior laws governing adoption, custody and the cessation of prenatal rights 31 Mar 87

David H Souter Associate Justice, US Supreme Court

3300 [It] is a simple scrivener's error.

Unanimous ruling that the court's duty was to "repunctuate" a 1916 statute that appeared to forbid small national banks to sell insurance to customers nationwide 7 Jun 93

3301 [The humor of parody] necessarily springs from recognizable allusion to its object through distorted imitation. Its art lies in the tension between a known original and its parodic twin.

Unanimous ruling that the rap group 2 Live Crew had infringed the copyright on Roy Orbison's rock classic "Oh, Pretty Woman" by recording its own rap version 5 Mar 94

John Paul Stevens Associate Justice, US Supreme Court

3302 Just as a single word is the skin of a living thought, so is a contract evidence of a vital, ongoing relationship between human beings.

Minority opinion in 5–4 ruling that upheld a major civil precedent that gave minorities the right to use a Reconstruction-era law to sue for private acts of racial discrimination 15 Jun 89

3303 The creation of a federal right to post bulletin boards and graffiti on the Washington Monument might enlarge the market for free expression, but at a cost I would not pay.

Dissenting opinion in 5–4 ruling that no laws could prohibit political protesters from burning the American flag 21 Jun 89

3304 Term limits. . . unquestionably restrict the ability of voters to vote for whom they wish. . . [but] may provide for the infusion of fresh ideas and new perspectives, and may decrease the likelihood that representatives will lose touch with their constituents.

Majority opinion in 5–4 ruling that despite advantages of limiting terms, the change can only be made by constitutional amendment 22 May 95

3305 Allowing individual States to craft their own qualifications. . . would thus erode the structure envisioned by the Framers. . . designed, in the words of the Preamble of our Constitution, to form a "more perfect Union."

ib

Potter Stewart Associate Justice, US Supreme Court

3306 I shall not today attempt further to define the kinds of material. . . but I know it when I see it.

Concurring opinion in 6–3 ruling that overturned ban on pornographic films 22 Jun 64

3307 This is an uncommonly silly law.

Dissenting opinion in 7–2 ruling stemming from the challenge of an 1879 Connecticut statute that prohibited the use of any drug, article, or instrument to prevent conception 7 Jun 65

A Wallace Tashima Federal Judge, Central District of California, Los Angeles

3308 The right of artists to challenge conventional wisdom and values is a cornerstone of artistic and academic freedom, no less than the rights of scientists funded by the National Institutes of Health.

Rejecting a law requiring the National Endowment for the Arts to "take into consideration general standards of decency" *NY Times* 10 Jun 92

Clarence Thomas Associate Justice, US Supreme Court

3309 Where the Constitution is silent, it raises no bar to action by the State or the people.

Minority opinion in 5–4 ruling that congressional terms may only be limited by constitutional amendment 22 May 95

3310 Government-sponsored racial discrimination based on benign prejudice is just as noxious as discrimination inspired by malicious prejudice. In each instance, it is racial discrimination, plain and simple.

Concurring opinion in 5–4 ruling that federal programs that classify people by race are presumably unconstitutional, a significant move against affirmative action 12 Jun 95

Vito J Titone Judge, NY State Court of Appeals

3311 In the context of eviction, a more realistic, and certainly equally valid, view of a family includes two adult lifetime partners whose relationship is long-term and characterized by an emotional and financial commitment and interdependence.

Majority opinion in 4–2 ruling that a gay couple who had lived together for a decade could be considered a family under New York City rent-control regulations *NY Times* 7 Jul 89

Earl Warren Chief Justice, Us Supreme Court

3312 The opportunity of an education. . . is a right which must be made available to all on equal terms.

Unanimous opinion that declared segregated schools unconstitutional 17 May 54

3313 The courts will require that defendants make a prompt and reasonable start. . . to admit to public schools on a racially non-discriminating basis with all deliberate speed.

Additional ruling in *Brown* v. *Board of Education* 17 May 54

3314 The mere summonsing of a witness and compelling him to testify, against his will, about his beliefs, expressions or associations is a measure of governmental interference.

Majority opinion in 6–1 ruling that imposed new judicial curbs on the investigative powers and procedures of congressional committees when legislative purposes conflict with individual, guaranteed 1st Amendment rights 17 Jun 57

3315 The freedom to marry has long been recognized as one of the vital personal rights essential to the orderly pursuit of happiness by free men.

Unanimous opinion that struck down interpretation of Virginia law against interracial marriage 12 Jun 67

Byron R White Associate Justice, US Supreme Court

3316 The confidential information was generated from the business and the business had a right to decide how to use it prior to disclosing it to the public.

Deadlock opinion in 4–4 ruling that a *Wall Street Journal* reporter and his associates purchased stocks and then in subsequent columns illegally increased their value 16 Nov 87

3317 The *Journal* has been deprived of its right to exclusive use of the information, for exclusivity is an important aspect of confidential business information and most private property.

ib

3318 A school must be able to take into account the emotional maturity of the intended audience in determining whether to disseminate student speech on potentially sensitive topics.

Majority opinion in 5–3 ruling that public school officials have broad power to censor school newspapers, plays and other "school-sponsored expressive activities" *NY Times* 13 Jan 88

3319 It is common knowledge that plastic garbage bags left on or at the side of a public street are readily accesible to animals, children, scavengers, snoops and other members of the public.

Majority opinion in 6–2 ruling that police may freely search garbage bags and other refuse containers left outside for collection l6 May 88

3320 We find no evidence that Congress intended to modify the nostrum to read, "crime does not pay, except for attorney's fees."

Majority opinion in 5–4 ruling that Government can freeze assets of many criminal defendants before trial without regard to whether the person will have enough money left to hire a defense lawyer 22 Jun 89

3321 Using a defendant's coerced confession against him is a denial of due process of law regardless of the other evidence in the record aside from the confession.

Minority opinion in a 5–4 ruling that introduction of an involuntary confession is no longer taboo but merely a technicality 26 Mar 91

3322 Today, a majority of the Court, without any justification. . . dislodges one of the fundamental tenets of our criminal justice system.

ib

3323 Ours is an accusatorial and not an inquisitorial system.

ib

3324 We would think that a prison inmate also could successfully complain about demonstrably unsafe drinking water without waiting for an attack of dysentery.

Majority opinion in 7–2 ruling that a prisoner does not have to become ill before bringing suit against sharing a cell with a heavy smoker—a decision that offered a notably generous interpretation of the 8th Amendment's prohibition against cruel and unusual punishment 18 Jun 93

Robert N Wilentz Chief Justice, NJ Supreme Court

3325 This is the sale of a child, or at the very least, the sale of a mother's right to her child, the only mitigating factor being that one of the purchasers is the father.

Unanimous opinion in 7–0 ruling that held that payment to Mary Beth Whitehead as a surrogate mother by William and Elizabeth Stern was illegal *NY Times* 4 Feb 88

3326 Criminals, convicted and punished, have paid their debt to society and are not to be punished further.

Majority opinion in 6–1 ruling that upheld that alerting communities to the presence of sex offenders and requiring them to register with police is the only exception to the guarantee of privacy for those who have served prison sentences; called "Meagan's Law" in rememberance of the murder of a New Jersey girl, Maureen Meagan, it was at odds with a Federal Judge Nicholas H Politan who had ruled in February 1995 that disclosure of the whereabouts of sex offenders was unconstitutional 26 Jul 95

Susan Webber Wright Judge, Federal District Court, Eastern District of Arkansas

3327 Our form of government. . . asserts as did the English in the Magna Carta and the Petition of Right, that even the sovereign is subject to God and the law.

Compromise decision issued in Little Rock AR holding that Paula C Jones' lawsuit alledging improper sexual advances by President Clinton would consitute a significant burden for the chief executive and should not go to trial until he leaves office *NY Times* 29 Dec 94

Criminology

Siddig Ibrahim Siddig Ali Islamic terrorist

3328 The water will be going everywhere—everything will be broken into smithereens, everything. The World Trade Center, compared with this, will be like a dwarf.

On secretly recorded plans to blow up Hudson River tunnels to intimidate US on its Middle East policies *NY Times* 18 Jun 95

Henry Allen essayist

3329 His villainy swells like a great carbuncular growth.

On books and films on FBI Director J Edgar Hoover *Washington Post* 23 Mar 93

Judy Amar commentator

3330 Crime-watch is just what they say it is—they watch you commit the crime and if you need help carrying things, they help you.

On "casual burglary" *20/20* ABC TV 25 Mar 88

Aldrich H Ames CIA agent

3331 I gathered up all that I had and gave it to them. . . a goldmine. . . the keys to the kingdom.

On spying for Russia while a member of the CIA, quoted by Michael Binyon *London Times* 18 Feb 95 reviewing *The Million Dollar Spy* BBC TV 18 Feb 95

Amnesty International capital punishment opponents

3332 Criminal codes do not sanction the raping of rapists or the burning of arsonists' homes.

On the application of a different standard when the crime is murder *NY Times* 4 Dec 94

Anon

3333 A highly placed sensitive source of known reliability was contacted and furnished items of personality.

On how an FBI agent would report a "black bag job" of surreptitious entry *NY Times* 23 Sep 80

3334 She ain't nothing but Maggie Strong,/ Everything she own, she got on.

Prison saying quoted by Jean Harris *Stranger in Two Worlds* Macmillan 86

3335 He just a suit-wearin' nobody. He so dumb he play chess with marbles.

On a parole officer *ib*

3336 If a man does not enjoy his own company, he is in deep trouble.

On a convict's "total helplessness" assessment of "the new Alcatraz" almost entirely devoted to solitary confinement *US News & World Report* 27 Jul 87

3337 If you can read/ Please heed this call/ There is no radio/ None at all.

Sign on automobile to discourage break-ins *NY Times* 10 Oct 88

3338 I ain't going to say it's fun. It's getting your anger out at somebody.

On youth gang that was "wilding" in terrorization of New York's Central Park, news summaries 30 May 89

3339 It's like stealing fruit. It's not cause you are hungry.
ib

3340 Hostile surveillance.
Police term for letting a suspect know he is being watched *Time* 7 Aug 89

3341 Snitches get stitches.
On prisoners who report others *NY Times* 1 Sep 90

3342 A full moon and a full gun makes for a night of fun.
Excerpted from computer communications of Los Angeles patrol cars *Time* 22 Jul 91

3343 Thumb therapy.
On punishment of prisoners who attack prison staff, quoted by Pete Early, author of *The Hot House* Bantam 92, radio station WAMU Washington 28 Feb 92

3344 A giant mausoleum adrift in a great sea of nothingness.
A convict writing to his mother on Leavenworth federal prison *ib*

3345 This is where the Bureau finds out if a man clangs when he walks.
On the Federal Prison Bureau's view of Leavenworth warden's need for "two brass balls. . . awfully damn big" *ib*

3346 He had more brains before breakfast than Al Capone had all day.
On Tony "Big Tuna" Accardo, a key figure in Chicago's Capone gang who avoided all prison convictions for more than 60 years *London Times* 29 May 92

3347 Murder is to S&M what rape is to sex.
On sadomasochistic practices, quoted by David France on fatal shooting of Egil Vesti by Bernard LeGeros whom he called his "executioner" *Bag of Toys* Time Warner 92

3348 It's recreational litigation.
On prisoners who sue on incidental matters *20/20* ABC TV 24 Sep 93

3349 Three strikes and you're out.
Proposing permanent imprisonment of repeated felons, quoted by President Clinton, State of the Union Address 25 Jan 94

3350 How do you tell the difference between the sociopathic killer and the innocent person? The sociopath has a better story.
Black humor among criminologists *Newsweek* 14 Nov 94

3351 It is beyond bizarre.
Lawyer commenting on Colin Ferguson, defendant certified as insane, who was allowed to act as his own attorney in fatally shooting six persons and wounding 19 on the Long Island Railroad *Nightline* ABC TV 10 Feb 95

3352 Purple Flower Power.
A "hippie-dippy" name for marijuana seed *NY Times* 19 Feb 95

3353 It was like saying you were kosher even though you had Chinese food in a refrigerator out in the garage.
On desire to rid one's house of the skunky smell of drying marijuana leaves *ib*

3354 Fifty-three crates furniture from Atlanta received in good condition—installed—no breakage.
Warden's telegram to US Attorney General after first prisoners arrived at Alcatraz for the period it was used as a high security federal prison 1934–1963, recalled in *NY Times* 19 Feb 95

3355 Did you ever hear of a Columbian necklace?
A drug-world term for cutting the throat and inserting the victim's tongue through the wound; introduced by defense in the O J Simpson trial in belief that a house guest had not paid for drugs 7 Mar 95

3356 There's no such thing as a drive-by knifing.
On the need for gun-control to curb the major weapon in violence, Station WAMU Washington 29 Mar 95

3357 A police state is well policed.
On Moscow's low crime rate during Communist rule, quoted by news commentator Daniel Schorr, radio station WAMU Washington 21 Apr 95

3358 One riot, one ranger.
On the lonesome, understaffed ranks of the Texas Rangers *NY Times* 27 Aug 95

3359 Dead man walking!
Prison guard's warning that a convicted man is approaching the death chamber, title of book and film, quoted by Sister Helen Pregean *Dead Man Walking* Random House 94

3360 Black Bull was a race horse/ The very best of his era,/ The earth shook when he ran/ Defending Don Juan N Guerra.
On a legendary drug trader's love for race horses *NY Times* 9 Feb 96

W H Auden poet

3361 After shaking paws with his dog (whose bark would tell the world that he is always kind), the hangman sets off briskly over the heath. He does not know yet who will be provided to do the works of Justice with.
On the workaday approach of a professional hangman *Terce* Oct 53, Edward Mendelson ed *W H Auden: Collected Poems* Vintage 91

3362 With a sigh the judge descends his marble stair; he does not know by what sentence he will apply on earth the Law that rules the stars.
ib

3363 The poet, taking a breather round his garden before starting his ecologue, does not know whose Truth he will tell.
ib

Richard B Austin Federal District Court, Chicago

3364 The sound of the clanging jailhouse door has a salutary effect on the defendant and the community.

On sentencing of union chief Jimmy Hoffa on conviction of fraud *NY Times* 18 Aug 64

James David Autry convicted murderer

3365 Do it like they used to do—take you out and hang you or cut off your head or whatever they want.

On facing Texas' sentence of death by lethal injection, news summaries 31 Dec 83

3366 It ain't manly to go in there and lay on a table and let them stick you in the arm with a needle.

ib

Kenneth Baker British Home Secretary

3367 When a young, innocent toddler is killed in a brutal way, then you are beyond the edge of evil, you are into the heart of darkness.

On the murder by two 10-year-olds of a Liverpool boy age 2 *Wall Street Journal* 7 Apr 93

Richard Bank Philadelphia public defender

3368 They've never met anybody who wakes up with an alarm clock every morning.

On disadvantaged clients *Wall Street Journal* 25 Sep 90

Richard Bauer Administrative Assistant, Washington State Prison

3369 It's a science that deals with math, momentum and distance. . . the height and weight of the inmate, the proper drop from the platform and, obviously, the right knot.

On carrying out the sentence of hanging *NY Times* 22 Mar 89

3370 We don't want this to be any more unpleasant than it has to be.

ib

William Beattie police informer

3371 I'll kill anybody, but I'm not into cutting them up.

Court testimony in racketeering trial of eight members of the Westies that he would commit murder but not dismemberment *NY Times* 22 Oct 87

Robert Leslie Bellem novelist

3372 A bullet can give a man a terrific case of indigestion.

Hollywood Detective Aug 50

Brenda Benson lottery winner

3373 This has certainly knocked the gilt off the gingerbread.

On the burglary of her home following disclosure that she had won £20 million in a national lottery *London Times* 12 Jul 95

Enzo Biagi Italian journalist

3374 With us, violence is an ancient evil that seals many destinies.

On Italian highway bandits who fatally shot the small son of a California family *NY Times* 4 Oct 94

3375 This land, famed for its history, beauty, art, suffers from an invincible cruelty that hides behind the oleanders, the sycamores, within the ruins, that vibrates on air scented with lemon blossoms and in the night.

ib

Eugene Bird Governor, Spandau Prison, Berlin

3376 Time stood still for him since 1941.

On former Nazi leader Rudolf Hess's death after 46 years imprisonment by Allied powers *USA Today* 17 Aug 87

Nelson Birdwell Sr murderers' grandfather

3377 I saw them go from babies to monsters.

On grandsons David and Bryan Freeman, neo-Nazi teenagers, who killed their parents and younger brother, news summaries 8 Mar 95

Dr Martin Blender psychiatrist

3378 He was bingeing on Twinkies.

"The Twinkie defense" that junk food affected the judgment of San Francisco city official Dan White in his fatal shooting of Mayor George Moscone and city supervisor Harvey Milk *The Times of Harvey Milk* PBS TV 13 Nov 85

Ralph Blumenthal reporter

3379 Garbage is still very much the Mafia's bag.

On organized crime's control of private carting for more than three decades *NY Times* 24 Jan 88

3380 The sketch. . . brought a rash of tips, mainly from former wives.

On search for serial bomber 18 Dec 94

Alfred Blumstein Criminologist, Heinz School, Carnegie Mellon University

3381 A lot of robbers have always been willing to kill you. . . [but] didn't have guns. Now they do.

On the 1990s' increase in murders *Washington Post* 23 Oct 95

Timothy Blunk convicted felon

3382 You dig a trench in your heart. You try to keep your humanity from slipping through your hands.

On being held in maximum-security federal prison at Marion IL *20/20* CBS TV 18 Mar 88

Gerald Boyle defense attorney

3383 He was a runaway train on a track of madness.

On Milwaukee's Jeffrey Dahmer, serial killer of 16 men, quoted by Anne E Schwartz *The Man Who Could Not Kill Enough* Birch Lane 92

Rick Bragg reporter

3384 For nine days....he handled her like a piece of glass, afraid her brittle psyche would shatter and leave him with the jagged edges of a case that might go unsolved....(and) people would have been left to wonder, blame, and hate, divided by race and opinion over what truly happened the night that she gave her babies to the lake.

On Union County SC Sheriff Howard Wells who persuaded Susan R Smith to confess that her two small sons were not kidnapped by a black man but drowned when she allowed her car to roll into a lake near Union SC *NY Times* 4 Aug 95

3385 Voters liked his plain-spokenness and the fact that he was neither a backslapper nor backscratcher.... [in a] case that had pitted a man who wants children against a woman who threw hers away.

On the sheriff and the defendant *ib*

3386 Before he needed help to go to the bathroom, he was a dangerous man. Another was a kidnapper; now he has trouble holding a spoon. Still another, whoses life was washed away on a river of whiskey, seems to have vanished inside a wizened little man...plucking weeds.

On Alabama's increasingly crowded prison for aged and infirm convicts, a portent of penal life in the future *NY Times* 1 Nov 95

Anthony Cave Brown author and biographer

3387 Harold Adrian Russell Philby. . . became quite possibly the greatest unhanged scoundrel in modern British history.

On the Foreign Office's Kim Philby exposure as a lifelong Soviet spy *Treason in the Blood* Houghton Mifflin 94

3388 Arthur Martin, the young Security Service officer. . . had been burrowing away. . . with clerkly diligence.

On surveillance of Philby *ib*

3389 The bullfrogs' chorus lasted many months. . . expanded from time to time by declarations by one or another of the golden lads who had drifted into Churchill's games of legerdemain, force, and fraud.

On "savage literary fighting" among writers analyzing Philby's defection *ib*

Freddie Cherokee Brown Bronx teenager

3390 Once they get a badge and a gun, they're the law. They got all the authority in the world.

On a black teen-ager's view of police in the Hunts Point section of the Bronx *NY Times* 18 Apr 93

Frederic Brown novelist

3391 Death is an incurable disease that men and women are born with; it gets them sooner or later. A murderer never really kills; he but anticipates.

The Screaming Mimi Dutton 1949, recalled on Brown's death 13 Mar 72

Jeremy Brown rape victim

3392 We will take your freedom from you today. We will go on and be happy. . . live productive lives. You will remain in a void, a darkness incapable of any mutuality or reciprocity. . . never know warmth or love or trust. We have persevered. . . overcome . . . survived. You can go to hell.

Addressing a convicted murderer who kidnapped, repeatedly raped and tortured her within 76 days of his parole and was permitted to cross-examine her in Rockland County NY Court *NY Times* 8 Sep 95

Lee P Brown Director, National Drug Control Policy Center

3393 You can't arrest your way out of the drug problem, you can't incarcerate your way out of the problem.

On continuance of drug traffic although one in every three black men in their 20s was in prison, on parole, or otherwise under the supervision of the criminal justice system, *Washington Post* 5 Oct 95

Robert M ("Bear") Bryant Assisstant Director, FBI

3394 It was a marvelous piece of insubordination.

On agents whose forbidden search of garbage resulted in the arrest of the CIA's Aldrich H Ames as a spy for Russia *Washington Post* 27 Jan 95

Ted Bundy serial killer

3395 Now you've got a straw. You're trying to fill up a broom. . . one of these days you might make it.

On being questioned in serial murders for which he ultimately received the death penalty, quoted by Stephen G Michaud and Hugh Aynesworth *The Only Living Witness* Linden 83

Tommy Busetta Sicilian gang member

3396 When finally I came out of the coma caused by strychnine crushed between my teeth, I understood that such a solution, that of dying, was not enough. Something more was required—to destroy the present reality of the Mafia.

On his attempted suicide in Brazil after fleeing Mafia war in Sicily in which ten relatives were killed *US News & World Report* 18 Jan 88

George Bush 41st US President

3397 One of our brave National Guardsmen may have actually been safer in the midst of the largest armored offensive in history than he would have been on the streets of his own hometown.

To anti-crime conference during the Persian Gulf War *Wall Street Journal* 8 Mar 91

Lincoln Caplan reporter

3398 A tall and commanding veteran with a boyish haircut and the eyes of an owl in a hawk's face, he wore G-man suits with wide lapels, and broad ties in stars and stripes.

On senior government prosecutor Roger Adelman in John W Hinckley Jr's trial for attempted assassination of President Reagan *New Yorker* 2 Jul 84

Ricardo Silvio Caputo serial killer

3399 I would rather have my body locked up and my mind free, than living as I was, with another identity, with my mind locked up and my body free.

On serial murders over a 20-year period as an Argentinian with 17 aliases, countless personas, and several prison escapes *NY Times* 11 Mar 94

Gregory Carey Professor of Behavior Genetics, University of Colorado

3400 We already have a true genetic marker, detectable before birth, that predicts violence. . . that's right, being male.

Time 17 Jan 94

John Casey NYC police officer

3401 It's 90 percent boredom and 10 percent sheer terror.

On Emergency Service United *NY Times* 11 Feb 85

Bernard Cawley NYC police officer

3402 After we calmed the ladies down, we had sex with them.

On raiding brothels, testimony at hearing on police corruption *NY Times* 28 Sep 93

3403 I used to tune people up. . . a police word for beatin' up people....We were taught it's us against them. Us were the cops and them were the public.

ib

Marvin J Cetron President, Forecasting International Ltd

3404 Superterrorists. . . will have more sophisticated weapons. . . and they will show a new willingness to use them.

Report to US Department of Defense on the use of nuclear, chemical and biological weapons in worldwide terrorism *International Herald Tribune* 2 Jan 95

3405 Motivated not by political ideology but by fierce ethnic and religious hatreds, their goal will be. . . the utter destruction of their chosen enemies.

ib

Raymond Chandler detective novelist

3406 Crime isn't a disease, it's a symptom. Cops are like a doctor who gives you aspirin for a brain tumor, except that the cop would rather cure it with a blackjack.

NY Times 1 Nov 87

3407 On nights like that. . . meek little wives feel the edge of the carving knife and study their husbands' necks. Anything can happen.

On women who kill in Chandler's short story "Red Wind" recalled on hundredth anniversary of Chandler's birth, *Washington Post* 11 Sep 88

Mark David Chapman convicted assassin

3408 As soon as I saw his picture on that album. . . I knew I was going to kill him.

On fatal shooting of entertainer John Lennon *Let Me Take You Down* with Jack Jones, Villard 92

3409 John Lennon fell into a very deep hole, a hole that was so deep inside of me that I thought by killing him I would acquire his fame.

Interview with Barbara Walters *20/20* CBS TV 4 Dec 92

3410 I turned to Satan, because I knew I wouldn't have the strength to kill a man on my own. I asked Satan to give me the power to kill John Lennon.

ib

Chen Chih-Yi Chinese-American gang member

3411 Every town where you see a Chinese restaurant, you walk in and tell them you are with United Bamboo. They will take care of you.

Tape-recorded conversation about driving from Los Angeles to Florida *US News & World Report* 18 Jan 88

Agatha Christie novelist and playwright

3412 Oh dear, I never realized what a terrible lot of explaining one has to do in a murder!

Spider's Web 56

3413 I like blood. Such a beautiful color.

Lines for a murder suspect in *The Unexpected Guest* *Country Life* 3 Mar 94

George Christie Director, Glyndebourne Opera

3414 I don't think burglars would take Myrtle too seriously.

On a black pug as an ineffective watch dog *Country Life* 2 Mar 95

Gerald Clarke biographer

3415 The Clutters unsuspectingly awaiting their fate... their killers racing across Kansas to meet them, Nemesis in a black Chevrolet.

Capote Simon & Schuster 88 on the murder of a farm family recounted by Truman Capote *In Cold Blood* Random House 66

Judy Clarke defense attorney

3416 Confusion is not evil and hopelessness is not malice.

On Susan Smith's state of mind the night she drowned her two infant sons *Washington Post* 23 Jul 95

Francis X Clines reporter

3417 Female convicts tend to talk more than males, the murderesses here more than the murderers elsewhere.

On the Bedford Hills NY Correctional Facilty for Women *NY Times* 24 Apr 93

3418 A combination of tough matriarch and easy touch.... Superintendent Lord long ago decided a talkative ship is better than a tight one.

On Bedford's Elaine A Lord *ib*

Mickey Cohen gangster

3419 I never killed a man that didn't deserve it.

Playboy May 84

Bobby Comfort convicted felon

3420 If I happened to be in a bar with Martin Luther King or Socrates or Jesus Christ—I'd be back in jail for parole violation, right?

To NY State Parole Board after breaking parole by "associating with known criminals," quoted by Ira Berkow *The Man Who Robbed the Pierre* Atheneum 87

3421 I have been honorable at all times in my line of work.

Letter to NY Appellate Judge Andrew Tyler on reversal of a prison sentence *ib*

John Conyer Jr US Congressman

3422 There is a certain amount of wimpishness about being against the death penalty. I mean, some of my colleagues say to me, "Fry them vermins, John. What's the problem, man?"

Washington Post 15 Dec 90

Michael Crowell Director, Death Penalty Information Center

3423 They carry their lives around under their arms.

On the indefinite futures of prisoners on death row, Station WAMU Washington 15 Dec 90

Jeffrey L Dahmer serial killer

3424 You remember your first one... where the whole nightmare started.

On recollecting in his confession at age 31 the hitchiker he killed in 1978 before going on to dismember 16 other men and boys before being arrested in Milwaukee 22 Jul 91 *Washington Times* 4 Feb 92

3425 I didn't want him to leave.

On the dread of loneliness that led him to kill and preserve his victims' bones and organs *ib*

John Deakin crime reporter

3426 He was a member of the largest identifiable group in the American population, then and now: the slobs. He could read and write... [but] had he lived, he would have watched television.

On Carl Austin Hall, convicted kidnapper and killer of Kansas City school boy Bobby Greenlease *A Grave for Bobby* Morrow 90

Alfred A Dellibovi Urban Mass Transit Administrator, Washington

3427 Nobody was ever raped by a graffito.

On the need for the NYC subway to be as safe from the criminal element as from graffiti *NY Times* 10 May 89

Izaias De Paulo composer

3428 The reason toads don't go to heaven is because they have big mouths.

Expressing citizens' neutral position in wars of drug gangs in São Paulo *NY Times* 11 Sep 87

Albert Desalvo convicted murderer

3429 I was like any other normal guy, trying to make out.

On the murder and mutilation of 11 elderly women betweeen June 1962 and January 1964, quoted by Gerald Frank *The Boston Strangler* New American Library 66

3430 I just put my hand on them and was finished .... I was so build [sic] up by the time I found a woman I just got near her and I was releaved [sic].

Confessional letter to police *ib*

David N Dinkins Mayor of New York

3431 Burned-out bullies with billy clubs—have crossed the line from being protectors to being avengers and have themselves become a public menace.

To rookie police after public protests against LA police brutality *NY Times* 10 Apr 91

Westley Allan Dodd convicted murderer

3432 If I... escape, I promise you I will kill and rape again, and I will enjoy every minute of it.

On why he felt it was important to be executed before he had "an opportunity to escape or kill someone else"; convicted of the rape and murder of three boys, he became the first person to die by hanging in the US in nearly 30 years *London Times* 5 Jan 93

Richard A Dollinger NY legislator

3433 We are going to fill this with...the greatest venom present in our society today: pure and simple revenge.

On displaying a hypodermic syringe on the floor of the NY State Senate with claim that restoration of the death penalty would kill not only convicted murderers but also a measure of civilization *NY Times* 7 Mar 95

John Douglas Director, FBI Psychological Profile Unit

3434 Asocial, asexual, a loner, withdrawn, from a family with problems, strong feelings of inadequacy from early in life, an underachiever. This obsession with weapons—a form of power—is an overcompensation for deep-rooted feelings....[and so] they compensate for a while by talking the talk, but after a while they have to go out and do something about it. Typically the time for violence is in the mid-20s. They look in the mirror and see they're going nowhere fast. This is an easily controlled and manipulated personality. They are looking for something to hang their hat on, some ideology. They have difficulty fitting into groups, but they are more mission-oriented, more focused.

On characteristics that matched the profile of Timothy McVeigh, principal suspect in the bombing of an Oklahoma City federal building *NY Times* 31 Dec 95

Kenneth Dover President, Corpus Christi College, Oxford

3435 My problem was one which I feel compelled to define with brutal candor: How to kill him without getting into trouble...a fellow from whose non-existence the college would benefit.

Quoted in "Death in the Cloister" an editorial citing Dover's autobiography *Marginal Comment* and Dover's conviction that he willed the death of historian Trevor Aston before Aston became a suicide in 1985 *London Times* 30 Nov 94

3436 I have been masquerading as a human being all my life.

ib

3437 I prefer nasty truths to silly lies.

ib

Michael Dowd NYC Police Officer

3438 Us was the cops and they were the public.

On how lax supervision and an ingrained police department culture allowed him to evolve from free drinks and pizza on his first day on the job into taking $8,000 a week to protect Brooklyn drug dealers *NY Times* 28 Sep 93

Robert Draper crime writer

3439 When a man got his face held down in a river, it tended to refresh his memory.

On Texas Rangers' "investigative techniques" *NY Times* 27 Aug 95

3440 Putting a milk bucket over a fellow's head and beating on it with a nightstick often yielded some useful information.

ib

David Durk NYC police commissioner

3441 Men who could have been good officers, men of decent impulse...were told in a hundred ways..."Go along, forget the law, don't make waves and shut up."

Testimony at hearings on police corruption *Guardian Weekly* 17 Oct 93

Alan Farnham reporter

3442 Homes, stuffed with VCRs and microwaves and giant-screen TVs, are just so many nutmeats waiting to be shelled.

Reporting on increase of suburban burglaries *Fortune* 28 Dec 92

Federal Bureau Of Investigation (FBI)

3443 [He was] a well respected hoodlum.

On crime family head John Gotti *New York* 23 Jun 86

Thomas Flanagan novelist

3444 No warrant sworn against him, [he] saunders through fashionable quarters, intricate fanlights, the wood freshly painted yearly, the glass polished by platoons of lads and skivvies.

On an assassin at large in London *The Tenants of Time* Dutton 87

3445 But now he lay alone, frightened, wide awake at two in the morning, seeing the great centerless web of black and grey, save for a sudden dab, a dab of red blood in Chelsea.

ib

George P Fletcher Professor of Law, Columbia

3446 Nothing focuses a man's mind like the thought he will hang in the morning.

Paraphrasing Samuel Johnson *Washington Post* 26 Feb 95 reviewing David Von Drehle's *Among the Lowest: The Culture of Death Row* Times Books 95

3447 They. . . refine their confined minds.

On inmates' ability to "hoodwink" correspondents and romance lawyers *ib*

3448 On the verge of dying, they find sources of life.

ib

James Alan Fox Dean, College of Criminal Justice, Northeastern University

3449 In all of their lives, they've never distinguished themselves. . . ordinary at school, at their jobs, with their friends, but at murder, they're extraordinary.

On serial killers *NY Times* 1 Jul 93

James M Fox Assistant Director, NY Bureau, FBI

3450 The don is covered with Velcro, and every charge stuck.

On murder and racketeering conviction of Gambio crime family boss John Gotti, formerly called the "Teflon Don" because charges didn't stick *NY Times* 3 Apr 92

Jimmy Fratianno convicted murderer

3451 There are different ways and different methods, I just had the talent to do things like that. I never made any mistakes.

On being a Mafia hit man *60 Minutes* CBS TV 31 Aug 87

3452 You meet a nice class of people.

ib

3453 Before I had to lie to stay alive. Now I have to tell the truth to stay alive.

On testifying against the Mafia in exchange for government protection *ib*

Mark Fuhrman detective, LA Police

3454 This job is not rules. . . we'll make them up later.

On a position seen as responsible for corruption and brutality in US police departments, including possible planting of evidence in the O J Simpson murder trial *Time* 11 Sep 95

Issac Fulwood Chief, District of Columbia Police

3455 Do you go hunting deer with machine guns? No, you use them to kill people.

On need for gun control, American Public Radio 14 Dec 90

William A Gavin Director, NY Bureau, FBI

3456 Well disciplined. . . well organized. You have to respect them for their trade, and then you have to put them in jail.

On gangs of immigrant Albanians and Yugoslavians who videotaped supermarkets before robbing them *NY Times* 17 Dec 94

Jean Genet novelist

3457 I recognize in thieves, traitors and murderers, in the ruthless and the cunning, a deep beauty—an engraved beauty—which I deny you.

The Thief's Journal Grove 64, quoted by biographer Edmund White who noted that "Genet insults the reader in order to prove his fraternity with the disinherited" Genet Knopf 93

3458 My conscience regretted wounding, insulting those who were the downtrodden expression of my dearest treasure: my homosexuality.

On robbing his sex partners *ib*

Jeffrey Taylor Gibbs LA attorney

3459 Ego rape is a fringe benefit of the police department.

Station WAMU Washington 20 Mar 91

Glen Gilbreath felon

3460 Old burglars never die, they just steal away.

On facing his 13th robbery charge at age 72 *Chicago Sun-Times* 26 Apr 58

John Gleeson US Attorney

3461 Murder is. . . the way in which discipline was maintained, in which power was obtained. It is the heart and soul of this enterprise.

Summation in conviction of Gambino crime family boss, John Gotti, *NY Times* 3 Apr 92

David Green Hamilton OH attorney

3462 Where else will you find so many unattended women with money and with their minds in other places?

On shopping mall robberies *Wall Street Journal* 10 Sep 87

Juan N Guerra patriarch of criminal dynasty

3463 He's one coyote and I'm a different coyote; he took his road and I took mine.

Commenting as a legendary figure in Mexico's drug trade on his nephew's arrest in sweep of a huge cocaine operation *NY Times* 9 Feb 96

3464 When you sin, do it with discretion.

On speaking in aphorisms seemingly for his nephew *ib*

John Guido Chief of Inspectional Services, NYC Police

3465 The solution is to have tight supervision and to preach, preach, preach that brutality is the wrong way to be a cop.

NY Times 6 May 85

Bruce Handy essayist

3466 Here was precisely the kind of teeming social canvas that the likes of Dickens, Thackeray, Balzac, Eliot, and Flaubert used to such great effect.

On the O J Simpson murder trial *Time* 16 Oct 95

3467 We met earthy Salvadoran maids, beadle-like cops, bumbling civil servants, stalwart limo drivers, beaten-down screenwriters manqué and, of course, comically obsequious houseguests.

ib

3468 Occupying the top of the social pecking order in this modern-day Middlemarch was the defendant himself, living a life that would be the envy of any 19th century man of leisure.

On O J Simpson's "pleasant days at the country club. . . nights lost in the social whirl. . . [and] getting paid to play even more golf" *ib*

Jean Harris convicted murderess

3469 Prison isn't the best place to exchange recipes and dust the piano. . . but the opportunity to. . . consider things that might have slipped by me outside while I dusted the piano.

On conviction for the fatal shooting of Scarsdale-diet doctor Herman Tarnower *Marking Time* Scribner 91

3470 To speak the truth is considered arrogance. To speak logic is to be considered a fool or at best a misfit.

on prison life

3471 Good is bad and black is white and decency and truth are held laughable.

ib

Mark Hatfield US Senator

3472 If one argues that a prisoner deserves whatever he or she gets in prison, then one must also be prepared to argue that society deserves what it gets when the prisoner is eventually released.

USA Today 12 Jan 83

Constance L Hays reporter

3473 If the hair is gray, con artists see green.

On the elderly as profitable prime targets for scams *NY Times* 21 May 95

Leona Helmsley hotel owner

3474 We don't pay taxes. Only the little people pay taxes.

Remark to a former housekeeper that became a byword at trial and conviction for tax fraud by "the Queen of Mean" *NY Times* 13 Jul 89

Dennis Henigan Director, Legal Action Project, Center to Prevent Hand Gun Violence

3475 The NRA has never seen a gun it didn't like.

On the National Rifle Association's resistance to gun control legislation APR 14 Dec 90

Gary L Henman Warden, US Penitentiary, Marion IL

3476 We used to separate them in each institution. Now we put all the rotten apples into one barrel.

On "the new Alcatraz" almost entirely devoted to solitary confinement *US News & World Report* 27 Jul 87

Rudolf Hess Nazi official

3477 [He is] the greatest son whom my nation has brought forth in the thousand years of its history.

On Adolf Hitler, recalled on Hess's death at 93, 45 years after his flight to Scotland in a personal attempt to make peace between Germany and Britain *Life* Oct 87

3478 I would never again put a bird in a cage.

Letter to his wife *ib*

Paul Hill convicted murderer

3479 If the government is going to insist on killing me, I'm not going to resist them.

On being sentenced to death for fatally shooting two persons at an abortion clinic CNBC 23 Feb 95

John W Hinckley Jr convicted felon

3480 I helped his presidency. After I shot him, his polls went up 20 percent.

On attempted assassination of Ronald Reagan *Kansas City Times* 1 Jan 84

J Edgar Hoover Director, FBI

3481 Public Enemy No 1.

Ranking devised in the 1930s for post office posters and news reports on criminals most sought by Hoover's G-men (government men), recalled on Hoover's death 2 May 72

J D Howard Mayfair Window Cleaning Co, London

3482 Our employees on the whole lead somewhat boisterous lives.

On necessity of police check of workers assigned to the Queen Mother's residence *NY Times* 2 Jan 90

James Oliver Huberty mass killer

3483 I'm going out to hunt humans.

Last words to his wife before killing 22 persons and wounding 19 at a San Diego CA McDonald's restaurant, news reports 18 Jul 84

Ice-T entertainer

3484 I'm 'bout to dust some cops off: Die, die, die, pig, die!

"Cop Killer," controversial song withdrawn from Ice-T's album *Body Count* because of its advocacy of the murder of police officers *Newsweek* 10 Aug 92

Il Messaggero Rome

3485 The abolition of the ritual raises the prospect of. . . a new, compartmentalized Mafia, formed of miniscule cells, where each boss knows only a few disciples.

On Sicilian mafiosi concern that *supergrasses* were infiltrating their ranks and by passing the "kiss of honor," the gesture by which Costra Nostra members recognized each other *London Times* 21 Feb 95

3486 *Son la stessa cosa di te* ("I am the same as you")

Secret mafia password

Jesse Jackson political leader

3487 Black on black violence now kills more in one year in America than died during all the history of lynching.

Christian Science Monitor 3 Nov 93

3488 There is nothing more painful to me. . . than to walk down the street and hear footsteps and start thinking about robbery—then look around and see somebody white and feel relieved.

International Herald Tribune 17 Dec 93

Joaquin Jackson Texas Ranger

3489 I don't care if she's 9 foot tall and meaner than a barrelful of snakes. He's not going to talk to her.

On sheriff's cold shoulder to women Rangers *NY Times* 27 Aug 95

3490 Women can do investigative work. . . . They've got this little thing called intuition.

ib

P D James novelist

3491 It is a jolly sight more interesting to have a clever cop, or a clever criminal. I want to be interesting, not realistic.

On why she never has dumb policemen in her books *London Times* 16 Sep 95

Duncan Jevons library thief

3492 I was interested in the information. . . in ideas. . . [but] it was pure greed.

On stealing 52,000 books—35 tons, worth £500,000—over a period of 30 years *London Times* 26 Aug 95

Sam Jones professional executioner

3493 Nothin' to it. . . no different to me executing somebody than goin' to the refrigerator and getting a beer out of it.

Quoted by Wilbert Rideau and Ron Wikberg's *Life Sentences* Times Books 92

Tamara Jones reporter

3494 Poisonous denial and odd formality was easily seen. . . witnesses referred to adultery as dating and incest as an affair. . . deaths became "the events," "the incident," or simply "what happened."

Reporting on Susan Smith's Union SC trial in the drowning of her two small sons *Washington Post* 30 Jul 95

Stephen M Kalish convicted smuggler

3495 General Noriega called me back and said I forgot my briefcase. I told him it was for him, and he smiled.

On cash and kickbacks paid to Panamanian General Manuel Antonio Noriega *NY Times* 29 Jan 88

Alfred Kazin reporter

3496 They had no language in common but snarls.

On drunks snatching apples from Korean fruit stands *New York* 19 Jan 87

John Kifner reporter

3497 Benny Ong Uncle Seven, International Adviser for Life of the Hip Sing Tong, the Godfather of Chinatown, lay in state at the Wah Wing Sang Funeral Home. . . surrounded by enough flowers to cover much of lower Manhattan.

On wake for a tong leader *NY Times* 21 Aug 94

3498 Joss sticks burned. . . and the old gangster's favorite dish, boiled chicken, was there to sustain him on his trip to the afterworld, along with the bribes that would get him past the devils along the way.

ib

Stephen King novelist

3499 The night roared like a lion with a poisoned spear caught in its throat.

On skullduggery in small-town America *Needful Things* Viking 91

Alfred Kinsey Founder, Institute for Sex Research, Indiana University

3500 The difference between a "good time" and "rape" often depends on whether the girl's parents are still awake when she arrives home.

Sex Offenders Harper & Row 65

Edward I Koch Mayor of New York

3501 You got to be pretty damn nice to get on this ferryboat.

On ferry converted to US's first floating prison for jail overflow *US News & World Report* 6 Apr 87

3502 These kids were taught to hate. And they are not going to be untaught by being called juvenile delinquents.

On parental responsibility for a synagogue's burning by boys 12 and 15 *NY Times* l9 Sep 88

Richard J Koehler NYC Corrections Commissioner

3503 Jail. . . costs too much and we get almost nothing for it, except they don't do a crime while they're in the box. And that's all we get.

On the futility of effective prison terms *NY Times* 19 Apr 87

C Everett Koop US Surgeon General

3504 Violence is every bit a public-health issue. . . as small-pox, tuberculosis and syphillis were in the last two centuries. . . it has indeed assumed the proportions of an epidemic.

LA Herald Examiner 20 Jan 85

Ted Koppel commentator

3505 Texas. . . the capitol of capital punishment.

On the execution of 87 persons since restoration of the death penalty in 1982 *Nightline* 16 Jan 95

Jack Kroll reporter

3506 [They were] the neon waterholes where urban animals clash by night.

Newsweek 10 Oct 77 on Manhattan bars in Judith Rossiter's *Looking for Mr Goodbar* Simon & Schuster 77

J Miller Leavy prosecuting attorney

3507 I didn't prosecute to deter. I prosecuted to punish. Sending her to the gas chamber didn't bother me at all.

On the successful 1953 conviction of Barbara Graham for murder of an elderly woman, a first in a case based exclusively on circumstantial evidence *NY Times* 6 Jan 95

John le Carré novelist

3508 The brown paper parcel. . . reminded him of the marriage service, "With this ring I thee wed; with this paper parcel, I return thee to society."

On personal possessions restored to him on release from Communist prison *The Spy Who Came in From the Cold* Bantam 63

3509 They. . . made him sign for it. . . all he had in the world. . . the most de-humanizing moment of the three months and he determined to throw the parcel away as soon as he got outside.

ib

Bernard Legeros NYC art dealer

3510 Once for the body and once for the soul!

On the two sadomasochistic shots that dispatched foreign fashion model, Egil Vesti, quoted by David France *Bag of Toys* Time Warner 92

Brian Leonard English Kennel Club

3511 You cannot afford to have a guard dog do what old guard dogs used to do.

On new law requiring prosecution of householders if their dogs bite burglars *London Times* 22 Aug 95

Fred Leuchter professional hangman

3512 Capital punishment, not capital torture.

Motto of the US's only specialist in the design and construction of execution devices, quoted by Stephen Trombley's *The Execution Protocol* Crown 92

C Day Lewis (Nicholas H Blake) writer

3513 Every collector is a potential criminal.

From *Minute to Murder* Holt Rinehart Winston 1947, recalled on Lewis' death 22 May 72

G Gordon Liddy Council to the Committee to Re-Elect the President

3514 My will was now so strong I could endure a long, deep flesh-charring burn without a flicker of expression.

On perfecting resistance to cigarettes pressed against his hand, preparing for keeping silent under any interrogations that might arise from the Watergate break-in which he was ploting to lead *Will* St Martin's 80

3515 [It is] an *Einsatzgruppe*, General.

To US Attorney General John N Mitchell on recruits for the Watergate break-in. *ib*

3516 Defeat the fear of death and welcome the death of fear.

On fending off other prisoners while awaiting trial on Watergate *ib*

London Times

3517 The reprieve granted to the old-fashioned policeman's helmet by Scotland Yard is a welcome victory for traditionalism over the modern impulse to sweep away all that is familiar.

"Old Hat" editorial 28 Nov 94 on what was to be but a brief reprieve on the domed hats of the British "bobby" 28 Nov 94

Martin Luster NY legislator

3518 This chamber has a long and honorable history but what we are about to do here tonight is to taint that history with fraud.

On belief that New York state's restoration of the death penalty is a fraud in making people feel safer *NY Times* 7 Mar 95

Ben Maddow screenwriter

3519 Crime is a left-handed form of human endeavor.

The Asphalt Jungle 1950 film recalled on Maddow's death *London Times* 2 Nov 92

Norman Mailer novelist

3520 It is virtually not assimilable to our reason that a small lonely man felled a giant in the midst of his limousines, his legions, his throngs, and his security.

On Lee Harvey Oswald's assassination of John F Kennedy *Oswald's Tale* Random House 95

3521 If such a nonenity destroyed the leader of the most powerful nation on earth, then a world of disproportion engulfs us, and we live in a universe that is absurd.

ib

3522 At rest in the vibrationless center of a dream, he has passed through the mightiest of the psychic barricades—he has killed the king.

ib

3523 The lie has always been Oswald's tool all his life... [and] the difficulty with closing the book on Oswald is that every time one shuts the door, a crack opens in the wall.

ib

3524 It was a dead whale decomposing on a beach.

On the Warren Commission's investigation of the assassination *ib*

Janet Malcolm writer

3525 The irredeemably serious mistakes that convicts have made, the antisocial acts that brought them to their predicament, form the dire background for the petty dramas played out in the foreground.

On prison life *New Yorker* 16 Oct 95

Peter Z Malkin Israeli secret agent

3526 Suddenly, shockingly, he let out a piercing scream... the primal cry of a cornered animal.

On the capture of Nazi executioner Adolf Eichmann *In My Hands* Warner 90

William Manchester biographer

3527 Looking for a doctrine... is like looking for bone in a polyp.

On lack of valid political thought in statements of Lee Harvey Oswald *The Death of a President* Harper & Row 67

3528 The men and women who surrounded President Kennedy were unacquainted with the maggoty half-world of dockets and flesh-peddlers... furtive men with mud-colored faces... bottle blondes whose high-arched overplucked eyebrows give their flat glittering eyes a perpetually startled expression... sordid walkup hotels with unread Gideon Bibles and tumbled bedclothes and rank animal odors... police connivance in petty crime... a way of life in which lawbreakers, law enforcement officers, and those who totter on the law's edge meet socially and even intermarry.

On the background of Oswald's assassin, nightclub owner Jack Ruby *ib*

3529 All police reporters know at least one Ruby.

On the worshipful presence of shadowy figures hanging around patrolmen and plain-clothes men *ib*

3530 He is usually overweight, middle-aged... puffy eyes... broad lapels... outrageous neckties... decorates his stubby fingers with extravagant costume jewelry... recognized by the spicy smell of his shaving lotion... the way he keeps touching officers... handing them things... combing his hair... like an oarsman sculling.

ib

Curtis Mayfield lyricist

3531 I'm your mama, I'm your daddy./ I'm that nigger in the alley./ I'm your doctor, when you need./ Want some coke? Have some weed.../ I'm your pusherman.

On dealing drugs, quoted from his album *Superfly*, *Newsweek* 7 Feb 94

James McCord CIA Senior Officer

3532 The Holy Spirit was talking to me but I was not listening.

To G Gordon Liddy, leader of the 1972 break-in of Democratic Party offices in the Watergate, on McCord's participation in the burglary and in subsequently destroying evidence, quoted by Liddy in *Will* St Martin's 80

Reginald McFadden convicted murderer

3533 Prison is all I know, Your Honor, I'm sorry to say. I've read books. I've read Shakespeare, but prison is all I know... [but] I think it is important to understand about anger. My anger has ate out my heart.

On kidnap and rape that occurred 73 days after he had convinced 14 psychiatrists he was worthy of parole after serving 25 years as a convicted murderer *NY Times* 8 Sep 95

Robert D McFadden reporter

3534 The old images seem like a caricature... the shadowy world of secret rituals, aging dons behind high-walled estates, the passion for vengeance and power over other men... the stuff of novels and movies and whispers on Mulberry Street.

On the changing criminal scene *NY Times* 11 Mar 87

3535 In a city of disconnected lives and romantic possibility, it was hardly a remarkable beginning.

On a wine-tasting party that was to lead a year later to Richardo Varela's fatal shooting of investment banker Sarah Auerbach *ib* 9 Apr 94

3536 A spring evening, a swirl of Beaujolais and conversation, a lovely separated woman and a lonely divorced man, strangers with savoir faire and talent, bruised but still open to a relationship.

ib

3537 With trickery, threats, precision timing and a dash bravado, two armed robbers invaded Tiffany's fabled emporium.

On the famous store's costliest robbery in its 157-year history *ib* 6 Sep 94

3538 They made off with about $1 million in jewelry—and videotapes that had recorded the whole escapade.

ib

James M McHaney US prosecutor at Nuremberg War Criminals Trial

3539 [It was] the most startling, and most succinct report on murder in the history of criminology.

On meticulous records kept by Nazi doctors and scientists of experiments in infecting concentration camp inmates with fatal diseases, 275,000 of whom died *NY Times* 26 Apr 95

Robert McKenna NYC Police Lieutenant

3540 A little kid comes in.... He says, "Daddy, do you steal money?" The cop's stomach tightens. Some cops cry silently. Others just wish it was a bad dream.

Quoted in Mollen Commission's study of "corruption in uniform" *NY Times* 7 Jul 94

Larry R Meachum Connecticut Commissioner of Correction

3541 An eye for an eye will make the whole world blind.

Paraphrasing Mohandas Gandhi in defense of the controversial rehabilitation of criminals *NY Times* 8 Nov 93

3542 You run the risk of becoming like what you fear and what you hate.

ib

James Meredith civil rights activist

3543 This was the face the southern Negro has been staring at through 350 years of history: the hard eyes, the fleshy face, the hard line of mouth... the face of the deputy sheriff.

On being ambushed during freedom march from Memphis to Jackson, to become the first African American enrolled in the University of Mississippi *Saturday Evening Post* 13 Aug 66

3544 [It is] the face of the man freed by an all-white jury after murdering a Negro, the face of those vicious young men carrying Confederate flags who hit civil rights workers with ax handles

ib

David Milch screenwriter

3545 When a criminal is forced to talk, you see in purer form than in any other person what is a very distinctive human trait: the capacity for self-deception and rationalization.

On his television drama "NYPD Blue" *NY Times* 26 Oct 93

3546 Nothing is ever a criminal's fault... [they] lie and believe their lies.

ib

3547 Lying is clearly not a trait on which criminals have a patent... it's really what allows each of us to get up in the morning.

ib

Elijah J Miller Jr attorney

3548 He slipped from despair into oblivion and entered hell with his eyes open.

Address to jury on how moral values led John E List to kill his wife, mother, and three children, then disappear for 18 years *NY Times* 3 Apr 90

Jerry Miller Director, National Center on Institutions and Alternatives, Arlington VA

3549 Prison works to reduce crime only if you don't let the inmates out.

Time 29 May 89

David B Mitchell Chief of Police, Prince George County MD

3550 There are a lot of long guns and short tempers.
On need for gun control NPR 14 Dec 90

Mollen Commission ethicists

3551 The problem of police corruption extends far beyond the corrupt cop... not only because of opportunity and greed, but because of a police culture that exalts loyalty over integrity.
On two-year investigation of New York City Police Commission *NY Times* 7 Jul 94

Dorothea Montalvo suspected murderess

3552 I used to be a very good person at one time.
On arrest after seven bodies were found in yard of her Sacramento CA rooming house *NY Times* 18 Nov 88

Dominick "Donny" Montemarano gang member

3553 I'm gonna explain to you a story.
Conversation secretly recorded by FBI and played at Mafia trial *NY Times* 26 Jan 86

Jack Moran Tulsa, OK City Prosecutor

3554 Being kissed is an occupational hazard of police work.
On policewoman who was kissed by a man "trying to get out of a ticket" *NY Times* 5 Mar 87

Robert M Morgenthau District Attorney for Manhattan

3555 When he was arrested, he had a warm body and he confessed that he was alive.
On insurance fraud indictment of Brooklyn man twice reported dead, *NY Times* 7 Nov 87

John Mortimer lawyer and playwright

3556 Criminals expect a little bit of spectacle before they are sent away to prison.
On retaining robes and wigs in British courtrooms *NY Times* 23 Aug 92

George Moscone Mayor of San Francisco

3557 Crime is an overhead you have to pay if you want to live in the city.
Newsweek 20 Dec 76

Dennis Murphy detective

3558 He ate only the people he really liked and wanted to keep with him.
Testimony in trial of Milwaukee serial killer and cannibalizer Jeffrey L Dahmer *Washington Post* 1 Feb 92

NY State Department of Correctional Services

3559 A combination of normal saline, sodium pentothal, pavulon and potassium chloride will be used progressively to cause death.
Instructions manual issued to Unit for Condemned Persons for execution by use of lethal drugs in resumption of the death penalty after 32 years *NY Times* 2 Sep 95

3560 Ladies and gentlemen, the physican in attendance has pronounced the inmate dead. . . . The execution is complete and the officers will now escort you out of the institution.
Announcement provided for security supervisors *ib*

The New York Times

3561 Her crime—wicked and fascinating—speaks so eloquently of our time, in ways we don't even want to talk about.
"The Ballad of John and Lorena" editorial on the trial of Lorena Bobbitt for severing her husband's penis 13 Jan 94

3562 Man's scariest fantasy of Feminine Revenge... [but] for women, it is horror mixed with the awful temptation to admire the crime.
ib

Galina Novikov Russian tourist

3563 He embraced me and then there was blood, blood, blood everywhere. It was like a bad movie. And I see it over and over.
On fatal mugging of a Moscow cardiologist during New York visit with his wife *NY Times* 2 Jul 90

Arthur Nye prosecutor

3564 Some of us have a compulsion for malted milk or a cold beer. He's got a compulsion to kill.
On trial of Donald Harvey in murders of 24 patients, and possibly 54, the worst serial murder case in US history *US News & World Report* 31 Aug 87

Edna O'Brien novelist

3565 He rose as she went through the gate and acted so deftly that the scream she let out got lost in her throat as a wail... and as she fell, he helped her down.
On the murder of a faithless mistress in O'Brien's novel *Casualties of Peace* Simon & Schuster 67

Geoffrey Paterson British Embassy, Washington

3566 The bird has flown.

Code message to career Soviet agent Kim Philby that two colleagues, Guy Burgess and Donald MacLean, had fled to Moscow, quoted by Philby *My Silent War* Grove 68

Robert Perry prosecuting attorney

3567 For a plot hatched in hell, don't expect angels for witnesses.

In summation to jury as prosecuting attorney at John De Lorean's conspiracy trial, news summaries 6 Aug 84

Laurence J Peter author and educator

3568 Prison will not work until we start sending a better class of people there.

Recalled on Peter's death 12 Jan 90

Kim Philby British spy

3569 It seemed a good idea to camp at the mouth of the lion's den for a short spell.

On occupying a house near the residence of the FBI's Assistant Director while acting as a Soviet spy inside Britain's Washington Embassy *My Silent War* Grove 68

3570 All but the tip of the cat's tail was now out of the bag.

On the discovery that Philby's involvement in Spain's civil war may have been financed by the Soviets *ib*

3571 It left a nasty little question.

ib

Alfred Pierrepont professional hangman

3572 My father could dispatch a man in the time it took the prison clock to strike 8—leading him from his cell on the first strike and having him suspended dead on the rope by the last strike. That seemed a very worthy ambition to me.

On his role as Britain's chief executioner, recalled on Pierrepont's death 10 Jul 92

3573 The fruits of my experience has the bitter aftertaste that I do not now believe that anyone of the hundreds of executions I carried out has in any way acted as a deterrent against future murder.

ib

Daniel Pinkwater essayist

3574 It... had to do with his unique bookkeeping system.

Reporting on a man convicted of embezzlement NPR 25 Sep 95

Luca Pistorelli Italian judge

3575 In the mental map of a *mafioso...* Sicily is the center of the world. He considers himself first of all a Sicilian who believes in God and loves his land, its traditions, its unwritten codes.

Quoted by Alexander Stille *Excellent Cadavers: The Mafia and the Death of the First Italian Republic* Pantheon 95

3576 Sicilianness is the essential and indestructible component of the mentality of every Cosa Nostra member, from the newest initiate to the boss of bosses.

ib

Michael Pollan gardener of the exotic

3577 This is America in the time of the drug war... [the] densely planted indoor table-top garden.

Reporting on home-grown marijuana as the "high tech, high crime Number 1 cash crop" *NY Times* 19 Feb 95

3578 The community's epicenter... is the CIA: Cannabis in Amsterdam.

ib

Katherine Ann Power peace activist

3579 I am surrendering to authorities today to answer charges that arise from... the deep and violent crisis that the Vietnam War created in our land.

On entering police custody after 23 years in hiding under an assumed name following a Boston bank robbery in which a policeman was killed *NY Times* 16 Sep 93

3580 At that time, the law was being broken everywhere: at the very top, an intransigent President defied international law as well as the express intentions of Congress; in Government services, Daniel Ellsberg leaked the Pentagon Papers in the hope that citizen scrutiny could hasten an end to the war; among the clergy, priests and nuns destroyed draft records; in neighborhoods, young men defied the draft.

ib

3581 I must answer this accusation from the past, in order to live with full authenticity in the present... with openess and truth, rather than shame and hiddenness.

ib

President's Commission on Organized Crime

3582 [Mob lawyers are] the life-support system of organized crime.

Wall Street Journal 12 Aug 85

Raymond Prinzen St Louis Police

3583 Nobody is going to steal Grandma's gun. It is no longer stashed in the bottom drawer.

On police round-up of 5,000 firearms *NY Times* 23 Oct 91

Mario Puzo novelist

3584 A lawyer with his briefcase can steal more than a hundred men with guns.

The Godfather Putnam 68

3585 He decided to wash his Cadillac. . . . It always helped him think when he was grooming the car. He remembered his father in Italy doing the same thing with donkeys.

On a gangster's preparation for a murder

3586 Chicago, that black sheep of their world. They had given up trying to civilize Chicago.

On crime families' control of American cities *ib*

3587 Revenge is a dish that tastes best when it is eaten cold.

ib

Jamin Raskin Associate Dean, American University Law School

3588 We've developed a culture of crime as entertainment, the criminal a celebrity. So this culture gives license to borderline personalities to go out and make themselves famous.

On assaults on the White House *Washington Times* 25 May 95

James Earl Ray convicted murderer

3589 I was in Tennessee 24 hours and got 99 years.

On beginning 20th year of sentence in assassination of Martin Luther King Jr *Life* March 88

Janet Reno US Attorney General

3590 Unless we are willing to invest in children early on, we will never be able to build enough prisons ever to begin to cope with the problem 13, 15, 18 years from now.

NY Times 16 May 94

Walter Reuther labor leader

3591 It does us no good to be the first city in America to achieve integrated looting.

On Detroit riots 31 Dec 67

Alan Richman reporter

3592 A young man enters wearing a multi-functional digital watch, a diamond-chip pierced earring, two gold chains, one gold bracelet and two gold rings—a jewelry store waiting to be robbed.

On survey of subway muggings *NY Times* 28 Jun 79

Sara Rimer reporter

3593 The case has become a national conversation.

On O J Simpson's televised trial *NY Times* 6 Feb 95

Benjamin Robinson mortician

3594 Death. . . is 25 cents. That's what a bullet costs.

On youthful shootings in Brooklyn *NY Times* 10 Mar 92

Carlos Robinson convict

3595 This ain't nothing but a circus, a big old zoo. We all animals now.

At Georgia State Prison on joining the first US chain gang in 30 years *Newsweek* 15 May 95

Delroy Ross gang member

3596 You got it—we mixed up in homicide and drugs. We sell drugs, and we kill.

Boast to undercover detective that murders were an integral part of selling drugs *NY Times* 15 Mar 88

3597 I put the gun up to his head and go, bam, bam bam, bam.

On circumventing bulletproof vests *ib*

Linda Russell mother of murderess

3598 She is lost in a sea of guilt and grief.

On her daughter, Susan R Smith, South Carolina woman who drowned her children but alleged that a black man had car-jacked them, news summaries 31 Dec 94

"Tom Mix" Santoro Mafia underboss

3599 Aw, give me a hundred years and get it over with.

To judge sentencing seven members of La Cosa Nostra's high commission *US News & World Report* 26 Jan 86

Richard Schlesinger CBS reporter

3600 What's going to kill you, old age or electricity?

Interviewing Harold LaMont Otey who fought a murder sentence for 16 years before becoming the first man electrocuted in Nebraska in 30 years *NY Times* 14 Dec 94

Gil Schultz Houston Police

3601 Homicide is so exacting. Two people know who did it. One ain't talking, the other can't.

Quoted by Clifford Irving *Daddy's Girl* Summit 88

Cosmo Scordato Italian priest

3602 Our work here is God's work. We are ants of history; day by day, a little at a time.

On fighting the Mafia in Sicily *National Geographic* Aug 95

General Rosso Serrano Director, Colombian Police

3603 We set out to hunt a tiger, and we found a pussycat.

On the surprising ease of apprehending the Cali cocaine cartel *Washington Post* 28 Aug 95

James Sewell Florida State University police

3604 He was the all-American boy murdering all-American girls.

On serial killer Ted Bundy *Newsweek* 6 Feb 89

Pamela Smart accessory to murder

3605 I'm sorry if I reacted wrong, but nobody gave me the 22-year-old widow's handbook.

On her arrest after her husband's murder by her 15-year-old lover *NY Times* 1 Apr 91

O J Simpson athlete and murder suspect

3606 Absolutely 100 percent not guilty!

Entering his plea on arraignment on murder of his wife *NY Times* 23 Jul 94

Perry Smith convicted murderer

3607 I thought he was a very nice gentleman. . . I thought that right up to the moment I cut his throat.

On the murder of a wealthy Kansas farmer, quoted by Truman Capote *In Cold Blood* Random House 66

3608 Phillipsburg, Kansas. Where the folks have a real cute jail. If you like jails.

ib

3609 They never did anything wrong to me—the way other people have all my life. Maybe they're just the ones who had to pay for it.

On the farm family he murdered *ib*

R C Smith writer

3610 Twenty-three German shepherds. . . sang out warnings with the baritone barking that burglars' nightmares are made of.

On calling on Scottish author Brian Plummer *New Yorker* 15 Feb 88

Clyde Collins Snow forensic anthropologist

3611 Unable to dissolve his marriage, he decided to dissolve his wife.

On a Chicago butcher who put his wife's body in a sausage vat filled with boiling potash, quoted by Christopher Joyce and Eric Stover's *Witnessing from the Grave* Little, Brown 91

3612 Although they speak softly, they never lie and they never forget.

On skeletons as evidence of crime *ib*

Robert Spagnoletti Assistant US Attorney

3613 He has an attitude the size of Montana.

On a convicted rapist *Washington Post* 18 Sep 94

Richard Speck convicted murderer

3614 If that one girl hadn't spit in my face, they'd all be alive.

To a columnist interviewing him 12 years after Speck confessed to killing eight student nurses *Chicago Sun Times* 31 Mar 78

Albert Speer Hitler aide and architect

3615 Boredom is the one torment of hell that Dante forgot.

On 20-year imprisonment of Nazi war criminal Rudolph Hess Spandau *The Secret Diaries* Macmillan 76

3616 [It was] a life unlived. . . the organization of emptiness.

ib

Lynne Stewart attorney

3617 [He has been taken] to a peculiarly inaccessible part of the world. . . to Middle America, to Noplaceville.

On her client, the blind Sheik Omar Abdel Rayman, convicted in bombing of the World Trade Center and transferred immediately from New York to a Springfield MO medical prison *Washington Post* 3 Oct 95

Joseph P Stinson screenwriter

3618 Go ahead, make my day!

Film dialogue for Clint Eastwood to a gunman holding him at bay in 1983 screenplay for *Sudden Impact* based on short story by Earl E Smith; his words were further popularized when used by President Reagan in urging Congress to vote a tax increase *Time* 18 Mar 85

Fred Stock Warden, Federal Prison, Atlanta

3619 There are a lot of dangerous people here. After all, that's why they're in prison.

On the growing number of assaults despite a ratio of one guard to every 6.9 prisoners *NY Times* 9 Feb 95

Nathaniel Sweeper drug dealer

3620 You don't kill nobody from across the street. You walk up to him, you kill him in the head.

To a fellow member of the New Vigilantes *NY Times* 15 Mar 88

Hunter S Thompson author

3621 [He was] Genghis Khan on an iron horse. . . flat out through the eye of a beer can and up your daughter's leg.

On a motorcycle gang leader *Hell's Angels* Random House 66

Kevin D Thompson bank robber

3622 This is a stickup, keep clam I have a gun give me some $100, $50, & 20 keep clam and no won will get harm. Thank you.

Holdup note written on back of his own paycheck stub that led to his subsequent arrest *NY Daily News* 10 Mar 88

Thomas Thompson author

3623 In a severely tailored blue dress that enhanced her thinness. . . eyeglasses dangling from a silver chain. . . sensible black walking shoes. . . waif-like hair cut inelegantly and let go to shades of sleet and snow, she was the woman who had graded everybody's English Lit exam since education began.

On Lilla Paulus as defendant in Texas murder trial of Dr John Hill *Blood and Money* Doubleday 77

Tommy G Thompson Governor of Wisconsin

3624 If keeping criminals off our streets means sending our prisoners to Texas, bye-bye. They're going South.

On clearing room for more convictions by joining ten other states in brokering to send 3,776 prisoners to Texas jails *NY Times* 9 Feb 96

Craig H Trout Federal Bureau of Prisons

3625 There are no nice guys at Leavenworth. They are all sharks, and when you put sharks together the stronger ones feed on the rest.

On Leavenworth Prison, quoted by Pete Earley *The Hot House* Bantam 92

Maurice Turner Chief of Police, District of Columbia

3626 Eventually, the turf will be divided, they will go out and sell their drugs, people will pay their drug bills on time, and we're not going to have all these shootings.

New Yorker 17 Apr 89

Unabomber (alledgedly Theodore John Kaczynski) terrorist

3627 In order to get our message before the public with some chance of making a lasting impression, we've had to kill people.

Letter to newspapers from an unknown person dubbed Unabomber because he sent his first bombs to university research institutions to protest industrial-technological progress as "a disaster for the human race" *Washington Post* 30 Jun 95

John P Vukasin Federal District Judge

3628 [He] is zero at his bones.

On John Anthony Walker Jr's sale of cryptographic secrets, quoted by John A Barron *Breaking the Ring* Houghton Mifflin 87

3629 Devoted to determining the wind direction and how he can make a profit from the coming storm. . . he represents the evil of banality.

ib

Adam Walinsky Police Corps lobbyist

3630 Our crime problem is only our race problem wearing a different face

NY Times 30 Oct 94

3631 The job of the police in America, at least for the last 30 years, is to keep "them" away from "us." Nobody wants to know how they do it. They just want it done.

ib

John Anthony Walker Jr convicted spy

3632 If I had access to it, color it gone.

On sale of secret material to Russian agents, quoted by John A Barron *Breaking the Ring* Houghton Mifflin 87

3633 K-Mart protects its toothpaste better than the US Navy protects its secrets.

Quoted on *The Spy Who Broke the Code* PBS TV 10 Apr 90

3634 I'm a great believer in KISS—keeping it simple, stupid.

On instructions for drop-offs of secret material *ib*

Wallis Duchess of Windsor

3635 Nothing like a murder in the country to cure what ails you.

Luncheon comment the day after the shooting of Long Island socialite Billy Woodward, quoted by Susan Braudy *This Crazy Thing Called Love* Knopf 92

Washington Times

3636 There's no crime like the present.

On one week's count of three persons jumping the White House fence *Washington Times* 25 May 95

Charles J Whitman mass murderer

3637 After my death, I wish an autopsy on me to be performed to see if there's any mental disorder.

Note written a few hours before killing his mother and his wife as well as 12 others and wounding 33 with rifle fire from a 27-story tower at the University of Texas, Austin, 1 Aug 66

Anthony Williams Deputy Director, Metropolitan Police, London

3638 I discovered this bloody great bucketful of money!

Admission of taking $8 mllion from a Scotland Yard secret fund to fight the IRA and using it instead to restore a highlands village *NY Times* 30 May 95

Geline Williams Hingham, MA prosecutor

3639 The hand that blessed, that married, that absolved of sin was the hand that fondled and penetrated.

On a priest's abuse of acolytes in several parishes *USA Today* 16 Mar 94

Howard Wilson US Prosecuting Attorney

3640 Some took a lot of gold, and some a little, but they all took.

On defendants accused of bribing millions of dollars for helping to obtain military contracts *NY Times* 12 Mar 88

Dr Otto Wolken Auschwitz prisoner-physician

3641 They acted like animals... that had tasted blood.

Testifying at trial of staff of Auschwitz concentration camp *NY Herald Tribune* 25 Feb 64

3642 Some guards and officials could not sleep well at night unless they had beaten someone to death during the day.

ib

Julia Wright confessed murderess

3643 Everything is all right. You can come home now. I have killed Fiona.

To her husband after fatally stabbing his mistress *London Times* 3 Dec 94

Peter Wright M-I5 Agent

3644 British Security Service defectors are false, lies are truth, truth lies and the reflections leave you dazzled and confused.

On the sense that he was uncovering disinformation or only what the Soviets wanted him to learn in investigation of art historian Anthony Blunt *Spycatcher* Viking 87

Robin Young reporter

3645 The tacky remnants of a traitorous life made more than $150,000 at Sotheby's in London yesterday.

On the autioning of personal effects of British spy Kim Philby who fled to Moscow in 1963 *London Times* 20 Jul 94

BUSINESS

Executives

Paul (Red) Adair Chair, Red Adair Co

3646 They couldn't find their ass with radar.

On competition from other oil-fire fighter companies *Forbes* 19 Jul 93

American Continental Corp

3647 Memorize the pitch until it flows from your mouth like carbon monoxide from the exhaust pipe of a Mack truck.

Confidential memo to salesmen of bonds that financed Charles H Keating Jr's ill-fated Phoenician Hotel, quoted on *Frontline* PBS 1 May 90

3648 The weak, the meek and ignorant are always good targets.

ib

John Edward Anderson Chair, Ace Beverage

3649 You need enough cash cows to feed your pigs.

On ownership of banks, insurance, and real estate to support Bel Air CA beverage distributor and other interests *Forbes* 17 Oct 94

Anon

3650 One hot dog can't like another hot dog.

On the relationship of Chrysler Executive Committee Chair Lee Iacocca and Chrysler President Robert Lutz *Fortune* 20 Apr 92

Stanley Bing columnist

3651 That gap between what I have and what I deserve is the bulwark of my status.

On the rationed space of corporate offices *Fortune* 21 Aug 95

Henry W Bloch Chair, H & R Bloch

3652 There was really nobody around to help the average person.

On 1955 establishment of chain for the filing of income tax *Forbes* 17 Oct 94

Warren Buffett Chair, Berkshire Hathaway, Investment Brokers

3653 It's pleasant to go to bed every night knowing there are 2.5-billion males in the world who have to shave the following morning.

On his profitable investment in Gillette blades *London Times* 9 Oct 93

3654 It is better to be approximately right than precisely wrong.

Fortune 4 Apr 94

Leo Burnett Chair, Leo Burnett Advertising

3655 Any fool can write a bad ad, but it takes a real genius to keep his hands off a good one.

NY Times 11 Apr 95

3656 We want consumers to say "That's a hell of a product" instead of "That's a hell of an ad."

100 Leo's: Wit and Wisdom from Leo Burnett NTC Business Books 95

3657 To swear off making mistakes is very easy. All you have to do is swear off having ideas.

ib

Philip Caldwell Chair, Ford Motor Co

3658 We redesigned everything but the air in the tires.

On developing a new line that included the Taurus that was to become the best-selling car in the US *Fortune* 3 Apr 95

James E Casey President, United Parcel Service

3659 Deft fingers! Deft fingers wrapping thousands of bundles! Neatly tied! Neatly addressed! Stuffed with soft tissue paper! What a treat! Ah, packages!

Quoted by Philip Hamburger *Mayor Watching and Other Pleasures* Rinehart 58

Wendall Chino President, Mescaleros Indian Tribe

3660 The Navajos make rugs, the Pueblos make pottery and the Mescaleros make money.

On $2-billion deal with nuclear utilities for land for radioactive garbage *US News & World Report* 8 Jan 96

Jack Kent Cooke sportsman and financier

3661 Tell them I'm worth $1.98.

Reply to *Forbes* survey on richest people in America *Washington Post* 21 Mar 93

3662 The good thing about being rich is when you drop a Tic Tac, you don't have to pick it up—until nobody's looking.

ib

E Gerald Corrigan Chair, Goldman Sachs

3663 We need more gray hair.

On the collapse of Britain's 233-year-old Barings brought on by a 28-year-old trader *NY Times* 6 Mar 95

Trevor Creed Director, International Design, Chrysler Corp

3664 It's one of our. . . corporate mantras.

On the addition of more "convenience features" to enhance sales appeal *NY Times* 9 Jan 95

3665 If we ever go above the Big Gulp. . . . that's when we get asked to put in a Porta Potti.

On inclusion of jumbo 7-Eleven "Big Gulp" cup holders *ib*

Joyce Culbert insurance analyst

3666 Take the best of the worst risks, charge the average of the worst risks, and make a ton.

On careful screening of drivers who can't get insurance *Fortune* 8 May 89

Gerald M Czarnecki Senior VP, Human Resources and Administration IBM

3667 Our view of corporate headquarters is that there should be as little of it as possible.

On abandonment of spacious country offices as icons of corporate life *NY Times* 13 Jan 94

3668 The big building on the hill is more and more a thing of the past.

ib

Arnold W Donald Chair, Monsanto Agricultural Co

3669 Have three people do five jobs but pay them like four.

Management philosophy *Fortune* 9 Sep 91

Pierre Samuel Du Pont II stockholder

3670 The thing about Du Ponts is that some are very, very rich and the others are just plain old rich.

On family retention of 15 percent of company stock *Forbes* 19 Oct 92

Joseph Durst real estate developer

3671 Never buy farther than you can walk.

Forbes 19 Oct 92

Ferdinand Eberstadt Partner, Dillion Read

3672 God appeared to us in the guise of Walter P Chrysler, and he offered to buy the Dodge Company.

On stock maneuver that swung control of Dodge stock to Chrysler, quoted by Robert Sobel *The Great Bull Market* Norton 68

Frederick Hudson Ecker Chair, Metropolitan Life

3673 I don't think anybody yet has invented a pastime that's as much fun, or keeps you as young, as a good job.

Recalled on Ecker's death at age 96 20 Mar 64

William T Esrey Chair, Sprint Corporation

3674 Are you going to eat lunch, or have your lunch eaten for you?

On aggressiveness in telecommunications *NY Times* 23 Aug 92

Benjamin Fairless President, US Steel

3675 You cannot add to the stature of a dwarf by cutting off the legs of a giant.

To House of Representatives Subcommmittee on Study of Monopoly Power, news reports 27 Apr 50

3676 This is a plant that will go on for 50 or perhaps 100 years to come, pouring steel into the ribs of our nation and wealth into its economic veins.

On opening of the Fairless Steel Works, Fairless Hills PA, recalled 40 years later when the plant was closed *Washington Post* 12 Apr 92

Harvard S J Fang agent for Asia, American Acres

3677 They pay $500 to buy the American dream. . . to hang on the wall and see it every day, their American dream.

On the sale of deeds to tiny parcels of land that make Chinese eligible for a US visa *NY Times* 29 Jan 93

Mohamed Al Fayed Chair, Harrods of London

3678 They think I'm a wog.

On British opinion that regards him as a "wily Oriental gentleman" *Vanity Fair* Sep 95

Marshall Field V investor

3679 They all started out with nothing in those days, and the biggest crooks won. I was just lucky to come from a line of successful crooks.

On his inheritance from 19th century business *Esquire* 28 Mar 78

Henry Ford II President, Ford Motor

3680 Most of the trouble with business. . . is not the product of evil intentions but of the enormous difficulty of carrying out the best intentions.

Sales Management 15 Jan 69

3681 My name is on the building.

Insistence on having the last word, recalled on Ford's death 29 Sep 87

3682 Sometimes you just don't like somebody.

On firing Lee Iacocca *ib*

Clive Francis British realtor

3683 I used to own two airplanes. Now I own a bicycle.

On heavy losses in the world's preeminent insurance market, Lloyds of London *NY Times* 27 Apr 93

Mike Frazier Director, Commercial Real Estate, General Electric

3684 When you get up in the morning, if you're not thinking of ways to make money, this isn't the place to work.

Fortune 21 Feb 94

Shiro Fujita President, NTT Data, Tokyo

3685 Just-in-time is the reason everyone is late.

On last-minute deliveries *Fortune* 20 Apr 92

William Henry Gates III Chair, Microsoft

3686 Like a hammer, they can be used to hit a nail or smash someone in the face.

On electronic networking *Fortune* 9 Aug 93

3687 If I'd had some set idea of a finish line, don't you think I would have crossed it years ago?

On being asked what he would shoot for after becoming one of America's 400 richest people *Forbes* 17 Oct 94

Lawrence Gladstone President, Sequins International

3688 In China, there are 500,000 women and children with needle and thread and sequins.

Acknowledging cheap labor while championing quality production by content employees *NY Times* 29 May 95

David D Glass CEO, Walmart

3689 They think we're offensive. So go ahead and be offensive.

On price wars *Fortune* 8 Feb 93

Roberto Goizueta CEO, Coca-Cola

3690 The moment avoiding failure becomes your motivator, you're down the path of inactivity. You stumble only if you're moving.

Fortune 1 May 95

John Grado President, Grado Laboratories

3691 God blessed me with good ears and my uncle taught me to listen.

On becoming a leading manufacturer of stereo headphones *Forbes* 5 Jun 95

Robert Greenleaf Director of Management Research, AT&T

3692 For the person with creative potential, there is no wholeness except in using it.

Servant Leadership Paulist Press 77

3693 Only to the extent that trustees give support when it is needed does the chief executive want a strong board.

ib

Thomas Haggai Chair, IGA Inc

3694 Cast your bread upon the waters, but wait until the tide is coming in to do it.

Fortune 7 Nov 88

Najeeb E Halaby CEO, Pan American Airways

3695 [It is] locked in a shrinking box, with the top, bottom, and sides all closing in at once.

On becoming head of financially-ill Pan Am *Fortune* Jan 70

Robert Half President, Robert Half Int

3696 A resume is a balance sheet without any liabilities.

Robert Half on Hiring Crown 85

Joyce Clyde Hall founder, Hallmark Cards

3697 [It is] the art of the masses.

On greeting cards as a billion-dollar a year business, recalled on Hall's death 29 Oct 82

Armand Hammer President, Occidental Petroleum

3698 When I work 14 hours a day, seven days a week, I get lucky.

Guardian Weekly 30 Dec 90

William Hewlett co-founder, Hewlett Packard

3699 Never try to take a fortified hill, especially if the army on top is bigger than your own.

On avoiding a head-on collision with IBM in mainframe computers *NY Times* 10 Mar 92

Jimmy Hoffa President, International Brotherhood of Teamsters

3700 I hope the worms eat his eyes out.

On hearing of President Kennedy's assassination 22 Nov 63, recalled on 20th anniversary of Hoffa's disappearance *NY Times* 23 Jul 95

3701 You will only get what you are big enough to take.

On labor unions and US business NBC TV 27 Jul 95

Soichiro Honda founder, Honda Motor Co

3702 My greatest achievement was in imitating American cars.

On visiting Ford headquarters at Dearborn MI *LA Times* 10 Oct 89

Johnnie Bryan Hunt Chair, J B Hunt Transport

3703 I was hungry once and once you're hungry, you're different.

On his background as a poorly educated truck driver before building a trucking company with sales projected at $900 million *Forbes* 19 Oct 92

Mel Hurtig Canadian publisher

3704 There will not be a Canada a generation from now if this agreement is signed.

On effects of trade pact allowing US to flood Canada with lower-cost products and cause plants to be relocated in US to escape higher taxes and production cost *NY Times* 13 Dec 87

Lee A Iacocca automobile executive

3705 I checked my wallet, and it was a little short of $40 billion.

On considering a take-over of General Motors *NY Times* 1 Jun 88

3706 Beyond the peaks, there's a valley.

On stock market automotive futures, Station WAMU Washington 22 Aug 95

Carl Icahn corporate raider

3707 When nobody wants something, that creates an opportunity.

On buying into Texaco and USX when both were troubled companies *Fortune* 5 Nov 90

Herman Jacobs pharmaceutical supplier

3708 It is not the mouse who is the thief, it is the hole that allows the mouse in.

On applying Talmudic principles to business *Forbes* 21 Nov 94

Llewellyn Jenkins President, American Bankers Assn

3709 A bank buys money like a grocer buys bananas—and then adds on salaries and rent and sells the product.

LA Times 14 May 82

John Justin Jr manufacturer

3710 God ain't making any more cowboys.

On importance of a new breed, "weekend cowboys," as major purchasers of Justin's Chippewa heavy-duty work-boots *US News & World Report* 9 May 94

Alfred Kahn Chair, Civil Aeronautics Board

3711 We thought an airplane was nothing but a marginal cost with wings.

On deregulation that failed to prosper airlines *NY Times* 2 Jan 91

Donald M Kimball Chair, PepsiCo Inc

3712 There's no place where success comes before work, except in the dictionary.

USA Today 21 Apr 86

Lane Kirkland President, AFL-CIO

3713 The founders of the American labor movement left us all with one central theme. . . Agitate, Educate, Organize.

To 1977 AFL-CIO convention, quoted by William Safire *Safire's Political Dictionary* Random House 78

3714 My pappy told me never to bet my bladder against a brewery or get into an argument with people who buy ink by the barrel.

Quoted by David Olive *Business Babble* Wiley 93

Ted Kleisner President, Greenbrier Hotel

3715 Anyone who doesn't work here and who is of working age, there's a reason they're not here.

On being the only significant private employer in West Virginia's Greenbrier county *Washington Post* 31 May 92

George L Knox VP for Public Affairs, Philip Morris Co

3716 The only permanent fixtures in New York City are Grand Central Terminal and the Empire State Building.

On reports that Philip Morris might relocate and cut its backing of the arts *NY Times* 5 Oct 94

Semon Emil Knudsen automotive executive

3717 Before you tell someone how good you are, you must tell him how bad you used to be.

Time 25 May 59

3718 Competition will bite you if you keep running. . . stand still, it will swallow you.

Citing advice from his father on entering automobile industry, quoted by Peter Collier and David Horowitz *The Fords* Simon & Schuster 87

Jerome Kohlberg Wall Street buy-out specialist

3719 An ethic is not an ethic, and a value not a value without some sacrifice for it. Something given up, something not gained.

Fortune 3 Jun 91

Ray Kroc founder, McDonald's

3720 Luck is a dividend of sweat. The more you sweat, the luckier you get.

Quoted by Penny Moser "The McDonald's Mystique" *Fortune* 4 Jul 88

3721 If they were drowning to death, I would put a hose in their mouth.

On competitors *ib*

Joseph F Kruy Chair, Cambex Corp

3722 When you compete with IBM, you go to bed with your clothes on.

Quoted by Norm Alster "Dancing in the Shadow of the Giant" *Forbes* 1 Apr 91

Mordecai Kutz Professor of Economics, Stanford

3723 There is only one truth, and many opinions. Therefore, most people are wrong most of the time.

On how viewpoints of stock can differ without contradicting basic information *Fortune* 3 Apr 95

Estée Lauder cosmetics tycoon

3724 I never thought I'd make it big. If I felt I had made it, I would be somewhere nice, like St Moritz, skiing.

Forbes 19 Oct 92

Charles Lazarus founder, Toys "R" Us

3725 When Mama went back to work, department stores were dead.

On successful specialization *Fortune* 23 May 88

Nick Leesom Singapore trader of Barings Futures

3726 There were days when I could lose 25- to 30-million pounds. . . days when I made 50 million.

On causing the collapse of the esteemed British firm *London Times* 11 Sep 95

3727 The first day that I asked for funding there should have been massive alarm bells ringing.

On lack of awareness in London headquarters *ib*

Samuel Jayson LeFrak Chair, LeFrak Organization

3728 Rather than reap two crops a year, I bring in 12. . . one each month when our rents are due.

On developing over 200,000 apartments *Forbes* 16 Oct 95

3729 He who has the gold makes the rules.

On a guiding principle engraved on a plaque in financier Armand Hammer's bedroom *Regardie's* Feb 91

Michael Levine Dean, Yale School of Management

3730 We thought the industry would be full of hungry piranhas....[but] this is shark and tuna country.

On economics compelling consolidation of airlines *NY Times* 2 Jan 91

John Long Manager, Shell, Romania

3731 This is a country of brown envelopes.

On bribes necessary to doing business in Romania *Washington Post* 3 Nov 93

Peter Lynch head of Fidelity Investments Magellan Fund

3732 I like to buy a company any fool can manage because eventually one will.

Fortune 28 Dec 92

General Douglas MacArthur US Army

3733 Acheson, I don't want to talk about those midgets!

To Secretary of State Dean Acheson when asked how he found big business after a lifetime of army service, quoted by David Acheson *Acheson Country* Norton 93

Cyril Magnin Chair, Joseph Magnin Co

3734 Never look at the doors closing behind you or you'll miss the ones opening ahead.

NY Times 31 Dec 89

Stanley Marcus Chair, Neiman Marcus Co

3735 You achieve customer satisfaction when you sell merchandise that doesn't come back to a customer who does.

Fortune 22 Mar 93

Forrest Mars Sr founder, Mars Inc

3736 I'm a religious man. I pray for Milky Way. I pray for Snickers.

Washington Post 12 Apr 92

Ramón Masip Vice President, Nestle Inc

3737 Sometimes you have to cut off a finger to save an arm.

On downsizing in the world's third largest food company *Fortune* 6 Sep 93

Peter McArthur British newspaper publisher

3738 Every successful enterprise requires three men—a dreamer, a businessman, and a son of a bitch.

Quoted by David Olive *Business Babble* Wiley 91

Jim McGroddy Chief of Research, IBM

3739 The spoken word was fleeting. . . not inspected as thoroughly as it should be. And the written word was very incomplete. And therefore not inspectable.

On the need to improve corporate communications *Fortune* 3 Oct 94

Peter Middleton Chair, Lloyd's of London

3740 They should be doing it, and they should be doing it for a more significant part of their day.

On executives who need to overcome the discomfort of thinking *NY Times* 3 Jan 93

William Moll Vice President, Research, Oil-Dri Corp, Chicago

3741 Cat litter has done for the cat what air conditioning did for Houston.

Quoted by Penny Ward Moser "Filler's the Name, Odor's the Game" *Fortune* 25 Apr 88

Gary Moss Vice President, Marketing Communications, Campbell Soup

3742 You can teach an elephant to dance, but the likelihood of its stepping on your toes is very high.

On the declining roll of advertising agencies as monarchs of marketing *Forbes* 15 Mar 93

Tom Murphy CEO, Capital Cities/ABC Inc

3743 If you hire mediocre people, they will hire mediocre people.

Fortune 6 May 91

Michael Murray Director of Human Resources, Microsoft

3744 If Microsoft were a car it would have a large gas pedal and a small but workable brake. It would not have a rear-view mirror.

On decision-making by small groups from the ranks of employees *Newsweek* 11 Jul 94

Bill O'Gara Ohio manufacturer

3745 Workers don't hang their brains on the door when they come to work anymore.

On cutting production hours through development of self-guided work teams and reviews *Forbes* 18 Jan 93

Kenneth Olsham Chair, Wells Rich Greene

3746 There are so many layers in producing ads that it's like cutting salami—you take a slice off here, you take a slice off there, and soon you have no salami.

On malaise in the world of advertising *Forbes* 27 Mar 95

Gretchen Park Director of Compensation and Benefits, Residential Services Corp

3747 Some take the "boiled-frog approach." People get used to hotter and hotter water.

On corporate struggle to define what makes people productive *International Herald Tribune* 25 July 92

Dennis Patrick President, Time Warner Telecommunications Unit

3748 We will be digital from the get-go. . . able to operate in a multimedia universe. . . voice, video and data.

On developing a wireless empire *NY Times* 20 Sep 93

John Peers President, Logical Machine Corp

3749 Kickbacks must always exceed bribes.

1,001 Logical Laws Doubleday 79

T Boone Pickens Chair, Mesa Petroleum

3750 Work eight hours and sleep eight hours and make sure they are not the same.

NPR 28 May 92

Pasquale Pistorio Motorola executive

3751 All I got was an armored car and a pay cut.

On transfer from $170,000 US post to $135,000-a-year job in Italy *Fortune* 7 Nov 88

James Preston CEO, Avon Products

3752 A bad reputation is like a hangover. It takes a while to get rid of, and it makes everything else hurt.

Fortune 10 Feb 92

Clarence B Randall CEO, Inland Steel

3753 Every man who has lived his life to the full, should, by the time his senior years are reached, have established a reserve inventory of unfinished thinking.

Sixty-five Plus Little, Brown 63

Sumner Redstone Chair, Viacom Inc

3754 There's a time for killing and a time for kissing.

To John Malone, Chair, Tele-Communications Inc on Malone's attempt to combine Viacom with cable movie channels *Forbes* 17 Oct 94

Walter Reuther President, United Automobile Workers

3755 Labor is not fighting for a larger slice of the national pie. Labor is fighting for a larger pie.

Quoted by Nelson Lichtenstein *The Most Dangerous Man in Detroit* Basic Books 95

James D Robinson III CEO, American Express

3756 Quality is the only patent protection we've got.

Fortune 20 Nov 89

3757 You have to manage for delivery of quality rather than quality itself

ib

David Rockefeller Jr President, Chase Manhattan Bank

3758 One thing this family does not need to do is make itself resented by thousands of more people.

On reluctance to join management, quoted by Peter Collier and David Horowitz *The Rockefellers* Holt Rinehart Winston 76

John D Rockefeller Jr philanthropist

3759 The secretaries here have an advantage I never had. They can prove to themselves their commercial worth.

To NY Chamber of Commerce 6 Apr 50, quoted by Peter Collier and David Horowitz *The Rockefellers* Holt Rinehart Winston 76

Nelson A Rockefeller statesman

3760 If the capitalist system has any way of getting things done, the Rockefeller brothers have access to it.

Quoted by A A Berle *Navigating the Rapids* Harcourt Brace Jovanovich 73

Steven J Ross CEO, Time Warner Inc

3761 You learn to say, "Hey Charlie, I don't want to talk business today. . . tell me what your problem is."

That is the important thing that is the guts of the business. . . in Hollywood or a funeral parlor.

On using a family-owned mortuary as the basis for Time Warner, world's largest media and entertainment company *NY Times* 21 Dec 92

3762 There are those who work all day; those who dream all day, and those who spend an hour dreaming before setting to work to fulfill those dreams. Go into the third category because there's virtually no competition.

Quoting death-bed advice from his father *ib*

Anthony J Rucci Vice President for Human Resources, Sears Co

3763 A compelling place to work does not mean a nice place to work.

On challenges of companies in the throes of cultural change *NY Times* 7 Jan 96

3764 We want people to feel some degree of anxiety, the stress of the achievement-oriented.

ib

3765 To produce, to hit performance targets and to take part in the transformation process. . . that's like saying, "Fly an airplane and change the wings on the plane while you're at it."

ib

Wolfgang Schmitt Chair, Rubbermaid Corp

3766 Innovation most of the time is simply taking A, B, C and D, which already exist, and putting them together in a form called E.

On designing new products *Fortune* 14 Nov 94

Howard Schultz President and CEO, Starbucks Coffee

3767 Retail is detail.

On building the largest US coffee-bar chain *NY Times* 14 Dec 94

Charles Scribner Jr Chair, Charles Scribner's Sons

3768 Nobody else was allowed in. . . [but] nowadays a sales conference resembles a Passion play: everybody is invited to participate and marvel at the drama.

On introducing new books *In the Company of Writers* Simon & Schuster 91

3769 Working with Hemingway was rather like being strapped in an electric chair. . . it would need just the flicking of a switch to ruin me.

On Ernest Hemingway *ib*

3770 First novels come out of people's lives and the lore of their families and friends.

ib

3771 Although we had quite a few private subscribers. . . it is difficult to get these reference books sold to individuals—how to get the oats to the horses? .

ib

C F Seabrook founder, Seabrook Farms

3772 The work consists in doing whatever the employer feels like asking at any moment of the day or night.

On advertising for workers in the 1920s *New Yorker* 20 Feb 95

3773 It doesn't matter how many PhDs you have, it's how many PhDs you have working for you that counts.

ib

John Seabrook former heir to Seabrook Farms

3774 It goes to show that you can't keep the old bulls and the young bulls in the same pasture.

On stormy relationship between his father and grandfather, founder C F Seabrook *New Yorker* 20 Feb 95

3775 It's like a birthmark. I used to try to conceal it.

On being identified as the heir to Seabrook Frozen Foods *ib*

3776 He fired and disowned my father and sold the business to spite him. . . so in fact my only inheritance is bitterness.

ib

3777 In spite of all the pain that creamed spinach cost my family, it is still the best creamed spinach you can buy.

ib

Jim Shoulders Oklahoma rancher

3778 If John Justin tells you a chicken is going to pull a wagon, then you saddle up that chicken, because that chicken will go ahead and pull.

On holding stock in John Justin Jr's highly successful manufacturing of heavy-duty work boots *US News and World* Report 9 May 94

Herschel Shostek telecommunications consultant

3779 Cellular calls are not cost based; they're insanity based.

NY Times 12 Nov 92

Sheldon Henry Solow builder

3780 We're in barracuda land. You can only get away with this once.

On the vastly profitable NYC office structure 9 West 57th St *Forbes* 19 Oct 92

Henry Steinway consultant to Steinway Inc

3781 The idea that your daughter is a schlumpf unless she plays the piano—William did more to invent that than anybody.

On his grandfather's promotion of Steinway pianos "Ain't It Grand" *Life* Jun 88

Donald J Trump financier

3782 [He is a] member of the Lucky Sperm Club.

On hotel heir Barron Hilton, quoted by John Heins "The Son Also Rises" *Forbes* 25 Jan 88

3783 If you're going to be thinking. . . you might as well think big.

Time 16 Jan 89

3784 [It is] the ultimate trophy in the world.

On owning New York's Plaza Hotel in what was to be a brief satisfaction *NY Times* 5 Jun 90

3785 A gambler is someone who plays slot machines. I prefer to own slot machines.

On opening of his Atlanta City Taj Mahal casino *Time* 9 Apr 90

Don Tyson CEO, Tyson Foods

3786 If you can take $20,000 in one-hundred-dollar bills. . . and tear them up. . . and it doesn't bother you, then you should go into the commodities market.

New Yorker 30 May 94

Hicks Waldron Chair, Boardroom Consultants Inc

3787 People do what you pay them to do, not what you ask them to do.

Quoted in study on executive salaries *Wall Street Journal* 17 Apr 91

Sam Walton Chair, Walmart

3788 We just got after it and stayed after it.

On building the Walmart chain of discount stores from nine in 1960 with $1.4 million in annual sales to 1,528 stores with $26 billion by 1990 *Made in America* Doubleday 92

3789 We were a flea attacking an elephant.

On competing with K-Mart *ib*

3790 We stay in the air and keep our ear to the ground.

On the fleet of a dozen planes developed from one used plane and his personal flying license *ib*

Louis Larrick Ward Chair, Russell Stover Candies

3791 There are only so many ways you can put chocolate, butter, cream, eggs, milk, fruit and nuts together—the real competition is in packaging.

Forbes 19 Oct 92

3792 Keep going forward, but keep your eye on the company in the rearview mirror.

ib

Thomas J Watson Jr Chair, IBM

3793 Lie dead in the water of any problem? Solve it quickly, solve it right or wrong.

Fortune 77

3794 If you solved it wrong, it would come back and slap you in the face and then you could solve it right.

ib

Richard L Weisman President, Stallwords Inc

3795 The only way not to read our ads is to close your eyes.

On installing advertising on rest-room doors *NY Times* 18 Feb 88

Jack Welch Chair, General Electric

3796 At Mt Sinai Hospital in New York, I have to get down on my hands and knees to sell one CAT scan; in China, a guy comes to lunch and orders a hundred.

Fortune 21 Feb 94

Leslie Wexler President, Victoria's Secret

3797 Women need underwear but women want lingerie.

On a luxurious atmosphere that brought annual sales from $7 million to $1.8 billion *Forbes* 5 Jun 95

3798 Narcissim is real. . . the key to the business.

ib

Gordon White Chair, Hanson Industries

3799 As always, we found a mix of pie-in-the-sky budgets and unpolished jewels.

On corporate purchases turning $3,000 into $90 billion *Fortune* 7 Nov 88

Robert C Wright President, NBC

3800 The economics of the network business today is roughly comparable to three hemophiliacs wandering around a razor factory.

Wall Street Journal 27 Dec 88

Sam Zell Zell/Merrill Lynch Real Estate

3801 Thou shalt not covet trophy properties. . . not buy at auction. . . not own old, outdated office space.

Commandments for real estate financing *NY Times* 10 Sep 95

3802 Rock Center. . . a jigsaw puzzle with an enormous number of moving parts, and the person who can see them all and know why they're moving and where they're moving will win.

On management of Manhattan's Rockefeller Center *ib*

3803 We were living out of the same checkbook.

On holding $500 million in assets with the late Robert H Lurie *ib*

Observers and Critics

Anatoli Adamishim Soviet Deputy Foreign Minister

3804 The Japanese will find out money isn't everything just as we found out armaments aren't everything.

Wall Street Journal 30 Jan 89

Emilio Ambasz journalist

3805 The large executive chair elevates the sitter . . . and it is covered with the skin of some animal, preferably your predecessor.

Smithsonian Apr 86

Susan Heller Anderson reporter

3806 Jowly and with wrinkles, she is still smiling gently.

On Elizabeth II's revised portrait at age 64 on a new five-pound note *NY Times* 7 Jul 90

Anon

3807 [The treasury] is subject to the banker syndrome, which is to foresee disaster but prefer inaction.

Non-governmental adviser to President Kennedy, quoted by Theodore C Sorensen *Kennedy* Harper & Row 65

3808 A desk is a dangerous place from which to view the world.

Sign on desk of American Express President Louis Gerstner *NY Times* 26 Jun 85

3809 You really can't be successful unless you've had at least one bankruptcy.

Quoted by Zenas Block, Professor of Management, NYU Graduate School of Business *Nation's Business* Jan 86

3810 The best fertilizer is the footsteps of the owner.

Texas rancher quoted by Hedley Donovan *Right Times, Right Places* Holt 89

3811 Boy, did he turn out to be an empty suit!

On style without substance *Fortune* 20 Nov 89

3812 The young Catholics came to Denver with the Ten Commandments and a $10 bill. . . determined not to break either one!

Restaurant manager commenting on Pope John Paul IIs visit on World Youth Day *NY Times* 13 Aug 93

3813 To have one's credit cards canceled is now akin to being excommunicated by the medieval church.

Reader's Digest Sep 93

3814 He wears granny glasses and puts out a granny car.

On Robert S McNamara's production of the Falcon for Ford Motor Co, quoted by Deborah Shapley *Promise and Power* Little, Brown 93

3815 Refrain from drinking water in the morning.

Warning to board members before annual meetings in Japan *NY Times* 28 Jun 94

3816 If you are not the lead dog, the view never changes.

Paperweight on the desk of Hospital Corp of America CEO Richard Scott *Forbes* 10 Oct 94

3817 The price to stay here is always equal to or greater than the price you paid to get here.

Sign in H-E-B supermarket's home office *ib* 17 Oct 94

3818 Sometimes you're the windshield, sometimes you're the bug.

On the fluctuating fortunes of automobile sales *ib* 21 Nov 94

3819 The Henry Ford of agriculture.

On Seabrook Farms founder C F Seabrook *New Yorker* 20 Feb 95

3820 It's the tequila effect.

On Mexico as a barometer of financial crisis for Latin America *Washington Times* 19 Mar 95

3821 We talk quality of life, they talk cheap underwear.

On small businesses pitted against Walmart *60 Minutes* CBS TV 30 Apr 95

3822 Is this the age of the informational?

On radio or television commercials that solve problems in using a product *NY Times* 3 Sep 95

Leonard M Apcar reporter

3823 He didn't have to climb the ladder; his family owned the ladder.

On Henry Ford II *Wall Street Journal* 30 Sep 87

Clement Attlee British Prime Minister

3824 Jungle red in tooth and claw.

On business take-overs, quoted by Anthony Sampson *Anatomy of Britain* Hodder & Stoughton 62

Isadore Barmash reporter

3825 The Christmas shopping season. . . concluded last night with a soft thud.

On 1990 recession *NY Times* 25 Dec 90

Warren Bennis Professor of Economics, University of Southern California

3826 Leaders are people who do the right things. Managers are people who do things right. . . a profound difference.

Fortune 19 Sep 94

3827 Leaders ask the what and why question, not the how question....[and] just when you start thinking you're really terrific, you start dictating to the market instead of listening to the customers.

On the peril of 20 to 25 years of success *ib*

Sallie Bingham heiress

3828 [I was] the face of the Other—that dark presence, invariably female, which intervenes between a man and control of the world.

On *Louisville Courier Journal* board on which she opposed her brother *A Family Memoir* Knopf 89

Alan S Blinder Professor of Economics, Princeton

3829 Economists have the least influences on policy where they know the most and are most agreed; they have the most influence on policy where they know the least and disagree most.

Hard Heads, Soft Hearts Addison Wesley 87

Richard Nelson Bolles consultant

3830 What Color is Your Parachute?

Title of job-hunting guide Ten Speed Press 72

Connie Bruck author

3831 [They believed that] any predator, no matter how small, was capable of swallowing any prey, no matter how large.

On corporate take-overs *The Predators' Ball* Simon & Schuster 88

Carnegie Endowment National Commission

3832 You can make fish soup out of an aquarium, but you can't make an aquarium out of fish soup.

On Eastern Europe's conversion from Communist central planning to democratic market economies *Time* special issue Fall 92

Connie Chung commentator

3833 City planners like the riches that come with the fishes.

On aquariums in shopping areas NBC TV 24 Feb 90

Francis X Clines reporter

3834 He suddenly swept through Tiffany's. . . to choose items the way Cézanne gathered apples and ewer for a still life.

On Gene Moore's 39 years as window decorator at Tiffany's *NY Times* 25 Dec 94

Country Life magazine

3835 Moor for your money.

On Scottish real estate 11 Aug 88

Douglas Coupland novelist

3836 McJob: A low-pay, low-prestige, low-dignity, low-benefit, no-future job in the service sector. Frequently considered a satisfying career choice by people who have never held one.

Generation X St Martin's 91

Ding Xinghao Director of American Studies, Institute of International Studies, Shanghai

3837 Japan's view is always a flying-geese format with Japan as the head goose.

On difficulties of cooperation *Wall Street Journal* 30 Jan 89

Phil Donahue TV host

3838 The breasts, the hallmark of our culture. You cannot sell anything in American without the breasts.

On implications of plastic surgery NBC TV Aug 90

David Herbert Donald biographer

3839 There was not enough money in death, she decided; people did not die fast enough.

On the mother of novelist Thomas Wolfe and her efforts to persuade her husband to switch from carving tomb stones to real estate investing *Look Homeward* Little, Brown 87

Peter F Drucker economist

3840 [It was] creative imitation, or entrepreneurial judo.

On Compaq Computer, superstar of personal computer boom *Fortune* 23 May 88

3841 Efficiency is doing things right. Effectiveness is doing the right things.

Quoted by Robert K Cooper *The Performance Edge* Houghton Mifflin 90

Walker Evans photographer and essayist

3842 People out of work are not given to talking much about the one thing on their minds. You only sense it by indirection, degrees of anger, shades of humiliation and echoes of fear.

On unemployment in the rural South *Fortune* Mar 61, reprinted in 50th anniversary issue 11 Feb 80

3843 Unemployment. . . has to be lived to be understood and felt. . . chronic indigestion, incipient stupefaction of the will, and hardening of the spirit.
ib

Alan Farnham reporter

3844 Linking computers is as easy as mating a cat and a Chihuahua.
On networking between companies *Fortune* 14 Jun 93

Doris Fleeson columnist

3845 [He was] better for Arkansas than 20 years of good cotton crops.
On Winthrop Rockefeller *Washington Star* 1 Sep 57

Malcolm Forbes publisher

3846 It is unfortunate we can't buy many business executives for what they are worth and sell them for what they think they are worth.
Quoted by David Mahoney *Confessions of a Street-Smart Manager* Simon & Schuster 88

Fortune magazine

3847 The class the dollars fell on.
On Harvard Business School Class of 1949, the first after World War II to complete four consecutive years of schooling, quoted in *NY Times* 4 Apr 86

Kennedy Fraser reporter

3848 Seeing Estée Lauder bustle into position. . . moving some jars and bottles a few inches this way or that was like seeing a brain surgeon scrub up.
"As Gorgeous As It Gets" *New Yorker* 15 Sep 86

3849 Here was a purposeful temple, a humming engineroom full of beauty.
On the Lauder manufacturing plant *ib* 17 Mar 94

Elizabeth Fried labor consultant

3850 That's rug-ranking—treating her as a perk like the size of his office or the quality of the carpet.
On basing a secretary's pay on her boss's status rather than her job *NY Times* 17 Mar 94

Bob Garfield *Advertising Age*

3851 If you make a small amount of the right kind of noise, the media will deliver you tens of hundreds of millions of dollars worth of free publicity.
On charges that Calvin Klein's underwear ads were pornographic *Newsweek* 11 Sep 95

Harold Geneen author

3852 In the business world, everyone is paid in two coins: cash and experience. Take the experience first; the cash will come later.
Managing written with Alvin Moscow, Avon 84

3853 Words are words, explanations are explanations, promises are promises—but only performance is reality.
ib

Mark Geren consumer analyst

3854 This is pick-pocket by computer.
On differences between store "sale" prices and the price registered by check-out scanners *Dateline* NBC TV 16 Dec 94

William Glaberson reporter

3855 Just off the highway. . . a great concrete box in an asphalt field. . . part small town, part big top. . . framed by name brands, where the lives of sometimes as many as 100,000 people intersect in a day.
"The Heart of the City Now Beats in the Mall" *NY Times* 27 Mar 92

Stephen A Grayser Professor of Marketing, Harvard Business School

3856 Poets of commerce.
On advertising copywriters *NY Times* 28 Apr 87

Joseph Grundfest Professor of Law, Stanford

3857 It's a privilege to address the distinguished gathering of unindicted business school graduates, their unindicted faculty, and friends.
To University of Southern California commencement while a member of the Securities Exchange Commission *US News & World Report* 1 Jun 87

Kathleen Hagenbart financial consultant

3858 What will $10,000 do under the mattress?
On educating women as investors *Christian Science Monitor* 22 Feb 88

Robert W Hall Professor, Indiana University School of Business

3859 If you can persuade your customers to tattoo your name on their chests, they probably will not shift brands.
On loyalty to Harley-Davidson motorcycles *NY Times* 31 Dec 90

John Ensor Harr author

3860 In the American lexicon, the Rockefeller name is as synonymous with great wealth as Benedict Arnold's with high treason.

The Rockefeller Conscience with Peter J Johnson, Scribner 91

3861 No one can tell the wealthy how to spend their money. One can only set examples.

ib

Paul Hawken author

3862 If you plan to start your own business, plan to fail. It's one sure way to succeed.

Growing A Business Simon & Schuster 89

Andrew Heller IBM executive

3863 Technology is like fish. The longer it stays on the shelf, the less desirable it becomes.

On protesting slow technical development *Fortune* 15 Jul 91

Nicholas P Heymann security analyst

3864 The crisis at Westinghouse began as a hangnail and turned into gangrene.

On bad loans made by Westinghouse Electric's credit subsidiary *Fortune* 4 Nov 91

Steven A Holmes reporter

3865 Marketers [are]. . . appealing directly to children and hoping that the "nag factor" will help move the merchandise.

On "kid-influenced spending" *NY Times* 8 Jan 95

David Horowitz biographer

3866 Rockefeller Center was the last big institution that the family controlled. Now they're just rich.

On Japanese purchase of 51 percent of Rockefeller Center *Newsweek* 13 Nov 89

David Howarth author

3867 American oil men, when they reported thefts, were horrified to see their employees returning without hands.

On Middle Eastern punishment *The Desert King* McGraw-Hill 64

Elbert Hubbard author

3868 Cold, passive, noncommittal, with eyes like codfish. . . minus bowels, passion or a sense of humor.

On American auditors, quoted by Anthony Sampson *Anatomy of Britain* Hodder & Stoughton 62

John Huey essayist

3869 Your ass was on the line. Your job was to kick ass and take names. These were the innumerable truths of leadership you learned as you progressed from Boy Scouts to Officer Candidate School to the Harvard B-school. . . and they worked. God was in his heaven, and the ruling classes. . . ruled.

On the changing patterns of corporate life *Fortune* 21 Feb 94

Ada Louise Huxtable critic

3870 It was an idea based on frugality and the most for the least. . . that great American institution, the five-and-ten.

On hundredth anniversary of F W Woolworth chain *NY Times* 8 Nov 79

3871 You can't buy happiness. . . but there was a time when you could get pretty close for a nickel or a dime.

ib

Juzo Itami film director

3872 Japan tried to adopt an international language, and the language it happened to choose was money.

Quoted by Anthony Sampson *The Midas Touch* Hodder & Stoughton 89

Elliott Jacques corporate psychologist

3873 An employee's place in the corporate hierarchy can be determined by the amount of time he is given to reach a goal without supervision; the longer the time, the higher the employee perceives his pay should be.

NY Times 17 Feb 85

John Klenert National Co-chair, Lesbian, Bisexual and Gay United Employees at AT&T

3874 We smash lavender ceilings!

On 250 companies that mirrored AT&T policy against discrimination in employment, comparable to "glass ceilings" limiting women *Washington Blade* 3 Mar 95

Stephen Koepp reporter

3875 Disney would like to see a mouse on every mantel and a duck in every drawer.

On the consumer-products division of the Walt Disney entertainment industry *Time* 25 Apr 88

Steve Kroft CBS correspondent

3876 Too complicated to explain, too difficult to ignore. . . the financial equivalent of genetic engineering.

On the role of derivatives in the fall of Britain's 233-year old Barings *60 Minutes* CBS TV 5 Mar 95

3877 [Derivatives] exist for the most part only on computer screens, the imaginary currency of cyberspace.

ib

Robert Lacey biographer

3878 Lee Iacocca has got his sweetest revenge, of course, from being a better Henry Ford than Henry Ford.

On Lee Iacocca's success in running Chrysler after being fired from the Ford Motor Company *Ford* Little, Brown 86

Patrick Leahy US Senator

3879 A few of the piglets may go hungry, some may get sat on, but the resilient and resourceful will survive.

On Walmart's impact on local businesses *Fortune* 21 May 94

S Robert Lichter reporter

3880 Big business has become television's favorite villain . . . [and] businessmen now make up the largest group of murderers on TV apart from gangsters.

Watching America Prentice Hall 91, written with Linda S Lichter and Stanley Rothman *Fortune* 15 Jul 91

Luz Lopez textile worker

3881 It doesn't feel like a factory. It feels good. It feels like the future.

On introduction of employee benefits in the traditionally impersonal garment industry *NY Times* 29 May 95

Archibald MacLeish statesman and poet

3882 Mr Morgan struck me as a healthy and childish Britisher probably inhabiting the early 19th century.

On financier J P Morgan, quoted by Scott Donaldson *Archibald MacLeish* Houghton Mifflin 92

Peter Marks reporter

3883 On the benches and under the sculptures, in the food court and by the fountain, sat the unsung of American mercantilism. Call them retail's bystanders.

On those who wait patiently while others shop *NY Times* 21 Feb 94

Brian Martin American Can Co spokesman

3884 Secure the name Priamerica.

Telephone call officially notifying corporate identity specialist Lippincott & Margulies of the end of a long search for a new corporate name *NY Times* 8 Mar 87

Alan Millstein editor *Fashion Network* Report

3885 Basically, Woolworth is a kennel club. Most of them are dogs.

On Woolworth ownership of short-lived mall stores such as a musical gift shop, a watch retailer, and women's casual apparel *Forbes* 14 Aug 95

Allen Nevins biographer

3886 He had not waited to become rich before becoming generous.

On John D Rockefeller *Study in Power* Scribner 53

New York magazine

3887 The Japanese were the first to be fixated on fax.

On report that half of all calls from Japan to US are by fax machines *Parade* 1 Jan 88

George Orwell author and futurist

3888 Advertising is the rattling of a stick inside a swill bucket.

Recalled on Orwell's death 21 Jan 50

Victor Palmieri business turnaround specialist

3889 Strategies are okayed in boardrooms that even a child would say are bound to fail. The trouble is, there is never a child in the boardroom.

Forbes 13 Sep 93

Terene P Paré reporter

3890 He does just about everything you can do with money except print it.

On General Electric CEO Gary Wendt *Fortune* 21 Feb 94

3891 The management hails from the Edith Piaf School of Business: *Je ne regrette rien.*

ib

Laurence J Peter business consultant

3892 The cream rises until it sours.

On the belief that every bureaucracy was inevitably made up almost entirely of people inadequate to their tasks *The Peter Principle* with Raymond Hull, Murrow 69

3893 Equal opportunity means everyone will have a fair chance of becoming incompetent.

When Things Go Wrong Morrow 84

3894 An ounce of image is worth a pound of performance.

NY Times 15 Jan 90

3895 Tabulatory Gigantism is an obsession with having a bigger desk than one's colleagues.

ib

Jane Bryant Quinn *Newsweek* columnist

3896 Half of them don't know what's going to happen tomorrow and the other half don't know they don't know.

On stock market predictions CNN 4 Apr 94

Roger Rosenblatt essayist

3897 In the streets of the cities and towns, people hustled in the lowering afternoons, extracting happiness from the lights that illuminated things on sale.
"The Season of Objects and Things" *US News & World Report* 12 Dec 88

Paul Saffo Institute for the Future, Menlo Park CA

3898 The rush and flow of events is like electronic heroin. And once you get it into your veins it's really hard to stop.
On the increasing number of people who straddle many time-zones in a disappearing 9-to-5 workday *Fortune* 20 Mar 95

3899 You'll figure out a way to interrupt yourself.
ib

Anthony Sampson author

3900 Accountants are the priesthood of industry; the more fragmented and diversified a company becomes, the more important becomes the man who can disentangle the threads of profitability that hold it together.
Anatomy of Britain Hodder & Stoughton 62

3901 The Whitehall mandarins switch from taxes to fish, but they remain within a single bureaucratic tradition; while in industry, the pyramids, pension rights, and organograms conspire to bind men with chains of gold to a single corporation.
ib

Serge Schemann reporter

3902 Russians have been learning that capitalism can be a piece of cake.
On the first public sales of shares in a state-owned enterprise, a bakery *NY Times* 14 Dec 92

Deborah Shapley biographer

3903 It glittered. . . a small, poisoned dagger.
On Robert S McNamara's Phi Beta Kappa key he reportedly wore "on days he wanted to be particularly fearsome" *Promise and Power* Little, Brown 92

Brinkley Shorts securities manager

3904 If you drop a dead cat off a tall enough building, he's going to bounce.
On the rise of beaten-down small stocks *Fortune* 7 Nov 88

Mary Ann Sieghart essayist

3905 A pension plan is dry bread today to ensure jam tomorrow.
London Times 2 Mar 94

Nancy Terry reporter

3906 A fine Scotch blend: two parts Locust Valley, Long Island WASP—pampered, patrician, and exceedingly preppie—and one part earthy Scot, with deep voice, hearty chuchkle, bawdy humor.
On publisher-sportsman Nelson Doubleday *Fortune* 5 Jan 87

Tom Wolfe novelist

3907 That's an electric doughnut. . . all I do all day is talk to other electric doughnuts.
A stock broker describes his telephone *The Bonfire of the Vanities* Farrar Straus Giroux 87

Memorable Advertising

AIDS Prevention

3908 Don't die of embarrassment!
On use of condoms for safer sex *NY Times* 11 May 87

Alka-Seltzer

3909 Husband: I can't believe I ate the whole thing!
Wife: You ate it, Ralph!
Television commercial ABC TV 73

American Booksellers Association

3910 The gift that can be opened again and again!
NPR 8 Sep 90

American Broadcasting Co

3911 Out is no place to be tonight!
On building an audience for *Love Among the Ruins* with Katharine Hepburn and Laurence Olivier *NY Times* 6 Mar 75

American Express

3912 Don't leave home without it!
On credit cards 88

American Home magazine

3913 *American Home* has an edifice complex.
On residential construction *Advertising Age* 18 Sep 61

American Safety Council

3914 There are a million and one excuses for not wearing a safety-belt. Some are real killers!
CBS TV 8 Aug 69

American Telephone & Telegram

3915 Let your fingers do the walking!

On the use of the telephone directory's yellow pages 62

3916 Ever hear a smile? Listen carefully next time you call someone you love!
Look 11 Jun 68

Arkansas Industrial Development Commission

3917 Arkansas requests the pleasure of your company!
On attracting industry *Newsweek* 6 Jun 66

Arpege

3918 Promise her anything, but give her Arpege!
Slogan coined in 1946 by Lanvin Parfums President Edouard L Cournaud and used throughout the 1950s and 60s

3919 No bottles to break—just hearts!
New Yorker 16 Dec 61

Avis Car Rental

3920 We're number 2! We try harder!
Motto 87

Barbados Tourist Board

3921 Just 21 miles long a smile wide!
New York 19 Jan 76

Bolla Wines

3922 Wine is a little like love. When the right one comes along, you know it!
CBS TV 26 Aug 73

Book Of The Month Club

3923 Handed to you by the postman, the new books you intend to read!
Slogan written in the late 1920s by one of BOMC's founders, Harry Scherman, regarded as a model of book salesmanship and the foundation of the club's success *NY Times* 12 Nov 69

3924 America's Bookstore.
Slogan 85

Brim Decaffeinated Coffee

3925 Fill it to the rim with Brim!
Advertisement 84

Bufferin

3926 How your headache begins is your business; how it ends, is ours.
ABC TV 26 Apr 67

3927 The greatest moment in any headache is when you realize it's over!
ib

Calvin Klein Jeans

3928 Nothing comes between me and my Calvins!
Advertisement 85

Cartier

3929 *Les* must be Cartier!
New Yorker 27 Apr 80

Charmin Toilet Tissue

3930 Please don't squeeze the Charmin!
Long-time ad featuring Dick Wilson as the storekeeper Mr Whipple *US News & World Report* 8 Jan 96

Chemical Bank-NY Trust Co

3931 When a woman's need is financial, her reaction is Chemical!
CBS TV 21 Jan 68

Chevrolet

3932 See the USA in your Chevrolet!
Singing commercial ABC TV 85

Chiffon Soapflakes

3933 You'll never get caught red-handed!
Radio commercial 25 Jan 65

Clairol Cosmetics

3934 Does she. . . or doesn't she?
On hair-coloring *Newsweek* 19 Aug 63

3935 O barefoot girl with chic of tan!
Vogue Jun 67

3936 Only her hairdresser knows for sure!
On hair-coloring advertised between 1964 and 1987 *ib*

Coca-Cola

3937 I'd like to teach the world to sing in perfect harmony!
"Give the World a Coke" lyrics by Dick Smith 71; one of the ten best known television jingles *NY Times* 21 Apr 90

Cosmopolitan Magazine

3938 I guess you could say I'm that *Cosmopolitan* girl!
Personification of readership over a 25-year period under Helen Gurley Brown's editorship *NY Times* 21 Apr 90

Coty Perfumes

3939 Want him to be more of a man? Try being more of a woman!
Life 7 May 65

Cunard Steamship Co Ltd

3940 Getting there is half the fun!
Advertising slogan for ocean voyages used throughout the 1950s

De Beers Consolidated Mines Ltd

3941 Diamonds are forever.
Slogan used in magazine advertising 1950s

Dilly Beans

3942 If your friendly neighborhood grocer doesn't have a jar, knock something off a shelf on the way out!
Slogan quoted in *Advertising Age* 31 Oct 60

Dupont

3943 Better things for better living through chemistry.
Slogan 84

3944 The difference between a shattered windshield and a shattered life.
On safety glass in automobiles *Newsweek* 19 Oct 87

Ebony magazine

3945 We're dreaming of a black Christmas!
On advertisements especially written for African Americans *NY Times* 30 Nov 67

Folger's Coffee

3946 The best part of wakin' up is Folger's in your cup!
Radio commercial 81

Ford Motor Co

3947 There's a Ford in your future!
Slogan originated for the 1928 Model-A, revived in 1945 and used frequently in the 1960s

Four Roses Whisky

3948 America's most gifted whisky!
Advertisement cited for sales effectiveness *Printer's Ink* 23 Dec 60

Friends Of Animals

3949 Extinct is forever!
On endangered species *NY Times* 29 Apr 73

General Electric

3950 Progress is our most important product.
Slogan introduced in 1950

3951 GE. . . We bring good things to life.
Television commercial 83

General Foods

3952 It sits as lightly on a heavy meal as it does on your conscience!
Television commercial for Jell-O NBC TV 3 Nov 63

Gordon's Dry Gin Ltd

3953 Is it true that English women make better wives? Decidedly yes—say English husbands!
Vogue 1 Apr 61

Greyhound Bus Lines

3954 Leave the driving to us!
Recalled on Monitor Radio 4 Sep 95

Hallmark Cards

3955 When you care enough to send the very best!
Slogan presented with Masterpiece Theater 77

Horn & Hardart Restaurants

3956 Less work for Mother!
Long-time slogan of a pioneer fast-food chain 1950s

IBM (International Business Machines)

3957 Working paper. . . not paper work.
On boxes of tabulating cards 1960s

3958 Create an impression beyond words!
On "executive model" electric typewriters Newsweek 8 Jun 64

Irish Export Board

3959 May you have the health of a salmon—a strong heart and a wet mouth!
Toast for Irish Highball, quoted in advertising news column *NY Times* 16 Dec 60

3960 Health and long life to you! The wife of your choice to you! Land free of rent to you, from this day forth!
Toast for Irish coffee *ib*

Kellogg's Rice Krispies

3961 Snap, crackle, pop!
Advertisement of the 1950s cited as one of the ten best known television jingles *NY Times* 19 Jun 89

Kentucky Fried Chicken

3962 Buy a bucket of chicken and have a barrel of fun!
Commercial 83

3963 We do chicken right!
ib

Kloster Cruise Ltd

3964 There's no law that you can't make love at 4 in the afternoon on Tuesday!
Quoted in *Forbes* 21 Nov 94

Liberty Mutual Life Insurance

3965 Don't find out by accident!
NBC TV 10 Apr 65

Lifecall

3966 I've fallen and I can't get up!
Television commercial on panic buttons for the elderly *US News & World Report* 15 Jun 92

3967 We're sending help immediately, Mrs Fletcher!
ib

Lipton Tea

3968 Lipton's gets into more hot water than anything!
Radio commercial, Summer 67

L&M Cigarettes

3969 Just what the doctor ordered!
On lower tar content, slogan 1953, cited by Bill Bryson *Made in America* Morrow 94

Guy Lombardo

3970 The sweetest music this side of heaven!
On Guy Lombardo's orchestra noted for New Year's Eve and every presidential inaugural from 1932 to 1977 *NY Times* 30 Dec 89

Lord & Taylor

3971 Taking the "if" out of "gift!"
On personalized shopping service *NY Post* 3 Dec 76

Lord West Dinner Jackets

3972 A woman's most important accessory—her escort!
Vogue 16 April 64

Maidenform

3973 I dreamed I stopped traffic in my Maidenform bra!
One of the best known of 210 Maidenform's "dream" ads appearing between 1949 and 1969 and resumed 11 years later *International Herald Tribune* 10 Jun 80

3974 I dreamed I was wanted in my Maidenform bra!
Maidenform slogan coupled with a Post Office Wanted Persons poster *ib*

Paul Masson

3975 We sell no wine before its time!
NBC TV 16 Nov 87

Maytag Washing Machines

3976 Maytag repairmen are the loneliest guys in town!
On lack of need for servicing CBS TV 9 Aug 69

McDonald's Hamburgers

3977 You deserve a break today!
Musical slogan cited in round-up of memorable ads *NY Times* 18 Jul 88

Meow Mix

3978 The cat food cats ask for by name!
Ralston Purina ad written by Jerry Della Femina *NY Times* 20 Nov 92

Metropolitan Life

3979 A child is someone who passes through our life, and then disappears into an adult.
Magazine advertisement written by Young & Rubican's Tom Thomas for television commercials Jun 74

Mexican Brewery

3980 The beer that made Milwaukee jealous!
Quoted by commentator Dave Garroway *Good Housekeeping* Feb 57

Miller's Beer

3981 If you've got the time, we've got the beer!
Cited as one of the best known television jingles *NY Times* 19 Jun 89

3982 It's it! And that's that!
Slogan replacing advertising that for 17 years had centered on the beer's "liteness" *NY Times* 3 Jul 91

3983 You don't say "beer" now, you say "lite." It's the beer that beer's become!
ib

National Association for the Handicapped

3984 A curb is a wall to a handicapped person.
NBC TV 8 Apr 75

National Book Committee

3985 A book can give you peace. Make you feel young again, or old and wise. A book can turn a dream into reality or reality into a dream.
Advertisement presented in cooperation with the Amer Library Association CBS TV 21 May 64

National Public Radio

3986 Opening a book opens a mind.
Public service announcement 1 Jul 95

New School For Social Research
NYC

3987 The New School—it will change your mind!
Television advertisement 14 Jan 80

New York Central Railroad

3988 A hog can cross the country without changing trains but you can't.
Advertisement protesting government restrictions on transcontinental rail travel, recalled on death of Chair Robert R Young 25 Jan 58

Old Golds Cigarettes

3989 Not a cough in a carload.
Slogan cited by Bill Bryson *Made in America* Morrow 94

Paine Webber Stockbrokers

3990 You have a friend at Paine Webber!
NBC TV 78

Pan-American Coffee Bureau

3991 Good coffee is like friendship: rich and warm and strong!
Life 28 Jul 61

Paramount News

3992 The Eyes and Ears of the World.
Slogan recalled when the last of the motion picture newsreels succumbed to television *Time* 29 Dec 67

Pepperidge Farm

3993 Pepperidge farm remembers!
Commercial stressing nostalgia in its products CBS TV 11 Jan 64

Pepsi-Cola

3994 Pepsi-Cola hits the spot,/ Twelve full ounces and that's a lot,/ Twice as much for a nickel, too,/ Pepsi-Cola is the drink for you!
Quatrain by Pepsi President Walter S Mack recalled on Mack's death *London Times* 21 March 90

Pepsodent

3995 You'll wonder where the yellow went!
Toothpaste commercial quoted by Martin Mayer *Madison Avenue USA* Harper 58

Pillsbury Flour

3996 Nothin' says lovin; like somethin; from the oven!
Television commercial 79

Pinkerton's Inc

3997 The eye that never sleeps!
Trademark of Pinkerton's Detective Agency that became the source of the term "private eye" *Forbes* 25 Sep 95

Plaza Hotel New York City

3998 The Rendez-vous is so romantic... it's downright dangerous!
On its supper club *New Yorker* 22 Oct 60

Prudential Life

3999 No one plans to fail. They just fail to plan.
NBC TV 20 Jan 93

Purdue Chickens

4000 It takes a tough man to make a tender chicken.
Slogan cited by Bill Bryson *Made in America* Morrow 94

Purina Dog Food

4001 All you add is love!
Advertisement addressed to "Four-Legged Epicures" *Time* 26 Apr 68

Red Cross

4002 The greatest tragedy is indifference.
Theme of the Greater New York area fund-raising prepared by Young & Rubicam as volunteer agency *NY Times* 9 Feb 61

Rolls Royce

4003 At 60 miles an hour the loudest noise... comes from the electric clock.
Advertisement regarded by David Ogilvy as the best "headline" he had devised for a client *Confessions of An Advertising Man* Atheneum 63

Schaefer Beer

4004 Schaefer is the one beer to have when you're having more than one!
Cited as one of copywriter John J Jordan Jr's best known jingles *NY Times* 18 Jul 88

Scott Paper Co

4005 The quicker picker-upper.
On Bounty papertowels 1980s

Seagram's Gin

4006 Dryest gin in town! Ask any Martini!
New Yorker 11 Mar 61

Shell Oil Co

4007 A child is an island of curiosity surrounded by a sea of question marks.
Time 20 Jan 61

Smith-Barney investment brokers

4008 We make money the old-fashioned way! We earn it!
Television commercial used from 1979 to 1986 and revived in 1995 *NY Times* 25 Aug 95

E R Squibb

4009 Adam and Eve ate the first vitamins, including the package!
Advertisement advocating balanced diet rather than reliance on vitamin pills *Saturday Review* 19 Apr 58

Tareyton Cigarettes

4010 We'd rather fight than switch!
A man with a cigarette and a black eye, cited as one of copywriter James J Jordan Jr's most memorable slogans *NY Times* 18 Jul 88

Teacher's Scotch Whiskey

4011 No Scotch improves the flavor of water like Teacher's!
Life 5 Aug 66

Tennessee Gas Transmission Co

4012 When I Grow Up: Sharp and clear the dreams of the young and always framed in gold.
Time 12 May 58

4013 Vision, the projected power of the mind, builds a better world for each generation.
ib

Texaco Oil

4014 You can trust your car to the man who wears the star!
Radio commercial 67

United Air Lines

4015 Fly the friendly skies of United!
Magazine advertisement 78

United Negro College Fund

4016 A mind is a terrible thing to waste!
Television commercial 77

US Travel Service

4017 Friendly Americans win American friends.
Slogan promoting the nation as a world tourist attraction *NY Journal-American* 10 Jul 63

Virginia Slims Cigarettes

4018 You've come a long way, baby!
Magazine advertisement allied with women's lib 76

Wisk Laundry Detergent

4019 Ring around the collar!
On getting white shirts clean *NY Times* 18 Jul 88

Winston Cigarettes

4020 Winstons taste good like a cigarette should!
Television commercial 78

Wendy's Hamburgers

4021 Where's the beef?
Fast-food advertisement featuring white-haired, lace-collared septuagenarian Clara Peller, cited as one of the most popular ads *Newsweek* 23 May 88

Wheaties

4022 The breakfast of champions!
Slogan on cereal boxes 1950s

Yardley's Lavender Scented English Soap

4023 The soap that's kept women in hot water for 200 years—and they've loved every minute!
NBC TV 22 Aug 73

EDUCATION

Educators and Students

Lord Adrian (Edgar Douglas Adrian) Master of Trinity College, Cambridge

4024 Trinity may one day become a cafeteria for the young, an almshouse for the old. But even if it becomes meanwhile no more than a dormitory, it will always be something to have fallen asleep to the sound of the fountain of Trinity.

At dinner tendered him by 40 Trinity men who had become members of Parliament *Holiday* Jun 59

Lamar Alexander US Secretary of Education

4025 If it's OK with the local school district and OK with the Supreme Court, then dollars will follow the child.

On federal aid to schools whether public, private or parochial *NY Times* 20 Apr 91

4026 [It is] a fox dressed as a duck at a duck-family reunion.

On opposing Goals 2000 legislation to fund states for local projects designed to raise educational standards *Christian Science Monitor* 8 Jun 95

Julian Anderson Director-General, County Headmasters Association

4027 The hall. . . has absorbed the smells of all the meals ever cooked. . . the clock is one of the most long chiming. . . so you are deeply conscious of time and smell.

On sitting the Oxford entrance exam in Keble College Hall *London Times* 4 Feb 95

4028 The exam sorts out if you have the beginnings of a brain that can think its way out of corners.

ib

Nelson Andrews Chair, Tennessee State Board of Education

4029 He's a raspberry seed in your wisdom tooth; he makes you think.

On Chester Finn, Professor of Education and Public Policy, Vanderbilt University, as chief architect of George Bush's role as the "education president" *US News & World Report* 15 Jul 91

Anon

4030 What do we want? Everything! When do we want it? Now!

A plea from student rebellions "Sixties and Seventies" *Illustrated London News* May 78

4031 We here at Loyola are straining every effort to develop a college that the football team can be proud of!

Quoted by Henry D Spalding ed *The Lilt of Irish Humor* Jonathan David 78

4032 If you promise not to believe everything your child says happens at this school, I'll promise not to believe everything he says happens at home.

Note to parents from an English schoolmaster *Wall Street Journal* 4 Jan 85

4033 To the initiated, it is my college that I mention first; to the stranger, if asked, I announce myself as a Cambridge man.

Cambridge-educated American quoted in *Discovering Britain and Ireland* National Georgraphic Society 85

4034 Traditionally, students don't arrive at Cambridge, they "come down."

ib

4035 Four you score; five you die.

A saying among Japanese students quoted by Willis Hawley, Dean, Vanderbilt University School of Education, meaning "if you sleep five hours a night, instead of four, you won't pass the exam" *Christian Science Monitor* 5 Jan 87

4036 To go to school and fenisch my Schooling without getting prenant.

Definition of the American Dream offered by a 15-year old Detroit pupil *Newsweek* 29 Jun 87

4037 The doctor said to abandon his code of ethnics.

Example of "creative confusion" cited by English Professor Dorothy Evslin of Westchester NY Community College *NY Times* 16 Jan 88

4038 He was arrested for. . . mister meaners.

ib

4039 They came on deck yielding guns.

ib

4040 She was frightened in the mist of her enemies.

ib

4041 It is the baby-boom echo.

On the rising enrollment of baby-boomers' children NPR 31 Aug 96

4042 Better dead than coed.

Protest on acceptance of girls at Deerfield Academy *ib* 1 Feb 88

4043 The educational value of French. . . in the hands of Henri Peyre, sometimes becomes so great that it cannot be purchased with the debased currency of the ordinary mind.

Yale Student Guide on Henri Peyre, Sterling Professor of French *NY Times* 10 Dec 88

4044 No duties, only opportunities.

Motto of Princeton NJ Institute for Advanced Study, quoted by Ed Regis *Who Got Einstein's Office?* Addison-Wesley 88

4045 Benno doesn't listen, and when he listens, he doesn't hear; and when he hears, he doesn't understand; and when he understands, he's against it.

Reported as a "taunting little ditty bandied about at Yale about President Benno Schmidt who was seen as headstrong, secretive and impulsive" in the days leading up to his resignation at age 50 after seven years in office *NY Times* 15 Jun 92

4046 Put each tub on its own bottom.

On Harvard's decentralization policy that came under scrutiny from its new president, Neil Rudenstine, seeking a more unified university *ib* 10 Feb 93

4047 Children's museums are ice cream with vitamin D in it.

Quoted by Diane Frankel, Director, National Institute of Museum Services *Washington Post* 14 Jan 94

4048 Japanese, a language so fiendishly complex that it has been described as the greatest barrier to human communication ever devised.

On US Ambassador Walter Mondale's withdrawal after one lesson in Japanese *NY Times* 5 Nov 95

Antioch College

4049 Verbal consent should be obtained with each new level of physical or sexual conduct.

Sexual harassment code formulated in response to "date rape" *Wall Street Journal* 6 Apr 95

4050 The request for consent must be specific to each act.

ib

Association of American Colleges

4051 It is a supermarket where students are shoppers and professors are merchants of learning.

Integrity in the College Curriculum report on weaknesses of undergraduate programs *NY Times* 11 Feb 85

4052 Fads and fashions, the demands of popularity and success, enter where wisdom and experience should prevail.

ib

Louis Auchincloss novelist

4053 The law of a boys' school is the law of the jungle. When you're strong, we're behind you, but if you're weak, we throw you to the boys.

The Rector of Justin Houghton Mifflin 64

Jacques Barzun Dean of Faculties, Columbia University

4054 Teaching is not a lost art, but the regard for it is a lost tradition.

Newsweek 5 Dec 55, also see Barzun's *Teacher in America* Liberty Press 80

4055 The test and use of man's education is that he finds pleasure in the exercise of the mind.

"Science and the Humanities" *Saturday Evening Post* 3 May 58

4056 Instead of trying to develop native intelligence and give it good techniques in the basic arts of man, we professed to make ideal citizens, supertolerant neighbors, agents of world peace, and happy family folk, at once sexually adept and flawless drivers of cars.

Quoted by David Alexander *NY Times* 21 Apr 91 reviewing Barzun's Morris Philipson ed *Begin Here: The Forgotten Conditions of Teaching and Learning* University of Chicago Press 91

Bernard Iddings Bell Chaplain, University of Chicago

4057 A good education is not so much one which prepares a man to succeed in the world, as one which enables him to sustain a failure.

Life 16 Oct 50

William J Bennett US Secretary of Education 1985–88; Director, Office of National Drug Control Policy 1989–90

4058 [The shortage of student loans] may require. . . divestiture of certain sorts—stereo divestiture, automobile diverstiture, three-weeks-at-the-beach divestiture.

NY Times 12 Feb 85

4059 If my own son. . . came to me and said, "You promised to pay for my tuition at Harvard; how about giving me $50,000 instead to start a little business?" I might think that was a good idea.

ib

4060 Our common language is. . . English. And our common task is to ensure that our non-English-speaking children learn the common language.

ib 26 Sep 85

4061 The elementary school must assume as its sublime and most solemn responsibility the task of teaching every child in it to read.

Report on elementary schools *ib* 3 Sep 86

4062 Certification…must begin to reflect our demand for excellence, not our appreciation of punishment.

ib

4063 Moving from undergraduate to graduate study. . . is frequently like being transformed from a college athlete into a sports statistician.

LA Times 25 Mar 87

4064 A great university was brought low by the very forces which modern universities came into being to oppose: ignorance, irrationality and intimidation . . . [and] the loudest voices have won, not through force of argument but through bullying, threatening and name-calling.

On Stanford's replacement of required freshman courses that cover the contributions of minorities *NY Times* 19 Apr 88

4065 Drug use is a misguided attempt to find meaning in life.

Christianity Today 11 Feb 91

4066 Our collective cultural task is to remember what we were and what we still are. If we once again get that right, then immigrants will fit in and flourish, as they always have. If we keep getting it wrong, then it won't matter where the people come from. For whatever their place of origin, they will be citizens without a culture and they will bear children without a future.

On accepting Cubans, Haitians and others *Washington Post* 4 Dec 94

John Betjeman poet

4067 Before the hymn the Skipper would announce/ The latest names of those who'd lost their lives/ For King and Country and the Dragon School./ Sometimes his gruff old voice was full of tears/ When a particular favorite had been killed./ Then we would hear the nickname of the boy,/ "Pongo" or "Podge" and how he'd play 3Q/ For Oxford and, if only he had lived,/ He might have played for England—which he did,/ But in a grimmer game against the Hun./ And then we'd all look solemn, knowing well/ There'd be no extra holiday today.

On his prep school during World War I *Summoned by Bells* John Murray 76

James H Billington Librarian of Congress

4068 It's a question of bringing out the music that's already there.

On becoming Librarian of Congress *NY Times* 18 Apr 87

4069 There is an overwhelming feeling. . . of being inside the memory of the human race. . . Mankind's largest repository of knowledge.

On the Library of Congress "Memory and Imagination" PBS TV 15 Aug 93

4070 [It is a] place to preserve, more than any other single place on this planet, the human heritage of thought and creativity of the past. . . [but] I see the Library of Congress in the future as an active catalyst for civilization, not just a passive mausoleum of the cultural accomplishments of the past.

ib

4071 Libraries put things together. . . providing a coherence that is creative and ongoing.

ib

4072 A library is where humanity celebrates and preserves the wonder and mystery of the human mind. . . temples of hope for the future of humanity, and that's what connects that record of anguish, achievement, and aspiration of the past with the possibilities of the future.

ib

4073 The future of civilization and the richness and the possibilities of civilization depend on that kind of magic moment that occurs uniquely and specially in libraries. . . the times when you take that last walk through the stacks where, having digested a lot of material, suddenly a rush of creative ideas comes to you in the present.

ib

Claude T Bissell President, University of Toronto

4074 The University still represents man's best attempt to realize a world where reason does not yield to the gusts of passions; where the instruction of the past is not brushed aside; where beauty is not an afterthought; where civility and respect for others dwell together with passionate conviction and high arguments.

"On Being a University President" address 1 Oct 70

4075 With all its defects, its tortured self-doubts, its endless hesitations, its constant cynical juxtaposition of the ideal and the actual, the university is the institution that reminds man most insistently of the need for the examined life.

At the University of Toronto sesquicentennial *Toronto Star* 16 Mar 77

Stephanie Black Yale undergraduate

4076 It's just a matter of your friends being blond, brunette, gay or straight. No big deal.

Quoted by Julie V Iovine, Yale faculty wife whose article drew widespread reaction "Lipsticks and Lords: Yale's New Look" *Wall Street Journal* 4 Aug 87

4077 It probably depends on what part of the country you're from, whether or not you're going to be surprised by two women making out in the library.

ib

Harry A Blackmun Associate Justice, US Supreme Court

4078 Think just a little bit about who you are and where you are going, about being a professional in the true sense, about values, and about heroes, and holding tightly to them. . . and when on occasion you encounter moments of discouragement, as you will, it will lift you over those moments and into the sunshine beyond.

Extemporaneous address to Harvard Law School *Harvard University Magazine* Jul 94

Allan Bloom Professor of Political Science, University of Chicago

4079 Education is the taming or demonstration of the soul's raw passions—not suppressing them or excising them, which would deprive the soul of its energy—but forming and informing them as art.

The Closing of the American Mind Simon & Schuster 87

Derek Bok President, Harvard

4080 I won't say there aren't any Harvard graduates who have never asserted a superior attitude. But they have done so to our great embarrassment and in no way represent the Harvard I know.

M Jun 84

4081 If you think education is expensive—try ignorance.

Town & Country May 79

4082 Education is always imperfect, and however much we may appear to be succeeding, there are vast unrealized opportunities in the future for us and serious flaws in our present.

Celebrity Register Gale 90

Eugene L Boyer President, Carnegie Foundation for Advancement of Teaching

4083 A poor surgeon hurts one person at a time. A poor teacher hurts 130.

People 17 Mar 86

4084 Scholarship surely means the discovery of knowledge. . . [but] also means the integration of knowledge, the application of knowledge. And scholarship also can be defined as the presentation of knowledge, as in great teaching.

To American Association of Higher Education *NY Times* 4 Sep 90

John Bracey Professor of Afro-American Studies, University of Massachusetts

4085 [It is] to push off into deep water from sinking sand.

On need to finance program for talented minority students *US News & World Report* 8 Jun 87

Kingman Brewster President of Yale 1963–77; US Ambassador to Britain 1977–81

4086 If I take refuge in ambiguity, I assure you that it's quite conscious.

On appointment as president *NY Herald Tribune* 13 Oct 63

4087 Universities should be safe havens where ruthless examination of realities will not be distorted by the aim to please or inhibited by the risk of displeasure.

Inaugural 11 Apr 64

4088 Maybe you are the "cool" generation. . . if coolness means a capacity to stay calm and use your head in the service of ends passionately believed in, then it has my admiration.

Baccalaureate 12 Jun 66

4089 The most fundamental value of a liberal education is that it makes life more interesting. . . [and] to think things which do not occur to the less learned and it makes it less likely that you will be bored with life.

NY Times 9 Nov 88

4090 [A liberal-arts education] makes the difference between the traveler who understands the local language and the traveler to whom the local language is a jumble of nonsense sounds.

ib

David Britt President, Children's Television Workshop

4091 Kids hit a wall and that wall is called fourth grade. At that moment, a kid shifts from learning to read to having to read in order to learn.

US News & World Report 24 Aug 92

Roscoe C E Brown Trustee, Brooklyn Public Library

4092 Here are enshrined the longing of great hearts and noble things that tower above the tide, the magic word that winged wonder starts, the garnered wisdom that has never died.

Inscription on facade of central building of Brooklyn Public Library 50

4093 While men have wit to read and will to know, the door to learning is the open book.

Above center door *ib*

4094 Farther than arrow, higher than wings, fly poet's song and prophet's word.

On side doors *ib*

4095 The world for men with all it may contain is only what is compassed by the mind.

ib

4096 With equal care weigh well the record of the wisdom and the folly of mankind.

On Eastern Parkway wing *ib*

Alan Bullock founder, St Catherine's College, Oxford

4097 I am just a scholarship boy who came to Oxford, got a double-first, founded a college and wrote a few books. There are a hundred who've done the same.

London Times 26 Nov 94

Florence Campbell Oxford undergraduate

4098 Humiliation, embarrassment and discomfort. . . that is sex at Oxford.

Expressing an undergraduate's viewpoint *London Times* 26 Oct 93

4099 Two minutes of gooey near-satisfaction followed by weeks of haunting guilt is so much more easily attained at Haagen-Däzs.

On preference for ice cream over sex *ib*

J W Carmichael Professor of Chemistry, Xavier University, New Orleans LA

4100 I could always drop people from a helicopter into Lake Pontchartrain and see how many drown.

But what we do is start from the shore and teach them how to swim.

On college prep courses that made Xavier second highest in US in producing black medical students *NY Times* 28 Mar 90

Brad Carter Chair, Religious Studies Dept, Southern Methodist University

4101 They wanted a great university without building a great university.

On National Collegiate Athletic Association's suspension of SMU's football program for repeated violations *NY Times* 5 Mar 87

4102 They knew a lot about football, but not a lot about academia. . . a colonial mentality. You alternate between being aggressively imitative of the more advanced institutions like the Ivy League or California.

ib

Corbin Cherubini Superintendent of Schools, Morgan GA

4103 It was educational apartheid.

On a separation of whites and blacks supposedly based on test scores but, through a process called "tracking," was found to be dishonestly administered *60 Minutes* CBS TV 5 Nov 95

Sara Cohen Yale, class of 1988

4104 The granola dykes. . . have old-fashioned utopian ideas about feminism.

Contrasting "crunchies" with "lipsticks" as Yale's radical-chic lesbians, quoted by faculty wife Julie V Iovine in widely discussed *Leisure and Arts* page article reporting that "suddenly Yale has a reputation as a gay school" *Wall Street Journal* 4 Aug 87

4105 What's wrong with a little bestiality?

Reaction to poster for GLAD (Gay and Lesbian Awareness Days) that were altered to read "Bestiality Awareness Day" *ib*

Johnnetta B Cole President, Spelman College

4106 I. . . have a sense of what you have done in order to get here. And because of that I'm just prepared to. . . declare you heroes and sheroes too.

At University of North Carolina commencement *NY Times* 29 May 95

James B Conant President, Harvard

4107 Secrecy and the pursuit of knowledge for its own sake are uneasy bedfellows.

President's Report Harvard University 1951–52

4108 A Harvard education consists of what you learn at Harvard while you are not studying.

Quoted in letters column *Time* 29 Sep 86

4109 I was one of the outstanding kibitzers of the age.

Quoted by James G Hershberg *James B Conant* Knopf 93

4110 Education is what is left after all that has been learnt is forgotten.

In his freshman diary *ib*

4111 [College is] the process of growing old for four years under the influence of so-called intellect.

ib

4112 You can't kill an idea by making martyrs of its disciples.

To Massachusetts legislature 9 Feb 48 *ib*

Rudolph F Crew Chancellor-designate, NYC Board of Education

4113 You're going to continue to ask me about control and I'm just going to talk to you about kids who can spell it, and exercise it....

NY Times 12 Oct 95

John Davis anthropologist

4114 The trouble with telling your life story is that it looks as if you had worked out some sort of plan. In fact, as you live it, life is a series of misadventures and fortuitous chances.

Refusing in-depth interview on becoming warden of All Souls College, Oxford *London Times* 24 Jun 94

Wylie H Davis Dean, University of Arkansas Law School

4115 He charmed us all right out of our mortarboards.

On Bill Clinton at 27 as an applicant appearing before a faculty appointments committee, quoted by David Maraniss *First In His Class* Simon & Schuster 95

Kim Doherty Easton MD teacher

4116 If you teach a child all the parts of a car and to drive a car and you hand him the keys. . . he thinks you want him to drive the car. . . teach him how the sex act works. . . then hand him a condom, he thinks you want him to have sex.

On distribution of condoms in public schools NPR 18 Oct 90

4117 Even if I was sexually active at one point, there's such a thing as secondary virginity, that from this point on I'm going to abstain.

ib

Margaret Doody Professor of English, Princeton

4118 Some professors for a very long time have seen students as a box of chocolates for their delectation.

Quoted by Dorothy Rabinowitz "Arms and the Man" *New York* 17 Jul 89

Otis C Edwards Assistant Professor of New Testament, Nashotah House Seminary

4119 To be loose with grammar is to be loose with the worst woman in the world.

Lecture 10 Jan 66

Albert Einstein physicist

4120 Education is that which remains if one has forgotten everything else he learned in school.

Out of My Later Years Thames 50

4121 Princeton is a wonderful little spot. A quaint and ceremonious village of puny demigods on stilts.

Philadelphia Aug 75

4122 Everything should be made as simple as possible but not simpler.

Newsweek 16 Apr 79

Dwight D Eisenhower 34th US President

4123 I became president of Columbia University and learned within 24 hours to be ready to speak at the drop of a hat.

To joint meeting of Philippine and US Chambers of Commerce 17 Jun 60

4124 Trustees were expected to be ready to speak at the passing of the hat.

ib

Aliu Babatunde Fafunwa Minister of Education for Nigeria

4125 A lot of people call me... the father of mother tongue.

On his one-man movement for early education in indigenous languages rather than colonial *NY Times* 23 May 91

John H Finley Jr Professor of Humanities, Harvard

4126 I'm not quite sure people want to have crystaline laughter falling like waterfall... at all hours. I should think it would be a little disturbing if you were taking advanced organic chemistry.

On enrolling women at Harvard *NY Times* 14 Jun 95

4127 God as humorist had in store for me the letter of recommendation as an art form.

On the resourcefulness necessary in writing letters of reference for several generations of Harvard men *ib*

J William Fulbright US Senator

4128 A tree whose roots are tampered with cannot grow.

On being relieved of the presidency of the University of Arkansas in a political shakeup after two years as the nation's youngest state university president 2 Jun 1941, recalled on Fulbright's death 9 Feb 95

Mary Futrell President, National Educational Association

4129 We've so over-regulated the schools that they're almost teacher-proof.

Fortune 7 Nov 88

John Kenneth Galbraith Professor of Economics, Harvard, also Ambassador to India

4130 [Economics] is a subject profoundly conducive to cliché, resonant with boredom.

At University of Arkansas 10 Jul 82

4131 On few topics is an American audience so practiced in turning off its ears and minds. And... none can say that the response is ill advised.

ib

4132 The commencement speech is not, I think, a wholly satisfactory manifestation of our culture.

At American University, Washington DC *Time* 18 Jun 84

4133 Speeches in our culture are the vacuum that fills a vacuum.

ib

John W Gardner US Secretary of Health, Education and Welfare

4134 We are all faced with a series of great opportunities—brilliantly disguised as insoluble problems.

Reader's Digest 9 Aug 65

Keith Geiger President, National Education Association (NEA)

4135 Our schools are improving. It's childhoods that are not.

Keynote address to NEA *NY Times* 5 Jul 91

4136 The United States... cannot continue to be the "911" emergency number for the rest of the world and refuse to be "911" for its own children.

ib

A Bartlett Giamatti President, Yale

4137 A liberal education is at the heart of a civil society, and at the heart of a liberal education is the act of teaching.

"The American Teacher" *Harper's* Jul 80

4138 Teaching is an instinctual art, mindful of potential, craving of realizations, a pausing, seamless process.

ib

4139 On a good day, I view the job [of president] as directing an orchestra. On the dark days, it is more like that of a clutch—engaging the engine to effect forward motion, while taking greater friction.

NY Times 6 Mar 83

4140 It is not enough to offer a smorgasbord of courses. We must ensure that students are not just eating at one end of the table.

ib

4141 There are many who lust for the simple answers of doctrine or decree. . . on the left and right. They are not confined to a single part of the society. . . terrorists of the mind.

Final baccalaureate address *ib* 26 May 86

4142 Being the president of a great university is a great privilege, and it's fascinating in many ways. But intellectually stimulating it's not.

Christian Science Monitor 16 Jul 87

Robert F Goheen President, Princeton

4143 If you feel that you have both feet planted on level ground, then the university has failed you.

Baccalaureate, news reports 23 Jun 61

4144 In the realm of ideas it is better to let the mind sally forth, even if some precious preconceptions suffer a mauling.

Commencement *ib* 18 Jun 66

Brigadier General Henry Graham Alabama National Guard

4145 Governor Wallace. . . please stand aside so that the order of the court may be accomplished.

To Governor George C Wallace on integration of the University of Alabama 11 Jun 63

Henry F Graff Professor of History, Columbia University

4146 This is a noble day on which to remember one of the great dropouts of Columbia, Alexander Hamilton.

On Columbia's bicentennial *NY Times* 11 Apr 87

Hannah Holborn Gray President, University of Chicago

4147 There was a perception that life—I won't say gray, that's hard for me—is beige.

On a guidebook's observation that "studying is the U of C student's favorite pastime" *Time* 28 May 84

4148 The university's characteristic state may be summarized by the words of the lady who said, "I have enough money to last me the rest of my life, unless I buy something."

Christian Science Monitor 25 Nov 86

4149 This is a university that is addicted to the life of the mind.

On U of C's hundredth anniversary *ib* 25 Feb 92

Germaine Greer journalist

4150 Libraries are reservoirs of strength, grace and wit, reminders of order, calm and continuity, lakes of mental energy, neither warm nor cold, light nor dark.

Excerpted in *NY Times* 24 Mar 91 from Greer's *Daddy, We Hardly Knew You* Fawcett 91

4151 The pleasure they give us is steady, unorgastic, reliable, deep and long-lasting. In any library in the world, I am at home, unselfconscious, still and absorbed.

ib

A Whitney Griswold President, Yale

4152 A Socrates in every classroom.

On his hopes for the Yale faculty *Time* 11 Jun 51

4153 If Carlyle could define a university as a collection of books, Socrates might have defined it as a conversation about wisdom.

Esssays on Education Yale University Press 54

4154 Could Hamlet have been written by a committee, or the Mona Lisa painted by a club? Could the New Testament have been composed as a conference report?

Baccalaureate 9 Jun 57

4155 Creative ideas do not spring from groups. They spring from individuals. The divine spark leaps from the finger of God to the finger of Adam.

ib

4156 Self-respect. . . comes to us when we are alone, in quiet moments in quiet places when we suddenly realize that, knowing the good, we have done it; knowing the beautiful, we have served it; knowing the truth, we have spoken it.

ib

4157 Books won't stay banned. They won't burn. Ideas won't go to jail. In the long run of history, the censor and the inquisitor have always lost.

NY Times 24 Feb 59

4158 The only sure weapon against bad ideas is better ideas.

ib

4159 A college education is a taste for knowledge, a taste for philosophy, a capacity to explore, question and perceive relationships between fields of knowledge and experience.

On revising Yale's curriculum *ib* 20 Apr 63

4160 The world is always upside down to a baccalaureate speaker. . . . Things have got to be wrong in order that they may be deplored.

ib

4161 He is like a fireman who sees six fires from the window, dashes out to extinguish one, and hopes somebody else will get the other five.

On being a university president *NY Herald Tribune* 13 Oct 63

Edith Hamilton classicist

4162 To be able to be caught up into the world of thought—that is educated.

Saturday Evening Post 27 Sep 58

4163 To rejoice in life, to find the world beautiful and delightul to live in, was a mark of the Greek spirit which distinguished it from all that has gone before. It is a vital distinction.

The Greek Way 1930 recalled on Hamilton's death 31 May 63

Kim Harris Gallaudet University student

4164 She won't listen to us and if we can't have a deaf president, we won't listen to her.

On opposition to appointment of a president who was not hearing impaired, a movement that succeeded in retention of the tradition of a deaf president *NY Times* 8 Mar 88

Vaclav Havel President of the Czech Republic

4165 Every education is a kind of outward journey.

Quoted by Bill Moyers *Healing and the Mind* Doubleday 93

S I Hayakawa US Senator and educator

4166 In a real sense, people who have read good literature have lived more than people who cannot or will not read.

Language and Thought in Action Harcourt Brace Jovanovich 78

4167 It is not true that we have only one life to live; we can live as many more lives and as many kinds of lives as we wish.

ib

Seamus Heaney poet

4168 For the honor, not for a living.

On post-Nobel laureate plans to continue to lecture for four months annually at Harvard *London Times* 13 Oct 95

4169 Like all teachers, I am filled with dread at the thought of it, but enjoy the action of it.

ib

Gregory P Heyman Collegiate School, NYC

4170 All kids, even mature, refined Collegiate boys, have sex even if they don't have a condom.

At 17, advocating distribution of condoms to his classmates and all students in private schools *NY Times* 26 May 92

Alford Houston-Buswall Headmaster, Harrodian School

4171 We have to learn not to be fazed by luxury.

On *de rigueur* lunch menus that included salade niçoise and tarte aux fruits *London Times* 21 Feb 95

Robert M Hutchins President, University of Chicago

4172 There is no reason why the University should be stuck with me at 51 because I was a promising young man at 30.

On resigning after 22 years as president and chancellor, news reports 8 Jan 51

4173 Why is it that the boy or girl who on Jun 15 receives his degree, eager, enthusiastic, outspoken, idealistic, reflective and independent, is on the following Sep 15, or even Jun 16. . . dull, uninspiring, shifty, pliable and attired in a double-breasted blue serge suit? The answer must be in the relative weakness of the higher education, compared with the forces that make everybody think and act like everybody else.

Farewell address *ib* 12 Feb 51

4174 Education is a kind of continuing dialogue, and a dialogue assumes, in the nature of the case, different points of view.

On academic freedom, testimony to House of Representatives loyalty committee *ib* 8 Dec 52

4175 It is not so important to be serious as it is to be serious about the important things. The monkey wears an expression of seriousness which would do credit to any college student, but the monkey is serious because he itches.

Quote 3 Aug 58

4176 It is the task of every generation to reassess the tradition in which it lives, to discard what it cannot use, and to bring into context with the distant and intermediate past the most recent contributions to the Great Conversation which has gone on from age to age.

"The Great Conversation" preface to "Great Books of the World" series *Encyclopedia Britannica* 59

4177 In the Middle West, the high school is the place where the band practices.

NY Herald Tribune 22 Apr 63

4178 The university is the terrestrial instrument which the author of our being has placed at our disposal for the purpose of getting us clothed and, when necessary, reclothed in our rightful mind.

On inauguration of Edward Levi as president of the University of Chicago, quoted by Harry S Ashmore *Unseasonable Truths: The Life of Robert M Hutchins* Little, Brown 89

4179 Colleges and universities will find themselves converted into intellectual hobo jungles. And veterans unable to get work and equally unable to resist putting pressures on colleges and universities will find themselves educational hoboes.

"The GI Bill, 50 Years On" editorial *NY Times* 22 Jun 94

Louis Johannot Headmaster, Institute Le Rosey

4180 I always try to meet and know the parents. . . it helps me to forgive their children.

Life 7 May 65

Stanley N Katz President, American Council of Learned Societies

4181 Guggenheim invented the prestige fellowship . . . [a] *Good Housekeeping* Seal of Approval. . . a cache that was invaluable.

On the John Simon Guggenheim Memorial Foundation *NY Times* 21 Oct 95

Neil L Rudenstine President, Harvard

4182 I wanted the very best turtle soup.

On becoming a graduate student at Harvard, recalled when he became its president *Harvard University Magazine* Jul 94

Evelyn Wood remedial reading specialist

4183 Eat a dish of rice kernel-by-kernel or take a spoonful to get a good taste?

On choosing to read slowly or rapidly with greater comprehension *NY Times* 30 Aug 95 in a nation where "faster is synonymous with better" *Time* 11 Sep 95

Critics

John F Akers Chair, IBM

4184 Each school can, once again, become what it was always meant to be—a building that has four walls with tomorrow inside.

Challenging the US to reduce the dropout rate of 4,000 students a day *Wall Street Journal* 20 Mar 91

Edward Albee playwright

4185 I am a Doctor. A.B. . . M.A. . . . Ph.D. . . . ABMAPHID!. . . a wasting disease of the frontal lobes.

Lines for a college professor in *Who's Afraid of Virginia Woolf?* Atheneum 63

Sally Bowman Alden Executive Director, Computer Learning Foundation

4186 Putting most of a school's computers in a lab is the equivalent of keeping most of its pencils in one room.

Fortune 14 Nov 94

Robert Anderson playwright

4187 All you're supposed to do is every once in a while give the boys a little tea and sympathy.

On the duties of a headmaster's wife *Tea and Sympathy* Broadway play 54

Anon

4188 A major cause of deterioration in the use of the English language is very simply the enormous increase in the number of people who are using it.

Quoted by Robert McCrum, William Cran, and Robert MacNeil *The Story of English* Viking 86

4189 The thicker the applicant, the thicker the file.

On private schools *New York* 23 Nov 87

4190 This door is alarmed.

Kentucky airport sign cited as an example of "dangerous language pollution" *NY Times* 5 Jan 88

4191 It is the soup that eats like a meal.

Television commercial *ib*

4192 Sidwell is a place where Episcopalians teach Jews how to be good Quakers.

On a Washington DC prep school *Washingtonian* Dec 88

Hannah Arendt philosopher

4193 [Education] is where we decide whether we love our children enough not to expel them from our world and leave them to their own devices, not to strike from their hands their chance of undertaking something new, something unforseen by us, but to prepare them in advance for the task of renewing a common world.

Between Past and Present Viking 77

Louis Auchincloss novelist

4194 The time from age 12 to 18 is when a human being becomes what he is going to be.

On formation of the future, address at Groton School 1982 Prize Day, quoted by Carol Gelderman *Louis Auchincloss: A Writer's Life* Crown 93

W H Auden poet

4195 A professor is one who talks in someone else's sleep.

Recalled on Auden's death 28 Sep 73

4196 The greatest educational problem of today is how to teach people to ignore the irrelevant, how to refuse to know things, before they are suffocated. For too many facts are as bad as none at all.

Quoted by Charles Osborne *W H Auden: The Life of a Poet* Harcourt Brace Jovanovich 79

Max Beerbohm humorist

4197 The nonsense which was knocked out of them at school is all put gently back at Oxford or Cambridge.

On undergraduates, recalled on Beerbohm's death 20 May 56

Griffin Bell US Attorney General

4198 By obtaining what she wants, she'd lose what she wants because it wouldn't be there.

On a woman applicant for the traditionally all-male Virginia Military Institute *Washington Times* 26 Sep 94

Kenneth Boulding British economist

4199 In a time Apocalyptic/ On the mountain Eucalyptic/ Full of thought Acropolyptic/ Stands the Hutchins Hutch./ In this intellectual attic/ Institutions Democratic/ Are studied by the Mode socratic/ With the Midas Touch.

On the Ford Foundation's Center for the Study of Democratic Institutions, Santa Barbara CA, quoted by Harry S Ashmore *Unseasonable Truths* Little, Brown 89

George Hambley Brown film producer

4200 How depressing for you to know that you failed with this talented child.

Rebuke to headmistresses who expelled his daughter, future *New Yorker* editor Tina Brown *London Times* 22 Jan 84

Matthew J Bruccoli biographer

4201 [He was] one of that legendary breed of headmasters whose schools were extensions of their own personalities.

On the Kent School's founder, Father Frederick Herbert Sill, OHC *James Gould Cozzens: A Life Apart* Harcourt Brace Jovanovich 83

Carnegie Foundation for the Advancement of Teaching

4202 Teachers must think for themselves if they are to help others think for themselves.

A Nation Prepared quoted in *NY Times* 16 May 86

4203 [They are] little more than human storehouses to keep young people off the streets.

On many of the public schools in large cities *An Imperiled Generations ib* 16 Mar 88

4204 No one notices if they drop out because no one noticed when they dropped in.

On student anonymity *ib*

Rachel Carson enviromentalist

4205 If a child is to keep alive his inborn sense of wonder, he needs the companionship of at least one adult who can share it, rediscovering with him the joy, excitement and mystery of the world we live in.

The Sense of Wonder Harper & Row 60

Lawton Chiles Governor of Florida

4206 Knowledge is the antidote to the poison of prejudice.

On augmenting a state law requiring public schools to teach holocaust history with a similar measure supporting black history *NY Times* 15 May 94

Winston S Churchill statesman

4207 Headmasters have powers at their disposal with which Prime Ministers have never yet been invested.

Recalled on Churchill's death 24 Jan 65

4208 Study history, study history. In history lies all the secrets of statecraft.

Quoted by James Humes *Churchill* Stein & Day 80

4209 I got into my bones the essential structure of the ordinary British sentence—which is a noble thing.

On studying remedial English for three school terms, quoted by William Manchester *The Last Lion* Little, Brown 83

William J Clinton 42nd US President

4210 We ought to just give you the money if you're eligible for it, and let you bring it here and get a good education.

At Carl Sandburg College, Galesburg IL, on simplifying government and educational grants 10 Jan 95

Roger Cohen journalist

4211 [They are] the "aliterate" Americans.

Reporting in the Educational Supplement of the *NY Times* on those who follow television, sports, and films but do not read, quoted by Edwin Diamond *Behind the Times* Villard 93

Jennett Conant wife of James B Conant

4212 Everything works out by formula; he'll compound his formula for running the university, and then stand over while it develops into substance.

On Dr Conant's approach as a chemistry professor to the presidency of Harvard, quoted by James G Hershberg *James B Conant* Knopf 93

Frank Conroy journalist

4213 [The Citadel] is Charleston's shrine to southern masculinity.

On Charleston SC's Citadel military academy *The Lords of Discipline* Houghton Mifflin 80 quoted in report of the first woman plebe who left within a few days *Newsweek* 28 Aug 95

James Gould Cozzens novelist

4214 Dr Holt's face was like something outstanding and lordly cut from a cliff. . . blue eyes, keen, haughty and wise, waited, ready to leap.

On headmaster patterned on Father Frederick Herbert Sill, OHC, founder of the Kent School, quoted by Matthew J Bruccoli *James Gould Cozzens* Harcourt Brace Jovanovich 83

4215 His. . . tangled blond eyebrows—these were a sandy, strong, blond, and similar hairs grew out of his massive nostrils—resembled somehow the illustrations in the fourth-form Caesar, showing a cross-section of the Gallic defenses—ditch, glacis, and a hedge of uprooted trees.

ib

4216 He was intensely solid; a considered, terrible energy.

ib

4217 For whatever it was disastrous or inexpedient for him to hear, he heard. Involved explanations, trembling evasions and artless falsehoods he could not hear. He roared for their repetition—a task beyond many a guilty conscience.

ib

David N Dinkins Mayor of New York City

4218 What good does it do to put a Harvard in Harlem if you can't walk to it without dodging bullets?

On announcing a $28-million program to identify the 40 most dangerous public schools *NY Times* 3 Mar 92

E L Doctorow novelist

4219 Someone. . . gets an MFA in writing, and immediately gets a job on another campus teaching other young people to get their MFA's in writing.

On the proliferation of teachers of composition, George Plimpton ed *Writers at Work* Penguin 88

Will Durant historian

4220 In my youth, I stressed freedom, and in my old age I stress order. I have made the great discovery that liberty is a product of order.

On need for more discipline in education *Time* 13 Aug 65

Marian Wright Edelman President, Children's Defense Fund

4221 Preventing that second child is what it's all about.

On New Futures School, Albuquerque NM, that provides nursery for infants so that young mothers can continue their educations *NY Times* 15 Mar 88

Susan Faludi journalist

4222 The over-all effect is that of a theme park for post-Cold War kids.

On profiling The Citadel military academy at Charleston SC *New Yorker* 5 Sep 94

E M Forester novelist

4223 They go forth with well developed bodies, fairly developed minds and underdeveloped hearts. An undeveloped heart—not a cold one. The difference is important.

On boys from British public schools *Life* 2 Apr 51

4224 Spoon-feeding in the long run teaches us nothing but the shape of the spoon.

London Observer 7 Oct 51

Felix Frankfurter Associate Justice, US Supreme Court

4225 Incurably cold, without radiation.

On James B Conant as president of Harvard, quoted by James G Hershberg *James B Conant* Knopf 93

Robert Frost poet

4226 Education is the ability to listen to almost anything without losing your temper or your self-confidence.

Reader's Digest Apr 60

4227 Education doesn't change life much. It just lifts trouble to a higher plane of regard.

Quote 9 Jul 61

4228 College is a refuge from hasty judgment.

ib

4229 Education is. . . hanging around until you've caught on.

Recalled on Frost's death 29 Jan 63

Brendan Gill essayist

4230 Neither Stuart Little nor Snow White and the Seven Dwarfs was likely to bring a blush to the cheek of even the primmest members of the Yale academic establishment.

On the passing over of novelist John O'Hare to confer honorary degrees on E B White and Walt Disney *A New York Life* Poseidon 90

Newton L ("Newt") Gingrich Speaker, US House of Representatives

4231 Princeton sent me a rejection letter so elegantly worded that I still think of myself as an alumnus.

Newsweek 9 Jan 95

Ruth Gledhill journalist

4232 Eton... an eerie... gothic incubator for Cambridge's intellectual elite.

London Times 21 Jan 95

Victoria Glendinning author and critic

4233 The earnest, grey-cardigan world of female academe was not for her.

On poet Edith Sitwell as guest lecturer at Oxford's Lady Margaret Hall and Somerville College *A Unicorn Among Lions* Weidenfeld & Nicolson 81

David Gonzalez reporter

4234 [His] parents toiled with their hands so he could work with his mind.

On blue-collar workers who support private education for their children *NY Times* 19 Aug 95

4235 An education grounded in tradition and values could sometimes make the difference between going to Yale and going to jail.

ib

Geoffrey Grigson journalist

4236 There she sits, a figure of learning, a Queen Victoria with brains, vast, booted, bosomy, comprised of elements which are intellectual, emotional, comfortable, romantic, olfactory, personal, universal.

On hundredth anniversary of the British Museum Reading Room *London Observer* 19 May 57

Gilbert M Grosvenor President, National Geographic Society

4237 If you don't know where you are, you're nowhere.

On NGS's establishment of $20-million foundation to fight ignorance of geography *Washington Post* 14 Jan 88

David Halberstam historian

4238 The overt teaching was that the finest life is service to God, your family and your state, but the covert teaching, far more subtle and insidious, was somewhat different: ultimately, strength is more important; there is a ruling clique; there is a thing called privilege... [and] the real world is going to remain that way and you might as well get used to it.

On New England prep schools *The Best and the Brightest* 69

Molly Haskell journalist

4239 The maiden schoolteachers who were the loving persecutors of my youth live on in my memory, tall and shapeless, brandishing female self-respect like a ruler.

"Paying Homage to the Spinster" *NY Times* 8 May 88

4240 The most interesting and inquisitive part of me is the legacy of the inviolable spinster within.

ib

Richard Hoggart journalist

4241 It's terribly difficult for anyone to get out of the Oxford-Cambridge feeling: like class itself in Britain, it's the last thing we let go after our clothes.

"The Listener" 2 Jun 60, quoted by Anthony Sampson *The Anatomy of Britain* Hodder & Stoughton 62

Rear Admiral Grace Murray Hopper US Navy

4242 A ship in port is safe: but that is not what ships are built for.

On exploring the future, address at Trinity College, Washington DC *Washington Times* 22 Jun 87

Robert Hughes art critic

4243 The choir of conservatives denouncing "well-subsidized left academics" as bludgers, whilst taking their own subsidies from various right-wing foundations, is truly one of the wonders of American intellectual life.

Quoted by Henry Louis Gates Jr *New Yorker* 19 Apr 93 reviewing Hughes' *Culture of Conservatives* Oxford 93

Walter Isaacson journalist

4244 He was something between an epitome and a parody.

On Harvard Professor William Elliott as Henry A Kissinger's mentor *Kissinger* Simon & Schuster 92

Maharani Of Jaipur Indian intellectual

4245 An open door is a very good thing, but don't keep your mind so open that your brains fall out.

Quoted by US Secretary of Education William J Bennett at commencement at The Citadel, Charleston SC *Time* 9 Jun 86

Claudia ("Lady Bird") Johnson

4246 The public comes in thousands and the scholars in trickles.

On the Lyndon B Johnson Presidential Library *A White House Diary* Holt Rinehart Winston 70

Quincy Jones jazz trumpeter and songwriter

4247 To try to talk to the young people who will run the future—in ten minutes—is a little like trying to put a cantaloupe in a coke bottle.

At Claremont College commencement *NY Times* 29 May 95

Tamara Jones journalist

4248 She felt that restless thrill, that fresh promise of fall when anything seems possible and the world can be kept within a fourth-grader's grasp.

On a teacher's reluctant retirement after 28 Septembers *Washington Post* 4 Sep 95

Thomas H Kean Governor of New Jersey

4249 The high school diploma is more a proof of age than it is any kind of achievement.

USA Today 5 Feb 91

John F Kennedy 35th US President

4250 The human mind is our fundamental resource.

To Congress on the state of education 20 Feb 61

4251 A child miseducated is a child lost.

State of the Union 11 Jan 62

4252 It might be said now that I have the best of both worlds. A Harvard education and a Yale degree.

On receiving an honorary doctorate *NY Times* 12 Jun 62

4253 I want to emphasize in the great concentration which we now place upon scientists and engineers how much we still need the men and women educated in the liberal tradition, willing to take the long look, undisturbed by prejudices and slogans of the moment, who attempt to make an honest judgment on difficult events.

At University of North Carolina 12 Oct 62

4254 Liberty without learning is always in peril and learning without liberty is always in vain.

At Vanderbilt University 19 May 63

4255 Modern cynics and skeptics... see no harm in paying those to whom they entrust the minds of their children a smaller wage than is paid to those to whom they entrust the care of their plumbing.

ib

Tracy Kidder journalist

4256 The task of universal, public, elementary education is still usually being conducted by a woman alone in a little room.

Quoted by Phyllis Theroux *NY Times* 17 Sep 89 reviewing Kidder's *Among Schoolchildren* Houghton Mifflin 89

4257 Public education rests precariously on the skill and virtue of the people at the bottom of the institutional pyramid.

ib

Edward Koch Mayor of New York

4258 Each diploma is a lighted match... [and] each one of you is a fuse.

At State University of NY *NY Times* 10 Jun 83

Charles Kuralt commentator

4259 If hope were an ocean, this month would bring its highest tide.

On September opening of schools *Sunday Morning* CBS TV 6 Sep 92

Jim Lehrer PBS commentator

4260 The diploma you are about to receive does not mean you are well-educated.... It means you have been opened up to a perpetual state of ignorance and thus a life-long hunger for more ideas, more thoughts, more challenges, more of everything.

At Southern Methodist University commencement 20 May 89

4261 Some of the dumbest people I know personally had degrees from one of America's finest institutions of higher learning.

At Williams College commencement 6 Jun 93

4262 They... took the diploma... said "Hey, hey, you know, I'm educated," and proceeded to never read another book, never entertain another fresh idea, and most tragically for their society and their country, never again paid much attention to anything other than themselves, to much of anything that was happening around them or to others.

ib

4263 You have not well-educated them... thank goodness... but you've gotten the lifelong process off to a great start.

To the faculty *ib*

Herman Leonard public finance specialist

4264 From the point of view of the family, the best thing to do is buy a Mercedes the day before you fill out the form.

On decreasing savings to qualify for scholarship aid *NY Times* 12 Jul 87

C S Lewis essayist

4265 The real Oxford is a closed corporation of jolly, untidy, lazy, good-for-nothing humorous old men, who have been electing their own successors ever since the world began and who intend to go on with it.

Quoted in Jan Morris ed *The Official Book of Oxford* Oxford 78

Wilmarth S Lewis Selections Committee, Yale

4266 Is God a Yale man?.

A traditional question rethought while considering a woman for president *NY Times* 24 Apr 77

London Times

4267 The insidious element of accent unifies them all.
On public schools 25 Sep 61

4268 The elevation to a Regius chair of a scholar of distinction should be the product of a process of consultation between Crown and gown. . . [but] unless the Crown's power is also used discreetly, there may tomorrow be no prerogative left to exercise.
"Crown and Gown" editorial on whether acadmeic appointments are "a Prime Minister's proper business" 15 Feb 95

4269 Whether it be Bangladesh or Britain, Dhaka or Dorchester, cheating is an art as old as the oldest classroom
"Copybook Technique" editorial 15 Jul 95

4270 Schools. . . have always been a bustling zoo for all sorts of creatures: swots, sneaks, bullies, sissies, milksops, greedyguts, oiks, thieves and—this complex species invariably—cheats.
ib

Archibald MacLeish poet and statesman

4271 [Students] remember very well a blue ironic eye behind a brightly polished eye-glass. . . and a voice which can crackle under a fool's complacence like dry wood under an empty kettle.
On Felix Frankfurter as a law professor, quoted by Scott Donaldson *Archibald MacLeish* Houghton Mifflin 92

Harold Macmillan Prime Minister of Britain

4272 The only industry when I was up was marmalade—which seemed somehow appropriate.
On industrialization of Oxford, quoted by Anthony Sampson *Anatomy of Britain* Hodder & Stoughton 62

Douglas Martin journalist

4273 They came to the Brooklyn Library's literacy program to begin at the beginning with Dick and Jane and Spot. Self-esteem is the reason they give, almost in unison.
On adult education *NY Times* 18 Jan 92

John Masefield Poet Laureate of England

4274 There are few earthly things more beautiful than a university. . . a place where those who hate ignorance may strive to know, where those who perceive truth may strive to make others see.
At American University commencement, Washington, 10 Jun 63

R B McCallum Master of Pembroke College, Oxford

4275 Fulbrght is responsible for the greatest movement of scholars across the face of the earth since the fall of Constantinople in 1453.
On US Senator J William Fulbright's sponsorship of Fulbright fellowships *Saturday Evening Post* 23 Mar 63

Thomas Merton Trappist monk

4276 October is a fine and dangerous season in America. . . a wonderful time to begin anything at all. You go to college, and every course in the catalogue looks wonderful.
Recalled on Merton's death 10 Dec 68

Richard Mitchell Editor, *The Underground Grammarian*

4277 I promise the students I will never ask them a question to which I know the answer. . . [and] in return for this you are going to promise never to tell me anything that I must already know.
NY Times 29 Apr 88

Robert Mitchum actor

4278 It was a finishing school—if you were there you were finished.
On a high school in Manhattan's Hell's Kitchen *NY Times* 14 Nov 85

Christopher Morley essayist

4279 Like a skilled diver they went through the outer film of sense with very little splash.
On how "images which sink deepest are often those we scarcely knew, at the time, we were noticing at all," preface to 11th Edition *Bartlett's Familiar Quotations* Little, Brown 1942, recalled on Morley's death 28 Mar 57

4280 One of the pleasures of this re-editing has been that one collaborator, by long experience with inquiries for the affable, familiar ghosts of print, knows acutely what readers want; and the other believes himself to know what they ought to want.
ib

4281 The English-speaking peoples are considered somber-minded, but they often have a way of making a joke when no one is listening. They even laugh at themselves, which makes it unanimous.
ib

4282 The job. . . is really that of sweeping the hearth of literature.
On editing *Bartlett's ib*

4283 [They are] the vitamins of speech.
On colloqualisms *ib*

4284 It is not easy to be a bottleneck for the flood of print.
Preface to 12th edition

Lewis Mumford critic

4285 [He was] as full of flavor as hickory smoke.

On geotechnic expert Benton MacKaye *Harvard University Magazine* Jul 94

National Commission on Excellence in Education

4286 If an unfriendly foreign power had attempted to impose on America the mediocre educational performance that exists today, we might have used it as an act of war.

A Nation at Risk quoted by Edward B Fiske on fifth anniversary of its publication "35 Pages That Shook the US Education World" *NY Times* 27 Apr 88

Newsweek magazine

4287 As chairman of the Rockefeller Brothers panel on education, he coined the phrase "pursuit of excellence"—and lived to shudder at its deterioration into a cliché.

On John W Gardner, US Secretary of Health, Education and Welfare 9 Aug 65

The New York Times

4288 Either stolen or loved to death.

"Miracle on Fifth Avenue" editorial on books most often replaced by NY Public Library 5 Oct 86

Richard M Nixon 37th US President

4289 [I was trying] to lift them a bit out of the miserable intellectual wasteland in which they now wander aimlessly around.

Memo marking a pre-dawn visit to student demonstration at the Lincoln Memorial 13 May 70, quoted by Fred Emery *Watergate* Times Books 94 [p 20]

4290 [H G Wells said] the military mind. . . is by definition mediocre because nobody with any real intellectual talent would submit himself to the military career and Wells, of course, has the feeling that the solution to all problems is education for everyone, and that's a terrible idea, especially for women.

To White House Chief of Staff H R Haldeman Chief of Staff in January 1972, quoted by Stephen E Ambrose in introduction to *The Haldeman Diaries* Putnam 94

4291 Violence or the threat of violence [must] never be permitted to influence the actions of judgments of the university community. Once it does, the community, almost by definition, ceases to be a university.

On tumult on college campuses 22 Mar 69

4292 From time immemorial expulsion has been the primary instrument of university discipline.

ib

Sean O'Faolain Irish writer

4293 It is really the undergraduate who makes a university, gives it its lasting character, smell, feel, quality, tradition. . . whose presence creates it and whose memories preserve it.

Harvard Alumni Bulletin 24 Oct 64

J Robert Oppenheimer physicist

4294 No man should escape our universities without knowing how little he knows.

Partisan Review Summer 67

John Osborne playwright

4295 I don't think one "comes down" from Jimmy's university. . . it's not even red brick, it's white tile.

Look Back in Anger Faber & Faber 57

Philip Duke of Edinburgh

4296 I'm only going to bother if you're permanently bottom.

On his children's school reports, quoted by Denis Judd "Prince Philip at 60" *Illustrated London News* Jun 81

General Colin L Powell Chair, US Joint Chiefs of Staff

4297 I remember the front door. . . the auditorium. . . the feeling that you can't make it. But you can.

On revisiting the South Bronx high school from which he graduated in 1954 *NY Times* 16 Apr 91

Anna Quindlen columnist

4298 School prayer. . . bears about as much resemblance to real spiritual experience as that freeze-dried astronaut food bears to a nice standing rib roast.

On efforts to return prayer to classrooms *NY Times* 7 Dec 94

4299 It was almost an insult to God, a rote exercise in moving your mouth while daydreaming or checking out the cutest boy in the 7th grade that was a far, far cry from soul-searching.

ib

Ronald Reagan 40th US President

4300 [He is the] best thing to happen to American education since the McGuffey Reader.

On William J Bennett as Secretary of Education *NY Times* 10 Aug 88

Harry Reasoner commentator

4301 It may be the most important commencement speech ever made.

On New York businessman who promised college scholarships to everyone who persevered in graduating from inner-city high school *60 Minutes* CBS-TV 28 Jun 87

Ed Regis journalist

4302 Geologists, biologists, and open-heart surgeons need not apply; such people have dirty hands.

On preference for pure mathmematics and theoretical physics at Princeton NJ Institute for Advanced Study *Who Got Einstein's Office?* Addison-Wesley 88

Bertrand Russell philosopher

4303 Oxford and Cambridge are the last medieval islands, all right for first-class people. But their security is harmful to second-class people—it makes them insular and gaga.

London Observer 4 Sep 60, quoted by Anthony Sampson *Anatomy of Britain* Hodder & Stoughton 62

Fran R Schumer journalist

4304 The fence around the principal's house was down. . . the initial tangible evidence of what the new principal would be like.

On Kendra Stearns O'Donnell, first woman principal of 216-year-old Phillips Exeter Academy *NY Times* 17 Oct 87

William Sherk neologist and author

4305 There must be hundreds of millions of people throughout the world who are sequilingual and don't even know what to call themselves.

On coining the word "sequilingual," those who speak one and a half languages *Toronto Star* 29 Dec 76

Edith Sitwell poet

4306 [It is] the arrival at my destination.

On receiving an honorary degree from Oxford University, quoted by Victoria Glendinning *A Unicorn Among Lions* Weidenfeld & Nicolson 81

Theodore R Sizer Chair, Department of Education, Brown University

4307 [It is an] enervating and bottom-aching journey of being talked at.

On high school curriculums *NY Times* 31 Oct 87

Theodore C Sorensen Counsel to Kennedy White House

4308 A rain of honorary degrees began to fall.

On publication of John F Kennedy's *Profiles in Courage* Kennedy Harper & Row 65

Leo Stein journalist

4309 The perfect method of learning is analogous to infection. It enters and spreads.

Journey Into the Self Crown 50

John Steinbeck novelist

4310 You can't bite the hand that sets a mortarboard on your head.

On refusing an honorary doctorate from his own university, Stanford, and other schools, Elaine Steinbeck and Robert Wallsten ed *Steinbeck* Viking 75

4311 My poison glands are still producing a very high test kind of venom and I'll resist being a classic until they plant me at which time I will automatically cease to be one.

ib

Kurt Vonnegut Jr novelist

4312 High school is closer to the core of the American experience than anything else.

Introduction to John Birmingham ed *Our Time is Now* Praeger 70

Donald Walker NY Public Library

4313 Read under dim spot-lamps in taxis or air shuttles, balanced on subways, carried on boardwalks and into bathtubs. . . they develop broken spines, pages like prune skin or go to their reward in the land of lost umbrellas.

On books most often worn out or stolen "Missing Book Lists Speak Volumes" *NY Times* 28 Sep 86

Wall Street Journal

4314 Experience even in the Communist world has stilled the dreams of the 1960s, but at least one place continues to revere them—the ivory foxhole, known as the American academy.

"The Stanford Mind" editorial on Stanford University as an example of institutions that "have caved into political pressure and cashiered its popular 'Western Culture' course requirement for freshmen" 22 Dec 88

Evelyn Waugh writer and critic

4315 We class schools. . . into four grades: leading school, first-rate school, good school and school.

Recalled on Waugh's death 10 Apr 66

4316 Oxford is simply a very beautiful city in which it is convenient to segregate a certain member of the young of the nation while they are growing up.

Quoted in Donald Gallagher ed *A Little Order* Little, Brown 81

Howard Webber publisher

4317 It is clear that the final lexicon exists only in the mind of God.

Concluding preface to *Webster's II New Riverside Dictionary* Houghton Mifflin 84

Jim White columnist

4318 The lecture theater—the place where information passes from the notebook of the lecturer to the notebook of the student without necessarily passing through the mind of either.

Comparing medical school lectures to anatomy labs *London Times* 13 Nov 92

Thornton Wilder playwright and novelist

4319 The process of learning is accompanied by alternations of pain and brief quickenings of pleasure that resemble pain.

The Eighth Day Harper & Row 67

Peregrine Worsthorne Editor, *London Sunday Telegraph*

4320 The difficult part is to teach him not to oversimplify, not to believe that he has the answers, above all not to believe that he can always tell the truth because so often there is no truth to tell.

To Kurt Hahn on educating boys at Gordonstoun, the Hahn-founded prep school in Scotland, quoted by Peter Vansittart *In the Fifties* John Murray 95

Frank Lloyd Wright architect

4321 Were I a Rockefeller, Ford, or DuPont. . . I would buy up our leading universities, close them, and hang out the sign: Closed by the beneficence of one, Frank Lloyd Wright.

American Scholar Spring 94

Jonathan Yardley critic

4322 [It is] the first spadeful of dirt on the casket of bilingualism.

On NY Board of Education's report that children learn more in programs conducted in English than in bilingual teaching *Fortune* 3 Apr 95

MEDICINE

Physicians and the Medical World

American Medical Association

4323 A physician may not ethically refuse to treat a patient whose condition is within the physician's current realm of competence.

Statement four years after outbreak of AIDS *NY Times* 13 Nov 87

4324 All patients, regardless of their sexual orientation, have a right to respect and concern for their lives and values.

"Health Care Needs of Gay Men and Lesbians in the US," report reversing a 13-year-old policy that sought to change homosexual orientation and often resulted "in ostracism and discrimination from some health professionals" *Washington Times* 22 Dec 94

Natalie Angier journalist

4325 After a brief, charming fantasy that the age of infectious disease was behind us, the entire medieval bestiary of scourges has returned with teeth bared and claws extended.

On reemergence of medicine's most contageous maladies *NY Times* 22 Aug 95

4326 To *P falciparum* any red blood cell can look like home.

On the opportunistic spread of malaria *ib*

Dr George Annas Boston University School of Medicine and Public Health

4327 Doctors are the last to accept that there is nothing left that medicine has to offer.

On AMA report that physicians' tend to ignore "living wills" on unduly sustaining life *US News & World Report* 4 Dec 95

4328 If you want control over your death, you have to stay out of the hospital.

ib

Anon

4329 A rash of dermatologists, a hive of allergies, a scrub of interns, a chest of phthisiologists, or, a giggle of nurses, a flood of urologists, a pride of proctologists, an eyeful of ophthalmologists, or a whiff of anestheologists, a staff of bacteriologists, a cast of orthopedic rheumatologists, a gaggle of laryngologists.

On "nouns of multitude" *Journal of the American Medical Association* Oct 64

4330 Nutritional sabotage.

Term used by Ethiopian relief workers for families who practice intentional malnourishment to gain admittance to shelters *NY Times* 9 Jun 85

4331 Bedpan mutuals.

Nickname for insurance companies that offer low premium malpractice insurance *Time* 24 Mar 86

4332 Required Request.

Title of New York state legislation directing hospitals to seek family permission for donations of organs and tissues *NY Infirmary/Beekman Downtown Hospital Newsletter* 31 Jul 86

4333 It's different from other diseases because you—and every patient—know the outcome from the start. . . death within two years, weighing perhaps 65 pounds, incontinent, in severe pain, with 80 percent experiencing mental changes.

Physician describing the ravages observed in most instances of AIDS *NY Times* 4 Oct 87

4334 AIDS telescopes what we all will go through. . . a chronic, progressive disease that will be painful to experience, painful to watch, expensive and ultimately fatal.

ib

4335 I want my son to have a new stereo, car, nose and chin.

Typical thinking among parents increasingly willing to provide cosmetic surgery *Wall Street Journal* 24 Sep 90

4336 Do not resuscitate.

Patient's formal designation (DNR) necessary on hospital charts to avoid emergency measures *NY Times* 4 Oct 90

4337 Here it is normal to become blind before you have white hair.

Tribal leader in Mali quoted in Rick Smolan ed *The Power to Heal* Prentice Hall 90

4338 [Its use] would be like jumping from the 20th floor of a building instead of the 22nd.

An official of the US Office on Smoking and Health commenting on cigarettes billed as chemical-free *US News & World Report* 28 Jan 91

4339 Give comfort care only.

Instructions for not medicating terminal patients, cited by Dr Samuel Gorovitz, Station WAMU Washington 11 Nov 91

4340 My doctor loses money when I get well.

Bumper sticker from foes of government health insurance *ib* 3 Feb 92

4341 Scales Are for Fish, Not for Women.

Banner carried by diet-resisters who trashed their scales in demonstration in Huntington W VA *NY Times* 12 Apr 92

4342 Document What You Do. Charge What You Document. If You Didn't Document It, You Didn't Do It.

Sign in Colorado surgeon's office instructing the staff to use care in its paperwork *Wall Street Journal* 8 Apr 93

4343 We're trying to add life to years, not years to life.

Unofficial motto of geriatrics specialists *Newsweek* 4 Oct 93

4344 Smoking cures cancer.

Bumper sticker 93

4345 You can teach a monkey to operate but you can't teach a monkey when not to operate.

On the sublety of medical training *McNeil-Lehrer Report* 20 Sep 94

4346 The Biting Edge of Medicine

Label for coolers transporting *Hirudo medicinalis*, the European medicinal leech produced by Leeches USA and Biopharm in Swansea, Wales *Washington Post* 24 Feb 95

4347 Drive-through deliveries.

Name-tag given hospitals that discharge women within 24 to 48 hours after giving birth *USA Today* 29 Jun 95

4348 If a physician is not up on it, he's down on it.

On keeping track of medical advances Station WAMU Washington 16 Sep 95

4349 A veterinarian is a doctor who can make a diagnosis without asking a question.

ib 16 Sep 95

4350 When you see the Golden Arches you are probably on the way to the Pearly Gates.

Physician's comment on McDonald's and other fast-food restaurants NPR 11 Nov 95

4351 Try to die as young as possible while living as long as you can.

On the objectivity of good health, quoted by Harold Cooper and Robert Bloomfield *The Power of Five* St Martin 95

Einar Areklett Manager, Karolinska Hospital, Stockholm

4352 Running a hospital is like running an opera house. You have a lot of Pavarottis.

Fortune 3 Apr 95

Dr Richard Asher British physician

4353 Look at a patient lying long in bed. . . a pathetic picture he makes. . . blood clotting in his veins, calcium draining from his bones, feces stacking up in his colon, flesh rotting on his buttocks and the spirit evaporating from his soul.

On complications of prolonged bed-rest *London Times* 1 Dec 94

Dr Vincent Askey President, American Medical Association

4354 I recommend frequent doses of that rare commodity—common sense.

The Land of Hypochondriacs address at Bakersfield CA 20 Oct 60

Dr Kenneth J Bart Director, National Vaccine Program, Department of Health and Human Services

4355 Immunization has become a privilege. . . [but] every child has a right to be vaccinated, just as everybody has a right to clean water.

On proposal for federal purchase of all childhood vaccines for free distribution to public *NY Times* 1 Feb 93

Abraham Bartell medical student

4356 Only after we had stared death in the face could we deal with the living.

On dissection of cadavers *NY Times* 23 Feb 91

Edwin Bayrd journalist

4357 It is moving the most weight the greatest distance for the longest time that you burn the most calories.

On the advantages of walking *Today's Health* Jul 79

Henry Bellamann screenwriter

4358 Where's the rest of me?

Lines for Ronald Reagan as an amputee in *King's Row* 1940, often quoted by Reagan during his presidency, news reports 30 Jan 88

Alan Bennett journalist

4359 Reprieved, I bike back home thinking of the people who are reprieved and do not bike back home, resolving to do better, work harder, behave.

On finding that a foot condition was not cancerous *New Yorker* 22 May 95

4360 It's such a precarious business, life's peaceful landscape suddenly transformed, what looked like green fields suddenly a swamp of anxiety.

ib

Dr David Blankenhorn University of Southern California

4361 The basic process that causes coronary artery disease can be reversed at the level of the artery wall—where the rubber meets the road.

Newsweek 29 Jun 87

Joshua Boger founder, Vertex Pharmaceuticals

4362 We have similar arrogance levels.

To a large drug company with whom he was seeking a partnership, quoted by Barry Werth *The Billion-Dollar Molecule* Simon & Schuster 94

Gordon Bonnyman Legal Aid Society of Middle Tennessee

4363 He was the dog that taught the pack to hunt.

On loopholes in medical costs closed by Tennessee's finance commissioner David Manning *Forbes* 25 Sep 95

Dr Lonnie R Bristow President, American Medical Association

4364 While we agree with his general diagnosis, we disagree with some of his treatment decisions.

On President Clinton's health care plan *NY Times* 30 Sep 93

4365 [It forces] a bureaucrat or an accountant to stand between patient and physician.

ib

4366 [Sexual assault] is shrouded in silence, caused by unfair social myths and biases that incriminate victims rather than offenders.

Statement warning of a "silent violent epidemic growing at an alarming rate and traumatizing the women and children of our nation" *Washington Post* 7 Nov 95

4367 The patient you are seeing today who is suicidal may have the root of the problem in a sexual assault years earlier.

ib

British Medical Journal

4368 Surgery can be extremely hazardous—and nobody in the [operating] theater is safe.

On mishaps to surgeons and patients *Washington Times* 2 Jan 89

4369 The amazed patient. . . was confronted with the hilarious sight of a dead mouse and an unconscious surgeon.

On a surgeon who, chasing a mouse, knocked himself out on the rim of the operating table *ib*

Dr Samuel Broder Director, National Cancer Institute

4370 We saw a young gay man with the most devastating immune deficiency we had ever seen.

On a day on Ward 3-B in June, 1981, the beginning of the AIDS epidemic *NY Times* 3 Jun 91

4371 Cancer cells. . . wander off and set up shop at new sites. . . replicate themselves in the territory of neighbors. . . are guilty of narcissism and colonialism.

Washingtonian Mar 95

4372 Women. . . demanded the right to have equal access to a tool of slow suicide.

On women rivaling men in the increase of smoking and lung cancer *ib*

Jane E Brody columnist

4373 The time to start protecting against the sun is the moment when we first can see it.

On avoidance of skin cancer *NY Times* 15 Apr 87

Dr Roderick Bronson Tufts University

4374 If curing heart disease and cancer means we get to die of Alzheimer's, we'll look back on them as our friends.

Fortune 21 Feb 94

Jerry Brown Governor of California

4375 You drink, you eat junk food, and you smoke an average of two packs of cigarettes a day—and when you get sick, you won't have to pay for it.

On government health insurance, quoted by David Brinkley NBC TV 13 Aug 80

Shannon Brownless journalist

4376 While they're at it, maybe they can figure out a way to make those #@!&* childproof aspirin bottles open.

On public panels to provide guidelines for physicians *US News & World Report* 18 Sep 95

Antole Broyard journalist

4377 When the cancer threatened my sexuality, my mind became instantly erect.

Intoxicated by My Illness Potter 92

George Bush 41st US President

4378 There is only one way to deal with an individual who is sick: with dignity, compassion, care, confidentiality and without discrimination.

On outlawing discrimination against people with AIDS *NY Times* 30 Mar 90

4379 We don't spurn the accident victim who didn't wear a seat belt. . . [or] reject the cancer patient who didn't quit smoking cigarettes. We try to love them. . . care for them. . . comfort them. We do not fire them. . . evict them. . . [or] cancel their insurance. Our goal is to turn irrational fear into rational facts.

ib

4380 Nationalized health would serve everyone . . . just like a restaurant that serves bad food, but in very generous proportions.

LA Times 8 Feb 92

Dr Robert Butler Mt Sinai Medical Center, NYC, President, National Institute on Aging

4381 Two of the worst pieces of advice an older person can receive, we've learned, are: What do you expect at your age? and take it easy.

Fortune 21 Feb 94

4382 If people are living longer, they should work longer.

On the "amber years" as a replacement for "golden years" years *Newsweek* 18 Sep 95

Joseph A Califano Jr Professor of Health and Public Policy, Columbia

4383 We only pay doctors to stick 'em and cut 'em. We don't pay them to talk to patients.

On the need to give nurses more opportunity and compensation for personal attention to patients, Station WAMU Washington 3 Feb 95

4384 Despite all our statistics, the death rate remains the same: it's one per person.

ib

Albert Camus writer

4385 Illness is a convent which has its rule, its austerity, its silences, and its inspirations.

Time 10 Jul 78

Jimmy Cannon sports columnist

4386 Dreaming with morphine after an operation, I believed the night climbed through the window and into my room like a second-story worker. . . . [It] had the dirty color of sickness and had no face at all as it strolled in my brain.

Quoted by Ira Berkow *Red* Times Books 86

Dr Arthur L Caplan Director, Center for Biomedical Ethics, University of Minnesota

4387 Drug companies. . . find out who their markets are early—in medical school—and they stay with them until they retire.

On favoritism behind the high costs of drugs *LA Times* 11 Apr 91

Dr William Castelli Director, Framingham Heart Study

4388 Has the magic bullet arrived? Is it the humble nut?

On discovery that nuts in the daily diet may lower risk of heart disease *NY Times* 4 Mar 93

4389 It looks like folks on nuts will do better than everyone else.

ib

Dr Leon Charash Chair, National Medical Advisory Board

4390 It is like giving a whole library when all you want is one book.

On discovery for adding genes to the body *NY Times* 6 Sep 90

Dr Tenzin Choedak Senior Physician to the Dalai Lama

4391 The cause of illlness is. . . not recognizing the meaning of selfishness.

Quoted in Rick Smolan ed *The Hero in the White Coat* Prentice Hall 90

Dr Aleksandr Chuchalin Russian Academy of Sciences

4392 It's not enough. . . to say that our life style accounts for these numbers. No life style could account for all of this.

On plunging life expectancy that, said a leading biologist, goes beyond "conception of children by drunken couples. . . [to] chemical and radioactive contamination of the environment" *NY Times* 2 Aug 95

Winston S Churchill statesman

4393 Nature is merciful and does not try her children, beyond their compass. It is only when the cruelty of man intervenes that hellish torments appear.

Recalled on Churchill's death 24 Jan 65

4394 If at any moment in the long series of sensations a grey veil deepening into blackness had descended upon the sanctum, I should have felt or feared nothing additional.

On being struck by a taxi in New York in 1931, quoted by William Manchester *The Last Lion* Little, Brown 83

Dr A J Clayton Canadian public health officer

4395 AIDS is a successful virus mutation, perhaps the first in recorded, written medical history, and we are thus dealing with a new disease.

NY Times 21 Nov 85

Hillary Rodham Clinton First Lady

4396 I hope. . . when our work is done, when the Congress has done what only the Congress can do to bring all of the disparate voices of America into these rooms to hammer out the choices that confront us, every American will receive a health security card guaranteeing a comprehensive package of benefits that can never be taken away under any circumstance.

To House of Representatives Ways and Means Committee on embarking on a health plan that was ultimately unacceptable 29 Sep 93

4397 People [should] know they are not being denied treatment for any reason other than it is not appropriate—will not enhance or save the quality of their lives. What this president. . . and I look forward to is a vigorous, honest debate, that sheds light and not just heat.

On accompanying her husband to deliver Health Security legislation to the Capitol Hill *Washington Post* 28 Oct 93

William J Clinton 42nd US President

4398 When doctors and nurses are forced to write out the same information six different times in seven different ways just to satisfy some distant company or agency, it wastes their time. . . and undermines the integrity of a system that leaves you spending more and caring for fewer people.

On seeking to end costly paper work *NY Times* 18 Sep 93

4399 Now it is our turn to strike a blow for freedom in this country. The freedom of Americans to live without fear that their own nation's health care system won't be there for them when they need it.

To Congress 22 Sep 93

4400 [We are] choking on a health care system that is not working.

On delivering Health Security legislation to Capitol Hill 27 Oct 93

4401 The face of AIDS is no longer the face of a stranger.

At Georgetown Medical Center over a decade after AIDS appeared 1 Dec 93

4402 [AIDS] is a problem which has diminished the life of every American. . . .[and] my job is to be a lightning rod.

ib

4403 Cigarettes and smokeless tobacco are harmful, highly addictive and aggressively marketed to our young people; the evidence is overwhelming. . . the threat is immediate.

On issuing an exectuve order to restrict advertising, promotion, distribution and marketing of cigarettes to teen-agers 11 Aug 95

Colette (Sidonie Gabrielle Colette) novelist

4404 Sufferers from a creeping illness who know their days are counted may say aloud, "I am in a hurry." Under their breath, they whisper, "I am pursued."

Quoted by A M Sperber *Murrow* Freundlich 86

Dr Robert C Collins Chair, Neurology Dept, UCLA

4405 The brain represents the furthest extent of biological evolution.

Fortune 3 Dec 90

George Howe Colt journalist

4406 Even those for whom this extraordinary scientific feat was familiar were awed into silence as the heart, making itself at home, slowly began to pump.

On receipt of a heart transplant by a six-week old "Dylan's New Heart" *Life* May 90

4407 As he grows, the six-inch scar on his chest fades like a thin white icicle melting from the warmth of his heart.

ib

Dr Alex Comfort British physician

4408 The idea of the human responsibility of the doctor has been present since medicine was indistinguishable from magic.

The Listener 29 Nov 51

4409 AIDS. . . the arrival of this disease totally alters the sexual landscape.

Quoted in *New Yorker* 7 Oct 91 in review of Comfort's *The New Joy of Sex* Crown 91

Dr Denton A Cooley cardiologist

4410 [Heart surgery is] changing a fan belt with the engine on.

Quoted by Richard Conniff "Profiles: Denton A Cooley MD" *Architectural Digest* May 87

Arthur J Cordell Adviser, Science Council of Canada

4411 Growth for growth's sake is the ideology of the cancer cell.

Time 29 Jun 70

Norman Cousins editor and lecturer

4412 Your heaviest artillery will be your will to live. Keep that big gun going.

Anatomy of an Illness Norton 79

4413 Laughter is a form of internal jogging. . . moves your internal organs around. . . enhances respiration. It is an igniter of great expectations.

On the therapeutic value of laughter *ib*

4414 Their illnesses intensified at the moment of diagnoses.

On the psychological effect of confronting knowledge *Wall Street Journal* 24 Apr 87

Dr Antonio Damasio Professor of Neurology, University of Iowa

4415 It's like a tornado that cuts a very narrow path, destroying buildings in a strip a hundred yards wide but leaving everything else standing.

On Alzheimer's disease effect on the brain *NY Times* 7 Sep 84

Dr Peter Davies Neuroscientist, Albert Einstein College of Medicine, Boston

4416 Any function that needs sustained reasoning is impaired; that's why Alzheimer's patients don't commit suicide.

NY Times 24 Sep 95

Dr James E Davis President, American Medical Association

4417 This is a landmark in the history of medical ethics. . . saying for the first time that. . . the physician may be required to violate patient confidentiality.

On AMA's overwhelming vote for physicians to warn sexual partners of patients with "this lethal disease, AIDS" *NY Times* 1 Jul 88

Anita Desai novelist

4418 Every sleep, every night, is an experience of nonbeing. . . that area of life where we drift where the darkness takes us, where we cannot guide our course.

NY Times 17 Sep 89, reviewing J Bernlef's novel on Alzheimer's disease *Out of Mind* David R Godine 89

4419 Those whose illness is a loss of self.

On Alzheimer victims *ib*

Dr W Richards Dickinson essayist

4420 Priesthood in medicine. . . is a state of mind. If its traditionalism is less militant now than it used to be, it is more complex, and more insidious.

Transactions American Clinical Association 62

4421 Study your patient. . . [and] from there build up the whole structure of your care, a broad structure, as broad as the measure of distress. Surely this is no denial of medical science, but its fulfillment.

ib

Dr William Dietz Professor of Pediatrics, Tufts University

4422 The fattest of the fat are getting fatter faster.

On increased obesity among young children *Newsweek* 6 Jun 88

Dr Noel Dilly Professor of Anatomy, St George's Medical School, London

4423 There's nothing like hands-on experience to discover how anything works.

On acquiring cadavers *London Times* 13 Nov 92

Dr Bruce H Dobkin Associate Clinical Professor of Neurology, University of California, Los Angeles

4424 In the dim light of my bathroom, I looked into a vial of a dozen oval, sky-blue sleeping pills. I was getting desperate.

On insomnia that strikes up to 15 percent of adults and 30 percent of the elderly *NY Times* 5 Feb 89

4425 I pulled out my rarely used bottle of Halcion with the anxiety of someone hesitant to plunge into the unknown

ib

Madeleine Duffield Matron, St Christopher's Hospice, London

4426 Deception is not as creative as truth; we do best in life if we look at it with clear eyes.

On honesty about terminal illness *Time* 5 Sep 88

4427 A hospital would insist on a strict diet for a dying patient but we serve chocolate cake. We make it possible to face the unsafety of death.

On the hospice philosophy *ib*

Dr Craig Dufresne Johns Hopkins Children's Center

4428 [It was like] clipping through a hard-boiled egg shell with toe-nail clippers.

On the thin, 2-inch band of bone that joined German-born twin brothers at their heads *USA Today* 11 Sep 87

Dr Paul J Edelson Professor of Epidemiology, Cornell University Medical School

4429 The real work of medicine starts when the drugs no longer work.

Newsweek 28 Mar 94

Dr Joycelyn Elders US Surgeon General

4430 Just because you have a condom, you are not going to have sex. Car insurance doesn't mean you're going to have a wreck.

On distribution of condoms in public schools *NY Times* 14 Sep 93

4431 We taught them what to do in the front seat of a car. Now it's time to teach them what to do in the back seat.

On driver education and sex education *ib*

4432 Sex is a wonderful, normal, and healthy part of our being, whether it is homosexual or heterosexual.

On homosexuals' suitability to adopt children, serve as scoutmasters, and have their needs addressed in school-based health clinics *Washington Times* 19 Mar 94

4433 Masturbation is something that perhaps should be taught.

At UN World AIDS Day 1 Dec 94 in a statement that, reported out of context, led to Dr Elders' dismissal by President Clinton *Washington Post* 10 Dec 94

4434 Yeah, they love little babies, as long as they're in somebody else's uterus.

To anti-abortion groups while serving as Clinton's appointee as director of the Arkansas Health Dept 1987–93 *ib*

4435 Get over your love affair with the fetus.

ib

Dr Samuel S Epstein Professor of Environmental Medicine, University of Illinois

4436 This is toxological Russian roulette.

On irradation of fruit to retard spoilage and kill organisms *NY Times* 21 Jan 92

Equal Employment Opportunity Commission

4437 Decisions about the employment of an individual with a disability cannot be motivated by concerns about the impact of the individual's disability on the employer's health insurance plan.

Ruling on fair employment practices *NY Times* 9 Jun 93

Dr Roger W Evans Director, Health Services Evaluation, Mayo Clinic

4438 It's like a car at a chop shop. Somebody's making a handsome fee off of processing the parts.

On sale of human organs and tissues for transplants *NY Times* 8 Jul 94

Walker Evans photographer and essayist

4439 The least one can do is drop dead, and apparently that is very often done.

On being diagnosed with "a modest edition of coronary thrombosis" quoted by Belinda Rathbone *Walker Evans* Houghton Mifflin 95

Dr Thomas H Fay Audiologist, Columbia-Presbyterian Medical Center, NYC

4440 The ears are the portal into the body and the damage done at the front door is merely the most obvious.

On $210-million program to muffle subway noise *NY Times* 6 Nov 86

Dr Jim Finnell Illinois farm veterinarian

4441 If it has fur, feathers or wool and it's sick, we treat it.

On four decades of veterinarian practice *Life* Oct 92

Dr Jeffrey Fischer Anatomic Clinical Pathologist, Helicon Foundation

4442 They don't need passports to travel.

On spread of bacteria *The Plague Makers* Simon & Schuster 94

Dr George Fister President, American Medical Association

4443 When has lasting greatness ever been achieved by one who sought greatness for itself rather than allowing it to move quietly upon him as he worked for others? It has never been done. It cannot be done.

To Southwest Surgical Conference, Mexico City 22 Apr 63

4444 What Dooley, or what Rush, or Kendall or Schweitzer set out to do anything but help his neighbor in the way he knew best?

ib

Anne Taylor Fleming journalist

4445 [We were] instant intimates, trapped in the surreal world of post-sexual procreation. . . and we are now hope junkies.

On participants in fertility clinics *NY Times* 1 Feb 89

4446 It's impossible not. . . to become biologically narcissistic.

ib

Dr Henry Flournoy obstetrician

4447 Every baby has turned into a ticking time bomb that can go off in your hand.

On malpractice suits *NY Times* 18 May 86

Arthur W Frank medical sociologist, University of Calgary

4448 The ultimate value of illness is that it teaches us the value of being alive.

At the Will of the Body Houghton Mifflin 91

4449 [Serious illness] leaves no aspect of life untouched. . . relationships, your work, your sense of who you are and who you might become, your sense of what life is and ought to be—these all change, and the change is terrifying....Illness takes away parts of your life, but in doing so it gives you the opportunity to choose the life you will lead, as opposed to living out the one you have simply accumulated over the years. For all loss, you have an equal opportunity to gain: closer relationships, more poignant appreciations, clarified values. [By choosing] how we experience illness, we can be more than victims.

ib

Dr Benjamin Freedman Canadian bioethicist

4450 The appropriate emotion is awe.

On the mix and match of animal genes and organs for use in humans *NY Times* 17 Dec 95

Dr Maurice Friedman Professor of Physiology, University of Pennsylvania Medical School

4451 It's highly reliable. The only more reliable test is to wait nine months.

On pioneering a test to determine pregnancy if a rabbit died after being injected with a woman's urine *NY Times* 10 Mar 91

Dr Michael Garavito University of Chicago Medical Center

4452 Aspirin blocks the front door and puts a bar across the door; then it physically stands in the door.

On the use of aspirin *USA Today* 1 Aug 95

Howard Gardner journalist

4453 To ask "Where in your brain is intelligence?" is like asking, "Where is the voice in the radio?"

Frames of the Mind: The Theory of Multiple Intelligence Basic Books 83

Dr John Garrow Professor of Human Nutrition, St Bartholomew's Hospital, London

4454 The suggestion must be. . . that the fat cells think "Good heavens we must hydrolyze the fatty acids." It is laughably improbable.

On introduction of a cream to shrink women's thighs *London Times* 23 Oct 93

Dr Frank Gawin Cocaine Treatment Director, Yale Medical School

4455 Early in use, all of the positive things that are said about cocaine are true. As use continues, all the negative things become true.

NY Times 17 Nov 86

Dr Stephen Jay Gould Professor of Biology, Harvard

4456 Genes do not plan and scheme. They do not act as witting agents of their own preservation.

Disputing the theory of species' inherent protection of each other *US News & World Report* 13 Apr 87

Maggie Green mother of murder victim

4457 Our son's future was stolen from him. . . [but] we saw a way to give that treasure to others.

On donating the vital organs of 7-year old Nicholas a few hours after he was shot to death while traveling with his parents in Italy *Life* Oct 95

4458 After seeing Nicholas. . . in intensive care, she shoved straws up her dolls' noses and in their mouths. And they all got better.

On 4-year-old Eleanor's healing therapy *ib*

4459 I have faith that Nicholas is out there somewhere. He has a spirit that is well-suited to heaven.

ib

Graham Greene novelist

4460 The secrets of the consulting room, my dear boy, are one-sided. . . the patient, though not the doctor, is at liberty to tell everything.

New Statesman 8 Oct 65

William Grigg US Food and Drug Administration

4461 If it sounds too good to be true, it probably is.

On miracle diets *Newsweek* 30 Apr 90

Dr Michael Grodin Director, Program of Medical Ethics, Boston University School of Medicine and Public Health

4462 For a baby that has no brain and is born dying, life for just another minute or day is not an appropriate goal; it's saying that it's the technology that has life, not the patient.

Decrying the daily cost of $1,464 to preserve a hopeless existence *NY Times* 24 Sep 93

Dr Claude Gubler personal physician to French President François Mitterand

4463 I was caught in a trap, submerged in a lie from which I could not get out until 15 years later.

On being sworn to secrecy by President Mitterand on the spread of the statesman's prostate cancer, quoted on Mitterand's death at age 79 *Washington Post* 17 Jan 96

Dr Karel Gunning President, League of Dutch Physicians

4464 Our society is moving very quickly from birth control to death control.

On Holland's adoption of a law permitting euthanasia *NY Times* 10 Feb 93

Learned Hand Senior Judge, 2nd Circuit, US Court of Appeals

4465 Pain, what we call agony. . . excludes, it concentrates, it minimizes the whole self; it takes over the whole being—there is nothing left but that.

On old age, quoted by Gerald Gunther *Learned Hand* Knopf 94

Blaine Harden journalist

4466 The creatures. . . [are] a dark brown, strong-jawed worm that squirm with gustatory delight in the presence of human flesh.

On the use of leeches as "living surgical aides" *Washington Post* 24 Feb 95

4467 The main therapeutic value. . . is in the sticky, brownish saliva they leave around their bite wound, which, curiously, is shaped like the corporate logo of the Mercedes-Benz motorcar company. The saliva contains a unique cocktail of anticoagulants, blood thinners and a local anaesthetic.

ib

Dr Steven Harris gerontologist, University of Southern California

4468 We grasp its side, we say aging is a wall. We grasp its trunk, we say aging is a snake. We grasp its leg, we say aging is a tree.

On "the great grey, elephantine mystery of aging" *Life* Oct 92

4469 Every time we grasp something new, our understanding of the elephant grows. . . . We're getting to know the nature of the beast.

ib

Dr Michael R Harrison University of California at San Francisco

4470 It. . . makes it clear that the fetus is a patient.

On successful major surgery on a fetus several weeks prior to birth *NY Times* 31 May 90

4471 Is it worth having an arm when you don't have one? Well, hell, yes.

On the possibility of fetus' limb transplants *London Times* 31 Aug 93

Ben Hecht journalist

4472 Doctors. . . are often as close mouthed as old-fashioned bomb throwers on their way to a rendevous.

Recalled on Hecht's death 18 Apr 64

Dr Henry Heimlich developer of the Heimlich maneuver

4473 They said that a maneuver was a procedure involving an expert movement, while a method involved a series of steps, as in a urinalysis, and I shouted, "Call it a maneuver!"

On the American Medical Association's naming of the technique for dislodging food caught in the throat *NY Times* 7 Jan 96

4474 My name, a proper noun, has now become an adjective modifier.

To language maven William Safire *ib*

Dr Donald Henderson epidemiologist

4475 AIDs has taught us humility. That one little virus has reminded us how much we still have to learn.

National Geographic Jul 94

Dr Charles S Hirsch NYC Medical Examiner

4476 [An] "independent" autopsy. . . that is the only kind of autopsy I know how to give, whoever I may be working for. That is my hallmark.

On need for examinations with no outside influences *NY Times* 28 Sep 88

Eric Hodges novelist

4477 A miracle drug is a drug that will do what the label says it will do.

Episode Atheneum 63

Dr Stephen A Hoffman Internist, Brigham and Women's Hospital, Boston

4478 A doctor tries to assume it from the outset, adjusting it as he goes on, as he would the fit of his white coat.

On demeanors appropriate to the individual patient "The Doctor As Dramatist" *Newsweek* 1 Feb 88

4479 Whether or not we're trying to be God's understudies, we always play to our audience... people expect it of us. Good bedside manner, in fact, is good theater.

ib

Dr Thomas Jeeves Horder British physician

4480 Inevitably the doctor... will spend his time keeping the fit fit, rather than trying to make the unfit fit.

Recalled on Horder's death 13 Aug 55

4481 It is the duty of a doctor to prolong life... not to prolong the act of dying.

To House of Lords 1936 *ib*

Dr James A Horne Professor of Psychophysiology, Loughborough University, Leicester, England

4482 [The function of sleep is to] repair the cerebral cortex from the wear and tear of consciousness.

On relationship of creativity to lost sleep *NY Times* 5 Jan 89

Robert Hughes critic

4483 Malt juice and pickled cabbage put Europeans in Australia as micro-chip circuitry would put Americans on the moon.

On successful conquest of scurvy during long sea voyages *The Fatal Shore* Knopf 87

Jayne Hurley Nutritionist, Center for Science in the Public Interest

4484 It's a heart attack on a plate.

On Fettuccine Alfredo *Washington Post* 14 Jan 94

John K Igelhart Editor *Health Affairs*

4485 [It is] something of an 800-pound gorilla.

On influence and pronouncements of the American Medical Association *NY Times* 20 Feb 90

Dr Marion Jenkins Attending Physician, Parkland Hospital, Dallas TX

4486 She nudged me and then with her right hand she handed me a good-sized chunk of the President's brain. She didn't say a word.

On Jacqueline Kennedy Onassis after President Kennedy's assassination *Time* 30 May 94

4487 She started kissing him. She kissed his foot, his leg, thigh, chest, and then his lips. She didn't say a word.

ib

Lucille Joel RN, Rutgers University

4488 The American ideal of a doctor was essentially a nurse.

On sentimental recollections of the kindly, caring, reassuring physician, quoted by George Will "The Dignity of Nursing" *Newsweek* 23 May 88

4489 If we live long enough, something wears out. I don't care how much oatmeal you eat.

ib

Cathy Johnson Transplant Coordinator, Methodist Hospital, Houston, Texas

4490 Let's make it a nicer day. Come on in and we'll give you a new heart.

On telephoning a cardiac patient in El Paso, Texas *NY Times* 11 Mar 88

Dr Stephen C Joseph NYC Health Commissioner

4491 It is the central knot in the seamless web of our problems.

On drug abuse *NY Times* 10 May 89

Dr John Kane Director, Lipid Clinic, University of California at San Francisco

4492 It's the Kitty Hawk of gene therapy.

On permanent reversal of inherited disease by altering genetic makeup of a patient's cells *NY Times* 1 Apr 94

Charles Kellner Editor, *Convulsive Therapy*

4493 It's more dangerous to drive to the hospital than to have the treatment.

On the safety of shock therapy for depression *USA Today* 6 Dec 95

Dr Jack Kevorkian Michigan physician

4494 My specialty is death.

On assisting suicides of the chronically ill *Time* 31 May 93

4495 It isn't assisted suicide on trial... it's your civilization and society.

On becoming the first person arrested under new Michigan law that made assisted suicide a felony *NY Times* 18 Aug 93

Dr David L Kirp Professor of Public Policy, University of California at Berkeley

4496 Many gay men feel both grateful and guilty to have remained alive... in a world peopled by ghosts.

On the fortunate half of the population of gay men in New York, Los Angeles, and San Francisco who did not die of AIDs in the 1980s *NY Times* 1 Oct 95

4497 Those who remain uninfected extracted little pleasure from living long enough to turn out all the lights.

ib

Verlyn Klinkenborg journalist

4498 This was a simple, if dramatic, exercise in medical geography.

On pinpointing AIDS epidemic *Washington Post* 15 May 94

Laurie Knipp wife of El Paso, Texas patient

4499 You get here and you realize there isn't a heart just sitting in the refrigerator.

On waiting for a transplant *NY Times* 11 Mar 88

Dr Melvin Konner anthropologist and physician, Emory University

4500 Before we become aware of them, [brain tumors] may already have drastically changed precisely that part of us that is capable of awareness. They are already at the center of who we are.

NY Times 21 Feb 88

4501 Brain tumors are lesions of the soul. Ultimately, of course, the mind is the organ of orgasm.

ib 29 Apr 90

4502 Deep in the brain a convergence occurs: something must happen to touch the soul.

ib

Dr C Everett Koop US Surgeon General

4503 [It is] the genocide of homosexuals.

On AIDS, Station WPIX TV, New York, 13 Apr 87

4504 If you have a monogamous relationship, keep it. If you don't have one, get it.

On keeping free of AIDS infection *US News & World Report* 4 May 87

4505 I expect everything all the time.

When asked if he anticipated criticism for the unprecedented mailing of an AIDS brochure to every US household *NY Times* 5 May 88

4506 Everything you and I look at, worry about, and talk about in reference to health will be a symptom of overriding tensions between our aspirations and our resources.

Esquire Jun 88

4507 The White House doesn't like the C word. But if you don't talk about condoms, people are going to die. So I talk.

On preventing AIDS *Time* 24 Apr 89

4508 I am the Surgeon General, not the chaplain, of all the people, and that includes homosexuals.

On objective rather than moral judgment *ib*

Glenn Kramon journalist

4509 For couples stranded in the desert of infertility ... [it] is an oasis.

On Dr Geoffrey Sher's Pacific Fertility Center Greenbrae, CA *NY Times* 19 Jun 92

Kurt H Kruger Medical Device Analyst, Hambrecht & Quist Co

4510 Without device intervention, one dies; with the device, one lives.

On implant of defibrillators to correct irregular heartbeat *NY Times* 24 Feb 93

4511 Never has the grip of death been so strong and success of device intervention so clear.

ib

Tony Kushner playwright

4512 KS, baby. Lesion Number One... the wine-dark kiss of the Angel of Death.

On Kaposi's Sarcoma, the purplish skin nodules that characterize a particularly virulent form of AIDS *Angels in America* Broadway play 93

Richard D Lamm Governor of Colorado

4513 The elderly have a duty to die and get out of the way.

On health care costs *NY Times* 1 Oct 93

Laurence Leamer journalist

4514 As long as she continued to sing out, and to add and subtract, the doctors kept cutting away, destroying larger and larger areas of her brain. From that day on, Rosemary was gone.

On lobotomy performed under a local anaesthetic on a daughter of US Ambassador Joseph Kennedy *The Kennedy Women* Bantam 94

David Leavitt novelist

4515 Illness moved into their house like an elderly aunt in a back bedroom. It lived with them. . . [and] sat at the kitchen table.

Equal Affections Weidenfeld & Nicolson 89

Dr Burton J Lee III personal physician to President Bush

4516 I'm a very careful listener to patients because patients generally are right.

NY Times 23 May 91

Trudy Leiberman Editor, *Consumer Reports*

4517 Give it a sniff test.

On detecting the absence of odors in choosing the best nursing homes NBC TV 23 Aug 95

Dr Jacques Leibowitch René Descartes University, Paris

4518 If the song of the T-4 orchestra were true, you would have an infection every other second.

On belief that T-cell destruction is neither necessary nor sufficient for development of AIDS *NY Times* 7 Jun 88

George Leonard journalist

4519 It is the toughest inhabitant of the body and the most tremulous, the furnace of animal passion and the seat of the most exquisite sensibilities. . . quick to take offense or alarm yet capable of profound composure.

On the heart, Rick Smolan ed *The Hero in the White Coat* Prentice Hall 90

4520 A slimy, throbbing mass of muscle entwined in its own veins and arteries, a tender, fearsome instrument of love and power—the heart!

ib

René Leriche physician

4521 Disease is like a drama whose first acts have been played before the lights have gone up on the stage.

"Qu'est-ce que la maladie?" *Journal de médecine de Bordeaux et du Sud-Ouest* Oct 50

Dr Linda Lewis Associate Dean of Student Affairs, Columbia University College of Physicians and Surgeons

4522 It takes a lot more than four years to become God, and you're certainly not God when you walk in the front door.

To medical students *NY Times* 28 Nov 93

Dr Rodolfo Llinas Professor of Neuroscience, NYU

4523 Light is nothing but electromagnetic radiation. Colors clearly don't exist outside our brains, nor does sound.

Time 17 Jul 95

4524 Sound is the relationship between external vibrations and the brain. If there is no brain, there can be no sound.

On the theory that there is no sound if a tree drops in the forest and no one hears it *ib*

London Times

4525 [It is a] passport to an unknown country.

On voluntary euthanasia cards 25 Feb 93

Dr Joanne Lynn Dartmouth Medical Center

4526 It is easier to get a heart transplant or cataract surgery than supper or a back rub.

On patients' fear of highly technological medical systems that exhausts their resources while ignoring pain *NY Times* 14 Feb 93

Dr Ruth Macklin Ethicist, Albert Einstein College of Medicine

4527 They're not donors, they're vendors. . . selling their gametes.

On the ethics women face in volunteering or selling eggs for the infertile *NY Times* 10 Nov 91

Dr William Maples CA Pound Human Identification Lab, Gainesville FL

4528 Truth wants to be discovered.

On the guiding principle in autopsies and exhumations *USA Today* 26 Oct 95

4529 Death to me is no terror of the night but a daylit companion. . . answerable to scientific inquiry.

ib

Dr Philippa Marrack National Jewish Center for Immunology and Respiratory Medicine, Denver

4530 [T-cells] are put together like a dinner from the menu at a Chinese restaurant.

On the variety of genes in a T-cell receptor vital to the immune system *US News & World Report* 2 Jul 90

Adam Mars-Jones anthologist

4531 I said I had cancer, which I do and I don't, I mean I do but that isn't the problem, and while I was saying cancer I thought, all the time my Gran was ill we never once said cancer, but now cancer is a soft word I am hiding behind.

On AIDS as a word that replaced the dread of cancer *Monopolies of Loss* Knopf 93

4532 I was curling up in the word's soft shade, soothed gratefully by cancer's lullaby. Cancer. What a relief. . . that I can live with.

ib

William Maxwell novelist

4533 She managed a flicker of recognition. . . [but] she didn't belong to us anymore. She belonged to her illness.

On visiting a terminally ill patient *Billie Dyer and Other Stories* Knopf 92

Marc O Mayer Analyst, Sanford C Bernstein Co

4534 One person prescribes a drug, another dispenses it, somebody else takes it and somebody else pays for it.

On lack of incentives to limit price increases of prescription drugs *NY Times* 11 May 91

Dr John L McClenahan physician

4535 It is because we have begun to act like merchants and in many instances to observe the same hours, that the public expects us to be regulated by the same restraints.

X-Ray Technician Vol XXXII 61

Carson McCullers novelist

4536 He was a man watching a clock without hands.

On terminal illness *Clock Without Hands* Houghton Mifflin 53

Dr John A McDougal physician

4537 If it looks good, tastes good and smells good, spit it out—it's a mistake.

On overly strict dieting, station WAMU Washington 4 Jun 94

Dr Peter Medawar Nobel Laureate in Immunology

4538 A virus is a piece of bad news wrapped in protein.

National Geographic Jul 94

Dr George Miller Professor of Pediatric Infectious Diseases, Yale University

4539 There might be an epidemic of diagnosis.

On a readiness to accept the possibility of a fatigue virus *NY Times* 28 Jul 87

Sigmund Stephen Miller medical researcher

4540 More organic food is sold than grown.

Symptoms: The Complete Home Medical Encyclopedia Crowell 77

Paul Monette journalist

4541 It's common among gay men now to say we're all 80 years old, our friends dying off like Florida pensioners.

Borrowed Time Harcourt Brace Jovanovich 88

4542 There's something nearly sacred. . . about being a wound dresser. To be. . . so close to the body's ache to heal. . . you are an instrument, and your engine is concentration.

ib

John Moore patient

4543 What the doctors had done was to claim that my humanity, my genetic essence, was their invention and their property.

On learning that physicians had sold cell lines taken from his spleen to a biotechnology company for $1.7 million, making him "essence-raped," the world's first patented man *Guardian Weekly* 1 Jan 95

4544 They viewed me as a mine from which to extract biological material. I was harvested. . . . [yet] genetic material extracted from human beings should belong to society as a whole, and not be patentable.

ib

Dr Jonathan D Moreno Professor of Bioethics, Health Science Center, State University of New York

4545 We require you to be the agents of a disintegration of a human body far more systematic and bloodless than that of the field of battle.

To medical students working with cadavers *NY Times* 23 Feb 91

Frederick Morris patient

4546 It was like a balloon of blood hanging out of my heart.

On an aneurism relieved by a heart transplant in 1973 that 22 years later made him Europe's longest surviving transplant patient *London Times* 23 Feb 95

Lance Morrow essayist

4547 A heart attack feels like this: A sickness suddenly surrounds the lungs, a sort of toxic interior glow—fleeting at first, lightly slithering, but returning a moment later, more insistent.

Heart: A Memoir Wagner 95

4548 The heart's signature had that hurried negligence of the 40th traveler's check you have signed while standing at the bank counter....[but] death presses like a vise, squeezing the margins until they threaten to meet in the center.

On climbing a hill on a bitterly cold night *ib*

Edward R Murrow commentator

4549 The sun was warm, the earth coming alive; there was hope and promise in the air. The occasion called for banners in the breeze and trumpets in the distance.

On the discovery of the polio vaccine Edward Bliss Jr ed *In Search of Light* Knopf 67

Marion Nestle Chair, Department of Nutrition, NYU

4550 It's. . . the 3,700-calorie-a-day problem.

On America's continued weight gain in its sedentary life style amid an abundance of food *NY Times* 17 Jul 94

Dr Donald Neuenshwander Chair, Medical Center Bank, Houston TX

4551 You can't be all things to all people. But you can be all things to people I select.

On the satisfaction of contributions to an organ bank *Time* 3 Dec 84

The New York Times

4552 The images lend a grim whiff of the Middle Ages to modern New York City hospitals. . . [but] shackling of the sick has no place in a city that would call itself humane.

"Where the Sick Lie in Chains" editorial opposing the shackling to beds of prisoners afflicted with AIDS 1 Nov 87

Herbert Nickens VP American Association of Medical Colleges

4553 The real danger is that AIDS could be labeled as a disease of people who are expendable.

Washington Post 5 Jun 91

Richard M Nixon 37th US President

4554 They told me I feel fine.

On physical examination at start of his second term *NY Times* 21 Dec 72

4555 My physical recovery. . . was not enough. A healthy vegetable is still a vegetable.

On the lack of wholeness that plagued him after resigning the presidency, quoted by Stephen E Ambrose *Nixon: Ruin and Recovery* Simon & Schuster 91, excerpted in *Time* 2 Apr 90

4556 To recover physically involves regaining the ability to get up in the morning; to recover spiritually requires restoring the will and desire to do it.

ib

Dr Gustav J V Nossal New England physician

4557 The system cannot know in advance what it may one day have to recognize. It simply has to arm itself with a vast collection of repertoire of recognition units. . . so that somewhere in the collection is a key for every possible lock.

On how the body successfully fights or fails, especially in regard to the AIDS virus *Boston Globe* 18 Oct 87

Dr Antonia Novello US Surgeon General

4558 In years past, R J Reynolds would have us walk a mile for a Camel. Today, it's time that we invite Joe Camel himself to take a hike.

On joining the American Medical Association in demand that the cartoon character Joe Camel be dropped from cigarette advertising because of its appeal to children *NY Times* 10 Mar 92

Dr Sherwin B Nuland Professor of Surgery, Yale

4559 Judgement, clinical intuition, decision making—the taste and smell, if you will, of a patient, his needs, the surroundings of the disease, and the pathophysiology of the process that has brought him to the doctor—these are the real ingredients of the art of cardiac transplantation.

Doctors Knopf 88

4560 That word, "harvest". . . implies that the earth is yielding up its treasures to nourish mankind. . . the performance of a worshipful act, the receiving of one of the benisons of a fructified soil. . . a gift of God's abundance. . . nourishment and life.

On the "harvesting" for transplanting of human organs *ib*

4561 There is one singular ingredient of the art of healing that should not be allowed to vanish. . . the transmission of a few encouraging words.

On "a joining between doctor and patient in which one human being is privileged to help another" *ib*

4562 Cancer cells behave like the members of a barbarian horde run amok—leaderless and undirected, but with a single-minded purpose: to plunder everything within reach.

How We Die Knopf 94

Dr William Osler Regius Professor of Medicine, Oxford University

4563 One finger in the throat and one in the rectum makes a good diagnostician.

London Times 10 Aug 93

Dr Ralph Pelligra Director of Medical Research, National Aeronautics and Space Administration

4564 We are children of gravity. Sagging skin and organs, varicose veins, arthritis, failing hearts—these all come from the lost battle against gravity.

National Geographic May 89

4565 [Gravity] has guided the evolutionary destiny of every plant and animal species and has dictated the size and shape of our organs and limbs.

ib

Dr George A Perera Professor, Columbia University College of Physicians and Surgeons

4566 Curiosity is the hallmark of scholarship and science, but it is also the hallmark of service.

Journal of Medical Education Vol XXXVIII 63

4567 Curiosity is not confined to the research laboratory; it is obligatory at the bedside as well. Only by being curious as to basic mechanisms, with a genuine regard for who is ill, how did he become so, and why this disorder or that sign or that symptom, can one become and remain a competent physician.

ib

Dr Galina M Perfilyeva Moscow public health expert

4568 As long as the most popular man in Russia is the Marlboro Man, we can't even begin to do much about the wretched health of the nation....[but] something immediate needs to be done.

On President Boris N Yeltsin's national ban on all tobacco and alcohol advertisements as an official acknowledgment of an alarming surge of illness and death *NY Times* 22 Feb 95

Dr Candace Pert pharmacologist

4569 Emotions are neuropeptides attaching to receptors and stimulating an electrical charge on neurons.

National Geographic Jun 95

Dr Chase Peterson VP, Health Sciences, University of Utah Medical Center

4570 He has gone from blue to pink.

On the first patient to receive an artificial heart *NY Times* 4 Dec 82

Dr Robert T M Phillips Deputy Medical Director, American Psychiatric Association

4571 People don't come into the world with a gun in their hand... with rage and anger in their heart. They learn it.

On tendencies toward violence *NY Times* 16 May 94

Dr Robert Plate British physician

4572 The first staggering fact about medical education is that after two and a half years of being taught on the assumption that everyone is the same, the student has to find out for himself that everyone is different, which is really what his experience has taught him since infancy.

British Medical Journal Vol II 65

4573 After being taught... not to trust any evidence except that based on the measure of medical science, the student has to find out for himself that all important decisions are in reality made almost at an unconscious level.

ib

Dr Henry Plotkin British physician

4574 Interest is the mother of intelligence.

The Nature of Knowledge Allen Lane 94

4575 Emotions are postcards from our genes telling us in a direct and non-symbolic manner about life and death.

The Nature of Knowledge Allen Lane 94

Dr Paul Rainsbury Director, Hallam Medical Center, London

4576 The hypothalamus... is the conductor of the endocrine orchestra. If the conductor is put out of tune, the rest of the endocrine orchestra, including the testicles, can be too.

On the role of stress in infertility *London Times* 22 May 92

4577 The pain of infertility... never killed anyone but it's left a lot of broken hearts.

ib

Ronald Reagan 40th US President

4578 I now begin the journey that will lead me into the sunset of my life.

Handwritten letter to "my fellow Americans" on being diagnosed with Alzheimer's disease five years after leaving office *Washington Post* 6 Nov 94

Barbara Reuter R J Reynolds Co

4579 [It is a] revolutionary nicotine delivery device.

Confidential memo on development of a cigarette that offered a satisfying dose of nicotine while reducing byproducts such as tar, quoted in Food and Drug Administration's efforts to regulate cigarettes as drug delivery devices *Washington Post* 9 Dec 95

Patrick Reynolds tobacco heir

4580 Am I biting the hand that feeds me?... the hand that has killed 10-million people and may kill millions more.

To Congressional hearing on the R J Reynolds Co founded by his grandfather *NY Times* 17 Jul 86

Frank Rich critic

4581 He inhabits a particular present-day Manhattan where the most prevalent form of party is a memorial service. . . where the sight of young men hobbling on canes is commonplace.

On Paul Rudnick's off-Broadway play *Jeffrey NY Times* 3 Feb 93

Marion Roach patient's daughter

4582 She was losing her mind in handfuls.

On her mother, a victim of Alzheimer's disease *Another Name for Madness* Houghton Mifflin 85

Dr David E Rogers Chair, NY State AIDS Advisory Council

4583 Those who are the sickest are the most likely to get care. . . . Your best ticket to care is being mortally ill.

NY Times 5 May 89

Dr Sol Rosen Deputy Director, Clinical Center, National Institutes of Health

4584 The hypothalamus is sometimes called the Board of Directors.

On that part of the brain that regulates bodily temperature, certain metabolic processes, and other autonomic activities NPR 2 Nov 91

Paul Rudnick playwright

4585 AIDS. . . the guest that won't leave. . . the one we all hate. But you have to remember: hey—it's still our party.

In his play *Jeffrey* whose cast included the AIDS-infected Olympic diver Greg Louganis *Time* 6 Mar 95

Mark Rutenberg President, Neuromedical Systems Inc

4586 What goes on in a lab is like looking for a needle in a haystack. The haystacks are enormous. And most have no needles.

On developing computerized search for abnormal cells *NY Times* 30 Sep 90

Dr Frank Ryan Fellow, Royal College of Surgeons

4587 Of the people who found the cure, 50 percent weren't even medically qualified. . . of the medical people involved, none were TB experts; the experts, you see, didn't believe it would ever be cured.

On developing a tuberculosis vaccine *NY Times* 1 Aug 93

4588 Success or failure will boil down to whether there is the will. . . to spend sufficient money to win the battle. It is likely to depend more on compassion than on molecular biology.

On finding a vaccine against AIDS *The Forgotten Plague* Little, Brown 93

Dr Albert Sabin researcher and government adviser

4589 A scientist who is also a human being cannot rest while knowledge which might be used to reduce suffering rests on the shelf.

On developing oral vaccine for polio *NY Times* 4 Mar 93

William Safire columnist

4590 A doctor with all those years of pre-med. . . is miffed at being lumped with insurance salesmen and bedpan bandits.

On use of the inclusive term "health care provider" *NY Times* 11 Apr 93

4591 Take a couple of euphemisms and call me in the morning.

ib

Dr Jonas Salk Salk Institute, San Diego CA

4592 Why did Mozart compose music?

On devoting his life to research *Time* 29 Mar 54

4593 Could you patent the sun?

When asked who owned the patent on polio vaccine *See It Now* CBS TV 12 Apr 55, quoted by Jane S Smith *Patenting the Sun* Morrow 90

4594 [There is] the possibility of giving everyone some hamburger, instead of sirloin steak to a few.

On widespread vaccinations *ib*

4595 I look upon it as ritual and symbolic. You wouldn't do unto others that which you wouldn't do unto yourself.

Comment 30 years after he had tested his polio vaccine on himself and colleagues *ib*

Dr Lee Salk Professor of Pediatric Psychology, NY Hospital-Cornell Medical Center

4596 In both structural and functional terms, Mr and Mrs Stern's role as parents to Baby M was achieved by a surrogate uterus and not a surrogate mother.

Defense report in suit for custody of a child by its biological mother *NY Times* 9 Feb 87

Dr Stephen Sallan pediatric specialist

4597 It's painful. . . a lot of love affairs end.

On treating cancer in children *Newsweek* 15 Aug 77

Dr Duncan Salmon cardiologist, Good Samaritan Hospital, Baltimore

4598 If you spend a lot of time knitting sleeves, you get good at knitting sleeves.

On medical specialties *Washington Post* 7 Nov 93

Dr Cecely Saunders founder of St. Christopher's, London, first modern hospice

4599 Deception is not as creative as truth. We do best in life if we look at it with clear eyes, and that applies to coming up to death as well.

On telling patients their true condition *Time* 5 Sep 88

4600 We must not lose the chance of making good on a great deal of untidiness in our lives, or of making time to pack our bags and saying, "Sorry, goodbye and thank you."

ib

Dr Béla Schick physician

4601 First the patient, second the patient, third the patient, fourth the patient, fifth the patient, and then maybe comes science. We first do everything for the patient; science can wait, research can wait.

I J Wolf ed *Aphorisms and Facetiae of Béla Schick* Waverly Press 65

Bruno Schiefer Director of Toxicology, University of Saskatchewan

4602 You just carry one little brick. You don't know if it is going to end up being a brick in the cathedral or simply a little piece to keep the outhouse from falling over.

On researching high incidence of multiple sclerosis in colder climates *NY Times* 19 Mar 85

Jeffrey Schmalz reporter

4603 To have AIDS is to be alone, no matter the number of friends and family members around. Then, to be with someone who has HIV, be it interviewer or interviewee, is to find kinship.

On being both a victim of AIDS and a reporter on it *NY Times* 7 Nov 93

4604 It's like knowing I will be killed by a speeding car, but not knowing when or where.

ib 28 Nov 93

4605 The ship is beginning to sink, the water is lapping onto the deck. I am eager for any lifeboat, however leaky.

On joining a nevirapine experimental group *ib*

Dr Joseph Schulman Director, Genetics and IVP Institute, Fairfax VA

4606 I don't see that... it's OK to reduce triplets to twins but not twins to singletons, especially because if I were doing abortions, I'd be reducing singletons to nothing.

On the ethics of "pregnancy reductions" *NY Times* 25 Jan 88

Dr Marvin M Schuster Johns Hopkins University School of Medicine

4607 The problem is in the gut.

On evidence that irritable bowel syndrome is not a psychosomatic disorder *NY Times* 2 Feb 88

Dr Albert Schweitzer medical missionary

4608 Here, at whatever hour you come, you will find light and help and human kindness.

Inscription on lamp outside his hospital at Lambarene, recalled on Schweitzer's death 4 Sep 65

4609 Pain is a more terrible lord of mankind than even death himself.

NY Times 27 Sep 87

Dr Gordon Seagrave the "Burma surgeon"

4610 All I wanted was plenty of jungle and thousands of sick people to treat.

On 40 years in Southeast Asia *NY Times* 29 Mar 65

Dr Hans Selye Director, Institute of Experimental Medicine and Surgery, University of Montreal

4611 Stress, in addition to being itself and the result of itself, is also the cause of itself.

Selye's First Annual Report on Stress 51

Dr Richard Selzer Professor of Surgery, Yale

4612 Pathologists... [are] cynical, jaded men who scorn your workaday carrion, and pant only after corporeal exotica much as the gourmet who despises porridge but would sell his father's name for a ragout of cuckoo tongue.

Confessions of a Knife Simon & Schuster 79

4613 What is the difference between a surgeon and an internist?... One is the stance of a warrior; the other, that of the statesman.

Letters to a Young Doctor Simon & Schuster 82

4614 Dwell upon his awakening. Say the word "recovery"... a winged word. The sight and sound of you at this time is balm in Gilead to him.

On anaesthetizing a patient *ib*

4615 Wet heat applied to human flesh has done more to ease the plight of the sick than all the surgery past and all that is to come.

On use of warm compresses *ib*

4616 A compress gives such an insinuating warmth... cooks the tissues gently, giving off a humid aroma, softening resistant fibers, drawing out poison, polishing and smoothing all the rough places of the body, much as footsteps and knees hollow the stones of an old church.

ib

4617 Man is albuminoid, proteinaceous, laked pearl; woman is yolky, ovoid, rich. Both are exuberant bloody growths.

"The Exact Location of the Soul" *Mortal Lessons* Simon & Schuster 87

4618 There are outposts where clusters of cells yet shine, besieged, little lights blinking in the advancing darkness. Doomed soldiers, they battle on. Until death has secured the premises all to itself.

On death taking over only gradually *ib*

4619 Wrinkles on a beloved's face, the body after death, are mortal lessons. He who shrinks from their contemplation is like a dandy sniffing a vinegar-soaked hanky lest he catch the rank whiff of the poor.

ib

4620 Halfway up a hillside is just where a hospital belongs-midway between a cathedral on the top and a jailhouse at the foot, in touch with both the sacred and the profane.

"Hospital: A Meditation" *NY Times* 1 May 88

4621 You could watch the smoke from the crematorium chimney rise and diffuse over the city as the dead insisted upon mixing with the living. The natural course is to be born, to flourish, to dwindle and to die. Yet the medical profession has encouraged people to think of the natural course as an adversary, to be fought off until the bitter end.

Time 31 Jul 89

4622 The more they drank, the less they ate, growing fleshless and bloated. . . some wearing the yellow livery of cirrhosis.

Down From Troy Morrow 92

4623 It was the masochism of hopelessness. The autopsy. . . did not show the real cause of his death—that life had sunk so deeply into him that it simply could not come back out again.

On his father, also a physician *ib*

4624 [The autopsy did not] reveal the cluster of whispers in the hollow of his right ear that might have told the painful secrets he kept; nor the echoes in his brain of the cries and moans of ten thousand sick. . . nor the whole beloved town moving slowly across his retina. Autopsies tell only the facts, never the truth.

ib

4625 The heart. . . heft it in your hand. It has the weight of a good-sized tomato, and so precisely fits the palm as to suggest that it was originally intended to sit there and that only on second thought did the Maker decide to hang it within a cage of ribs, perhaps to free the hand for playing the violin.

On the work of pathologists *ib*

Anne Sexton poet

4626 Don't send death in his fat red suit and his ho-ho baritone.

"May 30th" poem included in *Words for Doctor Y* Houghton Mifflin 78

Dr Richard Sharpe British physician

4627 It's. . . like trying to find out what is wrong with a car by looking at the exhaust.

On the lower sperm count of men born in the 1950s *London Times* 29 Aug 95

Dr Douglas Shenson Co-founder, International Committee for Medical Human Rights

4628 Here I thought is the seed of all the ruin.

On observing the intravenous flow of blood to an AIDS patient *NY Times* 28 Feb 88

4629 AIDS. . . an acronym that implies the very opposite of its nature. Many wouldn't speak of their relatives' diagnosis. A few abandoned them to the hospital. All expected secrecy.

On families of AIDS patients *ib*

4630 The transformation of this disease into a socially manageable entity starts in the doctor's office. I cannot, as yet, change my patient's prognosis, but I can alter his relationship to his illness. Once his damnation is sealed, the opportunity for creative intervention is defeated—and he wraps his world in profound secrecy and lives in unbounded anger.

ib

Dr Charles Sherrington British neurophysiologist

4631 Paradoxical though it may sound, the more skillful a demonstration experiment is performed the less from it do some students learn.

Preface to *Mammalian Physiology* recalled on Sherrington's death 4 Mar 52

Randy Shilts reporter, *San Francisco Chronicle*

4632 Single frames of tragedy in this and that corner of the world would begin to flicker fast enough to reveal the movement of something new and horrible rising slowly from the earth's biological landscape.

On mounting toll of AIDS deaths in November 1980 *And the Band Played On* St Martin's 87

4633 The patient mentioned that he was gay, but Gottlieb didn't think any more of that than the fact the guy might drive a Ford.

On Dr Michael Gottlieb's pioneer tracking of the AIDS virus *ib*

4634 [They] were guiding couples through the difficulties of maintaining relationships in the biggest sexual candy store God ever invented.

On psychotherapists *ib*

4635 You're left with a strange feeling that your life is over without it being quite finished.

On the stress of being HIV-Positive *60 Minutes* CBS TV 20 Feb 94

Alex Shoumatoff journalist

4636 [He imagined] this archetypical communicable disease traveling. . . in countless copulations, and like a swallowed dye pill illuminating all the liaisons danger uses, the thousands upon thousands of illicit premarital, extra-marital, interracial and homosexual encounters that must have taken place for it to spread as far as it has.

On the spread of AIDS *African Madness* Knopf 89

Dr Bruce Siegel President, Health and Hospitals Corp

4637 We used to have a monopoly on poor people.

On the public hospital system's loss of patients who opted for managed-care programs affiliated with private hospitals *NY Times* 30 Jun 94

Paul Siegel sociologist

4638 The lights went out and people were left to interact with each other.

On directing a study of sharp increase in births after blackout of eastern US *NY Times* 10 Aug 66

Dr Mark Siegler Director, Center for Medical Ethics, University of Chicago

4639 Patients will be afraid that their doctor may be a great believer in death with dignity when all they need is their asthma medicine.

On the changing course of medical ethics *NY Times* 23 Feb 88

Henry E Sigerist journalist

4640 Some have a urine-glass in their hands, others a stethoscope, yet one and all, from the shamans of primitive tribes, down to the scientific physicians of our own day, are inspired by the same will.

The Great Doctors Dover 71

Anthony Smith zoologist

4641 The brain of modern man, whatever its origins, is better than it need be, and rarely tapped for its true potential.

The Mind Hodder & Stoughton 84

4642 Liver, spleen, heart and guts are all intriguing, but cannot hold a candle to the brain. It is the most important thing on earth, for good or ill.

ib

Jane S Smith biographer

4643 Pranksters have been known to telephone these hopefuls in the middle of the night. . . with a phony Swedish accent that wouldn't pass muster at any hour if it were not the echo of so many months and years of hopeful calling into the void.

On chronic yearning for the Nobel Prize *Parenting the Sun* Morrow 90

Dr John E Smith Minnesota family practioner

4644 The golden age of medicine. . . seemed golden to me not for the harvested coin. . . but rather for the golden glow of approval that a good doctor-patient relationship radiated.

Writing in a medical journal eight years before allegations of sexual misconduct forced him to relinquish his practice *NY Times* 5 Nov 95

Dr Richard Smith Editor, *British Medical Journal*

4645 If you listen carefully to the patient, he or she will tell you the diagnosis.

London Times 10 Aug 93

Smokefree Educational Services

4646 You Give Them Money. . . They Give You Cancer!

Subway advertisement against cigarettes *New Yorker* 6 Jan 92

Dr Seymour Solomon Dean, Montefiore Medical Center, NYC

4647 Everyone is touching the elephant in a different place.

On the comprehensiveness of migraine research *Life* Feb 94

Susan Sontag philosopher and essayist

4648 Everyone who is born holds dual citizenship, in the kingdom of the well and in the kingdom of the sick. Although we all prefer to use only the good passport, sooner or later each of us is obliged, at least for a spell, to identify ourselves as citizens of that other place.

Illness as Metaphor Farrar Straus Giroux 78

Marietta Spencer social worker

4649 A genetic history—psychological as well as medical—is something like a child's washing instructions. When you buy a sweater, you want to know all about its fabric content.

On histories of birth families to accompany adoptions *NY Times* 3 Sep 89

Dr Ellen M Stevenson Columbia-Presbyterian Medical Center, NYC

4650 The normal complement after a weekend. The knife and gun club. The crack. The threats. The temper tantrums gone bad.

On hospital Monday mornings *NY Times* 7 Apr 93

Dr John Stone Professor of Cardiology, Emory University School of Medicine

4651 This is the room in which the body confesses... [where] surgical specimens are examined while the surgeon waits impatiently and the patient sleeps on.

On examination of quick-frozen specimens *NY Times* 7 Aug 88

4652 A person's life can be thought of as a series of stories, coalescing over time to form the most idiosyncratic novel ever written. The good doctor must learn to listen for the real messages in these stories.

ib 24 Sep 90 excerpted from *In the Country of Hearts: Journeys in the Art of Medicine* Delacorte 90

Dr Stephen Straus virologist, National Institutes of Health

4653 You have to start believing what they're describing.

On mysterious chronic fatigue syndrome *Time* 29 Jun 87

Dr Louis W Sullivan US Secretary of Health and Human Services

4654 [They are] promoting a culture of cancer.

On R J Reynolds' test-marketing of cigarettes aimed primarily at African Americans *NY Times* 19 Jan 90

Dr Theoralf Sundt surgeon

4655 The idea is to get in and out without the brain knowing you've been there.

On neurosurgery *60 Minutes* CBS TV 31 Dec 95

4656 Neurosurgeons know the brain like the streets of their towns.

ib

Dr. Adina Blady Szwajger Polish physician

4657 We already knew that there was less and less we could do to save lives; that instead we were becoming, more and more, bestowers of quiet death.

On children's hospitals in wartime Warsaw *I Remember Nothing More* Pantheon 91

Dr James M Tanner Institute of Child Health, University of London

4658 We are now moving from an era in which there were too many patients chasing too little growth hormone to an era in which there will be too much growth hormone chasing too few patients.

On increased development and sale of drugs for hormone deficiency *NY Times* 16 Jun 91

Mortin Thompson novelist

4659 Being born is a momentous thing full of purpose, full of magic, alive with destiny, and this is the place where it happened.

On modern hospitals *Not As A Stranger* Scribner 54

4660 They all had the look of a child in their eyes, bewildered and humble and expectant... probably dead now... long dead. All but the look. The look lived on.

On emergency room patients *ib*

4661 That's it, Doctor. Pneumonia! Enemy of the young, friend of the aged! That's how we kill 'em at the County.

On welfare patients *ib*

4662 They were doctors... the high priests of man's mightiest mystery: himself.

ib

4663 He felt towards his patients the pride, love, and delight which an architect feels passing a building he planned, which an engineer feels watching traffic pass over a a bridge he has mended.

ib

4664 The only human sign in that room of white tile... were the rolling eyes of the patients, supine on the table, that altar of human knowledge, and the patient's body, whose mysteries were about to be explored by minds that did not know the ultimate mystery of even the greatest lesser mysteries but would do all they could.

ib

4665 What they owed him was no more, and what he had done for them had no monument, and what they needed of him they took to someone else.

On the death of a physician *ib*

Dr Christopher Tietze Director, National Committee on Maternal Health

4666 It's because people may have had trouble finding their accustomed contraceptives, or just because it was dark.

On sharp increase in birth rate after blackout of eastern US *NY Times* 10 Aug 66

Dr James S Todd Executive VP, American Medical Association

4667 We have everything to gain and, oh, so much to lose if we start drawing lines in the sand while the ship of reform is still at sea.

On need for restraint in criticizing the efforts to perfect a viable national health care system *NY Times* 6 Dec 93

Dr E Fuller Torrey National Institutes of Health

4668 We carry it around in this box on our shoulders that's very inconvenient to research.

On the brain as the most difficult part of the body to study *National Geographic* Jun 95

Dr Paul Tournier physician and ethicist

4669 We who are the first to receive man into this world. . . have the great privilege of faithfully accompanying him right to his last drawn breath, to the very gates of death.

The Seasons of Life John Knox Press 63

4670 We have the great privilege of knowing that all this pathway has meaning, that its destination lies in that mysterious fullness which has been declared unto us.

Quoted at committal of ashes of Nelson A Rockefeller 19 Jan 79

Dr. Irving Townsend veterinarian

4671 We, who choose to surround ourselves with lives even more temporary than our own, live within a fragile circle, easily and often breached.

On pet care *The Once Again Prince* privately published 1986

4672 Unable to accept its awful gaps, we still would live no other way; we cherish memory as the only certain immortality, never fully understanding the necessary plan.

ib

Bernard Tresnowski Director, Blue Cross and Blue Shield Association

4673 In the past employers were like an absentee host who paid the bill but never showed up at the table; now they are intimately involved in planning the menu.

On new roles in determining medical benefits *Newsweek* 2 Jul 84

Dr Wilfred Trotter cardiac specialist

4674 Disease often tells its secrets in a casual parenthesis.

Quoted by Dr John Stone *In the Country of Hearts* Delacorte 90

US Surgeon General

4675 Warning: Quitting smoking now greatly reduces serious risk to your health.

One of the four warnings mandated by law to be printed on cigarette packets *NY Times* 12 Feb 86

4676 Surgeon General's Warning: Smoking Causes Lung Cancer, Heart Disease, Emphysema, and May Complicate Pregnancy.

Subsequent warning used in the 1990s

US News & World Report

4677 [It is] a fever lurking in the blood.

Reporting on Finnish study showing that AIDS virus can go unnoticed in conventional blood tests 12 Oct 87

Mona Van Duyn US poet laureate

4678 A life-renouncing meal of smoke.

On cigarettes *Washington Post* 5 Jan 93

Dr Abraham Verghese AIDS specialist

4679 [It had] strong resemblances to a secret society with me at its head and the various novitiates and initiates dispersed among the townfolk, disguised as bakers, shoe repairman, housewives, priests, waiters, blacksmiths, and publicans.

My Own Country Simon & Schuster 94

Loudon Wainwright Jr essayist

4680 The killer, in effect, had appeared in everyone's home—every medicine cabinet had become a potential hiding place for some life-threatening horror.

On contamination of Tylenol capsules *Life* Nov 82

Mike Wallace commentator

4681 Billfold biopsy.

On hospital's demand for insurance before accepting a patient *60 Minutes* CBS TV 17 Mar 85

4682 The "working poor"—too poor to have insurance, not poor enough to have Medicare.

ib

Dr Simon Wallis physician

4683 There is an immediate pleasure from having got it right.

On recognizing patterns to reach a correct diagnosis *London Times* 10 Aug 93

Michael Walters American Veterinary Medical Association

4684 They don't smoke. . . rarely travel by automobile. . . are less likely to be victims of street crimes.

On pets as good insurance risks *NY Times* 15 Feb 92

Sally Weinper Los Angeles attorney

4685 I want to smell the roses now because I may not be able to recognize them later on.

At age 54 after Alzheimer's claimed her mother and three aunts *Time* 3 Apr 95

Dr Kevin Welch dermatologist, University of Arizona Health Sciences Center

4686 Skin is sort of like an elephant. It never forgets a ray of sun that hits it.

Life Aug 92

Larry C White California attorney

4687 Cigarettes are the only products on the market (aside from weapons) that kill and injure when used as they are intended to be used.

Merchants of Death Beech Tree/Morrow 88

George Whitmore journalist

4688 Every walk in the park might be your last. Every rent check is a lease on another month's life.

On state of mind of AIDS patients *Someone Was Here* New American Library 88

Paul Willging Executive VP, American Health Care Association

4689 This is not what people refer to as the "welfare population." This is your Mom and Dad. . . tax-paying, middle-class people until they got sick.

On two-thirds of nursing home patients who received Medicaid assistance after exhausting their savings, half of them within the first year *NY Times* 12 Nov 95

Edward O Wilson Professor of Zoology, Harvard

4690 Genes hold the culture on a leash.

Sociobiology: The New Synthesis Belknap Press 75

John R Wilson journalist

4691 The most useful equipment for a successful surgeon is a pessimistic pathologist.

Hall of Mirrors Doubleday 66

Dr Jay Winsten Associate Dean, Harvard School of Public Health

4692 Yesterday's adolescent fist fight is today's adolescent shootout. Yesterday's black eye and injured pride is today's gaping exit wound with massive injuries. It's casting a pall of fear over the lives of American children.

NY Times 16 May 94

4693 We're inviting them to walk away from confrontation. What are we asking them to walk up to instead? We have to create a whole superstructure of activities in which they can compete and win.

ib

Harris Wofford US Senator

4694 The Constitution says that if you are charged with a crime, you have a right to a lawyer. But it's even more fundamental that if you're sick, you should have the right to a doctor.

Time 11 Nov 91

Marguerite Yoursenar novelist

4695 If we were not so afraid of pain, they would tell fewer lies.

On physicians *Memoirs of Hadrian* Farrar Straus Cudahy 54

Dr John Ziegler Director, AIDS Clinical Research Center, University of California

4696 Everybody who is infected will get sick. Everyone who gets sick will die.

Time 21 Dec 87

Dr Hans Zinsser Professor of Bacteriology and Immunology, Harvard Medical School

4697 Bacteria, protozoa, viruses. . . about the only genuine sporting proposition that remains unimpaired by the relentless domestication of a once free-living human species is the war against these ferocious little fellow creatures.

Quoted by Jane S Smith *Patenting the Sun* Morrow 90

4698 [They] lurk in the dark corners and stalk us in the bodies of rats, mice, and all kinds of domestic animals. . . fly and crawl with the insects, and waylay us in our food and drink and even in our love.

ib

Psychology and Psychiatry

Anon

4699 People don't smell dice on your breath or see card marks on your arms.

On the difficulty of detecting the compulsive gambler *NY Times* 29 Jun 90

W H Auden poet

4700 He is no more a person now but more a climate of opinion.

"In Memory of Sigmund Freud" 1939 Edward Mendelson ed *Collected Poems* Vintage 91

Dr Richard Berendzen President, American University 1980–90; Professor of Astronomy 1990–

4701 I could understand a quasar 15-billion light years away, but I couldn't understand the boy that's now within the man.

Comparing his professional competence to compulsion for placing obscene telephone calls *Washington Post* 7 Jun 90

Dr Steven Berglas Professor of Psychology, Harvard Medical School

4702 Arrogance, a sense of aloneness, the need to seek adventure, and adultery... [are] the core attributes of people who achieve stellar successes without the psychological bedrock to prevent disorder.

Time 4 Nov 91

Dr Leonard Berkowitz Emeritus Professor of Psychology, University of Wisconsin

4703 The finger pulls the trigger. But the trigger may also pull the finger.

On weapons as a stimulant to violence *Time* 8 May 95

Dr Frederick Berlin Director, Sexual Disorders Clinic, Johns Hopkins University

4704 He's afflicted with... a cancer of the mind.

Testimony at Jeffrey Dahmer's trial for murder and dismemberment of 17 men and boys in Ohio and Wisconsin *Washington Post* 4 Feb 92

Alan Berman Washington School of Psychiatry

4705 Adolescence goes to at least the age of 49.

Adolescent Suicide American Psychological Association 91

Dr Robert Bosnak psychiatrist

4706 When you pay attention to your dreams, you begin to inhabit a much larger part of your soul.

Life Sep 59

Dr Rosalind Cartwright Chair, Department of Psychology, Rush-Presbyterian Medical Center, Chicago

4707 Dreams are a metaphor in motion... the language of the night.

The Power of Dreams Discovery Channel 20 Jun 94

Dr Raymond B Cattell Professor of Psychology, University of Illinois

4708 Adolescence is the time when even the dullest clod knows that he possesses a soul and the genius that he lives in a perpetual adolescence.

An Introduction to Personality Study Hutchison University Press 50

William J Clinton 42nd US President

4709 I'm always smiling and try to make it look easy... [but] in some ways, while I'm gregarious, I may be more solitary than I appear.

On a background of "pain and agony" as the stepson of an alcoholic father *Newsweek* 30 Mar 92

4710 I struggle now for ways to reveal my true feelings that don't seem self-indulgent. It's a real hard thing for me to do, I confess.

ib

4711 One of the biggest problems I had in fully maturing was learning how to... express disagreement without being disagreeable.

ib

Dr Harold Cooper Chair, Advanced Excellence Systems

4712 The depth of your relaxation, your ability to let go, determines the height of your creativity.

Co-author with Robert Bloomfield *The Power of Five* St Martin's 95

Dr Antonio Damasio Neurologist, University of Iowa

4713 Consciousness is a concept of your own self, something that you reconstruct moment by moment on the basis of the image of your own body, your own autobiography and a sense of your intended future.

Descartes Error Putnam 94

Gayle Delaney Assistant Professor, California Institute of Integral Studies, San Francisco

4714 Lots of people dream of killing people when they have absolutely no intention of doing so.

Life Sep 95

4715 Dream therapy without dream interpretation is like orthopedics without X-rays.

ib

Dr James Eagan Director of Child and Adolescent Psychology, NY Hospital-Cornell Medical Center

4716 The view of the American Psychiatric Association is that once a patient, always a patient.

On the ethical belief that a professional therapist–patient relationship should never be breached, Station WAMU Washington 24 Aug 92

Joseph Epstein essayist

4717 Psychology wants to know what a man's problems are; character has to do with how he surmounts them.

Partial Payments: Essays on Writers and Their Lives Norton 89

Erik H Erikson psychoanalyst

4718 The fact that human conscience remains partially infantile throughout our life is the core of human tragedy.

Childhood and Society Norton 50

4719 [The] sense of identity provides the ability to experience one's self as something that has continuity and sameness, and to act accordingly.

On coining the term "identity crisis" *ib*

4720 Potentially creative men... often starve themselves socially, [and] erotically... in order to let the grosser needs die out, and make way for the growth of the inner garden.

Encounter Sep 66

Joan Erikson co-author with Erik H Erikson

4721 Lots of old people don't get wise, but you don't get wise unless you age.

At age 86, continuing expansion of psychological theories developed with her husband *NY Times* 14 Jun 88

4722 When it comes to understanding life, experimental learning is the only worthwhile kind; everything else is hearsay.

ib

Dr Frederic F Flasch psychiatrist

4723 Depression... is associated with endings, and because each ending involves starting over, depression is itself a new beginning.

The Secret Strength of Depression Lippincott 74

Dr Erich Fromm psychoanalyst

4724 There is... nothing in the patient I do not have in me.

Recalled on Fromm's death 18 Mar 80

4725 The scars left from the child's defeat in the fight against irrational authority are to be found at the bottom of every neuroses.

Man for Himself Rinehart 1947

Dr Jesse Geller Director, Yale University Psychological Services Clinic

4726 Whenever someone stays in psychotherapy beyond a reasonable limit—more than four years in psychoanalysis, for example—there's a collusion, conscious or unconscious, between the therapist and the patient, where the patient is gratifying some need of the therapist.

NY Times 18 Apr 93

Dr Kenneth J Gergen Professor of Psychology, Swarthmore

4727 Our identity is continuously reformed and redirected as we move through a sea of changing relationships.

US News & World Report 1 Jul 91

4728 Who and what we are is not so much the result of personal essence but how we are constructed in social groups.

ib

Dr Sam Goldstein psychiatrist

4729 They see life through mud-colored glasses.

On depression in children ABC TV 25 Jul 95

Dr Gerald W Grumet Director, Psychiatric Emergency Services, Rochester NY General Hospital

4730 The tattoo is typically an attempt to make permanent that which is fleeting... a pictorial quest for self-definition, easing one's sense of inadequacy and isolation... tangible promise of a final identity, the clarified picture of a diffused ego.

NY Times 21 Aug 90

Dr Peter Guggenheim psychiatrist

4731 You have to clean a good clock every three or four years... take out the innards, just like I do when I work with patients.

Forbes 25 Sep 95

Dr Manfred Guttmacher psychiatrist

4732 [It was] a rupture of the ego, an episodic discontrol.

Testimony at trail of Jack Ruby for slaying of Lee Harvey Oswald *NY Times* 11 Mar 64

Pete Hamill journalist

4733 Anybody who has a sense of confusion can benefit from a neutral person in their life.

On therapy, Station WAMU Washington 29 Mar 95

Sandra Harding National Association of Social Workers

4734 We need to weed out the worried well.

On patients who overuse psychotherapy *NY Times* 18 Apr 93

Dr Christopher Hardman psychoanalyst

4735 Psychoanalysis is the study of self-deception.
International Herald Tribune 22 Nov 85

Dr Leston Havens psychoanalyst

4736 The body... secures its sovereignty of our happiness by an unrivaled intimacy: we can never leave it, except in death and imagination, we are abjectly dependent on it for our greatest delights.
Making a Safe Place Harvard University Press 89

4737 Beware... of surgeons who thirst to operate. Away with medicines, they say, ... give me that knife. Many psychotherapists are no different... they thirst to explain.
ib

James Hillman psychologist

4738 Words, like angels, are powers which have invisible power over us... personal presences which have whole mythologies: genders, genealogies... histories, and vogues; and their own guarding, blaspheming, creating, and annihilating effects.
A Blue Fire Thomas Moore ed Harper 91

Robert Hughes critic

4739 The pursuit of the Inner Child has taken over just at the moment when Americans ought to be figuring out where their Inner Adult is.
Culture of Conservatives Oxford 93

Kathryn Hulme novelist

4740 The dark-veiled silhouette... that solitary form patroling without visible strain or vain glory a demented dreamland of fearful potential.
On a nursing sister on a psychiatric ward *The Nun's Story* Little, Brown 56

Dr Thomas Jensen Chair, Adolescent Psychiatric Unit, St Mary's Medical Center, Lewiston ME

4741 With the chemical changes that occur after puberty... he focuses on one negative thing, and he convinces himself that suicide is the only option.
On depression in teen-agers *NY Times* 1 Oct 95

4742 You could have a million things going right for you but if one thing is wrong, the depressed person completely loses perspective.
On cognitive distortion *ib*

Dr Virginia E Johnson Masters-Johnson Clinic, St Louis

4743 Intimacy is not an industry, it's not fast food.
On plethora of books on relationships, Station WAMU Washington 28 Mar 94

4744 Love means as many different things as there are people you ask.
ib

Jill Johnston reporter

4745 The inmates are ghosts whose dreams have been murdered.
On Bellevue Hospital's psychiatric wards *Paper Daughter* Knopf 85

Dr Carl Jung Swiss psychoanalyst

4746 The conscious mind allows itself to be trained like a parrot, but the unconscious does not—which is why St Augustine thanked God for not making him responsible for his dreams.
Psychology and Alchemy Princeton 53

4747 A man who has not passed through the inferno of his passions has never overcome them.
Memories, Dreams, Reflections Atlantic Monthly Press 62

4748 Neurosis is always a substitute for legitimate suffering.
Quoted by Dr M Scott Peck *The Road Less Traveled* Simon & Schuster 78

Maarten Klein patient

4749 I seem to lose words like another person loses blood. Everyday, every day there's something gone. It leaks everywhere.
On experiencing the early stages of Alzheimer's Disease, quoted by J Bernlef *Out of Mind* David R Godine 89

Komsomolskaya Pravda Communist youth newspaper

4750 One and the same person may be adjudged a schizophrenic in Moscow, a psychopath in Leningrad and healthy in Kharkov.
On diagnoses of mental health *NY Times* 24 Jan 88

John Kotre psychologist

4751 It has the temperament of a librarian, a keeper of memory's most important archives... fastidious ... guarding its original records and trying to keep them pristine.
On "the remembering self" *White Gloves: Ourselves Through Memory* Free Press 95

4752 Memory's archivist by day has a secret passion by night... seeking to generate conviction about what it thinks is true.
ib

Dr R D Laing British psychologist

4753 By... 15 or so, we are... a half crazed creature more or less adjusted in a mad world. This is normality in our present age.
The Politics of Experience Pantheon 67

Dr Jeremy A Lazarus Chair, American Psychiatric Association

4754 A patient's right to confidentiality survives death.
On Diane Wood Middlebrook's disputed use of tapes of psychiatric sessions in biography of the poet Anne Sexton *NY Times* 15 Jul 91

Anne Morrow Lindbergh essayist

4755 The habit of writing almost daily in my diary... probably saved my sanity. If I could write out moods which could be admitted to no one, they became more manageable, as though neatly stacked on a high shelf.
On surviving her infant son's kidnapping *War Within and Without* Harcourt Brace Jovanovich 80

4756 Brought to the aseptic light of the diary's white page, the giant toadstools withered.
ib

Andrew H Malcolm reporter

4757 A quiet... office steeped in woodgrains, books and stale grief... and, nearby, the requisite box of tissues.
On interviewing a psychiatrist *NY Times* 3 Jan 92

Janet Malcolm journalist

4758 Analysts... pick away at the scab that the patient tries to form between himself and the analyst to cover over his wounds. He keeps the surface raw, so that the wound heals properly.
Psychoanalysis: The Impossible Profession Knopf 81

4759 The house of psychoanalysis has many mansions, but some of Freud's followers... have not wanted to live in the main house and have built their own annexes and outbuildings.
On revisionist schools of Freudian thought *NY Times* 6 Nov 94

Dr Arnold J Mandell Professor of Psychology, University of California, San Diego

4760 Ourselves, our personalities... [come from] an orchestra of chemical voices in our heads.
Time 2 Apr 79

Mary McCarthy novelist

4761 All neurotics are petty bourgeois. Madmen are the aristocrats of mental illness.
The Group Harcourt Brace World 63

Candia McWilliam novelist

4762 Nannied. Lightly castrated, like princes in the ballet.
On victims of inferior child care *A Little Stranger* Doubleday 89

Dr Karl A Menninger Founder, Menninger Clinic, Topeka KS

4763 Unrest of spirit is a mark of life.
This Week *NY Herald-Tribune* 16 Oct 58

4764 Money-giving is a very good criterion... of a person's mental health. Generous people are rarely mentally ill people.
Newsweek 2 Nov 59

4765 Neurotic means he is not as sensible as I am, and psychotic means he's even worse than my brother-in-law.
Recalled on Menninger's death 18 Jul 90

Arthur Miller playwright

4766 How few the days are that hold the mind in place; like tapestry hanging on four or five hooks. Especially the day you stop becoming; the day you merely are.
Saturday Evening Post 1 Feb 64

Dr Timothy Miller clinical psychologist, Stockton CA

4767 People spend their lives honestly believing that they have almost enough of whatever they want. Just a little more will put them over the top; then they will be contented forever.
Time 28 Aug 95

National Institute of Mental Health

4768 Depression is the common cold of mental illness.
NY Times 14 May 86

The New York Times

4769 To be mad is not necessarily to be creative, or there'd be a Shelley on every corner.
"Making Art of Madness" editorial on the link between genius and madness 15 Oct 93

4770 To be creative is almost invariably to be diligent—and, manic-depressive or no, to swing high, swing low.
ib

Dr Jim Pivarnik Exercise Physiologist, Texas Children's Hospital

4771 Do they love to do it, or do they love to do it because I love it when they do?
On parental motivation *Newsweek* 10 Aug 92

Dr Theodore Reik psychoanalyst

4772 In order to be happy it is necessary to make at least one other person happy.
NY Times 1 Jan 70

4773 The secret of human happiness is not in self-seeking but in self-forgetting.
ib

Maria Riva biographer

4774 It took nearly 30 years to break her spirit, then destroy her mind. My mother and father were very thorough people.
On her father's mistress *Marlene Dietrich* Knopf 92

Ann Roiphe essayist

4775 In the office there was an old, soft and worn blue velvet couch, above which a hundred thousand dissected dreams floated in the peaceful, still air.
Recalling an interview with psychoanalyst Helene Deutsch *NY Times* 13 Feb 71

Dr. Milton Rokeach psychiatrist

4776 To say that a particular psychiatric condition is incurable or irreversible is to say more about our ignorance than about the patient.
The Three Christs of Ypsilanti Knopf 64

Dr. Theodore I Rubin psychiatrist

4777 I must learn to love the fool in me—the one who feels too much, talks too much, takes too many chances. . . [that] alone protects me against that utterly self-controlled, masterful tyrant who. . . would rob me of human aliveness, humility and dignity but for my fool.
Love Me, Love My Fool McKay 76

Dr Lee Salk Professor of Pediatric Psychology, Cornell Medical Center

4778 The attention you withhold from a young child will be demanded doubly when he is older.
What Every Child Would Like His Parents to Know McKay 72

John A Sanford priest-therapist

4779 The unconscious is not only the basement of our minds into which we place the discarded material of our own lives; its also the ocean out of which our conscious lives have sprung, and over which the ship of the soul sails its course through life.
The Kingdom Within Harper & Row 78

Marvin Schneider NYC Human Resources Administration

4780 There are many people on the street whose link with reality is knowing what time it is.
On the importance of keeping clocks in working order *NY Times* 15 Nov 92

Dr Edwin Schneidman psychologist

4781 One jumps from a place which has a reputation.
On 391 fatalities from San Francisco's Golden Gate Bridge in a 33-year period *Time* 24 Aug 70

Wilfrid Sheed journalist

4782 All the witches of London, New York and Sydney, Australia, held square dances in my head.
On addictions that destroy the ability to concentrate *In Love with Daylight* Simon & Schuster 95

R Z Sheppard journalist

4783 Freud's apostles begat apostates who in turn spawned heresies and a bemusing number of therapeutic sects, each claiming to have a piece of the true couch.
Time 18 Apr 88

4784 People once said they were "in" psychoanalysis, meaning they were committed to a long immersion. In a sense, they were writing their autobiographies.
ib 28 Sep 88, reviewing Peter Gay's *Freud: A Life for Our Time* Norton 88

Eileen Simpson journalist

4785 [The] black ink of anxiety spilled and spread, saturating the fabric of my life.
Orphans: Real and Imaginary Weidenfeld & Nicolson 87

C R Snyder Professor of Psychology, University of Kansas

4786 Many neurotic symptoms started out as normal excuses that were used so often they became a way of life.
NY Times 1 Sep 87

Anthony Storr journalist

4787 Creativity is one mode adopted by gifted people of coming to terms with, or finding symbolic solutions for, the internal tensions and disassociations from which all human beings suffer in varying degree.
The Dynamics of Creation Atheneum 72

William Styron novelist

4788 All capacity for pleasure disappears, and despair maintains a merciless daily drumming.
On depression *NY Times* 19 Dec 88

4789 Depression is a wimp of a word for a howling tempest in the brain.

Darkness Visible Random House 90

Lord Taylor Of Harlow (Stephen James Lake Taylor) physician

4790 Hypomania is an admirable human characteristic when it comes to getting things done.

NY Times 23 Feb 64

Robin Williams author and patient

4791 [Psychotherapy is] open-heart surgery in installments.

NY Times 25 Jan 88

Tennessee Williams playwright

4792 [It is] the sharp knife in the mind that kills the devil in the soul.

On frontal lobotomies *Suddenly Last Summer* New Directions 58

SCIENCE

Edwin E ("Buzz") Aldrin Jr, US astronaut

4793 Beautiful! Beaultiful! Magnificent desolation!

On joining astronaut Neil A Armstrong in man's first walk on the moon 20 Jul 69

Luis W Alvarez physicist

4794 Paleontologists. . . they're really not very good scientists. They're more like stamp collectors.

On debate on whether a large comet may have killed off dinosaurs 65 million years ago *NY Times* 19 Jan 88

American Library Association

4795 The computer is only a fast idiot. . . no imagination. . . cannot originate action. . . and will remain only a tool to man.

Prediction on the future of computers as seen in the Univac computer exhibited at NY World's Fair 64

Anon

4796 There was once a twin brother named Bright/ Who could travel much faster than light,/ He departed one day, in a relative way,/ And came home on the previous night.

On relativity *Newsweek* 3 Feb 58

4797 Here men from the planet Earth first set foot upon the moon, July 1969 AD. We came in peace for all mankind.

Plaque planted on the lunar surface by astronauts Neil A Armstrong and Edwin E Aldrin Jr 20 Jul 69

4798 [They were] iron men in wooden ships.

On early Arctic explorers *Buried in Ice* PBS TV 2 Feb 88

4799 The condor has been destroyed in order to save it.

On the capture of the last free-flying California condor for breeding in Los Angeles zoo NPR 9 Oct 90

4800 Let conversation cease. Laughter, take flight. This place is where death delights to aid the living.

Inscription on wall of NYC's autopsy morgue *New Yorker* 19 Jul 93

4801 Recycling is where the environment and the economy meet.

On recycling of motor oil by a California firm *National Geographic* Jul 94

4802 The moon will be our first stopping point on the cosmic highway. It should be called Exit I.

Suggestion in contest to rename the moon *US News & World Report* 19 Sep 94

4803 Language changes every 20 miles.

"Homo Loquens" editorial quoting a Ghanan proverb in commenting on American Association for the Advancement of Science paper that said that nearly 3,000 languages could become extinct over the next century *London Times* 24 Feb 95

4804 Bigger than big brother.

On use of cellular telephones in China *Christian Science Monitor* 31 May 95

4805 It may be a bit like watching paint dry, but it is scientifically interesting.

Comment from a director of Finland's Ranua Wildlife Park on plans to run a live internet video feed of a bear in hibernation *ib*

Neil A Armstrong US astronaut

4806 Houston. Tranquility base here. The Eagle has landed.

Message to earth from *Apollo II* lunar module after landing on the moon 20 Jul 69

4807 That's one small step for man, one giant leap for mankind.

On becoming the first man to walk on the moon; also reported as "That's one small step for a man" *ib*

4808 We landed on the Sea of Tranquility, in the cool of the early lunar morning, when the long shadows would aid our perception.

To joint session of Congress 16 Sep 69

4809 Man must understand his universe in order to understand his destiny.
ib

Renée Askins Founder, Wolf Fund

4810 A heart without a heartbeat.
On national parks devoid of wolves *NY Times* 11 Dec 94

John Aspinwall Howlett's Wild Animal Park, Canterbury

4811 Other tigers they know and humans they know are not on the menu.
Expressing belief that "faulty genes" rather than hunger caused a tiger to kill a keeper *London Times* 17 Feb 95

W H Auden poet

4812 In the company of scientists, I feel like a shabby curate who has strayed. . . into a drawing room full of dukes.
"The Poet and the City" 1962 in *The Dyer's Hand* Random House 69

4813 How happy the lot of the mathematician . . . judged solely by his peers. . . the standard so high that no colleague or rival can ever win a reputation he does not deserve.
"Writing" *ib*

J G Ballard novelist

4814 It is like God taking a photograph.
On the atomic bomb, quoted in film based on Ballard's Novel *Empire of the Sun* Simon & Schuster 84

Robert D Ballard Senior Scientist, Woods Hole Oceanographic Institution

4815 It is a quiet and peaceful place. . . the remains of this greatest of sea tragedies. . . forever may it remain that way—and may God bless these new-found souls.
On descending to the wreck of the *Titanic* 70 years after it sank with the loss of more than 1,500 passengers *NY Times* 10 Sep 85

4816 After years of gluttony the creatures starved and dropped dead at the table. . . having robbed the *Titanic* of her last touch of elegance.
On wood-boring organisms that devoured ornate panels of the ill-fated ocean liner *National Geographic* Dec 86

Lincoln Barnett reporter

4817 The quick harvest of applied science is the useable process. . . the shy fruit of pure science is Understanding.
On Einstein's completion of mathematical formula for the United Field Theory *Life* 9 Jan 50

Sharon Begley reporter

4818 It reached out of the rugged St Elias mountains like a finger from a polar deity, snapping and crackling as if the very earth had come down with creaky joints.
On Alaska's runaway glacier *Newsweek* 15 Aug 86

4819 The mind can store an estimated 100 trillion bits of information—compared with which a computer's mere billions are virtually amnesiac.
29 Sep 86

Howard Berkes reporter

4820 Wildfires burn green for fire-fighters.
On the high cost of protecting woodlands NPR 17 Sep 94

Lucien Biberman Associate Director, University of Chicago Military Research Lab

4821 Involvement in the development of atomic energy. . . left a deep scar on the moral fiber of this place.
NY Times 7 Jun 63

Jim Bishop columnist

4822 Archaeology. . . Peeping Tom of the sciences. . . sandbox of men who care not where they are going: they merely want to know where everyone else has been.
On undersea explorations *NY Journal-American* 14 Mar 61

Niels Bohr physicist, University of Copenhagen

4823 An expert is a man who has made all the mistakes, which can be made, in a very narrow field.
Recalled on Bohr's death 18 Nov 62

4824 When it comes to atoms, language can be used only as in poetry.
On Bohr's role as the father of the quantum theory *NY Times* 18 Oct 87

Roger Boisjoly US astronaut

4825 I knew we were in deep yogurt.
On controversial effect of weather on explosion of the space craft *Challenger Life* Mar 88

Frank Borman US astronaut

4826 A vast, lonely, forbidding expanse of nothing. . . like clouds and clouds of pumice stone.
Message from *Apollo 8* during the first manned orbit of the moon 25 Dec 68

4827 Exploration is really the essence of the human spirit.

To joint session of Congress *NY Times* 10 Jan 69

Diane Boyd naturalist

4828 In the bakery of life, I've got a really enormous cake.

On researching the ecology of wolves in the northern Rocky Mountains *Sports Illustrated* 18 Oct 93

Jack Bronowski journalist

4829 You will die but the carbon will not. . . [but] will return to the soil, and there a plant may take it up again in time; sending it once more on a cycle of plant and animal life.

"Biography of an Atom—and the Universe" *NY Times* 13 Oct 68

4830 Sooner or later every one of us breathes an atom that has been breathed before by anyone you can think of who has lived before us—Michaelangelo or George Washington or Moses.

ib

4831 The essence of science: ask an impertinent question, and you are on the way to the pertinent answer.

The Ascent of Man Little, Brown 73

4832 The most wonderful discovery made by scientists is science itself.

A Sense of the Future New American Library 77

Paul Brooks journalist

4833 You can murder land for private profit. You can leave the corpse for all to see, and nobody calls the cops.

The Pursuit of Wilderness Houghton Mifflin 71

Hugh Carlisle Counsel for Nuclear Initiatives Inspectorate

4834 A classic example of brains in neutral.

On failure to shut down potentially explosive machinery at a Nuclear Electronic plant *London Times* 14 Sep 95

Kenneth Carpenter paleontologist, Denver Museum of Natural History

4835 Tyrannossaurus was truly the Schwarzenegger of dinosaurs.

Likening the powerful forelimbs of a carnivorous dinosaur to Hollywood's Arnold Schwarzenegger *NY Times* 3 Jul 90

Rachel Carson environmentalist

4836 Over increasingly large areas of the United States, spring now comes unheralded by the return of the birds, and the early mornings are strangely silent where once they were filled with the beauty of bird song.

On the effect of insecticides and fertilizers *Silent Spring* Houghton Mifflin 62

4837 As crude a weapon as a cave man's club, the chemical barrage has been hurled against the fabric of life.

ib

Erwin Chargaff Professor of Biological Chemistry, Columbia

4838 Science is wonderfully equipped to answer the question "How?" but gets terribly confused when you ask the question "Why?"

Columbia Forum Summer 69

4839 Science is now the craft of the manipulation, substitution and deflection of the forces of nature. What I see coming is a gigantic slaughterhouse, an Auschwitz, in which valuable enzymes, hormones, and so on will be extracted instead of gold teeth.

ib

Georges Charpak physicist

4840 I can buy a new pair of shoes this afternoon.

On selection for the $1.2 million Nobel Prize for work on atom smashers *Washington Post* 15 Oct 92

Francis Collins Geneticist, University of Michigan

4841 [It is like] trying to find a burned-out light bulb in a house located somewhere between the East and West coasts without knowing the state, much less the town or street the house is on.

On genes responsible for specific illnesses *Time* 17 Jan 94

4842 The use of. . . technology for sex selection insults the reasons I went into genetics in the first place. Sex is not a disease, but a trait.

On selection process that could lead to abortion of fetuses with undesirable characertisitics or the wrong sex *ib*

Edwin G Conkling Professor of Embryology, Princeton

4843 Wooden legs are not inherited but wooden heads may be.

On the view that acquired characteristics can be inherited, recalled on Conkling's death 21 Nov 52

4844 Apparently the anti-evolutionist demands to see a monkey or an ass transfomed into a man, though he must be familiar enough with the reserve process.

ib

William Conway President, NY Zoological Society

4845 We want zoos to become conservation cows flowing with the sweet milk of support.

On raising funds for wild life presservation *NY Times* 25 Apr 95

Leon Cooper Professor of Science, Brown University

4846 A theory is a well-defined structure that we hope is in correspondence with what we observe. It's an architecture, a cathedral.

Quoted by George Johnson *In the Palace of Memory* Knopf 91

4847 To say that science is logical is like saying that a painting is paint.

ib

Jacques-Yves Cousteau oceanologist

4848 The best way to observe fish is to become a fish.

On Aqua Lung's use in undersea exploration *National Georgraphic* Oct 52

4849 We must plant the sea and herd its animals... for that is what civilization is all about—farming replacing hunting.

Interview 17 Jul 71

4850 A scientist... is a curious man looking through... the keyhole of nature, trying to know what's going on.

Christian Science Monitor 21 Jul 71

Colonel Richard O Covey US Air Force

4851 *Endeavour* has a firm handshake with Mr Hubble's telescope.

To Houston Mission Control on snaring the Hubble space telescope on $1.6 billion crippled spacecraft 357 miles above the earth *NY Times* 5 Dec 93

George B Craig Jr Professor of Entomology, Notre Dame

4852 They're trying to clean out the sea with teaspoons.

On the futility of zappers that kill 100 to 200 mosquitoes a night as compared to 60,000 produced by one female in half a summer *Wall Street Journal* 25 Jul 94

James Crocker Space Telescope Science Institute, Baltimore

4853 The Hubble... could detect fireflies in Tokyo.

On long-range capabilities of the Hubble space telescope *Washington Post* 14 Jan 94

Helena Curtis journalist

4854 You and I are flesh and blood, but we are also stardust.

On formation of the planet Earth *Biology* Worth 68, quoted in Worth's advertisement saluting Curtis' work *NY Times* 2 Aug 87

David Deamer Professor of Biology, University of California

4855 Origin-of-life work... [is] a primordial soup.

On researching self-reproducing molecules *Christian Science Monitor* 4 Apr 85

John Dewey Professor of Philosophy, Columbia University

4856 Every great advance in science has issued from a new audacity of imagination.

Recalled on Dewey's death 1 Jun 52

Jeanette Dezor journalist

4857 You can drop humans anywhere and they'll thrive—only the rat does as well.

Smithsonian May 86

Stuart Diamond reporter

4858 A supervisor... decided to deal with it only after the next tea break.

On mistaking a methyl isocyanate leak for a water leak with the resulting death of at least 3,000 persons 2 Dec 84 near Phopal, India, Union Carbide plant *NY Times* 28 Jan 85

Baba Dioum Sengalese conservationist

4859 We will conserve only what we love... love only what we understand... understand only what we are taught.

On raising funds for Kenya's National Animal Orphanage *NY Times* 25 Apr 95

Mildred Donlon Chemical Specialist, Advanced Research Projects Agency, US Department of Defense

4860 A singing canary on a chip.

On development of a biosensor to detect chemical weapons and sprays like canaries sensed poison gas in mines *US News & World Report* 3 Apr 95

Frank D Drake Professor of Astronomy, University of California

4861 The way we were going about it... was like looking for the needle by strolling past the haystack every now and then.

On limitations of range and duration of observation in search for life in outer space *Is Anyone Out There?* Delacorte 92

Alan Dressler Professor of Astrophysics, Carnegie Institution

4862 Most people are awed by the size of the universe and our being so small... [but] complexity resides not out there but here, in our biology and our minds.

Fortune 8 Oct 90

4863 The one idea that was too good to be true turned out to be too good to be true.

On discarding belief that there was an even spread of matter from the explosive moment of cosmic creation *NY Times* 3 Jan 91

René DuBois journalist

4864 In science the credit goes to the man who convinces the world, not to the man to whom the idea first occurs.

The Conquest of Tuberculosis Gollanz 53

Jack Dyer Director, Pioneer 10 Project

4865 Today, Neptune; yesterday, Pluto; tomorrow, on to the stars.

On the first unmanned spacecraft to leave the realm of known planets *NY Times* 14 Jun 83

Sylvia Earle President, Deep Ocean Engineering, Leandro CA

4866 Each fish has a personality... they aren't just tasty morsels to have with a lemon wedge.

On swimming with Grand Cayman Island's sergeant majors and yellowtails *Life* Dec 95

Paul Ehrlich Professor of Biological Studies, Stanford

4867 [The National Academy of Sciences] would be unable to give a unanimous decision if asked whether the sun would rise tomorrow.

Look 1 Apr 70

Albert Einstein physicist

4868 The grand aim of all science is to cover the greatest number of empirical facts by logical deduction from the smallest number of hypotheses or axioms.

Life 9 Jan 50

4869 Science without religion is lame, religion without science is blind.

Out of My Later Years Thames 50

4870 The most incomprehensible thing about the universe is that it is at all comprehensible.

The World As I See It Covici, Friede 1934, recalled on Einstein's death 18 Apr 55

4871 Some recent work by E Fermi and L Szilard... leads me to expect that the element uranium may be turned into a new and importance source of energy in the immediate future.

Letter of August 1939 telling President Franklin D Roosevelt of the possibility of an atomic bomb *ib*

4872 $E=mc^2$

Mathematical formula for theory of relativity that became synonymous with his name *ib*

4873 Politics are for the moment. An equation is for eternity.

ib

4874 The cosmic religious experience is the strongest and the noblest driving force behind scientific research.

ib

4875 General annihilation beckons.

On radioactive atmospheric poisoning, comment in rare television appearance, quoted by Eric F Goldman *The Crucial Decade—And After* Random House 60

4876 Now he's gone slightly ahead of me, leaving this strange world. That doesn't mean anything. For us believing physicists this separation between past, present, and future has the value of more illusion, however tenacious.

On the death of a friend a month before Einstein's death, recalled in *NY Times* 1 Dec 72

4877 Concern for man and his fate must always form the chief interest of all technical endeavors.... Never forget this in the midst of your diagrams and equations.

London Times 1 Jul 85

4878 [She has] the soul of a herring.

On Marie Curie, quoted by Susan Quinn *Marie Curie* Simon & Schuster 95

Kenan T Erim Professor of Classics, NYU

4879 Aphrodisias... a place haunted with memories in marble.

On two decades of digging through the city that the Emperor Augustus called the most beautiful in Asia *National Geographic* Aug 57

4880 Blind marble eyes stare up at the blue Anatolian sky... the face of a fellow man whose memory lives still in this bit of stone, a fellow man whose image we have resurrected from centuries of darkness.

ib

Edna Ferber novelist

4881 Science had married the wilderness and was taming the savage shrew.

On *Alaska Ice Palace* Doubleday 58

Timothy Ferris journalist

4882 History plays on the great the trick of calcifying them into symbols.

On decalcifying Galileo as a "devoted careerist with a genius for public relations" *Coming of Age in the Milky Way* Morrow 88

Klaus Fuchs physicist

4883 It was always my intention, when I had helped the Russians to take over everything, to get up and tell them what is wrong with their own system.

On arrest for sharing nuclear secrets, quoted by Robert Caldwell *Williams Klaus Fuchs, Atom Spy* Harvard 87

Birute M F Galdikas Canadian archaeologist

4884 A walk in the rainforest is a walk into the mind of God.

On studying orangutans *Reflections of Eden* Little, Brown 95

Paul H Gebhard Director, Kinsey Institute for Sex Research

4885 It is a crossing of a Rubicon in life history.

To American Association for Advancement of Science on the initial experience on sexual intercourse *NY Times* 30 Dec 67

David Gelernter Professor of Computer Science, Yale

4886 Straight ahead for the Hall of Stodginess. Dreariness upstairs to your right.

Reporting on American Museum of Natural History's image as a place of musty corridors and dreary dioramas *NY Times* 5 Mar 95

Harold M Gibson Chief Meterologist, NYC Weather Bureau

4887 Looking out the window is the most important thing if you want to know what's going on.

NY Times 30 Mar 84

Captain Robert L Gibson Commander of Spaceship *Atlantis*

4888 Houston, we have capture.

Message to ground controllers on an American space shuttle's first successful docking with a Russian space station in two decades *NY Times* 30 Jun 95

William Gibson author

4889 Cyberspace is where you are when you're on the telephone.

Quoted by *US News & World Report* editor Dick Sussman, Station WAMU Washington 21 Jun 94

Walter Gilbert Professor of Molecular Biology, Harvard

4890 To recognize that we are determined by a finite collection of information that is knowable will change our view of ourselves... the closing of an intellectual frontier with what we will have to come to know.

On how new knowledge of gene therapy alters the outlook on infinite human potential *Time* 17 Jan 94

Alfred G Gilman Pharmacologist, University of Texas Southwestern Medical Center, Dallas

4891 I secreted a hell of a lot of adrenalin and then that reached my adrenergic receptors and they responded via the G proteins.

On becoming a co-winner of the Nobel Prize for Medicine for discovery of how key molecular mechanisms help cells respond to signals from within the body and the outside world *Washington Post* 11 Oct 94

Peter Vilhelm Glob Danish archeologist

4892 His face wore a gentle expression—the eyes lightly closed, the lips pursed, as if in silent prayer... as though the man's soul had for a moment returned from another world, through the gate in the western sky.

On viewing a body buried for 2,000 years in a peat bog in Jutland *NY Times* 2 Jun 91

Walter Goodman critic

4893 Within the most demure pussy cat lurks a creature of the wild.

Reviewing television documentary *Cats: Caressing the Tiger* *NY Times* 9 Jan 91

Dick Gore Science Editor *National Geographic*

4894 [DNA is] the most celebrated chemical of our time, the master choreographer of the living cell and carrier of the genetic code.

Reporting on deoxyriobonuclaic acid as part of an explosion of knowledge that "utterly transformed the life sciences" *National Geographic* Sep 76

4895 If anything illustrates what has happened in biology, it is this profound new ability to take the very stuff of life out of the cell... isolate it in a test tube... dissect it, and probe the deep mysteries borne in its fragments.

ib

Stephen Jay Gould Professor of Paleontology, Harvard

4896 [It] seals our fate in... asserting specialness for human ancestry.

On Chinese scientists' discovery of fossils of *Yunnanozoon lividum*, a tiny half-a-billion-year-old creature showing vestigial traces of a spinal cord *NY Times* 5 Nov 95

4897 As for our place in the history of life, we are of it, not above it.

ib

Paul Graham Harvard graduate student

4898 The culture for making great software is slightly crazy people working late at night.

On US lead in software production *NY Times* 8 Nov 88

Ronald Graham Director, Mathematical Sciences, Bell Laboratories

4899 A creation of pure thought cannot be protected.

Predicting wide use of Norman Karmarkar's systems of equations that were sometimes too complex for the most powerful computers *NY Times* 19 Nov 84

Günter Grass novelist

4900 We of the long tails... of the presentient whiskers... of the perpetually growing teeth... the serried footnotes to man, his proliferating commentary. We, indestructible!

The Rat Harcourt Brace Jovanovich 87, quoted by Steven Erlanger "In New York, Rats Survive the Man Race" *NY Times* 2 Nov 87

Georgy Grechko Soviet cosmonaut

4901 During prolonged flights in the absence of gravity, human height increases.

On Yuri Romanenko's growth of two-fifths of an inch during ten and a half months in space *US News & World Report* 11 Jan 88

Celia Green environmentalist

4902 The way to do research is to attack the facts at the point of greatest astonishment.

The Decline and Fall of Science Hamish Hamilton 72

Harry W Greene Professor of Integrative Biology, University of California at Berkeley

4903 I've thought a gadzillion times it would be so cool for a short period of time to be a black-tailed rattlesnake, to know what it felt like.

On guess that many biologists share the same wonderment, *NY Times* 9 Aug 94

Susan Greenfield Fellow, Lincoln College, Oxford

4904 Bloodlusts, fates, the struggle of the individual against destiny. So much more exciting than spirogyra.

On abandoning the study of Greek in favor of science *London Times* 26 Dec 94

Gus Grissom US Astronaut

4905 Occasionally, I lie in bed at night and think now why in the hell do I want to get up on that thing?

Recalled when Grissom and two others were burned to death in an aborted takeoff of *Saturn I* 27 Jan 67

J B S Haldane geneticist

4906 The universe is not only queerer than we imagine, but queerer than we can imagine.

Quoted by Oliver Sacks *An Anthropologist on Mars* Knopf 95

Philip Hamburger journalist

4907 [Oppenheimer is] tense, dedicated, deeper than deep, somewhat haunted, uncertain, calm, confident, and full, full, full of knowledge, not only of particles and things but of men and motives, and of the basic humanity that may be the only savior we have in this strange world he and his colleagues have discovered.

On physicist J Robert Oppenheimer, Director of Institute for Advanced Study, Princeton NJ, quoted by Fred W Friendly *Due to Circumstances Beyond Our Control* Random House 67

James Hamilton-Paterson oceanographer

4908 Stately, funereal, mysterious, it spoke ultimately of... time's liquid correlative which gulps down objects, lives, all that was and will be.

The Great Deep: The Sea and Its Thresholds Random House 92

Larry D Harris Professor of Wildlife Ecology, University of Florida

4909 Stewardship of land should be based on the principle that resources are not given to us by our parents, but are loaned to us by our children.

LA Times 22 Jun 87

Stephen Hawking Lucasian Professor of Mathematics, Cambridge

4910 My goal is simple. It is a complete understanding of the universe, why it is as it is and why it exists at all.

Washington Post 15 Apr 88

4911 We see the universe the way it is because if it were different, we would not be here to observe it.

ib

4912 The ultimate triumph of human reason... to know the mind of God.

On what it would mean if humankind learned "why... we and the universe exist" *A Brief History of Time* Bantam 88

Harold Hayes conservationist

4913 Anthropomorphism has been an irresistible urge, from the mega-industry Walt Disney built around a mouse, backward to the ancient Egyptians' unusually high regard for the cat.

On "the troublesome phenomenon of the tendency to ascribe human characteristics to the animal observed" *Life* Nov 86

Dr Jack Horner Curator of Paleontology, Museum of the Rockies

4914 In the lifetime of one person, we went from figuring out where we came from to figuring out how to get rid of ourselves.

On the 80 years between Darwin's *Origin of Species* and the nuclear bomb *Time* 26 Apr 93

Peter Huber Fellow, Institute for Policy Research, NYC

4915 Telephones are something the oppressors of individuals have always hated.

Christian Science Monitor 31 May 95

Robert Jastrow Director, Goddard Institute for Space Studies

4916 The moon is a Rosetta stone of the planets.

Time 18 Jul 69

Donald C Johanson President, Institute of Human Origins, Berkeley CA

4917 There are no real surprises in the anatomy.

On the earliest known direct human ancestor, 3.2 million years old *NY Times* 22 Sep 94

George Johnson author

4918 Science. . . is not a description of the physical world, but a description of how the world interacts with the mind—and how experience is translated into the structures we call memories.

In the Palace of Memory Knopf 91

4919 Neurotransmitter turned on receptors, calcium came in through the membrane and activated calpain, calpain ate the cytoskeleton and caused the synapse somehow to change.

On points of transfer in memory retention *ib*

David Johnston geologist

4920 Vancouver! Vancouver! This is it. . .

Last words radioed from a point six miles below erupting volcano on Oregon's Mt St Helens *National Geographic* Jan 81

Steve Jones Department of Genetics and Bometry, University College, London

4921 Research is wonder.

When asked if research destroys wonder *London Daily Telegraph* 26 Oct 92

4922 [We were discussing the] evolution of penis size in Greek statues.

On a coffee break with colleagues *ib*

Michio Kaku Professor of Physics, City University of New York

4923 It's like using Scotch tape to pull together a mule, a whale, a tiger and a giraffe.

On scientific research *US News & World Report* 9 May 94

William M Kelso archeologist

4924 [It is] the archeology of poverty.

On excavation of slave quarters to place them in perspective to graciousness of 18th century Virginia *NY Times* 12 Sep 88

Murray Kempton journalist

4925 Elegance was for him its own absolution.

On atomic scientist J Robert Oppenheimer *Rebellions, Perversities and Main Events* Times Books 94

John F Kennedy 35th US President

4926 America has tossed its cap over the wall of space, and we have no choice but to follow it.

At dedication of Aerospace Medical Health Center, San Antonio TX, two days before Kennedy's assassination 22 Nov 63

Nikita S Khrushchev Soviet Premier

4927 It is not a question of mooning him but of demooning him.

On the prospect of a successful return of Russia's first man to reach the moon *NY Times* 8 Sep 62

4928 Our national emblem is already on the moon, but we don't want to place a coffin beside it.

ib

4929 We were sheep seeing a new gate for the first time. . . peasants in a marketplace.

On realizing Russia's capabilities for rocket warfare, quoted by Walter A McDouglass *The Heavens and the Earth* Basic Books 85

Nicola Khuri Lebanese physicist

4930 It's like looking for a needle in a haystack and finding the farmer's daughter.

Offering a definition for serendipity in a conversation with English physicist Stephen Hawking *Washington Post* 15 Apr 88

Martin Luther King, Jr civil rights leader

4931 As marvelous as the stars is the mind of the person who studies them.

Quoted by Alan Dressler *Voyage to the Great Attractor* Knopf 95

Charles Kuralt commentator

4932 It takes an earthquake to remind us that we walk on the crust of an unfinished earth.

Sunday Morning CBS TV 23 Jan 94

Edwin H Land chairman, Polaroid Corp

4933 On a sunny day in Santa Fe my little daughter asked why she could not see at once the picture I had just taken of her.

On devising the initial technolgy in an hour's walk, recalled on Land's death 1 Mar 91

Leon Lederman US Government researcher and Nobel laureate

4934 Congress, in its infinite wisdom, said "Oops, no."

On Washington's changing mood toward "big science" that led to abandonment of a $2 billion superconducting, supercollider proton smasher *NY Times* 26 Oct 93

Jorgen Lehmann Sahlgren Hospital, Gothenburg, Sweeden

4935 I must work completely independently. . . [with] my thoughts as delicate and as easily disturbed as a spider's web.

On developing anti-tuberculosis vaccine, quoted by Frank Ryan *The Forgotten Plague* Little, Brown 93

Richard C Lewontin Professor of Zoology, Harvard

4936 The requirement for great success is great ambition. . . for triumph over other men, not merely over nature.

Quoted by Jane S Smith *Patenting the Sun: Polio and the Salk Vaccine* Morrow 90

Alan Lightman physicist and novelist

4937 They are so beautiful, the equations. . . their precision and power.

On falling in love with physics *Good Benito* Pantheon 95

4938 The world buckled at its knees when Bennett took his first algebra course.

On a 13-year-old's discovery of math's mystical power to define and purify the problems of the physical world *ib*

4939 He gets the same feeling as seeing moonrise over trees.

On understanding an equation *ib*

Art Linkletter entertainer

4940 Thunder does all the barking, but it's lightning that bites.

A Child's Garden of Misinformation Geiss 65

London Times

4941 The funeral rites of other tongues are conducted in English.

"Homo Loquens" editorial on American Association for the Advancement of Science warning that nearly 3,000 languages could become extinct 24 Feb 95

Konrad Lorenz psychologist

4942 It is a good morning exercise for a research scientist to discard a pet hypothesis every day before breakfast. It keeps him young.

On Aggression Harcourt, Brace 66

Archibald MacLeish poet and statesman

4943 To see the earth as it truly is, small and blue and beautiful in that eternal silence where it floats, is to see ourselves as riders on the earth together, brothers on that bright lovliness in the eternal cold—brothers who know now they are truly brothers.

On space capsule *Apollo 8 NY Times* 28 Dec 68

Norman Mailer novelist

4944 Physics is the church, and engineering the most devout sinner.

Of a Fire on the Moon Little, Brown 69, quoted in Thomas Mallon's survey of literature on the first moon landing *NY Times* 16 Jul 89

Andrew Malcolm reporter

4945 An air of concern, a note of awe and a sense of futility.

On Chicago's view of Lake Michigan's 40-foot high eroding waves *NY Times* 5 Dec 86

Alan Nunn May British physicist

4946 162 micrograms of Uranium 233, in the form of acid, contained in a thick lamina.

Atomic formula given to Soviet agent two weeks before test explosion in New Mexico *Guardian Weekly* 6 Aug 95

David McCullough author and commentator

4947 [The Panama Canal was] the moon shot of its era.

A Man, A Plan, A Canal, Panama PBS TV 3 Nov 87

Robert D McFadden reporter

4948 A monster with the heart of a blizzard and the soul of a hurricane.

On one of the Atlantic seaboard's most powerful storms *NY Times* 14 Mar 93

Ron McNair Professor of Physics, Massachusetts Institute of Technology

4949 A tear-drop of green.

On viewing the earth from a space shuttle *Newsweek* 10 Feb 86

4950 One individual, peacefully and non-violently, standing between the gun and the seal... the harpoon and the whale... factory and the stream... can force his opponent into a decision and can make for change.

On the founding of Greenpeace conservation project *London Observer* 24 Dec 78

James A Michener author

4951 He had a good life and he stumbled his gigantic way through it with dignity and gentleness.

On prehistoric mastadons *Alaska* Random House 88

John Moffat physicist

4952 Any fundamental theory of physics is beautiful. If it isn't, it's probably wrong.

Bulletin University of Toronto 5 May 86

4953 Physics is imagination in a straight jacket.

ib

Hans Moravec Director, Mobile Robot Laboratory, Carnegie Mellon University

4954 Our machines... will mature... into something transcending everything we know—in whom we can take pride when they refer to themselves as our descendants.

Mind Children Harvard 88

Bruce Murray research scientist

4955 The quality of a civilization is measured not by what it has to do, but by what it wants to do.

Exploring Space Random House 91

4956 Space itself is not the final frontier. The mind is.

ib

J Robert Oppenheimer physicist

4957 I am not sure the miserable thing will work, nor that it can be gotten to target except by ox-cart. That we become committed to it as a way to save the country and the peace appears to me full of dangers.

On development of the atomic bomb, quoted in *In This Fabulous Century 1950–60* Time-Life Books 70

4958 A technically sweet problem.

On the hydrogen bomb, quoted by Peter Wyden *Day One* Simon & Schuster 84

4959 It wasn't so very dry. I can still feel the warm blood on my hands.

On being told that his investigation as a Communist Party member in 1954 was a dry crucifixion *ib*

4960 Typical of the physical scientist! To give up something very difficult so as to try the impossible.

On James B Conant's resignation as president of Harvard to become High Commissioner for Germany, quoted by James G Hershberg *James B Conant* Knopf 93

4961 Those two scorpions in a bottle.

On the US and Soviets in the early 1950s, quoted by Anthony Cave Brown *Treason in the Blood* Houghton Mifflin 94

Hal Osburn Texas Parks and Wildlife Development Department

4962 It's a win-win-win situation. Industry wins. The public wins. The environment wins.

On sinking of oil rigs as artificial reefs *Washington Post* 4 Sep 93

4963 A permanent artificial reef is born, and all the fish are thankful.

ib

Dennis Overbye physicist

4964 Cosmology is serious business and in our hearts we are nothing if not cosmologists, hanging in a cold cage sifting the ruthless jewels of existence.

On the scientific quest for the secret of the universe *Lonely Hearts of the Cosmos* HarperCollins 91

4965 Some day Sandage's atoms and those of everyone in that lecture hall would be splashed across space, stripped, and recombined in some as-yet-unborn star, or slumped into a black hole.

On astronomer Allan Sandage *ib*

4966 Sandage, a cosmic quipster, edgy as a razor, scat quick, and humorously dry as a lemon, standing on the lip of the stage as if it were the edge of eternity, one eye on the audience scanning for trouble, some hard fact, the other one gazing much farther.

ib

Jake Page editor and naturalist

4967 Humbling and exalting... the result of 30 years of voyeurism that ranks with the great scientific achievements of the 20th century.

Guardian Weekly 25 Nov 90 on Jane Goodall's study of the chimpanzees of Gombe *Through a Window* Houghton Mifflin 90

James K Page Jr journalist

4968 The most scientifically sophisticated society known to history insists on building on faults, floodplains, and evanescent beach fronts, and calls the inevitable disasters that occur "acts of God."

On earthquakes *Smithsonian* Jul 78

William Penney nuclear physicist

4969 Five or six will knock us out; to be on the safe side, seven or eight. I'll have another gin-and-tonic, if you would be so kind!

At Macmillan-Kennedy meeting in Bermuda on how many hundred-megaton bombs would be needed to destroy Britain, quoted by Alistair Horne *Harold Macmillan* Viking 89

Julio C Perla Florida zoo curator

4970 Our monkeys don't know what it means to escape because you can't escape from freedom.

On animals who had roamed at will prior to even greater freedom provided by Hurricane Andrew *NY Times* 22 Sep 92

Jacques Piccard oeanographer

4971 Slowly, surely, in the name of science and humanity, the *Trieste* took possession of the abyss, the last extreme on our earth that remained to be conquered.

On making a record 35,800-foot dive to a submerged ship *National Geographic* Aug 60

John E Pike Senior Analyst, Federation of American Scientists

4972 It's the triumph of silicon over steel.

On the computer chip's capabilities in processing instant information for planes, bombs, sensors and cruise missiles in the Persian Gulf War *NY Times* 21 Jan 91

Joel Primack Professor of Physics, University of California, Santa Cruz

4973 [It is] the handwriting of God.

On galaxies of the night sky *Newsweek* 4 May 92

Robert Pyle conservationist

4974 A gold curtain parts and a rain of golden sequins falls before you.

On the Monarch butterfly migration to Mexico *NY Times* 29 Nov 86

W V O Quine Professor of Philosophy, Harvard

4975 The totality of our so-called knowledge or beliefs, from the most casual matters of geography and history to the profoundest laws of atomic physics or even of pure mathematics and logic, is a man-made fabric which impinges on experience only along the edges.

Quoted by A J Ayer *Philosophy in the 20th Century* Random House 82

4976 Science is like a boat, which we rebuild plank by plank while staying afloat in it. The philosopher and the scientist are in the same boat.

Quoted by George Johnson *The Palace of Memory* Knopf 91

I I Rabi Professor at Large, Columbia University

4977 [People consider the scientist] a creature scattering antibiotics with one hand and atomic bombs with the other.

Comment of a Nobel laureate on appointment at Columbia *NY Times* 28 Oct 64

4978 Science. . . a great game. . . the playing field is the universe itself.

ib

4979 Red tape ran in his veins.

On working with James B Conant, quoted by Daniel J Hersh *James B Conant: Harvard to Hiroshima and the Making of the Nuclear Age* Knopf 93

Ayn Rand novelist

4980 The rocket rose slowly. . . a pale cylinder with a blinding oval of white light at the bottom, like an upturned candle with its flame directed at the earth.

On *Apollo II*, *The Voice of Reason* New American Library 88

Anne Raver reporter

4981 The beat of their powerful wings could be thunder. Or the thumping of your own excited heart.

On 500,000 sandhill cranes in a springtime visit to Nebraska *NY Times* 21 Mar 93

4982 Their honks and shrill cries and low guttural purrs mix in a joyous din that draws some ancient music up out of the soul.

ib

Roger Ray Director of Pacific Operations US Energy Department

4983 All they knew was that the sun came up twice that morning.

On residents of the Marshall Islands after a 1954 nuclear test *NY Times* 9 Jun 93

T R Reid journalist

4984 It was a seminal event of postwar science, one of those rare demonstratons that changes everything.

On the development of the microchip *The Chip* Simon & Schuster 85

4985 A circuit with 100,000 components could easily require a million different soldered connections. . . [but] the only machine that could make the connection was the human hand.

On the miniaturization of computer components *ib*

Arthur H Robinson Professor Emeritus of Cartography and Geography, University of Wisconsin

4986 The land masses look like wet, ragged, long winter underwear hung out to dry on the Arctic Circle.

On the aesthetics of projections by West German historian Arno Peters *NY Times* 25 Oct 88

Rustom Roy Professor of Engineering, Pennsylvania State University

4987 Little more than welfare queens in white coats.

On plethora of tax-supported research scientists *Newsweek* 14 Jan 91

Carl Sagan Professor of Astronomy, Cornell University

4988 Not explaining science seems to me perverse. When you're in love, you want to tell the world.

On writing about science *Washington Post* 9 Jan 94

4989 There is perhaps no better a demonstration of the folly of human conceits than this distant image of our tiny world.

On a space-voyager's view of earth *Time* 9 Jan 95

Jim St Pierre Director, Maine Woods Project, Wilderness Society

4990 That's the ghost of Christmases future.

On tree preservation NPR 21 Aug 93

Allan R Sandage Hole Observatory, Santa Barbara CA

4991 The greatest mystery is why there is something instead of nothing, and the greatest something is this thing we call life.

Quoted by Alan Lightman and Roberta Brawer *Through a Window* Harvard 90

4992 I am entirely baffled by you and me. Astronomy is a science in which you are not able to touch anything you study.

NY Times 12 Mar 91

4993 The study of origins is the art of drawing sufficient conclusions from insufficient evidence.

ib

David Sarnoff Chair, Radio Corporation of America (RCA)

4994 Freedom is the oxygen without which science cannot breathe.

Quoted by Emily Davie *Profile of America* Crowell 54

4995 Man is still the great miracle and the greatest problem on this earth.

First message sent with atomic-powered electricity 27 Jan 54 *ib*

4996 In most of the world, life is still an earth-packed floor, an empty bowl, and a premature death.

At Awards Dinner of National Institute of Social Science, quoted by Claudia ("Lady Bird") Johnson *A White House Diary* Holt Rinehart Winston 70

Susan Schiefelbein journalist

4997 Within our bodies course the same elements that flame in the stars.

The Incredible Machine National Geographic Book Service 86

David Schwartz US Geology Service

4998 They aren't little puppies. They are big, biting dogs and they each get unleashed every few hundred years.

On earthquakes originating from California's San Andreas Fault and its branches *National Geographic* Apr 95 *ib*

4999 There'll be a lot of wine on the ground.

On future damage to California vineyards *ib*

Richard Sharpe reproductive biologist

5000 If men were selected for breeding on the same criteria as farmyard animals, most would go to the slaughterhouse.

London Times 22 May 92

B F Skinner behavioral psychologist

5001 The real problem is not whether machines think but whether men do.

Contingencies of Reinforcement Appleton Century Crofts 69

5002 The mind seems to be merely the double of the person whose mind it is. . . a replica, a surrogate, a *doppelgänger*.

NY Times 13 Sep 87

Clyde Collins Snow forensic anthropologist

5003 The ground is like a beautiful woman. If you treat her gently, she'll tell you all her secrets.

On exploring the massacre of thousands of Mayan Indians in Guatemala in the early 1980s *Washington Post* 18 Dec 91

Bjarne Stroustrup Bell Laboratory scientist

5004 What I deal in is control of complexity.

On making computers work the way people think *Fortune* 8 Oct 90

Oleg Struin Soviet Commander in Antarctica

5005 I polarman. No problem for polarman.

Smithsonian Nov 84

Albert Szent-Gyorgyi Nobel laureate

5006 Discovery consists of seeing what everybody has seen and thinking what nobody has thought.

In Irving John Good ed *The Scientist Speculates* Basic Books 62

5007 Research is four things: brains... eyes... machine with which to measure and, fourth, money.

Recalled on Szent-Gyorgi's death 22 Oct 86

TASS, Soviet Press Agency

5008 The moon speaks Russian.

On message from *Luna 9*, first spacecraft to achieve a soft landing on the moon *NY Times* 6 Feb 66

Estevao Taukane Chief, Bakairi Indians

5009 We can't depend on smoke signals any longer.

On the use of cellular telephones in the southern Amazon to reach government officials in Brasilia *Christian Science Monitor* 31 May 95

Edward Teller atomic scientist

5010 I'm not worrying about the situation. I'm worrying about the people who should be worrying about it.

On Russia's development of nuclear weapons, quoted by Richard Rhodes *The Making of the Atomic Bomb* Simon & Schuster 86

5011 It's a boy.

Coded message from the Pacific to Los Alamos on the first successful dentonation of the hydrogen bomb *ib*

5012 The use of weapons is none of my business, and I will have none of it.

On being asked if the newly perfected hydrogen bomb should be used in the Korean War *ib*

John Von Neumann Fellow, Institute for Advanced Study,

5013 In England... he could have gone around among his students with his penis hanging out, and everyone would have been charmed by his eccentricity.

On the respect with which atomic scientist J Robert Oppenheimer was held, quoted by David Halberstam *The Fifties* Villard 93

Selman Waksman Professor of Soil Microbiology, Rutgers

5014 Doctors surrounding Ninotchka looked upon her... as a child Lazarus.

On a 9-year-old Russian girl who responded to streptomycin to survive tuberculous meningitis, quoted by Frank Ryan *The Forgotten Plague* Little, Brown 93

Wansworth Council village board

5015 [Canadian Geese] are the thugs of the bird kingdom.

On Britain's crisis with aggressive fowl *Country Life* 14 Apr 94

Jonathan Weiner naturalist

5016 [It is the] variations that we measure in millimeters that are the cornerstones of evolution.

The Beak of the Finch Knopf 94

Wang Wenghu Chinese conservationist

5017 Distant water cannot put out a nearby fire.

On difficulties of working from Beijing to protect the giant panda in the wild, quoted by George B Schaller's *The Last Panda* University of Chicago Press 93

Victor Weisskopf Professor of Physics, Massachusetts Institute of Technology

5018 A virulent case of collective mental disease.

Reflecting 40 years later on his pioneering work on the atomic bomb, quoted by Peter Wyden *Day One* Simon & Schuster 84

Edward O Wilson Professor of Science, Harvard

5019 The green prehuman earth is the mystery we were chosen to solve, a guide to the birthplace of our spirit.

Quoted by T H Watkins *Washington Post* 27 Sep 92 reviewing Wilson's *The Diversity of Life* Harvard 92

5020 A swamp filled with snakes may be a nightmare to most, but for me it was a ceaselessly rotating lattice of wonders.

On boyhood interest in water snakes and other biota *New Yorker* 12 Dec 94

5021 I was roused by the amphetamine of ambition.

On writing *Sociobiology* Belknap 75

5022 It came by a lightning flash like knowledge from the gods.

On the epochal 1953 discovery of the DNA molecule *ib*

H Boyd Woodruff microbiologist

5023 Each biological observation has an underlying chemical cause... in unravelling the latter, one could understand the other.

Quoted by Frank Ryan *The Forgotten Plague* Little, Brown 93

Harriet Zuckerman sociologist, Mellon Foundation

5024 It's a natural attraction of quality to quality.

On study showing that half of all US Nobel laureates studied with or worked under other Nobel laureates *Christian Science Monitor* 11 Oct 85

TRAVEL

Travelers on Traveling

Dean Acheson US Secretary of State

5025 A ship sailing does not seem a conveyance going from one place to another, but something going out of one's life to an unknowable bourne.

Morning and Noon Houghton Mifflin 65

5026 Even the longest holiday can be unraveled by a woman's tongue. . . I hung up while I had the advantage of mystery.

On telephoning his wife to propose an afternoon's excursion *Grapes From Thorns* Norton 75

James Agee novelist and essayist

5027 Whatever we may think, we move for no better reason than for the plain unvarnished hell of it. And there is no better reason.

"The Great American Roadside" *Fortune* 17 Dec 90

Edward Allen journalist

5028 On worn tires, you feel close to the ground, and there is a jangling, wounded kind of weariness, that only people who did not finish college can feel.

Straight Through the Night Soho Press 89

Anon

5029 The white man is an old woman in the Arctic.

Quoted by Ernie Lyall *An Arctic Man Hurting* 79

5030 One positive thing about crashes—they sure make flying safer.

Unidentified airline executive *Toronto Globe & Mail* 21 May 80

5031 Our kids die laughing.

Safe-driving brochure sponsored by Ortho Pharmaceutical Corp and Johnson & Johnson 87

5032 First in flight.

Slogan commemorating 75th anniversary of the Wright brothers at Kitty Hawk NC, used on NC state license plates 87

5033 The lonely vigil of the night is known only to men of courage.

Inscription on stone monument memorializing two snow-plow drivers killed in Colorado avalanches in 1970s *NY Times* 3 Mar 87

5034 I've never unbuckled a dead person.

Highway patrol officer commending use of seatbelts *The Daily Plant* New York City Hall 30 Aug 88

5035 An incident at altitude.

Standard in-house airlines term used prior to making public disclosure of plane crashes *Time* 2 Jan 89

5036 There are old pilots and bold pilots, but there are no old, bold pilots.

Quoted by Charles Kuralt *A Life on the Road* Putnam 90

5037 The lift is being fixed for the next day. During that time we regret that you will be unbearable.

Sign in a Bucharest hotel *Forbes* 15 Oct 90

5038 Cooles and Heates: If you want just condition of warm in your room, please control yourself.

Japanese information book on air conditioning *ib*

5039 The manager has personally passed all the water served here.

In an Acapulco hotel *ib*

5040 The flattening of underwear with pleasure is the job of the chambermaid.

Yugoslavian hotel *ib*

5041 There'll be carloads of Louises/ From Parisian stripteases/ Importing foul diseases/ Into Kent./ There'll be Swedes of a charmless candor/ Coming over to philander,/ Spreading Left-wing propaganda/ About wealth./ Belgian girls of vast proportions,/ Who have failed to take precautions,/ Driving over for abortions/ On the Health.

Ode to the Chunnel on opening of tunnel and influx of French to use nationalized health care *Newsweek* 22 Mar 93

5042 You couldn't know the difference with your eyes closed. Isn't that how cabbies drive anyway?

Taxi dispatcher's comment on a Brooklyn cab company's use of compressed natural gas as an alternate fuel *Fortune* 22 Mar 93

5043 Objects in mirror are closer than they appear.

Warning on rear-view mirrors of US cars 93

5044 Small dogs may, at the discretion of the conductor, be carried in the bus in the arms of passengers. The decision of the conductor will be final.

Lamppost sign for Londoners boarding buses *NY Times* 23 Jan 95

5045 I'm going to look at the horses.

On how to excuse yourself to go to the bathroom in Mongolia as quoted in background briefing book prepared for Hillary Rodham Clinton's visit *Washington Post* 8 Sep 95

5046 If we are away a long time, the dog's psychiatrist fees are so high it's less expensive to take the dog with us.

On animal accommodations when traveling *USA Today* 25 Oct 95

5047 We are everywhere.
Bumper sticker for gay rights NPR 22 Dec 95

Max Apple journalist

5048 She had not invented the motel, she had changed it from a place where you had to be to a place where you wanted to be.
On Molly Bryce's design of Howard Johnson motel chain *The Prophеteers* Harper & Row 87

Serge Aru President, Friends of the Deux Chevaux

5049 The Deux Chevaux is a part of France like the beret, the baguette and Camembert. It might not be pretty, but we have grown to love it.
On the phasing-out of the Citroën Deux, "valiant little companion of the road," described by reporter Steven Greenhouse as looking like "a cross between a camel and a frog and about as aerodynamic as an aardvark" *NY Times* 9 Mar 88

Associated Press

5050 At Newark International Airport, the Rev Salvatore Malanga had just begun Mass when a woman walked up to his altar and handed him a ticket.
AP daily report 15 Apr 85

Wilbert Awdry railroad buff

5051 A steam engine is the most human of all mechanical contrivances. Unless he is sitting in a siding with his fire drawn, he always has something to say.
London Times 14 Sep 91

5052 The diesel engine does not confide in anybody. . . .[while] an electric train. . . has the soul of a worm; you could cut it in half and it wouldn't mind.
ib

Russell Baker columnist

5053 A good bit of leather, whiskery jaws, helmets like round pots. . . . In the winter, black leather jackets; this time of year, black T-shirts.
On the motorcycle culture *NY Times* 23 Jun 87

5054 Are you fellows really as mean as you dress, or are you just a bunch of regular folks hopelessly devoted to a dynamic form of gasoline romance?
ib

5055 The true biker exults in laying down an onslaught of noise that loosens the wisdom teeth of passers-by and blows soup right out the bowl.
ib

Roland Barthes journalist

5056 Cars today are almost the exact equivalent of the great Gothic cathedrals. . . the supreme creation of an era, conceived with passion by unknown artists, and consumed in image if not in usage by a whole population which appropriates them as a purely magical object.
Mythologies J Cape 72

Stephen Bartoli Product Planning Manager, Chrysler Corp

5057 When we got to the ash receiver, we said, "Jeez, most people don't even use this thing."
On the first mass-market car without an ashtray *NY Times* 5 Jan 94

Richard Beeching Chair, British Transport Commission

5058 There is. . . no question of adopting Continental signalling systems, any more than we shall be serving *zabaglione* in the British dining cars.
Reply to "public talk as if derailments were infectious" *Punch* 14 Feb 62

Bill Bell Canadian Pacific engineer

5059 Always whistle *Moon River*. Calms you right down.
On difficult locomotive runs *National Geographic* Dec 94

Alan Bennett playwright

5060 Embassies abroad are invariably outposts of snobbery of one kind or another, where one is welcomed if one is "amusing" or a "celebrity" but not otherwise.
New Yorker 22 May 95

Bernard Berenson art collector

5061 [Xenodochiophobia is] the sinking feeling that in my travels often overcame me: of fear lest the inn or hotel at which we were to lodge would be sordid.
Rumor and Reflection Simon & Schuster 52

5062 I would wish the destination farther and farther away, for fear of what I should find when I reached it.
ib

John Betjeman poet

5063 Isn't abroad awful?
On travel outside England, quoted in *John Betjeman: A Life in Pictures* John Murray 84

Diane M Bolz essayist

5064 A map says. . . "Read me carefully, follow me closely, doubt me not. . . I am the earth in the palm of your hand."
Smithsonian Feb 92

Bubbles Brazil Gypsy Rights lobbyist

5065 Aw, you can't give up what's in the blood . . . .[or] describe what gets in you when the sun starts shining and you want to be done. I never met a traveler yet would deny what they were.

On wanderlust *NY Times* 20 May 88

George Bush 41st US President

5066 So what are you waiting for, an invitation from the President?

British television commercial in which Bush was a pitchman for American tourism *Washington Post* 28 Dec 91

Truman Capote novelist

5067 I had to go all the way to Europe to go back to my hometown, my fire and room where stories and legends seemed always to live beyond the limits of our town. And that is where the legends were: in the harp, the castle, the rustling of the swans.

A Capote Reader Random House 87

5068 The only scenery that bores me is any that I can't imagine purchasing a part of. . . and I instantly consider buying or building a house. A wandering waif—Madrid today, Mexico tomorrow.

On a woman known to be heiress Barbara Hutton in short story "Unspoiled Monsters" *Answered Prayers* Random House 87

5069 [She] never traveled; she merely crossed frontiers, carting 40 trunks and her insular *ambiente* with her.

ib

5070 Anybody becomes a confidante on a yacht cruise and I think I've lived through every screw she ever had in her life. . . an Arabian night's tale of a thousand and twelve.

On traveling with Pamela Harriman, quoted by Christopher Ogden *The Life of the Party* Little, Brown 94

Deirdre Carmody reporter

5071 The windjammer. . . tall ships from around the world whose very presence bespeaks man's centuries-old struggle against the inexorabilities of the sea.

On crafts assembled for the "tall ships" parade celebrating the Statue of Liberty's centennial *NY Times* 27 Jun 86

Agostino Cardinal Casaroli Vatican Secretary of State

5072 Weeds never die.

On world tours John Paul II *Tablet* London 8 Dec 90

Louis-Ferdinand Céline journalist

5073 A city without its concierge has no history and no taste. . . a soup with neither pepper nor salt.

Journey to the End of the Night New Directions 80

Carol Channing actress

5074 I've never been there but my baggage goes there.

To political convention delegates from Guam NPR 13 Jul 92

Charles Prince of Wales

5075 I'm biased because I know her, I've known her all my life.

Protesting the decommissioning of the royal yacht *Britannia* quoted by Jonathan Dimbley *The Prince of Wales* Morrow 94

Clementine Churchill wife of Winston Churchill

5076 Winston's a sporting man; he always gives the train a chance to get away.

On her husband's tardiness, quoted by William Manchester *The Last Lion* Little, Brown 88

Alan Clark British Minister of Trade

5077 VIP suites are windowless, and heavily sound-insulated. . . gently are we drawn into the nether world of deep jet-lag.

Diary entry at Heathrow *Mrs Thatcher's Minister* Farrar Straus Giroux 93

Francis X Clines reporter

5078 The travelers. . . felt threatened with terminal poshness of the soul.

On the luxuriousness of an Irish country house *NY Times* 20 Sep 87

Peter Collier biographer

5079 When he left the farm. . . one in five Americans lived in the city. When he died, the proportion was exactly reversed, largely because his Tin Lizzie had extended human range.

With David Horowitz on inventor Henry Ford *The Fords: An American Epic* Simon & Schuster 87

E H Cookridge journalist

5080 Kings and crooks, millionaries and refugees, big game hunters and smugglers, prima donnas and courtesans traveled on it; tycoons and financiers clinched their deals across its sumptuous dining tables; diplomats, spies and revolutionaries... moved secretively to their moments of history.

The Orient Express Random House 78

Jerry Della Femina advertising executive

5081 I have thousands of little shampoos from thousands of hotels and I don't even have hair.

On joining the majority of guests who take soap, shampoo and other small items *Wall Street Journal* 1 Nov 93

Don Delillo playwright

5082 A motel... represents a peculiar form of nowhere... you don't know quite where you are, and for a brief time, perhaps, not quite who you are.

NY Times 20 Dec 87

William O Douglas Associate Justice, US Supreme Court

5083 Freedom of movement is the very essence of our free society... once the right to travel is curtailed, all other rights suffer.

NY Times 23 Jun 64

Lawrence Durrell author and playwright

5084 Journeys, like artists, are born and not made. A thousand differing circumstances contribute to them, few of them willed or determined by the will.

Bitter Lemons Dutton 57

Shawn Dwyer wanderer

5085 This whole country is mine as far as I'm concerned. I got a piece. I got a right to go anywhere I want to go. And so that's what I do.

On riding transcontinental buses *NY Times* 27 Mar 94

Donald D Engen Director, Federal Aviation Administration

5086 The airports today are the bus stations of the 1950s... cut-offs... babies on their backs... the US flying.

Time 12 Jan 87

Walker Evans photographer and essayist

5087 [We went] down among the torn gum wrappers into the fetid, clattering, squeeling cars underground.

On taking pictures in the NYC subway, quoted by Belinda Rathbone *Walker Evans* Houghton Mifflin 95

Rita Fairfax Sedalia MO storekeeper

5088 If you're here and you don't have somebody to take you somewhere, you're here.

Quoted by Peter T Kilborn "Small Towns Grow Lonelier as Bus Stops Stopping" *NY Times* 11 July 91

E M Forster novelist

5089 Railway termini... are our gates to the glorious and the unknown. Through them we pass out into adventure and sunshine, to them, alas, we return.

Howards End 1910 recalled on Forster's death 7 Jun 70

Ian Frazier motorist

5090 It's possible to drive from here to California and stay at more or less the same motel the entire way.

In William Zinsser ed *They Went* Houghton Mifflin 91

Brendan Gill critic and essayist

5091 What Lindbergh was the first to do, by an act of superb intelligence and will, millions of us accomplish regularly with the expenditure of no more intelligence and will than is required to purchase a ticket and pack a bag.

On Charles A Lindbergh's transatlantic flight *Lindbergh Alone* Harcourt Brace Jovanovich 77

5092 The once-inimical Atlantic scarcely exists for the contemporary traveler: a glimpse of tame, pewter-colored water at the start or finish of a journey. The most that we are asked to face and outwit... is boredom.... [in a] sealed tube as snug as a night-nursery.

ib

Graham Greene novelist

5093 When a train pulls into a great city I am reminded of the closing moments of an overture.

Travels With My Aunt Viking 69

5094 My father, he never travelled further than central London. He travelled from one woman to another.

ib

5095 [I had a] feeling of exhilaration which a measure of danger brings to a visitor with a return ticket.

On a visit to Indochina, recalled on Greene's death *NY Times* 4 Apr 91

5096 I travel because I have to see the scene. I can't invent it.

On researching his novels *Newsweek* 15 Apr 91

Helen Gunn columnist

5097 I am always surprised when I see people so at ease with the grandeur in their midst that they no longer notice it, so colloquial with it that they cease to address it.

Country Life 13 Jul 95

5098 Holiday memories are always like this: the inconsequential pressed up against the momentous.

ib

H R Haldeman Nixon White House Chief of Staff

5099 He said. . . when you have too many spear-carriers along, you find that every time you turn around, they're sticking you in the ass with a spear.

On President Nixon's reluctance to travel with an overly large staff *The Haldeman Diaries* Putnam 94

Bob Hall automobile designer

5100 Since we only live some 70 or 80 years, it is both impractical and irresponsible to refuse the simple happiness the convertible brings.

Connoisseur Sep 90

Leslie Hanscom journalist

5101 It is a day consecrated to the itch to be elsewhere.

On the Fourth of July *Newsweek* 8 Jul 63

William Least Heat-Moon tourist

5102 Some little towns get on the map only because some cartographer has a blank space to fill.

Blue Highways Little, Brown 82

Dorothy Herrmann biographer

5103 Sure that no one had recognized him, he stood. . . gazing up at the machines he regarded as extensions of himself and remembering the miraculous journeys they had taken together.

On Charles A Lindbergh's visit to the Washington museum housing *The Spirit of St Louis* and *Tingmissartoq,* quoted in Herman's biographical *Anne Morrow Lindbergh* Ticknor & Fields 92

Benjamin L Hooks Executive Director, National Association for the Advancement of Colored People

5104 [Blacks] fought for the right to check into a hotel; today we are fighting to have enough money to check-out.

USA Today 30 Jun 86

Roger Horn safety lobbyist

5105 Airline passengers have less protection than cattle in a freight car.

On law limiting alcohol testing to railroad employees *NY Times* 18 Mar 90

Robert Hughes critic and historian

5106 Malt juice and pickled cabbage put Europeans in Australia as micro-chip circuitry would put Americans on the moon.

On the anti-scurvy diet during long sea voyages *The Fatal Shore* Knopf 87

5107 Some nails and beads pitched ashore, the calling cards of the South Pacific. Its waves. . . are overwhelming, toddering hills of indigo and mallachite glass, veined in their transparencies with braids of opaque white water, their spewmy crests running level with the ship's crosstrees.

On the Indian and Southern Oceans *ib*

Christopher Isherwood novelist

5108 I would have gone anywhere with anyone . . . wild with longing for the whole unvisited world.

On travel lust at age 23 in his short story "Mr Lancaster" *Down There on a Visit* Farrar Straus Giroux 61

Diane Johnson novelist

5109 [There are] those moments of travel ennui or traveler's panic we all have felt: the sheer inability to eat another wonton, the desperate wish to be transported by instantaneous space/time travel into one's own bed.

Natural Opium Knopf 93

Dr Alfred E Kahn Chair, Civil Aeronautics Board

5110 An uncomfortably tight oligopoly.

On airlines' deregulation *Washington Post* 19 Mar 89

Harold Katz President, Newburg NY Chamber of Commerce

5111 The Hudson Valley is a people sanctuary. We need a little protection, too.

On seeking the same laws applied to swamps and bird sanctuaries *NY Times* 1 May 71

Dr Benjamin H Kean Director, Parasitology Laboratory, New York Hospital

5112 [Eat lettuce] only if sterilized with a blowtorch.

On avoiding diarrhea in Mexico *NY Times* 26 Sep 93

Thomas Keneally novelist

5113 [It is] the always but never known place.

On Ireland as viewed by the its emigrees *Now and in Time To Be: Ireland & the Irish* Norton 92

Michael Kernan journalist

5114 Far ahead our inexorable headlight melted the blackness.

"Whistle Stops" *Washington Post* 3 Jul 88

5115 There are a lot of porches with chairs ranged on them, set at friendly angles as though conversing.

And when there aren't porches... the chairs have moved onto the lawns to talk. A town may have its grand square and its glittering strip, but its reality is the backyards and back alleys.

ib

5116 We're all together here... sealed up in this hurtling tube, immune to the dust devils outside.

ib

Douglas Kneeland journalist

5117 Out of their crowded interiors, heavy with luggage, thermos jugs and travel games, stained by drinks and popcorn and potato chips, spills America. Summer-struck, road-caught middle-America.

On vacationists arriving at motels *NY Times* 11 Jul 70

5118 The men, blinking their strained eyes behind sunglasses, easing the cramps in their weary legs under pastel slacks and plaid Bermuda shorts. The women, tight in the mouth, their hair windblown, their culottes wrinkled. The children, sullen, explosive-looking.

ib

Charles Kuralt commentator and essayist

5119 It isn't a question of safety. It's a question of fitness. At the end of a sentence is a period. At the end of a train is a caboose.

On the return of the railroad caboose *America Tonight* CBS TV 27 Dec 90

John Le Carré novelist

5120 They might have been anywhere—Berlin, London—any town where paving stones turn to lakes of light in the evening and the travel shuffles despondently through wet streets.

The Spy Who Came in From the Cold Bantam 63

Steve Lewins Gruntal Research

5121 The white-knuckle fliers will probably get scabs on their knuckles from wringing their hands. But they will fly.

On continuing use of commuter airlines despite crashes *USA Today* 15 Dec 94

Sinclair Lewis novelist

5122 My foreign traveling has been a quite uninspired recreation.... My real traveling has been sitting in Pullman smoking cars, in a Minnesota village, on a Vermont farm, in a hotel... listening to the normal daily drone of what are to me the most fascinating and exotic people in the world—the Average Citizens of the United States.

On accepting Nobel Prize, recalled on Lewis' death 10 Jan 51

5123 Friendliness to stranger... rough teasing... passion for material advancement and shy idealism... interests in all the world and their boastful provincialism—the intricate complexities which an American novelist is privileged to portray.

ib

Anne Morrow Lindbergh essayist

5124 It is so strange to leave this airport where we went off in the *Sirius* for the trip to the Orient and to Greenland... now in a silvered limousine of a plane, soft seats, small curtained windows, muffled noise, air conditioning, sky-hostesses.... It does not seem like flying to me.

On departing via commercial airlines from NYC's LaGuardia Field *War Within and Without* Harcourt Brace Jovanovich 80

London Times

5125 Passengers converged disgruntled—and, for once, found their neighbors avid to every detail of their trip.

"Justice at Sea" editorial on lawsuits for injuries sustained aboard the *Queen Elizbeth II* before completion of its remodeling 31 Jan 95

Sister Marie Raymond teacher

5126 If you die and go to hell you've got to go through Denver.

On Amtrak's bypassing of Cheyenne WY *NY Times* 20 Mar 91

Stuart Matthews President, Flight Safety Foundation

5127 If the public absolutely demands that flying be totally safe, you are going to have to ban flying.

NY Times 19 Dec 94

Jonas McGallaird chauffeur

5128 The old son of a bitch rode behind me for 40 years, and this is the first time he won't be able to talk back.

On chauffeuring for food executive C F Seabrook, then driving the hearse for his burial *New Yorker* 20 Feb 95

John McSweeney White House Travel Office

5129 It all looks like Peoria.

On presidential tours *Washington Post* 27 Feb 95

H L Mencken critic and essayist

5130 I know New Yorkers who have been to Cochin, China, Kafristan, Somaliland, and West Virginia, but not one who has ever penetrated the miasmatic jungles of Arkansas.

Recalled on Mencken's death 29 Jan 56

W S Merwin poet

5131 The knowledge of all that he betrayed/Grew till it was the same whether he stayed/Or went. Therefore he went.

"Odysseus" on complexities of modern man *Selected Poems* Macmillan 88

Michelin Guide

5132 We formally disrecommend the course to motorists not trained to the conduct of mountain.

Translation of warning on curving roads of the French alps, quoted by Ira Berkow *Red* Times Books 86

Dennis Miller American Airlines pilot

5133 What they're really saying is, "I am giving you my life and the life of my family."

On watching passengers board his plane *USA Today* 2 Nov 93

Henry Miller journalist and expatriate

5134 It is an air conditioned nightmare.

On US travel, recalled on Miller's death 7 Jun 80

François Mitterrand President of France

5135 I have always experienced the same shock, the same impression of entering the future through the window.

On air travel *Time* 25 May 84

Brian Moore novelist

5136 The messenger kicked down on the accelerator and his bike roared obedience.

On motorcyclist in *The Color of Blood* Dutton 87

Lance Morrow essayist

5137 Real travel is work and may profit from an edge of danger.

Time 31 May 82

5138 It is always one's self that one encounters in traveling: other people, of course, other parts of the world, other times carved into stone now overgrown by jungle—but still, always oneself.

ib

5139 Americans are weather junkies. They monitor it the way a hypochondriac listens to his own breathing and heartbeat in the middle of the night.

Fishing in the Tiber Holt 88

5140 Motels. . . are among the distinctive artifacts of American civilization.

Civilization Nov-Dec 94

5141 Staying in any of the chain motels beside the Interstate is like being sprayed lightly with Lysol, sealed in Tupperwear and stashed in the refrigerator for the night.

ib

Alastair Morton Co-Chair, Eurotunnel

5142 You are the first British sovereign in history to have returned safely from a foreign adventure by land.

To Elizabeth II after the opening of the first land link between England the Continent since the Ice Age *NY Times* 7 May 94

Daniel Patrick Moynihan US Senator

5143 The railroad is an early 19th-century development. The automobile is a late 19th-century adaptation. The airplane appeared nearly a century ago. Nothing has happened since.

Commending trains that may levitate magnetically above their tracks and move at more than 300 miles an hour safely, cheaply, cleanly, quietly, and efficiently *NY Times* 5 Apr 88

Herbert Muschamp critic

5144 At the heart of everything was the train station, the great temple to the restless movement of cosmopolitan life. . . a grand portal into the city. . . a magnificent temptation to leave it.

On European capitals *NY Times* 27 Mar 94

New Yorker magazine

5145 For Americans, the only thing akin to a *carta d'identita* is a driver's license, a brash, under-sized document confirming our national passion for speed, instability, and glittering chrome.

"Talk of the Town" 30 Nov 87

5146 The nervous little model I drive in Rome . . . buzzes angrily, like a bottled wasp. . . so small that—it's embarrassing to admit—after parking I occasionally lift it closer to the curb.

ib

The New York Times

5147 Reaching agreement to tunnel under the channel was itself a miracle; the digging was remarkable, too. And now, ever so routinely, there are tickets for sale.

"The Chunnel, at Last" editorial on opening of tunnel under the English Channel 13 Jan 94

Linda Niemann railroad brakewoman

5148 [It was] playing soccer with box cars.

Boomer University of California Press 90

Steve Norris Minister-in-Charge, London Transport

5149 You have your own company, your own temperature control, your own music and don't have to put up with dreadful human beings sitting alongside you.

On the privacy of the motor car, statement widely protested *London Times* 9 Feb 95

Jeff Obser journalist

5150 Coming to Prague felt to me as though some very kind god had suddenly turned off all the bizarre machinery. . . [and] what remained was only a charming old gramophone sputtering in the corner. . . playing an old orchestra tune, something curious and comforting.

Washington Post 2 Jan 91

Walter Percy photographer and essayist

5151 [New Orleans]. . . a most peculiar concoction of exotic and American ingredients, a gumbo of stray chunks of the south, of Latin and Negro oddments, German and Irish morsels, all swimming in a fairly standard American soup.

Signposts in A Strange Land Farrar Straus Giroux 91

Randy Petersen Publisher, *Inside Flyer*

5152 Miles is a sexy word. It gets a lot of attention.

On accumulation of frequent-flier miles as an alternate currency *NY Times* 21 Aug 94

David Quammen essayist

5153 The essence of travel is relinquishing full control over the texture and path of your own life—and one aspect of that relinquishment is a chronic shortage of decent reading.

Washington Post 6 Aug 95

Jonathan Raban critic and essayist

5154 The sea was the beginning of English journeys; it was the end of American ones.

In Jonathan Raban ed *The Oxford Book of the Sea* Oxford 92

Jonathan Rabinovitz reporter

5155 One month after New York City began a test of six new sidewalk toilets, going to the bathroom has become New York's latest tourist attraction.

NY Times 5 Aug 92

Dan Rather commentator

5156 The FAA is accused of making changes after counting tombstones.

On the Federal Aeronautics Authority's tardiness in ordering the same safety measures for cmmuter planes as it does for larger ones CBS TV 2 Mar 95

Alastair Reid essayist

5157 What haunts a foreigner is the thought of always having to move on, of finding in the places where he comes to rest, the ghosts he thought were left behind; or else of losing the sharp edge, the wry, surprised eye that keeps him extra-conscious of things.

Whereabouts North Point 87

Jesus Rengel reporter

5158 "The shufflers are here," someone yelled out, and all the regulars at Lagoda's Saloon looked up to see the end of an era.

On the last diesel-switching at South Amboy NJ where scores of commuters had always converged on a trackside bar *NY Times* 2 Jul 88

Sara Rimer reporter

5159 The Number 10 becomes a park bench moving through the city.

On free bus travel that expands the world of the elderly *NY Times* 29 Sep 87

Victor Ross NY Bureau of Traffic Operations

5160 This was not a day of *Titanic* proportions. Maybe just *Lusitania*.

On Labor Day congestion *NY Times* 5 Sep 84

5161 My expressway runneth over.

On tractor trailer with wine casks that split open on the Brooklyn-Queens Expressway *ib* 7 May 85

Salman Rushdie novelist

5162 How far did they fly? Five-and-a half thousand as the crow. Or from Indianness to Englishness, an immeasurable distance. Or, not very far at all, because they rose from one great city and fell to another.

On migrants from India *The Satanic Verses* Viking 89

John Russell critic and essayist

5163 The bedrooms are just large enough for a well-behaved dwarf and a greyhound on a diet.

On modern European hotels *NY Times* 4 Aug 77

Vita Sackville-West novelist and critic

5164 There is no greater bore than the travel bore. . . [and] what he has seen in Hong Kong.

Passenger to Teheran Moyer Bell 90

Eulalie Salley storekeeper

5165 We lived on Yankees in the winter and blackberries in the summer.

On Aiken SC as a sleepy Southern resort *National Observer* 22 Aug 66

Ross Sandler NYC Transportation Commissioner

5166 Some of our worst congestion is caused by people in $30,000 autos driving to $100,000-a-year jobs who leave an expressway to save $2.

NY Times 11 Oct 87

Bill Saporito Senior Editor *Time*

5167 From ticketing to bag claim, you fight to get upstream, only to become *sushi* at any moment to one of the airline grizzlies.

On discomforts of "bad attitudes at high altitudes" *Fortune* 3 Apr 95

5168 If a passenger can't read the newspaper of the person seated in front of him, add another row.

On greedy airlines management *ib*

5169 The hopefuls will be hovering around the counter like hummingbirds, trying to dip a beak in the first-class nectar.

On "frequent fliers" wanting to upgrade

5170 Airlines have resolutely stood by the overpromise and underdeliver strategy the way Fidel Castro clings to socialism.

ib

George F Scheer III essayist

5171 For two weeks I had been steadfastly cordial, the purpose of my trip being in part to meet people, and I was fast wearying of my own geniality.

Booked on the Morning Train Algonquin 91

5172 I looked forward to becoming reacquainted with the surly side of my nature.

ib

Vincent Scully Professor of Art History, Yale University

5173 One entered the city like a god; one scuttles in now like a rat.

On the demolition of New York's Pennsylvania Station, quoted by Ada Louise Huxtable *NY Times* 9 Nov 75

Robert Seigel commentator

5174 Not so much a gas guzzler, they'd have us believe, as a gas gourmet.

On introduction of the 1989 Cadillac NPR 7 Oct 88

Mary Lee Settle novelist

5175 She dreamed, lulled by the train, of getting off at heaven or New York City, whichever she got to first.

The Scapegoat Random House 80

Joe Sexton reporter

5176 Morning did not break so much as it creaked into being in Queens. . . daylight stretching out slowly across the concourse at Jamaica Center.

On the wake of a subway wreck *NY Times* 7 Jun 95

5177 With most of the city still in bed, this off-peak shift was on its way to start the city's day, operating by internal clocks that keep them routinely out of synch with almost everyone else.

On early morning commuters

5178 The J train wound with a certain wheezing ease through Queens and into Brooklyn. . . . Birds could be heard through the rumble, and graveyards and unopened schools flashed by outside the windows.

ib

Earl Shorris critic and essayist

5179 In the city, power walks; taxis are for those who meet other men's schedules.

Power Sits at Another Table Fireside 86

Theodore C Sorensen Counsel to the Kennedy White House

5180 We rarely missed a plane and barely caught most of them.

On JFK's campaigning *Kennedy* Harper & Row 65

Philip Spadaro ferry captain

5181 While everyone else is walking in all stressed, they walk in super-duper happy.

On water-borne commuters *New Yorker* 23 May 88

Michael Specter reporter

5182 The floor lady, or *dezhurnaya*, is part Big Nurse, part house mother, part cop and all Russian.

Reporting on a fixture of the Communist system that lives on, presiding over the morals and keys of hotel guests *NY Times* 24 Aug 95

5183 Nothing is scarier than a *dezhurnaya* with a bad attitude.

ib

Stephen Spender poet

5184 After the first powerful plain manifesto/The black statement of pistons, without more fuss/But gliding like a queen, she leaves the station.

"The Express" 1933, recalled on Spender's death 18 Jul 95

Vilhjalmur Stefansson essayist

5185 A land may be said to be discovered the first time a European, preferably an Englishman, sets foot on it.

Discovery McGraw-Hill 64

John Steinbeck novelist

5186 Once a journey is designed, equipped and put in process, a new factor enters and takes over. . . it has personality, temperament, individuality, uniqueness. A journey is a person in itself, no two are alike.

Travels With Charley Viking 62

5187 We find after years of struggle that we do not take a trip; a trip takes us.

ib

Paul Theroux journalist

5188 The journey, not the arrival matters; the voyage not the landing.

The Old Patagonian Express Houghton Mifflin 79

5189 Grin like a dog and wander aimlessly.

Advice for wayfarers *Riding the Iron Rooster: By Train Through China* Putnam 88

5190 Writing about good times is just boasting. . . they want to hear about the hitches.

Christian Science Monitor 14 Jun 92

5191 Travel's a fairly miserable business in which the journey is nothing but self-discovery is everything.

Quoted by Susan Stamberg *Talk* Random House 93

Alan Thompson observer

5192 It is a disturbing thought that the chamber pot—once a classless and functional object in the days of Victorian utilitarianism—is becoming our newest status symbol.

On British Rail's supply of chamber pots to First Class passengers, letter to *London Times* 19 May 76

Time magazine

5193 The old man puffed into sight like a venerable battle-wagon streaming up over the horizon.

On Winston S Churchill disembarking in New York *Time* 14 Jun 52

5194 [It is the] cataracts and Cadillacs syndrome.

On profusion of elderly drivers *Time* 16 Jan 89

Nevis Tramontin boat builder

5195 The best age for a gondola is seven years. Then she is like a woman of 35, polished, well curved and settled into herself.

At 70 on a lifetime of crafting Venetian gondolas, *NY Times* 15 Jul 91

Harry S Truman 35th US President

5196 [I am] feeling as good as an angel full of pie.

Postcard to a cousin in Missouri from Minnesota 1913, quoted by David McCullough *Truman* Simon & Schuster 92

John Updike novelist

5197 To the man travelling alone, his hotel room, first entered in rumpled clothes, with a head light from sleeplessness, looms as the arena where he will suffer insomnia, constipation, loneliness, nightmares, and telephone calls: his room will become woven into the deeper, less comfortable self that travel uncovers.

"Five Days in Finland at the Age of 55" *Odd Jobs* Knopf 91

5198 One's hotel room is a place one is always trying to leave and yet always returning to.

ib

Washington Post

5199 If it won't eat a Volkswagen, it's only surface distortion.

On local roads going to pot and pot-holes 22 Jan 88

Wellington Webb Mayor of Denver

5200 I've been thrown off four times. But. . . I'm going to break this horse and ride it.

On the much delayed opening of the $5-billion Denver International Airport *Washington Post* 19 Feb 95

Eudora Welty short story writer

5201 Writers and travelers are mesmerized alike by knowing of their destinations.

One Writer's Beginnings Harper & Row 84

5202 You could see a town lying ahead in its whole, as definitely formed as a plate on a table. And your road entered and ran straight through the heart of it; you could see it all, laid out for your passage through.

On the pre-expressway US *ib*

5203 Towns, like people, had clear identities and your imagination could go out to meet them.

ib

E B White essayist

5204 Commuter—one who spends his life/In riding to and from his wife;/A man who shaves and takes a train/And then returns to shave again.

"Commuter," *Prose and Sketches of E B White* Harper & Row 67

George F Will columnist

5205 In the 1950s, America was at the wheel of the world and Americans were at the wheel of two-toned (and sometimes even more-toned) cars, tail-finned, high-powered, soft-spring rolling sofas.

"Fifties Baseball" essay in Ken Burns and Geoffrey C Ward eds *Baseball* Knopf 94

5206 A Buick had. . . a grille that looked like Teddy Roosevelt's teeth when he was in full grin over some whomping big-stick exercise of American might.

ib

Robin Williams humorist

5207 The only people flying to Europe will be terrorists, so it will be, "Will you be sitting in armed or unarmed?"

US 3 Nov 86

Tom Wolfe novelist

5208 The more grim the subway became, the more graffiti these people scrawled on the cars, the more gold chains they snatched off girls' necks, the more old men they mugged, the more women they pushed in front of trains, the more determined was John Campbell McCoy that they weren't going to drive him off the New York City subways.

On en elderly New Yorker who for years commuted to Wall Street, quoted by Frank Conroy *NY Times* 1 Nov 87 reviewing Wolfe's *The Bonfire of the Vanities* Farrar Straus Giroux 87

Daryl Wyckoff humorist

5209 The airlines were always ending up like my beagle, 15 blocks from home and panting.

On bankruptcy of airlines that expanded routes too quickly after deregulation in 1978 *Time* 8 Oct 84

Melissa Zegans essayist

5210 You have to run ahead of people sometimes and try to kill them.

On catching cabs in Manhattan *NY Times* 18 Dec 86

The Eye of the Traveler

Dean Acheson US Secretary of State

5211 This is the ideal place to make you unable to remember what you came to forget.

On Antigua, David S McLellan and David C Acheson eds *Among Friends* Dodd Mead 80

James Agee novelist and essayist

5212 The Smokies. . . like seeing sunlight striding through waves, just before they topple.

On Tennessee's Smoky Mountains *A Death in the Family* McDowell Obolensky 57

Nelson Algren novelist

5213 Like loving a woman with a broken nose, you may well find lovelier lovelies. But never a lovely so real.

Chicago—City on the Make Doubleday 51

Anon

5214 Fly-over land, the midwest.

Jacket copy for J F Power's novel *Wheat That Springeth Green* Knopf 88

5215 Not the end of the world, but you can see it from here.

On midwest farm life *NY Times* 28 Feb 88

5216 Fort Worth is where the West begins, they say; Dallas is where the East peters out.

NY Times 17 Jan 94

5217 The most southern place on earth.

On the Mississippi Delta *Washington Post* 18 Apr 95

Peter Applebome reporter

5218 Rows of boarded-up red brick buildings. . . speak more eloquently than the living about the despair at the bottom of urban America.

On New Orleans' St Thomas housing project *NY Times* 28 Jan 91

Harvey Arden journalist

5219 Top-choice America, America cut thick and prime.

On Iowa *National Geographic* May 81

W H Auden poet

5220 An Eliot landscape where the spiritual air is "thoroughly small and dry." If I stay here any longer I shall either take to mysticism. . . or buy a library of pornographic books.

On the midwest, quoted by Charles Osborne *W H Auden: The Life of a Poet* Harcourt Brace Jovanovich 79

B Drummond Ayers Jr reporter

5221 Its sound. . . out on the broad marshes is the whisper of salt air brushing against reeds and down on the rickety docks is vowel clanging against vowel.

On the distinctive accents of Smith Island MD *NY Times* 8 Nov 87

5222 Watermen discuss the day's catch in the still-unadulterated patois of their Colonial English forebears.

ib

Jacques Barzun Dean, Graduate School, Columbia University

5223 The way to see America is from a lower berth about two in the morning. . . [with] nothing but the irrational universe with you in the center trying to reason it out.

God's Country and Mine Little, Brown 54

Jim Bishop columnist

5224 A busted pencil with 17 saloons and one church.

On his home-base of Sea Bright NJ, a description that stirred controversy in the area *Red Bank NJ Register* 28 Jul 87

5225 Sea Bright could never understand that it's possible to love an aging prostitute.

ib

Jim Black Sky West pilot

5226 We call it "office with a view."

On scenic rewards of six daily flights from Salt Lake to Jackson Hole WY CBS TV 2 Mar 95

5227 When it's dark and you can't see, altitude's your best friend.

On steep climbs after take-off

Maeve Brennan essayist

5228 [New York is] most cumbersome, most restless, most ambitious, most confused, most comical, saddest and coldest and most human of cities.

The Long-Winded Lady: Notes from the New Yorker Morrow 69

5229 She likes taxis. She travels in buses and subways only when she is trying to stop smoking. New York. . . the capsized city. . . half-capsized, anyway, with the inhabitants hanging on, most of them still able to laugh as they cling to the island that is their life's predicament. Amsterdam and London and Hong Kong are mysterious. . . .Rome and Berlin. . . [but] New York is not mysterious. New York is a mystery.

ib

Tom Brokaw commentator

5230 [The] physical and cultural remoteness. . . compels everyone to memorize almost every South Dakotan who has left the state and achieved some recognition.

Quoted by John Milton *South Dakota* Norton 77

5231 As a child I would pore over magazines and newspapers, looking for some sign that the rest of the world knew we existed.

ib

Holger Cahill journalist

5232 You could shoot a cue ball from the southern boundary of the state all the way to Canada and halfway to the North Pole.

On South Dakota *The Shadow of My Hand* Harcourt, Brace 56

Chris Calkins National Park Service

5233 Such a gentle place, for such a terrible war to have ended here.

On Virginia countryside that saw the Civil War Battle of Sailor's Creek *Life* Apr 95

5234 It is here that the will to kill and be killed gave out. Everybody just wanted to go home.

ib

David G Campbell Professor of Geography, Grinnel College

5235 Antarctica seemed to be a prebiotic place, as the world must have looked before the broth of life bubbled and popped into whales and tropical forests—and humans.

The Crystal Desert Houghton Mifflin 92

5236 During the short, erotic summer along the ocean margins. . . Antarctica seemed to be a celebration of everything living. . . transmuting sunlight and minerals into life itself, hatching, squabbling, swimming and soaring on the sea wind.

ib

Truman Capote novelist

5237 White clusters of grain elevators rise as gracefully as Greek temples.

On the Kansas planes *In Cold Blood* Random House 65

5238 This island, floating in river water like a diamond iceberg.

On Manhattan *A Capote Reader* Random House 87

5239 Danger! Men Working signs glitter in the sober shade of dwarfed Dickensian streets: Cranberry, Pineapple, Willow, Middagh. The dust of dynamited stone hangs its sentence in the air.

On Brooklyn Heights *ib*

5240 I sat looking at Manhattan and wondering what sort of ruins it would make.

ib

Archie Carr Zoologist, University of Florida

5241 A quiet so deep you could hear a wolf spider charge a cricket across the dry oak leaves.

On the night stillness of a live oak in a spanish moss forest *A Naturalist in Florida* Yale 95

5242 A big old live oak tree without moss is like a bishop without his underwear.

ib

William Cecil Vanderbilt heir

5243 George Vanderbilt never envisioned 700,000 people a year flushing his toilets.

Reporting on the plumbing needs of hordes of visitors to Biltmore House at Asheville NC *NY Times* 13 Dec 92

William J Clinton 42nd US President

5244 It was a beautiful night. . . for putting the pieces of life together and threading the past through today to tomorrow.

On a December 1968 student stroll from London's Festival Hall on the Thames to Westminster "for a brief conversation with Abe Lincoln, who stands in the square," letter quoted by David Maraniss *First In His Class* Simon & Schuster 95

Pat Conroy novelist

5245 You get the feeling that the 20th century's a vast, unconscionable mistake.

On Charleston SC *The Lords of Discipline* Houghton Mifflin 80

Alan Coren reporter

5246 The plangent reliquiae of pre-post-industrial Britain. . . *memento mori*, at one with Nineveh, Tyre and the Britain Can Make It Exhibition.

On junk sales and flea-markets *London Times* 20 Mar 92

Norman Cousins essayist

5247 The blood in the earth runs deep at Gettysburg, but the eye sees only an enchanted land.

On the Civil War battlefield in Pennsylvania "Visit to Gettysburg" *Saturday Review* 11 Jul 64

Brad Darrach essayist

5248 Up at 4, after a short sleep in bedrolls spread on the ground, they saddle their horses by moonlight and, fortified with scrambled eggs and throat-scorching coffee, lope off to the chaparral as dawn backlights the eastern ridges.

On cowboys herding cattle in Texas *Life* Sep 95

5249 The hired hands move on. . . working their way from Texas to Montana, nomads of the purple sage.

ib

Joan Didion novelist

5250 The famous new skyline, floating between a mangrove swamp and a barrier reef, had a kind of perilous attraction, like a mirage.

Miami Simon & Schuster 87

Maureen Dowd columnist

5251 She isn't a pregnant Indian.

Reporting on the public's idea of the 19-foot statue atop the US Capitol *NY Times* 17 Apr 93

5252 Since 1863, through all the decades in Washington when women were merely ornaments, this 19-foot tall warrior guarded the capital with her sword and shield and piercing gaze, a Joan of Arc for democracy. The Goddess of Freedom, and quite a hefty one, just shy of 15,000 pounds. . . giving the effect, close up, of a giant wrapped in her grandmother's quilt. . . and about to get her first bath in 130 years.

On cleaning the $23,000 figure at a cost of $750,000 *ib*

Stephen Drucker reporter

5253 It has felt like 5:30 pm in the lobby of the Algonquin Hotel for nearly 90 years now. . . chronic, romantic twilight.

On Manhattan's Algonquin Hotel *NY Times* 18 Jan 91

Lawrence Durrell novelist and playright

5254 The plums will be falling into the pool, the swallows will be darting through the garden, and the white owls will hoot from the stone tower late into the night.

To a prospective renter of Durrell's villa in France *NY Times* 21 Nov 90

Gretal Ehrlich essayist

5255 [Its] space is swept out daily, leaving a bone yard of fossils, agates, and carcasses in every stage of decay. Though it was water that initially shaped the state, wind is the meticulous gardener, raising dust and pruning the sage.

On Wyoming *The Solace of Open Spaces* Viking 85

Dwight D Eisenhower 34th US President

5256 The most beautiful region under God's blue sky.

On the rolling plains of his boyhood Kansas *NY Times* 29 Mar 69

Elizabeth II Queen of England

5257 [Manchester is] not such a nice place.

On a visit to St Petersburg State University, speaking to a Russian student who had studied at Manchester, a light-hearted exchange that raised hackles in Manchester *London Times* 20 Oct 94

Stanley Elkin novelist

5258 It wasn't a place, it was a pecking order.

On Miami's ethnic groups *Mrs Ted Bliss* Hyperion 95

5259 Lovers kneading lotions and sun block into one another's flesh like a sort of sexual first aid.

On Miami Beach *ib*

Dennis Farney reporter

5260 A grand hotel in the White Mountains that marks America at the crest of the American century.

On Bretton Woods NH's Mt Washington Hotel *Wall Street Journal* 29 Oct 92

Edna Ferber novelist

5261 We're rich as son-of-a-bitch stew but look how homely we are... we know about champagne and caviar but we talk hog and hominy.

A Texan's self-description *Giant* Doubleday 52

5262 Nature was the killer, like a living murderous enemy surrounding a stockade.

On Alaska *Ice Palace* Doubleday 58

5263 Mount McKinley, king of all the peaks on the North American continent, white-crowned in summer, white-robed in winter, looking in this mid-summer midnight like God's Valhalla—or a gigantic scoop of raspberry or orange sherbert.

ib

5264 [It] looked like a frosted picture postcard gone mad.

On Flemington NJ during the 1935 Lindberg kidnapping trial, quoted by Julie Goldsmith *Gilbert Ferber* Doubleday 78

Robin Finn reporter

5265 A natural habitat, where the unnatural runs rampant.

On Las Vegas as the US's gambling capital *NY Times* 29 Oct 90

M F K Fisher essayist and gourmet

5266 Garish... sort of grand... imposing in a funny, outlandish, extravagant way... a rather faded, beautiful old courtesan.

On Paris' *Gare de Lyon*, quoted by Susan Stamberg *Talk* Random House 93

Thomas Flanagan novelist

5267 History is the curse of this country... [and] when we take the train back to Dublin, I shudder—history closing in upon me like hedges.

The Tenants of Time Dutton 88

Janet Flanner ("Genêt") Paris correspondent *New Yorker*

5268 Paris was the capital of limbo.

On German occupation of the French capital, recalled on Flanner's death 7 Nov 78

5269 [They are] an apronful of lump sugar dumped on to the brown dustcloth which is the Attic Plain.

On cities of Greece, quoted by Brenda Wineapple *Genêt* Ticknor & Fields 89

Umberto Franzoi essayist

5270 A cradle stands at the foot of the bed as though it were the logical outcome of the whole seductive environment.

On the *Palazzo Don Rezzonico* in Venice *The Grand Canal* Vendome 94

Edward Gargan reporter

5271 The sun hung low like a pale yellow lozenge in a sky of hammered zinc.

On ice harvesting at New Bremen NY *NY Times* 10 Feb 85

Georgie Anne Geyer columnist

5272 Easter egg colors against the snow.

On Russian churches *Waiting for Winter to End* Brassey 94

Joseph Giovannini reporter

5273 [There is] a great tango of eye contact between men and women on the streets of New York.

NY Times 18 Oct 87

Antony Glenn essayist

5274 An elderly and aristocratic Britishwoman weeding in the pouring rain is one that should be seen by all those who wish to understand the British character.

Discovering Britain and Ireland National Geographic Society 85

Donald Goddard essayist

5275 The resident director makes a point of sleeping in every one of the hundred rooms, when unoccupied, of course.

On London's Goring Hotel *NY Times* 20 Nov 83

Vicki Goldberg biographer

5276 All London was blacked out; a pale moon counted the columns of St Paul's dome and shuddered in the waves of the Thames.

On photographing wartime London *Margaret Bourke-White* Harper & Row 96

5277 The hills lay like wrinkles on the face of the earth.

On North Africa from the air *ib*

Josh Greenfeld essayist

5278 New Jersey looks like the back of an old radio.

Penthouse Nov 78

Clyde Haberman reporter

5279 *Via Veneto*, that dowager of shopping streets.

"They Came, They Saw, Then They Sandblasted" *NY Times* 22 Dec 89

Katharine Hepburn actress

5280 First God made England, Ireland and Scotland. That's when he corrected his mistakes and made Wales.
Time 7 Aug 78

George Hill reporter

5281 Painted Virgins elbow to elbow... waiting like geishas to be carried off in thousands by pilgrims.
On Oberammergau's wood-carvings *London Times* 19 May 90

Charles H Hirshberg reporter

5282 An orgy of wholesomeness.
On National Tom Sawyer Days, Hannibal MO *Life* Apr 95

Christopher Hitchens essayist

5283 A local guide book brackets him with Pompeii as two local antiquities not to be missed.
On novelist Gore Vidal and the Amalfi coast *Vanity Fair* Nov 95

Marjorie Holmes essayist

5284 Hyacinths—whole hillsides painted with their blue, as if someone had dumped buckets of sky on them.
Reader's Digest Apr 91

Langston Hughes poet

5285 I went to San Francisco,/I saw the bridges high,/Spun across the water/Like cobwebs in the sky.
The Langston Hughes Reader Braziller 58

Robert Hughes poet and essayist

5286 Business as usual: the slow, noisy shuffling of packed bodies as in a stockyard whose animals are all looking to heaven.
On the Sistine Chapel's reopening after 8-year renovation *Time* 11 Feb 85

5287 They stand like idealized statues carved from the gross and hairy male protein of their former selves.
On the *Via Liturgica* where transvestites cruise *Barcelona* Knopf 92

5288 A stone book on which the whole theology of the Catholic faith is written... [but] the first cathedral to be saved by Shinto tourism.
On Barcelona's *Sagrada Familia* basilica PBS 12 Apr 93

Randall Jarrell Professor of English, University of North Carolina

5289 To Americans, English manners are far more frightening than none at all.
Pictures From An Institution University of Chicago Press 86

David J Jefferson reporter

5290 [In Los Angeles] the car is an extension of the self and the self is measured by abdominal tautness.
Wall Street Journal 9 Feb 89

Ward Just essayist

5291 An America diplomat goes to Berlin as a lover goes to Venice.
The American Ambassador Houghton Mifflin 87

Dan S Kaercher Editor, *Midwest Living*

5292 Bland, boring and beige.
On an outsider's perception of the American midwest *NY Times* 27 Apr 87

Michael Kaufman reporter

5293 A Siberian tiger ripples in a silent strut.
On the Bronx Zoo *NY Times* 21 Oct 68

Garrison Keillor essayist and humorist

5294 Such a beautiful city, people have to make excuses for not living here.
Broadcast from San Francisco 15 Dec 90

5295 I could see a future for Roanoke, if it had... hearty traditionalists... [and] people with enough holes in their underwear to make them careful crossing streets.
On Roanoke VA "Travels Through the Guilt Belt" *NY Times* 13 Mar 94

5296 If you owned Texas and you owned Hell, you wouldn't know which to live in.
Broadcast from Houston 18 Jun 94

Ted Kerasote naturalist

5297 The sun skidded along the horizon, tinting the frozen sea the color of wild roses.
On Greenland *Bloodties* Random House 93

Nicholas King essayist

5298 The Isenheim altar piece... the rock crystal of Alsatian piety.
On Colmar Cathedral *Wall Street Journal* 17 Mar 87

Charles Kuralt essayist

5299 Death... causes this blinding show of color... a fierce and flaming death.
On autumn in rural Vermont, initial broadcast of *On the Road* CBS TV 26 Oct 67

5300 A club on every corner. . . nowhere does the outsider feel as far outside as in Philadelphia.
Dateline America Harcourt Brace Jovanovich 79

5301 Barns back east have weather vanes. . . but out here farmers just look out the window to see which way the barn is leaning.
On Nebraska *ib*

5302 I am suspicious of Pleasantville NY. . . Sawmill, Arizona, is more my kind of town. Or Window Rock or Hermits Rest or Turkey Flat or Grasshopper Junction.
On Arizona *ib*

Sydney Lea poet

5303 The school bus was a mobile jonquil, a giant bud in February's gray.
On rural Vermont *Annual Report* University of Georgia Press 87

David Leavitt essayist

5304 Yardfuls of untrimmed grasses quivered slightly in the chill dusk light. . . warehouses passed us, then the stodgy upright brick backs of stodgy upright brick East London houses.
On a train's arrival in London *While England Sleeps* Viking 93

Paul Levy reporter

5305 His 'n her thrones. . . squat, upholstered. . . gilded. . . . The 20th century was a poor period for thrones.
On Buckingham Palace opened to the public for the first time *Wall Street Journal* 10 Aug 93

Charles A Lindbergh explorer

5306 Bleak mountain summits glow coldly against a deepening sky. A thin layer of cloud burns molten gold.
On approaching the Avalon Peninsula in the first transAtlantic crossing *The Spirit of St Louis* Scribner's 53

5307 The empire of night is expanding over earth and sea.
ib

Beverly Lowry novelist

5308 It was. . . a drama of night and time, history and splendor.
On an autumn sunset at Washington's Lincoln Memorial *NY Times* 14 May 95

Henry R Luce publisher

5309 Venice is a city that must be seen to be disbelieved.
Smithsonian July 87

Robert MacNeil commentator

5310 [It was] a late Friday afternoon in summer, the commuting of the rich, the cold gin and tonic, and the promise of tanned limbs in sea-blown bedrooms.
Reporting on President Kennedy's landing at Hyannis MA *The Right Place at the Right Time* Little, Brown 82

William Manchester biographer

5311 A hundred tons of gleaming machinery. . . the personal flagship of the American President.
On Air Force One *The Death of a President* Harper & Row 67

5312 The brightest light in the bruise-blue canopy was *Capella.* Always a star of the first magnitude. . . it rose majestically a thousand miles to the northeast, over Boston.
On the flight bearing the slain president's body from Dallas to Washington

Sister Maria Del Rey Maryknoll missionary

5313 Any washing south of the chin and north of the wrists takes place only when you fall overboard.
On river travel in China *No Two Alike* Dodd, Mead 65

Beryl Markham aviator

5314 An aeroplane invaded the stronghold of the stars. . . [and] trembled their flames like a hand swept over a company of candles.
On the sky over Nairobi *West With the Night* North Point 83

John Bartlow Martin essayist

5315 The city roared with life, traffic sped up the outer drive, trucks rumbled down Western Avenue, and elevated trains roared by overhead on the wondrous El, reared against the sky.
"To Chicago With Love" *Saturday Evening Post* 15 Oct 60

5316 Randolph Street in the theatrical district blazed with light. . . and always there was the wonderful lake, a limitless inland sea. Only yesterday some other young man got off a train from Indiana, longing for excitement and opportunity, and found it here.
ib

Bob McEnery essayist

5317 A city of several cities, divided by color, culture, and cash.
On Los Angeles CBS TV 18 Jan 94

Stryker McGuire journalist

5318 Sweetly endearing almost to the point of boredom. . . Connecticut with volcanoes.

On Costa Rica *Streets With No Names* Atlantic Monthly Press 91

Ted McLaurin essayist

5319 If indeed there exists a physical heaven, I hope it is patterned after North Carolina between the summer hours of 6 and 8 am.

Keeper of the Moon Norton 92

James A Michener novelist

5320 Spain. . . hangs like a drying ox hide outside the southern door of Europe proper.

Iberia Random House 68

5321 It disappeared. . . behind the headlands like a beautiful woman entering a night room.

On a pirate-held ship in the Caribbean *Chesapeake* Random House 78

5322 The ultimate source of the river. . . the unspectacular congregation of nothingness, the origin of purpose.

On the Susquehanna River *ib*

Arthur Miller playwright

5323 Years later. . . the relief sculptures of full-bodied, crowned goddesses. . . would bring back to me the silent tumult of those evenings when the nowness of life seemed alive around us.

On Angkor Wat and memories of his marriage to Marilyn Monroe *Timebends* Grove 86

Geoffrey Moorhouse essayist

5324 An outpost of God's Empire on the Tropic of Cancer.

On Calcutta's St Paul's Cathedral *Calcutta* Harcourt Brace Jovanovich 71

Lance Morrow essayist

5325 Melodrama and annunciation. . . the Book of Genesis enacted as an afternoon dream.

On Africa's wildlife and landscape *Time* 23 Feb 87

Rob Neillands reporter

5326 Gather up some of those names painted on regimental drums, add a few more gleaned from the war memorial on any village green .

On touring World War I's western front *London Times* 10 Jan 87

5327 From the city of Ypres to the fatal Somme, a *via dolorosa* for a whole generation.

ib

Jenny Newman novelist

5328 The world outside was wimpled in snow.

On wintry convent grounds *Going In* Hamish Hamilton 94

Eric Nicol essayist

5329 You can't miss it, the first Province on the left.

On British Columbia, Alan Walker ed *Still A Nicol* Ryerson Press 72

Jeff Obser essayist

5330 What remained was only a charming old gramophone spluttering in the corner. . . an old orchestra tune, something curious and comforting.

On Prague and the impression that "some very kind God" had suddenly turned off all the bizarre machinery" of other cities *Washington Post* 2 Jun 91

Georgia O'Keeffe painter

5331 It's a pity to disfigure such wonderful country with people of any kind.

On Texas 1916, quoted by Jack Cowart and Juan Hamilton *Georgia O'Keeffe: Arts and Letters* Little, Brown 87

Michael Parfit essayist

5332 A big old locomotive, hauling grain west across the plains. . . the Canadian Pacific, the steel spine of Canada.

National Geographic Dec 94

Norman Parkinson photographer

5333 I applied. . . for a private burial ground a hundred yards from the house. . . you might want to come back and do a bit of haunting.

On falling "totally in love" with Tobago *Guardian Weekly* 25 Feb 90

Ovid William Pierce essayist

5334 North Carolina begins with the brightness of sea sands and ends with the loneliness of the Smokies reaching in chill and cloud to the sky.

Quoted by Richard Walser *The North Carolina Miscellany* University of North Carolina Press 62

John Pilger journalist

5335 Bondi is to Australians what the Ganges is to Hindus.

On Australia's celebrated Plaga de Bondi beach *Guardian Weekly* 27 Sep 92

William Plummer reporter

5336 Great Sand Dunes National Monument. . . where the major industry is silence.

Reporting on Carmelite monks' battle to preserve their monastery's solitude *People* 30 Nov 92

Mario Praz essayist

5337 Entering the Royal Docks was like entering vast cathedrals. . . like privileged altars, like confessionals for all the languages of the world.

On the docklands of the Thames, quoted by John Russell *London* Abrams 94

J B Priestley playwright

5338 London. . . a changing pattern of sight and sound, with little bits of reality here and there, like currants in a vague and enormous pudding.

All About Ourselves Heinemann 56

5339 [It was] a Yorkshire mill town smelling of high morals and damp wool.

On Rutherford-by-the-Sea *Lost Empires* Little, Brown 65

Steven Prokesch reporter

5340 Beams of sunlight. . . pierce the blanket of gray clouds and fall to earth like ladders from heaven.

On islands of the Outer Hebrides *NY Times* 14 Dec 89

Libby Purvis reporter

5341 British resorts may be tacky but that is the way we like them.

On Great Yarmouth *London Times* 20 Feb 95

John Rechy novelist

5342 Forced laughter drowns the vomiting of the jukebox.

On a California beach bar *City of Night* Grove 63

Robert Reinhold reporter

5343 The faces. . . were a mirror of the modern American southwest. . . rooted in an ancient Indian and Spanish past and hurtling into the glittery American future.

On John Paul II's visit to Phoenix AZ *NY Times* 15 Sep 89

David Rieff sociologist

5344 [Miami is] not like America anymore. Neither is America.

Quoted by John Krich *NY Times* 23 Aug 87 reviewing Rieff's *Going to Miami* Little, Brown 87

Maria Riva biographer

5345 Her love affair with Paris was the longest liaison of her life.

On her mother *Marlene Dietrich* Knopf 92

5346 As with all of her amours, what she loved became hers by right of expanded emotion.

ib

Tom Robbins novelist

5347 [Seattle] is surrounded by the soft, the gray, and the moist, as if it is being digested by an oyster.

On a foggy, rainy day in the northwest US *Half Asleep in Frog Pajamas* Bantam 94

5348 The sky is all huckleberry and nasturtium, the color of God's linoleum.

On a sunset *ib*

Mort Rosenblum essayist

5349 From the beginning, the French soul has bobbed in the waters of the Seine. On its bridges love blooms, beneath them lives end. . . . It nourished Maupassant's pen and watered Monet's lily pond.

The Secret Life of the Seine Addison Wesley 94

5350 Only a few nylon ropes, a power cable and a garden hose connected us to the real world.

On cruising the Seine by barge *ib*

Carl Rowan essayist

5351 Tennessee summer days were not made for work: in fact, many a resident had doubted that they were made at all, but that they sprang to life from the cauldrons of hell.

South of Freedom Knopf 52

Robert Runcie Archbishop of Canterbury

5352 Churches on a myraid of postcards and calendars, set in gentle glades and gentle vales. . . an Englishness which has retained its potency when the uniforms of imperial glory are tattered and even ludicrous.

At University of Kent, December, 1980 in James B Simpson ed *Seasons of the Spirit* Eerdmans 83

George Santayana philosopher

5353 Boston is a moral and intellectual nursery always busy applying first principles to trifles.

Daniel Cory ed *Santayana: The Later Years* Brazillier 63

Uri Savir Israeli Consul General

5354 While Paris gets to your heart, London to your mind, and Jerusalem to your soul, New York gets into your veins, a lifeline that becomes part of you more than you become part of it.

NY Times 25 Apr 92

5355 New York has a life of its own, its own pulse, which beats just a bit faster than that of its inhabitants.

ib

Eric Sevareid commentator

5356 Paris lay inert, her breathing scarcely audible, her limbs relaxed, and the blood flowed remorselessly from her manifold veins.

On the fall of Paris in 1940 *Not So Wild a Dream* Atheneum 76

5357 Paris lay dying, like a beautiful woman in a coma, not knowing nor asking why.

ib

5358 [In this] corner of America...the spring is lovely beyond belief...and intensely green like France, the rivers small...crossed by bridges where small boys sit with pole and line, hook and worm.

Address at Decorah College, Decorah, Iowa, quoted by Raymond A Schroth *The American Journey of Eric Sevareid* Steerforth Press 95

Nathaniel Sheppard Jr reporter

5359 A beautiful, crisp fall day. . . under skies that were as pure as PTA punch.

On Chicago's welcome to Prince Charles *NY Times* 20 Oct 77

Marlise Simons reporter

5360 [Tramontin's gondolas are] wooden vessels as elegant as a swan, nimble as a reed and finely carved as a violin.

On Venice's veteran gondola builder Nevis Tramontin *NY Times* 15 Jul 91

Wesley W ("Red") Smith sportswriter

5361 Somewhere in the tree tops a pine warbler spoke. A chickadee identified himself. A pewee stated his name, rank and serial number.

On becoming a sportswriter turned bird-watcher, quoted by Ira Berkow *Red* Times Books 86

5362 Through the fragrance of wood fires burning under the elms. . . wreaths of morning mist curled up to be burned away by slanting rays of sunshine.

On Saratoga Springs NY

5363 The rhythmic throbbing of hooves could be heard from the track itself, where horses were working.

ib

Alexander Solzhenitsyn author

5364 The secret of the pacifying Russian countryside . . . is the churches. They lift their belltowers—graceful, shapely, all different—high over mundane timber and thatch.

Quoted by President Reagan at Danilov Monastery *NY Times* 5 Jun 88

Muriel Spark novelist

5365 Cleanliness and godliness shook hands with each other.

On Edinburgh's Morningside district of her childhood *Curriculum Vitae* Houghton Mifflin 93

Basil Spence architect

5366 The cathedral was cold and dead—like a head without eyes.

On a wartime visit to Chartres Cathedral, its glass safely stored away *Phoenix at Coventry* Harper 62

Wallace Stegner novelist

5367 You have to get over the color green; you have to quit associating beauty with gardens and lawns; you have to get used to an inhuman scale.

On appreciating the western US *NY Times* 15 Apr 93

John Steinbeck novelist

5368 It's not their unbelievable stature, nor the color which seems to shift and vary under your eyes, no, they are not like any trees we know. . . ambassadors from another time.

On the California redwoods *Travels With Charley* Viking 68

Robert Sullivan essayist

5369 Same old French Quarter. Still dirty, still loud, still there.

On New Orleans *Life* Apr 95

Deborah Tall essayist

5370 [It] bears the brunt of the Atlantic's mayhem.

On Ireland's west coast *The Island of the White Cow* Atheneum 87

Amy Tan novelist

5371 Snow is like a high-level official—doesn't come too often, doesn't stay too long.

On wintry Nanking *The Kitchen God's Wife* Putnam 91

Paul Theroux essayist

5372 The way to China was. . . across Asia's wide forehead and then down into one of its eyes, Peking....[The iron rooster] squawked and crowed. . . [and] shook itself along the tracks. . . a big clattering thing, with bells and whistles, that went its noisy and cocksure way westward, into the desert of Turkestan....The trip was so long and it had claimed so much of me that it stopped being a trip. It was another part of my life. It was almost axiomatic that the worst trains go through the most magical places....I thought I liked railways until I saw Tibet and then I realized that I liked wilderness much more.

Riding the Iron Rooster Putnam 88

Judith Thurman essayist

5373 The river of the great 19th-century landscapists, of Cole, Cropsey and Church...at the end of the summer…lies motionless under the haze as under a light coat of varnish.

On the Hudson River *House & Garden* Dec 84

Time magazine

5374 If luxury had a lap, Beverly Hills sits square upon it.

On Beverly Hills CA 21 Feb 64

Arnold Toynbee historian

5375 The immense cities lie basking on the beaches of the continent like whales that have taken to the land.

On Australia *East to West* Oxford 58

Stewart L Udall US Secretary of the Interior

5376 Beyond the noise and the asphalt. . . we yearn for the long waves and beach grass; we see white wings on morning air, and in the afternoon, the shadows cast by the doorways of history.

At dedication of Cape Cod National Seashore *NY Times* 5 Jun 66

Auberon Waugh essayist

5377 One does not have to travel far into Heathrow—surely one of the vilest major international airports in the world—before suspecting that the country has left its heart in its public toilets.

Brideshead Benighted Little, Brown 86

Gordon Webber novelist

5378 Little towns with their handfuls of buildings huddled close to the grain elevators, like medieval towns clustered around their cathedrals.

On the North Dakota plains *The Great Buffalo Hotel* Little, Brown 79

Weekly Telegraph London

5379 In this corner of the shires, elderly ladies in bullet-proof tweed still wobble down the lanes on dreadnought bicycles.

On the area of East Bergholt, Suffolk 10 Jan 94

Roger Welsch commentator

5380 The plains, at one time, had a patchwork geography, of which echoes remain. . . but that was all long ago, and soon everyone wanted to be not Polish, or Danish, or Czech—but Americans—200 per cent American!

Sunday Morning CBS TV 14 Feb 93

E B White essayist

5381 On any person who desires such queer prizes, New York will bestow the gift of loneliness and the gift of privacy.

"Here Is New York" *Essays* Harper & Row 77

5382 No one should come to New York to live unless he is willing to be lucky.

ib

5383 New York lay stretched in midsummer languor under her trees in her thinnest dress, idly and beautifully to the eyes of her lover.

Poems and Sketches of E B White Harper & Row 81

5384 In every street the glimpse he caught of some door or some vestibule or some window would stir his memory and call up the recollection of something in his life that once had been.

ib

P G Wodehouse essayist

5385 Into the face of the young man who sat on the terrace of the Hotel Magnifique at Cannes there had crept a look of furtive shame, the shifty, hangdog look which announces that an Englishman is about to talk French.

The Luck of the Bodkins Penguin 75

Tom Wolfe novelist

5386 The Rome, the Paris, the London of the 20th century, the city of ambition, the dense magnetic rock, the irresistible destination of all those who insist on being where things are happening.

On Manhattan *The Bonfire of the Vanities* Farrar Straus Giroux 87

James T Wooten reporter

5387 It is something so basic, so common, so typical, and so utterly undramatic that many visitors depart without realizing that what they are leaving behind. . . an almost perfect, pristine example of village life in the American South.

On Jimmy Carter's hometown of Plains GA *NY Times* 20 Dec 76

5388 The good and the bad. . . virtues and vices. . . warts and wisdom, gossip and gospel, saints and sinners, meanness and mirth, the dual personality with right and wrong sides of the railroad tracks—all those familiar elements of a small Southern town are the principle ingredients of Plains.

ib

HUMANKIND

FAMILY LIFE

Family Members

Dean Acheson US Secretary of State

5389 The father of the bride is a pitiable creature. . . always in the way—a sort of backward child—humored but not participating in the big decisions.

To Harry S Truman on Margaret Truman's engagement quoted by David McCullough *Truman* Simon & Schuster 92

5390 His only comfort is a bottle of good bourbon. Have you plenty on hand?

ib

Andre Aciman Professor of French, Princeton

5391 The velvety hush of their voices when we turned off the lights and drew closer to the radio almost whispering. . . as though the enemy were listening. . . it was the blackout that spelled our evenings together.

On Alexandria during the Suez War *Out of Egypt* Farrar Straus Giroux 95

Anne Princess Royal

5392 My feelings have always been somewhere between fairly irritated and very very grateful.

On male succession in British royal family *Illustrated London News* May 88

Anon

5393 There are only two lasting things we can leave our children: one is roots; the other is wings.

Quoted by Joseph Giordano "An Italian American Looks Back" *NY Times* 19 Dec 87

5394 Money isn't everything—but it sure keeps you in touch with your children.

Inscription on cushion in study of Constantine, exiled King of the Hellenes *London Times* 15 Apr 94

5395 She was living on earth and boarding in Glory.

On people who "can walk with kings and not lose the common touch," favorite sayings of a great-grandmother recalled by Walt Harrison in article on passive objection to segregation in Alabama *Washington Post* 8 Oct 95

Barbara Lazear Ascher sister of AIDS victim

5396 There were times when we seemed to live in a quiet darkness where Bobby was concerned. Until his impending death broke our hearts and let the light in.

Landscape Without Gravity Delphinium 93

Ellen Auerbach photographer

5397 I was not exactly my mother's dreamboat. She would have liked a fat—or at least, not scrawny—child with no mind.... [and she] used to say, "You just wait till you get into life, and then you will see." This meant that while I was now in paradise, hell would break out immediately.

On growing up in pre-World War I Berlin *NY Times* 28 May 95

Russell Baker columnist

5398 When you're the only pea in the pod your parents are likely to get you confused with the Hope diamond.

William Zinsser ed *Inventing the Truth* Houghton Mifflin 87

Consuelo Vanderbilt Balsan heiress

5399 It was her wish to produce me as a finished specimen framed in a perfect setting. . . dedicated to whatever final disposal she had in mind.

On being compelled by her mother to marry at 18 the Duke of Marlborough, quoted by James Brough *Consuelo Coward McCann* Geoghegan 79

Mary Catherine Bateson Professor of Anthropology and English, George Mason University

5400 When we speak we echo many voices.

On the influence of her parents Margaret Mead and Gregory Bateson *NY Times* 15 Nov 87

Lord Beaverbrook (William Maxwell Aitken) publisher

5401 I'm going to do the greatest thing I can for you. . . I'm not going to leave you my money.

To nephew Jonathan Aitken, quoted by Anne Chilshom and Michael Davies *Beaverbrook* Hutchinson 92

Alan Beck essayist

5402 A boy is Truth with dirt on its face, Beauty with a cut on its finger, Wisdom with bubble gum in its hair and the Hope of the future with a frog in its pocket.

"What Is a Boy?" leaflet by New England Life Insurance 56

5403 Little girls are the nicest things that happen to people.

"What Is a Girl?" *ib*

Menachem Begin Prime Minister of Israel

5404 My father and mother. . . were among the six million people whose. . . sacred blood. . . reddened the rivers of Europe from the Rhine to the Danube to the Volga because only because—they were born Jews. Nobody, nobody came to their rescue, although they cried out, "Save us! Save us!" *de profundis*, from the depths of the pit and agony.

At White House signing of Israeli peace accord 26 Mar 79

Brendan Behan playwright

5405 I am married to Beatrice Salkeida, painter. We have no children except me.

Recalled on Behan's death 20 Mar 64

Alan Bennett playwright

5406 Every family has a secret, and the secret is that it's not like other families.

Writing Home Random House 94

5407 Sex did not come up to the expectations of either of them, but before it was discontinued they had one quick child.

On writer Kenneth Grahame and his wife, Elspeth *ib*

Bernhard Prince of the Netherlands

5408 You need a tightrope walker's sense of balance—and an understanding wife.

On succeeding as consort and husband of Queen Juliana *Collier's* 6 Jun 54

Burton Bernstein composer's brother

5409 [He who had] always been larger than life turned out to be smaller than death.

At funeral for his brother, quoted by Humphrey Burton *Leonard Bernstein* Doubleday 94

Leonard Bernstein composer and conductor

5410 Ma, I want lessons!

At age 10 on inheriting an aunt's piano, recalled on Bernstein's death 14 Oct 90

5411 I didn't know a baton from a tree trunk.

On being told that he should become a conductor *ib*

Erma Bombeck columnist

5412 In general my children refused to eat anything they hadn't seen on TV.

Motherhood Hill 83

Julia Boswell matriarch

5413 Oh, Leona! Leona and cousin Fannie were sisters. His grandmother was they aunt. She was Leona Edwards' aunt. That was Rosa Parks' mother.

Explaining her husband's family relationship to the woman who emerged as the central symbol in desegregating Montgomery AL *Washington Post* 8 Oct 95

Marlon Brando actor

5414 We were all scorched. . . in the furnace that was our family.

On growing up with alcoholic parents *Brando* Random House 94

Pearl Buck novelist

5415 As I watched her at play. . . it came to me that this child would pass through life as the angels live in Heaven. The difficulties of existence would never be hers.

On her mentally retarded daughter *The Child Who Never Grew* John Day 50

5416 Our educational techniques for normal children have been vastly improved by what the retarded children have taught us.

ib

5417 Be proud of your child, accept him as he is. . . . They resemble us in more ways than they differ from us.

Parade 13 Nov 60

Carol Burnett comedian

5418 [This is to explain] just how your mom turned out to be the kind of hairpin she is.

Note to her daughters in *One More Time* Random House 86, quoted in *NY Times* 19 Oct 86

George Burns entertainer

5419 New Year's... the only thing we could afford that was really new.

On 1890s family life on Manhattan's lower East Side *NY Times* 31 Dec 88

Barbara Bush First Lady

5420 At the end of your life you will never regret not having passed one more test, winning one more verdict or not closing one more deal. You will regret time not spent with a husband, a child, a friend or a parent....[but] somewhere out in this audience may even be someone who will one day follow in my footsteps and preside over the White House as the president's spouse, and I wish *him* well.

At Wellesley College commencement *Washington Post* 2 Jun 90

5421 We had a household staff of 93. Next morning we woke up and it was George, me and two dogs—and that's not all that bad!

On leaving the White House *NY Times* 18 Oct 93

5422 Let me tell you: George is the best little dishwasher in Texas.

ib

5423 I'm one who thinks you ought to enjoy what you have and not worry about what you don't have so I "started home" right then—up here in my head—and went down to Texas to look for a house.

On realizing that 1992 was not running in her husband's favor NBC TV 4 Oct 94

Dorothy Walker Bush President's mother

5424 I don't want to hear anymore about the great I Am.

Forbidding her son, George, to speak of personal accomplishments, quoted by Margaret Garrard Warner "Bush Fights the 'Wimp Factor'" *Newsweek* 28 Oct 87

George Bush 41st US President

5425 I feel something that was between an affectionate hug and a kidney punch—the Silver Fox telling me to get going.

On his wife's prodding at his inaugural ceremony *NY Times* 21 Jan 89

5426 The American people love her because she's something she is and stands for something.

On Wellesley College students who felt Mrs Bush was unworthy of an honoray degree because she had not achieved status except as a wife, news conference 3 May 90

5427 My mother was like an army drill sergeant. Dad was the commanding general... but mother was the one day in and day out shaping the troops.

On the death of Dorothy Walker Bush 18 Nov 92

5428 I make the coffee, Barbara makes the beds, and we're right back to square one where we got married when we were 20 years old.

On retirement *People* 19 Jul 93

5429 I was Millie's co-owner. Then it was Barbara's husband, the author of the best-selling book. And now it's the father of the Governor-elect of Texas.

On his self-effacing multiple roles of dog owner, mate and parent *Newsweek* 12 Dec 94

5430 There is about our house, a need. The running, pulsating restlessness of the four boys as they struggle to learn and grow; their athletic chests and arms and legs; their happy noises as the world embraces them... all this wonder needs a counterpart.

Letter to his mother after the death of daughter Robin at age 3 quoted in the biography *Barbara Bush: A Memoir* Scribner 94

Prescott S Bush President's father

5431 How'd we do in "Claims no more?"

Oft repeated question to his son, George, on school report card ranking of "Claims no more than his fair share of time and attention" *Newsweek* 28 Oct 87

Albert Camus novelist

5432 Jacques had seen her ironing the single pair of pants that he and brother each had until he left to go off into the world of women who neither iron nor do laundry.

On himself as a boy *The First Man* Knopf 95

5433 [There are] fewer points in time throughout lives that are gray and featureless. Rememberance of things past is only for the rich.

The First Man Knopf 95

5434 All at once he knew the shame and... the shame of having been ashamed.

On realizing his lack of appreciation for his mother's work at home and beyond it as a domestic *ib*

5435 Poverty is a fortress without drawbridges.

ib

Mary Cantwell essayist

5436 I was living in a blizzard of bake sales and church suppers and bright bits of fabric that I was piecing into glory.

"Close to Home" on making quilts *NY Times* 5 Jan 89

5437 Like most parents I have double vision: I see the toddler at the same time I see the adult and too often the first effaces the second.

ib 17 May 90

Jimmy Carter 39th US President

5438 I've never won an argument with her; and the only times I thought I had I found out the argument wasn't over yet.

On wife Rosalynn *Reader's Digest* Mar 79

5439 I do not remember... his ever saying a complimentary word to me... but I hungered for some demonstration of my father's love. I worked my ass off and he took it for granted!

On his father Earl Carter *Always a Reckoning* Random House 94

5440 My family's depicted as hillbillies... saying shonuf.

On newspaper cartoons when he became President "a bias that still exists in our country, an underestimation of southerners" *Life* Nov 95

Rosalynn Carter First Lady

5441 Because he feels he can, he feels he should.

On President Carter representing the US in international negotiations *Life* Nov 95

5442 He tends to appear naive... I don't like it... but it's important for him to be that way.

On her husband as a negotiator *ib*

Whittaker Chambers former Communist spy

5443 When you understand what you see, you will no longer be children.

To his children *Witness* Random House 52

5444 You will know that life is pain, that each of us hangs always upon the Cross of himself. And when you know that this is true of everyone you will be wise.

ib

Charles Prince of Wales

5445 I put my hands between Mummy's and swore to be her "liege man of life and limb and to live and die against all manner of folks"—such magnificent medieval, appropriate words even if they were never adhered to in those old days.

Diary entry 1 July 69 on Charles' investiture at age 21 at Caernarvon Castle, quoted by Jonathan Dimbleby *The Prince of Wales* Morrow 94

5446 [I was faithful] yes, absolutely... until it became irretrievably broken down, after us both having tried. It's the last thing I wanted to happen.

To commentator Jonathan Dimbleby on marriage to Princess Diana in an interview watched by an estimated 12.7 million people on ITV 29 Jun 94

5447 She's been a friend for a very long time and will continue to be for a very long time.

On Mrs Camilla Parker Bowles to whom he had proposed marriage in 1972 *ib*

John Cheever novelist

5448 When I remember my family I always remember their backs... always indignantly leaving places.

Quoted by Susan Cheever *Home Before Dark* Houghton Mifflin 84

5449 Saving a letter is like trying to preserve a kiss.

Urging his son not to preserve letters he had written him, quoted by Ben Cheever ed *The Letters of John Cheever* Simon & Schuster 88

5450 To conceive a child, my father told me, is as simple as blowing a feather off your knee.

The Journals of John Cheever Knopf 91

Susan Cheever essayist

5451 When Tolstoy wrote that all happy families are alike, what he meant was that there are no happy families.

Treetops Bantam 91

Clementine Churchill statesman's wife

5452 It wasn't a funeral: it was a triumph.

On Winston S Churchill's burial, quoted by their daughter Mary Soames *Clementine Churchill* Cassell 79

Winston S Churchill statesman

5453 Death came very easily to her. She had lived such an innocent and loving life of service to others and held such a simple faith that she had no fears at all and did not seem to mind very much.

On the death of his nanny, Elizabeth Everest, quoted by William Manchester *The Last Lion* Little, Brown 83

5454 It is a gaping wound whenever one touches it and removes the bandages and plasters of daily life.

On the death of his young daughter Marigold *ib*

5455 She has done what she liked and now she has to like what she has done.

On the marriage of daughter, Sarah, to the comedian Vic Oliver quoted by Philip Ziegler *King Edward VIII* Knopf 91

Alan Clark British Minister of Trade

5456 I like in these tall Gothic rooms with all these beautiful possessions around me accumulated by my father and by my grandfather to nostalgicise.

On Saltwood, Clark's ancestral home *Mrs Thatcher's Minister* Farrar Straus Giroux 93

5457 Why am I still in the main so zestful?/I know but I don't like to say./In case the gods take it away.

ib

Andrienne Clarkson Canadian mother

5458 Other people are parallel. But my children come at me from right angles.

Interview on *Television Ontario* 31 Dec 87

Hillary Rodham Clinton First Lady

5459 To the family that raised me, the family I joined, and the family we made.

Dedication page of her book *It Takes a Village* Simon & Schuster 95

5460 There is no such thing as other peoples' children!

Newsweek 15 Jan 96

5461 "It takes a village to raise a child". . . a timeless reminder that children will only thrive if their families thrive and if the whole of society cares enough to provide for them.

NY Times 5 Feb 96 on the African proverb that supplied the title for her book *It Takes a Village* Simon & Schuster 95

William J Clinton 42nd US President

5462 He genuinely did love me and I genuinely did love him. It was himself that he didn't love.

On his stepfather's alcoholism *Newsweek* 30 Mar 92

5463 People don't stay in hell—it's intermittent hell that we all put up with. [It was] a home where either nothing happened or all hell broke loose.

On being a child in an alcoholic home *ib*

5464 Like a lot of men of his age and time he didn't have a lot of conversations until he began to die.

On significant talks with his stepfather during a six-week period when Clinton drove 266 miles every weekend from Georgetown University to Duke Medical Center where his stepfather was a cancer patient *ib*

5465 It was my log cabin.

On his earliest years in his maternal grandparents' home, seen as politically equivalent to Lincoln's log cabin, quoted by Meredith L Oakley *On the Make* Regnery 94

Ivy Compton-Burnett novelist

5466 We do not discuss the members of our family to their faces.

A House and Its Head 1935 recalled on Compton-Burnett's death 27 Aug 69

James B Conant President, Harvard University

5467 First Day of Winter for the Conant family!

Diary entry on dual hospitalization at age 72 of himself and his wife, quoted by James G Hershberg *James B Conant* Knopf 93

5468 2nd day of winter. Winter came on fast!

Diary *ib* 8 Jul 65

Pat Conroy novelist

5469 He made the mistake of letting a novelist grow up in his house remembering every violent act.

On his father as reflected in Conroy's *Prince of Tides* Station WAMU 4 Sep 95

Bill Cosby entertainer

5470 We have many things in common the greatest of which is that we are both afraid of the children.

On his wife Camille *Fatherhood* Dolphin 86

Tricia Nixon Cox President's daughter

5471 A day for tears. . . [but] we must not collapse in the face of the ordeal. We must not let him down.

Diary entry 6 Aug 74 after learning of Nixon's intent to resign, quoted by Fred Emery *Watergate* Times Books 94

Christina Crawford actress's daughter

5472 [Her] eyes were the eyes of a killer animal.

On her foster mother, actress Joan Crawford *Mommie Dearest* Morrow 78

Joan Crawford actress

5473 No wire hangers! No wire hangers!

On raiding the bedroom closet of her foster daughter, quoted by Christina Crawford *Mommie Dearest* Morrow 78

Robert Crawford poet

5474 My childhood passes on a bicycle/Down West Coats Road beneath our sycamore/That filters sunlight through the slow/Sidereal quiet of the suburb. . .

A Scottish Assembly Chato 90

Rosalee Cunningham welfare mother

5475 The way I brought my children up I don't want nobody to bring theirs up.

On six of her eight offspring who followed her into prostitution and drug use *Frontline: The Confessions of Rosalee* PBS TV reviewed in *NY Times* 23 May 95

Mario Cuomo Governor of New York

5476 I watched a small man with thick calluses on both hands work 15 and 16 hours a day. . . [and] bleed from the bottoms of his feet. . . [and] taught me all I needed to know by the simple eloquence of his example.

Recalling his immigrant father in address to Democratic National Convention 16 Jul 84

5477 I haven't taught people in 50 years what my father taught by example in one week.

On his father *Time* 2 Jun 86

5478 The tenements, stores and houses were cramped together. . . except for the occasional patches of flowers or tomato plants. . . reminders of the peasant life our parents had left behind.

On Italian immigrant families in Jamaica, Queens *Life* Jul 86

5479 Manhattan, the center of power and dreams. . . beckoned us to the land still beyond our reach—the America of college and success of people with diplomas on their walls, of men and women rushing to catch trains to places with lawns and trees, to houses without clotheslines on their roofs.

ib

5480 I am a trial lawyer. . . Matilda says that at dinner on a good day I sound like an affidavit.

On life with his wife and children *ib*

Louise Sevier Gidings Curry Mother of the Year

5481 Spoil your husband, but don't spoil your children—that's my philosophy.

NY Post 14 May 61

Bette Davis actress

5482 If you've never been hated by your child, you've never been a parent.

On publication of her daughter B D Hyman's book *My Mother's Keeper*, CBS TV 5 May 85

Patti Davis President's daughter

5483 I didn't have the balls to vote against my father but I couldn't vote for him.

On Ronald Reagan *Vanity Fair* Jul 91

Frank Deford essayist

5484 It was a big deal one day long ago in August when your father had cleaned his fingernails for the occasion and then you made him the proudest Dad in all the land.

On winning a soap-box derby *Sports Illustrated* 1 Aug 88

Charles de Gaulle President of France

5485 Now she is like all the rest.

To his wife on the burial of their mentally retarded daughter, quoted by Don Cook *Charles de Gaulle* Putnam 83

Diana Princess of Wales

5486 There's no better way to dismantle a personality than to isolate it.

On the coldness of the Royal Family, paraphrasing Brian Keenan *An Evil Casting* Viking 93

5487 There were three of us in this marriage so it was a bit crowded.

On Prince Charles and his relationship with Camilla Parker Bowles ABC TV 24 Nov 95

5488 I thought we were a very good team.

On public appearances with her husband *ib*

5489 I felt the whole country was in labor with me.

On the birth of her first child *ib*

5490 I adored him. Yes, I was in love with him. But I was very let down.

Acknowledging an affair with an officer who later sold his story for a book *ib*

5491 I'd like to be queen of people's hearts.

On continuing with charity work as an alternative to being Queen of England *ib*

5492 That's the trouble, she won't go quietly. Because I believe I have a role to fulfill and I have two children to bring up.

On pressing for a suitable title, work and financial settlement *ib*

Jasmine Diaz slum tenant

5493 They're just one of us. They live here with us. They're our neighbors.

On the rat-infested Morrisania area of the Bronx *NY Times* 22 May 95

Franco Diligenti father of quintuplets

5494 A little Mafia. . . if one committed a mischief the others would not tell.

On choosing separate schools for his children *Saturday Evening Post* 25 Jun 64

5495 A man who has raised quints has had enough of babies!

ib

Oliva Dionne father of quintuplets

5496 I ought to be shot!

On becoming in 1934 the father of the world's first quintuplets to survive birth and reach maturity, recalled on Dionne's death 15 Nov 79

Michael Dirda esayist

5497 One child eats sandwich but no soup; another only soup; middle son refuses everything preferring to toast a couple of frozen waffles. All demand dessert—the true goal of any meal.

On a lunch-break from working at home *Washington Post* 15 Oct 95

5498 I attempt to discuss school activities, homework, reading. Oldest son rolls eyes at ceiling. Beloved spouse says the latest Dick Francis book is pretty good.

ib

E L Doctorow novelist

5499 We live in the past to an astonishing degree the myths we live by, the presumptions we make. Nobody can look in the mirror and not see his mother or father.

On *The Waterworks* Random House 94, a novel on a century of New York life *NY Times* 5 Jul 94

Anthony Eden Prime Minister of Britain

5500 My mother preferred the simpler relationship which existed between donor and recipient to the more complicated one between mother and child.

Quoted by William Douglas-Home, Jennifer Brown ed *The Prime Ministers* Allen & Elwin 87

Edward Duke of Windsor

5501 We had a buttoned-up childhood in every sense of the word.

A Family Album Cassell 60

5502 It's hell to be. . . this much dependent on the ice-veined bitches.

Letter 22 Feb 52 to the Duchess of Windsor on financial support from the Royal Family, quoted by Michael Bloch *The Secret File of the Duke of Windsor* Bantam 88

5503 Ice in place of blood in the veins must be a fine preservative.

On his mother, Queen Mary *ib*

5504 What a smug stinking lot my relations are and you've never seen such a seedy worn out bunch of old hags most of them have become.

ib

Jill Eikenberry adolescent's mother

5505 You have a wonderful child but when he's 13, gremlins carry him away and leave in his place a stranger who gives you not a moment's peace.

On teen-agers *Parade* 12 Jul 87

5506 Two or three years later the gremlins will return your child and he will be wonderful again.

ib

Dwight D Eisenhower 34th US President

5507 We were very poor but the glory of America is that we didn't know it.

On growing up in Kansas *Time* 16 Jun 52

5508 Our pleasures were simple—they included survival.

On his childhood *At Ease: Stories I Teil My Friends* Doubleday 67

5509 That was and still is the great disaster of my life—that lovely, lovely little boy. . . and things never get back to the way they were.

On the death of his first son in 1920 *Ike* PBS TV 15 Oct 86

5510 Pull me up! Two big men—higher! I want to go. God take me!

Dying words to his son John and a physician at Washington's Walter Reed Hospital, quoted by John S D Eisenhower *Strictly Personal* Doubleday 74

Julie Nixon Eisenhower President's daughter

5511 Go through the fire just a little while longer. . . millions support you.

Note left on President Nixon's pillow 6 Aug 74 by his youngest daughter after learning of his intent to resign, quoted by Fred Emery *Watergate* Times Books 94

Elizabeth Queen Mother

5512 I commend to you our dear daughter: give her your loyalty and devotion: in the great and lonely station to which she has been called she will need your protection and your love.

Public statement 11 days after the death of King George VI news reports 17 Feb 52

Elizabeth II Queen of England

5513 I declare my will and pleasure that while I and my children shall continue to be styled and known as the House and Family of Windsor my descendants. . . shall bear the name of Mountbatten-Windsor.

Decree incorporating the family name of her husband Philip Mountbatten *NY Times* 9 Feb 60

5514 They are not royal. They just happen to have me as their aunt.

On the son and daughter of Princess Margaret and Lord Snowdon *London Daily Mail* 4 Oct 77

5515 Thank goodness he hasn't got ears like his father!

On seeing Prince Charles' son William for the first time *International Herald Tribune* 8 Jun 92

5516 We put on dressing-gowns and shoes and crouched in the window looking onto a cold misty morning.

Recalling her parents' coronation day 12 May 1937 *London Times* 25 Sep 93

Major Ronald Ferguson Duchess of York's father

5517 I only made one comment. It was "Be yourself," and she has continued to be.

On the marriage of his daughter to the Duke of York *People* 21 Sep 87

Dorothy Canfield Fisher essayist

5518 A mother is not a person to lean on but a person to make leaning unnecessary.

Recalled on Fisher's death 9 Nov 58

Geoffrey Fisher Archbishop of Canterbury

5519 Don't bother me, dear, I'm busy dying!

To his wife on suffering a stroke at age 85, quoted by Edward Carpenter *Archbishop Fisher* Canterbury Press Norwich 91

Sally Fitzgerald anthologist

5520 I had an aunt whom we called Aunt Car. . . the only one of my father's three maiden sisters who could drive.

To novelist Flannery O'Connor, Sally Fitzgerald ed *The Habit of Being: Letters of Flannery O'Connor* Viking 79

Kitty Burns Florey essayist

5521 My parents waited ten years for me; that's the way they always put it as if I were a late train to a place they desperately wanted to go.

"Thoughts of Home" *House Beautiful* Nov 95

Henry Fonda actor

5522 It isn't that I'm a weak father, it's just that she's a strong daughter!

On actress Jane Fonda quoted by Allen Drury *Cosmos Club Bulletin* Washington Oct 94

Anne McDonnell Ford heiress

5523 We'd have been much better off. . . putting sandwich boards on their backs reading "I'm the daughter of Henry Ford. . . worth this many million dollars. . . this is my telephone number."

Regretting her daughters' failed marriages to Europeans, quoted by Peter Collier and David Horowitz *The Fords* Simon & Schuster 87

Gerald R Ford 38th US President

5524 All my children have spoken for themselves since they first learned to speak and not always with my advance approval and I expect that to continue in the future.

On the spirit of realistic tolerance in acceptance of an articulate brood *NY Post* 13 Aug 74

Henry Ford II industrialist

5525 My grandfather killed my father. . . I know he died of cancer—but it was because of what my grandfather did to him.

On Henry Ford and Edsel Ford, quoted by Robert Lacey *Ford: The Man and the Machine* Little, Brown 86

5526 I wanted you to be able to see and hear from me personally just what I've decided to do about my estate.

Videotape addressed to his wife and children three years before his death *Fortune* 16 Jan 89

J Merrill Foster essayist

5527 America's lifestyle prepares us well....but it prepares us not at all for old age.

NY Times 31 Jan 88

5528 Her's was the home the family came to, a place of books a big old house where civility was spoken.

ib

Brenda Frazier debutante

5529 I was bred and trained to be married, run a household, give parties and rear daughters to have their own debuts, and sons to dance with a new generation of debutantes.

Quoted by Gioia Diliberto *Debutante* Knopf 87

Tad Friend essayist

5530 They conjure up those family Saturday nights. . . when I was freshly bathed, in my flannel pj's and angling not to be sent to bed. And when I had a monster crush on Mary.

On watching situation comedies especially *The Mary Tyler Moore Show Esquire* Mar 93

5531 I knew those people better than I knew anyone outside my family and I understood them better than I understood most people in my family.

ib

5532 I believed that. . . coffee sobers a drunk, that bald people are especially witty and that women look sexy in flared slacks. Sadly this information turned out to be false.

ib

Sam Frustaci septuplets' father

5533 We thought it might be fun to have twins.

On the largest multiple birth in US history *Time* 3 Jun 85

Ava Gardner actress

5534 I got along with the mothers of all the men I married. If only I'd gotten along half as well with the husbands, I'd still be married to as many of them as the law allows.

Ava Bantam 90

Romain Gary novelist

5535 You carry within you the poison of comparisons and you spend your days waiting for something you have already had and will never come again.

On his mother's overshadowing love, recalled on Gary's suicide 2 Dec 80

George VI King of England

5536 I was so proud of you and thrilled at having you so close to me on our long walk in Westminster Abbey, but when I handed your hand to the Archbishop I felt that I had lost something very precious.

On Princess Elizabeth's wedding quoted by Sarah Bradford *The Reluctant King* St Martin 89

Brigitte Gerney accident victim

5537 The crane... was cold metal right next to me. I said "Can you cut my legs off and take me out? I have two children. I have to live."

On being pinned down by a 35-ton construction crane on a Manhattan building site *NY Times* 15 Apr 86

John Paul Getty financier

5538 I sincerely regret all my divorces because I don't like anything to be unsuccessful.

On five marriages *Time* 24 Feb 58

5539 Keep killing my son.

To attorney Moses Lasky on Gordon Getty's attempts to take over the family trust, quoted by Thomas Petzinger Jr *Oil & Honor* Putnam 87

Elise Gibbs poet

5540 Four is too big for his breeches,/Knows infinitely more than his mother,/Four is a matinee idol/To two-and-a-half, his brother./Four is a lyric composer,/Raconteur extraordinaire,/Four gets away with murder,/Out of line and into hair.

Four Curtis Publishing Co 55

5541 Where Four is, there dirt is also,/And nails and lengths of twine,/Four is Mr Fix-it/And all of his tools are mine./Four barges into everything/(Hearts too) without a knock./Four will be five on the twelfth of July,/And I wish I could stop the clock.

ib

Newton L ("Newt") Gingrich Speaker US House of Representatives

5542 We are an American family with all the complexity of an American family.

On being lobbied on gay rights by his half-sister Candace; "Washington at its most bizarre," said Reuters News Service *Washington Post* 7 Mar 95

Ruth Bader Ginsburg Associate Justice US Supreme Court

5543 I pray that I may be all that she would have been had she lived in an age when women could aspire and achieve and daughters are cherished as much as sons.

Recalling her mother in speech accepting President Clinton's nomination to the US Supreme Court *NY Times* 15 Jun 93

Mikhail S Gorbachev President of Russia

5544 The whole family agreed that it was up to me to decide and that they were ready to share with me to the end whatever was ahead.

On house arrests at outset of attempted overthrow *Washington Times* 28 Oct 91 excerpting *The August Coup* HarperCollins 91

Robert Graves poet

5545 People long dead were talked about as familiarly as though they had only just left the room.

Robert Graves Viking 87

Reginald Green shooting victim's father

5546 We thought it important to give his future to someone who had lost theirs.

On donation of his 7-year-old son's vital organs after the child was killed by highway bandits who attacked the Bodega Bay CA family near Salerno Italy *USA Today* 5 Oct 94

Vartan Gregorian educator

5547 There she was in her bed. Dead. But nobody explained it to me. They told me later that she had gone to America.

On his mother's death in Iran when he was age 7 *New Yorker* 14 Apr 86

5548 Dignity is not negotiable. Dignity is the honor of the family.

ib

Gerald Cavendish Grosvenor Duke of Westminster

5549 He's been born with the longest silver spoon anyone can have but he can't go through life sucking on it.

On his son as heir to Britain's biggest real estate holdings *Guardian Weekly* 7 Mar 93

Allan Gurganus novelist

5550 I watched my mother. . . waste her life vacuuming for reasons that are still mysterious to me. Dust is not something we need to be deeply ashamed of since we are it.

New York 21 Aug 89

Donald Hall autobiographer

5551 My grandfather did not know the maiden names of either of his grandmothers. I thought that to be forgotten must be the worst fate of all.

String Too Short to be Saved Viking 61

5552 [It was] a time and place of affection and security—a high pasture of grass and ferns surrounded by birches, and it remains in my mind the best idyll of my 64 years.

On childhood summers with his grandparents on a New Hampshire farm *Life Work* Beacon 93

5553 They lived here. . . in love and double-solitude.

ib

Barry Hannah novelist

5554 I wish I'd had a heart. I didn't even cry at my wife's funeral—knew I should but I just couldn't. My children looked long and expecting at me.

Reading aloud on *Sunday Morning* CBS TV from his book *Bats Out of Hell* Houghton Mifflin 93

5555 I was like that as a little boy. Look on the worst things without a blink, eyes so dry they hurt. Something left out of me at birth. I began lying because there wasn't nothing in true life that moved me.

ib

Moss Hart playwright

5556 My grandfather. . . towered over my first seven years like an Everest of Victorian tyranny.

Act One Random House 59

5557 He accepted my father's dim presence in the house with the passing annoyance of a GI watching a jungle fungus grow on his boot.

ib

Helen Hayes actress

5558 There's a little vanity chair that Charles gave me the first Christmas we knew each other. I'll not be parting with that nor our bed—the four-poster—I'll be needing that to die in.

On auctioning furnishings of the Nyack NY house she shared with husband, Charles MacArthur *NY Times* 21 Oct 23

5559 Charles. . . looked upon the poor little red thing and blurted "She's more beautiful than the Brooklyn Bridge!"

On their infant daughter, Nancy Caldwell Sorel ed *Ever Since Eve: Personal Reflections on Childbirth* Oxford 84

5560 Life would shape her, not me. All we were good for was to make the introductions.

ib

Annie Henderson poet's grandmother

5561 Wash as far as possible, then wash possible!

On bedtime baths, quoted by granddaughter, writer Maya Angelou *I Know Why the Caged Bird Sings* Random House 69

Katharine Houghton Hepburn actress' mother

5562 If you want to sacrifice the admiration of many men for the criticism of one, go ahead and get married.

To her daughter, actress Katharine Hepburn, quoted by Anne Edwards *A Remarkable Woman* Morrow 85

John Hinckley Sr attempted assassin's father

5563 What do you say the first time you see your son after he has done the unthinkable? Why did you shoot the President, son?

On John Hinkley Jr's wounding of President Reagan *Breaking Point* Zondervan 85

5564 We told John we loved him. . . and that we intended to see things through together.

Reaffirming loyalty to his son *ib*

Herbert Hoover 31st US President

5565 Mrs Hoover and I always believed the incidents of our family life were our sole possession.

On reluctance to write about his personal life except to expel "myths," preface to *The Memoirs of Herbert Hoover* Vol II Macmillan 51

Mary Jarrell poet's wife

5566 Jarrell was not much a father. . . as an affectionate encyclopedia.

On her husband's role in addition to being consultant in poetry to the Library of Congress *Randall Jarrell's Letters* Houghton Mifflin 85

Basia Johnson heiress

5567 Slam the door in their face and give them not the dust from a penny.

Instructing her lawyers on division of multi-million dollar fortune with children of her late husband, pharmaceutical executive J Seward Johnson, quoted by Barbara Goldsmith *Johnson & Johnson* Dell 88

Lyndon B Johnson 36th US President

5568 My father would have enjoyed what you have so generously said of me—and my mother would have believed it.

On receiving an honorary degree from Baylor University 28 May 65

5569 I have a little house where I was born the son of a tenant farmer, a picture of which is hanging up in my bedroom because every night when I go to bed and every morning when I wake up I call it the "opportunity house."

Washington 27 Apr 64, Jack Shepherd and Christopher S Wren eds *Quotations from Chairman LBJ* Simon & Schuster 68

Erica Jong novelist

5570 My mother accepted Ken as she had never accepted anyone before. It may have been merely exhaustion.

On Jong's fourth husband *Fear of Flying* Holt Rinehart Winston 73

5571 Jewish lesbians are required to fall in love with women who remind them of their mothers. And in today's feminist times, are doctors or lawyers.

Fear of Fifty HarperCollins 94

Natasha Josefowitz poet

5572 My father died/many years ago,/and yet when something special/happens to me,/I talk to him secretly/not really knowing/whether he hears,/but it makes me feel better/to half believe it.

Is This Where I Was Going? Warner 81

Juliana Queen of the Netherlands

5573 Our child will not be raised in tissue paper! We don't even want her to hear the word princess.

On hiring a nurse for her first child *Ladies' Home Journal* Mar 55

Terry Kay father

5574 You ain't goin' to get rid of me. I'm in that pecan grove. I'm in the shape of your ear. I'm in the callus on your thumb.

Father speaking to a son *To Dance With the White Dog* CBS TV 5 Dec 93

5575 I'd like to be buried on a day like this. I'd like the sun to be shoveled in with me.

ib

Garrison Keillor humorist

5576 Lake Wobegon, where all the women are strong, the men are good looking, and all the children are above average.

Sign-off lines on *A Prairie Home Companion* radio show begun in 1974 *NY Times* 18 Feb 87

5577 [It is] the little town that time forgot that the decades cannot improve.

ib

5578 Night after night I stood barefoot on the cold bedroom floor looking out the window studying other people's happiness.

On his Minnesota boyhood *ib* 8 Dec 85

5579 From this dear children you should sense/The value of obedience./When I say "Don't," I mean "Postpone/Some naughtiness for when you're grown./For wicked flings and wild rampages/Are much more fun at later ages."

We Are Still Married Viking 89

Edward M Kennedy US Senator

5580 My brother... should be remembered simply as a good and decent man who saw wrong and tried to right it, saw suffering and tried to heal it, saw war and tried to stop it.

At requiem for Robert F Kennedy *NY Times* 9 Jun 68

5581 Dad, I'm in some trouble.

Informing his father of the drowning of a young secretary when the Senator's car went off a bridge at Chappaquiddick on Cape Cod, quoted by Peter Collier and David Horowitz *The Kennedys* Summit 84

5582 You're going to hear all sorts of things about me... terrible things.

ib

5583 She was a blessing to us and to the nation—and a lesson to the world on how to do things right, how to be a mother, how to appreciate history, how to be courageous.

At requiem for sister-in-law Jacqueline Kennedy Onassis 24 May 94

5584 No one else looked, spoke, wrote like her or was so original in the way she did things. No one we knew ever had a better sense of self. During those four endless days in 1963, she held us together as a family and a country in large part, because of her we could grieve and go on.

On John F Kennedy's assassination and burial *ib*

5585 Jackie was too young to be a widow in 1963 and too young to die now.

ib

5586 She was the most beautiful rose of all.

Announcing the death of his mother Rose Fitzgerald Kennedy at age 104 *Washington Post* 23 Jan 95

5587 She was ambitious not only for our success but for our souls.

At requiem for his mother *NY Times* 25 Jan 95

5588 With effortless ease she could bandage a cut... recite from memory... and spot a hole in a sock from a hundred yards away. Her character... was a combination of the sweetest gentleness and the most tempered steel.

ib

John F Kennedy Jr President's son

5589 The three of us have been alone for such a long time. We welcome a fourth person.

Toast to his sister Caroline's fiancé, Edwin Scholossberg *People* 4 Aug 86

5590 She was surrounded by her friends and family and her books and the things that she loved. And she did it her own way and we all feel lucky for that and now she's in God's hands.

On his mother Jacqueline who left NY Hospital to die at home without life supports *ib* 6 Jun 94

Joseph P Kennedy patriarch

5591 Jack doesn't belong anymore to just a family. He belongs to the country.

Comment a few weeks before his son's inauguration, quoted by Hugh Sidey *John F Kennedy President* Atheneum 63

5592 If there's anything I'd hate as a son-in-law it's an actor; and if there's anything I think I'd hate worse than an actor as a son-it-law, it's an English actor.

Tongue-in-cheek comment on Patricia Kennedy's marriage to Peter Lawford *ib*

5593 He may be President but he still comes home and steals my socks!

Quoted by Hugh Sidey *ib*

5594 He's a great kid. He hates the same way I do.

On son Bobby, quoted by Richard J Whalen *The Founding Father* New American Library 64

5595 You are still and always will be tops with me.

Cable to daughter, Kathleen, on her marriage to a Protestant, recalled on *The Kennedys* PBS TV 8 Nov 93

Rose Kennedy matriarch

5596 I looked on child-rearing not only as a work of love and duty but as a profession that was fully as interesting and challenging as any honorable profession and one that demanded the best that I could bring to it.

Times to Remember Doubleday 74

5597 They warned me I would lose my figure, be tied down for years to come, never escape the demands of such a large family. If I hadn't had the ninth, I would now have no sons.

Quoted by Barbara Gibson *Life With Rose Kennedy* Warner 86

5598 Eleven children without a father! How could that happen? Two boys in one family assassinated!

On the assassinations of sons, John and Robert, and the latter's large family *ib*

Elizabeth King officer's daughter

5599 He is the most even-tempered man in the Navy. He is always in a rage.

On her father, Admiral Eric Larrabee *Commander in Chief* Harper & Row 87

Henry A Kissinger US Secretary of State

5600 My family is soap!

On White House plans for him to contact relatives during visit to Germany, quoted by Walter Isaacson *Kissinger* Simon & Schuster 92

Tony Kronheiser *Washington Post* columnist

5601 Dig a pit, throw in the kids and ice cream, add chocolate sauce; an hour later take out and send home.

On how to give children's birthday parties NPR 6 Jan 95

Philip Larkin poet

5602 They fuck you up your mum and dad,/ They may not mean to, but they do./ They fill you with the faults they had/ And add some extra just for you.
But they were fucked up in their turn/ By fools in old-style hats and coats,/ Who half the time were soppy-stern/ And half at one another's throats.
Man hands on misery to man./ It deepens like a coastal shelf./ Get out as early as you can,/ And don't have any kids yourself.

"This Be the Verse" *Collected Poems* Farrar Straus Giroux 89

5603 [My parents' marriage] left me with two convictions: that human beings should not live together and that children should be taken from their parents at an early age.

Quoted by Richard Locke *Wall Street Journal* 19 Aug 93 reviewing Andrew Motion's *Philip Larkin* Farrar Straus Giroux 93

Norman Lear sitcom writer

5604 Edith, stifle yourself! Stifle!

Line for Archie Bunker to his wife *All in the Family* ABC TV series 73

Louise Heath Leber Mother of the Year

5605 There's always room for improvement you know—it's the biggest room in the house.

NY Post 14 May 61

Madeleine L'Engle novelist

5606 I love my mother not as a prisoner of arteriosclerosis, but as a person; and I must love her enough to accept her as she is now for as long as this dwindling may take.

The Summer of the Great-Grandmother Farrar Straus Giroux 74

5607 She seems to have had the ability to stand firmly on the rock of her past while living completely and unregretfully in the present.

ib

Sam Levenson humorist

5608 Insanity is hereditary—you get it from your children.

Diner's Club Magazine Nov 63

Anne Morrow Lindbergh essayist

5609 In the sheltered simplicity of the first days after a baby is born, one sees again the magical, closed circle, the miraculous sense of two people existing only for each other, the tranquil sky reflected on the face of the mother nursing her child.

Gift from the Sea Pantheon 55

5610 Time has not continued since that Tuesday night. It is as if we just stepped off into one long night or day.

Diary entry on the kidnapping of her infant son *Hour of Gold, Hour of Lead* Harcourt Brace Jovanovich 73

5611 He was such a gay, lordly, assured, little boy. . . . I could not bear to have him baffled, hurt, maimed by external forces. I hope he was killed immediately and did not struggle and cry for help—for me.

ib

5612 C's grief is different from mine and perhaps more fundamental.

On her husband, Col Charles A Lindbergh *ib*

5613 There is something very deep in a man's feeling for his son, it reaches further into the future. My grief is for the small, intimate, everyday person. His blue coat on a hook, his red tam, his blue Dutch suit, the little cobweb scarf we tied around his neck. . . .[and] in the pockets I found a shell, a "tee," and his red mittens. It was like touching his hand.

On revisiting her child's nursery *ib*

5614 The punctuation of anniversaries is terrible, like the closing of doors one after another between you and what you want to hold on to.

On annual rememberances of her infant son's kidnapping *Locked Rooms and Open Doors* Harcourt Brace Jovanovich 74

Charles A Lindbergh Jr aviator

5615 He makes fuzz come out of my bald patch!

On his first automobile ride with son Scott quoted by Leonard Mosley *Lindbergh* Doubleday 76

5616 He'd let me walk behind him with a loaded gun, at 7 use an axe. . . drive his Ford car anywhere at 12. . . . My freedom was complete, all he asked for was responsibility in turn.

Recalling his father, quoted by Brendan Gill *Lindbergh Alone* Harcourt Brace Jovanovich 77

Reeve Lindbergh aviator's daughter

5617 [They] drink in the solitude like water and breathe it out like air.

On parents Charles and Anne Lindbergh *The Names of the Mountains* Simon & Schuster 93

Beverly Lowry essayist

5618 At night. . . ever since I've had children I've measured the safety of house and self by the steady sound of other people's sleeping.

Crossed Over Knopf 92

Henry R Luce publisher

5619 It was a great big mysterious world filled with a thousand objects, pictures, keys, the frayed edges of the rug, the crack in the window pane, the photograph album exactly placed, the sound of the doorbell—just so year after year—each of these objects was woven with long threads into the pattern of life.

On growing up in China, quoted by Ralph G Martin *Henry and Clare* Putnam 91

Alison Lurie essayist

5620 The kitchen fills with smoke and the hot sweet ashy smell of scorched cookies. The war has begun.

On a wife's discovery of her husband's infidelity *War Between the Tates* Warner 74

Gen Douglas MacArthur US Army

5621 I take enormous pride in being able not only to call her my wife but to cite her as my best and bravest soldier.

At Murfressboro TN hometown welcome for Jean MacArthur *NY Times* 1 May 51

5622 I grew up with the sound of Dixie and the Rebel yell ringing in my ears. Dad was on the other side but he had the good sense to surrender to my mother.

On being born of a Virginia mother on an Arkansas army post *ib*

Archibald MacLeish poet and statesman

5623 God was Father's father.

On life with department store executive Andrew MacLeish, quoted by Scott Donaldson *Archibald MacLeish* Houghton Mifflin 92

5624 [I thought] about the flood of cool, clean water beating onto the sand. . . down between the cracked, dry boards to the beautiful clean bones that lie there.

On a rainy visit to his brother's military grave in Belgium *ib*

Harold Macmillan Prime Minister of Britain

5625 No one who has not experienced it, can realize the determination of an American mother defending one of her children.

On thwarting conversion to the Roman Catholic Church, quoted by Alistair Horne *Harold Macmillan* Vol I Viking 88

Thurgood Marshall Associate Justice, US Supreme Court

5626 Son, if anyone ever calls you a nigger, you not only got my permission to fight him, you got my orders to fight him.

Quoting his father recalled on Marshall's death *Washington Post* 25 Jan 93

Mary Queen Mother

5627 Her old Grannie and subject must be the first to kiss her hand.

On Elizabeth II's accession to the throne quoted by John Pearson *The Selling of the Royal Family* Simon & Schuster 84

5628 We are never tired and we all love hospitals.

Reply to a protest of weariness with public engagements *ib*

5629 This is a nice kettle of fish!

On abdication of her son Edward VIII, recalled on Queen Mary's death 24 Mar 53

André Maurois critic

5630 A successful marriage is an edifice that must be rebuilt every day.

Quoted by Jacob Brande comp *Speaker's Encyclopedia* Prentice Hall 55

Robert Maxwell publisher

5631 He broke a rule that I keep and want my children to live by—duty.

On firing his son when the young man failed to keep an appointment NPR 16 Mar 91

Mary McCarthy novelist

5632 My father was a romancer and most of my memories of him are colored I fear by an untruthfulness that I must have caught from him like one of the colds that ran around the family.

Intellectual Memoirs Harcourt Brace 92

Phyllis McGinley humorist

5633 Casualness... the rarest of virtues... is useful enough when children are small... important to the point of necessity when they are adolescents.

McCall's May 59

James Merrill poet

5634 A face no longer/Sought in dreams but worn as my own.

On noticing in his shaving mirror a resemblance to his father *New Yorker* 27 Mar 95

Liza Minnelli entertainer

5635 Whenever we were on a plane we had a family.

On life with her mother, Judy Garland, and father, Vincent Minnelli NBC TV 15 Jan 74

Bernard Law Montgomery Field Marshal, 1st Viscount Montgomery of Alamein

5636 They generally end in a row.

On family reunions, quoted by Nigel Hamilton *Monty* McGraw-Hill 87

5637 I like to see my family one at a time... every five or ten years.

ib

Brian Moore novelist

5638 We stood a small deputation of the living in that white field of death.

On a burial in a snowy cemetery *No Other Life* Doubleday 93

Alexander More-Nisbett Scottish schoolboy

5639 I am quite homesick... practically every second. I really want to see my nanny and my gamekeeper. And my parents.

On leaving his country house near Edinburgh to enter boarding school at age 8 *London Times* 22 Feb 91

5640 The problem of life really is that the good bits take about five seconds flat and the other bits about five million hours.

ib

Bob Morris essayist

5641 It's easier to change your outfit for the weekend than your mother and father.

On dressing to please parents *NY Times* 5 Mar 95

Toni Morrison novelist

5642 [We are] the people of the broken necks and fire-colored blood, of black boys hanging from the most beautiful sycamore trees in the world and black girls who have lost their ribbons.

Beloved Knopf 89

Lewis Mumford essayist

5643 So long before his work was done/He was the father, I the son.

On his son's death in World War II "Green Memories" quoted by Donald L Miller *Lewis Mumford* Weidenfeld & Nicolson 89

Jerrold Mundis essayist

5644 They raid by telephone with jarring suddenness. . . [and] the cyclic constancy of a mortgage. . . inevitable and relentness.

On seeking privacy from his family *Gerhardt's Children* Atheneum 76

Tema Nason novelist

5645 She's hooking her high-waisted corset stiffened with stays, sucking in her loose belly with the belly button swimming in fat and shoving in the flesh like it's the kishke of some unkosher animal.

On a young girl watching her mother dress in book based on the life of convicted spy Ethel Rosenberg *Ethel* Delacorte 90

5646 On her shoulders she hangs the heavy broad straps of her long brassiere, lifting and pouring her breasts into each cup like so much cotton wadding.

ib

Harold Nicolson diplomat and biographer

5647 His hair is like that of a golliwog and his clothes noticeable at the other end of Trafalgar Square.

Expressing astonishment that son Ben had a horror of being conspicuous, quoted by Philip Vansittart *In the Fifties* John Murray 95

5648 He was almost always in the same nondescript suit as though he never realized that other clothes were actually on the market.

ib

Frank Nixon President's father

5649 This boy is one of five that I raised and they are the finest I think in the United States. If you care to give him a lift, I would say the *Ohio State Journal* is still doing some good.

Letter commending Richard M Nixon's 1953 vice Presidential candidacy, quoted by Nixon *RN: Memoirs of Richard Nixon* Grossett & Dunlap 78

Hannah Nixon President's mother

5650 I am sure you will be guided right in your decision to place implicit faith in his integrity and honesty. Best wishes from one who has known Richard longer than anyone else, his mother.

Telegram to Dwight D Eisenhower after investigation of an alleged secret fund, quoted in *RN: Memoirs of Richard Nixon* Grossett & Dunlap 78

5651 He was the best potato-masher one could wish for.

On Richard M Nixon in the family-run store *Washington Post* 9 Jan 94

Richard M Nixon 37th US President

5652 President Johnson and I. . . were both born in small towns. . . and we're both fortunate in the fact that we think we married above ourselves.

News reports 5 Sep 69

5653 [He had] the poorest lemon ranch in California. . . [and] sold it before they found oil on it.

Recalling his father in farewell remarks to the White House staff 8 Aug 74

5654 I think of her two boys dying of tuberculosis, nursing four others. . . she was a saint.

On his mother *ib*

5655 I had come so far from the little house in Yorba Linda to this great house in Washington.

RN: The Memoirs of Richard Nixon Grosset & Dunlap 78

5656 My critics in the media called her "Plastic Pat." What they did not know was that her plastic was tougher than the finest steel.

On criticism of his wife *In the Arena* Simon & Schuster 90

Noor Queen of Jordan

5657 Our planning may leave something to be desired but our designs, thank God, have been flawless.

On birth of the fourth child in six years *Time* 10 Mar 86

Richard Olton suicide's uncle

5658 When I held you in my arms at your baptism. I wanted it to be a fresh start, for you to be more complete than we had ever been ourselves, but I wonder if we expected too much.

Eulogy for 18-year-old nephew, *NY Times* 15 Mar 87

Stewart O'Nan novelist

5659 I don't like coming home. It keeps me from being nostalgic.

Snow Angels Doubleday 95

Alexander Onassis heir

5660 My father loves names and Jackie loves money.

On Aristotle Onassis' marriage to Jacqueline Kennedy, quoted by Peter Evans *Ari* Summit 86

Christina Onassis heiress

5661 [She was] my father's unfortunate obsession.

On Jacqueline Kennedy Onassis, quoted by William Wright *All the Pain That Money Can Buy* Simon & Schuster 91

Jacqueline Kennedy Onassis First Lady

5662 In this room lived John Fitzgerald Kennedy with his wife Jacqueline Kennedy—during the two years ten months and two days he was President of the United States. January 20, 1961–November 22, 1963.

Inscription incised on White House mantlepiece *NY Times* 11 Jan 64

5663 Do you think seeing the coffin can upset me, Doctor? I've seen my husband die, shot in my arms. His blood is all over me. How can I see anything worse than I've seen?

To a physician at Parkland Hospital Dallas 22 Nov 63 quoted by William Manchester *The Death of a President* Harper & Row 67

5664 So now he is a legend when he would have preferred to be a man.

Thoughts after the President's funeral *ib*

5665 His high noon kept all the freshness of the morning—and he died then, never knowing disillusionment.

ib

Katherine D Ortega US Treasurer

5666 In the next year or so, my signature will appear on $60 billion of United States currency. More important to me, however, is the signature that appears on my life—the strong, proud, assertive handwriting of a loving father and mother.

NY Times 19 Aug 84

John Osborne playwright

5667 Disappointment was oxygen to them. The grudge that was their birthright, they pursued with passionate despondency to the grave.

On his family and the nourishing of a sentiment that he carried over to plays he wrote as Britain's "angry young man" *NY Times* 24 Dec 94

5668 I am ashamed of her as a part of myself that can't be cut out.

On his mother as a central figure in his plays and autobiographical account of suffocating values of lower middle-class English life *A Better Class of Persons* Dutton 81

Marguerite Oswald alleged assassin's mother

5669 Lee was such a fine, high-class boy... if he'd killed the President he would have said so. That's the way he was brought up.

On Lee Harvey Oswald as alledged assassin of President Kennedy *Time* 13 Dec 63

5670 Mr Johnson should remember that I am not just anyone and that he is only President of the United States by the grace of my son's action.

14 Feb 64 *ib*

Octavio Paz poet

5671 The tablecloth smelled of gunpowder.

On his father and grandfather's stories of bandits and generals *NY Times* 12 Oct 90

5672 I kept quiet:who was there for me to talk about?

ib

Alton Peters composer's son-in-law

5673 He was one hundred one years old. He just fell asleep.

On the death of composer Irving Berlin *Variety* 27 Sep 89

Philip Duke of Edinburgh

5674 Constitutionally, I do not exist.

On his role as Prince Consort *Illustrated London News* Jun 81

Noa Ben-Artzi Philosof Prime Minister's granddaughter

5675 Others... eulogized you but none of them ever had the pleasure I had to feel the caresses of your warm, soft hands, to merit your warm embrace reserved only for us, to see your half-smile that always told me so much, that same smile which is no longer frozen in the grave with you.

At funeral for the assassinated Israeli Prime Minister Yitzhak Rabin *NY Times* 7 Nov 95

Pablo Picasso painter

5676 You can touch them with your eyes.

Forbidding daughter Paloma to use his art materials as playthings, recalled by her WNBC TV 10 Dec 86

R W F Poole essayist

5677 Victorian central heating never did more than make the pipes gurgle... Drawing rooms were windswept steeps... bedrooms were deep frozen.

Country Life 9 Dec 93

James Pope-Hennessy biographer

5678 [She was] too Royal to marry an English gentleman and not Royal enough for Royalty.

On concessions made for Princess Mary of Teck who was engaged to the Prince of Wales and after his death became the fiancée and later the wife and consort of George V *Queen Mary* Knopf 60

V S Pritchett novelist

5679 Father couldn't tell a story to save his skin but he could be a story.

Guardian Weekly 4 Mar 90

5680 He passed his plate up and said as his own mother had before, "Just a little more." It should have been his epitaph.
On his father *ib*

Anna Quindlen columnist

5681 Maria and I are much alike. . . to love her requires me to love myself.
On daughter Maria at age 5 "Birthday Girl" *NY Times* 21 Nov 93

Nancy Reagan First Lady

5682 I think he'll be very happy there. I mean the view is pretty.
On selecting her husband's burial site at the Reagan Presidential Library, Simi Valley CA *International Herald Tribune* 6 Mar 95

Ronald Reagan 40th US President

5683 Seventy-five years ago I was born in Tampico IL in a little flat above the bank building. We didn't have any other contact with the bank.
On his birthplace *NY Times* 7 Feb 86

5684 Now here I am sort of living above the store again.
On the White House *ib*

5685 We were poor when I was young, but the difference then was the government didn't come around telling you you were poor.
Time 7 Jul 86

Ronald Reagan Jr President's son

5686 [It's] like asking a tomato how it feels to be red.
On being the son of the President of the United States *Washington Post* 17 Jan 89

5687 You're girded in neon tinsel, glopped on your head, and it's announced that you are henceforth a charter member of the First Family. It doesn't seem to matter what sort of family that actually is.
ib

5688 These are theater people, these are actors. That was like the greatest role they could ever have. The greatest audience. Playing to a packed house, wherever they went. And now it's over.
On his parents' departure from the White House quoted by Kitty Kelley *Nancy Reagan* Simon & Schuster 91

Janet Reno US Attorney General

5689 She was life itself to me. Whenever I ask myself what life was for or what the meaning of life was, I need only look over at her or call her if I was away. . . or in the last days reach over and hold her old gnarled hand, to know the answer.
On her mother *NY Times* 15 May 94

5690 Mother loved us hard and she spanked us hard.
New Yorker 15 May 95

5691 She could say "I love you" better than anyone I know. . . . [but] I take some small comfort today in knowing that Mother will not insult anyone or embarrass the family. She was responsible for the most excruciating moments of my life.
Eulogy *ib*

James B Reston journalist

5692 Age 17 is the point in the journey when the parents retire to the observation car. . . when you stop being critical of your eldest son and he starts being critical of you.
Saturday Evening Post 5 May 56

5693 Helping your eldest son pick a college is one of the great educatonal experiences of life. . . . Next to trying to pick his bride, it's the best way to learn that your authority, if not entirely gone, is slipping fast.
ib

Alina Fernandez Revuelta

5694 I don't like to think I hate my father. But I hate the system and my father is the system.
On stunning Cuban exiles by disclosing that she was Fidel Castro's daughter and wished to take part in Miami's Freedom Flotilla human rights protest *USA Today* 31 Aug 95

5695 They forgave me for being my father's daughter.
ib

Maria Riva biographer

5696 Never turn to your mother for help when she has just had an abortion.
On her mother *Marlene Dietrich* Knopf 92

David Rockefeller Jr heir

5697 We weren't allowed to discuss it. . . to gloat. . . [to] do anything. And so it was like a festering sore. Like a thing that was going to pop later on.
On his father's belief that talk about money was "not nice," quoted by Peter Collier and David Horowitz *The Rockefellers* Holt Rinehart Winston 76

5698 If you let it control you, then you become a philanderer instead of a philanthropist.
ib

Hope Rockefeller heiress

5699 Every one of us has thought at one time or another of getting away from the name. . . yet we all know deep down that there's no escape.
On the fourth generation cousins *op cit*

Laura Rockefeller heiress

5700 It's very hard to get rid of the money. . . . [but] one of the ways is to subsidize people who are trying to change the system and get rid of people like us.

On her inheritance *op cit*

Lucy Rockefeller heiress

5701 Being a Rockefeller is like being a cripple. No matter what you do with your crippled arm or leg it's still crippled. What you try to do is develop the rest in such a way that the disability is not really you.

op cit

Marion Rockefeller heiress

5702 There have been times in my life when I wanted to be a lamb almost just to raise the wool so I could card it and spin it and knit it into a blanket for myself.

op cit

Richard Rockefeller heir

5703 He and his brother feel that if you're down you should go and clean up your room and then you'll feel better. . . if they "clean up their rooms," they do feel better.

On his father David and Uncle Nelson *op cit*

Sharon Percy Rockefeller Governor's wife

5704 When you marry a Rockefeller you are an in-law but you often feel like an outlaw.

On conforming to example of Rockefeller wives as partner with West Virginia Gov John D ("Jay") Rockefeller IV quoted by John Ensor Harr and Peter J Johnson *The Rockefeller Conscience* Scribner 91

Eleanor Roosevelt Fisrt Lady

5705 When I looked at my mother-in-law's face after she was dead, I saw and understood many things that I had never seen before.

Quoted by Joseph P Lash *Eleanor and Franklin* Norton 71

5706 [I'd] been living in other people's houses and. . . in a public institution. . . . My next move was into a museum.

To Frances Perkins on going from the Governor's Mansion in Albany NY to the White House, quoted by Blanche Wiesen Cook *Eleanor Roosevelt* Vol I Viking 92

John Roosevelt President's son

5707 What they could do for the world was far more important than anything they could do for us.

On his parents Eleanor and Franklin D Roosevelt *New York* 14 Apr 95

Ethel Rosenberg Communist spy

5708 We know that a car could strike us and kill us but that doesn't mean we spend every minute being fearful about cars.

Writing from Sing Sing's death row to her two children, quoted by Louis Nizer *The Implosion Conspiracy* Doubleday 73

5709 Answer briefly that it is painless electrocution, which we believe will never come to pass, of course.

On what her husband should tell their children *ib*

5710 I am one vast vessel of pain. . . every inch of me beats with hurt.

After her small sons' visit to death row *ib*

5711 These saviours are actually proposing to erect a sepulcher in which I shall live without living and die without dying.

On government efforts to persuade her to avoid execution by testifying against her husband *ib*

5712 Eventually, too, you must come to believe that life is worth the living. Be comforted with that even now, with the end of ours slowly approaching, that we know this with a conviction that defeats the executioner!

Letter to her sons a few hours before being put to death for espionage, quoted by Robert and Michael Meeropol *We Are Your Sons* Houghton Mifflin 75

5713 Your Daddy who is with me in the last momentous hours, sends his heart and all the love that is in it for his dearest boys. Always remember that we were innocent and could not wrong our conscience.

ib

Artur Rubinstein pianist

5714 It took great courage to ask a beautiful young woman to marry me. Believe me, it is easier to play the whole of *Petrushka* on the piano.

Quoted by Samuel Chotzinoff *A Little Night Music* Harper & Row 64

5715 The result was magnificent. . . I became the father of two girls and two boys, lovely children—by good fortune they all look like my wife.

ib

Carl Sandburg poet

5716 I kissed my hand to the dim shape standing in the shadows under the porch, looking good-bye to her boy, and I keep a picture of one shaft of moonlight trembling near her face, telling of wishes farther than love or death, the infinite love of an old woman keeping a hope for her boy.

On saying farewell to his mother *Breathing Tokens* Harcourt Brace Jovanovich 78

Jean-Paul Sartre essayist

5717 Had my father lived, he would have lain on me at full length and would have crushed me.

The Words Braziller 64

Antonin Scalia Associate Justice US Supreme Court

5718 [In a big family] the first child is kind of like the first pancake. If it's not perfect, that's okay, there are a lot more coming along.

Newsweek 30 Jun 86

Walter M Schirra Sr astronaut's father

5719 You don't raise heroes, you raise sons. And if you treat them like sons they'll turn out to be heroes even if it's just in your own eyes.

NY Herald Tribune 3 Feb 63

Bobby Scott lyricist

5720 He ain't heavy, he's my brother.

Song title adapted as fund-raising slogan by Boy's Town, recalled on Scott's death *NY Times* 10 Nov 90

John Seabrook executive

5721 You can't keep the old bulls and the young bulls in the same pasture.

On stormy relationship between his father and grandfather, Seabrook Farms Founder C F Seabrook *New Yorker* 20 Feb 95

Gertrude Selzer essayist's mother

5722 Just because kittens are born in the oven does not make them loaves of bread.

On why a physician's son may become a writer instead of a doctor, quoted by Richard Selzer *Down from Troy* Morrow 92

Dolly Sinatra singer's mother

5723 I won't have you staying out until all hours singing in one of those night clubs.

On her son Frank's road house appearances at 21 quoted by Kitty Kelley *His Way* Bantam 86

5724 This one don't talk. She don't eat. What's she do?

On Frank Sinatra's marriage to 19-year-old Mia Farrow *ib*

Upton Sinclair novelist

5725 I just put on what the lady says. I've been married three times so I've had lots of supervision.

On what he wears at age 85 *NY Times* 7 Sep 62

Edith Sitwell poet

5726 It is like being with one's own family, if one likes one's own family.

On vists to Aldous and Maria Huxley, quoted by Victoria Glendinning *A Unicorn Among Lions* Weidenfeld & Nicolson 81

Ben Sonnenberg Jr son of PR pioneer

5727 I was subordinate to Sheraton, second to George II, and not so much fun as a cheerful chintz.

On his father's passion for furnishing his house on Manhattan's Gramercy Park *New York* 21 Jan 91

Stephen Spender poet

5728 When a child, my dreams rode on your wishes,/I was your son, high on your horse./My mind a top whipped by the lashes/Of your rhetoric, windy of course.

"The Public Son of a Public Man" *Time* 20 Jan 86

Jacqueline Stallone actor-director's mother

5729 I don't think he should get married again unless he finds a woman of intelligence, humor and background. And where is he going to find one of those?

On her son, Sylvester Stallone *Parade* 1 Jan 89

John Steinbeck novelist

5730 The impulse of the American woman to geld her husband and castrate her son is very strong.

Elaine Steinbeck and Robert Wallsten eds *Steinbeck: A Life in Letters* Penguin 76

5731 Thom seems to be a baby-shaped baby. . . he just eats and sleeps and shits but I can think of worse kids.

On his eldest son, quoted by Jay Parini *John Steinbeck* Holt 95

5732 You can't imagine how many clothes you have to put on a girl when the sole purpose is to get them off.

On his step-daughter's wedding *ib*

Alice Boyd Stockdale poet

5733 The girls from Mercer's School/All smile and nod,/And light flows multi-paned/Upon the altar,/Now. . . Behold the Body/and the Blood. . . /the Chalice and the host/are raised. I falter. . . /Lord You are the same,/We are Your flock,/and suddenly we're at home/in Castleknock.

On the family of US Ambassador Grant Stockdale *To Ireland With Love* Doubleday 64

Karen Tashjian architect

5734 I was feeling like the center of a wheel with two spokes missing. Then those two spokes were put in place and all of a sudden the wobble was gone.

On tracing her biological parents *NY Times* 30 Aug 93

Alice Taylor essayist

5735 The entire household revolved around the fire which provided warmth, cooking facilities, and a social center. . . the heart of every home and its warm glow was never extinguished while people still lived in the house.

On her childhood in rural Ireland in the 1950s *Quench the Lamp* St Martin 91

Denis Thatcher Prime Minister's husband

5736 Typical of Margaret. She produced twins. . . and avoided the necessity of a second pregnancy.

Quoted by Gail Sheehy "The Blooming of Margaret Thatcher" *Vanity Fair* Jun 89

5737 A pace behind her, old chap, a pace behind her.

On public appearances *Time* 14 Aug 89

Margaret Thatcher British Prime Minister

5738 The things I learned in a small town, in a very modest home, are just the things that I believe have won the election.

Tribute to her grocer-father and family life above the shop in the English midlands *New Yorker* 10 Feb 86

5739 Home is where you come to when you have nothing better to do.

On leaving office *London Times* 9 May 91

5740 If you want any help you ask for it at home. If you've got any problems you take them home. That's what family life is about.

Vanity Fair Jun 91

5741 Being Prime Minister is a lonely job. . . but with Denis there, I was never alone. What a man. What a husband. What a friend.

On her husband Denis Thatcher *The Downing Street Years* HarperCollins 93

Dylan Thomas poet

5742 Do not go gentle into that good night,/Old age should burn and rave at close of day;/Rage, rage against the dying of the light.

First stanza "Do Not Go Gentle Into That Good Night," written in 1951 as his father lay dying *Collected Poems 1934–52* New Directions 53

5743 And you, my father, there on the sad height,/Curse, bless me now with your fierce tears, I pray./Rage, rage against the dying of the light.

Final stanza *ib*

Dorothy Thompson columnist

5744 Children want to feel instinctively that their father is behind them as solid as a mountain, but, like a mountain, is something to look up to.

Ladies' Home Journal Jun 56

5745 She. . . had, never heard of inhibitions. If she had she would have been for them.

On her Aunt Lizzie, quoted by Peter Kurth *American Cassandra: The Life of Dorothy Thompson* Little, Brown 90

James Thurber humorist

5746 My once bickering, but now silent, family occupies a good square mile of space.

On visiting Green Lawn Cemetery, Columbus OH, quoted by Burton Bernstein *Thurber* Dodd Mead 75

Mame Thurber humorist's mother

5747 Now don't you dare drive all over town without gasoline.

Warning to her son James, quoted by columnist Russell Baker *NY Times* 12 Apr 90

Betty Toni student

5748 She is always warm like cotton. . . as smart as a computer. Sometimes as mean as a lion.

My Grandmother poem written in elementary school class on use of metaphors *NY Times* 4 May 85

William Trevor

5749 Both were charming in different ways. . . but their charming of one another their pride in one another their pleasing of one another: in later years it was hard to believe any of that had ever been there.

Field of Battle, on his parents' marriage, quoted by Merle Rubin *Christian Science Monitor* 10 Mar 94 reviewing Trevor's *Excursions in the Real World* Knopf 94

5750 They were victims of their innocence when chance threw them together and passion beguiled them leaving them to live with a mistake and to watch their field of battle expanding with each day that passed.

ib

Harry S Truman 33rd US President

5751 I wish you would send me a pair of your old breeches to hang on the bed, maybe I can have some luck.

Letter to a cousin while still childless after four years of marriage in the 1920s, quoted by David McCullough *Truman* Simon & Schuster 92

5752 It is a terrible—and I mean terrible—nuisance to be kin to the President of the United States.

Letter to his mother and sister two weeks after assuming the presidency in 1945, quoted in Truman's *Year of Decision* Doubleday 55

5753 I have found the best way to give advice to your children is to find out what they want and then advise them to do it.

CBS TV 27 May 55

5754 My father was not a failure. After all, he was the father of a President of the United States.

Mr Citizen Geiss 60

5755 It seems like there was always somebody for supper.

On life in the White House, quoted by Merriman Smith *The Good New Days* Bobbs-Merrill 62

5756 We're going to be buried out here. . . . because I may just want to get up. . . and stroll into the office. And I can hear you saying "Harry—you oughtn't!"

To his wife on plans for burial at the Truman Library, Independence MO *ib*

Margaret Truman President's daughter

5757 It's only when you grow up and step back from him, or leave him for your own career and your own home—it's only then that you can measure his greatness and fully appreciate it. Pride reinforces love.

To joint session of Congress on centennial of her father's birth 8 May 84

5758 I discovered as I wrote. . . a woman who kept her deepest feelings, her most profound sorrows, sealed from my view. . . invariably acts of love.

Forward to her biography of her mother *Bess W Truman* Macmillan 86

5759 This story. . . is about a woman who loved in spite of starting with the worst possible odds against this fundamental experience, a woman who might have become a creature with a heart of stone.

ib

John Updike novelist

5760 When she died he became the custodian of. . . a thousand tiny nuanced understandings of her, a more commonplace language of which he was now the sole surviving speaker.

The Short Life and Other Stories Hamish Hamilton 95

Thomas Vance Jr recovering addict

5761 When I saw her mother's swelling belly while we were lying on cardboard boxes on a train platform I knew I had to stop using.

On how the birth of his daughter saved him from being a homeless crack addict *NY Times* 11 Dec 92

Gloria Vanderbilt heiress

5762 I knew what I had to have before my soul would rest. I wanted to belong—to belong to my mother. And in return—I wanted my mother to belong to me.

Recalling a childhood marked by custody disputes between her mother and a paternal aunt *Once Upon a Time* Knopf 85

5763 She always lived off someone else's smile.

On her mother *Black Night White Knight* Knopf 87

Frederick Vreeland trendsetter's son

5764 Mom only liked to appear in public at full gallop.

On *Vogue* editor Diana Vreeland *NY Times* 15 Oct 95

Helen Walton magnate's wife

5765 I kept saying, Sam, we're making a good living. . . . [But] after the 17th store, I realized there wasn't going to be any stopping it.

On establishment of more than 1500 discount stores, quoted by Sam Walton *Made in America* Doubleday 92

Evelyn Waugh novelist

5766 Of children, as of procreation—the pleasure momentary, the posture ridiculous, the expense damnable.

Letter to Nancy Mitford 4 May 54

Orson Welles director

5767 [My mother] raised me with benign neglect.

Recalled on Welles' death 10 Oct 85

Eudora Welty novelist

5768 I. . . stormed up the stairs, pounding the carpet of each step with both hands ahead of me, putting my face right down in the cloud of the dear dust of our long absence.

On return home from a trip *One Writer's Beginning* Harvard 84

E B White essayist

5769 This small man, so challengingly complete and so devastatingly remote!

On his infant son *Letters of E B White* Harper & Row 76

Mary Beth Whitehead biological mother

5770 I gave her life. I can take life away.

To the couple she served as a surrogate mother but later sought to revoke the agreement *Washington Post* 14 Oct 86

Tennessee Williams playwright

5771 It was as if he had the intention of tearing it down from inside.

On the way that his father, C C Williams, always entered their St Louis apartment, quoted by Lyle Leverich *Tom* Crown 95

5772 A little Prussian officer in drag.

On his mother, Edwina Dakin Williams *ib*

James C Wright Jr Speaker, US House of Representatives

5773 That was the year when our family ate the piano.

On growing up during the 1930s Great Depression *NY Times* 10 Dec 86

Boris Yeltsin President of Russia

5774 We had to make love on the floor—that's why we got girls.

On the unfurnished home of his early marriage and birth of two daughters *60 Minutes* CBS TV 4 Apr 93

Observers and Critics

Mabell Airlie Lady-in-Waiting to Dowager Queen Mary

5775 As the cortege wound slowly along, the Queen whispered in a broken voice, "Here he is!" and I knew that her dry eyes were seeing beyond the coffin a little boy in a sailor suit.

On the 15 Feb 52 funeral procession of son George VI *Thatched With Gold* Hutchinson 62

5776 She was past weeping, wrapped in the ineffiable solitude of grief.

ib

Maya Angelou poet

5777 The thorn from the bush one has planted, nourished and pruned, pricks more deeply and draws more blood.

All God's Children Need Traveling Shoes Vintage 86

Allied Van Lines

5778 Moving-out is saying goodbye to your roses... to the room you brought your first-born home to... to the kitchen you finally—finally!—got fixed just the way you wanted it.

McCall's Oct 66

5779 Moving-in is discovering that your neighbor has a boy just your son's age... that there's a place out back where roses ought to thrive... that you don't have to buy new draperies after all!

ib

Anon

5780 Slow: Grandparents at Play.

Traffic sign in Orange Harbor FL mobile-home park *NY Times* 24 Sep 84

5781 [It is] the feminization of poverty.

Social workers' reference to matriarchial families 31 Oct 85

5782 Listen to me little fetus,/Precious *homo incompletus*,/As you dream your dreams placental/Don't grow nothing accidental!

"Every Parent's Nightmare" *Newsweek* 16 Mar 87

5783 Boomerang kids.

On increasing number of young adults who return home to live with their parents *NY Times* 12 Mar 89

5784 Deadbeat Dads.

On separated or divorced men who ignore child-support payments 31 May 92

5785 Nobody can hate each other the way a family can.

Publishing executive on the Hoiles-Hardie clan, owners of Freedom Newspapers, 25 dailies and 29 weeklies *Forbes* 19 Oct 92

5786 She graciously accepted the fact that her only grandchildren would have four legs, a tail and a bark.

Obituary notice of a woman whose children had dogs but not offspring *USA Today* 6 Nov 95

5787 My greatest accomplishment was in making a decent and honorable man out of my husband.

Obituary notice composed by a Utah woman *ib*

Violet Asquith Prime Minister's daughter

5788 In his solitary childhood and unhappy school days, Mrs Everest was his comforter, his strength and stay, his one source of unfailing human understanding.

On Winston S Churchill's nanny, Elizabeth Everest, quoted by William Manchester *The Last Lion* Little, Brown 83

5789 She was the fireside at which he dried his tears and warmed his heart. She was the nightlight by his bed. She was security.

ib

Louis Auchincloss novelist

5790 With her pale brow under her faded brown hair, she was like a rock washed clean by years of her husband's absences.

On the wife of a man busy with conventions, dinner committee meetings, "or simply at the office" *The Book Class* Houghton Mifflin 84

Bill Barol critic

5791 Thirtysomething (thur-tee-sum-thing)... adj or of relating to an extended period of young-adult self-absorption *viz*: "Oh shut up. Don't be so thirtysomething."

Definition of *Thirtysomething,* title of television drama on family life "Return of a Fine Whine" *Newsweek* 12 Dec 88

5792 [The] early 30s, the period when adult responsibilities start to crowd in and the inner voice that cries "Wait a minute, I'm really just a kid!" takes on a tinny, desperate edge.

ib

Donald Barr essayist

5793 It confuses the sprouting adolescent to wake up every morning in a new body. It confuses the mother

and father to find a new child every day in a familiar body.
NY Times 26 Nov 67

Laurence I Barrett essayist

5794 Barbara was the magistrate for misdemeanors while her husband judged felonies.
On the George Bush family *Time* 31 Jul 89

Joseph Barth King's Chapel, Boston

5795 Marriage is our last best chance to grow up.
Ladies' Home Journal Apr 61

Jim Bishop columnist

5796 Nobody understands anyone 18, including those who are 18.
Syndicated column 26 Apr 79

5797 Pause to dwell on the amount of love and treasure and patience parents poured into bodies no longer suitable for open caskets.
On teen-agers killed in automobile accidents *ib*

Mary Kay Blakely essayist

5798 Divorce is the psychological equivalent of a triple coronary by-pass.
Parade 12 Jul 87

5799 After... a monumental assault on the heart, it takes years to amend all the habits and attitudes that led up to it.
ib

David Blankenhorn Institute for American Values NYC

5800 Fatherlessness is the most destructive trend of our generation.
Fatherless America Basic Books 95

Hal Boyle columnist

5801 What ever happened to that old-fashioned Grandpa? The big-city Grandpa... is the life of every party and out to prove he is just as young as he ever was.
NY Journal-American 31 Jul 59

5802 No grandchild makes the mistake of calling him "Gramps"!
ib

Anthony Brandt essayist

5803 Other things may change us, but we start and end with the family.
"Bloodlines" *Esquire* Sep 84

5804 No matter how many years have passed, how many betrayals there may have been, how much misery... we remain connected even against our wills.
ib

Patricia L Brueckner poet

5805 Knowing children/Surfeited with everything/ Money could buy,/I rejoiced/At the children of poverty/Seeing their genius/At the invented games/ Out of everything/Confronting them/In their joyous world/Of bare toughness of life/Lightsweet voices/ Singing skip rope,/Throw the pie plate,/Pitch a stone/ At the crack in the street./Collect the broken bits of glass/And always,/Like a Jungian racial memory,/The elegant precisions of hopscotch.
Privately published 64

Gail Lumet Buckley sociologist

5806 Whites they pretended to ignore as they busily lived mirror-image white lives.
On a black family *The Hornes* Knopf 86

5807 Family faces are... mirrors. Looking at people who belong to us we see the past, present, and future.
ib

George Burns entertainer

5808 Happiness is having a large, loving, caring close-knit family in another city.
Newsweek Special Issue Winter/Spring 90

Robert Caro biographer

5809 To the people of East Tremont, East Tremont was family. In its bricks were generations.
On a NY neighborhood demolished for the Cross-Bronx Expressway *The Power Broker* Knopf 74

Adrienne Carr sociologist

5810 They hear with their hearts.
On the difficulty of advising foster parents on legal guidelines *NY Times* 1 Oct 87

Children's Defense Fund

5811 Will your child learn to multiply before she learns to subtract?
Poster on teen pregnancies *Christian Science Monitor* 13 Mar 86

Jerome Chodorow playwright

5812 The real secret of how to stay married... [is] keep the cave clean. They want the cave clean and spotless. Air-conditioned, if possible.
Anniversary Waltz with Joseph Fields Random House 54

5813 Sharpen his spear, and stick it in his hand when he goes... and when the bear chases him, console him when he comes home... tell him what a big man he is, and then hide the spear so he doesn't fall over it and stab himself.
ib

Winston S Churchill statesman

5814 Solitary trees, if they grow at all, grow strong, and a boy deprived of his father's care, often develops if he escapes the perils of youth, an independence and a vigor of thought which may restore in after life the heavy loss of early days.

Quoted by Lewis Mumford *Sketches From Life* Dial 82

John Ciardi critic

5815 Among the hopes of this world none shines more promisingly than the external resilience with which some children manage to escape into humanity from even the dreariest of parents.

Saturday Review 10 Aug 63

Francis X Clines reporter

5816 He sits at the kitchen table, which is the only authentic way to touch down at home in Queens.

On a man's return from prolonged hospitalization *NY Times* 16 Jun 79

5817 In sedan-chair backpacks... like little Popemobiles, they bear the terrible burden of being designer clones of the parents displayed for genealogical appreciation.

On baby boomers' children in Moscow 9 Sep 90

Colette (Sidonie Gabrielle Colette) novelist

5818 The faults of husbands are caused by the excess virtues of their wives.

Recalled on Colette's death 3 Aug 54

Peter Collier biographer

5819 The Ford Motor Company would... make them preeminent in the country's industrial aristocracy, but also divide them from themselves and one another and make the development of the Ford dynasty to come at once a comedy, a melodrama and a tragedy.

With David Horowitz in prologue to *The Fords* Simon & Schuster 87

5820 His grandfather was the solid object Henry would repeatedly run into, defining himself by the collision.

On Henry Ford and grandson Henry Ford II *ib*

5821 Henry had set out to save the company for the family and to purge it of personality. He had instead purged it of family and filled it with himself.

On Henry Ford II *ib*

5822 He was the dangling modifier of his father's fury.

On Henry Fonda's son, Peter, *The Fondas: A Hollywood Dynasty* Putnam 91

George Howe Colt essayist

5823 How many different things a family can be—a nest of tenderness, a jail for the heart, a nursery of souls.

Life Apr 91

5824 Families name us and define us, give us strength, give us grief. All our lives we struggle to embrace or escape their influence.... magnets that both hold us close and drive us away.

ib

Laurie Colwin essayist

5825 References, jokes, events, calamities... layer upon layer of the things daily life is made of. The edifice that lovers build is by comparison delicate and one-dimensional.

On "that family glaze of common references" *The Lone Pilgrim* Knopf 81

Henry Steele Commager historian

5826 It's awfully hard to be the son of a great man and also of a half-crazy woman.

On Robert Todd Lincoln *NY Times* 12 Feb 85

Cyril Connolly essayist

5827 Boys do not grow up gradually. They move forward in spurts like the hands of clocks in railway stations.

Enemies of Promise Persea Books 1939, recalled on Connolly's death 26 Nov 74

Rachael Cook critic

5828 The death of parents is really the death of childhood, a latent abandonment... one of the most painful aspects of middle age.

On John Updike's short stories *London Times* 26 Jan 85

Alistair Cooke commentator

5829 Tolerating your parents... will soon give way to the even more challenging occupation of tolerating your children.

At Smith College *A Commencement Address* Knopf 54

Jo Coudert essayist

5830 The divorced person... like a man with a black patch... looks rather dashing but the fact is that he has been through a maiming experience.

Advice from a Failure Stein & Day 65

Marcelene Cox columnist

5831 Our children await Christmas presents like politicians getting election returns... the Uncle Fred precinct and the Aunt Ruth district still to come in.

Ladies' Home Journal Dec 50

Quentin Crewe critic

5832 The children despise their parents until the age of 40, when they suddenly become just like them—thus preserving the system.

On the British upper class *Saturday Evening Post* 1 Dec 62

Alison Cross screewriter

5833 Gay parents don't make gay children any more often than straight parents.

Quoted by John J O'Connor reviewing Cross's screenplay *Serving in Silence: The Margarethe Cammermeyer Story, NY Times* 6 Feb 95

Brad Darrach essayist

5834 She organized the household like a small town and ran it like a mayor.

On the matriarch Rose Kennedy *Life* Mar 95

Robertson Davies essayist

5835 People marry most happily with their own kind. . . .[but] at an age where they do not really know what their own kind is.

A Voice from the Attic Knopf 60

Patrick Dennis humorist

5836 The Upsons lived the way every family in America wants to live—not rich but well-to-do.

On the 1930s and 40s *Auntie Mame* Vanguard 55

5837 [The Upsons] had the flat on Park and a house in Connecticut, a Buick sedan and a Ford station wagon; a boy and a girl; man and maid, town and country clubs, money and position.

On having "two of everything" *ib*

5838 Mrs Upson had two fur coats and two chins. Mr Upson had two passions—gold and business—and two aversions, Roosevelt and Jews.

ib

Peter De Vries humorist

5839 When I can no longer bear to think of victims of broken homes, I begin to think of the victims of intact ones.

Quoted by Robert Byrne and Teresa Shelton *Everyday is Father's Day* Atheneum 89

Stanley Elkin novelist

5840 Her children and their families were not bad people but insignificant beside the anguished memories of her Marvin.

On becoming a widow *Mrs Ted Bliss* Hyperion 95

5841 Some instinctive *baleboosteh* topism drew her to all the tamed arrangements of human domesticities.

On neighboring apartments *ib*

5842 There was something in Dorothy that made her throw herself on all the. . . welshers and four-flushers. . . a candidate for death by heartbreak.

ib

Delia Ephron essayist

5843 Joint-custody. . . allows the delicious contradiction of having children and maintaining the intimacy of life before kids.

Funny Sauce Viking 86

Nora Ephron essayist

5844 Summer bachelors like summer breezes are never as cool as they pretend.

NY Post 22 Aug 65

5845 Men who philander during the summer. . . are usually the same lot who philander during the winter.

ib

Thomas Everly columnist

5846 Don't leave Grandma in the attic. . . . She may not be there when you return.

On proper preservation of family pictures *Washington Post* 7 Nov 95

Toni Falbo essayist

5847 The only child is a world issue now.

On population control *NY Times* 13 Aug 84

Betty Freidan feminist

5848 As she made the beds, shopped. . . ate peanut butter sandwiches with her children. . . lay beside her husband at night—she was afraid to ask even of herself the silent question—"Is this all?"

The Feminine Mystique Norton 63

Erich Fromm essayist

5849 The very essence of motherly love is. . . to want the child's separation from self.

The Art of Loving Harper 56

Robert Frost poet

5850 You don't have to deserve your mother's love. You have to deserve your father's.

George Plimton ed *Writers at Work* Viking 63

5851 Home is the place where, when you go have to go there/ They have to take you in.

"Death of the Hired Man" 1914 recalled on Frost's death 29 Jan 63

5852 The greatest thing in family life is to take a hint when a hint is intended—and not to take a hint when a hint isn't intended.

Vogue 15 Mar 63

Lavinia Christensen Fugal Mother of the Year

5853 Love your children with all your hearts... enough to discipline them before it is too late.

Today NBC 3 May 55

5854 Praise your children... they live on it like bread and butter and they need it more than bread and butter.

ib

André Gide journalist

5855 Families, I hate you! Shut-in-homes, closed doors, jealous possessors of happiness.

Recalled on Gide's death 19 Feb 51

Brendan Gill essayist

5856 One catches a glimpse of a bizarrely laicized Holy Family with old Joseph safely put away and Christ and Mary in cozy rapture.... who could survive such serene effrontery?"

On Sara Delano Roosevelt's acceptance of the role of "historic mother" *A New York Life* Poseidon 90

Haim Ginnott psychologist

5857 The measure of a good parent is what he is willing not to do for his child. We help most by not helping.

Between Parent and Child Macmillan 65

Janet Gordon columnist

5858 The royal family is not an example to real Britons. We are an example to them.

To British readers *NY Times* 27 Sep 92

Peter Grose biographer

5859 [You] could not help but like him. With his brother, Foster, it was often precisely the opposite.

On Allen and Foster Dulles who served simultaneously as US Secretary of State and CIA Director *Gentleman Spy* Houghton Mifflin 94

Henry Anatole Grunwald essayist

5860 Home is the wallpaper above the bed... the dinner table... church bells... bruised shins of the playground, the small fears that come with dusk.

"Home is Where You Are Happy" *Time* 8 Jul 85

5861 [Home is] the streets and squares and monuments and shops that constitute one's first universe.

ib

Sydney J Harris columnist

5862 "Spacing" children... [means] parents have time to learn the mistakes made with the older ones—which permits them to make exactly the opposite mistakes with the younger ones.

Leaving the Surface Houghton Mifflin 68

Heloise (Heloise Cruse) columnist

5863 I think housework is the reason most women go to the office.

On her household help-and-hints column *Editor & Publisher* 27 Apr 63

Theodore M Hesburgh President, Notre Dame

5864 The most important thing a father can do for his children is to love their mother.

Reader's Digest Jan 63

Lord Hesketh (Thomas Alexander Fermor-Hesketh) member of the House of Lords and future Whip

5865 [He is] the bedrock on which the whole cathedral sits.

On Prime Minister Margaret Thatcher's husband, Denis, *Vanity Fair* Jun 91

Marjorie Holmes essayist

5866 A child's hand in yours?... You are instantly the very touchstone of wisdom and strength.

Calendar of Love and Inspiration Doubleday 81

Thomas Holmes essayist

5867 Catching a cold when a mother-in-law comes to visit... was mentioned so often that we came to consider them a common cause of disease.

Time 6 Jun 83

Fannie Hurst novelist

5868 A bad marriage... a bitter experience... but it is the better alternative.

Parade 18 Sep 60

McCready Huston novelist

5869 She invoked the understood silence of the long married.

The Platinum Yoke Lippincott 63

Dr Carl Jung psychoanalyst

5870 Nothing has a stronger influence on their children than the unlived lives of their parents.

Boston Magazine Jun 78

Ellen Karsh essayist

5871 A teenager... [is] holes in jeans, studs in ear... a cap on his head (backwards).

"A Teenager Is a Ton of Worry" *NY Times* 3 Jan 87

John R Kelly sociologist, University of Illinois Urbana-Champaign

5872 Dinner together is one of the absolute critical symbols in the cohesion of the family.

NY Times/CBS News poll *NY Times* 5 Dec 90

Jeane J Kirkpatrick US ambassador to UN

5873 Truth, which is more important to a scholar, has got to be concrete. And there is nothing more concrete than dealing with babies, burps and bottles, frogs and mud.

On how the rearing of three sons prepared her for the UN *Newsweek* 3 Jan 83

Ann Kent essayist

5874 Grief and greed are as inextricably entwined as love and marriage should be....[and] those terrible rows over who inherits what are not restricted to novels, soap operas or the families of the rich.

"The Bitter Inheritance of Bereavement" *London Times* 12 Aug 85

Marci Klein designer's daughter

5875 Every time I'm about ready to go to bed with a guy, I have to look at my Dad's name all over the guy's underwear.

On fashion's Calvin Klein *Newsweek* 11 Sep 95

George Levinger essayist

5876 A happy marriage is not so much how compatible you are but how you deal with the incompatible.

NY Times 16 Apr 85

John Lockwood legal counsel

5877 Mr Rockefeller was like a sun and the boys like the planets. If one of them got too close, he got burned; if he got too far away he spun off into space.

On John D Rockefeller and his five sons, quoted by Peter Collins and David Horowitz *The Rockefellers* Holt Rinehart Winston 76

Onnie Lee Logan Alabama midwife

5878 I don't be going there on no license. I be going there as a friend to help that husband deliver his baby.

On transcending state licensing in the delivery of every child born in a predominantly black Alabama township from 1931 to 1984 *NY Times* 13 Jul 95

London Times

5879 However great the provocations, the estranged wife of the future monarch should not debate in public his fitness and preparedness to rule.

"The Royal Individuals" editorial on Princess Diana's television interview on her marriage 22 Nov 95

Robert D MacFadden reporter

5880 Respectability. . . modest homes. . . fathers who hate drugs but sell tons of heroin, gambling czars who lose heavily on the horses, murderers who take offense at off-color language, and Runyonesque characters with funny nicknames who beat people to death with hammers.

Reporting on the home life of the underworld *NY Times* 11 Mar 87

Norman Mailer novelist

5881 The internal workings of her psyche were always condemned to hard labor. . . outrageous ego. . . self-deceit. . . bold loneliness and cold bones, those endless humiliations that burn like sores.

On "the dread Marguerite," mother of President Kennedy's alledged assassin, Lee Harvey Oswald, *Oswald's Tale* Random House 95

William Manchester biographer

5882 The ritualistic unfolding of a Chartwell day, from dawn to Kent's long blue twilight is for him a kind of private pageant.

On Winston S Churchill at his country home *The Last Lion* Little, Brown 88

5883 He never doubts—nor does anyone else sleeping beneath this roof that he alone is. . . playwright, producer, director, stage manager, and, of course hero of the performance.

ib

George R Marek biographer

5884 He gave. . . whatever love he could spare from the love of Beethoven.

On conductor Arturo Toscanini and his family *Toscanini* Atheneum 75

Margaret Mead anthropologist

5885 The wife in curlpapers is replaced by the wife who puts on lipstick before she wakens her husband...but having two bathrooms ruined the capacity to cooperate.

On changes in American marriages, recalled on Mead's death 15 Nov 78

5886 City dwellers to cliff dwellers. . . at least 50 percent would prefer at least one jungle between themselves and their mothers-in-law.

ib

Arthur Miller playwright

5887 To live on through something. . . gets more poignant as we get more anonymous.

On Willy Loman in *Death of a Salesman* who saw his son as "his masterpiece" *NY Times* 9 May 84

Lance Morrow essayist

5888 Mothers and small towns. . . can be suffocating like an interminable Sunday in an airless house.

Time 24 Dec 90

5889 Home is a place to run away from when the time comes.

ib

5890 Someone else's lights are burning inside upon someone else's Christmas tree and the child that once lived there is now a stranger in the skin of a middle-aged man. The house is someone else's now.

ib

5891 Everywhere you hang your hat is home. Home is the bright cave under the hat.

ib

Owen Morshead Windsor Castle librarian

5892 The House of Hanover, like ducks, produce bad parents.

To biographer Harold Nicolson, quoted by Philip Ziegler *King Edward VIII* Knopf 91

Faye Moskowitz essayist

5893 Adolescence. . . a 20th-century invention that most people approach with dread and look back on with the relief of survivors.

A Leak in the Heart Godine 85

Andrew Motion biographer

5894 Moaning and wringing her hands, she preceded her son through his life, loading him down with the constraints he dreaded but also embraced.

On poet Philip Larkin's mother *Philip Larkin* Farrar Straus Giroux 93

5895 The very things that in the past had most irritated him about them. . . turned suddenly round and became emblems of their most lovable qualities.

On Larkin's return to his parents' bombed-out home in Coventry *ib*

5896 By promising his life. . . he hoped he might be able to keep it for himself.

On Larkin's relationship to his mother and his girlfriend *ib*

J Herbert Mumm parent

5897 These days when a father says, "Son, I think it's time we had a little talk about sex," the reply is apt to be "OK, what did you want to know?"

Time magazine advertisement *NY Times* 18 Sep 94

Ogden Nash poet

5898 [As for] what makes a wife. . . no sooner has he learned how to cope with the tick than she tocks.

Marriage License Little, Brown 64

5899 Whenever you're wrong admit it; whenever you're right, shut up.

Recalled on Nash's death 19 May 71

5900 Parents. . . make children happy by giving them something to ignore.

ib

Richard J Needham columnist

5901 The first child is made of glass, the second porcelain, the rest of rubber, steel and granite.

Toronto Globe & Mail 25 Jan 77

The New York Times

5902 To be an American is to aspire to a room of one's own.

"Dream House" editorial 19 Apr 87

John J O'Connor critic

5903 [They] live in struggling luxury. . . shopping for a Daimler when you can only afford an Austin.

Reviewing *The Bretts* a television series on an American family *NY Times* 9 Oct 87

John O'Hara novelist

5904 In every marriage. . . the wife has to keep her mouth shut about at least one small thing her husband does that disgusts her.

Butterfield 8 Modern Library 1935 novel republished in 1994, quoted in review by Margo Jefferson *NY Times* 18 Jan 95

Dorothy Parker critic and humorist

5905 The best way to keep children home is to make it pleasant—and let the air out of the tires.

Quoted in *Utne Reader* Mar/Apr 91

Ivy Baker Priest US Treasurer

5906 Like two sides of a dollar bill, each different in design. . . her problem is to keep one from draining the life from the other.

On having a career and a family *Green Grows the Ivy* McGraw-Hill 58

J B Priestley playwright

5907 As we read the school reports on our children we realize a sense of relief that. . . nobody is reporting in this fashion on us!

Reader's Digest Jun 64

V S Pritchett novelist

5908 Private and family legends. . . [are] often the violent toys on the floor of memory.

New Yorker 19 Feb 79

Mario Puzo novelist

5909 A man who does not spend time with his family can never be a real man.

The Godfather Putnam 69

Anna Quindlen columnist

5910 The most powerful advertisement for alcohol may be sitting at the kitchen table. Or sleeping it off in the bedroom.

NY Times 6 Nov 91

5911 The average working couple have just enough time together to discover that they have run out of coffee and one of them forgot to mail the mortgage payment.

ib 2 Dec 92

5912 What was handed down from generation to generation was distance and silence.

ib 7 Dec 94

Radio Tokyo

5913 This afternoon at 4:15 at the Imperial Household Hospital, Her Highness, the Crown Princess, honorably affecting delivery, the honorable birth of a son occurred. The exalted mother and child are honorably healthy.

On birth of a prince second in line to the throne *Newsweek* 7 Mar 60

Randolph Ray Rector, Little Church Around the Corner, NYC

5914 Kindness is the life's blood the elixir of marriage. . . [and] makes the difference between passion and caring.

My Little Church Around the Corner Simon & Schuster 57

5915 Kindness is good will. Kindness says, "I want you to be happy."

ib

Ronald Reagan 40th US President

5916 It was supposed to be a few dollars to help them out. . . [but] now they can live apart. And it broke up the three-generational family.

On Social Security, quoted by Peggy Noonan *What I Saw at the Revolution* Random House 90

Joyce Rebeta-Burditt essayist

5917 Alcoholism isn't a spectator sport. Eventually the whole family gets to play.

The Cracker Factory Macmillan 77

Christopher Ricks critic

5918 If there was one thing worse than being married to a ruthless unsuccessful poet, it was being married to a ruthless, successful poet.

On Robert Frost *London Sunday Times* 7 Mar 71

Roxanne Robinson reporter

5919 The kitchen. . . as comforting as a family quilt.

On an upstate New York farm house *NY Times* 4 Apr 93

Anna Rosenberg US Assistant Secretary of Defense

5920 These boys are such different individuals with such different interests that if they had not been brothers, they would never have met.

On sons of John D Rockefeller *Fortune* Feb 55

Roger Rosenblatt essayist

5921 They cut their children loose like colorful kites and wish them an exciting flight.

On credit cards and supposed freedom *Time* 6 Oct 86

Philip Roth novelist

5922 A Jewish man with parents alive is a 15-year-old boy.

Portnoy's Complaint Random House 69

Bertrand Russell essayist

5923 The fundamental defect of fathers is that they want their children to be a credit to them.

NY Times 9 Jun 63

Maude Shaw nanny

5924 Your father's upstairs. You can call him "Mr President" now.

To Caroline Kennedy the day after elections, quoted by Ralph G Martin *A Hero for Our Time* Macmillan 83

5925 Your father's been shot. They took him to a hospital, but the doctors couldn't make him better.

On the President's death *ib*

5926 Patrick was so lonely in heaven. . . [but] now he has the best friend anyone could have.

On the infant who lived only a few hours after his birth three months before the assassination, quoted by William Manchester *The Death of A President* Harper & Row 67

5927 God. . . is making your father a guardian angel. . . and he's watching you and he's loving you and he always will.

ib

Randy Shilts journalist

5928 The new 5-B policy [was] that all patients designate their significant others who would have visiting privileges.

On "right of AIDS patients to define their families, not the hospitals" *And the Band Played On* St Martin 87

Jane Smiley comentator

5929 When people leave, they always seem to scoop themselves out of you.

On family reunions *Ordinary Love and Good Will* Ivy 89

Sports Illustrated

5930 Any parents who has ever found a rusted toy automobile buried in the grass or a bent sand bucket on the beach knows that objects like these can be among the powerful things in the world.

26 Dec 60

5931 [Toys] can summon up in an instant, in colors stronger than life, the whole of childhood at its happiest.

ib

Susan Stamberg commentator

5932 The tooth fairy has deep pockets.

On report from east Texas that children were getting as much as $50 for a lost tooth NPR 20 Jan 95

John Tarkow essayist

5933 It absorbs the second generation over a flame so high that the first is left encrusted on the rim.

On "this melting pot of ours" *NY Times* 7 Jul 85

Studs Terkel commentator and historian

5934 We're talking about generational continuity.

On passing down family stories Station WAMU Washington 2 Oct 95

Time magazine

5935 Hippies seem. . . like candidates for a very sound spanking and a cram course in civics—if only they would return home to receive either.

7 Jul 67

John Updike novelist

5936 Children are not our creations but our guests.

Quoted by Anatole Broyard *Around by Books* Random House 74

Peter Ustinov actor

5937 Parents. . . are the bone on which the puppy can shape its teeth.

Reader's Digest May 90

Alan Valentine essayist

5938 For thousands of years, father and son have stretched wistful hands across the canyon of time.

Fathers to Sons: Advice Without Consent University of Oklahoma 63

5939 Nothing endures except the sense of difference.

ib

Abigail Van Buren (Pauline Phillips) columnist

5940 Self-sacrifice and martyrdom. . . her banner is the tear-stained hanky.

On the "rocket-boosted mother-in-law. . . queen of melodrama" *McCall's* Sep 62

5941 Phony as a colic cure, transparent as a soap bubble. . . harmless as a barracuda. . . more wretched than wicked and needs more help than she can give.

ib

5942 Mid–40s. . . the compact car of her own breed: efficient, trim, attractive and in harmony with her times. . . stiff competition for the plain young matron who's overweight and underfinanced.

ib

Gore Vidal playwright

5943 All children alarm their parents, if only because you are forever expecting to encounter yourself.

Weekend play 68

W D Wall Professor of Educational Psychology, University of London

5944 Children grow well when their parents are growing well.

Quoted by Alison Stallibrass *The Self-Respecting Child* Thames & Hudson 77

Judith Wallerstein Center for the Family and Transition, Corte Madera CA

5945 Divorce is not just an episode. . . [but] a natural disaster that really changes the whole trajectory of a child's life.

US News & World Report 27 Feb 95

Anthony Ward-Thomas President, Ward-Thomas Removels, Battersea

5946 The male feels usurped in his role as home provider and therefore would rather be absent.

On husbands who disappear on moving day *London Times* 16 Feb 95

5947 [The two types of wives are] "generals," anxious to stamp their authority on the proceedings, barking orders and delivering reprimands; and "hens," who fuss round, busily scuttling from the house to the lorry, carrying one spoon at a time.

ib

Evelyn Waugh novelist

5948 Perhaps host and guest is really the happiest relationship for father and son.

Atlantic Mar 63

Rebecca West novelist

5949 She was like the embodiment of all women who have felt an astonished protest because their children have died before them.

On Queen Mary on the death of her son, George VI *Life* 25 Feb 52

E B White essayist

5950 The time not to become a father is 18 years before a world war.

The Second Tree from the Corner Harper 53

John W Whitehead essayist

5951 Children are the living messages we send to a time we will not see.

The Stealing of America Crossway 83

P G Wodehouse humorist

5952 Unlike the male codfish, which suddenly finding itself the parent of 3,500,000 little codfish, cheerfully resolves to love them all, the British aristocracy is apt to look with a somewhat jaundiced eye on its younger sons.

Richard Usborne ed *Wodehouse at Work* H Jenkins 61

5953 Aunt is calling to Aunt like mastodons bellowing across primeval swamps and Uncle James's letter about Cousin Mabel's peculiar behavior is being shot round the family circle.

The Inimitable Jeeves 1923, recalled on Wodehouse's death 14 Feb 75

5954 It is no use telling me that there are bad aunts and good aunts... sooner or later out pops the cloven hoof.

The Code of the Woosters 1938

Tom Wolfe novelist

5955 Sherman made the terrible discovery that men make about their fathers sooner or later....that the man before him was not an aging father but a boy, a boy much like himself, a boy who grew up and had a child of his own and, as best he could, out of a sense of duty and, perhaps love, adopted a role called Being a Father so that his child would have something mythical and infinitely important: a Protector, who would keep a lid on all the chaotic and catastrophic possibilities of life.

The Bonfire of the Vanities Farrar Straus Giroux 87

Diane Wolkstein story teller

5956 There's a thirst in their eyes.

On parents who accompany children to her sessions in Central Park *NY Times* 3 Jun 92

Zhao Ziyang Chinese Communist Party chief

5957 If I say one there will be two, and if I say two there will be three.

On limiting Chinese families to one child *NY Times* 23 Dec 88

5958 We all know if we say one it will only be approximately one.

ib

Philip Ziegler biographer

5959 They are a philoprogenitive lot.

On the 540 living and legitimate descendants of Queen Victoria *King Edward VIII* Knopf 91

LOVE

Peter Ackroyd biographer

5960 In the end it was human love, the love that he had dismissed in his writing as the consolation only of ordinary men, that rescued him from a lifetime of misery and isolation.

On the poet T S Eliot, quoted by Walter Arnold *Wall Street Journal* 3 Dec 84 as "the final irony of this supreme ironist" in reviewing Ackroyd's *T S Eliot* Simon & Schuster 84

Akihito Crown Prince of Japan

5961 As I continue/My talks with her,/I become aware/That, in my heart,/A window is opening.

"After the Decision on Betrothal" 31-syllable *waka* Marie Philimene and Masako Saito eds *Tomoshibi [Light], Collected Poems* Weatherhill Tokyo 91

Woody Allen comedian

5962 The heart is a resilient muscle.

NY Times 23 May 86

Yehuda Amichai poet

5963 You gave me a letter opener made of silver. Real letters aren't opened that way; they're torn open, torn, torn.

"Gifts of Love" *Selected Poetry* Harper & Row 86

Martin Amis novelist

5964 Like an adolescent, throbbing, gaping, my poor flat pines for a female presence. And so do I.

Money: A Suicide Note Viking 85

Anon

5965 Love instilled into solid materials by loving craftsmanship is the only creation of mankind to defeat time.

Inscription on library wall of Loyd-Paxton Gallery, Dallas TX *Architectural Digest* May 86

5966 How slow we are to learn that choosing to share one's life with someone involves accepting that one day the sharing must stop.

Obituary for a victim of AIDS *NY Times* 10 Sep 87

5967 Love is a basket with five loaves and two fishes. It's never enough until you give it away.

Sign in soup kitchen visited by Barbara Bush *Washington Post* 1 Feb 89

5968 Love for me is like the bubble in the stem of a wineglass.

Quoted by Samuel Hazo, Director, International Poetry Forum, Station WETA Washington 8 Jul 89

5969 Marriage is a romance in which the hero dies in the first chapter.

Quoted by Barbara Gowdy's *Falling Angels* Soho Press 90

Jean Anouilh playwright and novelist

5970 There is love, of course. And then there is love's enemy, life.

Ardele Dell 65

Elizabeth Ashley actress

5971 You remember the cities you passed through but not much about them. George was one of those cities.

On an ex-husband *W* 26 Jul 74

W H Auden poet

5972 Among those whom I like, I can find no common denominator, but among those whom I love, I can; all of them make me laugh.

The Dyer's Hand Random House 62

Ingrid Bergman actress

5973 A kiss is a lovely trick designed by nature to stop speech when words become superfluous.

Viva May 77

Pierre Berton humorist

5974 A Canadian is somebody who knows how to make love in a canoe.

The Canadian 22 Dec 73

5975 Selflessness is. . . the basic ingredient of true love. . . mix well with affection and respect and, without a dime in your pocket, you're rich.

16 Nov 73

Dr Smiley Blanton psychiatrist

5976 The woman who anxiously scans the face of her lover and reaches out with soothing hand to comfort him. . . is obeying the same kind of impulse that directs the heart to pump more blood to a wounded limb.

Love or Perish Simon & Schuster 56

Mary Bloom teacher

5977 I'm suffering, not for a lost family. . . not for lost friends. . . my house hasn't burned, I have food in the fridge and my car still starts even when it rains. But my dog is dead.

On loss of her sheepdog, Anyus *NY Times* 1 Jan 80

5978 Now I have. . . loneliness, an emptiness, a space on the floor near the bed where a tail once wagged, because she loved me, the way dogs do.

ib

Laura Blumenfeld reporter

5979 It was late and he came alone. He hovered in the portico, a swollen Romeo, his face a loose collection of lines and mottled puff.

On Senator Edward M Kennedy calling on Victoria Reggie who was to become his second wife *Washington Post* 20 Mar 92

Louise Bogan poet

5980 [Love] comes in at the eyes and subdues the body. An army with banners.

In Ruth Limmer ed *What the Woman Lived* Harcourt, Brace, Jovanovich 73

Gerald Brenan essayist

5981 In a happy marriage, it is the wife who provides the climate, the husband the landscape.

Thoughts in a Dry Season Cambridge University Press 57

Fanny Brice commedian

5982 Love is like a motor that's going, you have such vitality to do things, big things, because love is goosing you all the time.

Quoted by Norman Katkov *The Fabulous Fanny* Knopf 53

Anatole Broyard essayist

5983 There are few things more subtly distressing than an inappropriate gift from someone close to you.

NY Times 21 Jan 79

5984 One of the best things about love—the feeling of being wrapped, like a gift, in understanding.

ib

Richard Burton actor

5985 She is an extremely beautiful woman, lavishly endowed by nature with a few flaws in the masterpiece.

On actress Elizabeth Taylor at age 34 *Life* 24 Feb 67

5986 She has an insipid double chin, her legs are too short, and she has a slight potbelly. She has a wonderful bosom, though.

ib

5987 For two days we circled each other—very wary, very polite. On the third day, we had a fight. Then we knew that we were ourselves again.

On re-marriage to Elizabeth Taylor, recalled on Burton's death 5 Aug 84

E Jean Carroll essayist

5988 Every woman gets a number of great romances, and then no more. And when they're over, all you can do is remember or—if you're very foolish—go and revisit the old stud.

"Loves of My Life" *Esquire* Jun 95

Gabrielle ("Coco") Chanel designer

5989 Passion goes, boredom remains.

McCall's Nov 65

5990 I loved him, or thought I loved him, which is the same thing.

On her ten-year affair with Hugh Richard Arthur Grosvenor, Duke of Westminster, quoted by Axel Madsen *Coco* Holt 90

5991 There is a time for work, and a time for love. That leaves no other time.

ib

Paddy Chayefsky playwright

5992 Dogs like us, we aren't such dogs as we think we are.

Lines for Ernest Borgnine to Betsy Blair *Marty* United Artists 55

John Cheever novelist

5993 I have always been the lover—never the beloved, and I have spent much of my life waiting for trains, planes, boats, footsteps, doorbells, letters, telephones, snow, rain, thunder.

Quoted by Rhoda Koenig *New York* 28 Nov 88 reviewing Ben Cheever ed *The Letters of John Cheever* Simon & Schuster 88

5994 My love for you. . . seems as natural and easy as passing a football on a fine October day and if the game bores you, you can toss me the ball and walk off the grass and there will be no forlornness.

Letter to a male lover *ib*

Anna Chennault widow

5995 He came into my life as the warm wind of spring had awakened flowers, as the April showers awaken the earth.

On her marriage to General Claire Chennault *A Thousand Springs* Taplinger 62

Marcelle Clements essayist

5996 Of all parts of the body that can be caressed or kissed, the brow is the most accessible and the most mysterious, just as sensual as more celebrated body parts but less frightening. It hides only the mind.

NY Times 5 May 91

5997 Perhaps bangs are the chastity belt of the mind.

ib

William J Clinton 42nd US President

5998 I liked being around her, because I thought I'd never be bored being with her.

On his wife, Hillary *New Yorker* 30 May 94

5999 Once in a while she'll come in and say, "I want to talk about such-and-such." And you know, I might as well try to lift that desk up and throw it through the window as to change her mind.

ib

Nellie Connally Governor's wife

6000 He's still vain, arrogant and conceited. . . the three things I always wanted in a man.

On her husband, Texas Governor John Connally, quoted by Connally with Mickey Herskowitz *In History's Shadow* Hyperion 93

Cyril Connolly essayist

6001 There is no pain in life equal to that which two lovers can inflict on one another. . . its avoidance is the beginning of wisdom, for it is strong enough to contaminate the whole of our lives.

The Unquiet Grave Penguin 67

6002 On how that first true love affair shapes itself depends the pattern of our lives. When sexual emotion increases to passion, then something starts growing which possesses a life of its own and which, easily though it can be destroyed by ignorance and neglect, will die in agony and go on dying after it is dead.

Also quoted in *Time* 20 May 83

Noel Coward playwright

6003 Remembered friends who are dead and gone./ How happy they are I cannot know/ But happy am I who loved them so.

Unpublished poem in his own handwriting donated to Actors Fund auction during Coward's last visit to New York *Cosmopolitan* Mar 58

6004 Don't run after it. Don't court it. Keep it waiting off stage until you're good and ready for it and even then treat it with the suspicious disdain that it deserves.

Letter of advice on falling in love, quoted by Maria Riva *Marlene Dietrich* Knopf 92

John Gould Cozzens novelist

6005 Love conquers all—*omnia vincit amor*, said the gold scroll in a curve beneath the dial of the old French gilt clock. . . [and] on top of the dial. . . a smiling cupid perched, bow bent, about to loose an arrow.

Opening words of the novel *By Love Possessed* Harcourt, Brace 57

6006 *Omnia vincit amor*, the metal ribbon unchangeably declared. . . as the unseen mechanism. . . struck a first silvery stroke.

Concluding the novel *ib*

John M C Crum poet

6007 Now the green blade riseth/ from the buried grain,/ wheat that in dark earth/ many days has lain;/ love lives again, that/ with the dead has been:/ Love is come again like/ wheat that springeth green.

Quoted by novelist J F Powers *Wheat That Springeth Green* Knopf 88

Marlene Dietrich entertainer

6008 Once a woman has forgiven her man, she must not reheat his sins for breakfast.

Cosmopolitan Feb 80

Phil Donahue television host

6009 We are somewhere between the elephant seal and the marmoset monkey.

On human monogomy NBC TV 11 Aug 86

David Herbert Donald biographer

6010 Reconciliation came soon, but things were never quite the same again. They had learned how to hurt each other.

On the novelist Thomas Wolfe and set designer Aline Bernstein *Look Homeward* Little, Brown 87

Michael Drury essayist

6011 If you would stay loved. . . maintain a reserve of mind and heart. That is neither self-indulgence nor a conjurer's trick; it is a clause in one's moral contract with existence.

Advice to a Young Wife from an Old Mistress Four Directions Press 93

Doris Duke heiress

6012 After I've gone out with a man a few times, he starts to tell me how much he loves me. But how can I know if he really means it? How can I ever be sure?

Recalled on Duke's death, leaving an estate of more than a billion *NY Times* 29 Oct 93

Allen Dulles Director, Office of Strategic Services

6013 We can let the work cover the romance, and the romance cover the work.

To his mistress Mary Bancroft who was also his colleague in wartime Switzerland, quoted by Peter Grose *Gentleman Spy* Houghton Mifflin 94

Clover Todd Dulles wife of Allen Dulles

6014 If any woman can be called a lady while she is having an affair with a married man, Wally was that lady.

On her father and the Countess Wally Toscanini Castelbarco, quoted by Peter Grose *Gentleman Spy* Houghton Mifflin 94

Daphne du Maurier novelist

6015 For richer, for poorer doesn't mean whether you can afford TV or buy a car, but whether the person you marry grows in personality and character or falls away.

Quoted by Margaret Forster *Daphne du Maurier* Doubleday 93

6016 In sickness and in health means not just cherishing someone who may get pneumonia, but someone who gets sick with longing for someone else. By God and by Christ, if anyone should call that sort of love by that unattractive word that begins with "L," I'd tear their guts out.

On lesbianism, often a hidden theme of Du Maurier's work *ib*

Mamie Dowd Eisenhower First Lady

6017 I have but one career and its name is Ike.

Quoted by J B West *Upstairs at the White House* Coward McCann Geoghegan 73

Walker Evans photographer

6018 I've never been unfaithful to anything but my negatives.

On the three marriages of his photographic career, quoted by Belinda Rathbone *Walker Evans* Houghton Mifflin 95

William Faulkner novelist

6019 You don't love because, you love despite; not for the virtues, but despite the faults.

Quoted by Willie Morris "Faulkner's Mississippi" *National Geographic* Mar 89

Edna Ferber novelist

6020 There is something I want to say to you. I've wanted to say it for years. World, I love you. I have always loved you. . . or almost always.

In autobiography *A Kind of Magic* Doubleday 63

John Fowles essayist and novelist

6021 Passion destroys passion; we want what puts an end to wanting what we want.

The Aristos Little, Brown 64

Marilyn French novelist

6022 She turned, as always, to analysis. . . subject to the superstition that what the mind could understand couldn't any longer hurt the heart, that what the tongue could utter was in the hand's control.

On psychoanalyses *The Bleeding Heart* Summit 80

Robert Frost poet

6023 Love is an irresistible desire to be irresistibly desired.

Life Apr 92

Eduardo Galeano essayist

6024 We are all mortal until the first kiss and the second glass of wine.

The Book of Embraces Norton 91

Greta Garbo actress

6025 Oh what a brutal question!

On Cecil Beaton's proposal of marriage, quoted by Hugo Vickers *Cecil Beaton* Little, Brown 86

Peter Gay Sterling Professor of History, Yale

6026 A novelist like Nikolai Gogol. . . paid indirect tribute to love by his energetic exertions to evade it.

The Tender Passion Oxford 86

Brendan Gill essayist

6027 Strangers become friends, friends become lovers, lovers become husbands and wives and ex-husbands and ex-wives become strangers.

A New York Life Poseidon Press 90

Lillian Gish actress

6028 I knew such charming men; perhaps I didn't want to disillusion any of them.

On why she never married, recalled on her death at age 99 *NY Times* 1 Mar 93

Graham Greene novelist

6029 [He] listened with the intense interest one feels in a stranger's life, the interest the young mistake for love.

The Heart of the Matter Doubleday 51

6030 Each love affair was like a vaccine. It helped you to get through the next attack more easily.

Quoted by Ralph Novak *People* 14 Nov 88 reviewing Greene's *The Captain and the Enemy* Viking 88

6031 Women like war, periods of waiting. Waiting while a car is late, a dentist's appointment, a curtain to fall. For everyone one has ever loved, one has waited.

New Yorker 11 Apr 94

Lorenz Hart lyricist

6032 When love congeals,/ it soon reveals/ the faint aroma/ of performing seals.

Washington Post 1 Jan 88

Seamus Heaney poet

6033 It all came back to me last night, stirred/ By the footfall of your things at bedtime,/ Your head-down, tail-up hunt in a bottom drawer/ For the black plunge-line nightdress.

"The Skunk" *Selected Poems 1966–1987* Farrar Straus Giroux 90

Lillian Hellman playwright

6034 It was an unspoken pleasure that having. . . ruined so much and repaired a little, we had endured.

On her relationshp with Dasheill Hammett, recalled on Hellman's death 26 Nov 86

Katharine Hepburn actress

6035 He was a baked potato—solid and you can have them without salt or pepper or butter. I was a fancy dessert—mocha chip ice cream.

On her relationship with actor Spencer Tracy ABC TV 18 Sep 87

John Herman essayist

6036 It is strange, the stages by which you realize you are too late, you have swallowed the hook.

The Weight of Love Doubleday 95

Elisabeth Hermodsson Swedish poet

6037 His love for me/ was to let me/ love him;/ my love for him was to let him/ through me love himself.

Quoted by Anna G Jonasdottir's *Why Women Are Oppressed* Temple University Press 94

Olga Ivinskaya Pasternak's lover

6038 The greatest part of my conscious life has been devoted to you—and what is left of it will also be devoted to you.

To Boris Pasternak from the woman who inspired the troubled Lara in his novel *Doctor Zhivago*, quoted on Ivinskaya's death at age 83 *NY Times* 13 Sep 95

Claudia ("Lady Bird") Johnson First Lady

6039 Lyndon loved everybody, and a little bit more than half the world is women. . . [but] I do know he loved me most.

Life Apr 95

Michael Kaufman bookbinder

6040 Rolodexes and electronic notebooks may be fine for business contacts, but there are other kinds of numbers, and there will probably always be a demand for little black books.

NY Times 7 Jun 95

Heather Kirby essayist

6041 They were love letters written of extraordinary dedication, thoughtfully numbering and dating each one for the voyeurs of posterity.

On Christie's auction of 965 letters between Tsar Alexander II and Princess Catherine Dolgoruka *London Times* 19 Sep 84

Henry A Kissinger US Secretary of State

6042 Can you imagine what this man would have been had somebody loved him? Had somebody in his life cared for him? I don't think anybody ever did, not his parents, not his peers. There may have been a teacher but nobody knows, it's not recorded.

On Richard M Nixon, Kenneth W Thompson ed *The Nixon Presidency* University Press of America 87

6043 He would have been a great, great man had somebody loved him.

ib

Carole Klein biographer

6044 The irony of Tom's dying before her had not escaped her and she had no answer for this twist of fate any more than she had for the one that had brought them together.

On Aline Bernstein learning of the death of novelist Thomas Wolfe, her much younger lover *Aline* Harper & Row 79

6045 She had made his life less lonely, less tormented. She would hold on to that thought as she lived out her own life, in a world forever diminished.

ib

Dominique Lapierre essayist

6046 Even those who have been spared the direct consequences of the disease have become, consciously or unconsciously, more timid, more conformist, too nostalgic and slightly dull.

On AIDS *Beyond Love* Warner Books 95

6047 The price of exploring life's edges has simply become too high.

ib

David Leavitt novelist

6048 In a corner, not far but far enough from where we lay, grief crouched, fended off, at bay.

On lovers reunited during the Spanish Civil War *While England Sleeps* Viking 93

6049 I knew it would wait until we fell asleep before it pounced again; this time, however, when we woke in terror, we would at least not wake alone.

ib

6050 I had affairs that year. . . they meant something still.

ib

6051 Who touches the body, however fleetingly, also touches the soul.

ib

Ursula K Leguin novelist

6052 Love doesn't just lay there, like a stone, it has to be made, like bread; re-made all the time, made new.

The Lathe of Heaven Scribner 71

Felicia R Lee reporter

6053 Love can leave you reeling faster than a one-eyed cat in a fish market.

On covering the Woody Allen–Mia Farrow child custody hearings *NY Times* 28 Mar 93

Madeleine L'Engle novelist

6054 There are times when love seems to be over. . . [but] these desert times are simply the way to the next oasis which is far more lush and beautiful after the desert crossing.

Two Part Invention Farrar Straus Giroux 88

C S Lewis autobiographer

6055 A noble hunger, long unsatisfied, met at last its proper food.

On falling in love *A Grief Observed* Seabury 61

6056 No cranny of heart or body remained unsatisfied. Anger is the fluid that love bleeds when you cut it.

Letters to Malcolm Harcourt, Brace, Jovanovich 64

Sinclair Lewis novelist

6057 You are. . . a. . . a pudding. . . a bread pudding. . . made of the divine host.

To Dorothy Thompson, quoted by Peter Kurth *American Cassandra* Little, Brown 90

6058 If I ever divorce Dorothy, I'll name Adolf Hitler as correspondent.

On Thompson's preoccupation with German politics *ib*

6059 Why the hell did I have to marry a Roman senator?

On Thompson's column, books, and public speaking *ib*

Alexander Liberman autobiographer

6060 I've always felt that people who shared the same childhood language have the best chance of happiness together; Russian was our basic language for anything that was meaningful.

On speaking in Russian to Tatianna "for anything that was meaningful," quoted by Dodie Kazanjian and Calvin Tomkins *Alex* Knopf 93

Anne Morrow Lindbergh essayist

6061 Only a refound person can refind a personal relationship.

Gift from the Sea Pantheon 55

Walter Lippmann columnist

6062 I am like a man who has seen in his mind's eye the glories of this existence, but had wandered through endless corridors, looking into empty rooms, till suddenly you unlocked the gate to the real world.

To his wife Helen Byrne Armstrong, quoted by Ronald Steel *Walter Lippmann and the American Century* Little, Brown 80

Clare Boothe Luce playwright

6063 It's being together at the end that really matters.

Lines for *The Women* 1937 Broadway play, recalled in *NY Times* 31 Jan 88

6064 Women do generally manage to love the guys they marry more than they manage to marry the guys they love.

Quoted by Ralph G Martin *Henry and Clare* Putnam 91

Archibald MacLeish poet

6065 I think we have come out on the other side. . . meaning that we love each other more than we ever did when we loved each other most.

On 60 years of marriage, quoted by Scott Donaldson *Archibald MacLeish* Houghton Mifflin 92

William Manchester biographer

6066 A poem of womanhood.

On General Douglas MacArthur's wife, Jean *American Caesar* Little, Brown 78

Nelson Mandela President of South Africa

6067 She married a man who. . . became a myth; then the myth returned home and proved to be just a man after all.

On the breakdown of his marriage to Winnie Mandela *Long Walk to Freedom* Little, Brown 94

Mary McCarthy novelist

6068 On the wall of our life together hung a gun waiting to be fired in the final act.

On Philip Rahj *Intellectual Memoirs* Harcourt, Brace 92

Margaret Mead anthropologist

6069 [They possessed] as few primitive cultures did, the true kiss, that is, lip contact that is punctuated by a sharp implosion of the breath.

On her study of Samoan islanders, quoted by Jane Howard *Margaret Mead* Simon & Schuster 85

Gian Carlo Menotti composer

6070 Love is born of faith, lives on hope, and dies of charity.

Notes for the opera *Maria Golovin* Baldwin Mills 58

W S Merwin poet

6071 Here love/ Must wander blind or with mistaken eyes,/ For dissolution walks among the light/ And vision is the sire of vanishing.

Selected Poems Atheneum 88

6072 The knowledge of all that he betrayed/ Grew till it was the same whether he stayed/ Or went. Therefore he went / ....You grieve/ Not that heaven does not exist but/ That it exists without us.

ib

Edna St Vincent Millay poet

6073 I will control myself or go inside./ I will not flaw perfection with my grief./ Handsome, this day, no matter who has died.

Poem found among her papers at her death, a year after her husband's, quoted in memoir by Vincent Sheean *The World in Vogue* Viking 63

Donald L Miller biographer

6074 Catherine would have his afternoons; she would have the rest of his days.

On Sophia Mumford's condoning of her husband's affair with Catherine Bauer *Lewis Mumford* Weidenfeld & Nicolson 89

Czeslaw Milosz poet

6075 Let that little park with greenish marble busts/ In the pearl-gray light, under a summer drizzle,/ Remain as it was when you opened the gate./ And the street of tall peeling porticos/ Which this love of yours suddenly transformed.

Unattainable Earth Ecco 87

Toni Morrison novelist

6076 The mattress, curved like a preacher's palm asking for witnesses in His name's sake, enclosed them each and every night and muffled their whispering, old-time love.

Jazz Knopf 92

Lewis Mumford essayist

6077 At some point the appearance of another person on the horizon, comes like the first flapping of sails on a becalmed boat, when an offshore breeze breaks through the sleepy torpor and drives it again, out on the open sea.

Quoted by Donald L Miller *Lewis Mumford* Weidenfeld & Nicolson 89

6078 Every man, in his middle thirties, falls in love with his wife's opposite.

ib

6079 I reach for you and what do I touch? A housing expert. I call for you in the stillness of the night and what do I hear? The percentage of vacancies in Laubengang apartment houses in Germany as compared with cottages.

On Catherine Bauer's growing expertise in public housing *ib*

V S Naipaul novelist

6080 They went to the bathroom and got their teeth. They went down to the sitting-room and ate large pieces of cake.

On reconciliation of an elderly couple *Mr Stone and Knights Companion* Macmillan 64

Naruhito Crown Prince of Japan

6081 Masako-san, I will protect you for my entire life.

On proposing marriage to Masako Owada *NY Times* 20 Jan 93

Reinhold Niebuhr theologian

6082 The highest calling of a human being is unselfish love—to love without being loved back, without any self-interest.

Quoted by US President Jimmy Carter *Life* Nov 95

Anaïs Nin essayist

6083 Women see themselves as in a mirror, in the eyes of the men who love them.

Quoted by Bruce Bawe *NY Times* 5 Mar 95 reviewing Deirdre Bair's *Anaïs Nin* Putnam 95

Pat Nixon First Lady

6084 Even when people can't speak your language, they can tell when you have love in your heart.

Inscription for her gravestone next to President Nixon *NY Times* 28 Apr 94

Jacqueline Kennedy Onassis First Lady

6085 It was a very spasmodic courtship, conducted mainly at long distance with a great clanking of coins in dozens of phone booths.

On engagement to John F Kennedy, quoted by Doris Kearns Goodwin *The Fitzgeralds and the Kennedys* Simon & Schuster 87

William Paley broadcasting executive

6086 He had a habit of falling in love and wanting to tell his best friend—and his best friend was Irene.

On motion picture producer David O Selznick's divorce from Irene Mayer, quoted by David Thomson's *Showman* Knopf 92

Dorothy Parker humorist

6087 Scratch a lover, find a foe.

Ballad of a Great Weariness 1937 recalled on Parker's death 7 Jun 67

Boris Pasternak novelist

6088 At one o'clock we shall sit down to table,/ At three we shall rise,/ I with my book, you with your embroidery./ At dawn we shan't remember/ What time we stopped kissing.

To Lara, in life Pasternak's lover Olga Ivinskaya, *Dr Zhivago* Pantheon 58

6089 Even as reeds go down beneath/ the rough seas following a storm/ so every line of her had gone/ to the bottom of his soul.

To Lara, considered on Ivinskaya's death to be Pasternak's epitaph for her *US News & World Report* 25 Sep 95

Octavio Paz essayist

6090 Love is one of the answers humankind invented to stare death in the face: time ceases to be a measure, and we can briefly know paradise.

The Double Flame Harcourt, Brace 95

6091 Beyond happiness or unhappiness, though it is both things, love is intensity: it does not give us eternity but life, that second in which the doors of time and space open just a crack: here is there and now is always.

ib

6092 In love, everything is two and everything strives to be one.

ib

Anthony Powell essayist

6093 Self-love seems so often unrequited.
Quoted by Robert Hughes *Culture of Complaint* Oxford 93

Raine, Countess Spencer Stepmother of Princess of Wales

6094 Being in love is so slimming, but he still wants another sliver off the derriere.
On her engagement to Jean François, Conte de Chambrun *London Times* 14 May 93

P V Narasimha Rao Prime Minister of India

6095 Their bodies, like strangers meeting for the first time, introduced themselves to each other.
On lovers in his novel *The Other Half* a partially published novel written at age 74 that shocked India *NY Times* 20 Dec 95

Maria Riva biographer

6096 For four years, their secret affair blazed, flickered, smoldered, simmered, then flamed anew—only to repeat its erratic, agonizing pattern all over again.
On her mother's relationship with actor Yul Brynner *Marlena Dietrich* Knopf 92

Dorothy L Sayers novelist

6097 The only sin passion can commit is to be joyless.
Recalled on Sayers' death 17 Dec 57

Flora Scott-Maxwell essayist

6098 Love is recognition often of what you are not but might be. . . sears and it heals. . . is beyond pity and above law. . . can seem like truth.
The Measure of My Days Knopf 72

Erich Segal novelist

6099 Love is never having to say you're sorry.
Love Story Avon 70

David O Selznick film producer

6100 I. . . snore loudly, drink exuberantly, work excessively, and my future is drawing to a close. But I am tall and Jewish and I do love you.
Proposal of marriage to Irene Mayer *London Times* 12 Oct 90

Vincent Sheean journalist

6101 It was. . . love not only at first sight but at a glance.
On Dorothy Thompson's meeting with her first husband, Joseph Bard *Dorothy and Red* Houghton Mifflin 63

Randy Shilts *San Francisco Chronicle*

6102 People still think it's important whether or not somebody goes home to Jack instead of Jill.
On homophobia *Esquire* Jun 88

Elizabeth Taylor actress

6103 I fell off my pink cloud with a thud.
On her European honeymoon with Nicky Hilton *A Passion for Living* HarperCollins 94

6104 It isn't ring-a-dink any more.
On a divorcing her second husband, actor Michael Wilding *ib*

6105 I sat like a mongoose mesmerized by a cobra.
On marriage proposal from Hollywood producer Michael Todd *ib*

6106 I went from a weak man to a strong man. I've done that a couple of times.
On leaving Michael Wilding to marry Michael Todd *ib*

6107 We had more fun fighting than most people have making love.
On her marriage to Michael Todd *ib*

6108 I thought I could keep Mike's memory alive. But I have only a ghost.
On her failed marriage to Eddie Fisher after the death of Michael Todd *ib*

6109 We are stuck like chicken feathers to tar.
On resuming life with Richard Burton after divorcing him in 1974 and their remarriage the following year *ib*

Thelma, Viscountess Furness (Thelma Morgan) ex-mistress of the Prince of Wales

6110 She looked straight at me. . . one cold, defiant glance had told me the entire story.
On losing Edward VIII to Wallis Simpson *Double Exposure* Frederick Muller 59

Alexander Theroux essayist

6111 [It] somehow made her responsible, as time passed, for all she wasn't. And didn't mean. And couldn't be. And shouldn't have.
An Adultery Simon & Schuster 87

Caitlin Thomas poet's wife

6112 Ours was not a love story proper. . . more of a drink story because without the first-aid of drink it could never have got on to its rocking feet.
On her marriage to the poet Dylan Thomas *Washington Post* 2 Aug 94

Walter Thomas essayist

6113 A facility for words is a lover's greatest asset. They even work sometimes when money won't

. . . soothe when actions disappoint. . . excite or deflate, clarify or confuse.

Mirabella Feb 95

6114 Repartee is what you *wish* you'd said.

ib

Dorothy Thompson columnist

6115 He amuses me: the first requirement of a husband.

On Sinclair Lewis, quoted by Peter Kurth *American Cassandra* Little, Brown 90

6116 A new love and a new life cannot cure old wounds. . . I do but wall them up: segregate them: stop them spreading. But in cold weather they ache.

ib

Mortin Thompson novelist

6117 [There is in] a thunderclap of first love, a hunger which with feeding becomes a stronger hunger, a fulfillment, an added function of the very body it inexorably and imperishably enchants.

Not as a Stranger Scribner's 54

Alice B Toklas Gertrude Stein's companion

6118 She held my complete attention, as she did for all the many years I knew her until her death, and all the empty ones since.

Quoted by Muriel James *Hearts on Fire* Tarcher 91

6119 She was a golden brown presence, burned by the Tuscan sun and with a golden glint in her warm brown hair.

ib

Abigail Van Buren (Pauline Phillips) columnist

6120 If you think of him first, he will think of you first; that's a good marriage.

To Phil Donohue NBC TV 1 Mar 88

Gore Vidal novelist

6121 He was interested in love, not gender.

On Tennessee Williams *NY Times* 19 Dec 94

General Archibald Wavell British officer

6122 Love is like a cigar. If it goes out, you can light it again but it never tastes quite the same.

Recalled on Wavell's death 24 May 50

Rebecca West novelist

6123 His skin smelled of walnuts.

On being attracted to fellow journalist H G Wells *Guardian Manchester* 16 Mar 83

E B White essayist

6124 Nausea and love, the twin convulsions, one of the stomach, the other of the entire system sometimes called the heart.

On New York *Poems and Sketches of E B White* Harper & Row 81

Thornton Wilder playwright

6125 Many who have spent a lifetime in love can tell you less of love than the child whose dog died yesterday.

Quoted by Edmund Fuller *The Notation of the Heart* in Hirman Hayden and Betsy Saunders eds *The American Scholar Reader* Atheneum 60

Tennessee Williams playwright

6126 If you break the heel of your slipper in the morning, it means you'll meet the love of your life before dark.

Orpheus Descending 57

6127 My clock is my heart and my heart don't say tick, tick, it says love, love!

The Rose Tattoo John Gassner ed *Best American Plays: 1951–1957* Yale 58

6128 The strongest influences in my life and my work are always whomever I love. Whomever I love and am with most of the time, or whomever I remember most vividly. I think that's true of everyone, don't you?

NY Times 18 Mar 65

6129 We come to each other gradually, but with love. It is the short reach of my arms that hinders, not the length and multiplicity of theirs. With love and with honesty, the embrace is inevitable.

Preface to *The Theater of Tennessee Williams* Vol 1 New Directions 71

6130 There is something that happens between men and women in the dark that seems to make everything else unimportant.

A Streetcar Named Desire recalled on Williams' death 25 Feb 83

6131 I discovered a certain "flexibility" in my sexual nature. . . [but] any kind of promiscuity is a distortion of the love impulse.

NY Times 19 Dec 94

William Carlos Williams poet

6132 A profusion of pink roses bending ragged in the rain speaks to me of being loved. It is God's finger on man's shoulder.

The Collected Later Poems of William Carlos Williams New Directions 63

Shelly Winters actresss

6133 Security is when I'm very much in love with someone extraordinary who loves me back.

News summaries 9 Jul 54

Woodrow Wyatt

6134 A man falls in love through his eyes, a woman through her ears.

"To the Point" London *Sunday Times* 22 Mar 81

Maurice Zolotow critic

6135 The education of a woman's heart is a series of lessons with a series of men until she falls in love for the rest of her life.

Marilyn Monroe Harcourt, Brace 60

Franco Zeffirelli film director

6136 [I made] the classic error of falling in love where there was no possibility of its being returned. . . a humiliating, wretched feeling most of us experience some time.

Zeffirelli Weidenfeld & Nicolson 86

RELIGION

Diane Ackerman essayist

6137 To the Mexicans. . . Los Palomas are the souls of children who died during the past year, fluttering on their way to heaven.

On migrations of the Monarch butterfly *Life* May 87

James Agee novelist

6138 The night smelled like new milk; the air which exhaled upon them when they opened the side door of the Chapel was as numb and remote as the air of a cave.

On Good Friday at St Andrew's School near Sewanee TN *The Morning Watch* Riverside 50

6139 Without knowing it they hesitated, subdued by the stagnant darkness and its smell of waxed pine and spent incense. The gravel took all the light there was in the perishing darkness and shed it upward, and in the darkness among the trees below the outbuildings a blossoming dogwood flawed like a winter breath. There between spread hands the body and the blood of Christ was created among words and lifted before God in a threshing of triplicate bells.

On serving early morning mass *Let Us Now Praise Famous Men* recalled in *New Yorker* 18 Jul 88

Anon

6140 Do good and disappear.

Motto of a nursing order, quoted by Kathryn Hulme *The Nun's Story* Little, Brown 56

6141 It lacks heat and drive; it leaves a sour aftertaste of regret.

A Cistercian monk's ranking of resignation as the lowest degree of clinging to God's will *The Hermitage Within* Darton Longman Todd 77

6142 Here lie German soldiers. God has the last word.

Inscription on World War II monument at Le Cambe, France *NY Times* 13 May 84

6143 May the peace of Christ be with you always—and may you find it profoundly disturbing.

Priestly blessing *Catholics in America* CBS TV 10 Sep 87

6144 Good morals like good art begins with drawing a line.

ib

6145 Lord, that's enough now. Please stop it.

A young girl's reaction to an Alaskan earthquake, quoted by C D F Bryan *National Geographic Society* hundredth anniversary book Abrams 87

6146 O God, to those who have hunger, give bread, and to us who have bread give the hunger for justice.

Latin American prayer *Anglican World* Advent 93

6147 Turning on your tap is an act of faith.

All Things Considered NPR 13 Jan 94

6148 God is your co-pilot, change seats.

Marquee sign, Emmanuel Baptist Church, Manassas VA *Washington Times* 13 Oct 94

6149 You want to make God laugh? Tell him your plans.

Quoted by former NBC commentator John Chancellor on retiring at 67 only to learn that he had stomach cancer *International Herald Tribune* 17 Jan 95

Peter F Anson historian

6150 [Anglican monasticism is] a remarkable manifestation of the persistence of an urge for a closer union with God.

The Call of the Cloister SPCK 55

6151 After more than 300 years, it came up again like a seed buried in a stony ground and grew into a mighty tree.

On unsuccessful eradication by 16th century reformers *ib*

Brooks Atkinson drama critic

6152 I have no objection to churches so long as they do not interfere with God's work.

Once Around the Sun Harcourt, Brace 51

W H Auden poet

6153 God may reduce you on Judgment Day/To tears of shame,/Reciting by heart/The poems you would have written,/had your life been good.

Postscript to *The Cave of Making* from *About the House* Random House 65

Pearl Bailey entertainer

6154 People see God every day, they just don't recognize him.

NY Times 26 Nov 67

Karl Barth thelogian

6155 The Jews have the promise of God and if we Christians from among the Gentiles have it too, then it is only as those chosen with them, as guests in their house, as new wood grafted onto their old tree.

Time 25 Jun 65

Lord Beaverbrook (William Maxwell Aiken) publisher

6156 Pray? Well, no. You see, I leave all that to the moderator of the General Assembly of the Presbyterian Church in Canada.

85th birthday interview *NY Herald Tribune* 25 May 64

Hilaire Belloc essayist

6157 I always like to associate with a lot of priests because it makes me understand anti-clerical things so well.

Quoted by Robert Speaight *Life of Hilaire Belloc* Farrar Straus Cudahy 57

George Bennard lyricist

6158 I will cling to the old rugged cross,/And exchange it some day for a crown.

The Old Rugged Cross hymn 1913, recalled on Bennard's death *NY Times* 11 Oct 58

Alan Bennett playwright

6159 The liturgy is best treated and read as if it's someone announcing the departure of trains.

New Yorker 22 May 95

Edward M Berckman Episcopal priest

6160 We are meant to be addicted to God, but we develop secondary addictions that temporarily appear to fix our problems.

"Substitutes for God" *Living Church* 15 Feb 87

John Betjeman poet

6161 How long was the peril, how breathless the day,/In topaz and beryl, the sun dies away,/His rays lying static at quarter to six/In polychromatical lacing of bricks./Good Lord, as the Angelus floats down the road,/Byzantine St Barnabas, be Thine abode.

On St Barnabas Church, Oxford in *John Betjeman: A Life in Pictures* John Murray 84

Black Manifesto rightist statement

6162 We are. . . demanding of the white Christian churches and Jewish synagogues which are part and parcel of the system of capitalism that they begin to pay reparations to black people in this country.

Presented by James Foreman to Black Economic Development Conference, Detroit 26 Apr 69

6163 We are demanding $500 million. . . $15 per nigger.

ib

Eugene B Borowitz Rabbi, NYC Hebrew Union College

6164 The peculiar malaise of our day is air-conditioned unhappiness, the staleness and stuffiness of machine-made routine.

Quoted on poster distributed by Argus Communications 69

Gerald Brenan theologian

6165 Religions are kept alive by heresies, which are really sudden explosions of faith. Dead religions do not produce them.

Thoughts in a Dry Season Cambridge University Press 78

Jimmy Breslin novelist

6166 A man bristling with celibacy.

On a priest portrayed in Breslin's novel *He Got Hungry and Forgot His Manners* Ticknor & Fields 88

Victoria Bruner Des Moines therapist

6167 The skies open up and put people in our path to help us. God is a puppeteer.

On tracing details of her fiancé's death *Washington Post* 12 Nov 92

Martin Buber theologian

6168 God wants man to fulfill his commands as a humanity being and with the quality peculiar to human beings.

The Writings of Martin Buber Meridan 56

Ephraim Z Buchwald Orthodox rabbi

6169 We Jews are believers who are doubters. Doubt provokes questions, and we Jews are a questioning people.

Address at Manhattan's Central Synagogue *NY Times* 13 Sep 96

William F Buckley Jr columnist

6170 Either Waugh had to go, or else the ritual. . . . The Holy Spirit made His choice. Waugh went.

On Evelyn Waugh's death immediately after congregations were asked to participate in the "exchange of peace" (embracing or shaking hands) *NY Times* 19 Jan 92

Frederick Buechner poet and essayist

6171 Until you have read the story of Adam and Eve, of Abraham and Sarah, of David and Bathsheba, as your own story. . . you have not really understood it.

Now and Then Harper & Row 83

Sophy Burnham essayist

6172 Coincidence is God's way of performing miracles anonymously.

Angel Letters Ballentine 91

George Burns entertainer

6173 A good sermon should have a good beginning, and a good ending, and they should be as close together as possible.

Washington Post 22 Apr 95

Laura Burrough novelist

6174 There was a soft babble as of discreet mice.

On a Carmelite convent *Sister Clare* Houghton Mifflin 60

6175 The grandfather's clock. . . began to chime, dropping through the silent monastery six liquid silver strokes.

ib

George Bush 41st US President

6176 There is profound meaning in the physical beauty. . . a massive 300-million pound mountain of Indiana limestone created as an act of worship.

At dedication of Washington National Cathedral 29 Sep 90

6177 The rose window high above seems black and formless. But when we enter, and see it backlit by the sun, it dazzles in astonishing splendor. And it reminds us that without faith, we too are but stained-glass windows in the dark.

ib

Prescott Bush Jr business executive

6178 God just was.

On his parents' reluctance to discuss religion with him and his brother George *Newsweek* 19 Oct 87

Vannevar Bush Chair, MIT

6179 A belief may be larger than a fact because a faith that is overdefined is the very faith likely to prove inadequate to the great moments in life.

Science Is Not Enough Morrow 67

John Byrne President, NY Senate of Priests

6180 Rome wasn't unbuilt in a day.

On changes following Vatican II *NY Times* 17 May 68

Erskine Caldwell novelist

6181 That's God's little acre. . . and every year I give the church what comes off that acre of ground.

On dedicating land but neglecting to cultivate it and always hoping it wouldn't bring gold that had to be shared *God's Little Acre* Scribner 1933, the source for Broadway's longest running play, recalled on Caldwell's death 11 Apr 87

George Carey Archbishop of Canterbury

6182 She is an elderly lady who mutters away to herself in a corner, ignored most of the time.

On the Church of England, interview with *British Reader's Digest* Mar 91

6183 When you are in trouble you go to this granny and get a sort of eternal tap on the head, and everything is all right again.

ib

6184 The idea that only a male can represent Christ at the altar is a most serious heresy. It has flirted with the Delilah of paganism and danced with the Salome of communist ideology.

ib; see also *London Times* 18 Jan 93

6185 I believe with all my heart that the Church of Jesus Christ should be a church of blurred edges. . . a church of no walls where people can ask their hardest questions without reproach.

London Times 19 Mar 94

Jimmy Carter 38th US President

6186 I believe God has a purpose for individual lives as well as for the sweep of human events. . . . I was His in 1976. I am His in 1980. Now, let's eat supper.

On election and defeat *Liberty* Sep 81

Owen Chadwick Regius Professor of Modern History, Cambridge

6187 Deciding to be ordained is the knowledge that you dimly see your future and have the courage to embark on an irreversible way and feel that at least you commit yourself to help humanity in its suffering or its moral predicament.

In biography of the hundredth Archbishop of Canterbury *Michael Ramsey* Oxford 90

Dora Chaplin Associate Professor of Pastoral Theology, General Theological Seminary, NYC

6188 Our Lord said, "Feed my sheep"; he did not say, "Count them."

On undue emphasis on church attendance *The Privilege of Teaching* Morehouse-Barlow 62

Charles Prince of Wales

6189 Poetry is for everybody... but banality is for nobody.

Comparing new liturgies to Thomas Cranmer's work on the 500th anniversary of his *Book of Common Prayer London Daily Telegraph* 20 Dec 89

6190 We commend the "beauty of holiness," yet we forget the holiness of beauty.

ib

6191 If English is spoken in Heaven, God undoubtedly employs Cranmer as his speech writer.

ib

6192 How can we be lifted up by a sentence which itself needs lifting on a stretcher?

ib

Susan Cheever biographer

6193 His religious requirements—that the service come from Cranmer's rites in the old prayer book, that it take 33 minutes or less, that the church be within 10 minutes driving distance and that the alter be sufficiently simple so that it wouldn't remind him of a gift shop—limited his choice of parishes.

On her father John Cheever *Home before Dark* Houghton Mifflin 84

Winston S Churchill statesman

6194 He is the only six-penny item in a penny bazaar.

On recommending William Temple to be Archbishop of Canterbury, recalled in *London Times* 1 Jul 95

Alan Clark British Minister of Trade

6195 This degradation of the ancient form and language is a calculated act, a deliberate subversion by a hard core whose secret purpose is to distort the beliefs and practices of the Church of England.

On revisions of the Bible and Prayer Book *Mrs Thatcher's Minister* Farrar Straus Giroux 93

6196 I would gladly burn... those trendy clerics at the stake. What fun to hear them pinkly squealing!

ib

William J Clinton 42nd US President

6197 They would see someone whose belief in God and faith is as sincere and deep and genuine as theirs. And they would probably see someone who is, perhaps rightly or wrongly, much more humble in his Christian faith than many of them.

On what might be found in his soul *London Times* 21 Feb 95

William Sloane Coffin Jr Senior Minister, NYC Riverside Church

6198 Hope arouses, as nothing else can arouse, a passion for the possible.

Once to Every Man Atheneum 77

Shimon Cohen journalist

6199 There have never been any yarmulkes... until the Chief Rabbi walks in.

On the House of Lords' seating its first rabbi *NY Times* 10 Feb 88

Community of St Mary religious order

6200 Bear thyself with the reserve of Our Lady, that thou mayest be worthy of her name here and of her company hereafter.

Book of the Rule quoted in booklet marking the centennial of the Episcopal Church's oldest society for women *Into the Second Century* Peekskill NY 65

Harvey Cox Professor of Divinity, Harvard

6201 There has never been a better raconteur than Jesus of Nazareth himself.

The Seduction of the Spirit Simon & Schuster 78

Lawrence N Crumb librarian, University of Oregon

6202 Will you remember, every month,/Just to send a check (by the mailman),/Living in our trailer we'll be easy to reach,/Right down there in Pompano Beach./All through the May years, premiums paid,/Every time you've dunned;/Will you remember, when it's December—/O Church Pension Fund?

An Episcopal priest's meditation on financial security, privately published 89

Charles Curran Professor of Theology, Catholic University of America

6203 My God is a big God, yes she is!

On Vatican censure for his liberal views *US* 20 Oct 86

Richard Cardinal Cushing Archbishop of Boston

6204 As sons of Adam, they are our brothers. As sons of Abraham, they are the blood brothers of Christ.

Plea to Vatican Council II to disassociate the Jewish people with blame for the crucifixion *Saturday Evening Post* 17 Oct 64

Dalai Lama spiritual leader

6205 Sleep is the best meditation.
People 10 Sep 79

Anthony Dalla Villa

6206 What you are is God's gift to you: what you make of it is your gift to God.
Eulogy at Andy Warhol's requiem mass, St Patrick's Cathedral, NYC 1 Apr 87

6207 Death gives life its fullest reality.
ib

Dom Gregory Dix OSB, Anglican liturgist

6208 It is no accident that the symbol of a bishop is a crook, and the sign of an archbishop is a double-cross.
On ethics among prelates, letter to *London Times* 3 Dec 77

Judith Kaplan Eisenstein Jewish initiate

6209 Bat Mitzvah began not as feminism but as a dedication to something larger than life itself.
At age 82, recalling the ceremony in 1922 when she became the first woman to be Bat Mitzvahed, now widely observed as a counterpart to Bar Mitzvah for males *NY Times* 15 Feb 96

Robert Ellis Communications Director, Diocese of Lichfield

6210 For the Church to ignore religious TV advertising is like Caxton ignoring printing and St Paul ignoring boats.
London Times 22 Dec 92

Kennedy Fraser essayist

6211 Archbishops seemed to be the spiritual footmen of superstars.
On royal weddings *New Yorker* 4 Dec 95

Andre Frossard journalist

6212 A heavy, ironclad cruiser *Potemkin* steaming into harbor at St Peter's. . . a cavalry troop suspended in midcharge. . . a hurricane harnassed.
Recalling John Paul II's election to the papacy *New Yorker* 17 Oct 94

Rumer Godden novelist

6213 One of the most important things in her life were her keys. Waking, her life was bound by them, and sleeping, her thoughts were dogged by them and she had always the comfortable feeling of their weight by her side.
On a Mother Superior *Black Narcissus* 1939 novel never out of print, James B Simpson ed *Veil and Cowl* Ivan R Dee 94

Mikhail S Gorbachev Soviet premier

6214 Believers are Soviet people, workers, patriots, and they have the full right to express their conviction with dignity.
On promising a new law of freedom of conscience *NY Times* 30 Apr 88

David Hare essayist

6215 One enfeebled institution clinging to the other!
On the monarchy and the Church of England *New Yorker* 4 Dec 95

Ralph Peter Hatendi Bishop of Harare, Zimbabwe

6216 She may be Queen, she may be Prime Minister, she may be a doctor or a manager of a big business, but she will not mount the altar of sacrifice.
On women bishops, address at Lambeth Conference *Illustrated London News* Sep 89

Walter Farquhar Hook Vicar, St Peter's, Leeds, England

6217 Christian is my name, Catholic my surname.
Asserting the Anglican position of Biblical Apostolic, traditional belief *Country Life* 20 Dec 84

Iakvos Greek Orthodox Archbishop of North and South America

6218 The Jew is the eternal Protestant.
A History of the Jews Harper & Row 87

6219 We'd like the American public to know the Orthodox Church has come of age. The US is not a foreign land. It is our land.
On the first assembly of Russian, Greek, Serb and other Orthodox churches after 200 years in the US *NY Times* 9 Dec 94

William Cardinal Keeler President, National Conference of Catholic Bishops

6220 The most widely spoken language in the world is bad English.
On neutralizing gender, Station WAMU Washington 13 Dec 94

John Cardinal Krol Archbishop of Philadelphia

6221 All priests need a pat... gently and high or hard and low.

NY Times 4 Oct 79

Pio Cardinal Laghi Vatican Prefect of the Congregation for Catholic Education

6222 It is not only what we say as a church, it is the way we say it that can mean as much. On that we can improve. Nuance, it is everything.

NY Times 11 Dec 94

Henry Lewis Chaplain, University of Michigan Medical Center

6223 Call me Mister, call me friend,/A loving ear to all I lend,/But do not my soul with anguish rend,/Please stop calling me Reverend!

On "The Rev" as a title properly used only with a complete name *Time* 30 Nov 62

W R Matthews Dean, St Paul's Cathedral, London

6224 The church that marries the spirit of this age will find itself a widow in the next.

Recalled on Matthews' retirement 31 Dec 67

Arthur Miller playwright

6225 You people seem not to comprehend that a minister is the Lord's man in the parish... not to be so lightly crossed and contradicted.

The Crucible John Glassner ed *Best American Plays 1951–1957* Yale 58

Peggy Noonan essayist and critic

6226 True ecumenism was when the Italians and the Irish started speaking to each other.

Wall Street Journal 24 Dec 90

Paul Reeves Anglican Observer at the UN

6227 If... you bite and devour one another, take care that you are not consumed by one another!

At General Convention of the Episcopal Church, Phoenix AZ 14 Jul 91

Richard Rutt Bishop of Leicester

6228 The ordination of women is merely the ears of the hippopotamus.

On joining seven bishops and more than 700 clergy on leaving the Church of England to become Roman Catholics *London Times* 24 Feb 94

Robert Schuller Pastor, California's Crystal Cathedral

6229 I am a retailer of religion, an apostle of possibility thinking.

On his nationally televised ministry *Time* 18 Mar 85

Peter Steinfels reporter

6230 Praise for him was as thick as the slices of filet mignon.

On dinner honoring the Greek Orthodox Archbishop Iakovos during Constantinople's attempt to force his resignation *NY Times* 12 Nov 95

Walter Sundberg Northwestern Theological Seminary, St Paul MN theologian

6231 Going to bed with Episcopalians is like ecclesiastical necrophilia.

On conversations between Lutheran and Episcopal churches *Newsweek* 4 Mar 91

Margaret Thatcher British Prime Minister

6232 It would have been a little bit better to have been a little bit less.

On church attendance as a child *London Times* 10 May 93

6233 There'll be blood on the carpet of Lincoln Cathedral before he's finished.

To her Appointments Secretary on naming Brandon Jackson to be Dean of Lincoln, a portent of Jackson's prolonged discord with Lincoln's bishop and cathedral chapter *ib* 4 Mar 95

G M Trevelyan agnostic

6234 I am a flying buttress of the Church; I support it, but from the outside.

Quoted by David Cannadine *G M Trevelyan* Norton 93

Tim Unsworth sociologist

6235 [They followed] the yellow brick road that would ultimately invest them in the watered silk.

On the 30 percent of Roman Catholic archibishops who studied in Rome for doctorates in canon law *The Last Priests in America* Crossroads 91

William Wilson essayist and critic

6236 Barth's Church Dogmatics is... chewing a mouthful of bubble gum studded with broken glass.

An Incomplete Education Ballantine 87

Tom Wolfe novelist

6237 The bishop is black....it could just as easily been a woman or a Sandinista. Or a lesbian. Or a lesbian Sandinista.

On liberality of the Episcopal Church *The Bonfire of the Vanities* Farrar Straus Giroux 87

James Wood critic

6238 Newman had been a very Catholic Anglican and remained to the end of his life a very Anglican Catholic.

On John Henry Cardinal Newman *Guardian Weekly* 24 Oct 93 reviewing Newsome's *The Convert Cardinals* John Murray 93

John Yates Bishop of Gloucester

6239 No longer will a patron be able to announce his new parson to the bishop over the port; that surely can't be a bad thing.

On the House of Lords' termination of the lord of the manor's ancient right to pick the local vicar *London Times* 16 Jul 86

HUMOR

Alice Acheson wife of Dean Acheson

6240 It either stands or falls. . . not like a foreign country; he doesn't have to wait 25 years to see how the thing comes out.

On the furniture-making hobby of her husband, Secretary of State Dean Acheson, quoted by James B Reston *Deadline* Random House 91

Dean Acheson US Secretary of State

6241 My attempts to reply cause every Frenchman to take on a the look of a mastiff to the impertinences of a fox terrier.

On conversing in French *Sketches from Life* Harper 61

6242 Reading, as always, at your bidding,/ I wonder who the hell you're kidding?

Letter to the *Washington Post* on its report that Americans avoid scapegoats *Newsweek* 26 Jul 65

6243 Every subject was taken to pieces, sometimes put together again, and sometimes just left lying around.

On harness shop discussions in the Conneticut of the early 1900s *Morning and Noon* Houghton Mifflin 65

6244 We are all old and we are all eloquent.

On lengthy meetings of senior advisers, quoted by Henry Kissinger *White House Years* Little, Brown 79

James Agee novelist

6245 Like trying to put socks on an octopus!

On difficult conversations with the diffident *A Death in the Family* McDowell, Obolensky 57

Fred Allen comedian

6246 What's on your mind? If you'll forgive the overstatement.

Recalled on Allen's death 17 Mar 56

6247 Was she old? When they lit all of the candles on her birthday cake, six people were overcome with the heat!

Much Ado About Me Little, Brown 56

6248 Money talks—the only conversation worth hearing when times are bad.

ib

6249 I don't want to say Jack Benny is cheap, but he's got short arms and carries his money low in his pockets.

Quoted by Irving Fein *Jack Benny* Putnam 75

6250 Anybody who believes in astronomy was probably born under the wrong star.

McLean's 22 Aug 77

6251 Population explosion: when people take leave of their census.

Quoted by Leo Rosten *Infinite Riches* McGraw-Hill 79

6252 Filet of anchovy. . . they look like damp hyphens.

Quoted by Robert Taylor *Fred Allen: His Life and Wit* Little, Brown 89

Henry Allen humorist

6253 The color of Monday is like used Saran wrap. . . lumpy. . . [and] reminds you of the waiting room at a transmission shop.

Washington Post 22 Aug 94

6254 Wednesday doesn't judge like Sunday, blame like Monday, exhort like Tuesday, hurry you like Thursday, inflame like Friday, or overwhelm like Saturday.

ib 24 Aug 94

6255 Wednesday has an air of expecting something of you. Not demanding but expecting. . . [and] it is the cruelest day, breeding Thursdays out of dead Tuesdays.

ib

Woody Allen comedian

6256 The lion and the calf shall lie down together but the calf won't get much sleep.

On Biblical predictions of peace *New Republic* 31 Aug 74

6257 Love is the answer but while you're waiting for the answer, sex raises some good questions.

Time 15 Dec 75

6258 It's not that I'm afraid to die, I just don't want to be there when it happens.

Love and Death Samuel French 75

6259 I'm really a timid person. I was beaten up by Quakers.

Sleeper Random House 78

6260 I feel about New York as a child whose father is a bank robber. . . not perfect, but I still love him.

NY Times 20 Aug 92

Joseph W Alsop columnist

6261 It is a simple rule of thumb that with eight people at table you cannot have so much as one bore; with ten you can have half a bore; with 12 a whole bore; with 14 a bore and a half.

I've Seen the Best of It Norton 92

6262 The mindless rich, if very rich, also count as half bores.

ib

Kingsley Amis novelist

6263 There's no need to get out of bed for it; /Wherever you may be,/ They bring it to you free.

On death "Delivery Guaranteed" *Collected Poems* Viking 80

Christopher Andreae humorist

6264 Rumbustious. . . a glorious, wonderful, notable, promotable, old giant of a word! Go on, say it! Roll it round your teeth!

Christian Science Monitor 20 Aug 92

Maya Angelou poet

6265 [The age 40] with the authorized brazeness of a uniformed cop stomps no-knocking into the script, bumps a funky grind on the shabby curtain of youth, and delays the action. Unless you have the inborn wisdom and grace and are clever enough to die at 39.

"On Reaching 40" *Maya Angelou Poems* Bantam 86

Anon

6266 [She was] a Himalayan Marie Antoinette.

On the American heiress Hope Cooke, formerly Queen of Sikkim *New Yorker* 13 Apr 87

6267 Retirement? "Twice as much husband, half as much pay!"

Reader's Digest Apr 87

6268 Russian royalty partied with czars in their eyes.

Life Styles of the Rich and Famous WPIX TV 17 May 87

6269 There was a woman who didn't know her husband was a drunk until one night he came home sober.

Quoted by Phil Donohue NBC TV 1 Jun 87

6270 Pit-bulls' connuptial cavorting results in inbreeding; no wonder they're especially vicious at family gatherings.

Live at Five NBC TV 27 Jul 87

6271 As for those who don't love us, may God turn their hearts, and if he doesn't turn their hearts, may he turn their ankles so we'll know them by their limping.

Irish prayer quoted by President Reagan in tongue-in-cheek reference to Congress *USA Today* 9 Sep 87

6272 Upon my honor/ I saw a Madonna/ Standing in a niche/ Above the door/ Of a prominent whore/ Of a prominent son of a bitch.

On a dressing-room bungalow built for actress Marion Davies by her lover William Randolph Hearst; wrongly attributed to Dorothy Parker who said she would never rhyme honor with Madonna, quoted by Marion Meade *Dorothy Parker* Villard 88

6273 [Clare Boothe Luce]. . . a beautiful palace without central heating.

Quoted by biographer Sylvia Jukes Morris *NY Times* 31 Jan 88

6274 The man has all the ethnicity of Formica.

Denial that Superman is Jewish, quoted in cover story on 50th anniversary of the comic strip character *Time* 14 Mar 88

6275 When my therapist went away, I went into this Buddhism thing for two weeks and wound up chanting. I later realized it was somewhat related.

NY Times 23 Jul 88

6276 If you don't swing, don't ring.

Plaque on front door of *Playboy* publisher Hugh Hefner 28 Jul 88

6277 Feel safe tonight: Sleep with a cop.

Sign at Chambers Street Police Station NYC 27 Aug 88

6278 [An intellectual is] a person who takes more words than necessary to say more than he knows.

Definition frequently quoted by Dwight D Eisenhower, recalled by Hedley Donovan *Right Places, Right Times* Holt 89

6279 [He] could sell the Pope on financing a Mormon tabernacle.

On Thomas A Shaheen's indictment for use of phony certificates in attempted acquisition of an insurance company *Wall Street Journal* 1 Feb 89

6280 Dr Don, the Stone of Scone, it is gone!

Westminster Abbey verger to Dean Allen Don on the 1950 theft of the ancient Coronation stone *Christian Challenge* Nov 89

6281 The answer is maybe—and that's final.

On a pillow owned by heiress Doris Duke *New Yorker* 3 Sep 90

6282 There she is, living proof that the Indians slept with the buffaloes.

On a congresswoman known as "Buffalo Gal," quoted by Peggy Noonan *What I Saw at the Revolution* Random House 90

6283 Odds of meeting a single man: 1 in 23; a cute, single man: 1 in 529; a cute, single, smart man, 1 in 3,245,873; when you look your best, 1 in 9,729,528.

Cocktail napkin 90

6284 There once was a lawyer named Tex/ Who was sadly deficient in sex./ When arraigned for exposure/ He remarked with composure/ *De minimus non curat lex.*

On legal aphorisms, quoted by William Safire *Language Mavern Strikes Again* Doubleday 90

6285 The last shall be first.
Credo of London bootmaker *NY Times* 13 Jan 91

6286 Marriage is Alan's way of saying good-bye.
On the much-married Alan Jay Lerner *ib* 24 Feb 91

6287 Make money the modern way. Urn it!
Advertisement for undertakers and crematoriums *Wall Street Journal* 25 Apr 91

6288 It's difficult not to plant a tree at some time during the day.
On the British royal family PBS TV 22 May 91

6289 The buck *starts* here.
Sign at US Bureau of Printing and Engraving 92

6290 Have you ever been so close and yet so far away?
On watching money roll off the presses *ib*

6291 Reggie is to Kennedy what Gorham polish is to tarnished silver.
On Victoria Reggie's engagement to Senator Ted Kennedy *Washington Post* 20 Mar 92

6292 Denial is more than a river in Egypt.
CBS TV 18 Jul 92

6293 He was to sex what Columbus was to geography.
On researcher Alfred Kinsey, quoted by Garrison Keillor, American Public Radio 15 Aug 92

6294 Blooms mostly at night, varies in length, depending on owner... may wilt in chilly atmosphere.
Sign attached to condom "plant" on desk of US Surgeon General Joycelyn Elders *Washington Post* 16 Feb 93

6295 Escaping the draft again?
On President Clinton's state visit to Canada *Washington Post* 23 Feb 95

6296 Three interruptions make one conspiracy.
Quoted by Norman Mailer on cut-offs in broadcast interview on his book on Kennedy assassin Lee Harvey Oswald, Station WAMU Washington 1 May 95

6297 It's not the guards that keep changing, it's the ticket prices!
On tours of Buckingham Palace *London Times* 13 Sep 95

6298 Nouveau riche is better than no riche at all.
Sofa cushion at Merrywood, the Virginia home of housing developer Alan Kay *Washington Post* 28 Sep 95

6299 Here lies an atheist—all dressed up and no where to go.
Grave stone in a Derry NH churchyard NPR 11 Nov 95

6300 Good girls go to heaven. Bad girls go everywhere.
Needlepointed cushion in the office of *Cosmopolitan* editor Helen Gurley Brown *Washington Post* 31 Jan 96

Robert Anthony humorist

6301 Nostalgia isn't what it used to be.
Think Again Berkley Books 86

Peter Arno cartoonist

6302 Tell me about yourself—your struggles, your dreams, your telephone number.
Cartoon caption recalled on Arno's death 22 Feb 68

Louis Auchincloss novelist

6303 [It was] a giant phallic symbol to remind one that duty is never done.
On the chapel tower of a New England prep school *The Rector of Justin* Houghton Mifflin 64

W H Auden poet

6304 Sincerity always hits me like sleep... if you try to get it too hard, you won't.
Quoted by Charles Osborne *W H Auden: The Life of a Poet* Harcourt Brace Jovanovich 79

6305 My face... a wedding cake left out in the rain.
Quoted by Humphrey Carpenter *W H Auden* Houghton Mifflin 82

6306 Who am I now? An American? No, a New Yorker who opens his *Times* at the obit page.
Prologue at 60 Edward Mendelson ed *W H Auden: Collected Poems* Vintage 91

Murray Bail

6307 The British enunciate clearly... to penetrate the humidity and hedges, the moist walls and alleyways.
Homesickness Macmillan 80

Letitia Baldrige commentator

6308 Good listeners don't interrupt—ever—unless the house is on fire.
"The Art of Listening" *Town & Country* Sep 95

Billy Baldwin decorator

6309 She had a parure of emeralds.... She had the same thing in sapphires, and I guess that only God and Ailsa knew what else she had.
On Ailsa Mellon Bruce *Billy Baldwin* with Michael Gardine, Little, Brown 85

6310 She looked as though she smelled something terrible all the time.
ib

Lucille Ball entertainer

6311 The secret of staying young is to live honestly, eat slowly, and lie about your age.

Esquire Feb 93

Mary Bancroft OSS operative

6312 That Virgin Mary in pants.

On FBI Director J Edgar Hoover, quoted by Leonard Mosley *Dulles* Dell 78

Tallulah Bankhead actress

6313 I'm as pure as the driven slush.

Recalled on Bankhead's death 12 Dec 68

6314 Only good girls keep diaries. Bad girls don't have time.

ib

6315 Conventional sex makes me claustrophobic and the others give me either a stiff neck or lockjaw.

Playboy Dec 77

6316 You and I are the only constantly High Episcopalians I know.

To Tennessee Williams *New Yorker* 15 Jul 94

William Baring-Gould poet

6317 The limerick is furtive and mean;/ You must keep her in close quarantine,/ Or she sneaks to the slums/And promptly becomes/ Disorderly, drunk and obscene.

The Lure of Limerick Potter 67

Myrtie Lillian Barker humorist

6318 The idea of strictly minding our own business is moldy rubbish. Who could be so selfish?

On gossip *I Am Only One* Bobbs Merrill 63

Donald Barr Headmaster, Dalton School, NYC

6319 Consistency is only a kind of chastity of the head.

Who Pushed Humpty Dumpty? Atheneum 71

Jack Barry humorist

6320 The trouble with New York is it's so convenient to everything I can't afford.

Reader's Digest Dec 52

Alfred Baxter retired professor

6321 Prostate, prostate, burning right/ Up there where the plumbing's tight/ What in hell persuaded thee/ To plug the pipe through which I pee?/ In what ocean, on what land/ Grew the tissues of this gland?/ What dread ailment fed increase/ That caused my fluid flows to cease?

Lamentation penned from a Berkeley CA hospital that kept its author from attending the Bohemian Club's annual frolic *Washingtonian* Jan 91

Cecil Beaton photographer

6322 A pair of very long medieval shoes appeared, then a muffled figure and finally a huge, golden melon of a hat.

On poet Edith Sitwell's arrival by ambulance at a party in London *The Parting Years* Weidenfeld & Nicolson 78

6323 Edith was wheeled into place and given two strong martinis.

ib

Hilaire Belloc humorist

6324 A trick that everyone abhors/ In little girls is slamming doors.

Cautionary Tales recalled on Belloc's death 16 Jul 53

6325 We must assume the Lord knew best/ When he created Ivor Guest.

Unpublished lines on a fellow member of the Liberal Party *London Times* 28 Dec 93

6326 Grant, O Lord, eternal rest/ For Thy servant Ivor Guest./ Never mind the where or how/ Only grant that it be now.

ib

Saul Bellow novelist

6327 If he's forgiven her bagpipe tidders and estuary leg veins, she'd forgive his unheroic privates.

On imagining Billy Rose and an auditioning actress *The Bellarose Connection* Viking Penguin 89

Walter Benjamin humorist

6328 [It was] love at last sight.

On reconciliation and mutual forgiveness of New York City *Our New York* Harper & Row 90

Alan Bennett playwright

6329 We started off trying to set up a small anarchist community, but people wouldn't obey the rules.

Getting On 72

6330 Tom, a priest (although you would not guess it—actually maybe God would not guess it either).

On a meeting of Alcoholics Anonymous *New Yorker* 22 May 95

6331 She's a bore. Maybe that's what drove her to drink because as sure as hell it drives other people.

ib

6332 Colder than a greyhound's nostrils!

On royal palaces in screenplay for *The Madness of George III* 95

Lloyd Bentsen Jr US Senator

6333 Never mind the dog, beware of the owner.
Sign placed on property of Bentsen's 95-year-old father *Wall Street Journal* 20 Jul 88

Thomas Berger novelist

6334 Her features gargoyled with indignation.
On a character in his novel *Being Invisible* Little, Brown 87

Milton Berle entertainer

6335 I can't tell you his age but when he was born the wonder drug was mercurochrome.
On Danny Thomas NBC TV 8 Jan 91

6336 Sex at 84 is terrific, especially the one in the winter.
NY Times 28 Jul 92

Irving Berlin composer

6337 She's the hostess with the mostest on the ball!
Title and lyrics of a salute to US Minister to Luxemburg Pearl Mesta *Call Me Madam* musical 54

John Betjeman poet

6338 What more precious link between our two great countries than the linen drawers of the Master?
On inheriting Henry James' underwear, quoted by Brendan Gill *A New York Life* Poseidon 90

Mel Blanc actor

6339 Eh, What's up, Doc?
Lines for Bugs Bunny, recalled on Blanc's death 10 Jul 89

6340 Thufferin' thuccotash!
Frequent exclamation of Sylvester the cat *ib*

6341 I tawt I taw a puddy tat!
Lines for Tweetie the canary *ib*

6342 That's all, folks!
Stammering sign-off line for Porky Pig originated in 1935 and soon the signature for the entire Warner Brothers animated oeuvre *Time* 26 Feb 96

Roy Blount Jr humorist

6343 If he'd stayed in the Confederate army, he might've been killed and gone on to write *Gone With the Wind.*
On Mark Twain *Prairie Home Companion* 1 Dec 90

Hal Borland naturalist

6344 The owl, that bird of onomatopoetic name, is a repetitious question wrapped in feathery insulation especially for winter delivery.
Sundial of the Seasons Lippincott 64

Elizabeth Bowen novelist

6345 [She] looked like a high altar on the move.
Quoted by Victoria Glendinning *Edith Sitwell* Knopf 81

Alla Renee Bozarth Episcopal priest

6346 I received stipends ranging from nothing to not much.
Womanpriest Lura Media 88

Jimmy Breslin humorist

6347 They were married. . . by a priest who saw that the bride had her future well in front of her.
Table Money Ticknor & Fields 86

6348 The T-Bone Diner. . . a Greek rebellion against public health.
ib

David Brinkley commentator

6349 [It is] rhetoric that rolls like a freight train over a bridge.
On speechmaking of union czar John L Lewis *Newsweek* 13 Mar 61

6350 Marijuana is a growth industry.
NBC TV 7 Nov 80

6351 She agreed to marry him on condition he stop drinking, a promise he kept perhaps 50 times.
On heiress Evalyn Walsh McLean and Edward Beale *Washington Goes to War* Knopf 88

6352 If not a crime, at least a serious indiscretion.
On conservatives' viewpoint on women who give birth after age 40, Station WAMU 7 Nov 95

Leonard Brockington humorist

6353 I've ruined my constitution years ago, and I've been living on my by-laws ever since.
Quoted by J Francis Leddy at Canada Council dinner, Ottawa 14 Jun 82

Montgomery Brower reporter

6354 The entire scene resembles a fox concentration camp.
On one of 350 Russian state farms for breeding foxes for sale of pelts *People* 6 Apr 87

Edmund G Brown Sr Governor of California

6355 Why, this is the worst disaster since my election.
On the 1965 Watts riots, recalled in *NY Times* 21 Aug 94

John Mason Brown critic

6356 He talks at the drop of a pause.
On John Gunther *Esquire* Apr 60

6357 He's the best listener of any non-stop talker I know.

ib

6358 They're the Typhoid Marys of culture.

On clubwomen *ib*

Rita Mae Brown novelist

6359 I think of birth as the search for a larger apartment.

Starting from Scratch Bantam 88

Anatole Broyard critic

6360 When Harriet goes to bed with a man, she always takes her wet blanket with her.

On Iris Owens' *After Claude* Farrar Straus Giroux 73

6361 He is forever taking a stand on marshy ground.

On the hero of Gordon Webber's *The Great Buffalo Hotel* Little, Brown 79 *NY Times* 30 Jun 79

Art Buchwald columnist

6362 Everybody in this country who owns a gun also owns a typewriter. So my solution to the gun registration problem is to make everybody register his typewriter.

To law school commencement at Catholic University 7 May 77, quoted by William Safire *Lend Me Your Ears* Norton 92

6363 I have always wanted to write a pornographic book but I get so excited doing the research that I can never get around to the book.

ib

William F Buckley Jr columnist

6364 Idealism is fine, but as it approaches reality the cost becomes prohibitive.

Quoted by John Winocur *The Portable Curmudgeon* New American Library 87

6365 I would like to take you seriously but to do so would affront your intelligence.

ib

Gelett Burgess humorist

6366 Ah, yes, I wrote The Purple Cow/ I'm sorry, now, I wrote it!/ But I can tell you, anyhow,/ I'll kill you if you quote it.

The Purple Cow recalled on Burgess' death 18 Sep 51

George Burns entertainer

6367 If I have to cry, I think of my sex life; if I have to laugh, I think of my sex life.

Chicago Tribune 7 Nov 76

6368 It's nice to be here. When you're 99 years old, it's nice to be anyplace.

USA Today 20 Jan 95

6369 Sincerity is the secret of success. If you can fake that, you've got it made.

News summaries 31 Dec 95

6370 As a rule, an entertainer gets a standing ovation at the end of the show.

On an audience's spontaneous tribute as he approached his hundredth birthday ABC TV 19 Jan 96

Richard Burton actor

6371 It was white-tie-and-taco.

On a party given by ex-wife Elizabeth Taylor for the Mexican lawyer Victor Gonzaleza Luna *McCall's* Sep 85

Tony Burton reporter

6372 The endangered species was noted for its floppy ears, fluffy tail, pouty breast and stilt legs.

On bunny waitresses who were becoming extinct with closing of the last of the Playboy Clubs in New York, Chicago, and Los Angeles *NY Daily News* 29 Jun 86

6373 Its night-time habitat was dimly lighted caves where it attracted males draped in polyester, gold chains, and fantasy.

On Playboy Clubs *ib*

Barbara Bush First Lady

6374 He'll be calling me Thyroid Mary.

On diagnoses that her husband also had an overactive thyroid, news reports of 10 May 91

George Bush 41st US President

6375 It's a little unsettling to turn on the news and see Peter Jennings pointing to a diagram of a heart with your name on it! It isn't even Valentine's Day!

On public discussions of his health *NY Times* 8 May 91

6376 Welcome from the bottom of my previously fibrillating heart.

To White House guests a few days after being hospitalized *Newsweek* 20 May 91

6377 Why don't you just roll me under the table and let me sleep it off?

To Prime Minister Kiichi Miyazawa after fainting at a state dinner in Tokyo *Washington Post* 9 Jan 92

Robert C Byrd US Senator

6378 [It] betrays a mind whose thoughts are often so disorganized as to be unutterable—a mind in neutral gear coupled to a tongue stuck in overdrive.

On use of "y'know" in conversation *NY Times* 16 Jun 91

6379 I believe the senator has referred to floccinaucinihilphlification but did the Senator add "ism?"

On Daniel Patrick Moynihan's use of a word referring to the futility of making estimates on the accuracy of public data and regarded as the longest word in the

English dictionary rather than antidisestablishmentarianism 23 Jun 91

Erskine Caldwell novelist

6380 [He was] as persistent as snow in Alaska.
On fellow journalist Ralph Ingersoll, quoted by Vicki Goldberg *Margaret Bourke-White* Harper & Row 87

Hortense Calisher novelist

6381 Ms is a syllable which sounds like a bumble bee breaking wind.
On alternate use of Miss and Mrs *NY Times* 22 Sep 74

Albert Camus novelist

6382 Charm. . . a way of getting the answer "yes" without having to ask any clear question.
The Fall Knopf 88

Ray Capo Director of Sales and Administration, Woodlawn Cemetery, Bronx, NY

6383 These mausoleums were built long before they were needed. . . . You could lose your fortune and still have a real nice place to go.
New Yorker 28 Mar 94

Truman Capote novelist

6384 She suspected the sweet waters of her own crystalline reputation had been seweraged.
On a woman who thought she was depicted in a novel *Answered Prayers* Random House 87

6385 I may be a black sheep, but my hooves are made of gold.
Lines for fictional character Kate McCloud *ib*

6386 She looked like. . . a vulnerable, deceptively incapable child who had gone to sleep and awakened 40 years later with puffy eyes, false teeth, and whiskey on her breath.
On Dorothy Parker *ib*

6387 Mrs P had only one fault; she was perfect; otherwise, she was perfect.
On Babe Paley, quoted by Gerald Clarke *Capote* Simon & Schuster 88

6388 [She] looked as if she wore tweed brassieres.
On a character at La Cote Basque reportedly based on Pamela Harriman

6389 If Kate had as many pricks sticking out of her as she's had stuck in her, she'd look like a porcupine.
ib

6390 What Billie Holiday is to jazz, what Mae West is to tits. . . what Seconal is to sleeping pills, what King Kong is to penises, Truman Capote is to the great god Thespis!
On himself as an actor *ib*

Gretchen Carlson Miss America 1989

6391 When I go out on stage, I know it's all me.
On cosmetic surgery as "not sincere" *Washington Times* 12 Sep 88

Joyce Cary humorist

6392 What is there in the abstract? You might as well eat triangles and go to bed with a sewing machine.
The Horse's Mouth M Joseph 1944 recalled on Cary's death 29 Mar 57

John Cashman tour director

6393 Here lies John Cashman, who loved Greenwood so much he decided to stay.
Epitaph composed for Cashman's gravestone in Brooklyn's Greenwood cemetery *NY Times* 16 Oct 94

John Chancellor commentator

6394 It was a private occasion held mainly in public.
On a Washington visit by the Prince of Wales NBC 18 Jul 70

Raymond Chandler novelist

6395 It was a blond. A blond to make a bishop kick a hole in a stained-glass window.
Fairwell, My Lovely Lancaster 70

Gabrielle ("Coco") Chanel designer

6396 A woman of my age, if she has the luck to find a lover, cannot be expected to look at his passport.
On her World War II relationship with a German officer *Vanity Fair* Jun 94

6397 An old garlic clove like me? Who would want me?
Disclaiming lesbian affairs *ib*

Paddy Chayefsky playwright

6398 Religion has become so pallid recently, it is hardly worth while being an atheist.
The Tenth Man, Random House 61

John Cheever novelist

6399 Never put whisky into hot water bottle crossing borders of dry states or countries. Rubber will spoil taste.... Never make love with pants on.... [and remember] ecclesiastical dampness causes prematurely gray hair [when] kneeling in unheated stone churches.
A man's advice to his sons *The Wapshot Chronicle* Harper 57

6400 It was one of those rainy late afternoons when the toy department of Woolworth's on Fifth Avenue is full of women who appear to have been taken in adultery and who are now shopping for a present to carry home to their youngest child.

Characteristic irony recalled on Cheever's death *NY Times* 18 Jun 82

6401 The pain of death is nothing compared to the pain of sharing a coffeepot with a peevish woman.

On his wife Mary *The Journals of John Cheever* Knopf 91

Tom Cheney cartoonist

6402 You're right, they are delicious—but you never know where they've been.

Cartoon caption for tigers observing men *New Yorker* 13 Nov 96

Winston S Churchill statesman

6403 When the events took place which this society commemorates, I may say I was on both sides in the war between us and them.

To Order of Cincinnati on being born of an American mother *NY Times* 16 Jan 52

6404 Human beings may be divided into three classes. . . billed to death. . . worried to death. . . bored to death.

Quoted by William Manchester *The Last Lion* Little, Brown 88

6405 A dead bird does not leave its nest.

On being told that his fly was open *Guardian Weekly* 14 Mar 93

Ina Claire actress

6406 I do not want to sit here having some man look at that goddamned bridge. I want him to look at me.

On decorating a San Francisco apartment, quoted by Billy Baldwin *Billy Baldwin* with Michael Gardine; Little, Brown 85

Gregory Clark humorist

6407 Among porcupines, rape is unknown.

John Robert Columbo ed *Colombo's Canadian Quotations* Hurtig 74

William J Clinton 42nd US President

6408 [He is the first vice president to understand] the gestalt of a gigabyte.

On Albert A Gore Jr's assignment to develop a computer-driven "information superhighway" *Washington Times* 11 Apr 93

6409 [It is] the crown jewel of the federal prison system.

On White House safety precautions that even influence sending out for pizza *Vanity Fair* Jun 93

6410 I thought to myself, "That's a pretty good speech, but not good enough to give twice."

On TelePrompter that offered him the State of the Union message instead of the one he was delivering on health care *Newsweek* 4 Oct 93

6411 There isn't much job security in my line of work. I may need the skill.

On giving tours of the White House *Time* 11 Oct 93

6412 I have a quota, one saxophone play per country.

When asked to repeat a performance given for Russian President Boris Yeltsin *NY Times* 15 Jan 94

6413 There's a poll saying that 40 percent of the American people think Hillary's smarter than I am. What I don't understand is how the other 60 percent missed it.

Time 21 Mar 94

6414 The *Wall Street Journal* criticizing my wife for making money is like *Field & Stream* criticizing people for catching fish.

On investigation of Mrs Clinton's stock market gains, White House Correspondents dinner, C-Span 23 Apr 94

6415 By the time you're old enough to be standing up here, there will probably be a woman President saying, "Well, I've done a pretty good job appointing men to my Cabinet."

To participants in "Girls Nations" *NY Times* 22 Jul 94

6416 Being president is like running a cemetery; you've got a lot of people under you and nobody's listening.

At Galesburg IL *US News & World Report* 23 Jan 95

Jean Cocteau writer and playwright

6417 Regret cannot come. Lie to follow.

Telegram canceling a visit *Diary of An Unknown* Paragon 88

Richard Cohen columnist

6418 She has donated half her fee from *Playboy* to People for the Ethical Treatment of Animals. It would be only fair, then, if an owl donated its brain to her.

On nude pose of President Reagan's daughter, Patti Davis, 41, *Washington Post* 9 Jun 94

Bob Colacello biographer

6419 [She is] a kind of cross between the middle-aged Merle Oberon and the juvenile Elvis Presley.

On Imelda Marcos, quoted by Grace Glueck *NY Times* 9 Aug 90 reviewing Colacello's *Holy Terror* Harper-Collins 90

Colette (Sidonie Gabrielle Colette) author

6420 Don't eat too many almonds; they add weight to the breasts.

Gigi and Other Stories New American Library 63

Dr Alex Comfort physician and author

6421 Old stockings are... murder to untie quickly in an emergency.

On sexual bondage *The New Joy of Sex* Crown 91

John Connally Governor of Texas

6422 It's not a sin to be rich anymore—it's a miracle.

Time 18 Jan 88

Marc Connelly essayist

6423 [It was] a two-ton truck meetin' another two-ton truck... a collision on the highway.

On the immediate, intense attraction between Dorothy Parker and Charles MacArthur, quoted by Marion Meade *Dorothy Parker* Villard 88

6424 [He was] just a bird looking for the right twig to land on.

On Charles MacArthur *ib*

Dan Cook broadcaster

6425 It ain't over till the fat lady sings.

Reply countering Texas Tech PR man Ralph Carpenter who had exclaimed, "The rodeo ain't over till the bull riders ride," *RQ Winter* 85; a variation is "Church ain't out 'till the fat lady sings" *Southern Words and Sayings* Office Supply Co, Jackson MS 76

Alistair Cooke commentator

6426 Hers was a character as positive as a carving knife.

On Rosa Lewis of London's Cavendish Hotel *The Duchess of Duke Street* PBS TV 1 Dec 78

Charles Correll and Freeman Gosen humorists

6427 I'ze regusted!

Quoted by Melvin Patrick Ely's *The Adventures of Amos 'N' Andy* Free Press 91

Linda Coruzzi fashion executive

6428 TWA is the best contraceptive.

On birth control and travel, quoted by Dinah Prince "Marriage in the 80s" *New York* 1 Jun 87

Bill Cosby humorist

6429 The seven ages of man have become preschooler, Pepsi generation, baby boomer, mid-lifer, empty-nester, senior citizen, and organ donor.

Time Flies Dolphin 87

6430 I helplessly watched my body turn from a temple to a storefront church.

On overeating *ib*

6431 Proud men have gone to the brink of gangrene to maintain the interior fashion of their youth.

On adjusting a 40-inch waist to size 36 jockey shorts

Country Life magazine

6432 One fears an upsurge of bottom-pinching on the Tube.

"Fewer Hugs, Please—We're British" on fear that the fad for warm embraces ("as ubiquitous as the greeting kiss") would spread to liberties on public conveyances 16 Mar 95

Noel Coward playwright

6433 Certain women should be struck regularly, like gongs.

Private Lives 1930 recalled on Coward's death 26 Mar 73

6434 Mad dogs and Englishmen go out in the midday sun.

Song *Mad Dogs and Englishmen* 1931 *ib*

6435 The stately homes of England/ How beautiful they stand,/ To prove the upper classes/ Have still the upper hand.

Operetta 1938 *The Stately Homes of England ib*

6436 When Eve said to Adam, "Stop calling me Madame"/ the world became far more exciting/ which turns to confusion, the modern delusion/ that sex is a question of lighting.

At opening night at London's Cafe de Paris 21 Jun 54, quoted by Maria Riva *Marlene Dietrich* Knopf 92

Quentin Crisp humorist

6437 There was no need to do any housework at all. After the first four years the dirt doesn't get any worse.

The Naked Civil Servant Holt Rinehart Winston 68

Howard Crossman blackjack player

6438 I don't gamble. I invest with a risk.

On his expertise in Atlantic City casinos *NY City News* 8 Oct 78

Mart Crowley playwright

6439 Show me a happy homosexual, and I'll show you a gay corpse.

The Boys in the Band 1968

6440 What's the matter with your wife, she got lockjaw?

On fellatio *ib*

Richard Cardinal Cushing Archbishop of Boston

6441 Whenever I am having trouble with a woman, I call her "my dear."

Time 21 Aug 64

Helen Caldwell Cushman rejected wife

6442 I don't say she was above reproach. She was above self-reproach.

On photographer Margaret Bourke-White's marriage to Cushman's former husband, Erskine Caldwell, quoted by Vicki Goldberg *Margaret Bourke-White* Harper & Row 86

R G Daniels British magistrate

6443 The most delightful advantage of being bald—one can hear snowflakes.

Observer 11 Jul 76

Brad Darrach essayist

6444 Her hair, when it's not bleached, is taxidermic brown.

On actress Meryl Streep *Life* Dec 87

Robertson Davies novelist

6445 Prophecy consists of carefully bathing the inevitable in the eerie light of the impossible, and being the first to announce it.

Samuel Marchbanks' Almanack McClelland & Stewart 67

6446 Fanaticism. . . over-compensation for doubt.

The Manticore Penguin 72

6447 They kept mistresses. . . of such dowdiness they might almost have been mistaken for wives.

On men in a provincial town near Ottawa *What's Bred in the Bone* Penguin 85

Elmer Davis commentator

6448 Yesterday afternoon [the] Senator. . . wrestled with his conscience. He won.

On an unnamed senator, quoted by Fred W Friendly, *Due to Circumstances Beyond Our Control* Random House 67

Doris Day actress

6449 The really frightening thing about middle age is the knowledge that you'll grow out of it.

Quoted by A E Hotchner *Doris Day* Hall 78

Peter De Vries humorist

6450 The human brain is a device to keep the ears from grating on one another.

Comfort Me With Apples Little, Brown 56

6451 We all learn by experience, but some of us have to go to summer school.

The Tunnel of Love Penguin 82

John Diefenbaker Prime Minister of Canada

6452 Don't get me started on history because then you shall know the meaning of eternity.

Quoted by Tom Alderman *Canadian* 29 May 71

6453 I'm disturbed because the doctors tell me I'm as sound as a dollar.

Toronto Star 26 Apr 75

Art Dineen entertainer

6454 We will sell no wine before its time, that would be statutory grape.

The Art Dineen Show WCKY Cincinnati 15 Jul 88

E L Doctorow novelist

6455 I read big fat *Les Miserables* for weeks while I took the IRT to the doctor for my Wednesday allergy shots, I needed to know Jean Valjean lived a more miserable life than I did.

Lives of the Poets Random House 84 quoted in *NY Times* 5 Jul 94

Phil Donahue TV host

6456 Michaelangelo's David? Now there's a guy who works out.

On presenting a panel of male strippers *Donahue* NBC TV 20 Nov 87

6457 The mammary gland has become the hallmark of our culture.

ib Dec 91

Scott Donaldson biographer

6458 If there was a hole in the conversation, she darned it with her wit.

On Ada MacLeish *Archibald MacLeish* Houghton Mifflin 92

Hedley Donovan editor

6459 If Dan were a corporation, the Anti-Trust Division would break him up.

On editor and sociologist Daniel Bell *Right Places, Right Times* Holt 89

Joseph Dougherty humorist

6460 [The] six basic genetic building blocks are eating, sleeping, goofing off, work if you're lucky, sex if you're really lucky, and looking for a place to park.

Script for *Thirtysomething* television series quoted by John J O'Connor *NY Times* 30 May 89

Denzil Doyle commentator

6461 If Canada invented the wheel, it would drag it on a sled to be marketed in the United States.

Quoted by Jonathan Chevreau *Globe & Mail's Report on Business* Toronto Nov 85

Doris Duke heiress

6462 Forget the calendar; we're down to the hours.
On giving Tex McCrary a Bulgari clock on his 83rd birthday *Town & Country* Aug 93

David Eccles British Minister of Works

6463 The only sure guide to the sex of a pelican is another pelican.
NY Times 17 Feb 52

Osborn Elliott editor

6464 [Her] family background was so complicated that she insisted the only way it could be explained was that her grandfathers were sisters.
On German-born Liane Beebe *The World of Oz* Viking 80

Janet Flanner (Genet) columnist

6465 [Charles de Gaulle] was the most interesting of Frenchmen to all of France, to the French, and doubtless to himself. . . almost constantly.
Recalled on Flanner's death after nearly five decades as Paris correspondent for *New Yorker Newsweek* 20 Nov 78

6466 How can I tell until the last minute?
When asked if she would be sorry to die, quoted on *60 Minutes* CBS TV 30 Jan 94

Ian Fleming novelist

6467 [Horses are] dangerous at both ends and uncomfortable in the middle.
London Sunday Times 9 Oct 66

Gerald Ford 38th US President

6468 If Lincoln were living today, he would turn over in his grave.
On opposition's assertion that Lincoln would have become a Democrat *Time* 17 Feb 67

6469 Ronald Reagan doesn't dye his hair; he's just prematurely orange.
Esquire Jan 85

6470 It's the best public housing I've ever seen.
On the White House *Life* 30 Oct 92

Henry Ford II business executive

6471 A nice-looking place. I'd like to buy it.
On being jailed for drunken driving in Santa Barbara CA, quoted by Robert Lacey *Ford* Little, Brown 86

Dick Francis novelist

6472 A woman's favorite animals are a mink in the closet, a Jaguar in the garage, a tiger in the bed—and a jackass to pay for it all.
Comeback Putnam 91

Nancy Franklin humorist

6473 Over the years, things between me and my apartment deteriorated to the point where we barely acknowledged each other's existence.
On a situation in which "I kept waiting for it to change into something that it wasn't, and it kept waiting for me to give it the attention it deserved" *New Yorker* 16 Oct 95

6474 The exterior is unremarkable to the point of unnoticeability, like a bicycle that works but that nobody would ever think of stealing.
ib

6475 I put the twin bed in the other bedroom . . . [and] slept there when I was having a fight with myself.
ib

6476 I don't deliberately collect anything, but I automatically accumulate everything.
ib

Clement Freud humorist

6477 If you resolve to give up smoking, drinking and loving, you don't actually live longer; it just seems longer.
London Observer 27 Dec 64

Otto Friedrich editor

6478 The automotive industry. . . ignored charges that they were tampering with a way of life, not to mention the birth rate.
On halt of production of convertibles *Time* 22 Jul 85

Zsa Zsa Gabor actress

6479 A man in love is incomplete until he has married. Then he's finished.
Newsweek 28 Mar 60

6480 We were both in love with him. . . I fell out of love with him, but he didn't.
On ex-husband George Sanders Chicago *American* 4 Sep 66

6481 When I'm alone, I can sleep crossways in bed without an argument.
On being between marriages *Family Weekly* 7 May 76

6482 You're never too young to be younger.
Oui Jan 78

6483 Macho does not prove mucho.
Washingtonian Nov 79

6484 I have never hated a man enough to give his diamonds back.
Cosmopolitan Feb 80

Bob Garfield humorist

6485 Chain letters are the postal equivalent of intestinal flu; you get it and pass it along to your friends.
NPR 5 Oct 90

Robert Gepshell humorist

6486 When donkeys fly!
On the impossibility of what some cafe customers believed, spoken by the waitress Flo played by Polly Holliday in sitcom *Alice* CBS TV *Variety* 8 Sep 76

6487 Kiss my grits!
ib

Brendan Gill essayist

6488 They were names... which gave off a formidable hum for a long time after they were dropped.
On Wall Street, Locust Valley, Fishers Island and Kennebunkport *A New York Life* Poseidon 90

Newton L ("Newt") Gingrich Speaker, US House of Representatives

6489 Perseverance is the hard work you do after you get tired of doing the hard work you already did.
NY Times 12 Mar 95

Allen Ginsburg activist

6490 What if someone gave a war and nobody came?
Fall of America City Lights 72

Victoria Glendinning biographer

6491 "Taking at random the names of friends who have sat round its soft gold and peach-colored surface, it would murmur, Maynard Keynes, Virginia Woolf, George Gershwin, T S Eliot"... Osbert wrote in his old age, gracefully letting the table do his name dropping for him.
On Osbert Sitwell's dining room *A Unicorn Among Lions* Weidenfeld & Nicolson 81

Allan R Gold reporter

6492 A New York City judge has found Cityspire, a commercial and residential skycraper on West 56th Street, guilty of whistling and has sentenced it to shut up.
On Judge Gerald Denaro's order disallowing louvers in which wind created noise similar to air raid sirens *NY Times* 13 Apr 91

Samuel Goldwyn producer

6493 You ought to take the bull between the teeth.
"Goldwynism" recalled on Goldwyn's death 31 Jan 74

6494 Include me out.
Quoted by A Scott Berg *Goldwyn* Knopf 89

Ellen Goodman reporter

6495 Hef and his hutch took us from the era when Nice Girls Didn't to the era when Everybody Had To and on to the era when Everybody's Scared To.
On Hugh Hefner's Playboy Clubs *Washington Post* 2 Aug 88

Mikhail S Gorbachev Soviet Premier

6496 Oh, they are a crucial part of our military forces... the central bankers, and you have no idea how much damage they can do.
On group of elderly men marching at end of Moscow's May Day parade *NY Times* 25 Feb 88

6497 They say that Mitterrand has 100 lovers—one with AIDS, but he doesn't know which one; Bush has 100 bodyguards—one a terrorist, but he doesn't know which one; Gorbachev has 100 economic advisers—one is smart, but he doesn't know which one.
To reporters *Time* 10 Dec 90

George Stuart Gordon Vice Chancellor, Oxford University

6498 O Sir, of all men most polished, fastidious, graceful, whimsical and uproarous, I hereby... admit you and your whole crowd of ditto creations to the degree of Doctor of Letters.
Citation for honorary degree conferred on P G Wodehouse, recalled on Wodehouse's death 14 Feb 75

Albert Gore Jr US Vice President

6499 You get all the French fries the President can't get to.
On being Vice President *NY Times* 8 Apr 94

Robert Graham US Senator

6500 The only stock he invested in had four legs and a tail, so if it falls down you can pick it up.
On his father's investments *NY Times* 23 Oct 87

Robert Graves poet

6501 He found a formula for drawing comic rabbits:/ This formula for drawing comic rabbits paid,/ So in the end he could not change the tragic habits /this formula for drawing comic rabbits made.
"Epitaph on an Unfortunate Artist" quoted by Martin Seymour-Smith *Robert Graves* Holt Rinehart Winston 82

Paul Green screenwriter

6502 I'd love to kiss ya, but I just washed my hair.
Screenplay for Bette Davis in *The Cabin in the Clouds* based on H H Kroll's novel of the same name; cited by Davis as her favorite dialogue *Time* 16 Oct 89

Graham Greene novelist

6503 Her idea of fame was to be represented at Tussaud's. . . and I really believe she would have opted for the Chamber of Horrors rather than have had no image made of her at all.
Travels With My Aunt Viking 69

6504 She was an unconscious ventriloquist.
ib

6505 [I plan to] make love behind every high altar in Italy.
On eloping with Catherine Walston *London Times* 24 Sep 94

William Grimes reporter

6506 [They were] Falstaffian personalities. . . effortless charmers who radiated the warmth of a pizza oven.
On Vartan Gregorian and Timothy Healy as ebullient presidents of the NY Public Library *NY Times* 10 May 95

William Francis Guess commentator

6507 We were taught to be South Carolinians, Ca-ro-li-ni-ans, mind you, and not, please God, the Tarheel slur, Calinians.
In Eric Larrabee ed *American Panorama* NY University Press 60

Ben Guggenheim biographer

6508 Never make love to a woman before breakfast. . . it's wearing. . . [and] in the course of the day you may meet somebody you like better.
Quoted by Milton Lomask *Seed Money: The Guggenheim Story* Farrar Straus 64

Francis Hackett journalist

6509 In a diplomat's soul you may find iron ore, but it is usually oil—and in a whale of a diplomat you'll find the whole equipment—the blubber of charity, the whalebone of flexibility, the oil of commodity. A great diplomat is a regular Moby Dick.
Quoted by Roger B Merriman *Suleiman the Magnificent* Harvard University Press 1944, recalled on Hackett's death 25 Apr 62

Alan Hamilton reporter

6510 The assailant. . . is thought to be one of the nortorious Seven Dwarfs of Windsor. . . Spark, Myth, Fable, Diamond, Kelpie, Phoenix and Pharos, members of the feared royal corgi gang.
Reporting on the pet corgi that bit Queen Elizabeth, 6 Mar 91

George Hamilton actor

6511 She was just like a parakeet on Benzedrine.
On his talkative ex-wife, Alana Collins, *Vanity Fair* Jan 91

6512 What I've really always wanted was Walden Pond with a kitchen added on.
ib

William Hamilton novelist

6513 It was a fortune so big and abstract that instead of belonging to anyone, people belonged to it.
On an heiress in his book *The Lap of Luxury* Atlantic Monthly Press 88

6514 All they knew of its existence was the dew of checks regularly condensing in their mailboxes.
ib

Charles J Haughey Prime Minister of Ireland

6515 Deep down I'm a shallow person.
NY Times 20 Dec 87

Helen Hayes actress

6516 I decided long ago never to look at the right hand of the menu or the price tag of clothes—otherwise I would starve, naked.
Washington Post 7 May 90

Chic Hecht US Senator

6517 [There will not be a] nuclear suppository.
Opposition to dumping a nuclear-waste in Nevada *Wall Street Journal* 11 Aug 88

Howell Heflin US Senator

6518 You omitted perhaps one thing—that in 1974 I had a hemorrhoidectomy.
On a lengthy introduction *Newsweek* 20 May 91

Joseph Heller novelist

6519 In the long run, failure was the only thing that worked predictably.
Good As Gold Simon & Schuster 79

Lillian Hellman playwright

6520 He was getting over a four-day drunk, and I was getting over a four-year marriage.
On meeting her future lover Dashiell Hammett *Christian Science Monitor* 13 Oct 85

Ernest Hemingway novelist

6521 Wearing underwear is as formal as I ever hope I get.

Quoted by A E Hotchner *Papa Hemingway* Morrow 88

A P Herbert humorist

6522 "Death!" remarked Sir Thingummy Jig,/ "Bring me a pen and ink!/ Bring me a fair white writing pad, and/ something strong to drink./ And wrap a towel about my head and/ don't let anyone in,/ For I must write to *The Times* tonight and/ save the world from sin!"

The Saviours 1925 recalled in study of letters that averaged 300 a day over a 25-year period, *London Times* 12 Aug 95

C David Heymann biographer

6523 They started with separate beds in the same bedroom and ended with separate beds on separate continents.

On Jacqueline Kennedy and Aristotle Onassis *A Woman Named Jackie* L Stuart 89

6524 His dealings made Jack Kennedy look like Little Lord Fauntleroy. . . a many-faceted man whose relationships were not limited to the domestic front.

On Robert F Kennedy *Publisher's Weekly* 1 Mar 91

Robert Hughes critic

6525 The museum, a refurbished dame, was more or less pulled together: slip awry, flushed under the powder, panting somewhat, but ready.

On opening of expanded NY Museum of Modern Art *Time* 14 May 84

6526 A visitor furtively ran his finger over the marble nipple of a luscious demimondaine writhing naked among stone roses.

On Paris's *Musee d'Orsay* 8 Dec 86

6527 He was to ordinary male chauvinist pigs what Moby Dick was to whales.

On Pablo Picasso 20 Jun 88 *ib*

6528 Add Dallas to Callas and presto Phallus!

On Picasso's sensual attraction *ib*

Hubert Humphrey US Vice President

6529 I'm like the little boy who learned how to spell "banana" and never knew when to stop.

Quoted in William Safire ed *Lend Me Your Ears* Norton 92

Caroline Hunter essayist

6530 He will be the one displaying the most obvious sense of superiority.

On how to spot the butler "English Country Weekends" *M* Sep 84

Charles Hussey editor

6531 There are no coronets on their 24 male chromosomes.

On Britain's life peers whose titles die with them *NY Times* 25 Aug 63

Dr Wayne Isom surgeon

6532 He can sell you a dead horse and, when you come back to complain, sell you a saddle for it.

On the persuasivness of Cornell Medical School Dean G Tom Shires *NY Times* 24 Jan 88

Lee Israel tabloid editor

6533 He got a look from Dorothy that would have frightened horses in the street.

On Dorothy Kilgallen and a radio show host *Kilgallen* Delacorte 79

Clive James writer and broadcaster

6534 An anodyne divine who's put unction in your function.

On Robert Runcie, Archbishop of Canterbury *London Times* 14 Jul 88

Antony Jay Program Editor BBC

6535 You gave the world the guillotine/ But still we don't know why the heck/ You have to drop it on our neck.

On France's rejection of Britain as a member of the Common Market *Time* 8 Feb 63

6536 From now on you can keep the lot./ Take every single thing you've got,/ Your land, your wealth, your men, your dames,/ Your dream of independent power,/ And dear old Konrad Adenauer,/ And stick them up your Eiffel Tower.

ib

Daisy Mae Jeter essayist

6537 Nudists are very honest people.

NY Times 12 Feb 52

Lyndon B Johnson 36th US President

6538 The thorns are all in the next office, to the right.

To visitors to the White House rose garden outside the President's study 21 Apr 64

6539 The President ought to be as unsatisfied as a little boy's appetite.

On unnecessary expenditures in government 6 Oct 66

Erica Jong essayist

6540 Bigamy is having one husband too many. Monogamy is the same.

Fear of Flying Holt Rinehart Winston 73

6541 Jealousy is all the fun you think they had.
On lost lovers *ib*

6542 Zippers fell away like petals, underwear blew off in one breath like dandelion fluff.
On zipless passion *ib*

James H Kabbler III Chair, Bikkal Industries Ltd

6543 Heaven is an American salary, a Chinese cook, an English house and a Japanese wife. Hell is having a Chinese salary, an English cook, a Japanese house and an American wife.
Parade 1 Jan 89

E J Kahn essayist

6544 If the average age of all the people who have died above the centerfold of the page is higher than my age, I believe I am going to have a good day.
On reading obituaries at breakfast *About the New Yorker and Me* Putnam 78

George S Kaufman playwright

6545 Like the Arabs, I fold my tens and silently steal away.
On winning at poker, quoted by Scott Meredith *George S Kaufman and His Friends* Doubleday 74

6546 My God, Peggy, I thought we were both dead.
At age 71 on encountering an old friend *ib*

Garrison Keillor humorist

6547 It is our farewell performance and I hope the first of many.
At Radio City Music Hall *Christian Science Monitor* 15 Jun 88

6548 He had vanity that makes Donald Trump look like a nun.
On Mark Twain, American Public Radio 1 Dec 90

6549 Bankruptcy gave my life a simplicity it had never had before.
In short story entitled "Al Denny" *New Yorker* 11 Mar 91

6550 There are people you never guessed had any liquid in them at all.
On Christmas carolers NPR 14 Dec 91

6551 Adultery is hard on a small town because it can cause sudden population loss, and usually it's the wrong people who get run out.
"Travels Through the Guilt Belt" *NY Times* 13 Mar 94

6552 A gnawing sense of guilt makes them more willing to serve on committees.
ib

6553 You can no more become a Christian by going to church then you can become an automobile by sleeping in your garage.
Broadcast 26 Jun 94

Nancy, Lady Keith socialite

6554 Sometimes you get such a long run of good fortune that you think luck has your home number.
On her marriage to Leland Hayward *Slim* with Annette Tapert, Simon & Schuster 90

6555 The English really aren't interested in talking to you unless you've been to school with them or to bed with them.
ib

George F Kennan statesman

6556 The devil having been banished and virtue being triumphant, nothing terribly interesting can ever happen again.
On California's resemblance to heaven *Sketches from a Life* Pantheon 89

Florynce Kennedy feminist

6557 If men could get pregnant, abortion would be a sacrament.
Ms Mar 73

John F Kennedy 35th US President

6558 It was easy—they sank my boat.
To an Ashland WI youth who asked in 1958 how Kennedy became a war hero, quoted by Theodore C Sorensen *Kennedy* Harper & Row 65

6559 I have just received the following from my generous Daddy: "Dear Jack—Don't buy a single vote more than is necessary. I'll be damned if I'm going to pay for a landslide."
To Washington's Gridiron Club 15 Mar 58, quoted by Harold Brayman *The President Speaks-Off-the-Record* Dow Jones 76

6560 I asked each senator about his preferences for the Presidency—and 96 Senators each received one vote.
ib

6561 The Democratic Advisory Council has succeeded in splitting our party right down the middle—more unity than we've had in 20 years.
ib

6562 Policemen bending over a body in the alley say cheerfully, "Two of his wounds are fatal—but the other one's not so bad."
ib

6563 If we both pass away, I feel I shall have performed a great public service by taking the Vice President with me.

On testing cranberriers with Richard M Nixon in a 1959 visit to Wisconsin, quoted by Irving Bernstein *Promises Kept* Oxford 90

6564 I'm against vice in all forms.

On efforts to make him a 1960 vice presidential candidate, quoted by Ralph G Martin *A Hero for Our Time* Macmillan 83

6565 Do you realize the responsibilities I carry? I'm the only person between Nixon and the White House.

To a liberal supporter in 1960 presidential campaign, quoted by Theodore C Sorensen *Kennedy* Harper & Row 65

6566 I really don't think there's anything that I can say to President Truman that's going to cause him to change his particular manner. Perhaps Mrs Truman can, but I don't think I can.

On Harry S Truman's campaign profanity

6567 No President was ever prayed over with such fervor. Evidently they felt that the country or I needed it—probably both.

Postscript on letter to novelist John Steinbeck a few days after the 1961 Kennedy inauguration, quoted in Elaine and Robert Wallsten ed *Steinbeck* Viking 75

6568 Bobby wants to practice law, and I thought he ought to get a little experience first.

To Gridiron Club on appointment of his brother at age 35 to be Attorney General 11 Mar 61

6569 I just jumped in and hung on.

On sleeping in the Lincoln bed on his first night in the White House, quoted by Richard Reeves *President Kennedy* Simon & Schuster 93

6570 All he asks in return is merely for us to advertise his law firm on the backs of one-dollar bills.

On presidential advisor Clark M Clifford, recalled in *NY Times* 5 Apr 91

Rose Kennedy President's mother

6571 You have a breath that would make a maggot gag!

Quoted by her secretary Barbara Gibson *Donahue* NBC TV 30 Aug 90

Florence King biographer

6572 Devoid of body hair and whiskers, with undescended testicles and dimensions dolorous, he presents Wallis with a daunting task, but she, who has operated all her life on the shabby-genteel principle of "make do," does.

"Playing the Palace" *NY Times* 9 Jun 91 reviewing Anne Edwards' novel on the Duchess of Windsor *Wallis* Morrow 91

Henry A Kissinger US Secretary of State

6573 I do not stand on protocol. If you just call me Excellency, it will be okay.

On being asked if he should be addressed as Mr Secretary or Dr Secretary, quoted by Walter Isaacson *Kissinger* Simon & Schuster 92

6574 It's always a pleasure to introduce someone who also speaks with an accent.

On a foreign policy address by President Clinton *Newsweek* 13 Mar 95

Ronald Knox humorist

6575 A loud noise on one end and no sense of responsibility on the other.

On babies, recalled on Knox's death 24 Aug 57

Ernie Kovacs humorist

6576 Are you Abraham Lincoln?

On being told that the name of mystery guest Henry J Kaiser was associated with automobiles *NY Times* 27 Feb 91

Ron Kovic novelist

6577 Keep one hand on her tits and the other on your wallet.

To war veterans who retire to Mexico *Born on the Fourth of July* McGraw-Hill 76

John Cardinal Krol Archbishop of Philadelphia

6578 I posed for the portrait as an act of penance but threatened to give it to an institution for the blind.

On dissatisfaction with a portraitist *NY Times* 6 Nov 83

Carlton Lake humorist

6579 He decided he'd had his fill of cavities.

On Jake Schwartz taking leave of dentistry to found London's Ulysses bookshop *NY Times* 6 Sep 87

Ann Landers (Eppie Lederer) columnist

6580 Wake up and smell the coffee!

On get-with-it advice to 90 million readers of 1,200 newspapers *US News & World Report* 23 Oct 95

Lewis H Lapham biographer

6581 Born into the ranks of the equestrian class. . . I don't know how I could have avoided an early acquaintance with the pathologies of wealth.

Money and Class in America Widenfeld & Nicholson 88

6582 A pervasive feeling of gratified desire sustained a crowd of at least 400 people in a bubble chamber of collective euphoria.

On Truman Capote's Black and White Masked Ball *ib*

Philip Larkin poet

6583 I'm sure we shall recognize each other by progressive elimination, ie, eliminating all the progressives.

Letter to Barbara Pym, quoted by Hazel Holt *A Lot to Ask* Dutton 91

6584 Sex is too good to share with anyone else.

On collecting pornography, quoted by Andrew Motion's *Philip Larkin* Farrar Straus Giroux 93

Alan Lascelles humorist

6585 [It is as believable as] a herd of unicorns grazing in Hyde Park and a shoal of mermaids swimming in the Serpentine.

On a non-adulterous relationship between the Prince of Wales and Wallis Simpson, quoted by Philip Ziegler *King Edward VIII* Knopf 91

Gertrude Lawrence actress

6586 From 16 to 22, like Africa—part virgin, part explored... 23 to 35, like Asia—hot and mysterious... 35 to 45, like the USA—high-toned and technical... 46 to 55, like Europe—quite devastated but interesting in places.

Comparing women to geography, quoted by Margaret Forster *Daphne du Maurier* Doubleday 93

6587 From 60 upwards like Australia—everybody knows about it, but no one wants to go there.

ib

Norman Lear producer

6588 Where are the police when I need them? Probably frisking some topless waitress.

Archie Bunker in television sitcom *All in the Family* 72

6589 With credit you can buy everything you can't afford.

ib

John le Carré novelist

6590 A committee is an animal with four back legs.

Tinker, Tailor, Soldier, Spy Hodder & Stoughton 74

Oscar Levant humorist

6591 It's not a pretty face... but underneath this flabby exterior is an enormous lack of character.

Screenplay for Alan Jay Lerner's *An American in Paris* 51

6592 Self-pity. It's the only pity that counts.

Steve Allen Show NBC TV 29 Jun 58

6593 Besides incompatibility, we hated each other.

On divorcing Barbara Wooddell *Memoirs of an Amnesiac* Putnam 65

6594 The worst thing about having a mistress is those two dinners you have to eat.

The Unimportance of Being Oscar Putnam 68

6595 Chutzpah enables a man who has murdered his mother and father to throw himself on the mercy of the court as an orphan.

ib

6596 When I was young, I looked like Al Capone but I lacked his compassion.

Quoted by Sam Kashner and Nancy Shoenberger *A Talent for Genius* Villard 94

Gib Lewis Speaker of Texas House of Representatives

6597 This is unparalyzed in the state's history.

Malapropism quoted by William Safire *NY Times* 17 Sep 89

6598 This problem is a two-headed sword: it could grow like a mushing room.

ib

6599 There's a lot of uncertainty that's not clear in my mind.

ib

Joe E Lewis comedian

6600 I've never met a nymphomaniac I didn't like.

Parade 22 May 88

A J Liebling humorist

6601 The brain, like Rhineish wine, should be chilled, not iced, to be at its best. Women, however, are best at room temperature.

The Honest Rainmaker 53 reprinted by North Point Press 89

Life

6602 The wonder is that he found so much time to paint.

On Pablo Picasso's sex life Dec 68

London Daily Express

6603 It wasn't long before the heir presumptive became very presumptive. And the heir apparent became rather more apparent than he had been.

On photograph of young Prince Henry lifting Prince Charles' kilt *Time* 26 Dec 88

Alice Roosevelt Longworth President's daughter

6604 Dorothy is the only woman in history who has had her menopause in public and made it pay.

On columnist Dorothy Thompson, quoted by Vincent Sheean *Dorothy and Red* Houghton Mifflin 63

6605 My father always wanted to be the corpse at every funeral, the bride at every wedding and the baby at every christening.

On President Theodore Roosevelt, Cleveland Amory and Earl Blackwell ed *Celebrity Register* Harper & Row 63

6606 He looks just like the little man on the wedding cake.

On GOP President aspirant Thomas E Dewey, recalled on Longworth's death 20 Feb 80

6607 [I am] Washington's topless monument.

On her mastectomy *ib*

6608 I do wish he did not look as if he had been weaned on a pickle.

On Calvin Coolidge *ib*

6609 [He was] 90 percent mush and 10 percent Eleanor.

On Franklin D Roosevelt *Newsweek* 3 Mar 80

6610 [My attitude is] detached malevolence.

ib

Robert Lowell poet

6611 If there's a light at the end of the tunnel, it's the light of the oncoming train.

On an anxious view of the future, quoted by former wife Caroline Blackwood *NY Times* 15 Feb 96

Anita Loos playwright

6612 Lorelei would have met Henry Kissinger on a plane, where you can pick up more and better people than any other public conveyance since the stagecoach.

On the heroine of *Gentlemen Prefer Blondes NY Times* 26 Apr 73

Clare Boothe Luce essayist

6613 I was wondering today what the religion of the country is—and all I could come up with was sex.

Washington Post 9 Apr 82

6614 I was having no success at charming him, so I slayed him with pure intellectual superiority.

On dining with Prime Minister Edward Heath *NY Times* 31 Jan 88

6615 And, Lord, while Thou art up, grant Thy servant a double martini.

Addition to interminable intercessory prayers, quoted by Hedley Donovan *Right Times, Right Places* Holt 89

Peter Luke playwright

6616 In Bloomsbury, couples in squares live in triangles.

Bloomsbury 74

Russell Lynes essayist

6617 Any real New Yorker is a you-name-it-we-have-it-snob.

Town & Country Aug 65

6618 [His] heart brims with sympathy for the millions of unfortunates who through misfortune, misguidedness, or pure stupidity live anywhere else in the world.

ib

Dorothy Disney Mackaye editor

6619 "He [or she] never listens" is universal in the institution of marriage.

On 30 years of producing the *Ladies' Home Journal* column "Can This Marriage Be Saved?" recalled on Disney's death 5 Sep 91

Archibald MacLeish poet and statesman

6620 [He was] like a horse you could get along with if you came up beside him from the okay side.

On Robert Frost, quoted by Wallace Stegner *The Uneasy Chair* Doubleday 74

Harold Macmillan Prime Minister of Britain

6621 [Memorial services are] the cocktail parties of the geriatric set.

Comment in his 90s quoted by Alistair Horne *Harold Macmillan* Vol II Viking 89

6622 The thing to do was to get a hedgehog. So we went to Harrods, and we bought one.

On getting rid of cockroaches *ib*

Madonna (Madonna Ciccone) entertainer

6623 You don't have to have a language in common with someone for a sexual rapport. But it helps if the language you don't understand is Italian.

London Times 22 Oct 92

David Mamet playwright

6624 If the cat crawled into the oven and had kittens would that make them muffins?

On whether being born in Vermont makes a Vermonter *London Times* 15 Sep 93

Joseph L Mankiewicz screenwriter

6625 We all come into this world with our own little individual horns. If we don't blow them, who will?

Lines in *All About Eve* based on Mary Orr's short story *The Wisdom of Eve* screenplay 50

6626 Fasten your seat belts; it's going to be a bumpy night!

Lines for the fictional actress Margot Channing played by Bette Davis *ib*

6627 I never understand the process by which a body with a voice suddenly fancies itself as a mind but it's about time the piano realized it has not written the concerto.

ib

6628 So many people know me. Except me. I wish somebody would tell me about me.

ib

Thurgood Marshall Associate Justice, US Supreme Court

6629 What's shaking, Chiefy baby?

Customary greeting to Chief Justice Warren E Burger, quoted by Michael D Davis and Hunter R Clark *Thurgood Marshall* Birch Lane 92

Douglas Martin reporter

6630 At 200-plus degrees, it's easy to break the ice.

On meeting women in Turkish baths *NY Times* 10 May 91

Judith Martin ("Miss Manners") columnist

6631 One apologizes for the unfortunate occurence, but the unthinkable is unmentionable.

Advice to ignore embarrassments such as losing lingerie on the dance floor *Time* 5 Nov 84

Groucho Marx comedian

6632 You don't get paid for the right answers. But you do take the consequences for the wrong answer.

Likening a tax exam to television's *Truth or Consequences NY Times* 11 May 51

Carol Matthau actor's wife

6633 For God's sake, Walter, why don't you chop off her legs and read the rings?

To her husband's question on an actress's age *Among the Porcupines* Random House 92

Elsa Maxwell party-giver

6634 [It is] a stud book for mediocrities.

On the New York Social Register *Reader's Digest* Jul 64

Carson McCullers novelist and playwright

6635 You got to keep three eyes open all the time.

On running a carousel *The Heart Is a Lonely Hunter* Houghton Mifflin 67

Diana McLellan journalist

6636 Flowers, champagne, cigarettes and caviar were as vital to a model seduction as a nice new condom is today.

On Greta Garbo, Cecil Beaton and 1930s' "courtship and conquest among the beautiful and bisexual" *Washington Post* 10 Jul 94

Don McNeil *Breakfast Club* host

6637 Some people are like teabags—they don't know their own strength until they get in hot water.

ABC Radio 9 Sep 65

Marion Meade biographer

6638 She regarded him as a slice of packaged white bread, unambiguous and predictable.

On Dorothy Parker's attitude toward humorist Robert Benchley *Dorothy Parker* Villard 88

H L Mencken essayist

6639 [They] became Knights of Pythia, Odd Fellows, Red Men, Nobles of the Mystic Shrine, Knights Templar, Patriarchs Militant, Elks, Moose, Woodmen of the World, Foresters, Hoo-Hoos, Ku Kluxzers.

On American fondness for secret societies, quoted in Alistair Cook ed *The Vintage Mencken* Vintage 55

6640 For every degree there was a badge, and for every badge there was a yard of ribbon.

ib

6641 Along side this lowly washer of the dead, General John J Pershing newly polished would seem almost like a Trappist.

On a Maryland mortician burying a fellow lodge member *ib*

6642 Chamber of Commerce red hunters, WCTU smellers, Methodist prowlers, Baptist guardians. . . we have the national mentality of a police lieutenant.

Cited as typical Mencken that caused the *NY Herald Tribune* to call him "a specialist in sentences that could lacerate millions at a time" *ib*

6643 When the mercury is 95, I dine in my shirt sleeves and write poetry naked.

Quoted by Fred Hobson *Mencken: A Life* Random House 94

6644 Self-respect—the secure feeling that no one, as yet, is suspicious.

ib

6645 Bells will toll. . . fire engines will rush through the streets. . . cops will yell and shoot off pistols, and you will hear the news that I have been translated into an angel.

Writing 20 years before his death which, wrote Hobson, "came instead as sleet was falling in the depths of a silent midwinter night not unlike that January night 57 years before when his own father had died in the same house" *ib*

Don Meredith humorist

6646 The higher you climb the flagpole, the more people see your rear-end.
Life Jan 84

Merriam-Webster's Dictionary of English Usage 1969

6647 You do run the risk of giving some of your listeners the mistaken impression that they are smarter than you are.
On mistaking flout (to disregard contemptuously) with flaunt (to show-off), quoted by William Safire *NY Times* 1 Mar 95

Peter Mikelbank humorist

6648 The hangover was... maybe eight feet tall, all moths and cobwebs and grinning crazier than a dog about to tooth a postman. A shambling thing large enough to occupy its own bar stool.
"Cheers to Harry's Bar," a brief history of hangovers from a famed Paris saloon *Washington Post* 1 Jan 91

Terence J (Spike) Milligan humorist

6649 I shook hands with a friendly Arab. I still have my right hand to prove it.
A Dustbin of Milligan Dobson 61

6650 Money can't buy friends but you can get a better class of enemies.
Washingtonian Jan 86

Joseph Mitchell novelist

6651 You haven't cracked a smile since Christ left Cleveland.
"I Couldn't Dope It Out" short story in *Up In the Old Hotel* Pantheon 92

Ashley Montagu essayist

6652 The idea is to die young, as late as possible.
Town & Country May 79

Lord Moynihan (Antony Patrick Andrew Moynihan) *enfant terrible* of the House of Lords

6653 The ladies do all the work, and I just collect the money.
On ownership of a Philippine brothel called the Yellow Brick Road *Wall Street Journal* 9 Nov 93

Malcolm Muggeridge essayist

6654 Tranquilizers to overcome angst, pep pills to wake us up, life pills to ensure blissful sterility. I will lift up my ears unto the pills whence cometh my help.
New Statesman 3 Aug 62

6655 He is not only a bore but he bores for England.
On Anthony Eden *Newstatesmanship* Books for Libraries Press 70

Lewis Mumford essayist

6656 Given two Pope John's, I could become a Catholic; three might even turn me into a Christian.
My Work and Days Harcourt Brace Jovanovich 79

Edward R Murrow commentator

6657 It was the best piece of advice I ever ignored.
On not covering the Korean War, quoted by A M Sperber *Murrow* Freundlich 86

Vladimir Nabokov essayist and author

6658 It was like moving from one darkened house to another on a starless night during a strike of candlemakers and torchbearers.
On learning English, quoted by Brian Boyd *Vladimir Nabokov* Princeton 91

Ogden Nash poet and humorist

6659 Someone invented the telephone/ And interrupted a nation's slumbers/ Ringing wrong, but similar numbers.
In Ithiel de sola Pool ed *The Social Impact of the Telephone* MIT Press 77

6660 Here lies my past. Goodbye, I have kissed it./ Thank you kids. I wouldn't have missed it.
NY Times 20 May 95

Richard J Needham essayist

6661 In the unplanned economy, it's dog eat dog; in the planned one, both of them starve to death.
Toronto Globe & Mail 27 Oct 80

Newsday

6662 [He has had] a life that makes *The Prisoner of Zenda* seem like a Prudential Insurance Company training film.
On designer Oleg Cassini *NY Times* 27 Sep 87

Newsweek magazine

6663 Even her staunchest defenders concede that Nancy Reagan is more Marie Antoinette than Mother Teresa.
22 Apr 91

New Yorker magazine

6664 She gives the impression of being not so much an inscribed tablet. . . as a blackboard, restored to freshness after every lesson.

On Hope Cooke, former Queen of Sikkim, as volunteer guide for NYC walking tours 13 Apr 87

6665 She sometimes refers to her stint as a Himalayan potentate as though it were a junior year abroad that had got out of hand.

ib

6666 There are ghosts of old elevator men. . . [who] were saying "Drop the sons of bitches. Drop them."

On moving to new offices 11 Mar 91 *ib*

6667 The new *Joy* lovers are younger than the old ones, and they have been working out.

Review 7 Oct 91 on illustrations in Dr Alex Comfort's *The New Joy of Sex* Crown 91

6668 The old lover's member, rendered in full-page illustration, emerged as a blunt stub from a swamp of tufts at the southern swell of his paunch.

ib

6669 The new man's member fits like a dashboard accessory on his Greek body.

ib

The New York Times

6670 [Labor Day is] when people who haven't taken their vacations yet are viewed with thinly-veiled dislike by those who have.

"The Day When" editorial 2 Sep 85

6671 [The] decision. . . was the liturgical equivalent of changing the formula for Coke.

"Truth Keeps Marching" editorial on "The Battle Hymn of the Republic" and "Onward Christian Soldiers" being dropped from the Methodist hymnal 7 Jul 86

6672 A lot of places can beat it for livability; almost any place can beat it for civility; and as for affordability—don't ask.

"Joyful Noises for New York" editorial 27 Feb 91

Peggy Noonan Reagan White House speechwriter

6673 I'm just your basic bad Catholic. . . full of flaws that make for real interesting confessions.

What I Saw at the Revolution Random House 90

6674 The battle for the mind of Ronald Reagan was like the trench warfare of World War I. Never have so many fought so hard for such barren terrain.

ib

Flannery O'Connor novelist

6675 One old lady who wants her heart lifted up wouldn't be so bad, but you multiply her 250,000 times and what you get is a book club.

Quoted by John Leonard *Sunday Morning* CBS TV 27 Dec 92

Molly O'Neil reporter

6676 As flaky as last year's granola.

On theologian Matthew Fox *NY Times* 17 Mar 93

P J O'Rourke humorist

6677 Communism doesn't really starve or execute that many people. Mostly it just bores them to death.

Holidays in Hell Atlantic Monthly Press 88

6678 Government is to life what panty hose are to sex.

ib

George Orwell novelist

6679 Big Brother is watching you.

A recurring philosophy of government recalled on Orwell's death 21 Jan 50

6680 An embittered atheist does not so much disbelieve in God as personally dislikes him.

ib

Mitchell Owens reporter

6681 [Her] soft, husky voice is pitched somewhere between a whisper and a promise.

On interviewing Evangeline Bruce on her biography of Napoleon and Josephine *NY Times* 16 Mar 95

Parade magazine

6682 [She] clearly regards her prominent bust as one of her two most outstanding physical attributes.

On Dolly Parton 7 Feb 88

Dorothy Parker humorist

6683 If all the girls at Smith and Bennington were laid end to end, I wouldn't be surprised.

Quoted by Scott Meredith *George S Kaufman and His Friends* Doubleday 74

6684 He has a child by his first wife—I imagine he swam over her.

On a passionless marriage, quoted by Matthew J Bruccoli *James Gould Cozzens* Harcourt Brace Jovanovich 83

6685 What fresh hell is this?

Subtitle of biography by Marion Meade *Dorothy Parker* Villard 88

6686 [The Atlantic] crossing was so rough that the only thing I could keep on my stomach was the first mate.

ib

6687 Good work, Mary. We all knew you had it in you.

On birth of a child to Robert and Mary Sherwood *ib*

6688 It's difficult to get terribly interested in food I digested 45 years ago.

On being asked about menus of the Algonquin round-table *ib*

6689 Excuse my dust!

Epitaph recalled on interment of Parker's ashes in Baltimore *Washington Post* 21 Oct 88

6690 It just goes to show what God could do if He wanted to, and if He had the money.

On additions to Moss Hart's farmhouse, quoted in Robert Phelps with Jerry Rosco ed *Glenway Westcott Continuous Lessons* Farrar Straus Giroux 90

6691 She realizes she doesn't know as much as God; but feels she knows as much as God knew when He was her age.

On columnist Dorothy Thompson *ib*

6692 You can lead a whore to culture but you can't make her think.

On being asked to use the word "horticulture" in a sentence *NY Times* 8 Jan 93

Marion Parsonnet screenwriter

6693 If I'd been a ranch, they would have named me the Bar Nothing.

Spoken by Rita Hayworth in Parsonnet's screenplay for the 1946 film *Gilda*, recalled in *Washington Post* 6 Apr 89

S J Perelman humorist

6694 Here congregated tycooon and political nawab, screen idol and press overlord, rock star and capo of capos, secure in the knowledge that no losers were present.

On New York's 21 Club *NY Times* 15 Jan 78

6695 The luminati rubbed elbows with the cognoscenti, publishers rubbed knees with nascent lady novelists, male dress designers rubbed thighs.

ib

6696 The drumfire of epigrams and the bray of egotism were rising to sawmill pitch.

ib

6697 Button-cute, rapier-keen, wafer-thin, pauper-poor.

Self-description *Life* Feb 94

6698 A brunette Jane was lying there, half out of the mussed covers. . . as dead as vaudeville.

On a mystery novel *ib*

Joanna Pitman essayist

6699 One of those mouths permanently set at twenty past 8.

On a Japanese instructor in safe driving *London Times* 23 Oct 93

James Pope-Hennessy biographer

6700 I should classify her as An American Woman par excellence, were it not for the suspicison that she is not a woman at all.

On Wallis, Duchess of Windsor *A Lonely Business* Weidenfeld and Nicholson 81

Katherine Anne Porter novelist

6701 I have lost my husbands and lovers. . . because I have always talked too much at breakfast.

Quoted in Robert Phelps with Jerry Rosco ed *Glenway Wescott Continual Lessons* Farrar Straus Giroux 90

Anthony Powell novelist

6702 Books *do* furnish a room.

Title of novel Heinemann 71

General Colin L Powell Chair, Joint Chiefs of Staff

6703 The National Security Adviser and Secretary of State have not gotten on so well since Henry Kissinger held both jobs simultaneously.

Quoted by George P Shultz *Turmoil and Triumph* Scribner 93

George Price cartoonist

6704 I heard a bit of good news today. We shall pass this way but once.

Caption *Washington Times* 2 Jan 89

V S Pritchett essayist

6705 I shall never be as old as I was between 20 and 30.

NY Times 16 Dec 85

6706 He stood suddenly isolated in his autobiography.

On being interrupted in telling a long story, in D J Enright and David Rawlinson ed *The Oxford Book of Friendship* Oxford 91

Publisher's Weekly magazine

6707 He shows. . . Clinton as such a womanizer as to make Jack Kennedy seem celibate.

Review 12 Dec 94 of Ronald Kessler's *Inside the White House* Pocket 95

Barbara Pym novelist

6708 Everything must be put back in its proper disorder.

On housecleaning *Civil to Strangers* Dutton 87

Anna Quindlen columnist

6709 The clearest explanation for the failure of any marriage is that two people are incompatible; that is, one is male and the other female.

"Life in the 30's" *NY Times* 6 Jan 88

Don Quinn humorist

6710 'Taint't funny, McGee!

Spoken by Molly McGee in radio's longest running comedy *Fibber McGee and Molly* 1935–1956, recalled on Quinn's death *Time* 12 Jan 68

Dorothy Rabinowitz critic

6711 She wanted to make her life and career in Alaska or some other wild and strange place but managed essentially the same thing by marrying Lyndon B Johnson.

On a televised biography of Lady Bird Johnson *Wall Street Journal* 27 Jun 93

Michael Ramsey Archbishop of Canterbury

6712 Like false teeth, they irritate a bit but when you are used to them you find them serviceable.

On liturgical vestments, quoted by Owen Chadwick *Michael Ramsey* Oxford 90

6713 I approach it like an alcoholic his drink, secretly and often.

On finding ample time for reading *ib*

Lanfranco Rasponi publicist

6714 I am half Byzantine and half hillbilly.

On his parents Count Rasponi and Caroline Montague of Chattanooga TN *The International Nomads* Putnam 66

Ronald Reagan 40th US President

6715 Before I refuse to take your questions, I have an opening statement.

To a news conference *Washington Post* 2 Jan 89

6716 I'd recently lost my job. Before that I was living in public housing for a while.

Recalling his fear that he couldn't meet hospital bills 29 Mar 91

Walter Redfern humorist

6717 With fronds like these, who needs anemones?

On substituting palms for flowers *Puns* Blackwell 85

James B Reston reporter

6718 I felt like a beached whale at a medical convention.

On Peking hospital care after an appendectomy and acupuncture *Deadline* Random House 91

John Richardson essayist

6719 Her flamboyance made the Gabor sisters look like Little Women.

On Andre Reynolds' relationship with murder suspect Claus von Bulow *Vanity Fair* Nov 90

Maria Riva biographer

6720 They filled our hall like a monogrammed Stonehenge.

On the six closet-size wardrobe trunks used by her mother *Marlene Dietrich* Knopf 92

Joan Rivers entertainer

6721 More chins than a Chinese phone book.

On Elizabeth Taylor *People* 2 Dec 85

Roxanne Roberts reporter

6722 Needlepoint nametags, floor-length dresses and sashes across their formidable chests, an army with its very own generals and soldiers the likes of Susan B Anthony, Clara Barton, Grandma Moses and Ginger Rogers.

On the Daughters of the American Revolution *Washington Post* 12 Oct 90

Essie Robeson wife of singer Paul Robeson

6723 He has not only strayed but gone on a hike.

On her husband's extra-marital affairs, quoted by Martin Bauml Duberman's *Paul Robeson* Knopf 89

Rodman Rockefeller heir

6724 I was once referred to as "moneybags," I believe by a young DuPont, but I guess we all have our crosses to bear.

Quoted by Peter Collier and David Horowitz *The Rockefellers* Holt Rinehart Winston 76

George Romney business executive

6725 The way the Kennedys are overrunning Washington it's a good thing it was the Mormon Church and not the Catholic Church that practiced polygamy.

To Washington's Gridiron Club 11 Mar 61, quoted by Harold Brayman *The President Speaks Off-the-Record* Dow Jones 76

Andy Rooney humorist

6726 We had such a hangover, we were afraid we weren't going to die.

On drinking with Fred Astaire and Dick Powell NBC 25 Feb 95

6727 Age is nothing but experience and some of us are more experienced than others.

At age 74 *ib*

Ned Rorem composer

6728 People seldom change as they age, they just get more as they always were.

Memoir Simon & Schuster 94

Phyllis Rose essayist

6729 [For] a flea-market junkie... flirting is not good enough. Eying is not enough. I must possess... live with and contemplate... see at leisure, know in detail, change and be changed by what I possess.

On "flea market fever" *Mirabella* Feb 95

Rita Rudner humorist

6730 In a world where there are more women than men, it makes sense to recycle.

On remarriage as "ecologically responsible" *Guide to Men* Viking 94

Judy Rumbold reporter

6731 The groom wore the expression of a traumatized ferret; she went as white as six layers of scarlet blusher would allow.

On wedding of Raine, Countess Spencer, stepmother of Diana, Princess of Wales, and Count Jean-François de Chambrun *Guardian Weekly* 18 July 93

6732 With cheeks the color of nuked tomatoes and a complexion like liberally floured tripe, the enduring impression of the countess was a rag doll careerning at great speed through someone else's washline.

ib

Robert Runcie Archbishop of Canterbury

6733 Never has the line between exaggeration and untruth been more confidently negotiated.

On commendations on retirement *Guardian Weekly* 10 Feb 91

Morris (Morrie) Ryskind screenwriter

6734 They say a firing squad just hurts for a few seconds.

Quoted by Scott Meredith *George S Kaufman and His Friends* Doubleday 74

William Safire columnist

6735 Crisp... a splendid word, blessed with a great etymological pedigree that runs parallel to its onomatopoeia: the word's sound helps evoke its meaning.

"Crispy Crunchy" *Language Maven Strikes Again* Doubleday 90

6736 Whenever whom is required, recast the sentence. This keeps a huge section of the hard disk of your mind available for baseball averages.

NY Times 7 Oct 90

6737 The reason pandas have reduplicating names like Ling-Ling and Hsing-Hsing is that they can't hear well and zoo keepers have to call them twice.

2 Jul 95

Mark Schiff humorist

6738 When somebody says "The last thing I want to do is hurt you," it means they've got other things to do first.

NY Newsday 22 Feb 94

Phyllis Schlafly columnist

6739 Marriage is like pantyhose. It all depends on what you put into it.

Boston Globe 16 July 74

Edwin Schlossberg attorney

6740 He instructs Sartre in no uncertain terms to perform various acts upon himself.

Reaction of man whose humming annoyed Jean Paul Sartre *The Philosopher's Game* with John Brockman St Martin's 77

Elin Schoen feminist

6741 If men were meant to know all there is to know about women, there would be no such thing as 24-hour mascara.

Ladies' Home Journal Mar 79

Dr Richard Selzer surgeon and essayist

6742 All you have to do is drive out your nature with a pitchfork.

On celibacy *Taking the World in for Repairs* Morrow 86

6743 Proceed day by day, secure in the folk wisdom that one does not go blind in the absence of sex.

ib

6744 A nun alone was a sailboat; two, side by side, a regatta; three, a whole armada. These sisters did not walk; they skimmed, they hovered.

On Sisters of Mercy in full habit "Hospital: A Meditation" *NY Times* 1 May 88

6745 The black nose of a shoe would peek from beneath the hem, then dart back inside the flaring recesses, as though each was sheltering a family of mice.

ib

6746 With what wit and gallantry he returned to those laborious virgins a glimmer of their long-forsworn sexuality.

On his physician-father's good humored teasing *ib*

Garry Shandling comedian

6747 They said I was having a bad hair day.

On a statement of frustration originated by his publicists in June 1991, quoted by William Safire, *NY Times* 11 Jul 93

Lionel Shapiro humorist

6748 I've talked about myself long enough. Now you talk about me.

Quoted by Charles Lynch *You Can't Print That!* Hurtig 83

George P Shultz US Secretary of State

6749 A fact without a theory is like a ship without a sail. . . a boat without a rudder. . . a kite without a tail.

Concluding an address with an impromptu song to the tune of *Silver Dollar* while serving as director of the Office of Management and Budget *Time* 26 Feb 73

6750 A fact without a figure is a tragic final act, but one thing worse in this universe is a theory without a fact.

ib

Hugh Sidey columnist

6751 [He] climbed higher in the power circle than any other barber outside Seville.

On Milton Pitts who cut the hair of four Republican presidents *Time* 9 Jan 95

6752 Secretaries of State William Rogers and James Baker came in for their $25 trims along with free advice on world and national affairs.

ib

Thomas Simmons Professor of English, University of California at Berkeley

6753 The latest guerrilla action against socially acceptable behavior. . . yet another black fly on the baby-smooth skin of human decency.

On telephone answering machines *NY Times* 9 Aug 86

6754 I can't come to the phone right now—and I don't want to talk to you anyway.

Suggested recorded answer *ib*

Scott Simon commentator

6755 Do you suppose that Lassies sit around on their haunches talking about how to breed better trainers?

NPR 6 Aug 94

Frank Sinatra entertainer

6756 Between the two of us, we're older than one of the sphinxes.

At age 72 to Lionel Hampton age 78 *NY Times* 12 Sep 87

Edith Sitwell poet

6757 I have often wished I had time to cultivate modesty. . . but I am too busy thinking about myself.

Recalled on Sitwell's death 9 Dec 64

6758 He looked like a plaster goose on a stone toadstool. . . a bad self-portrait by Van Gogh.

On D H Lawrence *Taken Care Of* Atheneum 65

6759 [She] had the elegance and distinction of a very tall bird. . . and one would not have been surprised, at any moment, if she had preened her quills.

Self-description of herself as a young girl, quoted by Victoria Glendinning *A Unicorn Among Lions* Weidenfeld & Nicolson 81

6760 Osbert had mistaken an enlarged photograph of W J Turner for a map of Vesuvius.

On her brother Osbert Sitwell *ib*

Curtis Sliwa National Director, Guardian Angels

6761 She holds a black belt in karate and in cooking—she could kill you either way.

On his wife Lisa *NY Times* 25 Jun 86

Walter W ("Red") Smith sportswriter

6762 A strong unofficial move was on here tonight to get a Nobel prize for George Brett's proctologist.

On batter's return to 1980 World Series after hemorrhoid operation, quoted by Ira Berkow *Red* Times Books 86

Reggie Smythe cartoonist

6763 Middle age. . . takes only half as long to get tired and twice as long to get rested.

"Andy Capp" comic strip *Washington Post* 16 Sep 88

C P Snow novelist

6764 The gossips had been busy on Lady Ashbrook for a lifetime. . . [and] as she became older the more she was talked about.

A Coat of Varnish Scribner's 79

6765 If any visitors had called she would have greeted them in the armor of her caustic style.

ib

Albert Sonnenfeld Professor of French and Italian, University of Southern California

6766 A waste is a terrible thing to mind.

Paraphrasing an advertising slogan that "a mind is a terrible thing to waste" Station WAMU Washington 13 Feb 95

Muriel Spark novelist

6767 A short neck denotes a good mind... the messages go quicker to the brain.

The Ballad of Peckham Rye Lippincott 60

Ivor Spencer humorist

6768 The worst gaff a butler can make is to murder his employer. It makes it too difficult to get references.

Life Feb 74

Brent Staples essayist

6769 Canceled checks... will be to future historians and cultural anthropologists what the Dead Sea Scrolls and hieroglyphics are to us.

"Raw Meat for the Accountant" *NY Times* 15 Mar 87

6770 They tell all, even the state of the heart... the mournful Billie Holiday records acquired after the affair had crashed and burned beyond recognition. They are tasting life, but the government is tasting them.

On income taxes *ib*

Aianna Stassinopoulos biographer

6771 The queen of sequential monogamy.

On Elizabeth Taylor *New York* 25 Jul 83

Edward Steichen photographer

6772 On the day that God made Carl, He didn't do anything else that day but feel good.

On his brother-in-law, the poet Carl Sandburg, quoted by Harry Golden *Carl Sandburg* World 61

Gloria Steinem feminist

6773 A woman without a man is like a fish without a bicycle.

US News & World Report 27 Sep 93

George Steiner essayist

6774 His ability to jump into an upper bunk from a crouching position has left me with an untarnished image of pure carnal grace and discipline.

On a University of Chicago classmate *New Yorker* 23 Oct 89

Jennifer Steinhauer reporter

6775 Eyes speak and the message is not exactly from Hallmark.

On couples' disagreement on finances *NY Times* 28 May 95

Adlai E Stevenson Governor of Illinois

6776 The State of Illinois and its local governing bodies already have enough to do without trying to control feline delinquency.

On vetoing a bird-protection bill, recalled on Stevenson's death 14 Jul 65

6777 Anyone can become president of the United States. It's a risk we take.

ib

Lena H Sun foreign correspondent

6778 Men are willing to go to great lengths, as it were, for greater length.

On surgery for elongating the penis "A Growth Industry in China" *Washington Post* 17 Nov 91

Gloria Swanson actress

6779 [His injunction is] a compliment to my memory and an insult to my integrity.

On Aristotle Onassis's request that she forget their affair, quoted by Peter Evans *Ari* Summit 86

Stuart Symington US Senator

6780 I found out that he was a bachelor, as was his father before him.

On hiring a speechwriter, to Washington's Gridiron Club, quoted by Harold Brayman *The President Speaks Off-the-Record* Dow Jones 76

Terry Teachout biographer

6781 Life with a cat is in certain ways a one-sided proposition. Cats are not educable; humans are. Moreover, cats know this.

Washington Post 10 Nov 91

Sybil Thorndike actress

6782 Divorce? Never. Murder? Frequently.

On marriage *NY Times* 12 Sep 94

James Thurber humorist

6783 I used to wake up at 4 AM and start sneezing... must be an allergy to consciousness.

Life 14 Mar 60

6784 My drawings have been described as pre-intentionalist, meaning that they were finished before the ideas for them had occurred to me.

ib

6785 I think there's been a fall-out of powdered fruit-cake—everyone's going nuts.

ib

6786 I'm 65... but if there were 15 months in every year, I'd only be 48.

Time 15 Aug 60

6787 Women... deserve to have more than 12 years between the ages of 28 and 40.

ib

6788 If we went out on the street dressed the way we talk, we should be arrested for indecent exposure.

Recalled on Thurber's death 2 Nov 61

6789 Surely you don't mean by unartificial insemination!

To a woman who said she would like to have a child by him *ib*

6790 Even in a nightgown a wolf does not look any more like your grandmother than the Metro-Goldwyn lion looks like Calvin Coolidge.

On "Little Red Riding Hood" *Fables of Our Time* Harper 1940 *ib*

6791 The little girl took an automatic out of her basket and shot the wolf dead.

ib

6792 It is getting to be harder and harder to tell government from show business.

Quoted by Michael J Rosen *Collecting Himself* Harper & Row 89

Arturo Toscanini conductor

6793 I kissed my first woman and smoked my first cigarette on the same day. I have never had time for tobacco since.

Recalled on Toscanini's death 16 Jan 57

John H Trattner Center for Excellence in Government

6794 A prune is an experienced plum.

On government officials *NY Times* 12 Jul 88

James Traub essayist

6795 A voice as soft as chamois... the kind of posture they don't teach anymore... [and a] smile with which the perfect hostess greets the crashing faux pas.

On philanthropist Carroll Petris *New Yorker* 29 Dec 94

Calvin Trillin essayist

6796 The place they loved was at the point/ At which they quickly must anoint/ A saviour who could save the joint.

Tribute to Vartan Gregorian as president of the NY Public Library *NY Times* 5 Feb 89

Joan Tucker students' mother

6797 When my older son began his medical training he paid ten pounds for half a human skeleton... my younger son 20 pounds... my daughter 40 to 50 pounds. What better investment than a skeleton in the closet?

Letter to *London Times* 13 Jun 74

Frank Tuohy essayist

6798 The ballroom with portraits of the Queen and the Duke of Edinburgh was like being inside a stamp album.

Collected Stories Holt Rinehart Winston

Alice K Turner humorist

6799 Hell is the largest shared construction project in imaginative history.

The History of Hell Harcourt, Brace 94

United Press International wire service

6800 Britain withdrew the farthing from circulation as a coin of the realm because after 800 years it isn't worth a farthing any more.

Chicago Sun-Times 30 Jul 60

John Updike novelist

6801 A healthy male adult bore consumes each year one and a half times his own weight in other people's patience.

"Confessions of a Wild Bore" *Assorted Prose* Knopf 65

Gore Vidal novelist

6802 A wise career choice.

On Truman Capote's death *New York* 29 Oct 84

6803 The love that Ruth felt for Naomi... might well end in the joint ownership of a ceramics kiln in Laguna Beach.

On the Old Testament Book of Ruth *United States: Essays 1952–92* Random House 93

6804 I had never wanted to meet most of the people that I had met and the fact that I never got to know most of them took dedication and steadfastness on my part.

Palimpsest Random House 95

6805 Harold Acton has had a long and marvelously uninteresting life.

ib

David Von Drehle reporter

6806 Bulky, boxy, black—a hearse on steroids.

On presidential limousines *Washington Post* 18 Apr 94

Robert F Wagner Mayor of New York

6807 When in danger, ponder; in trouble, delegate; in doubt, mumble.

NY Times 17 Feb 91

Wall Street Journal

6808 Think it's tough to make a call to a small Pacific island? Not atoll.

10 Jul 85

Henry A Wallace US Vice President

6809 A coordinator is someone who can keep all his balls in the air while not losing his own.

On Nelson Rockefeller, quoted by Peter Collins and David Horowitz *The Rockefellers* Holt Rinehart Winston 76

Wallis Duchess of Windsor

6810 I've had a Christmas card from Mae West!

Letter to Duke of Windsor three weeks after his abdication *Wallis and Edward* Summit 86

6811 They certainly can arrange the damndest divorce laws!

On English courts *ib*

6812 The Duke is not heir-conditioned.

Quoted by Charles J V Murphy and J Bryan III *The Windsor Story* Morrow 79

6813 I would have thought you of all people could play the king!

On a bungled hand of bridge held by the Duke of Windsor, recalled in *London Times* 18 Jun 94

6814 I'm not a hedgehog you know!

To Archbishop Michael Ramsey on the crowded space in the royal burial grounds *Vanity Fair* Jun 86

6815 Looks like the Archbishop has been bitten by the tomb bug!

On learning that more burial space had been secured *ib*

6816 Why should he go to her coronation? He didn't go to his own.

On being asked if her husband, the former Edward VIII, would attend Elizabeth II's investiture, quoted by Caroline Blackwood *The Last of the Duchess* Pantheon 95

6817 In a litter of nine, one of the pups tends to turn out OK.

On John F Kennedy and his siblings *ib*

Andy Warhol artist

6818 She's gone to Bloomingdale's.

When asked about his mother's death, quoted by Ultra Violet *Famous for 15 Minutes* Harcourt Brace Jovanovich 88

T H Watkins biographer

6819 Surgeons. . . had wanted to have a look, presumably to satisfy their curiosity regarding the structure of an anarchist brain as opposed to, say, that of a Presbyterian.

On an autopsy that followed the assassination of a Chicago police chief *Righteous Pilgrim* Holt 90

Evelyn Waugh novelist

6820 Like German opera, too loud and too long.

On the Battle of Crete, recalled on Waugh's death 10 Apr 66

6821 [It was] a typical triumph of modern science to find the only part that was not malignant and remove it.

On Randolph Churchill in Clifton Fadiman ed *The Little, Brown Book of Anecdotes* Little, Brown 85

Chaim Weizmann President of Israel

6822 Einstein explained his theory to me every day, and on my arrival I was fully convinced that he understood it.

On transatlantic crossing with Albert Einstein, quoted by Nigel Calder *Einstein's Universe* Viking 79

Edward N West Canon Sacrist, Cathedral of St John the Divine, NYC

6823 Now I'll do some screaming to you and the next county!

On instructing a procession 9 Apr 86

6824 This is not an aphrodisiac service. We will have three thrones there and l8 waxworks over there. And you, Duckey, please pace out the procession while I shove the mayor.

On seating dignitaries *ib*

6825 The bishop is used to being pushed around and I will agitate someone to bring him forward.

ib

6826 Don't let them burst into athletics.

On controlling processions *ib*

6827 The clergy mentality is such that they think they need more room than they do. They sit broad.

ib

Mae West actress

6828 Sex is like a small business. You gotta protect it, watch over it. A matter of timing.

Newsweek 16 Nov 64

6829 I like a man in uniform and, honey, that one fits you grand.

To a Salvation Army captain in the 1926 play *Sex*, recalled in *TV Guide* 28 Feb 65

6830 Come up and see me sometime.

To Cary Grant in 1939 film *She Done Him Wrong ib*

6831 Sex hasn't changed. There's just more of it.
ib

6832 All discarded lovers should be given a second chance. But with somebody else.
The Wit and Wisdom of Mae West Putnam 67

6833 I generally avoid temptation. Unless I can't resist it.
ib

6834 When I'm good, I'm very, very good, but when I'm bad I'm better.
ib

6835 Too much of a good thing can be wonderful.
ib

6836 Old Father Time will turn you into a hag if you don't show the bitch who's boss.
ib

6837 I always figured, never leave yourself down to one man or one dollar.
ib

6838 Keep a diary and some day it'll keep you.
Time 11 Feb 80

6839 It isn't what I do, but how I do it. It isn't what I say, but how I say it.
Recalled on West's death 22 Nov 80

6840 It's better to be looked over than overlooked.
ib

6841 Between two evils I always pick the one I never tried before.
ib

6842 They used to call me Snow White but I drifted.
Quoted by Regina Barreca *They Used to Call Me Snow White* Viking 91

Rebecca West novelist

6843 If he really liked birds, he would have done better to preach to the cats.
On St Francis *This Real Night* Viking 85

6844 [His mind seemed to be like] a telephone exchange with not enough subscribers.
On Edward VIII, quoted by Victoria Glendinning *Rebecca West* Knopf 87

6845 She would know something about beds if anybody did, and I bought several; they are superb.
On a furniture sale staged by Lord Shrewsbury's mistress *ib*

6846 One had the impression that there were camels padding up and down the corridors.
On being hospitalized with wealthy Arabian patients at the London Clinic *ib*

6847 He is every other inch a gentleman.
On novelist Michael Arlen, quoted by Anne Chisholm and Michael Davie *Lord Beaverbrook* Knopf 93

E B White essayist

6848 Although you can take a nation's blood pressure, you can't be sure that the nation hasn't just run up a flight of stairs.
On public opinion polls, in Rebecca M Dale ed *Writings from the New Yorker 1925–76* HarperCollins 90

6849 I went to my dentist's for dinner. . . [and] my doctor and his wife were there too, so I was well covered in the event of sudden cavities or heart failure.
New Yorker 17 Dec 93

Ian White-Thomson Dean, Canterbury Cathedral

6850 A few days ago I received a communication addressed to T A Becket, Esq, care of the Dean of Canterbury. This must surely be a record in postal delay.
Letter to *London Times* 5 Feb 70

Thornton Wilder novelist

6851 [We were brought up in the] late foam-rubber period of American Protestantism.
On himself and his friend Robert M Hutchins, quoted at Hutchins' memorial service 20 May 77

Billy Wilder film producer

6852 Love-making is the red-tape of marriage.
Lines for Gary Cooper to Claudette Colbert in *Bluebeard's Eighth Wife* 1938, recalled by Vincent Canby *NY Times* 10 May 91

6853 If you give them food, it's a democracy. If you leave the labels on, it's imperialism.
Lines for a US Congressman discussing postwar relief in Europe *A Foreign Affair ib* 1938

6854 There was a maharajah who came all the way from India to beg for one of her silk stockings to strangle himself with.
Lines for the butler played by Erich von Stroheim speaking of fading screen star Norma Desmond, played by Gloria Swanson *Sunset Boulevard ib* 50

6855 I don't kneel—it bags my nylons.
Lines for Jan Sterling to Kirk Douglas on why she didn't attend church *Ace in the Hole ib* 51

6856 Just like Jell-O on springs.
Lines for Jack Lemmon watching Marilyn Monroe walk away from him on a railway platform *Some Like It Hot ib* 59

6857 Hey, Charlie, give me a bourbon and step on it.
Lines for a drunken Santa Claus pushing his way up to a Manhattan bar on Christmas Eve *The Apartment ib* 60

6858 I haven't formulated an opinion yet, but I've formulated a hunch.
Lines for Sig Ruman as a medical expert speaking to a patient, Jack Lemmon, suspected of insurance fraud *The Fortune Cookie ib* 1964

6859 I'd worship the ground you walk on, if you lived in a better neighborhood.

To Audrey Wilder *New Yorker* 21 Jun 93

George F Will essayist

6860 Any dictionary that says "uninterested" and "disinterested" are synonyms deserves to be brought before an uninterested judge.

On Merriam-Webster dictionaries *Christian Science Monitor* 16 Jul 87

Tennessee Williams playwright

6861 Sincere as a bird call blown on a hunter's whistle.

Stage directions for clergyman in *Cat On a Hot Tin Roof* New Directions 55

6862 Suspicion is the occupational disease of landladies.

"The Angel in the Alcove" in Tennessee Williams *Collected Stories* New Directions 85

John Winokur humorist

6863 He was not a raconteur but a conversational guerrilla fighter.

On critic George S Kaufman *The Portable Curmudgeon* New American Library 87

6864 You'll hear some pure 15th arrondissement mumbling and diphthonging, an arch but rough equivalent of Locust Valley lockjaw.

On upper-class Long Island accents *NY Times* 18 Jan 87

P G Wodehouse novelist and essayist

6865 I don't know anything that braces one up like finding you haven't got to get married after all.

Jeeves in the Offing Jenkins 60

6866 The right sort of people do not want apologies, and the wrong sort take a mean advantage of them.

The Man Upstairs Metheun 1914, recalled on Wodehouse's death 14 Feb 75

6867 She fitted into my biggest armchair as if it had been built round her by someone who knew they were wearing armchairs tight about the hips that season.

My Man Jeeves George Newnes *ib* 1919

6868 The lunches of 57 years had caused his chest to slip down to the mezzanine floor.

ib

6869 What a queer thing Life is! So unlike anything else, don't you know, if you see what I mean.

ib

6870 Tap his forehead first, and if it rings solid, don't hesitate. All the unhappy marriages come from the husbands having brains.

Advice on accepting a proposal of marriage *The Adventures of Sally ib* 1920

6871 Jeeves coughed one soft, low, gentle cough like a sheep with a blade of grass stuck in its throat.

The Inimitable Jeeves Doran 1923

6872 Aunt Agatha's demeanor was rather like that of one who, picking daisies on the railway, has just caught the down express in the small of the back.

ib

6873 If not actually disgruntled, he was far from being gruntled.

The Code of the Woosters Doubleday 1938

6874 Slice him where you like, a hellhound is always a hellhound.

ib

6875 Big chap with a small moustache and the sort of eye that can open an oyster at 60 paces.

ib

6876 Ice formed on the butler's upper slopes.

Pigs Have Wings 52

6877 A fishlike face has always been heriditary in the Wooster family. . . [but] Sleur de Wooster had the forethought to conceal himself behind a beard like a burst horsehair sofa.

Letter to *London Times* quoted by Kenneth Gregory ed *The First Cuckoo* Allen & Unwin 76

Tom Wolfe novelist

6878 He eased the revolver of his Resentment back into his waistband and told his Snobbery to go lie down by the hearth.

On discovering unexpected affection for an effusive hostess *The Bonfire of the Vanities* Farrar Straus Giroux 87

Ed Wynn comedian

6879 I bred my cast upon the waters.

On rehearsing plays for Mississippi showboats *Life* 1 Jul 66

Yevgeny Yevtushenko Russian poet

6880 It is much better to have the screaming sensitivity of the soul uncovered by any protective skin than to have tear-proof rhinoceros skin in combination with cold fish blood.

At Juniata College commencement *US News & World Report* 27 May 91

Henny Youngman humorist

6881 I once wanted to become an atheist, but I gave up—they have no holidays.

Book of Lists #2 Morrow 80

6882 My wife Sadie had plastic surgery—I cut up her credit cards.

ib

Mikhail S Zadanov Russian satirist

6883 It appears that there are four, although the cow was given a plan for five.

On board of scientific inquiry on how many nipples on a cow's udder *Washington Post* 31 Mar 88

WISDOM, PHILOSOPHY, AND OTHER MUSINGS

Lionel Abel essayist

6884 I have noted that persons with bad judgment are the most insistent that we do what they think best.

Important Nonsense Prometheus 86

Richard Adams biographer

6885 To hear good news—something of close personal concern, lying in the future—is like walking across country and coming in sight, for the first time, of a welcome destination—a friend's house, or a river or cathedral.

The Girl in a Swing Knopf 80

Edward Albee playwright

6886 Sometimes a person has to go a very long distance out of his way to come back a short distance correctly.

The Zoo Story Coward-McCann 60

Anthony Alvarado chancellor, NYC Public Schools

6887 You have to reach way into yourself and discover. . . your core that is you. . . [and] you are stronger and you know what you believe in and you don't get so distracted by all the garbage.

On ouster as chancellor *NY Times* 18 Jul 88

John Amatt biographer

6888 We do not conquer mountains. . . [for] the true conquest lies in penetrating the self-imposed barriers, those limitations within our minds.

On Sharon Wood, first woman to climb Mt Everest *One Step Beyond: Rediscovering the Adventure Attitude* Altitude 95

Maya Angelou poet

6889 There is nothing so pitiful as a young cynic because he has gone from knowing nothing to believing nothing.

PBS 28 Mar 88

6890 Lift up your faces, you have a piercing need/ For this bright morning dawning for you./ History, despite the wrenching pain,/ Cannot be unlived, but if faced/ With courage, need not be lived again.

Poem read at President Clinton's inauguration *NY Times* 20 Jan 93

6891 Here, on the pulse of this new day/ You may have the grace to look up and out/ And into your sister's eyes, and into/ Your brother's face, your country /And say simply/ Very simply/ With hope—/ Good morning!

ib

Stanley W Angrist critic

6892 The first rule of wing walking—never let go of what you are holding onto until you grab hold of something else.

On resigning from one job before securing another *Wall Street Journal* 20 Nov 91

Anon

6893 Death. . . a quiet person. . . kind of scary. . . does not say much but is very sharp and it is almost impossible to outsmart him.

American male undergraduate quoted in Robert Kastenbaum and Ruth Aisenberg eds *The Psychology of Death* Springer 75

6894 Although you would like to stay away from him, there's something about him that kind of draws you to him. You like him and fear him at the same time. I picture Death as being millions of years old but only looking about 40.

ib

6895 My soul has been tired for a long time. Now my feet are tired, and my soul is resting.

Aged African-American woman during Montgomery AL boycott of city buses, quoted by Paul Carter *Another Part of the Fifties* University Press 83

6896 The most visible creators I know of are those. . . whose medium is being. . . artists of being alive.

From a greeting card copyright by J Stone, Silverton OR 85

6897 If your lips would keep from slips/ Five things observe with care:/ Of whom you speak, to whom you speak,/ And How, and When, and Where.

The Duchess of Windsor's Commonplace Book, quoted by Michael Bloch *Wallis and Edward* Summit 86

6898 Heaven only hates people who love each other; it separates those who would be happy. Don't postpone pleasure.

Needlepointed inscription on pillow prized by Henry Ford II in retirement, quoted by Peter Collier and David Horowitz *The Fords* Simon & Schuster 87

6899 Never acknowledge and you won't be. Do naught and you'll be.

Forbes 5 Sep 88

6900 Give me a mediocre life. Do not let me be disturbed by any great thing.

Cited by novelist Robertson Davies as "the Canadian national prayer" *US News & World Report* 16 Jan 89

6901 Persistence and determination alone are omnipotent.

Framed saying in home of columnist Heloise Cruse, "high priestess of housework, the maven of the mundane" *NY Times* 19 Oct 89

6902 As he comes, so he goes.

Paris undertakers' rejection of burial clothes for the Duke of Windsor, quoted by the Duke's footman *NY Times* 21 Dec 89

6903 Everytime a person dies, a library burns.

Quoted by Edmund White, Fall 1990 *AIDS Quarterly* NPR 26 Nov 90

6904 Don't hang noodles from my ears.

Russian slang for being insincere *Newsweek* 26 Aug 91

6905 Only the grave straightens the hunchback.

Interpretation of the saying "you can't teach an old dog new tricks" *ib*

6906 The naked have sly devices.

On "necessity as the mother of invention" *ib*

6907 When there's no fish, a crab is a fish.

On "half a loaf is better than none" *ib*

6908 The first pancake is always a flop.

On perseverance *ib*

6909 Work isn't a wolf, it won't run into the woods.

On procrastination *ib*

6910 Anytime you see a turtle atop a fence post, you know it had some help.

On achievement, quoted by Alex Haley *US News & World Report* 24 Feb 92

6911 Les does not necessarily have the courage of his convictions. He has the courage of his conclusions.

On US Secretary of Defense Les Aspin *Washington Post* 21 Feb 93

6912 Good, better, best. Don't ever rest, until good is better and better is best.

US Attorney General Janet Reno quoting her mother *Washington Post* 21 Apr 93

6913 I am a soldier of happiness/ I don't like bullets/ You can kill my summer/ But my spring will survive.

Soldier of Happiness, the most popular song in war-ridden Bosnia *Time* 26 Jul 93

6914 You're not needed anywhere, not wanted anywhere, and not expected anywhere. Nobody cares what you do.

On homelessness, quoted by Elliot Liebow *Tell Them Who We Are* Free Press 93

6915 Mountain folk cannot live without guests any more than they can live without air. But if the guests stay longer than necessary, they choke.

Russian proverb quoted by Soviet Premier Mikhail S Gorbachev in concluding his first meeting with British Prime Minister Margaret Thatcher, quoted by Thatcher in *The Downing Street Years* HarperCollins 93

6916 To the heavens with a purse.

Latin inscription over cast-iron portal to Kykuit, the Rockefeller mansion near North Tarrytown NY *Christian Science Monitor* 19 May 94

6917 The secret of redemption is rememberance.

Sign at the exit of Israel's Yad Vashem memorial to the Holocaust *New Yorker* 14 Aug 95

6918 Women hold up half the sky.

A favorite saying of Mao Zedong, recalled in Bejing at the 4th World Conference on Women *USA Today* 29 Aug 95

Hannah Arendt historian

6919 Forgiving and promising enacted in solitude or isolation remain without reality and can signify to more than a role played before one's self....[otherwise] we would remain the victims of its consequences forever.

The Human Condition University of Chicago Press 58

6920 Thinking does not lead to truth. Truth is the beginning of thought.

Carol Brightmen ed *Between Friends* Harcourt, Brace 94

Fernando Arrabal essayist

6921 Insurgents have always belonged to the well-to-do classes, for they can see injustice clearly from the best seats in the stands.

The Tower Struck by Lightning Viking 88

Louis Auchincloss novelist

6922 He may be a hothouse plant, but he sees a great deal from his hothouse windows.

The Rector of Justin Houghton Mifflin 64

W H Auden poet

6923 I and the public know what all school children learn; those to whom evil is done do evil in return.

Time 14 Apr 80

6924 [Oscar] Wilde, after all, is important not as a writer—he couldn't write at all—but as a behaver.

Quoted by Alan Ansen, Nicolas Jenkins ed *The Table Talk of W H Auden* Ontario Review Press 90

6925 Blessed be all metrical rules that forbid automatic response, force us to have second thoughts, free from the fetters of Self.

Lines written in 1969, quoted by Nicholas Jenkins ed *By With, to and From Lincoln Kirstein* Farrar Straus Giroux 91

6926 You need not know what someone is doing to know if it is a vocation, you have only to watch the eyes... the same rapt expression, forgetting themselves in a function.

"Sext" Spring 54, Edward Mendelson ed *W H Auden: Collected Poems* Vintage 91

6927 Passing a slum child with rickets, I look the other way: He looks the other way if he passes a chubby one.

"Vespers" *ib*

6928 To long for certain letters is to be fully human, and to admit a common humanity.

Quoted by Vivian Gornick "Letters Are Acts of Faith: Telephone Calls Are a Reflex" *NY Times* 31 Jul 94

Harold Azine essayist

6929 Youth is a fast gallop over a smooth track to the bright horizon... the time of great expectations for yourself and expectations of others for you—to be fulfilled at an unspecified time called "Someday."

The House in Webster Grove NBC TV 16 Feb 58

6930 A mailbox is a symbol, a place in life... [that] says to the world, "a person lives here, one of individual form and soul, with the right of privacy and the mantle of dignity. This is his name. This is his home.

ib

6931 Happiness in the older years of life, like happiness in every year of life, is a matter of choice—*your* choice for yourself.

ib

6932 Happiness in old age is, more than anything else, preserving the privileges of privacy.

ib

6933 [Happiness is] to trim the day to one's own mood and feeling, to raise the window shade of your own bedroom an hour early and squander the hour in the morning sunshine, to drink your own tea from your own cup, to practice the little wisdoms of housekeeping, to hand a picture on the wall where memories can reach out to it a dozen times a day and to sit in your kitchen and talk to your friend.

ib

Richard Bach essayist

6934 Jonathan is that brilliant little fire that burns within us all, that lives only for those moments when we reach perfection.

On central metaphor in his best-seller *Jonathan Livingstone Seagull* Macmillan 70

6935 In the United States, Christmas has become the rape of an idea.

ib

6936 The more I want to get something done, the less I call it work.

Illusions Delacorte 77

Sheila Ballantyne essayist

6937 There is no irritant as painful as an ace up your sleeve that you can never use; it's the kind of thing that causes oysters to produce pearls.

Imaginary Crimes Viking 82

Julian Barnes essayist

6938 If you gave the full context, people thought you a rambling old fool. If you didn't give the context, people though you a laconic old fool.

Imagining Old Age Staring at the Sun Cape 86

Jacques Barzun Dean of Faculties, Columbia University

6939 Art distills sensation and embodies it with enhanced meaning in memorable form—or else it is not art.

The House of Intellect Harper 59

6940 Principle never forgives: its logic is to kill.

ib

Rick Bass Montanta rancher and writer

6941 It can be so wonderful, finding out you were wrong... ignorant... know nothing, not squat. You get to start over. It's like snow falling that first time each year.

Winter Houghton Mifflin 91

Margaret P Battin Professor of Philosophy, University of Utah

6942 In a society that can't agree when human life begins, it's no surprise that we have trouble deciding when it should end.

On euthanasia *LA Times* 2 Nov 91

Bruce Beaver poet

6943 I welcome the anonymity of the middle years,/ years of the spreading girth/ and conversational prolixity, /when the whole being loosens/ the stays of the thirties and/ lengthens out into paragraphs/ of perceptiveness where once/ had bristled the pointed phrase.

Letters to Live Poets South Head Press 69

Daniel Bell Emeritus Professor of Social Sciences, Harvard

6944 Wisdom is the tears of experience, the bridge of experience and imagination over time... the listening heart, the melancholy sigh, the distillation of despair to provide a realistic, if often despondent, view of the world.

At Brandeis commencement *NY Times* 27 May 91

Saul Bellow novelist

6945 Banality is the adopted disguise of a very powerful will to abolish conscience.

Quoted by columnist George Will *Newsweek* 25 May 87

6946 [Memoirs] keep the wolf of insignificance from the door.

Quoted by Lance Morrow *Time* 16 May 88

Alan Bennett playwright

6947 The majority of people perform well in a crisis and when the spotlight is on them; it's on the Sunday afternoons of this life, when the nobody is looking, that the spirit falters.

New Yorker 22 May 95

Bernard Berenson essayist and art historian

6948 Life has taught me that it is not for our faults that we are disliked and even hated but for our qualities.

The Passionate Sightseer Simon & Schuster 60

6949 [I would willingly stand at] street corners hat in hand begging passers-by to drop their unused minutes into it.

H Kiel ed *The Bernard Berenson Treasury* Simon & Schuster 62

6950 Any question that can be asked in a sentence can be answered in a sentence.

Quoted by Frederick Buechner *Now & Then* Harper & Row 83

Edward Bernays public relations pioneer

6951 Everybody is born with genius but most people only keep it a few minutes.

Quoted by dancer Martha Graham NPR 1 Apr 91

John Betjeman poet

6952 Now if the harvest is over/ And the world cold/ Give me the bonus of laughter/ As I lose hold

A Nip in the Air Norton 76, recalled on Betjeman's death *Time* 28 May 84

6953 History must not be written with bias, and both sides must be given, even if there is only one side.

First and Last Loves Murray 52

Stephen Birmingham biographer

6954 What is known as success assumes nearly as many aliases as there are those who seek it.

"Young Men in Manhattan" *Holiday* Mar 61

6955 Success is commonly regarded as an exclusively American product, and it is advertised on matchbook covers and in the back pages of adventure magazines, accessible by way of a high-school education or a new truss.

ib

6956 [Success] is thought by some to have a distinctly bitter taste, not unlike a mouthful of dimes. But its smell is generally conceded to be sweet.

ib

Jim Bishop columnist

6957 Courage is a good word. It has a ring. . . a substance that other people, who have none, urge you to have when all is lost.

NY *Journal-American* 14 Mar 59

6958 To have courage, one must first be afraid. The deeper the fear, the more difficult the climb toward courage.

ib

6959 The future is an opaque mirror. Anyone who tries to look into it sees nothing but the dim outlines of an old and worried face.

ib 15 Oct 59

6960 It is difficult to live in the present, ridiculous to live in the future and impossible to live in the past. Nothing is as far away as one minute ago.

ib 7 May 61

6961 At 19, everything is possible and tomorrow looks friendly.

ib 9 May 61

6962 Death is as casual—and often as unexpected—as birth. . . difficult to define as grief or joy. Each is finite. Each will fade.

Red Bank NJ *Register* 13 Aug 73

6963 Books, I found, had the power to make time stand still, retreat or flow into the future.

A Bishop's Confession Little, Brown 81

Lawrence Bixby essayist

6964 Each handicap is like a hurdle in a steeplechase, and when you ride up to it, if you throw your heart over, the horse will go along, too.

"Comeback from a Brain Operation" *Harper's* Nov 52

Shirley Temple Black actress and diplomat

6965 Make-believe colors the past with innocent distortion, and it swirls ahead of us in a thousand ways—in science, in politics, in every bold intention. It is part of our collective lives, entwining our past and our future. . . a particularly rewarding aspect of life itself.

American Weekly 25 May 58

Harry Blackstone Jr magician

6966 Nothing I do can't be done by a 10-year-old. . . with 15 years of practice.
Newsweek 16 Oct 78

Robert Bly poet

6967 You can't say to a dreamer, "Be careful!" You can only say, "Think as hard as you can, love as hard as you can, pray as hard as you can, and if it doesn't work, laugh as hard as you can."
Quoted by Benedict Reid *A Spirit Loose in the World* Harbor House West 93

Ronald Blythe novelist

6968 He longed to be lost but he couldn't bear not to be found.
On T E Lawrence *The Age of Illusion* Houghton Mifflin 64

6969 To be old is to be part of a huge and ordinary multitude. . . the reason why old age was venerated in the past was because it was extraordinary.
The View in Winter Harcourt Brace Jovanovich 79

6970 Death used to announce itself in the thick of life but now people drag on so long it sometimes seems that we are reaching the stage when we may have to announce ourselves to death. . . . It is as though one needs a special strength to die, and not a final weakness.
ib

6971 The ordinariness of living to be old is too novel a thing to appreciate.
ib

Geoffrey Bocca biographer

6972 Wit is a treacherous dart. It is perhaps the only weapon with which it is possible to stab oneself in one's own back.
The Woman Who Would Be Queen: A Biography of the Duchess of Windsor Rinehart 54

Humphrey Bogart actor

6973 The whole world is about three drinks behind.
Recalled on Bogart's death 14 Jan 57

Sissela Bok philosopher

6974 Liars share with those they deceive the desire not to be deceived.
Lying Random House 78

6975 We are all, in a sense, experts on secrecy. From earliest childhood we feel its mystery and attraction. . . the power it confers and the burden it imposes. . . how it can delight, give breathing space and protect.
Secrets Pantheon 83, quoted by Frank Trippett "The Public Life of Secrecy" Time 17 Jan 85

6976 While all deception requires secrecy, all secrecy is not meant to deceive.
ib

Erma Bombeck columnist

6977 Don't confuse fame with success. One is Madonna; the other is Helen Keller.
To Meredith College commencement *USA Today* 20 May 91

Hal Borland naturalist

6978 Summer is a promissory note, signed in June, its long days spent and gone before you know it, and due to be repaid next January.
NY Times 18 Jun 61

6979 Buds are the tree's hostages to the future—the promise a tree makes to itself that there will be a tomorrow, another year.
Barbara Dodge Borland ed *Twelve Moons of the Year* Knopf 79

Robert Boswell novelist

6980 Every man has a day in his life when nobody can defeat him.
Living to be a Hundred Knopf 94

John Malcolm Brinnin biographer

6981 Proximity is nine-tenths of friendship.
Truman Capote—Dear Heart, Old Buddy Delacorte 87

Alan Houghton Broderick autobiographer

6982 A man's life, for himself as for others, is like a fish gleaming in the waters: a flash, and it is gone, another flash and it reappears, until it is lost forever.
Casual Change Morrow 64

Joseph Brodsky poet

6983 Boredom speaks the language of time. . . to teach you the most valuable lesson of your life, the lesson of your utter insignificance.
At Dartmouth commencement *NY Times* 12 Jun 89

6984 The greatest thing a society can do to a citizen is leave him alone.
Quoted by Eliot Liebow *Tell Them Who I Am* Free Press 93

William F Buckley Jr columnist

6985 Friendship is strengthened by. . . that which ever so lightly elevates us from the trough of self-concern and self-devotion.

Gratitude Random House 90

Aureliano Buendia essayist

6986 The secret of good old age is simply an honorable pact with solitude.

Quoted by Philip Ziegler *Mountbatten* Knopf 85

James Branch Cabell novelist

6987 [Gallantry is] to accept the pleasures of life leisurely, and its inconveniences with a shrug.

Time 28 Jan 52

Italo Calvino essayist

6988 We all turn in our hands an old, empty tire through which we try to reach some final meaning, which words cannot achieve.

On observing a gorilla playing with a tire *Mr Palomar* Harcourt Brace Jovanovich 85

Albert Camus essayist

6989 The need to be right, the sign of a vulgar mind.

Recalled on Camus' death 4 Jan 60

Elias Canetti essayist

6990 The great writers of aphorisms read as if they had all known each other well.

The Human Province Seabury 58

Ethan Canin critic

6991 Time is but the thinnest bandage for our wounds.

The Palace Thief Random House 94

Mary Cantwell essayist

6992 I am not inclined to pry because I believe a certain ignorance attends the best friendships.

NY Times 13 Feb 92

Angela Carter essayist

6993 Comedy is tragedy that happens to other people.

Wise Children Farrar Straus Giroux 92

Gabrielle ("Coco") Chanel designer

6994 Speak badly of no one but yourself. At least you will be believed.

NY Times 29 Jul 67

6995 He who does not enjoy his own company is usually right.

ib

Charlie Chaplin actor

6996 There are more valid facts and details in works of art than there are in history books.

My Autobiography Simon & Schuster 64

Paddy Chayefsky playwright

6997 To keep his sense of virility bolstered, he throws a pass at some other woman. . . as much a part of the American scene as honeysuckle.

Marty Simon & Schuster 55

Alan Clark British Minister of Trade

6998 [After 45]. . . the bruising of repeated sexual rejection starts to show in the eyes.

Mrs Thatcher's Ministers Farrar Straus Giroux 94

Francis X Clines reporter

6999 A photograph really is not about the past. It is a premeditated continuation of the present.

NY Times 16 Jun 79

William J Clinton 42nd US President

7000 You realize that the time you have is limited, and you want to live like a laser beam instead of a shot gun.

On aging *US News & World Report* 20 Jun 92

Cyril Connolly essayist

7001 No one over 35 is worth meeting who has not something to teach us—something more than we could learn by ourselves, from a book.

The Unquiet Grave Penguin 67

Pat Conroy novelist

7002 Fantasy is one of the soul's brightest porcelains.

Beach Music Doubleday 95

Roger Cooper essayist

7003 Anyone who, like me, has been educated in English public schools and served in the ranks of the British Army is quite at home in a Third World prison.

On five years as a captive in Iran *Newsweek* 15 Apr 91

Julio Cortazar essayist

7004 A piece of me fell dead. . . on the tablecloth in the midst of the conventional phrases.

On hearing an indifferent allusion to television news of Jean Cocteau's death *A Certain Lucas* Knopf 84

Philip Crane US Congressman

7005 The quantity of his life finally exceeded its quality.

On the death at 94 of his father, syndicated columnist Dr George W Crane *NY Times* 19 Jul 95

John Culhane biographer

7006 This is the heart of the circus: successful acts of human skill and daring harmonized by the counterpoint of clownish failure.

The American Circus Holt 89

Robertson Davies novelist

7007 The world is full of people whose notion of a satisfactory future is... a return to the idealized past.

The Manticore Viking 72

7008 The art of the quoter is to know when to stop.

What's Bred in the Bone Viking 85

7009 [In] the Great Theater of Life... admission is free but the taxation is mortal. You come when you can, and leave when you must. The show is continuous.

The Cunning Man Viking 95

Andrew Delbanco Professor of English, Columbia University

7010 Meanings are to be made, not found. They are imposed on concrete facts; they do not inhere in them.

Facing Facts Oxford 94

Morarji Desai Prime Minister of India

7011 Form no habits except... telling the truth. All other habits enslave... and make one dependent and weak.

The Story of My Life Macmillan 74

David W Dunlap reporter

7012 Here, for the first time, was a moving, tangible link to a population that had been demeaned in life and forgotten in death.

On the discovery of a burial ground for black slaves on Manhattan's southern tip *NY Times* 28 Feb 93

Albert Einstein scientist

7013 Nationalism is an infantile disease... the measles of mankind.

Recalled on Einstein's death 18 Apr 55

7014 Perfection of means and confusion of goals characterize our age.

Out of My Later Years Greenwood 56

Paul Eldridge essayist

7015 History is the transformation of tumultuous conquerors into silent footnotes.

Maxims for a Modern Man Yaseloff 65

T S Eliot poet and playwright

7016 If you haven't the strength to impose your own terms upon life, you must accept the terms life offers you.

The Confidential Clerk Harcourt, Brace 54

Stanley Elkin novelist

7017 Now she was 82... [and] it was as if all the square feet and exact specs of the properties and registered deeds of her existence had at last been revealed to her.

On the central figure of his novel *Mrs Ted Bliss* Hyperion 95

Ralph Ellison novelist

7018 I am an invisible man... [but] a man of substance... flesh and bone, fiber and liquids—and I might even be said to possess a mind.

Opening lines of *Invisible Man* Random House 52, seen in terms of African-American liberation as a landmark, "seminal novel" at Ellison's death *NY Times* 17 Apr 94

7019 It is this which frightens me: who knows but that, on the lower frequencies, I speak for you?

Conclusion of *Invisible Man ib*

Louise Erdrich novelist

7020 Talk is an old man's last vice... [but] I got well by talking. Death could not get a word in edgewise, grew discouraged, and traveled on.

Tracks Holt Rinehart Winston 88

Bergen Evans Professor of English, Northwestern University

7021 Most of what passes as human wisdom is merely the post-examination gabble of the excited students trying to guess how the new lesson will explain the old questions.

Introduction to *Dictionary of Quotations* Delacorte 68

William Faulkner novelist

7022 Only the unrealized parts of our lives seem perfect. That's what keeps Paris green for us... something we are sure is there only we ourselves never fully realized it.

Quoted by Stephen Longstreet *We All Went to Paris* Macmillan 72

7023 Memory believes before knowing remembers. Believes longer than recollects, longer than knowing even wonders.

ib

Ian Fleming novelist

7024 Luck was a servant and not a master... had to be accepted with a shrug or taken advantage of up to the hilt.

On the philosophy of fictional Agent 007 *Forbes* FYI Nov 93

Peter Fleming humorist

7025 Pain... of all human experiences is... the most absorbing.

My Aunt's Rhinoceros Harp, Davis 56

7026 Pain is the only human experience which, when it comes to an end, confers a real if not a very high kind of happiness.

ib

Malcolm S Forbes publisher

7027 While alive, I lived.

Inscription for his memorial plaque *London Illustrated News* Spring 91

Robert Frost poet

7028 Not being crossed is the one thing that matters most in life.

Lawrence Thompson ed *Selected Letters of Robert Frost* Holt Rinehart Winston 64

John Kenneth Galbraith economist and statesman

7029 Money... ranks with love as man's greatest source of joy—and with death as his greatest source of anxiety.

Money: Whence It Came, Where It Went Houghton Mifflin 75

Jerry Garcia lyricist

7030 Once in a while you can get shown the light/ In the strangest places if you look at it right.

Lyrics for *Scarlet Begonias* 76, regarded as Garcia's philosophy as expressed through his rock band known as "The Grateful Dead" *NY Times* 10 Aug 95

Judy Garland actress

7031 We cast away priceless time in dreams, born of imagination, fed upon illusion, and put to death by reality.

Quoted by Anne Edwards *Judy Garland* Simon & Schuster 74

Brendan Gill essayist

7032 To the born wisecracker, uttering the one funny word too many is the last appetite that fails.

Introduction to *The Portable Dorothy Parker* Penguin 73

7033 Custom requires an exchange of piffling politenesses.

On "small talk" as "a high glass wall over which one climbs at one's peril" *ib*

Rumer Godden novelist

7034 Everyone is a house with four rooms... physical... mental... emotional... spiritual... [and] unless we go into every room every day, even if only to keep it aired, we are not a complete person.

A House With Four Rooms Morrow 89

Gail Godwin novelist

7035 All the corners of his days were filled in, as they are when someone has found the work that best suits his disposition.

Father Melancholy's Daughter Morrow 91

Paul Goldberger critic

7036 New York is an arrogant city... has always wanted to be all things to all people, and a surprising amount of the time it has succeeded.

The City Observed Random House 78

7037 Public enough to have a consistently high profile, private enough to have an aura of mystery.

On the place of the Rockefeller family in American life *NY Times* 6 May 94

7038 Snow... makes one think not of a clean slate, a glorious future, but of a happy past and never mind that the past never really was like that.

ib 11 Jan 96

7039 The pure whiteness that covered everything is soft, almost sensual, and we like to believe the past was that way, too, with no hard edges.

ib

Albert Gore Jr US Vice President

7040 It's a place where people know about it when you're born and care about it when you die.

On hometowns *NY Times* 10 Jul 92

Martha Graham dancer

7041 Age is the acceptance of a term of years... maturity the glory of years.

Christian Science Monitor 25 May 79

Robert Graves poet

7042 Intuition, the supra-logic that cuts out all routine processes of thought and leaps straight from problem to answer.

Five Pens in Hand Doubleday 58

Germaine Greer essayist

7043 Human beings have an inalienable right to invent themselves; when that right is pre-empted, it is called brain-washing.

London Times 1 Feb 86

Walter Gropius architect

7044 However often the thread may be torn out of your hands, you must develop enough patience to wind it up again and again.

On "inner devotion to the tasks you have set yourself" *NY Times* 8 Jul 69

Ramon Guthrie critic

7045 He was one of those people who are born knowing that they will never sleep again.

On novelist Sinclair Lewis, quoted by Peter Kurth *American Cassandra* Little, Brown 90

Sue Halpern essayist

7046 Privacy... is essential... not only to the souls of painters and poets, who thrive in solitude, but to the rest of us, too—individuals whose canvas is our lives.

Migrations to Solitude Pantheon 92

Dag Hammarskjöld UN Secretary General

7047 These notes... are signposts you began to set up after you had reached a point where you needed them, a fixed point that was on no account to be lost sight of.

Journal entry 1956 *Markings* Knopf 64

Moss Hart playwright and director

7048 Boredom is the keynote of poverty... its dark brown sameness.

Act One Random House 59

Vaclav Havel President of Czech Republic

7049 Hope is not a feeling of certainty, that everything ends well. Hope is just a feeling that life and work have a meaning.

Time 17 Sep 90

Samuel Hazo poet

7050 Expect nothing,/ and anything seems everything./ Expect everything, and anything/ seems nothing.

"The First and Only Sailing" from *Thank a Bored Lion* New Directions 59, quoted by Jane Alexander at Julliard School of Music commencement *NY Times* 30 May 94

7051 To live/ you leave your yesterselves/ To drown without a funeral./ You chart a trek where no/ One's sailed before./ You rig. You anchor up. You sail.

ib

Timothy Healy President, NY Public Library

7052 The library is one of the last decent, honorable things going... one of the great keeping places of the memories of man.

US News & World Report 5 Jun 89

Ben Hecht novelist

7053 There is hardly one in three of us who live in the cities who is not sick with unused self.

Child of the Century Simon & Schuster 54

Martin Heidegger Emeritus Professor of Philosophy, University of Marburg, Germany

7054 Thinking only begins at the point where we have come to know that Reason, glorified for centuries, is the most obstinate adversary of thinking.

Being and Time Harper & Row 62

Theresa Helburn theatrical producer

7055 One's lifework... grows with the working and the living. Do it as if your life depended on it, and first thing you know, you'll have made a life out of it.

A Wayward Quest Little, Brown 60

Joseph Heller novelist

7056 There was only one catch and that was Catch-22, which specified that a concern for one's own safety in the face of dangers that were real and immediate was the process of a rational mind.

Catch-22 Simon & Schuster 61

7057 If he flew them [the missions] he was crazy and didn't have to; but if he didn't want to, he was sane and had to.

On a pilot's paradox, his "catch–22" *ib*

7058 I know so many things I'm afraid to find out.

Something Happened Knopf 74

Cecil Helman essayist

7059 Almost every adult body now dances its daily *pas de deux* with the clock, and plays a physiological duet with the little machine tied to its wrist.

The Body of Frankenstein's Monster Norton 92

Ernest Hemingway novelist

7060 The world breaks every one and afterward many are strong at the broken places.

A Farewell to Arms Scribner 1929, recalled on Hemingway's death 2 Jul 61, chosen as frontispiece in Arthur M Schlesinger Jr's book on the Kennedy presidency *A Thousand Days* Houghton Mifflin 65

William A Henry III critic

7061 Definitions. . . tend to be 10 percent axiom and 90 percent hedging and exceptions.

In Defense of Elitism Doubleday 94

Alan Patrick Herbert Member of Parliament

7062 When we laugh, richly and gloriously, without restraint and bitterness, we. . . are as angels looking down on life, laughing at it but loving it.

Recalled on Herbert's death 11 Nov 71

Bruce Hershensohn essayist

7063 Creativity always dies a quick death in rooms that house conference tables.

NY Times 2 Apr 75

Russell Hoban novelist

7064 When Kleinzeit opened the door of his flat Death was there, black and hairy and ugly, no bigger than a medium-sized chimpanzee with dirty fingernails.

Kleinzeit, A Novel Summit 83

7065 Not all that big, are you, said Kleinzeit. Not one of my big days, said Death. Sometimes I'm tremendous.

ib

7066 Under the bed Death sat humming to itself. . . elsewhere Action lay in his cell smoking and looking up at the ceiling. . . . Why couldn't I have been Death or something like that. Steady work, security.

ib

Laura Z Hobson novelist and biographer

7067 A flick here, a flick there. . . no yellow armband, no marked bench in the park, no Gestapo. . . but day by day, the little thump of insult. . . the delicate assault on the stuff of a man's identity. That's how they did it.

On anti-semitism *Laura Z* Arbor House 83

Eric Hoffer essayist

7068 When people are free to do as they please, they usually imitate each other.

The Passionate State of Mind Harper 54

7069 Every new adjustment is a crisis in self-esteem.

The Ordeal of Change Harper & Row 63

7070 Hippies are merely tired minds in young faces.

NY Sunday News 4 Feb 68

Lena Horne entertainer

7071 Don't grow old without money, honey.

On retiring at age 62 *People* 7 Apr 80

Zora Neale Hurston essayist

7072 I have been in Sorrow's kitchen and licked out all the pots. Then I have stood on the peaky mountain wrapped in rainbows with a sword in my hands.

Dust Tracks on a Road Arno 69

Aldous Huxley novelist

7073 There are few who would not rather be taken in adultery than in provincialism.

Recalled on Huxley's death 22 Nov 63

7074 Facts. . . sitting on a wise man's knee may be made to utter words of wisdom; elsewhere they say nothing or talk nonsense, or indulge in sheer diabolism.

ib

William Ralph Inge "gloomy" Dean of St Paul's

7075 A man may build himself a throne of bayonets, but he cannot sit on it.

Quoted by Boris Yeltsin on attempted overthrow of Premier Mikhail S Gorbachev ABC TV 21 Aug 91

Pico Iyer essayist

7076 Punctuation is something more than a culture's birthmark; it scores the music in our minds, gets our thoughts moving to the rhythm of our hearts.

"In Praise of the Humble Comma" *Time* 13 Jun 88

7077 Silence is sunshine. . . company is clouds; silence is rapture. . . company is doubt; silence is golden. . . company is brass.

"The Eloquent Sounds of Silence" *ib* 25 Jan 93

Erica Jong novelist

7078 Divorce is my generation's coming of age ceremony—a ritual scarring that makes anything that happens afterward seem bearable.

Fear of Fifty HarperCollins 94

Dr Carl Jung psychoanalyst

7079 Death is a faithful companion of life and follows it like its shadow.

C G Jung Letters Vol 1 Princeton University Press 73

Stefan Kanfer essayist

7080 The aphorism is a personal observation inflated into a universal truth, a private posing as a general.
Time 11 Jun 83

7081 A proverb is anonymous human history compressed to the size of a seed.
ib

Helen Keller essayist

7082 Pink is a baby's cheek, a soft Southern breeze. Gray is a shawl around the shoulders. Brown is withered hands, warm friendly leaf mold, the trunks of aged trees. Lilac is the loved, kissed face. Yellow is the sun, the rich promise of life.
Expressing a sightless person's vision of color, 70th birthday interview *NY Times* 25 Jun 50

Virginia Clinton Kelley President's mother

7083 There's always a brighter side to a story. You just have to look. People get too busy sometimes.
On the death of her first husband a few months before the birth of the future President CNN 9 Jan 94

John F Kennedy 35th US President

7084 All of life is like that—systole and diastole.
Applying the heart's rhythms to a columnist's advice "not to try to do two opposite things at once," quoted by Theodore C Sorensen *Kennedy* Harper & Row 65

Jack Kerouac essayist

7085 We are beat, man. Beat means beatific, it means you get the beat.
Quoted by Herbert Gold "The Beat Mystique" *Playboy* Feb 88

Martin Luther King Jr civil rights leader

7086 Segregation is the adultery of an illicit intercourse between injustice and immorality.
NY Times 1 Jul 63

7087 Man must evolve for all human conflict a method which rejects revenge, aggression and retaliation. The foundation of such a method is love.
Accepting Nobel Peace Prize Oslo 11 Dec 64

7088 The tortuous road which has led from Montgomery to Oslo is a road over which millions of Negroes are traveling to find a new sense of dignity. It will, I am convinced, be widened into a superhighway of justice.
On tracing his protests onward from Montgomery AL *ib*

Stephen King novelist

7089 You have to start knowing yourself so well that you begin to know other people. A piece of us is in every person we can ever meet.
Night Shift Doubleday 78

Matthew Knight essayist

7090 We are all legends in our own minds.
Letter from Palm City FL, NPR 9 Sep 93

Alice Koller novelist

7091 Being solitary is being alone well. . . luxuriously immersed in doings of your own choice, aware of the fullness of your own presence rather than of the absence of others.
The Stations of Solitude Morrow 90

Antonina Konoplev Russian worker

7092 You pick up the soil and it's like holding your mother's hand.
On farming during time-off from a Soviet garment factory *NY Times* 9 May 88

Sheldon Kopp novelist

7093 Revenge is a form of nostalgia.
What Took You So Long? Science and Behavior Books 79

7094 Suicide can be a case of mistaken identity.
ib

Bernard Kops playwright

7095 Commit arson every day in your imagination, burn down the previous day's lies, have a little revolution now and again in your heart; try and help lonely people.
The Hamlet of Stepney Green play quoted by Peter Vansittart *In the Fifties* John Murray 95

John Kotre essayist

7096 The years we remember best. . . say a lot about who we are and why our life is turning out the way it is.
White Gloves Free Press 95

7097 By the age of 30 most of us have had the experiences that count in our lives, and by the age of 50 we are beginning to see their long-range consequences.
ib

Milan Kundera novelist

7098 A man possessed by peace never stops smiling.
The Book of Laughter and Forgetting Knopf 80

Louis L'Amour novelist

7099 There will come a time when you believe everything is finished. That will be the beginning.

Lonely on the Mountain Bantam 81

Edwin Herbert Land Founder, Polaroid Corp

7100 To a child, a photograph gives a permanent thing that is both outside himself and part of himself. He gets a new kind of security from every picture he takes.

Time 26 Jun 72

7101 As we grow older. . . a photograph makes permanent our own perception of a portion of that world.

ib

7102 I find each new person whom I meet a complete restatement of what life and the world are all about.

ib

Philip Larkin poet

7103 Perhaps being old is having lighted rooms inside your head, and people in them, acting.

"The Old Fools" *Collected Poems* Farrar Straus Giroux 89

7104 I know, none better, the eyelessness of days without a letter.

Quoted in *London Sunday Times* 5 Dec 93 review of Anthony Thwaite ed *Selected Letters of Philip Larkin 1940–1985* Farrar Straus Giroux 93

Richard Leakey Director, Kenyan Wildlife Service

7105 All life's important things take place above the knee.

After losing his feet and ankles in a plane crash *London Times* 7 Jul 95

Timothy F Leary psychologist

7106 Turn on, tune in, drop out.

Motto for the counter-culture *The Psychedelic Experience* sound recording by Folkways Records 66

John le Carré novelist

7107 People are very secretive—secret even from themselves.

London Observer 31 Dec 85

7108 [It is] a unique moment in history—perhaps no longer than the blink of a star—when to be a realist it is necessary also to be an idealist, when the improbable is happening every day and the impossible every week.

On *Glasnost* in US–Russian relations "Why I Came in From the Cold" *NY Times* 29 Sep 89

Harper Lee novelist

7109 Shoot all the bluejays you want, if you can hit 'em, but remember it's a sin to kill a mockingbird.

To Kill a Mockingbird Lippincott 60

Stanislaw Lem essayist

7110 Is it progress if a cannibal uses knife and fork?

Unkempt Thoughts St Martin's 62

7111 Watch out—it is not only a typographical error that can change rationalism into nationalism.

Holiday Sep 63

7112 To reach the source you have to swim against the current.

ib

7113 An apt aphorism half kills, half immortalizes.

Holiday Sep 64

7114 No snowflake in an avalanche ever feels responsible.

More Unkempt Thoughts Funk & Wagnalls 69

7115 Get out of the way of Justice. She is blind.

ib

7116 Most of the sighs we hear have been edited.

ib

Madeleine L'Engle novelist

7117 If you're going to care about the fall of the sparrow you can't pick and choose who's going to be the sparrow. It's everybody.

The Arm of the Starfish Ariel 65

7118 Yes. A good week. One can get through almost anything on the strength of one good week.

A Severed Wasp Farrar Straus Giroux 82

John Lennon musician

7119 All we are saying is, give peace a chance.

Popular protest song of the Vietnam war, recording copyright Northern Song Ltd 69

Max Lerner journalist

7120 I want to die young at an advanced age.

Washington Times 8 Jun 92

7121 I am neither an optimist nor pessimist, but a possibilist.

ib

Oscar Levant entertainer and wit

7122 Happiness isn't something you experience: it's something you remember.

Recalled on Levant's death *Time* 28 Aug 72

Margaret Lewerth novelist

7123 The truth is not always dressed for the evening.
Stuyvesant Square Dutton 87

C S Lewis essayist

7124 The greatest evil is not done in those sordid dens of evil that Dickens loved to paint. . . but is conceived and ordered (moved, seconded, carried and minuted) in clear, carpeted, warmed, well-lighted offices, by quiet men with white collars and cut fingernails and smooth-shaven cheeks who do not need to raise their voices.
Introduction to revised edition *The Screwtape Letters* Macmillan 61

7125 She's the sort of woman who lives for others—you can always tell by their haunted expression.
ib

7126 An explanation of cause is not a justification by reason.
Recalled on Lewis' death 22 Nov 63

7127 The long, dull, monotonous years of middle-aged prosperity or middle-aged adversity are excellent campaigning weather for the devil.
ib

7128 The future. . . everyone reaches at the rate of 60 minutes an hour, whatever he does, wherever he be.
ib

7129 It's so much easier to pray for a bore than to go and see one.
ib

7130 Extraordinary pride. . . [is] being exempt from temptation that you have not yet risen to the level of eunuchs boasting of their chastity!
In Kingsley Amis and Robert Conquest eds *Spectrum IV* 65

7131 I'd sooner live among people who don't cheat at cards than among people who are earnest about not cheating at cards.
ib

7132 All joy. . . emphasizes our pilgrim status; always reminds, beckons, awakens desire. Our best havings are wantings.
In W H Lewis ed *Letters of C S Lewis* Harcourt Brace World 66

7133 One can hardly say anything either bad enough or good enough about life.
ib

7134 As for wrinkles—pshaw! Why shouldn't we have wrinkles? Honorable insignia of long service in this warfare.
Letters to an American Lady Eerdmans 67

7135 Courage is not simply one of the virtues but the form of every virtue at the testing point.
Quoted by Cecil Connolly *The Unquiet Grave* Penguin 67

Beatrice Lillie actress

7136 The vows one makes privately are more binding than any ceremony or even a Shubert contract.
Every Inch a Lady 1927, recalled on Lillie's death 21 Jan 89

Anne Morrow Lindbergh essayist

7137 I observed the porcelain perfection of their smoothly ticking days.
On watching other women *Gift from the Sea* Pantheon 55

7138 If suffering alone taught, all the world would be wise, since everyone suffers.
Hour of Gold, Hour of Lead Harcourt Brace Jovanovich 73

7139 Men kick friendship around like a football, but it doesn't seem to crack. Women treat it like glass and it goes to pieces.
Locked Rooms and Open Doors Harcourt Brace Jovanovich 74

Charles A Lindbergh aviation pioneer

7140 It was a love of the air and sky and flying. . . lure of adventure. . . appreciation of beauty. . . beyond the descriptive words of men—where immortality is touched through danger, where life meets death on equal plane, where man is more than man, and existence both supreme and valueless at the same time.
On contemplating his first parachute jump *The Spirit of St. Louis* Scribner 53

7141 Life [is] a culmination of the past, an awareness of the present, an indication of a future beyond knowledge, the quality that gives a touch of divinity to matter.
"Is Civilization Progress?" *Reader's Digest* Jul 64

7142 If I had to choose, I would rather have birds than airplanes.
Recalled on Lindbergh's death 26 Aug 74

London Times

7143 London remains what it has been since its first stone was laid—a magnet for commerce and trade, a home for all races and conditions, and a mystery of extensive and peculiar tradition.
"Navel of London" editorial on the ancient "London Stone," an "umbilical milestone," a round-topped limestone pillow believed to have been an altar erected by Brutus of Troy 30 centuries ago 8 Jul 95

7144 After the Last Post and the two minutes of silence, in which even the traffic of London fell quiet, the throaty roar of the Lancaster bomber aimed as straight as a pathfinder down the Mall, recovered the lost world of 50 years ago more powerfully than words.

"Honor Due" editorial on half-century observance of the end of World War II 21 Aug 95

7145 The weekend drew the last great line under the greatest war and gave due honor to worthy pride and inconsolable grief.

ib

Barry Lopez essayist

7146 The perceptions of many people wash over the land like a flood, leaving ideas hung up in the brush, like pieces of damp paper to be collected and deciphered.

"The Country of the Mind" *Arctic Dreams* Scribner 86

Clare Boothe Luce playwright and legislator

7147 [Communism is] the opiate of the intellectuals . . . but no cure, except as a guillotine might be a cure for dandruff.

Newsweek 24 Jan 55

7148 *Courage* is the ladder on which all the other virtues mount.

Reader's Digest May 79

7149 A great man is one sentence. . . and it is always a sentence that has an active verb.

Recalled on Luce's death *Time* 19 Oct 87

7150 [Greatness means] to see, to say, to serve.

To Winston S Churchill *ib*

Henry R Luce publisher

7151 What I have most missed. . . [is] that I have never had. . . an American hometown. . . . I would give anything if I could say simply and casually, "Oskaloosa, Iowa."

On being born of missionary parents in Tengchow, China *Saturday Evening Post* 16 Jan 65

7152 Men cannot achieve wisdom by their own efforts nor goodness. Only a great event can change men—an event in their personal life, or their collective life.

Recalled on Luce's death 28 Feb 67

Russell Lynes essayist

7153 It is always well to accept your own shortcomings with candor but to regard those of your friends with polite incredulity.

Vogue 1 Sep 52

M magazine

7154 The straight arrow. . . folks who say what they mean, mean what they say, value honesty and integrity, believe not only in laws but in ethics too, and generally operate on principles, with a comfortable predictability.

"The Return of the Straight Arrow" theme of issue Aug 87

General Douglas MacArthur US Army

7155 Years may wrinkle the skin, but to give up interest wrinkles the soul.

NY Times 8 Jun 84

Shirley MacLaine actress

7156 Friendship. . . a ship on the horizon. . . and then as it moves on. . . dips out of your vision, but that doesn't mean it's not there.

Dancing in the Light Bantam 85

7157 We are not victims of the world we see. We are victims of the way we see the world.

ib

Archibald MacLeish poet and statesman

7158 You were a wonder to us, unattainable,/ a longing past the reach of longing,/ a light beyond our light, our lives/ perhaps/ a meaning to us./ Now,/ our hands have touched you in your/ depth of night.

Poem used on front page *NY Times* 21 Jul 69 following man's first moon walk, recalled by A M Rosenthal "The Moon Poem" *NY Times* 18 Jul 89

7159 To see the earth as it truly is, small and blue and beautiful in that eternal silence where it floats, is to see ourselves as riders on the earth together, brothers on that bright loveliness in the eternal cold—brothers who know now they are truly brothers.

On *Apollo 11*'s mission to the moon 25 Dec 69 *ib*

7160 It is when the human heart faces its destiny and notwithstanding sings—sings of itself, its life, its death—that poetry is possible.

On the nobility of old age, quoted by James B Reston *Deadline* Random House 91

Hugh MacLennan naturalist

7161 In the cathedral hush of a Quebec Indian summer with the lake drawing into its mirror the fire of the maples, it came to me that to be able to love the mystery surrounding us is the final and only sanction of human existence.

The Watch That Ends the Night Scribner 61

Harold Macmillan Prime Minister of Britain

7162 He was in one of those moods, preparatory to some creative effort, when the artist is anxious, nervous, dissatisfied with himself, and everyone else—a good sign on the whole.

On Winston S Churchill's address in 1950 to Consultative Assembly of European Nations *Tides of Fortune* Macmillan 69

Melvin Maddocks essayist

7163 Gossip is a misanthrope's documentary—life seen meanly through the keyhole of a third-rate hotel as if this were all there is.

"The Latest Inside Word on Gossip" *Christian Science Monitor* 10 Jun 87

7164 Gossip's first cousin, anthropology.

ib

Thomas Mallon anthologist

7165 We are all convinced of our own uniqueness, and all conscious of our own impermanence; the impulse to keep a diary begins at the point where the two forms of awareness intersect.

A Book of One's Own Ticknor & Fields 84

André Malraux novelist and critic

7166 Each man experiences deep within him the presence of destiny. . . [and] experiences—and almost always tragically, at least for certain moments—the world's indifference vis-a-vis himself.

The Walnut Trees of Altenburg J Lehmann, London 52

7167 The greatest mystery is not that we have been flung at random between the profusion of the earth and the galaxy of the stars, but that in this prison we can fashion images of ourselves, sufficiently powerful to deny our nothingness.

ib

Alberto Manguel essayist

7168 Because reading is a lonely vice, we frequently bring others into our reading. . . nudge them to listen, share our delight or disgust, judge our selection. Every reader is an anthologist who breeds readers.

"Sweet Are the Uses of Anthology" *NY Times* 23 Aug 87

Beryl Markham aviator and essayist

7169 When you can experience a physical loneliness for the tools of your trade, you see that the other things—experiments, irrelevant vocations, vanities you used to hold—were false.

Recalled on Markham's death 3 Aug 86

Douglas Martin reporter

7170 It spins around and around like an endless summer day, its 57 brightly painted horses snorting and gallopping toward the butterscotch heart of childhood.

On Central Park's carousel *NY Times* 13 Jul 91

7171 [It] sings of cotton candy. . . and daydreams. It is impossible not to smile on a carousel.

ib

John Masefield poet

7172 I wonder whether you ever think of the place of friendship in life; what determines it; what it is; what it has of destiny; what it is of design; what of momentary nearness, and passing mood; what of eternity.

Letter to Audrey Napier-Smith, D J Enright and David Rawlinson eds *The Oxford Book of Friendship* Oxford 91

7173 I have seen flowers come in stony places/ And kind things done by men with ugly faces,/ And the gold cup won by the worst horse at the races,/ So I trust too.

Lines from Masefield's 1926 novel *Odtaa*, quoted by David Vansittart on finding no epitaph on Masefield's stone in Westminster Abbey *In the Fifties* John Murray 95

Carol Matthau essayist

7174 We are not here to see through one another. We are here to see one another through.

Among the Porcupines Random House 92

William Maxwell novelist

7175 What is lacking is someone, anyone, of the older generation to whom you can turn. . . about some detail of the landscape of the past. There is no longer any older generation. You have become it, while your mind was mostly on other matters.

On turning 70 *Billie Dyer and Other Stories* Knopf 92

Mary McCarthy novelist

7176 Understanding is often a prelude to forgiveness, but they are not the same, and we often forgive what we cannot understand (seeing nothing else to do) and understand what we cannot pardon.

The Writing on the Wall and Other Literary Essays Harcourt Brace Jovanovich 85

Carson McCullers playwright

7177 She was afraid of all the Freaks, for it seemed to her that they had looked at her in a secret way and tried to connect their eyes with hers, as though to say, "We know you."

On a circus sideshow *The Member of the Wedding 1946*, Broadway play 50

Robert S McNamara economist and statesman

7178 Humanity must step up and take charge of its destiny.

On the threat of an over-populated world in which humankind declines, quoted by Deborah Shapley *Power and Promise* Little, Brown 93

Margaret Mead anthropologist

7179 Leisure does not automatically develop the soul. And this is a real dilemma of Americans.
Life 23 Aug 68

7180 The best way to learn is to learn from the best.
Blackberry Winter Morrow 72

7181 Never doubt that a small group of thoughtful committed citizens can change the world. Indeed, it's the only thing that ever has.
Utne Reader Mar/Apr 91

H L Mencken essayist

7182 It is the fate of man, I believe, to be wholly happy only once in his life.
Quoted by Fred Hobson *Mencken: A Life* Random House 94

7183 Of all escape mechanisms, death is the most efficient.
ib

Gian Carlo Menotti composer

7184 When I see darkness coming, I turn on the stage lights and don't worry about the cost of electricity.
On approaching the age of 70 *Time* 6 Jun 77

Melina Mercouri actress

7185 All any woman wants is to sleep with a man. It is simple. Life is simple.
NY Times 7 Mar 94

Thomas Merton Trappist monk

7186 When I reveal most I hide most.
Quoted by Donald L Miller in frontispiece of *Lewis Mumford* Weidenfeld & Nicolson 89

Harry Middleton essayist

7187 Mountains are the scribblings of time on the surface of the land.
On the Spine of Time Simon & Schuster 91

John T Miles Chaplain to First Family

7188 She was like a rubber ball. The harder life put her down, the higher she bounced.
Eulogy for President Clinton's mother, Virginia Kelley, *NY Times* 9 Jan 94

James M Minifie essayist

7189 History does not repeat itself; historians do.
Expatriate McClelland & Stewart 76

John Moore linguist

7190 Slang is a token of man's lively spirit ever at work in unexpected places.
Your English Words Lippencott 62

7191 Slang. . . is a kind of metaphor and metaphor, we have agreed, is a kind of poetry; you might say indeed that slang is a poor man's poetry.
ib

7192 Scientists will have rifled the secrets of the moon and of Mars long before they will know the secret and subtle workings of the myriad-minded force which shapes the course of the language.
ib

Olive Moore novelist

7193 Hatred is a passion requiring one hundred times the energy of love. Keep it for a cause, not an individual.
Collected Writings Dalkey Archive 92

Ted Morgan essayist

7194 The man has flair, and New Yorkers will forgive anything if you have flair.
On Manhattan realtor Donald J Trump *NY Times* 1 Jan 89

Robin Morgan feminist

7195 Only she who attempts the absurd can achieve the impossible.
Sisterhood is Global Doubleday 84

Toni Morrison novelist

7196 There is a loneliness that can be rocked. Arms crossed, knees drawn up. . . . It's an inside kind—wrapped tight like skin.
Beloved Knopf 87

7197 Then there is a loneliness that roams. No rocking can hold it down. It is alive, on its own. A dry and spreading thing that makes the sound of one's own feet going seem to come from a far-off place.
ib

Lance Morrow essayist

7198 Reading restores to the mind a stabilization of linear prose, a bit of the architecture of thought.
"The Best Refuge for Insomniacs" *Time* 29 Apr 91

7199 The contemplation of anything intelligent. . . helps the mind through the black hours. . . music like bright ice water. . . the memory of the serene Palladian lines of Jefferson's Monticello. These things realign the mind and teach it not to be petty.
ib

Anna Mary Robertson Moses
Grandma Moses

7200 I look back on my life like a good day's work, it was done and I am satisfied with it. I was happy and contented. . . knew nothing better and made the best out of what life offered. And life is what we make it, always has been, always will be.

My Life's History Harper 51

7201 What a strange thing is memory, and hope; one looks backward, the other forward. The one is today, the other is tomorrow.

ib

Malcolm Muggeridge essayist

7202 Human life in all its public or collective manifestations is only theater, and mostly cheap melodrama at that.

Guardian Weekly 25 Nov 90

Lewis Mumford critic

7203 One of the functions of intelligence is to take account of the dangers that come from trusting solely to the intelligence.

The Transformations of Man Harper 56

7204 I'm a pessimist about probabilities. . . an optimist about possibilities. Life contains both and if you don't see that there are tragic and irreparable elements in life, you're unable to understand the course of human development.

NY Times 6 Jul 77

Vladimir Nabokov novelist

7205 What counts in life is not the events that surround one but the reflection of those events in one's consciousness.

Novel With Cocaine written under the pseudonym M Ageyev Dutton 84

7206 All of a man's life—work, deeds, will, physical and mental prowess—is completely and utterly devoted to, fixed on bringing about one or another event in the external world, though not so much to experience the event in itself as to experience the reflection of the event on his consciousness.

ib

Shiva Naipaul essayist

7207 Life is like an ice cube. We, too, melt as we grow old.

An Unfinished Journey Viking 87

N Richard Nash screenwriter

7208 There are other dreams, Starbuck, little quiet ones that come to a woman when she's shining the silverware or putting mothflakes in the closet.

Lines for Katharine Hepburn in *The Rainmaker* Paramount 56

National Geographic Society

7209 Our first grand discovery was time. It abides in every niche of nature. . . traces the growing rings of trees and dwells in rocks that layer the earth. . . blossoms with every flower and butterfly, paces every heartbeat, and resounds in every tick of a clock.

Exhibition on the theme of Time, Washington, DC 92

7210 Humans have devoted more attention to measuring time than anything else in nature. Time flies. . . we kill time, waste time, lose time. Some of us make the big time. Some go to jail to do time.

ib

Richard J Needham essayist

7211 Laughter would seem a pleasant way to begin a man–woman relationship; a good way to maintain it; and the only way to conclude it.

Toronto Globe & Mail 17 Nov 80

Peter C Newman essayist

7212 When a nation's elite is less than three generations removed from steerage, it cannot afford too many pretentions.

Debrett's Illustrated Guide to the Canadian Establishment Metheun 83

New Yorker magazine

7213 The city is our lives together, what we have to offer each other, the offering and receiving that become at times almost indistinguishable, and amount to a third reality.

15 Mar 82

7214 The city is ambition and hubbub, buying and selling, greed and haste, but the real stuff of the city, that which makes it alive rather than dead, civilized rather than barbarous, a place of nourishment rather than of deprivation, is this third reality—the reality that comes of offering and receiving.

ib

The New York Times

7215 Fear and ignorance about AIDs can so weaken people's senses as to make them susceptible to an equally virulent threat: bigotry.

"AIDS and the New Apartheid" 7 Oct 85

7216 People addressed as Mrs, Mr, Miss and Ms are given a little fence, the gate to which they can open if they choose.

"Yo, Mary, Hey, Dave!" editorial on "America's reason for turning surnames, complete with Mrs, Mr, Ms, or Miss into artifacts rare as runningboards" 3 Jul 88

7217 Being invited to call them by their first name is a lot like being invited into the front yard.

ib

7218 Another deal of the cards, another roll of the dice, another pull on the one-armed bandit. And this year, maybe, the jackpot.

"365 Clean Pages" editorial 1 Jan 91

Harold Nicolson essayist

7219 Only one person in a thousand is a bore and he is interesting because he is one person in a thousand.

NY Times 2 May 68

7220 Williamstown is a small place and is very remote, and you will need someone within two hours' driving distance to whom you can say the first thing that comes into your head with no risk of being misunderstood.

To John Pope-Hennessy on his appointment to teach at Williams College, quoted by Pope-Hennessy *Learning to Look* Doubleday 91

Richard M Nixon 37th US President

7221 What starts the process really are laughs and slights and snubs when you are a kid. . . . But if you are reasonably intelligent and if your anger is deep enough and strong enough, you learn that you can change those attitudes by excellence, personal gut performance, while those who have everything are sitting on their fat butts.

Quoted by Tom Wicker *One Of Us* Random House 91

Dr Sherwin B Nuland Professor of Surgery, Yale

7222 Far from being irreplaceable, we should be replaced. Fantasies of staying the hand of mortality are incompatible with the best interests of our species and the continuity of humankind's progress.

How We Die Knopf 94

7223 The greatest dignity to be found in death is the dignity of the life that preceded it. Hope resides in the meaning of what our lives have been.

ib

Sean O'Casey playwright

7224 It's my rule never to lose me temper till it would be detrimental to keep it.

The Plough and the Stars play 1926, recalled on O'Casey death 18 Sep 64

7225 The secret of happiness is to find a congenial monotony.

NY Times 24 Apr 82

Flannery O'Connor novelist

7226 There is no quicker way to get out of a job than to prescribe it for those who have prescribed it for you.

On failing to escape writing a book *A Memoir of Mary Ann* Farrar Straus Cudahy 61

Clifford Odets novelist and screenwriter

7227 It's not what you are but what you don't become that hurts.

Lines for Oscar Levant in 1946 film *Humoresque*, quoted by Sam Kashner and Nancy Shoenbergs in frontispiece for Levant biography *A Talent for Genius* Villard 94

Sean O'Faolain essayist

7228 Imagination is a soaring gull, and opinions no more than a gaggle of ungainly starlings chattering angrily in a cornfield.

Quoted by Peter Vansittart *In the Fifties* John Murray 95

7229 Opinions breed anger, nourish hate, ossify the heart, narrow the mind.

ib

Aristotle Onassis shipping magnate

7230 If women didn't exist, all the money in the world would have no meaning.

Quoted by columnist Liz Smith *Baltimore Sun* 4 Apr 91

Jacqueline Kennedy Onassis First Lady

7231 After going through a rather difficult time, I consider myself comparatively sane. I'm proud of that.

To poet Stephen Spender who asked what she considered her greatest achievement *Time* 30 May 94

Yoko Ono musician

7232 Keep your intentions in a clear bottle and leave it on a shelf when you rap.

Chicago Tribune 25 Jun 78

Domingo Ortega poet

7233 Bullfight critics ranked in rows/ Crowd the enormous Plaza full;/ But only one is there who knows—/ And he's the man who fights the bull.

Bullfighter's poem frequently quoted by President Kennedy, cited by Theodore C Sorensen *Kennedy* Harper & Row 65

George Orwell novelist

7234 Doublethink means the power of holding two contradictory beliefs in one's mind simultaneously and accepting both of them.

1984 New Directions 74

7235 Human beings want to be good, but not too good, and not quite all the time.

Quoted by Michael Shelden *Orwell* HarperCollins 91

7236 In the metabolism of the Western world, the coal-miner is second in importance only to the man who ploughs the soil . . . a grimy caryatid upon whose shoulders nearly everything that is not grimy is supported.

Recalled by Tony Horwitz reporting on the closing of British mines *Wall Street Journal* 22 Dec 92

Dorothy Parker critic

7237 They sicken of the calm, who knew the storm.

Fair Weather 1928, recalled on Parker's death 7 Jun 67

7238 Sorrow is tranquility remembered in emotion.

Here Lies 1939 *ib*

C Northcote Parkinson essayist

7239 If there is one invention that has influenced freedom. . . it is the clock, the chiming hour and the pocket watch.

NY Law Journal 19 Dec 63

7240 The chief product of a highly automated society is a widespread and deepening sense of boredom.

NY Times 25 Sep 87

7241 [A committee] grows organically, flourishes and blossoms, sunlit on top and shady beneath, until it dies, scattering the seeds from which other committees will spring.

12 Mar 93

Boris Pasternak novelist

7242 All great, genuine art resembles and continues the Revelation of St John.

Dr Zhivago Pantheon 58

7243 Reality, like a neglected daughter, ran off half-dressed and presented legitimate history with the challenge of herself just as she was—from head to toe illegitimate and dowryless.

On the Russian revolution, unpublished letter *NY Times* 1 Jan 78

Gary Paulsen essayist

7244 In farming, all the luck in the world has to come every year.

Clabbered Dirt, Sweet Grass Harcourt Brace Jovanovich 92

Saint-John Perse (Alexis Saint-Léger Léger) essayist

7245 Life is beautiful as a ram's head painted red and nailed over a doorway.

Epigraph to Tennessee Williams' play *The Rose Tattoo* quoted by Williams *Memoirs* Doubleday 75

Eden Phillpotts essayist

7246 The universe is full of magical things, patiently waiting for our wits to grow sharper.

Paul Quinnett ed *Pavlov's Trout* Keeokee 94

Pablo Picasso painter

7247 You are wrong not to be married. It's useful.

Last words before dying, addressed to his doctor, quoted by Arianna S Huffington *Picasso* Simon & Schuster 88

Robert T Pirsig novelist

7248 We keep passing unseen through little moments of other people's lives.

Zen and the Art of Motorcycle Maintenance Morrow 74

David Plout critic

7249 Deathbed utterances, like suicide notes, are a powerful coinage stamped by an awareness that words can outlive us.

Quoted by J M Coetzee *Age of Iron* Random House 90

Ezra Pound poet and critic

7250 One of the pleasures of middle age is to find out that one was right, and that one was much righter than one knew at say 17 or 28.

ABC of Reading New Directions 60

7251 Any general statement is like a check drawn on a bank. Its value depends on what is there to meet it.

ib

7252 And the days are not full enough/ And the nights are not full enough,/ And life slips by like a field-mouse/ Not shaking the grass.

Lustra 1916, recalled on Pound's death 1 Nov 72

Anthony Powell essayist

7253 One of the worst things about life is not how nasty the people are. . . it is how nasty nice people can be.

A Dance to the Music of Time Scribner 51

7254 Growing old is like being increasingly penalized for a crime you haven't committed.

ib

V S Pritchett essayist

7255 We do not wish to be better than we are, but more fully what we are.

The Living Novel and Later Appreciations Random House 64

7256 We live by our genius for hope; we survive by our talent for dispensing with it.

ib

7257 Art, you know, deals with that side of people's lives where they are not aware of what they are taking in. . . of the judgments they are making.
Sunday Times London 10 Jul 88

William Proxmire US Senator

7258 Sunrise remains the world's best disinfectant.
NY Times 9 Sep 77

Anna Quindlen columnist

7259 Putting Up a Good Front. . . is a way of life. . . serene, good-humored and pleasant. So, too, are refrigerators, until you open the Tupperware.
NY Times 16 Dec 87

7260 Figuring out who you are is the whole point of the human experience.
ib 6 Sept 92

Howell Raines sportswriter

7261 Fly-fishing is to fishing as ballet is to walking.
Fly-fishing Through the Midlife Crisis Morrow 93

Ayn Rand novelist

7262 When there's sacrifice, there's someone collecting sacrificial offerings. Where there is service, there is someone being served.
Recalled on Rand's death 6 Mar 82

7263 The man who speaks to you of sacrifices speaks of slaves.
ib

Diane Rehm commentator

7264 "Never" and "always" are the two most inflammable words in human relationships.
Station WAMU Washington 6 Jul 93

Casey Robinson screenwriter

7265 Don't let's ask for the moon. We have the stars.
On coping with loneliness *Now Voyager* 1942 screenplay for Bette Davis recalled on Davis's death *Time* 16 Oct 89

John D Rockefeller Jr philanthropist

7266 Often a man gets into a situation where there's just one thing to do. . . so he goes ahead on the only course that's open and people call it courage.
Quoted by Peter Collier and David Horowitz *The Rockefellers* Holt Rinehart Winston 76

Andy Rooney commentator

7267 We're all proud of making little mistakes. It gives us the feeling we don't make any big ones.
Not That You Asked Random House 90

Eleanor Roosevelt First Lady

7268 Friendship with oneself is all important, because without it one cannot be friends with anyone else in the world.
Recalled on Mrs Roosevelt's death 7 Nov 62

Roger Rosenblatt essayist

7269 A dog's eyes search your face for a mystery as deep as God, asking nothing and everything the way that music operates.
Time 29 Jun 87

7270 The past is always dozing in the ice, waiting to alter the present.
US News & World Report 24 Oct 88

7271 Old ladies, I have believed all my life, are the highest form of human being on earth, the strongest, the most articulate, the top of the line.
Life Nov 90

Jean Rostand essayist

7272 A married couple are well suited when both partners usually feel the need for a quarrel at the same time.
Maxims for Marriage Hachette 64

Jane Rule feminist

7273 I may have to go on calling myself a lesbian into great old age, not because it is any longer true but because it takes such a long time to make a simple point that I have the right to be.
A Hot-Eye Moderate Naiad 85

Salman Rushdie novelist

7274 Our lives teach us who we are.
NY Times 12 Dec 91

Bertrand Russell philosopher

7275 Mathematics, rightly viewed, possesses not only truth but supreme beauty—a beauty cold and austere, like that of sculpture, without appeal to any part of our weaker nature, without gorgeous trappings of painting or music, yet sublimely pure, and capable of a stern perfection such as only the greatest art can show.
The Study of Mathematics 1902, recalled on Russell's death 2 Feb 70

7276 To know people well is to know their tragedy; it is usually the central thing about which their lives are built.
The Autobiography of Bertrand Russell 1914–72 Atlantic-Little, Brown 67

7277 Mathematics takes us still further from what is human, into the region of absolute necessity, to which not only the actual world, but every possible world, must conform.

ib

7278 The infliction of cruelty with a good conscience is a delight to moralists. That is why they invented Hell.

Skeptical Essays 1928 *ib*

7279 Next to enjoying ourselves, the next greatest pleasure consists in preventing others from enjoying themselves, or, more generally, in the acquisition of power.

ib

7280 Boredom is. . . a vital problem for the moralist, since half the sins of mankind are caused by the fear of it.

The Conquest of Happiness 1930 *ib*; also see *Life* 13 Feb 70

7281 One should as a rule respect public opinion insofar as is necessary to avoid starvation and to keep out of prison, but anything that goes beyond this is voluntary submission to an unnecesary tyranny.

ib

7282 Work is. . . altering the position of matter at or near the earth's surface relative to other such matter. . . [or] telling other people to do so. The first kind is unpleasant and ill paid; the second is pleasant and highly paid.

In Praise of Idleness and Other Essays Unwin Hyman 81

William Safire columnist

7283 A sense of duty is moral glue, constantly subject to stress.

On the abdication of Edward VIII *NY Times* 23 May 86

Carl Sandburg poet

7284 Acquaintance with death, sir/ comes by ice and is slow, sir/ comes by fire and is fast, sir/ comes by the creep of clock hands/ comes by the crash of split-seconds.

"Acquaintance With Death, Sir" *Collier's* 7 Dec 56

7285 Always a silence and content/ or evening bronze shadows/ and blue fog beyond fathoming/ goes with the unforgotten.

ib

7286 Not often in the story of mankind does a man arrive on earth who is both steel and velvet. . . as hard as rock and soft as drifting fog, who holds in his heart and mind the paradox of terrible storm and peace unspeakable and perfect.

Beginning address to joint session of Congress on 150th anniversary of birth of Abraham Lincoln 15 Feb 59

7287 Always the path of American destiny has been into the unknown. Always there arose enough of reserves of strength, balances of sanity, portions or wisdom to carry the nation through to a fresh start with ever-renewing vitality.

On 96th anniversary of Lincoln's Gettysburg address *NY Times* 20 Nov 59

7288 Birth is the starting point of passion,/ Passion is the beginning of death,/ How can you turn your back from birth?/ How can you say no to passion?/ How can you bid death hold off?/ And if thoughts come and hold you/ And dreams step in and shake your bones/ What can you do but take them and make them/ more your own?

"Fog Numbers" *Honey and Salt* Harcourt Brace Jovanovich 63

7289 Death comes once, let it be easy/ Ring one bell for me once, let it go at that./ Or ring no bell at all, better yet./ Sing one song if I die/ Sing *John Brown's Body* or *Shout All Over God's Heaven*./ Death comes once, let it be easy.

"Finish" *ib*

7290 The past is a bucket of ashes.

"Prairie" 1918 *The Complete Poems of Carl Sandburg* Harcourt Brace Jovanovich

7291 Study the wilderness under your hat and say little or nothing of how you are not unaccustomed to throne.

On being "a child of the wilderness" *Breathing Tokens* Harcourt Brace Jovanovich 78

7292 Write on the tomb of the mule, on the one vast historic repository containing all that remains of the mule these words: I builded railroads and I fought wars and I changed the land from a broken wilderness to a country filled with cities and crossed with rails; hitched to the iron scoops and shovels I dug the paths of civilization or whatever you call the thing you now have: now vast mules of steel, snorting steam and eating coal take my place; they obey more and they love less than I did the human hands that feed them.

"Mule" *ib*

7293 To see a fool you lock yourself in your room and smash the looking-glass.

Quoted by Stuart Berg Flexner *Listening to America* Simon & Schuster 82

7294 Out of the silent working of his inner life came forces no one outside himself could know, they were his secret, his personality and purpose; beside which all other facts of his comings and goings were insignificant.

On Abraham Lincoln, quoted by Penelope Niven on flypage of *Carl Sandburg* Scribner's 91

7295 Take up your cross and go the thorn way. If a sponge of vinegar is passed you on the end of a spear, take that too. Souls are woven of endurance.

Writing in his notebook while a traveling salesman in 1902 *ib*

7296 He has more ropes and tears in him than any other human clay pot I know of.
On Lincoln *ib*

7297 Only those who come to live with loneliness can come to know themselves and life. I go out there and walk and look at the trees and sky. I listen to the sounds of loneliness. I sit on a rock or a stump and say to myself, "who are you, Sandburg? Where have you been, and where are you going?"
To journalist Ralph McGill *ib*

7298 Before you go to sleep at night you say, "I haven't got it yet, I haven't got it yet."
On being asked by a reporter to identify the principal end in life *ib*

7299 When you're over 70, a day is an awful lot of time.
At 78 *ib*

7300 I have no strong will but I long ago decided that a deep enough desire, a big enough wanting, is better than the most boasted strong will.
ib

7301 Hope is an echo. Hope ties itself yonder, yonder.
Quoted by Charles Kuralt Sunday Morning CBS TV 20 Sep 92

George Santayana philosopher

7302 Friendship is almost always the union of a part of one mind with a part of another: People are friends in spots.
Recalled on Santayana's death 26 Sep 52

7303 There are books in which the footnotes or comments scrawled by some reader's hand in the margin are the more interesting than the text. The world is one of these books.
ib

7304 That life is worth living is the most necessary of assumptions, and, were it not assumed, the most impossible of conclusions.
The Life of Reason 1906 *ib*

7305 Fanaticism consists in redoubling your efforts when you have forgotten your aim.
ib

7306 Those who cannot remember the past are condemned to repeat it.
ib

7307 Perhaps the only true dignity of man is his capacity to despise himself.
The Ethics of Spinoza 1910 *ib*

7308 There is no cure for birth and death save to enjoy the interval.
Soliloquies in England 1922 *ib*

7309 Skepticism is the chastity of the intellect.
Skepticism and Animal Faith 1923 *ib*

7310 The young man who has not wept is a savage, and the old man who will not laugh is a fool.
Dialogues in Limbo 1926 *ib*

7311 The highest form of vanity is love of fame.
ib

7312 It is a great advantage for a system of philosophy to be substantially true.
The Unknowing from *Obiter Scripta* 1936 *ib*

7313 The trembling harmonies of field and cloud,/ Of flesh and spirit was my worship vowed./ Let form, let music, let all-quickening air/ Fulfill in beauty my imperfect prayer.
Last stanza of five verses of *The Poet's Testament* found among Santanya's papers and read at his funeral *Time* 27 Oct 52

Helen Hooven Santmyer novelist

7314 [Time was] an accordian, all the air squeezed out of it as you grew older.
. . . *And Ladies of the Club* Putnam 84, quoted in *Time* 9 Jul 84

William Saroyan novelist

7315 The greatest happiness that you can have is knowing that you do not necessarily require happiness.
New summaries 16 Dec 57

7316 Good people are good because they've come to wisdom through failure. We get very little wisdom from success, you know.
NY *Journal-American* 23 Aug 61

7317 Everybody has got to die, but I always believed an exception would be made in my case. Now what?
Telephone call to the Associated Press a few hours before his death 13 May 91

May Sarton novelist

7318 One must think like a hero to behave like a merely decent human being.
Quoted by Richard Locke *Wall Street Journal* 30 May 89 reviewing John le Carré's *The Russian House* Knopf 89

7319 It is only when we lose the connection between ourselves and other people that we begin to freeze up into despair. That connection has to be kept open whatever happens. . . by letters, by unexpected encounters, or by simply contemplating the points of light here or there.
Winter Thoughts 1982 recalled on Sarton's death *NY Times* 18 Jul 95

7320 Solitude is the salt of personhood. It brings out the authentic flavor of every experience.
Rewards of a Solitary Life 1990 *ib*

Jean-Paul Sartre philosopher

7321 Man can will nothing unless he first understands that he must count on no one but himself; that he is alone, abandoned on earth in the midst of his responsibilities, without help, with no other aim than the one he sets himself, with no destiny than the one he forges for himself on this earth.

On existentialism *Being and Nothingness* Philosophical Library, recalled on Sartre's rejection of the Nobel Prize for Literature *NY Times* 23 Oct 64

7322 When anyone speaks to me about Him today, I say, with the easy amusement of an old beau who meets a former belle, "Fifty years ago, had it not been for that misunderstanding, that mistake, the accident that separated us, there might have been something between us."

On abandoning belief in God *The Words* Braziller 64

7323 Like all dreamers, I mistook disenchantment for truth.

Les Mots Penguin 64

7324 [I want] to rid the passing moments of their fat, to twist them, dry them, purify myself, to give back at last, the sharp, precise sound of a saxophone note.

Nausea Penguin 65

7325 Hell is other people.

No Exit 1944 recalled on Sartre's death 15 Apr 80

7326 I think of death only with tranquility, as an end.

ib

7327 I refuse to let death hamper life. Death must enter life only to define it.

ib

7328 Freedom is what you do with what's been done to you.

ib

Thomas Savage essayist

7329 Cosmic upheaval is not so moving as a little child pondering the death of a sparrow in the corner of a barn.

Her Side of It Little, Brown 81

Francis B Sayre Dean, Washington Cathedral

7330 He had the courage to fail.

At memorial service for Adlai E Stevenson, quoted by James B Reston *Deadline* Random House 91

Dore Schary film producer

7331 The true portrait of a man is a fusion of what he thinks he is, what others think he is, what he really is and what he tries to be.

Heyday Little, Brown 80

Nancy Scheibner poet

7332 And you and I must be free. . . / not to kill ourselves with a nameless gnawing pain/ but to practice with all the skill of our being/ the art of making possible.

Poem written for her classmate, Hillary Rodham, used to conclude the future First Lady's address to 1969 Wellesley College commencement *Vanity Fair* June 93

Diana Jean Schemo reporter

7333 Their spidery red lines seem a map of grief's back roads.

On the eyes of the fire chief of Little Falls NY where six children died in a house fire *NY Times* 26 Dec 91

Richard Schickel critic

7334 The law of unintended consequences pushes us ceaselessly through the years, permitting no pause for perspective.

Time 28 Nov 83

Raymond A Schroth biographer

7335 To grow up in a North Dakota town, it seems, is an experience so radical—in the original meaning of that word, "root"—that it is more than a clue to the character of anyone who has survived.

The American Journey of Eric Sevareid Steerforth Press 95

Maurice Schumann French foreign minister

7336 The only lecture by Madam Curie that I was privleged to attend, even though I was incapable of comprehending it, extended my horizon forever after.

On being asked to name "the ten brains that gave the greatest amount of light during the first half of the 20th century," quoted by Janet Flanner *Paris Journal 1944–1965* Atheneum 65

7337 The men of my generation are essentially "survivalists," a fact that condemns them to tragedy but confers upon them a singular dignity.

ib

Jonathan Schwartz disc-jockey and novelist

7338 Most of us are only tuned in to distant stations where all kinds of things are happening to other people. We listen through the static to their heartbreaks as if we were in some well-protected receiving chamber.

Distant Stations Doubleday 79

7339 We are distant stations for anyone else who comes across our transmissions through our static. It's all one network; we're affiliates of the same conglomerate.

ib

7340 What about the fatty tissues of the soul? . . . What thoughts do I cut down on? What ideas should occur to me no more than twice a week?

ib

Martin Scorsese film director

7341 Suffering is a thing that people have to go through to be redeemed in life.

LA Times 10 Nov 91

Albert Schweitzer medical missionary

7342 At sunset... four hippopotamuses and their young, plodded along in our direction. Just then, in my great tiredness and discouragement, the phrase "Reverence for Life" struck me like a flash.

Recalling a 1915 African journey that provided his lifelong philosophy *World Book Encyclopedia* supplement 64

7343 "Reverence for Life" means my answering your kind queries; it also means your reverence for my dinner hour.

To a group of tourists, recalled on Schweitzer's death 4 Sep 65

7344 Example is not the main thing in influencing others. It is the only thing.

ib

7345 An optimist is a person who sees a green light everywhere, while the pessimist sees only the red stoplight. . . . The truly wise person is colorblind.

ib

7346 Reverence for life is the highest court of appeal.

ib

7347 The tragedy of life is what dies inside a man while he lives.

ib

7348 Hear our prayer, O Lord... for animals that are overworked, underfed and cruelly treated; for all wistful creatures in captivity that beat their wings against bars; for any that are hunted or lost or deserted or frightened or hungry; for all that must be put to death... and for those who deal with them we ask a heart of compassion and gentle hands and kindly words.

Prayer for animals *ib*

7349 I cannot grasp or understand the possibility that I have exerted an influence in our time. It haunts me like a secret on the final stretch of my life.

To Albert Einstein 20 Feb 55, quoted by Martine E Marty *NY Times* 27 Sep 92 reviewing Hans Walter Bohr ed *Letters, 1905–1965* Macmillan 92

Charles Scribner Jr publisher

7350 Reading is a means of thinking with another person's mind: it forces you to stretch your own.

Publisher's Weekly 30 Mar 84

Richard Selzer physician and author

7351 The gardens of my heart are not found in the country, nor even in small towns and villages. It is in great cities that the oasis of the spirit lie, in cities, bridged and tunneled, and with pavement planted.

Letters to a Young Doctor Simon & Schuster 82

Richard Sennett critic

7352 Authority... is itself inherently an act of imagination.

Authority Random House 80 *Newsweek* 5 May 80

Eric Sevareid commentator

7353 It is doubtful if this nation has ever before gone into officially proclaimed mourning... over the death of a private citizen, and this man the descendant of slaves. This is not the realization of a sick society but of a fundamentally healthy society trying desperately to cleanse itself of the one chronic, persistent poison in its body.

On riots following assassination of Martin Luther King Jr CBS TV 5 Apr 68

7354 The label on his life must not be a long day's journey into night. It must be a long night's journey into day.

ib

7355 The chief source of problems is solutions.

Reader's Digest Mar 74

7356 Man brings the laws of his own nature into space... [hence] the problem does not lie in outer space, but where it's always been: on terra firma in inner man.

On the death of rocket scientist Werner von Braun CBS TV 17 Jun 77

Peter Shaffer essayist

7357 Everything we feel is made of Time. All the beauties of life are shaped by it.

The Royal Hunt of the Sun Stein & Day 65

Ben Shahn painter

7358 Fame is like a smudge on your nose. You can't see it. Other people can.

Christian Science Monitor 11 Nov 72

George Bernard Shaw playwright

7359 The reasonable man adapts himself to the world; the unreasonable one persists in trying to adapt the world to himself. Therefore all progress depends on the unreasonable man.

Recalled on his death 1 Nov 50

7360 The world's best reformers are those who begin on themselves.

ib

7361 Don't trouble about it being the right side—the north is no righter than the south—but be sure it is really yours, and then back it for all you are worth.

Collected Letters Dan Laurence ed Dodd, Mead 65

7362 Never stagnate. Life is a constant becoming: all stages lead to the beginning of others.

ib

7363 The true joy of life [is] being used for a purpose recognized by yourself as a mighty one... being thoroughly worn out before you are thrown to the scrap heap... being a force of nature instead of a feverish, selfish clod of ailments and grievances.

ib

7364 You see things; and you say "Why?" But I dream things that never were, and I say "Why not?"

From his play *Back to Methuselah* recalled on Shaw's death 1 Nov 50; presidential campaign of Robert F Kennedy and quoted in funeral eulogy by his brother, Edward *NY Times* 9 Jun 68

7365 A perpetual holiday is a good working definition of hell.

Quoted by Charles Krauthammer *Time* 27 Aug 84

7366 We ought to have declared war on Germany the moment Mr Hitler's police stole Einstein's violin.

Quoted by Claude Rawson *NY Times* 20 Oct 91 reviewing Michael Holyroyd's *Bernard Shaw* Vol III Random House 91

7367 People are always blaming their circumstances for what they are... [but] the people who get on in this world are the people who get up and look for the circumstances they want, and, if they can't find them, make them.

Quoted by Danny Cox and John Hoover *Seize the Day* Career Press 94

Lord Shawcross (Hartley William Shawcross) Chief Prosecutor, Nuremburg War Criminal Trials

7368 The so-called new morality is too often the old morality condoned.

London *Observer* 17 Nov 63

Fulton J Sheen Auxillary Bishop of NY

7369 Jealousy is the tribute mediocrity pays to genius.

Quoted by Daniel P Noonan *The Passion of Fulton Sheen* Dodd, Mead 72

Gail Sheehy essayist

7370 Will your personal life story in Second Adulthood be conceived as a progress story or a decline story?

Quoted by Janet Maslin *NY Times* 18 Jul 95 reviewing Sheehy's *New Passages: Mapping Your Life Across Time* Random House 95

Carol Shields novelist

7371 There are chapters in every life which are seldom read.

The Stone Diaries Viking 94

Earl Shorris essayist

7372 The lion need not attack to differentiate itself from the lamb; the possibility of the lamb is sufficient.

Power Sits at Another Table Fireside 86

7373 Cities protect one's sense of power because they protect the ego from the vast scale of nature.

ib

Igor Sikorsky aviation engineer

7374 The work of the individual still remains the spark that moves mankind ahead even more than teamwork.

Recalled on Sikorsky's death *NY Times* 27 Oct 72

Beverely Sills opera singer

7375 A happy person is someone who has no cares; a cheerful one who has cares but is cheerful anyway.

NBC TV 13 Jan 77

Alistair Sim actor

7376 It was revealed to me many years ago with conclusive certainty that I was a fool and that I had always been a fool. Since then I have been as happy as any man has a right to be.

Time 30 Aug 76

Georges Simenon novelist

7377 I adore life but I don't fear death. I just prefer to die as late as possible.

International Herald Tribune 26 Nov 81

Isaac Bashevis Singer novelist

7378 The analysis of character is the highest human entertainment.

NY Times 26 Nov 78

7379 Whey you betray somebody else, you also betray yourself.

ib

7380 Our knowledge is a little island in the great ocean of nonknowledge.

ib 3 Dec 78

Edith Sitwell poet

7381 The aim of flattery is to soothe and encourage us by assuring us of the truth of an opinion we have already formed about ourselves.

Quoted by Elizabeth Salter *The Years of a Rebel* Houghton Mifflin 67

Sacheverell Sitwell autobiographer

7382 He had imprisoned his ambitions within such confined limits that the direst poverty could hardly have reduced them further: some pipe tobacco and two or three whiskies-and-sodas being his ordinary and unvarying demand.

On his former tutor, A B Brockwell, quoted by Sarah Bradford *Splendors and Miseries* Farrar Straus Giroux 93

7383 He had two or three needs that came in rotation with the seasons, a little coal in winter and a few hours of sun in summer; the price of the one, and the niggardliness of the other, formed, indeed, his two grumbles against life, and if only these could have been assured to him, he would not have minded his bare table or cold bed.

ib

7384 To have been alive and sentient is the great experience.

Self-epitaph *ib*

B F Skinner behavioral scientist

7385 I did not direct my life. I didn't design it. I never made decisions. Things always came up and made them for me. That's what life is.

Particulars of My Life Knopf 76

Suzanne Slesin essayist

7386 Chintz, it could rightly be said, is the basic black dress of the English-style interior.

"Floral Attributes" *NY Times* 14 Apr 85

Jane Smiley commentator

7387 The paramount virtue of looking right. . . is something you embrace, the broken plank you are left with after the ship has gone down.

A Thousand Acres Knopf 91

C R Smith essayist

7388 A problem is something you have hopes of changing. Anything else is a fact of life.

Publisher's Weekly 8 Sep 69

Lillian Smith novelist

7389 To believe in something not yet proved and to underwrite it with our lives: it is the only way we can leave the future open.

Foreword to *The Journey* World 54

7390 Man, surrounded by facts, permitting himself no surprise, no intuitive flash, no great hypothesis, no risk, is a locked cell.

Killers of the Dream Norton 1944, recalled on Smith's death 28 Sep 66

7391 The human heart does not stray too long from that which hurt it most. There is a return journey to anguish that few of us are released from making.

ib

Red Smith (Walter Wellesley Smith) columnist

7392 My life has been strawberries in the wintertime, and you can't ask for more than that.

Quoted by Ira Berkow *Red* Times Books 86

7393 Dying is no big deal, The least of us will manage that. Living is the trick.

ib

C P Snow novelist

7394 If you hear anyone talking to you about your own best interests, look out for yourself.

Quoted on *Who Said That?* BBC TV 11 Feb 58

7395 Civilization is hideously fragile [and] there's not much between us and the horrors underneath, just about a coat of varnish.

A Coat of Varnish Scribner's 79

Ralph W Sockman Minister, Christ Church, Methodist, NYC

7396 Whatever the right hand findeth to do, the left hand carries a watch on its wrist to show how long it takes to do it.

Triumph Over Time NBC 12 Jan 58

7397 Let us not bankrupt our todays by paying interest on the regrets of yesterday and by borrowing in advance the troubles of tomorrow.

ib

7398 The larger the island of knowledge, the longer the shoreline of mystery.

Recalled on Sockman's death 29 Aug 70

William Sockman minister's son

7399 Just as a wounded gull dismembered from the sky/ With sunlight on its wings swoops seaward down to die/ So after all the fishing cries and blind pursuits of noon/ Falls quietly the golden afternoon.

Look 21 Nov 61

7400 That all our failures may not be our fault/ Is all that we ask of victory.

Before suicide at age of 20 *ib*

Stephen Sondheim composer and lyricist

7401 Everything's coming up roses!

Song from the musical *Gypsy* 59

Susan Sontag essayist

7402 I was not looking for my dreams to interpret my life, but rather for my life to interpret my dreams.

The Benefactor Doubleday 63

7403 He who despises himself esteems himself as a self-despiser.

Death Kit Farrar Straus Giroux 67

7404 Interpretation is the revenge of the intellect upon art.

Quoted by Richard Lacayo, "Stand Aside, Sisyphus" *Time* 24 Oct 88

Muriel Spark novelist

7405 It is impossible to dissuade a man who does not disagree, but smiles.

The Prime of Miss Jean Brodie Lippencott 62

7406 If I have my life to live over again I should form the habit of nightly composing myself to thoughts of death. . . there is no other practice which so intensifies life.

Washington Times 13 Mar 94

7407 Death, when it comes, ought not to take one by surprise.

ib

Stephen Spender poet

7408 [Quality is] three parts natural grace, one part sense of period and two parts eccentricity.

Time 28 Jan 85

7409 Born of the sun they travelled a short while towards the sun,/ And left the vivid air signed with their honor.

I Think Continually of Those Who Were Truly Great, Collected Poems 1928–85 Random House 86

7410 What I had not foreseen/ Was the gradual day/ Weakening the will/ Leaking the brightness away.

What I Expected Was 1933, recalled on Spender's death 17 Jul 95

Elli Georgiadis Stassinopoulos novelist's mother

7411 Angels fly because they take themselves lightly.

Favorite advice to her daughter, Arianna Huffington *Time* 12 Sep 95

Wallace Stegner novelist

7412 Most things break, including hearts. The lessons of life amount not to wisdom, but to scar tissue and callus.

The Spectator Bird Doubleday 76

John Steinbeck novelist

7413 Men do change, and change comes like a little wind that ruffles the curtains at dawn, and it comes like the stealthy perfume of wildflowers hidden in the grass.

Sweet Thursday Viking 54

7414 Where does discontent start? You are warm enough, but you shiver. You are fed, yet hunger gnaws you. You have been loved, but your yearning wanders in new fields. And to prod all these there's time, the Bastard Time.

ib

7415 It is a common experience that a problem difficult at night is resolved in the morning after the committee of sleep has worked on it.

Recalled on Steinbeck's death 20 Dec 68

7416 Man, unlike any other thing, organic or inorganic in the universe, grows beyond his work, walks up stairs of his concepts, emerges ahead of his accomplishments.

ib

Gloria Steinem feminist

7417 A pedestal is as much a prison as any small space.

Playboy Oct 79

7418 Some of us are becoming the men we wanted to marry.

Chicago *Sun-Times* 27 Apr 81

7419 Feminism was blamed for the beef boycott. . . [but] feminism isn't responsible for divorce; marriage is responsible for divorce.

NY Times 9 Feb 95

William P Steven poet

7420 You cannot define talent. All you can do is build the greenhouse and see if it grows.

Time 23 Aug 63

Wallace Stevens poet

7421 In my room, the world is beyond my understanding: but when I walk I see that it consists of three or four hills and a cloud.

"On the Surface of Things" *The Collected Poems of Wallace Stevens* Knopf 54

7422 The most beautiful thing in the world is, of course, the world itself.

Quoted in Frank Doggett and Robert Buttle eds *Wallace Stevens* Princeton 80

George Steiner essayist

7423 [The] most important tribute any human can pay to a poem or a piece of prose he or she really loves. . . is to learn it by heart. Not by brain, by heart; the expression is vital.

Publisher's Weekly 24 May 85

Henry L Stimson statesman

7424 The only way to make a man trustworthy is to trust him.

Recalled on Stimson's death 20 Oct 50

Harry Stein essayist

7425 Envy is as persistent as memory, as intractable as a head cold.

Esquire Jul 80

Adlai E Stevenson statesman

7426 All progress has resulted from people who took unpopular positions.

At Princeton University 22 Mar 54

7427 There is nothing so fine as to be 21 and an American. One is for a fleeting instant—and the other is forever. So live—decently, fearlessly, joyously—and don't forget that in the long run it is not the years in your life but the life in your years that counts!

Coronet Dec 55

7428 With the supermarket as our temple and the singing commercial as our litany, are we likely to fire the world with irresistible vision of America's exalted purposes and inspiring way of life?

Wall Street Journal 1 Jun 60

7429 Freedom is not an ideal, it is not even a protection, if it means nothing more than the freedom to stagnate.

Putting First Things First Random House 60

7430 We have confused the free with the free and easy.

ib

7431 She would rather light candles than curse the darkness and her glow has warmed the world.

On Eleanor Roosevelt 7 Nov 62

7432 Man. . . doesn't like to read the handwriting on the wall until his back is up against it.

Quoted by James B Reston *Deadline* Random House 91

Tom Stoppard playwright

7433 Life is a gamble, at terrible odds—if it was a bet you wouldn't take it.

Rosencrantz and Guildenstern are Dead Grove 67

7434 Age is a very high price to pay for maturity.

ib

7435 The bad end unhappily, the good unluckily. That is what tragedy means.

ib

Mark Strand poet

7436 Not every man knows what he/ shall sing at the end,/ Watching the pier as the ship/ sails away, or what it will seem like/ When he's held by the sea's roar/ motionless, there at the end,/ Or what he shall hope for once it/ is clear that he'll never go back.

"The End" poem included in *The Continuous Life* Knopf 90

Mildred Witte Struven essayist

7437 A clay pot sitting in the sun will always be a clay pot. It has to go through the white heat of the furnace to become porcelain.

Quoted by her daughter Jean Harris *Stranger in Two Worlds* Macmillan 86

Glendon Swarthout essayist

7438 The whole deal [virginity] is simply not that monumental. . . nor do I think a girl's misplacing it somewhere is [as] catastrophic as the decline and fall of the Roman Empire.

Where the Boys Are Random House

Thomas Szasz essayist

7439 People often say that this person or that person has not yet found himself. But the self is not something that one finds. It is something that one creates.

The Second Sin Doubleday 73

7440 As the internal-combustion engine runs on gasoline, so the person runs on self-esteem: if he is full of it, he is good for the long run; if he is partly filled, he will soon need to be refueled; and if he is empty, he will come to a stop.

ib

Barry Targan essayist

7441 Adventure is hardship aesthetically considered.

Kingdoms State University of New York 81

Edward Teller physicist

7442 Life improves slowly and goes wrong fast, and only catastrophe is clearly visible.

The Pursuit of Simplicity Pepperdine University 80

7443 No endeavor that is worthwhile is simple in prospect; if it is right, it will be simple in retrospect.

ib

7444 My experience has been in a short 77 years. . . that in the end when you fight for a desperate cause and have good reasons to fight, you usually win.

To Israeli Institute for Advanced Political and Strategic Studies *Wall Street Journal* 8 Aug 86

Margaret Thatcher Prime Minister of Britain

7445 Why do you climb philosophical hills? Because they are worth climbing. . . . There are no hills to go down unless you start from the top.

Recalling childhood maxims *New Yorker* 10 Feb 86

Alexander Theroux essayist

7446 Silence [is] the unbearable repartee.

"I Sing the Parrot!" *Reader's Digest* May 83

Caitlin Thomas poet's wife

7447 Fearful as reality is, it is less fearful than evasions of reality... Look steadfastly into the slit, pinpointed malignant eyes of reality as an old-hand trainer dominates his wild beasts.

Not Quite Posthumous Letter to My Daughter Atlantic-Little, Brown 63

Dylan Thomas poet

7448 Oh, isn't life a terrible thing, thank God!

Under Milk Wood New Directions 54

Lewis Thomas physician

7449 The thing we're really good at as a species is usefulness.

On "one of the very important things that has to be learned around the time that dying becomes a real prospect" *NY Times* 21 Nov 93

7450 An epidemic of apprehension.

When concern is widespread, quoted by George F Will *Newsweek* 22 Jul 96

Marlo Thomas actress

7451 Women have gone through a real revolution ... they have started trusting one another.

US News & World Report 12 Oct 87

Dorothy Thompson columnist

7452 We all start as grazing land and end up as ploughed fields.

On the moods of a lifetime, quoted by Victoria Glendinning *Rebecca West* Knopf 87

Mortin Thompson novelist

7453 All life... is measureable only by minutes and hours won, the inevitable staved off, the doom prolonged.

Not as a Stranger Scribner's 54

Alvin Toffler essayist

7454 The wider any culture is spread, the thinner it gets.

The Law of Raspberry Jam St Martin's 64

7455 Future shock is... too much change in too short a time.

Future Shock Random House 70

7456 Loneliness is now so widespread it has become, paradoxically, a shared experience.

The Third Wave Morrow 80

Jackie Torrence novelist

7457 [I tested the water] to see if it came out white.

On segregated drinking fountains *US News & World Report* 13 Feb 89

H R Trevor-Roper Professor of History, Oxford

7458 History... is what happened in the context of what might have happened... the alternatives, the might-have beens.

History and Imagination Oxford 80

Garry Trudeau cartoonist

7459 [The US] is the only country where failure to promote yourself is widely considered arrogant.

Newsweek 15 Oct 90

Harry S Truman 33rd US President

7460 A robin hops around looking for worms... a mockingbird has no individual note of his own. A lot of people are like that.

Diary entry after spending time on the balcony he added to the White House, quoted by David McCullough *Truman* Simon & Schuster 92

Barbara W Tuchman historian

7461 The dignity of women does not have to be registered or authenticated or validated by entry into men's groups or activities.

Accepting award from Washington's Cosmos Club *Washington Post* 7 Feb 89

Charles Turner novelist

7462 A board in a step near the top sighed and then sang out, and sighed again as he lifted his weight. A heart set on melody was not to be outdone, he supposed.

The Celebrant Servant 82

7463 He had always responded to the violins in old houses, and only a boor would have called the sound a squeak.

ib

Ted Turner business executive

7464 Years ago, I came up with what I was going to say to an assassin if he came to shoot me.... "Thanks for not coming sooner!"

Time 6 Jan 92

Kenneth Tynan critic

7465 When I'm unhappy, I can't work. When I'm happy, I don't need to work. But when I don't need to work, I'm unhappy.

Tynan Right and Left Atheneum 67

John Updike novelist

7466 Life is. . . an overlong drama through which we sit being nagged by the vague memories of having read the reviews.

The Coup Knopf 78

Peter Ustinov playwright

7467 As for being a General, well, at the age of four with paper hats and wooden swords we're all Generals. Only some of us never grow out of it.

Romanoff and Juliet I Random House 58

Kurt Vonnegut novelist

7468 A flaw in the human character is that everybody wants to build and nobody wants to do maintenance.

Hocus Pocus Putnam 90

Marilyn Vos Savant columnist

7469 An error becomes a mistake when we refuse to admit it.

Parade 22 Nov 87

Francis H Wade Episcopal priest

7470 Ugly things should be called by ugly names.

On why a commission on racism voted to retain its name, report to convention of the Diocese of Washington 30 Jan 88

Wallis Duchess of Windsor

7471 You can never be too rich or too thin.

London Times 18 Jun 94

7472 If you are tired of shopping you are going to the wrong shops.

ib

Evelyn Waugh novelist

7473 Memories. . . are my life—for we possess nothing certainly except the past.

Quoted by Moss Hart in frontispiece to his autobiographical *Act One* Random House 59

Jack Weinberg student

7474 Don't trust anyone over 30.

A saying among students of the 1960s rebellions, quoted by Stuart Berg Flexner *Listening to America* Simon & Schuster 82

Rebecca West novelist

7475 It is sometimes very hard to tell the difference between history and the smell of skunk.

Quoted by Victoria Glendinning *Rebecca West* Knopf 87

Glenway Westcott essayist

7476 Unless one has learned to work in spite of extreme unhappiness, one will never accomplish much. One's lifetime will not be long enough.

Journal entry on Westcott's 51st birthday, Robert Phelps with Jerry Rosco ed *Continual Lessons* Farrar Straus Giroux 90

E B White essayist

7477 Like every great river. . . the moon belongs to none and belongs to all. . . holds the key to madness. . . controls the tides that lap on shores everywhere. . . guards the lovers who kiss in every land under no banner but the sky.

Rebecca M Dale ed *Writings From the New Yorker 1925–76* HarperCollins 90

Edmund White Visiting Professor in Creative Writing, Brown University

7478 Gay men have followed a very dramatic itinerary. . . repressed in the 50s, liberated in the 60s, exalted in the 70s and wiped out in the 80s.

Fall 1990 *AIDS Quarterly*, National Public Television 26 Nov 90

John W Whitehead essayist

7479 Children are the living messages we send to a time we will not see.

The Stealing of America Crossway 83

Howard Whitman essayist

7480 When you go to the raw, infectious weather of rumor and gloomy, bundle up with courage and confidence. You don't want to catch cold feet.

Reader's Digest Jan 71

George F Will columnist

7481 The worst feature of the 50s is that they were pregnant with the 60s.

"Daddy, Who Was Kerouac?" *Newsweek* 4 Jul 88

Tennessee Williams playwright

7482 The violets in the mountains have broken the rocks.

Inscription on Williams' gravestone *NY Times* 30 May 90 from his play *Camino Real* 53

A N Wilson novelist

7483 [There does] occur in human lives certain conjunctions which are conducive to evil; rather in the way that certain chemicals, harmless when left to themselves, turn into dangerous explosives when mixed.

The Vicar of Sorrows Norton 93

Ludwig Wittgenstein essayist

7484 Whereof one cannot speak thereon one must remain silent.

Recalled on Wittgenstein's death 29 Apr 51

Amy Witting essayist

7485 [Lust was] a weary hunt through rough bush after a half-seen animal, ending in a desert where it left you alone.

Marriages Penguin 90

P G Wodehouse humorist

7486 Fate was quietly slipping the lead into the boxing glove.

Very Good, Jeeves Doubleday 1930 recalled on Wodehouse's death 16 Feb 75

Herman Wouk novelist

7487 The beginning of the end of war lies in remembrance.

Words carved on the first monument to commemorate the Korean War *Washington Times* 28 May 90

Marguerite Yourcenar novelist

7488 We are so accustomed to viewing wisdom as a result of passion spent that it is difficult for us to recognize it as the hardest and most condensed form of ardor, the bit of gold born of the fire, and not of ashes.

Critical Introduction to Constantin Cavafy Gallimard 78

7489 There is no wisdom without courtesy, no sanctity without human warmth.

Quoted by Richard Locke *Wall Street Journal* 11 Aug 92 reviewing Yourcenar's *That Mighty Sculptor, Time* Farrar Straus Giroux 92

7490 Human speech is relayed to us from the past in stages—staggering along, infected with miscomprehensions, eaten away by omissions, and encrusted with additions.

ib

Maurice Zolotow critic

7491 In the lives of men and women who rise high in the world, there is a moment, while they are passing from obscurity to consequence, that is perhaps the most satisfying they will ever know. The difficulties of the old life are abandoned; the difficulties of the new life are unknown.

Marilyn Monroe Harcourt, Brace 60

COMMUNICATIONS AND THE ARTS

ARCHITECTURE

Architects on Architecture

Note: In the first section of *Architecture*, all of the following speakers are architects, unless otherwise noted.

Josep Anton Acebillo

7492 [It is] like adding arms to the Venus de Milo.

On continuing work on Barcelona's Sagrada Familia Cathedral *Time* 28 Jan 91

Mario Bellini

7493 A design career is a process of learning better and better what you know instinctively.

NY Times 25 Jun 87

Philip Bess

7494 The multi-use stadium is the civic icon of the late 20th century. . . the equivalent of a cathedral, proof in the citizens' minds that they're world-class cities.

Wall Street Journal 20 Mar 87

Douglas Cardinal

7495 It takes a tremendous amount of warriorship to believe in your vision.

On designing the Canadian Museum of Civilization *Time* 10 Jul 89

Walter Gropius

7496 Society needs a good image of itself. That is the job of the architect.

"Not Built In A Day" editorial *London Times* 13 Aug 92

Frederick Gutheim

7497 The winning design in the Franklin D Roosevelt competition is not architecture but literature. It should not be built.

On a minimalist memorial design, dubbed "instant Stonehenge," calling for large slabs with Roosevelt quotations *Washington Post* 31 Dec 60

Wallace K Harrison

7498 To work with great people and do beautiful buildings. For an architect, it was like being handed a meringue glaceé; it was almost too easy.

On Rockefeller Center, quoted by Victoria Newhouse *Wallace K Harrison, Architect* Rizzoli 89

7499 I had a lot to do with everything Nelson didn't.

On Governor Nelson Rockefeller and design of the state government mall at Albany NY

7500 I was always conscious of who I was: Mr Harrison, watch your step. I was the little friend called the architect.

ib

Philip Johnson

7501 The essence of a theater is elegance, just as the essence of a church is spirituality.

On Lincoln Center's NY State Theater *Newsweek* 4 May 64

7502 Six poets trying to write a poem.

On the design team for Lincoln Center, quoted by Edgar B Young *Lincoln Center* NYU Press 80

7503 It is the diary of an eccentric architect.

On his glass house, sculpture gallery, and visitors' pavilion, assembled on the 40-acre Johnson estate at New Haven CT *NY Times* 17 Sep 95

Louis I Kahn

7504 The brick was always talking to me, saying you're missing an opportunity.

On use of handmade, wood-fired bricks with teak, slate, and solid white oak in library at Philips Exeter Academy *NY Times* 23 Oct 72

7505 On a gray day it will look like a moth; on a sunny day like a butterfly.

On his design for the Yale Center for British Art *New Yorker* 15 Jun 92

Frederick Kiesler

7506 Colors of Rome: tomato-red turned musty; rose sienna burned to umber; orange-peel pink; all off-beat brown mulattoes; soft ochre to hard dirt; washed-off greens gone mustard; foul apricots cocoa-stained; burning cheeks and ivory foreheads; cool-sounding violets; no trumpet colors screaming.

Inside the Endless House Simon & Schuster 67

Jean-Philippe Lachenaud

Director of Architecture, Ministry of the Environment

7507 [It was] a 19th century parody of what the 18th century was thought to be.

On renovation of Gare d'Orsay as Musée d'Orsay of Paris *Time* 8 Dec 86

Charles Le Corbusier (Charles-Edouard Jeanneret)

7508 One has to be conceited, sanctimonious, sure of oneself, swaggering, and never doubting—or at least not let it show. One has to be a show salesman. *Merde, alors*!

Quoted by Charles Jencks *Le Corbusier and the Tragic View of Architecture* Harvard 73

Maya Lin

7509 I had an impulse to cut open the earth. . . an initial violence that in time would heal. The grass would grow back, but the cut would remain.

On designing Washington's Vietnam Memorial Wall *National Geographic* May 85

7510 Sculpture to me is like poetry, and architecture is like prose.

International Herald Tribune 11 May 94

Ludwig Mies Van Der Rohe

7511 Less is more.

On restraint in design *NY Herald Tribune* 28 Jun 59

7512 God is in the details.

Reversing words from an unnamed Japanese diplomat who remembered that "arms-control negotiators always used to say that 'the devil is in the details,'" *NY Times* 10 Jan 92

Charles W Moore

7513 The dreams which accompany all human actions should be nurtured by the places in which people live.

On need for buildings to reflect circumstance and place *NY Times* 17 Dec 93

Robin Nicholson

Vice President, Royal Institute of British Architects

7514 There are too many twiddly bits.

On the "grand Gothic garnish" in restoration of St George's Hall after a fire at Windsor Castle *NY Times* 28 May 95

Claes Oldenburg

7515 [He aims] to stir things up. . . to jump feet first into the kind of spaghetti Bolognese of red tape which clogs this country from one end to the other.

On designing a large foot on squished soggy pasta, suggestive of Prince Charles as architectural critic *NY Times* 13 Jan 91

J J P Oud

7516 If I was not optimistic, I would not be an architect.

Quoted in *NY Times* 4 Dec 94 from John Peter's *The Oral History of Modern Architecture* Abrams 94

I M Pei

7517 Let's do it right. This is for the ages.

On his design for the National Gallery's East Building as it soared beyond budget to a cost of $94.4 million *Washington Post* 27 Aug 95

7518 Architecture must have integrity, like a friend.

On the moral obligation, as a biographer put it, of fully executing geometry "the right way, all the way" *ib*

Richard Seifert

7519 Many of my buildings are condemned in advance.

London Observer 6 Aug 72

Philip Tilden

7520 I specialize in prying pearls from oysters.

On remodeling of large old houses *Country Life* 5 May 94

7521 Creeping fungus tracked down the cracks and crevices. . . an inroad into the very bones of a building. . . the cancer of the very body of every house.

On renovations at Chartwell, Winston S Churchill's country home *ib*

Robert Venturi

7522 [It is] drawing a moustache on a madonna.
On designing an addition to Oberlin College's 1917 Allen Memorial Art Museum *NY Times* 30 Jan 77

7523 A wing on a symmetrical Renaissance villa, like a bowler hat on a Venus, will never look correct.
ib

George White architect, US Capitol

7524 They have the words... but not the music.
On the difference between builder and an architect *Connoisseur* Apr 87

Colin St John Wilson

7525 Books are like wine: they belong in the basement—a point the French have failed to understand.
On his sprawling design of new quarters for the British Museum as compared to the four "open book" glass towers of the *Bibliothèque de France* *NY Times* 17 Sep 95

Frank Lloyd Wright

7526 The physician can bury his mistakes, but the architect can only advise his client to plant vines.
NY Times 4 Oct 53

7527 It comforted me to see the fire burning deep in the solid masonry of the house.
On massive central chimneys that became a hallmark of his home design, quoted by Meryle Secrest *Frank Lloyd Wright* Knopf 92

Bruno Zevi

7528 You will not need this honor but Italy does.
To Lewis Mumford on receipt of an honorary doctorate in architecture from the University of Rome, quoted by Donald L Miller *Lewis Mumford* Weidenfeld & Nicolson 89

Critics

Dean Acheson US Secretary of State

7529 The old house carried an assurance, typically Portuguese, that nothing was urgent.
On US Embassy residence in Lisbon *Sketches from Life* Harper 61

Kurt Andersen critic

7530 The requisite material was marble, the form was strictly neoclassical, the intended effect was stirring—Sousa in stone.
On Washington monuments *Time* 29 Jun 87

Douglas Anderson homeless person

7531 A dump spot, an eyesore... but if you saw this place up close, you would see it's a home, with a personal touch.
On his shack under the Franklin D Roosevelt Drive along the East River *NY Times* 28 Mar 93

Susan Heller Anderson reporter

7532 [It was] trampled by the be-ins of the 50s, invaded by the drug dealers of the 70s and defaced by the graffiti of the 80s.
On Central Park's 123-year-old Bethesda Terrace *NY Times* 3 May 87

Roger Angell critic

7533 The expensive Houston experiment... [is] a giant livingroom—complete with man-made weather and wall-to-wall carpeting... so totally, so drearily resembling the one just left.
On the $31.6 million Houston Astrodome, quoted by Ken Burns and Geoffrey C Ward ed *Baseball* Knopf 94

Lord Anglesey (George C H V Paget) land owner

7534 It is like living in a howdah on top of a white elephant which is being fed by someone else. And a very beautiful white elephant it is.
On continuing to live near his country house, Plas Newydd, after take-over by the National Trust *London Times* 22 Oct 94

Lord Annan (Noel Gilroy Annan) Chair, Board of Trustees, National Gallery

7535 [It is] like removing the lower jaw from someone's face.
On the demolishing of the lower terrace of the National Theater, letter to *London Times* 12 Dec 94

7536 [It is] a confection of gingerbread which ought to be under a glass shade on a giant mantlepiece.
On the Albert Memorial's restoration *London Times* 29 Jul 92

7537 You used to enter New York City like a king; now you slither in like a rat.
Quoted by Senator Daniel Patrick Moynihan on the difference between the old Pennsylvania Station, 1910–1963, and its successor, news reports 30 Sep 94

Anon

7538 The pile of bricks at the end of the of the line.
Comment on the St Pancras Station Hotel by those considering its reclamation *London Times* 10 Dec 94

7539 It ain't Wright!

Political slogan urging that no changes be made in the revival of Frank Lloyd Wright's design for a Madison WI civic center 24 Jun 95

7540 With I M Pei, you Pei and Pei and Pei.

On escalating costs of I M Pei architecture *Washington Post* 27 Aug 95

7541 It's no longer the mistake on the lake.

On the enthusiastic public reception given I M Pei's Museum of Rock and Roll on Lake Erie at Cleveland, Monitor Radio 2 Sep 95

Architectural Forum

7542 Remodeling. . . is building's stepchild and architecture's bastard.

"The Art That Science Forgot" Jan 60

Eric Arthur critic

7543 The saddest word in my books is "demolished."

Toronto: No Mean City University of Toronto Press 64

Blake Auchincloss novelist's son

7544 [It was] a blend of a villa for my father with vernacular Catskills for my mother.

On his parents' country house near Liberty NY designed by Peter Pennoyer for Louis and Adele Auchincloss, quoted by Carol Gelderman *Louis Auchincloss: A Writer's Life* Crown 93

Louis Auchincloss novelist

7545 A certain leaning to heaviness. . . is lightened by the profusion of verdurous lawns and hedges and by the glory of elm trees. God, as usual, has done a better job than man.

On the chapel of a New England prep school based on Groton *The Rector of Justin* Houghton Mifflin 64

7546 The great yellow towers of the Beresford . . . rose into the bare sky with the heavy placidity of an Aztec temple.

On looking west across Central Park *ib*

7547 [It was] a bribe to compensate so devoted an asphalt hound.

On his wife's inclusion of a spectacular library in their country house *Architectural Digest* Jun 89

7548 I would rather see the old reservoir on 42nd Street or the original Madison Square Garden than I would any of the lost wonders of the ancient world.

Quoted by Carol Gelderman *Louis Auchincloss* Crown 93

Warren R Austin US Representative to the UN

7549 If you're going to get this loan request through Congress, the building should have a dome.

On plans for the UN General Assembly building, quoted by Victoria Newhouse *Wallace K Harrison, Architect* Rizzoli 89

Kent S Barwick Executive Director, Municipal Art Society

7550 Who would have thought that in one fell swoop, they could saw off Grand Central Terminal from the rest of America?

On Amtrack's switching of all long distance trains to Manhattan's Pennsylvania Station some years after Barwick campaign to save the Beaux Arts landmark *NY Times* 2 Apr 91

Max Beerbohm critic

7551 There is much virtue in a window. It is to a human being as a frame is to a painting, as a proscenium to a play, as a "form" to literature. It strongly defines its content.

On comparing mill owners' windows and millworkers' windows in Lowell MA, recalled on exhibition of windows at Washington's National Building Museum *NY Times* 21 Mar 91

John Betejeman poet

7552 Snow falls in the buffet of Aldersgate station,/ Soot hangs in the tunnel in clouds of steam./ City of London! before the next desecration/ Let your steepled forest of churches be my theme!

Monody on the Death of Aldersgate Street Station recalled on Betejeman's death 19 May 84

7553 I like my churches blue with smoke and as baroque as possible.

London Church Times 25 May 84

Marcus Binney critic

7554 The memorial is not simply an overblown bauble, nor just a hymn to Victorian polychromy but a lasting and visible proclamation of the Prince Consort's belief that the future of Britain lay in an enlightened and creative interplay between the arts and manufactures—design and industry in modern parlance.

On the restoration of the Albert Memorial *London Times* 29 Jul 92

7555 The correspondence columns of *The Times* shook with thunder.

On opposition to British Railways' 1968 attempt to amalgamate two London terminals—Victorian architect Gilbert Scott's St Pancras Station and King's Cross 10 Dec 94

Maxwell Bloomfield Professor of History and Law, Catholic University

7556 With its evocation of past imperial grandeur, the Beaux-Arts tradition of an expansionist America [contributed to]. . . a mystique of the Court as a group of detached sages who are impervious to popular pressures.

On the US Supreme Court in Washington in Kermit L Hall ed *The Oxford Companion to the Supreme Court of the United States* Oxford 92

Richard Boston critic

7557 [It is] a dull grey building designed by a dull gray architect in a drab slab of a place where it's always raining.

On Robert Venturi's addition to London's National Gallery *Guardian Weekly* 7 Jul 91

7558 The pictures are much more important, and it does them proud. That's really all that matters in the end, as it did in the beginning.

ib

Maeve Brennan essayist

7559 The obliterating touch of the cement mixer is gradually smoothing this block into the bland expression that is the new New York.

On mid-town Manhattan "The View Chez Paul" *The Long-Winded Lady: Notes from the New Yorker* Morrow 69

Stephen G Breyer Judge, US Court of Appeals, Boston

7560 This most beautiful site in Boston does not belong to the judges, it does not belong to the lawyers, it does not belong to the Federal Government, it belongs to the people.

On the new federal courthouse on Boston's Fan Pier *NY Times* 15 May 94

Mary Brosnahan Executive Director, NY Coalition for the Homeless

7561 A place to cook. . . where friends can visit and lovers can stay overnight. . . a rejection of the institution of the shelters, where your soul is checked at the door.

On the rigged, makeshift structures set up by an estimated 15,000 of New York City's 90,000 homeless *NY Times* 28 Mar 93

7562 At the bare minimum, we're talking about a small, secure room with a door that locks.

On planning future housing for the homeless *ib*

J Carter Brown Director, National Gallery of Art

7563 This East building. . . is anybody's fantasy. Just like a piano, it can be played in a variety of keys.

On I M Pei's $94 million 1978 addition to Washington's National Gallery of Art *Sunday Morning* CBS TV 13 Sep 92

Patricia Leigh Brown reporter

7564 A grim symbol of the seeming permanence . . . of the disposessed. . . tucked into the city's most forlorn corners and tenuously echoing a remembered idea of home.

On shacks and lean-to's that constitute the homeless' "architecture of despair" *NY Times* 28 Mar 93

Kenneth L Burns critic

7565 The most recognizable building in America.

On the US Capitol, designed by an Englishman, inspired by a Russian church, decorated by Italian craftsmen and built in part by slaves, it is the nearest thing Americans have to a national temple *The Congress* PBS TV 4 Jul 90

Barbara Bush First Lady

7566 No other single building is so much a part of the American consciousness.

At 200th anniversary of the laying of the White House cornerstone *Washington Times* 24 Jan 92

Hugh Casson Provost, Royal College of Art

7567 Architects are cannibals, if they are not parrots.

American Scholar Spring 94

Jean Cau critic

7568 [It is] a horror made of cardboard, plastic and appalling colors, a construction of hardened chewing gum and idiotic folklore taken straight out of comic books written for obese Americans.

On the opening of Euro Disneyland in former sugar-beet fields east of Paris *NY Times* 13 Apr 92

Gabrielle ("Coco") Chanel fashion designer

7569 It's not houses that I love, it's the life I live in them.

Quoted by Annette Tapert and Diana Edkins *The Power of Style* Crown 94

Charles Prince of Wales

7570 If I had sat at these people's feet as often as disciples are supposed to. . . I would probably end up by developing architectural hemorrhoids.

Denying influence of a palace coterie of architectural "gurus" *NY Times* 10 Aug 87

7571 [I have an urge to] throw a proverbial royal brick through the inviting plate glass of pompous professional pride.

21 Feb 88

7572 [Lost in] a jostling scrum of office buildings . . . like a basketball team standing shoulder to shoulder between you and the Mona Lisa.

On what he saw as the wrecking of the London skyline and desecration of St Paul's Cathedral 13 Mar 88

7573 An academy for secret police.

On Colin St John Wilson's design of the new British Museum 12 Aug 93

7574 A nuclear power station in the heart of London.

On Denys Lasdun's Royal National Theater *London Times* 12 Dec 94

Winston S Churchill statesman

7575 The party system is much favored by an oblong form of chamber.

On retaining rectangular shape of the House of Commons in its post-war rebuilding *Time* 6 Nov 50

7576 It is easy for an individual to move through those insensible gradations from left to right, but the fact of crossing the floor [to change parties] is one which requires serious consideration. . . [and] I have accomplished that difficult process not only once but twice.

ib

Kenneth Clark critic

7577 If I had to say which was telling the truth about society, a speech by a Minister of Housing or the actual buildings put up in his time, I should believe the buildings.

Civilization Harper & Row 70

7578 He believed that he built very good Gothic, we believed that he built very bad.

On Victorian architect Gilbert Scott, *London Times* 10 Dec 94

Francis X Clines reporter

7579 [It is] a giant wine-colored altar of private tabernacles found surviving in the urban jungle.

On Manhattan's Hotel Chelsea *NY Times* 4 Feb 78

Alistair Cooke commentator

7580 To see the towering ceiling, to stand at black-and-white marble stalls in a Roman urinal about ten times the Roman scale. . . it made one's anatomy look awfully shabby.

On the men's lounge at Radio City Music Hall *The Americans* Knopf 80

7581 There is no more breathtaking example in the world of the style of decoration peculiar to the late 1920s and early 1930s. By now it has a name. It is a cult. . . called Art Deco.

On post-Depression acceptance of a new style *ib*

7582 [It is] a white jewel of 18th-century grace in wood.

On a colonial church in Litchfield CT *ib*

7583 What he missed was a porch to rock on, so after a squabble with Congress and the architects (who said the second floor would look like a big Missouri back porch) he had some construction done under the back portico. It looked like a big Missouri back porch.

On Harry S Truman's White House balcony *ib*

Henry F S Cooper Editor, *Yale Daily News*

7584 [They were] awaiting any barnacles of wisdom which might fall from the venerable craft anchored before them.

On Frank Lloyd Wright's visit to Yale undergraduates, quoted by Meryle Secrest *Frank Lloyd Wright* Knopf 92

Richard Cork critic

7585 Of all the memorials erected throughout Britain after the Great War, the Cenotaph is lodged most securely in the nation's heart. . . a receptacle for whatever emotions the viewers want to project on to its plain white surface.

On the Whitehall monument designed by Edwin Lutyens *London Times* 12 Nov 94

Coventry Cathedral Bishop and Provost

7586 The cathedral is to speak to us and to generations to come of the Majesty, the Eternity and the Glory of God. God, therefore, direct you.

To architects competing for commission to design Coventry Cathedral, quoted by Basil Spence *Phoenix at Coventry* Harper & Row 62

7587 The cathedral should be built to enshrine the altar. . . this should be the idea of the architect, not to conceive a building and to place in it an altar, but to conceive an altar and to create a building.

ib

Salvador Dali painter

7588 [It looks] the way an angel cooks a cathedral.

On the melted appearance of Antonio Gaudi's Barcelona Cathedral of the Sacred Family, quoted by Anatole Broyard *Aroused by Books* Random House 74

Thomas M Debevoise adviser to John D Rockefeller Jr

7589 The only conclusion the public can possibly reach is that Mr Rockefeller and his people have the biggest heads in the world.

Memo on press reports ("the most rampant boasting about size") during construction of Rockefeller Center, quoted by Peter Collier and David Horowitz *The Rockefellers* Holt Rinehart Winston 76

Anthony Depalma reporter

7590 A single five-pointed star is embossed above the doorframe. . . a bit of whimsy in the deadly business of keeping the sea from wrecking ships and stealing men's lives.

On Coney Island Light, the last US lighthouse run by a civilian keeper *NY Times* 13 Apr 91

Thierry Despont architect

7591 Neither one is less Frick than the other.

On the difference between Henry Clay Frick's 1870 Pittsburgh mansion and his 1905 Manhattan home *NY Times* 5 Nov 87

Patrick Deuchar Chief Executive, Albert Hall

7592 This hall was designed with a massive social snobbery which saw nothing wrong with treating different sections of the audience as first, second, third or fourth-class citizens.

On refurbishing of London's 120-year-old Albert Hall *London Times* 17 Sep 93

David Diaz reporter

7593 You can read the entire Vietnamese War in the faces of the crowds here.

On the dedication of Washington's Vietnam Wall NBC TV 5 May 85

Joan Didion writer

7594 [They are] toy garden cities in which no one lives but everyone consumes.

On shopping malls *NY Times* 27 Mar 92

E L Doctorow novelist

7595 A mansion would appear in a field. The next day it stood on a city street with horse and carriage passing by.

On the Manhattan of the late 1800s, quoted by Malcolm Jones Jr *Newsweek* 27 Jun 94 reviewing Doctorow's novel *The Waterworks* Random House 94

Arthur Drexler Director, Architecture and Design, Metropolitan Museum of Art

7596 History is written for the victors and what they leave out is the losers.

On the *Ecole des Beaux Arts* as countermodern architecture rather than postmodern *NY Review* 27 Nov 75

Stephen Drucker journalist

7597 This is England as only Dallas could build it.

On London's Hotel Lanesborough *Travel & Leisure* Apr 95

David W Dunlap reporter

7598 Broadway announces itself triumphantly. . . [and] begins its journey with a conquering swagger.

On Broadway's start in New York's center of international finance *On Broadway* Rizzoli 90

The Economist London

7599 The architects, many of whom live or work in Georgian terraces, are already protesting. The general public, many of whom live or work in concrete slabs, will applaud.

On Prince Charles' criticism of a "scrum of office buildings" obscuring St Paul's Cathedral *NY Times* 13 Mar 88

Edward Duke of Windsor

7600 [It is] Dickens in a Cartier setting.

On Jacobean-style Sandringham Palace in Norfolk, recalled in *Fortune* 25 Mar 91

Walker Evans essayist and photographer

7601 America's heritage of great architecture is doomed.

On the destruction of New York's Pennsylvania Station *Life* 9 Jul 63

7602 From east to west, the wrecker's ball and bulldozer are lords of the land.

ib

J Howard Farrar reporter

7603 It might easily be mistaken for a distinguished town hall that has retired to the country.

On Highclere Castle, ancestral home of the Earls of Carnarvon *Christian Science Monitor* 26 July 88

Lisa W Foderaro reporter

7604 Grand Central. . . one of those rare buildings where public use and landmark architecture intersect to form a sense of public ownership.

On installation in New York's Grand Central Terminal of a high-definition television screen that could raise $1 million a year *NY Times* 5 Nov 93

Benjamin Forgey critic

7605 The power of the wall, the sheer emotional force of great civic art in the right place at the right time. . . apt, simple, stunning. . . [a] great statement of sorrow and healing.

Opposing additions of a flag pole and statuary to the site of Washington's Vietnam Wall *Washington Post* 13 Feb 88

7606 [It] will be a relatively innocuous behemoth clad in the selfsame granite as its notable neighbor.

On Judicial Office Building adjacent to Washington's Union Station 4 Feb 89

7607 The roof was the big challenge. . . the. . . wonderful, repeated legerdemain of columns reaching just over the top of the curved concrete beam to grip it with the merest fingertip.

On Eero Saarinen's gravity-induced, catenary-shaped roof at Dulles Airport built in 1965 and extended three decades later 9 Sep 95

7608 Domes are to the nation's politics what skyscrapers are to its commerce. The difference is that we invented the skyscraper, and we adapted the dome.

On reviewing architectural photographer Eric Oxendorf's study of Washington, DC 21 Oct 95

Jeanette Friedman reporter

7609 In the misty cavern, in the naked rock, with lights piercing through the hiss and rush of compressed air, they are the tamers.

On drilling a third water tunnel for New York City *NY Sunday News* 23 Aug 87

7610 After the project is finished and the stainless-steel pipes are sealed away for the ages, deep in the metamorphic rock, no human will ever again see this astonishing place.

ib

Peter Fuhrham reporter

7611 [It is] a curving sleeve of glass and steel.

On Waterloo Station's terminal for channel trains *Forbes* 13 Mar 95

David Gelernter Professor of Computer Science, Yale

7612 Those bulldozers will be plowing calm dignity under and replacing it with glitz, hype and somersaults, and we will all be worse off for it.

On replacement of the Hayden planetarium at Manhattan's Museum of Natural History *NY Times* 5 Mar 95

Nancy Gibbs reporter

7613 Designed by an architect no one has heard of, in a city no one wants to live in.

Reporting on Donald Trump's Taj Mahal casino at Atlantic City, NJ *Time* 9 Apr 90

7614 The Taj actually looks edible, the work of a candymaker gone mad. . . a vast white meringue, iced with 70 fruit-flavored minarets.

ib

Brendan Gill essayist

7615 The big houses sat in self-congratulatory propinquity on their level green lawns. . . stout matrons seated elbow to elbow, implacably chaperoning a ball.

On a residential boulevard of Rochester NY *A New York Life* Poseidon 90

Paul Goldberger critic

7616 To step from a train platform into Grand Central's extraordinary concourse. . . is to feel in every fiber that you have arrived someplace important, to know that you have come into a great city and that great city has greeted you properly.

On the 75th anniversary of Grand Central Station as "one of the 20th century's greatest interior spaces," *NY Times* 2 Feb 88

7617 If architecture were opera, this would be the ultimate prima donna.

On I M Pei's Meyerson Symphony Center in Dallas *ib* 17 Sep 89

7618 The whole thing looks like a skyscraper in drag.

On San Francisco's Marriott Hotel *ib* 1 Apr 90

7619 [It is] Atlantic City with the volume turned up. . . with a booster shot made up of one part Las Vegas and one part Disneyland.

On Trump's Taj Mahal casino *ib* 6 Apr 90

7620 When a lion lays down with a lamb, one is always a bit suspicious of what the lion expects to get out of the deal.

On truce between Manhattan and builder Donald J Trump for West Side river-edge development *ib* 17 Mar 91

7621 The Salk Institute is a building that makes you want to caress concrete.

On Louis Kahn's Salk Institute for Biological Studies, La Jolla CA *ib* 23 Jun 91

7622 McKim's great temple is at once sinfully opulent and chillingly dry.

On Manhattan's Pierpont Morgan Library *ib* 3 Nov 91

7623 A whole philosophy of being: serenity on the outside, indulgence within.

On Thomas Jefferson's Monticello *ib* 25 Apr 93

7624 A country house in a corset. . . too tall, too tight, too unwilling to let go.

On John D Rockefeller's mansion, Kykuit, near Tarrytown NY *ib* 6 May 94

7625 In Israel, Corinthian columns do not a convincing courthouse make.

On classicism inappropriate to the West Israel *ib* 13 Aug 95

Peter Gordon Professor of Economics, University of Southern California

7626 There is this strange conceit among architects that people should live in what they design.

Newsweek 15 May 95

Lloyd Grossman BBC commentator

7627 Cathedrals of convenience, barns on steroids.

On supermarkets with pantiled roofs and white clock towers *London Times* 9 Sep 95

Stephen Hall journalist

7628 Grand Central Terminal... [is] a mecca, a national metaphor for bustle, a distinctly American structure—all rippling steel and Yankee ingenuity dressed up in 19th century French *habiliment*.

Travel and Leisure Nov 84

William L Hamilton reporter

7629 Meditation for most New Yorkers is thinking about their next apartment, the bigger one.

NY Times 9 Mar 95

George Hartman reporter

7630 The architectural profession gave the public 50 years of modern architecture and the public's response has been ten years of the greatest wave of historic preservation in the history of man.

"New Game in Town: Facademanship" *NY Times* 31 Aug 83

Henry-Russell Hitchcock writer

7631 A pilgrimage spot, the *Ile-de-France* of modern architecture.

On Frank Lloyd Wright's homes in Oak Park IL, quoted by Donald L Miller *Lewis Mumford* Weidenfeld & Nicolson 89

Christopher Hitchens journalist

7632 It... must be a revenge for the architectural horror with which the US government has disfigured Grosvenor Square.

On the British chancery in Washington *Vanity Fair* Aug 93

Joseph Hudnut Dean, Harvard School of Architecture

7633 This ponderous, huge monster has seized this unaffected and reticent man and holds him... in an eternal pillory of pomp and pretense.

On General Ulysses S Grant and his controversial tomb on Manhattan's Riverside Drive, recalled on Hudnut's death 17 Jan 68

John Huey journalist

7634 The Lazarus of American cities.

On Pittsburgh "The Best Cities for Business" *Fortune* 4 Nov 91

Ada Louise Huxtable critic

7635 A small white palace... a die-cut Venetian palazzo on lollypops.

On Manhattan's $7-million Huntington Hartford Gallery of Modern Art at Columbus Circle *NY Times* 26 Feb 64

7636 I got a terrible case of the Fountainblues.

On Miami Beach *ib* 15 Oct 70

7637 Water is the wine of architecture.

Quoted by Herbert E French *Of Rivers and the Sea* Putnam 70

7638 America the beautiful,/ Let me sing of thee;/ Burger King and Dairy Queen/ From sea to shining sea.

On the disapperance of landmark structures "Goodbye History, Hello Hamburger" *NY Times* 21 Mar 71

7639 A collection that lines and encloses the Mall like a brontosaurian marble boneyard.

On additions to the Smithsonian *ib* 6 Oct 72

7640 The daintiest big buildings in the world.

On the twin towers of the World Trade Center *ib* 5 Apr 73

7641 The soaring sweep of scarlet-boxed papers behind glass, holding what the shredder didn't get... is great architectural drama and calculated symbolism.

On the Lyndon B Johnson Library *ib* 30 Sep 73

7642 A solid gold turkey.

On the US Senate's Dirksen Office Building *ib* 23 Jun 74

7643 Born-dead, neo-penitentiary modern.

On Washington's Hirshhorn Museum *ib* 6 Oct 74

7644 The Met has done the wrong thing impeccably.

On the Metropolitan Museum of Art's Lehman wing *ib* 26 May 75

7645 New York, thy name is irreverence and hyperbole. And grandeur.

ib 20 Jul 75

7646 The murmurous sea of the huge reading room is still sanctuary for scholars and life's gentler failures... [in] great rooms of marble, carved wood, and bronze.

On the NY Public Library *ib* 6 Nov 75

7647 A city that is as heartbreaking in its beauty as it is in its poverty and decay. It is still a city of dreams—promised, built, and broken.

On New York *ib* 9 Nov 75

7648 The Empire State Building, of course, is a star in its own right, with an enduring, romantic charisma.

ib 1 Feb 76

7649 The tail totally wags the dog.

On the alliance of art and politics in presidential libraries *ib* 28 Oct 79

7650 The last of the solid marble bombs in the long line willed to the nation by the late Architect of the Capitol, J George Stewart... this born-dead behemoth.

On completion of the James Madison building at the Library of Congress *ib* 4 May 80

7651 An aesthetic slum.

On expansion of Manhattan's Museum of Modern Art *ib* 29 Jun 80

7652 The rigid rule of mediocrity through uneasy compromise with an uncertain past that has characterized the best and worst of Washington construction in our day will be broken.

On I M Pei's East Building to extend the National Gallery of Art *Washington Post* 27 Aug 95

Gyula Illyes poet

7653 A Turkish bath crossed with a Gothic chapel.

Voicing a poet's opinion of Budapest's ornate parliament on the Danube, recalled on Illyes' death 4 Apr 83

Simon Jenkins columnist

7654 The King commissioned it himself. . . royal megalomania with style.

On George IV's 9,000-guinea equestrian statue in Trafalger Square *London Times* 29 Apr 95

Barbara Piasecka Johnson heiress

7655 This is to show you the quality—not the quantity—of my money.

On paying $15 million for an 18th century cabinet for Jasna Polana, the lavish New Jersey mansion built with her late husband, Johnson & Johnson heir J Seward Johnson *Forbes* 16 Oct 95

Claudia ("Lady Bird") Johnson First Lady

7656 [It is like] a great beauty that you've seen at seven in the morning in an old bathrobe that's missing a few buttons.

On construction site of the National Wildflower Research Center at Austin TX *Life* Apr 95

William H Jordy critic

7657 Paestum is beautiful to me because it is less beautiful than the Pantheon. . . because from it the Parthenon came.

Reviewing Louis I Kahn's *In the Realm of Architecture* Rizzoli 91 *NY Times* 29 Dec 91

John F Kennedy 35th US President

7658 It may be the only monument we'll leave.

On preservation and developmental plans for Lafayette Square across from the White House, quoted by Arthur M Schlesinger *A Thousand Days* Houghton Mifflin 65

Michael Kimmelman writer

7659 It remains boundless and insurmountable, the Everest of museums. And me without a pickax.

Reporting on the expansion of the Louvre *NY Times* 28 Nov 93

7660 The Louvre has gone from vast to vaster.

ib

Bernard Levin writer

7661 The only passersby that can contemplate it without pain are those equipped with a white stick and a dog.

On post-war architecture *London Times* 31 Dec 83

Neil Locke interior designer

7662 We had to go to London to get the four thrones done. It's tough to find a good thronemaker these days.

On the $350-million palace of Brunei *International Herald Tribune* 22 Dec 83

Mark Loizeaux demolitionist

7663 We don't blow buildings up. We blow them down. We drop them.

On use of explosives in demolition *Smithsonian* Dec 86

London Times

7664 The place was built by the original Yuppie as. . . the first big luxury development for executive-style, riverside gracious living with nobs on.

"The Palace Hotel" editorial on turning Hampton Court into rental apartments 5 Aug 92

7665 What a grateful nation gave to the Duke of Marlborough in 1706 remains forever a treasure of the nation.

"The Battle of Blenheim" editorial on irresponsibility of the inheritor of the title in the maintenance of Blenheim Palace 9 Apr 94

7666 As usual. . . argument about heritage, taste and Church matters has mixed the maxium color with the minimum light.

"Blobby Between Mullions" editorial on the removal of Sherborne Abbey's Victorian window of Old Testament prophets, kings and patriarchs that one visitor described as "a collection of Mr Blobbies" 17 Jul 95

Walter Lowrie Episcopal priest

7667 In matters of taste, the Benedictines were the Episcopalians of the Roman Church.

Quoted by Judith Rice Millow *St Paul's Within the Walls*, Rome, published by William L Bauhan, Dublin NH 82

Russell Lynes essayist

7668 What had been a missionary church in a Philistine jungle began to look curiously like, and take on the airs and graces of, a cathedral of the new culture.

On the Museum of Modern Art's move from temporary quarters to its own building *Good Old Modern* Atheneum 73

John Major Prime Minister of Britain

7669 Grey, sullen, concrete wastelands... monuments to the failed history of socialist planning.

On public housing ghettos of Britain's inner cities *Guardian Weekly* 7 May 95

William Manchester biographer

7670 The house is a metaphor of its squire... complex... steeped in the past.

On Chartwell, Winston S Churchill's country home *The Last Lion* Little, Brown 88

7671 To him the essence of Chartwell is that it is completely, utterly, entirely English.

ib

Marsha Martin NYC Mayor's Office on Homelessness and Single Room Occupancy

7672 This isn't housing. There is no standard to evaluate a Sterno can in a cardboard box.

On shacks called "street architecture" on Manhattan's Lower East Side *NY Times* Mar 93

Rachel ("Bunny") Mellon arbiter of fashion

7673 Nothing should be noticed.

On deliberate understatement *Washington Post* 26 May 94

James A Michener novelist

7674 One of the world's strangest-looking serious buildings, a huge unfinished cathedral, a gaping wound in the heart of genius.

On Barcelona's Cathedral of the Holy Family *Iberia* Random House 68

Joseph Mitchell novelist

7675 Putting riveting tools in their hands was like putting ham with eggs.

On training Native Americans for skyscraper riveting *Up in the Old Hotel* Pantheon 92

Margaret Morton Associate Professor, Cooper Union School of Art

7676 The architecture of despair.

On the shanties of the homeless *NY Times* 28 Mar 93

Daniel Patrick Moynihan US Senator

7677 We've come full circle but the best remains the heart of the city, the greatest center of the greatest city, our Acropolis.

On New York's Rockefeller Center *Washington Times* 15 Mar 91

Lewis Mumford critic

7678 Despite the papal Gothic mask, [it is] a joyful creation... the last smile of skyscraper romanticism.

On New York Hospital, quoted in *Alumni Quarterly* Cornell University Medical College Dec 82

7679 No one has ever conceived of building a mirror on this scale.

On the UN Secretariat, quoted by Victoria Newhouse *Wallace Harrison, Architect* Rizzoli 89

Herbert Muschamp critic

7680 Rooms along the Fifth Avenue side command magnificent vistas of Central Park. Now that's intensive care.

On I M Pei's $200-million addition to Manhattan's Mt Sinai Medical Center *NY Times* 24 Sep 92

7681 Take two atriums. Call in the morning light.

ib

7682 The opposite of Hamlet in modern dress, St John's is the anxious modern hero in period costume.

On the hundredth anniversary of upper Manhattan's Cathedral of St John the Divine *ib* 20 Dec 92

7683 At last, a Fifth Avenue dress to go with a Fifth Avenue address.

On the 1994 remodeling of the Metropolitan Museum of Art *ib* 6 Apr 95

7684 The theater is... the frame around the picture, the cover of the book.

On reclaiming Broadway theaters *ib* 30 Jul 95

Allen R Myerson reporter

7685 The skyscraper was born and raised, and raised some more, in the United States, defining the nation's proudest cities, enshrining its largest corporations and giving airline pilots the willies.

NY Times 25 Jun 95

Eric P Nash reporter

7686 Majestic and intimate... [with] eight-inch posts for silk top hats and a Western Union telegraph key for calling messenger boys, you can practically hear the clop of a horse-drawn shay.

On Manhattan's Beaux-Arts building of the State Supreme Court's Appellate Division *NY Times* 4 Dec 94

The New York Times

7687 [It is] a cavernous suite with... an adjoining bathroom spacious enough to board a buffalo.

"Bruce Babbitt's Landscape" editorial on the new Secretary of the Interior operating out of "the biggest Cabinet office in Washington" in "a sprawling agency that makes the Balkans seem tidy by comparison" 1 Mar 93

7688 [It is like placing] a jewel in a swine's snout.

On building the lavish Jefferson Market Courthouse in 1877 in Greenwich Village, recalled on the first tolling of its two-ton bell since Admiral George Dewey's Manila Bay victory in the Spanish-American War; a graffiti painter daubed "to hell with Spain—Remember the Maine—1898" *ib* 1 Mar 95

Louis Nizer attorney

7689 Buildings made for day use seem resentful of nocturnal visitors. They express it in dampness and hostile echoes. The grandeur of the marble becomes sepulchre.

On the US Supreme Court reopened for a special night session in Rosenberg espionage case *The Implosion Controversy* Doubleday 73

Denis Noble Oxford physiologist

7690 This great cathedral of intellectual endeavor built up over the centuries is still intact. But the roof is badly leaking and the fabric is distinctly tatty.

To Parliament, quoted by James Atlas "Oxford Versus Thatcher's England" *NY Times* 24 Apr 88

Patrick O'Donovan reporter

7691 They appear to waste space as all good architecture does. You could carry a coffin down the stairs with perfect dignity, the mouldings are good and the doors thick enough to stop a horse.

On London's Harley Street *NY Times* 20 May 69

Jacqueline Kennedy Onassis First Lady

7692 Perhaps saving old buildings and having the new ones be right isn't the most important thing in the world—if you are waiting for the bomb—but I think we are always going to be waiting for the bomb and it won't ever come and so to save the old and to make the new beautiful is terribly important.

To painter William Walton 8 Jun 62 when the east and west sides of Lafayette Square were threatened with demoliton, recalled on her death *Washington Post* 29 May 94

7693 All our wildest dreams come true!

To David Finley, Chair, National Trust for Historic Preservation and the Commission of Fine Arts, on the General Services Administraton's decision to preserve Lafayette Square *ib*

Charles P Pierce journalist

7694 [It is a] tattered old dowager arena tucked into a backwater bend near to where the Charles River fouls the sea.

On the Boston Garden *NY Times* 21 Mar 93

Dan Pinck critic

7695 Frank Lloyd Wright ate clients for breakfast, other architects for lunch, and anyone who doubted that he was the world's greatest architect for dinner.

American Scholar Spring 94

Anthony S Pitch journalist

7696 No one knows why this building, shaped like a pregnant hexagon, came to be called the Octagon.

On Washington DC's Octagon House *Sightseers' Guide* Mino Publications 91

Fairfield Porter critic

7697 To ask the meaning of art is like asking the meaning of life: experience comes before a measurement against a value system.

New York 18 Jun 84

Frank J Prial journalist

7698 The view is traditional Manhattan airshaft.

On writer Robert Caro's office in "a nondescript building in midtown" *NY Times* 31 Mar 90

Malvina Reynolds lyricist

7699 They're all made out of ticky-tacky, and they all look just the same.

"Little Boxes" 1962 song on housing development south of San Francisco, recalled on Reynolds' death 17 Mar 78

Peter Rice engineer

7700 He talks the way he eats—in great, lusty mouthfuls, which suggest enthusiasm without discipline.

On architect Richard Rogers, quoted by Lincoln Caplan "Profiles: An Architecture of Possibilities" *New Yorker* 14 Nov 88

Nelson Rockefeller Governor of New York

7701 If there is anything more satisfying than dedicating a new building, it is dedicating eight new buildings.

On Albany's government mall *NY Times* 13 Mar 70

7702 Mean structures build small vision.

Defending high costs of Albany mall quoted by Peter Collier and David Horowitz *The Rockefellers* Holt Rinehart Winston 78

Richard Rodriguez critic

7703 In the modern city, it takes on the status of a cathedral, our Chartres, our Notre Dame, our marble museum of the soul.

On San Francisco's new Museum of Modern Art *MacNeil-Lehrer Report* 27 Feb 95

Jonathan Routh journalist

7704 [They are] small palaces, gleaming brass handrails, wonderful mosaic floors, walls of polished slate and marble, great mahogany and frosted glass doors to the cubicles, massive porcelain urinals.

On London's Guildhall Yard, quoted on the hundredth anniversary of the first public lavatory *London Times* 31 Jan 92

Witold Rybczynski essayist

7705 It is truly a place for self-presentation—of oneself, to oneself. A fitting sign of the self-absorbed 1980s.

On growing luxuriousness of bathrooms, quoted by Christopher Lehmann-Haupt *NY Times* 19 Nov 92 reviewing Rybczynski's *Looking Around* Viking Penguin 92

Carl Sandburg poet

7706 The skyscrapers stand proud./ They seem to say they have/ sought the absolute/ and made it their own./ Yet they are blameless, innocent/ as dumb steel and the dumber/ concrete of their bastions.

"Skyscrapers Stand Proud" *Poems 1950–67 Complete Poems of Carl Sandburg* Harcourt Brace Jovanovich 70

George Santayana essayist

7707 A building without ornamentation is like a heaven without stars.

Christian Science Monitor 14 Dec 90

William Seale historian

7708 To Americans, the dome is the architectural symbol of democracy.

On the US capitol and state capitals as seen in Eric Oxendorf's photographic study *Washington Post* 21 Oct 95

Walter F J M Scott Duke of Buccleugh

7709 He had the woods and plantation laid out to resemble the shadow of cumulous clouds cast on a sunny hillside.

On Scott's great, great grandfather, the 5th Duke of Buccleugh *Country Life* 5 Jan 95

Vincent Scully critic

7710 [Nature is] sacred once again on a windy slope in the Umbrian highlands, with the olives shimmering silver in the breeze and the heavy clouds riding above them.

On Assisi, birthplace of St Francis *Architecture: The Natural and the Manmade* St Martin's 91

Will Self journalist

7711 The motorways of today are our pyramids, our ziggurats, our great collective earthworks.

London Times 25 Sep 93

Richard Sennett Professor of Humanities, New York University

7712 The foundation of respect in our society is not having cash, but a place to live.

On the shacks of "Bushville" on Manhattan's Lower East Side *NY Times* 28 Mar 93

Fulton J Sheen Roman Catholic archbishop

7713 Our Lord. . . said that if men withheld their praise of him, "the very stones would cry out," which they did as, later, they burst into Gothic cathedrals.

These Are the Sacraments Hawthorn 62

Robert A E Stern critic

7714 The dialogue between client and architect is about as intimate as any conversation you can have because, when you're talking about building a house, you're talking about dreams.

"The Trend-Setting Traditionalism of Architecture" *NY Times* 13 Jan 85

Bayrd Still journalist

7715 [Rockefeller Center is] the tombstone of capitalism. . . with windows.

Mirror for Gotham University Press 56

Hans Stimmann Director of Building, Berlin

7716 We must bring this city back so that when we look in the mirror, we will know that it is our face. . . Berlin must look like Berlin.

On the need for an individuality different from Tokyo or Hong Kong *International Herald Tribune* 7 Feb 95

Lee Strobel Pastor, Willow Creek Community Church, South Barrington IL

7717 [St Paul's is] not very user-friendly.

Comparing his "megachurch" to Wren's masterpiece in London *NY Times* 20 Apr 95

John Summerson essayist

7718 We. . . begin evaluating the contents of a period of architecture on the assumption that in relation to the society that built it, it was right. Where the Victorians are concerned, it would be very much safer to begin. . . on the assumption that it was wrong.

Victorian Architecture Columbia University Press 70 quoted by Herbert Muschamp *NY Times* 6 Dec 92

Francis Henry Taylor critic

7719 The script might be the work of Victor Hugo executed by Cecil B De Mille.

On Le Corbusier's design for a pyramid-shaped World Museum for the League of Nations, quoted by Karl E Meyer *The Art Museum* Morrow 79

Margaret Thatcher Prime Minister of Britain

7720 Nearly 250 years of history... looked rather like a down-at-heel Pall Mall club... rather like a "furnished house to let," which in a way, I suppose it was.

On moving into 10 Downing St *The Downing Street Years* HarperCollins 93

Martha Thorne critic

7721 It's ridiculous... it's like trying to finish a Roman ruin.

On attempts to complete Antonio Gaudi's Church of the Sagrada Familia begun in 1883 in Barcelona *NY Times* 18 Oct 87

Time magazine

7722 [It resembles] an aluminum-and-marble houseboat run aground.

On *Chicago Sun-Times* headquarters 18 Jul 88

Donald Trump financier

7723 See that gold Cadillac down the street? That's the color I want those handrails. Gold. Cadillac Gold. Not yellow like a daisy.

On handrails in Manhattan's Trump Tower, quoted by Paul Trachtman *Smithsonian* Mar 95 reviewing Alexander Theroux's *The Primary Colors* Holt 95

Wolf Von Eckardt critic

7724 You can't see the foyer for the trees.

On E Kevin Roche's atrium in Manhattan's Ford Foundation headquarters *Horizon* Summer 71

7725 I M Pei's architectural hallelujah reminds me of the joyful white and gold domed naves of Bavarian baroque churches, where swallows twitter and swoop through theatrical sunbeams. It is that evocative.

On retracting his earlier reservations about the East Building additon to the National Gallery of Art recalled in *Washington Post* 27 Aug 95

Mark Wallington journalist

7726 [London railway stations are] a strange collection of Victorian landmarks, now stranded around the Monopoly board of the modern city like brick dinosaurs.

In *Britain* Jan 84

Peter Watson critic

7727 Empire even now is the umpire of taste.

On the "grand Gothic garnish" marking the restoration after a fire at Windsor Castle *NY Times* 28 May 95

P G Wodehouse critic

7728 Few of them were to be trusted within reach of a trowel and a pile of bricks.

On remodelers of Victorian houses *Country Life* 23 Oct 84

Tom Wolfe novelist

7729 [It is] the Versailles of American corporate culture.

On Manhattan's Four Seasons restaurant *NY Times* 14 Nov 92

Iran Wolfman journalist

7730 Home is where the altar was.

On remodeling of churches for apartments "Born-Again Churches" *NY Daily News* 15 Mar 87

ART

Painters and Sculptors

Georg Bazelitz artist

7731 I have trouble with beauty.

On the lasting influence of a childhood visit to bombed-out Dresden *NY Times* 21 May 95

7732 I've painted my wife a hundred times... but she always says, "Why don't you ever make me pretty?"

ib

7733 [Art plays] the same role as a good shoe, nothing more.

On efforts to find political or social meaning in art *ib*

7734 Art is... rejection of the old and the search for new beginnings.

ib

Constantin Brancusi sculptor

7735 Nothing grows in the shade of great trees.

On giving up his early studies with Auguste Rodin *Town & Country* Oct 95

Romare Bearden artist

7736 The canvas was always saying no to me.

On early attempts to perfect his work *Washington Post* 14 Mar 88

Thomas Hart Benton muralist

7737 The very thought of large spaces puts me in an exalted state of mind, strings up my energies, and heightens the color of the world.

On work as a muralist *Smithsonian* Apr 89

7738 The ordinary Missouri mule had more to do with the actual growth of the state than any of its favorite sons.

Defending a state house painting under fire for its study of the common life instead of prominent persons *ib*

Alexander Calder inventor of the mobile

7739 When everything goes right, a mobile is a piece of poetry that dances with the joy of life and surprises.

Sunday Morning CBS TV 5 Jan 92

Marc Chagall artist

7740 The artist cannot see himself but with age you see your own life... [and] one paints one's inside as if it were a still life.

"Chagall: Painter of the Poetic" *MD* Aug 80

7741 The title of "Russian painter" means more to me than any international fame... in my paintings there is not one centimeter that is free from nostalgia for my native land.

NY Times 7 Apr 85

7742 I needed Paris as a tree needs rain.

On gift that enabled him to study professionally *MD* Jun 87

Christo (Christo Javacheff) artist

7743 My art is like a marriage... for better and for worse.

On the complexity of wrapping buildings *NY Times* 12 Nov 91

Winston S Churchill statesman

7744 How do they paint one today? Sitting on a lavatory!

On Sutherland portrait afterwards destroyed by Lady Churchill, quoted by Roger Berthoud *Graham Sutherland* Faber & Faber 82

Salvador Dali artist

7745 There is only one picture which you continue all your life on different canvases, like frames on the real film of the imagination.

Vogue 15 May 50

7746 The magic of divine Dali, the illusionist, stands on a sheet of glass, lofted on steel poles.

Quoted by Ultra Violet (Isabelle Dufresne) "Goodbye, Dali—It's Been Surreal" *NY Times* 30 Jan 89

7747 I am the caviar of the irrational famine that reigns in the art world.

ib

Willem de Kooning artist

7748 Flesh was the reason oil painting was invented.

Pittsburgh International Museum *Bulletin* 80

Marcedonlo De La Torre artist

7749 The imagination... must be denied food so that it can work for itself.

NY Times 3 Feb 60

Stephen De Staebler artist

7750 What the clay wanted to do was more beautiful, and full of energy, than what I had in my own mind.

On his exhibiton at the San Francisco Museum of Modern Art *Wall Street Journal* 28 Jul 88

Jean Dubuffet artist

7751 Unless one says goodbye to what one loves and travels to completely new territories, one can expect merely a long wearing-away of oneself and an eventual extinction.

Recalled on Dubuffet's death 12 May 85

Raoul Dufy artist

7752 Nature, my dear sir, is only an hypothesis.

To a critic who questioned "the impossibly poetic blue" in Dufy landscapes, quoted by Alexander Theroux *The Primary Colors* Holt 95

Hans Magnus Enzensberger artist

7753 Culture is a little like dropping an Alka Seltzer into a glass—you don't see it, but somehow it does something.

NY Times 25 Jan 87

Jacob Epstein sculptor

7754 It is amazing how English women of no uncertain age fancy themselves dressed as Venus.

On women's fondness for decolletage for portraits *Epstein* Dutton 55

Helen Frankenthaler artist

7755 I follow the rules until I go against them all.

On translating large, lyrical abstracts from paintings to prints *Washington Times* 16 Apr 93

Albert Giacometti sculptor

7756 I'd have to put you on canvas. Then I might begin to see you a little.

Smithsonian Sep 88

Philip Guston artist

7757 I go to my studio every day, because one day I may go and the angel will be there. What if I don't go and the angel came?

Washington Post 7 Mar 91

Frederick E Hart artist

7758 Art must touch our lives, our fears and cares; evoke our dreams and give hope to the darkness.

Reflections privately published 94

Barbara Hepworth sculptor

7759 The strokes of the hammer on the chisel have to be in time with your heartbeat or pulse.

NY Times 5 Mar 95

7760 The left hand is the feeling hand, the right hand the executant.

ib

Al Hirschfeld sketch artist

7761 I was a sculptor. But that's really drawing—a drawing you fall over in the dark, a three-dimensional drawing.

85th birthday interview *NY Times* 21 Jun 88

7762 What I do, across all the years of staring at a blank piece of paper, is create a new problem every time, and then solve it to my own satisfaction.

ib

7763 I've always been interested in the insanities of people rather than nature; it would never occur to me to do the Grand Canyon.

9 Nov 91

Hans Hoffman artist

7764 The ability to simplify means to eliminate the unnecessary so that the necessary may speak.

Search for the Real MIT Press 67

Edward Hopper artist

7765 A nation's art is greatest when it most reflects the character of its people.

Quoted by Anatole Broyard *Aroused by Books* Random House 74

7766 It's probably a reflection of my own, if I may say, loneliness. . . . It could be the whole human condition.

On the subjects of his paintings *Washington Post* 25 Jun 95

7767 I can't do this house. . . don't want to paint this house. . . does nothing for me. . . no light and no air.

On his disdain for painting on commission *NY Times* 8 Sep 95

Peter Hurd artist

7768 He's a chair-fighter. . . can't get him to sit still. . . [but] he has a very paintable face. What I would call Texas Roman.

On the Lyndon B Johnson portrait commissioned by the White House Historical Association but later rejected by Johnson *Time* 8 Jul 66

Augustus John artist

7769 America is an orgy of color, noise, smartness, and multitudinous legs.

Recalled on John's death 31 Oct 61

Jasper Johns artist

7770 [I paint] things that are seen but not looked at.

On subjects such as the American flag, archery targets and the numbers zero through 9 *NY Times* 19 Jun 88

Nikos Kazantzakis author

7771 My entire soul is a cry, and all my work is a commentary on that cry.

Report to Greco Simon & Schuster 65

Rockwell Kent artist

7772 Sledgehammer sentimentality.

On his wholesome depiction of contemporary America *Washington Post* 6 Jun 93

Giuseppe Lund artist

7773 I just took the lovely generous cleavage of a lady of her age. . . that's really what you've got in the center of those gates.

Defending the fragile design of the Hyde Park gates erected by public subscription as a 90th birthday tribute to the Queen Mother *London Weekly Telegraph* 10 Jul 93

René Magritte artist

7774 If the spectator finds that my paintings are a kind of defiance of "common sense," he realizes something obvious. . . that for me the world is defiance of common sense.

NY Times 11 Sep 92

Henri Matisse artist

7775 When I started to paint I felt transported into a kind of paradise. . . [while] in everyday life, I was usually bored and vexed by the things people were always telling me I must do.

Quoted in *History of Modern Painting* Skira, Geneva 50

7776 I was driven on by. . . a force which I see today as something alien to my normal life. . . so I have been no more than a medium, as it were.

Dominique Fourcade ed *Henri Matisse* Hermann, Paris 72

7777 My canvases that are simply drawn... are more profoundly moving... like the tears of a child in its cradle. The others are like the screams of a whore in love.
Newsweek 25 May 87

7778 [It is] my drawing with scissors.
On his *papiers découpés,* largely developed by wielding scissors from a sick-bed when he was no longer able to stand *Christian Science Monitor* 14 Aug 86

7779 An old brush has vitality, it's a brush that has lived, that has had a life of its own.
Quoted by Rosamond Bernier *Matisse Picasso, Miro* Knopf 92

Joan Miró artist

7780 You have to abandon yourself to your work ... only then does your work contain you totally.
Quoted by Hayden Herrera's *Matisse* Harcourt Brace 93

7781 When you're out of willpower, you call on stubborness.
On continuing to work after surgery *ib*

7782 We Catalans believe you must always plant your feet firmly on the ground if you want to be able to jump up in the air.
Christian Science Monitor 27 Oct 93

7783 The fact that I come down to earth from time to time makes it possible for me to jump all the higher.
ib

7784 Express with precision all the golden sparks the soul gives off.
ib

Henry Moore sculptor

7785 Drawing and sculpture are the same thing... one an illusion of the other.
Illustrated London News May 78

7786 [Discipline in art is] a fundamental struggle to understand oneself, as much as to understand what one is drawing.
Recalled on Moore's death 31 Aug 86

7787 Sculpture is an art of the open air. I would rather have a piece of my sculpture put in a landscape, almost any landscape, than in, or on, the most beautiful building I know.
London Times 13 May 95

Robert Motherwell artist

7788 Every intelligent painter carries the whole culture of modern painting in his head... everything he paints is both an homage and a critique.
LA Times 31 Jul 77

7789 [Painting is] a state of anxiety that is obliquely recorded in the inner tensions of the finished canvas.
Time 29 Jul 91

Louise Nevelson artist

7790 A brook is beautiful... but I identify with the ocean.
Dawns and Dusks Scribner 76

7791 I began to stack my sculptures into an environment. It was natural. It was a flowing of energy.
ib

Georgia O'Keeffe artist

7792 Nobody sees a flower—really—it is so small—we haven't time—and to see takes time, like to have a friend takes time.
On magnifying of flowers and bleached bones *NY Times* 1 Nov 87

Claes Oldenburg artist

7793 I am for an art that does something other than sit on its ass in a museum!
London Times 29 Apr 95

Pablo Picasso artist

7794 When I was their age, I could draw like Raphael, but it took me a lifetime to learn to draw like them.
On an exhibition of children's drawings, quoted by Roland Penrose *Picasso: His Life and Work* Harper 58

7795 After me, you are the one who is opening a new door.
To Joan Miró *Christian Science Monitor* 27 Oct 93

7796 Sculpture is the best comment that a painter can make on painting.
On the complexity of his art *ib* 7 Apr 94

Eddie Pizzaro stone-carver

7797 We're not all perfect, but we can do something perfect.
On work as a stonecarver at New York's Cathedral of St John the Divine *NY Times* 14 Jul 90

Jackson Pollock artist

7798 You know more but I understand more.
To fellow painter Willem de Kooning, quoted by April Kingsley *The Turning Point* Simon & Schuster 92

John Roach muralist

7799 [It was a choice between] the Tennessee Switchback Kazoo Band and the London Philharmonic Orchestra. If what you want is the London Philharmonic, stick with me.

On his unsuccessful efforts to execute murals in the US Capitol *Washington Post* 5 Jan 94

Mark Rothko artist

7800 The people who weep before my pictures are having the same religious experience I had when I painted them.

On his nuanced, color-clouded works, quoted by James E B Breslin *Mark Rothko* University of Chicago 93

7801 I hope to paint something that will ruin the appetite of every son of a bitch who ever eats in that room.

On decorating Manhattan's Four Seasons restaurant *ib*

Anvar Saifoutdinov artist

7802 Life is not easy. I paint the memory of happiness.

Christian Science Monitor 19 Nov 92

Andres Serrano artist

7803 I had red and white and, quite frankly, I needed a third color to add to my palette. . . I turned to urine. . . a quite vivid and vibrant color.

On mixing urine with blood and milk as "life's vital fluids," a step that led to his controversial work of a crucifix immersed in urine *NY Times* 16 Aug 89

John Sloan artist

7804 Artists are the only people in the world who really live. The others have to hope for heaven.

Smithsonian Apr 88

Coosje Van Bruggen artist

7805 People saw me as the poison ivy climbing the big oak tree.

On collaborating with her husband Claes Oldenburg *London Times* 29 Apr 95

7806 We are pushing the parameters, using industrial materials, and we create doubt about whether this is art.

On producing commonplace objects enlarged up to 50 times in size *ib*

Andy Warhol artist

7807 In the future everyone will be famous for 15 minutes.

Washington Post 15 Nov 79

7808 I always wished I had died. . . because I could have gotten the whole thing over with.

On being shot by a former employee in 1969 *Newsweek* 9 Mar 87

7809 During the 1960s. . . people forgot what emotions were supposed to be. And I don't think they've ever remembered.

ib

7810 I'd like my own tombstone to be blank. . . Well, actually, I'd like to say "figment."

ib

7811 Fame is when you market your aura.

Quoted by Ultra Violet *Famous for 15 Minutes* Harcourt Brace Jovanovich 88

Andrew Wyeth artist

7812 I get excited by the shape of a person's nose, the tone of their eyes, or the way their back looks when they're turned away from me. That's my reason for painting.

National Geographic Jul 91

7813 [Mine] was the most imaginative, rich childhood you could ever imagine. That is why I have so much inside of me that I want to paint.

ib

Henriette Wyeth artist

7814 While she posed for me, there were times I could tell she wanted to be outside picking off the dead things. Things in the garden were going to hell without her.

On White House portrait of Pat Nixon, quoted by Julie Nixon Eisenhower *Pat Nixon* Simon & Schuster 86

N C Wyeth artist

7815 I feel so moved sometimes toward nature I could almost throw myself face down into a ploughed furrow.

On the fields and forests of Chadds Ford PA *National Geographic* Jul 91

7816 Never paint the material of the sleeve. Become the arm! Get your love into it.

ib

Elyn Zimmerman sculptor

7817 In a museum you can elect to go or not go. In a public scape the work inflicts itself on you.

On display of controversial, subsidized art *NY Times* 22 Sep 85

Photographers

Ansel Adams

7818 Not everybody trusts paintings but people believe photographs.

The Portfolios of Ansel Adams NY Graphic Society/Little, Brown 81

Richard Avedon

7819 He was the customer and I was the supermarket.

On *Vogue* editor Alex Liberman, quoted by Dodie Kazanjian and Calvin Tomkins *Alex* Knopf 93

7820 Glamour is the appearance of the possibility of achievement. . . salvation through magic.

New Yorker 21 Mar 94

7821 A red-headed force of nature, a wolf in chic clothing, the one flesh-and-blood woman in a world of exquisite creatures.

On the 1950s model Suzy Parker *ib* 13 Feb 95

Cecil Beaton

7822 He opened his blue eyes to stare long and wonderingly into the camera lens, the beginning of a lifetime in the glare of public duty.

Diary entry 1948 on photographing Prince Charles at the age of one month, recalled on Beaton's death 18 Jan 80

Robert Capa

7823 War is like an aging actress—more and more dangerous and less and less photogenic.

Quoted by John Hersey *Life Sketches* Knopf 89

Henri Cartier-Bresson

7824 [My camera is a] combination of the psychiatrist's couch, machine gun and a warm kiss.

Henri Cartier-Bresson: The Early Work NY Museum of Modern Art 87

7825 We are passive witnesses in front of an active world.

Life Dec 87

7826 A photographer is part pick-pocket and part tightrope dancer.

ib

Frank Deford

7827 She glances at the photo. . . the pilot light of memory flickers in her eyes.

On the 1930s German film director Leni Riefenstahl *Sports Illustrated* 4 Aug 86

Alfred Eisenstaedt

7828 The most important thing. . . is not clicking the shutter. . . it is clicking with the subject.

Witness to Our Time Viking 66

7829 I want to be a mouse in a mousehole.

On unobtrusiveness, recalled on Eisenstaedt's death 24 Aug 95

Walker Evans

7830 The portraits on these pages were caught by a hidden camera in the hands of a penitent spy and an apologetic voyeur.

On his reluctance to invade the poverty and privacy of sharecropper families *Cambridge Review* Mar 56

7831 I do like to suggest people sometimes by their absence. . . that an interior is almost inhabited by somebody.

Quoted by Belinda Rathbone *Walker Evans* Houghton Mifflin 95

7832 I am delighted with your plans to educate the Chase Bank. They have been educating me for so long now.

To Nancy Newhall on arranging a bank exhibit of Evans' work *ib*

7833 This lifting is, in the raw, exactly what the photographer is doing with his machine, the camera, anyway, always.

On stealing signs for a photographic record of his times *ib*

7834 Stare. It is the only way to educate your eye, and more. Stare, pry, listen, eavesdrop.

On perfecting his photographic skills in the sidewalk cafes of Paris *ib*

Hans Haacke

7835 I don't want to push myself into the foreground. The foreground should be my work.

On granting an interview with the provision that he would not be photographed *NY Times* 10 Dec 94

Horst (Robert P Horst)

7836 Sex was invented in America in the 60's. Before that, it didn't exist.

On trends in fashion photography *NY Times* 27 Feb 88

Andre Kertesz

7837 To feel is the *raison d'être.* The photograph is a fixed moment of such a *raison d'être,* which lives on in itself.

The Concerned Photographer Grossman 67

Jacques-Henri Lartigue

7838 The wonderful thing about fast sports is that one can live for a while in the fantastic domain of fractions of a second.

On photographing tennis players *Le Monde* 8 Nov 94 quoted in *Guardian Weekly* 25 Dec 94

7839 [It is] that indescribable whiff of air that has cooled down.

On the domain of perception and sensation in photography *ib*

Michael Lesy

7840 Even the dogs were docile, stiff and porcelain.

On photographing families at the turn of the century *Wisconsin Death Trap* Pantheon 73

Wright Morris

7841 The carriage, crossing a square, the pet straining at its leash, are momentarily detained from their destination.

On freezing subjects in a moment of time, James Alinder ed *Wright Morris: Photographs and Words* Matrix 91

7842 On these ghostly shades the photograph confers a brief immortality.

ib

Arnold Newman

7843 We don't take our pictures with cameras. We take them with our hearts. . . our minds.

Sunday Morning CBS TV 2 Aug 92

Norman Parkinson

7844 I am never bored when I am present.

On 50 years as a fashion photographer *NY Times* 15 Dec 87

Edward Steichen

7845 Photography records the gamut of feelings written on the human face, the beauty of the earth and skies that man has inherited and the wealth and confusion man has created.

Time 7 Apr 61

7846 Photography is a major force in explaining man to man. Every other artist begins [with] a blank canvas, a piece of paper. . . the photographer begins with the finished product.

Recalled on Steichen's death 25 Mar 71

7847 When that shutter clicks, anything else that can be done afterwards is not worth consideration.

ib

7848 Photography was conceived as a mirror of the universal elements and emotions of the everydayness of life. . . a mirror of the essential oneness of mankind.

Dialogue May 89

Vladmir Syomin

7849 I shoot photographs about the Russia that is beyond the fringes of our television civilization.

On award-winning pictures of "a Russia isolated by destroyed roads and vast woods" *NY Times* 30 Oct 95

Garry Winogrand

7850 I photograph to find out what something will look like photographed.

Cited by Richard Lacayo in review of Winogrand's work as "one of the world's most circular quotes" *Time* 16 May 88

Collectors and Curators

Walter H Annenberg publisher

7851 You are asking me to sell members of my family.

Rejecting a billion-dollar Japanese offer for his art collection *NY Times* 12 Mar 91

7852 I would never sell a member of my family because I want them to stay together.

On giving his collection to the Metropolitan Museum of Art *ib* 1 Apr 91

7853 I would get up out of my grave and hit the director over the head!

When asked his reaction were his paintings stored in the Met's basement *ib*

7854 I believe in strength to strength.

On selecting the Met because it ranked with the Louvre in having the world's most complete collection *ib*

7855 Only when you are moved by a painting should you buy it. Being moved is what collecting is all about.

Connoisseur Feb 91

Anon

7856 There's no real heaven in Jewish thought, and there's this feeling you must leave your good works on earth.

A senior official of the Metropolitan Museum of Art commenting on the generosity of Jewish donors, quoted by Anthony Sampson *The Midas Touch* Hodder & Stoughton 89

7857 Give it or get it.

On financial support expected of board members of the Metropolitan Museum of Art, quoted by Edwin Diamond *Behind the Times* Villard 93

Dore Ashton Head, Division of Art, Cooper Union NYC

7858 The words, dispersed everywhere, were after all part of his magic, as were the innumerable newspaper cuttings, magazine images, feathers, engravings, and pressed flowers that occupied the album of his imagination.

On Joseph Cornell's boxes and collages *A Joseph Cornell Album* Viking 74

Albert C Barnes Founder, Barnes Collection

7859 This mystic whom we have treated as a vagrant has proved his possession of a power to create out of his own soul and our own America, moving beauty of an individual character whose existence we never knew.

On African-American art in the US, recalled in *Christian Science Monitor* 26 Jul 93

Alfred H Barr Jr Curator, Museum of Modern Art NYC

7860 Except the American woman, nothing interests the eye of American man more than the automobile, or seems so important to him as an object of esthetic appreciation.

On exhibiting old automobiles parts, news summaries 31 Dec 63

7861 [Hopper's paintings] are like the edge of a stage beyond which drama unfolds.

On Edward Hopper, quoted by Anatold Broyard *Aroused by Books* Random House 74

Kathleen Weil-Garris Brandt Professor of Fine Arts NYU

7862 The changes were made at the request of the patron, namely the papacy... a chart of notions of decorum over time.

On removal of nearly half of the 40 breeches, loincloths and other draperies added after Michelangelo's death to his *Last Judgment* in the Vatican's Sistine Chapel *NY Times* 9 Apr 94

J Carter Brown Director, National Gallery of Art

7863 A great art collection is like a garden. A bit of pruning is necessary—though some blossoms fall.

Washington Post 9 Aug 89

7864 The point is to get them to take something away with them, and to have their eyes opened.

On visitors to the National Gallery *Celebrity Register* Gale 90

7865 I felt a rope had been attached to every limb and was being pulled by horses running in different directions.

On his surprise decision to leave the Gallery after 23 years *Washington Post* 2 Apr 92

Phillipe de Montebello Director, Metropolitan Museum of Art

7866 The Annenberg collection... magnificent, ravishing... an immeasurable addition.

On Walter H Annenberg's gift of impressionists and post-impressionists paintings *Newsweek* 28 Mar 91

George R Goldner Curator, J Paul Getty Museum

7867 No one wants to pay more than he should, but at the end of the day, the question is not how much you spent but whether you own the object.

Replying to charges that Getty bidding had inflated what was paid for Old Master drawings *NY Times* 23 Oct 88

Yasuo Goto Chair, Yasuda Insurance, Tokyo

7868 [I was] amused by the power and brightness... its courage and passion.

On purchasing Vincent Van Gogh's *Sunflowers* for £24.7 million, quoted by Anthony Sampson *The Midas Touch* Hodder & Stoughton 89

Armand Hammer petroleum magnate

7869 The art world is a jungle echoing to the calls of vicious jealousies and ruthless combat... but I have been walking in the jungles of business all my life, and fighting tooth and nail for pictures comes as a form of relaxation to me.

In his autobiography *Hammer, Witness to History* Simon & Schuster 87

7870 My Van Gogh is better than *Irises*. I have the whole garden.

On ranking Van Gogh's *Hospital at Saint-Ramy* over Van Gogh's *Irises* that brought £53.9 million at auction *Connoisseur* Jan 91

Walter Hopps Founding Director, Menil Collection, Houston

7871 Installing a museum exhibition is conducting a symphony orchestra.

New Yorker 29 Jul 91

7872 If I don't know where every single thing is going, within three inches, I'm not happy.

ib

7873 I think of myself as being in a line of work that goes back about 25,000 years... finding the cave and holding the torch.

ib

Thomas Hoving Director, Metropolitan Museum of Art

7874 The chase and the capture of a great work of art is one of the most exciting endeavors in life—as dramatic, emotional, and fulfilling as a love affair.

The Chase, the Capture Metropolitan Museum of Art 75

7875 You would appeal to. . . their desires to become a member of high society, and the highest society of all was to be on the board of the Met.

On raising money, quoted by Anthony Sampson *The Midas Touch* Hodder & Stoughton 89

7876 You would very simply lay out the most rational and important reasons why they should give their five million. . . and they would give it within, I'd say, six to ten seconds.

On financial contributions from board members *ib*

7877 It's pure social climbing. . . out of some wretched place into society.

ib

7878 Third wife, you know, the 30-year old beautiful, softic third wife, good tailor, fine houses, or two or three or four, a plane, a yacht: and then, art. Because art is the ultimate imprimatur that you are rich.

ib

7879 Frick, Morgan, the whole crowd of Robber Barons cleaned up their act through art.

ib

7880 The Met is in a sense the combination of the Vatican, Versailles, the Sultan's Court, and the Cave of Ali Baba.

Making the Mummies Dance Simon & Schuster 93

7881 You cannot dash around them, crawl over them, thrust a light to their eyes as you can do to storerooms, roofs, or the exteriors of a bunch of buildings.

On curators *ib*

Dominique-Charles Janssens artist

7882 *The Sunflowers* complicated everything.

On acquiring Vincent Van Gogh's house after the $39.9-million sale of his best-known painting *NY Times* 28 Sep 93

Michel Laclotte Director, The Louvre

7883 We have to choose once and for all where the future of the Gare d'Orsay will lie. . . with Cézanne, or is it to be with Camembert?

On decision to convert a Parisian rail terminal to a gallery instead of a showplace for produce and cheese *NY Times* 6 Jun 93

Paul Mellon philanthropist

7884 I never with confidence know,/ If Van Gogh is Van Gock or Van Gogh./ I admit to my shame,/ This chameleon name,/ Makes my hi-brows feel terribly low.

Toast at awards dinner at the National Gallery of Art, quoted by Claudia ("Lady Bird") Johnson *A White House Diary* Holt Rinehart Winston 70

7885 But a friend of mine said, off the cuff,/ You might say that his name was Van Guff,/ But regardless, I fear,/ What he did to his ear/ Was playing a little too rough!

ib

7886 [It was] just one more investment. . . one more prop for the scaffolding which held up his gigantic, intensive, mysterious ego.

On his father's founding of the National Gallery of Art *Washington Post* 7 Apr 92

Edward H Merrin antiquities dealer

7887 The price was quite reasonable. It just happened to be a lot of money.

On paying $2.09 million for nine-inch, 5,000-year-old Greek head *NY Times* 16 Jul 89

Thomas M Messer Director, Guggenheim Museum

7888 Individual and corporate support has kept us in the black. Not to mention cobalt blue, cadmium yellow, and burnt sienna.

On contributions for art acquired by the Chase Manhattan Bank *New York* 16 Nov 87

Michael King of Romania

7889 [I took] not even an ashtray.

On being sued for art works worth an estimated $500 million *NY Times* 14 Sep 93

Nell Minow President, Institutional Shareholders Inc

7890 If a company clerk takes money for something personal, it's embezzlement. If Armand Hammer does it, it's business judgment.

Connoisseur Jan 91

John Pope-Hennessy Director, Victoria and Albert Museum

7891 Dutch painting is too good to be studied only by the Dutch.

Learning to Look Doubleday 91

7892 The virus I caught at Oxford was emotional, and I have never recovered from it.

ib

7893 Objects mean more to me than people. . . not that I am frigid or reclusive, but that object-based relationships are more constant than human ones; they never change their nature and do not pall.

ib

Mikhail Pyotrovsky Director, The Hermitage

7894 No one has seen them for 50 years. No restorer has touched them in 70 years.

On exhibiting French Impressionists and Post-Impressionists held secretly since World War II *NY Times* 4 Oct 94

7895 I do not consider it a sin that art was taken away from Germany. The sin was to conceal it from people for so long.

Vanity Fair Mar 95

David Rockefeller banker

7896 I was born into wealth and there was nothing I could do about it. It was there like food or air.

Merchants and Masterpieces WETA TV 31 Dec 90

John D Rockefeller Jr banker

7897 I have never squandered money on horses, yachts, automobiles or other foolish extravaganzas. A fondness for these porcelains is my only hobby—the only thing on which I have cared to spend money.

Requesting his father to support the million dollar purchase of J P Morgan's collection of Ming and Ching vessels *NY Times* 31 Jul 94

Pierre Rosenberg Director of the Louvre

7898 We have too many tourists and I am afraid they have evicted the visitors, those who know the museum, who love the museum. I want to give the museum back to the visitors.

NY Times 6 Feb 95

7899 We have never seriously considered cleaning her.

On the Mona Lisa *ib*

Charles Saatchi Saatchi Gallery, London

7900 I'm not sure what today's young artists are putting in their porridge.

On the emergent generation of artists as "challenging, articulate and relevant" *London Times* 6 Dec 94

7901 [Sometimes art appears] tasteless, cynical and uncouth. I think it's because sometimes we all are.

ib

Norbert Schimmel philanthropist

7902 Always buy the piece, never the story.

NY Times 20 Aug 89

Charles Schreiber President, House of Heydenryk NYC framers

7903 If you notice the frame first when you look at a picture, we've made a mistake.

NY Times 28 Mar 91

Eugene M Schwartz advertising executive

7904 Collecting is the only socially commendable form of greed.

Confessions of a Poor Collector Fairleigh-Dickinson University 70

7905 It is a conduit for museums.

On the walls of his Park Avenue penthouse that changed as often as the institutions to which he gave *ib*

Robert Montgomery Scott President, Philadelphia Museum of Art

7906 My reaction is a combination of "shucks" and "hooray."

On learning of Walter H Annenberg's gift of 52 Impressionists and Post-Impressionists paintings to the Metropolitan Museum of Art *Newsweek* 25 Mar 91

Robert Storr Curator of Painting and Sculpture, Museum of Modern Art

7907 It's a letting go of distances.

On the necessity of establishing an intimacy and trust between artist and sitter *NY Times* 1 Jan 95

7908 A portrait allows you to stare at somebody as much as you like and satisfy your curiosity.

ib

Roy Strong Director, Victoria and Albert Museum

7909 It was just our historical bitchery in the past, but now it's on a megaplane.

On museum competition for Japanese funds *NY Times* 30 Sep 87

Gary Tinterow Engelhard Associate Curator, European Paintings, Metropolitan Museum of Art

7910 Our feeling was that 19th-century paintings would be more at home in a 19th-century space.

On $10-million renovation of the most widely visited galleries of Impressionist and Post- Impressionist paintings *NY Times* 16 Sep 91

Alice B Toklas companion to Gertrude Stein

7911 (It was) my first infidelity to Paris, and a big mistake.

On spending a winter in Rome during which paintings left her by Gertrude Stein were seized by the Stein estate, quoted by Janet Flanner *Paris Journal 1944–1965* Atheneum 65

7912 I am not unhappy about it. I remember them better than I could see them now.

At 84, *ib*

Peter Vansittart novelist

7913 David, you talk in metaphor.

To the curator David Sylvester who replied, "Always better than simile," quoted by Peter Vansittart *In the Fifties* John Murray 95

John Walker Director, National Gallery of Art

7914 It is true the women I love lack a third dimension but no one frowns on two-dimensional polygamy and infidelity for culture is justified.

On great portraits of women *NY Herald Tribune* 9 Jan 66

7915 Neither marriage, nor divorce is involved, jealousy is inconceivable. The lady is always waiting, is never impatient. . . never loses her beauty, and is indifferent to the age, wealth, and charm of her suitors. Conversations with her are apt to be one-sided, but arguments, criticisms, quarrels?—these are unthinkable. . . . And you can tell your wife all about it.

ib

7916 Once they begin spending Other People's Money they will never leave well enough alone.

On the escalating cost of I M Pei's East Building at the National Gallery of Art, recalled in *Washington Post* 27 Aug 95

Lila Acheson Wallace art patron

7917 A painting is like a man. If you can live without it, then there isn't much point in having it.

Recalled on Wallace's death 8 May 84

FASHION

Designers

Billy Baldwin interior designer

7918 [Rich Palm Beach clients] all wanted the same kind of different thing.

NY Times 20 Oct 85

7919 One of my favorite colors is no color at all.

3 May 87 *ib*

7920 His apartments were always delightful, but he had a heart of beige.

On designer Van Day Truex, Billy Baldwin with Michael Gardine *Billy Baldwin* Little, Brown 85

7921 Nothing-at-all is better than second-best. Never fill an empty space just to fill it. Second-best is expensive, while nothing costs nothing.

ib

7922 A young woman must be a debutante in Baltimore and a young married woman in New York City. An old woman must marry a European, preferably in Paris, and live the rest of her life there.

On old society's unwritten code, quoted by Annette Tapert and Diana Edkins *The Power of Style* Crown 94

Cristobal Balenciaga dress designer

7923 You don't have to have any taste at all. You are fitted by my fitter and that is it!

To fashion editor Diana Vreeland, who had asked, "Does one need great taste to wear your clothes?" *Country Life* 15 May 86

Geoffrey Beene dress designer

7924 The first two years weren't bad, then every disease we studied, I got.

On why he left medical school for Seventh Avenue dress designing *Celebrity Register* Gale 90

Manolo Blahnik dress designer

7925 About half my designs are controlled fantasy, 15 percent total madness and the rest are bread-and-butter designs.

W 25 Aug 86

7926 These are very dainty and super-refined, but really vile.

On shoes for winter 1986 *ib*

7927 Women are wearing tight and sexy clothes again. . . body-conscious mentality. . . revealing every bulge.

ib

7928 My shoes are special. . . shoes for discerning feet.

ib

Bill Blass dress designer

7929 When in doubt, wear red!

On dresses and accessories, news summaries 31 Dec 82

7930 Sometimes the eye gets so accustomed that if you don't have a change, you're bored. . . and that, I suppose, is what style is about.

W 25 Feb 83

7931 Real estate was interfering with his social life, so he sold it. And from then on he specialized in friendship; it became his profession.

On former real estate executive Jerry Zipkin as a society escort of celebrities *Vanity Fair* Sep 95

Marc Bohan designer

7932 Elegance is a yardstick, the art of knowing how much free rein one can allow one's imagination without overstepping the boundaries of classicism.

On furniture and interiors *Architectural Digest* Oct 94

Mario Buatta interior designer

7933 I like all the chairs to talk to one another, and to the sofas. . . not those parlor-car arrangements that create two Siberias.
On furniture placement *New York* 28 Jan 85

Pierre Cardin sportswear designer

7934 The jean! The jean is the destructor. . . a dictator! It is destroying creativity.
Parade 28 Jun 76

7935 I wash with my own soap—wear my own perfume. . . go to bed on my own sheets. . . have my own food products. . . I live on me.
On endorsements *Celebrity Register* Gale 90

Oleg Cassini dress designer

7936 Good shoulders. . . and a long waist are the most necessary . . . when it comes to wearing clothes.
In My Own Fashion Simon & Schuster 87

7937 I imagined her as an ancient Egyptian princess.
On designing for Jacqueline Kennedy Onassis as First Lady *ib*

7938 I would use the most sumptuous fabrics in the purest interpretations. . . [but] very little jewelry or other frills which would detract from the monastic simplicity of her wardrobe.
ib

7939 Fashion anticipates, and elegance is a state of mind. . . a mirror of the time in which we live, a translation of the future, and should never be static.
ib

7940 When I entered the White House through the front door and not the servants' entrance, the status and image of the American designer changed. . . [and] I wore a dinner jacket, not pins in my mouth.
ib

Gabrielle ("Coco") Chanel dress designer

7941 I love luxury. . . not in richness and ornateness but in the absence of vulgarity. . . the ugliest word in our language. I stay in the game to fight it.
Life 19 Aug 57

7942 Quietly, calmly, with great determination, I began working on *un belle collection*. . . [and] always I was smiling inside my head and I thought, I will show them.
On her come-back after World War II *New Yorker* 28 Sep 57

7943 There are no potato sacks among my dresses!
Protesting copies of *la mode Chanel ib*

7944 Luxury must be comfortable, otherwise it is not luxury.
ib

7945 Fashion is made to become unfashionable.
ib

7946 Look for the woman in the dress. If there is no woman, there is no dress.
ib

7947 It is the unseen, unforgettable, ultimate accessory of fashion. . . that heralds your arrival and prolongs your departure.
On perfume *NY Herald Tribune* 18 Oct 64

7948 Elegance is not the prerogative of those who have just escaped from adolescence, but of those who have already taken possession of their future.
McCall's Nov 65

7949 God knows I wanted love. But the moment I had to choose between the man I loved and my dresses, I chose the dresses.
Quoted by Marcel Haedrich *Coco Chanel* Pierre Belfond, Paris 87

7950 Work has always been a kind of drug for me, even if I sometimes wonder what Chanel would have been without the men in my life.
ib

7951 Fashion is not something that exists in dresses only; fashion is something in the air. It's the wind that blows in the new fashion; you feel it coming, you smell it. . . in the sky, in the street; fashion has to do with ideas, the way we live, what is happening.
Quoted by Alex Madsen *Chanel* Holt 90

7952 I adore you, but you dress women like armchairs.
To Christian Dior *ib*

7953 For a dress to be pretty, the woman who's wearing it must look as if she were nude underneath.
ib

7954 I was the first one to live the life of this century.
On designing casual sportswear and dresses for business *Vanity Fair* Jun 94

7955 Look how ridiculous these women are, wearing clothes by a man who doesn't know women, never had one, and dreams of being one.
On Christian Dior's "New Look" *ib*

7956 I like fashion to go down to the street, but I can't accept that it should originate there.
Quoted by Annette Tapert and Diana Edkins *The Power of Style* Crown 94

7957 Fashion changes—style remains.
ib

Angela Cummings jewelry designer

7958 I think of Bergdorf's as being something like pastel sapphires.

On Bergdorf-Goodman on Fifth Avenue *NY Times* 20 Aug 84

Lily Dache milliner

7959 When I was six I made my mother a little hat—out of her new blouse.

News summaries 31 Dec 54

7960 Glamour is what makes a man ask for your telephone number. But it is also what makes a woman ask for the name of your dressmaker.

ib

Hubert de Givenchy dress designer

7961 I absolutely believe my talent is God-given. I ask for a lot, but I also thank Him. I'm a very demanding believer.

W 12 Oct 79

7962 Hair style is the final tip-off whether or not a woman really knows herself.

Vogue Jul 85

Elsie de Wolfe (Lady Mendl) interior designer

7963 It's my color—beige!

On the Parthenon, recalled on de Wolfe's death 12 Jul 50

7964 If I am ugly, and I am, I am going to make everything around myself beautiful. That will be my life. To create beauty.

On pioneering in interior design, quoted by Ludwig Bemelmans *To the One I Love the Best* Viking 55

7965 Beautiful things are faithful friends, and they stay beautiful as they get older.

ib

7966 My lovely house, my lovely garden—I could steal for beauty, I could kill for it.

ib

Niels Diffrient industrial designer

7967 The less there is of a phone, the more I like it.

NY Times 16 Oct 86

7968 It looks like a golosh with electronics in it.

On a rubber Italian telephone *ib*

Christian Dior dress designer

7969 My dream is to save them from nature.

On his desire to make all women beautiful *Collier's* 10 Jul 55

7970 To manufacture emotion a man must have a working agreement with madness.

ib

7971 Zest is the secret of all beauty. There is no beauty that is attractive without zest.

Ladies' Home Journal Apr 56

7972 Women are the most fascinating between 35 and 40 after they have won a few races and know how to pace themselves.

ib Apr 58

7973 Since few women ever pass 40, maximum fascination can continue indefinitely.

ib

7974 My weakness. . . is architecture. I think of my work as ephemeral architecture, dedicated to the beauty of the female body.

Architectural Digest Oct 94

7975 I brought back the neglected art of pleasing.

ib

Henri D'Origny necktie designer

7976 When I do my designs, it is like writing music. My vocabulary is graphic, repetitive, geometric, with the base of equestrian elements.

On Hermès ties as male tribal totems *International Herald Tribune* 16 Jan 95

Freddie Fox milliner

7977 She is not a fashion plate, she is a monarch: you can't have both.

On criticism of Queen Elizabeth's "awful hats" *London Times* 6 Oct 84

Anne Fogarty dress designer

7978 If you adore her, you must adorn her. There lies the secret of a happy marriage.

Wife Dressing Messner 59

Suzie Frankfurt interior designer

7979 [Interior decorating] isn't about buying furniture and filling space. It's creating space.

Vanity Fair Jun 87

Jean-Paul Gaultier dress designer

7980 She was the first punk woman.

On dying his grandmother's hair pink after failing to read directions on how to turn it blue *NY Times* 31 Oct 86

Rudi Gernreich dress designer

7981 It was just a whimsical idea that escalated when so many crazy ladies took it up.

On designing the topless bathing suit *Chicago American* 26 Nov 66

Halston (Roy Halston Frowick) dress designer

7982 Trench coat, pants, and sunglasses... told everyone there's no need to dress up for the day.

On Jacqueline Kennedy Onassis, quoted by Annette Tapert and Diana Edkins *The Power of Style* Crown 94

Mark Hampton interior designer

7983 A nice, undercooked look—nothing too fake, nothing too rich.

On understated interiors *NY Times* 22 Nov 84

Norman Hartnell dress designer

7984 I despise simplicity. It is the negation of all that is beautiful.

On clothes for Queen Elizabeth *London Times* 30 Apr 85

Edith Head wardrobe designer

7985 A designer is only as good as the star who wears her clothes.

After wining eight Oscars for her work *Saturday Evening Post* 30 Nov 63

7986 You just put the minimum of beads on the maximum chassis.

On dressing actress Juliet Prowse *ib*

7987 I have yet to see one completely unspoiled star, except for the animals—like Lassie.

ib

Dolly Hoffman interior designer

7988 Taking the cream out of every glass of milk, that's the way I understand decorating.

W 10 Jul 89

7989 My whole idea of life is that French song *La Vie en Rose*—everything gentle.

ib

Calvin Klein clothes designer

7990 There's something incredibly sexy about a woman wearing her boyfriend's T-shirt and underwear.

People 24 Dec 84

7991 You have to take things to an extreme and then bring them back to reality.

On undulating length of skirts, quoted by Trish Hall, "As Women Balk, Fashion Rethinks the Mini" *NY Times* 9 Mar 88

Eileen ("Butch") Krutchik stationer

7992 I don't do glitz. I do reverse chic.

On customized invitations and announcements *NY Times* 21 Dec 85

Karl Lagerfeld dress designer

7993 She acquired taste the way others buy antiques... her approach to fashion was a kind of connoisseurship.

On Wallis, Duchess of Windsor *NY Times* 19 Sep 93

7994 Her best years started at an age when women of her generation thought it was already too late.

ib

7995 Crossing and uncrossing her skinny legs on a gilded front-row seat in a couture salon was her most important occupation.

ib

7996 She never wanted to be sexy, but in those days ambitions were different, and she was the most ambitious of them all.

ib

7997 Chanel is composed of only a few elements, white camellias, quilted bags, an Austrian doorman's jacket, pearls, chains, shoes with black toes. I use these elements like notes to play with... [and] Chanel has become part of the "collective unconscious."

Vanity Fair Jun 94

Ralph Lauren clothes designer

7998 I don't design clothes. I design dreams.

NY Times 19 Apr 86

Lucien Lelong dress designer

7999 You can impose what you will by force but Paris's *haute couture* is not transferable, either in a block or bit by bit. It exists in Paris or it does not exist at all.

On German attempt to transfer the Paris fashion world to Berlin, quoted by Antony Beevor and Artemis Cooper *Paris After the Liberation* Doubleday 94

Raymond Loewy industrial designer

8000 They looked like chrome-plated barges.

On automobiles of the 1950s, recalled on Loewy's death 14 Jul 86

Mainbocher (Main Bocher) dress designer

8001 To be well turned out, a woman should turn her thoughts in.

Vogue 1 Apr 64

8002 I have never known a really chic woman whose appearance was not, in large part, an outward reflection of her inner self.

ib

Bruce Oldfield dress designer

8003 The bump I was trying to hide could be the future king of England.

On designing maternity clothes for Diana, Princess of Wales *Life* May 82

William Pahlmann interior designer

8004 Ambiance is an unstudied grace. . . the grace of human dignity.

Insider's Newsletter 18 Jan 65

8005 With the exception of psychoanalysis, there is probably no other field of civilized endeavor in which the personalities of client and adviser are in such violent conflict or harmonious cooperation as interior decoration.

NY Times 11 Nov 87

Mrs Henry Parish II (Sister Parish) interior designer

8006 All decorating is about memories.

Architectural Digest May 81

8007 I *am* taste!

W 14 Jun 85

8008 It's me—shabby English.

On furnishing her 5th Ave apartment *NY Times* 21 Mar 86

Mary Quant dress designer

8009 Legs stay throughout a woman's life.

On the ageless appeal of miniskirts, quoted by Marilyn Bender *The Beautiful People* Coward-McCann 67

Nell Donnelly Reed (Nelly Don) dress designer

8010 [I want to] make women look pretty when they are washing dishes.

On adding frills to house dresses, first step in pioneering women's ready-to-wear clothing in the 1920s *NY Times* 11 Sep 91

Nettie Rosenstein dress designer

8011 It's what you leave off that makes it smart.

Recalled on Rosenstein's death 12 Mar 80

Yves Saint Laurent dress designer

8012 I wish I had invented blue jeans. They have expression, modesty, sex appeal, simplicity—all I hope for in my clothes.

New York 28 Nov 83

8013 Dressing is a way of life.

ib

8014 Isn't elegance forgetting what one is wearing?

ib

8015 She alone could have given to a pink the nerve of a red. . . a neon pink, an unreal pink. . . . Shocking Pink!

On Elsa Schiaparelli's signature color *Architectural Digest* Oct 94

Vidal Sassoon hair dresser

8016 We have come a long way from the youths who wore so much long hair it became a uniform—its own form of uniformity.

Quote 13 Apr 75

Elsa Schiaparelli dress designer

8017 Good design is always on a tightrope of bad taste.

Shocking Life Dutton 54

8018 Fashion is born by small facts, trends, or even politics, never by trying to make little pleated furbelows, by trinkets, by clothes easy to copy, or by the shortening or lengthening of the skirt.

ib

8019 A good designer is a sorceress who dispenses happiness.

ib

8020 That damn bitch who sold the same jacket for 35 years!

On Coco Chanel, quoted by Geoffrey Beene *Vogue* Feb 94

8021 The house sings with a feeling of abandon, throws its arms around you, hugs you, and whoever comes to it as a guest never wants to leave it.

On the 18-room, pre-World War II Schiaparelli mansion on Paris' rue de Berri *Architectural Digest* Oct 94

Frank Sinatra entertainer

8022 I have always been bewitched by shadows and contrasts—a bright bursting orange sun against a twilight blue sky, the rich shadow cast by a simple green leaf.

On launching a tie collection based on his paintings *USA Today* 21 Feb 95

Lord Snowdon (Antony Armstrong-Jones) photographer and furniture designer

8023 [It was] just as Henry V would have done it, if he'd had perspex.

On designing a clear perspex canopy for the investiture of Charles, Prince of Wales 1 Jul 69, quoted by Jonathan Dimbleby *The Prince of Wales* Morrow 94

Emanuel Ungaro dress designer

8024 Quality is the alchemy struck between a woman and her clothes, her attitude and her allure.

On wedding dress for the marriage of Raine, Countess Spencer, to the Count Jean-François de Chambrun *Guardian Weekly* 18 Jul 93

Valentina (Valentina Nicholaezna Sanina Schlee) dress designer

8025 Mink is for football games... please. Out in the fresh air, sit in it, eat hot dogs in it, anything. But not evening, not elegance, I beg of you.

Ladies' Home Journal Mar 58

Valentino (Valentino Garavani Valentino) dress designer

8026 Reds has guts... deep, strong, dramatic. A geranium red. A Goya red... to be used like gold for furnishing a house... for clothes, it is strong, like black or white.

"Red is the Color of Happiness" *Harper's Bazaar* Sep 92

Manufacturers and Merchandisers

Mary Kay Ash Chair, Mary Kay Cosmetics Inc

8027 If you think you can, you can. And if you think you can't, you can't.

To new recruits on the art of selling *NY Times* 20 Oct 85

Nancy Hilton President, Hilton Clothes Inc

8028 Pat them on the neck and say, "Good boy!"

On selling custom tailoring for men *Forbes* 19 Dec 94

Carolyn Moss Fashion Director, Macy's

8029 It has everyone reassessing their assets... not the answer to world hunger, but it puts a smile on your face.

On the Wonderbra and its offer of greater cleavage *NY Times* 28 Sep 94

Jo Snowden Ellis Bridal sales representative

8030 All someone has to make now is a morning suit with extralong sleeves for the father-of-the-bride's shotgun.

On wedding dresses for *enceinte* brides *US News & World Report* 25 Sep 95

Bernie Spitz President, Henry Hangers

8031 A garment well displayed is a sale half made.

On manufacturing hangers *NY Times* 27 Jun 87

Doug Tomkins Chair, Esprit Inc

8032 We sell the crayons—the customer makes something of it.

On Esprit's vivid colors and bold prints *Wall Street Journal* 11 Jun 85

Critics

Stewart Alsop commentator

8033 A fashionable gentleman who concerns himself with the fashions of gentlemen is neither fashionable nor a gentleman.

Newsweek 30 Jun 75

Anon

8034 Get the feel of fur—slam your hand in a car door.

Poster by animal rights group *NY Times* 26 Feb 91

8035 A scent that even a truck driver with a head cold could pick out.

On Giorgio perfume *International Herald Tribune* 11 May 92

8036 Gandhi meets Amadeus on Carnaby Street.

On Jean-Paul Gaultier's combinations of style *NY Times* 6 Jul 93

8037 No eulogies, no prayers, no Hebrew, the perfectly restrained Episcopalian service in a synagogue... [and] no mixed flowers.

On socialite Jerry Zipkins's funeral amid all white blossoms at Manhattan's Temple Emanu-El *Vanity Fair* Sep 95

8038 They're exceedingly rebarbative... totally affectless, entirely composed... [with] highly varnished demeanor that earned them the sobriquet "Ken and Barbie."

On the Manhattan glamour couple Frank and Nancy Richardson as the Barbie doll and her boyfriend *New York* 4 Sep 95

Brooke Astor socialite

8039 It may be good, expensive furniture for a yacht, but it looks terrible on land.

On discarding furnishings from her husband's yacht, quoted by Billy Baldwin with Michael Gardine *Billy Baldwin* Little, Brown 85

8040 People expect to see Mrs Astor, not some dowdy old lady, and I don't intend to disappoint them.

On dressing well *NY Times* 17 Nov 91

Sonja Bata shoe heiress

8041 Shoes hold the key to human identity. They tell you more than any other artifact about people's status, climate, work and culture.

On establishing the Bata Shoe Museum in Toronto, *Washington Post* 17 May 95

Cecil Beaton set designer

8042 [She reminded me of] the neatest, newest luggage, and is as compact as a Vuitton travelling case.

On Wallis, Duchess of Windsor *London Times* 18 Jun 94

8043 An elegant crane picking her way out of a swamp.

Recalling fashion editor Diana Vreeland *NY Times* 15 Oct 95

Lucius Beebe journalist

8044 A concentration camp of competitive celebrities.

On Manhattan's El Morocco *NY Herald-Tribune* 19 Apr 64

Marilyn Bender business writer

8045 Women all across the United States... memorized the high-fashion mathmematics of multiplying chic by subtraction.

On influence of Jacqueline Kennedy Onassis *The Beautiful People* Coward-McCann 67

Alan Bennett essayist

8046 Nuns now dress like nurses; gone the voluminous black, the starched coif, the twinkling rosy face; these days it's a nanny's uniform in a nasty shade of gray—papal policewomen.

New Yorker 22 May 95

Irving Berlin composer

8047 Oh for a dress again/ To caress again—in a dress again./ Covered up from head to your toe,/ We must hide what we'd like to show./ Oh, for a skirt again.

Unpublished lines sent to any army entertainer who complained of heavy woolen trousers *Washington Post* 12 Nov 88

8048 Just to flirt again—in a skirt again./ There's no romance when you dance/ Cheek to cheek and pants to pants./ Oh for an old-fashioned dress.

ib

Marilyn Bethany critic

8049 *Toile de Jouy* is to France what chintz is to England and patchwork calico is to the United States—the very fabric of a nation.

"Jouy to the World" *New York* 14 Oct 85

Roy Blount Jr critic

8050 Fashion matters considerably more than horoscopes, rather more than dog shows, and slightly more than hockey.

NY Times 24 Oct 93

Ruth Smith Brady reporter

8051 The bride appeared in a dress... the color of melted coffee ice cream... weightless, as if it could be blown across town as easily as tumbleweed.

On a wedding on Manhattan's upper East Side *NY Times* 18 Dec 94

Pope Brock essayist

8052 He was just out of school/ When a fall from a mule/ Left young Lobb barely able to hobble./ A blow this severe/ Might have nipped his career—/ But the boy was determined to cobble.

English Leather on London's John Lobb, "world's premier shoemaker where the elite have brought their feet... for lasts from the past" *GQ* Mar 86

8053 Those boots—what a hit!/ They were sturdy. They fit./ He made them in rapid succession,/ With a hollow heel/ Where a man could conceal/ His booty (if that's the expression).

ib

Anatole Broyard critic

8054 Chic is a convent for unloved women.

NY Times 10 Jan 88

Truman Capote novelist

8055 She had... a face beyond childhood, yet this side of belonging to a woman.

On Holly Golightly and New York's fashion world in Capote's novel *Breakfast at Tiffany's* Random House 58

Margaret Carlson journalist

8056 There remains after three decades greater fascination with what goes on top of a woman's head than what is in it.

On Jacqueline Kennedy Onassis' 1961 pillbox followed by Hillary Rodham Clinton's round blue hat with turned up brim 32 years later *Vanity Fair* Jun 93

Angela Carter novelist

8057 The habit of applying warpaint outlasts the battle.

Quoted by Joyce Carol Oates *NY Times* 19 Jan 92 reviewing Carter's *Wise Children* Farrar Straus Giroux 92

8058 It's every woman's tragedy that after a certain age, she looks like a female impersonator.

ib

Charla Carter critic

8059 *Tres* French, it's what a woman has when her looks are as appealing as her personality.
NY Times 14 Jun 91

John Chancellor commentator

8060 Blow-dried, horn-rimmed, and well dressed.
On first US visit by Soviet premier Mikhail S Gorbachev *NY Times* 10 Dec 87

Alan Clark British Minister of Trade

8061 It's being done up in what one might term Aggressor-Deviant mode.
On Christopher Selmes' London house *Mrs Thatcher's Minister* Farrar Straus Giroux 93

8062 Mad great black painted walls; a pink Francis Bacon with a youth's demi (only) detumescent penis blotchily prominent... but it remains a rather dud Edwardian building.
ib

Amy Fine Collins journalist

8063 The bottle and its label were sleek and generic, like her other inventions of the 20s, the little black dress, as simple as a maid's and as ubiquitous as a Ford.
On Coco Chanel and Chanel Number 5 *Vanity Fair* Jun 94

Judy Cooper novelist

8064 (Stilettos) say "I mean to crush you under my heels if it suits me."
London Times 13 Sep 95

8065 They are female macho. Delilah shoes, bitch-goddess stuff.
ib

Giles Coren journalist

8066 The... ease of access to both sexes' nether regions... apparently conciliated the sexual revolution.
On the development of the zipper or what Aldous Huxley in *Brave New World* saw as a facilitator of "unlimited copulation," quoted in *London Times* 20 Feb 95 reviewing Robert Friedel's *Zipper* Norton 94

Douglas Coupland commentator

8067 Decade Blending: In clothing: the indiscriminate combination of two or more items from various decades to create a personal mood: Sheila-Mary Quant earrings (1960s) + cork wedgie platform shoes (1970s) + black leather jacket (1950s and 1980s).
Generation X St Martin's 91

Laura Cunningham journalist

8068 You'll be in someone's apartment and you'll see they pour cream out of a cow creamer. Then you know you can let your hair down.
On "boviniacs" of excessive enthusiasm for the commonplace *NY Times* 28 Feb 87

Martha E Dailey reporter

8069 Beige remains above reproach... [it] doesn't try to be anything but beige.
Washington Post 25 Jul 88

Boni De Castellane journalist

8070 Women no longer exist, all that's left are the boys created by Chanel.
Vogue Dec 69

Leanda De Listle journalist

8071 "Caage" is an abbreviation of "casual"... ripped jeans that have gone at the knee rather than being fashionably slashed at the thigh.
On the demise of black tie *Country Life* 16 Feb 95

8072 "Caage" is best summed up by Ralph Lauren's interpretation of traditional English clothes are where Manhattan meets Melton Mowbray.
ib

Annabelle D'Huart Parisian model

8073 [Nine hours of sleep a night] is the best makeup.
NY Times 14 Jul 91

Helen Dudar journalist

8074 "Pretty"... a courageously spare adjective in a profession addicted to rich ribbons of words.
"Urbane Unity: Reinterpreting a New York Classic" *Architectural Digest* Nov 85

Owen Edwards journalist

8075 The sight of a naked male kneecap threatens the very fabric of power and probity.
On midtown Manhattan corporate offices where "a man in shorts can raise eyebrows and lower human tolerance" *GQ* Jul 95

8076 Only a few decades ago shorts were something a boy wore and dreamed of outgrowing... the stigmata of preadolescence.
ib

S S Fair essayist

8077 Pseudo-collagian... jojoba... mint tonic... glycolic acids and soothing marigold... sesame oil... shark liver oil and bone marrow ointment.

On the variety of "damage control" cosmetics for use at bedtime *NY Times* 1 Oct 95

8078 Covered. . . in pharmaceutical wildlife, I can proceed to the nether parts.

ib

Nick Foulkes journalist

8079 It is the sort of cloth on which empires are founded, or if not founded, at least the sort of stuff in which empire builders are dressed.

On Bedford cord as "riding breeches for the gentry, sturdy trousers for the working man and uniform for the military" *Country Life* 30 Mar 95

David France journalist

8080 A Giacometti coffee table and a cluster of 18th century sofas in her cool, silk-covered living room. . . the archetype of the burnished Upper East Side socialite.

On socialite Nancy Richardson's Park Avenue apartment *New York* 4 Sep 95

8081 At 51. . . her face is pale and tight and high, her blue eyes are dark and patrolling.

ib

8082 The trip was a turning point—a glimpse at tasteful affluence two or three orders of magnitude below what she had known.

On a tour of smaller houses on Long Island *ib*

Joseph Giovannini reporter

8083 [It] is a design statement about not making a design statement.

On comfortable sofas *NY Times* 2 Jun 88

Edward Gorey reporter

8084 Does fashion matter? Only to those who would bother to answer the question.

NY Times 24 Oct 93

C Z Guest (Lucy Douglas Cockrane Guest) socialite

8085 Style is about surviving, about having been through a lot and making it look easy.

Quoted by Annette Tapert and Diana Edkins *The Power of Style* Crown 94

8086 Style is what you are inside.

ib

Amor Abdel Haman store clerk

8087 The fez is dying out. . . like elegance itself.

On the maroon, brimless hat that was once the epitome of Morocco's old world courtesy and taste *NY Times* 22 Mar 95

Rosemary Hawthorne essayist

8088 Crises and social upheaval bring out fashions that show off the bosom, because when times are hard we need to feel that there is something soft to fall back on.

London Times 26 Dec 92

Katharine Hepburn actress

8089 When a man says he likes a woman in a skirt, I tell him to try one.

WETA TV Washington 27 Jun 94

Woody Hochswender reporter

8090 Mr Stallone confessed to being in frock shock after seeing half a dozen fashion shows.

Reporting on Sylvester Stallone's attendance at both of Karl Lagerfeld's fashion shows in Paris *NY Times* 24 Mar 91

John Homans critic

8091 She was quickly mythologized as a shark in Chanel, a figure of mystery and rumor, the definitive dangerous woman.

On British editor Anna Wintour's arrival at Condé Nast as the eventual replacement for Editor Grace Mirabella *In and Out of Vogue* Doubleday 95

Cathy Horyn reporter

8092 Only he could make a fortune making the intentional appear unintentional.

On Ralph Lauren's fashionable casualness, *Washington Post* 24 May 92

Kathryn Hulme novelist

8093 Once upon a time in the Congo she had caught herself looking at the colonial ladies sipping aperitifs on cafe terraces, to see what was being worn in the world that season.

The Nun's Story Atlantic-Little, Brown 56

8094 Utexleo, she whispered, recalling a handsome blockprint summer suit of Congolese cotton.

ib

Julie E Iovine essayist

8095 The furniture suite was the backbone of bedroom communities all across America. . . their pseudo-historical styling as close to the original as Spam is to roast pork.

"Farewell, My Suite" on inexpensive furniture popular after World War II *NY Times* 29 Jan 95

8096 The furniture suite is finally receding from the interior landscape.

ib

Richard Lacayo essayist

8097 Hip was deaf to the best, blind to the truth and dressed by Penney's.
"Is Anyone Hip?" *Time* 8 Aug 94

Alan Jay Lerner lyricist

8098 That's quite a dress you almost have on.
Spoken by Gene Kelly on Nina Foch's bare-shoulder gown in *An American in Paris* Metro-Goldwyn-Meyer 51

Stephanie Mansfield reporter

8099 Coifed into a Washington power helmet.
Reporting on Pamela Harriman's as US Ambassador to France *Washington Post* 26 Apr 88

Colin McDowell essayist

8100 When she speaks it is as if very thick olive oil is pouring vigorously over gravel.
On fashion editor Diana Vreeland *Country Life* 15 May 86

Janet Morgan biographer

8101 Upholstered in tartan, bursting with antlers.
On Balmoral's Victorian decore *Edwina Mountbatten* Scribner 91

Raymond Mortimer reporter

8102 The French chaise became lounge and took a Turkish name (sofa)—an evolution welcome to authors, invalids, and lovers.
On the evolution of the chaise lounge *NY Times* 20 Jan 52

Kathy Najimy actress

8103 The Condom Earring! Perhaps we are tired of being shy about something we literally cannot live without.
"From Pearls to Condoms" on drug-store sale of "Safe Ears" as protection from AIDS *NY Times* 10 Feb 91

Enid Nemy reporter

8104 They were wearing cotton Oxford button-down shirts, unobtrusive ties, three-button suits, hats and gloves. . . they were shopping for button-down shirts, unobtrusive ties, three-button suits, hats and gloves.
On Brooks Brothers' semi-annual sale *NY Times* 8 Jan 74

8105 Storing underwear in refrigerators. . . is far from unique in a city where pavements bubble and a moment's coolness is a blessing.
On summertime in small apartments 1 Mar 87

The New York Times

8106 Polyester. . . the word that defines tacky for all time.
"Prettier Poly" editorial 21 Mar 91

8107 "Polyester". . . said everything there was to say about motel strips, souvenir shops and duded-up crab shacks.
On Florida *ib*

Jaqueline Kennedy Onassis First Lady

8108 Yes, yes, yes, and yes!
On approving Oleg Cassinis designs sent to Washington, quoted by Cassini *In My Fashion* Simon & Schuster 87

8109 Put your brilliant mind to work for dresses I would wear if Jack were President of France.
Letter to Cassini *ib* 13 Dec 60

8110 [I don't want] fat little women hopping around in the same dress.
On the importance of exclusive designs *ib*

8111 You will amuse the poor President and his wife in that dreary *Maison Blanche.*
ib

Paul O'Neil essayist

8112 [She] dressed with impeccable dowdiness.
On Hollywood columnist Louella Parsons *Life* 4 Jun 65

Susan Orlean essayist

8113 Livingrooms are a lot like underwear: while their function is mostly personal, you always wonder what other people's look like, and what you might look like to somebody else.
New Yorker 16 Oct 95

P J O'Rourke humorist

8114 A hat should be taken off when you greet a lady and left off for the rest of your life.
New York 21 Dec 92

Suzy Parker fashion model

8115 I come from an average Ku Klux Klan family.
On her Texas childhood, quoted in *This Fabulous Century 1950–1960* Time-Life Books 70

Naveen Patnaik commentator

8116 That left shoulder really has an aura of its own; it holds everything together.
On wearing a sari *Connoisseur* Apr 66

8117 The sari's radiance, vigor and variety, produced by a single straight length of cloth, should make the West think twice about zipper, dart and shoulder pad.

ib

Michael Pick critic

8118 Grotesque and shabby armchairs. . . nuzzle up to the fire like decrepit bulldogs.

On George Bernard Shaw's study *The English Room* Harmony/Crown 85

8119 Unabashed fantasy garnished with nostalgia!

On Pandora Astor's London residence *ib*

James Pope-Hennessy Director, Victoria and Albert Museum

8120 An American Woman par excellence were it not for the suspicion that she is not a woman at all.

On Wallis, Duchess of Windsor, Suzy Menkes and Peter Quennell eds *A Lonely Business* Weidenfeld & Nicolson 81

Dawn Powell essayist

8121 Its function has always been solemnly medicinal—to provide delicious discontent.

On *Vogue NY Times* 3 Nov 63

8122 *Vogue* says here is what other people have and you haven't. . . where some go but never you. . . the lovely land of never, and you dream of it, but that's all.

ib

Orville Prescott critic

8123 [The men] drank wine by the quart, hardly ever bathed, wore periwigs and shoes with 4-inch heels. . . allowed sewage to accumulate in their cellars, and died young.

On the 17th century English court *NY Times* 1 May 51

Anna Quindlen columnist

8124 The purse is the mirror of the soul.

Syndicated column *NY Times* 16 Dec 87

8125 My closet looks like a convention of multiple-personality cases.

Newsmakers '93 Gale 93

Sally Quinn journalist

8126 Oh, to have sharpshooters on the roof—be still, my heart!

On entertaining VIP's in Georgetown *Washington Post* 6 Jan 95

Joan Rivers humorist

8127 She's in a hospital having her handbag surgically removed.

On Elizabeth II, rarely photographed when not carrying a purse *NY Times* 27 Feb 91

Diane Salzberg reporter

8128 "I got these in Zermatt; everyone wears them there." That one remark is worth the cost of the vacation.

On fashionable remarks on chic resorts *NY Times* 5 Feb 86

8129 You want them to know you are letting them know that you know what they know.

ib

Richard Severo reporter

8130 An indefatigible lamenter of a world that to him had become hopelessly wrapped in clear plastic.

On taste arbiter Russell Lynes *NY Times* 16 Sep 91

Laura Shapiro essayist

8131 Breasts came back after World War II. . . linked with dumb blondes in the most regrettable partnership since the sweet potato met the marshmallow.

Newsweek 20 Jan 92

Claudia Shear critic

8132 Fashion absolutely matters, but it doesn't matter absolutely.

NY Times 24 Oct 93

Edith Sitwell poet

8133 Most Englishwomen dress as if they had been a mouse in a previous incarnation.

Recalled on Sitwell's death 9 Dec 64

8134 Why not be oneself. . . if one is a greyhound, why try to look like a Pekingese?

ib

Sacheverell Sitwell poet

8135 His clothes were a little too tidily frayed.

On a former tutor, quoted by Sarah Bradford *Splendors and Miseries* Farrar Straus Giroux 93

Carmel Snow Editor *Harper's Bazaar*

8136 Your dresses have such a new look!

To Christian Dior on a full-skirted, post-war collection that became known as the New Look, quoted by Antony Beevor and Artemis Cooper *Paris After the Liberaton* Doubleday 94

Marie Tempest actress

8137 A very dignified Zulu walked at the head of a file of wives, the first of whom, a young girl, wore only a loin cloth, the next a primitive brassiere, and so on, till we came to the eldest, who was completely clad.

Letter to *The Times* Kenneth Gregory ed *The First Cuckoo* Allen & Unwin 76

Margaret Thatcher Prime Minister of Britain

8138 Why Marks & Spencer, of course. Doesn't everyone?

On being asked where she bought her underwear *London Times* 29 Jun 91

8139 Nearly 250 years of history... down-at-the heel... like a furnished house to let... which in a way I suppose it was.

On moving into the Prime Minister's residence *The Downing Street Years* HarperCollins 93

Laetitia Thompson high school student

8140 Please, Mr President, the world is dying to know, is it boxers or briefs?

To President Clinton on his preference in underwear; he replied, "Usually, briefs" and said later, "I can't believe she asked that question!" *Newsweek* 2 May 94

James Thurber humorist

8141 It might have been made by the American Can Company.

On wearing an ill-fitting suit *Alarms and Diversions* Harper 57

Paul Valéry poet

8142 A woman who doesn't wear perfume has no future.

Quoted by Axel Madsen *Chanel* Holt 90

Diana Vreeland Editor of *Vogue*

8143 Jeans are the most beautiful things since the gondola.

NY Times 14 Sep 80

8144 Fashion must be the intoxicating release from the banality of the world.

Newsday 24 Aug 89

8145 Bored with red—it would be like becoming bored with the person you love.

NY Times 1 Apr 90

8146 Style! It helps you get up in the morning!

15 Oct 95

Gene Weingarten reporter

8147 Plastic digital, thick as a brick and handsome as a hernia.

On President Clinton's $39 Timex Ironman Triathlon *Washington Post* 7 Mar 93

Helen Kravadze Williams social arbiter

8148 Smile pleasantly and as soon as possible, tell the story to a friend. It eases the pain.

Instructing her classes of diplomats and other officials on how to deal with a *faux pas Washington Post* 5 Jun 93

Tom Wolfe novelist

8149 The Sideburn Fairy... had been... visiting young groovies in their sleep and causing them to awake with sideburns running down their jawbones.

On the "funky chic" of men's hair styles in the 1960s and 70s *Mauve Gloves and Madmen, Clutter and Vine* Farrar Straus Giroux 76

8150 Pale yellow ties became the insignia of the worker bees of the business world.

On Wall Street "power" neckwear of the late 1980s *The Bonfire of the Vanities* Farrar Straus Giroux 87

8151 From 62nd Street to 96th there had arisen the hideous cracking sound of acres of hellishly expensive plate-glass mirror being pried off the walls of the great apartments.

On a junking fad of the 1970s *ib*

Jerry Zipkin socialite escort

8152 It was perfect—not a poinsettia in sight!

On Christmas at designer Bill Blass' country house *Vanity Fair* Sep 96

8153 They all call it in. I just sit here and it comes pouring in. This is shit central.

On being a purveyor of social news and gossip *ib*

FILMS

Actors and Actresses

Fred Allen

8154 You can take all the sincerity in Hollywood, place it in the navel of a fruit fly and still have room enough for three caraway seeds and a producer's heart.

Quoted in John Robert Colombo *Popcorn in Paradise* Holt Rinehart Winston 80

Mary Astor

8155 You had to see the face, the trademark with its trademark: Mary Pickford's dimples, Doug's grin, Erich von Stroheim's monocle, Mae Murray's pout.

A Life on Film Delacorte 71

8156 The face, the gimmicks, the appearance took the place of genuine emotion.

ib

Lauren Bacall

8157 Legends and special ladies don't work; it's over for them; they just go around being legends and special ladies.

On maintaining a fresh image, quoted by Judith Viorst *NY Times* 9 Oct 94 reviewing Bacall's biographical *Now* Knopf 94

Tallulah Bankhead

8158 They made me sound as if I'd been castrated.

On early "talkies" *People* 9 Feb 87

Theda Bara

8159 There is a little bit of vampire instinct in every woman.

On her success in early motion pictures, recalled on Bara's death 2 Apr 55

Brigette Bardot

8160 I have been very happy, rich, beautiful, much adulated, famous and very unhappy.

Interview on 50th birthday *London Times* 28 Sep 84

Ethel Barrymore

8161 There is as much difference between the stage and the films as between a piano and a violin; you can't get the virtuoso in both.

NY Post 7 Jun 56

Lionel Barrymore

8162 Half the people in Hollywood are dying to be discovered and the other half are afraid they will be.

Quoted by Boze Hadleigh *Hollywood, Babble On* Carol Publishing 94

Warren Beatty

8163 As a director, you want to be in control, but. . . you want to be a little bit out of control of being in control. Whereas, if you're an actor, you're trying as hard as you can to be out of control all the while that you also have to be in control of being out of control.

Vanity Fair Nov 91

Humphrey Bogart

8164 [Hollywood] hurts itself—as if General Motors deliberately put out a bad car.

Time 7 Jun 54

8165 John was one of the few souls around this clumsy place.

On Director John Huston *Reader's Digest* Nov 87

Ray Bolger

8166 How lonely it is going to be on the Yellow Brick Road.

On the death of his co-star, Tin Man Jack Haley, recalled on Bolger's death 15 Jan 87

Marlon Brando

8167 Sometimes you just get the feeling that here it is 11 o'clock in the morning and you're not in school.

On playing in Western films *NY Post* 11 May 59

8168 If you ain't talking about him, he ain't listening.

On actors, British *Vogue* Aug 74

8169 I could lick my weight in wardrobe women.

On personal health ABC TV 24 Mar 90

8170 It was actor-proof, a scene that demonstrated how audiences often do much of the acting themselves in an effectively told story.

On *On the Waterfront, Brando: Songs My Mother Taught Me* Random House 94

8171 It couldn't fail because almost everyone believes he could have. . . been somebody if he'd been dealt different cards by fate.

On his famous line, "I coulda been a contender!" *ib*

Richard Burton

8172 Be as vicious about me as you please. You will only do me justice.

On being interviewed for a cover story in *Time* 26 Apr 63

8173 The lure of the zeroes was simply too great.

On making more money in non-Shakespearean roles, quoted by Donald Spoto *A Passion for Life* HarperCollins 95

8174 A spoiled genius from the Welsh gutter, a drunk, womanizer; it's rather an attractive image.

Self-description recalled on Burton's death 5 Aug 84

Charlie Chaplin

8175 Baggy pants, big shoes, a cane and a derby hat. . . everything contradictory.

On his famous costume as "the little tramp" *My Autobiography* Simon & Schuster 64

8176 The moment I was dressed. . . I began to know him, and by the time I walked onto the stage he was fully born.

On his hobo impersonation *ib*

8177 A tramp, a gentleman, a poet, a dreamer, a lonely fellow, always hopeful of romance and adventure.

ib

8178 Desperately serious in an attempt to appear as a normal little gentleman. . . much in earnest about clutching my cane, straightening my derby and fixing my tie, even though I have just landed on my head.

On the theme of all his pictures *ib*

Irving S Cobb

8179 If it be true that when the curtain comes down on eternity, all men will approach the gates bearing in their arms that which they have given in life, the people of show business will march in the procession carrying in their arms the pure pearl of tears, the gold of laughter and the diamonds of stardust they spread on what otherwise might have been a rather dreary world.

Quoted by President Reagan *NY Times* 6 Dec 80

8180 When at last all reach that final stage door, I am sure the keeper will say, "Open, let my children in."

ib

Joan Crawford

8181 The night studio, quiet, shadowed, the vast equipment standing idle, the city of a million fantasies and as many combined talents, ready to spring into being at daybreak.

On "one of the most wonderous place in the world," quoted by Jane Kesner Ardmore *A Portrait of Joan* Doubleday 62

8182 We can skip childhood because I didn't have any.

Quoted by Alexander Walker *Joan Crawford* Harper & Row 83

8183 They promised me a rose garden and gave it to me. . . acre by acre.

On her first successes in Hollywood

8184 If you want to see the girl next door, go next door.

On non-conformity *ib*

8185 I found that incredible thing, a public.

ib

8186 Life deals from the bottom, sometimes, doesn't it?

ib

8187 They're going to be awful lonely with all those goddamn clippings.

On youngsters who took Hollywood for granted and soared but briefly *ib*

8188 You manufacture toys, you don't manufacture stars.

On inventing herself *ib*

8189 I never go out on the street unless I expect and anticipate and hope and pray that I'll be recognized. That someone'll ask for my autograph.

On maintaining glamour *New Yorker* 21 Mar 94

8190 When somebody says "There's Joan Crawford," I say, "It sure is!" and I'm very happy about it!

ib

Bette Davis

8191 "Playing our parts." Yes, we all have to do that and from childhood on, I have found that my own character has been much harder to play worthily and far harder at times to comprehend than any of the roles I have portrayed.

NY Herald Tribune 22 Jul 56

8192 To fulfill a dream, to be allowed to sweat over lonely labor, to be given a chance to create, is the meat and potatoes of life.

ib

8193 The money is the gravy.

The Lonely Life Putnam 62

8194 Evil people. . . you never forget them. And that's the aim of any actress—never to be forgotten.

On her favorite roles NY State Theater program Jun 66

8195 The best time I ever had with Joan Crawford was when I pushed her down the stairs in *Whatever Happened to Baby Jane?*

John Robert Colombo ed *Popcorn in Paradise* Holt Rinehart Winston 80

8196 You know what I'm going to have on my grave stone? "She did it the hard way."

CBS TV 5 May 85

8197 I am just too much!

Self-description ABC TV 30 Mar 87

8198 The statuette's rear reminded me of his. . . and thus his bottom has been immortalized.

On ex-husband Harmon Oscar Nelson for whom filmdom's highest award took its nickname *Time* 9 Apr 84

8199 No guts, no glory.

Inscription on favorite needlepoint pillow *NY Times* 15 Jul 94

8200 They had found the first bitch heroine!

On *Of Human Bondage* that made her a star *ib*

8201 I always thought that Jane was the kind who never washed her face; she just added more makeup everyday.

On *Whatever Happened to Baby Jane? ib*

Marlene Dietrich

8202 Robert Donat. . . what a waste! A bourgeois mind with such a face!

On starring with Robert Donat in *Knight Without Armour* quoted by Dietrich's daughter, Maria Riva *Marlene Dietrich* Knopf 92

Errol Flynn

8203 I heard them say wherever I went, like Ava Gardner said, "Look at Errol. Look at him. When he was young he was the best-looking thing I ever saw." Ava didn't mean it unkindly.

My Wicked, Wicked Ways Putnam 59

Greta Garbo

8204 I never said, "I want to be alone." I only said, "I want to be left alone."

Quoted by John Bainbridge *Garbo* Doubleday 55

8205 I tink I go home.

On being rejected for a pay raise by producer Louis B Mayer, quoted by Norman Zierold *Moguls* Coward, McCann 89

8206 To defend my achievement, I chose complete silence.

Quoted by Antoni Gronowicz *Garbo: Her Story* Simon & Schuster 90

8207 One day, there's a hand that goes over the face and changes it. You look like an apple that isn't young anymore.

At age 85 *Vanity Fair* Feb 94

8208 People think I am pair-annoyed.

Denying an affair with Cecil Beaton *New Yorker* 2 Oct 95

Ava Gardner

8209 Stardom. . . gave me everything I never wanted.

Ava: My Story Bantam 90

8210 If I could act, everything about my life and career would have been different. But I was never an actress—none of us kids at Metro were. We were just good to look at.

ib

Judy Garland

8211 I've never looked through a keyhole without finding someone was looking back!

On lack of privacy NBC TV 16 May 67

8212 Me the girl next door? They couldn't find the right house or the right door.

On film and television moguls, quoted by David Shipman *Judy Garland* Hyperion 93

Mel Gibson

8213 If I've still got my pants on in the second scene, I think they've sent me the wrong script.

Parade 27 Dec 92

John Gielgud

8214 It's very flattering to be enshrined in celluloid, but it isn't essential.

Quoted by Kenneth Tynan *Harper's Bazaar* Jul 52

Lillian Gish

8215 An emotional Detroit.

Defining Hollywood, quoted by James A Clapp *The City* Center for Urban Policy Research 84

8216 [He had] given films their form and grammar.

On director D W Griffith PBS TV 11 Jul 88

8217 I played with the best actors and tried never to be caught acting.

ib

8218 I never fell in love with an actor. I wanted to be with writers I could learn from.

ib

8219 You can't teach acting. You learn that from the human race.

ib

8220 Those little virgins, after five minutes you got so sick of them—to make them interesting was hard work.

On her frequent roles as an innocent heroine *ib*

Jackie Gleason

8221 Variety is an actor's courage.

Emmy Jan 83

Cary Grant

8222 Our factory. . . is called a stage. We make a product, color it, title it, and ship it out in cans.

Newsweek 3 Jun 69

8223 I pretended to be somebody I wanted to be until finally I became that person. Or he became me.

Parade 22 Sep 85

Katharine Hepburn

8224 The. . . star's ambition is to be admired by an American, courted by an Italian, married to an Englishman and have a French boy friend.

NY Journal American 22 Feb 54

8225 I'll welcome death—no more interviews!

Prime Time CBS TV 18 Oct 90

8226 For him, life was difficult, it was acting that was easy.

On Spencer Tracy, Station WETA TV Washington 27 Jul 94

8227 I said to myself: don't act, don't do anything. Let the audience hear the lines.

On Eugene O'Neill's *Long Day's Journey Into Night ib*

8228 I think I was born at a time that was enormously suitable for my personality.

ABC TV 26 Apr 95

Charlton Heston

8229 Men and women are very different species: women are not like men—thank God! And as my son said, "My Dad pretends to be people."

To Sally Jessy Raphael ABC TV 12 Dec 90

Dustin Hoffman

8230 If I'd seen me at a party, I'd never have gone up and met me.

On self-image *Dateline* NBC TV 8 Mar 95

Rock Hudson

8231 I always said it would kill me if they found out—and now it has.

On his public image and AIDS, Rock Hudson ABC TV 8 Jan 90

Boris Karloff

8232 It grossed $12 million and started a cycle of so-called boy-meets-ghoul horror films.

On *Frankenstein* recalled on Karloff's death 2 Feb 69

8233 The monster was indeed the best friend I could ever have.

Connoisseur Jan 91

Danny Kaye

8234 I arrived overnight. Over a few hundred nights in the Catskills, vaudeville, clubs and on Broadway!

Boston Globe 4 Mar 87

Bert Lahr

8235 I was typecast as a lion, and there just weren't many parts for lions!

On *The Wizard of Oz*, *New Yorker* 26 Jan 63

Veronica Lake

8236 You could put all the talent I had in your left eye and still not suffer from impaired vision.

On her brief film career of the late 1940s *Parade* 28 Mar 93

Charles Laughton

8237 For someone with a face like the back-end of an elephant, I haven't done badly.

Last BBC radio broadcast, quoted by Peter Vansittart *In the Fifties* John Murray 95

Harold Lloyd

8238 Cut the top off my head, but leave my feet. That's where the jokes are.

On cropping his films for television, quoted by Brendan Gill *A New York Life* Poseidon 90

Gina Lollobrigida

8239 Nothing in show business will ever top what I saw on television today.

On man's first walk on the moon, news reports 20 Jul 69

Sophia Loren

8240 My jewels were a diary of my life.

Reporting theft to police, news summaries 16 Jun 60

Myrna Loy

8241 Once you were with M-G-M. . . a constant saturation created this legendary kind of thing. We couldn't help becoming legends.

Myrna Loy: Being and Becoming Knopf 87

Shirley MacLaine

8242 I've made so many movies playing a hooker that they don't pay me in the regular way anymore. They leave it on the dresser.

Out On a Limb Bantam 83

8243 I've admired him for 35 years. . . someone who represents integrity, honesty, art, and on top of that stuff I'm actually sleeping with him!

On Oscar, her award as best actress of 1983 *People* 7 May 84

8244 On the stage you try to act real. On the screen you try to be real.

Dancing in the Light Bantam 85

Anna Magnani

8245 If you are joking me, I will get up immediately and kill you wherever you are.

To a reporter who notified her of receiving an Oscar for best performance by an actress 22 Mar 56

Liza Minnelli

8246 I was born, somebody took my picture and it just kind of continued.

Washington Post 9 Jul 88

8247 Reality is something you rise above.

NY Newsday 23 Feb 94

Paul Newman

8248 [He is] the only man I know who would double-park outside a whorehouse.

On Sidney Lumet as a director, quoted by Shaun Considine *The Life and Work of Paddy Chayefsky* Random House 94

Jack Nicholson

8249 She's like a delicate fawn, crossed with a Buick.

On actress Jessica Lange *Vanity Fair* Oct 84

Rudolf Nureyev

8250 It's time to do it before I get wrinkles and they have to photograph me through a mattress.

On making his first film *New Yorker* 25 Dec 92

Pat O'Brien

8251 You feel like a burglar sometimes—taking all that money for all that fun.

On acting *NY Journal American* 6 Dec 61

Gregory Peck

8252 "In his later years"—it's candid, accurate, and comfortable and allows for more to come.

Accepting the American Film Institute Life Achievement Award, NBC TV 21 Mar 89

Mary Pickford

8253 Adding sound to movies would be like putting lipstick on the Venus di Milo.

Recalled on Pickford's death 29 May 79

8254 You would have thought I murdered someone, and perhaps I had, but only to give her successor a chance.

On national furor when she bobbed her hair *ib*

Luise Rainer

8255 They don't need an actress here. What they need and want is a face and the camera to go around it.

On Hollywood's emphasis on glamour *New Yorker* 21 Mar 94

Ronald Reagan 40th US President

8256 Those last few days seem like something I read in a book, but with your wire to cling to, I get back to realization with a very satisfactory bump.

Replying from Des Moines in 1937 to a telegram asking Reagan to return to Hollywood to sign a contract with Warner Bros *Time* 17 Jun 85

8257 You were doing it for the audience to see what in their minds they always think a kiss is; now you see a couple of people start chewing on each other.

NBC TV 24 Mar 86

8258 Today they show everything and do everything!

ib

8259 No one "goes Hollywood"—they were that way before they came here. Hollywood just exposed it.

People 9 Feb 87

8260 That exchange—"Can you describe this?" "I can"—is at the heart of acting, as it is of poetry and of so many of the arts.

To Moscow's cultural and arts community *Washington Post* 1 Jun 88

8261 You get inside a character, a place, and a moment. You come to know the character. . . as a particular person, yearning, hoping, fearing, loving, a face. . . and you convey that knowledge. In acting. . . you become. . . more attentive to the core of the soul—that part of each of us that God holds in the hollow of his hand, and into which he breathes the breath of life.

ib

Mickey Rooney

8262 I was a 14-year-old boy for 30 years.

On the Hardy family series and subsequent type-casting *NY Journal-American* 15 Apr 58

Harold Russell

8263 I got into an argument with a block of TNT and lost.

On losing both hands in World War II and going on to the Oscar-winning role as a wounded veteran in *The Best Years of Our Lives,* the first person with a visible disability to appear in a major film *NY Times* 7 Aug 92

8264 I love the Oscar but I love my wife more. Although I've had the Oscar longer.

On selling the coveted award of the Academy of Motion Picture Arts and Sciences to pay his wife's medical expenses *ib*

Rosalind Russell

8265 Flops are a part of life's menu, and I've never been a girl to miss out on any of the courses.

NY Herald Tribune 11 Apr 57

George Sanders

8266 I am leaving because I am bored.

Suicide note 25 Apr 72

Frank Sinatra

8267 Bill, sometimes I wish someone would really hurt you so I could kill them.

To his friend William J Green, Chair, Clevepack Corp, a guest at Sinatra's fourth wedding, quoted by Kitty Kelley *His Way* Bantam 86

8268 President Reagan doesn't like me and George Schultz to be absent from the White House at the same time.

On excusing himself from the Friars Club annual roast *ib*

8269 I hope you live to be 400 years old and may the last voice you hear be mine.

On receiving honorary degree from Stevens Institute of Technology in his hometown of Hoboken NJ *ib*

Barbara Stanwyck

8270 To eat, survive and have a good coat.

On her trinity of goals on receiving American Film Institute Life Achievement Award *NY Times* 11 Apr 87

8271 The boy's got a lot to learn and I've got a lot to teach.

At age 32 on marrying actor Robert Taylor age 28 15 Jul 91

Maureen Stapleton

8272 I actually think my girdle should have won for technical achievement!

On nomination for an Oscar for her work in Airport *People* 13 Oct 95

Eric Stoltz

8273 I'm the token penis... to prove that the little women are heterosexual.

On his role in *Little Women W* Oct 94

Preston Sturges

8274 Now I've laid me down to die,/ I pray my neighbors not to pry/ Too deeply into sins that I,/ Not only cannot here deny,/ But much enjoyed as life flew by.

Self-epitaph recalled on Sturges' death 6 Aug 59

Gloria Swanson

8275 When I die, my epitaph should read: She Paid the Bills. That's the story of my private life.

Saturday Evening Post 22 Jul 50

8276 By rearranging his cards a bit... bluffing a bit... he had managed to win a hand... his ambition was to stay in the game and start winning pots.

On success of her lover Joseph P Kennedy as a Hollywood producer *Swanson on Swanson* Random House 80

8277 Arriving Monday... Arrange ovation.

Trans-Atlantic cable to Adolph Zukor, quoted in article on maintenance of Hollywood glamour *New Yorker* 21 Mar 94

Jessica Tandy

8278 They show parts of a man close up that a woman who's married 50 years has never even seen.

On modern films *Ladies' Home Journal* Apr 91

Elizabeth Taylor

8279 I have a woman's body and a child's emotions.

On her brief marriage at age 19 to Nicky Hilton *Time* 4 Jun 51

8280 Success is a great deodorant.

ABC TV 6 Apr 77

8281 [He is] the Frank Sinatra of Shakespeare.

On Richard Burton *NY Times* 6 Aug 84

8282 God has the most beautiful new angel!

On actress Audrey Hepburn's death *Life* Dec 93

8283 Fame can be a drag, almost a disease—you have to take mental medication.

ABC TV 26 Apr 95

Shirley Temple

8284 I class myself with Rin-Tin-Tin. At the end of the Depression, people were perhaps looking for something to cheer them up. They fell in love with a dog and with a little girl. . . . I think it won't happen again.

NY Post 13 Sep 56

Spencer Tracy

8285 Know your lines and don't bump into the furniture.

Favorite advice to young actors, recalled on Tracy's death 10 Jun 67

8286 This is a movie, not a lifeboat.

On equal billing with Katharine Hepburn *ib*

8287 There were times my pants were so thin I could sit on a dime and tell if it was heads or tails.

Quoted by Larry Swindell *Spencer Tracy World* 69

8288 Not much meat on her, but what's there is cherce!

On Katharine Hepburn *People* 17 Mar 86

8289 She projected all the passion of a Good Humor ice cream—frozen, on a stick, and all vanilla.

On Nancy Reagan in the 1950 film *The Next Voice You Hear* quoted by Kitty Kelley *Nancy Reagan* Simon & Schuster 91

John Wayne

8290 Courage is being scared to death and saddling up anyway.

Quoted by Edna Buchanan *Never Let Them See You Cry* Random House 92

Johnny Weissmuller

8291 Me Tarzan, you Jane.

Straightforward description of his acting style although never a part of screen dialogue, recalled on Weissmuller's death 20 Jan 84

Orson Welles

8292 I have the dignity of a nude at high noon on Fifth Avenue.

Quoted by Kenneth Tynan, Kathleen Tynan and Ernie Eban eds *Profiles* Harper Perennial 90

Shelly Winters

8293 He had the quality of sexual lightning.

On her co-star Montgomery Clift NBC TV 19 Jun 80

James Woods

8294 Give 'em a great story, make them come into the theater, give 'em the popcorn and the Coke, and hope that while they're sitting there, they might actually think about something.

On his role in *True Believer* as a 1980s burned-out lawyer rediscovering the principles of the 1960s *NY Times* 12 Feb 89

Writers, Producers, and Directors

Nelson Algren novelist

8295 I went out there for a thousand a week... worked Monday... got fired Wednesday. The guy that hired me was out of town Tuesday.

Writers at Work Viking 58

Jay Presson Allen screenwriter

8296 Working with him is like rolling in feathers.

On United Artists President John Calley *New Yorker* 21 Mar 94

Anon

8297 He'll make a very nice first husband.

A studio executive commenting on Elizabeth Taylor's marriage at 19 to hotel heir Nicky Hilton *Look* 10 Jul 56

8298 I cawn't take a bawth on the grawss with the banawnas.

A classmate's imitation of Elizabeth Taylor's English accent when she began elementary school in California, quoted by Donald Spoto *A Passion for Life* HarperCollins 95

Ingmar Bergman producer

8299 I loathe the play, but that is frequently a fruitful point of departure. Much better than when you love a play, I believe.

On Edward Albee's *Tiny Alice*, *Christian Science Monitor* 29 Jan 65

8300 [The camera] is so refined that it makes it possible for us to shed light on the human soul, to reveal it the more brutally and thereby add to our knowledge new dimensions of the "real."

NY Times 22 Jan 78

8301 I write scripts to serve as skeletons awaiting the flesh and sinew of images.

ib

8302 It's terribly important that art... shows how human beings humiliate each other, because humiliation is one of the most dreadful companions of humanity, and our whole social system is based to an enormous extent on humiliation.

John Robert Columbo ed *Columbo's Hollywood* Collins 79

8303 Born and brought up in a vicarage, you are bound at an early age to peep behind the scenes of life and death.

Celebrity Register Gale 90

Iris Blitch US Congresswoman

8304 I hope the Attorney General, in the name of American womanhood, will take the measures necessary to determine whether Miss Taylor and Mr Burton are ineligible for re-entry into the US on the grounds of undesirability.

To House of Representatives after Elizabeth Taylor divorced Eddie Fisher to marry Richard Burton, quoted by Donald Spoto *A Passion for Life* HarperCollins 95

Bertolt Brecht screenwriter

8305 A sewer, a chrysanthemum in a coal mine.

On writing scripts for Hollywood studios, quoted by Shaun Considine *The Life and Work of Paddy Chayefsky* Random House 94

Richard Brooks director

8306 [Hollywood] is filled with people who make adventure pictures and who have never left this place... religious pictures and they haven't been in a church or synagogue for years... pictures about love and they have never been in love—ever.

NY Post 7 Dec 60

Rita Mae Brown novelist

8307 You sell a screenplay like you sell a car; if someone drives it off a cliff, that's it!

Newsweek 19 Aug 85

James M Cain novelist

8308 They have done nothing to my books. They are right over there on the shelf exactly as I wrote them.

On how Hollywood handled his books *American Heritage* Jul 93

Erskine Caldwell novelist

8309 The building in which I work has wooden fire escapes.

On the "worst footnote" Hollywood could have, quoted by Dan B Miller *Erskine Caldwell* Knopf 95

Yakima Canutt director

8310 Chuck, you just make sure y'stay in the chariot! I guarantee yuh gonna win the damn race!

On filming Charlton Heston in *Ben-Hur*, quoted by Heston *In the Arena* Simon & Schuster 95

Frank Capra director

8311 Do not help the quick moneymakers who have delusions about taking possession of classics by smearing them with paint.

To Library of Congress on computer colorization of films *NY Times* 5 Aug 86

8312 There are no rules in filmmaking. Only sins. And the cardinal sin is dullness.

People 16 Sep 91

Raymond Chandler novelist

8313 If my books had been worse I should not have been invited to Hollywood, and if they had been any better I should not have come.

Quoted by F MacShane *The Life of Raymond Chandler* Dutton 76

8314 There is hope... that somehow the flatulent moguls will learn that only writers can write screenplays and only proud and independent writers can write good screenplays.

Quoted by David Pirie, Martin Seymour Smith ed *Novels and Novelists* St Martin's 80

8315 Methods of dealing with screenwriters are destructive of the very force by which pictures must live.

ib

Tom Clancy novelist

8316 Giving your book to Hollywood is like turning your daughter into a pimp.

On film treatment of his book *The Hunt for Red October*, *Guardian Weekly* 25 Dec 94

Leon Clore producer

8317 If Americans didn't speak English, we'd have no problem.

On marketing British films in the US *NY Times* 13 Jul 80

Jean Cocteau author and artist

8318 A film is a petrified fountain of thought.

Esquire Feb 61

Harry Cohn President, Columbia Pictures

8319 So we don't have another dame with big boobs on the lot, so what? We ain't got a star? We'll make one.

On Rita Hayworth's departure from Columbia Pictures *New Yorker* 21 Mar 94

Pat Conroy novelist

8320 It was like walking down the street with the Statue of Liberty.

On Manhattan pedestrians' recognition of Barbra Streisand, star of the film made from his book *Prince of Tides* Station WAMU Washington 4 Sep 95

Frank Cosaro director

8321 I approach each work, old or new, as... a clear, clean space. The most thumbnailed musical chestnut becomes virgin territory; no matter how rouged or battered by time, each time is the first time—for both of us.

Maverick Vanguard 78

George Cukor director

8322 [She was] in the perfect image of a star, and, as such, largely the creation of her own indomitable will.

Eulogy for Joan Crawford at memorial service by Academy of Motion Picture Arts and Sciences, quoted by Alexander Walker *Joan Crawford: The Ultimate Star* Harper & Row 83

Cecil B DeMille producer

8323 The person who makes a success of living is the one who sees his goal steadily and aims for it unswervingly; that is dedication!

Introduction to Mary Pickford's *Sunshine and Shadow* Doubleday 55

8324 Creation is a drug I can't do without.

NY Times 12 Aug 56

8325 The way to make a film is to begin with an earthquake and work up to a climax.

John Robert Colombo ed *Colombo's Hollywood* Collins 79

8326 Why should I let 2,000 years of publicity go to waste?

On films on the Bible *ib*

8327 A dozen press agents working overtime can do terrible things to the human spirit.

In *Sunset Boulevard* 1950 in which he played himself with lines written for him by Billy Wilder with Charles Brackett and D M Marshman Jr, quoted in *Smithsonian* Jun 92

Walt Disney cartoonist

8328 I love Mickey Mouse more than any woman I've ever known.

Penthouse Nov 84

8329 Fancy being remembered around the world for the invention of a mouse!

To his wife during his last illness, quoted by Leonard Mosley *Disney's World* Stein & Day 85

Sergei Eisenstein producer

8330 The most important thing is to have the vision... see and feel what you are thinking... grasp it. . . hold and fix it in your memory and senses. And you must do it at once.

On filming *Ivan the Terrible*, quoted by President Reagan in address to Moscow's cultural and arts community *Washington Post* 1 Jun 88

William Faulkner novelist

8331 Hollywood is the only place in the world where a man can get stabbed in the back while climbing a ladder.

John Robert Colombo ed *Colombo's Hollywood* Collins 79

Federico Fellini director

8332 Even if I set out to make a film about a fillet of sole, it would be about me!

On the autobiographical nature of films *Atlantic* Dec 65

8333 Cinema is an old whore. . . who knows how to give many kinds of pleasure. Besides, you can't teach old fleas new dogs.

ib

8334 I did not expect this. Actually, I did. But not for another 25 years.

On receiving an Oscar *London Times* 1 Apr 93

8335 The visionary is the only true realist.

Recalled on Fellini's death *USA Today* 1 Nov 93

8336 I always make the same film. I can't distinguish one from another.

Washington Post 1 Nov 93

8337 You start on a voyage; you know where you will end up, but not what will occur along the way. You want to be surprised.

On changing scripts as films progressed *NY Times* 1 Nov 93

8338 I discovered there existed. . . a country of wide-open spaces, of fantastic cities that were a cross between Babylon and Mars.

On influence of American films of the 1930s *ib*

8339 I was overwhelmed by the variety of the country's physical landscape and, too, by the variety of its human landscape.

On joining a traveling circus in Italy *ib*

8340 It was a chance to discover the character of one's country and, at the same time, to discover one's own identity.

ib

Richard Fleischer director

8341 The worse the disaster, the more hilarious it becomes.

Just Tell Me When to Cry Carroll & Graf 93

8342 After all, it's only moving shadows on a silver screen.

ib

John Ford director

8343 When you understand what makes a great Western painting, you'll be a great Western director.

To Steven Spielberg at age 16 *Forbes* 26 Sep 94

Earl Glick Chair, Hal Roach Studios

8344 I could take 200 A–1 pictures, colorize them, and turn them into solid gold.

On computer conversion of black-and-white films for use on color television *Time* 6 Oct 84

Samuel Goldwyn producer

8345 A wide screen just makes a bad film twice as bad.

Quote 9 Sep 56

8346 Having integrity. . . means being completely true to what is inside you—to what you know is right. . . what you feel you must do, regardless of the immediate cost of sacrifice. . . to be honorable and to behave decently.

NY Herald Tribune 10 Jan 60

8347 Without integrity no person is complete and without it, no book, no play, nothing written, nothing done by man has any real value.

ib

8348 Tell me how did you love my picture?

Recalled on Goldwyn's death 31 Jan 74

8349 The reason so many people turned up at his funeral is that they wanted to make sure he was dead.

On producer Louis B Mayer *ib*

8350 Why only 12? Go out and get thousands.

On recasting the *Last Supper ib*

8351 Every director bites the hand that lays the golden egg.

ib

8352 Where they got lesbians, we'll use Albanians.

To an associate who questioned the taste of filming Radclyffe Hall's 1928 book *The Well of Loneliness ib*

8353 Too caustic? To hell with the costs, we'll make the picture anyway.

ib

8354 You gotta take the sour with the bitter.

To director Billy Wilder, quoted by A Scott Berg *Goldwyn* Knopf 89

8355 We are dealing in facts, not realities!

Quoted by columnist Walter Winchell *ib*

Peter Guber producer

8356 She's the devil's candy.

On the role of Maria in Tom Wolfe's *The Bonfire of the Vanities* quoted by Christopher Lehmann-Haupt *NY Times* 18 Nov 91 reviewing Julie Salamon's *The Devil's Candy* Houghton Mifflin 91

Dashiell Hammett novelist

8357 Nobody ever created a more insufferably smug pair of characters!

On the couple Nick and Nora in his last novel *The Thin Man* played by William Powell and Myrna Loy in MGM's 1934 film of the same name *Smithsonian* May 94

Jack Hannah producer

8358 Mickey Mouse was the star in the early days, but he was too much Mr Nice Guy.

On the creation of Donald Duck *Wall Street Journal* 10 May 84

Ben Hecht playwright

8359 The honors Hollwood has for the writer are as dubious as tissue-paper cufflinks.

Charlie Harper 57

8360 People's sex habits are as well known in Hollywood as their political opinions, and much less criticized.

NY Mirror 24 Apr 59

Lillian Hellman playwright

8361 To understand Sam you must realize that he regards himself as a nation.

On Samuel Goldwyn, John Robert Columbo *Columbo's Hollywood* Collins 79

Margaret Herrick Librarian, Academy of Motion Picture Arts and Sciences

8362 It looks just like my Uncle Oscar!

On the gold statuette regarded as Hollywood's most coveted award *London Times* 1 Apr 93

Alfred Hitchcock director

8363 If I made Cinderella, the audience would immediately be looking for a body in the coach.

Newsweek 11 Jun 56

8364 The poloist, steeplechaser, speedboat racer, and the fox hunter ride for the thrill that comes only from danger. . . and for every person who seeks fear in the real or personal sense, millions seek it vicariously, in the theater and in the cinema. Give them pleasure—the same pleasure they have when they wake up from a nightmare.

On audiences *Asbury Park, NJ Press* 13 Aug 74

8365 Self-plagiarism is style.

Defending repetition of his filming techniques *London Observer* 8 Aug 76

8366 Blondes make the best victims. They're like virgin snow that shows up the bloody footprints.

CBS TV 20 Feb 77

8367 Some films are slices of life; mine are slices of cake.

John Robert Colombo ed *Colombo's Hollywood* Collins 79

8368 A good film is when the price of the dinner, the theater admission, and the babysitter were worth it.

ib

8369 In feature films the director is God; in documentary films God is the director.

ib

8370 Television has brought murder back into the home—where it belongs.

ib

8371 I never said actors are cattle. What I said was that actors should be treated like cattle.

ib

8372 What is drama but life with the dull bits cut out?

ib

8373 [This award is] meaningful because it comes from my fellow dealers in celluloid.

On the American Film Institute's Lifetime Achievement Award, recalled on Hitchcock's death 29 Apr 80

8374 Disney, of course, has the best casting. If he doesn't like an actor, he just tears it up.

Jon Winokur ed *The Portable Curmudgeon* New American Library 88

8375 One could not make a picture like *Psycho* without a sense of humor because one knew beforehand that you are going to put the audience through the ringer.

Instant Recall CBS TV 1 Oct 90

8376 Mystery is withholding information from the audience. Suspense is giving information to the audience.

ib

8377 The assembly of pieces of film to create fright is the central part of my job.

American Cinema WETA TV 23 Jan 95

John Huston director

8378 The directing of a picture involves coming out of your individual loneliness and taking a controlling part in putting together a small world.

NY Journal-American 31 Mar 60

8379 A work of art doesn't dare you to realize it. It germinates and gestates by itself.

Reply to tribute from Directors Guild of America *Variety* 26 Apr 82

8380 It's not color, it's like pouring 40 tablespoons of sugar water over a roast.

To Directors Guild of America on computer colorization of black-and-white film 13 Nov 86

P D James novelist

8381 [They] paid vast sums of money and never made the film, which is the best of both worlds.

On a film producer's purchase of James' novel *Innocent Blood, London Times* 1 Aug 92

Dorothy Jeakins costumer

8382 The canvas is the script and the designer is the painter.

On designs that won three Academy Awards *NY Times* 30 Nov 95

8383 No crimson, blue, green, violet... [but] mud colors—olive, nutmeg, clove, persimmon, faded red—the colors of real life... the oppressive quality in Dublin social life... lamplight and the dour color of a Dublin house.

ib

8384 In the middle of the night, I can put my world down to two words: "Make beauty"... my cue and my private passion.

ib

Herbert T Kalmus film executive

8385 You can't break up know-how by court order.

On a 1949 decree that Technicolor should not constitute a monopoly *NY Herald Tribune* 12 Jul 63

Joseph P Kennedy financier

8386 The picture business... is a new industry and a gold mine... like another telephone industry.

On his initial investment in motion pictures, quoted by Peter Collier and David Horowitz *The Kennedys* Summit 84

Fletcher Knebel novelist

8387 Hollywood, to hear some writers tell it, is the place where they take an author's steak-tartare and make cheeseburgers out of it.

Look 19 Nov 63 on co-authoring with Charles W Bailey II the novel *Seven Days in May* Harper & Row 62

8388 A bland dish is borne to the consumer on flaming swords while the London Philharmonic plays Wagner.

ib

8389 Upon seeing the film, they say, the author promptly cuts his throat, bleeding to death in a pool of money.

On co-authoring *Seven Days in May, Look* 19 Nov 63

Howard Koch screenwriter

8390 Play it, Sam! Play "As Time Goes By"!

Lines for Ingrid Bergman speaking to pianist Dooley Wilson in Koch and Julius and Philip Epstein's 1943 film *Casablanca, NY Times* 18 Aug 95

Jack Kroll director

8391 We used the neon waterholes where urban animals clash by night.

On filming *Looking for Mr Goodbar* on Manhattan's West Side *Newsweek* 10 Oct 77

Jesse Lasky producer

8392 I yearned to trespass on Quality Street.

On desire to produce better films *New Yorker* 21 Mar 94

David Lean director

8393 Making a movie is using a vast piece of machinery like a crane to draw a fine line; one person must control the machinery.

On the importance of a single, autocratic director *NY Times* 17 Apr 91

Barry L Levinson director

8394 The hell with the trains, the helicopters, the Mafia, the FBI, the car crashes, the pursuits, the stakeouts, the barricades... all of those things that we pump into movies because we're afraid to make movies about people.

On casting Dustin Hoffman as an autistic savant in *Rain Man, NY Times* 11 Dec 88

Art Linson producer

8395 We are the mayonnaise in the sandwich.

On the role of the producer *NY Times* 28 Sep 92

George Lucas film executive

8396 Art is the retelling of certain themes in a new light, making them accessible to the public of the moment.

NY Times 9 Jun 88

Sidney Lumet director

8397 I don't want life reproduced up there on the screen. I want life created!

NPR 18 Apr 95

Norman Mailer novelist

8398 Novels are like wives—you don't talk about them. But movies are different—they're like mistresses, and you can brag a bit.

Parade 1 Jan 89

Herman J Mankiewicz screenwriter

8399 There, but for the grace of God, goes God.
On Orson Welles *NY Times* 11 Oct 85

8400 There are millions to be grabbed out here and your only competition is idiots. Don't let this get around.
Cable to Ben Hecht on early days in Hollywood *NY Times* 8 Jan 93

Joseph L Mankiewicz screenwriter

8401 When you're in a cage with tigers, you never let them know you're afraid of them, or they'll eat you.
On working with Elizabeth Taylor and Richard Burton *Life* 19 Apr 63

8402 I've been on the beginning, the rise, peak, collapse and end of the talking picture.
Washington Post 1 Jun 86

8403 She did it the hard way—and she did.
On Bette Davis' suggested epitaph *NY Times* 15 Jul 94

8404 For her, life itself was a kind of acting.
On Elizabeth Taylor, WETA TV Washington 27 Nov 95

Arthur Miller playwright

8405 One day I was sitting in my studio and I thought of this story. It wanted to be a movie so I let it be a movie.
On *Everybody Wins, NY Times* 22 Nov 88

8406 You sit at your typewriter and out comes 60 people, and sandwiches and $2 million worth of equipment.
On writing for films *ib*

David Newman screenwriter

8407 He is our myth, the American myth.
On the comic strip figure Superman on which Newman collaborated for a Broadway musical and three screenplays *Time* 14 Mar 88

Mike Nichols director

8408 Style is beginning something in the manner which will make it necessary for things that happen later to happen.
Film Comment May 91

8409 Glamour is the glorious moment continued and absorbed into personality. In that sense, it's in defiance of time and death. . . to make up for something that isn't there—either anymore or at all.
New Yorker 21 Mar 94

8410 If you live in a glamorous way or become a glamorous person, what you're doing is sacrificing being for seeming. The first thing you check at the gate and give up forever is spontaneity.
ib

Dorothy Parker humorist

8411 Hollywood money isn't money. It's congealed snow.
Paris Review Summer 56

8412 It's going to be the best you can do, and it's the fact that it's the best you can do that kills you.
ib

8413 The only ism Hollywood believes is plagiarism.
Recalled on Parker's death 7 Jun 67

8414 He never went about with a begging bowl extended for the greasy coins of pity.
On Oscar Levant, quoted by Roddy McDowell *Double Exposure* Morrow 68

8415 He long ago said everything about everything—and what Oscar Levant says, stays said.
ib

Robert Parrish film editor

8416 It was a small town and all the business was the movies. . . a factory, and the factory made movies.
On taking up life in Hollywood at age 8 "about 400 yards from the Paramount Studios" *NY Times* 6 Dec 95

8417 If they ask if you own a horse, say yes. If they ask if you are a horse, say yes. And you'll learn how to do it that night.
Advice picked up from Laura Virginia Reese "a card-carrying movie mother" *ib*

S J Perelman essayist

8418 A dreary industrial town controlled by hoodlums of enormus wealth, the ethical sense of a pack of jackals and taste so degraded that it befouled everything.
On Hollywood *Paris Review* Spring 64

Jack Pierce director

8419 We would cut the top of the skull off straight across like a pot lid, hinge it, pop the brain in and clamp it tight.
On the makeup for the original Frankenstein *Connoisseur* Jan 91

Roman Polanski director

8420 Directing while acting is one less person to argue with.
NY Times 22 Feb 76

8421 Unawareness is the real mother of invention.
Newsweek 28 Mar 94

Gerald Posner screenwriter

8422 The only thing he got right was the date of Kennedy's death.

On Oliver Stone's direction of *JFK*, Station WNET Washington 20 Sep 93

J B Priestley playwright

8423 Its trade, which is in dreams of so many dollars per thousand feet, is managed by businessmen pretending to be artists and by artists pretending to be businessmen.

John Robert Colombo ed *Colombo's Hollywood* Collins 79

8424 The artist begins to lose his art, and the businessman becomes temperamental and overbalanced.

ib

John Sayles director

8425 With the MacArthur, it's a tightrope with a safety net under you.

On the MacArthur Foundation's "genius grants" *NY Times* 17 Jul 88

Dore Schary producer

8426 Behave as citizens not only of your profession but of the full world in which you live... indignant with injustice... gracious with success... courageous with failure... patient with opportunity... resolute with faith and honor.

To American Academy of Dramatic Arts *Atlantic* Oct 59

David O Selznick producer

8427 If they will only do their job... that is all that they are being overpaid for.

On filming *The Garden of Allah* quoted by Maria Riva *Marlene Dietrich* Knopf 92

Mack Sennett producer

8428 A mother never gets hit with a custard pie. Mothers-in-law—yes. But mothers—never.

On producing slapstick comedy *NY Times* 6 Nov 60

Jerome Siegel screenwriter

8429 I'm lying in bed counting sheep when all of a sudden it hits me... a character like Samson, Hercules and all the strong men I heard tell of rolled into one. Only more so!

Recalling his original idea for Superman *Time* 14 Mar 88

8430 Strange visitor from another planet, who came to earth with powers and abilities far beyond those of mortal men. Superman!

Traditional introduction of Superman *ib*

8431 Who can change the course of mighty rivers, bend steel with his bare hands, and... fights a never-ending battle for truth, justice and the American way!

ib

Sigurjon Sighvatsson producer

8432 In constructing the film as speculative fiction, the little known character of Jack Ruby might be better understood—his ties to organized crime, often volatile nature, and motivation behind the killing of Oswald.

On enlarging facts in the film *Ruby* on the slayer of Kennedy assassin Lee Harvey Oswald *NY Times* 27 Mar 92

John Singleton director

8433 [It would be an act of] artistic racism.

On possible withdrawal of the controversial *Boyz'n the Hood* that he directed *NY Times* 14 Jul 91

Edith Sitwell poet

8434 I do not want my troubles going all round London and being discussed in potato queues.

Cautioning Portuguese poet Alberto de Lacerda against discussing her difficulties in producing a script for Hollywood, quoted by Victoria Glendinning *A Unicorn Among Lions* Weidenfeld & Nicolson 81

8435 He shrieks like a regiment of horses that has been mowed down by cannon.

On scripts by Walter Reich *ib*

Helena Solberg director

8436 This persona is for me, as a Brazilian woman, both alluring and absurd, and for many Latin Americans so unreal and strange.

On directing and narrating the television documentary *Carmen Miranda: Bananas Is My Business NY Times* 6 Oct 95

8437 Carmen Miranda is forever part of our mythology.

ib

Oliver Stone director

8438 I am like you, living through this time, seeing the absurdity around me.

On "a society and a culture going to hell... an era gone amok" as seen in the screenplay of *Natural Born Killers, London Times* 22 Feb 95

François Truffaut director

8439 An actor is never so great as when he reminds you of an animal—falling like a cat, lying like a dog, moving like a fox.

New Yorker 20 Feb 60

Jamie Uys director

8440 White, black or brown... you like to see the funny side of the human condition... you don't see their color.

Reply to critics of Bushmen and apartheid in Uys' *The Gods Must Be Crazy, NY Times* 2 Feb 96

Jack Valenti President, Motion Picture Assn of America

8441 Choice is to the cable monopoly what sunlight is to the vampire.

On control of 40 percent of US cable subscriptions by a small group of five companies *US News & World Report* 11 May 87

Anthony Veiller screenwriter

8442 The calla lillies are in bloom again.

Lines for Katherine Hepburn in *Stage Door,* 1937 screenplay by Veiller and Morie Ryskind, recalled on Veiller's death 27 Jun 65, also see *The Movie Quote Book* Harper & Row 90

Josef Von Sternberg director

8443 Do not kiss my hand, Madame. You have permitted my camera to worship you and in turn you have worshiped yourself.

Cable to Marlene Dietrich after she starred in *The Blue Angel,* quoted by Maria Riva *Marlene Dietrich* Knopf 92

Andy Warhol painter and producer

8444 [It is] illogical, without motivation or character, and completely ridiculous. . . very much like real life.

On his film *Kitchen, Wall Street Journal* 7 Apr 87

Jack Warner producer

8445 I have a theory of relatives. . . don't hire 'em.

On studio visit from the father of the relativity theory, Albert Einstein, quoted by Stephen Farber and Marc Green *Hollywood Dynasties* Delilah Books 84

8446 You were very good playing a bitch-heroine, but you shouldn't win an award for playing yourself.

To Bette Davis *Time* 9 Apr 84

8447 No, Jimmy Stewart for governor. Ronald Reagan for best friend.

On typecasting *Newsweek* 20 Jul 87

Orson Welles director

8448 A film is never really good unless the camera is an eye in the head of a poet.

Quoted by John Robert Colombo ed *Colombo's Hollywood* Collins 79

8449 Don't let Ted Turner deface my movie with his crayons.

Death-bed request that corporate executives not be allowed to colorize *Citizen Kane* NPR 18 Feb 89

8450 The best damned toy-box any boy was ever given.

On film, recalled on death of filmmaker Federico Fellini *London Times* 1 Nov 93

Billy Wilder screenwriter

8451 Look at this street! All cardboard, all hollow, all phony, all done with mirrors. You know, I like it better than any street in the world.

Description of a Hollywood set for *Sunset Boulevard* written with Charles Brackett and D M Marshman Jr for Paramount Pictures 50 *National Geographic* Jun 92

8452 I am big! It's the pictures that got small!

Lines for the fading actress Norma Desmond as played by Gloria Swanson *Vanity Fair* Jun 91

8453 We didn't need dialogue then. We had faces!

ib

8454 Hindsight is always 20/20.

John Robert Colombo ed *Colombo's Hollywood* Collins 79

8455 I have a vast and terrible desire never to be a bore.

ib

8456 Keep it out of focus. I want to win the foreign-picture award.

ib

8457 You have Van Gogh's ear for music.

To actor Cliff Osmond, news reports 31 Dec 82

8458 In the real crucifixion scene. . . use real nails.

On the return to the Oberammergau Passion Play of Anton Lang who had played Christ and gone on to serve in the German SS in World War II, quoted by David Freeman "Sunset Boulevard Revisited" *New Yorker* 21 Jun 93

8459 Nijinski was the greatest dancer ever. . . ended up in a French nuthouse, thinking he was a horse. . . [but] don't worry, there's a happy ending. In the final scene, he wins the Kentucky Derby.

To Sam Goldwyn on proposing a film on Nijinski *ib*

8460 People worked harder. They saved their money so they could have a dress like Jean Harlow's or a doublebreasted suit like Adolphe Menjou's to wear on the wrong occcasion.

On film-goers *New Yorker* 21 Mar 94

Tennessee Williams playwright

8461 The profits were as good as the movie was bad.

On filming of his play *Suddenly Last Summer, Memoirs* Doubleday 75

William Wyler director

8462 It looked more like a field of heather than a field of heather.

On Hollywood's version of Yorkshire moors created for *Wuthering Heights, NY Times* 19 Feb 88

Franco Zeffirelli director

8463 You can make 200,000 versions of Romeo and Juliet but they will never be the same.
London Times 22 Feb 95

Critics

Gilbert Adair essayist

8464 [He] returns to the underground caverns of his nightmare as obsessively as the tongue will return to the tiny cavern vacated by a loose filling.
On producer Steven Spielberg *Illustrated London News* Mar 88

Henry Allen reporter

8465 Her hair lounges on her shoulders like an anesthetized cocker spaniel.
On Lauren Bacall at age 70 *Washington Post* 27 Oct 94

8466 Jason Robards... gave her the best drinking years of his life.
On Bacall's second marriage *ib*

8467 Numberless women have walked past mirrors hoping for a hint of Bacall's slinkiness.
ib

Anon

8468 Cannes... is 10,000 people for ten people who really count.
French publicist on stars of the Cannes Film Festival, *NY Times* 17 May 86

8469 [She] simultaneously brought a blush to my cheek and a yawn to my jaw.
On Elsa Lanchester at London's Cafe de Paris, quoted by Kenneth Tynan, Kathleen Tynan and Ernie Eban eds *Profiles* HarperCollins 88

8470 Basically a benign volcano.
On Bette Davis, remark that became the title of a television biography *Basically A Benign Volcano* ABC TV 31 Dec 89

8471 A brassy brunette with a body worth swimming a moat for.
On Mercedes Ruehl in *The Fisher King, Good Morning, America* ABC TV 27 Sep 91

David Ansen critic

8472 Clipped mustache... whiskey-coated growl, steely self-assurance, an aristocrat of sleaze.
On Paul Newman in *The Color of Money, Newsweek* 13 Oct 86

8473 The body-fat content of a 20-year-old sprinter, bone structure of a public monument and the eyes... well, we know about the blue eyes (which happen to be colorblind). The world has lost its quintessential romantic icon.
On death of Cary Grant 8 Dec 86

Cecil Beaton photographer

8474 She has a face that belongs to the sea and the wind, with large rocking horse nostrils and teeth that you know just bite an apple every day.
On photographing Katharine Hepburn, recalled on Beaton's death 18 Jan 80

Paul V Beckley critic

8475 The Entertainer... has set itself to scratching the dandruff out of the mane of life.
NY Herald Tribune 4 Oct 60

Melvyn Bragg biographer

8476 Those whom the gods want to destroy they first make megasuccessful.
Richard Burton Little, Brown 88

Louis Brooks journalist

8477 Every actor has a natural animosity toward every other actor, present or absent, living or dead.
Lulu in Hollywood Knopf 82

Vincent Canby critic

8478 [His acting] remains forever fixed in a time that never dates.
On Cary Grant *NY Times* 1 Dec 86

8479 Watching the non-dancing, non-singing Fred Astaire is like watching a grounded skylark.
On Astaire's dramatic roles 23 Jun 87

8480 [It] is a great uninterrupted grin... from ear to ear.
On film based on the comic strip *Dick Tracy* 15 Jun 90

8481 He doesn't have a heart of gold. It's pure film.
On 40 years of screenplays 20 Nov 92

Gabrielle ("Coco") Chanel designer

8482 Hollywood is the Mont Saint Michel of tit and tale.
Quoted by Paul Morand *L'Allure de Chanel* Hermann, Paris 76

Francis X Clines reporter

8483 Historians... despair that the 37th President may be offered meanly as a wet-snouted caricature of paranoia.
On portrayal of Richard M Nixon in Oliver Stone's *Nixon, NY Times* 19 Dec 95

8484 Old advisers and family friends are spewing expletives deleted.
Recalling the "expletives deleted" phrase frequently used to cover profanity in tapes from the Oval Office *ib*

Jean Cocteau novelist

8485 A giant with the look of a child, a lazy activeness, a mad wisdom, a solitude encompassing the world.

On Orson Welles *NY Times* 11 Oct 85

8486 Your name begins with a caress and ends with the crack of a whip.

To Marlene Dietrich *Sotheby's Preview* Oct 92

Alistair Cooke commentator

8487 The most flourishing factory of popular mythology since the Greeks.

On Hollywood *America* Knopf 73

Richard Corliss critic

8488 Born schizophrenic. . . for 75 years it has been both a town and a state of mind, an industry and an art form.

On Hollywood *Time* 3 Feb 86

8489 She knew how to fill a room with her magnificent arrogance.

On Bette Davis 16 Oct 89

8490 Independence born in neurosis, strength forged in professional and domestic combat, her man of the moment an irrelevance or a desperate burden.

On Davis' creation of "Hollywood's first and finest portrait of the thoroughly modern woman" *ib*

8491 To do Bette Davis was to heighten her performances till they swerved between tragedy and camp.

ib

8492 She served wit on a knife to Anne Baxter. . . [and] a rat on a plate to Joan Crawford.

ib

8493 Sensation. . . she could still cause one; she could still be one.

ib

8494 His camera taking his picture. . . is as cool as the star it captured in its glass.

On Buster Keaton directing the films in which he was also the comic lead *ib* 9 Oct 95

8495 He had a tinkerer's obsession. . . everything goes wrong so that everything moves perfectly.

ib

Noel Coward playwright

8496 Though we all might enjoy/Seeing Helen of Troy/As a gay cabaret entertainer,/I doubt that she could/Be one quarter as good/As our legendary, lovely Marlene.

Introducing Marlene Dietrich at London's Cafe de Paris, recalled in *London Times* 7 May 92

Bosley Crowther critic

8497 This reviewer is certainly happy to have only sons.

On Spencer Tracy in *Father of the Bride, NY Times* 19 May 50

8498 Believe it or not, it is a picture about two young people romantically in love—in love with each other, that is, not with a tractor or the Soviet state.

On *The Cranes Are Flying* 27 Mar 60

8499 The Russians have finally found romance!

ib

Michael Curtiz critic

8500 The lighting. . . [is] too Semitic.

On an overly symmetrical set, quoted by Sam Kashner and Nancy Schoenberger in the Oscar Levant biography *A Talent for Genius* Villard 94

Frank Deford essayist

8501 The pilot light of memory flickers in her eyes.

On Leni Riefenstahl looking at pictures of Berlin 1930 *Sports Illustrated* 4 Aug 86

Katherine De Mille wife of actor Anthony Quinn

8502 Your whole life doesn't have to be a pissing contest, you know.

On competitiveness, quoted by Quinn *One Man Tango* HarperCollins 95

Alice Demoree critic

8503 Mediocrity shuffles after banality in an unending process.

On the French cinema, BBC Radio 20 Aug 68

David Denby critic

8504 The whole thing can slip away between the white wine and the arugula salad.

On portraying upper-middle class marriage in *Heartburn, New York* 4 Aug 86

Jennifer Dunning critic

8505 [It was] one surging tide of summer polyster and lazy anticipation.

On audiences rising to greet Bob Hope at Valley Forge Music Fair *NY Times* 1 Jul 80

Ann Edwards biographer

8506 She responded with the kind of immediacy a trusted love could expect.

On Katharine Hepburn and the motion picture camera *A Remarkable Woman* Morrow 85

St John Ervine critic

8507 American motion pictures are written by the half-educated for the half-witted.

NY Mirror 6 Jun 63

Janet Flanner *New Yorker* columnist

8508 Her figure was mandolin rather than guitar.

On Bette Davis *Janet Flanner's World* Harcourt World Jovanovich 79

Peter B Flint critic

8509 He projected the image of an eager, bouncy terrier. . . walk jaunty and manner defiant.

On James Cagney *NY Times* 31 Mar 66

8510 The plots. . . were breathing spaces between the couple's champagne dance numbers.

On Ginger Rogers-Fred Astaire musicals 28 Apr 95

8511 In lavish settings all the walls, telephones and pianos were white, butlers always comic and love was the only concern.

ib

Alan Franks critic

8512 The child was a permanent fixture within him.

On Peter Sellers *London Times* 11 Feb 95

Sheilah Graham columnist

8513 No one has a closest friend in Hollywood.

The Rest of the Story Coward, McCann 64

8514 I have a strange feeling he will wake up one day and ask, "What movie am I in?"

On Ronald Reagan as US President *London Times* 22 Aug 81

Felix Gutierrez Vice President, Gannett Foundation

8515 The new stories about color again have nothing to do with black or white or yellow. The true color is green.

On financial success of films on interracial romance *NY Times* 31 Mar 91

Mollie Haskell essayist

8516 [Hollywood] is the propaganda arm of the American dream machine.

From *Reverence to Rape* Holt Rinehart Winston 73

Ben Hecht playwright

8517 Movie-makers are able to put more reality into a picture about the terrors of life at the ocean bottom than into a tale of two Milwaukeeans in love.

Recalled on Hecht's death 18 Apr 64

C David Heymann biographer

8518 Hollywood was a silver-nitrate finishing school for a whole generation.

On films of the 1930s as educators in table manners, decor, dress, how to kiss, laughter, tears, tragedy, happiness, and "how to be brave, evil and good" *Poor Little Rich Girl* Random House 83

Charles Higham biographer

8519 Louella came to coo relentlessly over the child who somehow survived the presence of this witch at her cradle.

On columnist Louella Parsons calling on Bette Davis' baby *Bette* Macmillan 81

8520 Hedda descended like a bird of prey in a feathered hat to bless the newborn.

On columnist Hedda Hopper *ib*

Stephen Hunter critic

8521 Stiff-upper-lipping it, they enjoy what might have been, what could have been, what would have been.

On a revival of Noel Coward's 1945 *Brief Encounter* with Celia Johnson and Trevor Howard *Baltimore Sun* 17 Apr 91

Clive James critic

8522 Marilyn Monroe was so minimally talented as to be almost unemployable.

Commentators Oct 73

8523 She was good at playing abstract confusion in the same way that a midget is good at being short.

ib

Edwin C Johnson US Senator

8524 [It is] an assault upon the institution of marriage . . . a powerful influence for evil.

On an out-of-wedlock birth to Ingrid Bergman and Roberto Rossellini as the basis of a bill for "the licensing of actresses, producers and films by a division of the Department of Commerce," news summaries 31 Dec 50

Pauline Kael critic

8525 Good movies make you care, make you believe in possibilities again.

Going Steady Little, Brown 70

8526 *Citizen Kane*. . . seems as fresh as the day it opened. It may seem even fresher.

The Citizen Kane Book Bantam 71

8527 Her only flair is in her nostrils.

On Candice Bergen *Time* 16 Apr 84

8528 I sat screaming silently.

On reading rave reviews of *The Silence of the Lambs, NY Times* 13 Mar 91

8529 A toupee made up to look like honest baldness.
On *Nothing in Common, New Yorker* 8 Sep 86

Stefan Kanfer critic

8530 A stagy, rigid interpretation. . . brought to life by the hypnotic performance of Bela Lugosi as the bloodthirsty count, whose three wives live in coffins.
On the 1931 *Dracula, Connoisseur* Jan 91

8531 Haunting dialogue, very little blood.
On Boris Karloff in *The Mummy ib*

Jack Kroll essayist

8532 Wrap up the 20th century; Fred Astaire is gone.
Newsweek 6 Jul 87

Doug Larson humorist

8533 It took only 50 years for movies to go from the silent to the unspeakable.
Reader's Digest Sep 93

Oscar Levant humorist

8534 Pound-cake beauty!
On chorus girls, quoted by Sam Kashner and Nancy Schoenberger *A Talent for Genius* Villard 94

8535 I knew her before she was a virgin.
On actress Doris Day's girl-next-door roles *ib*

Life magazine

8536 [She began] a slide into the rhinestones.
On Rita Hayworth's divorce from Aly Khan and Las Vegas marriage to singer Dick Haymes, quoted by Leonard Pitts *Glamour Girls of Hollywood* Sharon 84

London Times

8537 His pallbearers were to include Herbert Hoover, Cardinal Spellman, William Randolph Hearst Jr and Spencer Tracy. . . no clearer indication that the Mayer family had become American royalty.
On film producer Louis B Mayer 12 Oct 90

8538 She passed again and again that final test of stardom—not just to do something, but to stand there.
On death at age 90 of Marlene Dietrich 7 May 92

Clare Boothe Luce essayist

8539 Greta Garbo—a deer, in the body of a woman, living resentfully in the Hollywood zoo.
John Robert Colombo ed *Colombo's Hollywood* Collins 79

Norman Mailer novelist

8540 One of the worst great movies ever made.
On *JFK,* Oliver Stone's film on President Kennedy's assassination *Vanity Fair* Feb 92

Edward Marsh essayist

8541 "Technicolor" suffuses everything with stale mustard.
Ambrosia and Small Beer Harcourt Brace Winston 65

Federico Mayor Director General, UNESCO

8542 The art of cinema is the custodian of the 20th century's memory.
NY Times 28 Feb 95

Robert D McFadden reporter

8543 A musty smelling refuge that offered instant nostalgia.
On closing of Manhattan's Thalia theater that had shown classic films since 1931 *NY Times* 11 May 87

Marion Meade biographer

8544 Through the thirties, Hollywood was a combination kosher deli and El Dorado.
Dorothy Parker Villar 88

Bob Mondello critic

8545 Dreams are the cinema of the mind.
Reviewing *Paper Moon* NPR 17 Mar 89

Lance Morrow essayist

8546 His mouth addressed a woman's lips with the quivering nibble of a horse closing in on an apple.
On Humphrey Bogart *Fishing in the Tiber* Holt 88

Julian Muller advertising executive

8547 When you wrote your book you committed an act of art. When you sell film rights you commit merely an act of commerce.
To the author of *By Love Possessed* Harcourt Brace 57, quoted by Matthew J Bruccoli *James Gould Cozzens* Harcourt Brace Jovanovich 83

The New York Times

8548 Cary Grant was not supposed to die but was supposed to stick around, our personal touchstone of charm and elegance and romance and youth.
"Cary Grant's Promise" editorial 2 Dec 86

8549 The haircut's perfect and so is the suit and the cleft in the chin is heaven's thumbmark.
ib

8550 Icons from an era when screens were silver and silents were golden.

On exhibition of early films 27 Mar 88

8551 How sweet it is to see the stars arriving in full light of day in full evening fig. How swell the ladies in their straplesses and sunglasses!

"Silent Night, Oscar Night" editorial on timing Oscar festivities to coincide with Eastern seaboard's prime time viewing 1 Apr 92

8552 How great the gents in their vibrant vests! . . . Fame on the hoof!

ib

John Powers reporter

8553 It's too easy to inadvertently bruise their narcissism.

On profiling Dustin Hoffman and other stars *Washington Post* 5 Mar 95

8554 He is as reverent as a Zen master describing a tea ceremony, as filled with relish as an old salt recalling his first trip to the bordello.

On Dustin Hoffman on researching a role *ib*

Frederic Raphael reporter

8555 We all knew that the unspeakable things happened in talent once it had crossed the Rockies.

On Hollywood-bound writers *NY Times* 6 Jan 85

8556 They are often glowing with the effusive sentimentality to be found only among those who have stolen each other's ideas, deals and live-in companions.

On Hollywoodians *ib*

Rex Reed

8557 Elegant and golden as a buttery iceberg. . . skin white as winter and blue-gray eyes the color of Park Avenue at dawn.

On Jean Seberg, recalled on Seberg's death 8 Sep 79

8558 In Hollywood you don't have happiness, you send out for it.

Chicago Tribune 16 Oct 83

8559 It's hate at first sight.

On Goldie Hawn as a football coach in *Wildcats, Palm Beach Daily News* 6 Apr 86

8560 I don't think she ever remembered giving me the interview, but she sure remembered reading it!

On a May 1967 profile of Ava Gardner *US* 19 May 86

Maria Riva biographer

8561 It resembled a Victorian christening dress, done in spun sugar. . . [and] she looked like the village idiot dressed in a bassinet.

On her mother's costume in *The Scarlet Empress* as a young woman in 18th century imperialist Russia *Marlene Dietrich* Knopf 92

8562 He was leading a cast of European hams. . . each one with an accent as thick as old cheese.

On *The Garden of Allah* as directed by Poland's Joseph Schildkraut "who believed he was Rasputin dressed up as Stroheim" *ib*

8563 A beturbaned Basil Rathbone, ever so long-nosed British Empire, was petrified astride a wild Arabian stallion and Dietrich, meticulously coiffed, looked like a dress dummy from a Berlin department store.

ib

8564 Like meringue, its sticky sweetness hurt your back teeth.

On Marlene Dietrich in *The Flame of New Orleans ib*

Megan Rosenfeld critic

8565 It is the artistic equivalent of a white bread and mayonnaise sandwich.

On ABC's movie of the week *They've Taken Our Children Washington Post* 1 Mar 93

Mort Sahl humorist

8566 I used to go out exclusively with actresses and other female impersonators.

Heartland Harcourt Brace Jovanovich 76

Carl Sandburg poet

8567 It was the only newspaper job I ever had that allowed me to get plenty of sleep.

On reviewing films for the *Chicago Daily News*, quoted by Penelope Niven *Carl Sandburg* Scribner 91

Richard Schickel critic

8568 This is a soul with perpetual migraine attack.

On Vanessa Redgrave as Olive in *The Bostonians Time* 15 Oct 84

8569 [It was] a place for older people to get back in touch with the Gables, Grables and Garbos of their lost youth. . . [and] avoided the scuzziness of most revival theaters.

On the closing of Manhattan's Regency Theater, Letters to the Editor *NY Times* 14 Sep 87

8570 What would English literature—or, for that matter, English sexuality–have done without gamy gamekeepers, lurking unrepressed in the gorse, ready to help the privileged class assert its true, randy nature.

Reviewing E M Forster's *Maurice, Time* 12 Oct 87

Tom Shales reporter

8571 Bette Davis got most of her exercise by putting her foot down.

Washington Post 9 Oct 89

Gene Shalit

8572 Some films could only have been cast in one way: screen tests were given and the loser got the parts!

NBC TV 18 May 71

Irwin Shaw novelist

8573 Hope and despair and beauty and death were carried around the city in flat, round, shining cans.

On the Cannes film festival *Evening in Byzantium* Delacorte 73

Wilfrid Sheed

8574 Dietrich's career was. . . a prolonged feat of audacity.

On Marlene Dietrich *NY Times* 4 Oct 92

Clancy Sigal novelist

8575 Too many freeways, too much sun, abnormality taken normally, pink stucco houses and pink stucco consciences.

on Hollywood *Going Away* Houghton Mifflin 62

John Simon essayist

8576 She is absolutely sanitary: her personality untouched by human emotions, her brow unclouded by human thought, her form unsmudged by the slightest form of feminiity.

On Doris Day *Private Screenings* Macmillan 67

8577 Her figure. . . defies definition by the most resourceful solid geometrician.

On Judy Garland *ib*

Edith Sitwell poet

8578 I met Miss Mary Pickford, a confectioner's goddess of vanilla-flavored ice cream.

Taken Care Of Atheneum 65

Harry Smith commentator

8579 The Academy Awards—Hollywood's annual orgy of self-congratulations.

Good Morning America ABC TV 26 Mar 91

Donald Spoto biographer

8580 Conrad Hilton Sr married the most incandescent of the pack, Zsa Zsa Gabor.

On Hilton marriages in Hollywood—the patriarch to Zsa Zsa Gabor and son Nicky to Elizabeth Taylor *A Passion for Life* HarperCollins 95

8581 Being gay was worse than being Communist.

On Hollywood of the 1950s *ib*

8582 She was idle while he was an idol.

On actress Elizabeth Taylor's restlessness while husband Richard Burton was Broadway's leading man in *Hamlet ib*

Wallace Stegner novelist

8583 The life of the stars. . . full of romantic excess and riddled with delightful scandal. . . invaded the consciousness of dreaming shop girls all around the globe.

On the influence of films *NY Times* 24 Feb 85

Richard Taruskin Professor of Music History, University of California, Berkeley

8584 Why can't it just enter the nitrogen cycle with the other mammoths and mastodons of Soviet high-priestly culture?

On the Russian-made film *Ivan the Terrible, NY Times* 28 May 95

8585 [It should be]. . . left on its side with all the other musical theme park of superannuated tyranny.

ib

8586 This movie and this score. . . conveyed as poisonous a message as art has ever been asked to monger.

ib

Lowell Thomas commentator

8587 They only got two things right, the camels and the sand.

On *Lawrence of Arabia* recalled on Thomas' death 28 Aug 81

Time magazine

8588 When she. . . claimed that a certain actress was pregnant, the actress's husband hastened to prove her correct.

On columnist Louella Parsons 26 Nov 61

8589 Her writhing stare could reduce a rabid dog to foaming jelly.

On Margaret Rutherford in *Mrs John Bull* 24 May 63

8590 The monster with a lace-valentine soul.

On John Hurt in the title role of *The Elephant Man* 1 Oct 90

Kenneth Tynan

8591 What, when drunk, one sees in other women, one sees in Garbo sober.

On Greta Garbo *Curtains* Longmans Green 61

8592 The vengeful hag is played by Ingrid Bergman, which is like casting Eleanor Roosevelt as Lizzie Borden.

On Friedrich Durrenmatt's *The Visit* recalled on Tynan's death 26 Jul 80

8593 Pearl is a disease of oysters. Levant is a disease of Hollywood.

ib

John Updike novelist

8594 Jewish brains projected Gentile stars upon a Gentile nation and out of their own immigrant joy gave a formless land dreams and even a kind of conscience.

On films of the 1930s *Bech: A Book* Knopf 70

8595 It was one of history's great love stories, the mutually profitable romance which Hollywood and bohunk America conducted almost in the dark, a tapping of fervent messaes through the wall of the San Gabriel Range.

ib

Jack Valenti President, Motion Picture Association of America

8596 Choice is to cable monopoly what sunlight is to the vampire.

US News & World Report 11 May 87

Harriet Van Horne columnist

8597 Joan Crawford... would have made an exemplary prison matron, possibly at Buchenwald.

NY Post 29 Oct 78

Gore Vidal novelist

8598 Miss Georgia and Mr Shaker Heights.

On Joanne Woodward and Paul Newman *NY Times* 28 Sep 86

8599 As I move, graciously I hope, toward the door marked Exit, it occurs to me that the only thing I ever really liked to do was go to the movies.

Screening History Harvard 94

8600 Sex and Art... neither ever proved to be as dependable as the filtering of present light through that moving strip of celluloid which projects past images and voices onto a screen.

ib

Alexander Walker biographer

8601 She subsumed herself so completely into her roles that an archaeologist would have embarked on a useless quest if he sought the remains of her.

Joan Crawford Harper & Row 83

Barbara Walters commentator

8602 Mostly they grimace and bear it—to read you've been somewhere you've never been, with someone you've never known, saying things you never said.

On gossip columns as the price of fame ABC TV 26 Apr 95

Edmund White biographer

8603 From the movies we learn precisely how to hold a champagne flute, kiss a mistress, pull a trigger, turn a phrase... [but] the movies spoil us for life; nothing ever lives up to them.

Genet Knopf 93

Dwight Whitney reporter

8604 [She was] dressed in a peignor of beige lace... with a blonde wig above false eyelashes—a kind of Mt Rushmore of the cosmetician's art.

On interviewing Mae West *TV Guide* 28 Feb 65

Malcolm Willits memorabilia dealer

8605 It's the ultimate collectible on a film, other than freeze-drying the star.

On sale of Oscars *Wall Street Journal* 9 Jan 89

Alex Witchel journalist

8606 The voice, with its particular, peculiar accent of a place where everyone waltzes like a dream and wins at baccarat every night, is unchanged.

On Omar Sharif 30 years after the filming of *Dr Zhivago*, *NY Times* 12 Apr 95

FOOD AND DRINK

Chefs and Restaurateurs

James Beard cooking school director

8607 If ever I had to practice cannibalism, I might manage if there were enough tarragon around.

NY Times 24 Jan 85

Julia Child cookbook author

8608 These scareheads... they're going to kill gastronomy!

On over-emphasis on dieting by "the food police" *Town & Country* Dec 94

Richard Darcy Kastro Lounge, NYC

8609 A fine martini has a surface tension. It should stun, then cascade through your being.

New York 20 Dec 93

Anthony Debari Hoboken NJ baker

8610 If you take too long beating the eggs, the dough will get nervy on you and it will be damaged forever.

On making St Joseph's Day zeppole pastry *NY Times* 13 Mar 91

Martin Hehman Drake Hotel, Chicago

8611 As you get older you don't drink all night, so you want a drink that lets you know you had a drink.

"Martini Redux: Yuppies Take Up A Classic" *Time* 11 Jan 88

Joseph "Joe Dogs" Iannuzzi cookbook editor

8612 Any meal may be their last, so it better be a good one.

The Mafia Cookbook Simon & Schuster 93

8613 If they went out and hurt somebody or killed them, accidentally or whatever, they didn't want no red meat at all. No way, fuggeddaboudit.

ib

Howard Koch screenwriter

8614 Of all the gin joints in all the towns all over the world, she walks into mine.

Humphrey Bogart on Ingrid Bergman, screenplay for *Casablanca* 1943, recalled on Koch's death *NY Times* 18 Aug 95

8615 Here's looking at you, kid.

Bogart's casual toast to Bergman *ib*

Georges Lepre Ritz Hotel, Paris

8616 This wine is Mozart, that one is pure Wagner!

On his cellar *NY Times* 13 Oct 85

Ferand Point La Pyramide, Vienne, France

8617 Go into the kitchen to shake the chef's hand. If he is thin, have second thoughts about eating there; if he is thin and sad, flee.

NY Times 16 Jul 83

Marie Louise Point La Pyramide, Vienne, France

8618 In summer, a gentleman is never far from a bottle of chilled *Beaujolais.*

NY Times 10 Jul 86

Mechai Viravaidya Cabbages and Condoms, Bangkok

8619 Sorry we have no mints. Please take a condom instead.

Sign at his restaurant *NY Times* 13 Mar 94

Manufacturers, Merchandisers, and Promoters

Anon

8620 Oh, you middle classes, you are all basil and fettuccine!

A greengrocer quoted by the Prime Minister's cook who added that the basil and fettuccine is "now all coriander and lime" *London Times* 9 Dec 94

Bill Bryson cereal pioneer

8621 He hastened to the kitchen in nightshirt, boiled some wheat, rolled it out into strips, and baked it in the oven.

On John Harvey Kellogg's midnight response to a dream that showed him how to develop his "quiet obsession" for a flaked breakfast cereal *Made in America* Morrow 94

David Halberstam commentator

8622 He has seen the future and it is hamburgers.

On Ray Kroc's decision to buy and expand the original McDonald's *The Fifties* Villard 93

Judy Licht commentator

8623 [It is] the citadel of salads, the capital of cole slaw, the treasury of tortellini.

On Blue Ridge Farms' marketeting of "designer salads" under its own label, Dumont TV 7 Aug 86

David S Milligan President, Seagream Chateau and Estate Wines

8624 People like the fiery guts of a young port but we think it's infanticide.

On not serving unmatured wine, "Sailing Into Port" *NY Times* 27 Sep 87

Christian Pol-Roger vintner

8625 Champagne! In victory, one deserves it; in defeat, one needs it.

NY Times 31 Dec 88

Murray Riese fast-food mogul

8626 Why sell a sandwich for a 10-cent profit when you can sell a restaurant for $10,000?

On his turn-over of restaurants that reportedly changed the face of Manhattan *NY Times* 21 Jul 95

Bill Samuels Jr vintage bourbon maker

8627 If you can hold it on your tongue without blowing your ears off, it meets the test.

On greatness in bourbon *Connoisseur* Jul 91

Cathon Seydoux vintner

8628 We are Krugs making our Krug.

On champagne produced by his family in Mesnil and Paris' *Rue Coquebert* since 1868 *Country Life* 15 Dec 94

Barbara Smith Partner, Ark Restaurants Inc

8629 In most restaurants, one partner drinks, one takes drugs, one gambles and one tries to hold the business together.

On B Smith's success as a restaurant free of "conventional management" *NY Times* 11 May 88

Robert McG Thomas Jr reporter

8630 A sprinkling of matzoh meal, a pinch of salt and a dollop of schmaltmanship... a $2 million a year operation.

On Sylvia Weinberg's product that moved from her Bronx luncheonette into a $2 million a year business *NY Times* 2 Aug 95

Marty Thrasher President, Campbell Soup

8631 Most people tell us, "Don't touch the icon," but we're taking a calculated risk to contemporize our products.

On subtle redesign of the Campbell soup can *NY Times* 17 Nov 95

Clark Wolf restaurant consultant

8632 It's absolutely the butler culture. Men are considered more decorative... the catering equivalent of Donna Reed.

NY Times 13 Oct 95

Gourmets and Critics

David Acheson essayist

8633 [His] chemically rich bourbon formula was all but radioactive!

On mint juleps prepared by his father, US Secretary of State Dean Acheson *Acheson Country* Norton 93

Edward Albee playwright

8634 For the mind's blind eye, the heart's ease, and the liver's craw. Down the hatch, all.

George's toast to his wife, roles played by Richard Burton and Elizabeth Taylor *Who's Afraid of Virginia Woolf?* Atheneum 63

David Allen Suffolk butler

8635 Never cure a sow, Sir! . . . Never let a woman touch the brine if it's her time of the month, never let her touch it, Sir! And never let the sun shine on your brine, Sir!

On hams *London Times* 25 Nov 95

Maynard Amerine Professor of Ecology, University of California

8636 The fine wine leaves you with something pleasant; the ordinary wine just leaves.

Quoted by Clifton Fadiman *The New Joy of Wine* Abrams 90

Anon

8637 A nice cut off the joint, two vegs, a spot of cheese, and a bit of sweet.

A typical English meal cited by Janet Flanner *London Was Yesterday* Viking 75 and by Anne Edwards as Queen Mary's favorite menu *Matriarch* Morrow 84

8638 Hunger will break through stone walls and anything except a Suffolk cheese.

British Heritage Apr-May 86

8639 "They make a very small martini," her husband said dryly.

On NYC's Colony Club *NY Times* 1 Feb 87

8640 It is like pouring diamonds into a tulip.

Slogan for Dom Ruinart champagne 1 Mar 87

8641 Skinny cooks can't be trusted.

Life Jul 87

8642 [A gray squirrel] is a rat with good public relations.

On recipes featuring squirrel *London Times* 2 Nov 91

8643 When you've got your winter cabbage in your heart you feel secure.

Folk saying in Communist China *NY Times* 22 Nov 94

8644 It is the *National Inquirer* of food because no one admits eating it.

On Spam, "Capitol Reports" ABC TV 4 Dec 94

8645 Manifest pig-parts fully cooked; soldiers called it ham that didn't pass its physical.

ib

8646 The filling was like napalm; these pies can skin you alive.

British engineer who brought suit for 3rd-degree burns from a McDonald's apple pie *Fortune* 20 Mar 95

8647 The English didn't call it dressing, they called it belly pudding.

On turkey and dressing ABC TV 17 Nov 95

Fred Applebome novelist

8648 The Crab Palace is a quintessentially south Louisiana mixture of no-frills Formica decor and celestial Cajun cooking.

On crawfish étouffée at the Crab Palace near Lake Charles LA *NY Times* 20 Apr 93

Tony Aspler critic

8649 Winemaking is the world's second-oldest profession and, no doubt, it has eased the burden of the world's oldest.

Toronto Star 21 Sep 85

Lee Bailey cookbook editor

8650 My grandmother actually smelled like a cookie and that's enough to get any child's attention.

Lee Bailey's *Country Desserts* Potter 88

Robert Benton screenwriter

8651 It's the face powder that gets 'em but it's the baking powder that keeps 'em home.

Bonnie and Clyde screenplay written with David Newman Warner Bros 67

Mave Brennan essayist

8652 Small, inexpensive restaurants are the home fires of New York City.

The Long-Winded Lady Morrow 89

J Bryan III essayist

8653 The drink is slipping its little hand into yours.

On the start of a perfect weekend *Travel & Leisure* Jul 74

Edward Bunyard columnist

8654 There are two classes of pears—those that taste like hair-wash and those that do not.

"The Anatomy of Dessert" *Country Life* 16 Sep 93

Marian Burros critic

8655 It was love at first slurp.

On encountering egg-creams at age 13 *NY Times* 15 Jun 88

Barbara Bush First Lady

8656 I wrote in my diaries about. . . good meals that I have eaten and am wearing today.

Barbara Bush: A Memoir Scribner 94

George Bush 41st US President

8657 I do not like broccoli. And I haven't liked it since I was a little boy and my mother made me eat it. And I'm President of the United States, and I'm not going to eat any more broccoli!

On menus aboard Air Force One, a comment that greatly displeased the broccoli lobby *NY Times* 23 Mar 90

Truman Capote novelist

8658 Buddy, it's fruitcake weather!

Lines for Cousin Souk on late November in his native Alabama *A Christmas Memory* Random House 56

8659 The chic old blue-haired ladies. . . chew in mute chandeliered isolation.

On elderly diners at Paris' Hotel Ritz *Answered Prayers* Random House 87

Gabrielle ("Coco") Chanel dress designer

8660 I don't like food that talks back. . . after you've eaten.

On banishing the scent of onions from her kitchen, quoted by Claude Baillen *Chanel* Solitaire Gallimard, Paris 71

Winston S Churchill Statesman

8661 We lived very simply—but with all the essentials of life well understood and provided for—hot baths, cold champagne, new peas and old brandy.

On his farm in Surrey, quoted by William Manchester *The Last Lion* Little, Brown 83

8662 It's water—and exceedingly nasty it is.

When asked by his wife what he was drinking *Churchill: The Wilderness Years* PBS TV 28 Aug 86

Craig Claiborne critic

8663 If there is a single dish over which Southerners in New York, London or Paris seem united, it is fried chicken. . . [but] they rarely agree how to fry it.

NY Times 26 Mar 64

8664 He was the Michelangelo, the Mozart and the Leonardo da Vinci of French restaurants in America.

On NYC restauranteur Henri Soule 28 Jan 68

Alan Clark British Minister of Trade

8665 No lunch, keep the stomach empty and then, in the very last seconds before going into the chamber for prayers—skol!

On his custom of "a teeny slug of neat vodka" prior to a questions session in the House of Commons *Mrs Thatcher's Minister* Farrar Straus Giroux 93

Paul Claudel essayist

8666 A cocktail is to a glass of wine as rape is to love.

Quoted by William Grimes *Americana* Dec 92

Cyril Connolly humorist

8667 Oh the joy of lingering over port and brandy with men in red coats telling dirty stories while it snows outside.

On the hour after the fox hunt *Cyril Connolly: Journals and Memoir* Ticknor & Fields 84

Henry Craddock essayist

8668 Shake the shaker as hard as you can: don't rock it: you are trying to wake it up, not send it to sleep!

The Savoy Hotel Cocktail Book quoted in *GQ* Sep 90

8669 Drink your cocktail as soon as possible. Quickly, while it's laughing at you.

ib

8670 [It is] four "hookers" of whiskey, four teaspoonfuls of sugar, a dash of vermouth, and a raw egg, and is meant for four (if you can find four who'll drink it).

On the Los Angeles cocktail as compared to the Manhattan *ib*

Cuisine Et Vin De France

8671 You do not buy domaine Leflaive wines; you solicit the honor of exchanging money for them.

Connoisseur May 91

Curnonsky (Maurice Edmond Saillang) essayist

8672 Cuisine is when things taste like themselves.

Proposed by food critic Bryan Miller as a maxim for Andre Soltner of NYC's Lutece Restaurant *NY Times* 15 Nov 91

Alan Davidson Editor *Petite Propos Culinaries*

8673 If you subtract Elizabeth David from the scene. . . you have just foothills, there is no mountain.

On England's star chef Elizabeth David *International Herald Tribune* 1 Jun 92

Else de Wolfe (Lady Mendel) critic

8674 You can't build a meal on a lake.

Objecting to soup as a first course, Jane S Smith and Diana Vreeland Ed *Elsie de Wolfe* Atheneum 82

8675 Plates should be hot, hot, hot; glasses cold, cold, cold; and table decorations low, low, low.

ib

Dictionnaire D'Americanismes

8676 [It is] *un plat national*

French definition of apple pie *NY Times* 24 Sep 86

Stanley Elkin novelist

8677 Backrooms. . . smoke-filled. . . with a smell of testosterone hanging in the air like the balls of beer.

On the sameness of taverns the world over *Washington Post* 18 Apr 93 *The New Joy of Wine* Abrams 90

Clifton Fadiman critic

8678 To taste port is to taste a tiny atom of England and her past.

Any Number Can Play World 57

William Faulkner novelist

8679 No such thing as bad whiskey! Some. . . just happen to be better than others.

Quoted by James M Webb and A Wigfall Green *William Faulkner of Oxford* 65

M F K Fisher essayist

8680 With good friends. . . and good food on the board, and good wine in the pitcher, we may well ask: When shall we live if not now?

The Art of Eating Vintage 76

8681 [New England] oysters—straightforward, simple, capable of spirit but unadorned, like a Low Church service or a Boston romance.

Smithsonian Jan 88

8682 I loved to entertain people and dominate them with my generosity.

New Yorker 11 Jan 93

Indira Gandhi Prime Minister of India

8683 There is no politician in India daring enough to explain to people that cows can be eaten.

Recalled on Gandhi's death 31 Oct 84

William Grimes reporter

8684 A foul-smelling vegetable extract with the consistency of axle grease. . . dried mud with a touch of salt.

On Marmite, the yeast extract adored by Britain with buttered toast and tea *NY Times* 9 Apr 93

Alan Hamilton essayist

8685 [His] infamous pie of carrot, turnip, potato and parsnip, topped with white sauce and pastry was deeply unpopular.

On a Lord Woolton wartime Christmas recipe *London Times* 24 Dec 94

Herbert Hoover 31st US President

8686 I should have been glad to have humanity forget about alcohol. . . but this vehicle of joy could not be generally suppressed by federal law.

On repeal of prohibition near the end of the Hoover administration *Memoirs* Macmillan 51

8687 [It is] the pause between the errors and trials of the day and the hopes of the night.

Defining the cocktail hour, quoted by Richard Norton Smith *An Uncommon Man* Simon & Schuster 84

Donald Dale Jackson critic

8688 *Sic transit gloria dineri!*

On the decline of the diner *Smithsonian* Farrar Straus Giroux 54

Claudia ("Lady Bird") Johnson First Lady

8689 Appetite is the best sauce.
A White House Diary Holt Rinehart Winston 70

8690 We had a delicious dinner of too much.
On NYC's Plaza Hotel *ib*

George S Kaufman playwright

8691 God finally caught his eye.
Epitaph for a deceased waiter, quoted by Jon Winokur *The Portable Curmudgeon* New American Library 87

Michael Kernan essayist

8692 The sounds of a dining car. . . silver against silver, silver against china, ice in glass goblets, tiny insinuating tinklings in pleasant chorus.
"Whistle Stops" *Washington Post* 3 Jul 88

Henry A Kissinger US Secretary of State

8693 I'd do anything for caviar and probably did.
On visiting Moscow, quoted by Walter Isaacson *Kissinger* Simon & Schuster 92

Allan M Laing humorist

8694 Let us with a knowing wink/ Praise the Lord for food and drink,/ Who his choicest gifts doth send/ Unto them with cash to spend.
"A Grace for Black Market Turkey" *Guardian Weekly* 7 May 95

Andre Lee critic

8695 Defining Nutella. . . that comes in a jar. . . is a bit like describing Michelangelo's David as a large carved piece of marble.
On Italy's hazelnut-chocolate spread *New Yorker* 6 Mar 95

8696 [Nutella is] packed with more sugar and fat per ounce than Oprah Winfrey on an ice-cream binge.
ib

Paul Levy critic, *London Observer*

8697 Cathedrals to heart-burn!
On American restaurants in London *NY Times* 1 Feb 89

John L Lewis President, United Mine Workers

8698 Bread to a man with a family comes first—before his union, citizenship. . . church affiliation. Bread!
Saturday Evening Post 12 Oct 63

Penelope Lively journalist

8699 The waiters treated us with affectionate interests, as though attending the remnants of a dying species.
On "lunching ladies" *NY Times* 7 Mar 93

London Times

8700 His achievement was to transform a sticky, carbonized brown syrup, of somewhat vulgar appeal, from the status of a local, Southern beverage to a symbol of the missionary advance of contemporary American culture.
On Pepsi-Cola President Walter S Mack 21 Mar 90

8701 Wine has. . . inspired invention, animated religion, made men vociferous, nourished beliefs, kindled wrath, provoked love and lust and softened hard beds.
"Wine Merchants Uncorked" editorial 3 Sep 93

8702 Supermarket. . . rows of mutely complaisant bottles is the perfect antidote to encounters with wine merchants of rotund speech and hectoring mien. The customer—humble quaffer and cenophile alike—is underling no more.
ib

8703 Absinthe makes the heart grow fonder.
"Absinthe Galore" editorial on revival of absinthe as "the heady cocktail of madness, nostalgia and the lure of the forbidden" 28 Jul 95

Ronni Lundy essayist

8704 The process of making onion soup is somewhat like learning to love. . . commitment, extraordinary effort, time, and will make you cry.
Esquire Mar 84

William Manchester biographer

8705 He gives the empty bottle a glance, not of regret, but of affection.
On Winston S Churchill's regard for brandy as "essential to a stable diet" *The Last Lion* Little, Brown 88

Chico Marx entertainer

8706 Mustard's no good without roast beef.
Recalled on Marx' death 11 Oct 61

Carson McCullers novelist

8707 Nothing is so musical as the sound of pouring bourbon for the first drink on a Sunday morning. Not Bach or Schubert or any of those masters.
Clock Without Hands Houghton Mifflin 53

H L Mencken essayist

8708 [The cocktail is] the greatest of all the contributions of the American way of life to the salvation of humanity.
Americana Dec 92

Michael Mewshaw essayist

8709 A *tarte au citron*, a dessert to die for or, given its butterfat content, to die from.

On Parisian pastries *NY Times* 3 Mar 91

James Michener novelist

8710 Never ignore the mice, for it is they that will keep you alive in the starving time.

Alaska Random House 88

Bryan Miller critic

8711 If Sardi's were a play, it could be called a mystery, a tragedy and a comedy wrapped in one.

On momentary lapse of the best known restaurant in NYC's theater district *NY Times* 9 Dec 88

8712 In this job, to tell the truth, you eat a lot of bran.

On reviewing restaurants *Town & Country* Apr 92

Jack Milroy critic

8713 It needs a drop of water. All malts do—like a rose needs dew.

Malt Whiskey Almanac quoted in *London Times* 25 Nov 95

National Geographic magazine

8714 The French do not eat, they dine.

"Letters from France" Jul 89

8715 Passionate commitment. . . has given us a litany of towns that trumpet their specialty: Roquefort, Dijon, Bordeau, Cognac.

ib

Richard M Nixon 37th US President

8716 She insisted it was best only when she beat fresh outdoor air into the batter before putting it in the oven.

On his mother's angel food cake baked before dawn for sale in the family store *RN: The Memoirs of Richard Nixon* Grosset & Dunlap 78

Molly O'Neill columnist

8717 It's a smell that arises from something as basic as wheat, as resourceful as the human hand and as powerful as fire.

On the aroma of baking bread *NY Times* 25 Jun 95

8718 There is something eternal about the freshness a lemon imparts. . . . They make you pucker and gnash, but you can't stay mad at lemons for long.

On lemons in spring recipes 9 Jul 95

Dorothy Parker humorist

8719 Three be the things I shall never attain: Envy, content, and sufficient champagne.

Quoted by Marion Meade *Dorothy Parker* Villard 88

Frank Prial columnist

8720 Winespeak. . . can be traced to the Gothic piles of Oxbridge, where, in the 19th century, certain dons, addled by claret, bested one another in fulsome tributes to the grape.

NY Times 8 Jul 79

8721 A third-rate Medoc could transport even a redbrick lecturer in Greek to the Elysian Fields.

ib

Sam Rayburn US Speaker of the House

8722 These society women never serve chili.

On why he avoided parties, quoted by David Brinkley *Washington Goes to War* Knopf 88

Ken Ringle reporter

8723 William Jefferson Clinton. . . campaigned as a Southern fried Good Ole Boy who never met a doughnut he didn't like.

On President Clinton dining out *Washington Post* 1 Nov 93

George Rosenbaum reporter

8724 A bagel is a doughnut with the sin removed.

NY Times 25 Apr 93

Richard Sennett Professor of Sociology, NYU

8725 It is a neighborhood. . . of single bald men, in commerce and sales, not at the top but walking confidently enough to the delis and tobacco stands lining Third Avenue.

On Manhattan above East 14th Street *The Conscience of the Eye* Knopf 91

8726 All the food. . . is sold in small cans and single portions; it is possible in the Korean groceries to buy half a lettuce.

ib

Dr Howard M Shapiro physician

8727 Most husbands are saboteurs.

On wives who try to diet *NY Times* 29 Sep 93

Philip Shenon reporter

8728 Among his most popular dishes is seared kangaroo rump served with Tasmanian pepperberries.

On the Australian national symbol as a well liked but patriotically controversial item on menus *NY Times* 10 Jul 95

Neil Simon playwright

8729 The nimblest fingers on earth dispensed. . . endless nickels, shiny nickels, magical nickels that were slipped into slots on the wall, and before your very eyes, an Open Sesame roll came around the bend of a glass cubicle.

A final salute on the closing of the last Automat *NY Times* 11 Apr 91

Michael Stern anthologist

8730 Tapioca is the teddy-bear of desserts, an edible security blanket.

Square Meals Random House 87

Roy Strong columnist

8731 Trifle as it entered the Georgian age. . . bore no relation to how it left it. . . [and] reached its apogee in Edwardian England.

On a famed desert's embellishment "A Trifle Delicious" *Country Life* 30 Mar 95

Ted Tally screenwriter

8732 I ate his liver, with fava beans and a nice Chianti!

Lines for the character Hannibal Lecter in *Silence of the Lambs* 1991 Academy Award winner based on the novel of the same name from St Martin's 88, quoted in *USA Today* 27 Oct 92

Dylan Thomas poet

8733 I liked the taste of beer, its live, white lather, its brass-bright depths. . . the salt on the tongue, the foam on the corners.

Quoted by Constance FitzGibbon *The Life of Dylan Thomas* Atlantic-Little, Brown 65

Time magazine

8734 [They are] born to eat their words.

On authors of cookbooks 23 Nov 81

Calvin Trillin essayist

8735 Well brought up English girls are taught. . . to boil veggies for at least a month and a half.

Third Helpings Houghton Mifflin 83

Harry S Truman 33rd US President

8736 I don't much care for your law, but, by golly, this bourbon is good.

To US Supreme Court Justice William O Douglas after the court held Truman's seizure of steel mills to be unconstitutional, quoted by Robert J Donovan *Tumultuous Years* Norton 77

Wallis Duchess of Windsor

8737 People forget you or don't ask you as much if they don't think you can return the cutlet.

On entertaining, Michael Bloch ed *Wallis and Edward* Summit 86

8738 The guests can wait for dinner, but my chef doesn't wait for the guests.

Quoted by Suzy Menkes *The Windsor Style* Salem House 88

Howard Waxman Editor *Ice Cream Reporter*

8739 The relation between the human tongue, the human psyche and butterfat is not very complex. The first two love the third.

Newsweek 30 Nov 92

David Wheeler columnist

8740 A kitchen without a lemon is like a song without a tune.

"A Cultivated Table" *Country Life* 19 Jan 95

Healey Willan composer and organist

8741 English by birth,/ Irish by extraction,/ Canadian by adoption,/ Scotch by absorption.

Self-description quoted by William Littler, *Toronto Star* 11 Jan 80

LITERATURE

Writers and Editors

Dean Acheson US Secretary of State

8742 Among the thorns of the law and the thistles of politics and diplomacy we found some fruit that had retained its flavor, and, in some cases, its tartness.

On writing his memoirs *Grapes From Thorns* Norton 72

Peter Ackroyd biographer

8743 The whole of London is like a haunted house.

On the British capital as the ideal setting for mystery novels, Station WAMU Washington 17 May 95

Rita Adler novelist

8744 A little obscenity here, a dash of philosophy there, considerable whining overall, and a modern satirical novel is born.

Toward a Radical Middle Random House 69

James Agee essayist and novelist

8745 I used as a child in the innocence of faith. . . to serve. . . at earliest lonely Mass, whose words were thrilling brooks of music.

On the influence of Anglican liturgy on a budding writer, *Let Us Now Praise Famous Men* with Walker Evans, Houghton Mifflin 1941 recalled in *New Yorker* 18 Jul 88

8746 Half old master, half old maid.

On photographer Walker Evans, quoted by Belinda Rathbone *Walker Evans* Houghton Mifflin 95

Gay Wilson Allen Professor of English, NYU

8747 Writing biography is a one-way transaction in friendship.

On the positive aspect of his work on Walt Whitman, *NY Times* 8 Aug 95

Margaret Atwood novelist

8748 It was like trying to stuff a dead dog with rigor mortis into two plastic bags.

On the difficulties of writing, Station WAMU Washington 5 Dec 94

Louis Auchincloss novelist

8749 The critics... think I need a cramp.

On writing 22 books in 30 years, quoted by Tom Stevenson *Juris Doctor* Nov 73

8750 To... see the New York I know in depth... that's the heart of my work.

MD Mar 80

8751 Plenty of old boys and girls still take me to the hospital for their hysterectomies and prostates.

On his readers *Collected Stories* Houghton Mifflin 94

Richard Bach novelist

8752 Every writer has a family out there, a group of people who share his vision and his dream. If he persists, he will find them.

NY Times 21 Jul 85

Russell Baker columnist

8753 Life is a braided cord of humanity stretching up from times long gone, and... cannot be defined by the space of a single journey from diaper to shroud.

On biographical writing *Celebrity Register* Gale 90

Monica Baldwin autobiographer

8754 Problems... were lying, piled up like luggage, on the doorstep of my mind.

On the period between leaving a convent and beginning her biography *I Leap Over the Wall* Rinehart 50

8755 The Rip Van Winkle complex began to steal over me like cold ink into blotting paper.

On recalling 28 years as a cloistered nun *ib*

Julian Barnes novelist

8756 [A net is] a collection of holes tied together with strings. You can do the same with a biography.

On his part biography, part literary essay and fantasy *Flaubert's Parrot* Vintage 90

8757 I always think of memory as a left-luggage office.

Station WAMU Washington 28 Oct 91

John Barth novelist

8758 It has proliferated like *herpes simplex* of the gypsy moth.

On popularity of the creative writing seminar *NY Times* 16 Jun 85

Brendan Behan playwright

8759 I was driven to write by muraphobia—the dread of having to paint walls or doors or anything else... [and] the pen is lighter than the paint brush.

Recalled on Behan's death 20 Mar 64

Max Beerbohm essayist

8760 To be outmoded is to be a classic, if one has written well.

Quoted by Joseph Epstein *Partial Payments* Norton 88

Saul Bellow novelist

8761 The child in me is delighted. The adult in me is skeptical.

On being cited for the Nobel prize 21 Oct 76

Tahar Ben Jelloun novelist

8762 My wife is Arabic and my mistress French, and I maintain a relationship of betrayal with both of them.

On the polygamy of languages, interviewed on winning the *Prix Goncourt*, *NY Times* 22 Nov 87

Vance Bourjaily novelist

8763 Writing is... brain work, but there is something that feels to me like physiological involvement... a kind of contracting and relaxing moment going on in the front part of my head just behind the forehead as I write.

Thomas McCormick ed *Afterwords: Novelists on Their Novels* St Martin's 88

Elizabeth Bowen novelist

8764 Characters are not created by writers. They preexist and have to be found.

Quoted by Saul Bellow in Bellow's Nobel laureate's address, Stockholm 12 Dec 76

Ray Bradbury novelist

8765 You have to know how to accept rejection and reject acceptance.

Quoted by Richard North Patterson, Station WAMU Washington 5 Apr 95

John Braine novelist

8766 Being a writer in a library is rather like being a eunuch in a harem.

NY Times 17 Oct 62

Max Brand novelist

8767 There has to be a woman, but not much a one. A good horse is much more important.

On writing Westerns *NY Times* 16 Sep 85

Maeve Brennan *New Yorker* columnist

8768 The fewer writers you know the better, and if you're working on anything, don't tell them.

Time 1 Jul 74

Pearl S Buck Nobel laureate

8769 In a mood of faith and hope, my work goes on. A ream of fresh paper lies on my desk waiting for the next book. I am a writer and I take up my pen to write.

Autobiography 16 years after writing *The Good Earth* and becoming the first woman to receive the Nobel Prize for Literature *My Several Worlds* John Day 54

8770 I love people, my family, my children. . . but inside myself is a place whre I live all alone and that is where you review your springs that never dry up.

NY Post 26 Apr 59

8771 [I am] mentally bifocal.

On being born to American parents living in China, recalled on issue of a commemorative stamp honoring Buck *NY Times* 19 Jun 83

Anthony Burgess novelist

8772 They were written not merely for bread and gin but out of conviction that the manipulation of language to the end of pleasing and enlightening is not to be despised.

Recalled on Burgess's death *Guardian Weekly* 5 Dec 93

Robert Olen Butler novelist

8773 [It] hit with the abruptness of a bolt of bayou lightning.

On receiving the Pulitzer Prize for his *A Good Scent from a Strange Mountain* Holt 92 *NY Times* 20 Apr 93

James M Cain novelist

8774 It can't be taught. . . the only thing you can do for someone who wants to write is to buy him a typewriter.

Recalled on Cain's death 27 Oct 77

8775 [Every writer knows] that he has just so many of these ova in his belly, and indeed he is never sure that the latest one he produced will not be his last.

NY Times 6 Sep 87

Erskine Caldwell novelist

8776 I have slept with them in jails. . . eaten with them in freight cars. . . sung with them in convict camps. . . helped the women give birth to the living. . . helped the men cover up the dead.

On respecting the poor, quoted by Dan B Miller *Erskine Caldwell* Knopf 95

8777 New England isn't mountains and lakes and seashores, but an inhibited and repressed old wretch who is a witch if there ever was one.

"The Bogus Ones" short story written after his book *The Bastard* Heron Press 1929 was banned from his Portland ME book shop *ib*

8778 Writing is like smoking. . . addicted to it. . . my hobby, my vocation, my life.

London Daily Express 20 Nov 63

Taylor Caldwell novelist

8779 There was an air. . . in this casual room filled with stark sunlight, of greatness and simplicity.

On her initial meeting with editor Maxwell Perkins *The Final Hour* Scribner 75

Elias Canetti writer

8780 All that is demanded of you is to watch and listen. . . their marvelous variety alone rekindles your delight in the human race.

On cafes as suppliers of plots, quoted by Peter Vansittart *In the Fifties* John Murray 95

8781 I enjoy listening. I have always enjoyed listening. . . . I will be dead when I no longer hear what a person is telling me about himself. He may thus live forever.

ib

Truman Capote novelist

8782 I am at present sorta this side of civilization where the people think if you don't say "ain't" you just ain't right. . . and the double negative is accepted grammar.

Writing from rural Alabama to his high school English teacher in Connecticut, letter exhibited at NY Public Library Dec 87

8783 I don't like it myself when I am the sitter and not the portraitist: the frailty of egos! and the more accurate the strokes, the greater the resentment.
NY Times 16 Jan 66

8784 Don't just go to a pine cabin all alone and brood and write. You reach that stage soon enough anyway.
To young writers 8 Nov 79

8785 Finishing a book is just like you took a child out in the yard and shot it.
Quoted by Linda Botts ed *Loose Talk* Quick Fox 80

8786 Good writing is rewriting.
New York 28 Nov 84

8787 [It is] a poetic explosion in highly suppressed emotion.
On his first book *Other Voices, Other Rooms* 1948, quoted by Gerald Clarke *Capote* Simon & Schuster 88

8788 I built an oak and reduced it to a seed.
On in-depth research for *In Cold Blood ib*

Rachael Carson environmentalist

8789 The discipline of the writer is to be still and listen to what his subject has to tell him.
Recalled on Carson's death 14 Apr 64

Barbara Cartland novelist

8790 I'm the only author with 200 virgins in print.
Town & Country Dec 77

8791 I'm on my 544th book. No, no, wait, it's my 543rd. I've done four chapters.
At age 90 *London Times* 10 Jul 91

Raymond Chandler novelist

8792 The most durable thing in writing is style, and style is the most valuable investment a writer can make with his time.
Recalled on Chandler's death 26 Mar 59

8793 Technique alone is just an embroidered potholder.
ib

8794 All writers are a little crazy, but if they are any good they have a kind of terrible honesty.
NY Times 17 May 95

John Cheever novelist

8795 How can we describe the most exalted experience of our physical lives as if—jack, wrench, hubcap, and nuts—we were describing the changing of a flat tire?
Some People, Places and Things That Will Not Appear in My Next Novel Harper & Row 71

8796 A man's prose style is very responsive—even a glass of sherry shows in a sentence.
Accepting National Medal for Literature, recalled on Cheever's death 18 Jun 82

Agatha Christie novelist

8797 I am a writer, crime my beat, murder my specialty.
Parterns in Crime PBS TV 21 Jun 87

8798 If I could write like Elizabeth Bowen, Muriel Spark or Graham Greene, I should jump to heaven with delight, but. . . I have learnt that I am me, that I can do the things that, as one might put it, me can do.
Smithsonian Sep 90

8799 There's nothing immoral in my books, only murder.
NY Times 14 Oct 90

Winston S Churchill statesman

8800 The reason I can write so much is that I don't waste my essence in bed.
On the value of celibacy, quoted by William Manchester *The Last Lion* Little, Brown 88

Mary Higgins Clark novelist

8801 You go to the attic of your mind and rummage around and find something.
On contracting for a near-record amount to produce four mystery novels for Simon & Schuster, ABC TV 5 May 89

Jean Cocteau novelist

8802 Even poets cannot write their own life story. . . too many true lies, too many tangles.
Opium 1930, quoted by Ian McIntyre *Not Drowning But Weaving* Andre Deutsch 95

Barbara Cohen novelist

8803 Children since the beginning of time have matured by learning to cope with life as it is. . . the great task of childhood and the great theme of children's literature.
Recalled on Cohen's death 29 Nov 92

Joan Collins actress

8804 I'm the queen of the adjectives and adverbs.
Acknowledging her dependence on editorial help even while successfully suing to retain the $5-million advance on work that Random House deemed unsuitable *NY Times* 10 Feb 96

Cyril Connolly novelist

8805 I have always disliked myself at any given moment; the sum total of such moments is my life.

Quoted by Kenneth Tynan *Tynan Right and Left* Atheneum 67

8806 Better to write for yourself and have no public than to write for the public and have no self.

Recalled on Connolly's death 26 Nov 74

8807 An author arrives at a good style when language performs what is required of it without shyness.

ib

8808 The pram in the hallway is the enemy of promise.

On young writers *ib*

James Gould Cozzens novelist

8809 In the field of the philippic (sorry to send you to your dictionary again), I think you're gifted.

On Dwight Macdonald's review of a Cozzens novel, quoted by Matthew J Bruccoli *James Gould Cozzens* Harcourt Brace Jovanovich 83

8810 I haven't in years had the pleasure of reading so refreshingly venomous an outburst!

ib

Michael Creighton novelist

8811 Books aren't written, they're rewritten. . . one of the hardest things in the world to accept, especially after the seventh rewrite hasn't quite done it.

Writer's Digest Sep 86

Robertson Davies novelist

8812 I never liked just being me. . . didn't really feel there was any me to be.

On why he turned from acting to writing *NY Times* 5 Feb 95

8813 [As an author] you can play all the parts, arrange the scenery, be the whole show and nobody gets in the way.

ib

Simone De Beauvoir novelist

8814 I have to find a way of saying the truth without saying it; that is exactly what is literature after all, clever lies which secretly say the truth.

Quoted by Deirdre Bair *Simone de Beauvoir* Summit 90

Walter de la Mare novelist

8815 Until we learn the use of living words we shall continue to be waxworks inhabited by gramophones.

Recalled on De La Mare's death 30 Dec 72

Monica Dickens novelist

8816 It was like someone coming along after Christ and saying they were Christ, too.

On her family's belief that great grandchildren of Charles Dickens should not be writers, recalled on Monica Dickens' death 25 Dec 92

Joan Didion novelist

8817 Grammar is a piano I play by ear; I seem to have been out of school the year it was mentioned.

NY Times 5 Dec 76

Annie Dillard novelist

8818 Do not hoard what seems good for a later place in the book, or for another book, give it, give it all, give it now.

The Writing Life Harper & Row 89

8819 When you write, you lay out a line of words. . . a miner's pick, a woodcarver's gouge, a surgeon's probe. You wield it, and it digs a path you follow.

ib

8820 With your two bare hands, you hold and fight a sentence's head while its tail tries to knock you over.

ib

E L Doctorow novelist

8821 It's like driving a car at night. You never see further than your headlights, but you can make the whole trip that way.

On writing a novel, George Plimpton ed *Writers at Work* Penguin 88

8822 The work itself is hard and slow, and the writer's illumination becomes a taskmaster, a ruling discipline, jealously guarding the mind. . . until the book is done.

Washington Post 17 Apr 94

8823 There is no way out except through the last sentence.

ib

Stadford Dody biographer

8824 The room looked like an opium den at Walden Pond.

On writing an autobiography with actress Bette Davis, quoted by Charles Higham *Bette* Macmillan 81

Scott Donaldson biographer

8825 Never write a biography of anyone whose children are still alive.

On suit brought by family of John Cheever *Washington Post* 15 Sep 88

John Dos Passos novelist

8826 He seeks to put his grisly obsession into expressive form the way a bacteriologist seeks to isolate a virus.

On satirists *Occasions and Protests* Regnery 64

Margaret Drabble novelist

8827 I was the first writer I'd ever met.

On her early life in London *NY Times* 11 Sep 88

Daphne du Maurier novelist

8828 A character or an idea has to grow like a seed and take possession. . . [like] one's own development and passage through life.

Quoted by Margaret Forster *Daphne du Maurier* Chatto & Windus 93

John Gregory Dunne novelist

8829 If a writer does not respond to his own past—never mind that he may not understand it—then I suspect he can never be a very good writer.

Harp Simon & Schuster 89

8830 The writer is. . . essentially investigating himself. . . always trying to reprogram the responses to his own history.

ib

Marguerite Duras novelist

8831 [Writing] arrives like the wind. . . naked, mere ink, writing, and it passes by like nothing else in life, nothing except life itself.

Quoted by Alain Virocondelet *Duras* Dalkey Archive Press 94

Umberto Eco novelist

8832 Some men. . . take up with chorus girls. I wrote a novel instead.

On producing at age 50 two novels that sold millions *Washington Post* 19 Dec 93

Stanley Elkin novelist

8833 I don't believe less is more. . . [but] that more is more. . . that less is less, fat fat, thin thin and enough is enough.

On "minimalists" *NY Times* 3 Mar 91

8834 [Writing is] an exercise in sculpture, chipping away at the rock until you find the nose.

ib

8835 The 1st Amendment, freedom of speech, is. . . their absolute mandate and fiat, the most profound law by which they live, sworn to its service and leaving as little wiggle room as a Commandment.

Washington Post 18 Apr 93

Sumner Locke Elliott novelist

8836 When you have been secreting a part of yourself for 50 years, it's like fresh air suddenly coming into the room.

On his first novel on homosexuality after numerous plays and nine other books, recalled on Elliott's death 24 Jun 91

Ralph Ellison novelist

8837 All novels are about certain minorities: the individual is a minority.

George Plimpton ed *Writers at Work* Viking 63

Louise Erdrich essayist

8838 Here I am, where I ought to be. A writer must have a place where he or she feels this, a place to love and be irritated with.

"Where I Ought to Be" *NY Times* 28 Jul 85

Peter Evans biographer

8839 [He had] an accent that carried the longing cadence of exile.

On interviewing Aristotle Onassis for his biography *Ari* Summit 86

8840 The silence of the grave gagged the living; people who had talked with his incarnate approval became sepulchrally mute.

On continuing biography after Onassis's death in 1975 *ib*

William Faulkner novelist

8841 The problems of the human heart in conflict with itself. . . alone can make good writing because only that is worth writing about, worth the agony and the sweat.

Accepting Nobel Prize 10 Dec 50

8842 I didn't know myself what I had tried to do, how much I had succeeded. . . but we will be judged on the splendor of our failures.

On Malcolm Crowley's editing of a Faulkner anthology *NY Times* 17 Dec 50

8843 You catch this fluidity which is human life and you focus a light on it and you stop it long enough for people. . . to see it.

On story telling *National Geographic* Mar 89

Edna Ferber novelist

8844 The ideal view for daily writing, hour on hour, is the blank wall of a cold-storage warehouse. Failing this, a stretch of sky will do, cloudless if possible.

A Kind of Magic Doubleday 63

8845 Dislike, displeasure, resentment, fault-finding, imagination, passionate remonstrance, a sense of injustice—they all make fine fuel....Life can't ever really defeat a writer who's in love with writing.

ib

E M Forster novelist

8846 Beauty [is that] at which a novelist should never aim, though he fails if he does not achieve it.

Aspects of the Novel Harcourt, Brace 54

8847 The personality of a writer does become important after we have read his book and began to study it... [but] study is only a serious form of gossip. It teaches us everything about the book except the central thing.

Quoted by Nicola Beauman *E M Forster* Knopf 94

Pamela Frankau novelist

8848 [I felt] like a Ford being patted on the back by a Hispano-Suiza.

On meeting Rebecca West, quoted by Victoria Glendinning *Rebecca West* Knopf 87

Lucinda Franks novelist

8849 A writer in New York is a little bit like a tree falling in a forest. You're never sure if somebody's going to hear you.

NY Times 30 Jan 88

William Gaddis novelist

8850 [It is] a collaboration between the reader and the page.

USA Today 21 Feb 95 on publication of Gaddis' fourth book *A Frolic of His Own* Scribner 95

John Gardner novelist

8851 The truth of what you say is what really matters... the only importance of technique is that when you say it badly you haven't said it.

On Writers and Writing Addison-Wesley 94

William Gass novelist

8852 If you write badly enough you'll have an audience. If you write well enough, you'll have readers.

Washington Post 21 Nov 94

Theodor Seuss Geisel ("Dr Seuss") children's storybook writer

8853 You can get help from teachers, but you are going to have to learn a lot by yourself, sitting alone in a room.

On becoming a writer *NY Times* 21 May 86

8854 If I start out with the concept of a two-headed animal, I must put two hats on his head and two toothbrushes in the bathroom. It's logical insanity.

On his children's stories that combined the ridiculous with the logical, recalled on Geisel's death 25 Sep 91

Jean Genet novelist

8855 You feel emotions so strong that your whole life is shaped by them... [and] only by describing them... can you understand them... then I started to write.

On finding himself in prison at age 15, quoted by Edmund White *Genet* Knopf 93

8856 Talent is courtesy towards matter... giving song to that which was dumb.

ib

8857 My way of "possessing" the people I love [is to]... immure them alive in a palace of sentences.

ib

Martin Gilbert Fellow, Merton College, Oxford

8858 I often just go for a walk. The heath is full of authors walking about and looking serious.

On taking breaks from the 16-hour days of writing *NY Times* 11 Dec 94

Brendan Gill essayist

8859 I will try to cram these paragraphs full of facts and give them a weight and shape no greater than that of a cloud of blue butterflies.

Here at the New Yorker Random House 75

8860 We are all six years old... staring woebegonely out from the face of a middle-age.

On the never-lessening pain of rejection *ib*

Rumer Godden novelist

8861 A writer who never explored words, never searched, seeded, sieved, sifted through his knowledge and memory... dictionaries... thesaurus, poems, favorite paragraphs, to find the right word, is like someone owning a gold mine who has never mined it.

Book-of-the-Month Club News Sep 69

8862 To me and my kind, life itself is a story and we have to tell it in stories.

Quoted by Sonya Rudikoff *NY Times* 24 Dec 89 reviewing Godden's *A House With Four Rooms* Morrow 89

Gail Godwin novelist

8863 The characters that I create are parts of myself and I send them on little missions to find out what I don't know yet.

Station WAMU Washington 7 Mar 91

Nadine Gordimer novelist

8864 Your whole life, you are really writing one book... an attempt to grasp the consciousness of your time and place—a single book written from the different stages of your ability.

World Press Review Oct 87

8865 A writer is selected by his subject—his subject being the consciousness of his own era.

Recalled on announcement of Gordimer's designation for the Nobel Prize *NY Times* 4 Oct 90

Joanne Greenberg essayist

8866 The pencil company's great act of genius was to put an eraser on the other end of the pencil.

On revisions of manuscript *Writing* Feb 87

Graham Greene novelist

8867 I remember. . . the suddenness with which a key turned in a lock, and I found I could read—not just sentences. . . but a real book. Now the future stood around on bookshelves everywhere.

The Lost Childhood Eyre & Spottiswoode 51

8868 I began to write. . . the potential civil servant, the don, the clerk had to look for other incarnations.

ib

8869 I wonder how all those who don't write, compose or paint, can manage to escape the madness, melancholia and panic which is inherent in the human situation.

On creative work as therapy *A Sort of Life* Simon & Schuster 71

8870 The characters in my novels are an amalgam of bits of real people. . . . Real people are too limiting.

NY Times 26 Feb 78

8871 A writer's knowledge of himself, realistic and unromantic, is like a store of energy on which he must draw for a lifetime: one volt of it properly directed will bring a character alive.

Washington Post 20 Sep 88

8872 I have no talent; it's just a question of working, of being willing to put in the time.

NY Times 4 Apr 91

8873 Henry James. . . was my idol, but to say he influenced me. . . is like saying a mountain influenced a mouse.

ib

8874 Every creative writer worth our consideration is a victim: a man given over to an obsession.

Newsweek 15 Apr 91

Noah Greenfeld novelist

8875 It's as if there were a single Pulitzer Prize and it came with a black belt.

On winning Japan's most important literary prize, the Akutagawa Award *NY Times* 15 Feb 87

Allan Gurganus novelist

8876 [I tend to] embroider on the decent muslin truth.

Lines for title character in *Oldest Living Confederate Widow Tells All* Knopf 89

8877 When people are talking about what they love and what they fear, everybody's eloquent.

ib

8878 Stories only happen to the people who can tell them.

ib

8879 I'm not a writer who's ever going to be blocked. I have a lot to do, a lot to tell. I'm just typing as fast as I can.

New York 21 Aug 89

A E Guthrie Jr novelist

8880 Nouns and verbs are the guts of the language. Beware of covering up with adjectives and adverbs.

Recalled on Guthrie's death 28 Apr 91

Dashiell Hammett novelist

8881 It is the beginning of the end when you discover you have style.

Smithsonian May 94

8882 I keep these typewriters chiefly to remind myself I was once a writer.

ib

Jean Harris autobiographer

8883 It is spring as I begin to put the pieces of a book together. Six springs have gone by since Hy died. . . an open wound. But it's time the wound was attended to.

On writing as therapeutic recovery from conviction for killing her lover, "Scarsdale diet doctor" Herman Tarnower *Stranger In Two Worlds* Macmillan 86

Shirley Hazzard novelist

8884 The state that you need to write is the state that others are paying large sums to get rid of.

NY Times 25 Mar 80

Ben Hecht novelist

8885 Nothing can disappear like a book.

On belief that only the classics endure, recalled on Hecht's death 18 Apr 64

Ernest Hemingway novelist

8886 I used the word "and" consciously over and over the way Mr Johann Sebastian Bach used a note in music when he was emitting counterpoint.

On *A Farewell to Arms* Scribner 1929, quoted by Lillian Ross *Reporting* Simon & Schuster 64

James Herriot novelist

8887 I became a connoisseur of the sick thud that a rejected manuscript makes on the doormat.

On short stories returned by prospective publishers *Life* Mar 88

8888 If a farmer calls me with a sick animal, he couldn't care less if I were George Bernard Shaw.

On continuing his Yorkshire veterinarian practice after becoming a best-selling author *Washington Post* 24 Feb 95

George V Higgins novelist

8889 That was one hell of a damned long night.

On 17 years of writing 14 novels, all rejected until *Friends of Eddie Coyle* Knopf 72 *NY Times* 30 Jul 90

8890 In restrospect: thank God [for rejection]. All have been hunted down and destroyed by their author.

ib

Richard Holmes biographer

8891 A biography is like a handshake down the years that can become an arm-wrestle.

Sunday Times London 21 Oct 90

Alistair Horne biographer

8892 The short answer is: with quite a lot of whiskey.

On how he persuaded Prime Minister Harold Macmillan to be interviewed for his biography *NY Times* 5 Mar 89

8893 [He regarded me as] a cross between Boswell and Torquemada.

ib

Aldous Huxley novelist

8894 The proper study of mankind is books.

In his novel *Chrome Yellow* Doran 1922, recalled on Huxley's death 22 Nov 63

8895 Geniusness only thrives in the dark, like celery.

On fear he would lose his obscurity *Those Barren Leaves* Doran 1925 *ib*

Christopher Isherwood novelist

8896 A separate being, a stranger almost... [but] we still share the same skeleton... have in common the label of one name, and a continuity of consciousness.

On writing of his youth *Down There on a Visit* Farrar Straus Giroux 61

Shirley Jackson novelist

8897 [Writing is] a logical extension of the adolescent daydream... most clearly a way of making daily life into a wonderfully unusual thing instead of a grind.

Quoted by Judy Oppenheimer *Private Demons* Putnam 88

8898 No one... is surprised to find me putting the waffle iron away on a different shelf because... it has quarreled with the toaster.

On weaving "a fairy-tale of infinite complexity around the inanimate objects" *ib*

P D James novelist

8899 My genes are optimistic... at home with the world and find it a friendly place, and believe people are going to like them and help them along. On the whole, they know they can always get by.

At 73, on producing a dozen novels in 25 years *British Heritage* Apr 94

Erica Jong novelist

8900 A writer's house is... many-gabled... bricks are made not of clay but of imagination... windows are the writer's eyes... chimneys smoke with our desires, and its fires blaze with the trees we chop down in our secret gardens.

NY Times 30 Dec 93

Kitty Kelley biographer

8901 It takes a real pushy pants to do it.

On writing biographies of Jacqueline Kennedy Onassis and Frank Sinatra *Washington Post* 30 Oct 88

8902 With Sinatra, all people worried about was getting killed. That was easy compared with Mrs Reagan.

On writing *Nancy Reagan* Simon & Schuster 91, *Vogue* May 91

8903 She lied... she assumed another life... as her mother did. I always go back to the mothers... it's a key to us.

ib

Jamaica Kincaid novelist

8904 Lying is the beginning of fiction.

NY Times 7 Oct 90

Barbara Kingsolver novelist

8905 Something I have to say... something that's burning a hole in the pockets of my heart.

On why she writes *USA Today* 15 Jul 93

Alice Koller essayist

8906 After a time... of patiently watching for the thing in me that is the why of me, of letting it know that it can come out now, that it no longer need huddle frozen, inert, at least not for a while, the words would come.

On breaking writer's block *The Stations of Solitude* Morrow 90

Anne Lamott novelist

8907 Mental illnesses arrive at the desk like your sickest, most secretive relatives... pull up chairs in a semicircle around the computer... weird coppery breath, leering at you behind your back.

Bird by Bird: Some Instructions on Writing and Life Pantheon 95

Margaret Laurence novelist

8908 When I say "work" I only mean writing. Everything else is just odd jobs.

Quoted in Donald Cameron ed *Conversations with Canadian Novelists* Macmillan 73

Martha Weinman Lear novelist

8909 We are stunned by our own capacities for obsession.

On steady concentration while resident at New Hampshire's MacDowell Colony *NY Times* 6 Mar 88

8910 We quit early, as usual, and went back to our digs to check out the inner weather reports for tomorrow.

ib

Fran Lebowitz novelist

8911 I work so slowly that I could write in my own blood without hurting myself.

US 25 Aug 86

Harper Lee novelist

8912 *Mockingbird* has never been out of print and I am still alive, although very quiet.

On *To Kill A Mockingbird* Lippincott 60 *London Times* 26 Aug 95

8913 Introductions inhibit pleasure, kill the joy of anticipation, frustrate curiosity.

On her prejudice on prefaces *ib*

Christopher Lehmann-Haupt novelist

8914 Writing can only be done because you go into a kind of euphoria—your child is beautiful no matter how ugly.

On his first novel *A Crooked Man* Simon & Schuster 94 *Publisher's Weekly* 24 Oct 94

Sinclair Lewis novelist

8915 I don't mind Babbitt. I just can't stand the boisterous sense of humor he has like, "Hello, you old horse thief, how the hell are you?" and he slaps you on the back.

Interviewed at 65 *NY Times* 5 Feb 50

8916 I've spoken to Rotary clubs and invariably a Babbitt stands up and says, "I guess Mr Lewis will know now that Babbitt isn't Babbitt after all."

ib

8917 Our American professors like their literature clear and cold and pure.

"The American Fear of Literature" address on accepting 1930 Nobel Prize for Literature, recalled on Lewis' death 10 Jan 51

8918 Writers have a rare power not given to anyone else; we can bore people long after we are dead.

Civilization Mar 95

Anne Morrow Lindbergh novelist

8919 It was a sudden recognition of something... that has sometimes been coaxed out, often crushed, raised its head in rebellion, been forgotten about, hurt, smothered with false attention.

On Harold Nicolson's encouragment to continue writing *Locked Rooms and Open Doors* Harcourt Brace Jovanovich 74

8920 Writing... happens to be the lens of me... clarifying... enabling me to see things and to think, and to concentrate what's in me.

The Flower and the Nettle Harcourt Brace Jovanovich 76

8921 My life does not go well *without* writing. It is my flywheel... cloister... communication with myself and God... my eyes to the world... window for awareness, without which I cannot see anything or walk straight.

War Within and Without Harcourt Brace Jovanovich 80

8922 It is like milk in the breast. It won't keep.

On the need to be published

David Lodge novelist

8923 Literature is mostly about having sex and not much about having children; life is the other way around.

The British Museum Is Falling Down Penguin 89

Desmond MacCarthy biographer

8924 A biographer is a writer who's on oath.

Time 2 Jul 79

Norman Maclean novelist

8925 There's no bastards in the world who like to argue more than fishermen and not one of them corrected me on anything. That is my idea of a good review.

On fishermen's letters on his book *A River Runs Through It* Pocketbooks 76 when made into a film in 92 *Newsweek* 2 Nov 92

8926 I have accomplished what I set out to do through writing. I have put the pieces of myself together.

ib

Archibald MacLeish biographer

8927 A real writer learns from earlier writers the way a boy learns from an apple orchard—by stealing what he has a taste for and can carry off.

A Continuing Journey Houghton Mifflin 68

Naguib Mahfouz novelist

8928 I write because I have two daughters and they need high-heeled shoes!

On writing that led to the Nobel Prize *NY Times* 14 Oct 88

Norman Mailer novelist

8929 I set up a base camp on the slopes of mystery. . . [although] few who build a base camp have no ambitions to reach the summit.

On his study of President Kennedy's assassin *Oswald's Tale* Random House 95

Bernard Malamud novelist

8930 I write to know the next room of my fate.

Time 2 Jul 79

8931 I work with language. I love the flowers of afterthought.

George Plimpton ed *Writers at Work* Penguin 84

Janet Malcolm biographer

8932 [Biography] is the medium through which the remaining secrets of the famous dead are taken from them and dumped out in full view of the world.

London Times 27 Aug 93

8933 The biographer at work, indeed, is like the professional burglar, breaking into a house, rifling through certain drawers that he has reason to think contain the jewelry and money, and triumphantly bearing his loot away.

ib

William Manchester biographer

8934 Like Gladstone speaking to Victoria, he addressed me as though I was a one-man House of Commons. It was superb.

On Manchester's only meeting with Winston S Churchill, the subject of Manchester's *The Last Lion* Little, Brown 83

André Maurois novelist

8935 A great biography should, like the close of a great drama, leave behind it a feeling of serenity.

The Art of Writing Dutton 60

8936 We collect into a small bunch. . . the few flowers which brought sweetness into a life, and present it as an offering to an accomplished destiny.

Poem *ib*

Martin Mayer essayist

8937 I am by profession a snoop; by craft, a writer; by trade, a gossip.

Making News Doubleday 86

Mary McCarthy novelist

8938 [It is] the price one pays for the price *The New Yorker* pays one.

To Janet Flanner on work excerpted prior to book publication, quoted by Brenda Wineapple *Genet* Ticknor & Fields 89

David McCullough biographer

8939 I see the past as my territory. . . a foreign correspondent who goes there instead of to India or South America.

US News & World Report 22 Jun 92

8940 It's a way of saying a lot of things about a lot of things.

On biography of Harry S Truman as a metaphor for America *Washington Times* 20 Jul 92

8941 I work in a book. . . putting myself under a spell. And this spell. . . is so real to me that if I have to leave my work for a few days, I have to work myself back into the spell. . . almost like hypnosis.

NY Times 12 Aug 92

8942 I wanted to do a full biography, a mural instead of a Vermeer.

On his study of the young Theodore Roosevelt *ib*

8943 Painters often look at their work in the mirror because you can see flaws that you don't see looking straight at a canvas.

On reading his work aloud to his wife and having her read it back to him *ib*

James A Michener novelist

8944 The only place worth writing about is the human heart. . . that bleak and wonderful terrain. . . the principal responsibility of the novelist.

Authors Guild Bulletin Apr 64

8945 You always hope that next time you'll get it right and have something sensible to say.

ABC TV 3 Feb 88

8946 When people tire of the 48-minute television novel, they will yearn for a substantial book within whose covers they can live imaginatively for weeks.

The World is My Home Random House 92

8947 I use those long, dull openings to weed out the ribbon clerks.

ib

8948 I went to bed an author and awoke to find Ezio Pinza famous.

On Michener's *Tales of the South Pacific* as the basis of the Pinza role in the musical *South Pacific* first starring Mary Martin and bass baritone Ezio Pinza *ib*

8949 Writing is a job. Do it well, it's a great life. Mess around, its disappointments will kill you.

ib

Nancy Mitford essayist

8950 Everybody's real life is quite different... no dark secret, but everything's different from the facade.

To Evelyn Waugh 31 Jan 51, quotes as frontispiece in Charlotte Mosley Ed *Love from Nancy: The Letters of Nancy Mitford* Houghton Mifflin 93

Brian Moore novelist

8951 I don't like to answer questions in novels. I only like to ask them.

NY Times 12 Sep 93

Ted Morgan novelist

8952 The truth coin would not tarnish in his hand.

On the honesty of the author William S Burroughs *Literary Outlaw* Holt 88

Edmund Morris biographer

8953 The ideal attitude is mild affection.

On a biographer's best attitude toward biographees *US News & World Report* 3 Aug 87

8954 About six months ago, he stopped recognizing me. Now I no longer recognize him.

On Ronald Reagan's development of Alzheimer's disease during the years Morris was working on Reagan's authorized biography *Newsweek* 23 Jan 96

Wright Morris novelist

8955 Before they made tools, perhaps before they made trouble, men and women were busy at the loom of fiction looking for clues to becoming more human.

About Fiction Harper & Row 75

8956 American writers were... the first to intuit... that the catchall web of the vernacular reflected the mind at its conscious level. This new melodious tongue shaped the writer to a greater extent than he shaped the language.

ib

Toni Morrison novelist

8957 Oppressive language... drinks blood, laps vulnerabilities, tucks its fascist boots under crinolines of respectability and patriotism, as it moves relentlessly toward the bottom line and the bottomed-out mind.

On accepting the Nobel Prize *Sunday Morning* CBS TV 12 Dec 93

8958 We die. That may be the meaning of life. But we do language. That may be the measure of our lives.

ib

John Mortimer essayist

8959 Americans say what they think whereas with the English you have to deduct what they think from what they say.

NPR 7 Jan 93

Andrew Motion biographer

8960 The beautiful flower of art grows on a long stem out of often murky material.

On Philip Larkin as an anti-Semite, racist, misogynist, and greatly talented poet *NY Times* 10 Mar 93

8961 What I tried to do was to throw a very fine net over the bird, to examine it and ring it, and then let it go.

On his Larkin biography *Guardian Weekly* 11 Apr 93

Lewis Mumford essayist

8962 I can scarcely remember the time when writing... in the Grub Street sense, to earn porridge and pickles, was not part of my young life.

Quoted by Donald L Miller *Lewis Mumford* Weidenfeld & Nicolson 89

8963 The middle-aged vice of completeness and overcomprehensiveness has taken the place of my youthful vice of sketchiness and superficiality.

On two years of prolonged work on *The Culture of Cities ib*

Vladimir Nabokov novelist

8964 I have rewritten—often several times—every word I have ever published. My pencils outlast their erasers.

Recalled on Nabokov's death 7 Jul 77

8965 Beyond the seas where I have lost a sceptre,/ I hear the neighing of my dappled nouns,/ Soft participles coming down the steps,/ Treading on leaves, trailing their rustling gowns.

On love for the Russian language carried into exile, quoted by Lance Morrow "A Holocaust of Words" *Time* 2 May 88

8966 The demenagement from my palatial Russian to the narrow quarters of my English was like moving from one darkened house to another on a starless night during a strike of candlemakers and torchbearers.

Unpublished note from Nabokov archives quoted by Brian Boyd *Vladimir Nabokov: The American Years* Princeton 91

V S Naipaul novelist

8967 I am the kind of writer that people think other people are reading.

Radio Times 24 Mar 79

8968 An autobiography can distort. . . but fiction never lies. It reveals the writer totally.

NY Times 14 Oct 90

Nora Naish novelist

8969 It's not pornographic and neither is it a bodice-ripper.

At age 78 *London Times* 2 Jun 93 on her book *Sunday Lunch* Sinclair Stevenson 93

Howard Nemerov poet and novelist

8970 People read novellas, but they tend to live in novels.

A Howard Nemerov Reader University of Missouri Press 91

Richard M Nixon 37th US President

8971 Writing a book is the most intensive exercise anyone can give his brain. It provided the therapy to put Watergate behind me.

In the Arena Simon & Schuster 90

William Novack biographer

8972 I was the chauffeur. I was taking him where he wanted to go.

On collaborating on automotive executive Lee Iacocca's autobiography *NY Times* 13 Sep 87

Joyce Carol Oates novelist

8973 The use of language is all we have to pit against death and silence.

NY Times 16 Aug 87

Edna O'Brien novelist

8974 Suffering. . . can make for profundity, definitely.

Publisher's Weekly 18 May 92

8975 The unconscious. . . that's where the gold is, if there is any gold. . . the big room. . . unknowable, and only intermittently can we go into it.

NY Times 30 Aug 95

8976 Unless we look at dark and covered painful wounds, we can never heal them.

ib

Flannery O'Connor novelist

8977 I have been wasting my time all these years writing—my talent lies in a kind of intellectual vaudeville.

Sally Fitzgerald ed *The Habit of Being* Viking 79

8978 I don't talk about other writers' work because I don't know enough, and I am reluctant to talk about my own because I know too much.

ib

8979 Nobody likes to be caught on the tracks when the Dixie Special comes through.

On being compared to William Faulkner *New York* 21 Aug 89

Frank O'Connor novelist

8980 A novel. . . is the smallest number of characters in the least number of situations necessary to precipitate a given crisis.

Quoted by James Matthews *Voices: A Life of Frank O'Connor* Atheneum 87

Sean O'Faolain novelist

8981 In all art, about one tenth is skill and the rest is personality.

The Short Story Devin-Adair 51

8982 A short story, if it is a good story, is like a child's kite—a small wonder, a brief, bright moment.

NY Times 22 Apr 91

John O'Hara novelist

8983 I can think of only one other author I'd rather see get it.

On congratulating John Steinbeck on the Nobel Prize, quoted by Jay Parini *John Steinbeck* Holt 95

Laurence Olivier actor

8984 Your duty is clear. . . to open up them golden gates and let all the filth out.

On writing an autobiography *LA Times* 7 Nov 82

Michael Ondaatje novelist

8985 The first sentence of every novel should be: "Trust me, this will take time but there is order here, very faint, very human." Meander if you want to get to town.

In the Skin of a Lion Knopf 87

Jose Ortega Y Gasset novelist

8986 Biography is a system in which the contradictions of a human life are united.

Recalled on Ortega Y Gasset's death 18 Oct 55

Milorad Pavic novelist

8987 Talented or gifted writers? We should talk of gifted and talented readers.

NY Times 20 Nov 88

Walter Percy novelist

8988 The greatest service a novelist can do his fellow man is. . . to attack the fake in the name of the real.

Signposts in A Strange Land Farrar Straus Giroux 91

S J Perelman novelist

8989 My senses bruise easily, and when they are bruised, I write.

Recalled on Perelman's death 17 Oct 79

Katherine Anne Porter novelist

8990 Practice an art for love and the happiness of your life—you will find it outlasts almost everything but breath.

NY Times 16 Apr 95

J B Priestley playwright

8991 Irony is the whisky of the mind.

Margin Released Harper & Row 62

V S Pritchett short story writer

8992 Sometimes ordinary speech is banal. . . but if selected with art. . . can reveal the inner life, often fantastic, concealed in the speaker.

Guardian Weekly 4 Mar 90

E Annie Proulx novelist

8993 If you get the landscape right, the characters will step out of it, and they'll be in the right place.

Time 29 Nov 93

Alexandra Ripley novelist

8994 Yes, Margaret Mitchell writes better than I do. But she's dead.

On completing *Scarlett* Warner Books 91, sequel to *Gone With the Wind, Christian Science Monitor* 6 Sep 91

Ned Rorem autobiographer

8995 Diaries are written in the heat of battle, memoirs in the repose of retrospect.

Publisher's Weekly 11 Sep 94, contrasting his previous books to his autobiography *Knowing When to Stop* Simon & Schuster 94

Roger Rosenblatt essayist

8996 It is the journal Dorian Gray would have written had he been a sophomore. But that is unfair to sophomores.

NY Times 15 Dec 90 on Bret Easton Ellis' *American Psycho* Vintage 90

8997 [The main character] does things to the bodies of women not unlike things that Mr Ellis does to prose.

ib

Philip Roth novelist

8998 It's like hearing a faint Morse code. . . and I need quiet to pick it up.

On the concentration required for writing *NY Times* 11 May 81

8999 One page a day. If I produce more, it is too much. Less, it is not enough.

People 8 Apr 91

Salman Rushdie novelist

9000 I have now spent over a thousand days. . . trapped inside a metaphor.

Likening to a balloon adrift his months in hiding after Iranian death threat for writing *The Satanic Verses NY Times* 12 Dec 91

9001 Free speech is the whole thing. . . . Free speech is life itself.

ib

Bertrand Russell essayist

9002 The things one says are all unsuccessful attempts to say something else.

Quoted by A O J Cockshut *The Art of Biography in l9th and 20th Century England* Yale 84

William Safire columnist

9003 If the scene deals with war or politics, it is fact; if it has to do with romance, it is fiction; if it is outrageously and obviously fictional, it is fact.

Newsweek 31 Aug 87 on the "credibility quotient" of his Civil War novel *Freedom* Doubleday 87

Carl Sandburg biographer

9004 He was. . . a strange friend and a friendly stranger to all forms of life that he met.

Writing in 1925 of his plans for a biography of Abraham Lincoln *The Sandburg Range* Harcourt, Brace 57

9005 A biography, sirs, should begin—with the breath of a man when his eyes first meet the light of day—then working on through to the death when the light of day is gone.

Biography prose poem in *Honey and Salt* Harcourt Brace Jovanovich 63

9006 You can reverse. . . starting the life with a coffin, moving back to a cradle.

ib

9007 It's a book about a man whose mother could not sign her name, written by a man whose father could not sign his. Perhaps that could happen only in America.

On completing his study of Lincoln, recalled on Sandburg's death 22 Jul 67

9008 Writing biography will wear you down like no other literary work.

Quoted by Penelope Niven *Carl Sandburg* Scribner 91

9009 Ain't it hell the way a book walks up to you and makes you write it?—Don't you feel almost predestinarian?

To Amy Lowell who had completed two volumes on John Keats a few weeks before her death *ib*

9010 It is a batch of sausage ground to a fine point that needs only a little seasoning and wrapping in packages.

To the editor overseeing production of Sandburg's *The American Songbook* 1950 *ib*

9011 Am now reading what the hell I last wrote. . . so that where I take up again the transition will be smooth as an eel swimming in oil.

On resuming work on more Lincoln biography *ib*

9012 There's a weariness in the bones. . . . The heave and the haul, the slime and the scum of a long voyage, is still on me.

On his first vacation in 11 years *ib*

Erich Segal novelist

9013 The limelight is like sunshine at first, and then eventually you can get sunstroke from it.

USA Today 25 Aug 88

Richard Selzer essayist

9014 The moment a writer picks up his pen, he is no longer himself or entirely of this world.

Taking the World in for Repairs Morrow 86

9015 Upon my tombstone shall be engraved the words, "He kept busy."

On his dual life as physician and writer *ib*

9016 Between then and now. . . there is a chasm across which swings only the frayed rope-bridge of memory.

Down from Troy Morrow 92

9017 The writer attempts to bridge the wound of childhood with words, knowing all the while that, should the wound heal, he would no longer be a writer.

ib

9018 A tool. . . in surgery. . . a scalpel, in writing, a pen. In the use of one, blood is shed; in wielding the other, ink is spilled upon a page.

ib

9019 In surgery the tissues of the body are sutured; in writing, words are stitched into sentences. A surgeon can unmake himself by simply stopping. . . .[but] a writer cannot. . . . Once that third eye is opened, it can never be shut.

Publisher's Weekly 10 Aug 92

Maurice Sendak children's book author

9020 [Writing is] a little like a quiet explosion in your head.

Station WAMU Washington 24 Dec 91

Eric Sevareid news commentator

9021 At best, the journalist may infuse scene, person and idea with a certain artistry, provided that some portion of his nerve endings have caught the subterranean murmurings of the English language.

Preface to his autobiographical *Not So Wild a Dream* Atheneum 76

9022 Words themselves become beings, sentences become. . . natural vegetation to be guided by the gardener's hands.

ib

9023 Often during those eight months of horticulture I would wake suddenly in the night because my subconscious knew I had done injury to the plant with a misplaced comma, a pathetic sentiment, a not-quite-accurate quotation. It was then impossible to sleep until the page was retrieved, the remedy applied.

ib

Michael Shelden biographer

9024 There is nothing to be gained. . . looking for certain patterns where none exist. Every life is full of pieces that do not fit.

Introduction to *Orwell* HarperCollins 91

Norman Sherry biographer

9025 I contracted dysentery in exactly the same mountain village, living in the same boarding house as Graham Greene had done.

On desire "to experience. . . what my subject had experienced," quoted by Paul Hollander *Wall Street Journal* 23 Jun 89 reviewing Sherry's *The Life of Graham Greene* Viking 89

9026 You have to have a good horse if you're going to be a successful biographical jockey.

Publisher's Weekly 27 Feb 95

9027 I'll just not finish the last sentence.

On Greene's prediction that he would not live to see Volume II and Sherry would not see Volume III *ib*

Georges Simenon novelist

9028 Writing is not a profession but a vocation of unhappiness.

Malcolm Cowley ed *Writers at Work* Viking 58

9029 Born in the dark and in the rain. . . I got away. The crimes I wrote about are the crimes I would have committed if I had not got away.

Autobiography *The Man Who Wasn't Maigret* Harcourt, Brace 94

Muriel Spark novelist

9030 Stage fright? . . . Write on, regardless.

On beginning a new novel *International Herald Tribune* 30 May 79

9031 I take an eye here and a nose there.

On characters based on life models *Newsweek* 15 Aug 88

John Steinbeck novelist

9032 When it comes right down to it, nothing has changed. The English sentence is just as difficult to write as it ever was.

Letter to his editor a month after accepting the 1962 Nobel Prize, quoted by Jay Parini *John Steinbeck* Holt 95

9033 I'm not the young writer of promise anymore. I'm a worked-over claim.

ib

9034 For every flowering thought there will be a page like a wet and mangy mongrel. . . for every looping flight, a tap on the wing and a reminder that wax cannot hold the feathers firm too near the sun.

George Plimpton ed *Writers at Work* Viking 77

General Joseph Stilwell US Army

9035 Wrote and wrote, terrible. I am just scribbling to keep from biting the radiator.

On keeping a diary, quoted by Barbara W Tuchman *Stilwell and the American Experience in China* Macmillan 70

Peter Straub novelist

9036 I just got this dread object, the copy-edited manuscript!

On an author's most painful step towards publication *NY Times* 20 Jul 95

Jacqueline Susann novelist

9037 The people who read me can get off the subway and go home feeling better about their own crappy lives, and luckier than the people they've been reading about.

On Valley of the Dolls Simon & Schuster 66, *New Yorker* 14 Aug 95

Gay Talese biographer

9038 I was olive-skinned in a freckle-faced town.

On growing up Italian-American in Ocean City NJ quoted by Arthur Lubow *Vanity Fair* Feb 92 reviewing Talese's *Unto the Sons* Random House 92

Margaret Thatcher Prime Minister of Britain

9039 I depended on. . . letters, diaries, cuttings, conference reports and all the multifarious files where little bits of modern lives are written down and stored away.

Introduction to completing her memoirs *The Path to Power* HarperCollins 95

Paul Theroux essayist

9040 The difference between travel writing and fiction is. . . between recording what the eye sees and discovering what the imagination knows.

My Secret History Putnam 89

James Thurber humorist

9041 His faith in the good will, soundness, and sense of humor of his countrymen will always serve as his asbestos curtain.

On not getting burned from writing the truth *Newsweek* 4 Feb 57

9042 I don't believe the writer should know too much where he's going. . . . He runs into old man blueprint.

Malcolm Cowley ed *Writers at Work* Viking 58

9043 [Humorists] lead. . . an existence of jumpiness and apprehension. . . on the edge of the chair of Literature.

Preface to *My Life and Hard Times* Harper 1933 recalled on Thurber's death 2 Nov 61

9044 In the house of Life they have the feeling that they have never taken off their overcoats.

ib

9045 The little wheels of invention are set in motion by the damp hand of melancholy.

ib

9046 In his prose pieces he appears always to have started from the beginning and to have reached the end by way of the middle.

Analysis of his own writing in preface to *The Thurber Carnival* Harper 1945 *ib*

William Trevor novelist

9047 You are our characters' litmus paper, their single link with reality. They taste as you taste, they hear as you hear.

Excursions in the Real World Knopf 94

Diana Trilling essayist

9048 The lust for honesty in my family was ravaging and incurable.

On autobiographical writing *NY Times* 25 Oct 93

Barbara W Tuchman historian

9049 Without books, history is silent, literature dumb, thought and speculation at a standstill.

Washington Post 7 Feb 89

9050 [Books] are companions, teachers, magicians, bankers of the treasures of the mind... humanity in print.

ib

Scott Turow novelist

9051 It's a why dunnit, not a who dunnit.

Station WAMU Washington 3 Sep 90 on Turow's novel *The Burden of Proof* Farrar Straus Giroux 90

Anne Tyler novelist

9052 I write because I want more than one life; I insist on a wider selection. It's greed, plain and simple.

Civilization Mar 95

John Updike novelist

9053 [It] spoke to me of New York, sophistication, amusing adult misery, carefree creativity... nervous quiggles given permanence and celebrity by the intervening miracle of printer's ink... a super way to live, to be behind such a book.

On James Thurber's *Men, Women and Dogs* Harcourt, Brace 1943, as the book that most influenced Updike to become a writer *Hugging the Shore* Knopf 83

9054 He managed to win this prize for me. I feel like a heel having treated him so badly.

On Harry "Rabbit" Angstrom, the central figure in four novels, including *Rabbit at Rest* Knopf 90 that received a Pulitzer *Washington Post* 10 Apr 91

9055 Creativity... a delicate imp... should dwell under toadstools and garb itself in cobwebs and not be smothered beneath a great load of discriminatory judgments.

Odd Jobs Knopf 91

9056 It's not enough for a story to flow. It has to kind of trickle and glint as it crosses over the stones of the bare facts.

Quoted by NPR's Susan Stamberg *Talk* Random House 93

9057 It's the fading of Babbitt.

On decline of secret societies and men's clubs *Wall Street Journal* 9 Feb 95

Gore Vidal novelist

9058 Thanks, but I already belong to the Diners Club.

On rejecting membership in the American Academy of Arts and Letters *Smithsonian* Nov 92

Robert James Waller novelist

9059 The road versus responsibility, that's my theme... not that one is right and one is wrong, I'm just saying there's a conflict.

London Times 11 Sep 95 on *The Bridges of Madison County* Warner Books 92

Evelyn Waugh novelist

9060 Anyone can write a novel given six weeks, pen, paper and no telephone or wife.

Quoted by Joseph Epstein *Partial Payments* Norton 89

9061 I do not care to have Americans who have read my books interrupting my meal.

To novelist James A Michener in an Istanbul restaurant, quoted by Michener *The World Is My Home* Random House 92

9062 Style is not a seductive decoration added to a functional structure; it is the essence of a work of art.

Quoted by Peter Vansittart *In the Fifties* John Murray 95

9063 Lucidity, elegance and individuality... combine to form a preservative... the nearest approximation to permanence in the fugitive art of letters.

ib

Fay Weldon novelist

9064 Feeling dreadful... seems to be the human condition... normal and natural to be ridden by guilt, by jealousy and misery.

On readers who want to see the ideal life portrayed in fiction *New Yorker* 26 Jun 95

Eudora Welty novelist

9065 Writing fiction is an interior affair... put down little by little out of personal feeling and beliefs arrived at alone... over a period of time as time is needed.

The Eye of the Story Random House 77

9066 Fiction has, and must keep, a private address.

ib

Jessamyn West novelist

9067 Fiction reveals truths that reality obscures.

Reader's Digest Apr 73

9068 There is no royal path to good writing; and such paths as do exist do not lead through neat critical gardens, various as they are, but through the jungles of self, the world, and of craft.

Saturday Review 21 Sep 57

Rebecca West novelist

9069 All good biography, as all good fiction, comes down to the study of original sin... our inherent disposition to choose death when we ought to choose life.

Time and Tide 1941 quoted as frontispiece to Victorian Glendinning's *Rebecca West* Knopf 87

9070 If I had told all I know about the old blackguard he would have been asked to resign from all his clubs.

On writing a book on St Augustine *ib*

9071 E M Forster was a nice old cozy. Lytton Strachey's beard was an extension of his personality in the direction of doubt.

ib

9072 I have never been able to write with anything more than the left hand of my mind; the right hand has always been engaged in something to do with personal relationships.

On what she saw as her "sexual deprivation," letter to Elizabethan scholar A L Rowse

E B White essayist and novelist

9073 The essayist is a self-liberated man, sustained by the childish belief that everything he thinks about, everything that happens to him, is of general interest.

Essays of E B White Harper & Row 77

9074 The essayist can... pull on any sort of shirt, be any sort of person... philosopher, scold, jester, racounteur, confidant, pundit, devil's advocate, enthusiast.

ib

9075 Delay is natural to a writer. He is like a surfer—he bides his time, waits for the perfect wave on which to ride in... for the surge (of emotion? of strength? of courage?) that will carry him along.

George Plimpton ed *Writers at Work* Penguin 88

9076 I never submitted a manuscript with a covering letter or through an agent.... I believed in the doctrine of immaculate rejection.

ib

9077 Advice from this elderly practitioner is to forget publishers and just roll a sheet of copy paper into your machine and get lost in your subject. Write about it by day and dream about it by night.

To biographer Linda H Davis *New Yorker* 27 Dec 93

Edmund White biographer

9078 Biography... has become the revenge of little people on big people.

NY Times 7 Nov 93 on publication of his biography of Jean Genet *Genet* Knopf 93

Patrick White novelist

9079 Writing... the practice of an art by a polished mind in civilized surroundings.

The Prodigal Son 58, quoted by Peter Vansittart *In the Fifties* John Murray 95

9080 [Writing] became a struggle to create completely fresh forms out of rocks and sticks of words... to see things for the first time... to find the extraordinary behind the ordinary.

ib

9081 The soul remains anchored... a balloon tied to a bunch of bones.... Still, it will tug nobly.

ib

Elie Wiesel novelist

9082 Writing isn't an occupation, but a duty. I write as much to understand as to be understood.

Christian Science Monitor 24 Jun 81

9083 No one is as capable of gratitude as one who has emerged from the kingdom of night.

Recalling World War II imprisonment in accepting Nobel Prize for Peace *NY Times* 11 Dec 86

9084 The writer... opens himself to whatever is surrounding him and... causes others to open their eyes, and, sometimes, their hearts.

Writing Mar 87

9085 There's no business like Shoah business.

On writers who "reap the dividends of Auschwitz" *NY Times* 17 Dec 95

Mary Ann Wiggins novelist

9086 People who know me best detect a certain air of distracton from time to time.

On Station WAMU Washington 16 Oct 95 on working for five years on her novel *Eveless Eden* HarperCollins 95

Thornton Wilder novelist

9087 What interests one in a novel... is the quantity of glimpsed detail, the asides and the incidents along the way; not the over-all turn of events or the holocaust at the close or the happy ending.

Robert Phelps with Jerry Roscoe ed *Continuous Lessons: The Journals of Glenway Westcott 1937–1955* Farrar Straus Giroux 90

Tennessee Williams playwright

9088 I cannot write any sort of story unless there is at least one character in it for whom I have physical desire.

Quoted by Gore Vidal in introduction to Tennessee Williams *Collected Stories* New Directions 85

9089 I am never deliberately cruel. But after my morning's work, I have little to give but indifference to people.

New Yorker 15 Jul 94

9090 Sometimes I crack through the emotional block... but that is not long lasting. Morning returns, and only work matters again.

ib

A N Wilson novelist

9091 A blessing of my present state of mind is that I feel very close to the bishops: none of us believes in God.

Church Times London 1 Feb 91

Tim Winton novelist

9092 You can pull yourself up by your bootstraps but you've got to have some shoes first.
Station WAMU Washington 19 May 92

P G Wodehouse humorist

9093 I was writing stories when I was five. . . don't know what I did before that. Just loafed I suppose.
Quoted by Frances Donaldson *P G Wodehouse* Knopf 82

Tom Wolfe novelist

9094 Writers can't back off from realism, just as an ambitious engineer cannot back off from electricity.
US News & World Report 23 Nov 87

9095 Status is an influence at every level. . . all part of what I call plutography: depicting the acts of the rich.
Time 13 Feb 89 On his novel *The Bonfire of the Vanities* Farrar Straus Giroux 87

9096 Writers. . . are in the business of calling attention to themselves. My own taste is counter-bohemian.
On dressing as a "dandy" *ib*

9097 Writing a novel about this astonishing metropolis, a big novel, cramming as much of New York City between covers as you could, was the most tempting, the most challenging, and the most obvious idea an American writer could possibly have.
"Stalking the Billion-footed Beast" *Harper's* Nov 89

Marguerite Yourcenar novelist

9098 [I was] searching for a truth that is multiple, unstable, evasive, sometimes saddening. . . at first glance scandalous.
Dear Departed Memoir Farrar Straus Giroux 91

9099 [My goal was] specific reality. . . without which a "historical novel" is merely a . . . successful costume ball.
ib

9100 The nuance may seem delicate, but it is capital.
On not being Hadrian but becoming Hadrian in her book *Memoirs of Hadrian* Modern Library 84, quoted by Josyanne Savigneau *Marguerite Yourcenar* University of Chicago 93

Poets

Diane Ackerman

9101 I don't want to get to the end of my life and find that I lived just the length of it. I want to have lived the width of it as well.
Newsweek 22 Sept 86

9102 We ask the poet to teach us a way of seeing, lest one spend a lifetime on this planet without noticing how green light flares up as the setting sun rolls under, or the gauzy spread of the Milky Way on a star-loaded summer night, or what Beckett in *How It Is* calls "the fragility of euphoria among the sponges."
Excerpted in *NY Times* 10 Mar 91 from Ackerman's essay in Janet Sternburg ed *The Writer on Her Work* Vol II Norton 91

9103 [The poet] hoists things out of their routine, and lays them out on a white papery beach to be fumbled and explored.
ib

9104 An occasion, catalyst, or tripwire. . . permits the poet to reach into herself and haul up whatever nugget of the human condition distracts her at the moment, something that can't be reached in any other way.
ib

Anna Akhmatova

9105 Now let's sit together, two old people, in wicker chairs. A single end waits us. And perhaps the real difference is not actually so great?
On Robert Frost's visit to the Soviet Union, quoted by John Bayley *NY Times* 13 May 90 reviewing Roberta Reeder ed *The Complete Poems of Anna Akhmatova* Zephyr Press 90

Maya Angelou

9106 Poetry is music written for the human voice.
Quoted by Bill Moyers "The Power of the Word" PBS TV 15 Sep 89

John Ashbery

9107 Poetry [is]. . . going on all the time in my head and I occasionally snip off a length.
London Times 23 Aug 84

9108 I like poems you can tack all over with a hammer and there are no hollow places.
ib

9109 Experiences. . . I don't write about them, I write out of them.
NY Times 17 Aug 86

W H Auden

9110 The most decisive experience of my life so far.
On moving from England to New York in 1939, letter made public from NY Public Library's extensive Auden archive *NY Times* 28 Jul 94

9111 [Moving] has taught me the kind of writer I am—an introvert who can only develop by obeying his introversion. All Americans are introverts.
ib

9112 New York... is the only city in which I find I can work and live quietly. For the first time I am leading a life which remotely approximates to the way I think I ought to live. I have never written or read so much.

ib

9113 In others' eyes, a man is a poet if he has written one good poem. In his own he is only a poet at the moment when he is making his last revision to a new poem.

Recalled on Auden's death 28 Sep 73

9114 [In] Italian... you can't tell when you've written nonsense. In English you know right away.

Quoted by Charles Osborne *W H Auden: The Life of a Poet* Harcourt Brace Jovanovich 79

9115 Novels, even good ones, can be read simply to pass the time; music, even the greatest, can be used as background noise but nobody has yet learned to consume a poem: either one cannot read it at all, or one must listen to it as its author intended it to be listened to.

ib

9116 I always have two things in my head... the form looks for the theme, the theme looks for the form, and when they come together you're able to write.

ib

9117 Sometimes falling asleep at night, it feels warm.

On being aware of fame *New Yorker* 15 Dec 86

9118 Old, famous, loved, yet not a sacred cow.

Telegram to E M Forster's on his 80th birthday, quoted by Joseph Epstein *Partial Payments* Norton 89

9119 [I am in] deliberate avoidance of... visual imagery which has no basis in verbal experience and can therefore be translated without love.

Quoted by Lincoln Kirstein, Nicolas Jenkins ed *By, To, and From* Farrar Straus Giroux 91

9120 The word *Collected* suggests finality which, I hope anyway, is incorrect.

At age 52, objecting to a title, quoted by Edward Mendelson in preface to *W H Auden: Collected Poems* Vintage 91

John Betjeman

9121 That dear good man, with Prufrock in his head/And Sweeney waiting to be agonized,/ I wonder what he thought? Never says/ When now we meet, across the port and cheese,/ He looks the same as then, long, lean and pale,/ Still with the slow deliberating speech/ And enigmatic answers. At the time/ A boy called Jelly said, "He thinks they're bad"—/ But he himself is still too kind to say.

On his schoolmaster T S Eliot *Summoned by Bells* John Murray 76

9122 I made hay while the sun shone./ My work sold./ Now, if the harvest is over/ And the world cold,/ Give me the bonus of laughter/ As I lose hold.

"The Last Laugh" in *A Nip in the Air* Norton 76

Maxwell Bodenheim

9123 Poetry... the impish attempt to paint the color of the wind.

Quoted by Ben Hecht *Winkelberg* play 58

Louise Bogan

9124 [Your work] is carved out of agony as a statue is carved out of marble.

In *Achievement in American Poetry* Regnery 51

9125 [Poetry] is carved out of agony as a statue is carved out of agony.

ib

9126 The intellectual is... the fine nervous flower of the bourgeoisie.

Solicited Criticism Noontime Press 55

Joseph Brodsky

9127 Russia is my home... and for everything that I have in my soul I am obligated to Russia and its people. And—this is the main thing—obligated to its language.

NY Times 1 Oct 72

9128 Bad literature is a form of treason.

ib

9129 I was raised by... cold that, to warm my pain, gathered my fingers around a pen.

On being cited for the Nobel Prize *Time* 2 Nov 87

9130 Should we have been choosing our leaders on the basis of their reading experience and not their political programs, there would be much less grief on earth.

NY Times 9 Dec 87

9131 [Poet laureate]... a feather in the library's cap—or, rather, given the cloudiness of its mental operations, in its turban. (A turban looks like a cloud, yeah?)

On becoming the Library of Congress' Poet Laureate in residence *Washington Post* 31 May 92

9132 [Poet laureate] should be a bully pulpit from which to address the entire nation.

ib

9133 I sit at my desk/ My life's grotesque.

Citing his favorite poem written during his tenure *ib*

9134 [Washington is] lively, but on the whole it wasn't called Ground Zero for nothing.

ib

9135 [Poetry should be] in every room in every motel in the land.

On his successful campaign to provide poetry to travelers *NY Times* 15 Mar 94

9136 [Poetry is] our anthropological, genetic goal. . . linguistic, evolutionary beacon.

On hotel room volumes of poetry, many of which were stolen or purchased by guests *ib*

James Branch Cabell

9137 Poetry is man's rebellion against being what he is.

Jurgen 1919 novel recalled on Cabell's death 6 May 58

Charles Causley

9138 Edward FitzGerald sleeps/ Under this sheet of stone,/ Neat as never in life,/ Innocent, alone.

Boulge, elegy in the village of Boulge, England, for Edward Fitzgerald, translator of Omar Khayyam *Secret Destination: Selected Poems: 1977–88* Godine 90

9139 Flint-eyed, the church, the tower/ Shadow his page/ Thinly the Persian rose/ Frets in its cage.

Excerpted in *NY Times* 18 Mar 90

René Char

9140 A poet must leave traces of his passage, not proof.

Quoted by Josyane Savigneau *Marguerite Yourcenar* University of Chicago 93

John Ciardi

9141 The poet has to write by itch and twitch. . . intimately conditioned by all his past itching and twitching.

NY Times 2 Apr 86

Paul Claudel

9142 You explain nothing, O poet, but thanks to you all things become explicable.

Recalled on Claudel's death 23 Feb 55

Jean Cocteau

9143 A true poet does not trouble about the poetical. In the same way, a horticulturist does not scent his roses.

Quoted by Edith Sitwell *A Poet's Notebook* Little, Brown 51

9144 A poet is a liar who always speaks the truth.

Recalled on Cocteau's death 11 Oct 63

Cyril Connolly

9145 Poets arguing about modern poetry: jackals snarling over a dried-up well.

The Unquiet Grave Penguin 67

Gregory Corso

9146 We Germans have lost our readers—the Jews.

Evergreen Review No 16, 61

Rita Dove

9147 A good poem is like a bouillon cube. It's concentrated and it nourishes you when you need it.

Time 18 Oct 89

T S Eliot

9148 I was too slow a mover. It was much easier to be a poet.

On giving up college boxing *NY Herald Tribune* 11 May 58

9149 Genuine poetry can communicate before it is understood.

On Dante 1929, recalled on Eliot's death 4 Jan 65

9150 Sometimes to be a "ruined man" is itself a vocation.

The Use of Poetry and the Use of Criticism 1933 *ib*

9151 [Poetry] may make us. . . a little more aware of the deeper, unnamed feelings which form the substration of our being, to which we rarely penetrate; for our lives are mostly a constant evasion of ourselves.

Accepting 1948 Nobel Prize *ib*

9152 [I hope to write poetry] with nothing poetic about it. . . standing naked in its bare bones, or poetry so transparent that we should not see the poetry, but that which we are meant to see through poetry.

Unpublished 1933 address New Haven CT, quoted by Peter Ackroyd *T S Eliot* Simon & Schuster 84

9153 Words are perhaps the hardest medium of all material of art. One must simultaneously express visual beauty, beauty of sound, and communicate a grammatical statement.

On words as "perhaps the hardest medium of all material of art," Patricia C Willis ed *A Marianne Moore Reader* Viking 86

9154 [There are] two kinds of bad poets—the *faux mauvais,* those who have a spurt of writing in their youth, and the *vrais mauvais,* who keep on writing it.

ib

9155 [It was] the relief of a personal. . . grouse against life.

On "The Waste Land" 1922, Valerie Eliot ed *The Letters of T S Eliot* Harcourt Brace Jovanovich 88

9156 On some days he's a duller or/ brighter,/ He objects to both pencil and ink,/ Yet he bangs on an ancient typewriter,/ Without ever stopping to think.

In a letter of self-description found in a Hampshire attic *NY Times* 2 Nov 91

9157 To pass on to posterity one's own language, more highly developed... refined... more precise than it was before one wrote it, that is the highest possible achievement of the poet as poet.

"What Dante Means to Me" essay from *To Criticize the Critic* University of Nebraska 92 excerpted in *NY Times* 14 Jun 92

9158 Whichever Mr Auden is, I am not.

When asked if he was to be categorized as American or English *ib* 23 Jun 94

9159 In speech is both the highest level of consciousness and the deepest level of unconsciousness.

The Varieties of Metaphysical Poetry Harcourt Brace Jovanovich 94

9160 The human mind, when it comes to a terminus, hastens to look up the next train for almost anywhere.

ib

Paul Engle

9161 Verse is not written, it is bled;/ Out of the poet's abstract head./ Words drip the poem on the page;/ Out of his grief, delight and rage.

A Woman Unashamed and Other Poems Random House 65

Robert Frost

9162 I may not be equal to it but I can accept it for my cause—the arts, poetry—now for the first time taken into the affairs of statesmen.

Reply to President Kennedy's invitation to read at his inauguration *NY Times* 15 Jan 61

9163 The right reader of a good poem can tell the moment it strikes him that he has taken an immortal wound—that he will never get over it.

On the poetry of Amy Lowell, recalled on Frost's death 29 Jan 63

9164 [Style is] the mind skating circles around itself as it moves forward.

Quoted by Margaret Bartlett Anderson *Robert Frost and John Bartlett* Holt Rinehart Winston 63

9165 No tears in the writer, no tears in the reader.

ib

9166 Like a piece of ice on a hot stove the poem must ride on its own melting.

ib

9167 [A poem] can never lose its sense of a meaning that once unfolded by surprise as it went. It is only a moment here and a moment there that the greatest writer has.

ib

9168 An unromantic poet is a self-contradiction, like the democratic aristocrat that reads *The Atlantic Monthly*.

ib

9169 A poet never takes notes. You never take notes in a love affair.

Edward Connery Lathem ed *Interviews With Robert Frost* Holt Rinehart Winston 66

9170 [I hope to leave behind] a few poems that will be hard to get rid of.

On 80th birthday, quoted by Archibald MacLeish in introduction to *The Complete Poems of Carl Sandburg* Harcourt Brace Jovanovich 86

9171 To be a poet is a condition, not a profession.

Quoted on NPR 17 Jul 92

Christopher Fry

9172 Poetry is the language in which man explores his own amazement.

Time 3 Apr 50

Eduardo Galeano

9173 In the house of words was a table of colors. They offered themselves in great fountains and each poet took the color he needed: lemon yellow or sun yellow, ocean blue or smoke blue, crimson red, blood red, wine red.

The Book of Embraces Norton 91

Robert Graves

9174 A well-chosen anthology is a complete dispensary of medicine for the more common mortal disorders, and it may be used as much for prevention as cure.

On English Poetry Haskell 62

9175 A true poet writes because he must, not because he hopes to make a living from his poems.

Letter to *London Times* 30 Mar 62, Kenneth Gregory ed *The Second Cuckoo* Allen & Unwin 83

9176 He never considers himself affronted by neglect, and treats whatever money comes from the sale of his poems as laughably irrelevant to their making.

ib

9177 How to reconcile poetic principle with earning a livelihood is for him to settle, and no one else.

ib

9178 There are never more than four or five poets in any country at the same time who are worth reading, and all tend to be fanatically independent.

ib

9179 The poet is the unsatisfied child who dares to ask the difficult question which arises from the schoolmaster's answer to his simple question, and then the still more difficult question which arises from that.

Recalled on Graves' death 7 Dec 85

9180 Since the age of 15 poetry has been my ruling passion and I have never intentionally undertaken any task or formed any relationship that seemed inconsistent with poetic principles; which has sometimes won me the reputation of an eccentric.

The White Goddess Farrar Straus 1948 quoted in *New Yorker* 4 Sep 95

Seamus Heaney

9181 Between my finger and my thumb./ The squat pen rests; snug as a gun.

Selected Poems 1966–1987 Farrar Straus Giroux 90

9182 Nobel is one of the few magic words in the world. It blesses the art of poetry.

On winning the Nobel Prize *London Times* 13 Oct 95

Randall Jarrell

9183 A good poet is someone who manages, in a lifetime of standing out in thunderstorms, to be struck by lightning five or six times; a dozen or two dozen times and he is great.

NY Times 13 Jan 91

Stanley Kunitz

9184 The deepest thing I know is that I am living and dying at once, and my conviction is to report that dialogue.

NY Times 11 Mar 87

Philip Larkin

9185 [A poem] represents the mastering, even if just for a moment, of the pessimism and the melancholy, and enables you—you the poet, and you, the reader—to go on.

Recalled on Larkin's death 2 Dec 85

9186 [I look] like a balding salmon.

On his appearance *ib*

9187 Novels are about other people and poems are about yourself.

Collected Poems Farrar Straus Giroux 89

9188 I like to read about people who have done nothing spectacular, who aren't beautiful and lucky, who try to behave well in the limited field of activity they command, but who can see, in the little autumnal moments of vision, that the so called "big" experiences of life are going to miss them.

On novelist Barbara Pym, quoted by Joseph Epstein *Partial Payments* Norton 89

9189 The essence of [the poet's] gifts is to create the familiar, and it is from the familiar that he draws his strength.

Quoted by Richard Critchfield *An American Looks at Britain* Doubleday 90

9190 A poem is a sort of verbal device to preserve a feeling you have had, so that anyone who inserts the penny of his attention will receive that emotion neatly wrapped.

Anthony Thwaite ed *Selected Letters of Philip Larkin* Farrar Straus Giroux 93

9191 More and more I feel [the poet] should wander unnoticed through life, colorless and unremarkable, wearing ordinary clothes, smoking a common brand of cigarette, hair parted on the left, queueing for cheap seats.

Quoted by Andrew Motion *Philip Larkin* Farrar Straus Giroux 93

9192 You remind me of a Catholic priest, wondering why little ones aren't making regular appearances.

To his publisher *ib*

Peter Levi

9193 [It] is not a living wage: it is more like an enormous tip.

On the admission price to lectures, quoted by Claude Rawson *NY Times* 28 Apr 91 reviewing Levi's *The Art of Poetry* Yale 91

C Day Lewis (Nicholas H Blake)

9194 The aging poet is rebuked by his youth—by its happily spendthrift nature: so many concepts unrealized, so many images botched, so many poems that never grew to wholeness.

Foreword to *Selected Poems* Harper & Row 67

9195 The prodigality, the impatience, the wide-openness to joy and pain, the brave confidence of his earlier selves—these are what he envies now.

ib

C S Lewis

9196 Doubtless it is a rule in poetry that if you do your own work well, you will find you have done also work you never dreamed of.

The Allegory of Love Oxford 38 recalled on Lewis' death 22 Nov 63

Archibald MacLeish

9197 Journalism is concerned with events, poetry with feelings. Journalism is concerned with the look of the world, poetry with the feel of the world.

"The Poet and the Press" *Atlantic* Mar 59

9198 Journalism wishes to tell what it is that has happened everywhere as though the same things had happened for every man. Poetry wishes to say what it is like for any man to be himself in the presence of a particular occurrence as though only he were there alone.

ib

9199 To separate journalism and poetry, therefore—history and poetry—to set them up at opposite ends of the world of discourse, is to separate seeing from the feel of seeing, emotion from the act of emotion, knowledge from the realization of knowledge.

ib

9200 Anything can make us look, only art can make us see.

Poetry and Experience Riverside 61

9201 Poetry is the art of understanding what it is to be alive.

Recalled on MacLeish's death 20 Apr 82

9202 A poem should be palpable and mute/ As a globed fruit./ Dumb/ As old medallions to the thumb./ Silent as the sleeve-worn stone/ Of casement ledges where the moss has grown—/ A poem should be wordless/ As the flight of birds.

"Ars Poetica" *Collected Poems 1917–1982* Houghton Mifflin 85

9203 Recognize the great man's prior claims and shut up? And what if we can't shut up? Talk about the tragedy of the man who is ahead of his age: it is nothing to the tragedy of the man who comes after the man who is.

On critics' comments on MacLeish as influenced by T S Eliot, quoted by Scott Donaldson *Archibald MacLeish* Houghton Mifflin 92

9204 If the art of poetry is. . . the art of making sense of the chaos of human experience, it's not a bad thing to see a lot of chaos.

On his work in government *ib*

John Masefield

9205 My first book of verses, written mainly in six exciting weeks, consisted chiefly of ballads expressing a longing for sea air.

Recalled on Masefield's death 12 May 67

9206 Of 300,000,000 English readers, three read me and four criticize me.

Statement in 1958 quoted by Peter Vansittart *In the Fifties* John Murray 95

James Merrill

9207 What one wants in this world isn't so much to "live" as to. . . be lived, to be used by life for its own purposes.

New Yorker 27 Mar 95

9208 Here one is in Later Life, and it's perfectly pleasant really, not for a moment that garden of cactus and sour grapes I'd always assumed it must be.

At age 46, letter to a friend *ib*

W S Merwin

9209 The thing that makes poetry different from all of the other arts. . . [is] you're using language, which is what you use for everything else—telling lies and selling socks, advertising, and conducting law. Whereas we don't write little concerts or paint pictures.

On receiving the $100,000 Tanning Prize for Poetry *Washington Post* 30 Sep 94

Marianne Moore

9210 I do not write for money or fame. . . . One writes because one has a burning desire to objectify what it is indispensible to one's happiness to express.

At University of California 3 Oct 56, Patricia C Willis ed *The Complete Poems of Marianne Moore* Viking 86

9211 Omissions are not accidents.

On assembling all of her poems *ib*

9212 Subjects choose me. . . I lie in wait like a leopard on a branch-strained metaphor.

Quoted by Louis Untermeyer "Five Famous Poetesses" *Ladies' Home Journal* May 64

Ogden Nash

9213 My verse respresents a handle I can grasp in order not to yield to the centrifugal forces which are trying to throw one off the world.

Recalled on Nash's death 9 May 71

Pablo Neruda

9214 Peace goes into the making of a poem as flour goes into the making of bread.

Memoirs Farrar Straus Giroux 77

Mary Oliver

9215 Poetry happens because of life. . . [and] because of language. And poetry happens because of other poets.

On adding the National Book Award for *New and Selected Poems* Beacon 92 to her Pulitzer Prize *NY Times* 20 Nov 92

Octavio Paz

9216 Between what I see and what I say/ Between what I say and what I keep silent/ Between what I keep silent and what I dream/ Between what I dream and what I forget: Poetry.

Poem from 1976 cited by Swedish Academy of Letters in awarding Nobel Prize for poetry that consists "to a very great extent of writing both with and about words. . . [which through] surrealistically inspired thought, the words are endowed in this way with new, changeable and richer meanings" *NY Times* 12 Oct 90

9217 To me, a poet represents not only a region but the universe. Writers are the servants of language. Language is the common property of society, and writers are the guardians of language.

Interview on announcement of prize

9218 A writer has two loyalties. . . he belongs to the special tribe of writers. . . he also belongs to a culture, to his own country.

ib

9219 A writer is a descendant of other writers.
On influence of Eliot, Breton, Montale, Ungaretti, Calvino, and the French Surrealists *ib*

9220 The prize is not a passport to immortality but it does give a poet the possibility of a wider audience, and every writer needs a wider audience.
ib

Saint-John Perse

9221 Can the earthenwear lamp of the poet still suffice? Yes, if its clay reminds us of our own.
Accepting Nobel Prize *NY Times* 11 Dec 90

Ezra Pound

9222 How did it go in the madhouse? Rather badly. But what other place could one live in America?
On release after 13 years in St Elizabeth's Hospital, Washington DC, recalled on Pound's death 1 Nov 72

9223 [I am writing a] cryselephantine poem of immeasurable length which will occupy me for the next four decades unless it becomes a bore.
On "Cantos" which lay unfinished on his death *ib*

9224 Great literature is simply language charged with meaning to the utmost possible degree.
How to Read Harmsworth, London 1931 *ib*

9225 Music begins to atrophy when it departs too far from the dance;. . . poetry begins to atrophy when it gets too far from music.
ABC of Reading 1934 *ib*

9226 All America is an insane asylum.
On returning to Italy, quoted by Penelope Niven *Carl Sandburg* Scribner 91 *ib*

Pierre Reverdy

9227 Poetry has always been, and will always remain, the noblest outlet for a pained conscience facing a reality that is always hostile to man's divine dream of fullness, happiness, and freedom.
Le Gant de Crin quoted by Axel Madsen *Chanel* Holt 90

Carl Sandburg

9228 There is a formal poetry perfect only in form. . . . the number of syllables, the designated and required stresses of accent, the rhymes if wanted—they come off with the skill of a solved crossword puzzle.
"Notes for a Preface" *The Complete Poems of Carl Sandburg* Harcourt Brace Jovanovich 86

9229 The more rhyme there is in poetry the more danger of its tricking the writer into something other than the urge in the beginning.
ib

9230 In the spacious highways of books major or minor, each poet is allowed the stride that will get him where he wants to go if, God help him, he can hit that stride and keep it.
ib

9231 I am still studying verbs and the mystery of how they connect nouns. I am more suspicious of adjectives than at any other time in all my born days.
On receiving nearly a dozen honorary doctorates for biography of Lincoln *ib*

9232 Still traveling, still a seeker. I should like to think that as I go on writing there will be sentences truly alive, with verbs quivering, with nouns giving color and echoes.
On beginning at age 65 a novel that was to take him five years to complete *ib*

9233 [I am driven by the] ache to utter and see in word/The silhouette of a brooding soul.
"In Reckless Ecstasy" 1904 quoted by Penelope Niven *Carl Sandburg* Scribner 91

9234 Poetry is written out of tumults and paradoxes, terrible reckless struggle and glorious lazy loafing, out of blood, work and war and out of baseball, babies and potato blossoms.
ib

9235 [It is] a ballad pamphlet harangue sonata and fugue. . . an almanac, a scroll, a palimpsest, the last will and testament of Mr John Public, John Doe, Richard Roe, and the autobiography of whoever it was the alfalfaland governor meant in saying, "The common people will do anything you say except stay hitched."
On "The People, Yes" *ib*

George Santayana philosopher

9236 Pure poetry is pure experiment. . . memorable nonsense.
Helen Gardner ed *The New Oxford Book of English Verse* Oxford 91

May Sarton

9237 [Quietly I waited for the moment to come] when the world falls away, and the self emerges again from the deep unconscious, bringing back all I have recently experienced to be explored and slowly understood when I can converse again with my own hidden powers, and so grow, and so be renewed, till death to us part.
On the solitary life *NY Times* 18 Jul 95

Edith Sitwell

9238 The lust of the era I manage beautifully.
On writing on the 15th century *Time* 1 Dec 52

9239 The poet speaks to all men of that other life of theirs that they have smothered and forgotten.
Recalled on Sitwell's death 9 Dec 64

9240 Sometimes I see a giant lion-paw on my window sill, and my three Visitors still come—Her with the one tooth. . . . Her with the one eye, looking into the bleak future. . . . Her with the one ear, still waiting for some message from the Beyond.

On "the three Norms" described in her autobiography *Taken Care Of* Atheneum 65

9241 Soon. . . all will be over, bar the shouting and the worms.

ib

9242 She had not the look of one who has many acquaintances—not more, perhaps, than a few leafless flowering boughs and blackthorn boughs, and the early and remote flakes of the snow.

Self-description quoted by Victoria Glendinning *A Unicorn Among Lions* Weidenfeld & Nicolson 81

9243 Her only neighbor was the silence, and her voice had more the sound of a wood-wind instrument than a human voice. She was plain and knew it.

ib

9244 Accordant and discordant, youth and age,/ And death and birth./ For out of one comes all—/ From all comes one.

Last lines of Sitwell's poem *The Wind of Early Spring*, chosen as inscription on her gravestone *ib*

Jan Skacel

9245 Poets don't invent poems./ The poem is somewhere behind./ It's been there for a long time./ The poet merely discovers it.

Quoted by Eamonn McCabe *Guardian Weekly* 16 Dec 90

Stephen Spender

9246 [She] transforms everything into pure, hard edges.

On Edith Sitwell *World Within World* Harcourt, Brace 51

9247 Poems survive because people fall in love with them. They live because phrases, imagery, music, echoes, the idea of all the poems coalescing into a world single with the poet, hang about our hearts, become part of our lives.

London Observer 13 Dec 64

9248 [They are] that special band, the crew of voyagers, who have lived through so much.

On chronicling his "Old Gang"—the late W H Auden, C Day-Lewis, and Christopher Isherwood *Journals 1930–83* Random House 86

9249 He's still half with us/ Conniving slyly, yet he knows he's gone/ Into that cellar where they'll never find him,/ Happy to be alone, his last work done,/ Word freed from world, into a different wood.

On W H Auden "Auden's Funeral" *Collected Poems 1928–1985* Random House 86

9250 I have always wanted immortality since I was about 15. My bottom line has always been that if you wrote one poem that was still being read in a hundred years, that was really enough.

At age 85 *London Times* 24 Feb 94

9251 Poets are faced. . . with the problem of transforming into the comprehensive terms of the imagination the chaos of this politically obsessed world.

NY Times 18 Jul 95

Wallace Stevens

9252 The poet is the priest of the invisible.

Recalled on Stevens' death 2 Aug 55

9253 Poetry is a rich, full-blooded whistle, cracked ice crunching in pails, the night that numbers the leaf, the duet of two nightingales, the sweet pea, that has run wild, Creation's tears in shoulder blades.

Life 13 Jun 60

9254 Poetry is the supreme fiction, madame.

"A High-toned Old Christian Woman" in Helen Gardner ed *The New Oxford Book of English Verse* Oxford 91

Mark Strand US Poet Laureate

9255 My poems are less dark, fuller, longer, and they're not ashamed of being pretty.

On publication of *The Continuous Life* Knopf 90 that coincided with Strand's appointment as Poet Laureate *Washington Times* 19 Sep 90

Dylan Thomas

9256 Poetry. . . statements made on my way to the cemetery.

NY Times 17 Feb 52

9257 I had fallen in love with words. What mattered was the sound of them as I heard them for the first time on the lips of the remote and incomprehensible grown-ups who seemed, for some reason, to be living in my world.

Texas Quarterly Winter 61

9258 Words were, to me, as the notes of bells, the sounds of musical instruments, the noises of the wind, sea and rain, the rattle of milkcarts, the clopping of hooves on copples, the fingering of branches on a window pane might be to someone, deaf from birth, who had miraculously found his hearing.

ib

9259 I cared for the shapes of sound. . . made in my ears. . . in the colors of words cast on my eyes.

ib

Lionel Trilling

9260 The poet. . . may be used as a barometer, but let us not forget that he is also part of the weather.

The Liberal Imagination Viking 50

John Wain

9261 Poetry is to prose as walking is to dancing.
BBC interview 13 Jan 76

Derek Walcott

9262 The English language is nobody's special property. It is the property of the imagination.
Newsweek 19 Oct 92

9263 I'm just a red nigger who loves the sea,/ I had a sound colonial education, I have Dutch, nigger, and English in me,/ and either I'm nobody or I'm a nation.
"The Schooner Flight" regarded as Walcott's "personal identity card" *ib*

9264 Poetry. . . is perfection's sweat but most seen as fresh as the raindrops on a statue's brow.
NY Times 8 Dec 92

9265 The process of poetry is one of excavation and of self-discovery. The fate of poetry is to fall in love with the world, in spite of History.
ib

Alice Walker

9266 If there's the slightest little bubble coming up, I try to go with the bubble until it gets to the top of the water and then try to be there for it, so that I can being to understand what is happening down in the depths.
US News & World Report 3 Jun 91

Robert Penn Warren

9267 The poem is not a thing we see; it is, rather, a light by which we may see—and what we see is life.
On becoming the first US poet laureate 26 Feb 86

John Hall Wheelock

9268 It's almost two societies, the living and the dead, and you live with them both.
To National Institute of Arts and Letters *NY Times* 9 Apr 76

William Carlos Williams

9269 It isn't what he says that counts as a work of art, it's what he makes with such intensity of perception that it lives with an intrinsic movement of its very own to verify the authenticity.
On the work of a poet *The Later Collected Poems of William Carlos Williams* Random House 50

9270 It is difficult/ to get the new from poems/ yet men die miserably every day/ for lack/ of what is found there.
"Asphodel, That Greeny Flower" Christopher MacGowan ed *The Collected Poems of William Carlos Williams* Vol II, New Directions 88, also quoted by Susan Stamberg *Talk* Random House 93

Yevgeny Yevtushenko

9271 If you read the history of Russia, you will find that all the political/ social moments which changed our history began in poetry.
Christian Science Monitor 15 May 87

9272 Poetry was a kind of spiritual newspaper of the people.
On Soviet Russia *ib* 8 Mar 91

9273 I am longing for censorship—because nobody better than censors understood all the subtle nuances of poetry. Nobody appreciated us so highly.
ib

Critics

Dean Acheson US Secretary of State

9274 Gently, wisely. . . justly. . . but not the way to write biography!
On G M Young's *Stanley Baldwin* Hart-Davis 52, David S McClellan and David C Acheson eds *Among Friends* 80

Peter Ackroyd critic

9275 A triptych in which the presiding deities are Mother, England and Me.
On Noel Coward's memoirs London *Times* 1 May 86

Alison Adburgham critic

9276 The intimation of incest emerges from the imperceptible to the barely perceptible to the blindingly perceived.
On Gladys Parrish's *Madame Solario* Penguin 84 London *Times* 31 Dec 84

Henry Allen humorist

9277 Kahlil Gibran. . . died 60 years ago after writing the poetry that was read at everybody's first wedding.
Washington Post 25 May 91

Martin Amis essayist

9278 He. . . was obliged to wander the biological desert of middle-aged gaydom.
On Andy Warhol's diaries *NY Times* 25 Jun 89

Noel Annan Provost, King's College, Cambridge

9279 The sneer. . . he used like an oyster-knife, inserting it into the shell of his victim, exposing him with a quick-turn of the wrist, and finally flipping him over and inviting his audience to discard him as tainted and inedible.

On the critic F R Leavis *English Intellectuals Between the World Wars* Random House 91

Anon

9280 Little Christopher Isherwood, neat features, well brushed hair, the smile of a dirty-minded cherub.

London Observer 26 Feb 84

9281 I don't know if Mr Kissinger is a great writer, but anyone finishing this book is a great reader.

Book reviewer quoted by former US Secretary of State Henry Kissinger on publication of his 900-page *Diplomacy Washington Post* 11 Apr 94

Walter Arnold critic

9282 The supreme irony of this supreme ironist.

Wall Street Journal 3 Dec 84 on T S Eliot's life as seen in Peter Ackroyd's *T S Eliot* Simon & Schuster 84

Clive Aslet essayist

9283 Biography is now more or less a branch of psychiatry.

Country Life 10 Nov 94 on Jonathan Dimbleby's *The Prince of Wales* Little, Brown 94

9284 We expect the ticking movement of the human timepiece to be revealed.

ib

James Atlas critic

9285 A penumbra of somber dignity has descended over his reputation.

On Edmund Wilson *NY Times* 28 Jul 85 reviewing David Castronovo's *Edmund Wilson* Ungar 84

9286 To read Wilson. . . is to be instructed and amused in the highest sense—that is, be educated.

ib

9287 An account of some of these acts [makes] Henry Miller's crudest imaginations seem as chaste as a nun's diary.

On unexpurgated letters of James Joyce "Putting One Letter after Another" *ib* 15 Mar 87

9288 I doubt the garrulous archive bequeathed us by the tape recorder will prove as memorable as Henry James's thank-you notes.

On contemporary letter writers *ib*

W H Auden poet

9289 Some books are undeservedly forgotten; none are undeservedly remembered.

The Dyer's Hand Random House 68

Julian Barnes critic

9290 Books are where things are explained to you, life is where things aren't and I'm not surprised that some people prefer books.

ib

Bruce Barrer critic

9291 A five-year marrige to Ernest Hemingway roughly coincided with and bore more than a passing resemblance to World War II.

On Martha Gelhorn *Wall Street Journal* 9 Mar 93 reviewing *The Novellas of Martha Gelhorn* Knopf 93

Daniel Barshay critic

9292 He was John the Baptist to Lincoln's Christ.

On Walt Whitman, Station WETA Washington 30 May 91

Ann Beattie anthologist

9293 There are things that get whispered about that writers are there to overhear.

NY Times 1 Nov 87 on *Best American Short Stories* 1987 Houghton Mifflin 87

Reid Beddow critic

9294 Noonan. . . [has] the romanticism of a person who has read widely and deeply as a defense against life.

Washington Post 4 Feb 90 reviewing presidential speechwriter Peggy Noonan's *What I Saw at the Revolution* Random House 90

Max Beerbohm humorist

9295 He looked life straight in the face out of the corner of his eye.

On Beau Brummell, quoted by Joseph Epstein *Partial Payments* Norton 89

Hilaire Belloc essayist

9296 Just as there is nothing between the admirable omelette and the intolerable, so with autobiography.

Recalled on Belloc's death 15 Jul 53

Anatole Broyard critic

9297 A table in *Barchester Towers*. . . had more character than the combined heroes of three recent novels I've read.

Aroused by Books Random House 74 on Alvin Greenberg's *Going Nowhere* Simon & Schuster 71

Christopher Buckley novelist

9298 You won't go away hungry, but it's not quite satisfying; only a biography or autobiography gives you the hot meal.

On books on Congressman Newton L ("Newt") Gingrich *NY Times* 12 Mar 95

9299 Mr Amis is his generation's top literary dog. . . highly pedigreed, but his terrain is the junkyard of the human psyche.

On Martin Amis' novel *The Information* Harmony Books 95 *ib* 23 Apr 95

William F Buckley Jr critic

9300 These letters are a great exotic flower in modern literature.

NY Times 19 Jan 92 on Artemis Cooper ed *The Letters of Evelyn Waugh and Diana Cooper* Ticknor & Fields 92

Albert Camus novelist

9301 A novel is never anything but a philosophy put into images.

Recalled on Camus' death 4 Jan 60

Truman Capote novelist

9302 When God hands you a gift, he also hands you a whip. . . for self-flagellation.

Vogue Dec 79

9303 [You have] the morals of a baboon and the guts of a butterfly.

To critic Kenneth Tynan, quoted by Gerald Clarke *Capote* Simon & Schuster 88

Robert W Chapman essayist

9304 A quotation, like a pun, should come unsought and then be welcomed only for some propriety or felicity justifying the intrusion.

"The Art of Quotation" *Writer's Digest* May 77

9305 His ego can crack crystal at a distance of 20 feet.

On Russian poet Yevgeny Yevtushenko 18 Jun 82

William J Clinton 42nd US President

9306 Where books are preserved, studied and revered, human beings will also be treated with respect and dignity, and liberty will be strengthened.

At dedication of the University of Connecticut's Thomas J Dodd Research Center *NY Times* 16 Oct 95

Cyril Connolly humorist

9307 He could not blow his nose without moralizing on conditions in the hankerchief industry.

On George Orwell, recalled on Connolly's death 26 Nov 74

Sarah Booth Conroy columnist

9308 He has a face with some resemblance to a crumpled first draft.

On novelist Ross Thomas *Washington Post* 14 Jan 88

Basil Cottle humorist

9309 Graham Greene. . . had to be obscene to be believed.

Names Thames & Hudson 83

Robert Descharnes critic

9310 Biography is the advancing of various pieces on the chessboard of history.

Preface to Meredith Etherington-Smith's *The Persistance of Memory* Random House 92

Bernard De Voto essayist

9311 Novelists, whatever else they may be, are also children talking to children— in the dark.

The World of Fiction Houghton Mifflin 50

E L Doctorow novelist

9312 Someone. . . gets an MFA in writing, and immediately gets a job on another campus teaching other young people to get their MFA's in writing.

On the inbreeding of Masters of Fine Arts, George Plimpton ed *Writers at Work* Viking 88

David Herbert Donald Professor of American History, Harvard

9313 Their correspondence was a duet between tuba and piccolo.

On Thomas Wolfe and Aline Bernstein "Wolfe in Love" *NY Times* 11 Jan 87

Stanley Elkin novelist

9314 All books are the Book of Job. . . land-mined and unforgiving as golf greens.

"The Future of the Novel" *NY Times* 17 Feb 91

Michael Elliot essayist

9315 The very Chateau Lafite of whine.

Newsweek 5 Jun 94 recalling Betty Freidan's *The Feminine Mystique* Norton 63

Jane Emery critic

9316 Thin and neat as a furled umbrella!

Quoted by Peter Parker, *NY Times* 13 Sep 92 reviewing Emery's *Rose Macaulay* John Murray/Trafalgar Sq 92

D J Enright Professor of English, Warwick University

9317 Metaphysical lederhosen!
On German novels, quoted by Hermann Broch's *The Spell* Farrar Straus Giroux 87

9318 Clarity begins at home.
Washington Post 17 Dec 95

Joseph Epstein critic

9319 A woman bringing flowers to a church... middle-aged women running a tearoom... a vicar with an abstracted air being led by a wire-haired terrier... [all are] escapees from a Barbara Pym novel.
Partial Payments Norton 89

Peter Feibleman biographer

9320 The biggest difference between Lillian as a grown-up and Lillian as a child was that she was taller.
On novelist Lillian Hellman *Lily* Morrow 88

H L Foland Episcopal priest

9321 Something of a kook as well as a cook!
On M F L Fisher *Anglican Digest* IV Quarter 71

Roberto Friedman critic

9322 AIDS, the given subtext of any gay novel set in the 1990s.
Washington Post 3 Apr 94

Ann Geracimos critic

9323 Washington is a town where more people... contemplate writing a book than finish reading one.
Washington Times 29 Mar 89

Kaye Gibbons novelist

9324 I write about writers' lives with the fascination of one slowing down to get a good look at an automobile accident.
NY Times 7 Jan 90

Brendan Gill essayist

9325 Circumspect Boswells!
On books by Charles and Anne Morrow Lindbergh *Lindbergh Alone* Harcourt Brace Jovanovich 77

Victoria Glendinning biographer

9326 Her maiden voyage was a lonely one, and it lasted all her life.
On Edith Sitwell *A Unicorn Among Lions* Weidenfeld & Nicolson 81

Paul Gray critic

9327 His specialty is the varnished truth.
On novelist Philip Roth *Miami Herald* 14 Jun 87

Everett Groseclose critic

9328 It... makes a lovely doorstop!
Wall Street Journal 26 Nov 86 on James Clavell's *Whirlwind* Morrow 86

Donald Hall poet

9329 The sports column as Red Smith did it becomes a wildlife refuge for metaphor.
Ira Berkow ed *Red* Times Books 86

9330 I enjoyed my visit as one might enjoy walking a tightrope across the Crystal Palace.
On interviewing T S Eliot *NY Times* 14 Aug 92

Joshua Hammer critic

9331 More skeletons than a med-school anatomy class!
Newsweek 16 Sep 91 on the Anheuser-Busch beer family profiled by Peter Hernon and Terry Ganey's *Under the Influence* Simon & Schuster 91

Charles Handy business consultant

9332 Words are the bugles of social change.
Fortune 11 Feb 91

Shelby Hearon novelist

9333 They read as if they'd been recounted firsthand on the deepest porch in town.
NY Times 13 Dec 87 on Ferrol Sams' *The Widow's Mite and Other Stories* Peachtree 87

Ernest Hemingway novelist

9334 His talent was as natural as the pattern of dust on a butterfly's wings... [but] that he understood it no more than the butterfly.
On F Scott Fitzgerald *A Moveable Feast* Scribner 64

John Hersey novelist

9335 A gifted glassblower of language.
On the poet and critic I A Richards *New Yorker* 18 Jul 88

George V Higgins essayist

9336 Adults can read them to children without contracting diabetes.
On Beatrix Potter stories *NY Times* 30 Jul 90

Herbert Hoover 31st US President

9337 What this country needs is a great poem... something simple enough for a child to spout in school on Fridays.

To Christopher Morley, quoted by T H Watkins *Righteous Pilgrim* Holt 90

9338 Let me know if you find any great poems lying around.

ib

Richard Hough critic

9339 He would have been appalled. . . that his official biography ran to only a single volume.

On Louis Mountbatten, *London Times* 21 Jul 94

Margo Howard critic

9340 Man does not live by bed alone.

People 26 Mar 90 reviewing Sidney Biddle Barrows' *Mayflower Madam* Doubleday 90

Philip Howard columnist

9341 He was blocked for decades by a cabal of idiots.

On why Graham Greene never received a Nobel Prize, recalled on Greene's death 3 Apr 91

Richard Howard

9342 He may not deliberately teach but his excursions are tutelage.

On V S Pritchett as "the literature's greatest traveler" *Washington Post* 14 Jun 92

David Huddle Professor of English, University of Vermont

9343 You don't have to write all-out all the time, but you have to be ready to write all-out any time your story or your poem or your novel asks you to.

NY Times 31 Jan 88

9344 Like the cautious pitcher, the timid writer can spend a lifetime in the minor leagues.

ib

9345 Revision. . . a form of self-forgiveness.

ib

Robert Hughes critic

9346 Her pearly teeth: no stains or chips. . . which is remarkable, given that they have bitten off more than they can chew.

On Picasso biographer Arianna S Huffington *Time* 20 Jun 88

Elizabeth Janeway critic

9347 As long as mixed grills and combination salads are popular, anthologies will undoubtedly continue in favor.

Helen Hull ed *The Writer's Book* Harper 50

Margo Jefferson critic

9348 No narrator is more ruthless and full of longing than a child out to understand what his parents were like before he entered their lives.

NY Times 27 Aug 89

Alexandra Johnson critic

9349 Edith Sitwell, the Mother Goose of serious nonsense.

Christian Science Monitor 6 Oct 77

Daniel Johnson critic

9350 Tombstones of 800 pages. . . the staple of our intelligentsia.

On "the British vice of biography" *London Times* 2 Sep 95

William Jovanovich President, Harcourt Brace World

9351 The most important single thing in publishing is the English sentence, and the editor who cannot contemplate it again and again with a sense of wonder has not yet gained respect for the complexity of learning.

Now, Barabbas Harper & Row 64

Nora Joyce novelist's wife

9352 Well, Jim, I haven't read any of your books but they must be good considering how well they sell.

To her husband James Joyce, recalled on Joyce's death 12 Apr 51

Louis Kahn architect

9353 No one ever really paid the price of a book, only the price of printing it.

NY Times 23 Oct 72

Justin Kaplan anthologist

9354 [The essay] has been. . . squeezed to a shadow by the adjoining landmasses of the Article and the Review, not to mention its own dwarf love child, the Column.

Introduction *The Best American Essays 1990* Ticknor & Fields 90

John F Kennedy 35th US President

9355 The highest duty of the writer, the composer, the artist is to remain true to himself. . . . [for] in serving his vision of the truth, the artist best serves his nation

At dedication of Amherst College Robert Frost Library 25 Oct 63

9356 When power leads man towards arrogance, poetry reminds him of his limitations.

A portion of the address later believed to have inspired Sen J William Fulbright's 1966 reference to leadership's inclination to war as an "arrogance of power" *ib*

9357 When power narrows the area of man's concern, poetry reminds him of the richness and diversity of existence. When power corrupts, poetry cleanses.
ib

James J Kilpatrick essayist

9358 A whore may be naked, but a mistress is nude. We are talking class.
NY Times 12 Dec 93

Roger Kimball critic

9359 His subjects... bubble to life under the delicate inquisition of his pen.
On Brendan Gill *Wall Street Journal* 22 Oct 90

Stephen King novelist

9360 He is the Jane Austen of the political espionage story.
On Ross Thomas *NY Times* 19 Dec 95

Christopher Lehmann-Haupt critic

9361 Smothered in its crib with a patchwork quilt of cliches.
NY Times 5 Jan 89 on Loup Durand's *Daddy* Viking 88

9362 [He] seems happiest when he is trying to sculpture fog.
29 May 89 On Robert C Christopher's *Crashing the Gates* Simon & Schuster 89

9363 The only trouble with this book is that its covers are too close together.
9 Apr 92 On Florence King's *With Charity Toward None* St Martin 92

9364 This isn't bad; it's awful!
29 Jul 93 On Joe McGinniss biography of Sen Edward M Kennedy *The Last Brother* Simon & Schuster 93

Joseph Lelyveld critic

9365 His laughter... sparkled like a splash of water in sunlight.
On V S Pritchett at age 85 *NY Times* 16 Dec 85

John Leonard critic

9366 Good man, dull book... [from] an airless room on some other planet.
On James B Conant's autobiography *My Several Lives* Harper & Row 70 *NY Times* 4 Mar 70

9367 Cold obsessions, mixed... in a bowl, beat too lightly and baked too long.
On Gore Vidal's *Two Sisters* Little Brown 70 7 Jul 70

9368 Too many ironies in the fire.
ib

9369 Books fall from Garry Wills like leaves from a maple tree in a sort of permanent October.
15 Jul 79

9370 Flocks of multicolored anecdotes rise into the air on flapping wings, and, occasonally, a bee stings.
On Leonard and Mark Silk's *The American Establishment* Basic Books, 80 15 Sep 80

9371 A lollipop speaking baby talk.
On Suzanne Massie's *Land of the Firebird* Simon & Schuster 80, 8 Oct 80

9372 How's a reviewer to choose? Charm... fans... a hot topic, and a telephone call from a publisher who hasn't lied to you recently.
"Novel Ways to Get a Book Reviewed" 11 Nov 80

9373 The Chekhov of the suburbs.
On John Cheever *The Annual Obituary 1982* St Martin 83

9374 Bisexual bedroom behavior that would scandalize an Australian rabbit!
On *Primary Colors* by Anonymous, later identified as Joe Klein of *Newsweek*, purportedly on the 1992 Clinton presidential campaign *Sunday Morning* CBS TV 11 Feb 96

Bernard Levin columnist

9375 Mrs Barry... not only did the housekeeping... she did the eavesdropping as well.
On Wendy Barry's *The Housekeeper's Diary on the Prince of Wales, London Times* 8 Aug 95

Life magazine

9376 It... allows God to drop in for dinner and a skeptical old lady to laugh at him.
On Genesis' account of the elderly Sarah learning that she will give birth to a son 25 Dec 64

Wendy Lesser critic

9377 The English autobiographer... intimate and discreet... speaks to someone exactly like himself, who doesn't need to be told all the details.
NY Times 27 Nov 88

Eric Linklater biographer

9378 Wanting to know an author because you like his books is like wanting to know a goose because you like pate.
Washington Post 27 Nov 94

David Lodge novelist

9379 Literature is mostly about having sex and not much about having children; life is the other way around.
The British Museum is Falling Down Penguin 89

London Times

9380 Puddle-duck. . . insists on hatching her own eggs. . . a classic English non-conformist.

"Rabbit, Run On" editorial on centennial of a Beatrix Potter letter that transformed children's fiction 4 Sep 93

9381 A hundred years on, Peter Rabbit is still gently leading the very young from enchantment to reality.

ib

9382 The whirligig of literary fashion is reviving the reputation of. . . a chronic invalid who loved adventurous travel.

"Man of Two Worlds" editorial on Robert Louis Stevenson's centenary 3 Dec 94

William Manchester biographer

9383 By noon the cadences of his prose have begun to trot; by 1 pm they are galloping.

On Winston S Churchill dictating a manuscript *The Last Lion* Little, Brown 88

Alberto Manguel anthologist

9384 Because reading is a lonely vice, we frequently bring others into our reading, nudge them to listen, to share our delight or disgust, judge our selection.

On anthologies *NY Times* 23 Aug 87

9385 Old favorites are often sacred cows grown tough with age. . . [but] an anthologist lets himself be drawn. . . by a feeling of debt to the future.

ib

Janet Maslin critic

9386 The author's. . . role [is] social director aboard a lifeboat.

On Gail Sheehy, *NY Times* 18 Jul 95 reviewing Sheehy's *New Passages* Random House 95

David McCord critic

9387 These essays move as a quiet but observant Coast Guard cutter among the rocks and islands up and down the littoral of our life.

NY Times 27 Oct 68 on J B Priestley's *Essays of Five Decades* Little, Brown 68

Jane Mendelsohn *Village Voice* columnist

9388 Filled with dead writers laid out in their Sunday best.

Guardian Weekly 28 Mar 93 on Joyce Carol Oates ed *The Oxford Book of American Short Stories* Oxford 93

Suzy Menkes critic

9389 Lined with hard facts. . . stitched up with strong opinions.

London Times 11 Dec 84 on Colin McDowell's *Directory of 20th-Century Fashion* F Muller, London 84

Scott Meredith literary agent

9390 Most are more concerned about bringing in the bacon than in trying to rewrite the bacon.

On editors as father-confessors *LA Herald-Examiner* 27 Jan 81

Lorrie Moore novelist

9391 Literature. . . is lonely and waited for, brilliant and pure and frightened, a marriage of birds, a conversation of the blind.

NY Times 10 Jul 88 on Scott Donaldson's *John Cheever* Random House 88

9392 When biography intrudes. . . between reader and author, it may do so in the smallest of vehicles—photographs, book jacket copy, rumors—parked quietly outside.

ib

Marianne Moore poet

9393 To cite passages is to pull one quill from a porcupine.

On Ezra Pound, Patricia C Willis ed *The Complete Prose of Marianne Moore* Viking 86

Edmund Morris biographer

9394 Biography appeals to the child in all of us—that craving for "and then, and then."

NY Times 6 Nov 88

Andrew Motion biographer

9395 It suited him to receive the highest accolades by the lowest means. . . in keeping with the spirit of his poems.

On the postman's delivery of the Queen's Gold Medal for Poetry *Philip Larkin* Farrar Straus Giroux 93

Vladimir Nabokov novelist

9396 I read him for the first time in the early 40's, something about bells, balls, and bulls, and loathed it.

On Ernest Hemingway, recalled on Nabokov's death 7 Jul 77

9397 In pornographic novels, action has to be limited to the copulation of cliches.

NY Times 23 Feb 96

Howard Nemerov novelist

9398 People read novellas but they tend to live in novels.

A Howard Nemerov Reader University of Missouri Press 91

Newsweek magazine

9399 A rememberance of flings past.
14 Sep 64 on John Gunther's *The Lost City* Harper & Row 64

9400 Today's mud is served on fancy china at the Four Seasons.
On Kitty Kelley's biography of Nancy Reagan 22 Apr 91

Jack Newfield critic

9401 Koch has committed egocide with this book.
People 9 Apr 84 on Edward Koch's *Mayor* Simon & Schuster 84

The New York Times

9402 A New Yorker looks to Neil Simon for cheering up, Sigmund Freud for shocks…and Sir Thomas More for Utopia.
"New Yorkers by the Book" editorial mentioning volumes most frequently stolen from NY Public Library 4 Oct 86

9403 A Life of Malice Practiced on Principle .
Headline 15 Mar 88 for John Gross's review of Carol Felsenthal's biography *Alice Roosevelt Longworth* Putnam 88

9404 The Twains shall meet.
Editorial on discovery of second half of Mark Twain's manuscript of *Huckleberry Finn* 27 Feb 91

9405 Calling M F K Fisher. . . a food writer is like calling Mozart a tunesmith.
"The Gastronomical She" editorial 28 Feb 91

Lyubomir Nikolov Bulgarian writer

9406 They always arrive en masse: like a litter of porcupines, the soft underbellies and crackling needles, impaled on which tremble apples of what they know.
"The Poets Come to Iowa" Paul Engle, Rowena Torrevillas and Hualing Nieh Engle eds *The World Comes to Iowa* Iowa State University 87

9407 They slump on the green chairs, their backs hunched like the sagging spines of books that hold the unwritten poems of the world.
ib

Richard M Nixon 37th US President

9408 An English professor persuaded me to spend one of my summer vacations reading the works of Tolstoy. . . the best advice I had ever received.
US News & World Report 14 Apr 86

George Orwell essayist

9409 Good prose is like a window pane.
NY Times 27 Nov 88

9410 Autobiography is only to be trusted when it reveals something disgraceful.
Quoted by Michael Shelden *Orwell* HarperCollins 91

Grace Paley critic

9411 When people are talking about what they love and what they fear, everybody's eloquent.
New York 21 Aug 89

Jay Parini critic

9412 The macho heroes of his eight novels. . . are all out of the same denim.
NY Times 13 Sep 92

Dorothy Parker humorist

9413 The romance between Margot Asquith and Margot Asquith will live as one of the great love affairs of literature.
Quoted by Scott Meredith *George S Kaufman and His Friends* Doubleday 74

9414 [It] caused as much stir in literary circles as an incompleted dogfight on upper Riverside Drive.
On Ernest Hemingway's first collection of short stories, quoted by Marion Meade *Dorothy Parker* Villard 88

9415 As American as a sawed-off shotgun.
On Dashiell Hammett *ib*

Daniel Pennac French author

9416 The Reader's Bill of Rights: The right to not read, to skip pages, to not finish, to reread, to read anything, to escapism, to read anywhere, to browse, to read out loud, to not defend your tastes.
"The Reader's Bill of Rights" *Publisher's Weekly* 12 Sep 94

David Plout critic

9417 Deathbed utterances, like suicide notes, are a powerful coinage, stamped by an awareness that words can outlive us.
Wall Street Journal 26 Sep 90

Charles Poore critic

9418 The blaring modern city. . . looks, we gather, slightly like a used chariot dump in the suburbs of hell.
On a novel set in Oxford, *NY Times* 2 Nov 57

Katherine Anne Porter novelist

9419 Oh, poor Pearl Buck! No more bounce than a boiled potato!
On novelist Pearl S Buck, quoted by Glenway Westcott, Robert Phelps with Jerry Rosco eds *Continual Lessons* Farrar Straus Giroux 90

Peter S Prescott critic

9420 Restraint is what hits the remainder table.
Newsweek 26 Jun 89 on Norman Sherry's *The Life of Graham Greene* Viking 89

V S Pritchett essayist

9421 Comedy demands. . . a scholarly regard for the beauty of your malice.
New Statesman 15 Apr 66

9422 All writers—all people—have their store of private and family legends which lies like a collection of half-forgotten, often violent toys on the floor of memory.
New Yorker 19 Feb 79

9423 We grow tired of seeing our experience choked by the vegetation in our sentences.
Lasting Impressions Random House 91

9424 The Russian novelists of the 19th century owe everything to their response to the man or woman sitting alone in his room, to the isolation, inertia, the off-beat in human character.
Complete Collected Essays Random House 92

Joe Queenan journalist

9425 Mr Kurtz's heart is probably in the right place. It's just that his brain sometimes goes AWOL.
On Howard Kurtz's *Media Circus* Times Books 93 *Wall Street Journal* 6 May 93

Anna Quindlen columnist

9426 The murder of Dick and Jane. . . was a mercy killing of the highest order.
On pedestrian kindergarten stories replaced by Dr Seuss *NY Times* 28 Sep 91

9427 *Yertle the Turtle* is perhaps the most succint description of a bloodless coup in literature.
ib

9428 *The Cat in the Hat* is about all hell breaking loose with only a small fish to act as superego. The cat, of course, is pure id.
ib

Frank Rich columnist

9429 One of the dullest memoirs ever to lay waste to a forest.
On *Barbara Bush: A Memoir* Scribner 94 *NY Times* 15 Sep 94

Carol B Rinzler critic

9430 [She] has done for menopause what Philip Roth did for masturbation.
Comparing Barbara Raskin's *Hot Flashes* St Martin 87 to *Portnoy's Complaint* Random House 69, *People* 14 Dec 87

Marilynne Robinson novelist

9431 [These stories assume] for their characters a past of such density that it stands on the temporal landscape as stolidly as an empty house—promising comfort, needing care, full of habit and purpose somehow interrupted and abandoned.
On John Updike's *Trust Me* Knopf 87 NY Times 26 Apr 87

9432 It is trust that knits up the world in these stories, a stuff peculiarly liable to fraying and raveling.
ib

9433 In terms of divine attention, surely any sparrow fighting a down draft enjoys a priority over the dance of social spheres in the elderly towns of Massachusetts.
On Updike's interest in social climbing in New England *ib*

William Safire columnist

9434 [It] is a prime example of the new biography, a genre that exploded its tiny time pills of anecdote on each page to reflag the reader's interest.
NY Times 6 Sept 87 on *Man of the House* by House Speaker Tip O'Neill with William Novak Random House 87

Josyane Savigneau critic

9435 The vial of vitriol is never very far from the teapot.
Marguerite Yourcenar University of Chicago 93

Arthur M Schlesinger Jr historian

9436 He read partly for. . . the sheer joy of felicitous statement. He delighted particularly in quotations which distilled the essence of an argument.
On John F Kennedy *A Thousand Days* Houghton Mifflin 65

9437 He is, so far as I know, the only politician who ever quoted Madame de Stael on *Meet the Press.*
ib

Joe Sexton reporter

9438 The poets of Brooklyn. . . . sing the body electric, and write about paying the Con Ed bill.
On the subway, dynamos, steel, and granite as favorite subjects *NY Times* 16 Apr 95

R Z Sheppard critic

9439 Interviewees. . . have noms de casette.
Time 31 Jul 89 on sociological study entitled *Bird KS* Knopf 89

John Simon anthologist

9440 In the house of modern fiction, he is the atrium.
On essayist Italo Svevo *The Sheep from the Goats* Weidenfeld & Nicolson 89

Julia Llewellyn Smith critic

9441 Royal biographies were pastel-tined hagiographies. . . [but] Diana by contrast, looked like a portrait by Edward Munch.

London Times 21 Dec 93 on Andrew Morton's *Diana: Her Story* Simon & Schuster 92

Raymond Sokolov critic

9442 His growing sense of the short time left to him was like a muffled tattoo in the background.

On A J Liebling's last articles *Wayward Reporter* Harper & Row 80

Andrew Solomon humorist

9443 Being here is like being received at Elisnore the morning you finish Hamlet.

On polishing off Gore Vidal's *Palimpsest* Random House 95 shortly before a visit to Vidal's villa at Revello *NY Times* 15 Oct 95

9444 His epigrammatic discourse—bred in equal measure of imagination, affectation and brilliance—is delivered in a voice as rich and smooth and alcoholic as Zabaglione.

ib

Ronald Steel biographer

9445 Daisy Suckley. . . makes Henry James's novels seem wildly pornographic.

Civilization Mar 95 on the diary and letters of a "prim and dowdy lady of a genteel family of eroding means," a cousin of Franklin D Roosevelt, Geoffrey C Ward ed *Closest Companion* Houghton Mifflin 95

9446 She adored him, he adored being adored.

ib

John Steinbeck novelist

9447 A good writer always works at the impossible.

Recalled on Steinbeck's death 20 Dec 68

Frances Steloff bookseller

9448 Wise men fish here!

Sign at Steloff's Gotham Book Mart, quoted on her hundredth birthday, *NY Times* 30 Dec 87

Rod Serling actor

9449 Every writer is a frustrated actor who recites his lines in the hidden auditorium of his skull.

Vogue 1 April 57

Jean Strouse biographer

9450 She believed in facts the way some people believe in God.

On Mary McCarthy's autobiographical fiction, *NY Times* 24 May 92

A J P Taylor historian

9451 Power over words leads easily to a longing for power over men.

On the Russian Communist leader Leon Trotsky *From the Boer War to the Cold War* Penguin 95

Paul Theroux critic

9452 He was much more famous for not having won it. . . a magnificent annual failure, as the committee overlooked him year after year.

On Graham Greene's and the Nobel Prize *NY Times* 21 Apr 91

James Thurber humorist

9453 Long untrimmed essays grew up in the window boxes of his prose.

On Thomas Wolfe, Michael Rosen ed *James Thurber Collecting Himself* Hamish Hamilton 89

Alice B Toklas Gertrude Stein's companion

9454 You cannot tell what a picture really is or what an object really is until you dust it every day and you cannot tell what a book is until you type or proofread it. It then does something to you that only reading can never do.

Quoted by Diane Souhami *Gertrude and Alice* HarperCollins 91

Ivan Tolstoy critic

9455 Bringing out the details of the world is the highest happiness of the artist.

On Vladimir Nabokov *NY Times* 28 Feb 91

Calvin Trillin critic

9456 [They have] a shelf life somewhere between butter and yogurt.

On a plethora of new book titles *NY Times* 14 Jun 87

Anthony Tucker critic

9457 The little things and the great mingle, and somehow explain each other. That is what biographies are about.

On Mary S Lovell's *The Sound of Wings* Hutchinson 89 *Guardian Weekly* 29 Oct 89

John Updike novelist

9458 One of the last. . . of the great narrating English virgins.

Hugging the Shore Knopf 83 Citing a protagonist in Barbara Pym's *Excellent Women* Dutton 78

9459 A grateful, exuberant diner at life's feast.
On Edmund Wilson *New Yorker* 29 Nov 93

US News & World Report

9460 The face of American literature has freckles.
On the influence of Twain's *Huckleberry Finn* 22 Apr 91

Carl Van Doren biographer

9461 [He was] America telling stories.
On Sinclair Lewis, quoted by Harry E Maule and Melville H Cane *The Man from Main Street* Random House 53

Mark Van Doren poet

9462 [Dreiser] lacked everything but genius.
Quoted by Richard Lingeman *Theodore Dreiser* Putnam 90

Gore Vidal novelist

9463 American men do not read novels because they feel guilty when they read books which do not have facts in them.
Saturday Review 18 Jun 84

9464 Without question, the greatest jewel, the greatest zircon in the diadem of American literature.
On the death of Truman Capote *Palimpsest* Random House 95

Evelyn Waugh essayist

9465 Literature is simply the appropriate use of language.
Recalled on Waugh's death 10 Apr 66

Anthony Weller essayist

9466 They often seem less planned than vividly dreamt.
On Ian Fleming's James Bond novels *Forbes FYI* Nov 93

9467 He is almost always either the first real man in their lives or, unfortunately for them, the last.
On James Bond and his leading ladies *ib*

Rebecca West novelist

9468 *War and Peace* is a stodgy pudding of events mixed by a loveless, zestless boring egotist who wanted to write a big big book.
Civilization Nov-Dec 94

Donald E Westlake novelist

9469 The verbal equivalent of the pacing of a caged animal, interminably, tirelessly, between the bars on this side and the bars on that side.
NY Times 3 Jul 94 on Chief of Staff H L Haldeman's journal on the Nixon White House *Haldeman's Diaries* Putnam 94

E B White essayist

9470 Walden is the only book I own, although there are some others unclaimed on my shelves.
On *Walden* by Henry David Thoreau *New Yorker* 23 May 53

9471 Every man, I think, reads one book in his life, and this one is mine.
ib

9472 A sentence should contain no unnecessary words... for the same reason that a drawing should have no unnecessary lines and a machine no unnecessary part.
Elements of Style Macmillan 3rd edition 77

9473 Don't write about man. Write about a man.
Recalled on White's death 1 Oct 85

9474 The world likes humor, but treats it patronizingly; decorates its serious artists with laurel, and its wags with Brussels sprouts.
Quoted by Neil A Grauer *Remember Laughter* University of Nebraska Press 94

9475 If you ever got good, you'd be mediocre.
Advising James Thurber not to meddle with Thurber's writing style *ib*

Calder Willingham novelist

9476 Norman Mailer is a clown with the bite of a ferret.
Recalled on Willingham's death *London Times* 22 Feb 95

James Wolcott critic

9477 Ayn Rand took her last name from a famous make of typewriter, an apt choice for someone who herself became a word machine, a sacred monster of super, staccato output.
Vanity Fair Jun 89 on Nathaniel Branden's biography of Ayn Rand *Judgement Day* Houghton Mifflin 89

9478 Money for her was not a dirty pile of dead presidents but the shining sky-high symbol of man's unshackled mind.
ib

Geoffrey Wolff critic

9479 He folds sentences inside sentences... you start to get irritated; he pushes one inch further and you love it.
On novelist Stanley Elkin *NY Times* 3 Mar 91

James Wood critic

9480 Knighted, medalled, canonized, he is entitled ... to carry his 90 years with a swagger.
On V S Pritchett *Guardian Weekly* 4 Mar 90

9481 A high-priest of literature: instead, delightfully, he has the modesty of a low church curate whose parish is the world.

ib

Jonathan Yardley critic

9482 Vast seas of assembly-line prose.

Washington Post 24 Oct 93 on John Connally with Mickey Herskowitz *In History's Shadow* Hyperion 94

William Zinsser Editor-in-Chief Book-of-the-Month Club

9483 I always urge people to write in the first person. Writing is an act of ego and you might as well admit it.

On Writing Well Harper & Row 76

Maurice Zolotow critic

9484 In every life there is a week that requires 50 pages, and years that can be compressed into a few paragraphs.

NY Times 19 Oct 69

MUSIC AND DANCE

Artists and Entertainers

Roy Acuff country music star

9485 I reared back and sang it. . . like I was going for the cows in Union County.

On his 1953 Grand Ole Opry debut, recalled on Acuff's death 23 Nov 92

Marian Anderson African American contralto

9486 No matter how big a nation is, it is no stronger than its weakest people, and as long as you keep a person down, some part of you has to be down there to hold him down, so it means you cannot soar as you might otherwise.

Paraphrasing a statement on racial prejudice by Booker T Washington CBS TV 30 Dec 57

9487 Sometimes, it's like a hair across your cheek. You can't see it, you can't find it with your fingers, but you keep brushing at it because the feel of it is irritating.

Ladies Home Journal Sep 60

9488 I forgave the DAR many years ago. You lose a lot of time hating people.

Announcing her retirement nearly 25 years after the Daughters of the American Revolution had denied her use of Constitution Hall and she had sung instead at the Lincoln Memorial for a crowd of 75,000 *NY Times* 13 Dec 63

Louis Armstrong jazz trumpeter

9489 All music is folk music, I ain't never heard no horse sing a song.

NY Times 7 Jul 71

Fred Astaire dancer

9490 He writes for feet.

On George Gershwin, quoted by S N Behrman *People In A Diary* Little, Brown 72

Pearl Bailey entertainer

9491 There's a period of life when we swallow a knowledge of ourselves and it becomes either good or sour inside.

Chicago Tribune 7 Jul 78

George Balanchine choreographer

9492 If they were in medicine, everyone would be poisoned.

On the inadequacy of American ballet teachers *Newsweek* 4 May 64

9493 There are no sisters-in-law in ballet.

"Balanchine's Law" holding that ballet is not capable of portraying human relationships, quoted by Bernard Taper *Balanchine* Harper & Row 83

9494 [They are] poets of gesture.

On his dancers *Life* May 84

9495 Dance is music made visible.

Sunday Morning CBS TV 23 May 93

Mikhail Baryshnikov Artistic Director, American Ballet Theater 1980—89

9496 It was killing time because he knew time was killing him.

On Rudolf Nureyev's continued dancing while suffering from AIDS *New Yorker* 8 Feb 93

9497 A young girl must open her heart and mind. . . and learn from people who have never been as good as she already is.

Time 13 Feb 95

Thomas Beecham conductor

9498 In the first movement alone, I took note of six pregnancies and four miscarriages.

On hearing Bruckner's *Seventh Symphony*, recalled on Beecham's death 8 Mar 61

9499 [It sounds like] two skeletons copulating on a galvanized tin roof.

ib

9500 A very long work, the musical equivalent of the towers of St Pancras Station—neo-Gothic, you know.

On Elgar's *A-Flat Symphony* quoted by Neville Cardus *Sir Thomas Beecham* Collins 61

9501 Too much counterpoint; what is worse, Protestant counterpoint.

Manchester Guardian 8 Mar 71

Tony Bennett singer

9502 I was a tenor praying to become a baritone.

NPR 17 Mar 90

Irving Berlin composer

9503 Talent is only a starting point in this business.

Theater Arts Feb 58

9504 I love it, the way you love a child that you've had trouble with.

On one of several compositions for *Top Hat*, *NY Times* 19 Nov 74

9505 You don't have to stop yourself; the people who have to listen to your songs tell you to stop.

At age 75, quoted by Michael Freedland *Irving Berlin* Stein & Day 74

9506 My ambition is to reach the heart of the average American. Not the highbrow nor the lowbrow but that vast intermediate crew which is the real soul of the country.

Recalled on Berlin's death 22 Sep 89

Elise Bernhardt choreographer

9507 The whole place is choreography all the time.

On planning a ballet for presentation in Grand Central Station *NY Times* 9 Oct 87

Leonard Bernstein conductor

9508 If military strength is a nation's right arm, culture is its left arm, closer to its heart.

To National Press Club *NY Times* 14 Oct 59

9509 The deep magical aspect of conducting... is the mystery of... the conductor and orchestra bound together by the tiny but powerful split second.

The Joy of Music Simon & Shuster 59

J Henry ("T-Bone") Burnett entertainer

9510 If you don't have the freedom to fail, you don't have any freedom at all.

Quoted by Bill Flanagan *Written in My Soul* Contemporary Books 86

John Cage composer

9511 If my work is accepted, I must move on to the point where it isn't.

London Times 14 Aug 92

Maria Callas soprano

9512 My voice is not like an elevator going up and down.

On being asked to choose between *Traviata* and *Lucia* or *Tosca*, quoted by Irving Kolodin *The Metropolitan Opera* Knopf 67

Pablo Casals cellist

9513 The cello is like a beautiful woman who has not grown older, but younger with time, more slender, more supple, more graceful.

Time 29 Apr 57

9514 I am perhaps the oldest musician in the world. I am an old man but in many senses a very young man. And this is what I want you to be, young, young all your life, and to say things to the world that are true.

ib 23 Oct 73

Cabell ("Cab") Calloway band leader

9515 Women, horses, cars, clothes. I did it all.... It's called living.

Minnie the Moocher and Me Crowell 76

Eddie Condon jazz artist

9516 Notes I had never heard were peeling off the edges and dropping through the middle... trumpets like warm rain on a cold day... like daylight coming down a dark hole.

On first hearing jazz *NY Times* 17 May 64

9517 The choruses rolled on like high tide, getting wilder and more wonderful.

ib

James Conlon conductor

9518 Americans prefer foreigners and foreigners prefer foreigners.

On becoming the Paris National Opera's first American-born, Julliard-trained, principal conductor *NY Times* 7 Mar 95

Juan Carlos Copes dancer and choreographer

9519 Sometimes there is confusion that the tango is the steps. No. Tango is the feeling. It is one heart and four legs!

Smithsonian Nov 93

Aaron Copland composer

9520 You compose because you want to somehow summarize in some permanent form your most basic feelings about being alive.

Bill Moyers Journal Station WNET TV New York 14 May 76

Fernando Corena basso buffo

9521 *Arrivederci! Auf Wiedersehen!*
On the farewell performance to the 83-year-old Metropolitan Opera House before moving to Lincoln Center *NY Times* 16 Apr 66

Andrew Davis Musical Director, Glyndebourne Opera

9522 The best conductors are those who can get the most out of orchestras without saying a word.
Country Life 27 Oct 94

Miles Davis trumpeter and composer

9523 If a guy makes you tap your foot and if you feel it down your back, you don't have to ask anybody if that's good music or not.
Down Beat 2 Nov 55

9524 I always listen for what I can leave out.
On defining "cool," quoted in "Miles Ahead" editorial *NY Times* 29 Sep 91

Agnes De Mille choreographer

9525 Who am I?, the artists asks. And he devotes his whole life to finding out.
Dance in America Station WNET Washington 8 May 87

9526 [Her feet were] priceless little mummies... [and she] chuckled with a tiny sound like something very valuable breaking.
On ballerina Alice Markova *Portrait Gallery* Houghton Mifflin 90

9527 Ours is an up beat, a hurried, hasty beat.
On the essence of American dance *NY Times* 8 Oct 93

9528 I want one word on my tombstone—dancer.
US News & World Report 18 Oct 93

Placido Domingo tenor

9529 You carry the load for which you have the shoulders.
On the desire to sing *Tristan*, labeled by critic Jordan Bonfante as "the greatest voice killer of all" *Time* 27 Sep 93

Bob Dylan musician

9530 How does it feel/ To be without a home,/ Like a complete unknown,/ Like a rolling stone?
Like A Rolling Stone published by M Witmark & Sons 65

9531 I'd rather live in the moment than some kind of nostalgia trip... a real drug that people are mainlining... like it was morphine. I don't want to be a drug dealer.
On his fans' hope that Dylan would sing his old songs exactly as he recorded them *Newsweek* 20 Mar 95

Mafalda Favero soprano

9532 The spirit of Toscanini... made me sing, with those two deep eyes always fixed on me... so eloquent that one had to become excellent even if one was not.
Quoted by Mario Labrocca and Virgilio Boccardi *Arte di Toscanini* Turin 66

Leonard Feather entertainer

9533 Jazz without the beat... is a telephone yanked from the wall; it just can't communicate.
Show Jan 62

Eliot Feld choreographer

9534 Music has a certain kind of insistence that gives me the courage to go into a room with people.
NY Times 30 Apr 88

Jerry Garcia guitarist

9535 To the kids today, *The Grateful Dead* represents America... being able to go out and have an adventure.
On Garcia's musicians, seen by the *NY Times* as the embodiment of "psychedelic optimism" and the *Washington Post* as "the house band of counterculture" 10 Aug 95

Glenn Gould pianist

9536 For every hour that you spend in the company of other human beings you need X number of hours alone.
Quoted by Otto Friedrich's *Glenn Gould* Random House 89

Martin Gould composer

9537 I don't think you can do acquittal choreography.
On Agnes de Mille's desire to hang Lizzie Borden at the end of Gould's composition for dancing de Mille's *Fall River Legend* *NY Times* 9 Feb 94

Martha Graham choreographer

9538 Every dance is a kind of fever chart of the heart... it makes visible the interior landscape.
Recalled on Graham's death 1 Apr 91

9539 No artist is ahead of his time. He *is* his time; it is just that others are behind the time.
ib

9540 The theater was a verb before it was a noun.
NY Times 7 Apr 91

9541 The spine is the tree of life. Respect it.
ib

9542 Sometimes it's blood memory... not the blood your mother and father gave you... but that which stretches back two or three thousand years.

Blood Memory Doubleday 91

9543 I have never destroyed anyone who didn't want to be destroyed.

USA Today 2 Apr 91

9544 In the end it all comes down to the art of breathing.

Guardian Weekly 14 Apr 91

Adolph Green lyricist

9545 [He had] self-effacingly plotted my engagement extraordinaire at Uncle Len's Heavenly Haven for healthily well-fed young Hebrews.

On a drama counselor's introduction to Leonard Bernstein, quoted by Humphrey Burton *Leonard Bernstein* Doubleday 94

9546 I felt the fresh air of 1,000,000 windows opening simultaneously... that my life had been building towards a turning point.

ib

Dick Gregory entertainer

9547 [In] the Civil War Twist... the Northern part of you stands still while the Southern part tries to secede.

The Back of the Bus Dutton 62

Woody Guthrie entertainer

9548 You can't write a good song about a whorehouse unless you been in one.

Recalled on Guthrie's death 4 Oct 67

Buddy Guy jazz musician

9549 I wore out B-flat before I knew what it was.

On self-taught technique NBC TV 12 Aug 87

Oscar Hammerstein II lyricist

9550 The hills are alive with the sound of music,/ With songs they have sung for a thousand years!/ The hills fill my heart with the sound of music,/ My heart wants to sing every song it hears!

The Sound of Music title song for musical with Richard Rodgers, Williamson Music Inc 59

9551 There's nothing wrong with sentiment because the things we're sentimental about are the fundamental things in life.

Quoted by Stanley Gross *The World of Musical Comedy* Barnes 68

Edgar Yipsel "Yip" Harburg lyricist

9552 When I'm not near the composer I love, I love the composer I'm near.

On paraphrasing his song *When I'm Not Near the Girl I Love, 60 Minutes* CBS TV 5 Mar 78

9553 Magic... only happens when the words give destination and meaning to the music and the music gives wings to the words... [and] go places you've never been before.

Quoted by Harold Meyerson and Ernie Harburg *Who Put the Rainbow in the Wizard of Oz?* University of Michigan Press 93

9554 Writing songs of places I haven't been and people I haven't seen are the most exciting.

On penciling out "April in Paris" while seated at Lindy's on Broadway *ib*

9555 Negro rhythms and Hebraic melodies... a terrific combination, a fresh chemical reaction... a new sound in American theater music.

On Harold Arlen and George Gershwin *ib*

9556 A songwriter is really a journalist of the time with music.

ib

Jascha Heifetz violinist

9557 If the Almighty himself played the violin, the credits would still read "Rubinstein, God, and Piatigorsky," in that order.

On performing with pianist Artur Rubinstein and cellist Gregory Piatigorsky *LA Times* 29 Aug 82

Robert Helpmann choreographer

9558 The trouble with nude dancing is that not everything stops when the music stops.

On Broadway musical *Oh, Calcutta!* recalled on Helpmann's death 15 Mar 83

Hanya Holm choreographer

9559 Things go and push themselves into the foreground of the mind... [and it] begins to do acrobatics.

At age 90 on a half century of choreography for modern dance and Broadway musicals *NY Times* 27 Feb 91

Bart Howard composer

9560 The song just fell out of me.

On composing "Fly Me to the Moon" that was to earn a million dollars between 1954 and 1988 *NY Times* 19 Dec 88

Edward Jablonski composer

9561 The broad, long-lined, melody came to me... as if the Lord said, "Well, here it is, now stop worrying about it."

On the score for "Somewhere Over the Rainbow" that came to him while driving on Sunset Boulevard in Hollywood, quoted by Harold Meyerson and Ernie

Harburg *Who Put the Rainbow in the Wizard of Oz?* University of Michigan Press 93

Mahalia Jackson gospel singer

9562 It started. . . in the cotton fields. . . [and] men sellin' watermelons and vegetables on a wagon drawn by a mule, hollerin' "watermellllon" with a cry in their voices.

On the start of "soul" *Time* 28 Jun 68

9563 The man on the railroad track layin' crossties—everytime they hit the hammer it was with a sad feelin', but with a beat.

ib

9564 The Baptist preacher—he the one who had the soul—he give out the meter, a long and short meter, and the old mothers of the church would reply.

ib

9565 This musical thing has been here since America been here. . . is trial and tribulation music.

ib

Harry James band leader

9566 This very thin guy. . . had been waiting tables when suddenly he climbed onto the stage. . . [and] sang only eight bars when I felt the hair on the back of my neck rising.

On Frank Sinatra at age 22 in a New Jersey road house, quoted by Kitty Kelley *My Way* Bantam 86

Gwyneth Jones soprano

9567 I felt that the roof of Vienna's *Festspielhaus* would fly away and we would see God and all his angels.

On joining Shirley Verrett, Placido Domingo and Marti Talvela in Beethoven's *Ninth Symphony* quoted by Humphrey Burton *Leonard Bernstein* Doubleday 94

Fritz Kreisler violinist

9568 Well, gentlemen, shall we all now break our violins across our knees?

On hearing Jascha Heifetz for the first time, recalled on Heifetz's death 11 Dec 87

Wanda Landowska harpsichordist

9569 The first contract with a great work of art is. . . comparable to meeting the person who is going to play an important role in our life.

Denise Restout ed *Landowska on Music* Stein & Day 64

9570 Bach during the night. . . showed me a better way of fingering a passage in the 14th Goldberg variation.

On identifying the executant artist with the creative artist, quoted by George R Marek *Toscanini* Atheneum 75

9571 You play Bach your way, I play him his way!

To another harpsichordist *ib*

Alan Jay Lerner lyricist

9572 I sit down to write a lyric, and when I get up I'm usually about three pounds lighter.

NPR interview with Susan Stamberg *Talk* Random House 93

Oscar Levant pianist and humorist

9573 We had endless dialogues. I characterized it as exchanging his ideas with him.

On composer Arnold Schoenberg *Memoirs of an Amnesiac* Putnam 65

9574 Mine was the kind of piece in which nobody knew what was going on—including the composer, the conductor and the critics. Consequently, I got pretty good notices.

A Smattering of Ignorance Doubleday, Doran 1940 recalled on Levant's death 14 Aug 72

9575 Whenever anybody turns me down they tell me how talented I am. Talent's like a baby. Wrap it up in wool and it goes to sleep.

Levantics distributed by Warner Bros Studios *ib*

Frederick Loewe composer

9576 We could feel the movement in the structure of our work, and it wasn't termites.

On working with Alan Jay Lerner on *The Day Before Spring NY Times* 15 Feb 88

Lar Lubovitch choreographer

9577 [It was] wallpaper dance. . . flat, decorative and cold.

On experimental compositions reflecting preoccupation with mathematics and musical theory *US News & World Report* 2 May 88

Natalie Makarova ballerina

9578 It's nice to make people laugh, but it's even nicer to make people cry.

On switching from ballet to the role of the Grand Duchess Tatiana in *Tovarish London Times* 28 Oct 91

9579 [In ballet] the music drives you. . . in theater, you have to hear your own music inside.

ib

Marcel Marceau mime

9580 Do not the most moving moments of our lives find us all without words?

On silence and the art of the mime *Reader's Digest* Jun 58

9581 I have designed my style pantomimes as white ink drawings on black backgrounds, so that man's destiny appears as a thread lost in an endless labyrinth.

Wall Street Journal 19 Nov 65

9582 I have tried to shed some gleams of light on the shadow of man startled by his anguish.

ib

9583 Memory comes from what you witnessed as a child, not what you witness on TV and will forget in six months.

US News & World Report 23 Feb 87

Zubin Mehta conductor

9584 Although I am flexible and ready to take advice, I can't carry an umbrella of thoughts over my head that would distract me and affect my music making.

On not reading reviews *New York* 14 Jan 85

9585 The NY Philharmonic is just like any other. . . they have the spirit of kids, and if you scratch away a little of the fatigue and cynicism, out comes a 17-year old music student again, full of wonder, exuberance and a tremendous love of music.

ib

9586 He was basically the American Mozart.

On Leonard Bernstein *People* 7 Jan 91

Gian Carlo Menotti composer

9587 The artist's work never ends, never leaves him. He never closes the office and forgets about his job until the next morning.

NY Times 10 Jun 89

9588 [The artist] eats, sleeps, travels, makes love and all the while, in the back of his mind, the demon gnaws at his brain.

ib

9589 I've never met an artist's wife who didn't complain of being second.

Opera News Jun 91

9590 I moved to Scotland for a very simple reason: I wanted to live in a country where silence is not too expensive.

On 20 years' occupancy of a 17th century mansion near Edinburgh *Christian Science Monitor* 4 Dec 92

Olivier Messiaen composer

9591 I always hear what I have written as part of myself given sincerely, and it remains a part of me because it is a place where I have lived.

Recalled on Messiaen's death 27 Apr 92

Liza Minnelli entertainer

9592 Bleeding feet will bond us.

To fellow dancers NBC TV 2 Oct 91

Dimitri Mitropoulos Conductor, NY Philharmonic

9593 [He] didn't know a baton from a tree trunk.

On Leonard Bernstein at 20 *NY Times* 16 Oct 90

Thelonius Monk jazz musician

9594 Neon sleeping in puddles. . . a woman, feeling the city falling damp around her, hearing music from a radio, looks up and imagines the lives behind yellow-lighted windows: a man at his sink, a family round the TV, lovers drawing curtains, someone at his desk hearing the same tune.

On urban reflections of his music, quoted by Geoff Dyer *But Beautiful* Cape 91

Richard Morrison organist

9595 Sound surged from my toe!

On the Bradford Computing Organ, "the space age interloper" proposed for Oxford's Sheldonian Theater *London Times* 4 Feb 95

9596 English cathedral: rich, robust but not raucous. Trollope would have loved it.

ib

Arthur Murray dance instructor

9597 The man. . . treats the lady as though she were a china doll, holds her gently and is careful to see that she does not collide with every pillar, is more than often a man of fine sensibility.

On his instructors in ballroom dancing in 300 franchised studios grossing $25 million annually *NY Times* 4 Mar 91

Riccardo Muti Music Director, Philadelphia Orchestra

9598 In three notes, you must create a world.

To his musicians *Connoisseur* Jan 91

9599 I was afraid that if I read how to do it, I would no longer know how to do what I know how to do.

On rejecting a manual on conducting *ib*

9600 Loneliness is the first sacrifice of the conductor.

ib

Rudolf Nureyev dancer

9601 It's as though you felt a need to do something. . . and you cannot live without uttering this sentence or writing this piece of music. It just begs to manifest itself.

On talent as instinct leading to creativity *Dance* May 90

9602 My nationality is dance. My home is the stage.

On returning to Leningrad 28 years after defecting to the West *Guardian Weekly* 20 Dec 92

9603 There are those who bring something to this life which others can only observe. God gave it to me because I was lucky. And I never let go.

New Yorker 28 Dec 92

Luciano Pavarotti tenor

9604 They give all their love to opera; they think they are the ultimate judge of what is going to happen here, and that they have the right to applaud or boo. And if you want to know my opinion, they are right.

On regular opera-goers *London Times* 29 Sep 93

9605 The entire world of opera feels like an orphan after such a loss. . . a body without a soul.

On fire that destroyed the La Fenice Opera House in Venice *NY Times* 31 Jan 96

Oscar Peterson jazz pianist

9606 What happens on stage is my concern. What happens in the audience is theirs.

Down Beat Jan 91

Philippe Petit high-wire aerialist

9607 Piano and high wire are a very beautiful marriage.

On "Ascent: A Concert for Grand Piano and High Wire" that accompanied his walk 70 feet above nave of NYC's Cathedral of St John the Divine NY Times 6 May 86

Cole Porter composer

9608 I've done lots of work at dinner, sitting between two bores. I can feign listening beautifully. I can work anywhere.

Recalled on Porter's death 15 Oct 64

Elvis Presley entertainer

9609 I just have to jump around when I sing. . . ain't vulgar. . . just the way I feel.

Recalled on Presley's death 16 Aug 77

9610 I don't feel sexy when I'm singin'. If that was true, I'd be in some kinda institution as some kinda sex maniac.

ib

Sergey Sergeyevitch Prokofiev composer

9611 Bach—with smallpox.

On Igor Stravinsky's neo-classicism, recalled on Prokofiev's death 5 Mar 53

Jerome Robbins choreographer

9612 Dance is low on the totem pole of the arts, because you're not left with a painting. . . a book that will stay there, a score you can read.

International Herald Tribune 28 Dec 92

9613 [Dance is] like life, it exists as you're flitting through it and when it's over it's gone.

ib

Richard Rodgers composer

9614 All I really want is to provide a hard-working man in the blouse business with a method of expressing himself; if he likes a tune, he can whistle it, and it will make his life happier.

Recalled on Rodgers' death 30 Dec 79

Artur Rodzenski Conductor, NY Philharmonic

9615 I finally asked God whom I shall take and God said, "Take Bernstein."

On appointing Leonard Bernstein assistant conductor, his break-through to fame, quoted by Jean Peyser *Bernstein* Morrow 87

Ginger Rogers dancer

9616 Did you think I was your third leg?

To her longtime dancing partner Fred Astaire on their last meeting before Astaire's death NBC TV 29 Oct 91

Ned Rorem composer and essayist

9617 Music exists. . . only in motion. The good listener will hear it as the present prolonged.

Music from Inside Out Braziller 67

9618 Copland and Thomson were. . . the Rome and Avignon of American music.

On composers Aaron Copland and Virgil Thomson *NY Times* 10 Nov 85

9619 Too young to die? He led four lives in one, so he was not 72, but 288.

On Leonard Bernstein 21 Oct 90

9620 More than sex or love, appreciation is what humans crave and seldom get. So I am lucky in having always known what I wanted to be, in being able to be it, and in being acknowledged for being it.

At age 70 *Knowing When to Stop* Simon & Schuster 94

Mstislav Rostropovich conductor and cellist

9621 If I kiss, that's everything's gone absolutely clear what I say.

On affection that transcends language *NY Times* 11 Feb 85

9622 Impossible sit on ground and play cello! I must. . . ask chair. And that is how they recognize me. . . the chair was traitor.

On being recognized on visit to Berlin *London Times* 26 Feb 93

9623 He broke all records for the 880 yards hurdles for cellists.

On Benjamin Britten's performance of Rorem's first cello sonata *ib*

9624 Another day pass, I feel a guillotine is just tickling the back of my neck.

On increasing stressfulness *ib*

9625 Prokofiev told me people might be born with good musical taste but you have to clean it every day.

On advice from Russian composer Sergeyvich Prokofiev *ib*

Artur Rubinstein pianist

9626 Instead of dying, I broke with my weight the belt and fell heavily on the floor. . . . It was ridiculous. I went out in the street and there fell in love with life.

On an attempted suicide recalled on Rubinstein's hundredth birthday PBS 20 Jul 87

Carl Sandburg poet

9627 [It is] a chattel with a soul—a personal possession often owning its possessor—being quaint and quiet, dedicated to the dulcet rather than the diapason.

On the guitar that he played in appearances around the world, recalled on Sandburg's death 22 Jul 67

9628 [It is] a portable companion always ready to go where you go— a small friend weighing less than a fresh born infant—to be shared with few or many—just two of you in sweet meditation.

ib

Paul Schoeffler baritone

9629 Ze zum comes zu zink.

On linguistic hash of singing opera in English in an international opera house, quoted by Irving Kolodin *The Metropolitan Opera* Knopf 67

Diane Schuur entertainer

9630 I became a singer instead of a flyer—just a different way of flying.

On career as a blind jazz vocalist *20/20* ABC TV 2 Jul 87

Artie Shaw band leader

9631 I came out here because I figured I'd have to go 45 miles in any direction to get in trouble.

On retiring to Ventura County CA "60 miles from the center of Los Angeles if Los Angeles had a center" *NY Times* 18 Aug 94

9632 It was like cutting off a gangrenous arm. You miss it, but better to have one arm and have a life.

On giving up as "King of Swing" *ib*

Jean Sibelius composer

9633 The roof of my house is too low for you.

After Marian Anderson's private concert in his home, recalled on Sibelius' death 20 Sep 57

Frank Sinatra entertainer

9634 The mating call of a yak in heat!

On Marlon Brando's singing in *Guys and Dolls London Times* 3 Sep 94

Georg Solti Conductor, Chicago Symphony

9635 Mozart makes you believe in God—much more than going to church—because it cannot be by chance that such a phenomenon arrives into this world.

Time 22 Jul 91

Stephen Sondheim composer and lyricist

9636 You make music like you make a table.

On studying composition with Robert Barrow at Williams College *US News & World Report* 1 Feb 88

9637 People have lazy ears. Humble really means familiar.

ib

9638 Art tries to make order out of chaos, not just the chaos of the world, but the chaos of your own feelings and discombobulations.

NY Times 20 Mar 94

Bruce Springsteen entertainer

9639 The life of a rock and roll band will last as long as you look down into the audience and can see yourself, and your audience looks up at you and can see themselves.

Quoted by Robert Hilburn *Springsteen* Scribner 85

9640 You write the song just for yourself, but it's no good unless you play it for somebody else.

ib

Mariano Stabile baritone

9641 Maestro, I did not come here to let you hear how I sing Falstaff. I came here to let you hear if I possess the quality that one day I might be able to sing Falstaff.

To Arturo Toscanini's comment, "You sing too metronomically," quoted by George R Marek *Toscanini* Atheneum 75

Ringo Starr entertainer

9642 You know those little crawly things called beatles? Well, we're big beatles.

On his quartet's first visit to US, news reports 12 Feb 64

9643 Turn left at Iceland.
On how to get to America *ib*

Isaac Stern violinist

9644 He has been in the inner ear of every violinist since at least 1930.
On Jascha Heifetz *Time* 28 Dec 87

9645 What a feeling to be here amongst so many close friends.
On the Library of Congress' scores of Mozart, Brahms and other composers *Memory and Imagination* PBS TV 15 Aug 93

9646 There's a terrific quality of passion, tenderness, all of this, and you read the music and it shouts itself to you. . . . You get confirmation in the score. Now, where Brahms got the vision, you don't ask, you just accept.
ib

9647 Hurok knows six languages—and all of them are Yiddish.
On Sol Hurok, quoted by Harlow Robinson's *The Last Impresario* Viking 94

Leopold Stokowski conductor

9648 My man, you don't know your brass from your oboe.
To an offending musician, recalled on Stokowski's death 13 Sep 77

Igor Stravinsky composer

9649 The one true comment on a piece of music is another piece of music.
NY Review of Books 12 May 66

9650 I had a dream. . . about music critics. . . small and rodent-like with padlocked ears, as if they had stepped out of a painting by Goya.
London Evening Standard 29 Oct 69

9651 I need to touch music as well as to think it, which is why I have always lived next to a piano.
Today ASCAP Winter 75

9652 To see Balanchine's choreography is to hear music with one's eyes.
US News & World Report 2 May 88

9653 The trick is to compose what one wants to compose and to get it commissioned afterward.
NY Times 17 Oct 93

Jule Styne composer

9654 You write as well as who you write with.
On versatility in producing 2,000 songs with lyricists Sammy Cahn, Yip Harburg, Leo Robin, Stephen Sondheim and others *NY Times* 21 Sep 94

Joan Sutherland soprano

9655 [I will] become one of you out there.
To the Sydney Opera House audience at *Les Huguenots*, her final appearance 17 Sep 90, quoted by Norma Major *Joan Sutherland* Little, Brown 94

Twyla Tharp choreographer

9656 Dancing. . . like bank robbery. . . takes split-second timing.
Ms Oct 76

Michael Tippett composer

9657 I wrote one note today—but I crossed it out.
On his slow rate of composing *Guardian Weekly* 15 Jul 90

Arturo Toscanini conductor

9658 Madame, there are no stars in my performances. There are only stars in heaven.
On rehearsing with Geraldine Ferrar, recalled on Toscanini's death 16 Jan 57

9659 What I have heard today, one is privileged to hear only once in a hundred years.
On Marian Anderson's concert at the 1935 Salzburg Festival *ib*

9660 Madame, there you sit with that magnificent instrument between your legs, and all you can do is scratch it.
To a cellist *ib*

9661 For Strauss, the composer, I take my hat off; for Strauss the man I put it on again.
Recalling a meeting with Johann Strauss, quoted by George R Marek *Toscanini* Atheneum 75

9662 This must sound far away. Not too far—maybe Brooklyn.
On rehearsing trumpets for *La Bohème* by the NBC Orchestra *ib*

9663 I don't speak German, but when I conduct I speak all languages.
At a rehearsal in Bayreuth *ib*

9664 I am very sorry you were ever born; come to think of it, I am sorry I was born, to have to sit here and suffer.
To baritone Giuseppe Valdengo in *La Traviata ib*

9665 I was stupid, you were stupid, only Beethoven was not stupid.
On rehearsing Beethoven's *Seventh Symphony* for the last time *ib*

9666 With one more drop of blood perhaps we can come a little nearer to what Beethoven wanted.
On rehearsing the *Ninth Symphony ib*

9667 I began by hearing a performance of *Un Ballo in Maschere* at age four, up in the gallery, and I've finished by conducting it.
At age 87, quoted by Harvey Sachs *Toscanini* Lippincott 78

9668 To some it is Napoleon, to some it is a philosophical struggle, to me it is *allegro con brio.*

On Beethoven's *Eroica,* recalled on opening of the Toscanini archieve at NY Public Library *NY Times* 5 Apr 87

9669 If only your brains were so big!

On a mezzo-soprano's bosom *Washington Post* 8 Jan 88

Richard Tucker tenor

9670 My public doesn't like me in a role where I die in the second act.

On playing Lenski in Tchaikovsky's *Eugene Onegin* quoted by Irving Kolodin *The Metropolitan Opera* Knopf 67

Jay Ungar composer

9671 A Scottish lament written by a Jewish guy from the Bronx.

On *Ashokan Farewell,* fiddle tune that he composed as theme of PBS documentary *The Civil War New Yorker* 11 Mar 91

9672 When I first started hearing folk fiddling, it seemed to be all the parts I liked.

On writing his first hit, *Strike a Match and Light Another Marijuana Cigarette* as a member of a rock group called *Cat Mother and the All-Night News Boys*

Sarah Vaughn entertainer

9673 I listened to the trumpet to learn how to sing, not other singers.

Recalled on Vaughn's death NPR 7 Apr 90

Bobby Whalen entertainer

9674 If you haven't been baptized by hard times, you ain't never going to understand blues.

"Soundprint" Amer Public Radio 9 Dec 90

Meredith Willson composer

9675 Innocent, that was the adjective for Iowa. . . all I had to do was remember.

On writing *The Music Man,* quoted by Stanley Green *The World of Musical Comedy* Barnes 68

Charles Wuorienen composer

9676 [It is] the most civilized award ever invented.

On the MacArthur "genius" fellowships *NY Times* 17 Jul 88

Directors, Producers, Managers

Gerald Arpino Artistic Director, Joffrey Ballet

9677 We wanted to be dancer athletes and to prove that Americans could take the challenge, could become the Olympians of dance as well as the other great countries steeped in it for centuries.

On objectives pursued with Robert Joffrey *Christian Science Monitor* 4 May 88

Rudolph Bing Manager, Metropolitan Opera

9678 She will sing only if her husband conducts, so I accept the old Viennese saying that if you want the meat, you have to take the bones.

On Joan Sutherland *5,000 Nights at the Opera* Doubleday 72

9679 Miss Renata Tebaldi was always sweet and very firm. . . she had dimples of iron.

ib

9680 How nice the human voice is when it isn't singing.

Newsweek 1 May 72

9681 They have a disaster of the throat.

On singers *ib*

9682 [He was] like a moving couch covered in red plush.

On Lauritz Melchior in *Tannhauser,* quoted by Shirlee Emmons *Tristanissimo* Schirmer/Macmillan 90

9683 There's no addiction like the 8 o'clock curtain at the opera.

NY Times 7 Mar 95

Bonnie Brooks Director, Dance/USA, Washington

9684 Dance is like a suspension bridge held together with spider webs.

On financially sustaining her work *NY Times* 8 Jan 94

Corri Ellison linguist

9685 Our goal was to translate as little as possible but as much as necessary.

On operas in English for use on the 3,989 individual computer screens attached to seats at the Metropolitan Opera at a cost of $2.7 million *NY Times* 2 Oct 95

9686 My titles have few adjectives; they are simple but not simplistic.

ib

Sofiya N Golovkina Director, Moscow Choreographic School

9687 Our whole life is changing. . . but where creativity is concerned, where Russian ballet is at stake, this will not change.

NY Times 13 Jan 94

Robert Joffrey Founder, Robert Joffrey Ballet

9688 I gave them ballerinas in sneakers and modern dancers in toe shoes, jiving to Vivaldi and pirouetting to the *Beach Boys.*

Time 26 Dec 88

Alan Kayes Director, Artists and Repertory, RCA Victor

9689 Van Cliburn's career after the Tchaikovsky win was like an explosion in a piano factory.

On the devastating effect of Van Cliburn's surprise victory at the 1958 Tchaikovsky Competition in Moscow that left other young pianists asking, "Why not me?" *NY Times* 24 Oct 93

Lincoln Kirstein Co-Founder, NYC Ballet

9690 I don't have to tell you that Mr B is with Mozart and Tchaikovsky and Stravinsky.

To a NY State Theater audience a few hours after George Balanchine's death 30 Apr 83, Nicholas Jenkins ed *By With To & From: A Lincoln Kirstein Reader* Farrar Straus Giroux 91

9691 All imaginative kids have problems. . . but we're not offering a panacea for neurotics. It's hard enough to take care of broken bones.

On creating at the School of American Ballet a post of director of student life to deal with "everything that hasn't got to do with dancing" *NY Times* 9 Jan 91

9692 The whole thing about ballet. . . is that it is a language. The words are steps. It has its own grammar.

ib

9693 You can't have thoroughbreds without treating them like thoroughbreds. . . and so, finally, one can say we have very nice stables now.

On new quarters for school at Lincoln Center *ib*

Ardis Krainik Director, Chicago Lyric Opera

9694 I don't have a master plan because they're always developments in the middle that are even better than the master plan.

Time 7 Feb 94

Goddard Lieberson Producer, Columbia Records

9695 For a producer to ask a record company for money is immoral, for a record company to give it is ignorance.

On uniqueness of his underwriting of Irving Berlin's *Mr President* for Columbia Records and loaning its producers $200,000, quoted by Russell Sanjek *American Popular Music and Its Business* Vol III Oxford 88

George R Marek General Manager, RCA

9696 God was to him the one who created Mozart and Wagner and to whom one needed to speak sharply in the matter of inept clarinet-players.

On conductor Arturo Toscanini *Toscanini* Atheneum 75

9697 Music is a sleeping Snow White—existing for most only as undecipherable and inert signs on ruled paper until the interpreter awakens her.

ib

Robert Mayer Director, British Youth and Music Movement

9698 I look upon myself as a musical bricklayer with architectural aspirations.

New Yorker 21 Apr 80

André Mertens critic

9699 Singers' husbands! Find me stones heavy enough to place around their necks and drown them all!

Time 1 Aug 60

9700 In every prima donna there is a deep craving for security and comfort, linked with a fear of old age. This causes her to pick a man who is prepared to act as a permanent wet nurse.

ib

Lloyd Newson Director, DV–8 Theater

9701 It seems that if you're straight you can't bend your limbs.

On homophobic attitudes toward dance *London Times* 13 Sep 95

9702 Men police each other and if you break their narrow code you risk violence.

ib

James C Petrillo president, American Federation of Musicians

9703 If I was a good trumpet player, I wouldn't be here. I got desperate. I hadda look for a job. I went in the union business.

NY Times 14 Jun 56

Peter Mark Schifert artists' manager

9704 [He was] sort of Byronic, standing on the beach with the wind blowing. . . a very tormented guy. . . in a way he wanted to sleep with the world. It wasn't just sex but a deep hunger for connectedness.

On observing Leonard Bernstein prior to conducting his *Mass*, quoted by Merlye Secrest *Leonard Bernstein* Knopf 94

Beverly Sills Director, New York City Opera

9705 So long as it doesn't get to the point where you don't remember whose opera you're listening to, I'm willing to experiment.

On set design after becoming director of NYC Opera *Newsweek* 8 Oct 84

9706 I lived through the garbage, I might as well dine on the caviar.

On continuing as director *NY Times* 15 Oct 84

9707 Art is the signature of civilizations.
NBC TV 4 May 85

9708 The era of the old lady with the headache band and string of pearls is over. Her money has passed to the next generation, probably much diluted.
On opera patrons, quoted by John Dizikes *Opera in America* Yale 93

9709 Instead of the senior partner in the law firm, we have the junior partner—someone who still has to worry about the baby sitter, the parking and the dinner when he considers the price of his ticket.
ib

Michael Tilson Thomas Music Director, San Francisco Symphony

9710 What I want here is maximum expression with minimum dynamic change.
On approaching the prayerful adagio of Beethoven's *Ninth Symphony Washington Post* 8 Oct 95

9711 The best music has something eternally mysterious about it—you can never possess it or even fully know it. The score. . . [is] just a skeletal outline of the general area the piece inhabits. Don't play it the way it's written. . . play it the way it goes.
To the orchestra *ib*

Albert K Webster Manager Director, New York Philharmonic

9712 When the stars are ready to cross your path, you have to be able to grab them.
On 19-month search that led to choice of Kurt Masur as conductor *NY Times* 6 May 90

Critics

Joan Acocella critic

9713 *Swan Lake* says that life is not going to work out.
In keynote speech at conference on meaning and symbolism in ballet *Washington Post* 15 May 88

9714 [*Swan Lake*] glorifies our human ability to project an ideal, but takes account of our failure to achieve the ideal. *Swan Lake* is about the sorrow that's built into life.
ib

Vassilis Alexakis essayist

9715 No other musical instrument at rest produces quite as much silence as a closed piano.
Quoted by Joyane Savigneau *Marguerite Yourcenar* University of Chicago Press 93

Christine Amanpour critic

9716 They must go on like a bedroom slipper and do the work of combat boots.
On ballet slippers CNN 1 May 87

Maya Angelou poet

9717 I could crawl into the space between notes and curl my back to loneliness.
On music as a refuge *Gathered Together In My Name* Random House 74

Anon

9718 She is. . . the girl with a dimple in her voice.
Recalled on soprano Jessica Dragonet's death 18 Mar 80

9719 So vot can happen? He's a man, she's a duck!
On the Prince who loves a Swan Maiden in *Swan Lake Washington Post* 15 May 88

9720 Would it be possible to have Mr Taylor punctuate his speech with brilliant flashes of silence?
Disgruntled listener's letter on Deems Taylor's *sotto voce* commentary during opera broadcasts *NY Times* 26 Nov 89

9721 [You could] hear a mashed potato drop.
On Guy Lombardo and his orchestra *ib* 30 Dec 89

9722 This machine surrounds hate and forces it to surrender.
Inscription on a banjo, quoted by Joe McGinniss *Cruel Doubt* Simon & Schuster 91

9723 On Saturdays I get my black velvet dress out of its box. . . dress my hair and put a fresh flower in a vase beside me. After all, I am to spend the afternoon with dukes and duchesses.
An elderly woman's letter on listening to Metropolitan Opera broadcasts *Stereo Review* 73, quoted by Joan Dizikes *Opera in America* Yale 93

9724 He dazzles the ear as a diamond does the eye.
A London critic on violinist Jascha Heifetz *Vogue* Dec 94

W H Auden poet

9725 And when he sang in choruses/ His voice o'ertopped the rest,/ Which is very inartistic,/ But the public likes that best.
"The Choir Boy" Nicholas Jenkins ed *A Certain World* Viking 70

9726 People who attend chamber music concerts are like Englishmen who go to church when abroad.
Quoted by Charles Osborne *W H Auden: The Life of a Poet* Harcourt Brace Jovanovich 79

9727 The *Kyrie* seems marvelous. . . and then you realize he's going on with the thing to the bitter end.
On Bach, quoted by Nicolas Jenkins *The Table Talk of W H Auden* Ontario Review Press 90

Russell Baker columnist

9728 Nowadays Whitman would not hear America singing. He would hear Japanese technology singing.
On Walt Whitman were he alive today *NY Times* 2 Nov 91

Tallulah Bankhead actress

9729 Darling, I have gone mad over your back muscles. You must come and have dinner with me.

On watching Leonard Bernstein conduct, recalled on Bernstein's death *NY Times* 16 Oct 90

Clive Barnes critic

9730 No one could call her pretty, but only a fool would not call her beautiful.

On British Royal Ballet's Monica Mason *NY Times* 25 Apr 76

Felicity Barringer critic

9731 He lived and died in a gray world of unannounced concerts, unofficial recordings and unabashed public devotion.

On 50th birthday commeration of singer Vladimir Vysotsky as "official bard of the Gorbachev era" *NY Times* 27 Jan 88

Jacques Barzun Dean of Faculties, Columbia University

9732 Music, not being made up of objects nor referring to objects, is intangible and ineffable; it can only be... inhaled by the spirit: the rest is silence.

Pleasures of Music M Joseph 52

Cecil Beaton photographer

9733 What we were now seeing was the culmination of the development of dancing since it began.

On observing Rudolf Nureyev for the first time, recalled on Beaton's death 18 Jan 80

Hilaire Belloc humorist

9734 It is the best of all trades to make songs and the second best to sing them.

Recalled on Belloc's death 15 Jul 53

Anatole Broyard critic

9735 Women had been "only a bird in a gilded cage"... [but] when Miss Graham opened the cage, the bird became a bat out of hell.

On Martha Graham *Aroused by Books* Random House 74

Humphrey Burton biographer

9736 [They] were inveterate raiders of the bottom drawer.

On use of old material by collaboraters Leonard Bernstein and Edward Elgar *Leonard Bernstein* Doubleday 94

Robert Cantwell Professor of Music, Kenyon College

9737 [Country music] has never been anything but entrepreneurial and commercial, prospering in the one commodity which in America is ever in short supply—the past.

Bluegrass Breakdown University of Illinois Press 84 quoted by Tony Scherman *American Heritage* Nov 94

Truman Capote novelist

9738 The sweet anger of Armstrong's trumpet, the froggy exuberance... make Mississippi moons rise again, summon the muddy lights of river towns, the sound, like an alligator's yawn, of river horns.

On Louis Armstrong *The Dogs Bark* Random House 73

Mark Carrington critic

9739 Cliburn was a delicate grace note in the symphony that is civilization.

On Van Cliburn at the 1st Tchaikovsky International Piano Competition *Washington Post* 29 Sep 94

Robert Christian Editor *The Village Voice*

9740 It was Johnny who made buzz-saw definitely young, fast, and unscientific... made it speak, gave it shape, idiosyncrasy, and a sense of humor.

Recalled on Johnny Thunders' death 23 Apr 91

Kenneth Clark historian and critic

9741 Opera, next to Gothic architecture, is one of the strangest inventions of western man. It could not have been foreseen by any logical process.

Civilization Harper & Row 69

9742 When... in one burst of glorious music, the murderer, his mistress, his servant and the dying man all express their feelings, opera provides a real extension of human faculties.

On the beginning of Mozart's *Don Giovanni ib*

Catherine Clément critic

9743 All the women in opera die a death prepared for them by a slow plot, woven by furtive, fleeting heroes, up to their glorious moment: a sung death.

Quoted by Paul Robinson *NY Times* 1 Jan 89 reviewing Clément's *Opera, or the Undoing of Women* University of Minnesota Press 88

9744 The good priests with majestic voices would do what they really do... shove Pamina forcibly into the cubbyhole where Zarastro locks her up... beat up the Queen of the Night... kick Papageno... [but] the music would be no less divine; but it would then serve a more just cause.

On Clément's dream performance of *The Magic Flute ib*

9745 Oh voices, sublime voices, high, clear voices, how you make one forget the words you sing!

On putting across unappealing narratives *ib*

9746 Opera reveals its peculiar function: to seduce like possums.

ib

Hillary Rodham Clinton First Lady

9747 A man who loved "country" before "country" was cool.

On President Clinton's fondness for country music, news reports 27 Sep 95

Peter Conrad Professor of English Literature, Christ Church, Oxford

9748 Performance is a venture beyond the limits of life, reaching for the sky from which music first poured down like Apollo's sunlight.

A Song of Love and Death: The Meaning of Opera Poseidon 87

9749 Music is a song both of the senses and the spirit, and its genius for modulation and metamorphoses empowers it to represent a passage from one existence to the next.

ib

Alistair Cooke commentator

9750 Illiteracy must take on in her off-hours the powerful appeal that buttermilk has for a professional champagne taster.

On operatic soprano Helen Traubel's night club singing *America Observed* Knopf 88

Country Life

9751 One feels the essence of English culture rising from the grass like evaporating dew.

On the Glyndebourne Opera 27 Oct 94

9752 It would be wrong to call him tamed because one suspects that, as a former King's College organ scholar, he has never been that *farouche.*

On Andrew Davis, musical director of Glyndebourne Opera and the BBC Symphony's chief conductor *ib*

9753 Until this year, obtaining a ticket was as easy, for most people, as bottling sunlight.

On opening of Glyndebourne's larger hall *ib*

Noel Coward playwright and lyricist

9754 People are wrong when they say that the opera isn't what it used to be. It is what it used to be. That's what's wrong with it.

Recalled on Coward's death 26 Mar 73

Ben Crisler critic

9755 [His] peculiar slant on the dance. . . is the same as the Rockefeller perspective on oil.

On Arthur Murray's merchandising of ballroom dancing *NY Times* 4 Mar 91

Arlene Croce critic

9756 Mice raced through the wainscoting, animals gasped and died, caravans bearing shipments of marimbas blundered across pontoon bridges in the dark, whole cities were chopped to pieces by pneumatic drills, and the electronic equipment in the pit came down with gastritis.

On a Merce Cunningham dance program *Sight Lines* Knopf 88

9757 There should have been a sign over the City Center door: "If you have ears, prepare to plug them now."

ib

9758 What would the America of choreographers be without the America of crackpots?

ib

Will Crutchfield critic

9759 There is an utterly extraordinary halo of lush, quietly resonant string sound, bound together by the gentle connection between notes called *portamento.* . . as though a wordless chorus were ooh-ing.

On Leopold Stokowski's 1927 recording of Dvořák's *New World Symphony NY Times* 6 Jan 85

9760 Stokowski may have shaped it over years of meticulous rehearsal, but he did not carry it in his briefcase. It became a feature and a property not of the conductor but of the ensemble.

ib

Charlotte Curtis reporter

9761 Most of the sheet music was beige with age.

On the repertory for the popular Waltz Evenings at Boston's Sheraton Plaza Hotel *The Rich and Other Atrocities* Harper & Row 76

Brad Darrach essayist

9762 The hair was a Vaseline cathedral, the mouth a touchingly uncertain sneer of allure.

On Elvis Presley *Life* Winter 77

9763 Like a berserk blender, the lusty young pelvis whirled and the notorious git-tar slammed forward with a jolt that symbolically deflowered a generation of teenagers and knocked chips off 90 million older shoulders.

ib

9764 Out of the half-melted vanilla face a wild black baritone came bawling in orgasmic lurches.

ib

Gervase de Peyer clarinetist

9765 There is a lot of music. What is not available is the peace of mind to listen to it.

On classical music WETA Washington 23 Jun 90

John Dizikes critic

9766 It was a new opera house without walls.

On the opening of operatic archives *Opera in America* Yale 93

9767 He became "Mr Opera," but he remained subordinate to the opera, to the medium he presided over, unobtrusive, personally unremarkable, the ordinary leading to the extraordinary.

On radio host Milton Cross *ib*

Hugh Downs commentator

9768 I feel like a chihuahua at a convention of Great Danes.

On his status as an amateur composer *Parade* 8 Jul 90

Jennifer Dunning critic

9769 At the age of 83, a practiced pessimist.

On Lincoln Kirstein, founder with George Balanchine of the NYC Ballet *NY Times* 9 Jan 91

Marguerite Duras novelist

9770 Behind the dazzling fires of footlights no one is so beautiful as this ugly woman.

On Maria Callas, quoted by *Vogue* Dec 94 reviewing Alain Vircondelet's *Duras: A Biography* Dalkey Archive Press 94

David Edelsten critic

9771 Appalachian step-dancing. . . is a mixture of Scottish reel, tap, square, black and Indian. . . infectious. . . as example of that well-known fact that the best parties are often those that one least looks forward to.

Country Life 10 Aug 95

Albert Einstein physicist

9772 The fact that a man such as yourself is living among us compensates one for the many disappointments which one continuously experiences with the species *minorum gentium.*

Letter to Arturo Toscanini after he donated his time to conducting a benefit concert for a Palestinian orchestra, quoted by George R Marek *Toscanini* Atheneum 75

Dwight D Eisenhower 34th US President

9773 I like music with a theme, not all them arias and barcarolles.

To Leonard Bernstein on his White House rendition of Gershwin's *Rhapsody in Blue* 5 Apr 60, a remark that inspired Bernstein to compose a suite entitled *Arias and Barcarolles* in 1988, quoted by Humphrey Burton *Leonard Bernstein* Doubleday 94

Colin Escott biographer

9774 He could say to an audience of thousands what he couldn't say to someone sitting across the room.

On Hank Williams *Hank Williams* Little, Brown 94

Marshall Fishwick critic

9775 The Twist is a valid manifestation of the Age of Anxiety.

On a dance fad popularized by Chubby Checker at NYC's Peppermint Lounge bar *Saturday Review* 3 Mar 62

Bill Flanagan critic

9776 I call rock and roll all the subdivisions: folk and funk and fusion and everything else east of Lionel Ritchie, west of Miles Davis, north of George Jones, and south of Pete Seeger.

Written In My Soul Contemporary Books 86

Janet Flanner ("Genet") *New Yorker* columnist

9777 In her last Paris triumph. . . all that was left of Piaf was all that had ever counted—her immense, infallible voice, which rose to the roof, carrying its enormous, authentic outcry of banal phrases of anguish over lost loves, and poignant despair of happiness that would never arrive.

On Edith Piaf's death in 1963 *Paris Journal 1944–65* Atheneum 65

9778 She tottered—her thin legs supporting her in faltering obedience to her courage—across the stage to the microphone. . . and then her voice, that great remnant of her life, burst forth.

ib

Henry Ford II industrialist

9779 There should be music and the warmth of fellowship and, in this connection, a black jazz band playing *When the Saints Go Marching In* for a recessional, for I do not wish to be remembered only in a solemn fashion.

Tape-recorded funeral directions left in Ford's will *NY Times* 1 Oct 88

J William Fulbright US Senator

9780 It was less than half the cost of Lincoln Center and one day of the Vietnam War in 1966.

On the completion of Kennedy Center, quoted by Humphrey Burton *Leonard Bernstein* Doubleday 94

Ed Gardner entertainer

9781 Opera is when a guy gets stabbed in the back and, instead of bleeding, he sings.

On 1940s radio *Duffy's Tavern*, recalled on Gardner's death 17 Aug 63

Ronald Gelatt critic

9782 It is like the Renaissance rediscovering the ancient classics and holding them fast by means of the printing press. It marks an epoch in Western intellectual history.

On the opening of operatic archives *The Fabulous Phonograph* Appleton Century 66

David Gonzalez reporter

9783 [They were] gray-haired but still sharp in their shades, Ban-Lon shirts and white patent leather shoes. . . a musical bridge between black and white worlds.

On members of Jimmy Keyes' chorus *The Chimes,* singing at Keyes' wake the signature song *Sh-Boom* that opened up white radio stations *NY Times* 27 Jul 95

Anthony Haden-Guest critic

9784 [It is] an unprecedented aggregation of cultural clout.

On John Samuels' simultaneous chairmanship of NY City Center, City Opera and City Ballet "The Mysterious Mogul of Lincoln Center" *New York* 5 May 80

Alan Hamilton essayist

9785 He created a sound that to this day is redolent of bomber jackets, nylons and GI romance.

On World War II entertainer Glenn Miller killed in the Atlantic crash *London Times* 24 Dec 94

Richard Hell (Richard Meyers) punk-rock musician

9786 He played with a mesmerizing, casual fury, ripping chords from his guitar as if they were love letters he stopped himself just in time from sending.

On rock musician Johnny Thunders, recalled on Thunders' death 23 Apr 91

Donal Henahan critic

9787 Real folk music long ago went to Nashville and left no known survivors.

NY Times 8 May 77

9788 [It is an] attempt to embrace, in one tear-stained bear-hug, us, our children, God, our common dilemma. . . . Mahler, wherever he is, will appreciate the effort.

On Leonard Bernstein's *Mass* quoted by Meryle Secrest *Leonard Bernstein* Knopf 94

Manuela Hoeltherhoff critic

9789 He sounded so distant in the first act, I thought he was phoning it in from Italy.

On tenor Luciano Pavarotti in *Il Trovatore Wall Street Journal* 5 Oct 88

Stephen Holden critic

9790 A powerhouse rhythmic drive, a frisky pleasure in vocalizing, a workhorse energy and, above all, an astonishing musical fluency informed an unparalleled sense of musical balance and proportion.

On Ella Fitzgerald at 75 *NY Times* 25 Apr 93

9791 She taught America to see its popular song as more than a throwaway confection.

ib

9792 Life's complexities and problems were metaphorically faced and overcome in dazzling feats of scat improvisation.

ib

Leopold Holder President, NY Piano Center

9793 People fantasize that buying a piano will give them some Victorian ideal of life, with the family gathered around together. It's a totally emotional purchase.

On $800 million in annual piano purchases, marking its continuance as the most popular musical instrument in the US *Forbes* 27 Feb 95

Kathryn Hulme novelist

9794 The awesome antiphon [was]. . . the cry for mercy that was welling up at that moment to the Mother of God from every place where vowed ones lived behind walls.

On the singing of "*O dulcis Virgo Maria,*" *The Nun's Story* Little, Brown 56

Ludmila Ilieva voice student

9795 The opera was his house of worship, and I think he felt it was the natural place to die.

On voice coach Bantcho Bantchevsky, 82, who jumped to his death from an upper balcony during an intermission of Verdi's *Macbeth* at the Metropolitan Opera House, *NY Times* 29 Jan 88

Simon Jenkins critic

9796 Bells are still England's glory. . . [with] a jargon of gibs, gudgeons, sliders, sallies, prickings, hardstrokes and backstrokes.

London Times 24 Dec 94

9797 [Bells] encompass happiness and sadness. . . ring for marriages and royal occasions. . . toll the knell, not just the passing day, but the passing life.

ib

Michael T Kaufman reporter

9798 [They] walked with September eagerness.

On students entering 90-year-old Antonina Tumkovsky's class as she began her 46th year of teaching at NYC's School of American Ballet *NY Times* 9 Sep 95

Garrison Keillor entertainer

9799 Liberace was the step-father of glitz-rock. . . he fought hard against taste and sometimes he succeeded.

American Public Radio 20 Apr 91

9800 Second violins can play a concerto perfectly if they're in their own home and nobody's there.

30 Oct 93 *ib*

9801 Composers wrote so few notes for brass because after they've played for a while you can't hear them anymore.

ib

John F Kennedy 35th US President

9802 Reservations for inaugural concert, parade, ball are held for you.

Invitation to inaugural events to writers, artists, composers, philosophers, scientists and heads of cultural institutions with whom he hoped "to affect a productive relationship," Nicolas Jenkins ed *By With To & From: A Lincoln Kirstein Reader* Farrar Straus Giroux 91

9803 We believe that an artist, in order to be true to himself and his work must be a free man.

Introducing Pablo Casals at a White House dinner in November 1962 as the cellist broke for the first time a long silence of mourning for Spanish democracy, quoted by Arthur M Schlesinger Jr *A Thousand Days* Houghton Mifflin 65

9804 [It honors those] whose talent enlarges the public vision of the dignity with which life can be graced and the fullness with which it can be lived.

On reviving presentations of the Presidential Medal of Freedom *ib*

Jerome Kern composer

9805 What might unsympathetically be mistaken for brass is really gold.

Letter to critic Alexander Woollcott on Irving Berlin's genius for capturing the quintessential American mood, recalled on Berlin's hundredth birthday *US News & World Report* 9 May 88

9806 Irving Berlin has no place in American music. He *is* American music.

Recalled on Berlin's death at 101 22 Sep 89

9807 He. . . absorbs the vibrations emanating from the people, manners and life of his time and, in turn, gives these impressions back to the world—simplified, clarified and glorified.

NY Times 23 Sep 89

Ayatollah Ruholla Khomeini spiritual leader of Iran

9808 [Music is] no different from opium. . . [and] stupefies persons listening to it and makes their brain inactive and frivolous.

On banning music from radio and television *NY Times* 5 Jun 89

Anna Kisselgoff critic

9809 Her legs devour space.

On Darcey Bussell at 21 in Kenneth MacMillan's US premier of Benjamin Britten's ballet *The Prince of the Pagodas NY Times* 16 Mar 91

Henry A Kissinger US Secretary of State

9810 An art form of truly stupefying boredom. . . . As far as I could make out the girl fell in love with a tractor.

On Communist overtones in Chinese opera, quoted by Walter Isaacson *Kissinger* Simon & Schuster 92

Wayne Koestenbaum critic

9811 Flamboyance is to be appreciated. . . a salubrious force—a dangerous, sexually ambiguous energy without which no art dares call itself fine, without which no culture dares claim for itself a renaissance.

Guardian Weekly 29 May 94 reviewing Humphrey Burton's *Leonard Bernstein* Doubleday 94

Irving Kolodin critic

9812 The bulldozer could make its own way, unescorted by the jeep.

On Metropolitan Opera management passing from Edward A Johnson to Rudolph Bing in 1950 *The Metropolitan Opera* Knopf 67

9813 There would no longer be a wiser, more experienced head available to fend off disaster—the beginner's errors would be in the pit, the center of operatic authority from which there is no recourse.

On Bruno Walter's withdrawal as conductor *ib*

9814 The uncommon talent sought in vain for the uncommon appraisal that was its due.

On Maria Callas *ib*

9815 The inner core of hate erupted through the outer cloak of sanctity.

On the stabbing scene in *Tosca ib*

9816 Callas alone persuaded the viewer that she had not discovered the knife—the knife discovered her in her moment of extremity and need. . . and this Tosca had to use it, in a lightning-swift lunge, thrust, and shuddering rejection of her own act.

ib

9817 While a bad conductor can do more to spoil a performance than a bad singer, a good conductor can do more to ennoble it than a good singer.

ib

9818 The most bumptious, empty noise ever contrived!

On Leonard Bernstein's conducting of Gustav Mahler's *The Resurrection* quoted by Humphrey Burton *Leonard Bernstein* Doubleday 94

Charles Kuralt commentator

9819 Learning the Blues is a matter of turning what you feel into music. . . to touch the strings of a guitar so that they speak for you or make a trumpet say what's in your heart. Life is the usual teacher.

Sunday Morning CBS TV 29 Mar 92

C S Lewis novelist

9820 How tonic Beethoven is, and how festal—one has the feeling of having taken part in the revelry of giants.

Walter Hooper ed *Letters of C S Lewis to Arthur Greeves* Collier/Macmillan 86

Life magazine

9821 Rock 'n' roll is both music and dance. . . often heavily accented on the second and fourth beat. . . hollering helps and a boot banging on the floor makes it even better.

18 Apr 95

Alan Lomax musicologist

9822 Country music is folk music in overdrive.

Quoted by Tony Scherman *American Heritage* Nov 94

London Times

9823 Knight to Remember

Headline for Gerald Larner's review of *Falstaff* 6 Sep 93

9824 No star is too distant, no luminary too bright to escape the searing gaze of the Milanese.

"Maestro Muti" editorial on the reputation of Milan's La Scala Opera House "for making or breaking the best" 5 Jun 95

Allan MacEachen Canadian Minister of External Affairs

9825 A gentleman is a man who knows how to play the bagpipes but doesn't.

Canadian 21 Jun 75

Louis MacNeice poet

9826 The same tunes hang on pegs in the cloakrooms of the mind/ That fitted us 10 or 20 or 30 years ago/ On occasions of love or grief; tin pan alley or folk/ Or Lieder or nursery rhyme, when we open the door we find/The same tunes hanging in wait.

"Off the Peg" quoted by Muriel Spark "Footnotes to a Poet's House" *Architectural Digest* Nov 85

Jean Marsh actress

9827 If you don't believe (in God), you can suspend it while listening to Bach—and then go back to being an atheist.

Interview on "Desert Island" Station WETA Washington 2 Jul 88

General George C Marshall US Army

9828 He criticized everything but the varnish on the piano.

On Paul Hume's review of Margaret Truman as soloist, quoted by Margaret Truman *Bess W Truman* Macmillan 86

J D McClatchy poet

9829 Opera—its ecstasies and deceptions, its transcendent fires and icy grandeurs—is, above all, a stylized dramatization of our inner lives, our forbidden desires and repressed fears.

New Yorker 27 Mar 95

Carson McCullers novelist

9830 The music started. . . like a walk or march. Like God strutting in the night.

The Heart is a Lonely Hunter Houghton Mifflin 1940, recalled on McCullers' death 29 Sep 67

Marion Meade biographer

9831 His tongue, as efficient as a buzz saw when it came to slicing fools into small pieces, was a match for hers.

On critics Dorothy Parker and Deems Taylor *Dorothy Parker* Villard 88

George Melly critic

9832 It was a sentimental rather than an inspiring evening, a ritual rather than a happening. . . . Time was in the wings, glancing at his watch.

On Frank Sinatra's Albert Hall appearance on the eve of his 75th birthday *London Times* 7 Dec 90

Edna St Vincent Millay poet

9833 The Englishman foxtrots as he fox-hunts, with all his being, through thickets, through ditches, over hedges, through chiffons, through waters, over saxophones, to the victorious finish.

Recalled on Millay's death 19 Oct 50

Kenneth Miller essayist

9834 The piano's world encompasses glass-nerved virtuosi and stomping barrel-housers in fedoras; it is a world of pasture and storm, of perfumed smoke, of liquid mathematics.

"How to Buy a Piano" *Esquire* Apr 86

9835 No other acoustic instrument can match the piano's expressive range, and no electric instrument can match its mystery.

ib

9836 [The piano is] able to communicate the subtlest universal truths by means of wood, metal and vibrating air.

ib

Henry Mitchell critic

9837 The choirs left the main tune and soared two octaves past heaven in a descant to rattle the bones and surge the heart.

On dedication of nave of Washington DC's National Cathedral *Washington Post* 9 Jul 76

Bob Mondello critic

9838 *Rigoletto* is flawed. You get tired of it after about 50 years.

Station WETA Washington 3 Mar 91

Jim Mullen humorist

9839 She sings. . . acts. . . produces, and, at $350 a ticket, even scalps her own concerts.

On Barbra Streisand's come-back tour *People* 31 Dec 94

Ernest Newman

9840 She looks like an ox. . . moves like a cart horse. . . stands like a haystack.

Describing a typical operatic soprano *Time* 8 Oct 65

Newsweek magazine

9841 *La Sonnambula* is dull enough to send the most athletic sleepwalker back to bed.

On Bellini's opera 4 Mar 63

9842 The audience came out of its trance, transformed instantly from silence to cheers, from stillness to such vigorous applause that left and right hands might have been enemies.

On Rudolf Nureyev in *La Bayadère* 19 Apr 65

9843 And so it was good-bye at last . . . to that broad and angular face. . . to that tall, forceful figure, like a Rodin sculpture, carved out of a giant block of ebony. . . to those eyes which closed when she sang as if looking inward but which, when open, beamed warmth and quick response.

On Marian Anderson's farewell concert 26 Apr 65

New Yorker magazine

9844 [Their] expressions had gone beyond boredom to a sort of beatific madness.

On Budapest's gypsy musicians during the first postwar Grand Prix race in an Eastern European country 15 Sep 86

New York Times

9845 Who would want to butcher a cash cow—especially one that produces mystique as well as money?

"Art, Money and NY," NY editorial on considering revenues and leadership in the arts before cutting Dept of Cultural Affairs budget 29 May 95

Richard M Nixon 37th US President

9846 If I'm assassinated. . . have them play Dante's *Inferno* and have Lawrence Welk produce it.

On asking about Leonard Bernstein's *Mass* the day after it premiered in memory of President Kennedy, quoted by White House Chief of Staff H R Haldeman *Haldeman's Diaries* Putnam 94

People magazine

9847 Feet size 7-EEE was as broad as his appeal.

On the sale of costumes of the late Rudolf Nureyev 11 Dec 95

Henry Pleasants critic

9848 [She] could hold a note as long as the Chase National Bank.

On Ethel Merman *The Great American Popular Singers* Simon & Schuster 85, quoted in NY *Times* 16 Feb 85

9849 One small town boy, born at the right time, in the right place, in the right environment and under the right circumstances [represented the convergence] of all the musical currents of America's subculture: black and white gospel, country and western and rhythm and blues.

On Elvis Presley *ib*

Philadelphia Inquirer

9850 It was like Venus de Milo wearing a bra.

On Helen Traubel's false eyelashes in *Tristan and Isolde* quoted by Humphrey Burton *Leonard Bernstein* Doubleday 94

Adam Clayton Powell Jr US Congressman

9851 His personal blues are now finished. No more the problems of Beale Street. No more the irritations of Memphis. No more the vexation of the St Louis woman. No more the cynical "Love, Oh Love, Oh Careless Love."

Funeral tribute to WC Handy NY *Times* 3 Apr 58

Orville Prescott critic

9852 Romance is a kind of round-robin tournament, psychosis the hallmark of every experiment.

On the typical ballet troupe *NY Times* 13 Jan 52 reviewing Agnes de Mille's *Dance to the Piper* Atlantic Monthly Press 52

J B Priestley playwright

9853 Oh! to be a conductor, to weld a hundred men into one singing giant, build up the most gorgeous arabesques of sound, wave a hand and make the clamoring strings sink or a mutter, wave again and hear the brass crashing out in triumph.

Time 17 Jan 83

Donnie Radcliffe critic

9854 Battle, fired from the Metropolitan Opera for her temperament, last night was as sweet as the lime ice mold with berries and peaches.

On Kathleen Battle singing *Amazing Grace* and Mozart's *Alleluia* at a White House state dinner for Boris Yeltsin *Washington Post* 28 Sep 94

Cyril Ritchard actor

9855 Behind that cold, austere, severe exterior, there beats a heart of stone.

On Metropolitan Opera General Mgr Rudolph Bing *NY Times* 17 Sep 89

Paul Robinson Professor of Intellectual History, Stanford

9856 Operatic music is an opiate that lowers our critical guard and allows us to entertain views that our good liberal selves would disavow were they presented in naked prose.

NY Times 1 Jan 88 reviewing Catherine Clement's *Opera, or the Undoing of Women* University of Minnesota Press 88

9857 Opera. . . permits men to give voice to their homicidal misogyny, albeit in often disguised or distorted form.

ib

Edward Rothstein reporter

9858 The piano. . . has suffered one turn of the screw after another. . . and has emerged thoroughly scathed.

On decrease in piano sales due to the bicycle, automobile, and other popular diversions, *NY Times* 28 May 95

Carl Sandburg poet

9859 Songs are like people, animals, plants. They have genealogies, pedigrees, thoroughbreds, crossbreeds, mongrels, strays, and often a strange lovechild.

The American Songbag 1927, recalled on Sandburg's death 22 Jul 67

9860 The personal idiom of a corn shock satisfies me. So does the attack of a high note by an Australian mezzo-soprano.

"Personalia" *Poems of Carl Sandburg* Harcourt Brace Jovanovich 70

Wolfgang Saxon critic

9861 He was careful not to step on a single note of the overture.

On Milton Cross's disciplined commentary during 43 years of Metropolitan Opera broadcasts, *NY Times* 4 Jan 75

Artur Schnabel pianist

9862 Great music is music that is written better than it can be played.

Chicago Sun-Times 30 Dec 85

Harold C Schonberg critic

9863 Tenors are usually short, stout men (except when they are Wagnerian tenors, in which case they are large, stout men) made up predominantly of large, rope-sized vocal cords, large frontal sinuses, thick necks, thick heads, tantrums and *Amour propre*. . . a race apart.

Show Dec 61

9864 From his baton, from the tips of his fingers, from his very psyche flows some sort of electric surcharge that shocks a hundred-odd prima donnas into bending their individual wills to a collective effort.

The Great Conductors Simon & Schuster 67

9865 His vocal cords were kissed by God.

On Luciano Pavarotti *London Times* 20 Jun 81

9866 [It was] the greatest melange of styles since the ladies' magazine recipe for steak fried in peanut butter and marshmallow sauce.

On Leonard Bernstein's Kennedy Center performance of the Bernstein *Mass NY Times* 12 Sep 91

9867 [He has] a quality of grieving, suppressed excitement, something like that of a leashed Doberman Pinscher who sees a rabbit in the distance.

On composer/administrator William Schuman, recalled on Schuman's death 15 Feb 82

9868 When Callas carried a grudge, she planted it, nursed it, fostered it, watered it and watched it grow to Sequoia size.

On Maria Callas *The Glorious Ones* Times Books 85, quoted in NY *Times* 21 Aug 85

9869 [He has] a look of intelligence so pronounced it can almost be touched. . .

On the composer/administrator William Schuman, recalled on Schuman's death 15 Feb 92

9870 [It was] not unlike an eerie, throbbing voice. . . a cello lost in a dense fog and crying because it does not know how to get home.

On Leon Theremin's development of the first synthesizer 9 Nov 93

Richard Selzer essayist

9871 A small pure soprano. . . as though a white mouse were ringing a tiny silver bell.

On his mother's voice *Down From Troy* Morrow 92

George Bernard Shaw playwright

9872 German is. . . at an advantage. . . [but] English profanity, except in America, has not gone beyond a limited technology of perdition.

On the need of bad orchestras to be properly cursed, quoted by Harold C Schonberg *The Great Conductors* Simon & Schuster 67

9873 I did not. . . raise my voice when the opera was too loud for normal conversation.

On behaving well at a musical program, letter to *London Times* in Kenneth Gregory ed *The First Cuckoo* Allen & Unwin 76

9874 A lady came in and sat down very conspicuously in my line of sight. . . [but] I did not complain of her coming late and going early; on the contrary, I wish she had come later and gone earlier.

On a trespasser to enjoyment *ib*

9875 A tenor and a soprano want to make love but they're prevented from doing so by a baritone.

On opera's simplistic plots, quoted on *Texaco's Metropolitan Opera* broadcast 25 Feb 95

9876 Dancing is a perpendicular expression of a horizontal desire.

London Times 19 Aug 95

Bobby Short pianist

9877 [His was] a world of penthouses, chiffon and champagne.

On Cole Porter *NY Times* 23 Jul 90

Susan Stamberg commentator

9878 The relationship between an orchestra and conductor is a delicate thing. . . can be as solid as a 30-year marriage and fragile as a crystal wedding gift, as rocky as the road to the Reno divorce court.

On interviewing National Symphony Orchestra Director-designate Leonard Slatkin NPR 8 Sep 94

9879 The relationship involves artistry, leadership, obedience, ego, and the ability to surmount a number of very bad conductor jokes.

ib

Otis Stuart critic

9880 Performers live to be looked at; some. . . carry their own personal proscenium around with them.

On Rudolf Nureyev *Perpetual Motion* Simon & Schuster 95

9881 [He] appeared in the West like one of those snakeskin strangers in late Tennessee Williams—a man with a past, bashful but basking in his own beauty and trailing chaos in his wake.

ib

9882 [Nureyev was] rebel sexuality. . . the first gay hero everyone knew was gay [but] publicly refused to acknowledge his homosexuality.

ib

9883 Nureyev clearly missed his chance. . . to lend his inexhaustible resources to a cause other than Rudolf Nureyev.

ib

Robert Sullivan critic

9884 Creole songs, chain-gang dirges, missionary hymns. . . they blended into something wonderful called "jass."

On New Orleans jazz *Life* Apr 95

Bob Thaves humorist

9885 Ginger Rogers did everything he did backwards, and in high heels.

On Rogers' long partnership with Fred Astaire *Ginger* HarperCollins 91

Time magazine

9886 Nilsson. . . sang as though her lungs were made of the finest Swedish steel. . . her tone as silver-pure as a Nordic winterscape.

On Birgit Nilsson "age 48 and boatswain burly" in the title role of *Salome* who "was 16 and slinky-slim" 12 Feb 65

9887 Even John the Baptist would have lost his head.

ib

9888 Lady of Spain, I Abhor You. . . .

On the dread choice of many accordionists 28 May 90

Joanne Trollope critic

9889 Some musicians believe in God and all believe in Bach.

On music "that brings agnostics as close to God as they will get" in "The Choir" a BBC series *Country Life* 30 Mar 95

Harry S Truman 33rd US President

9890 You are an eight ulcer man on a four ulcer job.

Letter to *Washington Post* critic Paul Hume who was unenthused about Margaret Truman's concert *Time* 18 Dec 50

Arthur Vance Editor-in-Chief *Pictorial Review*

9891 It would take a double castrated pink-faced tenor voice to reach most of your musical settings.

On Carl Sandburg's "American Songbag," quoted by Penelope Niven *Carl Sandburg* Scribner 91

Herbert Von Karajan conductor

9892 The people responsible for our recording technology—which allows music to be spread—they are the ones who should win the Nobel Prize for Peace.

NY Times 22 Oct 82

Michael Walsh critic

9893 Seeing the show is an exercise in long-range planning.

On *Phantom of the Opera*, often a tough ticket to obtain *Time* 18 Jan 88

9894 So powerful are the designs that... one leaves humming the scenery.

On Metropolitan Opera production of *Lucia* 7 Dec 92

Deena Weinstein Professor of Sociology, DePaul University

9895 Heavy metal keeps culture honest by showing that its values and symbols have multiple, ambiguous and undecidable interpretations.

Quoted by Sean Piccoli *Washington Times* 31 Jul 92 reviewing Weinstein's *Heavy Metal: A Cultural Sociology* Lexington 92

9896 They see metal as a place where wisdom and goodness, where true beauty and power, all come together.

ib

Tennessee Williams playwright

9897 Jooking... that's where you get in a car and drink a little and drive a little and stop and dance a little to a juke box.

Orpheus Descending Broadway play 55

Tom Wolfe novelist

9898 Lenny treasures "the art of conversation"... monopolizes it, conglomerates it.

On Leonard Bernstein, quoted by Humphrey Burton *Leonard Bernstein* Doubleday 94

9899 Anyone who has spent a 3-day weekend with Lenny knows... the alternating spells of adrenal stimulation and insulin coma as the Great Interrupter, the Village Explainer, the champion of Mental Jotto, the Free Analyst, Mr Let's Find Out, leads the troops on a 72-hour forced march through the lateral geniculate and the pyramids of Betz.

New York 8 Jun 70

9900 No breathers allowed, until every human brain is reduced finally to a clump of seaweed inside a burnt-out husk and collapses, implodes, in one last crunch of terminal boredom.

ib 8 Jun 70

PRESS

Editors and Reporters

Selig Adler Managing Editor *NY Mirror*

9901 Get it set in type and then go get yourself a job.

On handing a printer the notice of the closing of Hearst's tabloid *Mirror* 15 Oct 63, quoted in James G Bellows and Richard C Wald *The World of Jimmy Breslin* Viking 67

Jack Anderson columnist

9902 I don't like to hurt people... but in order to get a red light at the intersection, sometimes you have to have an accident.

Newsweek 3 Mar 72

Joseph W Alsop Jr columnist

9903 Your feet, which do the legwork, are nine times more important than your head, which fits the facts into a coherent pattern.

On preparing his column "Washington Merry-Go-Round" *Newsweek* 7 Oct 74

9904 The notion that a newspaperman doesn't have a duty to his country is perfect balls.

On being questioned by the CIA *Time* 26 May 77

Anon

9905 One Englishman is a story. Ten Frenchmen is a story. One hundred Germans is a story. One thousand Indians is a story.

Notice in London newsroom *International Herald Tribune* news summaries 30 Oct 75

9906 The stakeout [is] the lowest form of journalism and a boring penance for their journalistic sins.

On vigil outside closed hearings on Iran-Contra arms sales investigation 20 Dec 86

9907 We are taking water slowly. Power almost gone. List increasing. Understand your situation similar.

Teletype message from Washington bureau to Manhattan headquarters of *NY Herald Tribune* on its last day of publication 23 Apr 65, quoted by Richard Kluger *The Paper* Knopf 86

9908 Morale good here, considering. Reports some drinking below decks, but crew still loyal and mutiny unthinkable. Some fear casting off in lifeboats on icy seas, unknown waters. May truth in print, and honesty in reporting, and integrity in publishing reign foreverrrrrrrrrrrr.

Conclusion of teletype message *ib*

9909 Wipe your knees before entering.

Needlepointed inscription on cushion in office of picture editor Robert E Gilka, quoted by C D B Bryan in *National Geographic Society's Hundredth Anniversary Yearbook* 87

9910 If your Mother says she loves you, check it out.

On verification of facts, motto of City News Bureau, Chicago, displayed on banner at its hundredth anniversary celebration NPR 15 Dec 90

9911 The ship of state is the only ship that leaks from the top.

Quoted by Clark M Clifford *Counsel to the President* Random House 91

9912 He who lives by the photo op dies by the photo op.

Comment from a photographer denied coverage of President Reagan's controversial visit 3 May 85 to a cemetery with graves of German SS members, quoted by Secretary of State George P Shultz *Turmoil and Triumph* Scribner 93

9913 Expletive deleted.

On profanity edited out of tapes of the Nixon White House, cited by Fred Emery *Watergate* Times Books 94

9914 We needed cannon fodder. Bodies to throw at stories.

On expanding *NY Daily News* under publisher Mortimer B Zuckerman *New York* 23 Oct 95

9915 There's nothing more powerful in the media than a black-and-white headline.

On the power of the traditional newspaper despite the addition of color pictures *ib*

R W Apple Jr Washington Bureau Chief *NY Times*

9916 Among those in the upper echelons of power, as well as those who court them and write about them, self-importance is an occupational disease.

On covering politics and government, *Washington Post* 28 Jun 94

Robert L Bartley Editor *Wall Street Journal*

9917 I don't put people in jail, I put them in the newspaper.

On reporting on government *Nightline* ABC TV 19 Apr 94

Theodore M Bernstein Asst Managing Editor *NY Times*

9918 If writing must be a precise form of communication, it should be treated like a precision instrument. It should be sharpened, and it should not be used carelessly.

NY Times 28 Jun 79

9919 I favor whom's doom except after a preposition.

Decision after years of ambivalence on the use of who and whom *ib*

Hubert Beuve-Méry Executive Editor *Le Monde*

9920 Journalism is contact and distance. Both are necessary.

Recalled on Beuve-Méry's death 6 Aug 89

Homer Bigart foreign correspondent

9921 You had crossed the submarine-infested Atlantic without sighting even a porpoise. A hell of a thing to have to confess to your grandchildren.

Reporting on World War II voyage that successfully avoided German U-boats, recalled on Bigart's death, *NY Times* 17 Apr 91

Jim Bishop columnist

9922 A newspaper is lumber made malleable. . . ink made into words and pictures.

Quill Oct 63

9923 [A newspaper] is conceived, born, grows up and dies of old age, all in a day.

ib

9924 A reporter. . . gets to know princes and presidents, popes and paupers, prostitutes and panderers. And always in the back of his head, there will be a dozen men and women he will never meet, and always, he will feel the poorer for it.

6 Sep 79

9925 He dropped pejoratives like subliminal seasoning.

On Alden Whitman's *NY Times* obituaries 11 Jun 80

9926 The reporter is the daily prisoner of clocked facts. . . he is expected to do his best in one swift swipe at each story.

A Bishop's Confession autobiography Little, Brown 81

Erma Bombeck columnist

9927 I was terrible at straight news. When I wrote obituaries. . . the only thing I ever got them to do was die in alphabetical order.

On her first newspaper job *Time* 2 Jul 84

9928 I was too old for a paper route, too young for Social Security and too tired for an affair.

On beginning her humor column *Time* 2 Jul 84

Artyom Borovik Afghanistan war correspondent

9929 We were specialists in the dynamite business. . . to blow up those old Empire State buildings of our mentality.

On implementing freedom of the press in the Soviet Union *NY Times* 3 Feb 91

Margaret Bourke-White photographer

9930 Nothing attracts me like a closed door. I cannot let my camera rest until I have pried it open, and I wanted to be first.

Portrait of Myself on pioneering in industrial photography for *Fortune* Simon & Schuster 63

9931 When I come into that narrow cell with its tiny cot and little coke stove and wash stand, I think that this is all I want in the way of luxury—that it's the best in the world—as long as I am doing work I want to do.

On covering World War II, quoted by Vicki Goldberg *Margaret Bourke-White* Harper & Row 86

9932 [Shelling is] intensely and horribly personal.

On war coverage *ib*

Benjamin C Bradlee Executive Editor *Washington Post*

9933 Oh, Kay, I'd give my left one for that.

To Katharine Graham on being offered the editorship of the *Washington Post*, quoted by Joseph C Goulden *Fit to Print* Lyle Stuart 88

9934 I will retire when anyone whose last name is Graham tells me to.

On grooming a successor *Washingtonian* Jul 88

9935 Carl loved the midnight glitter. Bob loved the midnight oil.

On assessing the post-Watergate careers of reporters Carl Bernstein and Bob Woodward, quoted by William Safire *NY Times* 1 Oct 95 reviewing Bradlee's *A Good Life* Simon & Schuster 95

9936 In the darkest hour, he gave the press its finest hour.

On President Nixon and Watergate *A Good Life* Simon & Schuster 95

9937 No one needs an editor like an editor.

Saluting Simon & Schuster's Alice Mayhew for her role in writing his biography *ib*

Helen Gurley Brown Executive Editor *Cosmopolitan*

9938 I care, I care a lot. . . and I am scared. So it's a combination of fright, caring and anxiety.

To American Magazine Conference on successfully reviving *Cosmopolitan* magazine 23 Oct 84

9939 I use to have sex all to myself. Now I have to share it with *Ladies' Home Journal.*

New York 28 Aug 95

Tina Brown Executive Editor *Tattler, Vanity Fair, New Yorker*

9940 When I took her on, *Tattler* was a rather dull, stodgy deb: I put her on a diet, got her into some good designer clothes, sent her to Barbara Daly to have her face done, introduced her to bad company—she went on drugs briefly (she's off them now)—and she made a very good marriage to Condé Nast.

On *The Tattler* after it became a Condé Nast magazine *London Sunday Times* 20 Feb 83

9941 As far as I could see, castles were always plaster, money was always funny, and the nuns came off the set for a fag.

On being an observer of facade and realism *Life's a Party* David & Charles Inc 84

9942 Once in a while you have to bite the hand that reads you.

To American Newspaper Publishers Association 13 May 91 on the need for shriller, harder-edge reporting to avoid loss of readers to television, quoted by Edwin Diamond *Behind the Times* Villard 93

9943 *Vanity Fair* is for the thinking rich, and *Town & Country* is for the stinking rich.

When asked the difference between Condé Nast and Hearst magazines, quoted by Thomas Maier *Newhouse* St Martin's 94

9944 It might pack a little more punch than sounding, as a couple of editors here thought, like a choleric colonel in Angmering-on-Sea.

Letter to novelist John le Carré suggesting that he reduce the length of a letter of protest *ib*

Malcolm W Browne foreign correspondent

9945 This war seemed to smell more of greasepaint than of death.

On news management in the Persian Gulf War *Time* 11 Mar 91

Sean Callahan reporter *Life*

9946 [She helped establish] the reporter as *sherpa.*

On priority of photographers with reporters as secondary staff, quoted by Vicki Goldberg *Margaret Bourke-White* Harper & Row 86

Cornell Capa photographer *Life*

9947 When we went on a job and had a researcher or writer to go with us, they were privileged to carry our equipment. The photographer was in charge. We were kings and princes.

Quoted by Vicki Goldberg *Margaret Bourke-White* Harper & Row 86

Liz Carpenter Washington newspaperwoman

9948 [I never hesitated] to charge hell with a bucket of water.

On serving as press secretary to Claudia ("Lady Bird") Johnson *NY Times* 26 Jul 87

Robert J Casey foreign correspondent *Chicago Daily News*

9949 It was, and is, the unspoken Hippocratic oath of the newspaperman that, though he may sell out everything and everybody else in the world, he will never sell himself.

Quoted by Martin Mayer *Making News* Doubleday 86

9950 A newspaperman can get even with anybody in the world if he lives long enough... quietly with a bouquet of roses in one hand and a sockful of night-soil in the other. And my friends and my enemies pass under my window.

ib

9951 He was an old-school reporter in an era when the motto of the profession was "all for none and no one for anybody."

On Chicago newspaperman Hildy Johnson *ib*

Turner Catledge Managing Editor *NY Times*

9952 The composing room has an unlimited supply of periods available to terminate short, simple sentences.

Memo to staff *Time* 20 Dec 54

9953 Hell, that's what the news is—an emergency... [and] we look at this as pretty much routine.

On the sinking of the *Andrea Doria ib* 6 Aug 56

Winston S Churchill statesman

9954 I affected the style of Macaulay and Gibbon, the staccato antitheses of the former and the rolling sentences and genitival endings of the latter; and I stuck in a bit of my own from time to time.

On writing *The Story of the Malakand Field Forces* assembled from frontier dispatches from India, quoted by William Manchester *The Last Lion* Little, Brown 83

Tony Clifton foreign correspondent

9955 In Vietnam, you went anywhere nerve or foolishness would take you.

On non-restrictive freedom to cover a war *Newsweek* 11 Feb 91

Francis X Clines reporter

9956 Death's sting has a new meaning now that *The Times* [of London] is including candid descriptions of human peccadilloes in the obituaries.

Reporting on British influence on handling of obituaries, *NY Times* 15 May 87

9957 Peter Utley, the newspaper's obituary editor... cheerfully checked with Primrose Palmer, his assistant. The late Archbishop from New Zealand sounded promising, it was agreed, but then again it was lunch time, and who knew what had been happening in some now-ending life.

On reporting deaths of interest *ib*

Ariel Cohen essayist

9958 I write a column. I tell everybody what to do. That's my job.

Washington Times 11 Oct 95

William Cohen reporter

9959 To say something without really saying something was a real test.

On interviews following closed hearings on Iran arms sales *NY Times* 20 Dec 86

Janet Cooke reporter

9960 My goal was to create Supernigger.

On her personal ambition in authoring a series on an 8-year-old heroin addict only to be unmasked as a fraud when it won a Pulitzer Prize *Washington Post* 9 May 96

Alan Coren Executive Editor *The Listener*

9961 It was like climbing the north face of the Eiger with a large gas stove strapped to your back.

On difficulties of editing BBC's 61-year old *The Listener* in the wake of dwindling constituency and clout *London Times* 14 Dec 90

Ken Crawford Washington Bureau Chief *Newsweek*

9962 Bring him in Friday afternoons, tip him upside down, and see what falls out of his pockets. That's where you'll find the best stories.

On how to work with veteran correspondent Teddy Weintal *Ben Bradlee: A Good Life* Simon & Schuster 95

Judith Crist reporter

9963 A lot of us hated each other and disliked editors. But that's family.

At staff reunion on 25th anniversary of the closing of the *NY Herald Tribune* American Public Radio 17 Dec 90

Allan Demaree Senior Editor *Fortune*

9964 A story should be miserly of a reader's time.

Fortune 6 Feb 95

9965 An editor should measure a story by insights per page.

ib

Hedley Donovan Editor-in-Chief *Life*

9966 "Bias" is what somebody has when you disagree with his or her opinion.

Right Time, Right Times Holt 89

Maureen Dowd columnist

9967 Wooing the press... is an exercise roughly akin to picknicking with a tiger. You might enjoy the meal, but the tiger always eats last.

On White House entertaining of the media *NY Times* 2 Jan 94

Michael Duffy White House correspondent *Time*

9968 It's the difference between covering checkers and chess.

Comparing the Bush and Clinton administrations *Time* 7 Feb 94

Martin Dunn Editor, *NY Daily News*

9969 It was a "Hey, Mabel!" story.

On pictures that cause reader to exclaim, "Hey, Mabel, look at this!" as exemplified by a photo vigil of an automobile stripped in four days to a bucket of bolts, *NY Times* 1 Nov 93

Walter Duranty foreign correspondent *NY Times*

9970 My first rule is to believe nothing that I hear, little of what I read, and not all of what I see.

Quoted by Whitman Bassow *The Moscow Correspondents* Morrow 88

Robert T Elson corporate biographer

9971 [He had]... awesome hypochondria... 12 yards of quivering mucous membrane.

On editor Ralph Ingersoll *Time Inc* Atheneum 68

Fred Emery Washington Bureau Chief *The Times* of London

9972 It was a story of botched government that went from the implausible to the unthinkable.

On the break-in of Democratic party headquarters *Watergate* Times Books 94

9973 John Dean... was Nixon's Ides of March... not so quick as Casca's thrust at Caesar but ultimately fatal.

On White House Special Counsel John W Dean III *ib*

9974 The faces of the Nixon women told it all.

On the Nixon family's departure from the White House 8 Aug 74 *ib*

Erik Emptaz Editor *Le Canard Enchaine,* Paris weekly

9975 Adultery is part of French culture.

Contrasting his country's attitudes to the attention that the US gives to political candidates' private lives *Wall Street Journal* 27 Feb 92

Janet Flanner foreign correspondent *New Yorker*

9976 It must be precisely accurate, highly personal, colorful, and ocularly descriptive.

On editor Harold Ross's requirements for Flanner's "Letter from Paris," recalled on Flanner's death 7 Nov 78

9977 I live in a steady conflagration of matches, easily burnt out, but always relighted.

On balancing deadlines of magazines and books, quoted by Brenda Wineapple *Genêt* Ticknor & Fields 89

Max Frankel Executive Editor *NY Times*

9978 What happened today is more important than what happened yesterday, and what happened this afternoon is more important than what happened this morning, and what happened the last hour is more important than what happened two hours earlier.

On keeping up with breaking news *Esquire* Mar 93

9979 If you move the meat counter when all they want is a piece of meat, there is hell to pay. But if you have a wonderful sale... a great new soup, you'd better stick it in the aisle somewhere where their eye catches it.

On running a newspaper like a grocery *ib*

9980 Relations between men and women are the most important thing in the world. Just as important as war.

On a new emphasis on people over international events *ib*

9981 To catch a trend at the right moment is the most important thing we do.

ib

9982 Hard news is what happens today. And hard-hard is why it happened and who made it happen.

ib

Guy D Garcia "People" Section Editor *Time*

9983 Celebrities are instant icons.

Time 29 Jun 87

Meg Greenfield Op-Ed Editor *Washington Post*

9984 True audacity is... to question the tired assumptions in which most politicians nest.

Newsweek 13 Nov 89

9985 We are the dreadful children from a previous marriage.

On President Clinton's first year in the White House *ib* 15 Feb 93

John Gunther foreign correspondent and essayist

9986 What interested me was what color a man gave to the fabric of his time.

On figures in the news *Procession* Harper & Row 65

Larry Gurwin foreign correspondent

9987 I wrote the nouns and Adam wrote the verbs.

On combining his knowledge of the Middle East with Adam Zagorin's experience of the area *Time* 6 Nov 95

David Halberstam foreign correspondent

9988 We are not your corporals. . . we are not going to take your word for anything that happens if there is the remotest chance we can see it ourselves.

To Gen Paul Harkins, commander-in-chief in Vietnam, on war coverage, quoted by Harrison E Salisbury *Heroes of My Time* Walker 93

William Haley Editor *The Times* of London

9989 Anything more done on the inside would be stultified unless we did the fundamental thing on the outside.

On abandoning its long-time custom of classified ads on the front page instead of news *NY Times* 3 May 66

Pete Hamill columnist

9990 There was no more exciting sound than dozens of typewriters clacking towards a deadline.

On the old fashioned city room as compared to the modern newsroom "as quiet as insurance companies" Station WAMU 29 Mar 95

9991 Alcoholics and newspapermen have the same desire for immediate reward.

ib

Richard Harwood Nashville *Tennessean*

9992 The city editor told the photographer to get out there and get a picture of that atom before they split it and then the two halves of it afterwards.

On first news of the atomic bomb developed at Oak Ridge TN quoted by Martin Mayer *Making News* Doubleday 86

Fred M Hechinger Education Editor *NY Herald Tribune*

9993 I narrow-mindedly outlawed the word *unique*. Practically every press release contains it. Practically nothing ever is.

NY *Herald Tribune* 5 Aug 56

Ben Hecht reporter

9994 We looked on the hopheads, crooks and gunsels and on their bawdy ladies as members of a family among whom we were privileged to move.

On crime reporting in Chicago *Charlie* Harper 57

9995 We trotted, coach-dog fashion, at the heels of the human race, our tails awag.

ib

9996 [I was]. . . as void of ambition as an eel of feathers. . . as in love with life as an ant on a summer blade of grass.

On being a cub reporter *Gaily, Gaily* Doubleday 63

9997 Chicago is a sort of journalistic Yellowstone Park, offering haven to a last herd of fantastic braves.

On cynical, hard-drinking, exuberantly emotional breed of newspapermen as seen in his play *The Front Page* writtern with Charles MacArthur in 1928, recalled on Hecht's death 18 Apr 64

Hugh Hefner Editor *Playboy*

9998 The interesting thing is how one guy, through living out his own fantasies, is living out the fantasies of so many other people.

On the 25th anniversary of the magazine *Newsweek* 1 Jan 79

Anthony Holden reporter

9999 If you hear an anecdote from one source, you file it away. If you hear it again, it may be true. The more times you hear it the less likely it is to be true.

International Herald Tribune 9 Jun 79

John W Huey Jr Managing Editor *Fortune*

10000 Forbes is that phenomenon, unique to our media-ocracy, known as the boutique candidate.

On publisher Steve Forbes as a wealthy presidential candiate with little chance of election *Fortune* 5 Feb 96

10001 [If a back-runner] shows well enough in Iowa or New Hampshire, they have at him. . . [and] the once charming prince sinks into a hopeless bog of amateurish gaffes and scandal.

ib

Aleksandr A. Illyin Deputy Editor *Pravda*

10002 You can't leap across an abyss in two jumps.

On the closing of the Communist Party's newspaper *Pravda* after collapse of the Soviet Union *NY Times* 13 Mar 92

William R Inge Anglican priest

10003 I have ceased to be a pillar of the Church and have become two columns in the *Evening Standard*.

On retiring as the "gloomy dean" of St Paul's to

become a newspaper columnist, quoted by Alfred Noyes *Two Worlds for Memory* Lippincott 53.

Walter Isaacson Managing Editor *Time*

10004 Bristling like a pine forest of first-person pronouns.

On an interview in which Henry A Kissinger took credit for the Nixon administration's entire foreign policy *Kissinger* Simon & Schuster 92

10005 If you ask often enough, people aren't going to say no. . . . After all, their own life is the most interesting topic in the world to them.

On persistence in obtaining interviews *Publisher's Weekly* 7 Sep 93

James O Jackson Moscow Bureau Chief *Time*

10006 There is an availability of sources unheard of in the past and a past that had not been heard of before. Now we do current events and history all at once.

On Russia after the fall of Communism *Time* 27 Jun 88

Herman Klurfeld columnist

10007 He was the king of the world and I was one of the assistant kings.

On gathering news items for a widely syndicated column and weekly broadcast of the 1930s and 40s, quoted by Neal Gabler *Winchell* Knopf 94

Ann Landers (Eppie Lederer) columnist

10008 The changes I've seen would twirl your turban!

On four decades of syndicated advice *New Yorker* 4 Dec 95

10009 Forty lashes with the wet noodle!

On meting out her favorite punishment *ib*

Alexander Liberman Art Director Conde Nast magazines

10010 Youth is everyone's dream.

On the enduring appeal of fashion magazines, quoted by Thomas Maier *Newhouse* St Martin's 94

A J Liebling Press Editor *New Yorker*

10011 People everywhere confuse what they read in newspapers with news.

New Yorker 7 Apr 56

10012 I can write better than anyone who can write faster, and I can write faster than anyone who can write better.

Recalled on Liebling's death 28 Dec 63

10013 [He indulges in metaphor] as sparingly as a Montclair housewife employs garlic.

On reporter Bert Andrews of the *NY Herald Tribune*, quoted by Richard Kluger *The Paper* Knopf 87

10014 Freedom of the press is guaranteed only in those who own one.

ib

10015 The press. . . is the weak slat under the bed of democracy.

Christian Science Monitor 23 Jan 95

Lin Binyan activist writer

10016 We have no right to be auditors in the courtroom of history.

On the need for straight-forward reporting, quoted by Jonathan D Spence *The Search for Modern China* North 90

10017 The people are the judges as well as the plaintiffs.

ib

Walter Lippmann columnist

10018 The newspaper is. . . the bible of democracy, the book out of which a people determines its conduct. . . the only book most people read. . . the only book they read every day.

Liberty and the News Transition Press 95

Peter Lisagor Washington Bureau Chief *Chicago Daily News*

10019 We became spear carriers in a great televised opera.

On covering President Kennedy's news conferences, quoted by Ralph G Martin *A Hero for Our Time* Macmillan 83

10020 It was like making love in Carnegie Hall.

ib

David Low British cartoonist

10021 Here lies a nuisance dedicated to sanity.

Self-epitaph recalled on Low's death 19 Sep 63

10022 In the bluff, counterbluff of world politics, to draw a hostile warlord as a horrible monster is to play his game. What he doesn't like is being shown as a silly ass.

ib

Andrew Malcolm columnist

10023 The most exciting thing is that. . . by selection and arrangement of words and sentences and language, rhythms, and patterns, can make somebody feel exactly the same thing somewhere else at another time, and cry.

On writing a *NY Times* human interest column *Publisher's Weekly* 17 Apr 87

Janet Malcolm *New Yorker*

10024 [A novelist] is a master of his own house and may do what he likes in it. A reporter is only a renter, who must abide by the conditions of his lease.

NY Times 19 May 93

10025 Every journalist. . . is a kind of confidence man, preying on people's vanity, ignorance and loneliness, gaining their trust and betraying them without remorse. . . the canker that lies at the heart of the rose of journalism.

London Times 27 Aug 93

Joseph L Mankiewicz screenwriter

10026 I always read my column to pass the time. . . minutes fly by like hours.

Lines for a columnist in *All About Eve* based on Mary Orr's short story "The Wisdom of Eve" screenplay 1950

Robert Manning Editor *Atlantic*

10027 Cynicism. . . deflects attention from our far more wide spread flaw, incorrigible sentimentalism.

On writers and editors, *NY Times* 12 Jun 82

Angus McKinney Deputy Editor, *British GQ*

10028 All editors are bastards. But he was a great bastard.

On the death of his boss Angus MacKinnon *Newsweek* 11 Sep 95

Grace Mirabella Editor *Vogue* 1971–88, Founder-editor *Mirabella* 1988

10029 They are in the communications business but they don't know how to communicate.

On the Newhouse penchant for firing people publicly without telling them privately *Washington Post* 5 Jul 88

Willie Morris essayist

10030 It was on a burnished morning of New York springtime.

On becoming editor of *Harper's* at age 32 *New York Days* Little, Brown 93

Andrew Neil Editor *London Sunday Times*

10031 The judges have gone collectively bonkers!

On the courts' refusal to stop the *London Daily Mirror* from infringing on exclusive rights to Margaret Thatcher's memoirs *London Times* 28 Dec 93

New Yorker magazine

10032 A fat man with little steel-rimmed spectacles, Liebling sat jiggling with silent mirth as he typed.

Recalling A J Liebling 11 Mar 91

Louella Parsons columnist

10033 Listen, dearie, I was at the top when you were a has-been practicing to be a never-was.

To rival Hedda Hopper *Hedda and Louella* CBS TV 12 May 85

10034 The only thing that would lift your face is an elevator.

On Hedda Hopper's claim that Parsons' "face-lift is unraveling" *ib*

Charles Pathé founder, Pathé News

10035 [Film] is the theater, the school and the newspaper of tomorrow.

On forseeing that the news presented as shorts in moviehouses had the potential it was to realize in television *International Herald Tribune* 12 Nov 95

Kenneth W Payne Managing Editor, *Reader's Digest*

10036 When it is not necessary to change, it is necessary not to change.

On condensing articles, quoted by John Heidenry *Theirs Was the Kingdom* Norton 93

Mike Pearl Editor *NY Post*

10037 Violence, sex, money, kids, animals.

On the five ingredients necessary for a tabloid's success *Newsweek* 29 Jun 87

Drew Pearson columnist

10038 I operate by sense of smell. If something smells wrong, I go to work.

Quoted by Oliver Pilat, *Harper's* Magazine Press 73

Westbrook Pegler columnist

10039 We all wind up as packaged goods.

On a sameness in philosophy and style of writing, quoted by columnist Murray Kempton *American Heritage* Feb 95

Suzanne Puddlefoot essayist

10040 The *Times* is a tribal noticeboard.

On Britain's most venerable daily, cited by Nigel Ross *Why Do We Quote?* Blandford 89

Anna Quindlen columnist

10041 Half of me has lived and the other half has watched me live, notebook in hand.

On meeting regular deadlines *NY Times* 1 Dec 88

Paige Rense Editor-in-Chief *Architectural Digest*

10042 I fear divorce more than fire.

On events that can destroy a story already on press *NY Times* 8 Nov 93

10043 I thank divorce for giving me a continuing supply of material.

ib

James B Reston Washington Bureau Chief *NY Times*

10044 He overwhelmed you with decimal points or disarmed you with a wisecrack.

On President Kennedy's news conferences, quoted by Ralph G Martin *A Hero for Our Time* Macmillan 83

10045 People know that we handle the news with care and will probably write their obituaries. This opens a lot of doors.

Deadline Random House 91

10046 He regarded the press as a conveyor belt that should carry, without question, any baggage he wanted to dump on it.

On President Johnson *ib*

Grantland Rice columnist

10047 When a sportswriter stops making heroes out of athletes, it's time to get out of the business.

Quoted by Ira Berkow *Red* Times Books 86

A M Rosenthal Executive Editor *NY Times*

10048 Nobody could go picking on the mayor unless we caught him fucking dead goats.

On covering City Hall, quoted by Joseph C Goulden *Fit to Print* Lyle Stuart 88

Harold Ross founding Editor, *New Yorker*

10049 We were willing to be digested, but we are not willing to be first supplied, then digested.

On rejecting *Reader's Digest* procedure of placing articles in other magazines before condensing them, quoted by John Heidenry *Theirs Was the Glory* Norton 93

10050 [We have] never been particularly impressed with the theory that any piece can be improved by extracting every seventh word, like a tooth.

ib

William Safire columnist

10051 Years of accessibility to influential newsmen is like money in the bank, enabling the prudent depositor to obtain shelter, or at least a sympathetic hearing, on rainy days.

On US Secretary of State Henry A Kissinger, *NY Times* 28 May 73

10052 I'm kicking them while they're up.

On criticizing officials in the ascendency *US News & World Report* 8 Feb 88

10053 An "innoculation story" is an authorized leak of just enough embarrassing information to justify a front-page story. . . but because the source is so forthcoming, there is full credit for candor.

On dealing with the White House *NY Times* 9 Feb 89

10054 They are private communications to the *cognoscenti*, phrases out of our literary past scribbled by our horseless headmen across a newspaper page, put in a bottle and thrown out to the sea of faces.

On literary allusions by headline writers 1 Dec 91

10055 What a joy it is to see really professional media manipulation.

On Secretary of State Henry A Kissinger's press relations, quoted by Walter Isaacson *Kissinger* Simon & Schuster 93

10056 An adage is not quite as graven in collective wisdom as a proverb or a maxim. . . not as legalistic as a dictum or as scientific as an axiom, or as sentimental as a homily or as corny as a saw, nor as formalized as a motto, but it is more rooted in tradition than an observation.

9 Jan 94

10057 The essence of an adage is age; sayings are coined and adopted all the time. An adage is an old saying. Any "old adage" is redundant and subject to execution before the Squad Squad.

ib

Adela Rogers St Johns reporter

10058 You ought to be the newspaperman's Dream Boy. And radio and TV and all. You are the Great American Story.

Letter in Jan 53 to Richard M Nixon on eve of inauguration as Vice President, quoted by Tom Wicker's *One of Us* Random House 91

Harrison E Salisbury foreign correspondent *NY Times*

10059 If a writer lacks the courage to go against the grain, he is in the wrong profession. He should take up bookkeeping.

Heroes of My Time Walker 93

Carl Sandburg poet

10060 I never was any good in synchronizing with editors or publishers, except when I was a police reporter, then I would have the murder in the paper before the corpse was cold.

Quoted by Penelope Niven *Carl Sandburg* Scribner 91

Paul Sann Managing Editor *NY Post*

10061 If you've got the story, tell it. If you don't have the story, write it.

Advice to reporters *NY Times* 24 Feb 94

Sydney H Schanberg New Delhi Bureau Chief *NY Times*

10062 The credibility gap in Saigon makes other such gaps look like hairline fractures.

On covering the Vietnam War *NY Times* 12 Nov 72

10063 Napalm is a forbidden word and is called soft ordnance.

ib

10064 [It is] the newspaper that interprets the establishment to the establishment; that tells the establishment what it is doing and how it should be done.

On the *NY Times Esquire* Mar 93

Robert B Semple Jr Editor Op-Ed Page *NY Times*

10065 The *Times* had given birth to a new baby called the Op-Ed page—so named because it appeared opposite the editorial page and not (as many still suppose) because it would offer views contrary to the paper's.

On 20th anniversary of Op-Ed *NY Times* 30 Sep 90

10066 It was as if the Gray Lady had hit the dance floor.

On receipt of 350,000 manuscripts over two decades *ib*

Elaine Shannon reporter

10067 The only kind of sources I don't have are optimists.

On covering both sides of the drug war *Time* 7 Mar 88

William Shawn Editor *New Yorker*

10068 New information resides nowhere until it has been identified, objectified, assembled, and communicated by one or another kind of reporter; and every reporter sets out on every quest more or less in the dark.

Introduction to Irving Drustman ed *Janet Flanner's World* Harcourt Brace Jovanovich 79

10069 [We are] never to publish anything, never to have something written, for a hidden reason: to promote somebody or something, to pander to somebody, to build somebody up or tear somebody down, to indulge a personal friendship or animosity, or to propagandize.

On the "essence" of the *New Yorker*, cited by Thomas Maier as "the single greatest loss in the takeover by S I Newhouse" *Newhouse* St Martin 94

George P Shultz US Secretary of the Treasury, later Secretary of State

10070 Put it in a book, stamp it "Top Secret" and leak it.

On how to handle significant news *NY Times* 2 Nov 73

Hugh Sidey columnist

10071 Patience was required, craftsmanship demanded, good humor expected.

On newspaper apprentices *Time* 9 Oct 89

Howard Simon Managing Editor *Washington Post*

10072 [Call him] Deep Throat.

On bestowing the pseudonym (based on the title of a 1972 pornographic film) for Watergate's best known anonymous source who spoke from a "deep background" of information, recalled on Simon's death 3 Jun 89.

Liz Smith columnist

10073 Gossip is just news running ahead of itself in a red satin dress.

Dallas Times-Herald 3 Aug 78

10074 Older people who. . . think the sun rises and sets in their ass. . . have to be killed off like dinosaurs.

New York 9 May 88

10075 Interest in gossip comes right after food, sex, and coming in out of the rain.

NBC TV 13 Jan 90

10076 I don't practice pocketbook journalism. I'm more coin purse.

On paying sources *ib*

Stephen G Smith Editor *Civilization* magazine

10077 Spin is a form of propaganda. . . telling the press what the news means when the press should be doing that itself.

On official Washington's willingness to offer a "spin" on news announcements *Civilization* Mar 95

Walter W ("Red") Smith columnist *NY Herald Tribune*

10078 [For me, writing is] like opening a vein and letting the words come out drop by drop.

Quoted by Richard Kluger *The Paper* Knopf 86

10079 You spend a lifetime learning to find your way to the dugout at Yankee Stadium. It would be a shame to waste it.

On decision not to leave sportswriting for the international beat, quoted by Ira Berkow *Red* Times Books 86

10080 Writing well always has been and always will be one of the most difficult of human endeavors. And it never gets easier.

ib

10081 Does everybody have to do something "significant"? I'll leave "significance" to the political writers.

ib

10082 I feel I've won one-and-a-half Pulitzers.
On his reaction to being asked as a Pulitzer prize winner to serve on the Pulitzer recommendations committee *ib*

10083 I need to feel room to be lousy once a week. . . you get gaited to a column as a trotter in a race.
On writing a daily column *ib*

10084 One of the beauties of this job is that there's always tomorrow. Tomorrow things will be better.
ib

John R Starr Managing Editor *Arkansas Traveler*

10085 The afternoon repeat of the morning mistake.
On the *Arkansas Democrat* as opposed to the *Arkansas Gazette* before the two newspapers merged, quoted by Meredith L Oakley *On the Make* Regnery 94

Edmond W Stevens reporter

10086 I got stuck with the story.
On covering the Soviet Union for 40 years *NY Times* 27 May 92

Richard Stolley Founding Editor *People*

10087 Young is better than old, pretty is better than ugly, TV is better than music, music is better than movies, movies are better than sports, and anything is better than politics.
Formula for editing, quoted by Mary W Quigley *Washington Journalism Review* Jul 88

C L Sulzburger *NY Times*

10088 [I like] keeping in with those who're out.
On establishing a relationship with Charles de Gaulle during the years he was not in power *London Times* 22 Sep 93

Herbert Bayard Swope Executive Editor *NY World*

10089 Nothing is more interesting than opinion when opinion is interesting.
On creating the first Op-Ed page and coining the term in the *NY World*, quoted by E J Kahn Jr *The World of Swope* Simon & Schuster 65

Evan Thomas White House correspondent *Newsweek*

10090 A stripper named Fannie Fox went swimming one night in 1974 on a drunken spree with House Ways and Means Chairman Wilbur Mills, thereby forever ending the zone of privacy that had protected the personal life of politicians.
Newsweek 26 Dec 94

Helen Thomas White House correspondent UPI

10091 There are no unacceptable questions, only unacceptable answers.
Quoted by Edward Bliss Jr *Now the News* Columbia University Press 91

Dick Thompson reporter

10092 My pen doesn't take pictures.
On interview with Soviet cosmonauts who didn't want to shave before being photographed *Time* 5 Oct 87

Edward K Thompson Managing Editor *Life*

10093 With that woman's capacity for self-delusion, she could have believed they couldn't have had the invasion without her.
On photographer Margaret Bourke-White's World War II coverage of Africa, quoted by Vicki Goldberg *Margaret Bourke-White* Harper & Row 86

James Thurber humorist

10094 He. . . used insults the way other people use simple declarative sentences.
On Alexander Woollcott *The Years With Ross* Atlantic Monthly Press 59

R Emmett Tyrrell Jr Editor *American Spectator*

10095 If you have a tabloid president, you're going to have a tabloid press.
On President Clinton ABC TV 26 Jul 94

Diana Vreeland Editor *Vogue*

10096 *Vogue* is the myth of the next reality.
Defining her magazine, quoted by Dodie Kazanjian and Calvin Tomkins *Alex* Knopf 93

10097 Youth went out to life, instead of waiting for life to come to them, which is the difference between the 60s and any other decades I've lived in.
ib

10098 I've never taken out more than two ribs.
On retouching photographs of models

10099 What sells is hope.
Quoted by Annette Tapert and Diana Edkins *The Power of Style* Crown 94

10100 Alex, I've known many White Russians, we've known a few Red Russians. But, Alex, you're the only Yellow Russian I've ever known.
To Condé Nast Art Director Alex Liberman after he failed to defend her dismissal, quoted by Thomas Maier *Newhouse* St Martin's 94

10101 Give 'em what they never knew they wanted.
On readers of fashion magazines, quoted by Grace Mirabella *In and Out of Vogue* Doubleday 95

John Wheeler Chair, Vietnam Memorial Fund

10102 It was the defining event. . . and remains a thousand degrees hot.

On the Vietnam War *Touched With Fire* Avon 85

E B White *New Yorker*

10103 When our phone rang just now. . . we thought, "Good! Here it comes!" But this old connection is broken beyond fixing.

On the death of editor Harold Ross *New Yorker* 15 Dec 51

10104 The phone has lost its power to explode at the right moment and in the right way.

ib

10105 Writing of the small things of the day, the trivial matters of the heart, the inconsequential. . . was the only kind of creative work which I could accomplish with any sincerity or grace.

On the accommodation of the *New Yorker* for his "impertinence and irrelevancies" *Washington Post* 7 Oct 85

10106 Sometimes in writing of myself—which is the only subject anyone knows intimately—I have occasionally had the exquisite thrill of putting my finger on a little capsule of truth, and heard it give the faint squeak of mortality under my pressure, an antic sound.

ib

10107 Commas fell with the precision of knives in a circus act, outlining the victim.

On the precise editing style of the *New Yorker* copy desk as a "marvelous fortress of grammatical exactitude and stylish convention" quoted by George Plimpton ed *Writers at Work* Penguin 88

Theodore H White reporter *Time*

10108 They had become more than a press corps—they had become his friends and, some of them, his devoted admirers. They. . . felt that they, too, were marching like soldiers of the Lord to the New Frontier.

On writers who covered John F Kennedy's campaign *The Making of a President 1960* Atheneum 61

10109 History can be approached as journeymen reporters generally do: as a study of men making up their minds, prisoners of their information, captives of events, forced in decision when scissored by clash, acting either clumsily or gracefully when hit by the unexpected.

The Making of a President 1968 Atheneum 69

10110 It was like walking through a field playing a brass tuba the day it rained gold. Everything was sitting around waiting to be reported.

On his book on the Kennedy campaign, quoted by Timothy Crouse *The Boys on the Bus* Random House 73

10111 When that book came out, it was like Columbus telling about America at the court of Ferdinand and Isabella.

ib

10112 When a reporter sits down at the typewriter, he's nobody's friend.

ib

10113 For those. . . lucky enough to break away from the pack, the most intoxicating moment comes when they cease being bodies in other men's command and find that they control their own time, when they learn their own voice and authority.

On becoming a foreign correspondent *In Search of History* Harper & Row 78

10114 I'd get into a room and disappear into the woodwork. Now the rooms are so crowded with reporters getting behind-the-scenes stories that nobody can get behind-the-scenes stories.

On his method of reporting, recalled on White's death 15 May 86

10115 When the tree begins to fall, for the first time you see how tall it is.

On Henry R Luce's withdrawal from active management of Time-Life publications, quoted by Ralph G Martin *Henry and Clare* Putnam 91

Alden Whitman reporter, *NY Times*

10116 An obit is. . . a picture. . . a snapshot. . . not a full-length biography. . . not a portrait. It's a quick picture.

W 18 Jul 80

10117 A good obit has all the characteristics of a well-focused snapshot, the fuller length the better. . . a quick fix on the subject, his attainments, his shortcomings and his times.

On pioneering the practice of personal interviews to personalize and energize later obituaries NY *Times* 5 Sep 90

William Whitworth Editor *Atlantic*

10118 All "little" magazines have the luxury of thinking the reader is the same person as their editors.

Christian Science Monitor 31 Jul 85

Russell Wiggins Editor *Washington Post*

10119 Always edit with your hat on.

On willingness to lose one's job to maintain editorial integrity, quoted by Hedley Donovan *Right Places, Right Times* Holt 89

Walter Winchell columnist

10120 If only when my epitaph is readied, they will say, "Here's Walter—with his ear to the ground as usual."

Quoted by Ed Weiner *Let's Go to Press* Putnam 55

10121 Broadway's mountain. Tough sledding on the way up—a toboggan on the way down.

Concluding item in Winchell's column in the last edition of his flagship newspaper *NY Daily Mirror* 16 Oct 63

10122 Gossip is the art of saying nothing in a way that leaves practically nothing unsaid.

Recalled on Winchell's death 20 Feb 72

10123 Today's gossip is tomorrow's headlines.

Quoted by columnist Liz Smith *Dallas Times-Herald* 3 Aug 78

10124 Social position is now more a matter of press than prestige.

Quoted by Neal Gabler *Winchell* Knopf 94

Bob Woodward *Washington Post*

10125 My Watergate reporting was very important for the country and for journalism and for subduing this rightist movement in American, tramping it down and saying, "Whoa!"

Wall Street Journal 3 Jan 88

10126 All good work is done in defiance of management.

On 20th anniversary of Watergate break-in CBS TV 17 Jun 92

10127 He much prefers thick ice.

On *Washington Post* publisher Don Graham's liking for controversy *Washingtonian* Aug 92

10128 There is a place for reporting that aspires to combine the thoroughness of history with the contemporaneity of journalism.

Introduction to his book on the first two years of the Clinton presidency *The Agenda* Simon & Schuster 94

Publishers and Management

Anon

10129 The public is interested in just three things: Blood, money, and the female organ of sexual intercourse.

A tabloid executive speaking to A J Liebling on the "yellow press" as it evolved in the hands of Pulitzer and Hearst *New Yorker* 12 Dec 94

Lord Beaverbrook (Maxwell William Humphrey Aiken) publisher

10130 What a fine title—Lord Thomson of Fleet! How did Northcliffe and Rothermere, Riddell and Lord Dalziel and I and some others give him an opportunity of taking that? . . . We could have been in before him.

On learning that Roy Thomson had been make a peer, quoted by Russell Braddon *Roy Thomson of Fleet Street* Collins 65

10131 I no longer control. I still dominate.

Letter to *Time* Inc founder Henry R Luce, John Robert Colombo ed *Columbo's Canadian Quotations* Hurtig 74

10132 Sow the seeds of discord! Sow the seeds of discord!

To his editors, quoted by Tim Heald *Weekend Toronto* 26 May 79

10133 It is time for me to become an apprentice once more.

At 85th birthday dinner two weeks before his death, quoted by A J P Taylor *Beaverbrook* Simon & Schuster 72

10134 Act justly, love money, walk briefly.

Personal motto quoted by Ann Chisholm and Michael Davies *Lord Beaverbrook* Knopf 93

Michael Berman Co-founder *George*

10135 Being John Kennedy's partner is a lot like being Dolly Parton's feet. . . nice but you tend to get overshadowed.

On launching a new monthly magazine with the slogan "Not just politics as usual" *New York* 18 Sep 95

Robert L Bernstein President, Random House

10136 A mountain range instead of a mountain.

On decentralized approach to book publishing, quoted by Thomas Maier *Newhouse* St Martin's 94

Fred Drasner Co-Publisher *NY Daily News*

10137 Mort's a lightning rod because he came in sideways.

On Mortimer B Zuckerman as a man of means rather than a man of the streets in purchase of the *Daily News*, quoted in *New York* 23 Oct 95

Donald E Graham Publisher, *Washington Post*

10138 We're turning our pages over to a man who has murdered people. But I'm convinced we're making the right choice between bad options.

On a serial killer known as Unabomber (Theodore Kaczynscki) and his demand for publication of a 35,000-word manifesto protesting an "unnatural industrial-technological society" *NY Times* 30 Jun 95

Katharine Graham Chair, *Washington Post*

10139 If we had failed to pursue the facts as far as they led, we would have denied the public any knowledge of an unprecedented scheme of political surveillance and sabotage.

On Watergate coverage *Washington Post* 5 Mar 73

10140 Here we were along with this... cow mess walking down a street and nobody came near it.

On initial reluctance of other newspapers to report on Watergate, quoted by Lawrence Leamer *Playing for Keeps in Washington* Dial 77

10141 [It is like] having Anwar el-Sadat... speak at a B'nai B'rith convention.

On presence of a critic, former Secretary of State William Rogers, at dedication of the newspaper's new building; Rogers responded with Thomas Jefferson's remark that "newspapers are an evil from which there is no remedy," quoted by Carol Felsenthal *Power, Privilege and The Post* Putnam 93

William Randolph Hearst publisher

10142 You furnish the pictures and I'll furnish the war.

To artist Frederic Remington on the Spanish American War, recalled on Hearst's death 14 Aug 51

10143 Puff Graham.

Terse notice to his newspapers to publicize evangelist Billy Graham *ib*

John Hoagland Jr Manager Christian Science Publishing Society

10144 It may be the jewel in the crown of the church but you have to have a crown to have a jewel.

On loss of $200 million since 1961 as a commitment to television that could not be retained *Time* 28 Nov 88

Michael J Klingensmith publisher *Entertainment Weekly*

10145 This magazine keeps people pop-culturally literate.

NY Times 6 Mar 95

Life magazine

10146 One of our functions is introducing the Vermonter and the Californian to each other... explaining America to Americans.

Quoted by Vicki Goldberg *Margaret Bourke-White* Harper & Row 86

Henry R Luce Co-founder Time Inc

10147 [A male researcher] would feel like a choir boy in the chorus of Minsky's burlesque. We invented most of the women who are here, because we invented a thing called the researcher.

On Time-Life's first decades when only men were editors, quoted by Ralph G Martin *Henry and Clare* Putnam 91

10148 Let all stories make sharp sense. Omit flowers. Remember you can't be too obvious. People talk too much about things they don't know.

To the first staff members *ib*

10149 The job of journalism was to foment and formulate. Facts should be married to imagination and passion.

On digested accounts of original reports *ib*

10150 [Explore] every corner of industry from the steam shovel to the board of directors.

To photographer Margaret Bourke-White on preparing the first issue of *Fortune* in 1929, quoted by managing editor John W Huey *Fortune* 21 Aug 95

10151 [Produce] the most dramatic photographs of industry that have ever been taken.

ib

Robert Maxwell publisher

10152 This is a sobering additional responsibility to take on 1,800 people's jobs and the survival of a monument.

On acquiring the *NY Daily News NY Times* 13 Mar 91

10153 When I pass a belt, I cannot resist hitting below it.

ib

Allen H Neuharth Founder *USA Today*

10154 We were frowned on by the establishment. Now they're stealing all our McNuggets.

On other newspapers' adoption of the jumbo weather map, regional news digests, and other features similar to popular innovations at McDonald's *Newsweek* 25 Apr 92

S I Newhouse publisher

10155 I'm not interested in buying funerals.

On closing newspapers that did not respond to a financial turn-around *Business Week* 26 Jan 76

S I Newhouse Jr publisher

10156 It's a little bit like trying to describe love.

Testimony in federal tax case on his motivation in acquring newspapers, quoted by Thomas Maier *Newhouse* St Martin 94

New York Publishers Association

10157 Give 'em nothing and do it retroactively.

Quoting advice from labor professionals in four-month newspaper strike *NY Times* 1 Apr 63

New Yorker magazine

10158 The *New Yorker* is no more a magazine about New York City than *Time* is a magazine about wristwatches.

Advertisement mailed to potential subscribers 5 Jan 89

New York Post

10159 Headless Body in Topless Bar.

Headline 15 Apr 83 that became a symbol of the newspaper's position as one of the last bastions of no holds-barred, spit-in-the-eye, tabloid journalism *Time* 23 May 88

The New York Times

10160 We do not omit the Mr in. . . references to a person convicted of crime or having an unsavory reputation.

NY Times Manual of Style and Usages Times Books 76

10161 Should the use of Mr in such cases seem ludicrously out of place, judicious editing and the use of pronouns or terms like the defendant or the suspect will solve the problem.

ib

10162 Until now, Ms has not been used because of the belief that it had not passed sufficiently into the language to be accepted as common useage.

ib

10163 All the corrections fit to print.

On decision to publicly acknowledge errors, interoffice memo 27 Jul 87

Eleanor Medill ("Cissy") Patterson Publisher *Washington Times-Herald*

10164 I wish I were still in Chicago so I could have that son of a bitch rubbed out.

On columnist Drew Pearson, quoted by David Brinkley *Washington Goes to War* Knopf 88 [p 186]

Lord Rothermere (Harold Sydney Harmsworth) Chairman London *Daily Mail*

10165 I buy wood pulp, process it and sell it at a profit.

Quoted by David Frost and Antony Jay *The English* Stein & Day 68

Arthur Hays Sulzberger Publisher *NY Times*

10166 [*The Times* is not a] Christmas tree from which roaming Santas might pluck packages at their will.

To reporters who wished to broadcast or write books about experiences as employees of the newspaper, quoted by Joseph C Goulden *Fit to Print* Lyle Stuart 88

Arthur Ochs ("Punch") Sulzberger Publisher *NY Times*

10167 These changes will not affect content or the quality of our product.

On switching to a six-column format *NY Times* 15 Jun 76

10168 [I was] a *Times* vice president in charge of nothing.

On joining the family-owned *New York Times* after World War II *New York* 30 Sep 91

10169 I've made my first executive decision. I've decided not to throw up.

To his sister after his first day as publisher, recalled as he stepped aside 28 years later for his son to take the job *NY Times* 17 Jan 92

Lord Thomson Of Fleet (Roy Thomson) publisher

10170 My favorite color? Gold!

On profitability of newspapers, John Robert Colombo ed *Colombo's Canadian Quotations* Hurtig 74

Mortimer B Zuckerman publisher *NY Daily News*

10171 I enjoy the *New York Post* as a comic book.

On competition among tabloids *New York* 6 Jun 94

Press Critics

Dean Acheson US Secretary of State

10172 The liturgical ending of all endeavors, a press conference.

On the conclusion of a Foreign Ministers meeting in Paris *Sketches From Life* Harper 61

10173 My small talk at dinner parties. . . is likely to run perilously close to slander. . . usually stimulated by the stuffed shirts, the pompous and pretentious, who multiply in Washington like algae in a summer pond.

Declining John Fischer's invitation to write a monthly column for *Harper's* 17 Dec 63, David S McLellan and David C Acheson ed *Among Friends* Dodd Mead 80

Henry Allen humorist

10174 They come to rest in Washington's mind. . . in the manner of statues that traffic circles get named after, with columnists perched on their shoulders like pigeons, cooing and squabbling.

On advisers to US Presidents *Washington Post* 3 Jan 89

Susan Heller Anderson reporter

10175 [He] often bit the hand he had kissed the night before.

Reporting on British cartoonist Mark Boxer *NY Times* 23 Jul 88

Peter Andrews essayist

10176 *USA Today* is like a bus schedule for people who can't get to the depot... doesn't give you much but tells you when the bus is leaving.

American Heritage Oct 94

10177 The ideal newspaper story is one that yokes celebrity with scandal in an action that can be simply stated.

ib

Anon

10178 The *NY Mirror*, 39, a partner in the Hearst Corporation, died yesterday at its home, 235 East 45th St, after a long illness. It is survived by a sister, the *NY Journal-American*.

A reporter's obituary on the closing of Hearst's Manhattan tabloid, quoted in *NY Times* 16 Oct 63

10179 [I applaud] the evocative quality of distant cultivated voices speaking in clearly modulated, often self-conscious tones.

On letters to *London Times* Kenneth Gregory ed *The First Cuckoo* Allen & Unwin 81

10180 Reporters are like alligators. You don't have to love them, you don't necessarily have to like them. But you do have to feed them.

White House source on plans for frequent press briefings during Tokyo economic summit *US News & World Report* 5 May 86

10181 Their readers are our customers; your readers are our shoplifters.

Bloomingdale advertising manager's reply to *NY Post* on his preference for advertising in the *NY Times*, quoted by Martin Mayer *Making News* Doubleday 86

10182 The velvet coffin.

On *LA Times* stodginess *Wall Street Journal* 7 Feb 89

10183 Cooking the news.

Journalistic terminology for practices such as *USA Today* requiring that a woman's photograph appear daily above the centerfold of the front page *Washington Times* 12 Apr 89

10184 You know you cannot bribe or twist/ Thank God, the British journalist,/ But seeing what the men still do/ Unbribed, there's no occasion to.

Quoted by Martin Mayer *The Greatest-Ever Bank Robbery* Scribner 90

10185 You've been fired on the front page of *The Times*!

A friend's telephone comment to Joni Evans on S I Newhouse Jr's failure to communicate directly with her on appointing a new publisher of Random House's signature imprint *New York* 5 Aug 91

10186 Tabloid terrorism.

Charge by aides of Governor Bill Clinton against sex scandal brought by the *Star* supermarket newspaper *NY Times* 2 Feb 92

10187 Preppy, tweedier-than-thou arrogance.

On editor Ben Bradlee, quoted by Carol Felsenthal *Power, Privilege and the Post* Putnam 93

10188 After you've worked in the White House, anything else is like playing poker with matchsticks.

Quoted by Liz Carpenter, press secretary to Claudia ("Lady Bird") Johnson, Station WAMU Washington 24 Nov 94

10189 Tabloid in a tutu.

Journalists' name for *NY Newsday*, Long-Island based daily that combined tabloid style with serious, in-depth coverage *NY Times* 15 Jul 95

10190 She's daring in her blaring.

On White House Correspondent Sarah McClendon CBS TV 8 Oct 95

10191 Sweeney and Mrs Sweeney are ambitious and expectant... they believe in God, the United States, and life... respect education and want the kids to have plenty of it.

An advertisement of the 1920s on typical readers of tabloids, recalled by John Chapman *Tell It to the Sweeneys* Doubleday 61, quoted in *New York* 23 Oct 95

10192 They look forward to a grapefruit for breakfast, their own homes, a little car, money in the bank, and a better future for the Sweeney juniors.

On desires of a few decades ago as compared, in Chapman's words, to "some of the Sweeneys [of the 1960s] who are buying Pierce-Arrows and Long Island estates" *ib*

Robert Sam Anson critic

10193 By the time he reached his 40th birthday, he'd passed through every station of the cross.

On Arthur Ochs Sulzberger Jr's jobs in all areas of work on the *NY Times* before becoming its publisher *Esquire* Mar 93

The Atlantic

10194 For 24 years he presided over these pages with discerning eccentricity.

Tribute to Charles W Morton, Nov 67

10195 Where ever he is—somewhere in Thurber Country with Mencken, Mr Dooley, DeVoto, and the other rare, ivory-billed woodpeckers of American letters—he is certain to be appalled by the food, outraged by the service, and unavoidably generous to the fellow at the gate.

ib

Ben Bagdikian critic

10196 Trying to be a first-rate reporter on the average American newspaper is like trying to play Bach's *St Matthew's Passion* on the ukulele: the instrument is too crude for the work, for the audience and for the performer.

American Heritage Oct 94

Russell Baker columnist

10197 [A newspaper is] a peeper, invader of privacy, scandal peddler, mischief-maker, busybody, a man content to wear out his hams sitting in marble corridors waiting for important people to lie to him, comic strip intellectual, human pomposity dilating on his constitutional duty, drum thumper on a demagogue's bandwagon, member of the claque for this week's fashion, part of next week's goon squad that will destroy it.

Life Apr 89

Max Beerbohm humorist

10198 Could not the outrage be averted? There sprang from my lips that fiery formula which has sprung from the lips of so many choleric old gentlemen, "I shall write to *The Times*!"

Kenneth Gregory ed *The First Cuckoo* Allen & Unwin 76

William J Bennett US Secretary of Education

10199 Your job is to have a successful conversation with the American people.

On press relations *Time* 19 Sep 88

Carl Bernstein reporter

10200 Ivana Trump, perhaps the single greatest creation of the idiot culture, a tabloid artifact if ever there was one.

New Republic 8 Jun 92

Aneurin Bevan Prime Minister of Britain

10201 I read the newspaper avidly. It is my one form of continuous fiction.

Recalled on Bevan's death 2 Jul 60

Joseph R Biden Jr US Senator

10202 The only thing worse than bad taste. . . would be for us to start to meddle in your 1st Amendment right to exercise your bad taste.

USA Today 11 May 87

Naomi Bliven critic

10203 If journalism comes in shades of yellow, Beaverbrook's was a pale buttercup.

On Lord Beaverbrook *New Yorker* 1 Mar 93 reviewing Anne Chisholm and Michael Davie's *Lord Beaverbrook* Knopf 93

Betty Boothroyd Speaker of the House of Commons

10204 Had I been an overworked social worker in Oldham, nobody would have written about it.

On leaving school at 16 to join the high-kicking Tiller Girls dance troupe *Washington Post* 29 Sep 93

Major General Patrick H Brady Deputy Commander, US 6th Army

10205 Some look on news as just another four-letter word, but I believe it is more useful to look at it as a C-letter word: chaos, confusion, contradiction, crime, corruption, color, catastrophe. It does not hurt if you add some S's—sex, sensationalism, state secrets.

On the military's press relations *Army* Sep 90, quoted in *NY Times* 3 Mar 91

Anatole Broyard critic

10206 John Aldridge has always seemed to me to be some sort of an organ transplant at *The Saturday Review*, one that never managed to revitalize the arteriosclerotic old body, but that, paradoxically, continued to thrive by itself.

Aroused by Books Random House 74

Warren Buffett Chair, Berkshire, Hathaway Inc

10207 [It is an] unregulated tollbooth.

On acquiring *Washington Post* stock *Washington Journalism Review* Jun 91

Barbara Bush First Lady

10208 Avoid this crowd like the plague. And if they quote you, make damn sure they heard you.

To Hillary Rodham Clinton on reporters covering the White House, *NY Times* 20 Nov 92

George Bush 41st US President

10209 These long penetrating lenses. . . cause us to wear T-shirts when we go swimming. . . because we don't want to be analyzed by the doctors from the *NY Times*.

To press on beach at Gulf Stream FL *NY Times* 15 Nov 88

10210 [It is] a modified limited photo op cum statement sans questions.

On photo sessions at which he spoke but did not take reporters' questions *ib* 26 Mar 89

10211 I hate to be secretive, to say nothing of deceptive, but I'm not going to tell you.

At Barranquilla, Colombia, reacting to criticism that his statement on a four-power conference pointed in one direction while his actions went in another *ib*

10212 I'm not going to discuss what I'm going to bring up. . . (and) even if I don't discuss it, I'm not going to discuss it.

On declining to elaborate on using US Navy to monitor South American drug traffic *ib* 16 Feb 90

10213 I can't go into the details of that, because some will think it is too much sleep and others will think it's too little sleep.

When asked if he had a good night's sleep *ib*

10214 I simply was not articulate enough to override a well-run opposition. . . and an often cynical and ugly press, an unaccountable press, the likes of which I've never encountered in 30 years in and out of public life.

Comment a year after losing to Bill Clinton for a second term *Washington Times* 21 Jan 94

10215 I do coffee. I do dog walking. I do windows. I do grandchildren. But I do not do press interviews, and that is a feeling of enormous liberation for me.

At forum sponsored by San Diego Chamber of Commerce *ib* 20 Nov 94

10216 He speaks for a bunch of...Chardonnay-sipping elitists.

On cartoonist Garry Trudeau's Doonesbury *Life* Oct 95

Jay Carr critic

10217 One of the things that will keep *The Front Page* burning bright as long as newspapers are alive is the myth that newspapermen are breezy and raffish. What other play has for so long fed the self-image of journalists?

Reviewing Broadway revival of Ben Hecht and Charles MacArthur's 58-year-old play *Boston Globe* 4 Dec 86

10218 They were fast-moving opportunists encased in cynicism and proud of it.

On Chicago reporters *ib*

10219 [Walter Burns] is the archetypal managing editor—ruthless, self-righteous, manipulative, downright maniacal if it means an exclusive, especially one that it can congratulate itself for on its own front page.

ib

Douglass Carter

10220 [It is a] fourth branch of government.

On the press quoted by Richard E Neustadt *Presidential Power and the Modern Presidency* Free Press 90

Jimmy Carter 39th US President

10221 There have been a few presidents in my lifetime who have been treated with kid gloves by the press. . . Roosevelt, Eisenhower, Kennedy, and Reagan. All the rest of us have been treated harshly.

Christian Science Monitor 5 Jun 87

10222 I never was able to form a reasonable relationship with the press.

ib

Alan Clark British Minister of Trade

10223 If you are Editor you can never get away for an evening. It's worse than a herd of dairy cows.

On dining with *London Times* Editor Charles Douglas-Home *Mrs Thatcher's Minister* Farrar Straus Giroux 93

Hillary Rodham Clinton First Lady

10224 I've always been a fairly private person leading a public life. . . always believed in a zone of privacy . . . [but] I feel after resisting for a long time I've been re-zoned.

On calling a news conference to discuss reports of her investments in Watergate land sales and in stock market commodities *NY Times* 23 Apr 94

10225 I can't be something other than what I am, and what I am is someone who wants to be part of helping to change this country.

Vanity Fair Jun 94

10226 I read things and hear stories about me. . . and I go, "Ugh, I wouldn't like her either."

On discussing her self-image with a group of women writers invited to a White House luncheon *International Herald Tribune* 11 Jan 95

10227 I have let other people define me. The stories come and go; I remain the same.

News conference 17 Feb 95

William J Clinton 42nd US President

10228 I have long since given up the thought that I could disabuse some of you of turning any substantive decision into anything but a political process.

Reply to ABC's Brit Hume who asked Clinton on the occasion of a Supreme Court appointment if he could disabuse the press of perceiving "a certain zigzag quality in the decision-making process" 14 Jun 93

10229 You guys have to compete with near-news. . . like. . . when we were kids, we'd drink near-beer.

To reporters aboard Air Force One on "too much information and too much sort-of quasi-information" *Washington Post* 24 Sep 95

Joanna Coles *The Guardian*

10230 He used letters like hand grenades.

On novelist Graham Greene's correspondence with newspapers, recalled on Greene's death 3 Apr 91

Cyril Connolly essayist

10231 The English language is like a broad river on whose banks a few patient anglers are sitting, while, higher up, the stream is being polluted by a string of refuse-barges tipping out the muck of Fleet Street and the BBC.

The Unquiet Grave Penguin 67

10232 Words today are like the shells and ropes of seaweed which a child brings home glistening from the beach, and which in an hour have lost their luster.

ib

10233 Literature is the art of writing something that will be read twice; journalism what will be read once.

Enemies of Promise 1930 recalled on Connolly's death 26 Nov 74

Gilbert Cranberg Professor of Journalism, University of Iowa

10234 The strongest desire is neither love nor hate. It is one person's need to change another person's copy.

Quoted by Hedley Donovan *Right Places, Right Times* Holt 89

John Crosby *NY Herald Tribune*

10235 He was truly a 14-carat son-of-a-bitch, no doubt about it. He looked like a cross between a weasel and a jackal and he was indeed a bit of both.

On fellow columnist Walter Winchell *Observer Review* 27 Feb 72, quoted by Neal Gabler *Winchell* Knopf 94

Charles de Gaulle President of France

10236 I addressed the press in the tones of the master of the moment and indeed, to judge from the questions that were put to me, all of them relating to what I would do in power, no one had the slightest doubt that I would soon be there.

Establishing the 4th Republic and gaining the elected office that had evaded him at the end of World War II 19 May 58, quoted by Don Cook *Charles de Gaulle* Putnam 83

Edwin Diamond essayist

10237 Beyond the adjustment of a sail here, and a rudder setting there, he steered the Times' editorials in new directions; some tacks were modest, others major, and all had the cumulative effect of moving the ship to starboard.

On *NY Times* publisher Arthur ("Punch") Sulzberger's "hidden hand" approach *Behind the Times* Villard 93

Diana Princess of Wales

10238 I love working with children. I simply treat the press as though they were children.

Life Feb 93

Shawn Doherty *Newsweek*

10239 One of the worst ordeals of a media age is trial by disclosure.

On investigation of candidates for public office *Newsweek* 27 Aug 84

Carl Dolmetsch Emeritus Professor of English, College of William and Mary

10240 [Their] idol had turned out to have feet not of clay but of mud.

On anti-semitism discovered in diaries of H L Mencken "Twilight of a God" *William and Mary Magazine* Summer 90

Jean Dutourd French Academy

10241 The Englishman is a religious animal... believes in those supernatural powers and intercessors between himself and the very high and very vague "something" which is the British soul... loves ceremonies, rituals, and monuments which surround him. *The Times* is all that at once.

On preface letters to *The Times* of London to *Le Premier Coucou,* French edition of *The First Cuckoo* Allen & Unwin 82

10242 [For the Englishman] *The Times* is the Holy Spirit, patron saint, intermediary through which he speaks to the Lord... the Church in which he makes his prayers ... the missal with which he recites his daily office.

ib

10243 Removal of the deaths column from the front page of *The Times* in 1966 was more affecting than the disappearance of the Commonwealth or the removal of the bas-reliefs from the Arc de Triomphe and their replacement *par des statues de Giacometti.*

ib

Dwight D Eisenhower 34th US President

10244 What the hell if I leave out verbs, hitch singular nouns to plural verbs and all that? They know what I mean, and that's what's important.

On the "dangling participles" that characterized Eisenhower news conferences, quoted by Michael R Beschloss *Eisenhower* HarperCollins 90

Elizabeth II Queen of England

10245 We are all part of the same fabric of our national society, and that scrutiny, by one part of another, can be just as effective if it is made with a touch of gentleness, good humor and understanding.

On press coverage of the royal family *Washington Post* 24 Nov 92

10246 Wisdom... is sometimes lacking in the reactions of those whose task it is in life to offer instant opinions on all things great and small.

ib

James Fallows editor *US News & World Report*

10247 Journalists live in the moment, and it is sobering to realize how soon after this moment most of them disappear.

On college students who could not identify the once-prominent Washington columnists Stewart and Joseph W Alsop, Jr *Washington Post* 18 Feb 96

Carol Felsenthal biographer

10248 She never lost sight of the fact that she headed a company with a newspaper as its heart and reporters as its lifeblood; that she was selling information, not widgets. She never lost her reverence for journalists, and in a way, she shared the typical editorial disdain for the "bean counters" who run newspapers.

On publisher Katharine Graham *Power, Privilege and the Post* Putnam 93

Marlin Fitzwater Reagan and Bush White House Press Secretary

10249 The tighest unwritten rule: The Press Secretary Stays Until He is Dismissed by the Press.

Call the Briefing! Times Books 95

10250 The premium is on patience and survivability because they will hold you at the podium until everyone has tried breaking you.

ib

10251 Spin is the weaving of basic truth into the fabric of a lie, the production of a cover garment that protects, or obscures, or deflects public examination.

ib

10252 [The press secretary stands between president and press] explaining, cajoling, begging, sometimes pushing both sides towards a better understanding of each other.

ib

Jeanne Fleischmann stockholder

10253 He wanted to buy it for his mother and put it on the coffee table. . . a classy thing to have, a status symbol.

On the Fleischmann family's sale of the *New Yorker*, to S I Newhouse Jr, quoted by Thomas Maier *Newhouse* St Martin's 94

Otto Friedrich Executive Editor Time

10254 Journalism and history, too, is what lives in that all too brief gap between the not yet known and that already forgotten.

"What Really Matters" *Time* 12 Oct 87

J William Fulbright US Senator

10255 A bombastic accusation, a groundless irresponsible prediction will usually gain a Congressman or a Senator his heart's content of publicity but a reasoned discourse. . . is destined for entombment in *The Congressional Record.*

On press attraction to "the high crimes and peccadilloes of persons in high places" *American Heritage* Oct 94

Neal Gabler biographer

10256 We embellish, distort, rearrange until what emerges is a kind of modern folklore—the equivalent of the myths the Greeks devised to appropriate their world, except that in America each of us gets to play Homer.

On biographies of the famous "The Gossip of Mount Olympus" *NY Times* 17 Apr 91

10257 Gossip today converts lives into long-running parables. . . [it] takes the famous, and in a weave of fact, half-truth, innuendo and projection, gives us sagas that can deify our fears, vent our prejudices, satisfy our envies and express our values.

ib

10258 By collecting gossipy anecdotes, we invade the celebrity's world. By shaping narratives around their peccadilloes, we assert our priority over them. It's the prose version of the strip search.

ib

10259 Walter Winchell. . . created a demand for juicy tidbits about celebrities and then spent more than 40 years attempting to satisfy it.

Winchell Knopf 94

10260 [It] steeped me in the vapors of tabloidia.

On reading the entire collection of Walter Winchell's columns in files of the *NY Mirror ib*

John Kenneth Galbraith educator

10261 Never write a newspaper article that depends on the placement of a comma.

Quoted by columnist Paul Gigot Station WAMU Washington 9 Dec 94

10262 While Herb appreciates virtue, his real interest is in awfulness.

On cartoonist Herb Block *Washington Post* 31 Dec 95

Suzanne Garment American Enterprise Institute

10263 "The press" is not a newsman with a microphone in his hand but a phalanx of equipment and people packed together and standing so close to the prey of the moment that he or she sometimes literally cannot move.

Scandal: The Culture of Mistrust in American Politics Times Books 91

10264 The press can even be a troop of guerrilla fighters lying in ambush, tape recorders camouflaged, to catch their ill-starred prey.

ib

David R Gergen Reagan White House press officer

10265 The single most important rule of damage control is to know all the damage before the rest of the world does.

NY Times 28 Sep 87

10266 When you're in a running story and you don't know where the bottom is, more often than not, it will fall out from under you.

ib

Newton Leroy ("Newt") Gingrich Speaker, US House of Representatives

10267 I start with an assumption that all human beings sin and that all human beings are in fact human. I assume that all reporters fit the same category.

Dismissing suggestions that his personal behavior compromised his crusade for stricter moral values *Washington Post* 19 Dec 94

10268 The media is the nervous system of a free society.

CBS TV 7 Apr 95

10269 We both own Mustangs... love policy... eat too much, and we both feel irritated with the Washington press corps.

On what he had in common with President Clinton *Newsweek* 10 Apr 95

Mary Elizabeth ("Tipper") Gore wife of US Vice President

10270 In politics, the media-friendly thing to say is, "Oh, no, the press didn't have anything to do with this. The press is wonderful!" I'm not going to say that. Because it's not true.

On coverage of the Clinton/Gore administration *NY Times* 5 Mar 95

Kenneth Gregory anthologist

10271 Only a few, however select, readers of *The Times* sit behind curtains and emphatic moustaches in Pall Mall. Indeed, of outrage-averting letters in this collection, scarcely more than a handful come from choleric old gentlemen of either sex.

Preface to The *First Cuckoo* Allen & Unwin 76

10272 [The letter-writer] rebukes sartorial unorthodoxy, admonishes heresies, ridicules pomposity... [and] sometimes he will release a theory explaining the universe.

ib

10273 The letters... are bulletins on the temper of civilization.

ib

10274 To read a Shavian letter over breakfast cleared one's mind for the day—or at least called forth curses on the man.

On George Bernard Shaw's correspondence over a period of 52 years, preface to Kenneth Gregory ed *The Second Cuckoo* Allen & Unwin 83

Alan Hamilton reporter

10275 The palace press secretary... Commander Richard Colville, an ironclad of silence, would verge on the apoplectic if a journalist had the temerity even to ring him up.

On Buckingham Palace press relations in the 1950s *London Times* 2 Jun 93

John Heidenry biographer

10276 Opinion makers... largely ignored it... [but] millions... often ignored the opinion makers.

On *Reader's Digest, Theirs Was the Kingdom* Norton 93

Harold L Ickes US Secretary of the Interior

10277 That great, overgrown lummox Colonel McCormick, mediocre in ability, less than average in brains, squirts sewage... at men whom he happens to dislike.

On *Chicago Tribune* publisher Robert McCormick *The Secret Diary of Harold L Ickes* Vol II Simon & Schuster 54

Lee Israel biographer

10278 Its front page was a virtual abattoir of murder most foul.

On Hearst's *NY Journal-American, Kilgallen* Delacorte 79

David Ives reporter

10279 It has arrived weekly like a string of perfect martinis.

On the 70th birthday of the *New Yorker NY Times* 16 Feb 96

Jerusalem Post

10280 *The Times* (of London) letters page is the last resort of the piquant, the idiosyncratic, the nutty, the dotty and the potty.

In Kenneth Gregory ed *The First Cuckoo* Allen & Unwin 81

George Jessel humorist

10281 He can be as warm as the first night of a love affair and as cold as the first night in a theater.

On columnist Walter Winchell, quoted by Neal Gabler *Winchell* Knopf 94

Claudia ("Lady Bird") Johnson First Lady

10282 Then the elevator door closed and I was safe and silent.

On retreating from interviews *A White House Diary* Holt Rinehart Winston 70

Lyndon B Johnson 36th US President

10283 The fact that a man is a newspaper reporter is evidence of some flaw of character.

Time 15 Apr 85

Stefan Kanfer essayist

10284 [They are] invasion of privacy swaggering in the trench coat of the 1st Amendment.

On supermarket tabloids *NY Times* 28 Apr 92

10285 Where tabloid print goes, tabloid television immediately follows, just as the thread obediently trails the needle.

ib

Garrison Keillor entertainer

10286 It reads like it was edited by two elderly sociologists, one of whom has been dead for many years.

On the *NY Times* NPR 17 Nov 90

10287 The press often sees cliff-hangers where there is no cliff.

At a dinner with President Clinton during Whitewater investigation *McNeil-Lehrer Report* PBS TV 15 Apr 94

John F Kennedy 35th US President

10288 I am reading it more and enjoying it less.

On the press, quoted by Press Secretary Pierre Salinger *With Kennedy* Doubleday 66

10289 The only way to confound the press is to win the war.

On Vietnam, quoted by Richard Reeves *President Kennedy* Simon & Schuster 93 and Calvin Tomkins *Alex* Knopf 93

Anne Morrow Lindbergh essayist

10290 How strange it was—a pair of unicorns meeting another pair of unicorns.

On two almost legendary couples dining together—Charles and Anne Lindbergh with the Duke and Duchess of Windsor *The Flower and the Nettle* Harcourt Brace Jovanovich 76

Clare Boothe Luce legislator and playwright

10291 Good journalism. . . is the effort to achieve illuminating candor in print and to strip away can't.

To Women's National Press Club 21 Apr 60

10292 No capital under the sun has a press corps. . . more eager to get the news, the news behind the news, and the news ahead of the news, the inside—outside-topside—bottomside news, than the Washington press corps.

ib

Archibald MacLeish poet and statesman

10293 Freedom of the press is only truly freedom of the press when it protects those who would destroy freedom of the press.

On serving as first curator of Nieman Fellows, quoted by Scott Donaldson *Archibald MacLeish* Houghton Mifflin 92

Harold MacMillan Prime Minister of Britain

10294 I read a great number of press reports and find comfort in the fact that they are nearly always conflicting.

London Observer 20 Dec 59

John Major Prime Minister of Britain

10295 Gossip dressed up as news. . . malice as comment, fiction as fact. *The Times* may be a changing but I am not.

London Times 5 Jun 93

Marya Mannes essayist

10296 [The newspapers are]. . . still the only effective screen against the morning features of the loved one, and as such perform a unique human service.

NY Times 22 Apr 60

10297 You can't line a garbage pail with a television set—it's usually the other way around.

ib

Stephanie Mansfield essayist

10298 A portly figure dwarfs the door frame. . . a bullish, larger-than-life presence, a Macy's Thanksgiving Day parade figure in a town full of dweebs, dorks, and deflated spectators.

On *NY Times'* R W Apple Jr *Lear's* Sep 93

Don Marquis essayist

10299 I got to seeing that column as a grave, 23 inches long, into which I buried part of myself every day.

Quoted by Karl E Meyer "Newspaper Columnists: Literature by the Inch" *NY Times* 18 Mar 90

H L Mencken critic

10300 [Journalism is] a fleeting thing, and the man who devotes his life to it writes history in water.

Quoted by Fred Hobson *Mencken: A Life* Random House 94

10301 [He was] a caboose with locomotive delusions.

On an overly ambitious assistant *ib*

Karl E Meyer Editorial Board *NY Times*

10302 Scrapbooks, the potter's field of journalism.

"Newspaper Columnists: Literature by the Inch" *NY Times* 18 Mar 90

Arthur Miller playwright

10303 A good newspaper... is a nation talking to itself.

London Observer 26 Nov 61

John Moody Rome Bureau *Time*

10304 [It is] like saying, "Gosh, things sure were better in 1000 AD than they were in the Stone Age."

On improvement in the Vatican's media relations *International Herald Tribune* 12 May 95

The New York Times

10305 Who owns history? The public servants who make it, or the people who hire them and to whom they are accountable?

Editorial on Presidential memoirs 19 Nov 63

10306 All the corrections fit to print.

Reversing its motto to underline its emphasis on accuracy 27 Jul 87

10307 For many people, the paper means Paris. To read it is to see again the silvery light, taste the *vin ordinaire* and wander the Left Bank.

On the hundredth anniversary of the *International Herald Tribune* 1 Oct 87

10308 It hangs on wooden racks in libraries in Lubumbashi and Kuala Lumpur. A breath of freedom, it greets the Aeroflot traveler arriving at the Copenhagen or Helsinki airport.

ib

10309 Where the Need to Know Meets the Need to Tell

Headline on report on the office of press secretary to the mayor of New York 22 May 92

Richard M Nixon 37th US President

10310 You won't have Nixon to kick around anymore.

To reporters the morning after he had lost the race to be governor of California 7 Nov 62

10311 [I am the first president to come to office] with the opposition of the major communications powers.

Memo to Chief of Staff H R Haldeman 9 May 71, quoted in Bruce Oudes ed *From the President* Harper & Row 89

10312 We simply have to... be as tough, ruthless and unfeeling as they are; otherwise, they will sink us without a trace.

ib

10313 Brutally chew them out and threaten them with extinction if they don't stop all leaks in the future.

To Haldeman on dealing with cabinet members and agency heads 22 Jun 71

10314 Don't get the impression that you arouse my anger. You see, one can only be angry with those he respects.

To the press at news conference during Watergate investigation 26 Oct 73

10315 One thing, Ron, old boy. We won't have to have any more press conferences, and we won't even have to tell them that either!

To White House Press Secretary Ronald L Ziegler two days before resigning the presidency, quoted by Nixon *RN: The Memoirs of Richard Nixon* Grosset & Dunlap 75

10316 The great concentration of power in the US today is not in the White House, the Congress or the Supreme Court. It's in the media. And it's too much.

Quoted by Robert Frost *I Gave Them a Sword* Morrow 78

10317 [For] those who write history as fiction on third-hand knowledge, I have nothing but utter contempt. And I will never forgive them. Never!

ib

10318 People in the media say they must look... at the President with a microscope... but boy, when they use a proctoscope, that's going too far.

NBC TV 8 Apr 84

Peggy Noonan Presidential speechwriter

10319 The proud old machines shook and made noise—they sounded like news.

On AP and UPI teletypes as compared to modern computers *What I Saw at the Revolution* Random House 90

Jacqueline Kennedy Onassis First Lady

10320 A newspaper reported I spend $30,000 a year buying Paris clothes and that women hate me for it. I couldn't spend that much unless I wore mink underwear.

NY Times 15 Sep 60

10321 [Jack] always told me to be more tolerant, like a horse flicking away flies in the summer.

On her husband's advice on newspapers, quoted by Ralph G Martin *A Hero for our Time* Macmillan 83

10322 I want minimum information given with maximum politeness.

To Press Secretary Pamela Turure *ib*

10323 The river of sludge will go on and on. It isn't about me.

On tabloids *Newsweek* 30 May 94

Paul O'Neil essayist

10324 [She interpreted] denials. . . as the great horned owl interprets the squeaking of distant mice.
On Hollywood columnist Louella Parsons *Life* 4 Jun 65

Leon E Panetta Clinton White House Chief of Staff

10325 She brings the perfect mixture of chicken soup and a kick in the butt that we need in this job.
On Evelyn S Lieberman as deputy press secretary *Washington Post* 12 Jan 96

Ezra Pound poet

10326 Journalism is the first draft of history.
Time 12 Oct 87

Todd S Purdum reporter

10327 He is rum raisin in a world of plain vanilla.
On Michael D McCurry as Clinton White House press secretary *NY Times* 6 Jan 95

Richard Reeves reporter

10328 The White House Press Room is an adult day-care center.
NY Times 21 Mar 76

Donald T Regan Reagan White House Chief of Staff

10329 In the Reagan administration, the leak was raised to the status of an art form.
For the Record Harcourt Brace Jovanovich 88

10330 When leaked slowly into the veins of the victim it kills public persona.
On bad publicity as "the most popular poison" *ib*

Abraham Ribicoff US Senator

10331 He will devote time and energy to the careful and honest checking of a rumor which he started.
On the Washington newsman, quoted by Harold Brayman *The President Speaks Off-the-Record* Dow Jones 76

Richard H Rovere critic

10332 It would like nothing better. . . than to hear of an armless worker, who, running his machine with his feet and hoeing his victory garden with his toes, produced more cartridge shells and bought more war bonds than anyone else in his factory.
On the *Reader's Digest* penchant for cheerfulness, quoted by John Heidenry *Theirs Was the Glory* Norton 93

Charles Scribner III publisher

10333 A divine abduction as painted by Reubens.
On Robert Maxwell's acquisition of the *NY Daily News*, *NY Times* 17 Mar 91

Scott Simon

10334 The boot camp of American journalism.
On the hundredth anniversary of Chicago's City News Bureau NPR 15 Dec 90

Alan K Simpson US Senator

10335 If the story "won't go away," there is only one reason for that. The media. Nothing more.
On prolonged interest in Anita Hill's testimony against Supreme Court Justice Clarence Thomas *Washington Post* 21 Jan 95

Frank Sinatra entertainer

10336 All day long, they lie in the sun, and when the sun goes down, they lie some more.
On Hollywood reporters *US* 16 Dec 85

Isaac Bashevis Singer novelist

10337 If Moses had been paid newspaper rates for the Ten Commandments, he might have written the Two Thousand Commandments.
NY Times 30 June 85

John Skow critic

10338 In journalistic terms, syndication is equivalent to ascending to heaven on a pillar of cloud.
On Erma Bombeck, "Erma in Bomburbia" Time 2 Jul 84

Walter W ("Red") Smith sports columnist

10339 My best girl is dead.
On closing of the *NY Herald Tribune* 15 Aug 66, quoted by Richard Kluger *The Paper* Knopf 86

Alexander Solzhenitsyn dissident

10340 Literature. . . cut short by the intrusion of force. . . is not merely interference with freedom of the press but the sealing up of a nation's heart, the excision of its memory.
Time 25 Feb 74

10341 Hastiness and superficiality are the psychic diseases of the 20th century, and more than anywhere else this disease is reflected in the press.
At Harvard commencement 7 June 78

Franklin Bliss Snyder President, Northwestern University

10342 The greatest privilege in our society is to be a purveyor of news.

To jounalism graduates, recalled on Snyder's death 11 May 58

Adlai E Stevenson politician

10343 An editor is one who separates the wheat from the chaff and prints the chaff.

Bill Adler ed *The Stevenson Wit* Doubleday 66

10344 I feel like that famous cow on the cold wintry morning who looked at the farmer and said, "Thanks for the warm hand."

To Washington's Gridiron Club 2 Mar 57 quoted by Harold Brayman *The President Speaks Off-the-Record* Dow Jones 76

Gay Talese essayist

10345 *Vogue* offers a kind of balmy escape for those thousands of female Walter Mittys who, under the hair dryer each week, can flip through the gossamer pages and perchance dream that they are flying their own Beechcraft toward some exotic spot far, far from Oshkosh. . . far, far from the Bronx.

"Vogueland" *Esquire* Jul 61

10346 On page 29 of this morning's newspaper are pictures of the dead. . . on page 1 are pictures of those who are running the world, enjoying the lush years before they land back on page 29.

New York—A Serendipiter's Journey Harper & Row 61

10347 Gloom is their game, spectacle their passion, normality their nemesis.

On journalists as "restless voyeurs" *The Kingdom and the Power* World 69

10348 A by-line is a testimony to being alive that day. . . and all the tomorrows of microfilm.

ib

Mother Teresa Catholic missionary

10349 Facing the press is more difficult than bathing a leper.

NY Times 2 Feb 90

Margaret Thatcher Prime Minister of Britain

10350 [We] must starve terrorists. . . of the oxygen of publicity on which they depend.

To American Bar Association 15 Jul 85

10351 [They] use freedom in order to destroy freedom.

On investigative reporting *NY Times* 19 Dec 87

10352 I rode an elephant and recoiled from the reptiles—an early portent of my relations with Fleet Street.

On a childhood visit to the London Zoo *The Path to Power* HarperCollins 95

10353 I came under savage and unremitting attack that was only distantly related to my crimes.

On attempts as Secretary of State for Education and Science to regulate costs of free milk for school children *ib*

10354 Politicians and journalists behaved as if the Four Hoursmen of the Apocalypse had just charged through the Bank of England.

On withdrawal of the pound sterling from an overvalued European exchange rate *ib*

Roger Thérond Editor-in-Chief *Paris-Match*

10355 It is our Dallas, our serial, and they are our Kennedys, and we didn't invent any of it.

On Monaco's royal family *NY Times* 28 Aug 84

Paul Theroux essayist

10356 It seems to do with ink and paper what morticians do with formaldehyde.

On the *New Yorker NY Times* 23 Sep 90

John Peter Toohey chief play reader for George C Taylor

10357 You keep saying it'll be a magazine about New York. Why don't you, for Crissakes, call it *The New Yorker*?

On naming the magazine founded by Harold Ross, quoted by Scott Meredith *George S Kauffman and His Friends* Doubleday 74

Harry S Truman 33rd US President

10358 To hell with them. When history is written they will be the sons of bitches—not I.

On criticism by what he called the "sabotage press" quoted by Margaret Truman *Bess W Truman* Macmillan 86

10359 I take orders from nobody, except photographers.

NY Times 24 Feb 94

Kenneth Tynan critic

10360 Pungent and artless, innocently sly, superbly explicit: what one would call low-falutin'.

On the *New Yorker* Kathleen Tynan and Ernie Eban ed *Profiles* HarperPerennial 90

Loudon Wainwright columnist

10361 [Its] formula called for equal parts of the decapitated Chinaman, flogged Negro, surgically explored peritoneum, and rapidly slipping chemise.

On *Life* at the half-century mark *The Great American Magazine* Knopf 86

James G Watt US Secretary of the Interior

10362 They kill good trees to put out bad newspapers.

Newsweek 8 Mar 82

Evelyn Waugh essayist

10363 Those in the know can usually discern an embryo truth, a little grit of fact, like the core of a pearl, around which have been deposited the delicate layers of ornament.

On newspaper accuracy *Scoop* Little, Brown 87

Ken Wells reporter

10364 Buckingham Palace might have been tempted to let sleeping dogs lie.

On a pet Corgi that bit Elizabeth II *Wall Street Journal* 6 Mar 91

Rebecca West novelist

10365 Journalism is the ability to meet the challenge of filling space.

Quoted by Jon Winocur *The Portable Curmudgeon* New American Library 87

Tom Wolfe novelist

10366 That great public bath, vat, spa, regional physiotherapy tank, White Sulphur Springs, Marienbad, Ganges, River Jordan for a million souls. . . the Sunday *New York Times.*

The Painted Word Farrar Straus Giroux 75

10367 [Tabloid reporters are] the farmers of journalism. . . [who] love the good rich soil. . . [and] like to plunge their hands into the dirt.

ib

10368 Before the mind can digest what the ears have just heard, an alarm puts the nervous system on red alert. A story!. . . a neutral event, a feeling as palpable as any recorded by the five senses. A story!

On "the feeling that journalists live for" *The Bonfire of the Vanities* Farrar Straus Giroux 87

Frank Zappa critic

10369 Rock journalism is people who can't write, interviewing people who can't talk, for people who can't read.

Loose Talk Warner Brothers 80

RADIO AND TELEVISION

Commentators

David Brinkley ABC

10370 A biased opinion is one you don't agree with.

CNN 16 Jan 95

10371 The broadcasting of news on television is the first truly new way of disseminating news since Gutenberg's inventions allowed the printing of newspapers in the 15th century.

David Brinkley Knopf 95

10372 We were young, former newspaper reporters trying to drive a new, highly complex machine that had arrived without an instruction book.

On the initial belief that television "was competing with newsreels and that news was whatever we could get on film and show, not tell" *ib*

10373 We've had everything from the back side of the moon to the bottom of the sea.

On the moon-walk as the most interesting event he had covered, Station WAMU Washington 7 Nov 95

Tom Brokaw NBC

10374 We are afflicted with the cancer of an ever shorter sound-bite.

On reducing speech to one-liners *NY Times* 23 Jan 92

10375 The nightly newscasts are still the great engines that drive broadcast journalism. . . for so geographically and culturally rich a country. . . a common denominator.

On television's unifying factor *Christian Science Monitor* 30 May 95

John Chancellor NBC

10376 The function of good journalism is to take information and add value to it.

Christian Science Monitor 18 Jun 90

10377 If I were a product on the shelf, I'd be in violation of food and drug laws.

On retiring at 65 after more than 40 years in broadcast journalism *Washington Post* 29 Jun 93

Charles Collingwood CBS

10378 If you want to make it, young man, dress British and think Yiddish.

Advice to Dan Rather *NY Times* 10 Sep 95

Richard Dimbleby BBC

10379 The moment of the Queen's crowning is come!

Whispered words at the climax of Elizabeth II's coronation, a terse, unprecedented eye-witness commentary from Westminster Abbey 2 Jun 53

Sam Donaldson ABC

10380 If you sent me to cover a pie-baking contest on Mother's Day, I'm going to ask dear old Mom why she used artificial sweetener or stole the apples!

On his trademark brashness *Newsweek* 2 Mar 87

Bob Edwards NPR

10381 They want their cousin in Moline to hear everything that they do.

On the selectivity of his news-centered "Morning Report" over the ubiquitous reporters on "All Things Considered," quoted by Thomas Looker *The Sound and the Story* Houghton Mifflin 95

Gabriel Heatter Mutual Radio Network

10382 Ah, there's good news tonight!

Customary beginning for news broadcasts on the Mutual network, ABC, and NBC, recalled on Heatter's death 30 Mar 72

Charles Hoff Chief, Jerusalem Bureau, CNN

10383 It's like a meat-packing plant that uses every piece of the animal.

On sharing information with poll-takers and other derivatives *Time* 6 Jan 92

Richard C Hottelet CBS

10384 FDR without radio is like Bach without a harpsichord.

On Franklin D Roosevelt's "fireside chats" NPR 8 Apr 95

Peter Jennings ABC

10385 He did his Arledgian dance rite... one of the great seducers of all time.

On ABC President Roone Arledge's talent for building a staff, quoted by Marc Gunther *The House That Roone Built* Little, Brown 94

Charles Kuralt CBS

10386 Think of our broadcasts as the spinach of the airwaves!

On children's letters to *Sunday Morning* CBS TV 10 Jun 90

Jim Lehrer PBS

10387 Journalism is caring where the fire-engines are going.

Interview on Station WAMU Washington 17 Feb 92

Rod MacLeish
Christian Science Monitor

10388 On looking closely, all have more acne.

On intensive coverage of persons in the news *Monitor Radio* 7 Mar 94

Bill Moyers CBS

10389 Television is the national campfire around which we spend our time.

LA Times 25 Dec 81

10390 Pollution of language spreads everywhere, like great globs of sludge crowding the shore of public thought.

US News & World Report 3 Jun 85

10391 A journalist is a professional beachcomber on the shore of other people's experience.

Time 13 Jun 88

10392 Our credibility had gotten so bad we couldn't even believe our own leaks.

Recalling the Johnson White House where he was press secretary during the Vietnam War PBS 2 Apr 90

Edward R Murrow CBS

10393 He mobilized the English language and sent it into battle.

On Winston S Churchill's wartime speeches, recalled on Murrow's death 23 Apr 65

10394 [Television] can teach... if humans are determined to use it to those ends. Otherwise it is merely lights and wires in a box.

Quoted by CBS News Director Fred W Friendly *Circumstances Beyond Our Control* Random House 67

10395 A lie can go around the world while truth is getting his pants on.

On McCarthyism, also attributed to Prime Minister James Callaghan, quoted by A M Sperber *Murrow* Freundlich 86

Dan Rather CBS

10396 It chewed me up inside... like trying to swallow barbed-wire-wrapped ball bearings.

On not being assigned to cover the Oklahoma City federal building bombing even though he was nearby at the time *NY Times* 10 Sep 95

Harry Reasoner CBS

10397 It faltered, slipped and fell.

On the shut-down of the *Minneapolis Times*, his former employer *Before the Colors Fade* Knopf 81

10398 I knew Dwight Eisenhower and Lyndon Johnson well, John Kennedy not well and Richard Nixon as well as I wanted to.

On covering the White House *ib*

Frank Reynolds ABC

10399 There is something much worse than a public official attempting to frighten a broadcaster, and that is a broadcaster who allows himself to be frightened.

ABC TV 21 Nov 69

10400 One day a cloud passed over the city and suddenly it was fall.

On begining a new broadcast season, recalled on Reynolds' death 20 Jul 83

Steve Roberts *US News & World Report*

10401 It was known as the fallopian jungle.

On the women's section of newsrooms before women's lib NPR 15 Dec 95

Morley Safer CBS

10402 Producers look for that cocktail of an American, someone who is at once sweet yet exuberant.

On television game shows 30 Aug 89

Diane Sawyer ABC

10403 A sonata for harp and jackhammer.

On co-anchoring *Prime Time* with Sam Donaldson *Time* 7 Aug 89

10404 Not eggs on our face, omelettes!

On how things can go wrong on *Prime Time*, quoted by Marc Gunther *The House that Roone Built* Little, Brown 94

Forrest Sawyer ABC

10405 There is a beast of war out there, an elephant we're trying to describe. . . [and] we're about at the toenail range.

On reporting from the Persian Gulf *Time* 4 Feb 91

Daniel K Schorr NPR

10406 The anecdote—selective, exaggerated or just wrong. . . is a potent weapon in the hands of the Gingrich revolutionaries.

On the House of Representatives and Speaker Newt Gingrich NPR 6 Mar 95

10407 True, half true, or untrue horror stories seem to be the stuff of revolution to the media age.

ib

Robert Seigel NPR

10408 Radio is a medium of many charms but permanency is not among them.

On hosting *All Things Considered* NPR 17 Sep 95

Eric Sevareid CBS

10409 Washington, DC. . . the greatest single news headquarters for the world since ancient Rome.

Not So Wild a Dream Atheneum 76

10410 A general journalist is a jack-of-all-trades and master of none, save the trade of being jack-of-all.

On "knowing just enough about almost everything to know when something hitherto unknown comes along," recalled on Sevareid's death 9 Jul 92

10411 This room is the sanctum sanctorum of American journalism. . . the Westminster Hall, Delphi, Mecca, Wailing Wall to everybody in this country having anything to do with the news business.

On the ballroom of Washington's National Press Club quoted by Raymond A Schroth, *The American Journey of Eric Sevareid* Steerforth Press 95

10412 The only hallowed place I know of that's absolutely bursting with irreverence!

ib

10413 Withdrawing a passport is censorship just as effective as wielding a blue pencil.

An observation that, barred by CBS, was placed in the *Congressional Record*, earning censure from CBS Chair William Paley *ib*

Scott Simon NPR

10414 The boot camp of American journalism.

On the hundredth anniversary of Chicago's City News Bureau NPR 15 Dec 90

Howard K Smith ABC

10415 The murder of a good reporter is more than the death of one man. It is the murder of truth.

On George Polk's death in Greece, quoted by Edward Bliss Jr *Now the News* Columbia University Press 91

Richard F Snow Editor, *American Heritage*

10416 Television has forever robbed the word Extra, Extra! of its urgency.

Editorial *American Heritage* Oct 94

Susan Stamberg NPR

10417 The voice gives life, as photographs and films cannot. . . wraps you in the aura of a person, starts pictures in the mind, makes connections to the heart.

Talk Random House 93

10418 [The NPR studio] in the middle of the night. . . is exactly like an intensive-care unit. The patient is a two-hour radio program... coffee the transfusion.

On assembling *Morning Edition* between 2:30 and 6 AM

John Cameron Swayze NBC

10419 Let's go hopscotching the world for headlines.

Customary introduction as anchor of *Camel News Caravan* 1949–56, quoted by Edward Bliss Jr *Now the News* Columbia University Press 91

Studs Terkel WFMT, Chicago

10420 Our society is a salad in which the fruits and vegetables keep their own flavor.

People 18 May 92

10421 Great interviews only begin when someone says something they have never heard themselves say before.

NPR 29 Jan 95

Arlene Violet Rhode Island Attorney General

10422 It's... open-mike therapy.

On taking calls from depositers turned away by closing of 45 Rhode Island banks and credit unions, *NY Times* 25 Feb 91

Mike Wallace CBS

10423 Vietnam fucked you, Mr President, and so, I'm afraid, you fucked the country. And you've got to talk about that!

To Lyndon B Johnson *Close Encounters* Morrow 84

10424 In almost any story, somebody's ox is gored. Abrasive... insistent, a proxy for the American public.

On his interviewing style *USA Today* 24 Sep 90

10425 I know my own Achilles' heels... all I have to do is frame them in questions to others... and give them a psychological excuse to reveal themselves.

Vanity Fair Nov 91

Walter Winchell NBC

10426 My fangs have been removed and my typewriter fingers rapped with the butt of a gun.

On network restrictions on discussion "of controversial issues in a biased and inflammatory manner," quoted by Neal Gabler *Winchell* Knopf 94

Zhang Qian Radio Orient, Shanghai

10427 They gave us our rice bowl and we don't want it broken.

On keeping broadcasts inoffensive to government *NY Times* 26 Apr 93

Personalities

Fred Allen entertainer

10428 Radio is about as lasting as a butterfly's breath.

Recalled on Allen's death 17 Mar 56

10429 Imitation is the sincerest form of television.

Emmy Fall 81

Steve Allen entertainer

10430 Is it larger than a bread box?

Favorite question in determining the occupations or products manufactured by guests on the long-running panel show *What's My Line?* CBS TV 3 Sep 67

Alan Bennett playwright

10431 The central character is a blank, a puzzle, and one which I hope the actor will solve for me. But now the actor is me and I don't know what to do.

On taking the major role in televised presentation of his play *Intensive Care New Yorker* 22 May 95

10432 Dressed from head to foot in red brocade... like an animated tandoori restaurant.

On being cast in a television production of *The Merry Wives of Windsor ib*

Candice Bergen actress

10433 Where else could so many of us go alone to be together?

On hosting *Great Television Moments* CBS 30 Oct 93

George Burns actor

10434 For forty years my act consisted of one joke. And then she died.

On his wife and partner, comedian Gracie Allen *Washington Times* 5 Dec 88

10435 My idea of a romance was being alone in a room with just me and Gracie and an audience of 1,500 people.

NY Times 31 Dec 88

10436 When the Man shows up at the door to return the pictures, you've got to go.

Referring, on the death of actress Lucille Ball, to vaudeville managers' practice of returning photographs when a booking was cancelled *NY Times* 19 Jun 89

Johnny Carson late-night show host

10437 We're more effective than birth-control pills.

Time 19 May 67

John Daly ABC

10438 Will the Mystery Guest sign in, please!

Introduction for celebrities whose identities were guessed by a blind-folded panel, highly popular Sunday evening panel show that ended a 17-year run 3 Sep 67

Phil Donahue NBC

10439 Television has as much right to be [at an execution] as it does at a four-alarm fire.

Newsweek 27 Jun 94

10440 [An execution as an] irrevocable, powerful act of the state is mandated by the people, it's paid for by the people and it is most certainly the business of the people.

ib

Jimmy Durante entertainer

10441 Good night, Mrs Calabash, wherever you are!

Sign-off line with his nickname for his late wife *Time* 11 Feb 80

Ralph Edwards television host

10442 Tonight, this is your life!

On greeting surprised guests whose past were profiled on the long-running *This Is Your Life*, *NY Times* 16 Apr 87

Garrison Keillor entertainer

10443 So many cars have signs that say "No Radio," you feel you've lost your audience before you start.

On broadcasting from New York, American Public Radio 31 Dec 90

Fulton J Sheen Auxiliary Bishop of NY

10444 It is time I pay tribute to my four writers: Matthew, Mark, Luke, and John.

On receiving an award for a devotional program that attracted thousands *NY World-Telegram & Sun* 24 Dec 54

10445 The community with which you deal is not. . . 42nd Street and Broadway, or Hollywood and Vine, the crusts on the great American sandwich. The meat is in between.

On viewers of mid-America, recalled on Sheen's death 10 Dec 79

10446 The big print giveth and the fine print taketh away.

On television contracts *ib*

Kate Smith NBC

10447 Thanks for listenin'.

Sign-off line that became Smith's signature along with *When the Moon Comes Over the Mountain* recalled on Smith's death 17 Jun 86

Burr Tillstrom puppeteer

10448 Here are the Kuklapolitans!

Introduction for pioneering television comedy that featured pixyish puppets Kukla, Ollie Dragon, Beulah Witch, Fletcher Rabbit, Werner Worm, and opera's Ophelia Ogglepuss, recalled on Tillstrom's death 7 Dec 85

Nancy Walker entertainer

10449 Comedians bones are set one-eighth-of-an-inch off—and whoever set those bones I want to give a letter of thanks!

Quoted in "Funny Woman" editorial on Walker's death, *NY Times* 27 Mar 92

Jack Webb actor

10450 It was Tuesday, January 11. . . cool in Los Angeles. . . and we were working the Day Watch. My partner's Frank Smith. My name is Friday.

Introduction for Detective Joe Friday of *Dragnet* quoted in *This Fabulous Century 1950–1960* Time-Life Books 70

10451 Just [give me] the facts, ma'am.

On interviewing witnesses *ib*

Mae West actress

10452 I could still do it; I still look like Mae West.

On the possibility of a television show in her old age, recalled on West's death 22 Nov 80

Oprah Winfrey ABC

10453 If there never had been a Phil, there never would have been a me.

On Phil Donahue's pioneering of topics such as abortion, lesbian nuns, transvestites, and incest *NY Times* 1 Feb 88

10454 I'd heard Jeff is a piranha. I like that. Piranha is good.

On replacing her agent with Chicago lawyer Jeffrey Jacobs *Forbes* 400 16 Oct 95

10455 I had to get rid of the slave mentality. He took the ceiling off my brain.

ib

Executives, Writers, Producers, Directors

American Cablevision

10456 Electronic shoplifting.

On use of electronic chips to obtain cable programs without payment *NY Times* 25 Apr 91

10457 Checkbook journalism.

On editors who pay for interviews, cited by CBS Producer Don Hewitt *Minute by Minute* Random House 85

Anon

10458 Our job. . . is to make the agony of decision-making so intense you can escape only by thinking.

On compelling people to be aware of social and legal issues, quoted by CBS News President Fred W Friendly in accepting American Bar Association Lifetime Achievement Award *NY Times* 12 Aug 92

Eugenia Bogdan Free Rumanian Television

10459 If television fails, the revolution falls.

On "videocracy" that provided the first revolution on live television *NY Times* 28 Dec 89

David Buksbaum CBS Program Director

10460 Cue the buffalo!

Calling for shotgun blasts to move a buffalo herd on a program of Americana produced for the first live trans-Atlantic telecast by space satellite, quoted by Av Westin *Newswatch* Simon & Schuster 82

Ken Burns filmmaker

10461 We are a people starved for self-definition.

On the success of his 11-hour PBS TV documentary *The Civil War*, *People* 7 Jan 91

Paddy Chayefsky playwright

10462 Television is an amusement park. . . we're in the boredom-killing business.

Lines for Peter Finch in *Network* United Artists 76

Columbia Broadcasting System

10463 Nobody is stopping Andy Rooney from speaking his mind. We're just stopping him from speaking it on CBS.

On barring a commentator for alleged racist and homophobic remarks *NY Times* 17 Feb 90

Louis Cowan producer

10464 I wanted to set up an event where people. . . would care what happened and not know until it happened what was going to happen.

On originating *The $64,000 Question*, quoted by Thomas A DeLong *Quiz Game* Praeger 91

Don Hewitt producer

10465 If you can catch someone violating "thou shalt not steal" by your violating "thou shalt not lie," that's a pretty good trade-off.

On using hidden cameras on *60 Minutes* to record dishonest practices *Washington Post* 30 Nov 92

Neal Marlens writer

10466 To write from our experience and to our experience is to write to the audience that's out there.

On a script for the 1960s *The Wonder Years* created with his wife, Carol *NY Times* 11 Apr 88

Howard Merrill producer

10467 All we have to is get these guilt-ridden, shame-filled people to tell these awful secrets to 25-million other people. . . and we are rich.

On originating *I've Got a Secret*, a mild forerunner of confessional television of the ilk of Phil Donohue, quoted by Thomas A DeLong *Quiz Craze* Praeger 91

Joseph H Ream Executive Vice President, CBS

10468 Because of the unique nature of broadcasting, it is important that, for the good of both the country and our own organization, there be no question concerning loyalty to our country of any CBS employees.

Memo requiring 2,500 employees to sign the same type of loyalty statements required of US civil servants *NY Times* 21 Dec 50

Lord Reith (John Charles Reith) Director General, BBC

10469 It was the brute force of monopoly that enabled the BBC to have become what it did; and to do what it did.

Quoted by Anthony Sampson *Anatomy of Britain* Hodder & Stoughton 62

10470 Somebody introduced Christianity into England and somebody introduced smallpox, bubonic plague and the Black Death. Somebody is minded now to introduce sponsored broadcasting.

To House of Lords, on commercialization *ib*

Montague John Rendell former Governor, BBC

10471 Nation shall speak unto nation.

Motto of BBC adopted in 1927, recalled on Rendell's death 5 Oct 50

Michael Schwartz News Director, KQED TV, San Francisco

10472 Television is the only neutral witness.

On provision of "more accurate information than accounts filtered through a reporter" *Newsweek* 1 Apr 91

Allan Sherman scriptwriter

10473 Reality was the great secret of their success. . . because it had the fresh smell of actuality—it was *happening* right before your eyes.

On crafting the highly popular *What's My Line* and *I've Got a Secret* quoted by Thomas A DeLong *Quiz Craze* Praeger 91

John B Sias President, ABC

10474 We're going to run that program come rain, blood or horse manure.

On controversial miniseries *Amerika*, about a peaceful Soviet takeover of the US *NY Times* 28 Jan 87

Henry Siegel LBS Communications

10475 I don't think anybody in our business is creative. What we do is copy something better than the next person.

NY Times 5 Sep 85

Critics

Kurt Andersen reporter

10476 They seemed irrelevant goofballs yelling "Theater!" in a crowded fire.

On agreements of producers and legislators to post warnings of violence in televised dramas *Time* 12 Jul 93

Anon

10477 Attack video.

On using television to publicize negative aspects of a political candidate's backgrounds *Newsweek* 19 Oct 87

10478 [They like] news that wiggles.

On preference of producers for action over stills, quoted by Hedrick Smith *The Power Game* Random House 88

10479 We made air on two nets tonight.

Bush White House lingo for presidential appearances on national television *Newsweek* 26 Feb 90

10480 He never made a mistake, either on the battlefield or before the cameras.

On General Norman Schwarzkopf III and the televising of the Persian Gulf War *US News & World Report* 11 Mar 91

10481 Between the soaps and the sitcoms/ When boredom is beginning to lower,/ Comes a lift in the day's occupation/ That is known as the peeper's hour.

On the prurient character of some late afternoon television *NY Times* 4 Aug 92

10482 Is this the age of the infomercial?

On commercials that spotlight the problems in using a product and tell how to use it *NY Times* 3 Sep 95

Russell Baker columnist

10483 He. . . looked her straight in the eye and saw daylight on the other side.

On a television interviewer *NY Times* 21 Jun 89

10484 In a police state. . . they lock you up, while in a democracy . . . they lock you out.

On CBS suspension of Andy Rooney for alleged racism and homophobia *ib* 17 Feb 90

10485 From now on, people would hunker in dim rooms, alone or in silent groups, which is the same thing, watching pictures flicker on electronic furniture.

On the advent of television *There's a County in My Cellar* Morrow 91

Peter Black critic

10486 To him the State Opening of Parliament was as delightful as hearing the first cuckoo.

Comparing the BBC's Richard Dimbleby's enthusiasm for royal ritual to a villager writing to *The Times* on signs of spring, *London Times* 20 Jan 95

Edward Bliss Jr critic

10487 Critics predicted death in infancy, but it lived, grew up, and became rich.

On NBC's *Today Show* that premiered 14 Jan 52 *Now the News* Columbia University Press 91

Daniel J Boorstin Librarian of Congress

10488 Nothing is real unless it happens on television.

NY Times 19 Feb 78

Frank Borman business consultant

10489 I don't think you can govern 250 million people with a TV set.

Former astronaut's comment on experimenting with an "electronic town hall" to gather "consensus by computer" *NY Times* 6 Jun 92

Patricia J Bowman plaintiff

10490 I'm not a blue blob.

On abandoning the "blue blob" of pasteboard anonymity that obscured her face during televised testimony as accuser in the William Kennedy Smith rape trial *NY Times* 20 Dec 91

10491 The police believed me; the prosecutor believed me; the State's Attorney believed me. There are millions of people out there who believe me. I believe me.

ib

David Brinkley commentator

10492 Johnny Carson leaving the *Tonight* Show is like Washington asking to get off the one dollar bill.

NBC TV 20 Apr 79

Susan Brownmiller feminist

10493 We are unalterably opposed to the presentation of the female body being stripped, bound, raped, tortured, mutilated and murdered in the name of commercial entertainment and free speech.

Against Our Will: Men, Women, and Rape Simon & Schuster 75

Anatole Broyard critic

10494 He talks about tearing off the porch to build a carport, a notion that makes you wonder whether. . . the TV set on its plastic wheels is all the porch he needs now.

NY Times 16 Mar 73 on the remodeling of a farm house in Curtis Harnack's *We Have All Gone Away* Doubleday 73

Tom Burke critic

10495 She speaks in gentle but perpetual italics.

On Imogene Coca *New York* 13 Mar 78

George Bush 41st US President

10496 These woolly animals give you a very hard time. They've bit me a time or two.

Warning Italian Prime Minister Giulio Andreotti of microphones at a photo session *NY Times* 5 Nov 91

John Carman critic

10497 He has a voice like Sunday morning. Deep, at ease, reassuring.

On Charles Kuralt as host on CBS TV's *Sunday Morning, Minneapolis Star* 7 Jan 81

Mark Carrington critic

10498 Walter Cronkite, that voice of seasoned reason.

On Cronkite's commentary on the 1st Tchaikovsky International Piano Competition *Washington Post* 20 Sep 94

Gabrielle ("Coco") Chanel designer

10499 Take this TV back. . . the programs on this one are really lousy!

Vanity Fair Jun 94

Cable News Network (CNN)

10500 It hit the redneck Riviera.

On hurricane damage in northwest Florida and barrier islands 6 Oct 95

Gerald Clarke biographer

10501 She required direction so extensive that it might more accurately have been called on-the-job training.

On Lee Radziwell's rehearsals for an acting debut *Capote* Simon & Schuster 88

Sarah Booth Conroy columnist

10502 Somehow the British seem to use actors whose faces have biographies still to be read, unlike so many Americans, whose plastic surgery has erased it all.

On *Masterpiece Theater*'s "Body and Soul" *Washington Post* 12 Feb 94

Alistair Cooke commentator

10503 [He is] some freak of climate—a tornado, say, or an electric storm that is heard whistling and roaring far away, against which everybody braces himself, and then it strikes and does its whirling damage.

On Walter Winchell, quoted by Neal Gabler *Winchell* Knopf 94

10504 He will pass into American folklore, and his memory will mushroom its own legends as easily as Paul Bunyan or John Henry or Johnny Appleseed, who also were actual men, ridiculously smaller and duller than the creatures they struck off from the imagination of the American people.

ib

Richard Corliss critic

10505 Caribbean blue eyes. The knowing mouth. A fine figure that stops just this side of martial artistry. These are the anonymous good looks of an afternoon actor.

On Alec Baldwin in soap operas *Time* 19 Mar 90

John Corry critic

10506 For an instant you worry that you will see them next in bed. . . [but] the mini-series goes from the wedding to breakfast the morning after. It still seems, though, like a narrow escape.

On television portrayal of Aristotle and Jacqueline Kennedy Onassis *NY Times* 1 May 88

Norman Corwin essayist

10507 Television tends to. . . make our political procedures a kind of National Trifle Association.

LA Times 9 May 81

David Cox critic

10508 "Bridging". . . means responding with what sounds like an answer to the question posed but which develops instead into a political broadcast about something else.

On interviews that veer out of control *London Times* 15 Feb 95

John C Danforth US Senator

10509 [Television] has locked candidates into ridiculous positions because only ridiculous positions can be compacted into 30-second commercials.

NY Times 18 Mar 90

Brad Darrach critic

10510 A voice that rasped like a blender full of rusty nails. A panoply of huge gleaming teeth that gleefully bit the necks off beer bottles.

Reporting on Lee Marvin in *M-Squad People* 14 Sep 87

Douglas Davis critic

10511 We arrive at dinner parties... with bloodshot eyes and brandishing bags of facts, names and anecdotes.

On gavel-to-gavel Congressional coverage by Cable Satellite Public Affairs *NY Times* 10 Jul 88

Anthea Disney Editor-in-Chief, *TV Guide*

10512 Television's biggest cheerleader and biggest critic.

Description of *TV Guide, NY Times* 18 Nov 91

Robert J Dole US Senator

10513 Today the Senate catches up with the 20th century.

On the admittance of television cameras 2 Jun 86, quoted by Edward Bliss Jr *Now the News* Columbia University Press 91

David Firestone critic

10514 A Queens hairdresser with an accent the size of Long Island.

On Fran Drescher in *The Nanny, NY Times* 18 Sep 94

E M Forster novelist

10515 The round plate that she held in her hands began to glow. A faint blue light shot across it, darkening to purple, and presently she could see the image of her son who lived on the other side of the earth, and he could see her.

The Machine Stops 1914, seen as a prediction of how telecommunications would develop, recalled on Forster's death 7 Jun 70

Mark S Fowler Chair, Federal Communications Commission

10516 Television is just another appliance... a toaster with pictures.

Nation 26 Oct 85

Bruce Jay Friedman novelist

10517 The most important thing about a TV set is to get it back against something and not out in the middle of a room where it's like a somber fellow making electronic judgments on you.

The Lonely Guy's Book of Life McGraw-Hill 78

Tad Friend critic

10518 We grew up whelmed in sitcoms as minnows are whelmed in the sea, in thrall to a new mass art form, a transcontinental, transsocietal in-joke that reaches up to 30-million people every half hour.

On situation comedies *Esquire* Mar 93

10519 Even the wittiest sitcom bypasses the brain and spears the emotions... really meant for children, or the child lurking in adults.

ib

10520 We are cradled in sitcoms, rocked in their warm lap, nursed from what Harlan Ellison calls "the glass teat."

ib

10521 Sitcoms are... old wine in a new bottle: Aristophanes and Molière wrote the sitcoms of their times.

ib

10522 Great character-driven sitcoms have become our fairy tales whereas high-concept comedies and bad character-driven sitcoms... are our fables.

ib

Marilyn Gardner critic

10523 "Entertain me" has become the insistent demand of restless Americans, who add, "and while you're at it, throw in a little violence."

Christian Science Monitor 23 Jun 94

10524 The criterion for TV news is "If it bleeds, it leads."

ib

Jeremy Gerard critic

10525 [Milton] Berle won for the television set what Caruso had done for the phonograph: one look, one listen, and you had to have one.

NY Times 11 Dec 90

Alan Goldberg critic

10526 Public Service Television is for the humor-impaired.

Washington Journalism Review Nov 83

Walter Goodman critic

10527 Fainting at the end of a scene, sure evidence of pregnancy in the theater.

On a televised presentation of Lorraine Hansberry's *A Raisin in the Sun* *NY Times* 1 Feb 89

10528 He crunches a glass in his hand, sure evidence of agitation in the theater.

ib

10529 Connoisseurs in an emporium of exotica.

On Bill Moyers and Dr David H Eisenberg as moderators of the television series *Healing and the Mind* 22 Feb 93

10530 The anonymity of Internet communication seems to be aphrodisiac.

"On the Information Highway, A Busy Red-Light District" 5 Jan 96

Jack Gould critic

10531 Prefab intellectuals.

On quiz show contestants who were coached on answers, *NY Times* 3 Nov 59

Meg Greenfield columnist

10532 Dr IQ himself—the host—was to today's game show what Homer was to Western literature.

On radio quiz show of the 1930s and 40s *Newsweek* 25 Aug 86

David Halberstam essayist

10533 Murrow. . . an innately elegant man in an innately inelegant profession. A rare figure, as good as his legend. . . his voice was steeped in civility, intelligence, and compassion.

On Edward R Murrow *Washington Post* 28 Dec 75

10534 The most important graduate school in America.

On the *Donahue* show *NY Times* 25 Feb 88

Alan Hamilton critic

10535 In the opulence of its set, its cast was remarkably adept. . . and it was richly endowed with character actors able, indeed anxious, to play cameo roles.

On initial telecasts from the House of Lords *London Times* 24 Jan 85

10536 Its plot is loose and tortuous and will take some time for its stars to emerge.

ib

10537 Royal messages have come a long way since George V interrupted his Christmas day lunch at Sandringham in 1932. . . barked a brief and gruff message of good cheer to the Empire and returned to his pudding.

ib

Gary Hart US Senator

10538 You can get awful famous in this country in seven days.

On television coverage of suppossed marital infidelity that abruptly ended his campaign for presidential nomination *NY Times* 7 Oct 84

Ben Hecht playwright

10539 Television. . . seems to be the last stamping ground of poets, the last place where I hear women's hair rhapsodically described, women's faces acclaimed in odelike language.

NY Herald Tribune 26 May 58

Kevin Helliker reporter

10540 In Britain, watching TV can be a crime.

On viewers who fail to obtain a license for their television sets *Wall Street Journal* 27 Sep 93

William A Henry III critic

10541 As deft and daring as Harold Lloyd. . . rubber-faced as Bert Lahr. . . as touching as Chaplin. . . more ladylike than Milton Berle.

On Lucille Ball *Time* 8 May 89

Philip Howard critic

10542 Television made him the national teddy-bear.

On poet John Betjeman *London Times* 5 Oct 95

Walter Isaacson biographer

10543 A floodlit American flag flying high over the ocher-and-red exterior of the Kremlin signified that, for the first time, a president of the United States had come to Moscow.

On television's favorite sign-off picture during Richard M Nixon's May 1972 summit *Kissinger* Simon & Schuster 91

Lyndon B Johnson 36th US President

10544 There's something indecent about that—dying on television.

On repeated showings of Senator Robert F Kennedy's assassination PBS TV 9 Apr 87

E J Kahn critic

10545 Looking at *60 Minutes* has roughly the impact on Hewitt that standing at the edge of an unruffled pool had on Narcissus.

On Don Hewitt, the veteran producer of *60 Minutes* "Your Ear on the Ball" *New Yorker* 19 Jul 82

Neal Karlen critic

10546 On paper it looked like a snorefest, but it worked.

On Garrison Keillor's use of the *Grand Ole Opry* as the pattern for *Prarie Home Companion* *NY Times* 27 Mar 94

Frederick Hiroshi Katayama critic

10547 Yuppies who bopped till they dropped in the disco 70s are staying home... [as] Saturday-night studs turned sofa spuds.

Fortune 23 May 88

Garrison Keillor entertainer

10548 Public radio is a ghetto of good taste.

Broadcast from Seattle 9 Feb 91

10549 They turn on television in rest homes because after you've watched it a while, death doesn't seem so awful.

1 Dec 91

N R Kleinfield reporter

10550 The country stopped... people didn't work... make phone calls... go to the bathroom... walk the dog.

On a jury ready to return its verdict only 24 hours after the end of nine televised months of the O J Simpson murder trial, *NY Times* 4 Oct 95

Elizabeth Kolbert reporter

10551 Outfitted with the austere elegance of a corporate boardroom, the museum positively demands... to be taken seriously... rather like taking a sitcom and removing the laugh track.

On the opening of Manhattan's Museum of Broadcasting *NY Times* 9 Apr 93

Charles Krauthammer essayist

10552 The acceptance speeches of Bill Clinton and Al Gore, orgies of self-revelation, mark the full Oprahtization of American politics.

On the influence of talk show host Ophrah Winfrey *US News & World Report* 10 Aug 92

10553 [The] Oprah-trained... demand... a psychic striptease.

ib

Louis Kronenberger writer

10554 In an automobile civilization, which was one of constant motion and activity, there was almost no time to think; in a television one, there is small desire.

Company Manners Bobbs-Merrill 54

Jean Lacouture biographer

10555 On television, de Gaulle had the eyes of an elephant; full of cunning and rancor, enormous wisdom and cold anger.

On France's president *DeGaulle the Ruler* Norton 92

10556 The face, which age had ceased to line... is now chiselled in planes, like the summit of some old mountain or Rodin's *Balzac*, made pink by the weather, twisted by invective, rounded when called upon to be paternal and joking.

ib

10557 [His] forearms... thrust forward, like tanks over the slopes of Abbeville.... this great solitary man's... astonishing oratorial talent suited so perfectly—and in so unexpected a way—the incomparable means of communication.

ib

Caroline Lang Senior International Editor, Macmillan

10558 People are taken for bigger imbeciles than they really are.

On prospects for successful book programs on television *NY Times* 10 Sep 90

Le Canard enchaîné Paris weekly

10559 On that contentious face, quarrelsome, grating, old age had already established its opening ruins.

On Charles de Gaulle's televised warning of the perils that awaited if he was not reelected, quoted by Janet Flanner *Paris Journal 1965–71* Atheneum 71

Charles Leerhsen critic

10560 The stages of grief in America now move quickly, it seems, from denial to CNN.

On basketball superstar Magic Johnson's disclosure that he was HIV-positive *Newsweek* 18 Nov 91

The Listener magazine

10561 [He is] the erotomaniac gleam at the tip of the phallic cigar.

On Groucho Marx *NY Times* 27 Oct 91

London Times

10562 The BBC will wear a brisk morning face.

On plans for Britain's first venture into programming at dawn 12 Apr 92

10563 Either the nation's depravity-threshold has fallen dreadfully low, or Constance Chatterley was not as black as she was painted.

"Bedtime Reading" editorial on the choice of *Lady Chatterley's Lover* for the BBC program "A Book at Bedtime" 11 Sep 89

10564 Agincourt was a doddle compared to what the BBC may be about to unleash... [and] the morning after will consist largely of people trying to avoid other people's eyes.

ib

Thomas Looker critic

10565 [That] thoroughbred of the public radio stables.

On *All Things Considered* on NPR *The Sound and the Story* Houghton Mifflin 95

Clare Boothe Luce essayist

10566 They only allow the missionary position on PBS.

On the boredom of a seduction scene in *Brideshead Revisited NY Times* 31 Jan 88

Harold Macmillan Prime Minister of Britain

10567 [The airport] is the place where television chooses to lurk. . . that hot, pitiless probing eye.

On interviews while traveling, quoted by Alistaire Horne *Harold Macmillan* Vol II Viking 89

William Manchester biographer

10568 It lay, tiny and incongruous, a flat plastic box from which assorted voices swelled and faded in concert while nine clay-faced men in dark suits bowed over it.

On a small radio aboard a flight to Japan transmitting to US cabinet members the news of President Kennedy's assassination *The Death of a President* Harper & Row 67

David Margolick columnist

10569 He took to Tinseltown like Gauguin to Tahiti.

On Newark attorney Roger Lowenstein who gave up a lucrative law practice to write a television crime series *NY Times* 8 Nov 91

Fletcher Markle critic

10570 The traffic lights at the CBC are forever amber.

On the Canadian Broadcasting Co *Toronto Life* Apr 78

Marshall H McLuhan Director, Center for Culture and Technology, University of Toronto

10571 Dullness is the only form which makes power acceptable or tolerable.

On "the solemn masks worn by top executives and their imitators" *Saturday Night* Feb 57

10572 The new electronic independence re-creates the world in the image of a global village.

The Gutenberg Galaxy University of Toronto Press 62

10573 The medium is the message.

Assessing the impact of television *Understanding Media* McGraw-Hill 64

10574 Vietnam was lost in the livingrooms of America and not on the battlefield.

On how "television brought the brutality of war into the comfort of homes" *Montreal Gazette* 16 May 75

10575 [They are] vidiots.

On those who watch television uncritically 30 May 81

Margaret Mead anthropologist

10576 [It is] the greatest invention since the novel.

On influence of television 31 Dec 74

Newton N Minow Chair, Federal Communicatons Commission

10577 When television is good, nothing is better. When it's bad, nothing is worse.

To National Association of Broadcasters *NY Times* 10 May 61

10578 You will observe a vast wasteland.

Inviting broadcasters to watch a full day's programming

10579 Worse than taking candy from a baby. . . it is taking precious time from the process of growing up.

On allowing television to monopolize a child's attention *NY Post* 19 Jun 61

Joe Morgenstern critic

10580 This glitz was as grim as glitz gets.

On debut of a television program based on the newspaper *USA Today NY Times* 1 Jan 89

Derek Morrah reporter

10581 A luster which no clouds could dim and no torrent could tarnish glowed at the heart of yesterday's tremendous events.

On the international televising of Elizabeth II's coronation *London Times* 3 Jun 53

10582 For the first time television brought many millions into the heart of that mystery, with consequences no one can measure, in this country and far beyond its shores.

ib

10583 Millions saw the culmination of the tremendous drama when St Edward's crown was uplifted in a majestic gesture by the Archbishop of Canterbury and descended gently in all its flashing splendor on the youthful brow, bowed to receive it.

ib

Lance Morrow essayist

10584 In sanctifying his memory, videotape became Kennedy's Parson Weems.

On comparing television's coverage of President Kennedy's assassination with the mythology of an 18th century preacher *Time* 14 Nov 83

10585 The reality of what the nation had lost was preserved with unprecedented, unthinkable vividness: his holographic ghost moving and talking inside every television set.

ib

Ken Mueller Museum for Television and Radio Broadcasting, NYC

10586 It was a guy speaking. . . right there in your livingroom. . . letting you know this is what's going on and what I think we ought to do about it.

On Franklin D Roosevelt's "fireside chats" *Washington Times* 18 Nov 94

10587 Radio was the theater of the mind.

On vaudeville and dramatic presentations that helped sell 4.4 million radios in 1929 *ib*

Malcolm Muggeridge essayist

10588 Salvadore Dali and Brendan Behan. . . were highly successful interviews, which I attribute to the fact that the former's English was totally incomprehensible, and the latter—God rest his soul—too drunk to utter.

Letter to *London Times* Kenneth Gregory ed *The First Cuckoo* Allen & Unwin 76

10589 Some politicians would walk barefoot from John O'Groat's to Shepherd's Bush if they were assured of a peak-viewing time appearance on arrival there.

On hiking the length of the British isles to gain publicity *ib*

The New York Times

10590 Radio let people see things with their own ears.

With Our Own Eyes editorial 30 Jan 86

10591 Millions drew up before the international hearth of television.

More War—and Less editorial on suspense of the deadline for Iraq's withdrawal from Kuwait 24 Feb 91

10592 The Bobbit case is like Madonna dressed in a legal brief: it just won't stop taking its clothes off.

"The Ballad of John and Lorena" editorial on trial of a Virginia manicurist who severed her husband's penis 19 Jan 94

10593 It takes us to some edge of ourselves that. . . is still capable of horror and wonder.

ib

10594 It is a sad day in Sitcomville.

"Mourning in Sitcomville" editorial on the death of Harriet Nelson, co-star with husband Ozzie and sons David and Ricky, "inhabitants of a mythic electronic community," in one of television's first situation comedies 5 Oct 94

10595 The night that Ricky was allowed to imitate Elvis. . . assured all the parents who took cultural signals from the Nelson livingroom that the hip-shaking menace from Memphis was a safe product to bring into their own homes.

ib

Richard M Nixon 37th US President

10596 American people don't believe anything until they see it on television.

On an estimated 80 percent of the population who get their news through television *Newsweek* 2 May 94

10597 [It] helped people see I wasn't just that Tricky Dick, meanspirited son-of-a-bitch.

On appearing on the "sock-it-to me" *Laugh-In* program in 1968 *Time* 13 Feb 95

Peggy Noonan essayist

10598 TV gives everyone a picture, but radio gives birth to a million pictures in a million brains.

On radio as the best training for presidential speechwriters *What I Saw at the Revolution* Random House 90

10599 He looked like a factory foreman running behind in stock.

On commentator Charles Kuralt *ib*

10600 Hours later. . . he'd lean into the camera cool and unflappable, perfectly urbane. TV is such a liar.

ib

10601 Now he is a statesman, when what he really wants is to be what most reporters are, adult delinquents.

On commentator Dan Rather as an anchor *ib*

10602 In Washington they were fighting for ideas, and here I was sailing from tedium to apathy with a side trip to torpor.

On dissatisfaction that sent her from network reporting to presidential speechwriting *ib*

10603 He's a terrific writer for broadcast, with that nice old courtly edge—he doesn't go somewhere, he's summoned by an intuition.

On commentator Bill Moyers *ib*

Matthew Parris columnist

10604 Three things. . . matter: how you appear, what you say, and when you say it. Think wardrobe, sound bite, and prime time.

"Greatest Show-offs on Earth?" reporting on the first six months of television cameras in the Commons *London Times* 27 Apr 90

10605 The Prime Minister. . . has relaxed. . . stopped shouting so much, often speaks softly. . . [and] smiles.

On Margaret Thatcher *ib*

10606 There was not much scope for vulgarizing the Commons: it was vulgar already.

ib

10607 John Major's tactics. . . did for a bland chancellor with a bland budget what the flavor enhancer monosodium glutamate does for frozen sprouts.

ib

10608 Tony Blair. . . released a barrage of abstract nouns of unprecedented duration and ferocity.

On a Tory MP's pride of Britain *ib* 22 July 94

10609 Never. . . have so many generalities been uttered with such passion by a single politician within one lunchtime. . . [as] Blair drove at gathering velocity round a track littered with the death-traps of policy-commitments, swerving to avoid every one.

ib

Dennis Patrick Chair, Federal Communications Commission

10610 By this action, we introduce the 1st Amendment into the 20th century.

On FCC's retirement of its 38-year-old fairness doctrine that required equal time for opposing views on controversial issues *US News & World Report* 11 Aug 87

Mike Peters cartoonist

10611 Do you want. . . the President's enlarged prostate on channel 2. . . benign polyp on 4 or a colonoscopy on 5?

Caption on the obsessive coverage of President Reagan's health *Newsweek* 12 Jan 87

Wesley Pruden columnist

10612 Phil Donahue. . . burns with a hard blue flame to be taken seriously by serious people.

Washington Times 18 Mar 94

Todd S Purdum reporter

10613 [He] speaks in sound bursts, not bites.

On Ken Bode as moderator of PBS *Washington Week*, *NY Times* 26 Jun 94

James Quello Federal Communications Commissioner

10614 I wouldn't be surprised if a big bolt of lightning came out of the sky and hit Howard Stern right in the crotch.

On objections to profanity on radio *Washington Post* 21 May 95

Anna Quindlen columnist

10615 Public television. . . the green vegetables of video viewing.

NY Times 30 Mar 91

Frank Rich columnist

10616 So much sex on television, so little time.

NY Times 13 Jan 94

David Richards critic

10617 We are peeping Toms without even leaving our livingrooms.

On the highly personal nature of programs on prominent persons, *NY Times* 14 Apr 91

John Robinson Chair, Survey Research Center, University of Maryland

10618 They watched television more, and they slept more. . . [a] post-industrious society.

On a five-hour gain in leisure time *NY Times* 2 Jan 88

Carl Sandburg poet

10619 The impact of television on our culture is. . . indescribable. There's a certain sense in which it is nearly as important as the invention of printing.

News summaries 30 Dec 55

Arthur M Schlesinger Jr historian

10620 [Television] has spread the habit of instant reaction and stimulated the hope of instant results.

Newsweek 6 Jul 70

Martin Schram critic

10621 Television. . . often cannot cover the passing of the torch without fanning the flames in the process.

New York 26 Mar 84

William Safire columnist

10622 Good capsule presentations. . . by men working from notes inside their heads.

On the 1960 Kennedy-Nixon presidential campaign debates *Lend Me Your Ears* Norton 92

Peter Schwartz Chair, Global Business Network

10623 While I don't regard television network news as a great source of information about events, I tune in regularly to find out what people believe is happening.

The Art of the Long View Doubleday 91

Tom Shales critic

10624 [It is] an animated smudge on the great lens of television.

Reviewing ABC TV's *20/20*, *Broadcasting* 12 Jun 78

10625 He submitted to ordeal by anchor.

On Dan Quayle's questioning by four television anchors on becoming George Bush's vice presidential nominee, *Washington Post* 18 Aug 88

10626 His bulls-eye interviewing style combines... Sugar Ray Leonard and Mikhail Baryshnikov... jabs, rejoinders and judicious interruptions: Koppel a cappella.

On Ted Koppel's *Nightline* quoted by Marc Gunther *The House That Roone Built* Little, Brown 94

10627 "Over America" will deserve a second look. But never, ever, ever will it deserve a second listen!

"Earplugs Over America" *Washington Post* 25 Feb 95

Hugh Sidey White House correspondent, *Time*

10628 It was through TV that the Kennedy profile, the sincere Kennedy tones, the Kennedy thoughts could get to the people.

On President Kennedy's pioneering use of televised news conferences as a new and highly penetrating way to keep in close touch with the country *John F Kennedy, President* Atheneum 63

10629 He did not have to run the risk of having his ideas and his words shortened and adulterated.

On the advantage of people seeing for themselves rather than reading presidential remarks *ib*

10630 This was the TV era, not only in campaigning, but in holding the presidency.

ib

10631 [Sam Donaldson] is television's sultan of splutter.

On ABC TV's White House correspondent *ib*

Hedrick Smith news analyst

10632 Calling on Helen, Sam, Andrea, Bill, or Mike... made them characters in the presidential TV serial... and projected Reagan as a patient father figure dealing with unruly children.

On President Reagan's use of a seating chart to befriend the press and convey familiarity at news conferences *The Power Game* Random House 88

David Souter Associate Justice, US Supreme Court

10633 [Cable television is] somewhere in between a newspaper and the telephone company.

On the place of "editorial discretion" in cable television and its regulation *NY Times* 13 Jan 94

Gloria Steinem feminist

10634 The same big TV antenna dwarfed each roof, as though life here could only be bearable if lived elsewhere in the imagination.

On revisiting the East Toldeo of her Ohio childhood *Revolution from Within* Little, Brown 92

David Stockman US Budget Director

10635 Reality for the boys came at 6 o'clock with the nightly news shows.

On White House emphasis on influencing political strategists through the major networks, quoted by Hedrick Smith *The Power Game* Random House 88

Norman Stone critic

10636 John Reith's was a comet of a life: a great, brilliant head, and a long tail of dust and ashes, that orbited on a wild ellipse through the British skies... [and] the great, brilliant head was the BBC, created between the wars by a Reith who was still remarkably young.

London Times 6 Sep 93 on Ian McIntyre's *The Expense of Glory* HarperCollins 93

10637 He appeared to the outside world as the ultimate in Athenaeum Man.

ib

10638 Reith [was] prancing about in ceremonial finery for the next generation... never finding anything sufficient for his energy.

ib

10639 He became, as someone told him, a Rolls Royce engine driving a wheelbarrow. And so did his country.

ib

John Walsh essayist

10640 He explained the niceties of English social protocol to viewers in Peoria.

On Alistair Cooke's role as a PBS televison host *Vanity Fair* Dec 92

10641 A gentle rumbling of slightly foggy sanity.

On explaining the US to the English *ib*

Andy Warhol artist

10642 Before I was shot I always suspected I was watching TV instead of living life. Right when I was being shot, I knew I was watching television.

NY Times 22 Feb 91

Byron R White Associate Justice, US Supreme Court

10643 [Television became] a hypodermic, an emotional bath.

On coverage of John F Kennedy's assassination, quoted by William Manchester *The Death of a President* Harper & Row 67

E B White essayist

10644 The voices of radio and television... move rapidly from selling to telling and back to selling again... dividing their allegiance.

Rebecca M Dale ed *Writings from The New Yorker 1925–76* HarperCollins 90

George F Will columnist

10645 Our *Iliad* has found its Homer.

On *The Civil War,* 11-hour PBS documentary *People* 7 Jan 91

10646 The first war of the wired world.

On the Pacific Gulf *Washington Post* 18 Jan 91

James Wolcott essayist

10647 William F Buckley Jr, so laid back that he seemed to be having a near-life experience.

On Buckley as moderator of CNN's *Firing Line* panel *New Yorker* 13 Feb 95

Jonathan Yardley critic

10648 Many put up with Huntley. . . as the price that had to be paid for Brinkley's servings of the tart, the irreverent and the mordant.

On NBC's *Huntley-Brinkley Report Washington Post* 15 Oct 95

10649 [He was] an endless delight to those of us who imagined ourselves to know what he was really saying.

On David Brinkley *ib*

Linda Yolestas

10650 That smirking half-smile of righteousness . . . lands its blow with the coolness of Carrara marble.

On Mike Wallace as interviewer *NY Sunday News* 14 Oct 84

Paul D Zimmerman

10651 The same cathode tube that has elevated an actor to the White House. . . has redefined, in largely show-biz terms, the standards by which we evaluate and embrace our public figures.

On the Reagan White House and televised hearings on Iran-contra arms sales *US News & World Report* 27 Jul 87

10652 Roosevelt, Churchill, Stalin and Hitler. . . starred in our neighborhood newsreels. . . their disembodied voices floated from our kitchen radios, their portraits populated our daily papers. But they didn't enter our homes, up close and personal.

On the pre-television era of World War II *ib*

SPORTS

Athletes and Players

Henry ("Hank") Aaron Atlanta Braves

10653 I've got a bat. . . I let the fellow with the ball do the fretting.

On pitchers, Geoffrey C Ward and Ken Burns eds *Baseball* Knopf 94

Dick Allen Chicago White Sox

10654 If the horses won't eat it, I won't play on it.

On astro-turf quoted by Geoffrey C Ward and Ken Burns *op cit*

Anon

10655 Golf matches are. . . won on the tee—the first tee.

Bobby Riggs ed *Court Hustler* Lippincott 73

10656 [It was] like a flash of white sewing thread coming up at you.

On Lefty Grove's fast ball, quoted by George F Will *Men at Work* Macmillan 90

Muhammad Ali (Cassius Clay) 3-time heavyweight champion

10657 Birds fly, waves pound the sand. I beat people up.

Job description *NY Times* 6 Apr 77

Arthur Ashe US Open Tennis champion

10658 Segregation. . . left me. . . forever aware of a shadow of contempt that lay across my identity and my sense of self-esteem. . . .only death will free me.

On integration *Days of Grace* Knopf 93

Ted Atkinson jockey

10659 I have a job riding horses but. . . the only people I work for are those two-dollar bettors on the rail.

NY Herald Tribune 19 Jan 59

Roger Bannister Olympic runner

10660 The earth seemed almost to move with me. . . .[as] I found a new source of power and beauty, a source I never knew existed.

On covering a mile in just under 4 minutes "The Joy of Running" *Sports Illustrated* 20 Jun 55

Lawrence Peter ("Yogi") Berra NY Yankees, 1946–63 (later manager and coach)

10661 I thank everybody for making this day necessary.

On induction into the Baseball Hall of Fame 7 Aug 72

10662 It gets late early out there.

On waning autumn sunlight at Yankee Stadium, Gorton Carruth and Eugene Ehrlich eds *Harper Book of American Quotations* Harper & Row 88

10663 Think! How the hell are you gonna think and hit at the same time?

Cited as a classic example of Berraism, "insight wrapped in a deceptively simpleminded observation," cited by Ralph Keyes *Nice Guys Finish Seventh* HarperCollins 92

William W ("Bill") Bradley NY Knicks, later US Senator

10664 There has never been a great athlete who died not knowing what pain is.

Quoted by John McPhee *A Sense of Where You Are* Farrar Straus Giroux 65

10665 A professional basketball player must. . . run six miles in a game, a hundred games a year—jumping and pivoting under constant physical contact.

Life on the Run Quadrangle/NYT Books 76

Chris Brewer defensive back, Denver Dynamites

10666 It's *Reader's Digest* football. Everything is condensed.

On playing under the modified rules of "arenaball" *Sports Illustrated* 20 Jul 87

Roy Campanella Brooklyn Dodgers

10667 You gotta be a man to play baseball for a living but you gotta have a lot of little boy in you, too.

NY Journal-American 12 Apr 57

Ty Cobb Detroit Tigers

10668 Baseball. . . a red-blooded sport for red-blooded men. . . not a pink tea, and mollywobbles had better stay out of it.

Recalled on Cobb's death 17 Jul 61

Jay Hanna ("Dizzy") Dean St Louis Cardinals

10669 There's a good example of testicle fortitude.

On a catch at the back of the outfield, recalled on Dean's death 17 Jul 74

10670 Son, what kind of pitch would you like to miss?

Favorite question for batters, quoted by Geoffrey C Ward and Ken Burns *op cit*

10671 They X-rayed my head and found nothing.

On being knocked out by a throw from a Detroit shortstop *ib*

Jack Dempsey World Heavyweight champion

10672 All the time he's boxing he's thinking. All the time he was thinking, I was hitting him.

On Benny Leonard *New Yorker* 13 May 50

Jesulin de Uerique Madrid toreador

10673 I kill two bulls, the taxman takes the proceeds of one.

On the economics of bull-fighting *Guardian Weekly* 1 Jan 95

Roberto De Vicenzo Argentine PGA senior

10674 Golf is like love—one day you think you're too old, and the next you can't wait to do it again.

St Petersburg Times 21 Feb 90

Joe DiMaggio NY Yankees

10675 I thought it was some kind of soft drink.

On being asked for a quote, George Plimpton ed *The Norton Book of Sports* Norton 92

10676 Your brain commands your body to "Run forward! Bend! Scoop up the ball! Peg it to the infield!" Then your body says, "Who, me?"

On announcing his retirement, quoted by Geoffrey C Ward and Ken Burns *op cit*

Ricky Ervins Washington Redskins

10677 [I am a] jackrabbit running in tall grass.

On his role as "change-up back" *NY Times* 10 Jan 92

Carl Ettinger skier

10678 Ski smarter. Learn how to fall. And remember that more people get killed riding bicycles.

NY Times 26 Feb 95

Darrell Evans Detroit Tigers

10679 I'm not old. . . just born before a lot of other people.

At age 40, baseball's oldest regular player *NY Times* 30 Sep 87

Steve Garvey Los Angeles Dodgers

10680 When nobody was listening, I applauded into my glove.

On the NY Yankees' Reggie Jackson's three consecutive home runs in final game of 1977 World Series, quoted by Ira Berkow *Red* Times Books 86

Rocky Graziano champion fighter

10681 I wanted to kill him. I like him but I wanted to kill him.

On classic brutal knock-out of Tony Zale after six rounds for 1947 world middleweight championship, recalled on Graziano's death 22 May 90

Kent Hill Houston Oilers

10682 The man who complains about the way the ball bounces is likely the one who dropped it.

US News & World Report 5 Oct 87

Jim ("Catfish") Hunter Oakland Athletics

10683 The sun don't shine on the same dog's ass all the time.

On losing out as a pitcher in a World Series game, quoted by George F Will *op cit*

Reggie Jackson NY Yankees

10684 Blind people came to the game just to listen to his fast ball.

On pitcher Tom Seaver *Sports Illustrated* 4 Jan 93

Michael Johnson US star sprinter

10685 The only one who can beat me is me.

Newsweek 31 Jul 95

Gary Kasparov world chess champion

10686 I. . . use a parachute and attack the back of a front.

NY Times 7 Oct 90

10687 We humans don't have in our head a fixed list; we feel the most important things.

On preparing for a landmark match against a computer 9 Feb 96

Billie Jean King women's tennis champion

10688 You're a child, still playing a game. . . . You're a superhuman hero. . . . No wonder we have a hard time understanding who we are.

Billie Jean Harper & Row 82

David Knight NY Jets

10689 Does football keep you from growing up? Oh, my God, yes! One hundred per cent, yes! I've even heard guys who I thought had no minds at all admit that.

Quoted by Rick Telander *Joe Namath and the Other Guys* Holt Rinehart Winston 76

Sandy Koufax LA Dodgers

10690 I'm retiring while I can still comb my hair.

At age 30, stunning the sports world with announcement that he was withdrawing, quoted by Geoffrey C Ward and Ken Burns *op cit*

10691 I don't regret one minute of the last 12 years but I think I would regret one minute too many.

ib

Rick Lancellotti Florida Marlins

10692 It's like they gave us a Mercedes without the keys but at least we got to sit in it!

On the opportunity to have been a replacement had the baseball strike ("the Seven Months War") lasted longer *Time* 10 Apr 95

Jeffrey Leonard San Francisco Giants

10693 To me anger is power and strength. I try to enter a game already teed off.

Sports Illustrated 24 Aug 87

Anne Morrow Lindbergh essayist

10694 One moonlit night. . . Charles and I. . . striking out on the smooth black ice, shadows of the bare trees veining the ice ahead. The cold air, the stars, the blue light of the moon. And across up the hill the puny yellow lights of men, in houses.

On ice-skating on Long Island *War Within and Without* Harcourt Brace Jovanovich 80

10695 [Underwater exploration is] a new and beautiful world—purple sea fans, luminous blue fish, yellow, black-and-white striped, gliding in and out of ferns, coral ranches, all moving to a rhythm we did not know or feel....One wears a boat, like a plane, and outside of that shell one has the whole sea, the whole sky for living space.

ib

Charles ("Sonny") Liston world heavyweight champion

10696 Someday they're gonna write a blues song just for fighters. . . slow guitar, soft trumpet and a bell.

Sports Illustrated 4 Feb 91

10697 The middle of a fighter's forehead is like a dog's tail. Cut off the tail and the dog goes all whichway 'cause he ain't got no more balance.

ib

10698 I'd rather be a lamp post in Denver than the mayor of Philadelphia.

On moving to Colorado after police harassment *ib*

Joe Louis world heavyweight champion

10699 He can run but he can't hide.

On challenging Billy Conn for boxing's heavyweight championship 19 Jun 1941, recalled on Louis' death 12 Apr 81; quoted by President Reagan after US attacks on Libya's Muammar Qaddafi 14 Apr 86

Marty Marshall heavyweight contender

10700 When I broke his jaw, he didn't even blink.

On an 8-round decision over Charles ("Sonny") Liston *NY Times* 25 Feb 64

Willie Mays NY Giants

10701 That was the perfectest throw I ever made.

On returning a ball that broke a tie with the Dodgers *NY Times* 18 Jan 52

Xavier McDaniel NY Knicks

10702 We'll be working 9 to 5. . . like those people in Pittsburgh working in those steelmines.

On NBA playoff with Chicago Bulls *Sports Illustrated* 4 Jan 93

John McEnroe US Open Tennis Singles Champion

10703 My greatest strength is that I have no weaknesses.

NY Times 20 Jun 79

Simon McNeill National Hunt jockey

10704 Very few jockeys wake up in the morning without something hurting.

London Times 28 Dec 93

Walt Michaels NY Jets

10705 Statistics are like loose women, once you get them you can do anything you want with them.

NY Times 17 Dec 78

Sandy Mitchell cricketer

10706 The fielders glare at me with a ghoulish hunger peculiar to cannibals.

Country Life 17 Aug 95

10707 [It is] amateur cricket in its purest, flannel-white incarnation.

ib

10708 Activity will be rigorously umpired.

ib

10709 Geneality is guaranteed.

ib

Jack Morris Detroit Tigers

10710 I don't talk to women when I am naked unless they are on top of me or I am on top of them.

On women sportswriters in locker rooms *Time* 15 Oct 90

Martina Navratilova Czechoslovakian tennis star

10711 At home there is no such thing as freedom of the press. In the US, no such thing as freedom from the press.

LA Times 2 Feb 87

Graig Nettles NY Yankees

10712 Some kids want to join the circus. . . . Others want to be big-league baseball players. . . . When I came to the Yankees, I got to do both.

Newsweek 6 Aug 90

Amos Otis Kansas City Royals

10713 Trying to sneak a pitch past Rod Carew is like trying to sneak the sunrise past a rooster.

On playing against the Minnesota Twins *Time* 18 Jul 77

John Jordan ("Buck") O'Neil Negro League star

10714 There is nothing in life like getting your body to do all the things it has to do on a baseball field. It's as good as sex. . . as good as music.

Quoted by Geoffrey C Ward and Ken Burns *op cit*

Satchel Paige American League's first black pitcher

10715 I—avoid fried meats, which angry up the blood.

"Master's Maxims" the sports world's commandments for longevity *Collier's* 13 Jun 53

10716 II—If your stomach disputes you, lie down and pacify it with cool thoughts.

ib

10717 III—Keep the juices flowing by jangling around gently as you move.

ib

10718 IV—Go very light on the vices, such as carrying on in society. The social rumble ain't restful.

ib

10719 V—Don't look back. Something might be gaining on you!

Cleveland Cavalier Coach Lenny Wilkens recalls "If you look back, someone will step on you" while the All Stars' Benny Bonds says "Don't look back, someone might be in front," cited by Ralph Keyes *Nice Guys Finish Seventh* HarperCollins 92

10720 Age is mind over matter. If you don't mind, it doesn't matter.

Recalled on Paige's death 8 Jun 82

10721 When a batter swings and his knees move, I can tell his weaknesses. . . [and] put the ball where he can't hit it.

ib

10722 That ball I threw was thoughtful stuff. . . knew just what it had to do.

ib

10723 I used my single wind-up, my triple wind-up, my hesitation wind-up, and my new wind-up, my step-and-pitch-it, my sidearm throw, and my bat dodger.

Recalling his first game *ib*

10724 I never threw an illegal pitch. The trouble is, once in a whle I toss one that ain't never been seen by this generation.

NY Times 9 Jun 82

Willie Pep heavyweight champion

10725 Naw, I'm not dead. I ain't even been out of the house.

Sports Illustrated 27 Jun 87

Gary Player golf champion

10726 If I had to choose between my wife and my putter, well, I'd miss her.

News summaries 31 Dec 91

Jonathan Raban author

10727 [England] seen from the sea, looks so withdrawn, preoccupied and inward—a gloomy house, all its shutters drawn, its eaves dripping, its fringe of garden posted against trespassers.

On sailing squall and current-ripped coastal waters *Life* May 87

Bobby Riggs Wimbledon and US tennis champ

10728 I was quick. . . agile. . . had the heart!

Recalling at age 77 the Wimbledon title won in 1939, the US championship in 1939 and 1941, and numerous senior titles *NY Times* 27 Aug 95

10729 I will not be remembered for winning Wimbledon on my first try, but there's the guy who lost to Billie Jean King in front of 90-million people!

ib

Phil (Scooter) Rizzuto NY Yankees

10730 No one had ever been booed at a Church's Communion Breakfast before but they started howling at me as soon as they found out I was filling in for Joe DiMaggio.

On fans' objection to a replacement on or off the baseball diamond *NY Times* 25 Feb 95

Jackie Robinson Brooklyn Dodgers

10731 There I was the black grandson of a slave, son of a black sharecropper, part of a historic occasion, a symbolic hero to my people. . . [but] I must tell you that it was Mr Rickey's drama, and that I was only a principal actor.

Recalling his role as the first major league black player in Branch Rickey's integration program, Ken Burns and Geoffrey C Ward *op cit*

10732 As I write this, 20 years later, and sing the anthem, I cannot salute the flag; I know that I am a black man in a white world. In 1972, in 1947, at my birth in 1919, I know that I never had it made.

ib

Raymond ("Sugar Ray") Robinson (Walker Smith Jr)

10733 The outcome of a fight will be determined by who wants it too much. . . [and] quicker to leave his game plan because he desperately wants to beat the other guy.

LA Times 2 Apr 85

Pete Rose Cincinnati Reds

10734 Playing baseball for a living was like having a license to steal.

Geoffrey C Ward and Ken Burns *op cit*

10735 Try to play it easy and ease off and the first thing you know, there you are, on the outside, looking in, wondering what went wrong.

ib

10736 I'd walk through hell in a gasoline suit just to play baseball.

ib

Tom Seaver NY Mets

10737 I was there when the flannel turned to double knit.

On joining the New York Mets in 1967, Tom Lane and Marty Appel eds *Great Moments in Baseball* Birch Lane/Carol 92

10738 Your arm is your best friend but in the end you've got to treat it as if it was your worst enemy.

On pitching, quoted by George F Will *op cit*

John S R Shad Chair, Federal Securities and Exchange Commission

10739 I don't know of any greater diversion from your usual concerns than sitting on the stoop of an airplane, looking down at the little tiny trees and houses down there and then jumping out. It really clears the mind.

On parachuting *M* Aug 87

O J Simpson American Football League All Star

10740 Fame vaporizes, money goes with the wind, and all that's left is character.

Quoted by Dick Belsky *Juice: O J Simpson's Life* HC Walck NY 77

Mike Smith jockey

10741 Who's the horse to beat? I've got to beat them all.

At 1994 Kentucky Derby a year after winning Eclipse Award as the best US rider *NY Times* 8 May 94

10742 I just tightened him up a little bit in the stretch and let him cruise on home.

On riding Holy Bull to victory in the $500,000 Grade I Haskell Invitational *ib* 1 Aug 94

10743 He keeps answering all the questions... clearly one of the greatest horses in America.

On fans who wondered if Holy Bull could redeem himself in the Derby *ib*

Warren Spahn Boston Braves

10744 Hitting is timing. Pitching is upsetting timing.

Speaking as "the winningest left-hander in the history of baseball"—so named and quoted by George F Will *op cit*

Mark Spitz US 1972 Olympic champion

10745 I swam my brains out.

On the unprecedented win of seven gold medals by one person, news summaries *ib* 31 Dec 72

Peter Stark luge sledder

10746 [I] collected the secrets of snow and ice the way other boys collected snakes and rocks... savored the power of ice heaves and avalanches like others... [and] keened after fighter planes and large guns.

On a Lake Placid luge sled *Driving to Greenland* Lyons & Burford 95

10747 Nothing frilly or baroque about it. You go straight, you go fast.

On a 30-meter flight from a Nordic ski jump in Ishpeming MI "Leaps of Faith" essay *ib*

10748 A spare, simple, elegant... knifelike bow and stern, and low, slightly sweeping deck... reminded me of the thinnest sliver of the new moon....painted light gray to mimic the skin tone of a narwhal calf.

On a native Greenlander's kayak on a three-day outing for harpooning narwhal whales *A Kindle of Strange Fish*

Lawrence Taylor NY Giants linebacker

10749 He's a cocky sumbitch. That's what makes him a great player.

On quarterback Phil Sims, quoted by Eric Pooley "True Blue: From Giants to Supermen" *New York* 26 Jan 87

Marian Tinsley checkers champion

10750 I am made in the image of God and that computer in the image of man.

On her advantage in playing checkers with a computer for championship stakes *Wall Street Journal* 15 Aug 94

Thomas J Watson Jr former Chair, IBM

10751 I'm no ball of fire but I hope I'm a glowing coal.

On stunt-flying *M* Oct 86

Ted Williams Boston Red Sox

10752 Nothing has as many variables and as few constants.

On hitting in baseball as the most difficult demand in sports *The Science of Hitting* Simon & Schuster 71

10753 It fought the wind, and it just kept on going into right center, toward the Red Sox bull-pen... it kept going and then out.

On the 521st and final homerun, quoted by Geoffrey C Ward and Ken Burns *op cit*

10754 Baseball gives every American boy a chance to excel. Not just to be as good as someone else, but to be better. This is the nature of man and the name of the game.

On 1966 induction into Baseball Hall of Fame *ib*

Yun Lou 1984 Chinese Olympic gymnast

10755 Suit too big. Grabbed pants instead of pommel.

On scoring low in pommel horse competition, news summaries 30 Jul 84

Coaches, Officials, and Owners

Aleksandr Adatov Russian baseball coach

10756 Throw to second, not first. Second is the one in the middle.

To a third baseman in game against the US Navy *NY Times* 12 Apr 89

Sparky Anderson Manager Detroit Tigers

10757 Nothing nobody does never hurts it.

On mismanagement of baseball *Newsweek* 6 Aug 90

Ray Benton US Open coach

10758 [He prefers] to stay in shape for tennis by playing tennis.

On managing US Open champion Jimmy Connors who rejected weight-lifting in favor of the game *Newsweek* 16 Sep 91

Lawrence Peter ("Yogi") Berra NY Mets coach and Manager 1965–75; NY Yankees Manager 64, 84, 85

10759 I just turned on the nonchalancy.

On nervousness at moving from the playing field to management *National Observer* 9 Mar 64

10760 It ain't over till it's over.

On the National League pennant race *NY Times* 15 Feb 87

10761 He's just naturally amphibious.

"It's Over for Yogi" editorial quoting Berra on Mickey Mantle's ability to hit left-handedly *ib* 1 Oct 89

10762 Baseball is 90 percent mental. The other half is physical.

Gorton Carruth and Eugene Ehrlich eds Harper *Book of American Quotations* Harper & Row 88

10763 If you can't imitate him, don't copy him.

On Frank Robinson's batting technique *ib*

10764 When you come to a fork in the road, take it.

Geoffrey C Ward and Ken Burns *op cit*

Kent Biggerstaff Pittsburgh Pirates trainer

10765 [It was] like putting just one more suitcase on the Queen Mary.

On weight gained by 240-pound Rick Reuschel *Sports Illustrated* 4 May 87

Pete Carril Princeton basketball coach

10766 The ability to rebound is inversely proportional to the distance one grew up from the railroad tracks.

On basketball as a game most artfully performed by poor boys from mean, urban streets *Time* 19 Mar 90

10767 You can't win with three-car garage guys. With two-car-garage guys, you got a chance.

On working with middle class and affluent students *ib*

Albert Benjamin ("Happy") Chandler Baseball Commissioner

10768 If Jesus was commissioner for six years and did a fair job, he couldn't get 75 percent of the votes.

On losing to Ford Frick in 1951 election as baseball commissioner *Sports Illustrated* 20 Jul 87

10769 A refreshingly ignorant sonofabitch. . . never carried anything heavier than a knife and fork in his whole life.

On NY Yankees' owner Del Webb *ib*

10770 He'd just. . . take what was coming. . . as simple as a goose going barefoot.

On manager Bill Veeck "if caught doing something tricky" *ib*

Penny Chutter Senior Coaching Director, Oxford University Boat Club

10771 A lightweight oarsman is like a corgi, forced to snap at the heels of the big men.

Country Life 30 Mar 95

Drew Coble umpire

10772 I felt like I was throwing God out of church.

On ejection of the Baltimore Orioles' Cal Ripken 7 Aug 89 *Time* 11 Sep 95

Mark Connor NY Yankees pitching coach

10773 When you lose your body, it's all arm.

On Charles Hudson's over-use of body and torso *NY Times* 14 Apr 87

Brian Cunnane US Merchant Marine Academy

10774 If it's true that losing builds character, then we have more characters than Disney and Warner Bros combined.

Sports Illustrated 1 Apr 91

Ralph Deleonardis umpire

10775 I blew it the way I saw it.

On a disputed call *Sports Illustrated* 27 Sep 93

Charlie Dressen Manager Brooklyn Dodgers

10776 The Giants is dead.

On the Dodgers' 1951 first place with the Giants 13 and a half games behind, a position later reversed recalled on Dressen's death 10 Aug 66

Leo Durocher Major League Manager

10777 You don't save a pitcher for tomorrow. Tomorrow it may rain.

On Brooklyn Dodgers *NY Times* 16 May 65

10778 There are only five things you can do in baseball—run, throw, catch, hit and hit with power.

On Chicago Cubs *Time* 16 Jul 73

10779 If you lose you're going to be fired, and if you win you only put off the day you're going to be fired.

Sporting News 11 Jun 84

10780 The nice guys are all over there. In seventh place.

Comparing Eddie Stanky's temperament to the last-place NY Giants as they emerged from their Polo Grounds dugout 5 Jul 46, often reported as "Nice guys finish last"; recalled on Durocher's death 7 Oct 91, also see Ralph Keyes *Nice Guys Finish Seventh* Harper-Collins 91

10781 That's a home run in an elevator shaft.

Frequent reaction to Phil Rizzuto's hitting a high pop-up Washington Post 1 Aug 94

10782 If he could cook, I'd marry him.

On Willie Mays' versatility to hit, run, and field *ib*

Chub Feeney President, National Baseball League

10783 We can't even beat the umpires. How are we going to beat the players?

On massive player walkout that laid waste to a full third of the 1981 season, recalled on the eve of another strike *NY Times* 31 Jul 94

A Bartlett Giamatti Baseball Commissioner

10784 [Baseball] because it is so much a part of our history as a people...has an obligation to the people for whom it's played.

On debarring Pete Rose from major league baseball for betting on games in which his own team had played *NY Times* 25 Aug 89

10785 [Baseball has] a purchase on our national soul.

"Giamatti Plays by the Rules" editorial quoting Giamatti in regard to Pete Rose *ib*

10786 The game begins in the spring, when everything else begins again, and it blossoms in the summer, filling the afternoons and evenings, and then as soon as the chill rains come, it stops and leaves you to face the fall alone.

On baseball as a game "designed to break the heart," to which Giamatti paid homage in his autobiography *Bart* Harcourt Brace Jovanovich 91

10787 You count on it, you rely on it to buffer the passage of time, to keep the memory of sunshine and high skies alive, and then, just when the days are all twilight, when you need it most, it stops.

ib

Walt Hriniak Chicago White Sox coach

10788 You don't lean into a pitch, you stride.

Wall Street Journal 27 May 94

Lee Hunt University of Missouri-Kansas City coach

10789 Recruiting is like shaving; miss a day, and you look like a bum.

Christian Science Monitor 3 May 88

Davey Johnson Cincinnati Reds manager

10790 I tell him something, and it goes in one ear, hits something hard and bounces back.

On reliever Rob Dibble *Sports Illustrated* 1 Aug 94

Charles E Kinney Jr Consultant, National Horse Show

10791 The humans can dismount and gripe... but, you know, the horse never really gets a chance to bitch.

On exhibition conditions at Madison Square Garden *New Yorker* 28 Nov 88

Bob Knight Indiana University basketball coach

10792 When my activities/ Are done here on earth,/ I hope I will be/ Buried upside down/ And my enemies can kiss my ass.

NBC TV 16 Mar 94

Chuck Knox LA Rams coach

10793 Most of my cliches aren't original.

Sports Illustrated 21 Sep 92

Vince Lombardi championship coach

10794 Winning is not everything—but making the effort is.

Statement frequently confused with Vanderbilt football coach Henry Russell "Red" Saunders who said some years earlier "Winning isn't everything; it's the only thing," George L Flynn ed *Vince Lombardi on Football* Vol I NY Graphics Society 73

10795 I wish to hell I'd never said the damn thing. . . . [what I meant was] the effort. . . having a goal. . . [and] I sure as hell didn't mean for people to crush human values and morality.

On his famous statement "Winning is . . ." quoted by James A Michener *Sports in America* Random House 76

10796 Football isn't a contact sports, it's a collision sport. Dancing is a contact sport.

ib

Wayne Lukas horse trainer

10797 I expected him to win. But that wasn't chopped liver out there that beat us.

On Tabasco Cat's narrow loss to Unaccounted For at Saratoga Springs NY Jim Dandy Stakes *NY Times* 1 Aug 94

Lester Mapes Judge, Westminster Kennel Club

10798 I'm an old man and if the competition was between me and some young stud-muffin, I'd say go ahead and pick the stud-muffin.

On judges' enthusiasm for new dogs *NY Times* 13 Feb 95

Fritz Marz former President, German Alpine Federation

10799 On the mountain, joy and sorrow are close companions.

On 11 mountain climbers who fell to their deaths in one of the Himalaya's worst accidents *International Herald Tribune* 17 Dec 94

Frank McGuire basketball coach

10800 In this country, when you finish second, nobody knows your name.

Quoted by James A Michener *Sports in America* Random House 76

Don Nelson Golden State Warriors coach

10801 I was pretty smart the first ten games and pretty dumb the last 20.

On agreeing to a $1-million buy-out after a clash with players that made him, in the words of sportswriter Tom Friend, "the latest coach unable to master Generation X" *NY Times* 14 Feb 95

Joe Paterno Penn State head coach

10802 Act like you expected to get into the end zone.

On how to behave after scoring a touchdown *NY Times* 4 Oct 94

Tom Penders University of Texas basketball coach

10803 The best way to save face is to keep the lower half of it shut.

On refusal to make predictions *Sports Illustrated* 25 Apr 88

Jerry Reinsdorf Chair, Chicago White Sox

10804 How do you know when George Steinbrenner is lying? When his lips are moving.

On the NY Yankees major owner *Newsweek* 6 Aug 90

Branch Rickey Manager, St Louis Cardinals, General Manager, Brooklyn Dodgers, Pittsburgh Pirates

10805 Baseball people are generally allergic to new ideas... numbers on uniforms... spikes on a new pair of shoes. But they will [get together] eventually. They are bound to.

On integrating major league baseball *Life* 2 Aug 54

10806 Luck is the residue of design.

NY Times 17 Nov 65

10807 Quality in quanity!

On the Cardinals' win of six pennants and four world champioships, recalled on Rickey's death 9 Dec 65

10808 Leo Durocher is a man with an infinite capacity for making things worse.

On the NY Giants manager *ib*

10809 What I need is more than a great player. I need a man that will take abuse, insults, in other words, carry the flag for the race.

On meeting Jackie Robinson for the first time in 1947 *ib*

10810 I want a ballplayer with guts enough not to fight back. You will symbolize a crucial cause. One incident, just one incident, can set it back 20 years.

To Robinson *ib*

10811 A baseball club in any city in America is a quasi-public institution, and in Brooklyn, the Dodgers were public without the quasi.

Protesting plans to move the Brookyn Dodgers *ib*

Bill Robinson NY Mets hitting coach

10812 A good hitting instructor is able to mold his teachings to the individual. If a guy stands on his head, you perfect that.

NY Times 27 Mar 94

Carlotta Robinson breeder of racing pigs

10813 Absolutely gorgeous and striking—and she was such a ham!

On Secretariat, fastest pig ever clocked *Sunday Morning* CBS TV 25 Oct 92

Pete Rose Cincinnati Reds Manager

10814 Whenever people tell me I have the body of a 30-year-old, I know I've got the brain of a 15-year-old. When you got both, you can play baseball.

LA Times 4 Apr 85

Henry Russell "Red" Sanders Vanderbilt University football coach

10815 Winning isn't everything, it's the only thing.

Quoted by Lee Green ed *Sportswit* Harper & Row 84; frequently attributed to Vince Lombardi who said "Winning is not everything—but making the effort to win is" quoted by George L Flynn ed *Vince Lombardi on Football* Vol I Graphics Society of New York 73

Wimp Sanderson Alabama University basketball coach

10816 I've been here so long that when I got here, the Dead Sea wasn't even sick yet.

On 32 years at Alabama *Sports Illustrated* 9 Mar 92

Lou Schultz trainer of Alaskan Huskies

10817 First you learn a new language, profanity; and second you learn not to discipline your dogs when you're mad, and that's most of the time when you're training dogs.

NY Times 15 Mar 80

10818 "No" is something you use a lot, and when you start using it you have a whip in your hands.

ib

10819 A good snow machine will cost $2,000 and last four to five years. With dogs, you've got regenerative powers. Snow machines don't have pups.

ib

George Steinbrenner NY Yankees owner

10820 Winning means everything! You show me a good loser and I'll show you a loser.

Newsweek 6 Aug 90

10821 I'm more of a Patton than an Eisenhower in the way I lead.
ib

Casey ("The Perfesser") Stengel professional baseball manager

10822 You done splendid!
Favorite accolade, quoted by Frank Graham Jr *Casey Stengel* John Day 58

10823 He's dead at the present time.
On the late Boston Braves outfielder Larry Gilbert a year after his death *Sport* Apr 66

10824 I'll sign anything but veal cutlets. My ballpoint pen slips on cutlets.
Reader's Digest Oct 67

10825 We got a lot from Johns Hopkins, but them we thought was from the college turned out to be from the clinic.
On trying to sign college players *Sporting News* 11 Apr 70

10826 Mister, that boy couldn't hit the ground if he fell out of an airplane.
On hiring Yogi Berra to coach the Mets after Berra managed the Yankees into the seventh game of the 1964 World Series "Joy in Mudville" *McCall* 70

10827 He'd fall in a sewer and come up with a gold watch.
On Yogi Berra *Baseball Digest* Aug 72

10828 Managing is getting paid for home runs someone else runs.
Recalled on Stengel's death 29 Sep 75

10829 Being with a woman all night never hurt no professional baseball player. It's staying up all night looking for a woman that does him in.
ib

10830 There comes a time in every man's life and I've had many of them.
Chosen for Stengel's gravestone *ib*

10831 There are three things you can do in a baseball game. You can win, or you can lose, or it can rain.
George Plimpton ed *Norton Book of Sports* Norton 92

10832 When a fielder gets the pitcher into trouble, the pitcher has to pitch himself out of a slump he isn't in.
Quoted by Charles Salzberg *NY Times* 5 Apr 92 reviewing Ira Berkow and Jim Kaplan eds *The Gospel According to Casey* St Martin 92

Eddie Sutton Kentucky basketball coach

10833 They want you to win 34 games—in a 32-game season.
On expectations of Wildcat fans *Christian Science Monitor* 3 May 88

Jerry Tarkanian University of Nevada at Las Vegas basketball coach

10834 Their cars are already paid for.
On preference for recruiting transfer students *US News & World Report* 25 Feb 91

Johnny Tocco trainer

10835 In the ring, Sonny was a killing machine.
On world heavyweight champion Charles ("Sonny") Liston *Sports Illustrated* 4 Feb 91

Daniel Topolski Coach, Oxford University Boat Club

10836 What I bring to this party is my competitiveness, a hate of losing, fear of losing.... [and its] humiliation.
On his role as "Mr Motivator" against Cambridge University as the arch-rival *Country Life* 30 Mar 95

10837 Most of all, I help them to focus on the light blue of Cambridge. Those are people that are going to stop them achieving their wish, their desire, their destiny.
ib

Alfred Vanderbilt sportsman

10838 Where do they get the money to come out here every day and bet?.... It's the money they save on neckties and razor blades.
On playing the horses, quoted by Ira Berkow *Red* Times Books 86

Bill Veeck Cleveland Indians, later Chicago White Sox president

10839 A winning team can bring a city together, and even a losing team provide a bond of common misery.
Thirty Tons a Day Viking 72

10840 Baseball is the only thing besides the paper clip that hasn't changed.
Recalled on Veeck's death 2 Jan 86

10841 He had a face that even Dale Carnegie would want to punch.
On club owner Walter O'Malley *ib*

10842 When there is no room for individualism in ballparks, then there will be no room for individualism in life.
ib

10843 No other city is so confident of its own preeminence that it could afford to take such an open delight in its own bad taste.
On affection for the NY Mets and Shea Stadium completed in 1964 *ib*

Philip Wrigley Chicago Cubs owner

10844 Baseball is now too much a business to be a sport and too much a sport to be a business.

Recalled on US Supreme Court 7–2 ruling that baseball is a sport not a business subject to anti-trust laws *NY Times* 19 Nov 53

Critics

Joey Adams humorist

10845 If you break 100, watch your golf. If you break 80, watch your business.

News summaries 31 Dec 82

Peter Alfano sportswriter

10846 Coverage of golf's most prestigious tournament... was filled with odes to Augusta, plus numerous shots of picture-postcard settings, bees pollinating and what the host... called "azaleas screaming at you and dogwoods whispering to you."

NY Times 17 Apr 84 on Augusta GA

Roger Angell *New Yorker*

10847 [It is] a tapestry of deceit and experience and efficiency.

Salute to pitcher Jim ("Catfish") Hunter, quoted by George Will *op cit*

10848 Perfection is admirable but a trifle inhuman... a stumbling kind of semi-success can be much more warming.

On a new standard for measuring the difference between Mets and Yankees fans *Once More Around the Park* Ballantine 91

10849 Yells for the Mets were also yells for ourselves... a wry, half-understood recognition that there is more Met than Yankee in everyone of us.

ib

10850 [The catcher] must be large, brave, intelligent, alert, stolid, foresighted, resilient, fatherly, quick, efficient, intuitive and impregnable... most of all... invisible.

ib

Anon

10851 Dice 'em, hash 'em, boil 'em, mash 'em! Idaho, Idaho, Idaho!

Football cheer, University of Idaho, quoted by Charles Kuralt *Dateline America* Harcourt Brace Jovanovich 79

10852 If God had meant Texans to ski, he would have made bullshit white.

Texas Observer 19 Sep 80

10853 A player on foot has no standing on the course.

Quoted by Alistair Cooke from a golf club rulebook *America Observed* Knopf 89

10854 A racetrack is a place where windows clean people.

Sampler on the wall of an ardent fan, President Clinton's mother *NY Times* 7 Jan 94

10855 He'd lost a yard off his heater.

On a pitcher whose fastball is slowing *Washington Post* 4 Oct 94

10856 We have to do everything now, from betting to drinking, on the sly. . . . [but] they haven't yet figured out how to ban human nature.

On racetracks in the Sudan *NY Times* 12 Dec 94

10857 [It is] about as well known as Siberian cow-chip tossing.

On R J Reynolds' annual Camel Trophy race at Grand Junction CO, the Olympics of Four-Wheel Drive *USA Today* 22 Feb 95

Richard Bak historian of black baseball

10858 Stearnes was detached, colorless, coolly efficient... the perfect embodiment of the Detroit assembly line, dependably delivering clutch plays in conveyor-like fashion.

Turkey Stearnes and the Detroit Stars Wayne State University Press 94

Marcus Berkmann writer

10859 Millions of innocent Britons believe that village cricket has been magically preserved from some golden age of sport to represent all that was once fine and fair about our great nation.

Country Life 17 Aug 95

10860 Professionalism has scuttled into the pavilion like a pregnant cockroach.

On 1990s cricket *ib*

Ira Berkow columnist

10861 The seat you'd invariably get in the grandstand at Comiskey would be perfect for counting the rivets in the steel girder in front of your nose.

On Chicago's Comiskey Park *NY Times* 11 Jul 88

10862 We've been calling baseball the national pastime for so long that it has integrated itself into our collective bloodstream.

8 Apr 91

10863 [It is] our second national anthem, at least.

On *Take Me Out to the Ballgame ib*

10864 It represents what our nation is all about, a combination of the old-time farmlike individual effort (the batter must do it alone) and industrial teamwork (the double play, or hitting the cut-off man for a play at the plate).

ib

10865 The crack of the bat, the cries of the crowd, the smell of the grass. . . represent the start of springtime with probably even more certitude than your average crocus or robin.

ib

10866 The Commissioner of Baseball had become like the queen of England, but without the handbag. And except for the pomp and ceremony he hasn't been missed.

On the year since Fay Vincent was ousted 1 Oct 93

Thomas Boswell Washington Post columnist

10867 Sports may be what Americans talk about best. With the most knowledge. The most passion. The most humor. The most capacity for cheerful change of mind. It has become one of our best ways of probing people, sounding their depths, judging their values.

On a common language in America *US News & World Report* 21 Jun 93

Margaret Bourke-White photographer

10868 [He introduced] the first pink-coated fox hunt ever to astonish an Indiana landscape.

On a wealthy manufacturer pictured in photo-essay on Muncie IN, quoted by Vicki Goldberg *Margaret Bourke-White* Harper & Row 86

Anthony Cave Brown foreign correspondent

10869 There was regal entertainment for the mission—a gazelle hunt, a splendid affair of swooping falcons, racing hounds, and death.

On entertainment of British diplomats at the Arabian court of Ibn Saud *Treason in the Blood* Houghton Mifflin 94

Kenneth L Burns anthologist

10870 Here is a game in which there is no clock, the defense holds the ball, though it has rigid rules, every park is different, the greatest heroes fail seven times out of 10, a game that's born in the spring dies in the fall. This is life.

On following his television documentary on the Civil War with an in-depth study of baseball *Washington Post* 4 Jul 94

10871 The team was called the Trolley Dodgers or just the Dodgers, after their devoted fans negotiated Brooklyn's busy streets.

On the Brooklyn Dodgers move to LA *ib*

10872 The team moved 3,000 miles away, leaving an empty hole in Flatbush . . . and an even emptier spot in the soul of every Brooklyn fan.

ib

10873 Baseball is the key to the emotional life of millions of people. . . it rewards study.

ib

Bob Carroll historian

10874 There was a "rightness" in the Green Bay Packer dynasty just as there is a "rightness" in a Beethoven symphony. . . an eternal truth in the New York Jets' Super Bowl III victory just as there is an eternal truth in David's victory over Goliath.

When the Grass Was Real Simon & Schuster 93

10875 There was beauty in a Johnny Unitas pass just as we find beauty in Dégas's dancers.

ib

Winston S Churchill statesman

10876 There's nothing better for the inside of a man than the outside of a horse.

On horseback riding, sometimes attributed to Ronald Reagan recalled on Churchill's death 24 Jan 65

Jimmy Cannon columnist

10877 A sportswriter is entombed in a prolonged boyhood.

Quoted in Jerome Holtzman ed *No Cheering in the Press Box* Holt 74

10878 The cruelty of Cobb's style fascinated the multitudes but it also alienated them. . . . in a climate of hostility, friendless by choice in a violent world he populated with enemies.

On Ty Cobb of the Detroit Tigers, quoted by Ken Burns and Geogrey C Ward *op cit*

10879 He was a parade all by himself, a burst of dazzle and jingle, Santa Claus drinking whisky straight and groaning with a bellyache.

ib

10880 Babe Ruth made the music that his joyous years danced to in a continuous party.

ib

10881 What Babe Ruth is, come down, one generation handing it to the next as a national heirloom.

ib

William J Clinton 43rd US President

10882 I identify with Babe Ruth. . . a little overweight and he struck out a lot. But he hit a lot of home runs because he went to bat.

Expressing hope that a baseball strike could be ended by 6 Feb 95, the hundredth anniversary of Babe Ruth's birth *US News & World Report* 6 Feb 95

Dennis Conner US skipper in America's Cup race

10883 Design has taken the place of what sailing used to be.

On coming to terms with the 1983 loss of America's Cup, recalled when it was regained *Time* 9 Feb 87

Alistair Cooke commentator

10884 Baseball. . . strikes me as a native American ballet—a totally different dance form. Nearly every move in baseball—the windup, the pitch, the motion of the infielders—is different from other games.

Paul Dickson ed *Baseball's Great Quotations* HarperCollins 91

10885 Next to a triple play, baseball's double play is the most exciting and graceful thing in sports.

ib

Bob Cooke columnist

10886 Rex Barney would be the league's best pitcher if the plate were high and outside.

NY Herald Tribune 10 Jan 50

Bill Cosby entertainer

10887 He would throw the right side of his body to one side of the field and the left side of his body kept going down the left side. And the defensive man didn't know who to catch.

On LA Bears' Hall of Fame running-back Gale Sayers *NY Times* 4 Oct 94

Bob Costas sportscaster

10888 Once I didn't speak to him for two months... didn't think it right to interrupt him.

On basketball commentator Dick Vitale *Sports Illustrated* 16 Nov 87

Country Life magazine

10889 There is such a long pause that one has the sensation of dealing with a bottle of barely animated ketchup; conversation comes out in dollops.

On Olympic horseman Capt Mark Phillips 3 Aug 95

Richard L Curry Judge, Cook County Circuit Court, Chicago

10890 Do those who schedule play time/ For the games of our national pastime/ Have the right to interfere with bedtime/ By starting the game at night-time/ Instead of the customary daytime?

Upholding the ban against lighting Chicago's Wrigley Field *Christian Science Monitor* 3 Apr 85

Arthur Daley sportwriter

10891 The question. . . is as easy to handle as a fistful of fish-hooks.

On the Brooklyn Dodgers' purchase of Jackie Robinson from Montreal, quoted by Ira Berkow *Red* Times Books 86

10892 Emily Post probably would recommend a ticker-tape parade. For confetti we can use shredded warrants of arrest.

On Charles ("Sonny") Liston's 1963 victory over Floyd Patterson for world heavyweight title, recalled in *Sports Illustrated* 4 Feb 91

Frank Deford sportswriter

10893 A jump to straddle, one leg up in an L; presses to a handstand, then a one-fourth pirouette and step-down; skips and steps, kicks again to a back flip-flop step-out; more steps and full turn backward; a body wave, dance steps, pose and aerial forward; side aerial to flip-flop step-out, leap; lies down on beam, does a Valdez through a back walkover to a knee perch, cartwheels to a stand; a back walkover to a handstand in the split position; two clip-flops, split leap, body waves; a round-off, double-twisting somersault dismount.

On Romania'a Nadia Comaneci, 14, Montreal Olympics' record-breaking gymnast 19 Jul 76 recalled in *Sports Illustrated* Fall 91

10894 It almost seemed as if the Statue of Liberty had gone on tour, turning in her torch for a Yonex racket.

On Martina Navratilova's return to her native Czechoslovakia to lead the US team in winning the Federation Cup tournament 4 Aug 86

10895 Surely it is no mere happenstance that the last two words of The Star-Spangled Banner are "Play ball!". . . some psychic connection between the anthem and the games Americans play.

ib Fall 91

Ron Fairly sportscaster

10896 Bruce Sutter has been around a while and he's pretty old. He's 35 years old. That will give you an idea of how old he is.

On NY Giants pitcher Bruce Sutter, quoted by George Will *op cit*

Alan Farnham reporter

10897 The young man hadn't hunted before and was unaware of the cardinal rule of Southern hospitality: Don't shoot the guests.

On hunting as big business *Fortune* 9 Mar 92

Marilyn Gardner journalist

10898 Bor-ing may represent the ultimate insult for any activity, especially one that captures the attention of billions of viewers in 194 countries.

On international televising of soccer *Christian Science Monitor* 23 Jun 94

10899 Too slow and—that dread word again—too boring. Bring on football's battering rams, viewers say, and its bruising pileups.

ib

10900 Nice sports finish last.

ib

William E Geist reporter

10901 The greatest honor a man can have—a candy bar named for him.

On Reggies, named for Oakland Athletics' Reggie Jackson CBS TV 4 Oct 87

William Grimes reporter

10902 The game looks only slightly more strenuous than lifting a gin and tonic.

On invitational tournament of US Croquet Assn *NY Times* 24 Jul 92

George V Higgins sportswriter

10903 A team without a World Series triumph since 1918 validates the writer's constant sense of insecurity, and thus proves he is sane.

On the Boston Red Sox *The Progress of the Seasons* Holt 89

10904 Baseball and the Red Sox... have sturdily remained, reliable and plain, nine young men on a level field, with bats and gloves and ball, an orderly and gracious world of bad tempers and foul language, precise rules and near riots, celebrations capped by requiems—and then we say: it's just a game.

ib

Charles Hirshberg essayist

10905 He wasn't a pitcher, he was Zeus, the mound was his Olympus, and the curve ball, that was his thunderbolt, streaking through space until it reached the plate, where it suddenly fell to earth.

On John Weiss as a 21-year old semi-pro reliever, "Faces of Baseball" *Life* May 90

10906 The hitter swung at Weiss's perfection and smashed it to hell. Over the fence it soared, out of the yard and across the street, which, to a relief pitcher, is hell indeed.

ib

David Huddle Professor of English, University of Vermont

10907 The crazy luck of baseball accounts for the vast role of spitting by its players: to spit is to change one's chemistry, to cast out the immediate past, to set oneself to face the future.

NY Times 31 Jan 88

Roger Kahn biographer

10908 Jackie Robinson did not merely play at center stage. He was center stage; and whenever he walked, center stage moved with him.

The Boys of Summer Harper & Row 72

Max Kase columnist

10909 [Truth makes] unscheduled appearances like a run in a girl's stocking.

On Casey Stengel's press statements *NY Journal-American* 9 Oct 60

Kitty Kelley biographer

10910 [The] baseball strike has pitted greedy owners against grasping players, killed one World Series, stymied the President, polarized Congress, disgusted the country and threatened to shut down the national pastime as we know it.

On the troubled winter of 1994–95 *NY Times* 25 Feb 95

10911 Joseph P DiMaggio... and with a P? What does it stand for? Paragon? And perfect silver hair... the face with the gentle folds of a basset hound.

On the Lotus Club awards dinner honoring Joe DiMaggio *ib*

William Kennedy novelist

10912 Hi-ho with the left, he cocks the Siffman amidships and crosses fast with a right to his knowledge box, but oh, now, didn't he get one back full in the domino case and down?

Use of 19th century writing style, quoted by Christopher Lehmann-Haupt *NY Times* 16 May 88 reviewing Kennedy's *Quinn's Book* Viking 88

Richard Kluger historian

10913 Baseball continually absorbed Red Smith, with the balletic movements of its players and its power to build suspense, so that ideally the outcome awaited the last pitch to the last batter in the bottom half of the last inning with the score tied, the bases loaded, the count full, and everybody on base running on the pitcher's delivery.

On columnist Red Smith *The Paper: The Life and Death of the NY Herald Tribune* Knopf 86

Charles Kuralt commentator

10914 Bart Giamatti understood that he was presiding over dreams and poetry in motion.

Tribute to former Yale University president who became Baseball Commissioner, news summaries 31 Dec 89

A J Liebling *New Yorker*

10915 Moore moved Ginaldi around the ring like a man shifting a picture on a wall as he looks for the exact place to hang it.

On Archie Moore meeting a mediocre opponent, Fred Warner and James Barbour eds *A Neutral Corner* North Point 90

10916 [It was like] a girl trying to get away from her date at the front door.

On heavyweight Ingemar Johansson backing away from Floyd Patterson *Newsweek* 26 Nov 90

Bernie Lincicome *Chicago Tribune*

10917 [Soccer] is a thrill-an-hour stomach knotter.

On joining other sportswriters on soccer-bashing *Christian Science Monitor* 23 Jun 94

Jean Lindamood Deputy Editor *Automobile*

10918 It's very much the boys' great adventure, He Man, Master of the Forest. . . also a test of your driving skills, your grace under pressure and your deodorant.

On the US Camel Trophy, an annual "Olympics of the Four-Wheel Drive," as R J Reynolds' Nabisco's "answer to the Marlboro Man" *USA Today* 22 Feb 95

Ed Linn biographer

10919 Boston knew how England felt when it lost India.

On Ted Williams' retirement in 1960 from the Boston Red Sox *Hitter* Harcourt, Brace 93

Franklin Loew Dean, Tufts University Veterinary School

10920 Time bombs on legs.

On pit bulls *Time* 27 Jul 87

London Daily Telegraph

10921 When someone of the Princess of Wales' pedigree elects to go to the dogs, it is a fair bet that a pack of status-conscious imitators will soon follow baying at her heels.

On Princess Diana's visit to Wembley stadium dog races 20 Apr 88

London Times

10922 What can they know of England who only England know?

"Cricket Mischief" editorial on criticism of non-English players 4 Jul 95

Robin MacNeil commentator

10923 You have only to name the fielders—wicket-keeper, slips, cover, square-leg, mid-off, mid-on, silly mid-off, and silly mid-on, to start them laughing. And try explaining the rules!

On why cricket is widely ridiculed by North Americans *Wordstruck* Viking 89

Bill Madden *NY Daily News*

10924 When you count the years you've worked with them, you have to do it in dog years—multiply by seven.

On the difficulties of covering owner George Steinbrenner and the Yankees *Newsweek* 6 Aug 90

Frank Mankiewicz Adviser to Reagan White House

10925 If Ronald Reagan had played guys in the movies who fixed football games, instead of playing in them, he would never have been elected president. But he played heroes and that's powerful as hell.

NY Times 9 Mar 88

10926 The Fighting Irish, the subway alumni, Knute Rockne, fresh-faced boys, the Four Horsemen—that's all absolutely classic American. Every American myth was there in Notre Dame football.

On Ronald Reagan's role in *Knute Rockne: All American* and the lines he spoke in the role of 1920 star George Gipp, "Some time when the team is up against it and the breaks are besting the boys, tell them to go out there with all they got and win just one for the Gipper" *ib* also *NY Daily News* 10 Mar 88

Martin Mayer critic

10927 Basketball is to Kentucky what Catholicism is to Vatican City.

Making News Doubleday 87

Tom McNichol reporter

10928 [*USA Today*] was the first daily paper to realize that quite a few sports junkies are actually statistics junkies.

With Margaret Carlson *Columbia Journalism Review* May/Jun 85

Mamoun a Mekki Secretary General, Sudanese Equestrian Federation

10929 The love we have for horses tames the hatreds that exist between us outside the clubhouse.

On the centuries-old veneration of horses in a Sudan racked by civil war *NY Times* 12 Dec 94

Jim Murray LA Times

10930 The world of sport now realizes it has gotten Charles ("Sonny") Liston to keep. It is like finding a live bat on a string under your Christmas tree.

On Liston winning the heavyweight championship over Floyd Patterson *LA Times* 24 Jul 63

10931 Pete Rose was as uncomplicated as a summer day, as instinctive as a hound dog. He was born to hunt, or, in his case, play baseball.

On Pete Rose as an extraordinary baseball hitter *Jim Murray: An Autobiography* Macmillan 93

10932 He never wanted to do anything else. He never could do anything else.

ib

10933 When Jack Nicklaus first came out on tour, he was—well, fat is the word you would want. . . . in silhouette, like something that should be floating over a Macy's parade.

ib

10934 Bill Russell. . . . was six-eleven but he had the moves of a startled zebra.

On the Boston Celtics *ib*

10935 Bear Bryant spoke in a deep rumble, the twang of his native Arkansas in a pitch that sounded like an underground explosion in a coal mine.

On Alabama's football coach *ib*

10936 Gentlemen, start your coffins!

On the Indianapolis 500 *Sports Illustrated* 16 May 94

10937 [Rickey Henderson] has a strike zone the size of Hitler's heart.

On Henderson as a player for Oakland A's and NY Yankees

10938 [John Wooden] was so square, he was divisible by four.

On a UCLA coach *ib*

10939 Once, when an official dropped a flag and penalized the Rams for having 12 men on the field. . . two of them were Bain.

On Bill Bain *ib*

10940 Outdoor pool sharks.

On golfers who are not athletes *ib*

10941 Norman Van Brocklin is a guy with the nice, even deposition of a top sergeant whose shoes are too tight.

ib

10942 To say Conrad Dobler plays football is like saying the Gestapo played *20 Questions.*

On a former guard for St Louis Cardinals

10943 Woody Hayes was consistent. Graceless in victory and graceless in defeat.

On Ohio State football coach *ib*

10944 It's not a town, it's a no-host cocktail party. If it were human, it'd be W C Fields. It has a nice, even climate. It's always winter.

On San Francisco *ib*

10945 Los Angeles is underpoliced and oversexed.

ib

10946 The trouble with Spokane is that there's nothing to do after 10 o'clock in the morning. But it's a great place to go for breakfast.

ib

William Nack essayist

10947 He was the undisputed heavyweight champion of the world—a 6'1½", 215-pound hulk with upper arms like picnic roasts, two magnificent 14-inch fists and a scowl that he mounted for display on a round, otherwise impassive face.

On Charles ("Sonny") Liston *Sports Illustrated* 4 Feb 91

Joseph Novitski writer and sailor

10948 She slid at first in the same kind of sudden, huge silence that fills the instant before an avalanche or the seconds just before an earthquake.

On severing of holding plates on a sailing ship *Wind Star* Macmillan 88

10949 [It] is a windless sound, as if the mountains were drawing in breath before letting it all out in a huge and rumbling sigh; one of those sounds that are not noise. . . felt more than heard.

ib

10950 The ship genuflected to the land, pivoting on the bow cradle as seawater bore her up from the stern.

ib

Susan Orlean reporter

10951 His face is turned up and pushed in, and has a dark mask, spongy lips, a wishbone-shaped white blaze, and the earnest and slightly careworn expression of a small-town mayor.

On Biff Truesdale, the boxer who won more shows that any other dog in 1994 *New Yorker* 20 Feb 95

10952 If I were a bitch, I'd be in love with Biff Truesdale.

ib

Phyllis Orlikoff Judge, Queens NY, Criminal Court

10953 'Twas Game Six of the Series when out of the sky,/ Flew Sergio's parachute, a Met banner held high./ His goal was to spur our home team to success,/ Burst Beantown's balloon claiming Sox were the best.

"And to All a 'Play Ball,'" ode written with law secretary Peter Kelly for the sentencing of actor Michael Sergio for parachuting into Shea Stadium during the World Series, front-paged in *NY Times* 20 Dec 86

10954 The fans and the players cheered all they did see,/ But not everyone present reacted with glee./ "Reckless endangerment!" the DA spoke stern./ "I recommend jail—there, a lesson he'd learn!"/ Though the act proved harmless, on the field he didn't belong./ His trespass was sheer folly and undeniably wrong.

ib

José Ortega Y Gasset essayist

10955 Wind, light, temperature, ground contour, minerals, vegetation, all play a part. . . they function, they act.

On relationship of habitat and hunters, Gerald Piel and Osborn Seberberg Jr eds *The World of René Dubos* Holt 91

Joe H Palmer Professor of English, University of Kentucky

10956 A man who would change Saratoga would stir champagne.

On the Saratoga Race Track *NY Times* 17 Jul 95

Joe Palmers sportswriter *New York Herald Tribune*

10957 Of course it's inhuman. And that stuff we were watching tonight—that's unchicken!

Comparing boxing to cockfighting, quoted by Ira Berkow *Red* Times Books 86

Westbrook Pegler columnist

10958 He could throw a lamb chop past a wolf.

On Lefty Grove, a remark sometimes attributed to Arthur "Bugs" Baer, Paul Dickson ed *Baseball's Greatest Quotations* HarperCollins 91

Harvey Penick golf pro and guru

10959 Face the ball plain, as if you are about to shake hands with someone on the other side of it.

On not twisting the body when making a long drive *Harvey Penick's Little Red Book* Simon & Schuster 92

Robert Peterson historian

10960 Only the ball was white.

Adopted as title of Robert Peterson 1970 groundbreaking book on black baseball recalled by David Conrads *Christian Science Monitor* 2 Jun 94

George Plimpton critic

10961 Good swearing is used as a form of punctuation. . . like a sprinkling of paprika.

Paper Lion Harper & Row 65

Jose Portal ophthalmologist

10962 It's as if they have an eye in the center of the brain.

On baseball hitters who don't favor either eye *Time* 19 Sep 88

Shirley Povich broadcaster

10963 At precisely 4:45 pm today, in Yankee Stadium, off came the 52-year slur on the ability of the Dodgers to win a World Series, for at that moment the last straining Yankee was out at first base, and the day, the game, and the 1955 Series belonged to Brooklyn.

On Brooklyn Dodgers first World Series win, defeating NY Yankees 2–0 to chalk up a record of taking four of seven games, news reports 4 Oct 55

Ronald Reagan 40th US President

10964 Two thousand years ago. . . . if a war was going on, they called it off.

On Olympic tradition in light of the Soviet withdrawal from the 1984 Olympics *Time* 21 May 84

10965 You gave new meaning to the term "capital offense."

On Washington Redskins' White House visit after Superbowl victory 3 Feb 88

Grantland Rice sportswriter

10966 Outlined against a blue-gray October sky, the Four Horsemen rode again. In dramatic lore they were known as Famine, Pestilence, Destruction and Death. These are only aliases. Their real names are Stuhldreher, Miller, Crowley, and Layden.

On Notre Dame's victory over Army, *NY Tribune* 19 Oct 1924, recalled on Rice's death 13 Jul 54

10967 A streak of fire, a breath of flame,/ Eluding all who reach and clutch;/ A gray ghost thrown into the game/ That rival hands may rarely touch.

"Spectral sobriquet" to football's "galloping ghost," Red Grange, recalled on Grange's death *Sports Illustrated* 4 Feb 91

Irving Rudd publicist

10968 His greatest dream is to die in his own arms.

On boxer Hector Camacho's ego *Sports Illustrated* 17 Aug 88

Budd Schulberg screenwriter

10969 I coulda had class! I coulda been a contender! Instead of a bum, which is what I am! Let's face it. It was you, Charley!

Lines for Marlon Brando blaming his brother for an abortive boxing career in *On the Waterfront* Columbia Pictures 54

George Bernard Shaw playwright

10970 What is both surprising and delightful is that the spectators are allowed, and even expected to join in the vocal part of the game. I do not see why this feature should not be introduced into cricket.

On baseball, recalled on Shaw's death 1 Nov 50

10971 There is no reason why the field should not try to put the batsman off his stroke at the critical moment by neatly timed disparagements of his wife's fidelity and his mother's respectability.

ib

Curt Simmons sportswriter

10972 Throwing a fast ball by Henry Aaron is like trying to sneak the sun past a rooster.

Sports Illustrated 19 Nov 73

Scott Simon commentator

10973 I remember Ernie Banks and his fine filigree-thin wrists flashing his bat at a fast ball and flicking it over Wrigley Field's ivy-robed walls—as vividly as I remember my first kiss.

NPR 23 Apr 94

Walter W ("Red") Smith sportswriter

10974 A yammer of radio announcers... a grouse of ballplayers... a conceit of managers... a dawdle of magnates... a braille of umpires and a bibulation of sportswriters.

A grouping of species *Sporting News* 4 Dec 76

10975 As a ballplayer, Dean was a natural phenomenon, like the Grand Canyon or the Great Barrier Reef.

Recalled on death of Dizzy Dean 17 Jul 74

10976 Ninety feet between home plate and first base may be the closest man has ever come to perfection.

Recalled on Smith's death 15 Jan 82

10977 [It was like] picking up quicksilver with boxing gloves.

On making sense of Casey Stengel's statements *ib*

10978 It was a hairy crowd, wrapped thickly in the skins of dead animals and festooned with derby hats, pennants and feathers of crimson and blue.

On a Harvard-Yale game, Dave Anderson ed *Red Smith Reader* Random House 82

10979 It wore the pelts of mink and beaver and raccoons. Indeed, counting the coon coats in any section of the Yale Bowl, you could be excused for assuming Coolidge was still President.

ib

10980 The jigs, or plugs, or tin squids, are cigar-sized gobbets of lead with feather tails which, it is optimistically hoped, will look edible to large stupid fish.

On carefully outfitted bait used by anglers at Martha's Vineyard, quoted by Richard Kluger *The Paper: The Life and Death of the NY Herald Tribune* Knopf 86

10981 [He] got integrity confused with geography.

On basketball scandals blamed on Yankees by coach Everett Case of North Carolina State, quoted by Ira Berkow *Red* Times Books 86

10982 It's no accident that of all the monuments left of the Greco-Roman culture, the biggest is the ball park, the Colosseum, the Shea Stadium of ancient times.

ib

10983 They overwhelmed one opponent, underwhelmed 12, and whelmed one.

On Vince Lombardi's Green Bay Packers *ib*

10984 Ernie Calvery is a gaunt, pale young case of malnutrition. But when he lays hand on that ball and starts moving, he is a whole troop of Calvery, including the pretty white horses. The guy is terrific, colossal, and also very good.

On a guard's role in Rhode Island State's overtime basketball win over Bowling Green in National Invitation Tournament *ib*

10985 [He] flings himself at right angles to the flight of the ball... the unconquerable doing the impossible.

On Jackie Robinson's play that won a National League pennant tie for the Brooklyn Dodgers *ib*

10986 [He was] a thin strip of darkness at the plate.

On Larry Doby, American League's first black player

10987 [It was] the saddest day in the year for the passel of young men whose fangs had been honed on major-league sirloins... and who had the naive notion that they'd never eat their way through to the other side of the cow.

On baseball rookies sent to minor leagues *ib*

10988 They called him the Splendid Splinter. No splinter now, he is the wholebolt of wood.

On Ted Williams at 6'3" and 205 pounds *ib*

10989 The fisher turned and ran for right field.

On a hooked salmon confronted by Ted Williams *ib*

10990 The reel was making the sweetest music this side of heaven... even a horse grazing across the river neighed approval.

ib

10991 Nobody circled the bases with the same pigeon-toed, mincing majesty.

On Babe Ruth, quoted by Peter Beilenson *Grand Slams and Fumbles* P Pauper Press 89

Tony Snow *Detroit Free Press* commentator

10992 Titanically dull... like watching an ant farm or observing a parking lot at closing time when shoppers are looking for their cars.

On soccer *Christian Science Monitor* 23 Jun 94

10993 No point... insufferably prissy... the ultimate low-tech, pre-industrial diversion.

ib

Gerald Strine columnist

10994 The Pats culda, shoulda and woulda been ahead of the Cowboys.

On the New England Patriots football team, Washington Post 7 Dec 78, an early usage of "shoulda, coulda, woulda," also used by Hillary Clinton in regard to financial transactions 22 Apr 94, cited by columnist William Safire *NY Times* 15 May 94

E M Swift journalist

10995 Howe has spent more than 30 years playing what he calls "religious hockey"—it's better to give than to receive.

"He Just Skates On and On" *Sports Illustrated* 21 Jan 80

Gayle Talbot journalist

10996 By talking in the purest jabberwocky he has learned that he can avoid answering questions and at the same time leave his audience struggling against a mild form of mental paralysis.

On Casey Stengel *San Francisco Call-Bulletin* 1 Feb 54

Robert McG Thomas Jr reporter

10997 Steve Carlton [was] a man of few words who let his slider do the speaking.

On Steve Carlton's 24-year career as his era's dominant left-handed pitcher *NY Times* 1 Aug 94

John Underwood reporter

10998 Snowboarders. Nineteen-sixties caricatures. Smelly hair and dirty mouths. Rings in their noses. Pot pipes in their pockets. And wild, erratic swoops down the mountain, ostensibly bowling over innocent skiers by the gross and cursing their downed, bloodied bodies for getting in the way.

On ski slope hippies *NY Times* 26 Feb 95

John Updike essayist

10999 The ball climbed on a diagonal line into the vast volume of air over center field. . . in the books while it was still in the sky.

On Ted Williams' last game *Sports Illustrated* 2 Oct 60

11000 Applause—no calling, no whistling, just an ocean of handclaps, minute after minute, burst after burst, crowding and running together in continuous succession, like the pushes of surf at the edge of the sand.

ib

11001 [He radiated] the hard blue glow of high purpose.

On Ted Williams, quoted by George Will *op cit*

11002 Williams is the classic ballplayer of the game on a hot August weekday before a small crowd, when the only thing at stake is the tissue-thin difference between a thing done well and a thing done ill.

ib

11003 He ran as he always ran. . . as if our praise were a storm of rain to get out of.

On Ted Williams' hitting a home-run, his 521st, in his last game *New Yorker* 22 Oct 60

11004 Our noise for some seconds passed beyond excitement into a kind of immense, open anguish, a wailing, a cry to be saved. But immortality is nontransferable. The other players. . . even the umpires. . . begged him to come out and acknowledge us. . . but he never had and did not now. Gods do not answer letters.

ib

George Vecsey columnist

11005 When the entire nation was watching him, he turned on the Stengelese. It was noblesse oblige.

On Casey Stengel, recalled on Stengel's death 29 Sep 75

11006 Waiting, waiting, waiting, waiting. . . these finicky packs of energy. . . wondering why all these two-legged types were wearing such expensive clothing in the mud.

On Kentucky Derby horses *NY Times* 8 May 94

11007 He turned the city into a playland one Sunday ever November. . . . [and] arranged for thousands and thousands of people, fat and skinny, young and old from dozens and dozens of countries, to romp through the five boroughs, a celebration of human will.

On Fred Lebow, originator of the New York City Marathon *ib* 10 Oct 94

Fay Vincent former Commissioner of Baseball

11008 Owners are fighting owners; owners are fighting the players' union; the union is fighting everything. And all the while there is no commissioner.

Comment a year after being ousted from office *NY Times* 1 Oct 93

Bucky Waters commentator

11009 They have the same role as the corpse at an Irish wake: Dress well and stay quiet.

On assistant coaches in basketball *Sports Illustrated* 20 Feb 89

T H White journalist

11010 The fisherman fishes as the urchin eats a cream bun—from lust.

Quoted by President Carter *An Outdoor Journal* Bantam 88

Ralph Wiley sportswriter

11011 Damage, specifically brain damage, is what boxing is all about. . . assault and battery with deadly weapons called the fists of man.

Serenity: A Boxing Memoir Holt 89

George F Will columnist

11012 The reviled boss, the Steingrabber, the man so many love to loathe.

On NY Yankees owner George Steinbrenner *Newsweek* 6 Aug 90

11013 Nonsense on stilts.

Discounting belief that baseball has "the pace of America's pastoral past" *Men at Work* Macmillan 90

11014 Baseball's fundamental trade-off is the purchase of opportunity by the coin of risk.

ib

11015 The crucial concept in baseball is the creation of opportunities.

ib

11016 Umpires should be natural Republicans—dead to human feelings.

ib

11017 Sport is the toy department of life.

Also attributed to Howard Cosell *ib*

Thomas Williams sportswriter

11018 [It was] the fish of his life that would make this moment, for better or for worse, forever a brilliant window.

On fishing in Quebec's Chibougaman Reserve, quoted by President Carter, *An Outdoor Journal* Bantam 88

Paul A Witteman sportswriter

11019 He rasps in a voice that is part James Cagney, part Peter Lorre, part Bethlehem PA.

On Princeton basketball coach Pete Carril *Time* 19 Mar 90

Stanley Woodward Executive Editor, *NY Herald Tribune*

11020 That is like blaming the Johnstown flood on a leaky toilet in Altoona.

On an Army coach who attributed a one-sided defeat by Michigan to the West Point center's failure to give the football a quarter-turn on the snap to the quarterback, quoted by Ira Berkow *Red* Times Books 86

Steve Wulf sportswriter

11021 There were three Bubbas, two Pookies, one Tookie, a Pork Chop, brothers Motorboat and Speedboat Jones. . . an Evers, a Chance and a lot of stinkers. . . large and incredibly small, ages old and older.

On minor league players who were to be replacements had a baseball strike continued *Time* 10 Apr 95

11022 Mama was Solar Slew, a daughter of Seattle Slew, but Papa was a rolling stone named Palace Music.

Tracing the lineage of Cigar, a top-ranking thoroughbred *ib*

11023 He is the nicest thing to happen to horse racing since Secretariat. . . . [and] can make even a casual visitor feel like Gulliver among the Houyhnhmns.

On Cigar's luck and dignity *ib*

THEATER

Actors and Actresses

F Murray Abraham

11024 When you get the big notices and the great modern parts and people applaud, just do Lear. Puts you right in your place.

On leaving his role as lawyer Roy Cohn on the closing of *Angels in America NY Times* 11 Dec 94

Andrew Allan

11025 It is impossible for an actor to pay the telephone bill when the telephone never rings.

Andrew Allan: A Self-Portrait Macmillan of Canada 74

Judith Anderson

11026 The lights go down and the pulse goes up.

On the theater, recalled on Anderson's death 3 Jan 92

Elizabeth Ashley

11027 Give me a great role. . . and it's like they've given you a magic bicycle.

Quoted by Dick Cavett on Ashley's performance in a revival of Tennessee Williams' *Suddenly, Last Summer NY Times* 8 Oct 95

Tallulah Bankhead

11028 If you really want to help the American theater, don't be an actress, dahling, be an audience!

Recalled on Bankhead's death 12 Dec 68

11029 Dahling Congressman Boykin: 10 AM is an unprecedented time for a child of the grease paint to cope with the sandman.

On being invited to speak at a fund-raising rally for a new civic auditorium in Washington DC *ib*

11030 There is less here than meets the eye.

On a revival of Maeterlinck's "Aglavaine and Selysette" *ib*

11031 In the theater only one man can count on steady work—the night watchman.

ib

Ethel Barrymore

11032 An actress. . . must have the face of Venus, the brains of Minerva, the grace of Terpsichore, the memory of Macaulay, the figure of Juno and the hide of a rhinoceros.

Quoted by George Jean Nathan *The Theater in the Fifties* Knopf 53

11033 I never let them cough, they wouldn't dare.

On controlling audiences during moments of high drama *NY Post* 7 Jun 56

Marlon Brando

11034 Performing with her was like trying to bite down on a tomato seed.

On Katharine Cornell *Brando* Random House 94

Fanny Brice

11035 Your audience gives you everything you need; there is no director who can direct you like an audience.

Quoted by Norman Katkov *The Fabulous Fanny* Knopf 52

Yul Brynner

11036 I am just a nice, clean-cut Mongolian boy.

On playing the title role in *The King and I, NY Post* 24 Sep 56

Carol Burnett

11037 An actress. I'd never said it out loud. . . [but] I came to life the times I wasn't me.

One More Time Random House 86

11038 I drifted off, dreaming of footlights every color of the rainbow.

After her first New York performance *ib*

Richard Burton

11039 A term of smelly tutorials and pimply lectures should effect a sharp cure.

On desire to lecture at Oxford, quoted by Melvin Bragg *Richard Burton* Little, Brown 89

11040 [I] will lecture to them until iambic pentameter comes out of their nostrils. . . [on] how privileged they are to speak and read and think in the greatest language invented by man.

ib

Carol Channing

11041 She played a nurse,/ She played a nun,/ She played a boy who was a fairy;/ She stopped the show,/ When she had to crow,/ And our hearts belong to Mary.

Lyrics to the tune *My Heart Belongs to Daddy* sung at Mary Martin's memorial service *NY Times* 29 Jan 91

Maurice Chevalier

11042 An artist carries on throughout his life a mysterious, uninterrupted conversation with his public.

Holiday Sep 56

Noel Coward

11043 They try to be clevah instead of watching me being clevah!

On talkative theater-goers *NY Mirror* 27 Nov 57

11044 My idea of heaven? Tonight at 8:30!

Quoted by commentator David Frost PBS TV 23 Jul 92

11045 Though we all might enjoy/ Seeing Helen of Troy/ As a gay cabaret entertainer/ I doubt that she could/ Be one quarter as good/ As our legendary, lovely, Marlene.

A first-night introduction for Marlene Dietrich, quoted by Patrick O'Connor *Dietrich Style and Substance* Dutton 91

Hume Cronyn

11046 The most magical moment in the theater is a silence so complete that you can't even hear people breathe. It means that you've got them.

Time 2 Apr 90

Bette Davis

11047 Wave after wave of love flooded the stage and washed over me, the beginning of the one greatest, durable romance of my life.

On her first curtain call *People* 21 Mar 77

11048 You can't say I didn't fall for you!

On collapsing on stage, quoted by Davis's daughter B D Hyman *My Mother's Keeper* Morrow 81

Edith Evans

11049 When you leave the theater, if you don't walk several blocks in the wrong direction, the performance has been a failure.

Quoted by Garson Kanin *Tracy and Hepburn* Angus & Robertson 70

John Gielgud

11050 Acting is. . . shame at exhibiting yourself, glory when you can forget yourself.

Quoted in Ronald Harwood ed *The Ages of Gielgud* Limelight 84

11051 Your English style will no doubt put all the other gentlemen to bed. I speak figuratively, of course.

On Cecil Beaton's decision to act in a production of *Lady Windemere's Fan*, quoted by Hugh Vickers *Cecil Beaton* Little, Brown, 85

11052 Now at least there will be one name I recognize.

On the christening of London's Globe Theater in honor of Gielgud *London Times* 4 Nov 94

Hermione Gingold

11053 I got all the schooling any actress needs. That is, I learned to write enough to sign contracts.

Look 4 Oct 55

Alec Guinness

11054 A superb tenor. . . a silver trumpet muffled in silk.

On John Gielgud, quoted by Ronald Harwood *The Ages of Geilgud* Limelight 84

Rex Harrison

11055 Whatever it is that makes a person charming, it needs to remain a mystery.

LA Herald Examiner 24 Jun 78

11056 Once the charmer is aware of a mannerism or characteristic that others find charming, it ceases to be a mannerism and becomes an affectation. And good Lord, there is nothing less charming than affectations!

ib

11057 Nobody is as interesting to spend an evening with as a really good part.

A Damned Serious Business Bantam 91

Helen Hayes

11058 I like my wrinkles, I call them my service stripes.

NBC TV 7 Jul 87

11059 An actress's life is so transitory—suddenly you're a building!

On Broadway theater named in her honor *ib*

Katharine Hepburn

11060 It was the first time I realized that the audience was not out to get me; in fact, they loved me. . . a delicious sensation.

On playing Coco Chanel on Broadway Station WETA TV Washington 27 Jul 94

Charles Laughton

11061 You are England, that's all!

To Laurence Olivier on his portrayal in the title role of Henry V, quoted by Julie Salamon *Wall Street Journal* 3 Apr 92 reviewing Donald Spoto's *Laurence Olivier* HarperCollins 92

Eva Le Gallienne

11062 I would rather play Ibsen than eat—and that's just what it amounts to.

Recalled on Le Gallienne's death 3 Jun 91

Jack Lemmon

11063 I won't quit until I get run over by a truck, a producer or a critic.

Newsweek 5 May 86

Beatrice Lillie

11064 They recognized something I'd known for years—I was a natural-born fool.

On audiences, recalled on Lillie's death 20 Jan 89

11065 Unless she starts to get bad very soon, people are just going to walk out.

On Elizabeth Taylor's well prepared reading of classic poetry in a benefit apperance, quoted by Donald Spoto *A Passion for Life* HarperCollins 95

James MacArthur

11066 What a wonderful sight, a full house—my mother would have loved it!

Speaking at the memorial service at New York's Shubert's Theater for his mother, Helen Hayes *NY Times* 19 Jun 93

Mary Martin

11067 They hadn't even started writing it, but it didn't matter; I knew that anything that had that song in it would be a hit.

On the impact of Rodgers and Hammerstein's "Some Enchanted Evening" for the 1949 musical *South Pacific* *NY Times* 26 Feb 87

11068 Give me four people and I'm on. Give me 400 and I'm a hundred times more on.

On her reaction to audiences *NY Times* 5 Nov 90

11069 I discovered I was happier in the air than on the ground. I probably always will be.

On her role of flying in *Peter Pan ib*

Raymond Massey

11070 I hope to see the day when a leading English actor. . . looks forward to his Canadian tour as a logical step in his career and not as a reason to apply to the Royal Geographical Society for an explorer's medal.

To Empire Club of Canada, recalled on Massey's death 30 Jul 83

Ethel Merman

11071 Oh, she's all right, if you like talent.

On Mary Martin after opening night of the 1949 musical *South Pacific*, *Theater Arts* Sep 58, recalled in *NY Times* 29 Jan 91

Bette Midler

11072 There comes a time when you have to let your clothes go out in the world and try to make it on their own.

On relinquishing mermaid costume worn in the 1970s *Clams on the Half Shell, People* 31 Aug 87

Jonathan Miller

11073 They are mechanized, common property. Other people have driven the joke before; it has cigarettes in the ashtray. You don't know where it's been, you don't know who the author is.

Comparing jokes to rental cars *London Times* 21 Mar 90

Robert Morley

11074 It is a great help for a man to be in love with himself, but for an actor it is absolutely essential.

London Times 8 Aug 95

Vanessa Redgrave

11075 I think there is some tiny proscenium arch racing through our genes.

On her family's theatrical dynasty *NY Times* 6 Jan 91

Ralph Richardson

11076 One can become a large, madly humming, demented refrigerator.

On keeping a role fresh through hundreds of performances *Time* 21 Aug 78

11077 He's a boring old scoutmaster on the face of it, but being that it's Shakespeare, he's the exaltation of all scoutmasters... the cold-bath king and you have to glory in it.

To Laurence Olivier on the title role in *Henry V*, quoted by Olivier in *Confessions of an Actor* Simon & Schuster 82

11078 Actors are the jockeys of literature. Others supply the horses, the plays, and we simply make them run.

Recalled on Richardson's death 10 Oct 83

11079 Acting is merely the art of keeping a large group of people from coughing.

ib

11080 *Hamlet*'s a cinch—just play it like a train, rush along through cuttings, stations and tunnels until you reach your destination. You must not get off at any of the stations along the way.

Advice to Albert Finney, quoted in John Goodwin ed *Peter Hall's Diaries* Harper & Row 84

11081 The characters... don't quite know who they are. But... we don't know exactly who we are, do we? We hardly know anybody else, really completely.... We're a mystery to ourselves, and to other people.

Quoted by John Russell *London* Abrams 94

11082 In music, the punctuation is absolutely strict... but our punctuations cannot be quite strict, because we have to relate it to the audiences. In other words, we are constantly changing the score.

ib

Cyril Ritchard

11083 Two thousand dear ladies. All very careful and diplomatic with one another. Ever so sweet and catty, you know.

On matinee audiences *Holiday* Sep 60

11084 I can hear that sweet-and-catty sound through the curtain while the house lights are still on. They all applaud with their gloves on, never too hard or too much.

ib

11085 They're busier watching each other than the show.

ib

Jason Robards

11086 All the abstract nouns that are involved become more real—forgiveness, pity, peace, love, hate, all become much deeper in the outcome.

On reviving role he played nearly 30 years earlier in Eugene O'Neill's *The Iceman Cometh NY Times* 23 Jul 85

11087 Acting is make-believe... if you make believe well enough, audiences make believe, too.

On being honored at the Library of Congress *ib*

Anna Russell

11088 The reason there are so few women comics is that so few women can bear being laughed at.

London Sunday Times 25 Aug 57

Rosalind Russell

11089 Flops are a part of life's menu and I've never been a girl to miss out on any of the courses.

NY Herald Tribune 11 Apr 57

Alastair Sim

11090 It was revealed to me many years ago with conclusive certainty that I was a fool and that I had always been a fool. Since then I have been as happy as any man has a right to be.

Time 30 Aug 76

Cornelia Otis Skinner

11091 It's as though some poor devil were to set out for a large dinner party with the knowledge that the following morning he would be hearing exactly what each of the other guests thought of him.

On opening night reviews *The Ape In Me* Houghton Mifflin 59

Maureen Stapleton

11092 A conversation with her was like talking to smoke.

On playwright Carson McCullers *NY Times* 2 Aug 92

11093 I loved her, but sometimes I thought she shouldn't be let out.

On actress Colleen Dewhurst

Barbra Striesand

11094 What does it mean when people applaud? . . . Should I give 'em money? Say thanks? Lift my dress? The lack of applause—that I can respond to.

Life 22 May 64

11095 They're called "angels" because they're in heaven until the reviews come out.

On financial backers *Playbill* Oct 69

Peter Ustinov

11096 Critics search for ages for the wrong word, which, to give them credit, they eventually find.

BBC Radio 1 Feb 52

11097 Laughter would be bereaved if snobbery died.

London Observer 13 Mar 55

11098 By increasing the size of the keyhole, today's playwrights are in danger of doing away with the door.

Christian Science Monitor 14 Nov 62

11099 After eating curry night after night, they deny the existence of asparagus.

Likening playwrights to "men who have been dining for a month in Indian restaurants" *ib*

Shelley Winters

11100 It's a sound you can't get in movies or television. . . the sound of a wonderful, deep silence that means you've hit them where they live.

Theater Arts Jun 56

11101 Stage nudity is disgusting, shameful and damaging to all things American. But if I were 22 with a great body, it would be artistic, tasteful, patriotic and a progressive religious experience.

News summaries 13 Sep 65

Estelle Winwood

11102 Don't worry about your looks. The very thing that makes you unhappy in your appearance may be the one thing to make you a star.

Recalled on Winwood's death 20 Jun 84

Ed Wynn

11103 A comedian is not a man who says funny things. A comedian is one who says things funny.

Time 1 Jul 66

Playwrights, Producers, and Directors

Edward Albee playwright

11104 One must let the play happen. . . let the mind loose to respond as it will, to receive impressions, to sense rather than know, to gather rather than immediately understand.

On his play *Tiny Alice National Observer* 5 Apr 65

11105 Good writers define reality; bad ones merely restate it.

Saturday Review 4 May 66

11106 Your source material is the people you know. . . [but] every character is an extension of the author's own personality.

ib

11107 American critics. . . like American universities . . . have dull and half-dead faculties.

To NY Cultural League 5 Nov 69

11108 You should always be surprised by awards and prizes, since you're always surprised when you don't get them.

On *Three Tall Women* that won him a third Pulitzer Prize *Guardian Weekly* 24 Apr 94

11109 It takes an entire life to write a play. . . three months to get it down on paper.

Parade 14 Aug 94

Maxwell Anderson playwright

11110 [They are] the Jukes family of journalists who bring to the theater nothing but their own hopelessness, recklessness and despair.

On critics *Saturday Evening Post* 13 Apr 57

11111 If you practice an art, be proud of it and make it proud of you. . . . It may break your heart but it will fill your heart before it breaks it, it will make you a person in your own right.

NY Herald Tribune 7 Mar 59

Robert Anderson playwright

11112 America is not playwright-conscious. . . . [It says] in all innocence, "I love to go see Lynn Fontanne. She always says such witty things."

NY Herald Tribune 5 Aug 56

11113 A playwright. . . is usually thought of as a slightly benighted child of nature who somehow did it all on a ouija board.

ib

11114 [It] is as though we were suddenly to say, "I'm tired of faces with two eyes and nose and a mouth."

On "clamoring for novelty" *ib*

11115 What we want. . . is not faces with three eyes, but more beautiful, strong, truthful, wise, humorous faces.

ib

11116 The mission of the playwright. . . is to look into his heart and write.

Theater Arts Mar 58

11117 You can make a killing in the theater but not a living.

NY Times 12 Jun 88

11118 Nobody asked you to be a playwright!

Sign over Anderson's desk *ib*

Jean Anouilh playwright

11119 Talent is like a faucet, while it is open, one must write.

NY Times 2 Oct 60

Boris Aronson set designer

11120 A propagandist theater after a revolution is like mustard after a meal.

NY Times 11 Oct 87

Cecil Beaton set designer

11121 Be daring, different, impractical, anything that will assert integrity of purpose and imaginative vision against the play-it-safers.

To set designers *Theater Arts* May 57

11122 I always hear the woman in the back of the dress circle who says she doesn't like blue.

On stage sets BBC TV 18 Feb 62

Mac Cole founder, Cole Carnival Shows

11123 The first carnival person was Christopher Columbus. . . didn't know where he was going. . . where he was. . . where he'd been.

Washington Times 18 Aug 89

Noel Coward actor, lyricist and playwright

11124 *Private Lives*. . . connoted to the public mind cocktails, evening dress, repartee and irreverent allusions to copulation, thereby causing a gratifying number of respectable people to queue up at the box office.

Recalled on Coward's death 26 Mar 73

11125 Coax it, charm it, interest it, stimulate it, shock it now and then if you must, make it laugh, make it cry, but above all. . . never, never, never bore the living hell out of it.

To playwrights on respecting public appeal *ib*

11126 Work is more fun than fun.

ib

11127 Someday I suspect, when Jesus has definitely got me for a sunbeam, my works may be adequately assessed.

Quoted by Cole Lesley *Remembered Laughter* Knopf 76

T S Eliot poet and playwright

11128 My greatest trouble is getting the curtain up and down.

Time 6 Mar 50

George Fearon publicist

11129 I told him "You should become known as the Angry Young Man." In fact, we decided then and there, that henceforth he was to be known as that.

On representing John Osborne's *Look Back in Anger* *London Daily Telegraph* 2 Oct 57

Peter Feibleman essayist

11130 There's a place where everybody wants to be insulted, and Lilly knew where it was.

On Lillian Hellman *New Yorker* 21 Jun 93

Harvey Fierstein playwright

11131 I assume everyone is gay, unless told otherwise.

Life Jan 94

Tyrone Guthrie producer

11132 Work can only be universal if it is rooted in a part of its creator which is most privately and particularly himself.

NY Times 27 Nov 55

Lorraine Hansberry playwright

11133 Though it be a thrilling and marvelous thing to be merely young and gifted in such times, it is doubly so—doubly dynamic—to be young, gifted and black.

NY Times 25 May 69

Moss Hart playwright and producer

11134 The only credential was the blindness to dream. . . feet embedded in the upper Bronx, eyes firmly set toward Broadway.

On contemplating a theatrical career *Act One* Random House 59

11135 That look of threatening benevolence.

On first-nighters *ib*

11136 The grapevine was apt to be hung with highly colored fruit of pure imagination.

On Broadway rumors *ib*

11137 The four most dramatic words in the English language: "Act One, Scene One."

ib

11138 The second act. . . is the soft underbelly of play writing.
ib

11139 There is no smile as bright as the smile of a box-office man the morning after a hit. . . as wide as the proscenium itself.
ib

Garson Kanin director

11140 It was one of the most important literary experiences of my life. . . some of the greatest prose in the English language, written by 18-year-old kids who couldn't spell.
Recalling his job as postal censor, quoted by Studs Terkel *The Good War* Pantheon 84

George S Kaufman playwright

11141 Massey won't be satisfied until he's assassinated.
On Raymond Massey's striving for the essence of the title role in *Abe Lincoln in Illinois* recalled on Kaufman's death 2 Jun 61

11142 Satire is what closes on Saturday night.
Quoted by Howard Teichmann *George S Kaufman* Atheneum 72

11143 I understand your new play is full of single entendres.
To Howard Dietz on his play *Between the Devil ib*

11144 A play isn't written. It's rewritten.
Quoted by Scott Meredith *George S Kaufman and His Friends* Doubleday 74

11145 You're not understudies. You're overstudies.
To over-rehearsed stand-in's

11146 Frank is a very painsgiving man.
On Kaufman's brother-in-law Frank Lieberman *ib*

11147 I saw the play under bad conditions. The curtain was up.
On playwright Alexander Woollcott

11148 There was laughter in the back of the theater, leading to the belief that somebody was telling jokes back there.
On Woollcott plays

11149 I'm going to patent an invention which will keep composers away from pianos at parties. . . [or] pianos away from composers.
ib

11150 Collaboration. . . is marriage without sex. . . the two people fly far above their talents.
ib

Howard Kolins Producer, Radio City Music Hall

11151 Imitation is the mother of theatrical inspiration. We change very carefully.
NY Times 4 Dec 94

Tony Kushner playwright

11152 I wanted to attempt something of ambition even if accused of straying too close to ambition's ugly twin, pretentiousness.
On *Angels in America NY Times* 21 Nov 93

11153 We organize the world for ourselves. . . reflect, refract, criticize, grieve over its savagery, and help one another to discern, amidst the gathering dark, paths of resistance, pockets of peace and places from whence hope may be plausibly expected.
ib

Lawrence Lagner co-founder, Theater Guild

11154 I have no interest in anything but genius, so please sit down.
To Tennessee Williams, recalled by Williams Memoirs Doubleday 75

Anita Loos playwright

11155 Tallulah never bored anyone, and I consider that humanitarianism of a very high order indeed.
Eulogy at Tallulah Bankhead's funeral *NY Times* 17 Dec 68

David Mamet playwright

11156 All of us write plays in our heads all the time. . . before we're going to visit our girl friend, before we're going to talk to a boss—we rehearse.
Quoted by Susan Stamberg *Talk* Random House 93

Arthur Miller playwright

11157 My works are a credit to this nation and. . . will endure longer than the McCarran Act.
On being refused a passport for supposed disloyalty *NY Herald Tribune* 31 Mar 54

11158 I have made more friends for American culture than the State Department. Certainly I have made fewer enemies, but that isn't very difficult.
ib

11159 The structure of a play is always the story of how the birds came home to roost.
Harper's Aug 58

11160 The best of our theater is standing on tiptoe, striving to see over the shoulders of father and mother.
National Observer 20 Jan 64

11161 The worst [of our theater] is. . . obsessive keyhole sexuality.
ib

11162 The job is to ask questions—it always was—and to ask them as inexorably as I can. And to face the absence of precise answers with a certain humility.
ib

11163 He worked awfully hard.

When asked to suggest his epitaph *60 Minutes* CBS TV 15 Nov 87

11164 If I knew, I would go there more often to find more.

When asked where his words originate *London Times* 12 Oct 95

Jonathan Miller playwright

11165 Directing is about two things: reminding people of what they know already and have forgotten, and persuading them to forget what they should never have known.

NY Times 1 Aug 82

Mike Nichols producer and playwright

11166 A sizeable number of people with severe respiratory infections... have... courageously made their way to the theater... the Discreet Choker and the Straight Cougher.

NY Times 2 Oct 77

J C Nugent playwright

11167 [He is] forcing gallons of saltwater through your fondest pretenses. Listing badly, you man the pumps, you head your nose into the gale, you mix up a new batch of metaphors.

On working with playwright James Thurber, quoted by Charles S Holmes *The Clocks of Columbus* Atheneum 72

11168 Next day, when you are patching your sails and cutting away wreckage, Thurber appears in a canoe, bearing fruit and flowers.

ib

Edna O'Brien novelist and playwright

11169 Writers really live in the mind and in hotels of the soul.

Vogue Apr 85

Sean O'Casey playwright

11170 Between the writing of plays, in the vast middle of the night, when our children and their mother slept, I sat alone, and my thoughts drifted back in time, murmuring the remembrance of things past into the listening ear of silence; fashioning thought to unspoken words, and setting them down upon the sensitive tablets of the mind.

Pictures in the Hallway Macmillan 1912, recalled in *NY Times* 16 Sep 56

11171 A heart-scald when you're writing, another in production, a terror during rehearsals.

On perfecting a play *ib* 28 Jul 94

11172 The novel is by far the easiest and most satisfactory work to do: when you're done, you're done.

28 Jul 94

Sean O'Faolain playwright

11173 I have learned in my 30-odd years of serious writing only one sure lesson: Stories, like whiskey, must be allowed to mature in the cask.

Atlantic Dec 56

Eugene O'Neill playwright

11174 I love every bone in their heads.

On critics *NY Times* 1 Dec 80

11175 [Her] love and tenderness... enabled me to face my dead at last and write this play—write it with deep pity and understanding and forgiveness.

On his wife Carlotta, recalled on Broadway revival of *Long Day's Journey into Night Christian Science Monitor* 1 May 86

11176 Little subconscious mind, say I each night, bring home the bacon.

Quoted by Kenneth Tynan *Tynan Right and Left* Atheneum 88

Joseph Papp playwright and producer

11177 You don't need a building... just a couple of planks and a dream.

On New York summer theater known as Shakespeare in the Park *Washington Post* 1 Nov 91

Harold Pinter playwright

11178 I no longer feel banished from myself.

On completing his first full-length play in 17 years *Newsweek* 18 Sep 95

J B Priestley playwright

11179 It is as if you had to devise a whole banquet out of rice pudding and stewed pears.

On realistic plays on contemporary England *The Art of the Dramatist* Heinemann 57

11180 I'm in the business of providing people with secondary satisfactions. It wouldn't have done me much good if they had all written their own plays.

At age 89 *Illustrated London News* Sep 84

Ringling Brothers, Barnum & Bailey Circus

11181 [We present] these snowy sovereigns from faraway frozen frontiers, ten towering titans of the tundra in an astounding array of ursine antics!

On polar bears who lumber through rings of fire *NY Times* 9 Apr 89

Billy Rose producer

11182 We've gotta use Canada for our backdrop, the moon and stars for our props, and Lake Erie for our swimming pool. . . bigger and more beautiful than any fountain in Versailles.

On Cleveland's Great Lakes Exposition, recalled in *Sports Illustrated* 15 Jun 92

Nicky Silver playwright

11183 I've never had a fist fight in my life. Of course the day is young.

On playwriting that exorcises inner ferocity *NY Times* 26 Feb 95

11184 I'd like to. . . have a big breakthrough, be the toast of the theater community for two years and then be bludgeoned to death by my bald lover.

ib

Tom Stoppard playwright

11185 Ambushing the audience is what theater is all about.

Newsweek 16 Jan 84

Lee Strasburg

11186 When Gielgud speaks the line, you can hear Shakespeare thinking.

On John Gielgud at 89 *London Times* 6 Apr 94

Elizabeth Swandos producer

11187 I like to explain La Mama as the Marx Brothers version of the United Nations.

On 25th anniversary of La Mama Experimental Theater *NY Times* 26 Oct 86

James Thurber playwright

11188 The theater is the primary evidence of a nation's culture.

NY Times 27 Jul 52

11189 The three-act play has sharp, concrete edges, rigid spacings, a complete dependence on time and more than a hundred rules, all basic.

Quoted by Charles S Holmes *The Clocks of Columbus* Atheneum 72

Jennifer Tipton lighting designer

11190 Light affects the same way music does. Wordlessly.

On illuminating drama and ballet *NY Times* 14 Apr 91

Mike Todd producer

11191 No gals, no gags, no chance.

On attending rehearsals for *Oklahoma!* in 1943, recalled on the 50th anniversary of the musical that ran six years, won a Pulitzer Prize, and was to have 750 revivals in 1993 *US News & World Report* 12 Apr 93

Wendy Wasserstein producer

11192 Interesting, exemplary, even sexy, but basically unhappy. The ones who open doors usually are.

On women's liberation movement as seen in her play *The Heidi Chronicles NY Times* 11 Dec 88

Margaret Webster producer

11193 You must not wear your heart on your sleeve for daws to pick at.

To Tennessee Williams on the out-of-town closing of his first professionally produced play *Battle of Angels NY Times* 17 Mar 57

Thornton Wilder playwright

11194 Many plays—certainly mine—are like blank checks; actors and directors put their own signatures on them.

NY Mirror 13 Jul 56

11195 A dramatist is one who believes that the pure event, an action involving human beings, is more arresting than any comment that can be made upon it.

In Malcolm Cowley ed *Writers at Work* Viking 58

11196 On the stage it is always now. . . that razor edge, between the past and the future. . . the essential character of conscious being and words are rising to their lips in immediate spontaneity.

ib

11197 The theater is supremely fitted to say: "Behold! These things are!"

ib

11198 The less seen, the more heard. The eye is the enemy of the ear in real drama.

On the bare stage prescribed for *Our Town, NY Times* 6 Nov 61

11199 I am not interested in the ephemeral—such subjects as the adulteries of dentists. I am interested in those things that repeat and repeat and repeat in the lives of millions.

ib

11200 I am like the woman charged with kleptomania, "I do steal, Your Honor, but only from the very best stores."

Recalled on Wilder's death 7 Dec 75

Tennessee Williams playwright

11201 I would not "make book" on the possibility that I will get up any morning and find it more inviting to live than write about living.

NY Times 17 Mar 57

11202 Writing as an escape from . . . being called a sissy by the neighborhood kids, and Miss Nancy by my father.

ib

11203 Spun forth at a speed that is incalculable to a length beyond measure.

On the emotional drive of playwrights *The Theater of Tennessee Williams* Vol 1 New Directions 71

11204 It's good for a writer to think he's dying. He works harder.

London Observer 31 Oct 76

11205 In my heart an inscrutable bird of dark feather seems to have built a nest which I can never quite dislodge, no matter how loudly I cackle or widely I grin.

"I Am Widely Regarded as the Ghost of a Writer" *NY Times* 8 May 77

11206 Maybe they were New York drama critics.

On being mugged in Key West *People* 7 May 79

11207 A country of endured but unendurable pain.

On the emotional environment of his characters *NY Times* 18 May 86

P G Wodehouse humorist and playwright

11208 Has anybody ever seen a dramatic critic in the daytime? Of course not. They come out after dark, up to no good.

NY Mirror 27 May 55

Critics

James Agate essayist

11209 He is. . . this generation's rightful tenant of this monstrous Gothic castle of a poem.

On John Gielgud's *Hamlet* recalled on 50th anniversary of the performance *London Times* 26 Dec 94

11210 Everybody died or got married or went mad more than competently. I left the theater humming.

On Laurence Olivier in *Richard III ib*

Kenneth Allsop *Picture Post*

11211 Lights flashed. Bells rang. Overnight "angry" became the code word. . . [for] irreverence, stridency, impatience with tradition, vigor, vulgarity, sulky resentment against the cultivated.

On the phrase "angry young men" that crystallized a mood of the early 1950s, quoted by William Safire *Safire's Political Dictionary* Random House 93

Anon

11212 Be light, stinging, insolent, and melancholy.

Favorite quotation that critic Kenneth Tynan posted above his desk *Tynan Right and Left* Atheneum 67

11213 Love your play. . . we only have problems with your main character, the second act and the ending.

A fan's comment on Wendy Wasserstein's *The Heidi Chronicles NY Times* 24 Jan 91

11214 To capture Friel is like shifting smoke with a pitchfork.

On the Abbey Theater's Brian Friel *ib* 29 Sep 91

11215 The crossroads of the circus, opera and magic.

On the *Folies Bergère ib* 30 Sep 93

Brooks Atkinson *NY Times*

11216 Good plays drive bad playgoers crazy.

Theater Arts Aug 56

11217 Ethel Waters, the flaming tower of dusky regality. . . knows how to make a song stand on tiptoe.

Recalled on Waters' death 1 Sep 77

11218 There is no joy so great as reporting that a good play has come to town.

Recalled on Atkinson's death 13 Jun 84

Clive Barnes *NY Times*

11219 Dialogue more tame than Wilde.

On Somerset Maugham's *The Constant Wife NY Times* 15 Apr 75

11220 As hard as the nails on a crucifix.

On Mildred Dunnock in *Days in the Trees ib* 28 Sep 76

11221 The mother is not dying exactly, but has reached a point in life where death is a familiar on the staircase.

ib

Mary Ellin Barrett lyricist's daughter

11222 High with a slight rasp, familiar, sweet. . . [and] after the wobbly first few bars, he seems at home up there, dropping 25 years, impish, with rumpled forehead and raised brows.

On "Oh, How I Hate to Get Up in the Morning" sung by her father, Irving Berlin, in a Broadway revival *Irving Berlin: A Daughter's Memoir* Simon & Schuster 94

Michael Billington *Manchester Guardian*

11223 He has made one of the most acclaimed comebacks since Lazarus.

On Edward Albee winning a Pulitzer Prize 30 years after earlier hits *Guardian Weekly* 20 Nov 94

Ben Brantley *NY Times*

11224 Basically a tempest in a martini shaker.

On Noel Coward's *Present Laughter ib NY Times* 9 Aug 95

11225 A stirring, bleating trumpet that fills the house.

On Betty Buckley singing as Norma Desmond in Andrew Lloyd Webber's Broadway production of *Sunset Boulevard ib* 28 Aug 95

John Mason Brown
Saturday Review

11226 He has ears he likes to bathe in sound.
On playwright Maxwell Anderson *Dramatis Personae* Viking 63

11227 The tick of his talk was measured, his words seeming to be spaced by minutes, but when he chimed he struck gaily.
On playwright Robert Sherwood as a grandfather clock at the Algonquin roundtable *The Worlds of Robert E Sherwood* Harper & Row 65

11228 The more one has seen of the good, the more one asks for the better.
"More Than 1,001 First Nights" *Saturday Review* 29 Aug 65

11229 Tallulah Bankhead barged down the Nile last night as Cleopatra—and sank!
NY Post 11 Nov 1937, recalled on Brown's death 16 Mar 69

11230 Most Hamlets look like the original interior decorator.
Time 1 May 39

11231 To many, dramatic criticism must seem like an attempt to tattoo soap bubbles.
Stagebill ib Dec 81

Anatole Broyard *NY Times*

11232 There is something about seeing real people on a stage that makes a bad play more intimately, more personally offensive than any other art form.
NY Times 6 Feb 76

Anthony Burgess essayist

11233 Life is a wretched gray Saturday, but it has to be lived through.
On Samuel Beckett's *Waiting for Godot, London Times* 10 Apr 86

Simon Callow actor and biographer

11234 Laughton does with acting what great creative artists attempt. . . to exalt the human soul and to heal the damaged heart.
Charles Laughton Grove 88

11235 He climbed down from the cross, pulled out the nails and made with uncertain steps for real life.
On wanting to be liked

Vincent Canby columnist *NY Times*

11236 The Upper West Side. . . a land of big, old-fashioned apartment buildings with doormen, high ceilings, waste space and psychiatrists on every floor.
On Woody Allen's *Central Park West NY Times* 7 Mar 95

11237 She. . . broke a bottle of champagne over the bow of the new Broadway season.
On Carol Burnett in *Moon Over Buffalo* 2 Oct 95

John Chapman critic *NY Daily News*

11238 Three and a half hours long, four characters wide, a cesspool deep.
On Edward Albee's *Who's Afraid of Virginia Woolf? NY Daily News* 15 Oct 62

Roger Cohen *NY Times*

11239 A young master of ceremonies in rimless spectacles was imbued with all the earnest sincerity of a marriage counselor.
On the *Folies Bergère NY Times* 30 Sep 93

Richard Corliss *Time*

11240 A dirge to incompatibility. . . a taste of exhumed ashes.
On Michael Hastings' play on T S Eliot's marriage *Tom and Vic Time* 25 Feb 85

11241 He spoke eloquently to the worst in ourselves.
On playwright John Osborne 9 Jan 95

William E Geist *NY Times*

11242 George, a camel, stepped on the foot of a Rockette; six sheep came off the elevator as three kings bearing gifts got on.
Reporting on "pandemonium backstage" at Radio City's Christmas show *NY Times* 29 Nov 86

11243 Human Christmas trees bumped into eight maids-a-milking at the water cooler and an elf came down with the flu.
ib

Wolcott Gibbs essayist

11244 The American theater is the aspirin of the middle classes.
Recalled on Gibbs' death 16 Aug 58

Brendan Gill *New Yorker*

11245 If it were better, it wouldn't be as good.
On Leonard Gershe's *Butterflies Are Free New Yorker* 1 Nov 69

11246 *The Iceman Cometh* is the most boring play ever written. . . *Long Day's Journey Into Night* easily the greatest.
On Eugene O'Neill *ib*

Mel Gussow *NY Times*

11247 He was a poet of the human heart.
On Tennessee Williams *NY Times* 26 Feb 83

Jesse Helms US Senator

11248 One cockroach in one's soup is one cockroach too many.

On the National Endowment of the Arts' grant for a drama depicting human mutilation *Washington Post* 26 Jul 94

William A Henry III critic

11249 A poet laureate of adolescent sexuality and middle-age longing.

On playwright William Inge *Time* 23 Jul 83

11250 A *cri de coeur* for the unassuageable pain of growing old before she has ever grown up.

On Shirley Booth in Inge's *Come Back Little Sheba ib*

George Hill travel writer

11251 Amateur dramatics on an epic scale.

On the Oberammergau *Passion Play, London Times* 19 May 90

Al Hirschfeld cartoonist

11252 They come to applaud their money.

On angels on opening night *NY Times* 21 Jun 88

Philip Johnson architect

11253 The essence of a theater is elegance, just as the essence of a church is spirituality.

On designing Lincoln Center's NY State Theater *Newsweek* 4 May 64

T E Kalem *Time*

11254 The laureat of the the outcast.

On Tennessee Williams *Time* 7 Mar 83

11255 He sometimes ran a purple ribbon through his typewriter and gushed where he should have damned.

ib

Garrison Keillor humorist

11256 It's a play that after you've been there for a short while, you wonder how long this is going to take.

On Edward Albee's *Three Tall Women, New York* 2 Jan 95

William Kennedy novelist

11257 [Her] presence reduced men into spittling, masturbating pigs.

On courtesan-actress Magdalena Colon, also known as La Ultima in *Quinn's Book* Viking 88

Walter Kerr *NY Times*

11258 Me no Leica.

On John Van Druten's *I Am a Camera* news summaries 31 Dec 51

11259 Hair mussed and with an innocent, indolent, irreverent look on its bright, bland face.

On musical comedy *NY Herald Tribune* 1 Sep 63

11260 Harpo Marx *looks* like a musical comedy!

ib

11261 His self-congratulatory chuckles could be sold as candy in the lobby.

On Vincent Price in *Darling of the Day NY Times* 11 Feb 68

11262 She won't let a line pass without making certain she's had it in for a private talk and perhaps tea.

On actress Catherine Burns *International Herald Tribune* 26 May 68

John David Klein commentator

11263 I saw this show under adverse circumstances—my seat was facing the stage.

On *Three Guys Naked from the Waist Down* Station WNET TV New York 5 Feb 85

Stewart Klein commentator

11264 I have seen stronger plots than this in a cemetery.

On *Break a Leg* WNYW TV New York 29 Apr 79

11265 [She] lives up to her name... as wooden as two trees.

On Marla Maples in *The Will Rogers Follies, NY Times* 20 Aug 92

John Lahr biographer

11266 To watch inspired laughter register with an audience is to be present at a great and violent mystery.

On comparing his father, Hollywood actor Bert Lahr, to British actor Barry Humphries *Dame Edna Everage and the Rise of Western Civilization* Farrar Straus Giroux 92

11267 What is released in the explosion of laughter is a deep contradictory thing that is both joy and pain, mischief and madness, pleasure and panic.

ib

11268 Anger was Lillian Hellman's oxygen.

On Peter Feibleman's play *Cakewalk* on his relationship with Lillian Hellman *New Yorker* 21 Jun 93

Bernard Levin *London Times*

11269 It may not only be the worst evening I ever spent in the theater but the worst evening anywhere.

On the Andrew Lloyd Webber 1978 musical *Evita, Quote, UnQuote* BBC program on Station WETA Washington 30 Sep 90

11270 Surely nanny told him in his pram that he could not have his cake before he had finished his bread and butter.

On Stephen Fry's desertion of his role in *Cell Mates London Times* 25 Feb 95

London Times

11271 [He] was the master of the epigram with a corkscrew for its tail.

"You Made It, Oscar, You Did" editorial on Westminster Abbey's dedication of a memorial window to Oscar Wilde 15 Feb 95

11272 Artists need neither rehabilitation by the Poets' Corner nor pardon by the Home Secretary. They live in their work.

ib

11273 Oscar is a modern man much more than a Victorian. . . and his boasts to the customs officer that he had only his genius to declare are in line with modern celebrity self-promotion.

On Oscar Wilde *ib*

William Manchester biographer

11274 Actors who have tried to play Churchill and MacArthur have failed abysmally because each of those men was a great actor playing himself.

Book of the Month Club News Jun 83

Joseph L Mankiewicz screewriter

11275 A playwright always speaks in italics.

Lines in *All About Eve*, film based on Mary Orr's short story *The Wisdom of Eve* 50

Clare McHugh reporter

11276 She never drank before a performance, but life after the curtain was an open bar.

On Maureen Stapleton *People* 23 Oct 95

Marshall H McLuhan essayist

11277 Why does a phone ringing on the stage create instant tension?. . . [It is the] intensity of electric polarity.

Quoted by Suzanne Keller, Ithiel de Sola Pool ed *The Social Impact of the Telephone* MIT Press 77

Herbert Muschamp *NY Times*

11278 Red-and-gold disease. . . an itch, the theater a place to scratch it. . . a yearning for the wider world.

Quoting "red-and-gold disease" coined by future director Lincoln Kirstein's mother when her son began haunting theaters *NY Times* 30 Jul 95

11279 The lights went down, the curtain went up. . . a place for the care and feeding of dreams.

ib

George Jean Nathan *NY Times*

11280 Criticism is the art wherewith a critic tries to guess himself into a share of the author's fame.

Recalled on Nathan's death 8 Apr 58

11281 He writes plays for the ages—the ages between 5 and 12.

On George Bernard Shaw *ib*

11282 Much of the contemporary English polite comedy writing suggests a highly polished and very smooth billiard table with all the necessary brightly poised cues, but without balls.

Quoted by Kenneth Tynam, Kathleen Tynan and Ernie Eban ed *Profiles* Harper & Row 90

New York Times

11283 Families That Play Together, Stage Together.

Headline on Benedict Nightingale's article on theatrical dynasties 6 Jan 91

11284 Too poor to go to college, he managed nonetheless to spill pure gold over Broadway and its offshoots and, indeed, over the entire American theater.

"Golden Gift" editorial on death of producer Joe Papp 1 Nov 91

Dorothy Parker critic and humorist

11285 Scratch an actor and you'll find an actress.

Recalled on Parker's death 7 Jun 67

Billy Rice humorist

11286 He's like the general run of people, only he's a lot more like them than they are themselves, if you understand me.

On playwright John Osborne *Spectator* 10 Jun 95

Frank Rich *NY Times*

11287 A dying volcano in final spluttering eruption under a Delta moon.

On Charles Durning's Big Daddy in Tennessee Williams' *Cat On a Hot Tin Roof* NY 22 Mar 90

11288 It moves at the leisurely pace of a contentious canasta hand.

On Ivan Menchell's *The Cemetery Club, NY Times* 16 May 90

David Richards *NY Times*

11289 Her voice has always sounded like heartbreak feels.

On Julie Harris *NY Times* 14 Apr 91

11290 Her powdery-white face remains triumphantly mutable. . . you can see in it the child, the flirt, the crusader or the crone.

ib

11291 The one-person play merely represents the high end of what has become a ravenous appetite for the low down.

On evening centering on Mark Twain, Emily Dickinson, Isak Dinesen, Lillian Hellman and other personages

Tim Richardson critic

11292 For Agatha Christie fans, there is nothing like a good murder to refresh the soul.

Reviewing Christie's *The Unexpected Guest*, *Country Life* 3 Mar 94

Lloyd Rose critic

11293 When that bold instrument sounds through the theater, everything on stage fades and vanishes.

On Maria Callas recordings incorporated in Terrence McNally's play *Master Class* with Zoe Caldwell as Callas, *Washington Post* 22 Sep 95

Richard Rosen critic

11294 Hers is the great gift of Inner Silliness.

On Andrea Martin in *My Favorite Year NY Times* 29 Nov 92

11295 A gentle childlike perversity whose intent is not to instruct or shock, but simply to make you laugh

ib

John Russell critic

11296 Here was an achievement that would last as long as there were people alive who had seen it.

On Edith Evans as the nurse in *Romeo and Juliet* and Lady Blacknell in *The Importance of Being Earnest* London Abrams 94

11297 For those who had grown up and grown old with them, these players. . . had served as landmarks in human experience.

On the generation of Edith Evans, Peggy Ashcroft, Sybil Thorndike, Laurence Olivier, Ralph Richardson, Rex Harrison, and John Gielgud *ib*

Saturday Review

11298 [She is] the Lizzie Borden of the midwest.

On *Chicago Tribune* critic Claudia Cassidy, quoted in Earl Blackwell ed *Celebrity Register* Simon & Schuster 73

Spectator magazine

11299 The public has consistently supported it. . . with "bottoms on seats" to use his own earthy phrase.

On Peter Hall's enthusiasm for a national British theater 10 May 80

Time magazine

11300 [Her] appearance suggests an overstuffed electric chair.

On actress Margaret Rutherford *Time* 2 Feb 62

11301 Her writhing stare could reduce a rabid dog to foaming jelly.

ib 24 May 63

11302 While tragedy moves from sanity toward madness, comedy moves from madness toward sanity.

On contemporary drama *ib* 22 Jan 65

11303 Man, as they see him, is a creature trapped betwen two voids, prenatal and posthumous, on a shrinking spit of sand he calls time.

On Beckett, Ionesco, Genet, Pinter, Osborne and other European dramatists who use "the World as a metaphor of dread" *ib* 8 Jul 66

Kathleen Tynan critic's widow

11304 Hawk-nosed, as thin as a heron, with a voice like a run-down foghorn.

On director Tony Richardson *Vanity Fair* Feb 92

Kenneth Tynan *London Observer*

11305 A good many inconveniences attend playgoing in any large city, but the greatest of them is usually the play itself

NY Herald Tribune 17 Feb 57

11306 The sheer complexity of writing a play always had dazzled me.

On why he became a critic *NY Mirror* 6 Jun 63

11307 No theater could sanely flourish until there was an umbilical connection between what was happening on the stage and what was happening in the world.

Recalled on Tynan's death 26 Jul 80

11308 [He has] slack, surly lips, on which words sit lovingly.

On Charles Laughton, Kathleen Tynan and Ernie Eban ed *Profiles* HarperPerennial 90

11309 His smile is that of a small boy jovially peeping at life in a nudist colony.

ib

11310 Though every actor's ambition is to stop the show, his instructions are that it must go on.

ib

11311 His uniqueness lies in the fact that he is greater than the sum of his parts.

On John Gielgud *Harper's Bazaar* Jul 52 *ib*

11312 Dame Edith Evans. . . suggests a crested wave of Edwardian eccentricity vainly dashing itself on the rocks of contemporary life.

ib

11313 She brings with her an aura of cigarettes stubbed out in pots of cold cream.

On Julie Harris in 1952 Broadway production of John Van Druten's *I Am a Camera ib*

11314 Watching her is like being present at a successful audition for the role of a theatrical immortal.

On monologuist Ruth Draper's 1952 London appearance *ib*

11315 When he hits a friend over the ear with a revolver-butt, he does it as casually as he will presently press the elevator button on his way out.

On James Cagney's gangster roles *ib*

11316 As I shamble aghast into the prime of life, I wonder what kind of dossier the Greatest Critic of Them All is compiling for me, Up There.

On Tynan's 40th birthday *Tynan Right and Left* Atheneum 67

11317 A relationship with Laurence Olivier is akin to that of a tugboat nudging an ocean greyhound into harbor.

ib

11318 If a play does anything—either tragically or comically, satirically or farcically—to explain to me why I am alive, it is a good play. If it seems unaware that such questions exist, I tend to suspect that it's a bad one.

ib

11319 A good drama critic. . . perceives what is happening in the theater of his time. A great drama critic also perceives what is not happening.

ib

11320 A critic is a man who knows the way, but can't drive the car.

Civilization Sep 96

Peter Ustinov playwright and critic

11321 By increasing the size of the keyhole, today's playwrights are in danger of doing away with the door.

Christian Science Monitor 14 Nov 62

Patricia Volk novelist

11322 A dark theater in a small town is like a corpse in the living room. It's dead and it's there.

On the revival of the Sharon CT Playhouse *NY Times* 30 Jul 95

E B White critic

11323 The critic leaves at curtain fall / To find, in starting to review it / He scarcely saw the play at all / For starting to review it.

NY Times 19 Sep 65

Walter Winchell columnist

11324 I can't go to Shubert openings. So I wait three nights and go their closings.

On being barred from Shubert-owned theaters, recalled on Winchell's death 20 Feb 72

11325 Who am I to stone the first cast?

On why he usually praised a season's initial show, quoted by Peter Hay Broadway *Anecdotes* Oxford 90

11326 South Terrific!

On opening night of the musical *South Pacific* recalled by its author, James A Michener *The World Is My Home* Random House 92

Alex Witchel essayist

11327 The voice. . . could sell you a thousand acres of swampland and leave you begging for more.

On Alec Baldwin in revival of Tennessee Williams' *A Streetcar Named Desire, NY Times* 20 May 92

Andrew L Yarrow *NY Times*

11328 Mr Crawford has grown accustomed to his face.

On the three layers of foam latex worn by Michael Crawford in *Phantom of the Opera, NY Times* 1 Feb 88

Maurice Zolotow *Theater Arts*

11329 Miss Verdon displays a series of variations on the derrière that is practically hypnotic to any healthy, red-blooded American drama critic.

On Gwen Verdon *Theater Arts* Jul 55

11330 There is no more offensive act of theatrical rudeness than coming late to a performance.

ib Feb 58

INDEX BY SOURCES

Note: Numerals refer to quotation numbers, not page numbers.

A

B

C

G

H

I

J

K

L

M

N

O

P

Q

R

T

U

V

Y

Z

INDEX BY SUBJECTS

Note: Numerals refer to quotation numbers, not page numbers.

C

D

E

F

M

T

U

V

KEY LINE INDEX

Note: This is not an exhaustive index but a selection of some of the most quotable lines to direct readers to closer examination in fuller context. Numerals refer to quotation numbers, not page numbers.

A

B

C

D

E

F

G

H

I

O

P

Q

R

S